Florida

a Lonely Planet travel survival kit

Nick Selby
Corinna Selby

Florida

1st edition

Published by
Lonely Planet Publications
Head Office: PO Box 617, Hawthorn, Vic 3122, Australia
Branches: 155 Filbert St, Suite 251, Oakland, CA 94607, USA
               10a Spring Place, London NW5 3BH, UK
               71 bis rue du Cardinal Lemoine, 75005 Paris, France

Printed by
The Bookmaker Pty Ltd
Printed in Hong Kong

Photographs by
All photographs by Nick Selby & Corinna Selby unless otherwise noted
Bill Bachmann   Kim Grant
Jan Butchofsky-Houser   Dave Houser
Kenneth Dreyfuss   Cheyenne Rouse
National Park Service / Everglades National Park
Florida Department of Commerce representing:
Karen Aldhizer   F Eric Tourney

Front cover: Miami Beach lifeguard station, Nick Selby
Title page: alligator billboard, Kenneth Dreyfuss

Published
January 1997

Although the author and publisher have tried to make the information as accurate as possible, they accept no responsibility for any loss, injury or inconvenience sustained by any person using this book.

National Library of Australia Cataloguing in Publication Data

Selby, Nick.
Florida.

1st ed.
Includes index.
ISBN 0 86442 374 8.

1. Florida – Guidebooks. I. Selby, Corinna.
II. Title. (Series: Lonely Planet travel survival kit).

917.590463

text & maps © Lonely Planet 1997
photos © photographers as indicated 1997
climate charts compiled from information supplied by Patrick J Tyson, © Patrick J Tyson, 1997

Nick Selby

Nick Selby was born and raised in New York City. He worked for five years as a sound engineer, but after 3½ years in a seven-foot-by-seven-foot cubicle mixing music for an American soap opera *(Guiding Light)* he decided that anything – anything – would be a step up.

In 1990 he took a job as a morning DJ at Warsaw's first privately owned radio station, Radio Zet, and soon afterwards did a stint as a creative director at a multinational advertising agency (a post from which he was unceremoniously sacked).

With another American expat, he set up a small publishing company in St Petersburg, Russia, and in 1992 he wrote *The Visitor's Guide to the New St Petersburg*. Since then, he's traveled throughout Southeast Asia, all too little of Australia, written Lonely Planet's *St Petersburg city guide* and co-authored *Russia, Ukraine & Belarus – a travel survival kit* and *Miami city guide*.

Corinna Selby

Corinna Selby was born and raised in Munich, Germany. As soon as she could afford it, she set out traveling through Europe, and spent a year in Portugal. After making more money back home, she traveled to Southeast Asia, where she spent the next two years traveling with a minuscule backpack. When she wasn't working as an English teacher in Tainan, Taiwan, or as an illegal art merchant in Japan, she spent her time perfecting a suntan, becoming familiar with the local flora and trying to do as little as possible.

Corinna returned to Germany to study English and Spanish translation, and to work in various departments of Munich's *Süddeutsche Zeitung*. After graduation she traveled to Eastern Europe, Russia, Cuba, back through Asia, down to Australia, and finally, to the USA.

Corinna is the co-author of Lonely Planet's *Miami city guide*.

From the Authors

Special thanks from both of us to Nick's father, Bernard Goldstein, for coming through in the clinch – every clinch.

In Miami, a million thanks as usual to Melanie Morningstar, Eugene Patron, Scott Silverman and Michael Aller, and to Jeanne Sullivan, José Lima, Bonnie Clearwater, Mitchel Kaplan, Les Standiford and Rebecca Terrell. Thanks also to Carolyn Dganogly for making us look *so* good, and especially to Tom Brosnahan.

Throughout the state of Florida, thanks to: Duncan McIntosh, Jacky Smith-Klein, Jack Dunlavey, Robin Knight and Rosetta Stone Land at the excellent Florida Division of Tourism; Beth Barrett, Liz Heath and Toby Pyle at Hostelling International; Kevin Sherman at the HI Key West Hostel; Sandra Warnock and Robert Magill at the HI Clearwater Beach Hostel; Charlotte Maas at Florida Youth Hostels; Floyd Creamer at Floyd's Crew House; and Linda Polansky at the HI Clay Hotel & International Hostel.

Also thank you Antony, Melanie, Max and Tabs, Monzi and Jason; Laura Hildebrand at the Lee County Visitor & Convention Bureau; Eugenio Nigro and Herman Morfin – and especially Charlie – at Walt Disney World; Michelle Brent, Tara Schroeder, Mitchell Martin and the Creatures of Delight Crew in Tampa; Ron and Amy Richter in Gainesville; Dan Ryan in Daytona Beach; Steve Cornman and Debby Nation, Gaja, Capt Dave @AugLink, Frank Sladish, Jr, Cathy and Phil (congrats!), Nadine Bernstein and the St John's County Library in St Augustine; Francine Mason and Scott Anthony in Fort Lauderdale; Danielle Saba Courtenay in Orlando; Lorna Meehan on Amelia Island and Scott Proffitt and the staff of the Main Bookshop in Sarasota, and Andy Metzger and John Daniels in Pensacola.

At Lonely Planet, thanks very much to Laini Taylor, Ann Neet, Beth Eilers, Greg Mills, Eric Kettunen, Carolyn Miller, Carolyn Hubbard and Caroline Liou, Hugh D'Andrade, Beca Lafore and Alex Guilbert, and the whole crew at LP UK, especially Charlotte Hindle and Jennifer Cox.

And personal thanks to Angela Wilson, Marlies Arnold, Maria 'Mutti' Jungwirth, Amy Portnoy and Joe Bornstein, the Artilleriestraße, Nattie, Tara, Pirate, Siamesey, Tom, Nancy, John and Ben.

From the Publisher

This 1st edition was edited by Laini Taylor and Jeff Campbell, and was proofed by Michelle Gagne with a smidge of help from Tom Downs. Mapping was executed by Beca Lafore with the assistance of Chris Salcedo and the coordinating prowess of Alex Guilbert, and illustrations were drawn by John Fadeff, Suzanne Bennett and Hugh D'Andrade. Beca coordinated layout, while Hugh designed the cover and helped with the color wraps. Thanks as always to overseers Scott Summers, Carolyn Hubbard and Caroline Liou.

Warning & Request

Things change – prices go up, schedules change, good places go bad and bad places go bankrupt – nothing stays the same. If you find things better or worse, recently opened or long since closed, please tell us and help make the next edition even more accurate and useful.

We value all of the feedback we receive from travelers. Julie Young coordinates a small team that reads and acknowledges every letter, postcard, and email, and ensures that every morsel of information finds its way to the appropriate authors, editors, and publishers. Everyone who writes to us will find their name in the next edition of the appropriate guide and will also receive a free subscription to our quarterly newsletter, *Planet Talk*. The very best contributions will be rewarded with a free Lonely Planet guide.

Excerpts from your correspondence may appear in updates (which we add to the end pages of reprints); in new editions of this guide; in our newsletter, *Planet Talk*; or in the Postcards section of our Web site. Please let us know if you don't want your letter published or your name acknowledged.

Contents

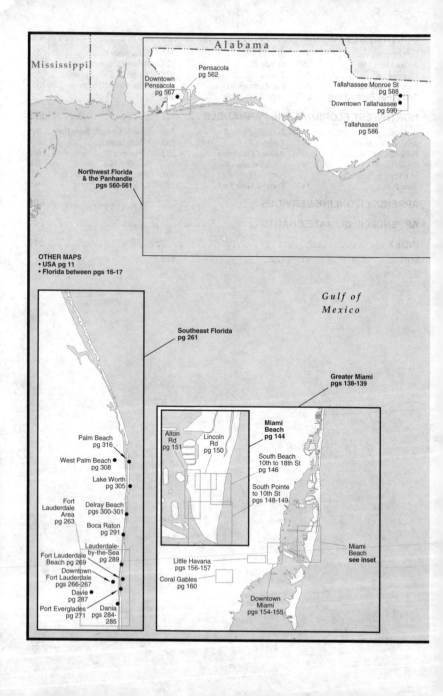

Mississippi

Alabama

Downtown
Pensacola
pg 567

Pensacola
pg 562

Tallahassee Monroe St
pg 588

Downtown Tallahassee
pg 590

Tallahassee
pg 586

**Northwest Florida
& the Panhandle
pgs 560-561**

OTHER MAPS
• USA pg 11
• Florida between pgs 16-17

*Gulf of
Mexico*

**Southeast Florida
pg 261**

**Greater Miami
pgs 138-139**

Palm Beach
pg 316

West Palm Beach
pg 308

Lake Worth
pg 305

Fort
Lauderdale
Area
pg 263

Delray Beach
pgs 300-301

Boca Raton
pg 291

Lauderdale-
by-the-Sea
pg 289

Fort Lauderdale
Beach pg 269

Downtown
Fort Lauderdale
pgs 266-267

Davie
pg 287

Port Everglades
pg 271

Dania
pgs 284-
285

Alton
Rd
pg 151

Lincoln
Rd
pg 150

**Miami
Beach
pg 144**

South Beach
10th to 18th St
pg 146

South Pointe
to 10th St
pgs 148-149

Little Havana
pgs 156-157

Coral Gables
pg 160

Miami
Beach
see inset

Downtown
Miami
pgs 154-155

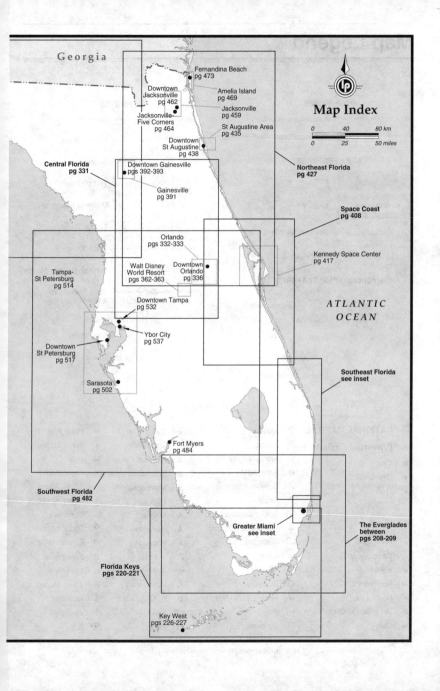

Map Index

Georgia

Fernandina Beach
pg 473

Downtown
Jacksonville
pg 462

Amelia Island
pg 469

Jacksonville
pg 459

Jacksonville-
Five Corners
pg 464

St Augustine Area
pg 435

Downtown
St Augustine
pg 438

Northeast Florida
pg 427

Central Florida
pg 331

Downtown Gainesville
pgs 392-393

Gainesville
pg 391

Space Coast
pg 408

Orlando
pgs 332-333

Kennedy Space Center
pg 417

Walt Disney
World Resort
pgs 362-363

Downtown
Orlando
pg 336

Tampa-
St Petersburg
pg 514

Downtown Tampa
pg 532

ATLANTIC
OCEAN

Ybor City
pg 537

Downtown
St Petersburg
pg 517

Sarasota
pg 502

Southeast Florida
see inset

Fort Myers
pg 484

Southwest Florida
pg 482

Greater Miami
see inset

The Everglades
between
pgs 208-209

Florida Keys
pgs 220-221

Key West
pgs 226-227

0   40   80 km

0   25   50 miles

Map Legend

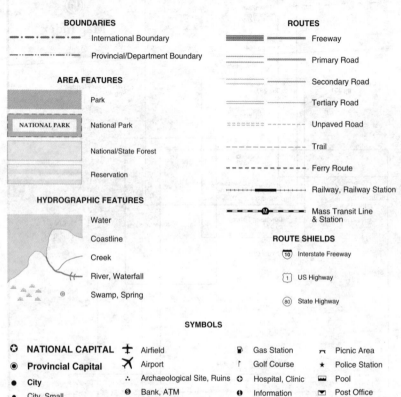

BOUNDARIES

— · — · — · — · — International Boundary

— · · — · · — · · — Provincial/Department Boundary

AREA FEATURES

Park

NATIONAL PARK National Park

National/State Forest

Reservation

HYDROGRAPHIC FEATURES

Water

Coastline

Creek

River, Waterfall

Swamp, Spring

ROUTES

Freeway

Primary Road

Secondary Road

Tertiary Road

Unpaved Road

Trail

Ferry Route

Railway, Railway Station

Mass Transit Line & Station

ROUTE SHIELDS

10 Interstate Freeway

1 US Highway

80 State Highway

SYMBOLS

✪ **NATIONAL CAPITAL**

◉ **Provincial Capital**

● **City**

● City, Small

● Town

■ Hotel, B&B

▲ Campground

⌂ Hostel

⌇ RV Park

▾ Restaurant

▾ Bar (Place to Drink)

▪ Cafe

✈ Airfield

✈ Airport

∴ Archaeological Site, Ruins

⑤ Bank, ATM

⚾ Baseball Diamond

⚲ Beach

⚹ Border Crossing

● Bus Depot, Bus Stop

⊟ Cathedral

⌒ Cave

✝ Church

⚲ Embassy

↝ Fishing, Fish Hatchery

⌣ Foot Bridge

✿ Garden

⛽ Gas Station

⚑ Golf Course

✪ Hospital, Clinic

❶ Information

⚟ Lighthouse

☀ Lookout

⚐ Mission

⚑ Monument

▲ Mountain

🏛 Museum

← One-Way Street

⚀ Observatory

🅿 Parking

▲☘ Park

)(Pass

⊓ Picnic Area

★ Police Station

⊟ Pool

✉ Post Office

⚐ Skiing, Alpine

⚐ Skiing, Nordic

⚓ Shipwreck

✦ Shopping Mall

🎦 Stately Home

✡ Synagogue

☎ Telephone

◼ Tomb, Mausoleum

⚑ Trailhead

⚐ Winery

🐗 Zoo

Note: not all symbols displayed above appear in this book.

Introduction

For a destination known throughout the world for its beaches and theme parks, the 'real' Florida surprises and astounds those who set out to find it. On just the other side of massive attractions like Disney World, Miami's South Beach and the Kennedy Space Center, travelers in Florida have the opportunity to see some of the most beautiful, rugged, challenging and bizarre natural attractions in the USA.

And it's accessible. The real Florida is where you'll be if you stay on the turnpike one extra exit in any direction from Orlando, Miami, Tampa or any other major city – off the beaten path in a state where a designated historic district can be as young as 50 years old or older than 400. You *can* get away from tourist traps in a state that was developed specifically for tourists, and be off on your own in the land of Crackers, anglers and alligators, manatees and mangroves, sink holes, springs and swamps.

The first European settlement in the New World was right here in St Augustine, by the Spanish in 1565, and over the next 300 years Florida found itself at the epicenter of a struggle for control of the New World. With British at the north and French at the west, the world's three superpowers skirmished constantly – and when America became a power of its own, it too joined the fight over the continent's tropical paradise.

In the end, Florida was ceded to the US by a Spain that was taking beatings around the world, one of the last feathers in the cap of a now creaky superpower has-been. It was their fault, really, for not attempting to settle the area more aggressively. If the

11

Spanish had gotten out and explored the territory they'd lucked onto, they never would have let it go.

Florida's settlement was accomplished only after American money was put up by developers to lure enough workers to battle the state's desperately difficult terrain, and after the army had thoroughly dispossessed the Indians who had called the territory home. Throughout the late-19th and early-20th centuries, certain groups of these Indians gave US Army Indian fighters a run for their money – and the Seminole people have never officially surrendered.

The contrast between nature and development in Florida is shocking, but the horrifying construction of high-rise developments and water-sucking, sprawling golf courses is offset by easily accessible spots of such lush beauty you wouldn't be surprised if Ricardo Montalban himself popped out from behind a palm tree and handed you a piña colada in a hula glass.

The theme parks of central and southwest Florida set the worldwide standard, and are the primary reason the state has become so popular with international travelers. And down on South Miami Beach, arguably the world's hippest photo backdrop, the mix of communities – straight and gay, white and Latin American, fabulous models and barrel-bellied Central Europeans – gives the place a feeling of tolerance that is refreshing to anyone. Add great diving along the Keys' coral reefs; eco-tourism in the Everglades' mangrove swamps and sawgrass flats; rafting, tubing, boating and every other conceivable water sport in the Atlantic Ocean, Gulf of Mexico, or in one of Florida's 30,000 rivers and lakes, and Florida is an easy place to promote.

Reports of violence and mayhem from the early years of the 1990s, combined with a lack of information about the state's interior, make it no wonder that this real Florida was a place visitors avoided for so long. That was a mistake. With spring-fed rivers so clear you can easily make out details 60 feet under water, pristine state parks and wonderfully weird tourist attractions as goofy as anything Disney could dream up, the real Florida is truly where the action is. Goofy? You bet. Head for psychic fulfillment at Cassadaga, the nation's only township made up entirely of spiritualists. Or look into the rich history of a different type of fulfillment at one of the nation's only bordello museums in Yahoo Junction (that's right, *Yahoo Junction*). See an underwater performance of dancing mermaids and mermen at Weeki Watchee (yes, *Weeki Watchee*). Watch residents of a state that saw about as much action as Wisconsin in the Civil War stage fantastically complex Civil War re-enactments. And grab a bag of Bull's potato chips in the city of Spuds (uh-huh, *Spuds*).

So when your last nerve is trounced by a bright-faced teenager urging you to 'have a Disney day' (they really say that), it's nice to know that even in the heart of Walt Disney World, the real Florida is as close as a 40-minute drive.

Facts about Florida

HISTORY
Early Inhabitants

It's generally accepted that the first people to inhabit America came from East Asia, over a land bridge to Alaska across what is now the Bering Strait. This land bridge was related to recurrent Ice Ages, during which the sea level was lower. There is some disagreement about the time at which migrations took place – estimates range from as early as 35,000 years ago, to somewhere between 12,000 and 13,000 years ago. The oldest undisputed evidence of human occupation in any part of the Americas is from about 12,000 years ago. Until recently most believed that the indigenous population of the Florida peninsula migrated down the North American continent over the next 10,000 years.

Another theory holds that the first inhabitants made their way north from South and Central America. Regardless of their origins, these Paleo-Indian hunter-gatherer groups arrived in Florida about 10,000 to 9000 BC.

While there was settlement throughout the state, the highest concentration of groups was in coastal areas, as it remains today. In the late Archaic period, about 3000 BC, populations were heaviest in

---

Who Were the Seminole?

The native group that today has the most name recognition in Florida, the Seminole, was not a single tribe, and nor did it exist when the first Europeans landed in Florida. Instead, the Seminole began as a collection of breakaways from other Indian tribes as well as runaways – slaves and others.

The name Seminole is a tricky one: the Florida Department of State says that it derives from the Spanish *cimarrone*, while most historical texts say that it was a Creek Indian word *sim-in-ole* or *sem-in-ole*; in any case, in both languages it means 'wild one' or 'runaway' or even 'one who camps at a distance', and reflects the origins of the Seminole nation.

The Muskhogean Indians once existed all around the Gulf Coast of the present-day USA. A subgroup, the Creek Confederacy, settled in Georgia and Alabama and had gained in number and strength by the turn of the 19th century, when skirmishes with the ever-encroaching Americans escalated into mass killings on both sides. Andrew Jackson enlisted the help of the American-friendly Lower Creeks against the Upper Creeks in the Battle of Horseshoe Bend, March 27, 1814, and all but wiped them out. The surviving Red Sticks, a faction of the Upper Creeks, escaped south into still-Spanish Florida where they were joined by other groups of Indians escaping similar treatment. The Seminole welcomed them, as well as runaway slaves, with open arms.

All these groups eventually became the Seminole and Miccosukee nations, and though technically in Spanish territory, they were far from safe from Andrew Jackson's purges. Partly in the interest of reclaiming escaped black slaves living among the Seminole, the Americans continued to pursue the Indians across the border. See Seminole Wars, later in this chapter. ■

the Panhandle, northeast and southwest portions of the state, and around present-day Tampa. Shell middens – mounds – are evidence of settlements, and are made up of the shells of snails, mussels and oysters in such riotous abundance that one wonders how it was possible to eat just that many shellfish. Seeing it for yourself is the only way to even get a grasp on the quantities. See the Southwest Florida chapter for information on Mound Key, whose shell mounds reach heights of 30 feet and were dense enough to provide the foundation for an entire village.

By 600 to 500 BC, more defined cultures began to develop ceramic, shell and copper items, and, in the northeast of the state, the St John's River villages had sand burial mounds and highly developed village life that for the first time showed signs of dependence on agriculture – corn – as opposed to hunting.

Florida's Indians

Because little written history exists of the various groups of natives in Florida, most information comes from the period after European settlement. But it seems clear that by the time the first Europeans arrived in the 16th century, several distinct groups of Indians had settled in the region.

The largest northern group were the Timucuan, described as being very tall (it is said that height was inbred, by mating the tallest males and females) and very beautiful (if we can believe the illustrations by early Spanish explorers, the men were handsome and the women stunning – but they also sure do look white, so we take these pictures with a grain of salt).

The 20,000 or so Calusa were the largest group on the southwest part of the peninsula. There's tantalizing speculation as to the origin of the Calusa's hatred of the Spaniards which suggests contact earlier than is recorded, but one thing is clear: the Calusa didn't much care for the Spanish, and were highly demonstrative of their animosity, as you'll see.

Other groups included the Tequesta (also sometimes spelled Tekesta) who lived at the southern tip of the peninsula between the 10,000 Islands and present-day Miami; Ais and Jeaga on the southeast coast; Tocobaga, on the Gulf Coast north of the Calusa; and the 25,000 Apalachee that occupied the eastern end of the Panhandle.

Spanish Exploration

Juan Ponce de León, an explorer who had sailed on Christopher Columbus' second voyage (1493) and had taken part in the Spanish siege of Puerto Rico (1506-7), sailed northwest from Spanish settlements in the Caribbean and wound up running smack into central Florida's Atlantic coastline, probably near present-day Cape Canaveral, in 1513. In honor of Pascua Florida, the Easter Feast of Flowers, Ponce de León named this new land Florida.

Ponce de León didn't see anyone on the shore of what he thought was an island (but claimed the land for Spain just in case) and began trying to find a way to sail around it. After making his way around the Florida Keys, he ended up at San Carlos, near present-day Tampa, where he was welcomed by the Calusa with arms – not open ones, just arms.

The Calusa attacked until he sailed away, but Ponce de León had discovered a good source of fresh water and, he presumed, a line on all the riches the area undoubtedly held. He made for Spain (on the way back out of Florida he discovered the arid keys west of Key West and named them *Las Tortugas* for the huge numbers of turtles there – see the Dry Tortugas in the Florida Keys chapter).

King Ferdinand V named Ponce de León governor of Florida in 1514, but he was unable to return to the land until 1521, when he brought settlers, animals and missionaries back to San Carlos. You can guess what the Calusa did. Ponce de León died shortly thereafter in Cuba as a result of a poison arrow wound. But this did not discourage the Spanish, who were convinced – based on their experiences in South America and the recent discoveries in Mexico – that Florida was a land of untold mineral wealth.

Searching for the fabled 'fountain of youth', Juan Ponce de León was the first European to set foot on the continental USA, in 1513.

the diaries of Narváez's treasurer, Núñez Cabeza de Vaca, who survived among the Indians for eight years before rejoining his own people in Mexico City. Much more successful was the 4000-some-odd-mile reconnoiter by Hernando de Soto in 1539. De Soto explored a huge area of the southeastern USA, and when he died in 1542 he was buried in the Mississippi River.

The French & British Sniff Around

Over the next 20 years, the Spanish were still unable to make a permanent settlement in Florida. Meanwhile the British and French were sniffing around the region looking for minerals and possible colonial lands.

Despite the Spanish claim on the region, the French sailed in in 1562 under the command of Jean Ribault and established a colony on Parris Island, at the southern end of present-day South Carolina. It failed, and Ribault's deputy, René de Laudonnière, pushed on to establish Fort Caroline in 1564 on the St John's River near present-day Jacksonville. Never one to let the French pull a fast one, Spain's King Philip II sent Pedro Menéndez de Avilés to stomp the French and establish a fort of his own.

In 1565 Menéndez arrived at Cape Canaveral with about 1500 soldiers and settlers, who made their way north and established St Augustine – named for the day on which they arrived on the Florida coast, August 28, the Feast Day of Saint Augustine, Bishop of Hippo. St Augustine was

After Ponce de León's death, several other attempts were made by the Spanish to suss out just what it was that Florida – the area now encompassing much of the present-day southeastern USA – had to offer. Attempts were made by the feckless Pánfilo de Narváez, who blew it in 1528 and lost everything – that is, four ships, 400 men (including himself) and 80 horses. Despite the disaster, though, much understanding about the land was gained from

---

That's Dedication

When the first Europeans arrived in Florida, they could not have imagined a less welcoming place. Aside from hostile natives and the unforgiving and unforgivable heat, the land itself was swampy, overgrown and fraught with dangers. Early settlers had to contend with alligators, poisonous snakes, thick undergrowth and vegetation, and perhaps worst of all, biting insects in such prodigious quantities that it seemed to the explorers they had arrived in hell itself.

As humankind pushed southward in Florida, workers related stories about black clouds of mosquitoes that swarmed from sunrise to sunset. And the swamp conditions throughout the state, especially in the south, made reclaiming land a nightmare.

As we look at Florida today, with its winding ribbons of asphalt and urban sprawl it's easy to forget just how recently much of the state was uninhabitable by any but the most dedicated backwoods travelers. ∎

established on September 4 – the USA's first permanent European settlement.

Menéndez and his troops headed north and were whupped but good by the French; the Spaniards retreated south to St Augustine. Soon after, the French, in an effort to fight *fuego* with *feu*, launched a fleet to take on the pesky Spaniards. But the French fell victim to one of Florida's famous coastal storms, and their fleet was destroyed. Menéndez, no shirk when it came to opportunism, immediately forged north to the relatively unpopulated French fort and destroyed it. Menéndez executed all prisoners, as well as survivors from the French fleet washed ashore south of St Augustine – in all, almost 600 were butchered, giving the inlet its name: *matanzas*, or slaughter.

And so it was that a full 50 years before the Pilgrims lurched up to Plymouth Rock, and 40 before even the establishment at Jamestown, Florida was finally settled for the Spanish by Menéndez.

It would become to North America what Poland is to Europe: the flattest piece of land between battling superpowers. Before it was ceded to the US by Spain in 1821, the area was occupied by several armies – a total of eight flags have flown over Amelia Island.

A Good Christian Colony

In addition to chasing away Frenchmen and seeking to get rich, Menéndez also sought to convert the Indians to Christianity and generally show them what swell folks the Spanish were. His goal was to establish a territory-wide series of missions, forts and trade posts.

All did not go as planned. Missionaries were murdered, and Indian uprisings became as common as one would expect when a new force comes in and tells you that everything you believe in is wrong, and in any case it belongs to them. To make matters worse, in 1568 a new bunch of Frenchmen showed up to avenge the deaths at Fort Caroline; they were assisted by turncoat Timucuans who led them right into the fort.

Menéndez regained control of the situation in a method still common today: he

threw money and people at it. He tidied up problems that were delaying his supply lines from Cuba, and offered highly attractive conditions to settlers, who came in droves. St Augustine became a bustling and wealthy trading town.

French & British Colonization

The French and the British were both making overtures to settle the New World, or at least keep their hands in. In 1584, Elizabeth I granted Sir Walter Raleigh a charter to settle lands in North America. His colony, on Roanoke Island in North Carolina's Outer Banks, is remembered today as the Lost Colony for the mysterious disappearance of its settlers.

Meanwhile, Spanish St Augustine was under constant pressure from the Brits: the city was attacked and burned by British troops led by Sir Francis Drake in 1586. Later, in 1702, the British came back again and laid siege to the city for 52 days, burning it down – but the Castillo de San Marcos fort held (see St Augustine in the Northeast Florida chapter).

The Jamestown, Virginia settlement of 1607 (which generally gets Anglocentric textbook honors for being the first European settlement in the New World, despite St Augustine) was a problem-plagued English colony, with half the party dying during its first winter.

Meanwhile the French were wondering how to get their hands on the Louisiana territory, which they would claim in the late 17th century.

From Settlement to Colony

As St Augustine grew, and life gained a degree of normalcy, incentives were shelved. Even the original missionary activities were starting to work, and Spain was forging relations with Indians throughout the territory. With a few notable exceptions near the turn of the 17th century, including rebellions by Guale and Ais Indians, Florida was humming right along. It was still a very dangerous place, fraught with the peril of Indian or European attacks, fires set either by invading armies

Miami's Vizcaya Museum & Gardens

Florida oranges

Seminole Tribal Fair in Hollywood

Flamingos at Miami's Metrozoo

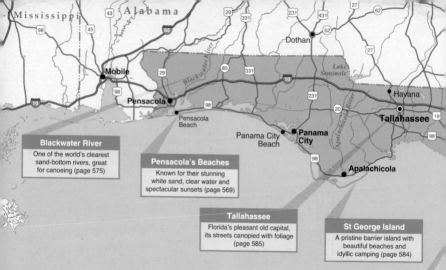

Blackwater River

One of the world's clearest sand-bottom rivers, great for canoeing (page 575)

Pensacola's Beaches

Known for their stunning white sand, clear water and spectacular sunsets (page 569)

Tallahassee

Florida's pleasant old capital, its streets canopied with foliage (page 585)

St George Island

A pristine barrier island with beautiful beaches and idyllic camping (page 584)

Ichetucknee Springs

A group of sparkling springs perfect for a lazy afternoon innertube float (page 400)

Busch Gardens

Florida's scariest roller coasters in an Africa-themed amusement park (page 541)

Venice Beach

Best place in the state to gather shark's teeth (page 512)

Gulf of Mexico

Florida

| 0 | 40 | 80 km |
| 0 | 25 | 50 miles |

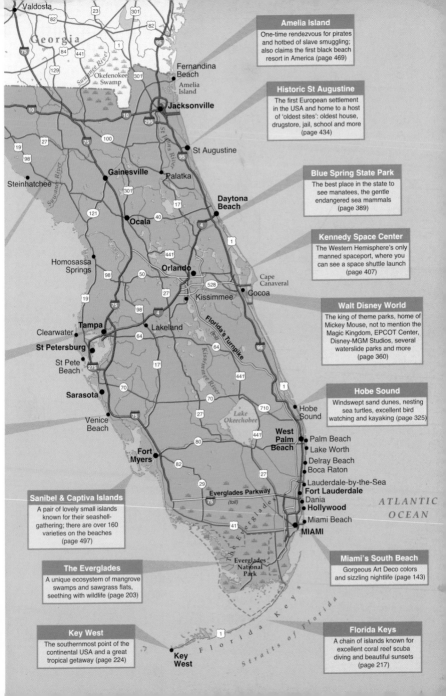

Amelia Island
One-time rendezvous for pirates and hotbed of slave smuggling; also claims the first black beach resort in America (page 469)

Historic St Augustine
The first European settlement in the USA and home to a host of 'oldest sites': oldest house, drugstore, jail, school and more (page 434)

Blue Spring State Park
The best place in the state to see manatees, the gentle endangered sea mammals (page 389)

Kennedy Space Center
The Western Hemisphere's only manned spaceport, where you can see a space shuttle launch (page 407)

Walt Disney World
The king of theme parks, home of Mickey Mouse, not to mention the Magic Kingdom, EPCOT Center, Disney-MGM Studios, several waterslide parks and more (page 360)

Hobe Sound
Windswept sand dunes, nesting sea turtles, excellent bird watching and kayaking (page 325)

Sanibel & Captiva Islands
A pair of lovely small islands known for their seashell-gathering; there are over 160 varieties on the beaches (page 497)

The Everglades
A unique ecosystem of mangrove swamps and sawgrass flats, seething with wildlife (page 203)

Miami's South Beach
Gorgeous Art Deco colors and sizzling nightlife (page 143)

Key West
The southernmost point of the continental USA and a great tropical getaway (page 224)

Florida Keys
A chain of islands known for excellent coral reef scuba diving and beautiful sunsets (page 217)

Pensacola pelicans

Spaceship house, Pensacola Beach

Haitian boats in Miami River loaded with bikes

Dancers at Seminole Tribal Fair

Wild berries

Yet another gator billboard

or drunken card-players, and a sense that it could all end at a moment's notice.

The population of St Augustine was mainly soldiers and traders, and the city limits at the time were far smaller than they are today. As the Indians and settlers began to pair off (and as prostitution became more common), the Indians found themselves looking at the business end of a slew of new diseases. These diseases would, over the next 100 years, finish what the early explorers had started, and exterminate all but a smattering of Florida's once-thriving Indian population.

Superpower Shift

During the 17th century the shape of the world superpowers was altered, with Spain losing control of many of its colonies and possessions and Britain and France gaining élan. While the British and French sent troops and explorers scurrying all over the new territories, the Spanish seemed perfectly content to maintain their itsy-bitsy settlements at St Augustine and at Pensacola, at the western end of the state.

The Brits, who by the end of the 17th century had well-established colonies in the northeast, were continually pressing the Spanish on the southern boundaries of the British territory. In 1670 a demarcation line was established on what are roughly the present-day borders of Georgia and South Carolina, but the line was taken more as a suggestion than a rule, and the Brits repeatedly ran raids into the Spanish territory – either overtly or covertly.

To the west, the French were quickly establishing colonies along the Mississippi River, trying to link up the south with their new Canadian territories. Alliances between the powers were formed as quickly as they were scrapped – and they were scrapped as soon as they were formed.

Throughout the 18th century the very proximity of the British in Georgia, the French in Louisiana and the Spanish in Florida raised tensions. By 1700 there were 12 British colonies, and the British were definitely setting their sights on Florida. In 1732, James Oglethorpe settled Savannah, Georgia, and after a trip to England for supplies and armaments, attacked St Augustine in 1740. That attack, which laid siege to the city for 27 days before Oglethorpe's troops ran out of supplies and were forced to retreat, led to the construction of tiny Fort Matanzas, at the southern end of St Augustine. While the Spanish repelled the attack again, their position had become one under constant pressure from the British.

French & Indian War

As pressure on Spain mounted, so too did the friction between the other two big boys in the fray, England and France. As the two began feel the urge to stretch their legs to the west and east respectively, hostilities broke out between them in 1754. Known as the French & Indian War for the French alliance with Indian groups against the British, it was the first war between European powers fought outside of Europe.

Choosing the marginally lesser of two evils, the Spanish jumped in on the side of France in 1761, to which England replied, 'Fine, and by the way we hope you liked Havana, 'cause we just took it.' In the First Treaty of Paris (1763) ending the seven-year-long war, Spain was offered a swap of Cuba for Florida, and they jumped at the chance.

American Revolution

England had tried to force the 13 colonies to float the cost of its war with France, in the form of new taxes. As George Bush realized, that's not the best way to win votes in America, and higher taxes, including tariffs on just about anything that Americans held dear, a hated Stamp Act, and taxes on iron goods, precipitated a break from England. America's rallying cry was 'No taxation without representation' (taxation imposed on the colonists while they had no ability to plead their own case to the Court of St James). Today, of course, content in their ample congressional representation, Americans happily chip in and pay all new taxes.

Officially declared in 1776, the American Revolution barely affected Florida, which remained avidly loyalist. Florida's governor at the time invited other loyalists to move down to the region.

But after just 20 years of British rule – during which time Florida developed a social structure the Spanish had never succeeded in creating – the Second Treaty of Paris (1783, ending the Revolution) returned Florida to the hands of Spain.

US Expansion

The northernmost portion of the state was becoming quite alluring indeed to expansionist Americans toward the end of the 18th century; in 1795 some Georgian hotheads attacked the San Nicolás mission in present-day Jacksonville; they held it for several months before being beaten back to Georgia. And in 1800 Spain finally gave up the Louisiana Territory to Napoleon, who promptly gave it up to the Americans!

A little later, the strategic location of Amelia Island, northeast of Jacksonville – that is, off the mainland – became key. In 1807-08 President Thomas Jefferson imposed his wildly unpopular Embargo Act, which banned the importation of French and British products, and prohibited slave importation – and Amelia Island became black market central.

As the superpowers – and the USA was fast on its way to becoming one, at least in this region – squared off for what was to become the War of 1812 (1812-15), the Spanish ended up allied with the British against the US and France. The War of 1812, aside from being a power struggle between the Americans and British, was an aggressive campaign of US expansion, north into Canada, westward across the plains, and south into Florida.

The 1814 Battle of Horseshoe Bend, in Alabama, proved pivotal for Florida. There, notorious (though, to his compatriots, heroic) Indian-hunter Andrew Jackson (1767-1845) defeated the Creeks in an overwhelming massacre of a victory, and then took half of their huge territory for the US. It also provided him with an excuse to chase fleeing Creeks into Spanish Florida under the guise of defense. In late 1817

Jackson instigated the First Seminole War; see below.

As the US sent more and more troops into the region on Indian-hunting and Spanish-harassing missions, the pressure became too much for Spain. It had gradually lost its grip on the East Florida settlements – Amelia Island was a Sodom-like den of smuggling, piracy, prostitution and debauchery – and the Spanish government's inability to adequately supply and police the area led to its decision to cede the territory to the US in 1819.

But an itchy King Ferdinand the VII of Spain began to waiver. After the US told the Spanish to give up and get out or face US troops, a renegotiated treaty, specifying among other things that the US would assume Spanish debt in the region, was signed, and the Spanish finally gave up control of Florida in 1821. The debts, by the way, were never repaid. And who do you think was made governor of the new American territory? Yep, Jackson himself.

Seminole Wars

The treaty signed in 1814 at the end of the Battle of Horseshoe Bend opened to white settlers some 20 million acres of land in the region owned by the Creeks. Tensions, as one would imagine, ran very high, and skirmishes broke out periodically; there were a total of three Seminole Wars.

The first, instigated by Andrew Jackson, began in 1817, when Indians in the Miccosukee settlement of Fowltown had the audacity to respond to an attack by whites, killing about 50, including some women and children. Enter Jackson, who late that year stormed through Florida with a force of 5000, destroying Seminole villages and, while he was at it, engaging in a totally unsanctioned attack on Pensacola (he actually took it, but the US gave it back – see the Pensacola entry).

Jackson was elected President of the USA in 1828, and the extermination of the American Indian was accelerated by his Indian Removal Act of 1830. The Treaty of Moultrie Creek of 1823 and the Treaty of Payne's Landing of 1832 were both signed by *some* Seminole, who agreed to give up their Florida lands and move west to reservations, but the provisions of the treaties were flouted by both sides. When the US began moving troops in 1835 to enforce the Treaty of Payne's Landing, Osceola, a Seminole leader, planned an attack on an army detachment. Major Francis Dade and 108 of his men were ambushed by the Seminole as they marched between Tampa and Fort King – only three survived. The attack is accepted as the beginning of the Second Seminole War, which lasted seven years.

The war dragged on for so long because it was fought guerrilla-style in swamps and hammocks by the Seminole, versus the traditional European tactics employed by US soldiers. Creek Indian warriors from Alabama were engaged to fight for the US, in exchange for promises of federal protection of their families while they were away fighting. (Not surprisingly, they returned to pillaged homes and were interned in camps and gradually forced west.)

Osceola was captured on October 27, 1837, as he approached US Major General Thomas Jesup, commander of the Florida troops, both traveling under white flags. Jesup snatched Osceola, who later died at Fort Moultrie in South Carolina.

By 1842, thousands of Seminole had been displaced, marched to reservations in the west by army troops. As the war wound down, the surviving Florida Seminole took refuge in the Everglades. Despite their relegation to the swamps, the Seminole weren't really left alone, and in 1853 they were actually outlawed – a law proclaiming Indians illegal in the state of Florida called for their removal to any place west of the Mississippi River.

In 1855, a party of surveyors were killed after they encroached on Seminole territory. The resulting backlash became the Third Seminole War, which ended after Chief Billy Bowlegs agreed to go west (he was paid) in 1858. He and about 100 Seminole did migrate, but about 200 or 300 refused to acknowledge the agreement, and retreated into the Everglades. There was never a full treaty ending the war, and some

Seminole leader, Osceola

Seminole today say that they are technically still at war with the USA.

Statehood & the Civil War

With the Indians out of the way, Florida became the 27th state admitted to the Union on March 3, 1845, only to secede 16 years later with the onset of Civil War. Admitted to the Union as a slave-owning, agricultural state, Florida seceded from the USA along with the Confederacy on January 10, 1861.

The US Civil War (1861-65) was brought on by a number of issues, but a few stand in the foreground. There was a profound debate over the moral and economic issues surrounding slavery. In the 19th century, public opinion against it – and in favor of 'free labor' – in the Northern states and in England was quickly rising. Compounding this issue were the distinct economic differences between the Northern and Southern states.

Northern states, while maintaining an agrarian base, were moving quickly to manufacturing and industry. The South depended on selling raw materials, principally cotton, to manufacturing nations, like Britain, but the North, in order to protect its fledgling industry, was in favor of instituting trade tariffs.

Additionally, the introduction of new territories to the USA through westward expansion potentially introduced a tilt in the balance of power between free and slave states within the US Congress. That issue was underscored with the admittance of California in 1850 as a free state.

Florida's Role Aside from providing troops, Florida's role in the Civil War was mainly one of supplying the ever-growing food needs of the Confederate war machine. As Yossarian explained to Milo in *Catch-22*, troops just can't eat cotton (even when chocolate covered), and since cotton was the South's main crop, the Confederate army pressed Florida's citrus and cattle farmers into heavy overtime.

All did not go well. Cattle ranchers and packing plants were heavily overburdened. Florida cattle were so valuable to the Confederate effort that the Union's attentions focused on Florida in an effort to cripple the South – the largest battle of the war held on Florida soil, at Olustee, began as a Union effort to cut off beef supplies.

A Tenuous Florida Connection

While Florida saw some action in the Civil War, none of it was decisive to the outcome of the war. But Florida's claim to fame was this: after shooting Abraham Lincoln (who was not from Florida) at the Ford Theatre in 1865, John Wilkes Booth (also not a Floridian), leapt from the president's box and, when landing on the stage, broke his leg. Also not from Florida was the good Dr Samuel Mudd, who patched up Booth's leg enabling him to make his escape from Washington. *But*, poor Dr Mudd – who hadn't the foggiest idea what was going on when he fixed the assassin's leg – found himself arrested on charges of aiding and abetting the assassin; his ass was hauled – you guessed it – to Florida. Fort Jefferson in the Dry Tortugas, to be precise.

Mudd served out his sentence well, and was pardoned after he showed 'great courage and compassion' treating victims of a yellow fever outbreak at the fort in 1867. ■

Battles of the Civil War in Florida included:

Santa Rosa Island – October 9, 1861. 1200 Union soldiers captured Fort Pickens at Pensacola.

St John's Bluff – October 1 to 3, 1862. A Union flotilla carrying about 1500 troops on ships steamed into the mouth of the St John's River, and after being joined by infantry forces at Mount Pleasant Creek and landing forces at Mayport, the Confederates got out of Dodge.

Fort Brooke – October 16 to 18, 1863. Under cover fire from two Union ships, the Union marched to the Hillsborough River and captured the *Scottish Chief* and *Kate Dale*.

Olustee – February 20, 1864. After a fine start sacking several Confederate encampments, Union General Truman Seymour's troops ran into the decidedly unimpressed Brigadier General Joseph Finegan and 5000 of his closest friends. Finegan broke the Union line but allowed the troops to retreat to Jacksonville in this, the largest battle in Florida.

Natural Bridge – On March 6, 1865 near St Marks, Major General John Newton went after Confederate troops that had attacked at Cedar Keys and Fort Myers. The Union army advanced and tried to cross the river at Natural Bridge, but the Confederates (Home Guard as well as a 'Baby Corps' of adolescent boy cadets) held their position.

At the end of the war, Tallahassee was the only Confederate state capital that hadn't fallen to Federal troops.

Reconstruction

The Civil War was one of the bloodiest conflicts in the history of modern warfare, and wounds ran incredibly deep. From early on in the conflict until his assassination, President Abraham Lincoln (1809-65) had been putting together a framework for reconstruction of the Union, the 10% Plan. Under the plan, the Union would give federal recognition to states in which as few as 10% of the populace had taken oaths of loyalty to the USA – a plan designed to grant political viability to dependable groups (in the Union's opinion) as quickly as possible.

But with Lincoln's assassination, all bets were off and a political void opened;

Florida was ruled by martial law under Union troops. Any semblance of a state government disappeared right after the war – Florida's governor, John Milton, blew his brains out, preferring death to Reconstruction, and the state was run by troops carrying out orders from Washington. In the confusion that followed, dozens of factions struggled for power – from labor organizers to the Ku Klux Klan, an organized gang of white supremacists who began a campaign of violence against blacks that continues to this day.

But as the federal government established and maintained order, the return to normalcy progressed. Farmers scrambled to reestablish their businesses and Florida blacks, though freed technically from slavery, found themselves working for the same plantations as before, now as hired hands. As businessmen and former politicians struggled to recreate a state government, arguments arose at every level on the role of blacks in the state and the level of freedom and recognition they would receive – and this was not contained to Florida: throughout the country, a consensus on how to reestablish state and local government and on what platform was proving far more difficult than had been expected.

President Andrew Johnson, a Southerner and former slave owner who succeeded Lincoln, devised a Reconstruction plan that compromised between Lincoln's 10% plan and the more radical proposals that were filtering in from the South. While his Presidential Reconstruction granted many concessions, it was absolutely firm that the states' constitutions ratify the 13th Amendment, abolishing slavery, before re-admittance.

The major issue was black suffrage, something the Southern states were loathe to grant, but under the congressional Reconstruction plan, martial law was eventually imposed to install it. When Florida was re-admitted to the Union in 1868, it had technically granted the vote to blacks, but the state's new constitution was carefully worded to ensure that it did not get a

Railroads in Florida

Railroads quite simply were the most important factor in the development of Florida, and as demand grew, several cropped up around the state. Most people associate railroads in Florida with Henry Flagler, who owned the Florida East Coast (FEC) Railway, but Flagler was a latecomer.

Henry B Plant (1819-1899) was probably the biggest player in the railroad scene; his Plant Railroad System ran up the southwest coast and across the state, connecting with steamships between Tampa, Key West and Havana. By the time he sold his railroad empire in 1902, his system included or connected with a network including the East Florida Railway from Jacksonville to the St Mary's River, the Savannah, Florida & Western Line and the Louisville & Nashville line running across the Panhandle.

After the land bust in 1926, service throughout the state became less and less in demand, and several lines folded. WWII breathed life into John Williams' Seaboard Air Line Railway for a while, but business stayed slow even after a merger of competing rail lines in the late 1960s. The beginning of the end was the arrival in 1971 of Amtrak, which gobbled up remaining companies, cut service and raised prices. The merger of the remaining lines, Seaboard Coast Line and the Chessie System, created the CSX Corporation in 1980.

Today railroad museums pop up here and there throughout the state, and if you do find a functional line – like the Seminole Gulf Railway in Fort Myers, it's probably only being run as a tourist attraction, for dinner and mystery rides, as opposed to straight transport. ■

Henry Morrison Flagler, the Rockefeller of Flordia

'negro government'. After federal troops left, discriminatory laws were enacted – including one forbidding a black man to testify at a white man's trial – and a poll tax was imposed which kept droves of black and poor white voters away from the voting booth.

The new Florida government began what in many ways continues to this day: an agenda of pro-business, pro-development activities to open up Florida's natural resources to exploitation at the expense of social programs, which have always been almost non-existent. While schools went underfunded and overcrowded, developers and tourists were enticed to the area – the former by unbelievably and criminally cheap land prices (25¢ an acre was not unheard of), and the latter by the hotels and resorts built by the former.

Development

At the end of the 18th century, real estate developers were creating holiday resorts throughout the state. As Florida's agricultural trade – especially citrus and cattle – expanded, the need for railroads increased, and as communications advanced, the ability to shuttle tourists to hitherto remote areas of the state became feasible.

The first trans-state railroad had been constructed just prior to the Civil War by David Yulee (the first Jewish member of the US Senate), but sadly it remained open for only about a month, running from Fernandina Beach to Cedar Key before being rerouted north during the war. After the war, railroads popped up throughout the state, and much of Florida was finally connected to the Atlantic coast railroads and thus with the Northern states for the first time.

Henry Flagler Developer Henry Flagler (1830-1913), who made his money as a partner of John D Rockefeller in Standard Oil, is considered by many to be the most important single force in the development of Florida as a holiday destination. Flagler, whose real estate career began in Westchester County, New York, became convinced that the Atlantic coast of Florida was the perfect playground for the rich and famous, and by gum, he was the man to bring them there. He began by buying up existing railroad between Jacksonville and St Augustine, and from that beginning created what would become the Florida East Coast Railway, that would eventually traverse the entire length of the state's east coast from Jacksonville to Key West.

Flagler built resorts in each of the railway's main terminals beginning in St Augustine, where he constructed the Ponce de León Hotel (now Flagler College) and helped spur a boom of resorts in the area. The railroad extended southward; Flagler had planned to make the southern terminus in Palm Beach, where he built an even more lavish resort, Royal Poinciana Hotel, to which he added on the Palm Beach Inn, now known as The Breakers.

After a record freeze in 1895 that shocked tourists and stunned the fledgling Florida citrus industry, Flagler took Julia Tuttle up on her offer to extend the FEC to Miami and eventually to Key West across Flagler's crown jewel, the Overseas Highway. The highway connected Key West to the mainland over a series of causeways, but it wasn't profitable and was destroyed by a hurricane in 1935. The foundations of the FEC's bridges were incorporated in the second incarnation of the Overseas Highway, the road that exists today, over the next several years.

Another major contributor to the development of South Florida was Addison Mizner (1872-1933), who in the years just after WWI would become a favorite architect of rich vacationers and homeowners in Palm Beach and especially Boca Raton, where Mizner developed most of his Mediterranean style, pastel-colored mansions. Mizner was wiped out in the land bust of 1926.

Spanish-American War

The USA showed the world it was a power to be reckoned with during the 10-week-long Spanish-American War in 1898. As Cuba struggled for independence from

Spanish rule, and as reports drifted back of Cuban farmers being gathered into prison camps, newspapers like William Randolph Hearst's *New York Journal* began a propaganda campaign of 'yellow journalism' which successfully riled the American public. The stories ostensibly supported the 'humanitarian annexation' of Cuba, which perhaps not coincidentally would have been a culmination of the USA's Manifest Destiny – a doctrine that held that the USA was destined to control all North America – and a happy windfall to US businessmen.

President William McKinley resisted intervention, but when the battleship *Maine* was destroyed in Havana harbor, McKinley declared war on Spain; Congress ratified the declaration on April 25.

The main fighting took place in two theaters: the South Pacific and Cuba. After handy victories in Manila and Guam, US army and volunteer regiments landed in Cuba in late June, including the Rough Riders (who actually had to leave all their horses in Florida), led by Leonard Wood and Theodore Roosevelt. Bully.

As the military buildup began, many Florida towns – especially Tampa, Key West and Miami but also northern cities like Jacksonville – saw land-office business as people poured into the region and lined up to receive plots of homesteading land. As reports filtered back to the Northern states about conditions in Florida, it was gaining a reputation as a paradisiacal location affordable to all: tourists came in droves. South Florida experienced something of a mini-boom as a result of the military buildup and of becoming the most important staging area for the fight in Cuba.

The Spanish-American War itself was something of a letdown to war buffs; the Spanish surrendered on July 17.

Social Conditions

Since the Civil War, tensions between black and white settlers in Florida had remained high, and blacks probably rightly felt nervous when federal troops withdrew from Florida. As the developers began to move into Florida, conditions for the poor grew

worse with railroad and land barons practically buying the state outright. Government was rife with corruption, land deals were questionable and social services were maintained at an appallingly low level.

But as farmers and workers began to organize, a distinct anti-developer mood began to slowly infiltrate the state's political system, and the organization and collective protests of farmers, blacks and women in conjunction with a strong populist movement resulted in the election to Governor of Napoleon Bonaparte Broward in 1905.

Elected as a populist, anti-developer/pro-little-guy candidate, Broward would actually follow through with many social programs, including child labor laws, an inspired education system, labor law reforms and new jobs. Unfortunately, his theories on how to create new jobs were the very cause of the destruction of the Everglades: it was he who initiated drainage and canals throughout the Everglades in a successful effort to expose mucklands necessary for growing sugar.

WWI & the Roaring '20s

Once again war would become a boon to Florida; by the time the USA entered WWI in 1917, Florida had again been built up with a large naval presence at Key West, Pensacola, Tampa and Jacksonville. By the time the war was over, Florida had thousands of new permanent residents. The WWI boom, especially in Miami, would continue and lead the state into the '20s with great momentum.

At the imposition of Prohibition (the ban on sale or use of alcohol in the USA), Florida became a smuggler's haven with lots of unguarded coastline, convenient proximity to Cuba and Puerto Rico, and an endless supply of imbibers not just on the beaches of Florida but in other states as well.

Miami especially never took much to Prohibition; Al Capone himself moved in to grab a piece of the action, and Miami Beach became one constant party, packing in the gamblers, drinkers and funsters.

The entire state was in the midst of an enormous boom the likes of which had never been seen in the USA on such a huge scale. Hundreds of thousands of people were migrating to Florida, and land prices soared. Railroads and roads were being built as if there were no tomorrow, and cities were expanding at staggering rates.

Land Bust

In a manner similar to the stock markets of the '20s, margin buying of land was the ticket in Florida, where shysters could buy land at incredibly small down payments and shuck it onto settlers at huge profits. With such buying and construction, transport was ever more important, and several disasters – among them a debilitating rail strike and a sunken supply ship in Miami harbor, blocking the entrance to the Miami River and keeping other boats from dropping off *their* loads – were straining the limits of existing communications.

But the end came in a flash: a major hurricane hit South Florida in late 1926, wiping out construction, killing 400 and injuring thousands. In the aftermath, the hordes of people who thought that they were getting the deal of a lifetime found the catch – deadly storms – and pulled out but quick, taking their money with them. Land prices plummeted, banks folded like books and as if to hammer the nails in the coffin, the area was hit by another devastating hurricane and several smaller storms a little more than a year later.

Great Depression

Florida businesses pretty much followed the national trend during the Great Depression after the stock market crash of 1929. As banks failed, businesses failed, and many of Florida's rich developers ran home with their tails between their legs. As Florida had already been in the midst of a state depression after the land bust, it was strongly affected by the Depression, and in need of more federal bail-outs than most other states.

Florida was a major supporter of Frank-

Cuban Revolutions

While most people peg the influx of Cubans to the rise of Castro in 1959, Cubans have been flocking to Miami – and Florida – for over a century. The first large wave of immigration was in 1868, when socialist-minded cigar workers fleeing the Ten Years' war made Key West sort of an 'enlightened masses tobacco combine'.

Those enlightened masses, educated about the struggle in Cuba as they were, began demanding more and more money and benefits at a time when the economy was in a downturn. Cigar maker Vicente Martínez Ybor practically single-handedly squashed Key West's cigar industry by moving his factory to Tampa and steaming in Cuban laborers from Havana.

The move to Miami began during the Spanish-American War, but took off after Cuban independence and really soared after regular aviation between Miami and Havana was established in the late 1920s.

From then until Castro's Revolution – despite intrigue and the murderous Batista regime – were the swinging days of the Cuban-American relationship. Gamblers and hot shots poured into Cuba on hourly flights from Miami, and wealthy Cubans poured right back at Miami to buy clothes and American products.

What ended this reign has played a key role in US attitudes towards Cuba and Cubans to this very day.

Most people agree that Fulgencio Batista, whose regime controlled Cuba for almost 30 years, was a horrible gangster who terrorized a nation. And at the time, it seemed the best hope of losing him was to back his adversaries, a coalition headed by Fidel Castro that had been trying for years to oust Batista.

In late 1958 President Eisenhower announced an arms embargo against the Batista government, which was interpreted by many to be tacit US support for Fidel Castro and

lin Delano Roosevelt. When elected president, Roosevelt made his way to Miami to thank South Florida for its support, and during that visit, in a speech at Bayfront Park, a would-be assassin took several shots at the president-elect (who wasn't hit).

In Roosevelt's first '100 Days' he called an emergency session of Congress, the result of which was the creation of dozens of government agencies that would have a profound effect on the state and the nation as a whole. As a part of Roosevelt's 'New Deal', the Works Progress Administration (WPA) and the Civilian Conservation Corps (CCC) were created. The CCC worked to restore state and national parks and the WPA sent armies of workers to construct buildings, roads, dams, trails and housing. Other federal programs included Social Security, which gives money to the elderly and infirm (memo to Republicans: if you don't like it, give yours back). It was the largest campaign of government-created jobs ever in the USA, and while critics at the time called it busy work, projects by both the WPA and CCC stand today, many as national landmarks.

WWII
But the most effective means of jump-starting the American economy was, again, military. After the Japanese attack on Pearl Harbor, Hawaii, on December 7, 1941, the USA began work on their war machine. But what set the area abuzz and ensured Florida's role in national security was U-Boat activity off the Florida coast. In early 1942, U-boats were sinking US freighters at an alarming rate.

Though it sounds cruel, a good war was just what the state needed. Almost overnight Florida was turned into one of the biggest war factories and training grounds in the Union. Almost every US pilot who flew in WWII trained in Florida; the Army's anti-U-Boat school was in Miami; Key West's naval base overflowed with sailors.

But the area was also the beneficiary of

his revolutionary coalition. Castro had made a formal promise to the coalition to hold free elections as soon as they took power.

Batista abdicated on January 1, 1959. There is some dispute as to just how forthcoming Castro was about his intentions, but over the next year and a half, Castro broke his promise of free elections, consolidated his power, and in a move that would set the tone of the next three decades, nationalized business – including major US-owned businesses – and property without compensation.

Fidel Castro, fomenting revolutionary fervor

The US responded by canceling its Cuban sugar quota, and Castro, pressed for cash, turned to the Great Soviet Market. In the ultimate thumb-nose to the USA, which was reaching the height of its Cold War with the Soviets, Castro had allied himself with Moscow. ∎

increased demand for agricultural products, and Florida's farmers were raking in the big bucks. During the war, Florida's citrus production was the highest in the nation.

1950s

And as the war ended, soldiers and sailors who trained here returned to the region and those with wartime jobs ended up settling. Once again, Florida was on the beginning of a boom initiated by war.

In the 1950s, Miami Beach had another boom, as it began to be known as the 'Cuba of America'; see the Miami history section for details on the gambling and the gangsters.

In 1954, Leroy Collins became the first southern Governor to declare racial segregation 'morally wrong'.

Orange and cotton growing was becoming huge business in northern Florida, and as the aerospace industry moved into Florida near the end of the '50s, an entire 'Space Coast' was created to support the high-fallutin' goals of the National Aeronautics & Space Administration (NASA) in their race to beat the Russkies into space – see the Space Coast chapter for a full history of the US space program.

Cuba & the Bay of Pigs

After the 1959 Cuban revolution, Miami and South Florida became flooded with anti-Castro immigrants, who, in gathering to arrange a counterrevolutionary (CR) force, managed to establish a permanent Cuban community in Miami.

A group of exiles formed the 2506th Brigade, sanctioned by the US Government, which provided help in the form of weapons and CIA training for the purpose of launching an attack on Cuba (memo to would-be Cuban dictators: enlist for your opponents the help of the CIA).

In April, 1961, the CRs launched an attack against the beaches at Playa de Giron: the Bay of Pigs. But warning somehow leaked to the Cubans – a *New York Times* correspondent says he heard about the impending attack weeks before it happened – and the pathetic, half-baked, poorly planned and badly executed attack was little more than an ambush.

And to add insult to injury, President Kennedy, when the magnitude of the botch-up became clear, refused to send in air cover or naval support in the name of 'plausible deniability'; the first wave of CRs was left on the beach with their cheese in the wind – no reinforcements or supplies arrived. The CRs were all captured or killed (though all prisoners were released by Cuba about three months later).

Kennedy vs Krushchev

Kennedy and the CIA both looked rather silly after the fiasco, and that is probably why Kennedy stood his ground so firmly during the event that brought the world to the brink of nuclear war: the Cuban Missile Crisis.

Smelling blood after the Bay of Pigs fiasco, the USSR's General Secretary Nikita Krushchev began secretly installing missile bases in Cuba. By some stroke of luck – or perhaps by accident – the CIA managed to take photographs of the proceedings, which were shown to Kennedy on October 16, 1962.

The Kennedy administration debated what to do about it, and for almost a week after Kennedy was shown the photos, the Soviet embassy denied the existence of the bases.

On October 22, Kennedy went on national television and announced that the USSR was installing missiles on Cuba, 90 miles south of Key West; that this was a direct threat to the safety and security of the country. He announced a naval 'quarantine' of Cuba (a nice euphemism for a naval blockade, which would have been an act of war) and further, that any attack on the USA from Cuba would be regarded as an attack by the USSR.

Tensions mounted and a flurry of letters passed between Washington and Moscow, beginning with 'Well, okay, we *do* have missiles but they're there as a deterrent not an offensive threat' and culminating in two offers from the Soviets to end the stalemate.

The first, dated October 26, agreed to

remove the missiles in exchange for a promise by the USA not to attack Cuba. The second, on October 27, tied the removal to the USA's removal of similar sites it had in Turkey.

Publicly, Kennedy responded to the first offer; it was announced that the USA would not invade Cuba, and the Soviets began removing their missiles. Several months later, and with markedly less fanfare, the US removed its missiles from Turkey.

Miami's Cuban population swelled as Cubans emigrated to the USA. A special immigration center was established to handle the overflow in Miami's Freedom Tower – the Ellis Island of the South.

In the mid-'60s, the 'freedom flights' running between Miami and Havana were bringing in huge numbers of Cuban refugees, and this was creating high tensions between blacks and Cubans.

A major development in the 1970s was the introduction to Florida of something that would change the face of the state's tourism market forever: Walt Disney World. Around this massive entertainment center and resort spurted hundreds of thousands of tourist-related jobs in service industries. Hangers-on and imitators also moved in.

Mariel Boatlift

In the late 1970s, as Florida's economy began to recover from the oil crisis and recession, Fidel pulled a fast one and opened the floodgates, allowing anyone who wanted to leave Cuba access to the docks at Mariel. Before the ink was dry on the proclamation, the largest flotilla ever launched for non-military purposes set sail (or paddle) in practically anything that would float to cover the 90 miles between Cuba and Florida. The Mariel Boatlift, as the largest of these would be called, brought 150,000 Cubans to Florida, including an estimated 25,000 prisoners and mental patients that Ol' Frisky Fidel had cleverly decided to foist off on the US. The resulting economic, logistical and infrastructural strain on South Florida only added to still-simmering racial tensions, which would explode on May 17, 1980 in

The 90-mile waterway between Cuba and Florida sees heavy refugee traffic.

Liberty City, a Miami neighborhood – see the Miami chapter for information on the Liberty City Riots.

Also in the late 1970s, Florida distinguished itself by becoming the first state to reinstate the death penalty, and Tampa became the first place where a Led Zeppelin concert turned into a major riot. Music, then, must have really irritated Florida judges, and one of them rang in the 1980s by declaring a 2 Live Crew album 'obscene' and banning its sale within the state.

1980s

In the 1980s, Florida was gaining recognition as an economic powerhouse both in banking and drug dealing – which despite an unsavory reputation happened to be a major force in the rejuvenation of South Florida. Jacksonville was becoming an insurance capitol, and tourism was playing an ever more important role statewide. Key West, rescued from bankruptcy after the Depression, was becoming an area as romantic to tourists as Paris, and terrorist activity targeting Americans abroad in the mid-'80s put Florida in the very enviable position of being America's holiday spot – 'nearby, easy to get to, no passports required and they talk good English like us'.

While technology began to boom throughout the country, the Space Coast and its support industries in the Central Florida corridor between the Kennedy Space Center and Orlando began to gain importance as simulation technology businesses set up shop. See the Orlando section and Space Coast chapter for more information.

'Cocaine,' Robin Williams once said, 'is God's way of telling us we're making too damn much money,' and if ever a nation was making too much money it was America in the '80s. All that blow had to come from somewhere, and Miami's excellent Caribbean location made it a major source of America's incoming drugs. As pink-clad detectives made the whole thing look sexy on *Miami Vice* (see the Miami chapter), South Florida was looking more and more like an armed camp. I-95 and US Hwy 1 were patrolled by officers from an alphabet soup of agencies, and were empowered to stop pretty much anyone they wanted to who fit 'drug runner profiles'. The Conch Republic was one form of public protest against this (see the Key West chapter), but more serious problems were developing in Miami and Ybor City, where drug use and displacement of the poor were becoming more and more of a problem.

By the late 1980s, Miami Beach had risen to international Fabulousness on a comet of big-name models and movie stars coming to the area to be 'seen', and the rest of South Florida was riding on its coattails.

But Florida entered the 1990s bumpily, with Hurricane Andrew - the most expensive storm ever to hit the USA – devastating South Florida in 1992 (see the Miami section). Coup and chaos in Haiti led to waves of refugees washing up on South Florida's shores, and upheaval in Cuba lead to several new waves of Cuban raft refugees as well. And Florida leapt to the national spotlight in the abortion fight when, in 1993, Dr David Gunn was shot dead by Paul Hill outside a Pensacola abortion clinic.

Haitian Coup

In late September 1991 the Haitian military led by Lieutenant General Raoul Cedras overthrew the government of constitutionally elected President Jean Bertrand Aristide. The US response was economic sanctions, to be removed only after the return of Aristide to power.

Under Cedras' leadership, Haitian armed forces, which at that time were given extreme legal and institutional autonomy, were responsible for law enforcement and 'public safety'. As human rights abuses – beatings, torture, executions and 'disappearances' – escalated, refugees began to flee to the relative (they thought) safety of the USA in anything that would float. Many refugees ended up in Little Haiti, and as many as possible were rounded up by INS for deportation. Signs posted throughout Miami urged people 'Don't Be a Snitch' by reporting Haitians you might see on the street to the police, but rather to point them in the direction of Little Haiti.

For the next three years, media images of Haitians being rounded up by the US Coast Guard permeated local media: in the first seven months of 1992 alone, the UN High Commissioner for Refugees (UNHCR) said that the US Coast Guard had intercepted and detained at Guantanamo Bay, Cuba, a total of 38,315 Haitians fleeing their country. Of those, only 11,617 were given the INS stamp of approval as 'potentially qualified for political asylum'.

As pressure mounted from Haitian groups in Miami, which pointed out the historical carte blanche given any Cuban who manages to wash up on US soil, the US Supreme Court upheld a detestable Bush-administration policy that allows the Coast Guard to return refugees it has intercepted on the high seas directly to their home country without the benefit of an asylum hearing. Which the Coast Guard immediately set to.

Through a series of maneuvers (including, some say, covert payment of a cool $1 million by the USA to Cedras) Aristide was returned to power. Cedras resigned, and was granted political amnesty. For the second time in a century, the US sent troops to Haiti to restore democracy.

Which allowed the Clinton Administration to say to the rest of the Haitians who were being held at Guantanamo Bay, in essence, to 'please go home now, you no longer have a claim of asylum as your country is again a model democracy.' As if to accentuate the divergent treatment of Haitians and Cubans, Clinton made that move the day after agreeing to allow some 20,000 Cubans at Guantanamo entry to the USA.

Cuban Affairs

With the fall of the Soviet Union in 1991 the USA's relationship with Cuba entered a new era. The loss of Soviet imports of fuel, and purchases of sugar and tobacco crippled the Cuban economy, and the USA began work on a *coup de grâce*: further isolation of Cuba from the international community which they expected would lead to Castro's downfall. The USA, which many now say precipitated the fall of the Soviet Union in a spending, not an arms, race, turned up the pressure on a broke Fidel Castro through a number of measures.

The funniest of these was Radio and TV Martí, a Reagan-era project that lasted through to the Clinton administration. In 1985 Martí began wasting about $50,000 a day on broadcasts of American 'cultural offerings' – *Days of Our Lives, Kate & Allie, Cheers* and *Lifestyles of the Rich & Famous* – between 3 and 6 am from a blimp hovering off the Keys. Yes, a blimp.

In some of the finest of Cold War justifications, Martí was considered to be a high priority to show US determination –

despite the fact that Cubans didn't know about it, didn't watch it, didn't have the equipment to watch it and even if they had, the Cuban government jammed the broadcasts anyway. *The Nation* magazine said that less than 1% of Cubans had seen Martí.

On a far more serious note, the US in the early 1990s put a stop to instant acceptance of Cuban refugees in an effort to keep the simmering hotheads in Fidel's court rather than on the streets of Miami. As anti-Castro demonstrators continually stepped up pressure, and as Cuba sank deeper into debt and more desperate for hard currency, the USA started its death watch, with pundits predicting the imminent fall of Castro.

February Shootdown

They'd be disappointed, at least up through late 1996, by a Castro that kept fighting back. But Castro may have made things far more difficult for himself by authorizing the shooting-down of two American planes in February, 1995, flown by pilots of Brothers to the Rescue.

Brothers to the Rescue is a Miami-based group of pilots that patrol the waters of the Caribbean looking for refugee rafters. Part of a group of rabid anti-Castro Miami-based Cubans who characterize their work as 'humanitarian aid', BTTR claims to have been responsible for the rescue of thousands of rafters and boat people. It

---

The Brothers, the CIA & the FBI?

Many people in Miami, and several newspaper and internet e-zine articles say that Brothers to the Rescue is certainly a CIA-backed operation. But a CIA spokesperson we spoke with (less spooky than you'd think) called such claims 'errant nonsense' and said that there was 'no truth whatsoever' in claims that CIA backs BTTR, though he went on to say cryptically that it was 'entirely possible' that there 'may have been some law enforcement connection' with the group and that we should maybe check with the FBI.

The FBI?

After a long tour through the FBI's infuriating phone system (with its EZ-listening hold music), a spokesperson said that the FBI doesn't engage in the support or non-support of any group, but then seemed to contradict that by saying that the FBI could not comment on whether they have offered any support to Brothers to the Rescue. Maybe yes maybe no.

Spook-backed or not, with rampant speculation in South Florida media and local scuttlebutt, BTTR has certainly found itself at the center of an international brouhaha of Ludlumesque proportions. ■

claims that rafters are shot at by Cuban patrol boats and helicopters.

After BTTR planes skirted in and out of Cuban airspace as part of a flotilla and airborne demonstration, they were fired upon and downed by Cuban Air Force planes. The US Government's outrage over the attack raised one of the biggest stinks since the Bay of Pigs.

The Helms-Burton Bill, which Clinton signed into US Law, increases sanctions against Cuba. It ended regular flights between Miami and Havana, and put the ixnay on many business deals that had been in the works between US and Cuban companies. But what has raised the ire of the international community – especially the EU and Canada – are the outrageous provisions in the law that give US citizens the right to sue for damages from foreign users of their former property that was confiscated by the Castro government after the 1959 revolution, and that bar foreigners with investments in Cuba from travel within the USA.

Essentially, the US has decided that it has the power to force other governments to go along with its own 'it's-my-ball-and-I'm-going-home' policy, and foreign governments are hopping mad about it.

Though the foreign governments are doing nothing to stop their citizens from traveling and doing business with Cuba, it is clear from any visitor to Cuba that the situation there is dire. Miami's Cuban population is watching with great interest the events that will unfold at the close of the century.

Crime against Tourists
Another thing that didn't exactly cause Florida's image to shine in the early '90s was a heavily publicized spree of foreign-tourist-related crimes in 1993. With several shootings and many robberies, the state was in a panic that it would lose its tourism market, which was fast becoming the state's most important industry. In May 1993, one of Great Britain's top tour companies quoted polls showing that Miami was perceived as the most dangerous desti-

nation in the world, followed by North Africa, Kenya and Turkey.

But the state bounced back, helped by heightened security, ever-brighter tourist attractions and the creation of a Tourist Police Force. Attacks against tourists have been substantially and considerably reduced.

Florida Today
Miami and Orlando are still the powerhouse tourism draws, but other cities – notably Key West, Fort Lauderdale, Tampa, St Petersburg, St Augustine and Pensacola – have been seeing more business than ever.

Theme parks account for much of the draw to regions outside the southeast: while Disney's still decidedly the king of the hill, tough competition from Universal Studios Florida, Sea World and Busch Gardens and smaller entries like Wet 'n' Wild and even Splendid China are packing them in. And more and more people are discovering just how accessible the state and national parks, like the Everglades, Ichetucknee, Blue Spring, Jonathan Dickinson and Hobe Sound, can be.

And while Florida's famed agriculture- and developer-friendly government still has a long way to go, the demand for more ecologically minded reforms have been given a shot in the arm by involvement from the federal government.

Some visitors are complaining that SoBe and Miami are getting overcrowded; that the boom is 'done'. And there may be some truth in that. But regions throughout the state are seeing renovation, renewal and a new lease on life.

GEOGRAPHY
Though some 'ban-*Catcher in the Rye*'-caliber school reformers have requested the shape be made less phallic on US school maps, it is safe to say that Florida has a shape very similar to what you'll see if you crook your left arm with your fist pointing to the right and make a thumbs-down sign. The Panhandle is called that because it's a handle-like strip of land jutting off to the northwest. The northern borders are

Alabama and Georgia, and the state's other borders are the Atlantic Ocean and the Gulf of Mexico on the east and west respectively.

The coasts are buttressed by natural barrier islands. The waterways between the barrier islands and the mainland were deepened and widened by the Army Corps of Engineers to create a sheltered inland route from Miami to Virginia: the Atlantic Intracoastal Waterway, one of the country's most important commercial and recreational waterways. A similar waterway, the Gulf Intracoastal Waterway, is found along the Gulf Coast.

Florida's terrain is mainly flat, with coastal lowlands, and slightly hilly in the center, though you won't find anything over 350 feet above sea level in Florida. The south-central portion of the state is all wetlands and reclaimed wetlands. As nature intended it, the sheet-flow ecosystem of water from the Kissimmee River fed Lake Okeechobee at the southeast center of the state, which then overflowed feeding sheets of fresh water to the Everglades. But nature was overruled in South Florida, and the Kissimmee was dammed, diked, canaled and diverted – see the Everglades chapter for more information.

Florida's a big state (though only the 22nd largest in the country): it's over 600 miles from Miami to Pensacola. Key West is closer to Havana than Miami, and the state capitol in Tallahassee is 239 miles from Tampa, which, by the way is almost 200 miles from St Augustine.

GEOLOGY

On the face of it, geologically speaking, Florida's not much to jump up and down about. It's essentially an enormous arched slab of porous limestone. But when the seas receded and exposed the Florida peninsula – recently enough that dinosaurs never made it here – the limestone caused some interesting things to happen.

First, the salt water that saturated the limestone was forced out by freshwater from rainfall. Decaying plant matter washed into the ground by rainfall created a carbonic acid, which ate away at the limestone, forming tunnels and caverns and eventually entire underground freshwater systems of rivers and streams.

These systems are aquifers, and while there are several, the entire system is the Florida Aquifer, the source of the state's fresh water supply.

Weaknesses and cracks in the limestone, combined with the pressure of the circulating water, result in springs, of which Florida has hundreds, if not thousands. And those same weaknesses are responsible for sinkholes, amusing when they're not on your property, which occur when the carbonic acid eats away at a section of limestone that's not thin enough to become a spring. When enough stone is dissolved, entire sections of ground simply . . . sink into, well, a hole. One of the best examples of a fascinating Florida sinkhole is the Devil's Millhopper just north of Gainesville.

CLIMATE

The area's warm weather may have been the only reason anyone would have dreamed of inhabiting the place at all.

Ideal conditions in the south of the state exist between December and May, when temperatures average between 59°F and

Florida Rain

There's a cats-and-dogs quality to Florida rain that'll be unfamiliar to anyone who hasn't spent time in the tropics. And it comes on quickly. In summer, rainstorms are preceded by inhuman rises in humidity, closely followed by fantastically ominous clouds which sweep in and reduce daylight to twilight in a matter of minutes. The rain – copious doses of fist-sized raindrops – has a ferocity that floods streets in minutes and causes drivers to pull over and cower; the thunder sounds as if the end of the world is upon us.

But the rains rarely last very long, and the weather – and the raindrops – are so warm that they can actually be refreshing. Afterwards, cool breezes make it all seem very much worth it. ∎

75° (15°C to 24°), and average rainfall is a scant 2.01 inches. But in the north, the winter months are cool and, in recent years, downright cold – not just Florida cold: northern Florida had several nights in 1996 with temperatures going into the teens °F.

Summer everywhere in the state can be summed up as very hot and humid with thunderstorms at 3 pm. June is the rainiest month with an average of 9.33 inches, and temperatures average between 75°F and 88° (24°C to 31°). August is probably the hottest month, with average temperatures between 77°F and 89° (25°C to 31°), but with all these temperatures you have to take into account the heat index, a product of heat and humidity. If feels a *lot* hotter than 89° when there's 90% humidity!

See the Climate Charts appendix for more detailed information.

ECOLOGY & ENVIRONMENT

While this will sound grim, keep in mind that things are improving and that government is now taking an active role in limiting and repairing damage and managing land use.

The *Encyclopedia of Florida* says that Florida's state motto, *In God We Trust*, was 'evidently taken from the inscription on American currency.' In that spirit lies the fundamental philosophy behind Florida's environmental and ecological policies. the destruction of vast tracts of Florida's natural balance came as a direct result of the government's encouragement.

From the mid-1800s, when developers 'discovered' the paradise of South Florida, the state government supported irresponsible large-scale agricultural projects and real estate development. The destruction of the Everglades began in an effort to create jobs, by controlling the flow of water from Lake Okeechobee and draining significant portions of wetlands to expose mucklands perfect for sugar farming.

While the Florida Aquifer has the ability to supply unbelievably large quantities of water, ground contamination from sources like pesticides, heavy metals, sewage and gasoline (that leaks from underground storage tanks) has drastically affected the quality of Florida's drinking water in many areas of the state. Similarly, Florida's rivers, streams and lakes have been polluted to the extent that largemouth bass is inedible from several lakes. Mercury levels in the Everglades are startlingly high.

While beaches are relatively clean, the coast has seen high levels of bacteria at certain times. Health authorities monitor conditions and are rather good about letting people know when limits are exceeded.

FLORA
Mangroves

Mangroves are halophytes, trees that grow in saltwater conditions. Located where the land meets the sea, they stabilize the shoreline and reduce inland flooding during storms, simply because they're there and therefore less sand and dirt can be washed away. Silt builds up, forming more and more land; eventually the mangroves are strangled by the very land they've created and die. Another special quality of mangroves is that their seeds sprout while still on the tree.

There are about 50 different species of mangroves around the world, and three of them can be found in Florida. The red mangrove *(Rhizophora mangle)*, sometimes also called walking tree, drops salt-filtering aerial prop roots, which make the plant look as if it's propped up on stilts. Their leaves are deep green on top and lighter green underneath.

The black mangrove *(Avicennia germinans)* has *pneumatophores* or 'breathing roots', which grow upwards and take oxygen into the system. This kind of mangrove excretes salt through its leaves, which are dark green with white salt crystals on them.

The white mangrove *(Laguncularia racemosa)* does not have a root system like the other two, and looks more like a run-of-the-mill tree. Its leaves are light green; they excrete salt through glands at their base.

Hammocks

Hammocks are tracts of forested land that rise above adjacent marshes, pineland, prairie or swamp. In South Florida they're often tropical hardwood forests, usually very dense, filled with shade-loving and air plants. Common plant species include gumbo-limbo (Bursera simaruba), pigeon plum (Cocoloba diversifolia), soldierwood (Colubrina elliptica), crabwood (Psychotria undata) and white stopper (Eugenia axillaris), which is the bush that produces that skunk aroma you keep smelling all over South Florida and drives you crazy because you can't understand where it comes from.

Sea Oats

Sea oats (Uniola Paniculata) get their name from the large plumes that they produce, but they're far from oats. They're protected vegetation in Florida because they trap wind-blown sand and thereby stabilize sand dunes. It's illegal to interfere with them in any way.

Sea Grapes

Sea grapes (Coccoloba uvifera) are coastal landscape plants native to Florida that stand up to wind and salt water. They have large, round leaves, and produce a small, purple edible fruit that braver people eat or make into jelly.

Pine Flatwoods

Pine flatwoods usually don't have very rich soil, and are home to mainly slash pine and saw palmetto, though sometimes cabbage palms (see below) grow in these as well.

Spanish Moss

The most surprising thing about Spanish moss (Tillandsia usneoides), the ubiquitous, armpit-hair-like frilly stuff that's attached to trees in the northern areas of the state, isn't what it isn't – a moss – but rather what it is: an air plant that's a member of the pineapple family. That's right, pineapple. Its seeds have tiny, little parachutes which carry them from tree to tree. In some areas of the state, notably Tallahassee and on St George Island, Spanish moss can get so thick and tangled that it jumps from treetop to treetop across roads, creating a 'canopy'.

Sawgrass

Sawgrass is the main vegetation in the Everglades, but grows wherever it's wet. It's rough, firm, stiff and green; fine teeth-like edges give it its name.

Strangler Figs

The rope-like roots that you'll see growing on cypress trees or cabbage palms are the strangler fig (Ficus aurea), whose seeds start growing as an air plant. As the strangler fig grows, it sends off roots, which wrap around the trunk of its host, eventually literally strangling and killing it.

Palms

There are many species of palms in Florida, which are tropical evergreen trees and shrubs with branchless trunks and fanned leaves in clumps at their top. The most common palms you'll run into are:

Cabbage palm (Sabal palmetto)
Tall and sometimes bent at fantastic angles, as on Lincoln Road Mall in Miami Beach.

Coconut palm (Cocos nucifera)
The classic desert-island fantasy, tall and gracefully curved, these do indeed produce coconuts. It's rare to find mature fruit in Florida, as landscapers hack them off as soon as they're large enough to hurt someone if the fruit should fall during a windstorm. If you do find one large enough (it's about the size and shape of an American football), hack off the top with a machete and use a straw to drink the juice. You'll sometimes see this offered from carts on the street in Miami's Little Havana.

King palm (Archontophoenix alexandrae)
Native to Australia, this is the knobby-trunked beast that can reach heights of up to 75 feet.

Royal palm (Roystonea regia)
Native to South Florida and Cuba, these enormous and very straight-growing palms have a white trunk and very long foliage. They line Palm Beach's Royal Palm Way.

Sago palm (Cycas revoluta)
Short trunked with leaves fanning out like a Japanese fan, these look as if they're playing a game of cards.

Yellow butterfly/areca palm (Chrysalidocarpus lutescens) Native to Asia, these grow in clumps of several plants which look as if they're racing their siblings to attain maximum height. Curved trunks, lush leaves.

Flowering Plants

Some flowering plants and trees which you're most likely to encounter in Florida (not necessarily native ones) include:

Allamanda – White or pink, trumpet-shaped flower; toxic.

Bougainvillea – A vine with clusters of red, pink, white or orange flowers.

Cassia – Also called golden or pink shower tree, depending on the color of the flowers, which appear before the leaves of the tree do.

Cup of Gold – An eight- to 10-inch-diameter flower, opens white and turns bright yellow; toxic.

Frangipani – An evergreen shrub with delicious smelling white, pink or red flowers, instantly recognizable to anyone who's ever seen a movie or TV show featuring somebody getting off a plane in Hawaii.

Hibiscus – A big, delicate, trumpet-shaped flower in red, white, yellow or pink, each flower blooms only for one day.

Ixora – Red, sometimes white clusters of starlike flowers, an evergreen perennial.

Jacaranda – Purplish-blue bell-shaped flowers on a tree with fernlike leaves, one of our absolute favorites.

Oleander – Pink, white, red or yellow flowers, a very toxic shrub.

Royal Poinciana – Also called flame tree with reddish-orange flowers, also a favorite of ours.

Spider lily – Actually you'll see many different kinds of lilies, we just particularly like the smell of this one, it's white and spider-like and toxic.

Fruit Trees

Throughout Florida you'll run into orange, grapefruit, lemon, lime and tangerine groves – see Economy below. And when you wonder why all the fruit you see in Publix and Winn Dixie sucks, it's because the good stuff is sent up north! There are also wild banana, mango and papaya trees almost everywhere you go. Most people are a little touchy about strangers walking up to their trees and snatching fruit, so ask first.

FAUNA
Crocodolians

Crocodilians are the world's largest living reptiles, and two species are native to the USA: the American alligator (*Alligator*

Mississippiensis) and the American crocodile (*Crocodylus acutus*). Crocodiles are very rare in Florida, so if you see a crocodilian here it's probably an alligator. This can be considered a good thing by visitors: crocs are the more aggressive of the two.

Alligators The name derives from the Spanish *el lagarto*, the lizard. They are carnivorous; hatchlings eat insects, frogs, small fish, snails and the like. As they grow, they move on to bigger game, but they're never above small snacks like a cricket or grasshopper. Alligators' jaws close on reflex: when open (the muscles to open their mouths are far weaker than those that close them), their closing mechanisms are triggered by anything touching the inside of their mouths.

When that something is edible, the alligator clamps down upon it, raises its head and gulps – swallowing prey small enough in one gulp, and crushing and tearing larger prey repeatedly until swallowable. Stories of alligators dragging prey underwater to drown it are hooey.

Appearance Alligators indeed look like long and scary lizards. Males grow to between nine and 12 feet, females six to eight feet; the largest found in Florida was a terrifying 17½ feet. Alligators generally live to an age of 30 to 35 years in the wild, longer when raised in captivity.

Young alligators are black with bright stripes and blotches of yellow on their backs, and cream-colored bellies. As they grow older they lose the stripes, but the stomach remains light-colored. It's said that Indians believed rubbing a gator's stomach would make it fall asleep – volunteers?

Alligators have a broad snout – the most obvious difference between alligators and crocodiles, which have narrow ones – and a socket in the upper jaw hides their fourth tooth, which is visible on crocs. There's nothing external to distinguish male and female alligators to the casual observer.

Alligators have large corneas, which enhance their night vision; they can see underwater, too: transparent, protective membranes cover their eyes when submerged.

Habitat Alligators are usually (but not exclusively) found in fresh water – shallow lakes, marshes, swamps, rivers, creeks, ponds and man-made canals. American alligators are found primarily in Louisiana, Florida and southern Georgia. They're a common sight sunning themselves along Florida riverbanks, and, more rarely, you could catch a glimpse of the lazy reptiles swimming across rivers and streams.

Gators are warm-weather fans, and will rarely feed when the temperature dips below 68°F; their metabolism slows considerably in cold weather. But gators are cold-blooded and can die when the temperature is over 100°F. To cool themselves, alligators sit on riverbanks or in the shade with their mouths wide open, which dissipates heat.

In the Everglades, where deep, open water is limited, females live in ponds, venturing into open areas for breeding. Males prowl, and during mating season make house calls on many ponds searching for female companionship. Nesting occurs in June and July, hatching in August.

In the winter dry season, alligators become a crucial factor in the survival of many species by digging 'gator holes' – artificial ponds. They dig with their mouth and legs, sweeping out mud and vegetation with lashes of their tails. As the hole fills with water, the gators keep it free of vegetation with further tail-lashing housekeeping. When the dry season comes, gator holes are often the only source of fresh water around for many other animals, and many come to hang out. Rent, however, can be expensive: some of the visitors become gator dinner.

Threats to Alligators While alligator eggs and infants are eaten by raccoons, otters and sometimes even other alligators, generally speaking humankind is alligators' only natural enemy. Formerly abundant in the wild in Florida, hunting and the draining of wetlands killed an estimated 10 million

from the late-19th century until the Mason-Smith Act, which banned the sale of endangered species, was passed in 1969. Alligators had been considered endangered since the mid-1940s. Thanks to protection, the alligator population has recovered to

Alligator Attacks

Generally speaking, alligators don't pose a threat to humans, and they attack from hunger, not maliciousness. But certain activities will cause alligators to become aggressive.

The most common mistake people make is feeding alligators, which is about as stupid as climbing a zoo fence to pet a cute saber-toothed tiger. When humans feed alligators, the gators naturally begin to associate humans with food – and if you're not holding out a cheeseburger, an alligator used to being fed by people might then consider making a snack of your arm. It is illegal in Florida to feed alligators.

Alligators – males and females – are also very protective of their young, and will descend upon any threat to any young alligator, not just their own, with great vigor. Acts seen as threatening can be as inadvertent as coming between a parent and child, say, in a canoe. The chief warning that you've behaved offensively is a loud hissing sound – a call for assistance, answered by other gators with as much enthusiasm as cops to an 'officer down' radio call. Get away as fast as possible and don't look back until you're safe – in a bar. ■

KIM GRANT

such an extent that it was re-classified as 'threatened' in 1985. It is still illegal to hunt or molest alligators in the wild, and strict penalties apply to violators.

Other threats to alligators include cars and loss of habitat.

Crocodiles The crocodile is classified as an endangered species. While there have never been as many crocs as alligators in Florida, there are only an estimated 400 to 500 left and in the wild, and their numbers are not substantially increasing.

Crocodiles are more aggressive than alligators, and will attack humans with less provocation. They can be smaller than alligators, but range in size from three to 15 feet; again, males are larger than females. Crocodiles nest on marl banks, porous sand or shell beaches.

American crocodiles prefer coastal, brackish and salt water habitats (but they can live in fresh water), their snouts are more tapered and triangular than those of alligators and their fourth tooth is exposed. Their bodies are grayish-green, with a light-colored underside; young crocs have dark bands on their back and tail.

Adult crocodiles feed at night in the water. They eat fish, crabs, birds, turtles, snakes and small mammals. In daytime they rest in creeks or in dens that they build within vegetation.

Nests – which you really don't want to approach, okay? – are found near deep water. Eggs are laid in April and May, and after hatching in July and August, mothers carry their newborns to the water in their mouths.

As with alligators, humans are their only natural enemies, though smaller crocs fall victim to the same attacks as smaller alligators.

Turtles

Florida turtles, both sea and land, are either threatened or endangered species, protected by state and federal law. The (relatively) most common sea turtle found in Florida is the loggerhead sea turtle (*Caretta caretta*) (threatened). Also seen, but far more rarely, are the green sea turtle (*Chelonia midas*) and, even more rarely, leatherbacks (*Dermochelys coriacea*), the largest of the sea turtles. Both the green sea and leatherback turtle are endangered. Disturbing turtle nests or possession of live or dead turtles can result in fines or imprisonment.

Nesting Florida's beaches are a perfect nesting ground for sea turtles. Nesting occurs from May to September.

Turtles swim ashore at night, preferably onto a wide beach, and pull themselves forward using their foreflippers to find a suitable (the drier the better) area for nesting. They hollow a pit with their front flippers, which helps them settle into the sand, and then dig a cylindrical cavity of about 20 inches with their rear flippers.

The turtle raises its hind flippers and releases two to three eggs at a time; she'll lay about 100 in all, each about the size of a ping pong ball. The eggs have a leathery shell, which ensures that they don't break when they hit the sand. The turtle covers the eggs with sand, using her front flippers, and returns to the water. Green sea and leatherbacks return after about two weeks, but loggerheads never return to the nest.

The eggs fall victim to raccoons and other small animals that dig them up for food. Surviving to hatching is really a matter of luck, and only one in 10,000 turtles will reach maturity.

Hatching Hatching occurs after about 60 days. Baby turtles orient themselves by moonlight to find the water, and here is yet another instance of humankind's development leading to tragedy for nature: turtle hatchlings are frequently disoriented by the lights from the condominiums and hotels that line the beaches, and often walk off in the wrong direction. Volunteers in Turtle Watch programs throughout the state (see especially the John D MacArthur State Park section in the Southeast Florida chapter and the Canaveral National Seashore section in the Space Coast chapter) stand by at hatching time and try to point the turtles in the right directions, employing any method they can – including flashlights and search lights – to get them into the sea.

Manatees

The Florida manatee *(Trichechus manatus)* is a subspecies of the West Indian manatee. Also called the sea cow, the Florida manatee is another endangered species. Once abundant throughout the tropical and subtropical Caribbean waters, today there are only between 1500 and 2200 left in the wild.

Manatees have large, plump, grayish-brown bodies with two small forelimbs and a tail shaped like a beaver's. They have a large, flexible upper lip that's covered with small whiskers. Manatees range in size from about nine to 12 feet, and weigh between 1000 to 2500 pounds.

They are herbivores, and consume 10 to 15% of their body weight daily. After 13 months of pregnancy they give birth to only one calf – every two to five years. They have no natural enemies except man.

Dolphins

The most common dolphin species in Florida is the bottle-nosed dolphin *(Tursiops truncatus)*, which isn't as shy as a common dolphin. It's very easy to see them throughout Florida, even in Biscayne Bay! If you're canoeing or kayaking in the Everglades and notice playful critters leaping out of the water alongside your boat, you may have run into a bottle-nosed, or into a porpoise – look for the long snout (bottle-nosed) or no snout (porpoise).

To identify individual bottle-nosed dolphins, look at their dorsal fin – when dolphins fight (and they do, so get those Flipper images out of your head) they take chunks out of their fins; every dorsal fin is shaped differently.

Florida Panthers

The beautiful Florida panther *(Felis concolor coryi)* has been on the endangered species list since 1973. Only about 30 to 50 remain in the wild. The reasons for their decline are hunting, habitat loss and cars and trucks. Because they're so rare, in-breeding has lead to genetic defects.

In 1982 they became the official mammal of Florida. Panthers are large, light-brown, sleek and very elegant cats. They're solitary animals that grow to about seven feet long, four feet high and weigh up to 150 pounds. They feed on deer, hogs, raccoons and sometimes even alligators.

Three kittens is an average litter; the gestation period is about three months.

The few that are left are found primarily in South Florida, in the Everglades and Big Cypress parks. Sadly, the only opportunity most visitors will have to see one is in a zoo, or dead on a roadside.

Birds

Pelicans are large brown birds that live to an average age of about 30 years. They weigh five to eight pounds, and eat about half of their body weight in fish a day. They're also positively prehistoric looking, resembling pterodactyls, and are hilarious, especially when they've grabbed a fish and are carrying it around in the sack beneath their chins.

There are several types of herons in Florida, long-necked wading birds who fold their necks over their backs in flight. Throughout the state you'll see snowy egrets and great white herons, along with ibis, and the pink and orange roseate spoonbill. You'll only see pink flamingoes in a zoo.

Our national symbol, bald eagles are an endangered species; there are only about 600 pairs of them left in Florida. Adults have a white head and tail, the body is dark and the eyes, bill and legs are yellow. They grow to about three feet high and can reach a wingspan of eight feet. They're visible in several Atlantic coast state parks, but you'll have to wait around for a while.

Wood storks, large wading birds with a dark featherless head, a stout bill, and a five-foot wing span, have been classified as endangered since 1985, victims of wetlands draining.

Coral Reef

Florida's coral reef is the largest in North America and the third largest in the world.

Bubba: Manatees' Biggest Threat

Manatees are shy and utterly peaceful mammals, and humankind is their only natural threat. Pollution is a problem, but their biggest killers are boaters, and of those, the worst offenders are pleasure boaters. Manatees seek warm, shallow water, and feed on vegetation. Unfortunately for them, South Florida is surrounded by just such an environment, along with one of the highest concentrations of pleasure boats in the world.

Despite pleas from environmental groups, wildlife advocates and the local, state and federal governments which have declared many areas Manatee Zones, some pleasure boaters routinely exceed speed limits and ignore simple practices that would help protect the species.

After grabbing a bite, manatees float up for air, and often float just beneath the surface chewing and hanging around. When speedboats zoom through the area, manatees are hit by the hulls and either knocked away or pushed under the boat, whose propeller then gashes the mammal repeatedly as the boat passes overhead. Few manatees get through life without propeller scars, which leave slices in their bodies similar to the diagonal slices on a loaf of French bread.

And yet some boaters don't see this as a problem. They consider manatees to be stupid ('cause so many git kilt') and, if you can believe this, a cause of reduced property values. 'Guy moves into a $4 million house down in the Grove,' said one reprehensible boater named Norm, who runs a water taxi service in Miami, 'and he wants to take his boat up to Miami to eat at Hard Rock. Then you say he can only go 5 mph to save a manatee? He'll move somewhere else.'

There are several organizations throughout the state that rescue and rehabilitate injured manatees, but they're fighting what would appear to be a losing battle. The two largest are Sea-World in Orlando and Seaquarium in Miami. See the Central Florida and Miami chapters for more information. ■

Corals belong to the Cnidarias family; they look like plants but they're actually animals. Individual members of coral (polyps) attach themselves to reefs and form a coral colony by producing calcium carbonate. The sea fans and whips found here – the ones that make it all seem like plant life – are unique to coral reefs in this area.

Coral reefs are to the underwater world what sea oats (see later) are to sand dunes: their rigidity catches sand and protects the shoreline from erosion by violent seas or storms. Coral reefs have an ecological diversity equal to, if not greater than, an entire tropical rainforest, and are home to thousands of varieties of plant and animal life, many with symbiotic relationships.

To exist, coral reefs require very stable warm temperatures and pure water, conditions threatened on several fronts. Storms and radical temperature shifts have affected the area. The purity of the water may have been threatened by a decline in freshwater in Florida Bay, a result of diverting water from the Everglades. In an effort to rebalance the salinity in Florida Bay, 'fresh' – that is, non-saline – water was pumped into the bay. But that water was full of agricultural runoff, including phosphates and nitrates – which disturbed the area's ecological balance.

All this, combined with humankind's meddling – boaters carelessly dropping anchor or running aground on coral, swimmers, divers and snorkelers standing on it or taking pieces of it, fishing and overfishing, and 'nutrient' – that's sewage to you and me – being pumped into South Florida water from the Florida Keys (where the sewage is only partially treated before being pumped directly into the ocean) – is killing the coral in the Keys. It has already long since died in areas to the north.

GOVERNMENT

With the exception of its long and proud history of open and seemingly encouraged graft, corruption and conflict of interest dating to Spanish explorers and pirates of all nationalities, the Florida state government is a miniature replica of the US federal government. (The US government at least has the decency to attempt to hush up such activities.) The US legislature is made up of the bicameral Congress – the Senate and the House of Representatives. The Senate has two senators from each of the 50 states, while the 435-member House has one or more members from each state, depending on the state's population. Florida, the fourth-most-populous state in the USA, has 23 representatives.

The US judicial branch is headed by the Supreme Court, which consists of nine justices who are appointed for life by the Pres-

---

The Florida Lottery

Florida has no state income tax and relies heavily on tourists (who pay a hotel tax), consumers (who pay state sales tax) and lottery players to support itself. The Florida Lottery is an unbelievably crafty dodge that brings in hundreds of millions of dollars a year to the state by promising – and sometimes even delivering – huge payoffs. While we think lotteries unconscionably suck money from the poor, the Florida Lottery is too big to ignore.

All lottery games are variations of the centuries-old numbers racket, in which the player picks numbers and hopes to match them to those chosen at random (at least in official games) on live television by large-breasted women supervised by hulking thugs. Buy tickets at supermarkets, liquor stores and even in video stores.

Some games include:

Lotto Choose six from 48 numbers
The weekly Lotto drawing has a minimum payoff of $7 million – and if no one wins it the pot is increased weekly until someone does.
Fantasy 5 Pick five from 26 numbers
Monday to Friday, payoffs start at $20,000.
Scratching Games Laminated cards you scratch to see if you've won. Prizes range from another ticket to a billion gezillion dollars. Win for Life is a scratch-off game which pays off winners at the rate of $1000 a week for the rest of their lives. ■

---

ident and approved by the Senate. The executive branch consists of the President, elected to four-year terms, the 14-member Cabinet and various assistants.

The Florida legislature is also a bicameral body made up of a House of Representatives and a Senate. Bills are introduced by representatives, and go through several sub-committees before being argued and amended on the floor of the House, which then passes it on to the Senate, which sends it through several subcommittees, and argues and amends it further. They're then sent back to the House for even *further* amendment, and, finally, to the Governor, who can sign it into law or veto it. About half of all bills die in the process.

The capital is in Tallahassee, in the northwest central section of the state, a geographical compromise reached when Florida had two capitals, St Augustine and Pensacola.

ECONOMY

Florida's economy relies heavily on tourism, its most lucrative and important business. But Miami's status as gateway to Latin America has also made it a powerhouse in international business: over 400 multinational companies have operations in Miami, and 150 have their Latin American headquarters here, including AT&T, Sony, Toshiba, Apple, American Airlines, UPS, Eastman Kodak and Texaco.

Miami customs processes 40% of all US exports to Latin America and the Caribbean. The city is also establishing itself as an international banking center: over 100 international banks call it home.

Other important economic activities in the state include sugar production; the $8 billion-a-year citrus industry which produces much of the country's frozen concentrated orange juice, bottled juice, grapefruit sections and citrus salad; electronics, programming and simulation technology, space exploration and space-related industry.

Minerals are important to Florida's economy as well. In fact, Florida mines about a quarter of the world's phosphate. Other minerals include limestone, peat, zircon, dolomite and sulfur. Oil and gas exploration continues in the Big Cypress National Preserve, but drilling is heavily restricted if not impossible. But there is oil and gas drilling in about 20 fields in Florida.

POPULATION & PEOPLE

The latest figures estimate Florida's population is just under 14 million, up from 11.9 million in 1990 and 9.5 million in 1980.

An astounding 45.1% of the population of Miami is foreign born: Cubans are the largest group, followed by Canadians, Haitians, Germans and Jamaicans.

Most of the population in the state is concentrated in coastal cities, and the largest of those are in the south: more than a quarter of the state's population lives south of Alligator Alley (Hwy 84/I-75).

There are two federally recognized Indian tribes in Florida with reservations; the Seminole Tribe of Florida (☎ 954-966-6300), with reservations in Hollywood, Big Cypress National Preserve and Brighton, and the Miccosukee Tribe (☎ 305-223-8388), with a reservation on the Tamiami Trail. The 1990 census showed that there were about 36,000 Native Americans living in the state of Florida. These also include Florida Creek Indians, in the Panhandle, descendants of Creeks from Alabama and Georgia.

Gambling, usually bingo, is held on Indian reservations (the Miccosukee have a bingo hall along the Tamiami Trail), and cultural celebrations are held throughout the state throughout the year. These, along with souvenir shops and airboat-ride franchises and the reprehensible alligator wrestling shows at the Miccosukee Cultural Center are, sadly, the only contact travelers normally make with Florida's Indians.

EDUCATION

Florida's public grade schools and Florida's students fall short of the national average in many areas, notably in Scholastic Aptitude Tests (SATs), the criterion for college and university admissions in the USA, and in the level of students that drop out before graduation. That's not surprising: Florida spends less than almost any other state on its education system, though they spend more than any other state on prison construction. As one local said, 'you can't blame the state for that; they're executing prisoners as quickly as they can!'

The US education system places children in classes (grades) based on age and performance from first to 12th grade. Generally speaking, normally progressing pupils are placed in a grade number five less than their age: 1st grade begins at age six, 12th grade at age 17, etc.

Florida has several state and private universities; the major players are the University of Florida in Gainesville, University of Miami, Florida International University in Miami and Florida State University in Tallahassee.

ARTS

Much of the state's arts – with the exception of local crafts, which can be found all over – emanate from South Florida, the vast majority from Miami. Over the past decade, Miami's gentrification and redevelopment have resulted in an explosion of artistic and cultural activity, and it's coming from all demographic sectors. Many artists who were formerly based in other areas of the country, notably the northeast, headed down there to take advantage of lower real estate prices and the increase in quirky and affluent visitors.

The influx of foreigners to the area has resulted in a boom in Caribbean and South American art as well.

Literature

While inroads are being made in poetry and experimental fiction, the Miami literature scene remains primarily a hotbed of mystery, scandal and detective novels. But no list of Florida writers would be complete without mention of Florida's best known: Ernest Hemingway, Marjorie Kinnan Rawlings and Zora Neale Hurston.

Rawlings' books contain beautiful descriptions of rural Florida life. She's best known for *The Yearling*, the story of Jodie Baxter's love for a fawn that alienates the boy from his family, but Rawlings is also author of books including *Cross Creek*, which describes her home in a town near Gainesville, and *Jacob's Ladder*.

Ernest Hemingway, known as much – in Florida, anyway – for his drinking in Key West bars as for his distinctive style and riveting tales of moral dilemmas, lived in that city during one of his most fertile periods. It was there that he completed many of his best loved works, including *A*

Farewell to Arms. Key West is rife with Hemingway-o-belia; see the Florida Keys chapter for more information.

Author of seven books, Zora Neale Hurston (1903-60) is best known for *Their Eyes Were Watching God*, her 1937 novel about an independent black woman in rural Florida. Hurston, born in Eatonville, also compiled Southern black folklore. See the Central Florida chapter for more info.

Poetry Of the emerging poets, most notable are Jefferey Knapp and Adrian Castro (mainly spoken word performances), Campbell McGrath (*American Noise* and *Capitalism*), Michael Hettich (*Small Boat* and *Immaculate Bright Rooms*), John Balaban (*Blue Mountain* and *Words for My Daughter . . .*) and Ricardo Pau-Llosa (*Cuba*).

Suspense/Thriller South Florida has over a dozen major suspense/thriller writers, and more are coming up every day. The heavy hitters include Carl Hiassen whose books (*Stormy Weather, Skin Tight, Native Tongue* and *Strip Tease*) offer snarling satires of South Florida and especially its tourists and developers; Pulitzer Prize-winning *Miami Herald* columnist Edna Buchanan (*Miami, It's Murder, Suitable for Framing, Nobody Lives Forever*), Paul Levine, whose attorney Jake Lassiter and ex-coroner-sidekick traipse through intricate psychological suspense in books like *Mortal Sin, To Speak for the Dead* and *Night Vision*; Les Standiford, whose eco-thriller *Spill* is in the process of being made into a movie, and whose other novels star building contractor John Deal in *Deal to Die For, Done Deal* and new *Book Deal*; and the quintessential grizzled Miami author Charles Willeford, best known for *Miami Blues* and author of almost two dozen other titles including *The Way We Die Now* and *Sideswipe*.

James W Hall's Florida Keys-based mysteries include *Mean Hightide, Beginning Algebra, Buzz Cut* and *Hard Aground*; and surprise, surprise, even Jimmy 'Margaritaville' Buffet has gotten into the act, with novels including *Jolly Man, Tales from*

Margaritaville, and the boring *Where is Joe Merchant?* Dan Wakefield is another well-known South Florida writer, author of books including *Going All the Way* and *Starting Over* in addition to the nonfiction *New York in the '50s*.

Never to be forgotten, of course, is Elmore Leonard, author of dozens of books including *Swag, The Moonshine War, Get Shorty, Gold Coast, The Switch* and *Maximum Bob*.

Les Standiford is also the director of Florida International University's highly regarded creative writing program, which has spawned several new literary up-and-comers, notably Vicky Hendricks (whose *Miami Purity* was her Master's thesis) and Barbara Parker, author of *Suspicion of Innocence* starring Miami lawyer Gail Connor. The university publishes *Gulf Stream*, a national magazine of poetry and literature.

Humor Also incredibly well known is Dave Barry, the humorist whose columns are syndicated throughout the world. He's the author of books including *Dave Barry Is Not Making This Up, Dave Barry Turns 40, Dave Barry's Only Travel Guide You'll Ever Need* and *Dave Barry's Greatest Hits*.

Music & Theater
While classical music has a local hero in the innovative New World Symphony, and some local bands are gaining recognition, the biggest story in Florida is Latin- and Caribbean-influenced music, including salsa, reggae, merengue, mambo, rhumba, cha-cha-cha and calypso. The big stars are Gloria Estefan, Celia Cruz, the androgynous Albita, Giolberto Santa Rosa, Willy Chirino and Jerry Rivera, and dance bands like Los Van Van, who perform in all-night *bailable* dance concerts.

The best times to see ensemble Cuban bands – with up to 20 musicians and singers – is during special celebrations, like the Calle Ocho Festival (see the Facts for the Visitor chapter).

And then there's classical. Every once in a while you hear of an idea so absolutely sensible and so totally reasonable that you kick yourself for not having thought it up yourself: Miami's New World Symphony is one of those. Established in 1987, the NWS is described as a 'learning and performing experience for gifted graduates of the most prestigious music schools' – it is a collection of the best and the brightest young (usually in their 20s) musicians in the country spending about three years of postgraduate time performing with the symphony in concerts around the country and the world.

The members live in absolutely tiny rooms in a renovated Deco hotel near the Bass Museum, and spend pretty much all their waking hours either talking about, rehearsing, jamming or otherwise being involved with the performance of music. The energy level in the dorms is enough to guarantee a good concert, so by the time these people get into the fantastically renovated Lincoln Theatre for a concert – whoa, Nelly, hold on to your hat. See the Miami chapter for further information.

Throughout the state, regional orchestras, such as the Florida Symphony and the Jacksonville Symphony, perform classical

---

Naked Came the Manatee
The biggest news to come out of the Miami literature scene in recent days is *Naked Came the Manatee*, which began as a series by 13 of Miami's best known writers in *Tropic* magazine in the Sunday *Miami Herald*.

The story involves the discovery (by a character much like Marjory Stoneman Douglas) of two metallic canisters that landed in Biscayne Bay after a skiff crashed into a manatee. Both canisters turn out to contain what appears to be the head of Fidel Castro.

The book, by authors including Les Standiford, Carl Hiassen, Dave Barry, Paul Levine, Edna Buchanan, James W Hall, Vicky Hendricks, John Dufresne and Elmore Leonard, will be published by Putnam; the royalties are being donated to charity. ∎

concerts regularly; performances and venues are listed in the text.

Dance

There are 46 nonprofit dance organizations registered with the Metro-Dade (Miami area) cultural affairs council alone, and the state has thousands of dance-related businesses like studios, schools and production companies, and the mix of American, African, Cuban, Haitian, European and Latin American cultures is obvious in the productions you'll see throughout the state. The two biggest players in the state are the Miami City Ballet and the Miami-based Florida Dance Association, which holds and coordinates performances throughout the state.

Art

In the mid-1980s, artists began to discover South Beach and Miami was a place where they could get much more space, and live far cheaper, than in other art centers like New York and Los Angeles. While there are small pockets of artists in other Florida cities, among them St Augustine and Ybor City in Tampa, the art scene in Florida is very Miami-centric.

The SoBe Boom was almost single-handedly responsible for the injections of cash that have fueled the art boom in South Beach. As recently as the early 1980s, Miami's art scene was virtually nonexistent, and today, though the lack of many major galleries or a truly world-class museum is still an issue, the arts market can definitely be described as fledgling.

Real-estate developers encouraged the arts by incorporating local artists' projects in the designs of private and public spaces, like the Margulies sculpture garden which includes works by Richard Serra, Isama Noguchi, Mark di Suivero and Jonathan Borofsky, now on long-term loan to the campus of Florida International University. The South Florida Art Center (an artist-run organization) bought and leased buildings to provide affordable studios and exhibition space in the mid-'80s, which significantly helped to revitalize Lincoln Road. And the Museum of Contemporary Art (MoCA), designed by Charles Gwathmey, is an excellent example of a fusion of urban and cultural planning, placing a civic and cultural center within a residential and commercial area.

Established Miami artists today include Susan Banks, Carol Brown, Robert Thiele, Marilyn Gottlieb-Roberts, Sheila Friedman and Salvatore La Rosa. Transplants, artists well-known in other markets who have now made their homes in Miami, include Jack Pierson, Felix Gonzalez-Torres, Robert Juarez and Kenny Scharf.

Another major impact on Miami's art community has been the influence of Cuban and Latin American artists like Felix Gonzalez-Torres, Jac Leirner, Ernesto Nero, Gabriel Orozco, Jorge Pardo, Jose Bedia (perhaps best known), Tomas Sanchez, Consuelo Castaneda, Teresita Fernandez, Maria Martinez-Canas and Wilfredo Lam.

Film

At the turn of the century, before Hollywood, California was the shoe-in for world film central, places like Jacksonville and even Hollywood, Florida, were cranking out films. These days, with Florida being as hot as it is, filmmakers are flocking back to the area: in the last few years Miami Beach was featured in staggeringly successful films including *The Bodyguard*, *The Specialist*, *Ace Ventura: Pet Detective*, *True Lies*, *Get Shorty* and *Bird Cage*.

But from the beginnings of film the state has been the backdrop for some of USA's most beloved classics, like *The Cocoanuts* (the Marx Brothers' first feature); *Where the Sidewalk Ends*, filmed entirely at Miami Studios; *Citizen Kane*, which used the South Florida coastline as the setting for Xanadu, the largest pleasure palace in the world; *Key Largo* with Bogie and Bacall (though it was shot on sound stages in Hollywood, California); *The Barefoot Mailman* (see the Books section in the Facts for the Visitor chapter); and three Bond films: *Dr No*, *Live and Let Die* and *Goldfinger*.

The ballroom dancing scenes in *Cocoon* made St Petersburg's Coliseum famous for

15 minutes or so. *Caddyshack* shows the darker side of golf in Fort Lauderdale, and who among us will ever forget Rob Lowe's hilarious performance in *Illegally Yours*, shot in and around historic St Augustine?

For a wonderful glimpse of Miami Beach at its lowest point, rent a copy of *Black Sunday*, which features a car and foot chase through South Beach of the early 1980s – as witnessed by thousands of octogenarians in beach chairs.

Alec Baldwin played a total sicko in *Miami Blues*, based on the book by Charles Willeford, but by that time everyone in the world knew where Miami was, due to a television phenomenon: *Miami Vice*.

If you watch the show today (it's available in many of the larger video rental shops) you'll see the Beach at the turning point from Scuzzball Alley to Fabulous beach spot. The series was filmed mainly in Miami Beach, but it's hilarious to see the way the action would jump to spots throughout the city that no film could possibly get away with today, now that the layout of the place is so universally recognizable.

The annual Miami Film Festival and the Miami Beach Film Society (see the Special Events section in Facts for the Visitor and the Miami Entertainment section) showcase the works of some of the area's rising talent as well as classics. Other (much smaller) film festivals are held throughout the state and are mentioned in the text where appropriate.

Independent filmmaking is slowly making inroads, and foreign productions are streaming into South Florida so quickly that the Miami Film Commission has placed an 'Express Permit Application' form online (see the Online Services appendix).

Architecture

Florida's architecture can be referred to as 'prosaic', but we'd rather call it 'spectacularly unspectacular'. With very few exceptions – notably Key West, Miami's Art Deco District, Ybor City in Tampa, and the historic districts in Pensacola and especially St Augustine – the architecture you'll

run into is run-of-the-mill post-1950s urban sprawl. Buildings that don't look like shopping centers are probably condos – highrise monsters that line the coasts.

There are several exceptions. The Spanish Colonial and Revival styles, predominant in St Augustine and Pensacola, resemble more the grand buildings of Mediterranean Spain, with archways, adobe, wood and terra-cotta tile, than the relatively stark version of Spanish mission architecture found in the USA's Southwest. A perfect example, we hate to say it, is taste-bastion Donald Trump's Mar-A-Lago in Palm Beach.

Pockets of Victorian and Queen Anne pop up here and there, recognizable by their riotous colors and gee-gaws, gingerbread, towers, doo-dads and hoo-has. If you feel as if you've just walked into an expensive soap shop – or a B&B – it's probably a Victorian.

Cracker architecture, also called Florida Vernacular, is classic pioneer homesteading architecture with a twist: enormous sun porches. Early 'single pen' houses, simple boxes with porches, were later expanded by adding a wall either straddling the existing chimney (saddlebag) or adjacent to the wall opposite the fireplace (double pen). Cracker homes run from quaint to enormous, and are wood inside and out.

While famous for three distinct architectural styles – Mediterranean, towering skyscrapers and Art Deco – Miami is made up mainly of boom-era construction vibrant pockets of style here and there.

Of its three notable styles, Miami Beach is best known for its collection of Art Deco buildings. In the course of researching this book we became convinced of only one thing: a group of architects discussing Art Deco will undoubtedly behave in the same manner as would a group of economists discussing . . . anything.

Few agree on anything except the derivation of the term, a contraction of the title of the 1925 Parisian *Exposition Internationale des Arts Décoratifs et Industriels Modernes*, in which a strong emphasis was placed upon decorative arts.

The Exposition wasn't the starting point, but rather was the dawn of a style that combined many forms – predominantly turn of the century and pre-World War I European movements such as Art Nouveau, Arts & Crafts, the Vienna Secession and Italian Futurism, and the more geometric Modernism.

Today the term loosely refers to the product of the morphing of many styles in decorative and applied arts as well as architecture that occurred *essentially* between the 19-teens and 1940s.

Deco can be broken into three distinct categories, European, Northeast/WPA and 'Tropical' Art Deco.

European Art Deco Art Deco in Europe, which was fairly short-lived, had a lot to do with the Exposition itself, and was a play on classical Greek, Roman and Egyptian decorations using more modern materials like sandstone, steel and frosted glass in an almost cubist manner – plain lines as opposed to the froufrou associated with architecture of the time. Good examples are the Palais Chaillot, at the Trocadero in Paris, and Miami's main post office at 13th St and Washington Ave. It maintains the austerity of a government building while achieving a modern look.

Northeast/WPA This is a category that's almost absent on Miami Beach but is seen mainly in the northeastern USA as well as in any project associated with Roosevelt's Works Projects Administration (WPA). It is characterized by heavy overtones of socialist ideals in concrete and granite, with lots of stainless steel and socialist frescos and big relief sculptures of workers – a perfect example is New York's Rockefeller Center. This never caught on down here: there's no place for socialism in this bourgeois vacationland.

'Tropical' Art Deco The Deco of Miami Beach relied less on the implied meaning of decoration and more on simple geometric forms and colors, which worked well with the harsh sunlight to create interesting façades. It's important to note that the colors you now see are more garish than they originally were – earlier, many of the buildings were white with only a color trim, and more pastels were used as opposed to the neon coloring of today, which look very pretty but are essentially island color.

This branch of Deco – thrown up in Boom-era construction – is often asymmetrical and inexpensively constructed of masonry and stucco with applied color. This is unlike the other two, richer styles of Deco, which relied on the color of the materials like the pinkish hue of sandstone or the pink, brown or gray of granite.

It's also interesting to note that the value of these buildings on Miami Beach is based more on the sheer number of protected historic buildings: individually, the inexpensively constructed houses would be worth far less.

SOCIETY & CONDUCT

'People in New York and Los Angeles,' said *Miami Herald* columnist Eugene J Patron, 'have a lifestyle. Floridians have a life.' Northerners are often pleasantly surprised when interacting with Floridians (at least outside Miami), who tend to be more laid-back and friendly. Southern hospitality is as good as its reputation, but one must remember that in Florida, the farther *north* you go the farther *South* you get. The Panhandle may as well be Alabama, while Miami may as well be Newark, New Jersey.

Outside the major cities, especially in rural areas, Floridians tend to be more 'conservative' in that their politics and attitudes are old-fashioned and right wing. In rural areas travelers should avoid behavior or dress that may be considered offensive – American flag T-shirts or pants are a definite no-no, as they're considered to be a desecration of the American flag. It's also not a good idea for women to wear revealing clothing or go braless. Gay and lesbian travelers in these areas should do their best to behave as 'straight' as possible – and all travelers should avoid public displays of affection.

Rednecks, who refer to themselves as just that, can be found in many areas of northern Florida, easily identified by their foul and racially derogatory language. It's best to leave them in peace to wallow in their ignorance. It is possible that travelers may hear remarks directed at Cubans, Jews, blacks, Asians and native Americans, but racially motivated crimes are rare.

RELIGION

The state's residents are predominantly Christians, but there are significant numbers of Jews in Florida as well. Many are transplants from the northeastern USA but a healthy number of Russian-Jewish and Cuban-Jewish immigrants live in Miami and South Florida. Many of Florida's Jews are Reform, who do not adhere as strictly to the religious and social teachings of the Torah as do the Orthodox. The area is also the home of the Florida branch of the Chabad Lubovitchers, a faction of Judaism that proselytizes within the Jewish faith: if a long-haired, bearded man dressed in a black suit and white shirt and wearing a hat or *yarmulke* asks you a) if you're Jewish and b) to step inside a recreational vehicle, you've just met a Lubovitcher.

Afro-Caribbean religions, practiced mainly in South Florida, include *Santeria*, a synchronism of the West African Yoruba religion with Catholicism. It was brought to Cuba by black slaves who settled there, and is primarily practiced in Cuba. Voodoo is Yoruba as practiced by Haitians. Both of these religions practice animal sacrifice as a token of fidelity to the gods and spirits, and it's not uncommon to come upon animal remains at various places around Miami, like along the Miami River, in parks and, strangely, near the Bass Museum.

Candomblé is an African religion as brought to northeast Brazil.

LANGUAGE

'One of the nicest things about Miami,' goes an old joke, 'is how close it is to the USA.' Indeed, while English is the predominant language in the USA, Miami's proximity to countries that have tended to generate mass refugee migrations has resulted in an above-average number of non-English speaking, and some may say intentionally unassimilated, foreigners.

It's a somewhat unique situation in the USA. While pockets of foreigners have gravitated to other large cities, notably New York, Chicago and Los Angeles, there seems to be a higher degree of linguistic assimilation there than here, where as some put it, 'Them Cubans just won't talk English like everybody else.'

Visitors can get away with English only, but to do that is to essentially write off experiencing a huge chunk of Miami culture and life. While we've never had cause to speak the Creole patois, we found that our Spanish was indispensable when we lived here.

Spanish is the main language in almost every shop, café, coin laundry and restaurant in Little Havana, and in a surprising number of businesses elsewhere in the city.

The Voodoo Squad

Each weekday morning, members of the janitorial staff at the Metro-Dade Courthouse at 1351 NW 12th St in Miami patrol the grounds outside the building as part of the Voodoo Squad. According to an article in the *Miami Herald*, they're on the lookout for the remains of voodoo rituals performed by family members of those in custody in an effort to sway the outcome of trials.

Objects they encounter on a regular basis include dead goats, roosters, chickens and lizards with their mouths tied (though sometimes a cow tongue tied with twine is substituted), voodoo powder, corn kernels, cakes and eggs. ∎

Floridisms

The sheer size of the USA means that different regions have different accents and terminology to such an extent that people from different parts of the country have trouble communicating: a Bostonian asking for a 'tonic and a grinder' in New York would get a puzzled look, and then receive a glass of tonic water and a meat grinder instead of a cola and a large sandwich. Pick up a copy of Lonely Planet's *USA Phrasebook* for more – sometimes hilarious – information.

You'll hear generic Southern vernacular as well as slang peculiar to Florida. Have a nice day.

Anymore – In the South, 'anymore' is used to refer to present as well as past tense, meaning both 'any longer' ('I don't love you anymore') *and* 'nowadays' ('We used to take US Hwy 1 but anymore we take I-95').

Bubba – Standard Key West catch-all greeting or reference, 'Hey, Bubba, howzit goan?'

Chickee – Thatched hut, derived from Indian word for house. Pseudo-Chickees are usually found in picnic areas in parks, but real chickee huts suitable for sleeping are found in the 10,000 Islands in the Everglades.

Conch – Native Key West resident; see the Key West chapter for information on the Conch Republic.

Cracker – Named for the sound of the cracking whips of cattle drivers, this is a term for white native Floridians whom you'd otherwise call rednecks. It can be pejorative if you need it to be.

CST – Cuban Standard Time – Miami excuse – implying that Cubans are always late: 'Sorry, I'm on CST.'

Gorby – Derogative Key West term for tourists.

Parrothead – Jimmy Buffet fan

Snowbird – Vacationing northerner

Touron – Derogative Key West term for tourists.

Y'all – Contraction of 'You all', generic reference to one or more, eg 'Y'all ain't got no grits in Germany?'

YUCA – Cuban Yuppie – **Y**oung **U**rban **C**uban **A**merican ■

See the Facts for the Visitor section for Spanish menu information.

Spanish

Books When you go, take along Lonely Planet's *Latin American Spanish Phrasebook* by Anna Cody, which is comprehensive and compact. If you're planning on romancing some Latin types, the absolute finest resource for you is *Hot Spanish for Guys and Girls* and *Hot Spanish for Guys and Guys*, both published by BabelCom Books (New York), and both containing an amazing number of useful phrases from 'I'd like to hold your hand' to 'lick around the edges.'

Pronunciation Spanish has five vowels: **a**, **e**, **i**, **o** and **u**. They are pronounced something like the highlighted letters of the following English words: f**a**ther, **e**nd, mar**i**ne, **o**r and tr**u**th. The stress is placed on the syllable with an accent over it (México = MEH-hiko) or the second to last syllable (hasta luego=AH-sta loo-EH-go).

Useful Words & Phrases

yes	*sí*
no	*no*
good/OK	*bueno*
bad	*malo*
best	*mejor*
more	*más*
less	*menos*
very little	*poco* or *poquito*

Greetings & Civilities

hello/hi	*hola*
good morning/day	*buenos días*
good evening/night	*buenas noches*

see you later	*hasta luego*	bus	*gua gua* or *autobús*
goodbye	*adiós*	train	*tren*
pleased to meet you	*mucho gusto*	taxi	*taxi*
please	*por favor*	toilet	*sanitario*
thank you	*gracias*		
you're welcome	*de nada*	**Numbers**	
excuse me	*perdóneme*	0	*cero*
		1	*un, uno* (m), *una* (f)
Buying		2	*dos*
How much		3	*tres*
does it cost?	*¿Cuanto cuesta?*	4	*cuatro*
I want . . .	*Quiero . . .*	5	*cinco*
What do		6	*seis*
you want?	*¿Qué quiere?*	7	*siete*
Do you have . . ?	*¿Tiene . . . ?*	8	*ocho*
Is/are there . . . ?	*¿Hay . . . ?*	9	*nueve*
I understand.	*Entiendo.*	10	*diez*
I do not understand.	*No entiendo.*	11	*once*
Do you understand?	*¿Entiende usted?*	12	*doce*
Please speak slowly.	*Por favor hable*	13	*trece*
	despacio.	14	*catorce*
		15	*quince*
Getting Around		16	*dieciséis*
street	*calle*	17	*diecisiete*
avenue	*avenida*	18	*dieciocho*
corner (of)	*esquina (de)*	19	*diecinueve*
block	*cuadra*	20	*veinte*
to the left	*a la izquierda*	30	*treinta*
to the right	*a la derecha*	40	*cuarenta*
straight ahead	*adelante*	50	*cincuenta*
Where is . . . ?	*¿Donde está . . . ?*	100	*cien*
the bus station	*el terminal de*	200	*doscientos*
	gua gua	500	*quinientos*
the train station	*la estación del*	1000	*mil*
	ferrocarril	1,000,000	*millón*

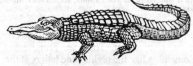

Facts for the Visitor

PLANNING

When to Go

See the Climate section in Facts about Florida for specifics on temperature and rainfall. While Florida used to be thought of as a winter destination, many areas in the northern reaches of the state, notably St Augustine, Gainesville, Tallahassee and the Panhandle, are booming summer destinations. And even in South Florida, the boundaries of the 'season' have been blurred by the stampede of models, of photo and film shoots and of huge numbers of people moving to the area, both from the US and abroad.

The advantage of coming during the early summer, despite the higher temperatures and increased rainfall, is that you get more of the place to yourself.

The Orlando area is a year-round destination, though there is heavy rainfall in summer. It is always crowded, especially during holidays, so reserve early if you plan to go there.

The hurricane season – from June 1 to November 30 – can be a perfectly pleasant time to visit, but you've got to be aware that one little hurricane can ruin a holiday. See the Dangers & Annoyances section for more information.

Miami and the southern part of the state are most visited in the winter, when it's pleasantly warm and the humidity isn't too high, so be prepared for higher prices and larger crowds. In summer, humidity and mosquitoes can be a problem (especially if you plan a trip into the Everglades), but the advantages are fewer people and cheaper prices. Also keep in mind that sometimes summertime is the only time to see certain things – turtles, for example, lay their eggs on Florida's beaches from May to August.

In the Panhandle and the northern part of the west and east coast, summer is considered high season. Winter gets quite cool, and the waters aren't really warm enough for swimming. But again, certain events happen just during that period – manatees, for example,

seek the warm water springs throughout the northern part of the state in the winter, whereas in summer chances to see those fellows are slim outside South Florida.

What to Bring

What to bring depends very much on where and when you go. Generally, if you come here in summer, you'll need light clothing (it hardly ever gets cool enough for a sweater), but you'll need to be prepared for sudden downpours. Keep in mind, this is a first-world destination, so anything you might forget is readily available. Here is list of things we suggest you pack (some of these may only be seasonal).

In the summer, clothes should be really light, but bring a pair of light-weight long pants and a sweater to fend of mosquitoes and no-see-ums (see the Dangers & Annoyances section). If you plan on going north in winter, bring slightly heavier clothes.

Key on the list at any time is suntan lotion. Bring lots of this stuff (see the Dangers & Annoyances section again), as well as good sunglasses and mosquito repellent (and/or a mosquito net with no-see-um netting). Swimming and snorkeling gear, a rain poncho or umbrella (especially in summer), a day backpack for hiking trips or other excursions, solid shoes (if you're a walking kind of person) and flip-flops or sandals (sometimes the sand on the beaches really heats up) will definitely make your trip more pleasant.

See the Outdoor Activities chapter for the equipment you'll need to bring for hiking, canoeing, kayaking or backpacking in the wilderness.

Florida is a very casual place, until it's not. Minimal requirement is a pair of cut-off jeans and a bathing suit, with an optional set of in-line skates, but people wear just about anything they want. That casualness, however, is a tricky bugger: Cubans in the Miami area, for example, dress very fashionably for a night out, and for South Beach, Palm Beach, Boca Raton, Sarasota or Tampa nightlife, you're really going to want to dress to the nines.

Toiletries, hygiene and first-aid products are readily available, and Florida is an inexpensive place to buy clothes, so plan on leaving with more than you arrived with.

Maps

Free maps to the state of Florida are easy to come by; the *Official Transportation Map of Florida* is a free road map that's probably better than most commercial maps that cover the same area. It's available through the Florida Tourism Industry Marketing Corporation (FTIMC) and through some larger convention & visitors bureaus. Members of the American Automobile Association (AAA) can receive free Florida maps from their local AAA office.

For city maps, many conventions & visitors bureaus and chambers of commerce will either hand them out or sell them cheaply, usually for $2.25 to 3.50. Those maps are probably made by the *Dolph Map Co*, which covers every major city in the state. Their maps usually sell for $2.95 in bookshops, gas stations and map shops – the ones the visitors bureaus and chambers sell will have local advertising on the back.

Hikers and backpackers can purchase topographical maps from specialty map shops like A World of Maps (☎ 954-776-3679), 6820 N Florida Ave, Tampa, FL 33604; A Galaxy of Maps (☎ 954-267-9000), 5975 N Federal Hwy Suite 116, Fort Lauderdale, FL 33308; the Map & Globe Store (☎ 904-385-8869), 537-E Scotty's Lane, Tallahassee, FL 32303; or directly from the US Geological Survey (☎ 303-236-7477), Map & Book Sales, Denver, CO 80225. A list of maps is available upon request. Many camping stores and national park and national forest ranger stations sell USGS maps of their immediate area. The maps most useful for hikers are the 1:62,500 scale (approximately one inch to one mile).

Boaters, canoers and kayakers can buy the National Oceanic & Atmospheric Administration's Coast & Geodetic Survey maps directly from the Distribution Division N/CG33, National Ocean Service, 6501 Lafayette Ave, Riverdale, MD 30737.

For getting off the beaten path, DeLorme's *Florida Atlas & Gazetteer* ($16.95, scale 1:150,000) is the best all-round source for really tiny roads, though it's useless for navigating in cities. It also has listings – some totally dated but others useful – of campgrounds, historic sites, parks, natural features and even scenic drives.

THE BEST

1   Miami's South Beach
2   Canoeing in the 10,000 Islands
3   Exploring (and picking strawberries) in old St Augustine
4   Broiling on the beaches of Pensacola
5   Collecting shark's teeth on Venice Beach
6   Manatee-watching at Blue Springs
7   Lunch at the Florida House Inn on Amelia Island
8   Tubing and canoeing on the Blackwater River
9   Viewing a shuttle launch
10 And (we hate to say it) Walt Disney World

THE WORST

10 Jacksonville
9   Public transport
8   Rednecks
7   Seething golf courses enveloping the state
6   JJ's Heritage Café, St Augustine ('Number thirty*seven* . . . ')
5   The horror of Hwy 192 in Kissimmee
4   Miami INS
3   Hurricanes, tornadoes and mosquitoes
2   Urban sprawl eating at the Everglades
1   Big white cars with Palm Beach County plates and shriveled retirees driving 5 mph

TOURIST OFFICES
Local Tourist Offices

Many towns don't have tourist offices per se – this function is often performed by local chambers of commerce or, in larger cities, the convention & visitors bureau (sometimes called a visitors & convention bureau and abbreviated in this book as CVB/VCB). They can provide you with local information about what to see and do, make hotel reservations for you and generally point you in the right direction.

And one handy and under-known service performed by CVB/VCBs is that if you're just stuck in a place and don't know what to do with yourself, you can call them and ask that they set up an itinerary for you. They'll try to tailor the itinerary to your needs (travel with kids, eco-tourism, organized tours, etc). But note that CVB/VCBs vary in usefulness from place to place. The address and telephone number of each chamber of commerce and/or other tourist offices are given in the Orientation & Information headings under each town.

If you're in a town with unhelpful, useless or hateful chamber or CVB/VCB personnel, and you just don't know whom to turn to for information, the next best bet is the research desk at the main branch of the public library. They're able to tell you about local organizations that specialize in whatever you're interested in. In this book, we list them as often as possible, and we've found that when no one else came through, the library did.

State Tourist Offices

The Florida Tourism Industry Marketing Corporation (formerly the Florida Division of Tourism – it's been privatized and now it's the FTIMC) will send you, upon request, a shiny, colorful folder of propaganda about the state put together by a bunch of overworked people. These brochures, which are usually free, are updated annually and contain addresses and telephone numbers of chambers of commerce, hotel lists and other very useful information. If you have a specific need or question, state tourist offices may be able to answer them or refer you to the appropriate office.

FTIMC offices include the following:

Campbellton Welcome Center
    5885 Hwy 231, Campbellton, FL 32426,
    three miles north of Campbellton on Hwy
    231 (☎ 904-263-3510, fax 904-263-3510).

Capitol Welcome Center
    Capitol, Plaza Level W, Tallahassee,
    FL 32399-2000 (☎ 904-488-6167)
Coral Gables Welcome Center
    2701 Le Jeune Rd, Suite 406, Coral Gables,
    FL 33134 (☎ 305-442-6926,
    fax 305-442-6929)
Jennings Welcome Center
    Route 2, Box 20, Jennings, FL 32053,
    four miles north of Jennings on I-75 S
    (☎ 904-938-2981, fax 904-938-2981)
Pensacola Welcome Center
    PO Box 17842, Pensacola, FL 32505,
    18 miles west of Pensacola on I-10 W
    (☎ 904-944-0442, fax 904-944-0442)
Tallahassee Welcome Center
    PO Box 1100, Tallahassee, FL 32302-1100
    (☎ 904-487-1462)
Yulee Welcome Center
    PO Box 339, Yulee, FL 32097,
    seven miles north of Yulee on I-95 S
    (☎ 904-225-9182, fax 904-225-9182)

Tourist Offices Abroad

For information on Florida from the UK, contact the FTIMC (☎ 0171-727-1661), 18/24 West Bourne Grove, 4th floor, London W25 RH. Call them to order their Florida Information Pack, or call the 24-hour hotline at ☎ 0891-600-555 for information on Florida tours. To get their information pack by mail, send a £2 check made out to ABC Florida to PO Box 35, Oxton OX14 4XF.

Other international offices include the following:

Brazil
    Alameda Campinas, 433-9 Andar SP,
    Sao Paulo 01404-901 (☎ 11-285-5167,
    fax 11-251-0438)
Canada
    121 Bloor St E, Suite 1003, Toronto,
    Ontario M4W 3M5, Canada
    (☎ 416-928-3139, fax 416-928-6841)
Germany
    Schillerstraße 10, 60313 Frankfurt am Main
    (☎ 069-131-0732, fax 069-131-0647)
Japan
    Belvedere Kudan Building, No 204, 2-15-5,
    Fujimi, Chiyoda-ku, Tokyo 102
    (☎ 3-5276-0260, fax 3-5276-0264)

The city of Miami has an information office in Germany; contact Dieter Jacobs PR

(☎ 069-465-566), Bergerstraße 436, 60385 Frankfurt am Main. Miami's Latin American information office is in Miami (!), run by JHJ & Associates (☎ 305-670-0231), 9200 S Dadeland Blvd, 603, Miami, FL 33156.

VISAS & DOCUMENTS
Passport
With the exception of Canadians, who need only proper proof of Canadian citizenship, all foreign visitors to the USA must have a valid passport and many also require a US visa. It's a good idea to keep photocopies of these documents; in case of theft, they'll be a lot easier to replace.

Visas
A reciprocal visa-waiver program applies to citizens of certain countries who may enter the USA for stays of 90 days or less without having to obtain a visa. Currently these countries are Andorra, Austria, Belgium, Brunei, Denmark, Finland, France, Germany, Iceland, Italy, Japan, Liechtenstein, Luxembourg, Monaco, the Netherlands, New Zealand, Norway, San Marino, Spain, Sweden, Switzerland and the UK. Under this program you must have a roundtrip ticket on an airline that is participating in the visa-waiver program; you must have proof of financial solvency and sign a form waiving the right to a hearing of deportation, and you will not be allowed to extend your stay beyond the 90 days. Consult with your travel agent or contact the airlines directly for more information.

Other travelers (except Canadians) will need to obtain a visa from a US consulate or embassy. In most countries the process can be done by mail, but in others, notably Turkey, Poland and Russia, you'll need to go in person to the nearest American consulate or embassy.

Your passport should be valid for at least six months longer than your intended stay in the USA, and you'll need to submit a recent photo with the application. Documents of financial stability and/or guarantees from a US resident are sometimes required, particularly for those from third-world countries.

Visa applicants may be required to 'demonstrate binding obligations' that will insure their return back home. Because of this requirement, those planning to travel through other countries before arriving in the USA are generally better off applying for their US visa while they are still in their home country rather than while on the road.

The validity period for US visitor visas depends on what country you're from. The length of time you'll be allowed to stay in the USA is ultimately determined by US immigration authorities at the port of entry.

Visa Extensions Tourist visitors are usually granted a six-month stay on first arrival. If you try to extend that time, the first assumption will be that you are working illegally, so come prepared with concrete evidence that you've been traveling extensively and will continue to be a model tourist. Extensions are manhandled by the US Government Justice Department's Immigration & Naturalization Service (INS) at 7880 N Biscayne Blvd in Miami (☎ 305-536-5741), and at 400 W Bay St, Room G18, in Jacksonville (☎ 904-232-2624). Get there early, bring along a good, long book and pack a lunch.

Travel Insurance
No matter how you're traveling, make sure you take out travel insurance. This not only covers you for medical expenses and luggage theft or loss but also for cancellation or delays in your travel arrangements (you might fall seriously ill two days before departure, for example), and everyone should be covered for the worst possible scenario, such as an accident that requires hospital treatment and a flight home. Coverage depends on your insurance and type of ticket, so ask both your insurer and your ticket-issuing agency to explain the finer points. STA Travel offers a variety of travel insurance options at reasonable prices. Ticket loss is also covered by travel insurance. Make sure you have a separate record of all your ticket details – or better still, a photocopy

of your ticket. Also make a copy of your policy, in case the original is lost.

Buy travel insurance as early as possible. If you buy it the week before you fly, you may find, for instance, that you're not covered for delays to your flight caused by strikes or other industrial actions that may have been in force before you took out the insurance.

If you're planning to travel a long time, the insurance may seem very expensive – but if you can't afford it, you certainly won't be able to afford a medical emergency in the USA.

Driver's License & Permits

Bring your home driver's license if you intend to rent a car; visitors from some countries may find it wise to back up their national license with an International Driving Permit, available from their local auto club, for a nominal fee, though note that your foreign driver's license *is* valid in the US. An IDP is not a license but rather an official translation of yours (valid for one year, and you still need to carry your license), and while the major rental companies are used to seeing foreign licenses, local traffic police are more likely to accept an IDP as valid identification than an unfamiliar document from another country.

Automobile Association Cards

If you plan on doing a lot of driving in Florida, it would be beneficial to join your national automobile association (just be sure that it's cheaper to join your organization at home than the $56 it will cost to join AAA for a year, including the one-time sign-up fee). Members of the American Automobile Association (AAA) or an affiliated automobile club can get car rental and sightseeing admission discounts with membership cards.

More important, it gives you access to AAA road service in case of an emergency (from locking your keys in the car to having major engine problems).

Hostelling International Card

About half of hostels in Florida are members of Hostelling International/American Youth Hostel (HI/AYH). HI was formerly the International Youth Hostel Federation, or IYHF. You can purchase membership on the spot when checking in, although it's probably advisable to purchase it before you leave home. The advantage of having one of these cards is that you'll get about a $2 to 3 discount off the nonmember rate. Surprisingly, though, some non-HI hostels, such as ones in Miami and St Petersburg, will also extend a discount to HI cardholders. Go figure.

Student & Youth Cards

If you're a student, get an international student ID (ISIC) or, not as good, bring along a school or university ID card to take advantage of the discounts available to students. You can get an ISIC from offices of Council Travel around the world on proof of enrollment. The ISIC can get you substantial discounts at museums and tourist attractions and on some airfares.

Seniors' Cards

British Railways and the American Association of Retired People issue identification cards for seniors, usually people over 55. These are absolutely key in Florida, where almost all major attractions, most hotel chains and some smaller hotels offer seniors' discounts. They can be substantial – up to 20% off on a room. You'll also save on some transport, including airfare.

Other Documents

If you could on the best of days be mistaken as being under 30, carry a photo ID card with your age on it – a major ID like your national identity card or your driver's license. Anyone who appears to be under 30 is asked for ID at bars and nightclubs.

EMBASSIES & CONSULATES
US Embassies Abroad

US diplomatic offices abroad include the following:

Australia
   21 Moonah Place, Yarralumla ACT 2600
   (☎ (6) 270 5900)

Austria
    Boltzmanngasse 16, A-1091, Vienna
    (☎ (1) 313-39)
Belgium
    Blvd du Régent 27, B-1000, Brussels
    (☎ (2) 513 38 30)
Canada
    100 Wellington St, Ottawa, Ontario 1P 5T1
    (☎ 613-238-5335)
Denmark
    Dag Hammarskjolds Allé 24, Copenhagen
    (☎ 31 42 31 44)
France
    2 rue Saint Florentin, 75001 Paris
    (☎ (1) 42 96 12 02)
Germany
    Deichmanns Au 29, 53179 Bonn
    (☎ (228) 33 91)
Greece
    91 Vasilissis Sophias Blvd, 10160 Athens
    (☎ (1) 721-2951)
India
    Shanti Path, Chanakyapuri 110021,
    New Delhi (☎ (11) 60-0651)
Ireland
    42 Elgin Rd, Ballsbridge, Dublin
    (☎ (1) 687 122)
Israel
    71 Hayarkon St, Tel Aviv (☎ (3) 517-4338)
Italy
    Via Vittorio Veneto 119a-121, Rome
    (☎ (6) 46 741)
Japan
    1-10-5 Akasaka Chome, Minato-ku, Tokyo
    (☎ (3) 224-5000)
Korea
    82 Sejong-Ro, Chongro-ku, Seoul
    (☎ (2) 397-4114)
Mexico
    Paseo de la Reforma 305, Cuauhtémoc,
    06500 Mexico City (☎ (5) 211-00-42)
Netherlands
    Lange Voorhout 102, 2514 EJ, The Hague
    (☎ (70) 310 92 09)
New Zealand
    29 Fitzherbert Terrace, Thorndon,
    Wellington (☎ (4) 722 068)
Norway
    Drammensvein 18, Oslo (☎ (22) 44 85 50)
Russia
    Novinskiy Bulvar 19/23, Moscow
    (☎ (095) 252-2451)
Singapore
    30 Hill St, Singapore 0617 (☎ 338-0251)
South Africa
    877 Pretorius St, Box 9536, Pretoria 0001
    (☎ (12) 342-1048)

Spain
    Calle Serrano 75, 28006 Madrid
    (☎ (1) 577 4000)
Sweden
    Strandvagen 101, S-115 89 Stockholm
    (☎ (8) 783 5300)
Switzerland
    Jubilaumsstrasse 93, 3005 Berne
    (☎ (31) 357 70 11)
Thailand
    95 Wireless Rd, Bangkok (☎ (2) 252-5040)
UK
    5 Upper Grosvenor St, London W1
    (☎ (0171) 499 9000)

Foreign Consulates in Florida

All of the consular offices in the state are in the greater Miami area. Check the Miami white pages in the telephone book under Consulates for diplomatic representation in the city. Embassies are located in Washington, DC, the US capital. Be patient: Miami is considered a cushy post by the always-hardworking diplomatic set, and some consular offices have ridiculously limited hours and act as if you're really interfering with their day if you ask for things like their help. Dress neatly and be polite. Most consulates are in Miami, but a few are in Coral Gables (all are area code ☎ 305).

Consulates include the following:

Argentina
    800 Brickell Ave, PH 1 (☎ 373-7794)
Austria
    1454 NW 17th Ave, Suite 200 (☎ 325-1561)
Bahamas
    25 SE 2nd Ave, Suite 818 (☎ 373-6295)
Bolivia
    25 SE 2nd Ave, Suite 545 (☎ 358-3450)
Brazil
    2601 S Bayshore Drive, Suite 800
    (☎ 285-6200)
Canada
    200 S Biscayne Blvd, Suite 1600
    (☎ 579-1600)
Chile
    1110 Brickell Ave, Suite 616 (☎ 373-8623)
Colombia
    280 Aragon Ave, Coral Gables
    (☎ 448-5558)
Costa Rica
    1600 NW 42nd Ave, Suite 300
    (☎ 871-7485)

Dominican Republic
    1038 Brickell Ave (☎ 358-3220)
Equador
    1101 Brickell Ave, M 102 (☎ 539-8214)
El Salvador
    300 Biscayne Blvd Way (☎ 371-8850)
France
    2 S Biscayne Blvd, Suite 1710
    (☎ 372-9798)
Germany
    100 N Biscayne Blvd (☎ 358-0290)
Guatemala
    300 Sevilla Ave, Suite 210, Coral Gables
    (☎ 443-4828)
Honduras
    300 Sevilla Ave, Suite 201, Coral Gables
    (☎ 447-8927)
Israel
    100 N Biscayne Blvd, Suite 1800
    (☎ 358-8111)
Italy
    1200 Brickell Ave (☎ 374-6322)
Jamaica
    25 SE 2nd Ave, Suite 842 (☎ 374-8431)
Mexico
    1200 NW 78th Ave, Suite 200 (☎ 716-4979)
Netherlands
    801 Brickell Ave, Suite 918 (☎ 789-6646)
Nicaragua
    8370 W Flagler St, Suite 220 (☎ 220-6900)
Paraguay
    2800 Biscayne Blvd, Suite 700
    (☎ 573-5588)
Peru
    444 Brickell Ave, Suite 135 (☎ 374-1305)
Portugal
    1901 Ponce de León Blvd, Coral Gables
    (☎ 444-6311)
South Korea
    201 S Biscayne Blvd (☎ 372-1555)
Spain
    2655 Le Jeune Rd, Suite 203, Coral Gables
    (☎ 446-5511)
UK
    1001 S Bayshore Drive, Suite 2110
    (☎ 374-1522)
Uruguay
    1077 Ponce de León Blvd, Suite B,
    Coral Gables (☎ 443-9764)
Venezuela
    1101 Brickell Ave, Suite 901 (☎ 577-3834)

Australian and New Zealand citizens may contact the British or Canadian consulates for emergency assistance, as neither country maintains consular offices in Miami.

CUSTOMS & IMMIGRATION

Most international flights land in either Miami or Orlando. You'll pass first through immigration – which checks your passport and visa – and if they're happy about *everything*, they'll pass you through to the next section, where you clear customs.

US customs allows each person over the age of 21 to bring one liter of liquor and 200 cigarettes duty free into the USA. US citizens are allowed to import, duty free, $400 worth of gifts from abroad while non-US citizens are allowed to bring in $100 worth. US law permits you to bring in, or take out, as much as US$10,000 in American or foreign currency, travellers cheques or letters of credit without formality. Larger amounts of any or all of the above – there are no limits – must be declared to customs.

Due to Miami's infamous popularity as a drug-smuggling gateway, customs officers in Miami are known to be . . . let's call them *thorough* in their examination of backpackers and other travelers who may fit the profile of what they call a 'mule', or someone ferrying narcotics. They may also not be very polite, but you should be, and you should dress neatly and carry a large wad of cash or travellers cheques and credit cards – or show signs of prosperity lest they think you're here to work illegally.

Both customs and immigration officers have the right to drag you into a room for questioning, or worse; Corinna's even been hauled into the back room here in Miami, and she's got a green card! Her tip:

Be as polite as you can. I was detained, it turned out, to verify that my resident visa was still current, but no one told me that – they just said, 'Follow me.' The immigration officer in the holding area told me to 'sit down and shut up,' and when I asked why I was being detained, he told me that if I wanted to make things difficult for myself, I could keep asking questions. I left four hours later.

If you are taken back there, one thing to make certain of is that a representative of your airline (who can call your relatives and get you information) knows you're there and who you want told of your predicament.

HIV & Entering the USA

Anyone entering the USA who is not a US citizen is subject to the authority of the Immigration & Naturalization Service (INS), who can keep someone from entering or staying in the USA by excluding or deporting them, meaning they have the power to prevent entrance or to return a visitor from whence they came. Being HIV-positive is not a grounds of deportation, but it is a grounds of exclusion, and the INS can refuse to admit HIV-positive visitors to the country.

Although the INS does not test people for HIV when they try to enter the USA, the form for the non-immigrant visa asks: 'Have you ever been afflicted with a communicable disease of public health significance?' The INS will try to exclude anyone who answers 'yes' to this question.

If you do have HIV but can prove to the consular officials you are the spouse, parent or child of a US citizen or legal resident (green-card holder), you are exempt from the exclusionary rule.

For legal immigration information and referrals to immigration advocates, visitors may contact the National Immigration Project of the National Lawyers Guild (☎ 617-227-9727), 14 Bacon St, Suite 506, Boston, MA 02108; and the Immigrant HIV Assistance Project, Bar Association of San Francisco (☎ 415-267-0795), 685 Market St, Suite 700, San Francisco, CA 94105. ∎

MONEY

Costs

You can really achieve whatever amount of luxury or penury you're striving for: youth hostels and cheap hotels abound, and there are good choices for every price range from backpacker to business traveler.

Getting here is sometimes stunningly cheap, especially from the UK or Germany, which are rife with package deals. It's also cheap from the US, especially if you take a Greyhound or drive here. See the Getting There & Away chapter for more information.

Florida rental cars tend to run cheaper than in most other states: rates start at around $20 a day (or $1.99 per hour, with no minimum, at Value; see Getting Around for more information) or $100 a week, but you have to seek those out; an average rate can be figured at $25/140.

Accommodation rates range widely in the state and, as with so many things here, depend a lot on when and where you go. Generally you'll probably find the cheapest beds in the state in the Orlando/Kissimmee area, where competition is so fierce that motel room rates start at about $20. Youth hostels are the cheapest option if you're traveling alone (rates start at $12 for a bed in a dorm), and hotel prices range anywhere from $25 to, well, anything really.

The cheaper end restaurants usually have breakfast for about $1.50 to 4, lunch can be $3 to 5 and dinner $4 to 7. A Big Mac costs $1.50 to 2. A beer in a supermarket is $1 (a six-pack $3 to 7, depending on the brand) and in a bar $2 to 3.50. A quart of milk in a supermarket will cost about $1.29, a loaf of bread anywhere from $1.09 to 2.09. Local phone calls are 25¢ at pay phones, and newspapers are 50¢ to $1 – and note that sales tax is charged on newspapers in Florida. Out-of-town newspapers sell for as much as they can get: the *Süddeutsche Zeitung* costs about $3 in Miami, British papers are about $2 and the Sunday *New York Times* is $4.

Carrying Money

Don't leave money – in any form – lying around in your room. Preferably, keep it in several different places on your person and in your baggage. When you go out, carry what you'll need in your pockets (but avoid eye-catching wallet bulges) with the rest tucked away under your clothing. A money belt is best (and the best of those are leather and inside your pants, against your skin – but remember to keep enough money in your pockets so you won't have to pull down your pants to buy a Pepsi, okay?).

Currency

The American dollar is divided into 100 cents with coins of one cent (penny), five cents (nickel), 10 cents (dime), 25 cents (quarter), and relatively rare 50 cents (half dollar). There are two examples of even rarer $1 coins; both of them were unpopular and only one of them is still in common circulation: the Susan B Anthony dollar, used almost exclusively at post office stamp machines and toll booths as change. This coin was rejected because it looks and feels almost exactly like a quarter. There's talk of a new $1 coin (gold and larger this time).

Bank notes are called bills. Be sure to check the corners for amounts, as they're all the same size and color! Circulated bills come in denominations of $1, $2 (rare), $5, $10, $20, $50 and $100.

In March 1996, the US Treasury introduced a new $100 bill, featuring a larger, off-center portrait of Benjamin Franklin. The older $100s will stay in circulation for the foreseeable future.

There are three straightforward ways to handle money in the US: cash, US$ travellers cheques and credit cards, with the proliferation of ATMs (automated teller machines, see below) facilitating the process.

Travellers Cheques

Travellers cheques are virtually as good as cash in the USA; most establishments (not just banks) will accept them just like cash. The major advantage of travellers cheques over cash is that they can be replaced if lost or stolen. But changing travellers cheques denominated in a foreign currency is rarely convenient or economical (though it's much easier than it used to be).

Get larger denomination US$100 cheques, as you may be charged service fees when cashing them at banks.

Automated Teller Machines (ATMs)

You can often withdraw money straight from your bank account at home. Most ATMs accept bank cards from the Plus and Cirrus systems, the two largest ATM networks in the USA. Honor is another popular network.

You can also easily obtain cash from bank ATMs with a Visa or MasterCard and a PIN (personal identification number).

The disadvantage of credit card cash advances is that you are charged interest on the withdrawal beginning immediately until you pay it back.

Credit Cards

Major credit cards are widely accepted by car rental agencies and most hotels, restaurants, gas stations, shops, and larger grocery stores. The most commonly accepted cards are Visa, MasterCard (Eurocard) and American Express.

In fact, you'll find it hard to perform certain transactions without a credit card – it's virtually impossible to rent a car

---

Bucks, Sawbucks, Portraits & Yards

Americans have a lot of nicknames for their money, as they do for everything else. Some have interesting etymologies, like 'two bits', a once-common name for a 25¢ piece or quarter (think of the jingle in old cartoons and movies *shave and a haircut/two bits*). It's named after the Spanish *bit*, worth at one time about 12.5¢. Some nicknames, like a 'portrait of Franklin', are more obvious.

Other nicknames draw from dated exchange rates (like 'pound' for $5). Others draw from typically imaginative analogies – 'sawbuck' ($10) is so named because a Roman numeral 10 (X) resembles a sawbuck or sawhorse. And still others are colorful gangster lingo – 'G' is short for grand ($1000); 'C-note' for $100.

But things get murky when you look for the origin of the 'buck' (which is also short for 'sawbuck' but that isn't the root of this slang). Some say that it's trapper terminology: skins were classified as 'buckskins' or 'bucks' and 'does', the former being larger and therefore more valuable. Other stories say that priests were called 'bucks', and they could always be counted on for a handout, but that sounds pretty silly. As do words like 'smacker', 'clam', 'simoleon' and 'yard'.

As with a lot of slang terms, we'll probably never really be sure about the origins. ■

without one. Even if you loathe them and prefer to rely on travellers cheques and ATMs, it's a good idea to carry one (Visa or MasterCard are your best bets) for emergencies. See the Dangers & Annoyances section below for some important warnings, though.

Currency Exchange

The best advice for people who need to exchange a foreign currency for US$ is to do so at home, before you arrive. Exchange rates are generally poorer in the US than at home. For example, when banks in Munich were routinely charging DM1.41 for $1, banks in the US were charging as much as DM1.53 for $1.

If you must change money in the states, you're probably best off at a real bank as opposed to an exchange office. Barnett Bank (☎ 800-553-9026) offers foreign exchange services in all its branches, and it has branches all through the state. Somewhat worse rates are available at some branches of NationsBank (☎ 800-367-6262) and SunBank (☎ 305-591-6000), the state's two other big banks. Shop around if you have time.

Private exchange offices generally offer the least competitive rates and charge the highest commissions on transactions. There are private exchange offices in larger cities, especially those popular with foreign tourists, and at all the major theme parks and many attractions. There are also foreign exchange desks in drugstores, record shops and so on.

Exchange Rates These are particularly volatile, but *at press time* exchange rates were as follows:

Australia	A$1	=	US$0.77
Canada	C$1	=	US$0.73
Germany	DM1	=	US$0.68
France	FF1	=	US$0.20
Hong Kong	HK$10	=	US$1.30
Japan	¥100	=	US$0.93
New Zealand	NZ$1	=	US$0.68
Singapore	S$1	=	US$0.71
UK	£1 =		US$1.54

Daily exchange rates are listed in *The New York Times, Wall St Journal* and *International Herald Tribune*. You can also get up-to-the-second exchange rates, if you're so inclined, on the internet from the United Nations, Koblas and Q&A – see the Online Services appendix.

Note that the exchange rates listed in newspapers and on the web are those for chunks of currency; actual street exchange rates will always be lower (unless you bring in a suitcase full of cash).

Tipping

Tipping is a US institution that can, initially, be a little confusing for foreign visitors. Waitstaff at restaurants, bartenders, taxi drivers, bellhops, hotel maids and others are paid a mere stipend. Owners, and indeed American culture, expect that customers compensate these people directly: the tips are actually part of their salary.

So tipping is not really an option; the service has to be absolutely *appalling* before you should consider not tipping. In a bar or restaurant a tip is customarily 15% of the bill; a tip for outstanding service in a restaurant is 20% (for a standard tip, double the tax and add a smidge). You needn't tip at fast-food restaurants or self-serve cafeterias. Hotel maids should be tipped about $1.50 a day, unless they don't deserve it. Tip daily, as maids rotate shifts.

Add about 10% to taxi fares even if you think your driver should be institutionalized. Hotel porters who carry bags a long way expect $3 to 5, or add it up at $1 per bag; smaller services (holding the taxi door open for you) might justify $1, but we don't think so. Valet parking is worth about $2, to be given when your car is returned to you.

Consumer Taxes

In this book, we list base prices, onto which you must add tax, unless otherwise indicated. In Miami the consumer (value added) tax is 6.5% (6% state and .5% local) on goods and services, with additional taxes of 5% on hotel accommodations (11.5% total tax on hotels). Rental cars in the state carry the 6% state sales tax plus local taxes and a

Florida state road surcharge of $2.05 a day. City taxes vary from city to city, so ask.

POST & COMMUNICATIONS
Mail
Mail within the USA generally takes two to three days, and mail to destinations within Florida from one to two days – except in St Augustine, where delivery time ranges from three days to never. Not to sound like a postal pamphlet, but it *does* help speed delivery to put the correct zip (postal) code on the envelope. If you know the address but not the zip code, you can find a list of them at the post office, or on the internet (see the Online Services appendix).

To Europe, allow at least a week, and up to two weeks at peak times of the year like Christmas. If you have the correct postage, you can drop your mail into any official blue mail box, which are found many places, like shopping centers and street corners. The times of the next mail pickup are written on the inside of the lid of the mail box.

Postal Rates Currently, rates for 1st-class mail within the USA are 32¢ for letters up to one ounce (28 grams; 23¢ for each additional ounce) and 20¢ for postcards.

International airmail rates (except Canada and Mexico, which are slightly cheaper) are 60¢ for a half-ounce letter, 95¢ for a one-ounce letter and 39¢ for each additional half ounce. International postcard rates are 40¢. Aerogrammes are 45¢.

Parcels airmailed anywhere within the USA are $3 for two pounds or less, increasing by $1 per pound up to $6 for five pounds. For heavier items, rates differ according to the distance mailed. Books, periodicals and computer disks can be sent by a cheaper 4th-class rate.

Receiving Mail You can have mail sent to you care of General Delivery at any post office that has its own zip (postal) code. It's best to have your intended date of arrival (if the sender knows it) clearly marked on the envelope. Mail is usually held for 30 days before it's returned to the sender.

Miami Beach South
  13th St at Washington Ave
  General Delivery, Miami Beach, FL 33139
Orlando downtown
  46 E Robinson St
  General Delivery, Orlando, FL 32802

Alternatively, have mail sent to the local representative of American Express or Thomas Cook, which provide mail service for their clients.

Telephone
All phone numbers within the USA consist of a three-digit area code followed by a seven-digit local number. If you are calling locally, just dial the seven-digit number. If you are calling long distance, dial 1 + the three-digit area code + the seven-digit number.

If you're calling from abroad, the international country code for the USA is '1'.

Phone Alphabet
Many businesses use letters instead of numbers for their telephone numbers in an attempt to make them snappy and memorable ('Dial M-A-T-T-R-E-S – and leave off the last 'S' – that's the 'S' for 'Savings'.'). Sometimes it works, but sometimes it's difficult to read the letters on the dial pad. If you can't read the letters, here they are:

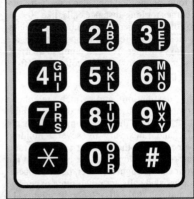

The 800 and new 888 area codes are designated for toll-free numbers within the USA and sometimes from Canada as well. Some can be called from anywhere in the USA, others are only used within the state. Those that are state specific are indicated in the text. Some long-distance carriers will allow you to call an 800 or 888 number collect from overseas.

The 900 area code is designated for calls for which the caller pays at a premium rate, usually only available from a private phone. They have a reputation for being sleazy operations – a smorgasbord of phone sex and psychic hotlines at $2.99 a minute.

Directory assistance can be reached locally by dialing either ☎ 411 or ☎ 555-1212; this is free from most pay phones but can cost as much as 50¢ from a private phone. For directory assistance outside your area code, dial 1 + the three-digit area code of the place you want to call + 555-1212. For example, to obtain directory assistance for a toll-free number, dial 1-800-555-1212. For all other out-of-state numbers, toll charges will apply on calls to directory assistance; from a pay phone it's usually 75¢.

Pay Phones Local calls usually cost 25¢ at pay phones. Almost all hotels (especially the more expensive ones) add a service charge of 50¢ to $1 for each local – and sometimes even toll-free – call made from a room phone, and they also have hefty surcharges for long-distance calls, like 50% on top of their carrier's rates. Public pay phones, which can be found in most lobbies, are always cheaper. You can pump in quarters, use a phone card or make collect calls from pay phones.

Long-distance rates vary depending on the destination and which telephone company you use. There are literally hundreds of long-distance companies in the US, and rates vary by several hundred percent – call the operator (☎ 0) for rates information. Don't ask the operator to put your call through, however, because operator-assisted calls are much more expensive than direct-dial calls. Generally, nights (11 pm to 8 am), all day Saturday and from 8 am to 5 pm Sunday are the cheapest times to call. Discounts also apply in the evenings from 5 to 11 pm daily. Daytime calls (Monday to Friday from 8 am to 5 pm) are full-price calls within the USA.

Debit Cards A new long-distance alternative is phone debit cards, which allow purchasers to pay in advance, with access through an 800 number. You call the 800 number, enter your card number, then enter the number you're calling, and the service tells you how much time you have left on your card before the call's put through. In amounts of $5, $10, $20 and $50, these are available in airports, post offices, some youth hostels and from Western Union and some other sources – even MTV has gotten into the phone card act. Shop around. The best rates we've been able to find (but you should double-check us when you get here) with these debit cards for domestic calls has been through GTI Telecommunications (☎ 800-364-9292), which gives a flat domestic rate of 25¢ per minute. For calls to Europe, we liked GlobalLink (☎ 305-538-1558), which has rates on a $20 pre-paid card of 78¢ per minute to the UK; 87¢ per minute to Germany and most of continental Europe; $1.37 per minute to Australia and New Zealand and 59¢ to 78¢ on calls to Canada. GlobalLink has an office at 865 Collins Ave in Miami Beach. Most of the hostels in the state sell phone cards.

International Calls To dial an international call direct from the Miami area, dial 011 + country code + area code (dropping the leading 0) + number. Treat Canada as a domestic call. From a pay phone, dial all those numbers before inserting coins; a recorded voice will come on telling you how much to put in the phone after you dial the number. For international operator assistance and rates dial ☎ 00.

As a general rule it's cheaper to make international calls at night, but this varies with the country you're calling. The exact cost for making an overseas call from a pay phone will depend on the long-distance company and the country in question. For calls from a private phone to Australia and Europe, typically the cost should be about $1.50 for the first minute and $1 for each subsequent minute. Other continents usually cost about twice that.

Collect & Country Direct You can call collect (reverse charge) from any phone. There are an increasing number of providers, but beware that there really is a difference in price, so check before your dial. The main players at the time of writing were AT&T (☎ 800-225-5288, or 800-CALL-ATT) and MCI (☎ 800-265-5328, or 800-COLLECT). During our research, MCI was always more expensive than AT&T. You can also just dial ☎ 0 and then the area code and number (omitting the 1

that normally precedes the area code, eg, 0+212+123-4567), but local telephone carriers are generally the most expensive option of all.

A collect call on a weekday using AT&T from Miami (☎ area code 305) to New York (☎ area code 212) cost about $1.75 for the first minute and 30¢ for each additional minute. That same call through MCI cost $1.89 for the first minute and 39¢ for each additional minute.

But if you're calling a country outside the USA, it *may* pay to use that country's country direct number (see the chart), which will connect you with an operator in the country you wish to call. At any rate, to use an American carrier to call overseas you can't use services like CALL-ATT or 800 COLLECT, you need a live operator.

Cheaper Collect Calls

Want to get your family really mad at you? Use MCI to call them collect in Australia. Sometimes the savings of using country direct service over AT&T and MCI are substantial.

Take that call to Australia, for example. AT&T reaches out and touches your wallet for $7.69 for the first and $1.48 for each additional minute. MCI has comedic celebrities on TV telling you how cheap an astounding $8.92/$1.71 for each additional minute is. And now the clincher: Telstra Australia Direct charges $3.80 (A$5.29) for the first and $1.64 (A$2.29) for each additional minute. 'Onya, Tonya! Make the call last only a few minutes and you're saving quite a bit over the US competition.

But it's not always the case. Take (of course) the UK. BT Direct charges $15.50 (£10.15) for the first and $2.40 (£1.54) for each additional minute, while AT&T charges $6.29/1.24 and MCI $8.30/1.12. BT's probably still trying to make up for all they lost when they changed their logo to that indeterminately sexed fanfare trumpet player.

Long-distance carriers are always changing their rates, so be sure and check who's cheapest during your stay before you make the call. Sometimes, the whole thing comes out about the same. Take Germany: AT&T wants $6.42/1.29, MCI gets $8.38/1.36 and Deutschland Direkt charges $8.57 (DM12.44) for the first but only 99¢ (DM 1.44) for each subsequent minute.

One other advantage of country direct service is that you can use your telephone company charge card from home. Telstra says that its cards are cheaper than collect calls.

Country Direct Service numbers are:

Australia	☎ 800-682-2878	Japan	☎ 800-543-0051
Austria	☎ 800-624-0043	Netherlands	☎ 800-432-0031
Belgium	☎ 800-472-0032	Norway	☎ 800-292-0047
Denmark	☎ 800-762-0045	New Zealand	☎ 800-248-0064
France	☎ 800-537-2623	Portugal	☎ 800-822-2776
Germany	☎ 800-292-0049	Singapore	☎ 800-822-6588
Greece	☎ 800-443-4437	Spain	☎ 800-247-7246
Hong Kong	☎ 800-992-2323	Sweden	☎ 800-345-0046
Ireland	☎ 800-562-6262	Taiwan	☎ 800-626-0979
Italy	☎ 800-543-7662	United Kingdom	☎ 800-445-5667

Fax & Telegram

Fax machines are easy to find in the USA, at shipping outlets like Mail Boxes, Etc, photocopy services and hotel business service centers, but be prepared to pay high prices (over $1 a page within the US, $4 or more to Europe and elsewhere). Prices for incoming faxes are usually half the outgoing domestic rate – about 50¢ a page.

Telegrams can be sent by Western Union (☎ 800-325-6000). You can charge telegrams to a credit card or (and Western Union doesn't exactly go around shouting this out) be billed directly at your home address or hotel. To be billed, you'll have to sound like a solid citizen, request it and insist when the operator says you need a credit card.

Telegrams are delivered generally within five hours inside the USA; overseas deliveries are not under the control of Western Union, which immediately sends the message overseas for delivery by your local company.

E-mail & Internet Access

E-mail is quickly becoming a preferred method of communication, and in many cities, notably New York, London, Helsinki and San Francisco, there are public terminals in restaurants and cafés. Not here yet.

Hotel business service centers may provide connections, and trendy restaurants and cafés sometimes offer internet service as well, though the latter hasn't caught on here as much as in other parts of the country.

Florida internet providers offer the usual services and flood the net with ads and cheap shots at getting business, but there are gems out there. We list useful websites in an appendix in the back of the book:

some are just excellent. Probably the best web search engine for finding documents on specific subjects is Alta Vista (http://altavista.digital.com/).

Some Florida internet providers include the following (all are prefaced by http://www.):

Boca Raton	wrld.net
Cocoa	digital.net
Fort Lauderdale	compass.net; aksi.net; netrunner.net; netpoint.net
Fort Myers	coco.net; tntonline.com
Gainesville	afn.org; digi-net.com; renegade-bbs.com
Jacksonville	jax-inter.net; net-magic.net
Orlando	accessorl.net; iag.net; netpass.com; oo.com; bridge.net
Miami	bridge.net; gate.net; shadow.net
Palm Beach	flinet.com; magg.net
Pensacola	amaranth.com; gulf.net
St Augustine	aug.com; oldcity.com
Tallahassee	freenet3.scri.fsu.edu; vistech.net
Tampa	intnet.net; packet.net

Note that many hotels are using digital PBX systems, which do not provide a dial tone that standard modems can 'hear', so if you're going to be staying in a few places, it's worth checking out a converter, available from electronics outlets like Radio Shack.

BOOKS

Most of the books listed here are available locally, some nationally and internationally. One of the best publishers of books on Florida and its regions is Pineapple Press, PO Drawer 16008, Southside Station, Sarasota, FL 34239. See the Facts about Florida chapter for works by local writers. For more difficult-to-find books we list the International Standard Book Number (ISBN) to assist you in a bookshop or library search.

Guidebooks One of our favorites is Frank Zoretich's *Cheap Thrills Florida – The Bottom Half* (Pineapple Press) written by an admittedly very stingy man, containing lots of real cheap things to do around here. If you're coming with kids, Lonely Planet's *Travel with Children* is a must-read for preparation and strategy, and don't miss the excellent *Places to Go with Children in Miami & South Florida* by Cheryl Lani Juárez and Deborah Ann Johnson (Chronicle Books), which is indispensable in keeping the little darlings calm and entertained. If you're sailing or boating around the state, two books stand out: *A Gunkholer's Cruising Guide to Florida's West Coast* by Tom Lefenstey (ISBN 0-8200-0127-9) and *Florida Under Sail* by Janey and Gordon Groene (ISBN 1-56626-088-8).

Flora & Fauna David W Nellis' *Seashore Plants of South Florida & the Caribbean* by Pineapple Press is a gorgeous book, with color photos throughout and very good and interesting descriptions of everything. A more scholarly and complete – yet accessible – guide is Ralph W Tiner's *Field Guide to Coastal Wetland Plants of the Southeastern United States*, University of Massachusetts Press, which has well-organized descriptions and line drawings. It's probably best to get *The Audubon Society Book of Water Birds* by Les Line, Kimball L Garrett and Ken Kaufman from a library – it's a coffee table-size book large and heavy enough to kill someone with and published with the usual impeccable quality of an Abrams book – astounding photography and great information but expensive.

Backcountry Travel For getting out in nature, don't miss Marjory Stoneman Douglas's classic *The Everglades: River of Grass* (Pineapple Press), which should be required reading for those heading out into the 'Glades. Also check out Susan D Jewell's excellent *Exploring Wild South Florida* (Pineapple Press) and Allen de Hart's *Adventuring in Florida* (The Sierra Club). *The Green Guide, Florida* by Marty Klinkenbergh and Elizabeth Leach (ISBN 1-56626-025-6) is good on details and practicalities for travel in state parks and wilderness. If you'll be canoeing, a fine investment is *The Canoe Handbook* by Slim Ray (ISBN 0-8117-3032-8), which has very good instructions and illustrations to teach good canoeing technique for one or more. *A Canoeing & Kayaking Guide to the*

Streams of Florida by Elizabeth F Carter and John L Pearce (ISBN 0-89732-033-6) is well-written and has lots of maps.

Architecture *Deco Delights* by Barbara Capitman, and *Miami: Architecture of the Tropics*, edited by Maurice Coulot and Jean François Legune are two excellent books on Art Deco architecture.

History The best book on Florida history is *The New History of Florida* (University Press of Florida, ISBN 0-8130-1415-8), edited by Michael Gannon and written by Gannon along with many experts in Florida history. The book is a concise and complete, beautifully written, flawlessly edited masterpiece of a good read – actually reading more like a novel then a history in many chapters. Another great read, though it's a bit more stilted, is *Adventures into the Unknown Interior of America* (ISBN 0-8263-0656-X) by Cabeza de Vaca and translated by Cyclone Cavey, describing the doomed expedition of Pánfilo de Narváez, the first European to thoroughly explore Florida (see the History section of Facts about Florida).

The standard work on the history of Florida, available in every Florida library, is the ever-so-dry *A History of Florida* by Charlton W Tebeau (pronounced TEE-bow); though it's patchy on pre-European history, many state history texts are as well, and Tebeau's book has been the classic reference for years. For a breezier read than all of the above, Michael Gannon's *Florida: A Short History* (University Press, ISBN 0-8130-1168-X) is a very good bet. Briefer yet, there's a good, quick history in *The Florida Handbook* by Allen Morris (Peninsular Publication Company, ISBN 0-9616-000-5-5).

Jonathan Dickinson's Journal (ISBN 0-912451-00-9) is the very interesting story of Quaker trader Jonathan Dickinson's shipwreck in 1696 near Hobe Sound and his journey home. The *Ybor City Story*, translated by Eustasio Fernandez and Henry Beltran is a good overall history of the development of Tampa.

NEWSPAPERS & MAGAZINES

There is usually at least one place in every city, town or village that carries, besides the local papers, national papers like *The New York Times*, the *Wall Street Journal*, *USA Today* – if you can't find a newsstand that carries whatever you're looking for, try a supermarket like Publix or one of the larger hotels. Speaking of newsstands, note that in Florida, they're almost nonexistent outside the big cities, having been replaced by steel boxes on streetcorners. We hate it, too.

The paper with the largest circulation in the state is the *Miami Herald*, the flagship of the Knight Ridder newspaper group. It's available in many cities around the state, though they've been scaling back circulation lately to cut costs.

For excellent, unbiased and thoughtful coverage of international news, pick up a copy of the *Christian Science Monitor*. *Time* and *Newsweek* magazines are also available in supermarkets, bookshops and newsstands.

In cities around Florida look for local tabloids, like *New Times* and *XS*, which have features, hard-hitting investigative journalism, comics and, of course, totally perverted and thoroughly enjoyable personal and classified advertisements.

Spanish & Overseas

See the Miami section for more. The *Miami Herald* publishes *el Nuevo Herald*, an excellent Spanish daily (in fact, if you speak Spanish, you should look here first for coverage of Latin America). *El Diario Américas* is another Spanish language daily available throughout South Florida.

Most major Western European newspapers are available at good newsstands.

RADIO

All rental cars have radios. Most stations have a range of less than a hundred miles, so if you're driving, you'll constantly have to change stations. In South Florida, Spanish-language broadcasts are common, and in major cities there's usually a good mix of rock, disco, Top 40, dance, adult contemporary and EZ listening, and usually there's at least one AM all-news station, at least in South Florida.

NPR, National Public Radio, is an excellent source of balanced news coverage with a more international approach than most US stations. Their news programs, *All Things Considered* and *Morning Edition*, are three-hour, evening and morning news programs that take the time to cover stories in a way that commercial radio simply can't. On Saturday mornings, *Car Talk* with Click and Clack, the Tappit Brothers, deals with cars and car problems – it's a funny and very popular show, and great if you're driving. And on Sunday mornings, *Prairie Home Companion* with Garrison Keillor is an excellent old-style variety show that levels a humorous, wry eye at American culture.

In most cities in Florida you'll also have the opportunity to listen to hate and political radio, featuring fat blabbermouths and convicted felons touting conservative political values. And Christian radio is big in the rural areas.

British news junkies or those who appreciate neatly clipped accents will appreciate broadcasts of the BBC news on shortwave. While there's generally news on the hour and half-hour throughout the day, pinning down exact frequencies or broadcast times is very difficult – even the venerable Beeb can't give a totally straight answer:

The nature of short wave is extremely unpredictable. The schedules, and some of the frequencies, change twice a year (beginning of April and end of October for the USA) to take into account changes in propagation conditions and shifts in listening habits.

Sound like a cop out? Yeah, well we don't see *you* bouncing signals off the ionosphere, now do we? You can get a complete program (sorry, programme) guide from the BBC by writing to PO Box 76, Bush House, Strand, London WC2B 4PH, or calling ☎ 0171-257-8165, fax 0171-257-8252; see the Online Services appendix for e-mail. Currently BBC broadcasts include the following frequencies and hours but check when you're here:

Frequency (kHz)	Time (GMT)
5965	5 to 7 am
5975	4 to 10 pm
9515	7 to 11.20 am
11865	8 to 11 am
15220	9 am to noon

Television

Because of the popularity of American television around the world, you'll find few surprises on TV. American television is a hodgepodge of talk shows, cop shows, dramas, melodramas, sit-coms, soap operas, game shows and commercials. Despite pressure from the US Congress to clean up what it considered to be inappropriate content or subject matter on daytime TV's talk shows (even Geraldo was talking ethics as we write), the genre is in no immediate danger, and American TV can still be an interesting place to spend an afternoon.

The five major broadcast television networks in the USA are ABC, CBS, FOX, NBC and PBS. Of them, FOX shows the most sensationalistic – but also the most groundbreaking – TV shows: it was FOX that syndicated *The Simpsons*, *Married with Children* and *The X-Files*. And FOX recently stunned the broadcast world by outbidding all contenders for the coveted NFL football coverage – something on which networks spend more money than news. CBS, ABC and NBC all show a mix of quasi-current films, news and news magazine shows and sit-coms, as well as dramatic programming like *ER*. ABC, CBS and NBC broadcast national news at 6.30 pm eastern standard time (EST).

PBS, the Public Broadcasting System, shows mainly educational programs, classical music and theater presentations, foreign programs and films (usually uncensored) and excellent current affairs shows like *Newshour with Jim Lehrer*. And the best part of it all is that it's mostly viewer supported – there are no standard commercial interruptions, but rather a list of corporate sponsors is read at the end of each program.

On local Florida TV stations, gore springs eternal: the local news motto is 'If it bleeds, it leads.' Local TV stations are cleaning up their acts in response to public outcry that news programs show too much violent video and concentrate on the negative, but most of the local news stuff is as sensationalistic as a British daily newspaper.

Cable TV is available at almost every hotel, which gives you access to, at the very least, ESPN (sports), CNN and CNN Headline News, the Weather Channel, Comedy Central, and some offer premium channels like HBO and Showtime (feature films).

PHOTOGRAPHY & VIDEO
Film & Equipment

Print film is widely available at supermarkets and discount drugstores throughout the state. Color print film has a greater latitude than color slide film; this means that print film can handle a wider range of light and shadow than slide film. However, slide film, particularly the slower speeds (under 100 ASA), has much better resolution than print film. Like black & white film, the availability of slide film outside of major cities is rare or is found at inflated prices. We found that for sharpness and vivid colors and ease of commercial developing, the two widely available slide films around are by Fujichrome: Velvia and Provia. Unlike Kodachrome, which is easy to screw up and must usually be sent out by developing places, these films are developed using the standard E-6 process, and it's virtually idiot-proof. And while Kodachrome when used and developed correctly is certainly fine film, these are just more user-friendly.

For certain subjects, like Indian petroglyphs, carry high-speed (400 ASA) film to avoid using a flash, which is not permitted at these sites.

Film can be damaged by excessive heat, so don't leave your camera and film in the car on a hot summer's day and avoid placing your camera on the dash while you are driving.

It's worth carrying a spare battery for your camera to avoid disappointment when your camera dies in the middle of nowhere. If you're buying a new camera for your trip, do so several weeks before you leave and practice using it.

Processing

Drugstores are a good place to get your film cheaply processed. If it's dropped off by noon, you can usually pick it up the next day. A roll of 100 ASA, 35-mm color film with 24 exposures will cost about $10 to get processed.

If you want your pictures right away, you can find one-hour processing services in the yellow pages under Photo Processing. The prices tend to creep up to the $13 to 15 scale, so be prepared to pay dearly. Many one-hour photo finishers operate in the larger cities, and a few can be found near tourist attractions.

Technique

Many parts of Florida experience over 220 days of sunshine annually, so there's plenty of light for photography. However, when the sun is high in the sky, photographs tend to emphasize shadows and wash out highlights. It's best to take photos during the early morning and the late afternoon when light is softer. This is especially true of landscape photography. Always protect camera lenses with a haze or ultraviolet (UV) filter. A polarized filter can dramatically emphasize cloud formations in mountain and plains landscapes.

Video

Overseas visitors who are thinking of purchasing videos should remember that the USA uses the National Television System Committee (NTSC) color TV standard, which is not compatible with other standards (Phase Alternative Line or PAL; Système Electronique Couleur avec Mémoire or SECAM) used in, respectively, Europe, Asia and Australia; and France and some parts of Africa, unless converted. Unless you have a double or multi-format VCR, it's best to keep those seemingly cheap movie purchases on hold until you get home.

X-Ray Inspection

All passengers on flights have to pass their luggage through x-ray machines. Technology as it is today doesn't jeopardize lower speed film, but it's best to carry film and cameras with you and ask the x-ray inspector to visually check your camera and film.

TIME

Except for the western section of the Panhandle, the entire state is in US eastern time zone, three hours ahead of San Francisco and Los Angeles, and five hours behind GMT/UTC. West of the Apalachicola River, the Panhandle is in the US central time zone, one hour behind the rest of the state, two hours ahead of San Francisco and Los Angeles and six hours behind GMT/UTC. When it's noon in Miami, it's:

9 am in Los Angeles and San Francisco
11 am in Pensacola and Panama City
5 pm in London
6 pm in Munich, Frankfurt and Berlin
1 am in Beijing, midnight in summer Beijing
    (when Beijing ignores daylight savingstime)
4 am in summer Sydney, 2 am in winter Sydney
6 am in summer Auckland, 4 am in
    winter Auckland

ELECTRICITY

Electric current in the USA is 110-115 volts, 60 Hz AC. Outlets may be suited for flat two- or three-prong plugs. If your appliance is made for another electrical system, you will need a transformer or adapter; if you didn't bring one along, check Radio Shack or another consumer electronics store.

WEIGHTS & MEASURES

Americans continue to resist the imposition of the metric system. Distances are in feet, yards and miles; weights are in ounces, pounds and tons. Gasoline is measured in US gallons, about 20% smaller than the Imperial gallon and equivalent to 3.79 liters. Temperatures are given in degrees Fahrenheit: from C° to F° multiply by 1.8 and add 32; from F° to C° subtract 32 and multiply by 5/9. See the inside back cover of this book for more conversions.

LAUNDRY

There are coin laundries in almost every city in the state except Palm Beach. Generally, the cost is $1.25 to wash and either a flat rate (like $1.25) to dry or dryers that cost 25¢ for between five and 10 minutes.

HEALTH

Florida is a typical first-world destination when it comes to health. For most foreign visitors no immunizations are required for entry, though cholera and yellow fever vaccinations may be required of travelers from areas with a history of those diseases. There are no unexpected health dangers, excellent medical attention is readily available and the only real health concern is that, as elsewhere in the USA, a collision with the medical system can cause severe injuries to your financial state.

Hospitals and medical centers, walk-in clinics and referral services are easily found throughout the state of Florida.

In a serious emergency, call ☎ 911 for an ambulance to take you to the nearest hospital's emergency room. But note that ER charges in the USA are stellar: Mount Sinai Hospital in Miami, a good hospital, charges a *minimum* ER fee of $276, and that's just the flagfall. There are additional charges for x rays, casting, medicines, analysis . . . *everything*, so the cost of a visit can easily top $1000. That's just slightly above average in Florida. The moral: don't get sick or hurt in the USA without insurance!

Predeparture Preparations

Make sure you're healthy before you start traveling. If you are embarking on a long trip, make sure your teeth are in good shape. If you wear glasses, take a spare pair and your prescription. You can get new spectacles made up quickly and competently for well under $100, depending on the prescription and frame you choose. If you require a particular medication, take an adequate supply and bring a prescription in case you lose your supply.

Health Insurance A travel insurance policy to cover theft, lost tickets and medical problems is a good idea, especially in the USA, where some hospitals will refuse care without evidence of insurance. There are a wide variety of policies and your travel agent

---

These Backward Americans

Americans write short format dates in the reverse order from the rest of the world, in month-day-year (not day-month-year). So 4/3/97 is April 3rd, not March 4th.

Numbers are written with a comma to separate powers of 10, and a period (full stop) separates decimal places: such as, 10,256.33.

American light switches are 'on' in the *up* position.

Also, the 1st floor in the USA is the ground floor, the 2nd is the European 1st, and so on.

And we drive on the right, as in *correct* side of the road. ■

---

will have recommendations. International student travel policies handled by STA Travel and other student travel organizations are usually good value. Some policies offer lower and higher medical expenses options, but the higher one is chiefly for countries like the USA with extremely high medical costs. Check the fine print.

Some policies specifically exclude 'dangerous activities' like scuba diving, motorcycling and even trekking. If these activities are on your travel agenda, avoid this sort of policy.

You may prefer a policy that pays doctors or hospitals directly, rather than your having to pay first and claim later. If you have to claim later, keep *all* documentation. Some policies ask you to call back (reverse charges) to a center in your home country for an immediate assessment of your problem.

Check whether the policy covers ambulance fees or an emergency flight home. If you have to stretch out, you will need two seats and somebody has to pay for it!

Travel Health Guides Lonely Planet's website (see the Online Services appendix) has an excellent section on travel health, and we include updates on new techniques and health issues of interest to travelers in our newsletter, *Planet Talk*, available by free subscription worldwide – see the back of this book for more information. There are a number of books on travel health:

Staying Healthy in Asia, Africa & Latin America, Dick Schroeder (Chico: Moon Publications, 1994): Though not specifically oriented toward North American travel, this is probably the best all-round guide. It's compact but very detailed and well organized.

Travelers' Health, Dr Richard Dawood (New York: Random House, 1994): This is comprehensive, easy to read, authoritative and highly recommended, but rather large to lug around.

Where There Is No Doctor, David Werner (Macmillan, 1994): This is a very detailed guide, more suited to those working in undeveloped countries than to travelers.

Travel with Children, Maureen Wheeler (Lonely Planet Publications, 1995): This offers basic advice on travel health for younger children.

Medical Kit While all this stuff is easily available throughout the state in pharmacies like Eckerd or Walgreens, it's useful to carry a small, straightforward medical kit, especially if you're going off the beaten path. This should include:

- Aspirin, acetaminophen or Panadol, for pain or fever
- Antihistamine (such as Benadryl), which is useful as a decongestant for colds, and to ease the itch from allergies, insect bites or stings or to help prevent motion sickness
- Antibiotics, which are useful for traveling off the beaten track, but they must be prescribed and you should carry the prescription with you
- Kaolin preparation (Pepto-Bismol), Immodium or Lomotil, for stomach upsets
- Rehydration mixture, to treat severe diarrhea, which is particularly important if you're traveling with children
- Antiseptic, mercurochrome and antibiotic powder or similar 'dry' spray, for cuts and grazes
- Calamine lotion, to ease irritation from bites or stings
- Bandages, for minor injuries
- Scissors, tweezers and a thermometer (airlines prohibit mercury thermometers)
- Insect repellent, sunscreen lotion, chapstick and water purification tablets

Basic Rules

Care in what you eat and drink is the most important health rule; stomach upsets are the most likely travel health problem (between 30 and 50% of travelers in a two-week stay experience this), but the majority of these upsets will be relatively minor. American standards of cleanliness in places serving food and drink are very high.

Water Bottled drinking water, both carbonated and noncarbonated, is widely available in the USA. In many places in Florida, the water is of a poorer quality than you're probably used to, unless you're from Leningrad or London: it's bad tasting and in some extreme cases can cause stomach upset. We live here and drink only bottled water. Many Publix supermarkets have filter machines that give a gallon of clean sweet water for 25¢. Buy a resealable one-gallon jug for about 69¢ and reuse it.

Everyday Health

Normal body temperature is 98.6°F or 37°C; more than 4°F or 2°C higher indicates a 'high' fever. The normal adult pulse rate is 60 to 80 per minute (children 80 to 100, babies 100 to 140). You should know how to take a temperature and a pulse rate.

Respiration (breathing) rate is also an indicator of illness. Count the number of breaths per minute: between 12 and 20 is normal for adults and older children (up to 30 for younger children, 40 for babies). People with a high fever or serious respiratory illness (like pneumonia) breathe more quickly than normal. More than 40 shallow breaths a minute usually means pneumonia.

Travel- & Climate-Related Problems

Motion Sickness Eating lightly before and during a trip will reduce the chances of motion sickness. If you are prone to motion sickness, try to find a place that minimizes disturbance, for example, near the wing on aircraft or near the center on buses. Fresh air usually helps, while reading or cigarette smoke doesn't. Commercial anti-motion sickness preparations, which can cause drowsiness, have to be taken before the trip commences; once you feel sick, it's too late. Ginger, a natural preventative, is available in capsule form.

Jet Lag Jet lag is experienced when a person travels by air across more than three time zones (each time zone usually represents a one-hour time difference). It occurs because many of the functions of the human body are regulated by internal 24-hour cycles called circadian rhythms. When we travel long distances rapidly, our bodies take time to adjust to the 'new time' of our destination, and we may experience fatigue, disorientation, insomnia, anxiety, impaired concentration and loss of appetite. These effects will usually be gone within three days of arrival, but there are ways of minimizing the impact of jet lag:

- Rest for a couple of days prior to departure; try to avoid late nights and last-minute dashes for travellers cheques or your passport.
- Try to select flight schedules that minimize sleep deprivation; arriving in the early evening means you can go to sleep soon after you arrive. For very long flights, try to organize a stopover.
- Avoid excessive eating (which bloats the stomach) and alcohol (which causes dehydration) during the flight. Instead, drink plenty of noncarbonated, nonalcoholic drinks such as fruit juice or water.
- Avoid smoking, as this reduces the amount of oxygen in the airplane cabin even further and causes greater fatigue.
- Make yourself comfortable by wearing loose-fitting clothes and perhaps bringing an eye mask and ear plugs to help you sleep.

Sunburn Use a good sunscreen and take your time – don't try to become a bronzed god or goddess on the first day (or for that matter, for the first week). Most doctors recommend sunscreen with a protection factor of 40 for easily burned areas like your shoulders and, if you'll be on nude beaches, areas not normally exposed to sun, like breasts and genitals.

If all that isn't enough to convince you, think about this: *no* one wants to have sex with someone with bright pink, festering skin who says 'Ouch!' when they're hugged.

Heat Exhaustion Dehydration or salt deficiency can cause heat exhaustion. Take time to acclimatize to high temperatures and make sure that you get enough liquids. Salt deficiency is characterized by fatigue, lethargy, headaches, giddiness and muscle cramps. Salt tablets may help. Vomiting or diarrhea can also deplete your liquid and salt levels. Anhydrotic heat exhaustion, caused by the inability to sweat, is quite rare, but unlike the other forms of heat exhaustion it is likely to strike people who have been in a hot climate for some time, rather than newcomers. Again, always carry – and use – a water bottle on long trips.

Heat Stroke Long, continuous periods of exposure to high temperatures can leave you vulnerable to this serious, sometimes fatal, condition, which occurs when the body's heat-regulating mechanism breaks down and body temperature rises to dangerous levels. Avoid excessive alcohol intake or strenuous activity when you first arrive in a hot climate.

Symptoms include feeling unwell, lack of perspiration and a high body temperature of 102°F to 105° (39°C to 41°). Hospitalization is essential for extreme cases, but meanwhile get out of the sun, remove clothing, cover with a wet sheet or towel and fan continually.

Infectious Diseases
Diarrhea A change of water, food or climate can all cause the runs; diarrhea caused by contaminated food or water is more serious, but it's unlikely in the USA. Despite all your precautions you may still have a mild bout of travelers' diarrhea from exotic food or drink. Dehydration is the main danger with any diarrhea, particularly for children, where dehydration can occur quite quickly. Fluid replacement remains the mainstay of management. Weak black tea with a little

sugar, soda water or soft drinks diluted 50% with water are all good. With severe diarrhea a rehydrating solution is necessary to replace minerals and salts. Such solutions, like Pedialyte, are readily available at Eckerd and other pharmacies throughout the state. The cost is around $5 per treatment, and you need from one to two treatments per day.

Hepatitis Hepatitis is a general term for inflammation of the liver. There are many causes of this condition: poor sanitation, contact with infected blood products, drugs, alcohol and contact with an infected person are but a few. The symptoms are fever, chills, headache, fatigue, feelings of weakness and aches and pains, followed by loss of appetite, nausea, vomiting, abdominal pain, dark urine, light-colored feces and jaundiced skin, and the whites of the eyes may turn yellow. Viral hepatitis is an infection of the liver, which can have several unpleasant symptoms, or no symptoms at all, with the infected person not knowing that they have the disease. The discovery of new strains has led to a virtual alphabet soup, with hepatitis A, B, C, D, E and a rumored G. Hepatitis C, D, E and G are fairly rare.

Tetanus Tetanus is difficult to treat but is preventable with immunization. Tetanus occurs when a wound becomes infected by a germ that lives in the feces of animals or people, so clean all cuts, punctures or animal bites.

HIV/AIDS Any exposure to blood, blood products or bodily fluids may put an individual at risk for HIV/AIDS. Infection can come from practicing unprotected sex or sharing contaminated needles. Apart from abstinence, the most effective preventative is always to practice safe sex using condoms. It is impossible to detect a person's HIV status without a blood test.

HIV/AIDS can also be spread through infected blood transfusions; most developing countries cannot afford to screen blood for transfusions, though the blood supply in the USA is now well screened. It can also

be spread if needles are reused for acupuncture, tattooing or body piercing.

A good resource for help and information is the US Center of Disease Control AIDS hotline (☎ 800-343-2347). AIDS support groups are listed in the front of phone books.

Cuts, Bites & Stings
Cuts & Scratches Skin punctures can easily become infected in hot climates and may be difficult to heal. Treat any cut with an antiseptic such as Betadine. Where possible avoid bandages and Band-aids, which can keep wounds wet.

Bites & Stings Bee and wasp stings are usually painful rather than dangerous. Calamine lotion will give relief, and ice packs will reduce the pain and swelling. Bites are best avoided by not using bare hands to turn over rocks or large pieces of wood.

First Aid See Snake Bite in Dangers & Annoyances below for information on what to do if you're bitten by a snake.

In the case of spiders and scorpions, there are no special first-aid techniques, but you should call Poison Control (call ☎ 800-282-3171, which will connect you with the nearest Poison Information Center, check the front of the phone book or ask the operator) for advice. Use ice on minor bites, but visit a doctor if an unusual reaction develops.

If you are hiking a long way from the nearest phone or other help, and you are bitten or stung, you should hike out and get help, particularly in the case of snake and spider bites. Often, reactions are delayed for up to 12 hours, and you can hike out before then. It is recommended to hike with a companion. For more information on some of these bugs and reptiles, see Dangers & Annoyances later in this chapter.

Ticks Ticks are a parasitic arachnid that may be present in brush, forest and grasslands, where hikers often get them on their legs or in their boots. The adults suck blood from hosts by burying their head into skin, but they are often found un-attached and can simply be brushed off. However, if one has attached itself to you, pulling it off and leaving the head in the skin increases the likelihood of infection or disease, such as Rocky Mountain spotted fever or Lyme disease.

Always check your body for ticks after walking through a high-grass or thickly forested area. If you do find a tick on you, induce it to let go by rubbing on oil, alcohol or petroleum jelly, or press it with a very hot object like a match or a cigarette. The tick should back out and can then be disposed of. If you get sick in the next couple of weeks, consult a doctor.

TOILETS

The USA is one of the worst countries in the world when it comes to the availability of public toilets; few cities have them, and when they do they're usually near, say, a beach or a public park, and not in the middle of the city where you'd need them. The only alternative is to ask permission to use the restrooms in restaurants and hotels, and, less frequently, businesses. In cheaper restaurants, or ones near heavily trafficked areas, there may be a 'customers only' policy in place – a sign will usually say so at the front door. Fear not – even in these places a polite request of 'May I use your bathroom, please' will more often than not lead to permission. Gas stations and fast-food places almost always have public toilets, but the best revenge is using the ones in five-star restaurants and hotels. Something about that five-star toilet paper . . . .

RECYCLING

Traveling in a car seems to generate lots of cans and bottles. If you'd like to save these for recycling (hint, nudge, wink, poke), you'll find recycling centers in the larger towns. Materials accepted are usually plastic and glass bottles, aluminum and tin cans and newspapers. Some campgrounds and a few roadside rest areas also have recycling bins next to the trash bins, so look out for those.

Perhaps better than recycling is to reduce your use of these products. Many gas stations and convenience stores sell large plastic insulated cups with lids, which are inexpensive and ideal for hot and cold drinks. You can usually save a few cents by using your cup to buy drinks.

Despite the appearance of many large cities, littering is frowned upon by most Americans. Travelers need to respect the places they are visiting even though it may seem that some locals think it's OK to trash their territory. Some states have implemented anti-littering laws (which impose fines for violation) to try to curb the problem. When hiking and camping in the wilderness, take out everything you bring in – this includes *any* kind of garbage you may create.

WOMEN TRAVELERS

Women often face different situations when traveling than do men. If you are a woman traveler, especially a woman traveling alone, it's not a bad idea to get in the habit of traveling with a little extra awareness of your surroundings.

Women must recognize the extra threat of rape, which is a problem not only in urban but also in rural areas. The best way to deal with the threat of rape is to avoid putting yourself in vulnerable situations. Conducting yourself in a common-sense manner will help you avoid most problems. It's said that shouting 'Fire!' may draw assistance more effectively than yelling 'Help!'

If despite all precautions you are assaulted, call the police; in any emergency, telephoning ☎ 911 will connect you with the emergency operator for police, fire and ambulance services.

Men may interpret a woman drinking alone in a bar as a bid for male company, whether you intended it that way or not. If you don't want the company, most men will respect a firm but polite 'no thank you'.

Don't hitchhike alone, and don't pick up hitchhikers if driving alone. If you get stuck on a road and need help, it's a good idea to have a pre-made sign to signal for help. At night avoid getting out of your car to flag

Toilets

For a country with a worldwide reputation for outspoken, sometimes coarse and even foul-mouthed language, it's an amazing phenomenon that very few Americans can bring themselves to utter the word for the porcelain appliance into which they empty their bowels and bladders.

In decades past, for ladies and gentlemen to refer to anything vaguely personal was to open themselves to scorn and embarrassment – even today, American television commercials hawk 'bathroom tissue', not toilet paper.

So Americans don't have toilets. They have (and these are just a few of

NICK SELBY

Powder Rooms

the euphemisms you will come across in your travels) a/the rest room, facilities, comfort station (?!?), commode, john, latrine, head, powder room, little girl's/boy's room, bathroom, way station and potty.

Even to natives, it can be confusing. As an old Southern legend has it, a woman of 'old-fashioned' values wanted to make certain that the campsite in which she would vacation had a toilet on the premises. She tried writing her question in a letter to the management, but kept coming up against that awful word, which she could not bring herself to commit to paper. She finally settled upon 'BC', short for 'Bathroom Commode', and wrote to the manager: 'Does your campground have a BC on the premises?'

The manager couldn't figure out what on earth she meant, and after showing the letter around he finally decided she must mean the local Baptist Church. He wrote back,

'Madam,

Unfortunately, the nearest BC is located six miles from the campsite. It is a lovely BC, with seating for 175 people, and on Sundays the organ sounds are quite spectacular. I haven't been able to go much lately, as my advancing age makes it difficult, but that's not for lack of desire. Perhaps when you arrive, we can go together . . . . ' ∎

down help; turn on your hazard lights and wait for the police to arrive. Be extra careful at night on public transit, and remember to check the times of the last bus or train before you go out at night.

The Associated Press reported in June 1996 that a new drug, Rohypnol, a tasteless sedative 10 times more powerful than Valium, was being added to women's drinks in Florida bars by the men who bought them; the women were sedated and raped. Never accept drinks proffered by strangers in bars.

To deal with potential dangers, many women protect themselves with a whistle, mace, cayenne pepper spray or some self-defense training. If you do decide to purchase a spray, contact a police station to

find out about regulations and training classes. Laws regarding sprays vary from state to state, so be informed based on your destination. One law that doesn't vary is carrying sprays on airplanes – because of their combustible design, it is a federal felony to carry them on board.

The headquarters for the National Organization for Women (NOW; ☎ 202-331-0066), 1000 16th St NW, Suite 700, Washington, DC 20036, is a good resource for any woman-related information, and they can refer you to state and local chapters. Planned Parenthood (☎ 212-541-7800), 810 7th Ave, New York, NY 10019, can refer you to clinics throughout the country and offer advice on medical issues. Check the yellow pages under

Women's Organizations & Services for local resources.

GAY & LESBIAN TRAVELERS

Florida, especially Miami's South Beach, is a key spot for gay and lesbian tourism in the USA: over $83 million of the $17 billion gay travel market was spent in Miami in 1995.

Florida would appear to be a very gay-friendly destination, but outside the major cities, it's probably not wise to be as out as one would be in, say, Miami, Fort Lauderdale, Key West or even Orlando. In rural areas especially, gay travelers may find hostility or open rudeness, but gay-bashing episodes are not common in Florida. Still, it pays to use caution in strange situations.

Outside South Beach and Key West there are cities with gay and lesbian bars and clubs and community centers, but there aren't any 'gay neighborhoods' of the type that one would find in New York or San Francisco.

In this book we list gay and lesbian resources wherever possible. On the internet, a very useful page is QueerAmerica (see the Online Services appendix for website), which lists gay and lesbian resources and community groups within specified area codes – enter yours and it will spit out as many as it knows. If we don't list something and they don't either, call the local public library's reference desk and ask them – they will usually be able to come up with something. Other good sources are college and university campuses.

Also on the internet, check out the Queer Resources Directory (see the Online Services appendix) for hundreds of links to gay and lesbian travel and other information resources.

For people with online capabilities, America Online (AOL) hosts the Gay & Lesbian Community Forum. This is also the online home of the National Gay/Lesbian Task Force (NGLTF), the Gay & Lesbian Alliance Against Defamation (GLAAD), Parents-Friends of Lesbians and Gays (P-FLAG) and other regional, state and national organizations. Michelle Quirk,

host of AOL's Gay & Lesbian Community Forum, can be contacted at quirk@aol.com.

National resource numbers include the National AIDS/HIV Hotline (☎ 800-342-2437), the National Gay/Lesbian Task Force (☎ 202-332-6483 in Washington, DC) and the Lambda Legal Defense Fund (☎ 212-995-8585 in New York City, 213-937-2727 in Los Angeles).

Books *The Out Pages*, an excellent book filled with listings of gay-owned or -friendly businesses in Miami and South Florida, is available at many local bookshops and gay/lesbian-owned businesses. For information on those, contact the SoBe Business Guild (☎ 305-234-7224). National guidebooks with sections on South Florida are *The Women's Traveler*, providing listings for lesbians, and *Damron's Address Book* for men, both published by the Damron Company (☎ 415-255-0404, 800-462-6654), PO Box 422458, San Francisco, CA 94142-2458, and the Gay Yellow Pages (☎ 212-674-0120), PO Box 533, Village Station, NY 10014-0533, which has a Southern Edition, covering areas from Washington, DC, south to the US Caribbean ($5).

DISABLED TRAVELERS

Travel within the USA is becoming easier for people with disabilities. Public buildings (including hotels, restaurants, theaters and museums) are now required by law to be wheelchair accessible and to have available toilet facilities. Public transportation services (buses, trains and taxis) must be made accessible to all, including those in wheelchairs, and telephone companies are required to provide relay operators for the hearing impaired. Many banks now provide ATM instructions in Braille, and you will find audible crossing signals as well as dropped curbs at busier roadway intersections.

Larger private and chain hotels (see Accommodations for listings) have suites for disabled guests. Main car rental agencies offer hand-controlled models at no extra charge. All major airlines, Greyhound buses and Amtrak trains will allow service animals to accompany passengers and will frequently sell two-for-one packages when attendants of seriously disabled passengers are required. Airlines will also provide assistance for connecting, boarding and deplaning the flight – just ask for assistance when making your reservation. (Note: Airlines must accept wheelchairs as checked baggage and have an onboard chair available, though some advance notice may be required on smaller aircraft.) Of course, the more populous the area, the greater the likelihood of facilities for the disabled, so it's important to call ahead to see what is available.

Be sure to contact local public transportation providers at least two weeks before you intend to be in town to arrange for Special Transportation Services (STS) if you'll require them.

Organizations

There are a number of organizations and tour providers around the world that specialize in the needs of disabled travelers. In Australia, try *Independent Travellers* (☎ 08-232 2555, fax 08-232 6877) at 167 Gilles St, Adelaide, SA 5000; and in the UK, *RADAR* (☎ 0171-250-3222) 250 City Rd, London, or *Mobility International* (☎ 0171-403-5688). The following is a list of organizations within the USA:

Twin Peaks Press
    publishes several useful handbooks for disabled travelers, including *Travel for the Disabled* and the *Directory of Travel Agencies for the Disabled*; PO Box 129, Vancouver, WA 98666 (☎ 202-694-2462, 800-637-2256)
Access
    The Foundation for Accessibility by the Disabled; PO Box 356, Malverne, NY 11565 (☎ 516-887-5798)
Information Center for Individuals with Disabilities
    Fort Point Place, 1st Floor, 27-43 Wormwood St, Boston, MA 02210 (☎ 617-727-5540, TTY 345-9743, 800-248-3737)
Mobility International USA
    advises disabled travelers on mobility issues, and runs an exchange program; PO Box 3551, Eugene, OR 97403 (☎ /TDD 503-343-

1284, fax 503-343-6812; see the Online Services appendix)
SATH
    Society for the Advancement of Travel for the Handicapped; 347 5th Ave No 610, New York, NY 10016 (☎ 212-447-7284)
Moss Rehabilitation Hospital's Travel Information Service
    1200 W Tabor Road, Philadelphia, PA 19141-3099 (☎ 215-456-9600, TTY 456-9602)
Handicapped Travel Newsletter
    a nonprofit publication with good information on traveling around the world and US government legislation (subscriptions are $10 annually); PO Drawer 269, Athens, TX 75751 (☎ /fax 903-677-1260)

SENIOR TRAVELERS

Though the age at which senior benefits kick in changes from place to place, travelers from 50 years and up (though more commonly 65 and up) can expect to receive cut rates at such places as hotels, museums and restaurants. Some national advocacy groups that can help seniors in planning their travels are the American Association of Retired Persons (AARP; ☎ 202-434-2277, 800-424-3410), 601 E St NW, Washington, DC 20049 (for Americans 50 years or older); Elderhostel (☎ 617-426-8056), 75 Federal St, Boston, MA 02110-1941 (for people 55 and older, and their companions); and the National Council of Senior Citizens (☎ 202-347-8800), 1331 F St NW, Washington, DC 20004. Grand Circle Travel (☎ 617-350-7500, fax 350-6206) offers escorted tours and travel information in a variety of formats and distributes a useful free booklet, *Going Abroad: 101 Tips for Mature Travelers*. Contact them at 347 Congress Street, Boston, MA 02210.

Visitors to national parks and campgrounds can cut costs greatly by using the Golden Age Passport, a card that allows US citizens aged 62 and over (and those traveling in the same car) free admission to all the country's national parks and a 50% reduction on camping fees. You can apply in person for any of these at any national park or regional office of the USFS or NPS, or call ☎ 800-280-2267 for information and ordering.

FLORIDA FOR CHILDREN

Florida is very kid-friendly – it's hard not to be with all those beaches (watch out for the topless spots if that sort of thing bothers you and you'll have a great time). There are museums specifically targeted to children's interests in many large cities and even in some smaller ones. Cities with outstanding children's museums – like science and technology, circuses and zoos – are Orlando (of course), Miami, Tampa, Fort Lauderdale, Sarasota, Boca Raton (believe it or not), St Augustine, Key West and West Palm Beach.

In this book we list as often as possible attractions that kids might like, as well as the prices for children for admission to attractions. There's almost never an extra charge for kids in hotels.

Most cities also have zoos, which in Florida can be quite good. And Lion Country Safari in West Palm Beach is definitely a fun stop.

Discovery Zone (☎ 800-282-4386) is a chain of indoor playgrounds that kids and parents absolutely adore – the kids because DZs are filled with ramps, ball rooms, rope ladders, swings, tunnels, slides and trampolines; the adults because there are usually other kids there to entertain yours, and you can sit down, for god's sake. Admission to DZs is $5.99 per child (adults don't pay, but adults are also not admitted without a child), and they're open daily. DZ has branches in such cities as Clearwater, Fort Myers, Jacksonville, Kendall, Pembroke Pines, Pensacola, Sarasota and Tallahassee.

Many McDonald's, some Burger King and all Pollo Tropical restaurants have kids play zones that do a good job of emulating DZ, and a kids' meal at the fast-food places is a very cheap admission to a good, safe playground. There are also public playgrounds in every city, especially along the beaches, and there are public toilets and water fountains at most of them.

Every sizable Florida city has a municipal swimming pool with organized programs and free swim periods. The Police Athletic League in many cities is a great source for weekend and after-school programs.

Pick up Lonely Planet's excellent *Travel with Children* by Maureen Wheeler (1995) for general information and encouragement.

Ask at your hotel about babysitters.

If you really need a day (or a week) of peace, there are a variety of cool programs that'll take the kids off your hands. The US Space Camp is a fantastic week-long educational program for kids interested in science and space exploration; see the Space Coast chapter under Titusville.

The nonprofit Newfound Harbor Marine Institute's Sea Camp programs are another rad and fun educational option for kids in the Florida Keys. Most science museums and even some art museums offer sleepover programs for kids, who can spend a night or a weekend within the museum with staff that run exciting camplike programs. And almost every state park has some sort of ranger-led program specifically for kids, even if not every day. Campfire programs are a favorite, with rangers organizing storytelling for campers, but even the simplest of nature walks are very popular with kids.

And Disney's Discovery Island Kidventure provides childcare in the form of an afternoon eco-adventure on Disney's island zoological preserve; see Walt Disney World in the Central Florida chapter.

If you're stuck for ideas on what to do with the kids, contact the nearest Convention & Visitors Bureau, who would be more than happy to help you work out an itinerary.

USEFUL ORGANIZATIONS
American Automobile Association

AAA, with offices in all major cities and many smaller towns, provides useful information, free maps and routine road services, like tire repair and towing (free within a limited radius), to its members. Members of its foreign affiliates, like the Automobile Association in the UK, are entitled to the same services; for others, the basic membership fee is $39 per annum, plus a one-time initiation fee of $17 (still an excellent investment for the maps alone, even for nonmotorists). Its nationwide toll-free roadside assistance number is ☎ 800-222-4357.

National Park Service (NPS) & US Forest Service (USFS)

The NPS and USFS administer the use of parks and forests. National forests are less protected than parks, allowing commercial exploitation in some areas (usually logging or privately owned recreational facilities).

National parks most often surround spectacular natural features and cover hundreds of square miles. A full range of accommodations can be found in and around national parks, from luxury campgrounds to budget motels. Contact individual parks for more specific information. National park campground and reservations information can be obtained by calling ☎ 800-365-2267 or writing to the National Park Service Public Inquiry, Department of the Interior, 18th and C Sts NW, Washington, DC 20013.

Current information about national forests can be obtained from ranger stations, which are also listed in the text. National forest campground and reservation information can be obtained by calling ☎ 800-280-2267 or writing to the National Park Service at the address above. General information about federal lands is also available from the US Fish & Wildlife Service (☎ 404-679-7289), whose Georgia office fields Florida-related questions.

Golden Passports Golden Age passports are free and allow permanent US residents 62 years and older unlimited entry to all sites in the national park system, with discounts on camping and other fees.

Golden Access passports offer the same to US residents who are legally blind or permanently disabled.

Golden Eagle passports cost $25 annually and offer one-year entry into national parks to the holder and accompanying guests. You can apply in person for any of these at any national park or regional office of the USFS or NPS, or call ☎ 800-280-2267 for information and ordering.

DANGERS & ANNOYANCES
Crime

In 1992 and 1993, several highly publicized incidents of attacks on tourists in Miami made headlines all over the world. Since then, attacks against tourists have been substantially and considerably reduced. In fact, of the 8.7 million tourists who stayed in unincorporated Dade County in 1995, there were 134 reported robberies; in 1993, the 'really bad year', there were 391 robberies.

You'd still do well to use caution.

The cities of Florida generally have lower levels of violent crime than larger, better known cities such as Washington, DC, New York and Los Angeles. Nevertheless, violent crime is certainly present, and you should take the usual precautions, especially in the cities.

Always lock cars and put valuables out of sight, whether leaving the car for a few minutes or longer, and whether you are in towns or in the remote backcountry. Rent a car with a lockable trunk.

Be aware of your surroundings and of who may be watching you. Avoid walking dimly lit streets at night, particularly if you are alone. Walk purposefully. Exercise particular caution in large parking lots or parking structures at night. Avoid unnecessary displays of money or jewelry. Split up your money and credit cards to avoid losing everything, and try to use ATM machines in well-trafficked areas.

In hotels, don't leave valuables lying around your room. Use safety deposit boxes or at least place valuables in a locked bag. Don't open your door to strangers – check the peephole or call the front desk if unexpected people are trying to enter.

Highway Robbery & Carjacking

Official police cars have flashing blue *and* red lights; if any other vehicle attempts to pull you over, using any other means, keep driving and get to a well-lighted area like a gas station and call the police. And that's what you should do if someone rams your car from behind – forget about stopping to exchange insurance information, just get to someplace safe and call the police. Don't stop for 'stranded' motorists.

Carjacking is a relatively new activity, in which someone approaches you at a stop light, points a gun at you and orders you out of the vehicle, which they then drive off. Police say that resisting a gun-wielding person is not wise; just follow instructions and hope for the best.

Credit Card Scams

When using phone credit cards of any sort, be aware of people watching you, especially in public places like airports. Thieves will memorize numbers and use them to make lots of international calls. Shield the telephone with your body when punching in your credit card number. Use touch-tone key pads to avoid having to actually say aloud your credit card number in a public place – the walls do have ears.

Don't give your credit card number out over the phone – people can charge anything they want if they have your name, card number and expiration date. Destroy any carbons generated by a credit card sale.

Never *ever* give out personal information over the phone to someone who's called you. No legitimate company representative would ever call and ask for your social security number, credit card number or expiration number or anything else.

Hotels customarily ask for a credit card imprint when you check in to cover incidental expenses. Make certain that this is destroyed if not used.

Enter a '$' sign before – and make certain there's a decimal point in – numbers written in the 'total' box on a credit card slip – we've heard reports of Japanese tourists being charged $1500 for a T-shirt instead of $15.

Hurricanes

A hurricane is a concentrated system of very strong thunderstorms with high circulation. The 74- to 160-mph winds created by a hurricane can extend for hundreds of miles around the eye (center) of a hurricane system. Floods and flash floods caused by the torrential rains it produces cause addi-

tional property damage, and perhaps most dangerous of all, hurricanes can cause a storm surge, forcing the level of the ocean to rise between four and 18 feet above normal: the 13- to 18-foot storm surge caused by a category-4 hurricane like Andrew would have easily destroyed the entire City of Miami Beach – and the nine- to 12-foot surge caused by Hurricane Opal did destroy much of the coast of the Florida Panhandle in 1995.

Which is exactly why Floridians are very hurricane conscious: school children participate in hurricane evacuation drills and take preparedness classes, and all Floridians have committed to memory facts and statistics on meteorological phenomena matched perhaps only by San Franciscans' knowledge of plate tectonics theory.

The Saffir/Simpson scale breaks hurricanes into five levels of intensity, based on the speed of circular wind intensity. Storms circulate counterclockwise in the northern hemisphere.

Some hurricane and storm terminology:

Tropical Depression
  Formative stage of a storm. This is an organized cloud system with winds of less than 39 mph.

Tropical Storm
  Strengthened tropical depression. This is an organized system of powerful thunderstorms with high circulation, and wind speeds between 39 and 73 mph.

Category-1 Hurricane
  Winds between 74 and 95 mph. This primarily effects plants, small piers and small crafts, and it can produce a storm surge of between four and five feet, flooding coastal roads. Note that a category-1 hurricane is still a hurricane and not to be treated lightly.

Category-2 Hurricane
  Winds between 96 and 110 mph. This causes major damage to plants, and trees can be uprooted. Mobile homes, roofs, doors and windows are damaged or destroyed. Six- to eight-foot storm surge.

Category-3 Hurricane
  Winds between 111 and 130 mph. Large trees are uprooted and knocked over; mobile homes and small buildings near the coast and signs are destroyed; roofs, windows, doors

and building structures damaged. Nine- to 12-foot storm surge cuts off coastal escape routes three to five hours before the storm.

Category-4 Hurricane

Winds between 131 and 155 mph. Mobile homes, plants, trees and signs are ripped up and destroyed; roofs, windows and doors damaged; major structural damage to buildings. Thirteen- to 18-foot storm surge cuts off coastal escape routes three to five hours before the storm.

Category-5 Hurricane

Winds above 155 mph. Destruction of buildings and roofs. Eighteen-foot storm surge cuts off coastal escape routes three to five hours before the storm.

Every year during hurricane season, which is from June 1 to November 30, storms form over the Atlantic Ocean and the Gulf of Mexico and gather strength – and some roll right over Florida. Some years – notably 1992, when Hurricane Andrew flattened the land, decimating the city of Homestead just south of Miami – are worse than others. In 1994, there was no major hurricane activity in the state.

Hurricanes are deadly. They can throw cars and trucks. And as anyone can attest who saw the carnage left behind in the City of Homestead after Hurricane Andrew, it can wipe out communities leaving little more than flat land, felled trees and broken gas lines.

Hurricanes are generally sighted well in advance and there's time to prepare. When a hurricane threatens listen to radio and television news reports. Give credence only to forecasts attributed to the National Weather Center (shortwave radio listeners can tune to 162.55 MHz), and dismiss anything else as a rumor. You can also call the National Hurricane Center (☎ 229-4470, option 1) for hurricane tracking information. There are two distinct stages of alert:

Hurricane Watch

This is given when a hurricane *may* strike in the area within the next 36 to 48 hours.

Hurricane Warning

This is given when a hurricane is likely to strike the area.

If a hurricane warning is issued during your stay, you may be placed under an evacuation order. Hotels generally follow these orders and ask guests to leave. The Red Cross operates hurricane shelters, but they're just that – shelter. They do not provide food. You must bring your own food, first-aid kit, blanket or sleeping bag and, hey, bring a book. Ask at your hotel or hostel for more information as to the logistics of evacuation.

If you're determined to sit out a hurricane warning, you will need at the very least:

- Flashlight
- As much fresh drinking water as possible (storms knock out water supply)
- Butane lighter and candles
- Canned food, peanut butter, powdered or UHT milk
- Cash (ATMs don't function)
- Portable, battery-powered radio

Stay in a closet or other windowless room. Cover yourself with a mattress to prevent injury from flying glass. Taping windows does not stop them from breaking but it does reduce shatter. For a full list of tips on preparedness, check on page 29 in the Miami white pages telephone directory.

Tornadoes

For a brief period after a hurricane, as if to add insult to injury, conditions become just ducky for a tornado. A tornado watch is generally issued as standard operating procedure after a hurricane, but actual twisters have popped up in Miami as recently as late 1995. There's not much you can do about this except be aware of the situation and follow the instructions of local radio and television stations and police.

Ocean Safety

Florida's Atlantic coastline isn't for the most part very rough, but there are a few areas of rough surf, and rip tides and undertows can occur. And the entire coast is dangerous before and after storms, when it is inconceivably stupid to go in the water.

The most important thing to keep in the water is your calm. Even if you're stuck in what seems like a bad rip tide, you're just a few minutes away from an easy swim back to shore. We watched in horror as two panicked swimmers made the wrong choice – to fight a riptide. That they lived through the experience was a miracle. Use your head: Human vs Ocean is no contest.

Riptides Rips, rip currents or riptides are fast-flowing currents of water within the ocean, moving from shallow areas out to sea. They are most common in conditions of high surf, forming when water from incoming waves builds up near the shore – essentially, when the waves are coming in faster than they can flow back out.

The water then runs along the shoreline until it finds an escape route out to sea,

Plotting a Hurricane

Scientists and National Weather Center (NWC) meteorologists now closely observe tropical depressions over the ocean and gulf as they become tropical storms and are finally upgraded to hurricanes. But plotting a hurricane's path is a tricky biz – in fact, it can't really be done.

In 1995, Miami television and NWC meteorologists predicted that Hurricane Erin was headed for a touchdown right in the center of the city. Miami and Miami Beach neighborhoods were evacuated and shelters sent out pleas for volunteers and supplies. Local television news teams gleefully ran around looking for driving rain ('Well, Patricia, it isn't coming down quite yet, but it's looking *very* ominous indeed . . . . '), waiting for something awful to happen while a mild degree of panic set in among local residents who had not evacuated. And then . . .

Nothing.

At least, nothing in Miami, where it rained a little. That evening a startlingly clear, star-filled sky, combined with a gentle breeze across the bay, made conditions lovely for a stroll on the beach.

The storm had suddenly veered due-north, catching northern Florida residents totally by surprise – in fact, many South Florida residents who had listened to news reports and evacuated their homes actually drove into the eye of the storm!

As Erin continued over land, it socked the Florida Panhandle with a wallop that knocked out power, destroyed houses as if they had been built from matchsticks and caused millions of dollars in damage.

About a month later, the second half of the one-two punch slammed the Panhandle as Hurricane Opal came through and flattened almost all of Panama City Beach, ripping down condominium apartment buildings, actually tearing up highways, houses and hotels; the city of Pensacola Beach was still under several feet of sand when we visited in the late fall, and Panhandle tourism officials estimate that the area's tourism industry won't return to normal before summer of 1997.

What this illustrates is the danger of becoming lulled into a false sense of security (or of panic) by mustachioed television personalities with complicated Doppler Radar charts and satellite imagery.

Hurricanes are much like the proverbial 800-pound gorilla: they set down wherever and whenever, they want. ∎

NICK SELBY

Ravages of Hurricane Opal

usually through a channel or out along a point. Swimmers caught up in the current can be ripped out to deeper water. Here's where that Don't Panic thing comes in.

Though rips can be powerful, they usually dissipate 50 to 100 yards offshore. Anyone caught in one should either go with the flow until it loses power, or swim parallel to shore to slip out of it. Trying to swim against a rip current can exhaust the strongest of swimmers.

Undertows Undertows are common along steeply sloped beaches when large waves backwash directly into incoming surf. The outflowing water picks up speed as it flows down the slopes. When it hits an incoming wave, it pulls under it, creating an undertow. Swimmers caught in an undertow can be pulled beneath the surface. Again, see Rule No 1. Go with the current until you get beyond the wave.

Jellyfish Take a peek into the water before you plunge in to make certain that it's not jellyfish territory. These gelatinous creatures with saclike bodies and stinging tentacles are fairly common on Florida's Atlantic coast. They're most often found drifting near the shore or washed up on the beach. The sting of a jellyfish varies from mild to severe, depending on the variety. But unless you have an allergic reaction to their venom, the stings are not generally dangerous.

The Portuguese man-of-war is the worst type to encounter. Not technically a jellyfish, the man-of-war is a colonial hydrozoan, or a colony of coelenterates, rather than a solitary coelenterate like true jellyfish.

Its body consists of a translucent, bluish bladderlike float, which generally grows to about four to five inches long. A man-of-war sting is very painful, similar to a bad bee sting, except that you're likely to get stung more than once from clusters of incredibly long tentacles, containing hundreds of stinging cells. Even touching a man-of-war a few hours after it's washed up on shore can result in burning stings.

If you do get stung, quickly remove the tentacles and apply vinegar or a meat tenderizer containing papain (derived from papaya), which act to neutralize the toxins. For serious reactions, including chest pains or difficulty in breathing, seek medical attention.

Snakes
Five of Florida's native snakes are venomous. The first four are members of the *Crotalidae* family (pit vipers), which inject venom that destroys the red blood cells and the walls of blood vessels. The coral snake is in the family of *Elapidae*, which produce venom that paralyzes the victim, whom they then begin to nibble. Before you freak out, we'd just like to let you know that in all the time we have spent in Florida we have never come across a poisonous snake.

The diamondback rattlesnake *(Crotalus adamanteus)* is the largest (and most dangerous) of the pit vipers. They can grow to be eight feet long. They have a big, heavy, brownish body, marked with dark (almost black) diamond shapes, set off by yellowish white borders. They usually rattle before they attack.

The pygmy rattlesnake *(Sistrurus miliarius)* is much smaller (from 1½ to two feet). They're grayish brown with round black and reddish orange markings. They also rattle before an attack, but their rattles are so quiet one can usually only hear it when it's very close. Their poison usually isn't fatal.

The copperhead snake *(Agkistrodon contortrix)* is only found in the northwestern section of Florida, and they're not very aggressive. They grow to about four feet and have an hourglass-shaped head. They too are grayish brown with chestnut-colored bands; the head is more copper-toned.

The cottonmouth (sometimes also called water moccasin) *(Agkistrodon piscivorus conanti)* is named for the white interior of its mouth. This olive green to brown snake with a dark stripe from its eyes to jaws grows to about five feet, and it has a heavy body ending in a thin, pointy tail. They live near lakes and streams and are very venomous.

The coral snake *(Micrurus fulvius)*, a relative of the cobra, is small and deadly: its poison is the most potent of any North American snake. They look very pretty – their slim body has sections of black and red divided by thin orange yellow stripes. They can easily be mistaken for the harmless scarlet king snake. To keep them apart, remember this little rhyme: Red touch yellow, kill a fellow; red touch black, good for Jack. Fortunately for us, they're very shy and generally nocturnal.

Snake Bite In the unlikely event of a bite by a poisonous snake, the main thing to do is stay calm – that's easy for us to say. If you can get to a telephone, call ☎ 800-282-3171, which will connect you with the nearest Poison Information Center. If you can, find a ranger.

If you're alone, stave off panic with the knowledge that snakebites don't, no matter what you've seen in the movies, cause instantaneous death. But they are dangerous and you need to keep a good, clear head on your shoulders.

Wrap the bitten limb tightly, as you would a sprained ankle, and then attach a splint. Get medical help as soon as possible, and if it's at all possible, bring along the dead snake for identification – but *do not* attempt to catch the snake if there's *any* chance of your being bitten again. Sucking out the poison and attaching tourniquets has been widely discredited as treatment for snakebites, so do not apply ice, a tourniquet, elevate the limb or attempt to suck out the poison yourself. Instead, keep the affected area below the level of the heart and move it as little as possible. And do not ingest alcohol or any drugs. Antivenoms are available in hospitals.

Sharks

Shark attacks off Miami Beach happen a couple of times a year, and there are more sharks out there than you would like to think. But other than staying out of the water, there's not much one can do about it, so, like, don't go see *Jaws* right before you come, OK?

Alligators

It's pretty unlikely that you'll even see an alligator in cities, but it's been known to happen. Alligators generally only eat when they're hungry – not as a punitive measure – unless they're feeling attacked. Things alligators like: small animals or things that look like them, such as small children or people crouching down real small to snap a photo. Things alligators don't like: you.

Alligators are fairly common in suburban and rural lakes, and they move around, but generally mind their own business. 'Nuisance alligators' – those which eat pets or livestock, become the bailiwick of the police, but generally speaking the best thing to do with an alligator is stay away from it completely.

Call the police at ☎ 911 if you see an alligator in a city. They'd probably want to know about it, hmm?

Biting Insects

Florida has about 70 types of mosquitoes and other biting insects like deer flies and fleas. They're bloody annoying, but there are some steps you can take to minimize your chances of getting bitten in the first place. Most larger Florida cities have mosquito-control boards that supervise spraying to reduce the problem, but in low-lying cities like St Augustine, the problem can be bad, especially in summer.

Prime biting hours are sunrise and sunset. Cover up, wear long pants, socks and long-sleeved shirts. The better brands of insect repellent in the USA are OFF! and Cutter for city use and industrial-strength products like REI Jungle Juice or any repellent that contains a high percentage of DEET for more severe situations like the Everglades or in the backwoods. A wonderful accident, Avon Skin So Soft is a moisturizer that happens to be excellent at repelling mosquitoes.

Treating Bites One of the best things about being in Florida is that aloe vera grows wild. If you've been bitten, grab an aloe vera leaf, break off a piece, squeeze out the juice and rub it on bites – great stuff. Calamine lotion, available at all drugstores, is what Nick's parents swore by – and he hated them for it! Pink globs all over your skin and the itch stays anyway – but it must work for some people, so try it if you want to.

Tiger Balm, available in better drug and health food shops, reduces itch and swelling from bites – rub it on the bite and try to control yourself from scratching for about five minutes and the itch should be gone. If that doesn't work for you, try cortizone cream, also available at all drug stores. Antihistamine tablets are also said to work.

Panhandlers & the Homeless
The waves of refugees from poor countries, in addition to the waves of refugees from the northeastern US, has resulted in a high percentage of homeless people and panhandlers in South Florida. This is a very touchy issue, and all we'll do is tow the official Lonely Planet line: don't encourage them – it only helps to make visitors an easy mark. If you're really concerned, you can volunteer at a homeless shelter, or donate to homeless relief programs at local churches and synagogues.

LEGAL MATTERS
Florida law tends to be tougher than in most northern states when it comes to drug possession or use. It's less strict in the far south of the state than in the north – in Miami the police are more tolerant than in, say, St Augustine, where someone arrested for carrying a pot pipe makes the newspaper. But 1995 and 1996 saw an increase in police raids on nightclubs, and dozens of people were arrested on minor drug charges. It's illegal to walk with an open alcoholic drink – including beer – on the street, unless you're on Panama City Beach. If you're driving, all liquor has to be unopened (not just sealed, but new and untouched) and, technically anyway, stored in the trunk of the car.

See below for the severe penalties in Florida for drinking and driving.

If you are stopped by the police for any reason, bear in mind that there is no system of paying fines on the spot. For traffic offenses, the police officer will explain your options to you. Attempting to pay the fine to the officer is frowned upon at best and may lead to a charge of bribery to compound your troubles. Should the officer decide that you should pay up front, he or she can take you directly to the magistrate instead of allowing you the usual 30-day period to pay the fine.

For those of you who missed every cop movie ever made: everyone arrested legally has (and is given) the right to remain silent, to make one phone call and to representation by an attorney. If you don't have a lawyer or family member to help you, call your embassy. The police will give you the number upon request. You are presumed innocent until proven guilty.

Note that police officers in Florida are allowed to search you if they have 'probable cause' – an intentionally vague condition that can be defined almost as 'if they want to'. They may be able to (this means probably are able to) search your car as well, under many different circumstances. There is no legal reason to speak to a police officer if you don't wish to (though they may try to offer you compelling reasons to do so, such as handcuffs, if they wish to speak with you and you ignore them).

Florida law carries the death penalty for capital crimes.

Driving Laws
As we went to press, speed limits in the USA were in a state of flux, the states having been set free from federal regulation of the speed limit. Currently, Florida is determining new speed limits on its roads, but as we write, the maximum permissible speed is 70 mph on interstate highways and between 55 and 65 mph on state highways unless otherwise posted. You can drive five mph or so over the limit without much likelihood of being pulled over, but if you're doing 10 mph over the limit, you'll be caught sooner or later.

Speed limits on smaller highways are 55 mph or less, and in cities they can vary from 25 to 45 mph.

Watch for school zones, where speed limits can be as low as 15 mph during school hours – and these limits are strictly enforced: Nick once got a ticket for $127.28 (!) for going 24 mph in a school zone. Seat belts must be worn in most states. Motorcyclists must wear helmets.

Drinking & Driving

The USA is one of the least tolerant countries in the world when it comes to drunk driving, and the concept of drunk is a fairly loose one: maximum permissible blood alcohol content in the state of Florida is .08%.

While alcohol levels vary from person to person, generally speaking, if you have *one* beer, you're pushing the legal limit. If you're pulled over and an officer suspects you're drunk, you'll be given a 'field sobriety test'. If you fail, you're placed under arrest immediately. In the police station you're offered a breath test. Refusal isn't admission of guilt, but if you think it helps, you're nuts – they'll undoubtedly find some charge on which to hold you even longer. If you fail a breath test, your license is immediately suspended pending a hearing, and you're fined a minimum of $250 and maximum of $500 for a first offense. Depending on alcohol level or whether you've had an accident, this fine could easily reach $5000.

During festive holidays and special events, road blocks are sometimes set up to deter drunk drivers.

For more information on other car-related topics, see the Getting Around chapter.

BUSINESS HOURS & HOLIDAYS

Office hours in Florida are generally 9 am to 5 pm, though there can be a variance of half an hour or so. In large cities, a few supermarkets will be open 24 hours a day. Shops are usually open from 9 or 10 am to 5 or 6 pm, but are often open until 9 pm in shopping malls, except on Sundays, when hours are noon to 5 pm. Post offices are open Monday to Friday from 8 am to 4 or 5.30 pm, and some are open Saturday from 8 am to 3 pm. Banks are usually open Monday to Friday from either 9 or 10 am to 5 or 6 pm. A few banks are open Saturday from 9 am to 2 or 4 pm. Basically, hours are decided by the individual branch so if you need specifics give the branch you want a call.

National public holidays are celebrated throughout the USA. Banks, schools and government offices (including post offices) are closed and transportation, museums and other services are on a Sunday schedule. Holidays falling on a Sunday are usually observed on the following Monday. The current national holidays are the following:

New Year's Day	January 1
Martin Luther King, Jr, Day	3rd Monday in January
Presidents' Day	3rd Monday in February
Easter	a Sunday in April
Memorial Day	last Monday in May
Independence Day	July 4
Labor Day	1st Monday in September
Columbus Day	2nd Monday in October
Veterans Day	November 11
Thanksgiving	4th Thursday in November
Christmas Day	December 25

CULTURAL EVENTS

The USA is always ready to call a day an event. Retailers remind the masses of coming events with huge advertising binges running for months before the actual day. Because of this tacky overexposure some of these events are nicknamed 'Hallmark Holidays' after the greeting card manufacturer. In larger cities with diverse cultures, traditional holidays of other countries are also celebrated with as much, if not more, fanfare. Some of these are also public holidays (see above) and therefore banks, schools and government buildings are closed.

January

Chinese New Year This begins at the end of January or the beginning of February and lasts two weeks. The first day is celebrated with parades, firecrackers, fireworks and lots of food.

February

Valentine's Day February 14. No one knows why St Valentine is associated with romance in the USA, but this is the day of roses, sappy greeting cards and packed restaurants. Some people wear red and give out 'Be My Valentine' candies.

March

St Patrick's Day March 17. The patron saint of Ireland is honored by all those who feel the Irish in their blood – and by those who want to feel Irish beer in their blood. Everyone wears green, stores sell green bread, bars serve green beer and towns and cities put on frolicking parades of marching bands and community groups.

April

Easter Observers of this holiday go to church and often paint eggs, which are usually hidden (by the 'Easter bunny') for children to find. Chocolate eggs and bunnies are also eaten. Travel during this weekend is usually expensive and crowded. Incidentally, Good Friday is not a public holiday and often goes unnoticed.

Passover This is celebrated either in March or April, depending on the Jewish calendar. Jewish families get together to partake in the traditional Seder dinner, which commemorates the exodus of Jews from their slavery in Egypt.

May

Cinco de Mayo This celebrates the day the Mexicans wiped out the French army in 1862. Now it's the day on which all Americans get to eat lots of Mexican food and drink margaritas.

Mother's Day This is held on the second Sunday of the month with lots of cards, flowers and busy restaurants.

June

Fathers Day Held on the third Sunday of the month, it's the same idea, different parent.

July

Independence Day More commonly called the Fourth of July, lots of flags are flown, barbecues abound, parades storm the streets of many towns, fireworks litter the air and ground – all to commemorate America's Declaration of Independence.

October

Halloween October 31. Kids and adults both dress in costumes. In safer neighborhoods, children go door to door 'trick-or-treating' for candy, and the adults go to parties to act out their alter egos.

November

Day of the Dead This is observed in areas with Mexican communities on November 2. This is a day for families to honor dead relatives, and people make breads and sweets resembling skeletons, skulls and such.

Election Day Held on the second Tuesday of the month, this is the chance for US citizens to perform their patriotic duty and vote. Even more flags are flown than on July 4 and signs with corny photos of candidates decorate the land.

Thanksgiving This is held on the last Thursday of the month. A day to give thanks, and ostensibly commemorating the short-lived cooperation between the original Pilgrims and Native Americans at the harvest, this most important family gathering is celebrated with a bounty of food and football games on TV. The following day is declared by retailers as the biggest shopping day of the year with everyone burning off pumpkin pie by running shopping relays through the malls. The day before Thanksgiving is the heaviest travel day in the country.

December

Chanukah This is an eight-day Jewish holiday commemorating the victory of the Maccabees over the armies of Syria and the rededication of their temple in Jerusalem. The date of Chanukah changes year to year, as it's tied to Kislev 25 to Tevet 2 in the Hebrew calendar, a nonlunar system. Generally, it's sometime in December.

Christmas – The night before the December 25 is as much of an event as the day itself, with church services, caroling in the streets, people cruising neighborhoods looking for the best light displays and stores full of procrastinators.

Kwanzaa – This seven-day celebration, held from December 26 to 31, is based on an African holiday that gives thanks to the harvest. Families join together for a feast and practice seven different principles corresponding to the seven days of celebration.

New Year's Eve – December 31. People celebrate with little tradition other than dressing up and drinking champagne, or staying home and watching the festivities on TV. The following day people stay home to nurse their hangovers and watch college football.

SPECIAL EVENTS

There are special events all the time in Florida; the Florida Division of Tourism has a complete list, updated annually, and each city's CVB/VCB or chamber publishes a list of its own celebrations.

January

FedEx Orange Bowl (Miami) See December, below, for information on the New Year's Eve Orange Bowl Parade, a Miami tradition. The Orange Bowl football classic is a major college football game at the Orange Bowl Stadium (☎ 305-371-4600).

Florida Citrus Bowl Classic (Orlando) The Citrus Bowl is also a college football game; they play at the Florida Citrus Bowl Stadium on or close to New Year's Day (☎ 407-849-2020).

Hall of Fame Bowl (Tampa) This football match takes place in the Tampa Stadium on January 1 (☎ 813-874-2695).

Circus Festival (Sarasota) Performers, acrobats, magicians and artists get together here in Ringling Country during the first week of January at the Sarasota County Fairgrounds (☎ 941-352-8888).

Art Deco Weekend Festival (Miami) This is held the second week in January, and 1996 became the first year in recent memory when it didn't rain on this parade – arts & crafts stalls line the east side of Ocean Drive, food stalls and the usual block party types. When it doesn't rain, it's great (☎ 305-672-2014).

Martin Luther King, Jr, Festival Actually festival*s*, Martin Luther King's birthday is celebrated in different towns throughout the state, sometime in mid-January.

Miami River Blues Festival Late January along the Miami River, near Tobacco Road, you can hear plenty of blues music (☎ 305-374-1198).

February, March & April

Miami Film Festival This international film festival is held the first two weeks of February at the Gusman Center for the Performing Arts (☎ 305-374-2444).

Edison Festival of Lights (Fort Myers) This festival celebrates the famous inventor, arts & crafts are sold and at the end there is a parade of lights; it takes place during the first two weeks of February (☎ 941-334-2550).

Speed Weeks (Daytona) This is a three-week auto race celebration beginning in early February, leading up to Daytona 500 at the Daytona International Speedway (☎ 904-253-7223).

Florida State Fair (Tampa) During the second week of February, fruits, vegetables and arts & crafts are sold at the Florida State Fairgrounds (☎ 813-621-7821).

Carnaval Miami There are festivals and parties throughout this nine-day event at the beginning of March, including a Miss Carnaval contest, Carnaval Night concerts at the Orange Bowl, an in-line skating contest and jazz concerts at South Beach, a Latin drag queen show and a Calle Ocho cooking contest (☎ 305-644-8888).

Calle Ocho Festival (Miami) The culmination of Carnaval Miami, the Calle Ocho Festival is a great time in Little Havana, with lots of concerts, giveaways and Cuban food on the second Sunday in March (☎ 305-644-8888).

Bike Week (Daytona) Lawyers, Hells Angels, speed heads, accountants and other suits from all over the state saddle up and get together for this wild party, based around motorcycle races at the Daytona Speedway (☎ 904-255-0981). First week in March.

Sanibel Shell Fair (Sanibel Island, near Fort Myers) This is a four-day celebration with all things shells; it's been happening since 1937 and starts the first Thursday of March (☎ 941-472-2155).

Festival of the States (St Petersburg) This 70-year tradition offers competitions, music performances, an antique car show and the like; it takes place from late March into early April (☎ 813-898-3654).

Springtime Tallahassee This is one of the largest festivals in the state – those ubiquitous arts & crafts are sold, and there is a balloon rally and music entertainment. It lasts for about four weeks from March into April (☎ 904-224-1373).

Fort Lauderdale Seafood Festival One of Florida's uncountable seafood celebrations, this is a great opportunity to taste local fish, oysters, crabs and regional cooking during the first week of April (☎ 305-463-4431).

Kissimmee Jazz Festival This music festival lasts for two days and takes place during mid-April at Kissimmee Lakefront (☎ 407-846-6257).

May & June

Fun 'n' Festival (Clearwater) Sport contests, musical events and lots of action on the beach and in town mark this festival, which starts after Easter and continues into May (☎ 813-462-6531).

Conch Republic Celebration (Key West) The founders of this island nation are toasted in true Key West style; it starts in April and lasts into May (☎ 305-296-0123).

Fiesta of Five Flags (Pensacola) The arrival of the Spanish is celebrated the first week of June, complete with reenactments and Spanish food and music (☎ 904-433-6512).

Cross & Sword (St Augustine) The story of the settlement of Florida is staged late June to early September in the amphitheater at Anastasia State Recreation Area (☎ 904-471-1965).

International Orchids Fair (Kissimmee) All kinds of orchids are on display and for sale toward the end of June at A World of Orchids (☎ 407-396-1881).

July, August & September

America's Birthday Bash (Miami) This excellent fireworks and laser show with live music and celebrations draws crowds of over a hundred thousand. It's held July 4th at Bayfront Park (☎ 305-358-7550).

Hemingway Days Festival (Key West) The best thing about this festival, held the last week in July, is the Hemingway look-alike contest, but there are also short story competitions and more (☎ 305-294-4440).

Annual Miami Reggae Festival One of the largest reggae events in the country, this is held in the first week of August at Bayfront Park (☎ 305-891-2944).

Festival Miami This annual concert series at the Gusman Concert Hall at the University of Miami campus in Coral Gables runs from mid-September to mid-October (☎ 305-284-3941).

October & November

Fantasy Fest (Key West) This is one of many Florida Halloween celebrations, but it's perhaps the most outrageous, with drag queens and other wacky entrants (☎ 305-296-1817).

Miami Book Fair Held in the second week of November, this international book fair is among the most important and well attended in the USA, with hundreds of nationally known writers joining hundreds of publishers and hundreds of thousands of visitors. The last three days of the eight-day fair is a street fair. If you're in town, it is absolutely mandatory (☎ 305-237-3258).

Lincolnville Festival (St Augustine) This festival features ethnic foods, live entertainment and arts & craft shows during the first weekend in November (☎ 904-829-8379).

December

Winterfest Boat Parade (Fort Lauderdale) This parade features almost a hundred decorated boats, cruising up the Intracoastal Waterway in the beginning of the month (☎ 305-767-0686).

Grand Illuminations (St Augustine) The entire historic district is lit with tens of thousands of little lights – you'll feel as if you're in a fairy tale. There are also reenactments and other shows and events. December until the first week in January (☎ 904-824-9550).

Orange Bowl Parade (Miami) The annual New Year's Eve blowout is the enormous Orange Bowl Parade: floats, clowns (professional and unintentional), a folkloric dance competition, a queen and a whole lot of other stuff. It would seem that all of Miami turns out for it at the Orange Bowl Stadium, and afterward, the AT&T Big Orange celebration at Bayfront Park has a fireworks salute (☎ 305-371-4600).

WORK

Foreigners are not allowed to work legally in the USA without the appropriate working visa, and recent legislative changes are specifically targeting illegal immigrants, which is what you will be if you try to work while on a tourist visa.

Miami and much of southeast Florida has been ground zero for large numbers of refugees from the Caribbean area, notably Haiti and Cuba, so INS checks are frequent. Local businesses are probably more concerned here than anywhere outside Southern California and Texas when it comes to verifying your legal status. See Visa Extensions in the Visas & Documents section for warnings on longer stays.

ACCOMMODATIONS
Reservations

The cheapest bottom-end motels may not accept reservations, but at least you can call them and see if they have a room – even if they don't take reservations, they'll often hold a room for an hour or two.

Chain hotels will all take reservations days or months ahead. Normally, you have to give a credit card number to hold the room. If you don't show and don't call to cancel, you will be charged the first night's rental. Cancellation policies vary – some let you cancel at no charge 24 hours or 72 hours in advance; others are less forgiving. Find out about cancellation penalties when you book. Also make sure to let the hotel know if you plan on a late arrival – many motels will rent your room if you haven't arrived or called by 6 pm. Chains often have a toll-free number (see below), but their central reservation system might not know about any local special discounts. Booking ahead, however, gives you the peace of mind of a guaranteed room when you arrive.

Some places, especially B&Bs, won't accept credit cards and want a check as a deposit before they'll reserve a room for you.

Camping

While less convenient than in Europe, Florida offers plenty of camping opportunities. There are three types of campsites available in the state: privately owned, public and undeveloped. Both privately owned and public campgrounds – usually located within or close to state parks – are clean and generally speaking very safe, and both usually have hot showers and sewage hookups for recreational vehicles (RVs). Your fellow campers will be an interesting mix of foreigners and generally speaking rural Americans – American city dwellers tend to camp less than rural dwellers.

Undeveloped campgrounds are what they are anywhere in the world: backwoods areas in which camping is permitted. These include riverbanks, fields within state or national parks or forests and other backwoods areas. Undeveloped campsites, obviously, have no running water, toilets or any other facilities, and generally accommodate only tent camping, not RVs or vans; see the Outdoor Activities chapter for more information.

Public campgrounds, while more Spartan than their private counterparts (there are usually no swimming pools, laundry facilities or other niceties) can nevertheless be the most fun of all: in addition to an inexpensive place to crash, park rangers usually operate some sort of entertainment or educational programs at least once a week, like campfire talks or organized nature walks. We give samples of ranger-led programs in the text, where available. Public campgrounds usually accommodate tents, RVs and vans.

Privately owned campgrounds are the most expensive option, and are usually located several miles from town. Most are designed with RVs in mind, but there is almost always a small section reserved for tenters. Fees are several dollars higher than in public campgrounds. The advantages in privately owned campgrounds are amenities: swimming pool, laundry, shuffleboard, restaurant, convenience store and bar, and in better ones, a lake with boating and fishing.

Undeveloped Campgrounds Camping in an undeveloped area, such as along the Florida National Scenic Trail, in the Everglades, Big Cypress National Preserve, Ocala National Forest or along rivers like the Blackwater River, whether from your car, canoe or just backpacking, entails basic responsibility. See the Outdoor Activities chapter for proper outdoor etiquette.

Public Campgrounds These usually have toilets, drinking water, fire pits (or charcoal grills) and picnic benches. Some don't have drinking water. At any rate, it is always a good idea to have a few gallons of water with you if you are going to be out in the boonies. These basic campgrounds usually cost between $7 and $20 a night. More developed areas may have showers or recreational vehicle (RV) hookups. These will cost several dollars more.

Costs given in the text for public campgrounds are per site. A site is normally for two people and one vehicle. If there are more of you, you'll need to pay more, and if there are more than six of you, you'll need two sites. Public campgrounds often have seven- or 14-night limits; the Everglades and Dry Tortugas have a 14-night per-stay limit, up to 30 days per calendar year per person.

Private Campgrounds Kampgrounds of America (KOA) is a national network of private campgrounds with sites in or near most Florida cities, and as they are uniformly equipped serve as a benchmark for privately owned campgrounds in quality and price. All KOA sites have a pool, laundry, restaurant, bar, games area (shuffleboard, volleyball and the like) and tent, RV/van sites and Kamping Kabins – small log cabins that have air conditioning and sometimes full kitchens. Kamping Kabins come in one- and two-bedroom flavors and average about $30 a night throughout the state. Sites in KOA campgrounds average $17 to 22, with electricity, cable TV and sewage hookups costing several dollars more for RVs. The cost is higher in places like Miami and the Keys.

You can get a directory of KOA sites by calling or writing: KOA (☎ 406-248-7444), PO Box 30558, Billings, MT 59114-0558. Most KOA campsites have toll-free 800 numbers, and all accept reservations. We list other privately owned campsites in the text, and magazines and coupon books from welcome centers and tourist information booths will give listings as well.

Hostels
Hostels are not just for youth; rather, they're places where travelers of all ages can get a cheap bed and exchange travel tales and information on where to do what.

There are hostels in Key West, Miami Beach, Clearwater, St Petersburg, Fort Lauderdale (though this may close; it was up for sale and its future unclear as we went to press), Orlando, Kissimmee, a brand new entry in Indialantic (near the Kennedy Space Center) that opened after our deadline, Daytona Beach (not recommended) and St Augustine. On the Panhandle, we've heard of a new hostel in the city of Ponce de León, north of Panama City Beach.

About half of Florida's hostels are affiliated with Hostelling International/American Youth Hostels (HI/AYH; HI is managed by International Youth Hostel Federation, or IYHF). Affiliated hostels offer discounts to HI/AYH members and usually allow nonmembers to stay for a few dollars more.

It's important to note that while HI/AYH hostels all maintain that organization's standards, some private hostels meet or exceed them. Don't pass on a place just because it is or is not an HI hostel: check out the rooms, and speak to travelers staying there before paying.

HI/AYH hostels expect you to rent or carry a sheet or sleeping bag to keep the beds clean. In all hostels there are information and advertising boards, TV rooms and lounge areas. Most hostels have a common kitchen, available to everyone staying there. There will be a common room where travelers can get together and hang out, and most of the time there are coin-operated laundry facilities (about 50¢ for the dryer and $1 for the washing machine). Books and games are often available.

Top Five Hostels

Floyd's Hostel & Crew House Fort Lauderdale; non-HI. For safety, cleanliness and attitude almost as much as for value, which is phenomenal.

Clay Hotel & International Hostel Miami Beach; HI member. The location is only surpassed by the setting: a Spanish Mediterranean villa once occupied by both Desi Arnaz and Al Capone – great traveler information and atmosphere.

St Augustine Hostel Non-HI. Perfect location, very friendly and helpful staff, and have we mentioned location?

Clearwater Beach International Hostel The newest HI member. Fantastic perks like canoes and bicycles, great staff, great beach and a pool.

HI Orlando Resort HI member. If it weren't for their location, for which you need a car, they'd be even higher. Pool, spotless rooms, four miles from Disney, very friendly. ■

Independent hostels may offer a discount to AYH or IYHF members. They often have a few private single/double rooms available, although bathroom facilities are still usually shared.

Dormitory beds cost about $11 to 15 a night. Private rooms – also available – are in the upper $20s for one or two people, sometimes more. Dorms generally have between four to eight single beds, mostly bunkbeds, and are often segregated by sex (some have mixed rooms). You'll usually have to share a bathroom.

Alcohol may be banned in some hostels. Reservations are accepted and advised during the high season – there may be a limit of a three-night stay then.

Motels

Motels, a creation of the 1950s, are relatively inexpensive hotels designed for short stays by motorists (the name is a contraction of 'motor hotel'), travelers, and trysts, usually by television evangelists.

A typical mid-range Florida motel is a one- or two-story building with a large parking lot often located just off a highway exit, near airports or along major roads. The entryway will smell like old coffee and have discount coupon and pamphlet racks against a wall.

Motels are usually about 10 years old, and some rooms show that more than others; the more rundown ones might have old cigarette burns in the sink or a scruffy carpet, but they're usually clean enough. The better – not necessarily the more expensive – ones can be spotless.

Rooms have private bathrooms, and towels, washcloths and soap are provided. There will be either one or two double or queen-size beds, and there is almost always color cable TV. Some offer pay-per-view movies ($5.95 to 8.95 per movie), and many have free HBO or Showtime (see TV under media in this chapter). All have air-conditioning.

Breakfast is rarely included – though many motels offer free coffee and doughnuts in the morning – and there are almost always soda and snack vending machines

and free ice (wash that ice bucket before you fill it up).

Daily maid service is standard, and you should leave a tip if the service is good (see Tipping, this chapter).

Bottom End These rooms, advertised as '$19.99', are the cheesiest offering, only to be explored by budget travelers. Mattresses are saggy, decor is preposterous and the cleanliness is absolutely minimum – that means clean sheets and towels. The cheapest national chain, and a noticeable step up in quality, is *Motel 6* (☎ 800-466-8356). Rooms are small and very bland, but the beds are usually OK, every room has a TV and phone (local calls are free) and most properties have a swimming pool. Rooms start in the $20s for a single in smaller towns, in the $30s in larger towns. They usually charge a flat $6 for each extra person. Motel 6s are pretty basic but offer reasonable value for money.

Mid-Range From $29.95 to about $50, motels are actually perfectly pleasant: furniture and televisions are newer; there may be a clock radio, a fridge and a microwave, the decor is better (though where they bought that painting is beyond us) and carpets are newer. Several motel chains compete with one another at this price level. The main difference between these and Motel 6 rooms is the size – more space to spread out in. Beds are always reliably firm, a 24-hour desk is often available and little extras like free coffee, a table, cable or rental movies, or a bathtub with your shower may be offered. If these sorts of things are worth an extra $10 or $15 a night, then you'll be happy with the *Super 8 Motel* (☎ 800-800-8000), *Days Inn* (☎ 800-329-7466) or *Econo Lodge* (☎ 800-553-2666). Not all of these have pools, however – Super 8 Motels, especially, have a good number of properties lacking a pool. Best Westerns (☎ 800-528-1234) in Florida vary greatly in quality.

Top End The larger and more expensive chain places, in the $45 to 80 range, make a motel almost as nice as a hotel – clean and fresh rooms and lots of amenities, like better soap, shampoo, conditioner, in-room safes, more towels and more space. Usually a buffet continental breakfast is included, and cafes, restaurants or bars may be on the premises or adjacent to them. The swimming pool may

be indoor, with a spa or exercise room also available. Very good are the *Quality Suites* (☎ 800-228-5151), *Comfort Inns* (☎ 800-228-5150) and *Sleep Inns* (☎ 800-627-5337). *Rodeway Inns* (☎ 800-228-2000) fall at the lower end of this category.

Hotels

As motels struggle to capture more of the business travel market, the differences between them and hotels is blurring, but hotels are still a different breed. Hotels are traditionally located within cities, and try to offer better service than motels. This means that there will be doormen, valet parking, room service, a copy of *USA Today* in the morning, laundry and dry cleaning, a pool and perhaps a health club, a business center and other niceties. Which come at a price, to be sure: want a shirt washed? Six bucks. And so on.

The basic hotel room differs little from the basic motel room except that it's reasonable to expect newer, cleaner stuff in hotels. The surprising thing is that the most really expensive hotels – the Hyatts and Sheratons of the state – are usually not any nicer than a high quality motel room, and usually cost more than twice as much.

The exceptions are privately owned smaller hotels in out-of-the-way places or unique settings, and larger hotels in larger cities, which have reduced their prices and increased their services to compete with better motels and resorts. And specialty hotels – like the Marlin, Casa Grande and La Voile Rouge in Miami Beach, the Breakers in Palm Beach and the Ritz-Carltons anywhere – offer decadence and a hotel experience that's worth it if you can afford it.

Chain-owned hotels in Florida include:

Hilton	☎ 800-445-8667
Holiday Inn	☎ 800-465-4329
Marriott	☎ 800-228-9280
Radisson	☎ 800-333-3333
Ritz-Carlton	☎ 800-241-3333
Sheraton	☎ 800-325-3535

Private Hotels There are, of course, non-chain establishments in all price ranges. Some of them are quirky historical hotels,

---

> **Rack Rates**
>
> The 'rack rate' a hotel offers is the standard, 'person-walks-in-off-the-street' price. It is not by any means necessarily the actual final price, as all prices are negotiable in American hotels.
>
> This is especially true in the larger, more expensive places. Sometimes a simple 'do you have anything cheaper' will result in an immediate price reduction. Sometimes, in chain places, it may help to walk to the telephone booth in the lobby and call that chain's toll-free reservation number and ask for specials. At other times, the toll-free line may quote you a price that's just much higher than that particular hotel can offer.
>
> Always try both whenever possible. For example, a room at a Marriot Residence Inn was listed with a rack rate of $129 a night on the toll-free number, but when we showed up at the desk and questioned it, we were quoted $79 for the *same* room.
>
> It's never bad form to negotiate in an American hotel, and the savings can be substantial if you do. ∎

full of turn-of-the-century furniture. Others are privately run establishments that just don't want to be a part of a chain. In smaller towns, complexes of cabins are available – these often come complete with a fireplace, kitchen and an outdoor area with trees and maybe a stream a few steps away.

Bottom End & Mid-Range The bottom end for hotels is about $70 a night throughout the state, usually Holiday Inns and Marriotts. These will offer basic amenities, room service and restaurants and nightclubs.

Top End Full-service hotels, with bellhops and doormen, restaurants and bars, exercise rooms and saunas, room service and concierge, are found in the main cities. Aimed at those on expense accounts, prices range from about $90 to 150 per room per night.

Resorts
Resorts in Florida are everything you'd want if you're looking for a place in which you can spend an entire holiday without leaving the grounds. They offer good service and add-ons like golf, tennis, water sports, health clubs, several pools, game rooms, activities for kids and adults, restaurants, cafés and sometimes even convenience stores and Pizza Huts. Resort prices are higher than hotel prices – count on at least $100 and usually around $200 a night for these places – and all the activities except those for kids are usually extra.

B&Bs
Bed & breakfast inns in Florida really try hard, usually successfully, to provide personal attention, excellent rooms, great service and local advice, and on many occasions, the owners are absolutely lovely people. The B&B concept – spending a night or so in someone's house as opposed to a hotel – is a very nice one, and the several we've stayed in were definitely worth the price. But defining them is tricky business, so we've resorted to this catchall, which we're sure you'll find accurate as you travel the state:

This charming (Victorian house/Key West mansion/Art Deco delight/Spanish Colonial villa/ renovated turn-of-the-century hunting lodge) is run by a lovely (American/English/German/ Uruguayan) (husband-and-wife team/gay couple) who make certain that all of the rooms, which feature (four-poster beds/sleek modern beds), coffeemakers, (TV and telephone/no TV or telephone) and (fireplaces/wood-burning stoves), are in ship shape. The four (dogs/cats) that live here are named (Harris, Tudor, Rex and Fluffy/Calvin, Siamesey, Pirate and Tom), and breakfast is a (full hot affair with pancakes, waffles, omelets and bacon/continental affair with freshly made muffins, breads and cakes, fruit) and coffee and tea. In the afternoon there's (a free cocktail hour/ free wine and beer). Out (front/back) there's a lovely (veranda/screened-in porch/sundeck), and there's (not) a pool and Jacuzzi. Room rates range from $69 to 179 a night.

FOOD
Florida's smorgasbord of multicultural cuisine can leave some visitors scratching their heads. The first thing that at least Europeans will scratch their heads over is the unbelievable quantity of food you get at American restaurants. A plate of food in the states, especially in Florida, groans under its own weight. Two light eaters may do perfectly well to share one entrée – though some restaurants charge a 'sharing fee', usually about $1 to 2.

Most important, you'll see dolphin on the menu in many restaurants throughout the state. This is dolphin *fish* and not the friendly and protected sea mammal. The other name for dolphin fish is mahi mahi.

Alligator tail is served in some restaurants (mainly in boring deep-fried nuggets, which may as well be Chicken McNuggets, but it's also served marinated and grilled, which is gorgeous) and is not from protected alligator but from those raised on federally licensed alligator farms.

Florida cuisine is a mixture of Amercan Southern, Cuban, Spanish, Caribbean, African and European foods, not to mention the bounteous gifts of the sea. There are also strong representations of French, Mexican and even English cuisine, along with Asian foods. Chinese food in Florida is generally poor, but Thai and Japanese are usually very good, sometimes excellent. Korean, Malaysian, Indonesian and Indian restaurants are very rare, and when you do find them they will be very expensive. The most common foreign cuisine is Italian, which has been considerably Americanized to include dishes that have never seen the light of day in Italy (like veal Parmagiani: breaded fried veal covered with melted mozzarella cheese and tomato sauce).

Highlights to look out for are Jamaican jerk dishes – heavily spiced, marinated and grilled dishes usually of chicken but also beef and fish. Creole dishes, usually shrimp but also chicken, have a tomato-based sauce with peppers, garlic, onions and celery served on rice (shrimp in a sauce – you'll like it). Jambalaya is a tomatoey rice dish usually featuring ham or sausage, onions, garlic and peppers.

Gumbo is derived from the Bantu word for okra. Its only consistent property is that it's a stewlike substance served over rice. The stew is thickened first with browned flour and then with either okra (a slimy vegetable) or filé powder, made from sassafras leaves. There are lots of variations on gumbo: the most popular is shrimp and crab, but look out for more exotic varieties like squirrel and oyster (!), duck and sausage, or z'herbes, a vegetarian version.

Note that Haitian and Cuban dishes sometimes use goat, which can be stringy.

Bagels
A bagel is a disk-shaped bread product made from heavy dough that has been boiled and then baked. The result is a substantial and chewy roll with a uniquely textured coating – the closest comparison would be a real Bavarian *Brez'n*, but that's not really it. Just eat one. Originally ethnic Jewish, the bagel has insinuated itself into the American menu and can now be bought in most big cities from coast to coast. They are usually offered in plain, sesame, poppy, onion, garlic, combinations of the previous and, more rarely, salt. They're available in any diner and in most restaurants that serve breakfast, but

several bagel specialists have opened in the state.

Fast Food
Burger places like McDonald's, Burger King, Wendy's and Checker's sell medium-size hamburgers, and toppings are usually free (at Wendy's you put them on yourself at a salad bar). Ketchup packets and other condiments are free.

In big cities, check prices – sometimes fast food is more expensive than cheap local restaurants; this is especially true in Miami. But generally speaking, big fast-food places – primarily McDonald's, Burger King and Denny's (see below) – have the cheapest breakfasts by far.

Other fast-food chains in Florida include Taco Bell, with excellent and very cheap Mexican-style food, Subway (great and huge sandwiches), Larry's Sub Shops (even better sandwiches, though harder to find), KFC (Kentucky Fried Chicken) and more upscale entries like Denny's (open 24 hours), Shoney's, Bennigans and Cracker Barrel for bland American food. Chilis has excellent Southwestern fare, Red Lobster has seafood, Pollo Tropical serves chicken with a Cuban twist, Boston Market and Kenny Rogers serve roasted chicken and Waffle House has excellent breakfasts 24 hours a day.

Look in discount coupon booklets for coupons to fast-food places – usually two-for-one deals or reduced-price combination meals – and remember that all fast-food places honor their competitor's coupons: a coupon for two Burger King Whoppers for the price of one will be happily accepted by McDonald's, which will give you two Big Macs. And the thing even extends to other kinds of fast-food places like KFC, where if you walk in with a coupon for a Whopper, fries and a drink, you can turn it into a three-piece chicken meal with fries and a drink. Poof!

Vegetarian Food
Vegetarianism is catching on in a big way in the US, and in the cities non-meat-eaters will have an easy time. In rural areas, though,

it can be more difficult, with meat playing a key role in most Southern cooking. Ask twice if something contains meat – some Crackers don't consider things like sausage seasoning, bacon bits or chicken to be meat! Salad bars are a good way to stave off hunger, and many restaurants serve large salads as main courses.

American Food

'Standard' American food is so influenced by the cuisines of other countries around the world that it's difficult to nail down other than the obvious: hamburgers. But modern American cooking can be summed up as combining American portions and homegrown foods with foreign sensibilities and techniques; there are many styles of American cooking that borrow heavily from French, Italian (which is probably the most popular foreign food in the USA), Asian and, to a lesser extent, Turkish and Greek. These listings from Pan Coast and Embers Restaurants in Miami Beach are a sample of typical high-end, foreign-influenced American food:

A salad of mixed greens, sautéed wild mushrooms, Roquefort and pine nuts with roasted red pepper vinaigrette dressing and a main course of oven-roasted five-spice chicken in mushroom sauce with herb-roasted potatoes and roasted vegetables.

Appetizers of crab cakes and steamed citrus-scented artichoke and a main course of bourbon-glazed filet mignon or four double chops of rack of lamb.

Cuban Food

Cuban food is common in the southern section of the state but available throughout it. The most common Cuban foods are pork, beef, rice, beans, eggs, tomatoes and lettuce, and rice, lemon and orange. *Yucca* (manioc or casava) is a starchy root vegetable that can be boiled or baked. Garlic and onion, rather than spices and chile peppers, are used for seasoning. Another common seasoning in Floridian Cuban food is *mojo*, a garlic citrus sauce. Common accompaniments are rice (*arroz*), black or red beans (*frijoles negro o rojo*), yucca and, especially,

plantains – a larger cousin to the banana, served fried. When done right, fried plantains are crispy outside and sweet and starchy inside. The darker the plantain, the sweeter the fruit.

Cuban Specialities The most common dish offered at Cuban restaurants is *carne asada* (roasted meat), usually *puerco asado* (roast pork) or *carne de cerdo* (pork). Other dishes include *bistec* (steak), *arroz con pollo* (chicken and rice), *ropa vieja* (literally 'old clothes' but actually shredded skirt steak stew served with rice and plantains) and *filete de pescado* (fish fillet).

Other seafood includes *calamar* (squid), *camarones* (shrimp), *jaiba* (small crab), *langosta* (lobster), *mariscos* (shellfish) and *ostiones* (oysters).

Meat and poultry include *bistec* or *bistec de res* (beefsteak), *cabra* (goat), *cabrito* (kid, or small goat), *chorizo* (spicy pork sausage), *cordero* (lamb) and *jamón* (ham).

Sandwiches Sandwiches available at *loncherias* (snack bars) are interesting, made by slicing Cuban loaves lengthwise, filling them with ingredients and toasting (and mushing) them in a *plancha* – a heated press. The biggies include the *Cubano* (pork or ham and cheese, sometimes with mustard and pickles, depending on how much you look like a *gringo*), *pan con lechón* (extra crispity-crunchy pork and *mojo*), *palomilla* (steak sandwich with fried onions) and *media noche* or 'midnight' (ham, cheese and roast pork on a roll).

Desserts Most desserts (*postres*) are small afterthoughts to a meal; they include *arroz con leche* (rice pudding), *crepa* (crêpe, a thin pancake), *flan* (custard, or crème caramel), *galletas* (cookies/biscuits), *gelatina* (jello), *helado* (ice cream), *pastel* (pastry or cake) and watch out for that *tres leches* (literally 'three-milk' cake, actually a glucose-tolerance-test disguised as a pudding).

Tea & Coffee The big players are *café con leche* (coffee with hot steamed milk or half-

and-half), *café con crema* (coffee with cream, served separately), espresso served in thimble-size shots (also called 'zoom juice'), *té de manzanilla* (chamomile tea) and *té negro* (black tea).

Fruit & Vegetable Drinks

Pure fresh juices *(jugos)* are popular all over Miami and readily available: the fruit is normally squeezed before your eyes. Every fruit and a few of the squeezable vegetables are used – ever tried pure beetroot juice?

Licuados are blends of fruit or juice with water and sugar. *Licuados con leche* use milk instead of water. Possible additions include raw egg, ice and flavorings such as vanilla or nutmeg.

Aguas frescas or *aguas de fruta* are made by mixing fruit juice or a syrup made from mashed grains or seeds with sugar and water. They are served chilled and are refreshing.

Southern Food

Southern cuisine is heavy on fat and meats; typical specialties include biscuits – similar to scones – and mashed potatoes, collard greens (served with hot-pepper infused vinegar) and black-eyed peas, all of which are prepared with chunks of pork or ham in them. Main courses include fried chicken, roasted ham, pork in any variety of ways (including that favorite light snack, pickled pigs' feet) and gravies with cornbread, a dry cakelike bread made from yellow cornmeal. If you're here on New Year's Day, have a plate of black-eyed peas for good luck in the coming year (every restaurant will be serving them); it's a Southern tradition.

Perhaps the biggest shock comes in the form of grits, a corn-derived white glop that's peculiar to the South. (Waitress to Corinna: 'Ya'll ain't never trahd no *grits* before? Ya'll ain't *got* no grits in Jermunee? Well, whadda ya'll *eat* in Jermunee?') Treat it as a hot cereal and add cream and sugar, or treat it as a side dish and add salt and pepper. It is served in lieu of potatoes at breakfast, and it's best when totally smooth and very hot.

Barbecue

Barbecuing is a Southern tradition that has been entirely deconstructed in the hands of Australians, who can't even get the fire going right and who depend on the women to cook while the men drink beer and give (faulty) instructions. Barbecue consists mainly of seasoned pork, chicken and baby-back ribs cooked over an open flame – brutal but, we have to admit, delicious. Barbecue is served with sweet-and-tangy sauce that has smoky overtones, and the idea is that the meat is cooked and smoked simultaneously, so that by the time it's done, the meat falls off the joints and bones. Whatever. There are many places in Florida to experiment with this cuisine, and the best of them are in small towns with cheesy signs. One sure-fire way to tell if it's good or not is the number of police cars, fire trucks, ambulances and vehicles parked in front – if it's packed, it's good. Purists say that the proper pronunciation is *bubbuh-kyu*.

The best chain place we found in the state – at least for ribs – is Sonny's, with branches all over the northern section of Florida. Even if you don't partake, buy a bottle of their Sonny's Sweet BBQ sauce to take with you, and put it on everything – we even use it on toast.

Seafood

Florida has over 8000 miles of coastline, so it's no surprise seafood is on many menus. Most common are grouper, dolphin (mahi mahi), tuna, salmon and swordfish, all served grilled, deep fried or blackened – thrown into a white-hot frying pan filled with black pepper so that the outside is burned to a crisp while the inside is cooked to medium. One sure-fire indicator of a town's sophistication is the availability of non-deep-fried foods – in some towns, everything, up to and perhaps including the check, is fried. Another Florida favorite is stone crab, indigenous to southern Florida and available in the winter only. Florida lobster doesn't hold a candle to Maine lobster, so if you like the latter, avoid the former. Many towns along the southwest and the Panhandle, especially the Apalachicola area, have 'raw bars', where raw clams and oysters are served on the half shell. Be careful, make certain everything's fresh before digging in (it usually is *very* fresh, but food poisoning isn't any fun, so look before you gulp).

Supermarkets

To the first-time visitor, an American supermarket is as daunting and over-the-top as a visit to the set of *American Gladiators* would be to Mahatma Gandhi: large enough to house a regulation football field, American supermarkets are one-stop shopping extravaganzas that stock everything you'd ever need in every room of the house plus the garage, the garden and in many cases the office. It's everything from auto parts to garbage cans, electronics to fully stocked pharmacies, school supplies to contraceptives, and fresh produce, seafood, meats, wine and beer. Most all supermarkets have bakeries, but you can also choose from over 100 types of packaged breads. Some supermarkets also have full-service delicatessen counters, and fewer have full-service cafés or restaurants.

The biggest supermarket chains in the state are, in approximate order of size, Publix, Winn Dixie and Hyde Park. There is free coffee at all Publix supermarkets, in the big stainless steel percolator near the entrance. Also note that soda machines selling cans of soda are almost always cheaper at supermarkets and outside K-Marts, where cans of cold soda sell for about 35¢.

Meals

Breakfast Breakfast in America is heavier than in many other countries, though Brits and Irish will feel right at home tucking into eggs, toast, bacon, ham or sausage and fried potatoes (either home fries – fried chunks with onions and sometimes bell peppers – or hash browns – shredded potatoes fried with any combination of stuff). Europeans looking for their traditional breakfasts (cheeses, ham, salami and assorted breads) will have no luck here at all outside Orlando

and Miami: we watched as a traveler asked for a turkey sandwich in a deli at breakfast time, and when he inquired 15 minutes later as to why it was taking so long, he was told that he'd have to wait because he'd 'ordered an unorthodox breakfast'.

'Continental breakfast' is a euphemism for anything from a donut and a cup of coffee (we can see the legions of French eating *that* on the Continent) to a European-like spread of cheese, bread, muffins and croissants, but usually no meats.

Many of the more upscale fast-food places, and some steak houses in Orlando, have all-you-can-eat breakfast buffets for around $9.95. Be suspicious of these, and calculate how much the same thing would cost you at a Waffle House or a diner, where your meal would be made to order, would probably be cheaper, and your eggs don't sit in a huge vat to be picked (and breathed) over by dozens of tourists before you get to them.

Lunch Lunch, in terms of ritual, is traditionally the least important meal in the USA; many office workers have it at their desks, and most people simply grab something on the run – which is precisely why America has the best sandwiches in the world: we know how to eat on the fly.

Sandwiches here are usually packed with stuff, including fresh vegetables, meats (like roast beef, ham and turkey), cheeses and condiments, and except for cheese, everything on top is free. Subway and Larry's Subs routinely offer sandwiches with any of the following: lettuce, tomato, onion, peppers, hot peppers, oil, vinegar, salt, pepper, mayonnaise, ketchup and mustard at no extra charge.

Because of this, many fine restaurants (and some not-so-fine ones) offer drastically reduced prices at lunchtime. You can get at lunch a meal for $5 that would cost $15 or more at dinner. Also in this category are early-bird dinners, offered from around 4 to 6 pm, which try to lure customers in for early trade by offering similar discounts.

Dinner Dinner is the main, and most social, meal of the day in the USA. Americans tend to eat at about 7 to 8 pm. It's the time when restaurants are the most expensive and the most crowded, and the time when the largest meals are eaten.

DRINKS

The soft drinks available in Florida are the same as everywhere in the world, so suffice it to say that there are no surprises when it comes to bottled or carbonated soft drinks. Smoothies are drinks made from yogurt and fresh fruits blended into a shake. A shake, by the way, is fast-blended ice cream, milk and flavoring, usually chocolate, vanilla or strawberry. The biggest surprise for many non-Latin foreign visitors is *guarapo*, or sugar cane juice. Cappuccino and European espresso are available in more upscale restaurants, but note that Starbuck's hasn't made any real inroads in Florida yet.

Alcohol

The strictly enforced drinking age in Florida is 21. Carry a driver's license or passport as proof of age to enter a bar, order alcohol at a restaurant or buy alcohol. Servers have the right to ask to see your ID and may refuse service without it. Minors are not allowed in bars and pubs, even to order nonalcoholic beverages. Unfortunately, this means that most dance clubs are also off-limits to minors, although a few clubs have solved the under-age problem with a segregated drinking area. Minors are, however, welcome in the dining areas of restaurants where alcohol is served.

Beer and wine are sold in supermarkets in Florida, while harder stuff is sold in liquor stores. One shocking sight in Florida is the drive-thru liquor stand, where customers pull through, order a bottle and zip away. There are several chain liquor stores in Florida, among them Walgreens, a pharmacy/liquor store, and regional chains like ABC.

Beer Commercially available American 'beer', for lack of a better term, is weaker and sweeter than its equivalent around the world, perhaps to encourage drinking more of it. Indeed, the marketing of 'light' beer – with fewer calories than regular beer – stalled until marketers were able to convince the public that 'less filling' meant that one could suck down many more beers on the same stomach.

Beer in the USA comes in cans and bottles. Bottles range from ponies (8 ounces) to standard 12-ounce, to long-neck (12-ounces as well, but the neck of the bottle is longer), to 32-ounce (one quart) bottles. American beer also comes in 12- and 16-ounce (one pint) cans. Bottles and cans are generally sold in bundles of six (six-packs) or 12 or in 'cases' of 24.

The major brands are manufactured by Anheuser Busch – Budweiser and Michelob – followed by Miller and its products, including Miller Genuine Draft and Lite. A six-pack of standard American beer sells for between $3 and 5 in supermarkets. You can visit the Anheuser Busch Brewery in Jacksonville (see the Northeast Florida chapter) or sample the wares at the Anheuser Busch Hospitality Center at SeaWorld, in Orlando (see the Central Florida chapter).

One new fad in American beerdom is 'ice' brewed beer. Ice brew implies a 'cold filtration process', but it adds up to beer with about 5.5% alcohol. Meanwhile, microbrewed beers are made by smaller companies with limited production. They can be excellent and taste much like their European counterparts. The biggest microbrews are Samuel Adams (Boston) and Anchor Steam (San Francisco) – both are gaining popularity so quickly that their 'micro' status will probably come under challenge. There are about a dozen microbrewers in Florida, and we try to mention them in the text where possible. Microbrews and ice brews cost between $5 and 8 a six-pack.

Wine Wine is also available in supermarkets, and foreign visitors will often find that wine from their home country is cheaper here – many Australian wines are about 20% less in Florida than at home. But while perfectly drinkable wine is available in supermarkets, connoisseurs will do far better in proper liquor stores, which sell a better range of higher-end wines from the USA and around the world.

ENTERTAINMENT
Performing Arts
The biggest center for music, dance and theater in the state is Miami, though Fort Lauderdale, Tampa and the Palm Beaches are noteworthy centers for performing arts. See the individual chapter sections for information on performing arts available.

Cinema
Americans have been known to make a movie or two, and every Florida city has at least one chain theater. American movie houses have taken the as-many-as-possible approach to cinemas, and the quaint one-movie cinema is practically extinct – look for five-, six-, nine-, 11- and up to 18-plex cinemas.

The best place to look for a cinema is in the nearest shopping mall. Prices are usually very cheap – from $2.50 to 3.25 in the afternoon before 4 pm and between $5 and 7 in the evening. Miami has several independent film outlets that offer smaller budget, foreign or cult films, but outside that city, expect only mass-appeal Hollywood films with few exceptions.

The main cinema chains in Florida are AMC and Cobb.

Bars
Bars in Florida range from down and dirty to as chic as one could expect. The prices range accordingly.

Most American bartenders (except in the tonier places that spend money on automatic pourers) free-hand pour in a manner that would make British publicans blanch. A 'shot', ostensibly one ounce, is often larger than that. American custom says that you tip the bartender for each drink – generally $1 – and that (except in very crowded nightclubs) you place your cash on the bar and leave it there while you drink.

'Happy hours', usually a lot longer than an hour – sometimes all day – are periods in which drink prices are reduced, some-times substantially. Deals are usually two or even three for the price of one. 'Ladies' nights', a clever ploy to lure horny, thirsty males by using women (who drink free) as bait, are usually held once a week.

Nightclubs
Nightclubs in Florida are found in all larger cities, and in almost all you'll have to dress for the occasion – especially in Miami, where you'd better dress and look as if you own the place or forget even getting in. In Miami Beach, competition is so fierce that nightclubs literally open and close every day.

In larger clubs, entry fees are between $10 and 12; in Orlando, admission to hootcha-terias like Church St Station and Pleasure Island is about $15, while local clubs charge less than average to try and draw people away from their huge competitors.

In most cities, bars turn into nightclub-ish places in the evenings, with live music of some sort or another, or contests.

Gay and lesbian nightclubs generally have live performances that range from drag shows, dating games and amateur nights to strippers.

SPECTATOR SPORTS
Sports in the USA developed separately from the rest of the world, and baseball (with its clone, softball), football and basketball dominate the sports scene, both for spectators and participants. Football and basketball, in particular, are huge.

In professional basketball, the excellent Orlando Magic is lamenting the loss of Shaquille O'Neal, their 42-foot-tall super-star, who signed as a free agent with the LA Lakers (and with Hollywood: he's embarked on an acting and producing career as well) at the end of the 1995-96 season. But the Magic is still by far the most popular team in the state, while the Miami Heat have been slogging along for years in the NBA playing competent if unspectacular, ball.

Florida has three NFL football teams: the winning Miami Dolphins, the greedy Tampa Bay Buccaneers and the upstart Jacksonville Jaguars. If you've ever wondered whether it was true that the word fan derives from 'fanatic', attend a Florida pro football game. And if you think that's bad, wait till you see the fanaticism associated with *college* football: the state has several good college teams, chief among them the University of Miami Hurricanes and the FSU Seminoles.

Baseball is so embedded in the country's psyche that, despite its complex rules, the difficulty and expense of maintaining playing fields with an irregular configuration, and labor-management problems at the highest professional levels, it continues to flourish. Many of the most meaningful metaphors in American English and even political discourse – such as 'getting to first base' or the recently debased 'three strikes and you're out' – come from the sport. Softball, which requires less space than baseball, draws more participants, both men and women, than any other organized sport in the country.

Many professional baseball teams come to the warmth of South Florida for spring training, from March to April, and minor-league teams play here throughout the baseball season, from May to October.

Jai alai, a fascinating and dangerous Spanish game in which teams hurl a *pelota* – a *very* hard ball – at over 150 mph can be seen (and bet on) in stadiums around the southern part of the state.

Soccer has made limited inroads, mostly among immigrants, but it has failed as a spectator sport and is likely to remain a minor diversion for at least the next few years.

THINGS TO BUY

Other than handicrafts and art in the cities, there's not really a big 'Florida product'. The main thing to buy here, especially if you're coming from Europe or even Australia, is clothing and consumer goods, all of which are cheaper than at home.

Crapola

Tourist crap stands abound in major cities and in gas stations along highways. The big offerings are 'funny' T-shirts, lacquered alligator heads (they're real, culled from alligator farms) and other standard schlocky tourist stuff that can be found around the world.

Large Specialty Chain Stores

There are several large specialty retailers in the state. When we're shopping for something, we usually call the big shops first, as their prices give us a good idea for price comparison with other places. Check the ads in the local newspaper for specials and sales. Many of these stores have more than one location in any given town, so ask when you call about the one nearest you. The larger clothing specialty stores are below, in Shopping Malls.

Sports Authority sells sporting goods, golf clubs, bicycles, running, hiking, climbing equipment and a small selection of backpacks.

Circuit City sells a decent range of electronics, computers, appliances and other gizmotronics.

Incredible Universe in Miami has taken the PT Barnum approach to selling electronics – balloons for the kids, big bright colors and a veritable three-ring circus of bleeping things.

Wal-Mart, K-Mart and Sears exist to be one-stop shopping centers for just about anything you'd need, from padlocks to plates, diapers to garbage disposals (pronounced 'dispose-all' in the South) and everything in between. If you need something, any of one of them will probably have it.

Eckerd is a chain of pharmacies around the state, some open 24 hours. Walgreens is a chain of (get this) combination pharmacy/liquor stores throughout the area, so if you should ever need a pint of whiskey *and* a bandage, stop here.

Car Max, a division of Circuit City, is a unique used car dealership, based on flat, non-negotiable prices on late-model used cars. If you're looking for a good (or at least expensive) used car, call their corporate offices at ☎ 804-727-0427 for a list of shops around the country.

Shopping Malls

Massive shopping malls have so saturated the shopping scene here that it's difficult to find many items without entering one. And the insidious nature of the malls and the huge shops is that lower wages lead to higher employee turnover: in Sports Authority, a major sporting goods chain, we com-

Cheaper in the States

While you won't find Vegemite anywhere (Publix does, however, stock Marmite and sometimes even Bovril), the USA has the best prices in the world (with the possible exception of Hong Kong) on some items. They include the following:

- Jeans – New blue jeans in the USA (like unwashed Levi's 501s) start as low as $24.
- Sunglasses – Ray Bans can be had for as low as $40.
- Zippo lighters – These babies start at about $12.
- Running shoes – You can get a good pair of name-brand running shoes starting at $40.
- Camping equipment – Everything costs less here.
- Computers – Though you may get hit with an import tax when you get home, the USA is definitely a great place for computers: take the price in UK£ and switch the symbol to $ and you're about right. As we went to press, a 75 MHz multimedia Pentium desktop with monitor could be yours for about $1200.
- Cameras – We got a good quality new Minolta 400 series Maxxum for just about $350, including two lenses.
- CDs and musical instruments – The average price for a new CD release is between $12 and $14; musical instruments, especially items like DATs, ADAM and digital samplers, are in the same category as computers.

Note that if you're buying electric or electronic appliances here (like coffee grinders, telephones, tape recorders, CD players, etc), you may need a step-down transformer (not adapter) to allow the thing to work in Europe or Australia. Check the power requirements on the back – if it says 120-240V, 50-60 Hz, you're set; you'll need only an adapter to change the shape of the plug. If it says 120V only, you'll need the transformer. If you're buying to bring it back to Japan, you'll always need a step-up transformer to turn the wimpy Japanese 100V current into something useful. ■

plained to a manager that we couldn't find one person who could tell us whether they had tents with no-see-um netting. 'Well,' he told us, 'we train them as best we can for the wage we pay them.'

The major shops in malls are generally clothing (Neiman-Marcus, Saks Fifth Avenue, Gap, Burdines) and general merchandisers (Sears, K-Mart, Wal-Mart, JC Penney), while all malls will have a food court (a collection of fast-food joints), a Sunglass Hut, shoe shops, some specialty jean and women's clothing shops and bookshops.

Factory Outlet Malls

Factory outlet malls are shops that sell old or overstocked items that the manufacturer is, for some reason, trying to get rid of. It could be last season's gear, it could be ugly as sin or it could be damaged or 'irregular'. Most of the time, though, the prices in a true factory outlet like Sawgrass Mills or Augustine Outlet Stores can be up to 70%

lower than retail. They're usually located several miles from a major city.

Thrift Shops

Thrift and second-hand shops can be found in most Florida cities. Most are affiliated with churches or relief organizations, to which items are donated. The organizations sell the donated items – usually very inexpensively – to raise money. The items range from books (usually about 50¢ a piece) to appliances to clothing. Clothing, while used, is always clean, and some absolutely fantastic vintage stuff can be had with a little digging.

The biggest are outlets of Goodwill, the Salvation Army and St Vincent de Paul. And of course, the best selection and the biggest scores are to be had in the more affluent neighborhoods, where donations are made more frequently and are of far higher quality than in other places.

It's unbelievable – a friend found a pair of Pucci original pants in amazing condition for $10 in a Palm Beach thrift shop. Also on offer at these places are cameras, movie cameras, film editors, bicycles and sometimes even cars. Check in the local yellow pages under Thrift Shops for listings.

Flea Markets

True flea markets are bazaars, usually held on weekends in huge parking lots, where merchants from all over the state get together to sell *stuff* from tables. Prices are negotiable and you should always bargain. In some cities, like Kissimmee, organized regular flea markets occur daily during the tourist season. Prices at these are higher.

EMERGENCIES

Dial ☎ 911 for police, fire and ambulance emergencies – it's a free call from any phone. Check the inside front cover of the Miami white pages for a slew of emergency numbers.

If you're robbed, report the theft to the police on the non-emergency numbers. You'll need a police report in order to make an insurance claim back home.

If your credit cards, cash cards or travellers cheques have been stolen, notify your bank or the relevant company as soon as possible. For refunds on lost or stolen travellers cheques (not cards) call American Express (☎ 800-221-7282), MasterCard (☎ 800-223-9920), Thomas Cook (☎ 800-223-7373) or Visa (☎ 800-227-6811).

To report lost or stolen credit cards, call American Express (☎ 800-528-4800), Visa (☎ 800-336-8472), MasterCard (☎ 800-826-2181), Diners Club (☎ 800-234-6377) and Discover (☎ 800-347-2683).

Foreign visitors who have lost their passports should contact their consulate. Having a photocopy of the important pages of your passport will make replacement much easier.

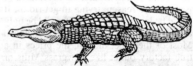

Outdoor Activities

Florida is about the outdoors; from broiling on the beach to jumping out of a plane over it. With so much water, the opportunities for swimming, snorkeling, scuba diving, canoeing and kayaking are almost unparalleled.

The road traveler in Florida is faced with some of the world's most monotonous highways: endless ribbons of shimmering, straight blacktop lined on either side with such a uniform dark-green blur that it would appear that there's absolutely nothing on either side of you until you get to the next major city. But the truth is that just off the major roads lies an astonishing array of wilderness areas, thousands of rivers and lakes, and the opportunity to view subtropical flora and fauna unseen anywhere else in the continental USA.

Even just stopping off for a day of canoeing in a state park will give you a look at Florida that most visitors miss out on.

Though each pursuit has specialized gear shops (usually the best source for local information), Lauderdale Sports in Fort Lauderdale is probably the best overall sporting superstore in the south of the state, though the more poorly equipped (and staffed) Sports Authority has more stores around the state.

HIKING & BACKPACKING

There is perhaps no better way to appreciate the beauty of Florida – its beaches, parks and scenic trails, peaceful hammocks and marshes – than on foot and on the trail. Taking a few days' (or even a few hours') break from the highway to explore the great outdoors can refresh road-weary travelers and give them a heightened appreciation of the scenery which goes whizzing past day after day. Some travelers will experience one good hike and decide to plan the rest of their trip around wilderness or hiking areas.

Florida National Scenic Trail (FNST)

With 880 miles of completed trail out of a planned 1300, the FNST is maintained by the Florida Trail Association, an all-volunteer organization that maintains this and other trails throughout the state.

But the FNST is far from completed: there are significant gaps in south central Florida and in the western Panhandle. When completed, the trail will run from Big Cypress National Preserve at the northern end of the Everglades National Park, north, around Lake Okeechobee, through the Ocala National Forest and straight up through the central part of the state, then curve west and extend to the Gulf Island National Seashore near Pensacola.

Maintenance in the portions of the trail that exist today is unpredictable. In some sections it's terrible due to flooding and mud, and in others it's great. There are organized campsites in certain sections, not in others; the same can be said for water. When hiking the trail, you should be prepared to bring everything you'll need, and be entirely self-sufficient.

For information and a trail map, call the Florida Trail Association (☎ 352-378-8823, within Florida 800-343-1882), or write to PO Box 13708, Gainesville, FL 32604-1708.

National Parks

Unless you have a few days to get into the backcountry of a national park, or are visiting during non-tourist season (between Memorial Day and Labor Day), expect hiking in national parks to be crowded.

Travelers with little hiking experience will appreciate well-marked, well-maintained trails in national parks, often with toilet facilities at either end and interpretive displays along the way. The trails give access to the parks' natural features, and usually show up on NPS maps as nature trails or self-guided interpretive trails. These hikes are usually no longer than two miles.

Most national parks require overnight hikers to carry backcountry permits, available from visitors centers or ranger stations, which must be obtained 24 hours in advance and require you to follow a specific itinerary. While this system reduces the chance of people getting lost in the backcountry and limits the number of people using one area at any given time, it may detract from the sense of space and freedom hiking can give. In backcountry areas of the Everglades and Big Cypress, you'll have to have an interview with a ranger to determine if you're an experienced wilderness explorer or a misinformed yahoo. For more information, call the NPS at ☎ 800-365-2267.

Treading Lightly

Backcountry areas are composed of fragile environments and cannot support an inundation of human activity, especially insensitive and careless activity. A good suggestion is to treat the backcountry like you would your own backyard – minus the barbecue pit and those kids.

A new code of backcountry ethics is evolving to deal with the growing numbers of people in the wilderness. Most conservation organizations and hikers' manuals have their own set of backcountry codes, all of which outline the same important principles: minimizing the impact on the land, leaving no trace and taking nothing but photographs and memories. Above all, stay on the main trail, stay on the main trail, and, lastly, even if it means walking through mud or crossing a patch of snow, *stay on the main trail*.

Wilderness Camping Camping in undeveloped areas is rewarding for its peacefulness, but presents special concerns. Take care to ensure that the area you choose can comfortably support your presence and leave the surroundings in better condition than on arrival. The following list of guidelines should help.

• Bury human waste in cat holes dug six to eight inches deep. The salt and minerals in urine attract deer; use a tent-bottle (funnel attachments are available for women) if you

are prone to middle-of-the-night calls by Mother Nature. Camouflage the cat hole when finished.

• Use soaps and detergents sparingly or not at all, and never allow these things to enter streams or lakes. When washing yourself (a backcountry luxury, not a necessity), lather up (with biodegradable soap) and rinse yourself with cans of water as far as possible away from your water source. Scatter dish water after removing all food particles.

• It's recommended to carry a lightweight stove for cooking and to use a lantern instead of a campfire.

• If a fire is allowed and appropriate, dig a hole and build a fire in it. On islands or beach areas, build fires below the high tide line. Gather sticks no larger than an adult's wrist from the ground. Use only dead and down wood, do not twist branches off live or dead and standing trees. Pour wastewater from meals around the perimeter of the campfire to prevent the fire from spreading, and thoroughly douse it before leaving or going to bed.

• Designate cooking clothes to leave in the food bag, away from your tent.

• Burn cans to get rid of their odor, then remove them from the ashes and pack them out.

• Pack out what you pack in, including all trash – yours *and* others'.

Safety

The major forces to be reckoned with while hiking and camping are the weather (which is uncontrollable) and your own frame of mind. Be prepared for unpredictable weather – you may go to bed under a clear sky and wake up in the midst of a thunderstorm the likes of which you haven't seen since you watched Moby Dick. Afternoon thunderstorms are very common in the summer. Carry a rain jacket at all times. Backpackers should have a pack-liner (heavy-duty garbage bags work well), a full set of rain gear and food that does not require cooking. A positive attitude is helpful in any situation. If a hot shower, comfortable mattress and clean clothes are essential to your well-being, don't head out into the wilderness for five days – stick to day hikes (actually, in summer, you'll just have to wait until about half past three for the hot shower, courtesy of one of Florida's spectacular thunderstorms).

Highest safety measures suggest never hiking alone, but solo travelers should not be discouraged, especially if they value solitude. The important thing is to always let someone know where you are going and how long you plan to be gone. Use sign-in boards at trailheads or ranger stations. Travelers looking for hiking companions can inquire or post notices at ranger stations, outdoors stores, campgrounds and youth hostels.

Fording rivers and streams is another potentially dangerous but often necessary part of being on the trail. In national parks and along maintained trails in national forests, bridges usually cross large bodies of water (this is not the case in designated wilderness areas, where bridges are taboo). Upon reaching a river, unclip all of your pack straps – your pack is expendable, you are not. Avoid crossing barefoot – you don't know where that bottom's been. Bring a pair of lightweight canvas sneakers or Tiva-style sandals for crossing to avoid sloshing around in wet boots for the rest of your hike.

Using a staff for balance is helpful, but don't rely on it to support all your weight. Don't enter water higher than mid-thigh; once higher than that your body gives the current a large mass to work against.

If you should get wet, wring your clothes out immediately, wipe off all the excess water on your body and hair and put on any dry clothes you (or your partner) might have.

People with little hiking or backpacking experience should not attempt to do too much, too soon, or they might end up being non-hikers for the wrong reasons. Know your limitations, know the route you are going to take and pace yourself accordingly. Remember, there is absolutely nothing wrong with turning back or not going as far as you originally planned.

What to Bring

Equipment The following list is meant to be a general guideline for backpackers, not an 'if-I-have-everything-here-I'll-be-fine' guarantee. Know yourself and what special things you may need on the trail; consider the area and climatic conditions you will be traveling in.

- Boots – light to medium weight are recommended for day hikes, while sturdy boots are necessary for extended trips with a heavy pack. Most importantly they should be well broken in and have a good heel. Waterproof boots are preferable.
- Alternative footwear – thongs or sandals or running shoes for wearing around camp and canvas sneakers for crossing streams.
- Socks – frequent changes during the day reduce the chance of blisters, but are usually impractical.
- Subdued colors are usually recommended, but if hiking during hunting season, blaze orange is a necessity.
- Shorts, light shirt – for everyday wear; remember that heavy cotton takes a long time to dry and is very cold when wet.
- Long-sleeve shirt – light cotton, wool or polypropylene. A button-down front makes layering easy and can be left open when the weather is hot and your arms need protection from the sun.
- Long pants – heavy denim jeans take forever to dry and hey, this is the sub-tropics. Sturdy cotton or canvas pants are good for trekking through brush, and cotton or nylon sweats are comfortable to wear around camp.
- Rain gear – light, breathable and waterproof is the ideal combination, but it doesn't exist no matter what those catalogs say. You need plastic, not GoreTex for the kind of rains you'll get in Florida. We use Rainbird 2000 ponchos, which fold into their front pockets and crush down to very small sacks that are good for pillows. If nothing else is available, use heavy-duty trash bags to cover you and your packs.
- Hat – a cotton hat with a brim is good for sun protection.
- Bandanna or handkerchief – good for a runny nose, dirty face, unmanageable hair, picnic lunch and flag (especially a red one).
- Small towel – one which is indestructible and will dry quickly. Check in any sporting goods store for camping towels.
- First aid kit – should include, at the least, self-adhesive bandages and adhesive tape, disinfectant, antibiotic salve or cream, gauze, small scissors and tweezers. An Ace-type bandage couldn't hurt either.
- Knife, fork, spoon and mug – a double-layer plastic mug with a lid is best. A mug acts as eating and drinking receptacle, mixing bowl

and wash basin; the handle protects you from getting burned. Bring an extra cup if you like to eat and drink simultaneously.

- Pots and pans – aluminum cook sets are best, but any sturdy one-quart pot is sufficient. True gourmands who want more than pasta, soup and freeze-dried food will need a skillet or frying pan. A metal pot scrubber is helpful for removing stubborn oatmeal, especially when using cold water and no soap.
- Stove – lightweight and easy to operate is ideal. Most outdoors stores rent propane or butane stoves; test the stove before you head out, even cook a meal on it, to familiarize yourself with any quirks it may have.

- Water purifier – optional but really nice to have; water can also be purified by boiling for at least 10 minutes.
- Matches or lighter – waterproof matches are good and having several lighters is smart.
- Candle or lantern – candles are easy to operate, but do not stay lit when they are dropped or wet and can be hazardous inside a tent. Outdoors stores rent lanterns; test it before you hit the trail.
- Flashlight – each person should have his or her own and be sure its batteries have plenty of life left in them. We like Petzl headlamps and MagLite because they're both almost indestructible and have slots for spare bulbs.

Global Positioning System

The Global Positioning System (GPS) was developed by the US military. It involves 24 satellites operating in six orbital planes at an altitude of 12,500 miles, which put out coded signals to be received by small units on earth. With the magic of computer chips that can solve several sets of simultaneous equations the readings produce, these instruments can determine their absolute location with surprising precision. In English, this little piece of gizmotronics tells you:

- Where you are on earth (within about 50 to 100 meters)
- Where you've been
- Where you're going (bearing, distance from any specific destination)
- How fast you're going
- When you'll get there
- What your altitude is above sea level
- And, of course, the time

As soon as I saw one I began to invent various justifications I could come up with for spending *however much it would cost* – I knew I *had* to have one, especially with Lonely Planet's Stan Armington (author of *Nepal Trekking Guide*) showing his off and talking about how a *Hitchhiker's Guide to the Galaxy* is close to being a reality. I finally went with the relatively inexpensive and very small Garmin GPS-40, which cost $329 at a Florida sporting goods shop.

If you know where you want to be you can enter the coordinates (latitude and longitude culled from, say, a good atlas or map) and the Garmin will show you an electronic 'highway' (a graphical representation of a road going off into the horizon): if the 'road' bends left, you turn left at the same angle – the idea being that as long as you keep the electronic 'road' on the screen pointing straight, you're going towards your destination. I've now used it for practice in Germany, throughout Russia and in the Florida Everglades, where it's an invaluable piece of gear.

Annoying features are that coverage changes depending on where you are – city readings are usually not very accurate and vertical readings are fantasy: while in the Alps, I once got a reading of 119 meters below sea level. Finally, they're not as easy as you'd hope – they have a terminology all their own and it takes a good while to get the hang of it.

As a guideline, a GPS will come in handy for those traveling in remote areas without roads – if you're hiking, biking, canoeing, flying or parasailing. And if you'll be traveling anywhere off the beaten track in the Everglades, these gizmos are choice gear.

Just don't think that it acts as your *only* orienteering tool – unless you've spent a lot of money and/or had a lot of experience with them, bring along a good compass as well for critical measurements. ■

- Sleeping bag – goose-down bags are warm and lightweight, but worthless if they get wet; most outdoors stores rent synthetic bags.
- Sleeping pad – this is strictly a personal preference. We hardly ever use them but a friend swears by ThermaRest pads, which fill up with air when unrolled and behave as an air mattress. Use a sweater or sleeping bag sack stuffed with clothes as a pillow.
- Tent – make sure it is waterproof, or has a waterproof cover, and has no-see-um – not just mosquito – netting, and know how to put it up *before* you reach camp. Remember that your packs will be sharing the tent with you.
- Camera and binoculars – don't forget extra film and waterproof film canisters (sealable plastic bags work well).
- Compass, GPS and maps – each person should have his/her own.
- Eyeglasses – contact-lens wearers should always bring a back-up set.
- Sundries – biodegradable toilet paper, small sealable plastic bags, insect repellent, sun screen, lip balm, unscented moisturizing cream, moleskin for foot blisters, dental floss (burnable and good when there is no water for brushing), sunglasses, deck of cards, pen or pencil and paper or notebook, books and nature guides.

Food Keeping your energy up is important, but so is keeping your pack light. Backpackers tend to eat a substantial breakfast and dinner and snack heavily in between. There is no need to be excessive. If you pack loads of food you'll probably use it, but if you have just enough you will probably not miss anything.

Some basic staples are: packaged instant oatmeal, bread (the denser the better), rice or pasta, instant soup or ramen noodles, dehydrated meat (jerky), dried fruit, energy bars, chocolate, trail mix and peanut butter or honey or jam (in plastic jars or squeeze bottles). See kayaking below for information on freeze dried meals. Don't forget the wet-wipes, but be sure to dispose of them properly or pack them out.

Books
There are quite a few good how-to and where-to books on the market, usually found in outdoors stores, or bookstores' Sports & Recreation or Outdoors sections. Chris Camden's *Backpacker's Handbook* (Ragged Mountain Press, 1992) is a beefy collection of tips for the trail. *How to Shit in the Woods* (Ten Speed Press, 1994) is Kathleen Meyer's explicit, comic and useful manual on toilet training in the wilderness.

Maps
A good map is essential for any hiking trip. NPS and USFS ranger stations usually stock topographical maps that cost $2 to $6. In the absence of a ranger station, try the local stationary or hardware store.

Longer hikes require two types of maps: USGS Quadrangles and US Department of Agriculture-Forest Service maps. To order a map index and price list, contact the US Geological Survey, PO Box 25286, Denver, CO 80225. For general information on maps, see also the Facts for the Visitor chapter. For information regarding maps of specific forests, wilderness areas or national parks, see the appropriate geographic entry.

ROCK CLIMBING
In a state with no mountains, or even hills to speak of, this heading may strike you as odd. Well, hell. There isn't any *real* rock climbing in the state, but the Eden Roc Resort in Miami Beach (☎ 531-0000, see the Miami Beach Places to Stay section in the Miami chapter) has a 23-foot-high indoor rock climbing complex. Contact the Eden Roc for information on their rock climbing-only memberships.

BICYCLING
It's not as if there's a lot of excitement in Florida biking: the state's as flat as a pancake. That said, there are plenty of bicycle trails in and around cities, in city, county, state and national parks, and railtrails – bicycle paths on the trackbeds of former railway lines – pop up here and there: in Tallahassee, Gainesville and along the southwest coast. In cities, especially cities like Miami Beach, Fernandina Beach on Amelia Island, St Augustine, Tallahassee, Pensacola and Pensacola Beach, Key

West and others, a bike is a great way to get around, and rentals are readily available. Note that in state parks, four bicyclists will pay more to enter than eight people in a car – generally admission for pedestrians and cyclists is $1 each.

Information
Members of the national League of American Bicyclists (LAB; ☎ 410-539-3399, 800-288-2453), 190 W Ostend St, Suite 120, Baltimore, MD 21230, may transport their bikes free on selected airlines and obtain a list of hospitality homes in each state that offer simple accommodations to touring cyclists. The LAB also publishes an annual *Almanac* that lists contacts in each state, along with information about bicycle routes and special events. Bicycle tourists will also want to get a copy of the *Cyclosource Catalog* listing books and maps and *The Cyclist's Yellow Pages*, a trip-planning resource, both published by Adventure Cycling Association (☎ 406-721-1776), 150 E Pine St, Missoula, MT 59802.

Laws & Regulations
Trail etiquette requires that cyclists yield to other users. Helmets should always be worn to reduce the risk of head injury, but they are not mandated by law. National parks require that all riders under 18 years wear a helmet.

HORSEBACK RIDING
Horseback riding is not as popular in Florida as in other areas of the country, and it tends to be expensive. Rates for recreational riding start around $15 per hour or $25 for two hours, though the hourly rate falls rapidly thereafter and full-day trips usually cost around $75 with a guide. Experienced riders may want to let the owners know, or

else you may be saddled with an excessively docile stable nag. Horse country in Florida is just southwest of Gainesville, and riding is more popular in the central section of the state than in any other – see the sections on the Paynes Prairie State Preserve, Devil's Den and Ocala in the Central Florida chapter for information.

CANOEING
Florida's covered with and surrounded by water, and there are canoeing opportunities practically everywhere you go. The best opportunities for canoe adventures are in the Everglades, where the 99-mile Wilderness Waterway, and trips around the 10,000 Islands, offer fantastic opportunities for canoeists.

But for standard paddles of an hour or several, many state and county parks offer canoe rentals, and private concessionaires operate in or near ones that don't. Generally speaking, the rentals are between $4 and 7 an hour, or $10 and 15 for four hours and from $20 to 25 for a full day or 24 hours. Many of the trails are very easy going paddles, and rangers are invariably helpful in letting you know how to see the most wildlife, and, if necessary, giving a paddling lesson.

What to Bring
Things you'll need to bring for individual backcountry canoe trips (obviously the overnight stuff is only if you plan to camp):

- Good, sightable compass and/or GPS
- Good flashlight (we like Petzl headlamps and Mini Mag brands)
- Nautical charts and tide chart
- Tent with no-see-um – not just mosquito – netting
- Sleeping bag
- One gallon of water per day, preferably in heavy-duty or army surplus water containers, not store-bought one-gallon jugs
- As much food as you'll need plus an extra day per person
- A solid plastic sealable cooler, like a Coleman or Eskimo – *not* Styrofoam – for food storage
- Portable cooking stove, pot and utensils

- Avon Skin-So-Soft or industrial-strength insect repellent like REI Jungle Juice
- Sunscreen, sunglasses and a hat
- Strong plastic garbage bags – Hefty brand lawn bags are nice
- Biodegradable toilet paper and a small spade to dig waste pit
- Binoculars (to see route markers) and camera
- Dry change of clothes for *when* you fall in the water
- Good shoes or boots

Packing

If you'll be traveling in a canoe, the idea that you have to take as little as possible can take a back seat to the important stuff: a) being comfortable when you get where you're going, b) not cheating yourself on meals, which are very important, and c) having the right equipment to make it possible to avoid getting yourself into trouble.

When we go we pack as much as we can – food and gear – into sealable coolers and use a trick encouraged by North American Canoe Tours in Everglades City: fill cleaned-out half-gallon milk jugs with water and freeze them; block ice lasts longer than cubes and as it melts you get cold drinking water. If you play your cards right and keep everything sealed tightly, you can make several of those last for two to three days.

One thing we skimp on is clothes: we know we're going to get wet, and pack as little as possible – but we always make certain to pack lightweight long pants, lightweight long-sleeved shirts and clean, dry socks and underwear. Keep these in the plastic garbage bags. Heavy duty Ziplock brand freezer bags are good for wallets and anything small that you don't want to get wet.

Speaking of things getting wet, expect that everything will and be pleasantly surprised with whatever doesn't. That said, take preventative steps to protect the most important of your assets, which in approximate order are: sleeping bag, tent, clothes and expensive electronics like your camera. Wrap these well in the heavy-duty garbage bags, remove the air from them, tie them off twice and place them in a backpack.

We tie everything – backpacks, coolers, water jugs – to each other in a daisy chain (that is, lines between each piece of gear, not tying everything together in a clump) and then tying one end of it to the inside of the canoe. In the unlikely event that you flip, it's nice to know you'll still have your stuff, and if you do flip, having all of your stuff safely tied, yet in the water enables you to right the craft much faster.

SEA KAYAKING

This quiet, unobtrusive sport allows you to visit unexplored islands and stretches of coast and view marine life at close range. Sea kayaks, which hold one or two people, are larger and more stable than whitewater boats, making them safer and easier to navigate. They also have storage capacity so you can take them on overnight or even up to week-long trips. Imagine paddling to a secluded beach on one of the Gulf Coast or Everglades islands and setting up camp for a week – one rad guy we met says that he books passage on day cruises to the Bahamas and takes his kayak and gear as carry-on, and once there he just paddles off into the sunset!

What to Bring

In terms of what you're bringing, kayaking is similar to backpacking. There is enough room in a Sea Lion sea kayak for seven days' worth of supplies – if you're very good at packing. You're going to want the same type of stuff that you'd want on a canoe trip, but the idea is to scale everything down. Also, you can use the kayak's sealable hatch in place of the heavy and bulky plastic cooler, which saves on space. But you're still going to have to sacrifice them bananas: freeze-dried food is the order of the day for overnights.

If you've yet to sample it, you may be in for a shock: freeze dried food, available from several companies, actually tastes a lot better than you'd expect (but it's not, like, *great* or anything). Companies like Natural High and Richmoore make a huge array of dishes. Some you dump into a pot of boiling water, and with some you add the water directly to the bag. For side dishes, like green beans or corn, expect to pay about $1.50 a bag. For breakfast items like – get this – a cheese omelet, it's about $2.50, and for full dinner meals including a main course and a side dish that's said to feed two but probably only feeds 1½, expect to pay from $4.99 (for things like beef stew and chicken teriyaki) to $5.99 (for more upscale stuff like honey lime chicken and whole grain rice).

Lauderdale Sports (☎ 954-436-4186) at 11249 Pines Blvd in Fort Lauderdale is the best place we've found in South Florida to buy the stuff. (Actually in terms of knowledgeable staff and stock it's the best sports superstore in South Florida, making Sports Authority look like chumps.)

You'll also be able to take with you smaller, one-gallon bottles of water, or a collapsible water container, as you're able to seal the boat. But you'll need to economize on size on things like your tent, stove, sleeping bag – actually anywhere you can. The trick is to take only exactly what you need, and in the smallest form possible.

SURFING
The surfing in Florida isn't much to speak of if you've been to Costa Rica, California or Hawaii, but there is surfing along the entire Atlantic coast. Surf shops may be loathe to rent out boards, because of insurance problems, but they will usually sell you a board and buy it back at the end of the day for about $15 less than you paid for it . . . Get it? Wink wink.

WINDSURFING
Though you can put-in at any beach or public boat launch, there are few places that rent windsurfing equipment, making it necessary for serious boarders to have their own. Beginners and casual boarders will find relatively calm conditions and rental facilities at Biscayne Bay, near the Rickenbacker Causeway, and in resorts. Generally speaking the best places for windsurfing are along the southeast and southwest coasts, though it's popular in the northeast as well; local weather forecasts give wind and surf conditions.

SCUBA DIVING & SNORKELING
To dive in Florida you need to have at least an Open Water I certificate, for which you'll need at least five open water dives (one skin dive and four scuba dives). You'll also need to work in the pool before even getting to the water. If you push yourself, and the weather and seas are right, you can certify in three days.

For information on dive courses and standards, contact the Professional Diving Instructors Corporation (PSIC; ☎ 717-342-9434), PO Box 3633, Scranton, PA 18505, or the National Association for Underwater Instruction (NAUI; ☎ 714-621-5801, 800-553-6284), PO Box 14650, Montclair, CA 91763.

Quick one- to three-day courses can get you into shallow waters to see the underwater world. This is especially satisfying in places like the Florida Keys, where the protected coral reefs house a rich marine environment close to the surface. Local dive shops are the best resources for equipment, guides and instructors. *Scuba Diving* and *Sport Diver* are widely available magazines dedicated entirely to underwater pursuits.

The best deal in the state for certification is at the HI International House in Fort Lauderdale, which can get you certified in as little as three days, weather and seas permitting, for $135 per person.

If you don't have the time, money or desire to dive deep, you can often rent a snorkel, mask and fins for under $10 an hour. In touristy spots such as South Beach, people set up equipment rental stands along the beach. If you'll do it more than three times, it pays to invest $25 or so in an inexpensive mask and snorkel from a place like Lauderdale Sports or Sports Authority.

FISHING

Saltwater fishing in Florida is an obsession, and every city along the coast has a marina packed with charter fishing boats. Freshwater fishing, or more specifically, bass fishing, is as much a Florida tradition as grits or speeding. There are complex limits on catches in Florida; licenses are issued and fees and validity set on a county by county basis. Fishing boats are available at practically every marina in the state.

SAILING

There are sailboats for charter at marinas throughout the state, with or without crew. Prices are vary unbelievably, depending on the size of the boat, the season, the mood of the owner, and your experience in these matters. See also the Getting Around chapter for suggestions on how to hook up with crew positions.

TENNIS

There are municipal tennis courts in almost every Florida city; check in the blue pages section of the telephone directory under Parks Department for local numbers.

All resorts and many hotels have courts as well. You also may be able to get time on the courts at college or university campuses by asking.

GOLF

Golf courses can be found all over the state of Florida, and those that golf say it's some of the best in the country. In many ways that's an unfortunate development. Golf courses waste colossal amounts of water for irrigation, and run-off from fertilizer poisons the very source of the state's fresh water supply: the Florida Aquifer. Golf courses also take up huge tracts of land, and environmentalists charge that the damage to local flora and fauna is unforgivable. The development in Florida associated with golf courses – condominium and resort development – add to the damage.

For these and other reasons, we don't list golf courses in this book. There are many sources for information on golfing in Florida – practically every pamphlet handed out by CVB/VCBs and chambers of commerce list all golf courses in the area, as golfers tend to be affluent.

HOT-AIR BALLOONING

Floating above the state in a wicker gondola has its attractions, given the scenery, but it's not cheap at the relatively few locations that offer it commercially. Most

Barracuda Danger
Do not eat barracuda in Florida no matter what size – they may carry ciguatera toxin (CTX), produced by microscopic alga. This is eaten by smaller fish and travels up the food chain and accumulates in larger fish, who pass it on to humans. It can cause severe illness with symptoms including diarrhea, nausea, cramps, numbness of the mouth, chills, headaches, dizziness and convulsions. Don't believe local legends about weight or cooking tests using a dime in the boiling water – this toxin can be deadly. ■

flights leave at dawn or at sunset and go 1000 to 2000 feet above the ground. They're available in the southwest, but pop up almost everywhere; check in local airports, where people will know of balloonists in the area. One-hour flights for two people typically cost $125 to 165.

SKY DIVING

If jumping out of a plane and falling at a speed of 150 miles per hour before opening your chute 3000 feet above the ground sounds fun, then you should head to South Florida. There are skydiving companies that set up shop at airports around the state – just drive into any airport and ask at the information desk or tower.

Skydive Miami (☎ 245-6160, 759-3483) will get you trained and pushed out of the plane on your first jump ('the most fun you can have with your clothes on') in one day for $129. If you saw the movie *Drop Zone* with Wesley Snipes, you've seen these folks in action – one of their former employees trained Snipes for the film, and most of the jumps – including the huge one allegedly over Washington, DC – were filmed here. They're at HGAA (see below); open every day all year in daylight hours, call the day before.

ULTRALIGHTS

South Florida is an aviation center, and hundreds of small planes fill the skies each day. Ultralight aircraft, in fact, became so popular down here that Dade County built a field specifically for the tiny planes at Homestead General Aviation Airport (HGAA; ☎ 247-4883). Ultralights are small aircraft that are regulated but require no pilot's license to fly. Lessons cost about $75 an hour, and you'll need 10 to 12 hours of training before you can fly solo. Contact the Light Aircraft Flyers Association (☎ 460-3356) for information about lessons, upcoming events, or just show up at the field on the second Saturday of each month for their Fly-In and Social Day at HGAA, where there's barbecue breakfast and lunch, talk of flying and, if the weather's good, flying.

SINGLE-ENGINE PLANES

If you've got a pilot's license you can usually stop into any decent airport and rent a plane to get yourself an orientation of the area. The price for a single-engine plane is usually between $50 and 100 an hour including fuel. You'll usually have to go up with the owner and let them see that you're capable of flying safely, which will give you the opportunity to ask about must-see attractions, local regulations, etc.

JET SKIS & MOTORBOATS

Jet skis and motorboats kill manatees and fish, rip sea plants and protected sea grass from the bottom (destroying the manatees' food supply), scare swimmers, annoy locals and result in several deaths a year. Florida waters are very shallow and tricky to navigate. Many areas of it are protected Manatee Zones. You can rent these hateful machines in various places around the state, and we wish you wouldn't.

Getting There & Away

AIR

Airports

The state's major international airports are Miami International Airport (MIA) and Orlando International Airport (MCO/ORL). But Fort Lauderdale's international terminal (FLL) has become, over recent years, a very popular place for inexpensive flights to land. If you've got a really cheap deal to Miami, you may be landing in Fort Lauderdale, about 30 miles north.

Three other airports that are seeing increased international traffic are Tampa/St Petersburg (TPA), Daytona Beach (DAB) and Jacksonville (JAX), which are becoming important domestic hubs as well.

Most cities in the rest of the state have regional airports, and offer connecting service to other US cities; these include Palm Beach (PBI, actually in West Palm Beach), Tallahassee (TLH), Gainesville (GNV), Fort Myers (RSW) and Pensacola (PNS).

In other locations, the airports are usually municipal and, while they support a small amount of commercial traffic, are geared more to private aviation. These can range from the sparkling new air strips at St Augustine to dirt strips.

With the exception of major tourist destinations like Miami, Fort Lauderdale, Palm Beach and Orlando, there is rarely public transportation between airports and downtown; you're at the mercy of car rental, taxis or, more rarely, shuttle services. In this book we list as many options as we've found and state average taxi fares.

Airlines

Aero Costa Rica	☎ 800-237-6274
Aero Mexico	☎ 800-237-6639
Aero Peru	☎ 800-777-7717
Aerolinas Argentinas	☎ 800-333-0276
Air Canada	☎ 800-776-3000
Air France	☎ 800-237-2747
Air Jamaica	☎ 800-523-5585
Air New Zealand	☎ 800-262-1234
Alaska Airlines	☎ 800-426-0333

America West	☎ 800-235-9292
American Airlines	☎ 800-433-7300
Avianca Airlines	☎ 800-284-2622
British Airways	☎ 800-247-9297
British West Indies Airlines	☎ 800-247-9297
Canadian Airlines	☎ 800-426-7000
Caribbean Airlines	☎ 800-566-1980
Continental	
(domestic)	☎ 800-525-0280
(international)	☎ 800-231-0856
Delta Air Lines	
(domestic)	☎ 800-221-1212
(international)	☎ 800-241-4141
Gulfstream Int'l Airlines	☎ 800-992-8532
Haiti Trans Air	☎ 800-394-5313
Hawaiian Airlines	☎ 800-367-5320
Japan Airlines	☎ 800-525-3663
KLM	☎ 800-374-7747
Ladeco Chilean Airlines	☎ 800-825-2332
LAN Chile	☎ 800-735-5526
LAPSA-Air Paraguay	☎ 800-795-2772
Mexicana Airlines	☎ 800-531-7921
Nicaraguense de Avacion	☎ 800-831-6422
Northwest	
(domestic)	☎ 800-225-2525
(international)	☎ 800-447-4747
Qantas Airways	☎ 800-227-4500
Transbrazil Airlines	☎ 800-872-3153
TWA	
(domestic)	☎ 800-221-2000
(international)	☎ 800-892-4141
United	
(domestic)	☎ 800-241-6522
(international)	☎ 800-631-1500
USAir	☎ 800-428-4322
Varig Brazilian Airlines	☎ 800-468-2744
Viasa-Venezualean Airways	☎ 800-468-4272
Virgin Atlantic	☎ 800-862-8621

Buying Tickets

Numerous airlines fly to the USA, and a variety of fares are available; in addition to a straightforward roundtrip ticket, you can also get a Round-the-World ticket or a Visit USA pass (see Air Passes below). So rather than just walking into the nearest travel agent or airline office, it pays to do a bit of research and shop around first. Consult reference books and check the travel sections of magazines like *Time Out* and *TNT* in the

UK, or the Saturday editions of newspapers like the *Sydney Morning Herald* and *The Age* in Australia. Ads in these publications offer cheap fares, but don't be surprised if agents happen to be sold out when you contact them: they're usually low-season fares on obscure airlines with conditions attached.

The plane ticket will probably be the single most expensive item in your budget, and buying it can be intimidating. Research the current state of the market and start shopping for a ticket early – some of the cheapest tickets must be bought months in advance, and some popular flights sell out quickly. Talk to other recent travelers – they may be able to stop you from making some obvious mistakes.

Note that high season in the USA is mid-June to mid-September (summer) and the two weeks around Christmas. The best rates for travel to and in the USA are found November through March – except for major holidays, especially Thanksgiving (the third Thursday in November), which account for the heaviest travel days of the year.

Call travel agents for bargains – airlines can supply information on routes and time-tables; however, except at times of fare wars, they do not supply the cheapest tickets. Airlines often have competitive low-season, student and senior citizens' fares. Before you buy, confirm the fare, the route, the dates and any restrictions on the ticket.

Cheap tickets are available in two distinct categories: official and unofficial. Official ones have a variety of names, including advance-purchase fares, budget fares, Apex and super-Apex. Unofficial tickets are simply discounted tickets that the airlines release through selected travel agents (not through airline offices). The cheapest tickets are often nonrefundable and require an extra fee for changing your flight. Many insurance policies will cover this loss if you have to change your flight for emergency reasons. Return (roundtrip) tickets usually work out cheaper than two one-way fares – often *much* cheaper.

Use the fares quoted in this book as a guide only. They are approximate and based on the rates advertised by travel agents and airlines at press time. Quoted airfares do not necessarily constitute a recommendation for the carrier.

If traveling from the UK, you will probably find that the cheapest flights are being advertised by obscure bucket shops whose names haven't yet reached the telephone directory. Many such firms are honest and solvent, but there are a few rogues who will take your money and disappear, to reopen elsewhere a month or two later under a new name. If you feel suspicious about a firm, don't give them all the money at once – leave a deposit of 20% or so and pay the balance on receiving the ticket. If they insist on cash in advance, go elsewhere. And once you have the ticket, ring the airline to confirm that you are booked on the flight.

You may decide to pay more than the rock-bottom fare by opting for the safety of a better-known travel agent. Established firms like STA Travel, which has offices worldwide, Council Travel in the USA or Travel CUTS in Canada are valid alternatives, and they offer good prices to most destinations.

Once you have your ticket, write down its number, together with the flight number and other details, and keep the information somewhere separate. If the ticket is lost or stolen, this will help you get a replacement.

Remember to buy travel insurance as early as possible.

Getting Bumped

Airlines try to guarantee themselves consistently full planes by overbooking, knowing that some passengers will not show up. When everyone who's booked actually does show up, some passengers can be 'bumped' off the full plane, but they are usually compensated for the inconvenience. Getting bumped can be a nuisance because you have to wait around for the next flight, but if you have a day's leeway, you can really take advantage of the system.

When you check in at the airline counter, ask if they will need volunteers to be bumped, and ask what the compensation will be. Depending on the desirability of the flight, this can range from a $200 voucher toward your next flight to a fully paid roundtrip ticket. Be sure to try and confirm a later flight so you don't get stuck in the airport on standby. If you have to spend the night, airlines frequently foot the hotel bill for their bumpees. All in all, it can be a great deal, and many people plan their trips with a day to spare in order to try for a free ticket that will cover their next trip.

But be aware that, due to this same system, being just a little late for boarding can get you bumped with none of these benefits.

Flying Standby

When flying standby, call the airline a day or two before the flight and make a 'standby reservation'. This way you get priority over all the others who just appear and hope to get on the flight the same day.

Air Passes

Visit USA Passes Almost all domestic carriers offer Visit USA passes to non-US citizens. The passes are actually a book of coupons – each coupon equals a flight. The following airlines are representative of the kinds of deals available, but it's a good idea to ask your travel agent about other airlines that offer the service.

Continental Airlines' Visit USA pass can be purchased in conjunction with an international airline ticket anywhere outside the USA except Canada and Mexico. All travel must be completed within 60 days of the first flight into the USA or 81 days after arrival in the USA. You must have your trip planned out in advance. If you decide to change destinations once in the USA, you will be charged $50. High-season prices are $479 for three coupons (minimum purchase) and $769 for eight (maximum purchase).

Northwest offers the same deal, but it gives you the option of flying standby.

American Airlines uses the same coupon structure and also sells the passes outside of the USA, excluding Canada and Mexico. You must reserve flights one day in advance, and if a coupon only takes you halfway to your destination, you will have to buy the remaining ticket at full price.

Delta has two different systems for travelers coming from abroad. Visit USA gives travelers a discount, but you need to have your itinerary mapped out to take advantage of this. The other option is Discover America, in which a traveler buys coupons good for standby travel anywhere in the continental USA. One coupon equals one flight. Only two transcontinental flights are allowed – Delta prefers that your travels follow some sort of circular pattern. Four coupons cost about $550, 10 cost $1250. Children's fares are about $40 less. Coupons can only be purchased in conjunction with an international flight, Canada and Mexico excluded.

Round-the-World Tickets Round-the-World (RTW) tickets have become very popular in the last few years. Airline RTW tickets are often real bargains and can work out to be no more expensive or even cheaper than an ordinary return ticket. Prices start at about UK£850, A$1800 or US$1300.

The official airline RTW tickets are usually put together by a combination of two airlines, and they permit you to fly anywhere you want on their route systems as long as you do not backtrack. Other restrictions are that you must usually book the first sector in advance and cancellation penalties apply. There may be restrictions on the number of stops permitted, and tickets are usually valid from 90 days up to a year. An alternative type of RTW ticket is one put together by a travel agent using a combination of discounted tickets.

Although most airlines restrict the number of sectors that can be flown within the USA and Canada to four, and some airlines black out a few heavily traveled routes (like Honolulu to Tokyo), stopovers are otherwise generally unlimited. In most cases a 14-day advance purchase is required. After the ticket is purchased, dates can be changed without penalty and tickets can be rewritten to add or delete stops for $50 each.

The majority of RTW tickets restrict you to just two airlines. British Airways and Qantas Airways offer an RTW ticket called

Air Travel Glossary

Air Shuttles – these are short domestic flights between major cities in which you can buy a ticket right at the gate at the time of the flight. This very often operates in conjunction with ticketless travel – and means you should arrive early at the gate to assure yourself a seat and travel without extra baggage.

Apex – Apex, or 'advance purchase excursion' is a discounted ticket that must be paid for in advance. There are penalties if you wish to change it.

Bucket Shop – An unbonded travel agency specializing in discounted airline tickets.

Bumping – Just because you have a confirmed seat doesn't mean you're going to get on the plane – see the Getting Bumped section.

Cancellation Penalties – If you must cancel or change an Apex ticket there are often heavy penalties involved, but insurance can sometimes be taken out against these penalties. Some airlines impose penalties on regular tickets as well, particularly against 'no show' passengers.

Check In – Airlines ask you to check in a certain time ahead of the flight departure (usually two hours on international flights). If you fail to check in on time and the flight is overbooked the airline can cancel your booking and give your seat to somebody else.

Confirmation – Having a ticket written out with the flight and date you want doesn't mean you have a seat until the agent has checked with the airline that your status is 'OK' or confirmed. Meanwhile you could just be 'on request'.

Direct Flight – Rather than nonstop, these flights have brief layovers at intermediate cities on long domestic flights; for example a one-hour 'stop' in Chicago on a New York-San Francisco flight. While better than changing planes, this still adds a considerable amount of time to your flight, but may save you money.

Discounted Tickets – There are two types of discounted fares – officially discounted (see Promotional Fares) and unofficially discounted. The lowest prices often impose drawbacks like flying with unpopular airlines, inconvenient schedules, or unpleasant routes and connections. A discounted ticket can save you other things than money – you may be able to pay Apex prices without the associated Apex advance booking and other requirements. Discounted tickets only exist when there is fierce competition.

Full Fares – Airlines traditionally offer 1st class (coded F), business class (coded J) and economy class (coded Y) tickets. These days there are so many promotional and discounted fares available from the regular economy class that few passengers pay full economy fare.

Lost Tickets – If you lose your airline ticket an airline will usually treat it like a travelers' check and, after inquiries, issue you with another one. Legally, however, an airline is entitled to treat it like cash and if you lose it then it's gone forever. Take good care of your tickets.

No Shows – No shows are passengers who fail to show up for their flight. Full-fare passengers who fail to turn up are sometimes entitled to travel on a later flight. The rest of us are penalized (see Cancellation Penalties).

Nonstop Flights – the most ideal way to fly is not to change planes or stop at all along the way, this is only called 'nonstop' and is often confused with flying direct. Nonstop is becoming harder to come by on longer flights, and therefore pricier.

On Request – An unconfirmed booking for a flight; see Confirmation.

Open Jaws – A return ticket where you fly to one place but return from another. If available this can save you backtracking to your arrival point.

Overbooking – Airlines hate to fly empty seats and since every flight has some passengers who fail to show up they often book more passengers than they have seats. Usually the excess passengers balance those who fail to show up but occasionally somebody gets bumped. If this happens guess who it's most likely to be? The passengers who check in late.

Promotional Fares – Officially discounted fares like Apex fares which are available from travel agents or direct from the airline.

Reconfirmation – At least 72 hours prior to departure time of an onward or return flight you must contact the airline and 'reconfirm' that you intend to be on the flight. If you don't do this the airline can delete your name from the passenger list and you could lose your seat. You don't have to reconfirm the first flight on your itinerary or if your stopover is less than 72 hours. It doesn't hurt to reconfirm more than once.

Restrictions – Discounted tickets often have various restrictions on them – advance purchase is the most usual one (see Apex). Others are restrictions on the minimum and maximum period you must be away, such as a minimum of 14 days or a maximum of one year. See Cancellation Penalties.

Standby – A discounted ticket where you only fly if there is a seat free at the last moment. Standby fares are usually only available on domestic routes.

Ticketless Travel – a new method used by low-fare domestic airlines where you buy tickets over the phone or through an agent, and pick up the boarding pass at the gate with picture identification. It's a very convenient and inexpensive way to travel, unless you have luggage to check – then you wait in a baggage check line *and* the boarding gate line – or are late for the flight, in which case you could end up bumped. Try to go with only carry-ons for these flights.

Tickets Out – An entry requirement for many countries is that you have an onward or return ticket, in other words, a ticket out of the country. If you're not sure what you intend to do next, the easiest solution is to buy the cheapest onward ticket to a neighboring country or a ticket from a reliable airline which can later be refunded if you do not use it.

Transferred Tickets – Airline tickets cannot be transferred from one person to another. Travelers sometimes try to sell the return half of their ticket, but officials can ask you to prove that you are the person named on the ticket. This is unlikely to happen on domestic flights, but on an international flight tickets may be compared with passports.

Travel Agencies – Travel agencies vary widely and you should use one that suits your needs. Some simply handle tours, while full-service agencies handle everything from tours and tickets to car rental and hotel bookings. A good one will do all these things and can save you a lot of money but if all you want is a ticket at the lowest possible price, then you really need an agency specializing in discounted tickets. A discount ticket agency, however, may not be useful for things like hotel bookings.

Travel Periods – Some officially discounted fares, Apex fares in particular, vary with the time of year. There is often a low (off-peak) season and a high (peak) season. Sometimes there's an intermediate or shoulder season as well. At peak times, when everyone wants to fly, all discounted fares may be higher or there may simply be no discounted tickets available. Usually the fare depends on your outward flight – if you depart in the high season and return in the low season, you pay the high-season fare. ■

Airport Security

After several incidents of terrorism on US soil, including bombings in Oklahoma City, Atlanta and on (as was suspected at the time of writing) TWA Flight 800 from New York to Paris, new airport security measures were being devised. These measures are expected to include the obvious – X-raying of all checked as well as hand luggage, increased detection technology to spot plastic explosives, more careful hand searches, roving packs of dogs sniffing your bags and psychics sensing your vibes – and are expected to mean that the security screening process for passengers will take up to 15 minutes for international flights to or from the USA. ∎

the Global Explorer that allows you to combine routes on both airlines to a total of 28,000 miles for US$2999 or A$3099.

Qantas also flies in conjunction with American Airlines, Delta Air Lines, Northwest Airlines, Canadian Airlines, Air France and KLM. Qantas RTW tickets, with any of the aforementioned partner airlines, cost US$3247 or A$3099.

Canadian Airlines offers numerous RTW combinations, such as with Philippine Airlines for C$2790, which could include Manila, Dubai, Pakistan and Europe; another with KLM could include Cairo, Bombay, Delhi and Amsterdam for C$3149; and a third with South African Airways could include Australia and Africa for C$3499.

Many other airlines also offer RTW tickets. Continental Airlines, for example, links up with either Malaysia Airlines, Singapore Airlines or Thai Airways for US$2570. TWA's lowest priced RTW, linking up with Korean Air, costs US$2087 and allows stops in Honolulu, Seoul, Tel Aviv, Amsterdam and Paris or London.

Air Travelers with Special Needs

If you have special needs of any sort – a broken leg, dietary restrictions, dependence on a wheelchair, responsibility for a baby, fear of flying – you should let the airline know as soon as possible so that they can make arrangements accordingly. You should remind them when you reconfirm your booking (at least 72 hours before departure) and again when you check in at the airport. It may also be worth ringing round the airlines before you make your booking to find out how they will handle your particular needs.

Airports and airlines can be surprisingly helpful, but they do need advance warning. Most international airports can provide escorts from check-in desk to plane where needed, and there should be ramps, lifts, accessible toilets and reachable phones. Aircraft toilets, on the other hand, are likely to present a problem; travelers should discuss this with the airline at an early stage and, if necessary, with their doctor.

Guide dogs for the blind will often have to travel in a specially pressurized baggage compartment with other animals, away from their owner, though smaller guide dogs may be admitted to the cabin. Guide dogs are not subject to quarantine as long as they have proof of being vaccinated against rabies.

Deaf travelers can ask for airport and inflight announcements to be written down for them.

Children under two travel for 10% of the standard fare (or free, on some airlines), as long as they don't occupy a seat (but they don't get a baggage allowance, either). 'Skycots' should be provided by the airline if requested in advance; these will take a child weighing up to about 22 pounds. Children between two and 12 can usually occupy a seat for half to two-thirds of the full fare, and they do get a baggage allowance. Strollers can often be taken on as hand luggage.

Arriving in the USA

Even if you are continuing immediately to another city, the first airport that you land in is where you must carry out immigration and customs formalities: if you're on a connecting flight from, say, London to Orlando via Miami, you will still have to take your bags through customs in Miami.

Passengers aboard the airplane are given

standard immigration and customs forms to fill out. The cabin crew will help you fill them out if you have any questions, but the forms are quite straightforward. After the plane lands, you'll first go through immigration. There are two lines: one for US citizens and residents and the other for nonresidents. Immigration formalities are usually straightforward if you have all the necessary documents (passport and visa). Occasionally, you may be asked to show your ticket out of the country, but this doesn't happen very often.

After passing through immigration, you collect your baggage and then pass through customs. If you have nothing to declare, there is a good chance that you can clear customs quickly and without a luggage search, but you can't rely on it. After passing through customs, you are officially in the country. If your flight is continuing to another city or you have a connecting flight, it is your responsibility to get your bags to the right place. Normally, there are airline counters just outside the customs area that will help you. Also see the information under Customs in Facts for the Visitor.

Baggage & Other Restrictions
On most domestic and international flights you are limited to two checked bags, or three if you don't have a carry-on. There could be a charge if you bring more or if the size of the bags exceeds the airline's limits. On some international flights the luggage allowance is based on weight, not numbers. It's best to check with the individual airline if you are worried about this.

The Price of Terrorism
Due to heightened security measures, there are no luggage lockers or stands in the airport or in bus or train stations. There are lockers at most youth hostels, most hotels (for their guests) and at the Depot in Key West, next to the Greyhound Station. For information on airport security, see the Facts for the Visitor chapter. ∎

If your luggage is delayed upon arrival (which is rare), some airlines will give a cash advance to purchase necessities. If sporting equipment is misplaced, the airline may pay for rentals. Should the luggage be lost, it is important to submit a claim. The airline doesn't have to pay the full amount of the claim; rather, they can estimate the value of your lost items. It may take them anywhere from six weeks to three months to process the claim and pay you.

Smoking Smoking is prohibited on all domestic flights within the USA. Many international flights are following suit, so if you smoke, be sure to call and find out. (Incidentally, the restriction applies to the passenger cabin and the lavatories but not the cockpit.) Most airports in Florida, and many in the USA, prohibit smoking (there's still smoking allowed in Orlando's airport). True smokers might consider joining a frequent flyer lounge (about $200 a year), which permit smoking even in airports that ban it. Other perks are free soft drinks, snacks, newspapers and magazines, TV and telephone/fax access and cheap alcoholic drinks.

Illegal Items Items that are illegal to take on a plane, either checked or as carry-on, include aerosols of polishes, waxes, and so on; tear gas and pepper spray; camp stoves with fuel; and divers' tanks that are full. Matches should not be checked.

Within the USA
The *New York Times*, *Los Angeles Times*, *Chicago Tribune*, *San Francisco Examiner* and other major newspapers all produce weekly travel sections with numerous travel agency ads. Council Travel (☎ 800-226-8624) and STA Travel (☎ 800-982-9947) have offices in major cities nationwide.

The magazine *Travel Unlimited*, PO Box 1058, Allston, MA 02134, publishes details of the cheapest air fares and courier possibilities.

Fares are incredibly varied. For example, an economy roundtrip ticket from Los Angeles to Miami is (as we write) between

$250 and almost $400 with a 14- or 21-day advance purchase requirement – it depends on which airline you fly. Sometimes the fare increases if you don't spend a Saturday night at your destination. If you book less than 21 days in advance, fares go up – sometimes way up, to around $600 to 800. Still, nothing determines fares more than demand, and when things are slow, regardless of the season, airlines will lower their fares to fill empty seats. There's a lot of competition, and at any given time any one of the airlines could have the cheapest fare.

The most expensive fares are those booked at the last minute – cheap standby fares are not normally offered. Some airlines price their one-way tickets at half the price of their cheapest roundtrip; others may charge much more than half of a roundtrip ticket for a one-way ticket.

Cuba: Who Can Go?

Generally, travel to Cuba for Americans is heavily restricted to the point of being next to illegal. Americans who want to get a license to visit Cuba must fall into one of several categories:

- Conference attendees
- Research
- Educational programs
- Religious groups
- Freelance journalists *on assignment*

If you can fit yourself into one of these categories, you may be able to get a license. At last report the flights went daily from Cancun and four times a week from Nassau. Roundtrip airfares were $165 from Nassau and $175 from Cancun. Marazul Tours adds a $35 registration fee to these prices. Americans eligible for a US government license to visit Cuba should contact Marazul Tours Inc (☎ 201-319-9670, fax 201-319-9009), Tower Plaza, 4100 Park Ave, Weehawken, NJ 07087, which operates the charter flights from Miami to Havana described above. Marazul also books reservations throughout Cuba – their brochure is most informative. ■

Major hubs for airlines serving Florida are Atlanta and Dallas, but most airlines fly directly to Miami and Orlando.

To/From Abroad

Bahamas The main airlines running between Miami and the Bahamas are American and Gulf Stream. Typical roundtrip fares are $130 to Nassau and up to $240 roundtrip to the farther islands. Travel by Design (☎ 305-673-6336, 800-358-7125) in Miami Beach specializes in this stuff, and they are a great source of information about getting around the Bahamas – from flying to mail boats. See the Miami chapter for more information.

Cuba At the time of writing, charter flights between Miami and Cuba had been discontinued indefinitely. Americans able to obtain US government permission to visit Cuba can use special charter flights between Miami and Havana via either Cancun Mexico or Nassau, the Bahamas.

Anyone in Florida who wants to visit Cuba without the major hassle of obtaining US government permission can easily do so through the Bahamas. Cuban Airline's Nassau-Havana flight operates three times a week ($130/175 one way/roundtrip, plus $15/27 tax), a useful connection for blockade runners. Book with Havanatur Bahamas (☎ 809-328-7985, fax 809-361-1336), PO Box N 10246, Nassau. Cuban tourist cards are sold at the airline desk in Nassau.

Other Caribbean Miami's the Gateway to the Caribbean, and the vast majority of flights to Caribbean destinations are serviced by American Airlines, with daily service to many destinations, including San Juan, Puerto Rico, Santo Domingo, Dominican Republic, Montego Bay, Jamaica, St Maarten and Barbados. Prices change dramatically, and last-minute deals are always a possibility. In Miami, see a good discount travel agent like Travel By Design for the latest prices. Following are the lowest published fares (one way/roundtrip) – remember that these will be higher than you'll likely pay:

Destination	Price
Barbados	$350/450
Montego Bay	$175/250
Puerto Rico	$250/345
Santo Domingo	$185/300
St Maarten	$350/450

Central & South America Miami is the main US/Latin American gateway, and MIA is served by everyone and his brother's airlines. Deals are sometimes incredible – like the $199 roundtrip to/from Caracas that has been offered several times in the last couple of years; check with discount brokers in Latin America for the best deals, which come and go quickly. By scheduled air, the highest roundtrip tickets are $300 to 450 from San Jose, Costa Rica; $450 from Managua, Nicaragua and Guatemala City, Guatemala; $950 to 1100 from Rio de Janeiro; and from Caracas, Venezuela $180 to 280 in June, $250 to 300 in January.

Canada Travel CUTS has offices in all major cities. The *Toronto Globe & Mail* and *Vancouver Sun* carry travel agency ads; the magazine *Great Expeditions* (PO Box 8000-411, Abbotsford, BC V2S 6H1) is also useful.

Most connections between the US Pacific Northwest and Canada are through Vancouver, BC. Both Portland and Seattle have frequent and inexpensive flights to Vancouver, which is serviced by both Air Canada and Canadian Airlines. Between Miami/Orlando and Toronto you could expect a high-season/low-season ticket price of C$220/340, to/from Vancouver C$420/675.

UK & Ireland Check the ads in magazines like *Time Out* and *City Limits*, plus the Sunday papers and *Exchange & Mart*. Also check the free magazines widely available in London – start by looking outside the main railway stations.

Most British travel agents are registered with the ABTA (Association of British Travel Agents). If you buy a ticket from an ABTA-registered agent who then goes out

of business, ABTA will guarantee a refund or an alternative.

London is arguably the world's headquarters for bucket shops, which are well advertised and can usually beat published airline fares. Two good, reliable agents for cheap tickets in the UK are Trailfinders and STA Travel. Trailfinders produces a lavishly illustrated brochure including air fare details.

Note that in the UK some incredible deals can be had: for example, in January you can get a roundtrip air ticket from London to Miami and Orlando for as low as £209; while in June and July, the price goes as high as £465.

Good travel agents in London include the following:

Campus Travel
    174 Kensington High St, London W8
    (☎ 0171-938-2188)
    28A Poland St, London W1
    (☎ 0171-437-7767)
STA Travel
    86 Old Brompton Rd, London SW7
    117 Euston Rd, London NW1
    (☎ 0171-937-9962)
Trailfinders
    42-50 Earl's Court Rd, London W8 6TF
    194 Kensington High St, London W8
    (☎ 0171-937-5400)
Travel Cuts
    95A Regent St, London W1 (☎ 637-3161)

The Globetrotters Club (BCM Roving, London WC1N 3XX) publishes a newsletter called *Globe* that covers obscure destinations and can help you find traveling companions.

Continental Europe It takes between eight to 10 hours to fly nonstop between Miami and the continent. The primary European airlines serving Miami and Orlando are British Air, SAS, Finnair, Air France, Lufthansa, Delta and United.

In Amsterdam, NBBS is a popular travel agent. In Paris, Transalpino and Council Travel are popular agencies. The newsletter *Farang* (La Rue 8 á 4261 Braives, Belgium) deals with exotic destinations, as does the magazine *Aventure du Bout du Monde* (116 rue de Javel, 75015 Paris, France).

From Paris, the highest scheduled airfare prices hover at about FF3000. In June/January, other scheduled prices are Dfl 1650/1289 from Amsterdam; FIM4600/4000 from Helsinki; ESP99,000/93,000 from Madrid; and DM1550/1175 from Munich or Frankfurt.

Australia & New Zealand There is no direct service from Australia or New Zealand to Florida; you'll have to change planes and/or carriers in Los Angeles, the US hub for Qantas and Air New Zealand. With the advent of long-range 747-400 aircraft, most services now overfly Hawaii, so at least the Pacific is covered in one mighty leap.

In Australia and New Zealand, STA Travel and Flight Centres International are major dealers in cheap air fares; check the travel agency ads in the Yellow Pages and call around. Qantas flies to Los Angeles from Sydney, Melbourne (via Sydney or Auckland) and Cairns. United flies to San Francisco from Sydney and Auckland (via Sydney) and as well as to Los Angeles.

The cheapest tickets have a 21-day advance-purchase requirement, a minimum stay of seven days and a maximum stay of 60 days. Typical Apex roundtrip fares vary from A$2000/2400 from the Australian east coast and NZ$2500 from Auckland. Full-time students can save A$80 (US$59) to A$140 (US$103) on roundtrip fares to the USA.

Asia Hong Kong is the discount plane ticket capital of the region, but its bucket shops can be unreliable. Bucket shops in places like Bangkok and Singapore should be able to come up with the best deals in Southeast Asia. Ask the advice of other travelers before buying a ticket. STA Travel, which is dependable, has branches in Hong Kong, Tokyo, Singapore, Bangkok and Kuala Lumpur. Many if not most flights to the USA go via Honolulu, Hawaii. There are no direct flights to Florida; you will need to change planes and/or carriers once you get to the US.

United Airlines has three flights a day to Honolulu from Tokyo with connections to West Coast cities like Los Angeles, San Francisco and Seattle. Northwest and Japan Airlines also have daily flights to the West Coast from Tokyo; Japan Airlines also flies to Honolulu from Osaka, Nagoya, Fukuoka and Sapporo.

Northwest Airlines flies to Honolulu from Hong Kong, Bangkok, Manila, Seoul and Singapore, with connections to the West Coast. Korean Air and Philippine Airlines also have flights from a number of Southeast Asian cities to Honolulu, with onward connections on domestic airlines to Florida.

Leaving the USA

You should check in for international flights two hours early. All passengers will need to present photo identification on check-in.

During check-in procedures, you will be asked questions about whether you have packed your own bags, whether anyone else has had access to them since you packed them and whether you have received any parcels to carry. These questions are for security reasons.

Departure Taxes Airport departure taxes are normally included in the cost of tickets bought in the USA, although tickets purchased abroad may not have this included. There's a $6 airport departure tax charged to all passengers bound for a foreign destination. However, this fee, as well as a $6.50 North American Free Trade Agreement (NAFTA) tax charged to passengers entering the USA from a foreign country, are hidden taxes added to the purchase price of your airline ticket.

LAND

Most travelers not arriving by air come by bus or private vehicle. Train is a little-used option. Florida is served by three main interstate highways that connect it with the north and the west; I-95 is the main East Coast interstate, extending from Miami to Maine; I-10 extends from Jacksonville due west across the South all the way to Los

Angeles; I-75 runs west from Miami across Alligator Alley and then due north to Michigan.

Bus

Greyhound (☎ 800-231-2222, see the Online Services appendix for website) is the main bus system in the USA, and it plays an important transportation role in Florida. As the only scheduled statewide bus service, Greyhound is the carless traveler's best friend, serving all major cities and many smaller ones. But bus travel can often be tiring, inconvenient and expensive, so look at all your options before deciding.

Greyhound only serves places along its main routes, and getting to places off those routes is impossible without a car. Buses tend to be few and schedules are often inconvenient. And fares are relatively high: bargain air fares can undercut buses on long-distance routes; in some cases, on shorter routes, it can be cheaper to rent a car. However, very long distance bus trips are often available at bargain prices by purchasing or reserving tickets three to seven days in advance. Then, once you've arrived at your far-flung destination, you can rent a car to get around.

Bus travel, of course, gives you the chance to see some of the countryside and to talk to some of the inhabitants that travelers by air or private car might miss. Then again, bus travel can subject you to conversation with some of the inhabitants that travelers by air or private car might miss – it can be a mixed blessing. And Greyhound stations are generally very sleazy places; solo travelers may feel uncomfortable in them. For these reasons, traveling by car is definitely recommended, if it's at all possible. However, details of major bus routes will be given in the text if you have the time or inclination to see the Greyhound side of travel.

Meal stops are made on long trips; you pay for your own simple food in inexpensive and unexciting cafés. Buses have on-board lavatories. Seats recline, ostensibly for sleeping, but a couple of days in a Greyhound seat

is a memorable experience. Smoking is not permitted aboard Greyhound buses.

In an effort to boost sagging ticket sales, Greyhound offers a series of incentive fares to a variety of locations around the country. These change frequently; as we went to press they were wrapping up a $79 to any-where fare. Regular published Greyhound fares from Miami to some other major US destinations include:

Destination	Price	Duration
Atlanta	$69	16 to 18 hours
Chicago	$89	33 hours
Dallas	$99	30 hours
Las Vegas	$149	61 hours
Los Angeles	$119	59 hours
New Orleans	$79	20 hours
New York	$89	26 hours
San Francisco	$149	75 hours
Washington, DC	$130	23 to 24 hours

Note that these travel times can vary dramatically depending on the time of day you leave, the route you take and other factors. For example, the New York run can be as short as 23 hours.

AmeriPass Ameripass is an unlimited travel pass available to anyone (not just non-US residents). It's available in seven-day ($179), 15-day ($289), 30-day ($399) and 60-day ($599) time periods, and unless you're going to be doing a whole lot of travel, it's probably not worth it.

Train

Amtrak (☎ 800-872-7245, see the Online Services appendix for website) has been, since 1971, the US national railway system, claiming that 'There's something about a train that's magic.' It connects Florida with cities all over the continental USA and Canada, and two main routes serve Florida – the Silver Service from New York and the *Sunset Limited* train from Los Angeles.

The pricing structure is hugely complex and based on the date you're traveling – the date, not just the time of the year, as the prices can change radically from one day to the next. You should always ask Amtrak if you can get a better deal by leaving a couple of days later or earlier. But generally speaking, in the winter months it's cheaper to go northbound, and more expensive to go southbound, and vice versa in spring. The cheapest period, generally speaking, is summer.

On all Amtrak trains, each adult can bring one or two children from two to 15 at half price. Seniors aged 62 and over get a 15% discount on tickets. There are two types of seating: airline-style seats ('There's something about a train that's painful . . . ') and cabins, which come in four flavors: single, double, family (which sleeps two adults and two children under 12) and first-class singles or doubles (which include all meal service, and we're sure the food's just yummy). Cabins are always a surcharge, and the surcharge changes depending on the date you're traveling.

If you're coming here by train from anywhere except Los Angeles, you will at some point have to connect with Amtrak's Silver Service: the *SilverMeteor* and *SilverStar* trains that run between New York City and Miami and Tampa. The *SilverMeteor* runs directly to Miami via Orlando; the *SilverStar* splits after Orlando: half the train's cars head to Miami and the other to Tampa. Travel time from New York City to Miami is 27 hours; to Orlando 22 hours; to Tampa 28 hours. You can pick up the Silver Service at any spot on the route, which has stops in Washington, DC, Virginia, North Carolina, South Carolina, Georgia and Florida. The *SilverStar* leaves New York City's Penn Station at 10.10 am daily, the *SilverMeteor* at 4.05 pm.

The cheapest time to take the Silver Service is between April 1 and mid-June, when Amtrak runs a special roundtrip fare between NYC and Miami of $158 including a stopover, or $148 without the stopover. If you want a cabin, it will be extra. A standard/first-class single cabin is an extra $59/150 (for a total cost of $207/298 without a stopover), a double is an extra $99/249 and a family cabin is an extra $249.

The most expensive time to go is in the winter: in December, the roundtrip fare without stopover is anywhere from $146 to 326, and standard/first-class cabins are $65/165 extra for singles, $109/275 for doubles and $275 for a family.

On the route from Los Angeles, the *Sunset Limited* train runs three times a week (currently on Sunday, Tuesday and Friday), passing through Phoenix, Tucson and El Paso to New Orleans and across the Panhandle to Florida's east coast, where it turns south to Miami. Prices and peak times on this route differ from the Silver Service run, and depending on availability, a roundtrip ticket on this route can cost less – sometimes significantly – than a one way. The peak season is from July to December. During the off-season, the price from LA to Miami is $279 one way and from $276 to 558 roundtrip depending on availability – the more seats available when you order, the lower the price. In peak season, the cost is $578 one way and between $318 and $1156 roundtrip.

The other option is the *AutoTrain*, which runs between Lorton, Virginia (near Washington, DC) to Sanford, Florida (near Orlando). The trains leave both stations at 4.30 pm daily, arriving the following morning at 9 am.

On the AutoTrain you pay for your passage, your cabin and your car separately. In the summer, a couple traveling with a mid-size sedan would each pay a roundtrip fare of $121, an economy double cabin would be $105 each way, a first-class double cabin $237 each way and the car $131 each way.

But a southbound one-way fare for two people with the same car in December would be $95 each for passage plus the standard/first-class double cabin $184/446, and the car $210. And in March the one-way southbound journey is $74 each for the fare, $84/184 for the cabin and $131 for the car.

Stopovers & RailPasses RailPasses and Explore USA tickets are available and priced by zones of the country; we're listing only East Coast ticket prices here for space reasons. Call Amtrak to sort all this out.

Some specials allow you to make Miami

a stopover. The peak season is from June 17 to August 18. At the time of writing, a 30-day Explore USA ticket for the entire eastern portion of the USA is $158 off-peak and $208 in peak season, including unlimited (but scheduled) stopovers. But this is not a rail pass; it's a glorified roundtrip ticket, and you have to know exact dates and stops before you buy the ticket.

The only full-fledged rail pass at the time of writing was available to non-US citizens only. USA RailPass offers unlimited transit on the East Coast for $185 for 15 days/ $240 for 30 days off-peak, $205/ 265 peak.

Car

Drivers of cars and riders of motorbikes will need the vehicle's registration papers, liability insurance and a valid driver's license. Visitors from countries that don't use the Latin alphabet may want to buy an optional international driver's permit (IDP) in addition to their domestic license. Note that the IDP is not a license but a translation of yours, and European visitors should have no problem using their home license in the USA. For information on buying or renting a car, see the Getting Around chapter; for information on using a driveaway (driving a car for someone else) see the sidebar.

TOURS

Tours of the USA are so numerous that it would be impossible to attempt any kind of comprehensive listing; for overseas visitors, the most reliable sources of information on the constantly changing offerings are major international travel agents like Thomas Cook and American Express. Probably those of most interest to the general traveler are coach tours that visit the national parks and guest ranch excursions; for those with limited time, package tours can be an efficient and relatively inexpensive way to go.

A number of companies offer standard guided tours of Florida, usually by bus and including hotel accommodations. Any travel

---

A Free Car

Want a free car? Try Auto Driveaway of San Francisco (☎ 415-777-3740) or New York (☎ 212-967-2344). People who want their car moved from city A to city B leave the car with this organization, and as long as you're willing to drive there at an average rate of 400 miles per day and pay for the gas (the first tank's free), the car's yours. To qualify, drivers (not passengers) must be 21 years old and have a valid driver's license and one other form of ID. Non-US citizens can use an international driver's license, but they must show a valid entry visa and passport as well. They require a $300 to 350 refundable cash or travellers cheque deposit, and a $10 nonrefundable registration fee. ■

---

agent can tell you about these and arrange air, train or bus tickets to get you to the beginning of the tour.

Green Tortoise

The wheatgrass-green buses of Green Tortoise (☎ 415-956-7500, 800-867-8647), the USA's most noteworthy alternative to Greyhound, ply the roads of the West Coast, down through Latin America, up to Alaska, and cross the country in various routes. The trips from San Francisco to the East Coast take between 10 and 14 days, and prices vary.

The buses have comfortable beds, and all food is prepared by the group. On some days you camp out, there are side field trips and a general merry pranksters atmosphere.

Unfortunately, they don't go to Florida. But they do go as close as New Orleans, from where you can easily hop one of the five daily Greyhound buses to Pensacola ($30/60) or the daily 22-hour direct bus to Miami ($82/133).

Green Tortoise runs trips from San Francisco to Boston via New Orleans in April, May and September. Fares for the 11-day journey to New Orleans (14 days to Boston) range from $380 to 430 including meals.

AmeriCan

AmeriCan Adventures (☎ 310-390-7495, 800-864-0335, fax 310-390-1446), 6762A Centinela Ave, Culver City, CA 90230, offers seven- to 21-day bus trips to different parts of the USA, including trips through Florida. Their American Explorer holiday, 28 days across the USA for $1139 in low season and $1269 from July to August, cruises out along the Panhandle on the way to New Orleans, and their Confederate Trail package includes stops in Orlando, Miami and Cape Canaveral as well as St Augustine – it's a 21-day journey that costs $689 in low season and $809 in July and August.

For worldwide sales contact them at their UK headquarters (☎ 01892-512700, fax 511896), 64 Mt Pleasant Ave, Tunbridge Wells, Kent TN1 1QY.

SEA

Crewing

Fort Lauderdale may be the yacht capitol of America, and every year hundreds of captains are looking for crew – professional or unpaid – to help them get their boats from here to wherever they're going. In May to June they're taking them to Europe; in summer they're heading to New England, the Mediterranean and, less frequently but gaining in popularity, the West Coast of the USA and Alaska. At other times they could be heading just about anywhere. Boats leave for South American, Asian and Australasian destinations year round. Best of all, it's legal for foreigners to work on a boat that's leaving the USA.

Boats also leave from other marinas and ports, of course; check locally for more information.

Getting a slot on a boat is a very interesting way to get yourself transport and perhaps even some spending money for wherever you'll get to. Many people have been getting around the world like this for years and don't see any reason to stop. Don't get it wrong – it's hard and serious work that requires concentration, dedication, common sense and the ability to work and live with others in close quarters. Those that do it say they wouldn't do anything else.

Information Sources Crew placement agencies are located all over Fort Lauderdale, and they will, for a fee, match up crew and boat owners. Inquire when in Fort Lauderdale at crew houses or marinas.

The best sources for information are crew houses in Fort Lauderdale, essentially hostels or guesthouses populated primarily by people looking for work. Floyd's Crew House is an excellent source of information. See the Fort Lauderdale Places to Stay section for crew house listings. Boat owners call crew houses when they have something up, and they also go to Fort Lauderdale's premiere unofficial crew agency – the three-ring binder book at Smallwood's Uniform Shop (☎ 954-523-2282), 1001 SE 17th St at 10th Ave in Fort Lauderdale. Owners come here and write what their requirements are and wait for crew to get in touch. It's open Monday to Friday from 7.30 am to 5.30 pm, Saturday from 9 am to 3 pm, closed Sunday.

Failing that, a good place to start is in one of the many sailing magazines to get an idea of trends and conditions. Try *Showboats*, *Cruising World* and *Sail* magazines, which run ads and classifieds.

Women Crew The crew world is a tight one, and both Floyd at Floyd's Crew House and management at Smallwood's say that they have not in many years heard of a woman being the subject of unwanted advances from boat owners. But as with all jobs, it's a possibility. Floyd says that most people can tell on the first interview the type of services that the owner is going to want, and that it will become clear very quickly if they will include the personal kind. Interview carefully and ask around about the owner before taking on an assignment.

How Long? An experienced hand can pick up work at any time of the year within a week or two; in winter the jobs go to the more experienced workers but there's plenty of work for everyone. Inexperienced hands looking for volunteer work will also hook up in about that long. Floyd says that consistently about 95% of those coming for work get it if they're serious.

What to Bring As little as possible: everything you'll need will be provided except a toothbrush, toothpaste and a hairbrush – so travel as lightly as you can. You'll of course need travel documents and, if necessary, visas for your destination country.

WARNING

This chapter is particularly vulnerable to change – prices for international travel are volatile, routes are introduced and can-

celed, schedules change, rules are amended, special deals come and go. Airlines and governments seem to take a perverse pleasure in making price structures and regulations as complicated as possible, and you should check directly with the airline or travel agent to make sure you understand how a fare (and ticket you may buy) works.

In addition, the travel industry is highly competitive and there are many lurks and perks. The upshot of this is that you should get opinions, quotes and advice from as many airlines and travel agents as possible before you part with your hard-earned cash. The details given in this chapter should only be regarded as pointers and cannot be any substitute for you own careful, up-to-date research.

Getting Around

AIR

Flying within Florida is sometimes convenient if you're trying to save time (it's over 600 miles from Miami to Pensacola, so time is definitely a factor), but the cost is usually higher than driving. Most airlines that operate in Florida are flying small commuter planes, so expect propellers!

There is service between all major cities in Florida. See individual city sections for specific information on routes and prices. The main airlines operating within the state are:

American Airlines	☎ 800-433-7300
Delta	☎ 800-221-1212
Continental	☎ 800-525-0280
USAir	☎ 800-428-4322
Northwest	☎ 800-225-2525
American Trans Air	☎ 800-435-9282
Air South	☎ 800-247-7688
Gulf Stream	☎ 800-992-8532

Charter Flights Charter flights are available at almost any airport in the state; rates are negotiable, but count on $90 an hour flying time in small planes, much more in larger planes, and remember that you have to pay the pilot for the return flight, not just for your one way. In this book we list the airport telephone number for the major cities; in smaller cities, check in the Blue Pages section of the telephone directory under 'municipal airport' or 'city airport', or just drive out there and speak to the pilots.

BUS
Greyhound

Greyhound (☎ 800-231-2222; Greyhound International in the UK at ☎ 01342-317-317; see the Online Services appendix for website) has bus service between all major Florida cities. Individual city sections within this book will generally list the telephone number and address of the local Greyhound depot. For specific route and fare information, call Greyhound. Some fares (one-way/roundtrip) and travel times between Miami and other Florida cities are listed below.

Destination	Price	Duration
Cocoa Beach	$38/76	5½ to 9¼ hours
Daytona Beach	$35/70	6 to 7 hours
Fort Lauderdale	$5/10	½ hour to 1 hour
Jacksonville	$49/9	7 to 10 hours
Orlando	$33/66	5 to 11 hours
St Augustine	$53/106	7 to 9 hours
Tampa	$29/39	7 to 8 hours
West Palm Beach	$5/10	two hours

TRAIN
Amtrak

Amtrak (☎ 800-272-7245, see the Online Services appendix for website) can be used for intra-Florida transport if you're heading to a destination on its routes (but not between Miami and Palm Beach, which is covered by Tri-Rail – see below), but it's an expensive way to get around and you'll do better to take a bus or sometimes even fly. Special discount fares (which are only offered on a space-available basis) usually cost the same one way and roundtrip. And for destinations that require Amtrak connecting bus service, like Daytona, Tampa, Clearwater and St Petersburg, the cost of the bus can be higher than a local taxi.

There are two trains a day on the Silver Service line from Miami up Florida's east coast, and on Sunday, Tuesday and Friday there's a third – the Sunset Limited – which heads up Florida's east coast and cuts west from Jacksonville.

Tri-Rail

Tri-Rail (☎ 800-874-7245, TDD 800-273-7545) is a commuter rail system that runs between three counties – Dade, Broward and Palm Beach – in southeastern Florida. The double-decker trains are a marvel of cleanliness, and at least for the time being, they're very cheap. For longer trips, however, it takes about four times longer than driving.

Fares are calculated on a zone basis, and the route spans six zones. The costs for a one-way ticket are one zone $2, two zones $3, three zones $4, four zones $4.50, five zones $5, and six zones $5.50. So the most you'll ever pay is for the ride between Miami and West Palm Beach, which is $5.50 one way, $9.25 roundtrip. A Tri-Rail station at Miami International Airport is expected to open in early 1997, but as we went to press, no further information was available on it.

The Tri-Rail stations are Miami International Airport, Tri-Rail/Metrorail Transfer Center (in Hialeah), Golden Glades, Hollywood, Fort Lauderdale Airport, Fort Lauderdale, Cypress Creek, Pompano Beach, Deerfield Beach, Boca Raton, Delray Beach, Boynton Beach, Lake Worth, Palm Beach Airport and West Palm Beach.

CAR & MOTORCYCLE

By far the most convenient and popular way to get around the state is by car – in fact, in many cities it's nearly impossible to get by without one. Even if you're in a small town like St Augustine, getting to a supermarket will undoubtedly require a car or an expensive taxi. Motorcycles are very popular in Florida, and with the exception of the rain in the summer, conditions are perfect: good flat roads and warm weather.

Overseas visitors: Unless you're coming here from Saudi Arabia or Indonesia, American gasoline prices are a gift from heaven. But remember to always use self-service islands, as full-service ones cost 25 to 50¢ more per gallon.

Road Rules

Americans drive on the right (and yes, that also means *correct)* side of the road and pass on the left. Right turns on a red light are permitted after a full stop. At four-way stop signs, the car to your right has the right-of-way. Flashing yellow lights mean caution; flashing red lights are stop signs. Speed limits in the city are between 15 and 45 miles per hour. Be especially careful in school zones, which are limited to 15 mph when the lights are flashing, and on causeways, which – no matter how fast cars actually

---

The US Highway System

There are five main categories of roads in Florida: Interstate highways are usually high-speed, multilane roads that cross several states; odd-numbered roads generally go in a north-south direction, even-numbered ones generally go east-west (in this book interstates are abbreviated as, for example, I-95 or I-4). US highways are smaller roads that nonetheless cross several states; they are lined with businesses and have stop lights (and are abbreviated in this book as, for example, US Hwy 1). State roads are about the same size as US highways, and county roads are smaller still (both are abbreviated simply as 'Hwy', such as Hwy 84). Finally, there are city streets.

Most roads in Florida are excellent for driving, motorcycling, bicycling or even in-line skating: flat, smooth, well maintained and well signed.

Note, though, that bicyclists and wheelchair-bound travelers using the roads will often become angry at the distinct lack of shoulders on the roads. ∎

---

travel – are limited to no more than 45 miles an hour. Speeding tickets are outrageous: for example, if you're clocked at 50 in a 40 mph zone, the fine is over $127. Radar detectors are legal in Florida (hint nudge wink).

Florida police officers are merciless when it comes to speed limit enforcement; see Legal Matters in the Facts for the Visitor chapter for more information on speed limits and what to do if you're pulled over.

All passengers in a car must wear seatbelts; all children under three must be in a child safety seat (the rental car companies will rent you one for about $5 a day). The fine for not wearing a seatbelt can be as high as $150.

Parking

Always park in the shade if possible, and it may pay to invest in a windshield shade – even a cardboard one – to filter sunlight. Cars heat up to an unbelievable temperature very quickly.

Outside cities, park wherever you want to within reason. It's always illegal and

towable to park in designated handicapped parking spaces or in front of a fire station, fire plug, taxi stand or police station. Believe it or not, in many cases it's also illegal to park in front of a church.

In cities, parking is often a challenge, especially in places like Miami, Miami Beach, Coral Gables, St Augustine, Ybor City in Tampa and Key West. In those places, look for metered parking or, if none is available, city or private parking lots. In city lots, parking is generally about 75¢ an hour; in private lots the sky's the limit, especially during special events.

Valet parking is available at many finer restaurants and in front of hotels in Miami Beach and in Miami. It's usually at least $10.

There's always free parking in supermarkets and shopping malls, and it's usually available for a small (about $2 to 5) fee at stadiums and theme parks.

Floridians are generally careful about not knocking over bikes parked on the street, but there aren't many motorcycle-only lots.

Towing

If your car is towed by the police, call the nearest police station and ask them which company they use. The tow will cost at least $50 plus the cost of the ticket to unimpound your car. It's not fun, and the location of the towing contractor is seldom convenient.

Theft

Car theft is a popular sport in Miami and throughout South Florida, where boats to the Caribbean are waiting to ship yours off to somewhere other than your garage. If you own a car, it may pay to invest in an anti-theft device like the Club, but note that in Miami some car thieves have found a simple yet effective method of getting around that: they hacksaw through your steering wheel.

Obviously, don't tempt thieves by leaving your keys in the car or your doors unlocked, and remove valuables from plain sight before leaving your vehicle.

So if, despite all precautions, you come back and find your car gone, call the cops on a non-emergency number to see if they're responsible. If it turns out your car is stolen, call ☎ 911 and report the theft immediately.

Breakdown

Most rental cars are covered for breakdown; see your rental agreement for a toll-free breakdown number. Depending on the company, they'll be either out soon or next to soon. If they can't get to you until the next day, ask if your motel costs can be covered. Even if they say no, keep the receipts for motel and food while you wait and take the matter up with a manager when you return the car – you may get reimbursed, or at the very least a coupon for a free rental next time.

If you break down in a privately owned vehicle, check in the yellow pages under 'towing', or if you're on the road, get to a pay phone and call ☎ 411 for directory assistance and ask them for one – if they argue with you and say they can't, ask for a supervisor and explain your situation and they'll usually look one up in the yellow pages for you. AAA members can call ☎ 800-222-4357 and a tow truck will be sent out but quick.

It may pay to rent or buy a cellular telephone, especially if you'll be traveling to remote areas. Most rental car agencies rent phones for about $3 a day plus expensive air time (about $1.50 a minute).

Car Rental

All major car rental companies in the USA have offices throughout Florida. Rates go

The Holocaust Memorial

Downtown Miami skyline

Wolfsonian Foundation

Vizcaya with Brickell Ave in the background

Exotic offerings at a West Indian market

The brighter the better

Little Havana's colorful residents

Living large in Miami

Long Drive? Kinsey Milhone to the Rescue

On long drives, and there are lots of those in Florida, one of the best ways of passing the time once the conversation's all used up is to listen to – believe it or not – books on tape. Almost all best-selling books are also released on tape, read by actors or sometimes even the authors themselves – we love mystery and suspense novels on tape for longer voyages. Books on tape generally run from two to five hours and take up four to six standard tape cassettes.

Cracker Barrel sort of rents books on tape, and the service is great. While they don't technically rent them, they do sell them – for about $40. When you return them – to any Cracker Barrel in the USA – they refund your money minus a $2 per week per tape 'service fee'. Wink wink.

Cracker Barrel is a national chain of restaurants and 'general stores', usually just off a major interstate highway: homey, hokey recreations of old Western supply houses that have awful gravy and lots of candy, knick-knacks and Americana.

In Florida, Cracker Barrel has restaurants in Gainesville, Daytona Beach, Fort Myers, Fort Pierce, Kissimmee, Ocala, Orange Park, Orlando, Palm Coast, Pensacola, Stuart, Tallahassee and West Palm Beach. ∎

---

up and down like the stock market, and it's always worth phoning around to see what's available. Booking ahead usually ensures the best rates – and booking ahead can be from the pay phone in the rental office to the company's 800 number. Sometimes the head office can get you a better price than the branch office, so always call ahead. If you're a member of a frequent-flyer club, be sure to check and see whether the rental company has a deal with your airline.

Major rental companies in Florida include the following:

Alamo	☎ 800-327-9633
Avis	☎ 800-831-2847
Budget	☎ 800-527-0700
Dollar	☎ 800-800-4000
Enterprise	☎ 800-325-8007
Hertz	☎ 800-654-3131
Thrifty	☎ 800-367-2277
Value	☎ 800-468-2583

Rates Rates in Florida for some reason tend to be lower than in most of the rest of the country; typically a small car might cost $23 to 45 a day or $129 to 179 a week. On top of that there will be a 6% state sales tax, $2.05 a day Florida road surcharge and $9 or 10 a day for each insurance option you take – plus local taxes.

Generally speaking, the best deals come on weekly or weekend rental periods. At the time of writing, the lowest rates consistently seem to come from companies like Alamo, Budget, Enterprise and Value, and the highest from Avis and Hertz, though there are always specials and the best bet is to shop around carefully. The same car can vary in price from operator to operator by as much as $20 a day or $75 a week. Note though, that Avis has more offices than any other company in Florida, and usually does not impose drop-off charges within the state; we have picked up cars in Pensacola and dropped them off in Tampa or Jacksonville or Miami at no extra charge. If you're planning on dropping off at a different location than the one you picked up from, check and make certain that there won't be any penalty.

Most car rental companies here include unlimited mileage at no extra cost – be sure to check this point, as you can rack up hundreds of miles even just in the city, and at 25¢ per mile, this could be an unhappy surprise.

Age & Credit Requirements Most operators require that you be at least 25 years of age and have a major credit card in your own name. Some will let you get away with the age thing by paying outrageous surcharges, but renting without a credit card – if you can even accomplish it – will require a large cash deposit, and you'll have to work things

Fill 'Er Up?

When you rent a car, the agent will no doubt cheerfully inquire whether you'd like to buy the fuel from them at a 'special discounted rate', usually a few cents per gallon below street prices. Isn't that nice? The reason they're so keen to provide this service is that the amount of gas left in the tank when you return a rental car is a crucial profit center for car rental companies. When you rent, you'll probably be offered the opportunity to buy the full tank from the operator at a slightly discounted rate. Unless you're the kind of person who can calculate *exactly* how far a tank will get you in a car you're not used to, and can run on fumes all the way back to the airport, this is a bad idea: there are no refunds on unused fuel.

If you bring it back with the tank half full, congratulations: you've just paid *twice* the going street rate for the gas.

If you don't buy gas from them, be certain to return the car with a full tank of fuel; if you let the company refill the car for you, the price is outrageous – generally $2.99 but sometimes as much as $3.99 a gallon. And, of course, filling stations near rental car places are few and far between. ■

---

out well in advance with the company. It's hard to do, and even if they let you, you will be treated with great suspicion!

Insurance Note that in Florida, liability insurance is not included in rental costs. Some credit cards cover Loss/Damage-Waiver (LDW – sometimes also called CDW, or Collision/Damage Waiver), which means that you won't have to pay if you damage the car itself, but liability insurance means that you won't have to pay if you hit someone and they sue you. If you own a car and have insurance at home, your liability insurance may extend to coverage of rental cars, but be *absolutely* certain before driving on the roads in the litigious USA. Also, if you opt out of the LDW, be certain that your credit card will really cover you for it.

Motorcycle Rental

See the Miami chapter for information on Rolling Thunder (☎ 305-668-4600, 800-851-7420, fax 305-441-0519) in Coral Gables that rents late-model Harley David-son motorcycles. CruiseAmerica (see below) rents Honda and Triumph Cruising bikes from their Miami and Orlando offices; they cost about $170 a day/980 a week in high season from January to May, and $133/750 from May 1 to December 31.

RV Rental

Renting a recreational vehicle (RV) makes sense if you meet one of two conditions: a) you're rich or b) there are several of you. If either are so, an RV can be a great way to get out into Florida. They're surprisingly roomy and flexible, and even the smaller ones can sleep four comfortably – as long as you're all close friends. If you're not, don't despair: many RV campsites are large enough to accommodate the RV and still leave room for a tent outside.

The downside is that you'll need transport when you get where you're going – at an average highway gas consumption of between eight to 10 miles per gallon, RVs are not exactly a good method of city transport. You can, of course, get a bicycle rack or, if you also have a car, a tow-hitch to bring that along, but note that that makes your already dismal gas mileage even worse.

CruiseAmerica (☎ 800-327-7799) is the largest and best known of the nationwide RV rental firms. They have a huge variety of rentals available. The smallest – 22 to 24 feet with two double beds and a dinette that converts to a single bed, a bathroom with shower and a full kitchen – cost $723 a week in low season (from April to June and from August to mid-December) and $837 in high season, including insurance and an electrical generator. A thousand miles are included; after that you're billed at 29¢ a mile. The Recreational Vehicle Rental Association (☎ 703-591-7130, 800-336-0355) publishes *Who's Who in RV Rentals*, a directory of rental agencies around the USA, Canada and Europe for $7.50, and *Rental Ventures*, which lists campgrounds that accommodate RVs ($3, or $2.50 when purchased with the directory). You can order by telephone or send a check payable to RVRA for the purchase price of the publications you're looking for to RVRA, 3930 University Drive, Suite 100, Fairfax, Virginia 22030.

Buying a Car or Motorcycle
One possible way to beat the high cost of renting a car is to buy a used vehicle on arrival and then sell it when you leave. If you go this route, it helps either to have a bit of the auto mechanic in you or to find a mechanic you can trust; you won't get much return value on a 'lemon' or a gas guzzler. Don't ask yourself, 'Do I feel lucky?' because even minor repairs could cost well over $100.

Any used car owner who won't bring or let you take the car to a mechanic is hiding something. While you're there, tell the mechanic how much the seller wants for it, and if things look good, ask them to run an emissions test – it's no good finding out after you've bought it that the car won't pass state emissions levels. As a general idea of how much you'll spend on that, Shorty & Fred's Garage (☎ 305-672-1047) in Miami will check out a car for $48 and run an emissions test for $39.95.

Once you've bought the car, you must buy a rather costly auto insurance policy (generally $500 to 800 a year depending on your age and driving record) and take the smog certificate and proof of insurance, along with the ownership title and bill of sale, to any office of the Department of Motor Vehicles (DMV). Check in the blue government section of the white pages under Florida State Department of Highway and Motor Vehicles for full listings.

It normally takes a full morning or afternoon to get your auto registration (waiting to speak with, as one comedian put it, staff who 'look as if they were raised in the trunk of a Buick'), which will cost anywhere from 7 to 12% of the cost of the car.

As your departure from the USA approaches, you must set aside time to sell the car, perhaps also laying out additional money to place a classified ad in a newspaper.

If you don't object to a little wind, you might consider buying a motorcycle, which is cheaper than a car and tends to be easier to sell. But note that motorcycle insurance costs more, that my mother says it's too dangerous, and that helmets for yourself and any passengers are required by Florida law, which is strictly enforced.

BICYCLE
If you can stand the heat, Florida's not a bad place for cycling. Absolutely flat roads make it easy going, and the benefit of a bicycle is that once you get where you're going you have transportation as well. Helmets are not required under Florida law, but they're a good idea, as are highly reflective everything you can think of – Floridian drivers are not used to seeing bicyclists, and the more you can do to inform cars of your presence, the better chance you have of getting where you're going.

If you do get tired of biking, you can pack your bike. Most international airlines, and all flights within Florida, allow you to bring along a bike at no extra charge as check-in luggage, or they charge a fee (about $50) if it's in addition to your carry-on limit. Bike boxes usually cost $10 to 15 if you buy them from an airline, Greyhound or Amtrak.

You'll have to remove the handlebars and pedals to box it (you may be able to get away with bagging it). Greyhound and Amtrak charge $10 extra for your boxed bike – Amtrak only takes them on trains that have baggage cars.

Organizations The League of American Bicyclists, 190 W Ostend Ave, Suite 120, Baltimore, MD 21230-3755, publishes an annual *Almanac* that lists bicycle resources for each state in the USA. It costs $30 a year to join the league. State organizations include the Florida Bicycle Association, PO Box 16652, Tampa, FL 32687-6652, and the Office of the State Bicycle/Pedestrian Coordinator, Florida Department of Transportation (☎ 904-922-2935), 605 S Suwannee St, MS 82, Tallahassee, FL 32399-0450.

Bike Florida, sponsored by the Sunshine State Games Foundation (☎ 352-955-2120), is the best all-round source for information about bicycling in the state. They'll help you plan itineraries, assist with reservations for accommodations and counsel you on the realities of a bike trip through Florida. Write them at 1330 NW 6th St, Suite D, Gainesville, FL 32601.

Bike Florida is also a seven-day ride (averaging 50 miles a day) held annually in late June that goes throughout the state from a starting city to the city that's hosting that year's Sunshine State Games, an amateur, Olympic-style athletic competition that attracts about ten thousand athletes a year. Contact Bike Florida for more information.

Within Cities Many cities in Florida have outlets for bicycle rentals – at hostels, hotels, resorts or bike shops. Sports Authority, Sears, K-Mart, WalMart and Lauderdale Sports all carry bicycle parts, so if you're in a town without a bike shop there's still reason to hope.

Bicyclists are charged $1 each for admission to most state parks.

Especially in Miami Beach, where everyone we know has had a bicycle stolen, make certain to lock your bike. If you can remove the front tire and take it with you, do it. Also remove the seat if it's got a quick-release height adjust. Use a sturdy U-type lock, not a chain and padlock.

HITCHING

Hitchhiking in the USA is a rather dangerous proposition, and it's therefore less common in the USA than in other countries. That said, if you do choose to hitch, the advice that follows should help to make your journey as fast, if not as safe, as possible. Officially, hitching is legal, except on interstate highways, but it *is* frowned upon by law enforcement and you can expect to be hassled by them if they see you. Hitch on the on-ramp, not on the highway. It helps to look neat and carry a neatly printed sign with your destination. Lots of baggage, two or more men or groups of three of any sex slow you down substantially. Women should think very carefully about hitching, especially if alone but even in groups of two or more.

Universities have ride-sharing programs, as well as bulletin boards, especially at the end of semesters and during school holidays. Check when you come for rides to or near where you're headed.

In Fort Lauderdale and in several of Florida's larger counties there are share-a-ride programs designed to assist commuters, but they can act, in a pinch, as the American equivalent of the German *Mitfahrzentrale* – a central source that pairs up drivers and passengers. You'll have to chip in for gas and tolls, and it usually doesn't work for very long distances.

BOAT

There's not much in the way of getting around Florida by boat except for very limited water taxi service within Miami and Fort Lauderdale (see those chapters' Getting Around sections for more information), but Florida is a world center for two major categories of boat transport: crewing aboard privately owned yachts and, of course, the fast-growing cruise ship industry. See the Getting There & Away chapter for information on crewing.

Cruise Ships

Miami The Port of Miami is the largest cruise ship port in the world, with over three million passengers a year. You can take cruises for anywhere from one day to the very common three-day Bahamas cruises; to four-day to one-week trips to ports of call like San Juan, Puerto Rico, St Thomas, St John and St Martin; to top-end round-the-world voyages. Ships leave from the

Port of Miami Cruise Passenger Terminals on Dodge Island.

Rates change almost daily, and there are any number of discounts that apply – even quoted fares when you call are subject to discounts just for the asking . . . so ask. Port charges are not included in most of these prices.

The major cruise operators include the following:

Carnival Cruise Lines (☎ 305-599-2600, 800-327-7276) This most popular line does three-night tours on the *Extasy* from Friday to Monday to Nassau, Bahamas; an inside cabin (category four) was at the time of research $449, or suites from $879. A four-night cruise (from Thursday to Monday on the *Fantasy* to the Bahamas starts at $399/869.

Norwegian Cruise Line (☎ 305-447-9660, 800-327-7030) Three-night tours aboard the *Leeward* to the Bahamas run from $329 to 1189; four-night voyages to Mexico run from $449 to 1439.

Royal Caribbean Cruise Line (☎ 305-539-6573, 800-327-6700) A three-night Bahamas weekend on the *Nordic Empress* runs from $629 to 1869; a four-night cruise is $779 to 2029 and the seven-night Eastern Caribbean aboard the *Grandeur of the Seas* is $1399 to 3999.

Discovery Cruise Line (☎ 305-467-5777, 800-937-4477) Day cruises out of Miami can be had for $75 (standard), $90 (superior), $100 (double) or $135 (suite) to the Bahamas; they leave on Monday, Tuesday and Thursday to Saturday on the *Discovery Sun*. Cruise times vary, but their casino (which is why most are here) usually opens 45 minutes after departure. You can also do a 'cruise' n' stay package' for one to four nights; rates here depend on location and nights, from $99 to 309.

Port Everglades The second-largest port after Miami, Port Everglades (☎ 954-523-0252), at 18050 Eller Drive in Fort Lauderdale, offers a very similar range of cruises by the same companies and several others. They include:

Celebrity Cruises	☎ 800-437-3111
Princess Cruises	☎ 800-421-0522
Cunard Line	☎ 800-528-6273
Holland America Line	☎ 800-426-0327
Royal Olympic Cruises	☎ 800-368-3888
SeaEscape	☎ 800-327-2005

Port Canaveral As the closest port to Orlando, Port Canaveral (☎ 407-783-7831) has been gaining popularity since Scandinavian World Cruises (☎ 954-474-3707) made its home base here in 1982. Since then, it's become one of the largest three- and four-night cruise ports in the world, and today it's a bustling cruise and cargo port with a great recreation area attached.

Carnival Cruise Lines' *Fantasy* runs three- and four-night Nassau and Freeport, Bahamas, cruises every Monday and Friday, and Premiere Cruise Lines' *Star/Ship Oceanic* (yes, the Big Red Boat – can you imagine having to tell your sailor buddies that you're captain of something called a Big Red Boat?) runs to Nassau and Port Lucaya, Bahamas, on Monday and Friday, and the *Star/Ship Atlantic* covers the same route on Thursday and Sunday. When Disney Cruise Lines begins service in 1998, the *Disney Magic* and the *Disney Wonder* will sail from here as well.

Port of Palm Beach The Port of Palm Beach (☎ 561-842-4201), north of West Palm Beach, is a much smaller affair, with far fewer regularly scheduled sailings. Palm Beach Cruise Lines (☎ 561-845-7447, 800-841-7447) offers six-hour gambling cruises three to five miles off the Atlantic Coast on Monday, Wednesday, Friday and Sunday aboard the *Viking Princess*. On Tuesday, Thursday and Saturday, the *Princess* heads out to the Bahamas at 8.30 in the morning and returns at midnight; you'll have about 3½ hours on the beaches over there, with gambling on the way there and back.

The Bahamas cruise costs $79 on Tuesday and Thursday, $89 on Saturday, plus port charges on all days of $36 per person. The gambling cruises cost between $39 and 49 plus $15 per person port charges.

LOCAL TRANSPORT

Local bus service is only available in larger cities; generally bus fare is between 75¢ and $1.25. Transfers – slips of paper that allow you to change buses – are from free to

25¢. Bus fare in Florida is paid as you board (you always board through the front doors), and usually exact change is required, though some buses accept $1 bills.

Wheelchair-bound passengers should contact the local bus company to inquire about special transport services. Most buses in Florida are wheelchair-accessible, though some bus companies offer individual transit services in addition to regular service for those with physical or mental disabilities. See the Facts for the Visitor chapter for information on organizations that assist with travel for the handicapped. Operating hours differ from city to city, but generally buses run from about 6 am to 10 pm.

Miami & Miami Beach

HIGHLIGHTS

- Bake on the beaches!
- The exotic aromas and tastes of the Fruit & Spice Park
- Venetian Pool, the world's most beautiful public swimming pool
- Performances by the nation's brightest young musicians at the New World Symphony
- Holocaust Memorial, one of the most moving memorials we've ever seen
- Metrozoo, a 754-acre natural-habitat zoo
- Leaping killer whales and dolphins at Miami Seaquarium
- Hands-on science and cheap stargazing at the Museum of Science & Space Transit Planetarium
- Excellent exhibits at the Museum of Contemporary Art
- Cigars, 'zoom juice' and fiery Cuban music in Little Havana

- *pop Miami 373,000, Miami Beach 93,000, Greater Miami 1.9 million*
- ☎ *305*

It used to be called 'God's Waiting Room'. And even today, if you mention Miami Beach to someone who hasn't been here or read about it lately, they might be able to conjure up a blurry memory of octogenarians mingling poolside while Aunt Sadie implored them to wait half an hour before going into the water. But to the arbiters of Fabulousness, SoBe (the inevitable contraction of 'South Beach') has been the Fabulous Spot in the USA since the early 1990s.

The boom, which began in the late 1980s, brought renovation and the restoration of the city's Deco District, but over-zealous developers were given a very short leash by local preservation groups who made certain that the Deco look wouldn't be demolished in favor of the high-rise monstrosities that line the beaches to the near north.

Today, Miami Beach is what you make of it: trendy or not, at the end of the day it's a great stretch of white sand beach lapped by clear blue water, on an island squarely between the Atlantic Ocean and downtown Miami, which sits only a causeway (and several lifestyle light years) to the west.

And the Greater Miami Area, which includes Coral Gables, Miami, Coconut Grove and other cities, as well as unique and distinctive neighborhoods like Little Havana and Little Haiti, is as much a melting pot as the USA's founding fathers could have envisioned.

HISTORY
The City's Beginnings
In 1895, a record freeze enveloped most of the north of Florida, where Henry Flagler's railroads were disgorging thousands of rich and powerful northerners who were coming to stay at his hotels and resorts. The freeze wiped out citrus crops and sent vacationers scurrying, and legend has it that Julia Tuttle (who owned large tracts of property here and had approached Flagler with the offer of partnership in exchange for the extension of his railroad to Miami, which he'd refused) went into her garden at Fort Dallas, snipped off some flowers and sent them to Flagler, who hightailed it down to Miami to see for himself.

Julia Tuttle - the mother of Miami

What he saw was a tropical paradise that was very warm indeed. Flagler and Tuttle came to terms, and Flagler announced the extension of his railroad. At that, thousands of people whose livelihoods had been wiped out by the big freeze, including citrus growers and service industry workers like doctors and merchants, began to head down to Miami in anticipation of the boom that was to come. Passenger train service to Miami began April 22, 1896. In that year the city of Miami incorporated and development kicked off. The wave peaked during WWI, when the US military established an aviation training facility here.

After WWI, the first full-fledged Miami boom (1923-25) was fueled not just by the area's idyllic beachfront location and perfect weather, but also by gambling and the fact that it never really took to the idea of prohibition – though it was illegal, liquor flowed freely throughout the entire Prohibition period.

But the boom was cut short by a devastating hurricane, which was immediately followed by statewide recession and national depression.

In the mid-1930s, a mini-boom saw the construction of Miami Beach's famous Art Deco buildings, and this reasonably prosperous period continued until 1942, when a German U-Boat sank an American tanker off Florida's coast. The ensuing freak-out created a full-scale conversion of South Florida into a massive military base, training facility and staging area.

Postwar Era & the 1950s

After WWII, many of Miami's trainee soldiers returned and settled; the city was maintaining its pre-war prosperity.

In the 1950s, Miami Beach had another boom, as the area began to be known as the 'Cuba of America': gamblers and gangsters, enticed by Miami's gambling, as well as its proximity to the fun, sun and fast times of Batista-run Cuba, moved in en masse. After the Castro coup in Cuba in 1959 Miami's Cuban population swelled – a special immigration center was established to handle the overflow in Miami's Freedom Tower – the Ellis Island of the South.

Racial Tensions

Blacks were relegated to an area north of downtown known as Colored Town, later Overtown, but in the 1950s, as the city grew, many were displaced to the federal housing projects at Liberty City, a misnomer if ever there was one.

In 1965, the two 'freedom flights' that ran every day between Miami and Havana disgorged over 100,000 Cuban refugees. Sensing the tension that was building up between blacks and Cubans, Dr Martin Luther King, Jr pleaded with the two sides not to let animosity lead to bloodshed.

But riots broke out, skirmishes and acts of gang-style violence occurred. In 1968, a riot broke out after two white police officers arrested a 17-year-old black male, stripped him naked and suspended him from his ankles from a bridge.

In 1970, the 'rotten meat' riot began when

blacks picketed a white-owned shop they had accused of selling spoiled meat. Between 1970 and 1979, there were 13 other race-related violent confrontations.

The Mariel Boatlift (see History in the Facts about Florida chapter) brought 150,000 Cubans to Florida, and the resulting economic, logistical and infrastructural strain on South Florida only added to still-simmering racial tensions, which would explode on May 17, 1980, when four white police officers, being tried on charges that they beat a black suspect to death while he was in custody, were acquitted by an all-white jury. When the verdict was announced, severe race riots broke out all over Miami, and lasted for three days. The Liberty City Riot resulted in 18 deaths, $80 million in property damage, and 1100 arrests.

1980s

In the roaring 1980s, the area gained prominence as the major East Coast entry port for drug dealers, their product, and the unbelievable sums of money that went along with them. A plethora of businesses – both totally legitimate concerns as well as drug-financed fronts – and buildings sprung up all over Miami, and the downtown was completely remodeled. But it was still a city being reborn while in the grip of drug smugglers: shootouts were common, as were gangland slayings by cocaine cowboys.

The police, Coast Guard, Drug Enforcement Agency, Border Patrol and FBI were in a tizzy trying to keep track of it all.

And then it happened: *Miami Vice*.

The show, which starred Don Johnson and Philip Michael Thomas as Crockett and Tubbs, two outrageously expensively – and yet pastel – clad narcotics detectives driving around in a Ferrari Testarossa and million-dollar cigarette boats – was responsible for Miami Beach rising to international attention in the mid-1980s. The show's unique look, its slick soundtrack and music video-style montages glamorized the rich life lived in South Florida, and before long people were coming down to see it.

By the late 1980s, Miami Beach had risen to international Fabulousness. Celebrities

Hurricane Andrew

On August 24, 1992, Hurricane Andrew, with sustained 140 mph winds and gusts of up to 170 mph, slammed down over Homestead. By the time the hurricane had passed, it was the costliest disaster to ever hit the USA.

Andrew Stats
Deaths: 52
Industry destroyed: tropical fruit, lime and nursery industries
Property damage: $30 billion
Evacuees: 300,000
Residents who permanently left the area: 100,000
Homes damaged: 77,000
Homes destroyed: 8000
Mobile homes damaged: 10,500
Mobile homes destroyed: 8900
Apartments damaged: 27,800
Apartments destroyed: 10,700
People left homeless: 175,000
Top wind speed: clocked at 163 mph before the meter at the National Hurricane Center broke.

(Sources: Florida Department of Community Affairs, Division of Emergency Management and *Wire*.)

It wasn't worse because a) people had had time to prepare and evacuate, and b) the hurricane – while a Category 4 storm – was obliging enough to keep on moving and not sit on the area. But had the storm been 20 miles farther north when it hit land (as was expected), the storm surge surely would have destroyed Miami Beach – see the Dangers & Annoyances section in the Facts for the Visitor chapter for complete hurricane information. ■

were moving in, photo shoots from all over the world were being shot here, and the Art Deco District, having been granted federal protection, was going through a renovation that turned the city into a showpiece of fashion and trendiness.

The Area Today

The area is riding the peak of a boom that's been going on for the past several years. Andrew barely affected the tourist

MIAMI

industry, which is the city's economic backbone. And despite highly publicized crimes against tourists in 1993, Miami is now the third most popular city for international tourists after Los Angeles and New York. Greater Miami saw 11.6 million visitors in 1993.

How long the boom will last is debatable. On the one hand, more people than ever are coming. On the other, there are distinct murmurs amongst the European and super-model crowd that South Beach is in danger of imploding and getting – gasp – passé.

Locals are not worried. After the film, TV and European fashion shoots, the Stallones and Schwarzeneggers, Sharon Stones and Madonnas, Versaces, and the thousands of oh-so-trendy people who swarm the chic neon-emblazoned cafés and boutiques of SoBe leave, South Beach will still be here, and better than ever.

ORIENTATION

The City of Miami covers an enormous, sprawling area that's subdivided into neighborhoods and sections and is adjacent to several cities. Miami is on the mainland, while the City of Miami Beach is on a thin barrier island about four miles east, across Biscayne Bay – locals call it the Billion Dollar Sandbar.

Downtown Miami

Downtown Miami is a fairly straightforward grid, with Flagler Ave as much the main drag as any. The downtown area is divided by the Miami River, crossed by the newly renovated Brickell Ave Bridge and continues on the south side of the river.

The north-south divider is Flagler St; the east-west divider is Miami Ave; prefixes are given to streets – N, W, S, E, NW, NE, SW, SE – based on that street's position relative to the intersection of Flagler St and Miami Ave.

Most avenues and streets are numbered: avenues begin at 1 and count upwards the farther east and west they are from Miami Ave, so E 1st Ave would be one block east of Miami Ave, while W 42nd Ave would be 42 blocks west of Miami Ave. Streets are numbered similarly, increasing in number

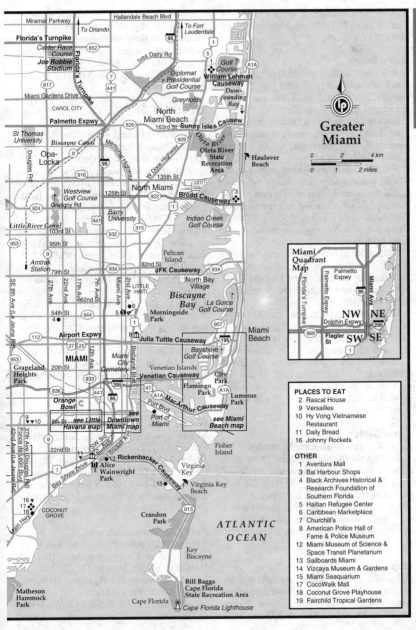

Greater Miami

LP

0   2   4 km
0   1   2 miles

Miami Quadrant Map

	Palmetto Expwy	
Florida's Turnpike	Palmetto Expwy	Miami Ave
	NW	NE
968	Dolphin Expwy	295
Flagler St		SW SE

PLACES TO EAT
2 Rascal House
9 Versailles
10 Hy Vong Vietnamese Restaurant
11 Daily Bread
16 Johnny Rockets

OTHER
1 Aventura Mall
3 Bal Harbour Shops
4 Black Archives Historical & Research Foundation of Southern Florida
5 Haitian Refugee Center
6 Caribbean Marketplace
7 Churchill's
8 American Police Hall of Fame & Police Museum
12 Miami Museum of Science & Space Transit Planetarium
13 Sailboards Miami
14 Vizcaya Museum & Gardens
15 Miami Seaquarium
17 CocoWalk Mall
18 Coconut Grove Playhouse
19 Fairchild Tropical Gardens

MIAMI

progressively the farther north or south of Flagler St, so N 1st St would be one block north of Flagler, etc.

Miami Beach

In this book, despite common practice, we break Miami Beach up into two distinct regions: South Beach (or SoBe) and Northern Miami Beach.

Streets run east-west and avenues run north-south, but the avenues are named, not numbered, and there are no directional sectors like NW or SE.

South Beach, on the widest section of the island, has a grid which mostly runs due north-south and east-west, except for curving bits of Alton Rd and the fact that Washington and Collins Aves and Ocean Drive run at a 20° angle northeast to the main grid system.

Lincoln Road is pedestrian-only between Washington Ave at the east and Alton Rd at the west; the strip is called Lincoln Road Mall and would seem to be perpetually under construction.

South Pointe is below 5th St at the southern tip of Miami Beach, directly across Government Cut from Fisher Island.

Northern Miami Beach is divided by narrow Indian Creek, which separates Collins Ave on the thin strip of land at the east from the residential districts at the west. The northern border of Miami Beach is 96th St.

Coral Gables

Coral Gables is essentially bordered by Calle Ocho at the north, Sunset Drive (SW 72nd St/Hwy 986) at the south, Le Jeune Rd (SW 42nd Ave/Hwy 953) at the east and Red Rd (SW 57th Ave/Hwy 959) at the west. US Hwy 1 slashes through at a 45° angle from northeast to southwest. Avenues here run east-west, while streets run north-south.

Maps

All rental car companies are required by law to hand out decent city and area maps when you rent a car – Alamo's isn't bad at all. Rand McNally, AAA and Dolph Map

Company make area maps of Miami. Freebies are usually not very good as they're simplified to the point of being totally inaccurate. You can get somewhat usable free maps from the Greater Miami & the Beaches Convention & Visitor's Bureau (see below).

INFORMATION
Tourist Offices

The Greater Miami & the Beaches Convention & Visitor's Bureau (☎ 539-3063, 800-933-8448, 800-283-2702) is at 791 Brickell Ave in downtown Miami. They operate a tourist information center at Bayside Marketplace (☎ 539-2980), 401 Biscayne Blvd.

The Art Deco Welcome Center (☎ 531-3484) at 1001 Ocean Drive, run by the Miami Design Preservation League, has tons of Deco District information. The Miami Beach Chamber of Commerce (☎ 672-1270) has an office at 1920 Meridian Ave.

The Black Archives Historical & Research Foundation of South Florida (☎ 636-2390) in Liberty City at 5400 NW 22nd Ave, Building B, has information about black culture and can arrange tours of Liberty City and other areas of the city.

The Coral Gables Chamber of Commerce (☎ 446-1557) at 50 Aragon Ave has that city's absolutely excellent tourist maps and other information.

Money

Barnett Bank has branch offices all over Miami and Miami Beach. Some private exchange offices include American Express (☎ 358-7350) at 330 Biscayne Blvd, Thomas Cook (☎ 374-0655) at 155 SE 3rd Ave, SunTrust (☎ 591-6000) at 777 Brickell Ave and Lincoln Road at Alton Rd and Chequepoint (☎ 538-5348) at 865 Collins Ave.

Post & Communications

The two main post offices on the Beach are at 13th St at Washington Ave (General Delivery, Miami Beach, FL 33139) and 71st St at Versailles (General Delivery, Miami Beach, FL 33141).

Nonmembers of SoBeNET (☎ 674-7007, see the Online Services appendix) can rent a computer station for e-mail transfer at a nominal printing cost.

Anyone who's anyone in Miami has a cellular telephone, and you can rent one as easily as you buy a soda from a soda machine. That's right, there are cell phone rental *vending machines* in many airport car rental offices. There are also cell phone rental places in larger hotels. You should make certain that you only have to pay for air time (not equipment rental), and find out if there's a daily minimum – it's usually about three minutes. Note that airtime on rentals is far more expensive than on normal cell phones – count on about $1.25 to $2 a minute on local and incoming calls, and much more for long distance outgoing calls.

Travel Agencies

We've used Travel by Design (☎ 673-6336, 800-358-7125) at 1436 Washington Ave, just around the corner from the Clay Hotel & International Hostel on many occasions, they do cut rate flights and sell Lonely Planet books. Pilar Tours (☎ 538-7026), is a discount travel agent specializing in cruises and some discount flights. Council Travel (☎ 670-9261, 800-226-8624, see the Online Services appendix) has a Miami office at 9100 S Dadeland Blvd. Travel Now is another agency that has two offices, at 1600 Collins Ave (☎ 532-7243) and at 14374 Biscayne Blvd (☎ 919-9000).

Bookstores

The best locally owned bookshops are the two branches of Books & Books, at 933 Lincoln Road on Miami Beach (☎ 532-3222) and at 296 Aragon Ave in Coral Gables (☎ 442-4408). The shops are host to visiting authors, discussions, poetry readings and, in Miami Beach, there's even a café. There is an excellent selection of literature, fiction and Florida-related books. It's open Monday to Thursday from 10 am to 10 pm, Friday and Saturday from 10 am to midnight, Sunday from 10 am to 9 pm.

Books by Us (☎ 532-6011) at 1665 Michigan Ave opened just as we went to press. The concept is great: books and readings by local writers in an intimate shop/café.

In downtown Miami the Downtown Book Center (☎ 377-9938) at 215 NE 2nd Ave, has a good selection and lots of Lonely Planet books.

Other than those, there is an excellent Borders (☎ 935-4712) at 19925 Biscayne Blvd in Aventura, with a café and an enormous Florida selection.

Periodicals & Foreign Press The News Cafe (☎ 538-6397) at 800 Ocean Drive has a separate 24-hour newsstand between the restaurant and the bar. They've got a good selection of international (from countries considered to be fashionable) and domestic press, and some paperbacks.

You can get dailies from practically every Spanish-speaking country at a couple of places: in downtown Miami, try the newsstand that sets up just across the street from the Gusman Performance Center at 174 E Flagler St, and the larger more permanent one at the corner of SE 1st St and SE 2nd Ave.

Libraries

The Miami Public Library (☎ 375-2665, 375-5184) has an enormous Florida room containing thousands of books on all aspects of Florida life, history and travel, as well as a large video and audio-tape library.

A good branch of the library is on Miami Beach (☎ 535-4219) at 2100 Collins Ave, open Monday and Wednesday from 10 am to 8 pm, Tuesday and Thursday to Saturday from 10 am to 5.30 pm, closed Sunday.

Media

The *Miami Herald* is the city's major daily. *Wire* is the (free) paper of record to find out where to play on the Beach, with the most up-to-date club listings and a club calendar. Great coverage of local issues, along with superb listings of restaurants, a club/pub/ bar/theater/cinema/special events calendar and reviews is the *New Times*, available free around town. On Fridays the Herald features a pullout section called *Weekend*, which has movie and music reviews and listings, gallery information for Miami and surrounding areas, comedy and a whole lot of other stuff.

The *Miami Herald* publishes *el Nuevo Herald*, an excellent Spanish daily. *El Diario Américas* is another Spanish language daily. Most major Western European newspapers are available at good newsstands.

NPR is at 91.3 FM.

Campuses
The two major players in the area are the state-run Florida International University (FIU) and the University of Miami (UM).

FIU, a state university with a liberal arts core curriculum, is the larger of the two, with enrollment of over 26,000 students. Their University Park campus is located on US Hwy 41 (west of Calle Ocho) between SW 107th Ave and Florida's Turnpike. The North Campus is located off US Hwy 1 at NE 151st Street.

Founded in 1925, UM's Coral Gables campus is on 260-acres within the City of Coral Gables. The university has a total enrollment of about 13,000 full- and part-time students.

Gay & Lesbian
The club scene is ever changing (during the research for this book, four closed) so check below for listings papers that give absolutely up-to-date information during your trip.

Information In an emergency, call the Switchboard of Miami (☎ 358-4357). The Lesbian, Gay & Bisexual Community Center (☎ 531-0366) is an excellent (if under-funded) resource for information and referrals at 1335 Alton Rd in Miami Beach. The South Beach Business Guild (☎ 234-7224) represents businesses that are owned by or friendly to gay men, lesbians and bisexuals.

In the *Miami Herald*, Eugene J Patron writes the weekly *Out & Around* column, which covers happenings and events of social or political significance in the metropolitan area. *twn* is a local weekly newspaper focusing on gay and lesbian community issues.

Lips is a lesbian-oriented monthly newspaper with a very good calendar section; *Pride* is a biweekly gay listings magazine; *Hotspots* is much flashier and packed with ads from discos to straightforward classifieds for prostitutes. *Scoop* is Hotspots' main competitor. *She Times* is another monthly lesbian-oriented paper.

Gay & Lesbian Bookstores The Gay Emporium (☎ 534-4763) at 720 Lincoln Road, sell gay and lesbian literature, as well as postcards, gifts, flags, magazines, condoms, leather and video rentals, etc. *Lambda Passages* (☎ 754-6900) way north at 7545 Biscayne Blvd sells gay and lesbian books and videos.

Film & Photography
Of the many places to develop and buy film in the area, we think that the best are on Miami Beach: Tropicolor at 1442 Alton Rd (☎ 672-3729) and 1657 Washington Ave (☎ 538-1183), and LIB Color Labs (☎ 538-5600) at 851 Washington Ave.

Laundry
On the Beach, the folks at the coin laundry at 510 Washington Ave (☎ 534-4298) are very friendly, they're open daily from 6 to 2 am. Mark's Dry Cleaning (☎ 538-6275) is 'at the breezy corner of Alton Rd and 20th St'.

Medical Services
The Stanley C Myers Community Health Center (☎ 538-8835), 710 Alton Rd, is a public clinic that charges based on your income. You'll need to get there early (they're open Monday to Friday from 7.30 am to 4.30 pm, closed Saturday and Sunday) as lines to this walk-in clinic are usually very long. You'll need to bring ID and US citizens should bring proof of residence and income. If you're foreign born, bring your passport and I-94 card.

Check in the yellow pages under Physicians or Clinics to find a doctor, or call the Dade County Medical Association (☎ 324-8717) Monday to Friday from 9 am to 5 pm. Look in the yellow pages under Dentists to find one of those, or try 1-800-DENTIST (☎ 800-336-8478), a free referral service.

In a serious emergency, call ☎ 911 for an ambulance to take you to the nearest hospital's emergency room. Mount Sinai Medical Center (☎ 674-2121) at 4300 Alton Rd is considered to be the best in the area.

Dangers & Annoyances

If you encounter any problems with hotels, restaurants or businesses during your stay, you aren't powerless; you have a couple of options other than the police. For incidents that occur anywhere in Miami Beach, contact Michael Aller (☎ 673-7010, emergency beeper 886-4795), the City of Miami Beach's lovable Tourism & Convention coordinator.

Unsafe Areas There are a few areas considered by locals to be dangerous, and racism – overt or implied – may be responsible for some, like Liberty City, a predominantly black neighborhood in northwest Miami, or Little Haiti. We've never had any problems in either, but in these and other reputedly 'bad' areas, you should avoid walking around alone late at night, use common sense and travel in groups.

Any deserted area, like below 5th St in Miami Beach or the area near the Greyhound station in downtown Miami, is more dangerous at night, as are areas under causeways and bridges from Miami, where homeless people and some refugees have set up shantytowns.

If you're considering sex on the beach, realize that it's not a very original idea: police patrol as do muggers.

Use caution when changing money – muggers have been known to hang around at exchange offices looking for victims.

Bad Service Service in some Miami Beach restaurants can be atrocious. Petulant and pouty wanna-be models of both sexes are employed at practically every Ocean Drive restaurant as 'hosts' and waitstaff. There's nothing much you can do about it except keep your dignity and remember: real models don't have to hand you a menu.

MIAMI BEACH

Most people come here for the beaches and the clubs and bars, but there are other compelling attractions within the City of Miami Beach that you should really try and see during your stay. And happily the attractions within the City of Miami Beach are easy to get to and between, so a day spent seeing what the Beach has to offer is one very well spent.

In addition to Cubans and a decidedly Latin flair, large numbers of Jews have settled here over the last 50 years. In fact, there's a **Cuban-Jewish Congregation** (☎ 534-7213), in a building that looks just like something out of Bedrock, at 1700 Michigan Ave.

Deco District

The Art Deco Historic District, one of the largest areas in the USA to be placed on the National Register of Historic Places, is in the very heart of South Beach. Its unique hotels and apartment buildings have now been renovated with a decidedly colorful flair, the façades painted with pastel pinks, blues and greens that make for a walk into the roaring '20s or an unguided tour of the very best in American kitsch, depending on your views.

The listing on the Register is what protected the area from attempts by the city and developers to raze significant portions of what was in the 1980s a crime-ridden collection of crumbling eyesores populated by drug-crazed lunatics, Cuban refugees and elderly residents.

The listing was fought for by Barbara Baer Capitman in 1976 after she heard plans by the City of Miami to raze several historic buildings in what is now the Omni Mall.

But Leonard Horowitz, a co-founder of the MDPL, played a pivotal role in putting South Beach back on the map, by painting the then drably painted Deco buildings in shocking colors like pinks, lavenders and turquoises.

The Deco District is bounded by Dade Blvd at the north, 6th St at the south; the Atlantic Ocean at the east and Lenox Court (half a block east of Alton Rd) at the west.

MIAMI

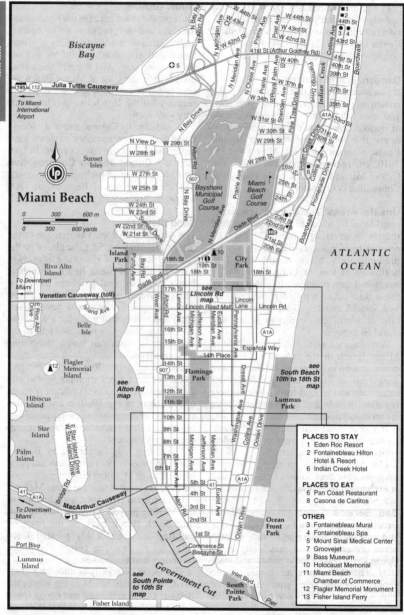

Biscayne Bay

195 112 **Julia Tuttle Causeway**

To Miami International Airport

Miami Beach

0   300   600 m
0   300   600 yards

Sunset Isles

Bayshore Municipal Golf Course

Miami Beach Golf Course

Rivo Alto Island

To Downtown Miami

Venetian Causeway (toll)

Island Park

City Park

ATLANTIC OCEAN

Belle Isle

see Lincoln Rd map

Lincoln Road Mall

Flagler Memorial Island

Hibiscus Island

see Alton Rd map

Flamingo Park

Española Way

see South Beach 10th to 18th St map

Star Island

Palm Island

Lummus Park

41 A1A **MacArthur Causeway**

To Downtown Miami

Port Blvd

Lummus Island

Fisher Island

see South Pointe to 10th St map

Government Cut

Ocean Front Park

Commerce St
Biscayne St

Inlet Blvd

South Pointe Park

Pier

PLACES TO STAY
1   Eden Roc Resort
2   Fontainebleau Hilton
    Hotel & Resort
6   Indian Creek Hotel

PLACES TO EAT
6   Pan Coast Restaurant
8   Casona de Carlitos

OTHER
3   Fontainebleau Mural
4   Fontainebleau Spa
5   Mount Sinai Medical Center
7   Groovejet
9   Bass Museum
10 Holocaust Memorial
11 Miami Beach
    Chamber of Commerce
12 Flagler Memorial Monument
13 Fisher Island Ferry

It contains an estimated 800 buildings, and the best thing about them is scale in general: most are no taller than the palm trees. And while the architecture is by no means uniform – you'll see examples of Streamline, Moderne and Mediterranean Revival as well as Art Deco – it all works well together, giving the entire district the feel of a small village.

Highlights in the Deco District include examples of Streamline, like the Avalon, Essex, Chesterfield, Carlyle, Leslie, The Tides, Cardozo and Breakwater Hotels; Mediterranean including most buildings along Española Way but especially the Clay Hotel & International Hostel, the Old City Hall at 1130 Washington Ave, the Wolfsonian Foundation building, Edison Hotel, Casa Casaurina (Versace's house) the Fernwood at 935 Pennsylvania Ave, and the Regal at the corner of 11th St and Pennsylvania Ave; Parc Vendome at 736 13th St; Depression Moderne (the post office); and the Neo-Classical Revival Betsy Ross Hotel. Other highlights are the Coral House at the corner of 9th St and Collins Ave, and the lovely courtyard inside the Mermaid Guest House.

Ocean Beach Historic District & South Pointe

Because the boundaries of the Deco District only extended as far south as 6th St, the area from there to South Pointe at the island's southern tip was, as the developers like to say, 'in play'.

In February 1996, the city designated most of the area an historic district, but not before the developers managed to get many of their projects grandfathered in, meaning that they were given variances due to the fact that they were in the process of building when the regulations were passed.

So while construction will continue in the area, **South Pointe Park** is a wonderful place to spend a sunny afternoon. It's got a nice little playground, a fishing pier from which kids (illegally) dive into Government Cut, a short boardwalk and an excellent stretch of beach that's less crowded during the week than the beaches

to the near north (though on weekends it's positively overrun by Latin American families, see Beaches, below).

The graffitied Miami Beach logo on the pastel pink **water tower** at the intersection of Jefferson Ave and Alton Rd is classic 1980s Miami Beach.

Ocean Drive

A walk along Ocean Drive from north to south is a safari through the trendy. To the right are the hotels and sidewalk cafés that seem to want to spill into the street itself. And vehicular traffic would appear to be limited to vintage roadsters, '63 Mustangs and grandiose Harley Davidsons.

Fashion plates will want to head immediately for the Miami Beach residence of Gianni Versace, **Casa Casaurina** (1930), at No 1114, a flashy three-story Spanish-Mediterranean palace.

But the fashionably impaired needn't worry; despite the Drive's undeniable chic, it's definitely a come-as-you-are affair: the minimum requirement is a pair of cut-off blue jeans, a tee-shirt and an optional pair of in-line skates.

Get your bearings while checking out the interior of one of the Beach's finest Deco treasures by heading to the **Park Central Hotel** – with it's Vampire LeStat room as described in Anne Rice's *Tale of the Body Thief* – at 640 Ocean Drive. Take the elevator to the sundeck on the top floor and gaze out over the city.

A good time to visit the roof is around 4 pm, when the huge luxury cruise ships chug through Government Cut channel on their way to the Caribbean; the roof offers a stunning view of the ships against the Miami skyline and the beach.

Cruising the Drive, a former SoBe tradition where people would drive the length of the Drive in search of a good time, is now illegal.

Washington Ave

Other than the Wolfsonian Foundation and the clubs and restaurants, there's not much to see on Washington. An exception, believe it or not, is the 1937 **post office**

MIAMI

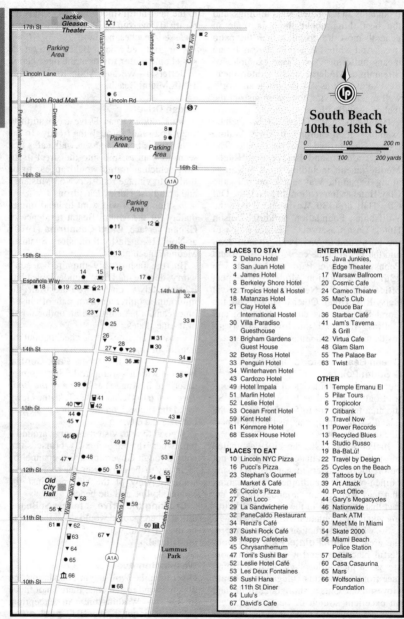

**South Beach
10th to 18th St**

| 0 | 100 | 200 m |
| 0 | 100 | 200 yards |

PLACES TO STAY
2 Delano Hotel
3 San Juan Hotel
4 James Hotel
8 Berkeley Shore Hotel
12 Tropics Hotel & Hostel
18 Matanzas Hotel
21 Clay Hotel &
   International Hostel
30 Villa Paradiso
   Guesthouse
31 Brigham Gardens
   Guest House
32 Betsy Ross Hotel
33 Penguin Hotel
34 Winterhaven Hotel
43 Cardozo Hotel
49 Hotel Impala
51 Marlin Hotel
52 Leslie Hotel
53 Ocean Front Hotel
59 Kent Hotel
61 Kenmore Hotel
68 Essex House Hotel

PLACES TO EAT
10 Lincoln NYC Pizza
16 Pucci's Pizza
23 Stephan's Gourmet
   Market & Café
26 Ciccio's Pizza
27 San Loco
29 La Sandwicherie
32 PaneCaldo Restaurant
34 Renzi's Café
37 Sushi Rock Café
38 Mappy Cafeteria
45 Chrysanthemum
47 Toni's Sushi Bar
52 Leslie Hotel Café
53 Les Deux Fontaines
58 Sushi Hana
62 11th St Diner
64 Lulu's
67 David's Cafe

ENTERTAINMENT
15 Java Junkies,
   Edge Theater
17 Warsaw Ballroom
20 Cosmic Cafe
24 Cameo Theatre
35 Mac's Club
   Deuce Bar
36 Starbar Café
41 Jam's Taverna
   & Grill
42 Virtua Cafe
48 Glam Slam
55 The Palace Bar
63 Twist

OTHER
1 Temple Emanu El
5 Pilar Tours
6 Tropicolor
7 Citibank
9 Travel Now
11 Power Records
13 Recycled Blues
14 Studio Russo
19 Ba-BaLú!
22 Travel by Design
25 Cycles on the Beach
28 Tattoos by Lou
39 Art Attack
44 Post Office
44 Gary's Megacycles
46 Nationwide
   Bank ATM
50 Meet Me In Miami
54 Skate 2000
56 Miami Beach
   Police Station
57 Details
60 Casa Casaurina
65 Mars
66 Wolfsonian
   Foundation

(☎ 531-3763) at 1300 Washington Ave, a Depression Moderne building with an enormous dome on the south corner.

At the corner of 17th St is the imposing **Temple Emanu El Synagogue** (☎ 538-2503), which holds services Sunday to Thursday at 8 am and 5.30 pm, Friday at 8 am and 6 pm, and Saturday at 9 am and 6 pm. North of 17th St on the west side of Washington Ave is the **Miami Beach Convention Center**, home to huge auto and boat shows.

Lincoln Road Mall
'The Road', a wide, pedestrian-only stretch of sidewalk, is the Beach's cultural epicenter, with galleries every hundred feet or so, and sidewalk cafés filled with off-duty models trying to relax.

Highlights include the **Miami City Ballet** (where you can watch rehearsals through the picture window), the **Colony Theatre** and the **Lincoln Theatre** – a Deco delight that is home to the New World Symphony. See the Entertainment section for information on those venues.

Monthly **Gallery Walks** take place on alternating Saturday nights. These are very popular with locals and visitors alike: most of the Road's galleries hold openings during these, and many give away wine and snacks and you can spend several hours popping into them before heading out for a late-night snack or a club. See the Entertainment section.

Every Sunday from November to March there's a **Farmer's Market** on the Road between Euclid and Meridian Aves. If you've got kids, note that the Lincoln Road Partnership has arranged kids' activities during the Farmer's Market: meet at the fountain in front of World Resources Café (☎ 534-9095), 719 Lincoln Road.

Free, golf-cart-drawn trams shuttle up and down the Road between Washington Ave and Alton Rd.

Española Way
Designed as a 'Spanish village' in the early 1920s, Española Way's (pronounced ess-pahn-YO-la) most prominent feature holds a special place in our hearts: the Clay Hotel & International Hostel – formerly the home of none other than Desi Arnaz, who also had a club here, and Al Capone's S&H Gambling Syndicate which had a casino in the middle wing (now rooms 128 to 138).

The most striking section is the short block between Washington and Drexel Aves, which is lined with – well, there's no other word but adorable – Spanish-style buildings. It was on this street that Desi himself started the rhumba phenomenon. Nothing like the rhumba . . . .

Beaches
For a city beach, Miami Beach is one of the best around. The water is relatively clear, and relatively warm, the sand relatively white and best of all, it's wide and certainly long enough to accommodate the throngs. The throngs, by the way, are generally rather considerate in that there's usually not lots of litter or broken glass in the sand, but do use caution when walking barefoot.

The most crowded sections of the beach are, of course, in South Beach – from about 5th St to 21st St. Weekends are more crowded than weekdays, but except during special events it's usually not too difficult to find a quiet spot. The beaches north of 21st St – especially the one at 53rd St, which has a playground and public toilets – are more family-oriented.

Latin Families For some reason, Latin American families – predominantly Cuban – tend to congregate between 5th St and South Pointe. In this area topless bathing is unwise and can be considered offensive.

Gay The gay beach centers around 12th St, across from the Palace Bar & Grill. It's not like there's sex going on (there isn't); it's just a spot where gay men happen to congregate. There's Fabulous volleyball Sunday afternoons at 4 pm, packed with fun and fun-loving locals.

Nude Nude bathing is legal at Haulover Beach, north of Miami Beach. The area you're looking for is at the northern end of the park between the two northernmost parking lots. The area north of the lifeguard tower is predominantly gay; south of it is straight. There's no sex allowed on any of these beaches and you will get arrested if you're seen trying to get to the bushes.

The Boardwalk There's a boardwalk running from 21st St all the way north to 46th St, and another running for several blocks from South Pointe Park to the north.

The Promenade The Promenade is a wavy ribbon of concrete at the Beach's westernmost edge (just east of Ocean Drive) that runs from 5th St to almost 16th St. If you've ever looked at a fashion magazine, you've seen it: it's *the* photo shoot site. All through the day and late into the night, this is where in-line skaters, bicyclists, roller skaters, skateboarders and motorized skateboarders, dog walkers, yahoos, locals and tourists mill about and occasionally bump into each other.

Bass Museum

The Bass Museum (☎ 673-7530) is a wonderful surprise at 2121 Park Ave, directly behind the Miami Beach Public Library, west of City Park. Selections from its permanent collection rotate through the galleries on the ground floor, while a widely varying array of visiting exhibitions rotate through other halls on the ground and 2nd floors. The star of the show here is the tapestry collection, to which the paintings play a definite second fiddle.

The South Gallery (to the left from the main entrance) contains *The Tournament* – said to be one of the finest examples of tapestry in an American museum.

The museum is open Tuesday to Saturday from 10 am to 5 pm, Sunday from 1 to 5 pm, closed Monday. On the second and fourth Wednesday of the month the museum is open from 1 to 9 pm. Admission is $5 for adults, $3 for senior citizens and students. For special exhibitions admission is $7/5. On the second and fourth Wednesday of the month, from 5 to 9 pm, admission is by donation only (which can be nothing, if you like).

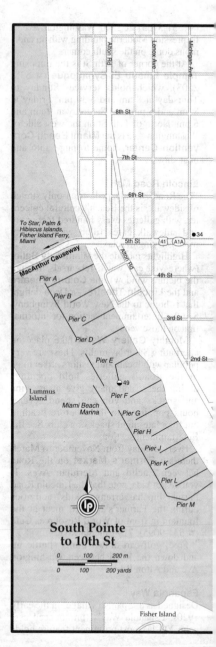

South Pointe to 10th St

MIAMI

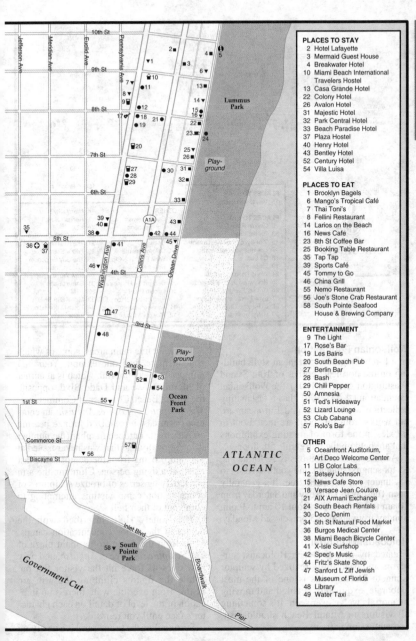

PLACES TO STAY
2 Hotel Lafayette
3 Mermaid Guest House
4 Breakwater Hotel
10 Miami Beach International
   Travelers Hostel
13 Casa Grande Hotel
22 Colony Hotel
26 Avalon Hotel
31 Majestic Hotel
32 Park Central Hotel
33 Beach Paradise Hotel
37 Plaza Hostel
40 Henry Hotel
43 Bentley Hotel
52 Century Hotel
54 Villa Luisa

PLACES TO EAT
1 Brooklyn Bagels
6 Mango's Tropical Café
7 Thai Toni's
8 Fellini Restaurant
14 Larios on the Beach
16 News Cafe
23 8th St Coffee Bar
25 Booking Table Restaurant
35 Tap Tap
39 Sports Café
45 Tommy to Go
46 China Grill
55 Nemo Restaurant
56 Joe's Stone Crab Restaurant
58 South Pointe Seafood
   House & Brewing Company

ENTERTAINMENT
9 The Light
17 Rose's Bar
19 Les Bains
20 South Beach Pub
27 Berlin Bar
28 Bash
29 Chili Pepper
50 Amnesia
51 Ted's Hideaway
53 Club Cabana
57 Rolo's Bar

OTHER
5 Oceanfront Auditorium,
   Art Deco Welcome Center
11 LIB Color Labs
12 Betsey Johnson
15 News Cafe Store
18 Versace Jean Couture
21 AIX Armani Exchange
24 South Beach Rentals
30 Deco Denim
34 5th St Natural Food Market
36 Burgos Medical Center
38 Miami Beach Bicycle Center
41 X-Isle Surfshop
42 Spec's Music
44 Fritz's Skate Shop
47 Sanford L Ziff Jewish
   Museum of Florida
48 Library
49 Water Taxi

MIAMI

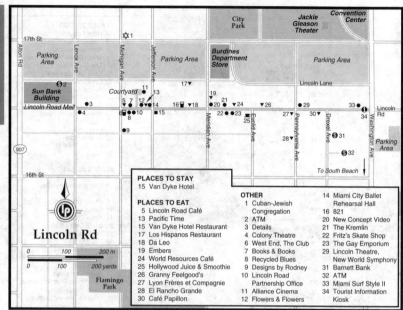

PLACES TO STAY
15 Van Dyke Hotel

PLACES TO EAT
5   Lincoln Road Café
13 Pacific Time
15 Van Dyke Hotel Restaurant
17 Los Hispanos Restaurant
18 Da Leo
19 Embers
24 World Resources Café
25 Hollywood Juice & Smoothie
26 Granny Feelgood's
27 Lyon Frères et Compagnie
28 El Rancho Grande
30 Café Papillon

OTHER
1   Cuban-Jewish
    Congregation
2   ATM
3   Details
4   Colony Theatre
6   West End, The Club
7   Books & Books
8   Recycled Blues
9   Designs by Rodney
10 Lincoln Road
    Partnership Office
11 Alliance Cinema
12 Flowers & Flowers

14 Miami City Ballet
    Rehearsal Hall
16 821
20 New Concept Video
21 The Kremlin
22 Fritz's Skate Shop
23 The Gay Emporium
29 Lincoln Theatre,
    New World Symphony
31 Barnett Bank
32 ATM
33 Miami Surf Style II
34 Tourist Information
    Kiosk

Wolfsonian Foundation

In a foreboding Mediterranean-style building on the northeast corner of 10th St and Washington Ave (No 1001), the Wolfsonian Foundation (☎ 531-1001) has a fascinating collection of American and European art, but works from this pool are meted out in trickles in the form of rotating exhibitions that are held on the museum's 5th floor.

Admission to exhibitions is $7 for adults, $5 for seniors, students and youth aged six to 18, under six admitted free. It's generally open Tuesday to Thursday and Saturday from 10 am to 6 pm, Friday from 10 am to 9 pm, Sunday from noon to 5 pm, closed Monday.

Holocaust Memorial

Created by Miami Beach Holocaust survivors and beautifully realized by sculptor Kenneth Treister, this is one of the most elaborate, exquisitely detailed and moving memorials we've ever seen. It's something all visitors to Miami Beach should visit, and admission is free.

There are five main areas, some of which contain more than one exhibit. Your first glimpse at the memorial, which is at corner of Meridian Ave and Dade Blvd, opposite the Miami Beach Chamber of Commerce, is *The Sculpture of Love & Anguish*: an enormous arm cast in oxidized bronze bearing an Auschwitz tattooed number (the number is intentionally one that was never issued at the camp) rising from the depths – the last reach of a dying person. Climbing the arm is a terrifying series of bronze sculptures of concentration camp victims attempting to climb out of their hell.

The Lonely Hall, inscribed with the names of the major concentration camps, leads from the dome to the main plaza of *The Sculpture of Love & Anguish*, and only now does its force hit the visitor full on. While the figures climbing the arm are visible from over the wall, there's no indication of the level of detail on each character's face until you're inside.

Surrounding the bronze arm is a terrifying

gathering of statues from *The Beginning* to *The Final Sculpture*. Words can barely describe the power these sculptures possess.

As you exit, through the dome again, turn right and walk past The Arbor of History, a colonnade of Jerusalem stone topped by vines, and on the wall is a series of photographs etched in black granite. Beneath the photographs are captions, by Professor Helen Fagin, the Memorial's historian, along with a summarized history of the Holocaust.

The memorial (☎ 538-1663, see the Online Services appendix) is open from 9 am to 9 pm daily.

Sanford L Ziff Jewish Museum

The Sanford L Ziff Jewish Museum of Florida (☎ 672-5044) is dedicated to exhibits of the history of Jews in Florida. Their mainstay is *MOSAIC: Jewish Life in Florida*, which features thousands of fascinating items from Russian *samovar* kettles to photographs, business cards, documents and other products of Jewish-owned or -run companies.

The museum is open Tuesday to Thursday and Saturday and Sunday from 10 am to 5 pm, Friday from 10 am to 3 pm, closed Monday. Admission is free on Saturday, on other days it's $4 for adults, $3 for senior citizens and students, or a flat fee of $9 per family. It's at 301 Washington Ave.

Mid & Northern Miami Beach

Once you pass 21st St on Collins Ave heading north, you're entering the world of 1950s and '60s Miami Beach – a series of monstrous high-rise hotels that line Collins Ave north of the 20s. So with a few notable exceptions – like the lovingly restored **Indian Creek Hotel** at 2727 Indian Creek Drive – from there up to the city limits is a never-ending string of high-rise condominiums, hotels and apartment buildings.

As you approach the **Fontainebleau Hilton Resort & Towers**, just before Collins Ave makes its little jog to the left, you see in front of you what appears to be two magnificent pillars, through which the Fontainebleau pool is visible. As you

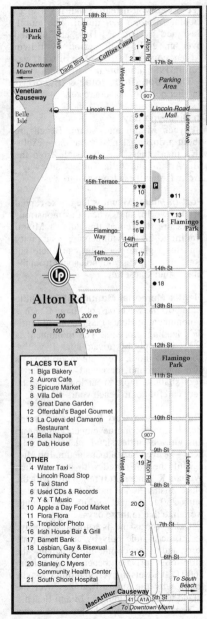

Alton Rd

PLACES TO EAT
1 Biga Bakery
2 Aurora Cafe
3 Epicure Market
8 Villa Deli
9 Great Dane Garden
12 Offerdahl's Bagel Gourmet
13 La Cueva del Camaron Restaurant
14 Bella Napoli
19 Dab House

OTHER
4 Water Taxi - Lincoln Road Stop
5 Taxi Stand
6 Used CDs & Records
7 Y & T Music
10 Apple a Day Food Market
11 Flora Flora
15 Tropicolor Photo
16 Irish House Bar & Grill
17 Barnett Bank
18 Lesbian, Gay & Bisexual Community Center
20 Stanley C Myers Community Health Center
21 South Shore Hospital

get closer, you'll realize that it's a spectacular *trompe-l'oeil* mural. The mural, designed by Richard Hass and painted over an eight-week period by Edwin Abreu, covers 13,016 sq feet of what was before 1986 a big blank wall.

The **Eden Roc Hotel & Resort** is another notable '50s-era resort.

In Biscayne Bay
Between Miami and Miami Beach are about a dozen islands, some more exclusive than others but all visible from the MacArthur and Julia Tuttle Causeways. We're listing these from east to west.

Port of Miami Miami is the cruise capital of the world, and when the monstrous liners are docked at the Port of Miami waiting to fill up with people, it's a pretty amazing sight to see. You can't help but notice the ships as you look south from the MacArthur Causeway.

Flagler Memorial Monument On a little island off the west coast of Miami Beach is a monument to Henry Flagler, one of Florida's leading pioneers. The monument is accessible only by private boat. If you've got one of those, there are mooring posts available around the island. The water is very shallow, more so at low tide, so be very careful not to beach yourself!

Fisher Island Carl Fisher, one of the Beach's pioneering developers, bought up this glorious little island, planning to die here – he even built a mausoleum. But after a while he got bored with it, and when William K Vanderbilt II fell in love with the place, Fisher traded the island for Vanderbilt's 250-foot yacht *and* its crew. Things were like that in those days.

Today, the island is a totally exclusive resort, accessible only by air and private ferry, and the condominiums which line the mile-long private beach range from $600,000 hovels to over $6 million. Maybe that's why the sun still shines over the island when it's raining on Miami Beach.

You can stay here, at the Inn at the Fisher Island Club (☎ 535-6097); see Places to Stay, below.

The island is usually open only to paying guests and residents, but you can arrange a tour if you're especially persistent. The *Eagle, Flamingo* and *Pelican* ferries leave from the Fisher Island Ferry Terminal off the MacArthur Causeway just west of the Coast Guard Station every 15 minutes around the clock.

Hibiscus, Palm & Star Islands Hibiscus, Palm and Star Islands are three little bastions of wealth – though far less exclusive than Fisher Island – just west of Miami Beach. There aren't too many very famous people living there now – just very rich ones – though Star Island boasts Miami's favorite star, Gloria Estefan, whose estate is at the eastern end. Palm Island was for a short time infamous for its local resident Al Capone.

Star Island is the farthest east, accessed by the little bridge almost opposite the Fisher Island Ferry terminal.

Watson Island The island nearest to downtown Miami, just east of the mainland, is the grungiest of the lot. Watson Island is home to **Chalk's International Airlines** (☎ 371-8628/9), which claims to be the oldest-running international airline. But in 1998, the expected relocation of Parrot Jungle to the island will change things considerably. Stay tuned.

Pelican Island On weekends you can take a free ferry from the causeway west of North Bay Village, about two miles west of 71st St in Miami Beach, to little Pelican Island. It's just a pleasant little place to have a picnic and look at the dozens of pelicans that congregate on and around the island.

MIAMI – DOWNTOWN
Miami's downtown skyline is considered one of the nation's most beautiful, or at least most colorful. At night, the towering skyscrapers are lit in neon, and the most unmistakable symbol of downtown is the IM Pei-designed **NationsBank Tower** (1987) at 100 SE 2nd St. The building is

illuminated every night, and on special events, the lighting – on seven visible faces of the building – can be custom lit with a combination of seven colors per face. Other neon comes courtesy of the Metromover's rainbow-illuminated track

For a downtown, Miami is not exactly the most exciting you'll encounter. Most of the streets are lined with shops selling electronics, luggage and clothing to Latin American visitors, and the place dies very quickly after 5 pm, when the office towers disgorge their yuppies.

Metro-Dade Cultural Center
The Mediterranean-style Cultural Center is sort of a one-stop shopping center for culture. The 3.3-acre complex holds two museums and the city's excellent public library. The complex is at 101 W Flagler St (Metromover stop: Government Center). A combination ticket for both the Historical Museum and Center for Fine Arts is $6 for adults, $3.50 for children.

Historical Museum of Southern Florida
This is one of our favorite museums, and it's excellent for kids. The Historical Museum (☎ 375-1492, see the Online Services appendix) has displays covering 10,000 years of Florida history. All the exhibits have excellent explanatory materials, all in English and Spanish. Count on spending about an hour to 1½ hours here.

Downstairs is a temporary exhibition hall, *La Plaza Theater*, which has new exhibitions every three to four months.

Admission is $4 for adults, $2 for children aged six to 12. On Monday the admission is waived – they still suggest the $4 donation, but you can give what you want. It's open Monday to Wednesday and Saturday from 10 am to 5 pm, Thursday from 10 am to 9 pm, Sunday from noon to 5 pm.

Center for the Fine Arts
This museum (☎ 375-3000) does rotating exhibitions of fine arts. When we visited they were finishing up *Caribbean Visions: Contemporary Painting & Sculpture* by French, Dutch and Spanish-speaking Caribbean artists. Contact the museum for a schedule of what's on when you visit.

Admission is $5 for adults, $2.50 for students and seniors, children under 12 free. It's open Tuesday, Wednesday and Friday from 10 am to 5 pm, Thursday from 10 am to 9 pm (free admission 5 to 9 pm), Saturday and Sunday from noon to 5 pm, closed Monday.

Wolfson Campus
The Wolfson Campus of the Miami-Dade Community College (☎ 237-3000) at 300 NE 2nd Ave has two art galleries of rotating exhibitions, the Centre Gallery and the Frances Wolfson Gallery. Both are open Monday to Friday from 10 am to 6 pm; admission is free.

Bayfront Park
Bayfront Park (☎ 358-7550), a freight port during the first Miami boom in the 1920s, is today a calm bit of green downtown, essentially between the Hotel InterContinental and Bayside Marketplace. There are two performance venues here: the AT&T Amphitheater (home to Fourth of July and New Year's Eve festivities) and the smaller, 200-seat South End Amphitheater (the site of Bayfront Park After Dark, a free entertainment series). See the Entertainment section. The park also houses a monument to the astronauts killed in the 1986 explosion of the space shuttle *Challenger*.

Bayside Marketplace
Bayside Marketplace (☎ 577-3344) at 401 Biscayne Blvd (it actually runs from NE 4th to NE 9th Sts) is a shopping mall that hordes of tourists just adore, with a bunch of little tourist shops, some restaurants – including a Hard Rock Cafe – and a *Miami Queen* paddlewheel cruise (☎ 445-7821) around Biscayne Bay Friday to Sunday at 2, 4 and 6 pm. Whee.

Bayside is also home to free concerts every day of the year; see the Free (or Cheap) & Outdoors in the Entertainment section below for more information.

This is also the main stop for the Water Taxi, which runs shuttle service to many

MIAMI

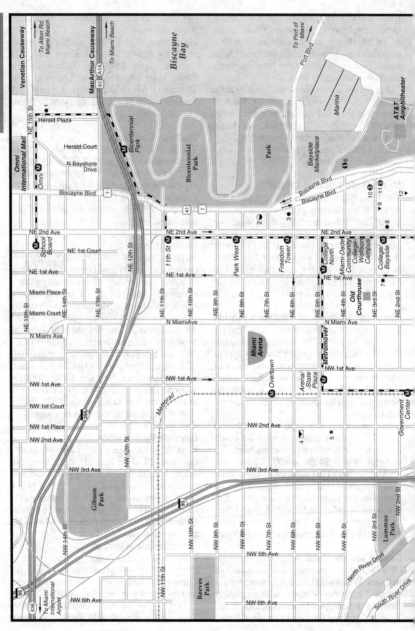

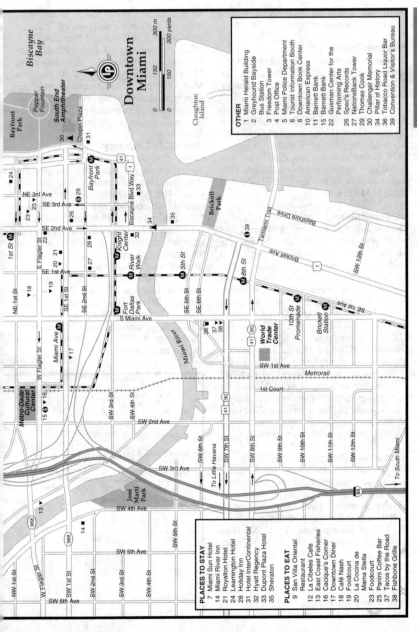

Biscayne Bay

Bayfront Park

Pepper Fountain

South End Amphitheater

Downtown Miami

300 m
300 yards
0   150
0   150

Claughton Island

Brickell Park

Brickell Ave

Bayshore Drive

Tamiami Trail

SW 12th Ave

SE 1st Ave

10th St Promenade

Brickell Station

World Trade Center

SW 1st Ave

Metrorail

1st Court

SW 6th St
SW 7th St
SW 8th St
SW 9th St
SW 10th St
SW 11th St
SW 12th St

To Little Havana

To South Miami

SW 6th Ave
SW 5th Ave
SW 4th Ave
SW 3rd Ave
SW 2nd Ave

José Martí Park

NW 1st St
SW 1st St
SW 2nd St
SW 3rd St
SW 4th St
SW 5th St
SW 6th Ave

W Flagler St

Metro-Dade Cultural Center

Miami River

Fort Dallas Park

S Miami Ave

Knight Center

River Walk

SE 5th St
SE 6th St

5th St
8th St

SE 2nd Ave
SE 1st St
Miami Ave
W Flagler St

NE 1st St
1st St
E Flagler St
SE 1st St
SE 2nd Ave
SE 3rd Ave

NE 3rd Ave

Chopin Plaza

Bayfront Park

Biscayne Blvd Way

OTHER

1 Miami Herald Building
2 Greyhound Bayside Bus Station
3 Freedom Tower
4 Post Office
5 Miami Police Department
6 Tourist Information Booth
8 Downtown Book Center
10 American Express
11 Barnett Bank
15 Barnett Bank
22 Gusman Center for the Performing Arts
26 Spec's Records
27 NationsBank Tower
29 Thomas Cook
30 Challenger Memorial
34 Pillar of History
36 Tobacco Road Liquor Bar
39 Convention & Visitor's Bureau

PLACES TO STAY

7 Miami Sun Hotel
14 Miami River Inn
21 Royalton Hotel
24 Leamington Hotel
28 Holiday Inn
31 Hotel InterContinental
32 Hyatt Regency
33 Dupont Plaza Hotel
35 Sheraton

PLACES TO EAT

9 San Villa Oriental Restaurant
12 La Cibeles Cafe
13 East Coast Fisheries
16 Cacique's Corner
17 Downtown Diner
18 Café Nash
19 Foodcourt
20 La Cocina de Mama Stella
23 Foodcourt
25 Panini Coffee Bar
37 Tacos by the Road
38 Fishbone Grille

downtown hotels as well as to Miami Beach (see Getting Around).

Freedom Tower

At 600 Biscayne Blvd, Freedom Tower's fame comes from the fact that it was the 'Ellis Island of the South': the immigration processing center for almost half a million Cuban refugees in the 1960s. The building, built in 1925, was for 32 years the home of the *Miami Daily News*. It was placed on the National Register of Historic Places in 1979. Today, despite renovation, it is abandoned, and looms over Biscayne Bay near the entrances to the Port of Miami and Bayside Marketplace.

US Courthouse

The coquina headquarters of Miami's first major post office (1931) later became the Miami Courthouse, because it was, in a kinder, gentler time, large enough to accommodate the needs of the US Government prosecutors. As crime increased, the Feds outgrew the building and now occupy the nearby Federal Building. Today it's open to visitors at 300 NE 1st Ave (☎ 536-4131). The reason to stop here is to get a look at Denman Fink's *Law Guides Florida Progress*, a mural depicting Florida in the 1930s, including a Cuba-bound Pan Am Clipper. The building is open Monday to Friday from 9 am to 5 pm; the mural is in the main courtroom (2nd floor) that also boasts hardwood furnishings like hewn-wood benches, and beautiful arched windows.

Brickell Ave Bridge

The Brickell Avenue Bridge, which crosses the Miami River south of downtown, reopened after a $21 million renovation which took several years and is more beautiful than ever. But its claim to fame now is the 17-foot bronze statue by Cuban-born sculptor Manuel Carbonell of a Tequesta warrior and his family atop the towering *Pillar of History* column at the center of the east side of the bridge.

Brickell Ave continues south from downtown across this bridge, where it becomes lined with office towers and some hotels.

There's nothing really to see in this area, with the possible exception of Tobacco Road, a small collection of bars that line S Miami Ave, including *Tobacco Road Liquor Bar* (☎ 374-1198) at No 626, open from 11.30 to 5 am every day. It's something of a Miami tradition (it has Miami's first liquor license and has been here for over 80 years and was a speakeasy during Prohibition) to stop in for a drink while you're here.

Miami City Cemetery

The original cemetery of the City of Miami was established in July 1897, and you can still visit if that's the sort of thing you like to do. The 9000-plus-grave cemetery has separate white, black and Jewish sections; Julia Tuttle was the 13th burial and she's got a front and center gravesite. Luminaries include many mayors and politicians, about 90 Confederate dead as well as veterans from all wars in the 20th century.

The cemetery is at 1800 NE 2nd Ave, not the friendliest part of town. The cemetery manager, Clyde Cates, suggests that if you want to visit you call him a day in advance and leave a message on his answering machine at ☎ 579-6938. Clyde will give visitors an informal tour.

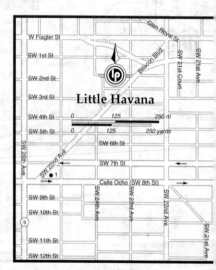

MIAMI

Cates recommends only visiting during the day: take Biscayne Blvd to NE 18th St and turn west to the cemetery, to avoid getting lost in the back streets. It's open Monday to Friday 7.30 am to 4 pm, and admission is free.

LITTLE HAVANA

After the Mariel Boatlift (see the History section in Facts about Florida), the section of town to which Cuban exiles had been gravitating for years exploded into a distinctly Cuban neighborhood, now known as Little Havana. The borders of Little Havana are arguable, but for the purposes of this book, we're saying that they're *really roughly* SW 13th St at the south, SW 3rd St at the north, SW 3rd Ave at the east and SW 37th Ave at the west. Note that while the Cuban influence is strongest in the southwest quadrant of the city, it's pervasive throughout Miami.

Spanish is the predominant language here, of course, and you will absolutely run into people who speak no English; see the Language section in the Facts about Florida chapter for some key phrases, or pick up Lonely Planet's *Latin American Spanish Phrasebook*.

The heart of Little Havana is Calle Ocho (KAH-yeh AW-cho), Spanish for SW 8th St (actually it's Spanish just for 8th St, but what the hell). The entire length of Calle Ocho is lined with Cuban shops, cafés, record stores, pharmacies, clothing (and, most amusing, bridal) shops, teeming with action. Calle Ocho runs one way from west to east for most of the length of Little Havana.

But while the wall-of-sound-style speakers set up outside places like Power Records are blasting salsa and other Latin music into the street, Little Havana as a tourist attraction is an elusive bugger. It's not concentrated like a Chinatown or a Harlem; it's actually not really a tourist attraction at all. It's just a Cuban neighborhood, so except for during the occasional street fair or celebration, you shouldn't expect, like, Tito Puente and Celia Cruz leading a parade of colorfully attired, tight-trousered men and slinky, scantily-clad women in a Carnaval or anything like that. More likely you'll see old men playing dominos.

Which is exactly the attraction the area holds: it's real, it's not putting on airs for anyone, and it could not care less whether you see it or not. So you should definitely go.

The famous green sign reading *Republic*

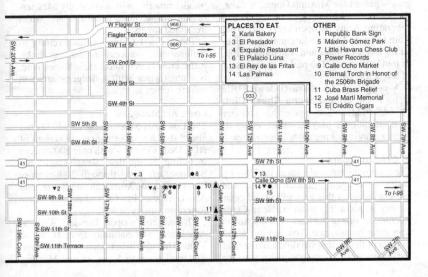

PLACES TO EAT	OTHER
2 Karla Bakery	1 Republic Bank Sign
3 El Pescador	5 Máximo Gómez Park
4 Exquisito Restaurant	7 Little Havana Chess Club
6 El Palacio Luna	8 Power Records
13 El Rey de las Fritas	9 Calle Ocho Market
14 Las Palmas	10 Eternal Torch in Honor of the 2506th Brigade
	11 Cuba Brass Relief
	12 José Martí Memorial
	15 El Crédito Cigars

MIAMI

Bank Welcomes You to Little Havana is on Calle Ocho just east of where SW 22nd Ave shoots off to the northeast.

Calle Ocho

Cuban **botanicas** can be found along Calle Ocho selling Santeria-related items like perfumed waters named for properties you may desire, like 'Money' or 'Love me', or the more esoteric 'Keep Dead Resting'.

And you'll want to stop for a guarapo, a café con leche or a thimbleful of zoom juice (espresso) and maybe a little pastry or something. See the Places to Eat section for proper restaurant listings, including the famous Versailles restaurant and an excellent Vietnamese (?!) offering. But for a quick something, try the Calle Ocho Market at No 1390, Karla Bakery at No 1842 (great-smelling and -tasting pastries that always make a line form) or El Rey de las Fritas at No 1177.

Máximo Gómez Park

The scores of elderly Cuban men playing dominoes here is an example of good government at work: this is a program for senior citizens run under the auspices of the Little Havana Development Authority. The park – named for Máximo Gómez y Baez, the Dominican-born chief of the Cuban Liberating Army, is open every day from 9 am to 6 pm. This is a fascinating place to sit for a few minutes and watch the action, or join in yourself. The park is at the corner of SW 15th Ave.

A couple of doors (east) down Calle Ocho is the **Little Havana Chess Club** (☎ 643-3622), where somewhat younger men sit indoors playing either chess or dominos and smoking a whole lot of cigars.

El Crédito Cigars

Cigar smoking has really taken the USA by storm once again. Ernesto Curillo, the present owner of this very successful cigar factory is, according to an article in *Cigar Aficionado*, one of the leaders of the American cigar renaissance. You can just stand in front of the picture window looking in at the dozen or so Cuban *tabaqueros* who are

hand-rolling cigars, or go in to smell (it's pretty . . . shall we say, aromatic) and buy. They're really nice about letting people take photos, so ask if you want one. It's at 1106 Calle Ocho (☎ 858-4162), open Monday to Saturday from 7.30 am to 6 pm, closed Sunday.

Cuban Memorial Blvd

For two blocks along SW 13th Ave south of Calle Ocho are a series of monuments to Cuban patriots and freedom fighters (read: Anti-Castro Cubans). The eternal flame at the corner of Calle Ocho is the **Eternal Torch in Honor of the 2506th Brigade** to the counterrevolutionaries who died during the botched Bay of Pigs invasion (see the History section in the Facts about Florida chapter). Other monuments include the huge brass map of Cuba, 'Dedicated to the ideals of people who will never forget the pledge of making their Fatherland free,' and a bust of José Martí.

CORAL GABLES

Coral Gables is a lovely, if pricey, city that exudes opulence and comfort. A gaggle of architects and planners under the direction of George Merrick designed the city to be a 'model suburb', with a decidedly Mediterranean theme, huge gateways, and wide, tree-lined streets.

Today Coral Gables, while exciting to multinational corporations and the diplomatic crowds that make their homes here, is a quiet place with a fledgling arts and culture scene.

Lowe Art Museum

The Lowe Art Museum (☎ 284-3535) has one of the largest permanent collections of art in Dade County – with over 8000 pieces including antiquities, Renaissance and Baroque art; 18th- through 20th-century European and American sculpture and Asian, African, Pre-Columbian and Native American entries as well.

The museum's open Tuesday, Wednesday, Friday and Saturday from 10 am to 5 pm, Thursday from noon to 7 pm, Sunday from noon to 5 pm, closed Monday.

Architectural Disneyland

George Merrick envisioned what would be called today an 'Architectural Disneyland' filled with theme areas; the idea was to bring people into a place that felt 'old'. He created a Dutch South African Village (6612, 6700, 6704 and 6710 SW 42nd Ave and 6705 San Vicente St) modeled after 17th-century Dutch colonists' farmhouses; a tiny Chinese Village, (one block between Sansovino Ave, Castania Ave, Maggiore St and Riviera Drive); a Florida Pioneer Village (4320, 4409, 4515, 1520 and 4620 Santa Maria St) that looks a lot more like New Hampshire than Miami; and the absolutely stunning French Normandy Village (on the block between SW 42nd Ave, Viscaya Court, Viscaya Ave and Alesio Ave).

Merrick lost the family fortune after the Depression, and the City of Coral Gables, which had been incorporated in 1925, went bankrupt. Eventually the city's finances were sorted, and Coral Gables grew with Miami but always seemed to attract more money and less attention.

In fact, Coral Gables is one of the few places in metropolitan Miami that's lovely to walk in: the banyan trees that shelter the winding streets actually provide good relief from the sun, and it's relatively safe. ∎

Admission is $5 for adults, $3 for seniors and students. It's at 1301 Stanford Drive, two blocks north of the University Metrorail Station on the Coral Gables campus of the University of Miami.

Biltmore Hotel

From practically anywhere in Coral Gables you can see the 315-foot-high tower of the Biltmore Hotel (☎ 445-1926), the city's crown jewel, at 1200 Anastasia Ave. The historic landmark hotel, which opened in 1926, has a history that reads like an Agatha Christie novel on speed – a story of murder, intrigue, famous gangsters and detectives set against an Old World European-style backdrop.

Al Capone had a speakeasy here, in what's officially called the Everglades Suite but what everyone – even the hotel management privately – calls the Capone Suite. It was in that room that the owner of just one of the spirits said to haunt the hotel, Fats Walsh, was murdered.

The hotel's architecture is referred to as Mediterranean-revivalist; the tower is modeled after (but not a replica of) the Giralda bell tower at the Cathedral of Seville in Spain.

The Biltmore's pool – the largest hotel pool in the continental USA – deserves special mention. It may not have as stunning a setting as the Venetian Pool (see below), but it is one of the most beautiful in the world. There's a café out there, and you can sit poolside with an espresso.

And don't miss Storytelling at the Biltmore every Thursday at 7.30 pm in front of the fireplace in the upper lobby. It's free, and you'll hear stories of ghosts, celebs who've stayed here, the construction of the hotel and lots more.

There is, of course, a lot more information about the place – not least of which is the mainstage productions of the Florida Shakespeare Theatre (see Theater in the Entertainment section) – its health clubs, 10 tennis courts, Sunday brunches, Cigars under the Stars, etc etc, so contact the hotel when you're in town.

Venetian Pool

What with all that building around here, a large quarry was formed. Somebody came up with the absolutely brilliant idea of making the world's ugliest hole in the ground the world's most beautiful swimming pool, which the Venetian Pool (☎ 460-5356) definitely is. It's listed on the National Register of Historic Places, and on our personal list of favorite places in Miami.

It's a spring-fed pool with caves, waterfalls and Venetian-style moorings that's just absolutely fantastic. It's large enough to have a kiddie area, space for laps and

MIAMI

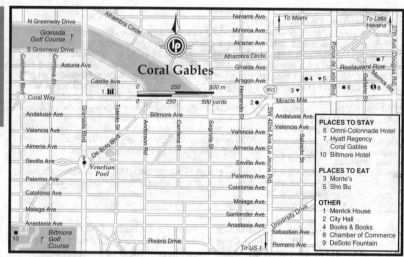

PLACES TO STAY
6 Omni-Colonnade Hotel
7 Hyatt Regency
   Coral Gables
10 Biltmore Hotel

PLACES TO EAT
3 Monte's
5 Sho Bu

OTHER
1 Merrick House
2 City Hall
4 Books & Books
8 Chamber of Commerce
9 DeSoto Fountain

room under the big waterfall to just romp around. Different sources come up with different figures, but we're settling on this: the pool holds 820,000 gallons of water. During the winter, the pool's drained and refilled every other night, in summer every night. The water's recycled through a natural filtration process.

It's at 2701 DeSoto Blvd just next to the DeSoto Fountain, about two blocks south of Coral Way. Free parking is available. Admission is $4 for adults, $3.50 for teens aged 13 to 17, kids $1.60; Coral Gables residents (with ID) pay $3/2/1.60. Token-driven lockers are available for $1.50. No refunds due to weather.

The pool has horribly complicated opening hours that change four times a year; call them for specific hours. Sometimes they're closed on Monday, but they are open year round on Saturday and Sunday from 10 am to 4.30 pm.

City Hall

Coral Gables City Hall, at the intersection of Biltmore and Coral Ways, is just a neat 1920s building. It's housed meetings of the City Commission since February 29, 1928 – the first commission was made up of Merrick, ET Purcell, Don Peabody, the city's first mayor EE Dammers and the interestingly named Wingfield Webster. Upstairs there's a tiny display of Coral Gables Public Transport from the mid-20th century, and rotating photograph and art exhibits, and oh, yes, look up at Denman Fink's *Four Seasons* ceiling painting in the tower, as well as his framed untitled painting of the underwater world on the 2nd floor landing. It's at 405 Biltmore Way.

Merrick House

There's not much to see here at the residence of the Merricks in Coral Gables (1899); in fact the place is mostly used for meetings and receptions by local clubs. But it's a lovely house (☎ 460-5361) and if the burly and friendly caretaker's around he'll let you wander through for $2 for adults, 50¢ for kids Sunday and Wednesday from 1 to 4 pm. The big draw is the well-maintained organic garden, which has some of the original fruit trees planted at the turn of the century like king oranges, copperleaf and bamboo. It's at 907 Coral Way, and there's good signs pointing the way.

Fast horses at Calder Race Course

Pitts Special, Weeks Air Museum

Banana trees, Fruit & Spice Park, Miami

Eyeing the tourists in Miami

Welcome!

Deco detail

Washington Ave

Angels at Vizcaya

The ubiquitous South Beach pastels

Fontainebleau's trompe-l'oeil mural

Watertower & Entrances

Still in restoration, the Alhambra Watertower (1931) where Greenway Court and Ferdinand St meet Alhambra Circle, looks for all the world like a lighthouse.

Merrick had planned a series of elaborate entry gates to the city, but the bust dried up most of the planning. Of the ones around, worth noting are: Country Club Prado (1927, at Calle Ocho and the Prado Country Club); the Douglas Entrance, *La Puerto del Sol* (1927; at Calle Ocho and Douglas Rd); and the Granada Entrance (Calle Ocho at Granada Blvd).

COCONUT GROVE

Site of the first major settlement in the Miami area, Coconut Grove was, for a time in the 1960s and '70s, a big-time bohemian hangout, but it's evolved – if that's the word – into a highly commercialized area whose main attraction (other than the excellent Coconut Grove Playhouse, see the Entertainment section) is now the CocoWalk shopping center, a stylized shopping mall with some restaurants, shops and a cinema. There are a couple of attractions worth the trip.

Barnacle State Historic Site

Opposite the Playhouse, this 1891 pioneer residence (☎ 448-9445) owned by Ralph Monroe is open to the public on weekends. Admission is $1 for everyone. It's at 3485 Main Hwy, open Friday to Sunday (except Christmas) with guided tours at 10 and 11.30 am and 1 and 2.30 pm. During the week it's for groups only.

Coconut Grove Exhibition Center

This is the sight of conventions and special events, like the monthly Coconut Grove Cares (☎ 444-8454) antique and jewelry show (see the Things to Buy section for more information).

MIAMI – SOUTHEAST
Miami Museum of Science & Space Transit Planetarium

What a total treat for kids – and we were pretty enthralled, ourselves! The Miami Museum of Science (☎ 854-4247) and Space Transit Planetarium (☎ 854-2222) share a building at 3280 S Miami Ave, very close to the grounds of the Vizcaya Museum & Gardens (see below), at Miami's southern city limit.

Both the museum and the planetarium are open daily from 10 am to 6 pm (ticket sales end at 5 pm), closed Christmas and Thanksgiving. There are separate cash booths for each. Admission for the Museum of Science is $6/4 for adults/senior citizens and children aged three to 12. The planetarium costs $5/2.50 or $6/3 for laser shows. On Friday and Saturday nights from 8.15 to 10 pm there is access to the planetarium's telescopes for $1 (for free Saturday night stargazing, see the Southern Cross Astronomical Society listing, below). Spanish speakers can use audiophones for simultaneous Spanish- language broadcast of planetarium shows, but there's a $20 deposit required for the gear.

A combination ticket is $9/5.50.

Museum of Science This is one of the finest science museums in Florida – and Florida has some good ones – for hands-on and just plain creatively fun exhibits. Among the draws: their virtual-reality basketball game, in which you compete with very tall and very talented cyberplayers.

But it's much more than geek-stuff: there are excellent exhibitions on creepy crawlers – insects as well as frogs and butterflies; the Body in Action; Everglades and coral reef exhibits in huge showcases with excellent written and audio descriptions (push the button for the audio); and the Slanted Room, which we'll leave to your imagination.

Outside is the Wildlife Center, open during good weather, where you can touch a tortoise, and see exotic birds – if you get there soon enough you may be able to get a look at their rehabilitated Bald Eagle, before they return it to the wild. There are frequent dinosaur exhibits as well. And don't miss their exhibition of Dangerous Animals of South Florida.

Even the museum store is entertaining and prices are pretty reasonable.

Space Transit Planetarium

There are no major surprises here, though the free Friday and Saturday space lectures and $1 telescope-viewing sessions hold a special place in the budget traveler's heart. The planetarium does movies, star shows and laser shows, including a daily 40-minute *Best of Pink Floyd* show at 2 pm, and the 44-minute *The Planets*, showing continuously from 2 pm to close.

Southern Cross Astronomical Society

Every Saturday night, weather permitting, members of the Southern Cross Astronomical Society (☎ 661-1375) set up telescopes for their Friendly Saturday Night at Metro-Dade-run Bill Sadowski Park (☎ 255-4767), SW 176th St and SW 79th Ave. There are free astronomy lessons and just plain stargazing between 8 and 10 pm. They also hold special events throughout the year; call for more information. Parking is $2 per car.

Vizcaya Museum & Gardens

This opulent palace was built in 1916 by James Deering. It's an Italian Renaissance-style villa (it was used as the setting for the splendid dinner party in *Ace Ventura: Pet Detective)* and filled with 15th- to 19th-century furniture and decorative arts, but unless you're a real early-20th-century Miami-Faux Venetian architecture or furniture buff, we can't for the life of us justify the admission prices of $10 for adults, $5 for children aged six to 12 ($1 AAA discount).

Okay, okay . . . there *are* undeniably stunning gardens, complete with beautiful fountains. Out back, a stone gondola in the center of the docking area acts as a break-water, and there's a charming gazebo. The pool is to die for, and there are canals running everywhere. There are narrow trails through the grounds as well.

Tours of the 1st floor, which are included in the price, are available from 10 am to 2 pm; they start every 15 to 20 minutes. All

the rooms are roped off, though you can peek in.

The museum (☎ 250-9133) is at 3251 S Miami Ave; tickets can be bought daily from 9.30 am to 4.30 pm, once inside you can stay in the house until 5 pm, the gardens until 5.30 pm.

Key Biscayne

The Rickenbacker Causeway ($1 toll) links the mainland with Key Biscayne via Virginia Key. The main attraction of Key Biscayne is the **Bill Baggs Cape Florida State Recreation Area** (☎ 361-5811). All of the 494-acre park's exotic plants – including about half a million Australian pines – were destroyed during Hurricane Andrew, and the park is in the process of replanting with natives. But all walkways and boardwalks have been replaced, and there are nature trails and bike paths.

The 1845 **Cape Florida Lighthouse** (☎ 361-8779) at the park's southern end should be able to reopen the staircase to allow visitors to climb to the top in July 1996. It's got a 1st-order lens (the scale of lighthouse lenses, since you asked, was developed by French physicist Augustin Jean Fresnel (1788-1827), who devised a beehive-like reflecting lens sized from 1st through 6th orders. 1st, the largest, is used at seacoasts, while 6th is used in harbors).

The official address is 1200 S Crandon Blvd; take the causeway to the very end and follow the signs. Admission is $3.25 per carload up to eight people, pedestrians and cyclists $1 per person. The park's open daily from 8 am to sundown.

Crandon Park & Hobie Beaches, public beaches on a five-mile stretch of white sand, are out here as well.

Miami Seaquarium

While the advertised star of the show at this excellent 37-acre aquarium (☎ 361-5705) is Lolita, the killer whale, we were far more impressed with what a genuine effort these great folks are making to preserve, protect and explain aquatic life. Case in point, their Manatee Presentation & Exhibit, where West Indian manatees are brought after

MIAMI

Marine Mammal Rescue Team

Seaquarium's manatee exhibit is made possible by Seaquarium's excellent Marine Mammal Rescue Team, whose divers, animal experts and veterinarians patrol the waters of South Florida and respond to reports of stranded manatees, dolphins and whales in the wild.

Team members were overjoyed on June 29, 1992, when the offspring of their male manatee Romeo (he's been here since 1957) and female Acacia (rescued by the team in 1990) was born. Little Indi weighed in at 75 pounds.

Indi became the first captive-bred manatee to become eligible for a release program. After a month in a 'soft-release' program – a secured natural habitat with minimum human contact to teach the manatee to learn to feed on sea grass – Little Indi was released into the wild.

There are only about 1800 of the endangered West Indian manatees left in the world, and the program is dedicated to preventing their extinction. While the program has been very successful, mankind – especially pleasure boaters – continues to threaten the species' existence.

As if to highlight the inhumane practices in designated manatee zones, a hit-and-run boater killed Little Indi near the Julia Tuttle Causeway. His body was found on November 18, 1995 with propeller gashes from head to tail. ∎

being injured by boat propellers. The manatees are nursed back to health and some are released. There are usually between five and eight manatees here: Juliet has been here since the late 1960s.

The shark presentations at Shark Channel are great for little kids if the sharks are hungry. Other shows include Splash of the Islands with Atlantic bottle-nosed dolphins, and Salty's Sea Scoundrels with Salty the Sea Lion.

Seaquarium's at 4400 Rickenbacker Causeway. The park is open daily from 9.30 am to 6 pm, tickets have to be bought before 4.30 pm though, $18.95 for adults, $13.95 for children aged three to nine, $16.95 for seniors. There's a AAA discount of 15%, and ISIC holders get $3 off.

Parking is $2. Wheelchairs and strollers can be rented for $4 (no deposit) and a kennel is available at no cost.

Virginia Key Beach This is a lovely city park with picnic tables, barbecue grills and relative peace and quiet. Parking is $2.

MIAMI – SOUTHWEST
Equestrian Center

Kids go crazy over this center (☎ 226-7886) at Tropical Park (Bird Rd at the Palmetto Expressway) where each weekend purebred horses perform free. You'll see show, quarter and rodeo horses. It's on the grounds of the Metro-Dade Police Stables. The park is usually open from 8 am to sunset, weather permitting.

Metrozoo

While it took a decisive hit from Hurricane Andrew, Miami's Metrozoo (☎ 251-0403, TDD 857-6680, sign language interpreters (five days in advance) 670-9099) is open and operating. Before Andrew this enormous sprawling natural habitat zoo (300 developed acres out of 754 total) was one of the top 10 in the USA, and they're looking to reclaim the title. They'll probably succeed: they've got 900 animals from over 260 species and as of late 1995, they've even got koala and a pair of Komodo dragons! There are nice waterfalls right outside the entrance and, once inside, the picnic area is to your left.

For a great orientation tour, get on the Zoofari Monorail for one complete circuit. The monorail's four stops are (1) in front of the amphitheater, (2) the Asian elephant, Wings of Asia and PAWS (the children's zoo, petting area, shows and rides section), (3) in front of the pygmy hippo, Egyptian geese and Arabian oryx, and finally (4) at the northernmost area of the zoo, home to

Colobus monkeys, black rhinoceros and African elephants.

PAWS is amazing: in the petting area, kids can play with pot-bellied pigs, Eld's deer (it looks like a white tail), sheep, a ferret, snakes (which are brought out by staff for the kids to touch), a monitor lizard and more. Elephant rides run continually throughout the day, and the Ecology Theater does shows at 11 am and 1 and 3 pm.

Don't miss the constantly changing wildlife shows in the Amphitheater daily at noon, 2 and 4.30 pm.

Remember where you parked! Metrozoo's enormous parking lot is as confusing as those at major theme parks, so keep track of your car.

The zoo is at 12400 SW 152nd St; take Florida's Turnpike Extension to the Metrozoo exit at SW 152nd St. The zoo's open daily from 9.30 am to 5.30 pm (tickets must be bought before 4 pm), ticket prices including tax are $8 for adults, $4 for children aged three to 12. Wheelchair rentals are $6 ($10 deposit), single/double strollers $4/7 ($10 deposit). Video cameras can be rented for $6 an hour (two-hour minimum, $20 deposit and a drivers license or passport required), and video tapes cost $4.

Gold Coast Railroad Museum

Just near the entrance to Metrozoo is the Gold Coast Railroad Museum (☎ 253-0063), and if you're at all interested in trains it's worth checking out. They've got over 30 antique railway cars, including the *Ferdinand Magellan* Presidential car, used by US Presidents Roosevelt, Eisenhower, Truman and even Ronald Reagan (for whom the thing was outfitted with three-inch-thick glass windows and armor plating). You have probably seen this train: it's the one in the photograph of newly elected president Harry Truman, which shows him standing at the rear holding a newspaper bearing the famous erroneous headline: *Dewey Defeats Truman*.

The museum's at 12450 SW 152nd St, open Friday to Sunday from 11 am to 4 pm. Admission is $4 for adults, $1 for kids

under 10 (kids under three are free). Admission includes a train ride, which lasts about 20 to 25 minutes (two miles). Trains leave every hour on the hour between noon and 4 pm.

Weeks Air Museum

Air and history buffs will be delighted with this museum – despite the damage it received from Hurricane Andrew, it's definitely open for business, and has been for a long time. What's nice about this, as compared to other air museums, is that it's truly a history of aviation, not just military aviation, as is often the case. The staff is knowledgeable and dedicated – there's always someone out on the floor to answer questions.

The museum (☎ 233-5197) is in the Tamiami Airport, 14710 SW 128th St. It's open daily from 10 am to 5 pm. The cost is $6.95 for adults, $5.95 for seniors, $4.95 for children aged 12 and under.

From Miami, take Hwy 836 west to Florida's Turnpike, go south to exit 19 (120th St), then west on 120th St for about two miles to 137th Ave (Tamiami Airport). Turn left (south) and enter the airport, then follow the signs.

Fairchild Tropical Gardens

The USA's largest tropical botanical garden, the Fairchild (☎ 667-1651) is 83 acres of lush greenery with lakes, streams, grottos and waterfalls. To call it a tourist attraction detracts from its purpose, which is the serious study of tropical flora by the garden's more than 6000 members.

The garden's absolutely excellent visitor pamphlet sets out three trails, with very good and easy-to-follow self-guided walking tours. Signs inside the gardens are very clear. There's a 40-minute tram orientation tour of the entire park, or you can set out on your own. Plan on spending 30 minutes for the Palmetum Walk; 45 for the Upland Walk, and at least an hour for the Lowland Trail, which goes from the rainforest in the southeast of the park, up around the lakes and ends at Hammock Lake.

The park is at 10901 Old Cutler Rd; take

US Hwy 1 south to SW 42nd Ave (Le Jeune Rd) south to Cocoplum Circle, turn south on Old Cutler Rd for two miles. The gardens are open daily from 9.30 am to 4.30 pm, closed Christmas. Admission is $8 for adults, free for members and children under 12.

Parrot Jungle & Gardens
Far southwest of Miami is Parrot Jungle (☎ 666-7834), which is more than a parrot show. The lush gardens, set in a hardwood hammock with over 1200 varieties of exotic and tropical plants like heliconias and bromeliads, are home to alligators and crocodiles, orangutans, chimps, tortoises and the very pink flamingoes from the intro sequence on *Miami Vice*. Their parrot show is held five times a day; highlights include trained (as in bicycle riding and roller skating) parrots, macaws and cockatoos.

The park is open every day from 9.30 am to 6 pm, tickets on sale until 5 pm. Admission is $11.95 for adults, $10.95 for seniors over 62, $7.95 for children aged three to 10. It's at 11000 SW 57th Ave; take I-95 south to US Hwy 1, and go five miles south to SW 57th Ave, turn left and go three miles to SW 111th St. Note that in 1998, Parrot Jungle expects to move to Watson Island, which will make it a much more major player in the city's tourism market.

Fruit & Spice Park
The Preston B Bird & Mary Heinlein Fruit & Spice Park (☎ 247-5727) is the only public garden of its kind in the USA. It's a very romantic place to go with a date – a 20-acre public facility that shows over 100 varieties of citrus, 50 of bananas, 40 of grapes and a whole bunch of exotic tropical fruits, plants and spices. There's also a nice poisonous plant area. Best of all, after walking through the paths smelling all that, you can buy exotic offerings at the Redland Gourmet & Fruit Store. We'd advise against the durian (which looks like a jackfruit, tastes like sugary fertilizer and smells like an aged corpse), but you can choose from pomello, rambutan, lychees, breadfruit, tamarind and seeds, spices, jellies and jams.

The park also offers an enormous range of classes and activities, from a Banana Workshop to tours of local commercial farms to Chainsaw Etiquette (we swear!) to Tropical Wine Making (all $10), to a Florida Keys Fruit Safari which visits private gardens in the Florida Keys ($25).

It's at 24801 SW 187th Ave (Redland Rd). The park is open daily from 10 am to 5 pm. Admission to the park is just $1 for adults, 50¢ for kids. Tours of the park are given Saturday and Sunday at 1 and 3 pm; the cost for all tours is $1.50/1.

To get there, take US Hwy 1 to SW 248th St, go west, and turn left on SW 187th Ave, and the park's on the left hand side of the road. Stop for a heavenly cinnamon bun at Knauss Berry Farm (☎ 247-0668), 15980 SW 248th St.

Monkey Jungle
In 1933, an animal behaviorist named Joseph Du Mond released six monkeys into the wild, and their descendants – now over 60 of them – are the highlight of Monkey Jungle (☎ 235-1611), which also features orangutans, chimpanzees and King, the lowland gorilla. The big show of the day is during the feedings, when the Java monkeys dive into the pool for fruit and treats.

Monkey Jungle is at 14805 SW 216th St. To get there, take Florida's Turnpike Homestead Extension to exit 11 and head west for five miles. Admission is $10.50 for adults, $9.50 for seniors and active military and $5.35 for children aged four to 12. It's open daily from 9.30 am to 5 pm; the ticket office closes at 4 pm. While you're out here, you really should go just a mile further to Burr's Berry Farm (☎ 251-0513), 12741 SW 216th St in Goulds, for some of the world's best strawberries.

MIAMI – NORTHEAST
With a few notable exceptions Northeast Miami is an absolutely uninteresting industrial section of town, packed with warehouses and dust. It's not a very appealing

place to head for, unless you're after some specific sights.

The American Police Hall of Fame & Police Museum

An American police officer is killed every 57 hours. This museum (☎ 573-0070, see the Online Services appendix) is dedicated to memorializing cops who have died in the line of duty – nearly 6000 as we went to press.

It's located in a boxy building with a highly visible and dramatic eye-catcher: a 1995 Chevy Caprice Classic police car on the side wall fronting Biscayne Blvd. While the museum has some fun items like the cop car from the movie *Blade Runner*, interesting gangster memorabilia and a huge display of confiscated weapons, it's mainly a memorial. The murdered officer's name, rank, city and state are engraved in the white Italian marble that makes up the main floor, where there's also an inter-denominational chapel.

But kids love the gore and the descriptions of the execution devices: you can have a seat in the gas chamber and the electric chair, but alas, you can only stand next to the guillotine ('please do not place your head beneath the blade'). You can work a crime scene as a detective, and there's a holding cell here as well.

The museum's at 3801 Biscayne Blvd, open daily from 10 am to 5.30 pm. Admission is $6 for adults, $4 for seniors and $3 for students and children.

Little Haiti

Haitians are the third-largest group of foreign-born residents in Florida after Cubans and (strangely) Canadians, and Little Haiti is the center of Haitian life in Miami. As with Little Havana, Little Haiti has absorbed waves of refugees during times of Haitian political strife (see History in Facts about Florida).

Little Haiti is a colorful neighborhood that is trying very hard, though with limited success, to make itself a tourist attraction. The **Haitian Refugee Center** (☎ 757-8538) at 119 NE 54th St is a community center dedicated to disseminating information about Haitian life in Haiti and in Miami. They are also a good resource for information about community events. The opening of the **Caribbean Marketplace** (☎ 751-2251), a combination tourist attraction and legitimate flea market at 5925-27 NE 2nd Ave has not taken off as planned, but with the growth of the nearby Miami Design District, the prospects are getting rosier all the time. The market is open Monday to Saturday from 10 am to 9 pm, Sunday from 10 am to 7 pm.

Haitian **botanicas** (which sell voodoo-related items) are worth visiting for beautiful bottles, beads and sequined banners with voodoo symbolism – while they may seem expensive ($100 to 200), they're far cheaper here in Little Haiti than at some art galleries around the USA, where the banners are selling as art.

There's a pretty bitchin' live music venue here in Churchill's (☎ 757-1807) at 5501 NE 2nd Ave – see the Entertainment section.

The **Tap Tap**, basically a colorfully painted group taxi mounted on a pickup truck (the name is onomatopoeic: think of the sound of a third-world truck engine), is a free shuttle between NE 2nd Ave and 36th St to NE 2nd Ave and 59th St from Friday to Sunday.

In 1996, as we went to press, the Roots & Culture Foundation was planning the first of what it hopes will be annual Roots & Culture Celebrations, with Haitian music, dance, art and food. A five-block section of N Miami Ave – from 54th to 59th St – was to be cordoned off for the free festival. It was scheduled for May 21, Haiti's Flag Day, commemorating Haiti's emergence as an independent nation in 1804.

Design District

Billed in the 1960s as 'the Square Mile of Style,' the area has been a center to the interior decorator and designer industry for about 30 years – with showrooms like Country Floors, David and Dash, Lord Jay, EG Cody and Concept Casual – and is located in a neighborhood called Buena

Vista. Since about 1993, the neighborhood has been going through something of a renaissance, as owners have ended their 'trade only' sales policy in favor of one that is 'courtesy to the trade and retail'.

People are pegging it as a 'new South Beach' because conditions are very similar to those just before the SoBe Boom: higher rents in more fashionable neighborhoods are forcing creative people to move over. Already the area is home to artists and their studios and galleries, film companies, photographers and dancers – basically anyone who needs lots of space for not a lot of money.

To see the place in its best light, go over on the second Saturday of the month when all the studios and galleries stay open for sort of a gallery walk. They do proper gallery walks as well, on the second Friday evening of the month.

Stop in at the *Piccadilly Garden Lounge* (☎ 573-8221) at 35 NE 40th St for coffee and light meals in their lush little courtyard.

At the northern end of the Design District, the **Florida Museum of Hispanic & Latin American Art** (☎ 576-5171) is one of the few museums in the country to be dedicated solely to the culture of Hispanic and Latin Americans. They have 11 rotating exhibitions per year (the museum's closed in August). A great time to visit is during one of their free Opening Nights, held the second Friday of the month (the same night as Design District gallery walks), which feature local, national and international artists, and, oh, yes, free cocktails from 6 to 10 pm. After you reread that sentence, we'll continue.

Nice, huh? The museum's at 1 NE 40th St; admission is $2 for adults, $1 for senior citizens over 58, students and children aged six to 12.

Museum of Contemporary Art (MOCA)

The Museum of Contemporary Art (☎ 893-6211, see the Online Services appendix) has moved to a brand new and much larger space in the city of North Miami. The museum, which runs excellent rotating exhibitions of contemporary art by local,

national and international artists, is also beginning a new permanent collection featuring the works of artists including Ian Hamilton Finlay, Quisqueya Henriques, Alex Katz, James Rosenquist and others.

To get to the museum, take I-95 to NE 125th St, and go east for 1½ miles; MoCA's at 770 NE 125th St. From Biscayne Blvd, take 123rd St west for one mile, and it will become 125th St. The museum is open Tuesday to Saturday from 10 am to 5 pm, Thursday from 10 am to 9 pm, Sunday from noon to 5 pm, closed Monday. Admission is $4 for adults, $2 for students and seniors; children under 12, city of North Miami residents and MoCA members get in free.

MIAMI – NORTHWEST
Liberty City & Overtown

From the birth of Miami, blacks were only permitted to live in the northwest quarter of downtown called Colored Town. Later the name was changed to Overtown – it was 'over the tracks'. Overtown was pretty well decimated by construction of freeways and bypasses. There's a locally famous mural of prominent black Miamians on the side of the **Lyric Theatre** at 819 NW 2nd Ave.

Liberty City, farther north and west, is a misnomer. Made infamous by the Liberty City Riots in 1980 (see the History section above), the area is very poor; crime is higher than in other areas of the city. And while plans exist to renovate the area by creating a village of cultural and tourist attractions, the prospects of that happening in the near future looked grim as we went to press.

In the 1950s, whites, fearing 'black encroachment' on their neighborhoods, actually went so far as to build a *wall* at the then border of Liberty City – NW 12th Ave from NW 62nd to NW 67th Sts – to separate their neighborhoods. Part of the wall still stands, at NW 12th Ave between NW 63rd and 64th Sts.

For information on Liberty City, Overtown and other areas significant to black history, contact the exceedingly helpful Black Archives History & Research Center of South Florida (☎ 636-2390) open from

9 am to 5 pm Monday to Friday (from 1 to 5 pm for specific research projects) in the Caleb Center at 5400 NW 22nd Ave.

ACTIVITIES

See the Outdoor Activities chapter for information on Skydiving and Ultralight aircraft opportunities in the area.

Bicycling

See Getting Around for information on biking around the city. Gary's Megacycles (☎ 534-3306) at 1260 Washington Ave rents bicycles for $3.50/10/35 an hour/day/week, open Monday to Friday from 9.30 am to 7 pm, Saturday from 9 am to 6 pm and Sunday from 10 am to 4 pm. Cycles on the Beach (☎ 673-2055) at 1421 Washington Ave has rentals for $3/15/40, open Monday to Saturday from 10 am to 9 pm, Sunday from 10 am to 7 pm. The Miami Beach Bicycle Center (☎ 674-0150) at 601 5th St does bike rentals for $3/14/50. It's open Monday to Saturday from 10 am to 7 pm, Sunday from 10 am to 5 pm. All of these shops sell bicycles as well.

Skating & Running

In-line skating is one of the most popular forms of transportation here. Everyone seems to have a pair of blades, and the streets are excellent for it. Be careful on Washington Ave and remember that there are very few shops that will allow you in with skates on around here. We usually tuck a pair of thong-type sandals in the back of our jeans to wear when we have to carry our skates. Running is also very popular, and the beach is a very good one for joggers as it's flat, wide and hard-packed.

Skate rental is easy but expensive: Skate 2000 has two locations on the beach, one at 1200 Ocean Drive, Suite 102 (☎ 538-8282), entered on 12th St, the other at 420 Lincoln Road, Suite 385 (☎ 538-8244). Rentals are $8 an hour, $24 for 24 hours, including all protective gear. On Sunday from 10 am to noon they give free skating lessons. You'll have to give them a $100 deposit (either cash or credit card).

South Beach Rentals, a booth on the Promenade around 8th St, rents skates for $8.50 an hour, $24 for 24 hours. The most expensive option is Fritz's Skate Shop (☎ 532-0054) at 117 5th St. It's $8 an hour, but the $24 daily does not include a $15 overnight fee; they have a second location at 726 Lincoln Road (☎ 532-1954).

Surfing

There's not a whole lot of surfing here, but there's some, and X-Isle Surf Shop (☎ 673-5900) is the only surf shop on the Beach, at 437 Washington Ave. They rent boards for $25 a day, weekly rates negotiable, and used boards sell for about $50 to 250, new ones $350 to 500. It's open Monday to Friday from 10 am to 7 pm, Saturday from 10 am to 6 pm and Sunday from noon to 6 pm.

Kayaking & Canoeing

There is something absolutely magical about kayaking through the mangroves, and places where you can are as close as Haulover Beach or South Miami. And the best thing about it is that you don't need any lessons and you can rent all the equipment you need very easily and cheaply. We've tried out Urban Trails Kayak Co (☎ 947-1302) on the bay side opposite Haulover Beach at 10800 Collins Ave, a very friendly outfit that rents one-person kayaks for $8/20 for one hour/four hours, two-person kayaks for $15/35, including paddles, lifejacket and instructions. There are 19 islands along the Intracoastal Waterway, many with barbecue facilities, and on some you can camp for nothing (an overnight kayak rental is $25 one-person, $45 two-person). It's open every day from 9 am to 5 pm.

Sailboards Miami (☎ 361-7245) rents one-person kayaks for $13 an hour, two-person kayaks for $18 an hour. See the Windsurfing section below for directions and the address.

Windsurfing

The only place we found to rent was Sailboards Miami (☎ 361-7245) which does short- and long-board rentals for $20 an hour, $37 for two hours, and holds two-hour 'guarantee-to-learn' windsurfing lessons for $49 for adults, $59 for kids. Private lessons are $25 an hour. They're in the right place for it: Hobie Island, the first right turn after the tollbooths for the Rickenbacker Causeway to Key Biscayne, where the water is calm. It's open daily from 10 am to 6 pm.

Swimming

The excellent T-shaped Flamingo Park Swimming Pool (☎ 673-7750), is open to the public daily from 8.30 am to 1 pm and 1.30 to 6 pm in winter, and admission is free. In the summer, the pool is open Monday to Friday from noon to 8 pm, Saturday and Sunday from 8.30 am to 8 pm. Admission in summer (yes, admission in the off-season, not the high season) is $1.25 for adults and 75¢ for seniors and children. The pool is between Jefferson and Michigan Aves and 11th and 12th Sts, parking adjacent to the pool. See Coral Gables for the Venetian Pool.

The rest of the really good pools, unfortunately, are at hotels, and hotel pools are restricted to hotel guests and club members. Now we'd *never* ever suggest breaking the policies of a hotel, but the best ones are at the Raleigh, as curvaceous as a 1930s Hollywood vixen at 1775 Collins Ave; the Fontainebleau where James Bond said 'Now this is the life'; and the Delano at 1685 Collins Ave – so swank that there's classical music piped in under the water that you can only hear when you're submerged (!).

ORGANIZED TOURS

With over 400 registered historic landmark buildings and 800 buildings, it's very hard not to have an interesting walk through the Deco District. The Miami Design Preservation League (☎ 672-2014) runs 90-minute **walking tours** of the Art Deco District every Saturday at 10.30 am. No reservations are required, but you should show up about 15 minutes early. The tours leave from the Oceanfront Auditorium at 1001 Ocean Drive and the cost is $6. During February and March the tours can get crowded, but during the rest of the year there are usually groups of 15 to 20 people.

On the first and third Sunday of each month, the MDPL offers two-hour **bicycle tours** (☎ 674-0150) in conjunction with the bike shop at 601 5th St, at the corner of Washington Ave. They leave at 10.30 am and the cost is $10 including a bicycle rental or $5 if you have your own.

Between September and late June every year Dr Paul George (☎ 858-6021) does about 70 different walking tours and boat and train tours of Dade county, in conjunction with the Historical Museum of South Florida. They're $10 for museum members, $15 for nonmembers. Dr George also offers private tours by appointment, though unless you're with a group it's going to be very expensive: two-hour tours start at about $100. Write to him at 1345 SW 14th St, Miami, FL 33145.

For an interesting – if somewhat expensive – view of the city, you can take a spin over the city with an **air tour** from Chalk's International Airlines (☎ 371-8628/9). The half-hour tours fly all around Miami, Miami Beach, Key Biscayne and the surrounding areas for $39.50 per person. Tours depart their Watson Island airport on Saturdays at 1.45 pm.

For tours outside the city, including the Everglades, the Keys, Orlando and other areas, Miami Nice Excursions (☎ 949-9180) does shuttle bus and guided excursions. They offer a wide range of tours and services.

PLACES TO STAY
Camping

This is really not the place for camping but there are some interesting opportunities around. Urban Trails Kayak Co (see Activities, above), rents kayaks, and you can paddle to one of the 19 nearby islands, on some of which you can camp for nothing.

Kobe Trailer Park (☎ 893-5121) is the closest you'll get in a commercial campsite to Miami Beach; it's at 11900 NE 16th Ave in Miami. Tent sites for two people, one tent, with electric hookup, cost $20 year round, friendly staff.

The KOA campsite in North Miami Beach closed recently, leaving *Miami-Homestead-*

Everglades KOA (☎ 800-562-7732) as the only KOA campsite in the area (which means there's a pool, game room, shuffleboard, bike rentals, laundry facilities, etc). Tent sites cost $24.95 in high season, 'less' in low season. It's at 20675 SW 162 Ave at 200th St in Homestead.

Miami Beach

From bottom end to top dollar, the Beach has the greatest variety of places to stay in the area. But the information in this section is extremely volatile. From the start of our research for this book to the finish, the prices we quote here rose by an average of $5 per night, the only exception being the youth hostels, whose prices remained stable throughout our research.

Hostels The *Miami Beach International Travelers Hostel* (☎ 534-0268, fax 534-5862) has just a little less of everything than the competition, but that applies to prices as well – it's the cheapest hostel bed in town with dorm bunks at $12 for HI members, $14 for nonmembers. Rooms are a tad worn, and air conditioning only operates between 9 pm and 9 am unless you pay an additional $4 per room per day. They have basic private rooms for $34.60 for one or two people (no HI-member discount) including tax. The hostel's a block and a half from the beach at 236 9th St, just east of Washington Ave. You'll need to show an out-of-state university ID, HI card, US or foreign passport with a recent entry stamp, or an onward ticket, but these rules are only strictly enforced when the place is very crowded – you will always need ID, though. They accept Visa and MasterCard for reservations only, payment is in cash or travellers cheques.

Perhaps the most beautiful hostel in the USA, the Beach's most established place is the HI-member *Clay Hotel & International Hostel* (☎ 534-2988) at 1438 Washington Ave at the corner of Española Way. Set in a 100-year-old Spanish-style villa, the Clay has clean and comfortable dorm rooms (four bunk beds) for $13 per night or $78 per week including taxes. They also have decent private rooms for $30 single, $33

double, $39 deluxe, and a $2 extra charge for a private bathroom. Private rooms all increase by $5 in winter. All of the above prices are reduced by $1 for HI and ISIC cardholders, and the seventh night is always free. The hostel has an excellent kitchen, awesome garden, a message board and a small bookshop. It's a definite travelers' hangout and information exchange center. Staff is very friendly, if a little harassed due to sheer volume, and helpful. They accept Visa and MasterCard, but not American Express. There's a great bar downstairs with food and drinks.

The most expensive dorm room is darn worth the extra $1 they charge. Perfectly located one block from the beach at 1550 Collins Ave and sporting an Olympic-size swimming pool, barbecue area and patio and a full kitchen, the *Tropics Hotel & Hostel* (☎ 531-0361; fax 531-8676) has dorm beds (four to a room) for $14 a night or $84 a week. Dorms are spotless. The Tropic's private rooms ($40 a night or $240 a week) are also quite nice, some with great views of the pool and what's in it at the moment. Air conditioning works until 8 am. They accept MasterCard and Visa, but not American Express.

Hotels – bottom end The *Henry Hotel* (☎ 672-2511) has large, comfortable and cleanish rooms with attached bathrooms, refrigerators, hot plates and ceiling fans for $105 a week. Staff is pleasant, and the rooms are perfectly adequate. It's at 536 Washington Ave, next to the Sports Café.

For about the same price – in fact they have a few cheaper rooms – the family-run *Matanzas Hotel* (☎ 673-9417) is not a bad option. The rooms are similar in style and quality to the Henry, but the location is a bit nicer, on the western end of Española Way at No 506. Rooms, which have fridges, stoves and ceiling fans, are $120 a week with a private bathroom and $100 a week ($14.30 a day) with a bathroom shared between two rooms.

Hotels – middle There are plenty of places on the beach where you can get away with paying less than $50 a night, even in winter. But there are major differences in quality – – shop around carefully before committing, and always check the rooms before you sign in. Even at the height of the high season, you've got a choice, and don't let anyone convince you otherwise. Also note that true Deco style is small by modern standards, so the more landmark Deco a hotel is, the smaller its rooms are likely to be.

The *Berkeley Shore Hotel* (☎ 531-5731) at 1610 Collins Ave is a lovely Art Deco box with a très swirly façade; staff is pleasant enough, and they're in the process of renovating the rooms, which currently are a bit worn but clean and cost $35 a day, $180 a week in summer, $50 a day in winter. The same management runs the cheerier *James Hotel* (☎ 531-1125) about two blocks away at 1680 James Ave, which has clean and large rooms for the same prices. In both these hotels, the rooms have full kitchens, bathrooms, air conditioning, television, telephones and free parking.

The *San Juan Hotel* (☎ 538-7531, fax 532-5704) at 1680 Collins Ave has surprisingly clean rooms, all with kitchens with microwaves. Rooms are $39 a night, $259 a week in summer, $50 to 60 a night in winter.

The *Kenmore Hotel* (☎ 674-1930, fax 534-6591) at 1050 Washington Ave (corner of 11th St) is close enough to the scene and the beach but just across the demarcation point for screaming partiers on the west side of Washington Ave. And, it's across the street from the police station. It's got a helpful and efficient staff and a very distinctive Deco look, with a wavy concrete wall and figure-eight-shaped pool. What's more, it's pretty cheap: rooms are $39 to 59 in summer, $59 to 79 in winter. There are more expensive deluxe rooms, and weekly rates are available as well.

Family-run *Villa Luisa Hotel* (☎ 672-9078, fax 673-9737) has very clean and cheerful rooms, some with an ocean view (actually a slice of the ocean sandwiched between two buildings). It's geared to students and young long-term residents, with rooms for $40 a night, $200 a week in

summer, $80 a night, $300 a week in winter. All the rooms have air conditioning, full kitchens and bathrooms. It's at 125 Ocean Drive.

The lovingly restored *Essex House Hotel* (☎ 534-2700, 800-553-7739, fax 532-3827) at 1001 Collins Ave, with its very cool lobby, is a very friendly place with helpful staff and large rooms. And if you're feeling flabby, you can use the South Beach Gym at 1020 Ocean Drive (in the Clevelander Hotel) where hotel guests get a $7 discount on day passes at $8 a day. Rooms are $75 to 95, suites $125 in summer, and $125 to 145, suites $175, in winter.

We like the *Winterhaven* (☎ 531-5571, 800-395-2322, fax 538-3337). Even though the hallways aren't much to look at at all, the rooms themselves are very sweet, with mosquito netting, ceiling fans and Mediterranean antique furnishings. Rooms are $45 to 85 in summer, $75 to 115 in winter. The hotel's at 1400 Ocean Drive.

Two friends from Germany stayed at and enjoyed the *Fairfax Apartment Hotel* (☎ 538-3837), an old and slightly crumbling but clean and perfectly pleasant hotel at 1776 Collins Ave, with rooms from $50 to 75 in winter.

The *Brigham Gardens Guesthouse* (☎ 531-1331, fax 538-9898) at 1411 Collins Ave is a charming guesthouse set in a beautiful lush, green garden populated by tropical birds. The large and airy guestrooms (most with kitchens and bathrooms) have convertible futon sofas, and all the rooms have communicating doors. There's a barbecue area out back. They're $50 to 95 a day, $295 to 575 a week in summer, $75 to 125 a day, $375 to 775 a week in winter. This place is very similar in style and personality to its friendly competitor next door, the *Villa Paradiso Guesthouse* (☎ 532-0616, fax 667-0074) at 1415 Collins Ave which charges about $5 more per day and about the same on weekly rates (they say the rates are negotiable, so speak with management). At both these guesthouses, the clientele is predominantly, but not exclusively, gay.

The funky old *Bentley Hotel* (☎ 538-1700, fax 532-4865) at 510 Ocean Drive has functional rooms with decent ocean views in some. Rooms are $50 to 75 a night, $150 to 175 a week in summer, $55 to 95 a night, $190 to 225 a week in winter. There's very limited free parking.

The cute little *Penguin Hotel* (☎ 534-9334, 800-235-3296, fax 672-6240) at 1418 Ocean Drive has pleasant, clean and large-ish rooms (fridges available free on request) and nice enough staff. They have a little café and lounge downstairs. Rooms are $63 to 93 a day, $380 to 450 a week in summer, $93 to 133 a day, $580 to 650 a week in winter; suites are $123 in summer, $173 in winter. All prices include continental breakfast. Just up the road at 1440 Ocean Drive is the beautifully renovated *Betsy Ross Hotel* (☎ 531-3934, fax 531-5282), with its unique mix of Deco and colonial styles on the beachfront. The location at the end of the beachfront promenade makes for really nice ocean views, and the Italian restaurant downstairs looks more expensive than it is (see Places to Eat). Rooms are $86 to 116 in summer, $116 to 161 in winter, suites are $156 in summer and $246 in winter.

Island Outpost, a management company that runs several local hotels, including the Marlin and Casa Grande, runs the *Kent Hotel* (☎ 531-6771, 800-688-7678, fax 531-0720) at 1131 Collins Ave, which has the cheapest prices of the company's properties. But you still get most of the same perks as in the others, though the rooms are somewhat smaller. They're priced from $65 to 95, suites $140 (negotiable) in summer; $95 to 115, suites $160 to 175 in winter. There are hammocks in the garden.

The *Park Central Hotel* (☎ 534-7520, fax 534-7520, 800-727-5236, reservation fax 534-3408) at 640 Ocean Drive is one of the classic SoBe hot spots; its rooftop deck a must-see even if you're not staying here. Rooms, which are small, are $65 to 130 a night in summer, $125 to 225 in winter. The LeStat Room (No 607), while heavily booked, is no extra charge – it was available for $175 per night when we called in April 1996. There's a nice café downstairs in the lobby.

Two hotels owned and operated by the same management company straddle the corner of Ocean Drive and 7th St. The northernmost one, at 700 Ocean Drive, is the *Avalon Hotel* (☎ 538-0133, 800-933-3306), in a gorgeous Streamline building (1941), and perhaps known more for its trademark white-and-yellow 1955 Lincoln convertible (it's parked out front) than for its rooms, which are very pleasant and clean. Rates run from $69 to 140 in summer, $95 to 175 in winter including continental breakfast and, they say, no hidden service charges. The *Majestic Hotel*, just south of 7th St at 680 Ocean Drive, is similar in everything – decor, price and service – to the Avalon, but in a toss up, the Avalon would win with slightly better everything.

We spent about a month at the *Mermaid Guesthouse* (☎ 538-5324), which recently was bought and beautifully renovated by a charming and lovely Uruguayan couple, Anna and Gonzolo. It's got a stunning and lush tropical garden that feels more like Bali than Miami Beach. The hosts are wonderful and friendly, rooms are absolutely great – all have four-poster beds with mosquito nets, hugely colorful walls and mermaids everywhere. None of the rooms have TVs (though they do have phones and private baths). Say hi to Molly the cat. We can't recommend this place enough: rooms are $75 to 85 in summer, $95 to 105 in winter. The rooftop apartment is $150. It's at 909 Collins Ave.

The very nice new owners of the *Beach Paradise Hotel* (☎ 531-0021, fax 674-0206, 800-258-8886) deserve a shot at it; their rooms are very clean and nice, looking a lot more like LA than Miami. Prices are $75 to 150 a night in summer, $90 to 175 in winter, weekly rates are negotiable. There's free Showtime, parking available and they have a nice lobby café. It's at 600 Ocean Drive.

The *Century Hotel* (☎ 674-8855) at 140 Ocean Drive is a darn nice hotel far south enough to keep things quiet even on weekends. Rooms range from $75 to 175 in summer, $125 to 275 in winter. There's a cool bar downstairs, the Lizard Lounge.

The *Ramada Resort* hotel (☎ 865-8511,

800-272-6232) at 6701 Collins Ave is $79 to 99 in summer and $125 to 155 in winter depending on the view. It may say something that Hostelling International held their convention at this hotel in 1994, but we're not sure what.

The *Colony Hotel* (☎ 673-0088, 800-226-5669, fax 532-0762) is another Deco landmark, with friendly staff, interesting rooms with teeny televisions but nice touches like potpourri. Prices are $89 to 200 a night in summer and $119 to 200 in winter, including continental breakfast. There's free Showtime, parking is $14 a day and Discover cards are not accepted. It's at 736 Ocean Drive.

Island Outpost runs the *Leslie Hotel* (☎ 534-2135, 800-688-7678, fax 531-5543) at 1244 Ocean Drive, where attentive and helpful staff go the distance – this means that baby-sitting services are available. It has many of the same perks as the Marlin (towels, flowers, TV/VCR, etc), but the Leslie is ever so slightly less luxurious. Spotless as is usual with IO's hotels, the relatively (when compared with the Marlin) simple rooms are $95 to 115, suites from $190 in summer, $135 to 150, suites from $250 in winter.

Our favorite beachfront sign is the one on the *Breakwater Hotel* (☎ 532-1220, 800-454-1220, fax 532-4451, see the Online Services appendix), and the newly renovated rooms here are pretty nice too, ranging from $99 to 169 in summer and $109 to 189 in winter. Their bitchin' penthouse suite is $299/450. Rooms have funky tropical decor, and about half have – get this – remote controlled air conditioner thermostats. The pool-view rooms can get loud at night; it's quietest and cheapest in back. Pay-per-view movies are $6.95. It's at 940 Ocean Drive, and there's a nice Italian restaurant downstairs.

Hotels – top end The fabulously renovated *Indian Creek Hotel* (☎ 531-2727, fax 531-5651) is a delightfully serene place with excellent service and very friendly staff. When our family came to visit us in Miami, we put them up here. The spotless rooms

have been painstakingly restored to their Deco glory. The hotel, at 2727 Indian Creek Drive, is far enough out of the madness 10 blocks south to be a restful retreat from the Fabulous, but close enough to be just a two-minute drive (or 10-minute walk) from the action. The pool out back is really nice, and the Pan Coast restaurant downstairs is one of our favorites (see Places to Eat). Singles/doubles/suites are $80/90/150 in summer, $100/110/190 in winter.

The elegant *Hotel Lafayette* (☎ 673-2262, fax 534-5399) is at 944 Collins Ave – the one with the French advertising kiosk. It's a quiet kind of place for quiet kinds of people – classical music, no loud parties and a break from the Fabulous world of SoBe. This is one of the best values in its price range not just for the rooms (which are very beautifully done, have fresh flowers daily and really nice bathrooms) but also for the service. The owners will help you plot excursions, pack you a picnic lunch and help you work out all aspects of day and even onward trips. They'll try to get your hometown newspaper, too. Their doubles are $105 to 125 in summer, $135 to 165 in winter, and suites are available as well.

Singer Gloria Estefan's *Cardozo Hotel* (☎ 535-6500, 800-782-6500) at 1300 Ocean Drive looks a bit more expensive than it is: its large rooms (many with hardwood floors and all with TV/VCR and hand-made furniture) are $110 to 135, suites $195 to 360 in summer; $120 to 145, suites $210 to 385 in winter. Downstairs is the Allioli Restaurant (see Places to Eat).

The gloriously renovated *Eden Roc Resort* (☎ 531-0000, 800-327-8337, see the Online Services appendix) at 4525 Collins Ave is giving the Fontainebleau Hilton a run for its money. With little extras like an indoor rock climbing complex, an Olympic (if not as cool as the Fontainebleau's) pool, and their newly remodeled spa and health club, it's a great place to get away to. Room rates run from $120 to 225, penthouse $1000 in summer, and $195 to 325, $1500 in winter.

To enter the hot spot of the second, the *Delano Hotel* (☎ 672-2000, 800-555-5001) at 1685 Collins Ave, you need to walk past two hyper-tanned beefcake doormen in white. Once inside, the self-congratulatory staff will allow you to get one of their slick, sparse and minimally appointed rooms for $130 to 175 a day (note: while the bay is one mile west, they refer to the cheapies as 'bay view') in summer, $175 to 225 in winter; the cuter poolside bungalows are $350/450. This place is in demand (Madonna had a birthday do here and owns a piece of the Blue Door restaurant downstairs), so reserve early.

The *Fontainebleau Hilton Hotel & Resort* (☎ 538-2000, 800-548-8886) is probably the most recognizable landmark on the Beach. It opened in 1954, and was taken over by Hilton in 1978. Now it's got three buildings surrounding the absolutely fantastic swimming pool. It's a stylish act all the way, with every conceivable amenity. Room rates in the summer range from $155 to 260 single and $180 to 285 double. Packages during the winter include the Bounceback, which works out to $139 per night per room including breakfast; one-week packages including breakfast, parking and oooh, a drink, are $1020/1170. The Towers Level, the newest addition to the place with keyed entry, concierge service and a bunch of other extras is $270 to 300 single, $295 to 325 double. The hotel is at 4441 Collins Ave.

Tucked away and accessed through its lush courtyard, the *Hotel Impala* (☎ 673-2021, 800-646-7252, fax 673-5984) at 1228 Collins Ave, is a European-style hotel with rooms that have oversize bathtubs, TV, VCR, stereo with CD player, etc. The place is lovely to look at, and the staff manages to create an atmosphere that's elegant but not arrogant. Room rates include continental breakfast and are $159 in summer, $189 in winter, suites $225 to 315 in summer, $269 to 369 in winter.

And in a recess at 834 Ocean Drive, the *Casa Grande Hotel* (☎ 531-8800, 800-688-7678, fax 531-5543) is a great deal for the admittedly high price; service is exquisite and rooms are beautiful, all with TV, VCR, CD/stereo, full kitchens, and tons of luxurious perks, like turndown service each evening and chocolates or flowers on your pillow. All the furniture's Indonesian, there're laundry and room services, staff is perfect, etc . . . . In summer, per night: studios are $150, one bedrooms $200, one bedrooms with ocean view $225; in winter it's $175/225/250. They also have two- and three-bedroom suites for up to $1000 a night, call for more information. Valet parking is $10.

The elegant, Mediterranean-style *Ocean Front Hotel* (☎ 672-2579, fax 672-7665) is a pleasure to write about. It's chic but not pompous, exclusive but not pretentious, and expensive but not really that expensive when you look at what you get. Twenty-two of their 27 rooms have an ocean view, and if you're really wanting to part with some cash for a treat the penthouse suite is almost sinfully luxurious, complete with rooftop terrace, a Jacuzzi and some beautiful furniture. Their pricing scheme is straight out of Kafka, but the least expensive rooms with ocean views are $150 to 175 (single or double) and without a view is $125 to 155. Other rooms range from $190 to 365, and the penthouse is $385 in summer, $425 in winter – other room rates only change by about $5 or so between summer and winter. It's at 1230-38 Ocean Drive.

For a treat or special occasion, the Caribbean-flavored rooms at the landmark *Marlin Hotel* (☎ 673-8770, 800-688-7678, fax 673-9609) are well worth the steep price tag of $200 to 325 a night year round (but this is negotiable in summer) including continental breakfast, as the service is superb, the place astonishingly clean, the rooms are all unique, and the location at 1200 Collins Ave is right in the thick of things. All rooms (actually they're suites) have TV, VCR and stereos (with a CD collection), a small book collection, kitchens, bathrobes and beach towels, all-natural soaps and shampoos and evening turndown service. Look for the vintage pink Caddy convertible outside. They have a rooftop patio for parties, but no pool.

You can also stay at the *Inn at the Fisher Island Club* (☎ 535-6097) on exclusive Fisher Island. Room rates range from $330 to $1295 a night, though they do offer a honeymoon package starting at $940 for three nights, double occupancy.

Miami

Unless you're here on an expense account or with a rich friend who's paying, the city of Miami isn't really the best place: what's here are mainly the big chains, a couple of notable and relatively cheap hotels, and the rest are flop houses that we don't recommend at all. The chain hotels here – Sheraton, Hyatt, Holiday Inn, InterContinental – offer no surprises whatsoever. They all have business centers, concierge service, expensive dry cleaning, restaurants and 'nightclubs' where industrial transmission cog salesmen named Dieter and Hans-Joachim boogie the night away, waving fists with the thumbs-up sign up and down on the dance floor.

For what you get for your dollar, in terms of proximity to the action and just plain neighborhood ambiance you will do far, far better staying on the Beach than in the city, but hey, if you're game, so are we.

Hotels – bottom end We really like the *Miami Sun Hotel* (☎ 375-0786, 800-322-0786) at 226 NE 1st Ave, which is surprisingly clean and tidy and perfectly located for a downtown hotel. It's also got friendly service, lots of gleaming white tile in the lobby, and very clean, if small, rooms. There's a café downstairs. Rooms range from $35 to 55 year round.

Royalton Hotel (☎ 374-7451) is slightly run down, but they keep it clean, and we love that old-fashioned elevator. Year round, singles are $42.50, doubles $49.50, triples $58. It's at 131 SE 1st St.

The *Leamington Hotel* (☎ 373-7783) at 307 NE 1st St is not a bad option; year-round prices here are $39.40 single, $45 double, $50.65 triple, and they, too have one of those old-fashioned elevators. Rooms are clean and nice.

Hotels – middle The *Miami River Inn* (☎ 325-0045, see the Online Services appendix) is a charming place right on the river at

119 SW South River Drive (between SW 1st and 2nd Sts). If we had to stay downtown and you were paying, this is where we'd do it. They have lovely rooms, six cats and excellent and friendly service. Rooms run from $49 to 89 in summer, $69 to 129 in winter.

Of the big chain hotels, the *Holiday Inn* (☎ 374-3000, 800-465-4329) at 200 SE 2nd Ave is the cheapest option downtown. They have a special summer rate of $59 (standard) and $89 for a 'king-size room' including two breakfasts; rooms normally range from $79 to 149, suites from $150 to 375.

The utterly unexciting *Dupont Plaza Hotel* (☎ 358-2541, 800-432-9076, 800-327-8480), on the site of the groundbreaking of the original city of Miami, is yet another standard business hotel option. A one-bedroom apartment is $95, so why would anyone want standard hotel rooms, which range from $99 to 105 (but ask for the corporate rate of $85)? Prices include two breakfasts; suites are $125 to 450. It's at 800 Biscayne Blvd Way.

Hotels – top end Other downtown options include the *Sheraton* (☎ 373-6000, 800-325-3535) at 495 Brickell Ave, which has rooms on the corporate floor from $119 to 144, and, if you're stupid, you can ask for a standard room priced from $144 to 184.

There are two Hyatts (☎ 800-233-1234) in the area, the *Hyatt Regency* (☎ 358-1234), downtown at 400 SE 2nd Ave, and *Hyatt Regency Coral Gables* (see below). Rooms downtown range from $135 to 160 per night.

Coral Gables

The *Hyatt Regency Coral Gables* (☎ 441-1234), 50 Alhambra Plaza, charges $149 to 217 per night. They are everything you'd expect from a Hyatt: we treated ourselves to a stay here and had a very nice time indeed, thank you very much.

The *Hotel InterContinental* (☎ 577-1000, 800-327-0200) at 100 Chopin Plaza has standard rooms for $159 to 189 and deluxe or superior rooms are $199 to 289.

The *Biltmore Hotel* (☎ 445-1926, 800-

727-1926, 800-228-3000) has rooms from $159 to 199 in low season, $179 to 219 in high season; one-bedroom suites $269 to 299/349, honeymoon and Eisenhower suites $399/449, and the tower suite (the Capone) is always $1800 a night. It's at 1200 Anastasia Ave, Coral Gables.

PLACES TO EAT
Miami Beach
There's a bounty of restaurants on the beach, catering to absolutely every style and budget. You can get by incredibly cheaply if you stick to Cuban and fast food, and you may be in for some new taste treats. Try local favorites like guarapo (sugar cane juice), Cuban coffee (respectfully referred to by SoBe locals as 'zoom juice') and *café con leche*, but don't expect some kind of chi-chi Seattle stuff: this is an over-sweetened (they put sugar in for you unless you specifically tell them not to) industrial-strength product, and Western palates may find the stuff ghastly. Whatever you're in the mood for, you'll find it on South Beach.

Coffee Bars This is not Seattle, or even Atlanta, when it comes to the coffeehouse scene, but there are a few alternatives to the reprehensible-to-Seattlites 'zoom juice' served at the Cuban places around town. *Aurora Cafe* (☎ 534-1744) at 1205 17th St has excellent espresso and cappuccino plus exotic coffees from around the world, a very slick yet unpretentious space and a

little library packed with lefty publications. They also do some food as well.

Starbar Café (☎ 674-7070), aside from having the best iced coffee and cappuccino on the beach ($1.75 to 3) and a really wonderful, starfishy atmosphere, swell staff and clean toilets, serves up whopping sandwiches (about $5.95), and an enormous bowl of miso soup with noodles and wok-fried vegetables for $3.75. They also do decent salads for $5.95. It's at 1360 Collins Ave, open Sunday to Thursday from 9 am to midnight, Friday and Saturday from 9 to 2 am.

Hollywood Juice & Smoothie (☎ 538-8988) isn't really a coffeehouse (though they do serve cappuccino and espresso), but we think it's a great place, so here it is: great fruit shakes and smoothies for $3.25 to 4.50, wheatgrass juice for $1.75 an ounce, and healthy sandwiches. It's at 704 Lincoln Road.

Java Junkies (☎ 674-7854) at 1446 Washington Ave, corner of Española Way, does all sorts of coffee miscegenation as well as the usual espresso ($1.50), cappuccino ($2.50), rolls, pastries and buns. Pseudo-nouveaux bohemian hangout.

The *8th St Coffee Bar* (☎ 672-7500) at 760 Ocean Drive has been highly recommended.

Markets For a (somewhat) moderately priced picnic of extraordinary delights, hit two shops on Alton Rd: the grand gourmet hangout *Epicure Market* (☎ 672-1861) at 1656 Alton Rd for some of their excellent delicatessen items, prepared Italian sauces and pasta dishes (they'll heat them up for you if you want) for $5 to 8, and then up the street a block or so to *Biga Bakery* (☎ 538-3335) at 1710 Alton, where you can choose from some of the best bread in the USA – rosemary reggiano ($7.50), their incredible onion rye ($4.75) and heavenly black olive ($6.25). The prices are a bit high but the loaves are large and delicious.

For natural foods, the huge 5th St Natural Food Market (☎ 535-9050) was in the process of opening when we were researching, probably worth checking out; it's at 1011 5th St at Michigan Ave. We

One artist's interpretation of the effects of zoom juice on the central nervous system

liked the smaller but still well-stocked Apple A Day Food Market (☎ 538-4560) at 1534 Alton Rd.

Budget – American *Hamburg* (☎ 672-5344) at 214 Española Way has excellent hamburgers. A quarter-pound beef, turkey or veggie burger is $2.95, half-pound is $3.95, fries are 92¢. They have sandwiches and other entrées as well, like grilled chicken breast for $5.45, but they're most beloved for their burgers and the fact that they're open every day from 11 to 5 am (and they deliver until late), a good place to head after a concert or a night of clubbing and pubbing.

Great Dane Garden (☎ 535-0120, fax 535-6314) at 1542 Alton Rd, has healthy and delicious sandwiches (no red meat) for $3.25 to 3.75, soups for $2.25 and $2.50 and salads from $3.50 to 6.25. They bake their fabulous breads daily, and they'll deliver within one hour for a $1.25 fee.

The mega-hip sandwich folks at *Tommy to Go* (☎ 674-8755, fax 674-9046) serve up healthy huge hero sandwiches, from simple offerings like roast beef and cheese ($4.25) to downright suspicious, like grilled vegetables with chèvre ($5.75). Fun and friendly staff. It has takeout and limited daytime delivery only, no eat-in. It's at 458 Ocean Drive and is open from 7.30 am till 9.30 to 11 pm depending on business and season.

Despite its frog name, baguettes and pretentious translations *(cornichons*=french pickles), *La Sandwicherie* (☎ 532-8934) is as American as a failed S&L. Which means that it has great – and great big – sandwiches; create your own for $4 to 7, salads from $5 to 7. There's no beer or alcohol but they do have fruit juices and sodas. It's at 229 14th St, in the alley (which does smell a bit ripe now and then). They have about four stools and a small sandwich bar. The place is open from noon to 5 am every day, and they'll deliver between noon and 3 pm.

The *Villa Deli* (☎ 538-4552, fax 673-6404) has been around forever, and it deserves to be: great cheap eats, breakfast (eggs, grits or potatoes, bagel or toast, cream cheese or butter, coffee or tea) for

$1.98, after 10 am and on Sundays it's $2.48. Lunch and dinner are similarly cheap, with sandwiches from $4.95 to 7.50, and a dinner combo from 3 to 7 pm for $5.95. It's at 1608 Alton Rd.

Granny Feelgood's (☎ 673-0408) at 647 Lincoln Road serves mainly vegetarian food. Though they do let a little chicken and turkey slip in here and there, you'll *never* see red meat on the menu. Their portions are simply breathtaking, and *two* can fill up on their $6.95 Thai salad, which is loads of veggies and some grilled sliced chicken topped with a peanut sauce. The waiters could technically slap a $1.50 'sharing' charge on you, but they rarely do in practice. They also have great breakfast specials for about $3, and soya pancakes for $2.95. It's a great, friendly place with good service and definitely worth hitting. They also have a juice bar and outdoor café, open Monday to Thursday from 9.30 am to 10 pm, Friday and Saturday to 11 pm, Sunday to 9 pm.

The Light (☎ 531-2721) is a wonderful vegan and vegetarian restaurant that opened just before we went to press. They have daily specials but some menu items include sweet & sour vegetables (tempeh, mushroom, celery and broccoli) or potato, soy, carrot, onion, tomato and eggplant stew for $7; vegetable rice for $2.50 and desserts like apple crisp, banana (soy) cream pie and strawberry pie for $2.50. The address is 901 Pennsylvania Ave, but it's at the corner of 9th St and Washington Ave, through the municipal parking lot.

The *News Cafe* (☎ 538-6397) at 800 Ocean Drive is an absolute South Beach landmark, though over the years the prices have gone up and the service has gone down. It's trendy enough to be painful, but it's open 24 hours. Their famous dish is their tomato bruschetta ($5.50), perfect with an iced tea for a light snack while watching the skaters wiggle by down Ocean Drive; also try their plain omelet ($5) or pasta dishes from $6.25 to 9.75. They add a 15% tip to all checks.

Budget – Cuban *La Cueva del Camaron Restaurant* (☎ 672-7680) at 1120 15th St

Just Say 'No! No!' To Tipping Twice
There's an insidious plot afoot in many Miami-area restaurants: a 15% tip is included in the bill. Of course, the staff may not go to heroic lengths in order to point this out to you – if you forget to check, and leave a cash tip as well, staff gets tipped twice. Unless you're feeling inordinately philanthropic, are a show-off or were *really* happy with the service, make absolutely certain that you're not tipping twice by examining the bill before you pay. ∎

east of Alton Rd is a family-run restaurant specializing in dad's shrimp Creole ($8.95) but with daily specials of chicken, steak, liver and onions or pig's feet with beans and rice for – hold on to your hat – $1.95. Other main courses are $2 to 6. It's a very nice place, and they have a $1.99 breakfast special that's a great buy, with eggs, bacon or ham, café con leche and Cuban toast. They're open Monday to Friday from 7 am to 7 pm, Saturday 7 am to 5 pm, closed Sunday. Just down Alton Rd at No 1439 is the *Chicken Grill* (☎ 672-7717), serving up grilled chickens for $6.99 and a leg/thigh with rice and beans for $3.29. There's a window counter serving zoom juice (30¢) and café con leche ($1), and the restaurant's open from 8 am to 11 pm, closed Sunday.

Closer to the center of town at 820 Lincoln Lane North (one block north of Lincoln Road, just west of Meridian Ave) the *Los Hispanos Restaurant* (☎ 531-3786) is a tiny, hidden-away local hole-in-the-wall with dependable specials from $4 to 7, all served with rice, beans and plantains. Baked chicken is $3.99, grilled cheese sandwich $1.30 and breakfast specials go from $1.25 to 1.99. Smoking section to the left (ha ha). It's open Monday to Friday from 7 am to 6 pm, Saturday from 7.30 am to 4 pm, closed Sunday.

The 24-hour café con leche market has been cornered by *David's Café* (☎ 534-8736), at 1058 Collins Ave at 11th St. They also have not-awesome Cuban food in the $3 to 6 range and an OK breakfast for $2 – it's really here as an emergency stopgap when you're starving at 3.15 am and don't want pizza.

At 941 Lincoln Road Mall, near the corner of Michigan Ave and just near Books &

Books, the *Lincoln Road Café* (☎ 538-8066) is another long-time Cuban spot famous for its infuriatingly slow service and reliably decent food. Skip the glucose-tolerance-test-sweet *tres leches* ($2.50) in favor of their *arroz con leche* (rice pudding) ($2). Sit outside here during Gallery Walks drinking coffee and save yourself some cash over the trendy nearby competition.

We would be remiss in our duties to omit the SoBe landmark *Mappy Cafeteria* (☎ 532-2064), with its excellent (though slow) service, good food and a killer location right at 1390 Ocean Drive that assures cameo appearances in movies shot in the neighborhood – like *The Specialist* and *Miami Blues*. The prices are higher than most other Cuban places, but it's worth a visit: reliably good breakfast specials go from $2.75 to 4, decent fish and seafood from $8 to 12, meat and chicken $5 to 8, good Cuban sandwiches $3 to 4.50. It's open daily from 7 am to 11 pm.

Budget – Mexican The battle of the burrito has come to South Beach, with extremely worthy contenders and a couple of wanna-be's (including a Taco Bell at 1665 Washington Ave). After lengthy consideration, we've decided that *San Loco* (☎ 538-3009) at 235 14th St between Washington and Collins Aves has the best burrito in town, hands-down. They serve up terrific and overstuffed burritos ($2.75 to 5.75), enchiladas ($3.50 to 5) and tacos ($1.50 to 4) in the restaurant, where really lovely staff take good care of you. They also don't throw bushels of cilantro at the food. They're open Sunday to Thursday from 11 to 5 am, Friday and Saturday from 11 to 6 am. Excellent salads are $3.75 to

5.75, and beer and sodas $1 to 2.75. No credit cards are accepted.

If you love cilantro, you'll love *El Rancho Grande* (☎ 673-0480), where they put it in absolutely everything they serve. It's a comfortable and cozy sit-down and more formal affair than San Loco, and it has great lunch specials with main courses from $3.49 to 6, and fajitas from $7.99 to 9.99. All the food is served in terra cotta dishware, burritos come smothered with two types of melted cheese and sour cream, along with rice and beans and guacamole, but salads are a bit mean-portioned. Prices almost double at dinner time. It's at 1626 Pennsylvania Ave (near Lincoln Road Mall), closed for lunch on Saturday and Sunday.

Budget – pizza Washington Ave is lined with pizzerias selling slices and pies, and pizza can be had all over South Beach. Most places are open way late on weekends. Pizza Hut (☎ 672-1900), Little Caesar's (☎ 531-4494) and Dominos (☎ 531-8211) all deliver, but if you want a pie you should do your best to try some of the beach's excellent homegrown product before resorting to the white-bread chains. For a real Italian-style pizza, head for the Sports Café (see Middle – Italian, below). We think that for delivery pizza, the *Bella Napoli* (☎ 672-1558) restaurant at 1443 Alton Rd is the best on the beach; they sell large (18-inch) pies for $7.50 (!) and a large pie with garlic, mushrooms, peppers and onions is $11.90. There's a $1 delivery charge and a $5 minimum order on deliveries, or you can eat in the restaurant, though it's a bit threadbare. It's open Monday to Friday from 11 am to 11 pm, Saturday and Sunday noon to 11 pm.

Some of Washington Ave's better slice offerings include: *Ciccio's Pizza* (☎ 534-7155) at No 1405, with a $2.99 special for two slices and a medium soda, $9 large pies, or one large pie with one extra topping and four cokes for $10.50. It's open Sunday to Thursday from 10 to 3 am, Friday and Saturday from 10 to 6 am. *Pucci's Pizza* (☎ 673-8133) at No 1447 does $2 slices and $11 large (18-inch) pies, and is open Sunday to Thursday from 11.30

to 4.30 am, Friday and Saturday from 11.30 to 6 am. *Lincoln NYC Pizza* (☎ 672-2722) at No 1595 has the two-slices-and-a-medium-drink deal for $3.50, plain large pies $10. Open daily 10 to 5 am.

Da Leo Pizza Via (☎ 538-0803) at 826 Lincoln Road has traditional Italian-style pizzas priced from $7 to 11.

Budget – bagels This is the New York Jewish capital of the Southern USA, and bagels are everywhere. *Brooklyn Bagels* (☎ 534-7373) at 941 Washington Ave, has darn good bagels for about $1.50 with cream cheese; add a cup of coffee and that's the breakfast special, 7 to 11 am, for $1.99.

The chi-chiest entry is *Offerdahl's Bagel Gourmet* (☎ 534-4003) at 1500 Alton Rd, which has cream cheeses flavored with such exotic ingredients as scallions, sun-dried tomatoes and strawberries and other toppings like honey, whipped peanut butter, etc. Any of the above, and more, on a bagel is $1.90 to 2.70, butter only is 80¢, and a bottomless cup of coffee is $1.10. If you're an idiot, you could pay $1.30 to have a *larger* bottomless cup. They were discussing a name change as we went to press.

Middle – American *LuLu's* (☎ 532-6147) is another of our favorites, and we're very thankful that the fire which totaled it in late 1995 wasn't bad enough to keep it from re-opening. It's a kitschy, wonder bread, Americana, Elvis-and Be-Bop setting where you can get the best dang chicken-fried-steak ($7.95) and blackened chicken ($8.95) south of the South. It's a very fun place, sit anywhere, smoke anywhere, have a Black-ened Voodoo or Dixie beer and kick back. It's at 1053 Washington Ave.

Fifty feet up Washington Ave at No 1065 is the *11th St Diner* (☎ 534-6373), an original Art Deco diner trucked down from Wilkes-Barre, Pennsylvania, renovated and serving really good three-egg omelets ($4.25), sandwiches ($2.50 to 6.25), and American favorites like fried chicken and meat loaf from $7.25 to 14.95. It's open 24 hours, every day. Service is usually pretty slow – it's cheerful enough, though – and don't forget that they include the tip in your check. There's an excellent mural in the smoking section.

The Strand (☎ 532-2340) is a posh place with many expensive items but there's one key exception when they do special dinners: meatloaf for $6.75. It's not every night, so call first. See the Entertainment section's nightlife calendar for information on weekly magic shows with Michael Hayes. It's at 617 Washington Ave.

Middle – Asian *Charlotte's* (☎ 672-8338) at 1403 Washington Ave has very good Chinese food, and it's a fine local hangout. Our favorites are their curry shrimp ($8.95) and Singapore fried noodle ($8.95).

Sushi's a happening thing on South Beach, and our favorite place for it is *Sushi Hana* (☎ 532-1100) at 1131 Washington Ave. The place is cavernous, but there are four traditional *tatami* tables in back, and service is usually very friendly (if rushed). There's free (and great) salad when you sit down. Sushi/roll combinations (big enough for two people to share) are $15.50. *Sushi Rock Café* (☎ 532-2133) at 1351 Collins Ave also has excellent sushi and darn good service at slightly higher prices for sushi, slightly lower for combinations and temaki rolls. *Toni's Sushi Bar* (☎ 673-9368) at 1208 Washington Ave is said to be good (and it's certainly crowded); à la carte sushi is $1 to 2.25, sushi entrees run from $12 all the way up to the gigantic sushi-boat at $60. They also do more expensive seafood dishes for $12.95 to 18.95.

World Resources Café (☎ 534-9095) at 719 Lincoln Road does a Thai-based world cuisine menu, with inexpensive appetizers ($3 to 4) and curries ($5 to 6) along with more expensive fare. It's a great place to be on weekends, Gallery Walks and on full moon days for their rotating and eclectic outdoor entertainment schedule. *Thai Toni's* (☎ 538-8424) at 890 Washington Ave is renowned for its more expensive specialties, but the service is excellent and the place itself very chic.

Our friends tell us that *Yeung's Chinese Restaurant* (☎ 672-1144) at 954 41st St delivers for a $1 charge some pretty respectable food – though some dishes, like vegetable dumplings ($4.75) and shredded duck with Chinese veggies and rice noodles ($9.95) are better than others, like crispy chicken ($8.95).

Middle – Cuban Gloria Estefan's *Larios on the Beach* (☎ 532-9577) deserves special mention in a category of its own. Fight through the crowds to get at the hostess (they don't pretentiously stand outside flagging people in) and apply for a table (no reservations accepted). The atmosphere is better than the food (which is good but not outstandingly so) and it's definitely worth it once. Try the paella ($38 for two people, takes 45 minutes) or the less expensive fish Creole ($8.25). Otherwise, you can squeak out for under $20 or so for two people by getting three or four appetizers (like the huge Cuban sandwich for $4.35) and one drink each. It's at 820 Ocean Drive.

Middle – European The *Dab Haus* (☎ 534-9557) at 825 Alton Rd has excellent German food like bratwurst, currywurst and knoblauchwurst for $5.95; Sauerbraten for $8.95 and pork and chicken schnitzel for $7.95. They also do crêpes – we like the mushrooms, potatoes, red cabbage and cheese for $7.75.

Stephan's Gourmet Market & Café (☎ 674-1760) just south of the Clay Hotel at 1430 Washington Ave is a market bursting with fresh and delicious Italian produce, cheeses, meats and spices, and the kinda sexy dining room has a special that's a very good deal on a date: $21.25 (including tax) for dinner for two with bread, an entree that changes nightly, salad and a bottle of wine. Nice penne with sautéed mushrooms in goat cheese sauce.

Renzi's Café (☎ 531-0480) at 1400 Ocean Drive at the Winterhaven Hotel, does Ocean Drive Italian with funny waiters, but it's only moderately priced for lunch – it gets expensive at dinner: pastas at lunch $6.50 to 7.95, at dinner $9.50 to 13.95; main courses run from $9.95 to 12.95 at lunch, $12.95 to 19.95 at dinner.

The Raleigh Bar & Restaurant (☎ 534-1775) is a gorgeous place to come before or after trying to gain access to their pool; it's also rather reasonable considering the FQ (Fabulous Quotient) of the place: for lunch main courses like roasted vegetables Provençal go for $7.50, tuna burger with ginger soy sauce $13 but grilled jumbo shrimp gazpacho $7.50. Sunday Brunch is a chi-chi affair (wild mushroom omelet with fresh herbs and goat cheese at $9.50) and dinner gets very expensive. It's a nice place, though, at 1775 Collins Ave.

The *Booking Table Restaurant* (☎ 672-3476) at 728 Ocean Drive does a filling and terrific surf & turf sampler appetizer ($8.95) that has salmon steak and chicken breast, and rosemary chicken pizzas (they're small and $8.95), but their dinner prices are just a tad high at $12.95 (grouper or dolphin) to $15 (tuna and salmon steak). They include a 15% tip in your check.

Lyon Frères et Compagnie (say that 10 times fast) (☎ 534-0600) is one of the Lincoln Road Mall's main meeting points. It's a combination gourmet market, chi-chi coffee joint, wine bar and French salad bar/café that has seats inside (no smoking) and outside on the sidewalk. There are free wine tastings most Friday evenings. Salads are sold by the half pound, and are $2.50 to 6 (careful construction is key to escaping cheaply). Their pre-wrapped sandwiches are 'European' (accurate if that means 'small') and cost $3.95. Focaccia is $4.95. Saturday and Sunday brunch is currently a good deal with an omelet for $3, but staff say the price should rise soon. It's at 600 Lincoln Road.

Café Papillon (☎ 673-1139) at 530 Lincoln Road is a good place to stop for lunch along the Road – soup and half a large sandwich is $5.95, and Italian sandwiches (like tomato, mozzarella, basil, oil and vinegar) are about $5. Newspapers on sticks, casual, if close, atmosphere.

One of the Beach's hottest spots, the *Van Dyke Hotel Restaurant* (☎ 534-3600) at 846 Lincoln Road serves adequate food in a very chic setting that's usually packed to the rafters and taking over half the sidewalk.

Service is very friendly, and even efficient, and if you could just get rid of the models preening, posing and prodding each other it would be a better place to eat their $6 to 9 burgers and chicken burgers, $8.75 open roast beef sandwich, and the house specialty, eggplant parmagiana, for $8.25. There's nightly jazz upstairs. Watch that included tip.

The Paramount (☎ 535-8020) at 1040 Lincoln Road, is a local favorite with imaginative food and reasonable prices. Appetizers are great, like toasted yellow pepper risotto cakes with pesto shrimp ($5.95), main courses like lasagna ($9.95) and grilled tuna with caper lime butter $13.95.

Middle – Haitian & Caribbean *Tap Tap* (☎ 672-2898) at 819 5th St is a charming and interesting place that should be seen if you're here. It's a wonderful place to have a drink – try Haitian Babencourt Rum, available in several grades. There's unique Haitian hand-made furniture and murals throughout the restaurant, and live music and other entertainment rotates through often – check the *New Times* or *Wire* for more information.

Mango's Tropical Café (☎ 673-4422) at 900 Ocean Drive next to Titi's Taco's just unveiled their incredible new Haitian tropical mural that goes all around the room and over the bar – their specialty is the Caribbean-style jerk chicken wings, an order of 10 is $5, 20 is $10; also try Cassie's chef soup (chicken, shrimp and veggies with noodles) for $6.95.

Middle – Italian It's a local's favorite, it's definitely our favorite, and the only reason *Sports Café* (☎ 674-9700) is in the Middle category as opposed to Budget is out of respect. This unpretentious and comfortable café's unfortunate name disguises a family-run place that feels as if you've walked into a Roman café – not a slicked up American version of a Roman café but a real one! When you sit down they give you freshly baked bread with a spiced extra-virgin olive oil dipping plate. The homemade pastas are simply the best we've ever had in the USA and maybe even in Italy (and we like our pasta!); simple pasta dishes like basil-tomato sauce are $6.95, lasagna $7.25, and daily specials from $7.25 to 8.95 – don't miss their crab ravioli in pink cream sauce topped with freshly ground Romano cheese and black pepper. Their pizza is made Euro style – smaller, thinner crust and a different method of layering the toppings – and it's first rate. Can it get better? Yup. Suave and attentive service, a good and inexpensive wine list and fish and chicken specials as well. They accept Visa/Mastercard, travellers cheques and cash, and are open from 11 to 1 am daily. It's at 538 Washington Ave.

PaneCaldo Restaurant (☎ 538-1440) at 1440 Ocean Drive (beneath the Betsy Ross Hotel), has authentic Italian food in a sophisticated setting; do try the excellent *ravioli d'aragosta allo Zafferano* (home-made lobster ravioli in a saffron cream sauce) ($10.50), and the very nice *tagli-atelle integrali vegetariane* (whole wheat pasta with a tomato-onion-spinach sauce) ($8.95). When you sit down they give you a sample of three types of breads with various dipping plates, like crushed olives and chopped tomatoes. Appetizers are $2.75 to 7.50, salads from $3.50 to 6.50.

Da Leo (☎ 674-0350) is darn worth trying; tables spill outside in the evenings, and people seem both happy and well fed; generous portions of pastas run $6.95 to 7.95, main courses $9.95 to 15.95. It's open for $7.95 set lunch (make-your-own salad, two pastas and a soup) from November to May, dinner year round, at 819 Lincoln Road.

Osteria del Teatro (☎ 538-7850) at 1443 Washington Ave has an expensive but very good Italian menu, but if you get there before 7.30 pm there's a fixed price $16 dinner that's worth every penny.

Middle – Mexican Everything on the menu at *Tita* (☎ 535-2497) is under $11; we liked the vegetarian burrito ($7.50) and the jalapeño smoked chicken breast with the works (vegetables, rice, beans and gua-camole) ($8.75). It's a small place (54 seats) with an industrial Mexican, earthy kind of feel to it. It's at 1445 Pennsylvania Ave.

Top End – American *Embers* (☎ 538-0997) at 1661 Meridian Ave is a reincarnation of the Embers from Miami Beach's 1940s heyday, and the atmosphere is very chic. The current owners bought up the recipes from the former ones – like one for the dressing on the famous Embers salad ($5), and the cuisine is sort of New-Age-classic-American with appetizers like crab cakes ($9.95), steamed citrus scented artichoke ($7.95), and main courses like David's signature bourbon-glazed filet mignon and the four double chops of their rack of lamb, both at $26.95. Pasta is somewhat cheaper, like rigatone at $14.95. There are specials on Mondays and Wednesdays.

Top End – Chinese *Chrysanthemum* (☎ 531-5656) at 1248 Washington Ave is open for dinner only. They serve quite a variety of fish and seafood dishes, like shrimp Imperial (with cashew nuts and bamboo shoots) for $13 and crispy fish in lemon sauce for $11.80, but also orange and garlic frog legs for $14.95 and duck for $13.80. On their menu they indicate which meals are low-calorie ones.

The *China Grill* (☎ 534-2211) at 404 Washington Ave may be expensive, but it's the place to bring a date you want to impress. Food is served family-style (well, maybe *wealthy* family-style) in large bowls intended to be shared. Menu items include grilled dry-aged Szechwan beef ($26.50 for one person, 46 for two), sizzling whole fish ($22/34), grilled rosemary scallops ($23) and wasabi crusted grouper ($22). For the cheapest and best deal they have, show up between 6 and 7 pm for their pre-event dinner for $24.96 per person including an appetizer and two of five entrees (but not tax or tip).

Top End – French *Les Deux Fontaines* (☎ 672-7878) is at the Ocean Front Hotel, 1030-38 Ocean Drive. Open for lighter lunch fare and more substantial dinners, this patio restaurant sits above Ocean Drive – close enough to people-watch but far enough away to keep the riff-raff away from your *saumon au papilotte*. It's a nice spot to have some paté and bread ($5.35) or escargot ($7.80) and a glass of wine at lunch. At dinner time, prices shoot upwards, though like the hotel in which it's located, it's not as expensive as it looks or feels – main dinner courses average about $15 per person without wine, tax or tip. Decent wine list (French and American).

Joe's Stone Crab Restaurant (☎ 673-0365) at 227 Biscayne St is as close as Miami Beach gets to a world famous restaurant. It's been around since 1913, and open only during stone crab season from October 15 to May 15. There's seating politics but at the end of the day it's just reliably excellent stone crab and seafood dishes. At a price, to be sure: medium stone crab claws (six per order) are $16.95; 'selects' (seven per order) are $21.95, and large (five per order) are $28.95 – and if your appetite is robust, you can easily polish off two orders per person.

Top End – Pan-Asian/Caribbean *Pan Coast Restaurant* (☎ 531-2727) at the wonderful Indian Creek Hotel is one of our absolute favorite places to eat: if you have one splurge in Miami Beach (dinner for two with wine will run about $60), we say do it here. The intimate (there are only about eight tables) restaurant is supervised by chef Mary Rohan, who calmly walks out of the kitchen now and then to bursts of applause from diners. Two things that are always on the menu are: the tempura shrimp with mustard-miso sauce ($9) and the mache greens-sautéed wild mushrooms-Roquefort-pine nuts salad with roasted red pepper vinaigrette dressing ($8). For main courses, which change twice a week, there are dishes like oven-roasted five-spice chicken, in mushroom sauce with herb-roasted potatoes and roasted vegetables ($15) or sautéed swordfish with watermelon-papaya-ginger salsa, mango-basil sauce and spicy chips ($18). But Mary's always willing to cater to vegetarians, and as the above dishes indicate, she does it imaginatively. Three thumbs up!

Nemo Restaurant (☎ 532-4550) at 100 Collins Ave has a very interesting Asian menu with oyster-miso soup ($6), wok-charred salmon and sprout salad and, that old Asian stand-by, pan-roasted chicken with mashed potatoes and dried cranberry dressing, both for $16.

Top End – Thai *Pacific Time* (☎ 534-5979) at 915 Lincoln Road has excellent Thai and other Pacific Rim food in a very elegant setting. They also do a lot of fundraising and community-minded projects, but service can get a tad snooty. Best deal is their prix-fixe dinner for $19.95 per person (between 6 and 7 pm), with scallion pancakes, grilled ginger chicken and Tahitian crème brulée.

Top End – Seafood *South Pointe Seafood House & Brewing Company* (☎ 673-1708) at 1 Washington Ave on Government Cut in South Pointe Park, is a very slick seafood restaurant with attentive service and very good food. Their lunch menu is the same as the dinner menu, but lunch dishes are about $5 cheaper. Wash everything down with some of their excellent beers that are microbrewed on the premises (see the Bars section under Entertainment).

Kerry Simon, the chef at New York's Plaza Hotel during the reign of Ivana Trump, runs the lovely *Max's South Beach* (☎ 532-0070) at 764 Washington Ave. Even if you're not up for the rather pricey main courses (like the $11 hamburger) or the specialties like salmon tandoori, black beans and Cayenne onion rings ($19.95) it's still a great place to stop in for one of their excellent Black Tie or 007 Martinis ($6.75).

Top End – other *Allioli* (☎ 538-0553) at 1300 Ocean Drive is in the same building as the Cardozo Hotel (see Places to Stay), both owned by Gloria Estefan. They provide a romantic, elegant and softly lighted atmosphere, while serving Spanish food with Italian/Cuban influence. For lunch roasted chicken with rice and vegetables is $9.50, churrasco $12.90 and their sandwiches $5.25 to 6.95. For dinner you'll have to part with a little more, pastas are $10.50, paellas $14.95 to 18.95 and meat and seafood $14.95 to 22.

Fellini Restaurant (☎ 532-8984) has good Italian food in a very nice atmosphere and prices aren't outrageous either: entrées run from $11.50 (grilled chicken with grilled veggies) to $14 (grilled salmon with veggies) to $19 for medallions of beef with porcini mushrooms and mashed potatoes. It's at 860 Washington Ave.

Casona de Carlitos (☎ 534-7013) at 2232 Collins Ave may not be as good as a restaurant actually *in* Buenos Aires, but for a *parrillada* (Argentinian barbecued side of beef) you could do a whole lot worse than this one at $29.95 for two people. Argentinian food is heavy on the red meat – another favorite is their barbecued filet mignon at $19.95.

The *Leslie Hotel Café* (☎ 538-5386) is good for snacks and sandwiches, even if it is really yellow and the prices are all totally odd. For a decadent splurge, the Skyy Hyy is a neat idea – two shots of Skyy vodka, an ounce of sevruga caviar, with a sashimi tuna-ponzu dipping sauce for $23.69. Sandwiches are a little more reasonable; mojo marinated grilled chicken on Caesar salad $8.93, and Angus burger with cheddar and fries is $6.78. It's at 1244 Ocean Drive.

Miami

Most places downtown cater to the 9 to 5-ers, and therefore close early, and most are closed on Sunday.

Downtown – foodcourts There are two good foodcourts offering a variety of Chinese, Mexican, Indian, pizza, sandwiches, etc, all for $1 to 6; the better of the two is at 243 E Flagler St, the other at 48 E Flagler St (upstairs), where you'll also find a *Granny Feelgood's* (see the Miami Beach Budget section above).

Downtown – cafés & restaurants *Pi's Place Restaurant* (☎ 539-7097) at the NationsBank Tower at 100 SE 2nd St is open for snacks and lunch Monday to Friday from 11.30 am to 2.15 pm. You can get a decent lunch for less than $5, and the view of downtown is pretty slick.

Café Nash (☎ 371-8871) at 37 E Flagler St, inside the Seybold Building Arcade is a fairly small place which seems to be quite popular among the business people downtown. They are open for breakfast and lunch only, omelets $3.25 to 4.95, lots of different salads $3.25 to 7.50, sandwiches $2.95 to 6, platters including two side orders $4.50 to 7.50.

The black-and-white checked *Downtown Diner* (☎ 375-8077) at 4 SW 1st St smelled darn good when we were there. Continental breakfast is $1.99; two eggs, potatoes, bacon or sausage, toast and coffee is $2.99; sandwiches $4.95 to 6.95 and platters (including two side dishes) are $5.95 to 7.95. It's open Monday to Friday from 7 am to 4 pm, Saturday from 8 am to 2 pm.

La Cocina de Mama Stella (no telephone) is extremely small: there are maybe five tables outside and the kitchen is more or less outside as well, but the food looks and smells fantastic, though the staff's English is extremely limited. Cuban dishes all cost $4.99. It's next to the Royalton Hotel at 121 SE 1st St.

Panini Coffee Bar (☎ 377-2888) is an indoor/outdoor café, French-ish and trendy by downtown standards. They serve coffees and pastries (60¢ to $2.95), as well as sandwiches on wide French bread ($4.75 to 5.75), salads ($2.50 to 5.95) and soup by the cup/bowl ($1.95/2.95), and are at 16 NE 3rd Ave, open Monday to Saturday from 8 am to 6 pm.

We walked by *La Cibeles Café* (☎ 577-3454) at 105 NE 3rd Ave and it looked worth a try; they do Cuban dishes from $4.25 to 6.95. The *San Villa Oriental Restaurant* (☎ 371-9359) at 230 NE 3rd St does Phillipino, Chinese, Japanese, Singaporian, Korean, Thai, Malay and Indonesian food cheaply: lunch is $2.50 to 5.95, dinner $5.95 to 8.50 and seafood dishes $10.95. It's open daily from 10 am to 10 pm (at least).

Cacique's Corner (☎ 371-8317) is another Cuban place at 100 W Flagler St near the downtown bus center. Platters (including three side dishes) are $4.50 to 8.95, chicken sandwiches $3.25, Cuban sandwiches $3.50.

The inevitable *Hard Rock Cafe* (☎ 377-3110) at 401 Biscayne Blvd in Bayside Marketplace is perhaps known more for the gigantic rotating electric guitar on its roof than for its food, which is perfectly fine (some is great) and not as expensive as we would have thought: enormous and excellent sandwiches like the VLT (veggie, lettuce and tomato) for 6.99, smoked barbecue beef on a pretzel roll $8.50 and full entrees from $8.99 to 16.99. It's open from 11 to 2 am daily. Also in the Bayside Marketplace (actually near the flag entrance to it) is *Las Tapas* (☎ 372-2737), which is said to have excellent little samplers of Latin foods.

Tobacco Road Liquor Bar (☎ 374-1198) at 626 S Miami Ave has been around for over 80 years. It's primarily known as a blues spot, but they also do good burgers with a variety of toppings from mundane (cheese) to strange (eggs) for $5 to 8. Home-made ice cream. It's open every day from 11.30 to 5 am. Next door is *Tacos by the Road* (☎ 579-0059) at No 638 which does an admirable selection of tacos ($3.21), burritos ($4.59 to 4.99), and nachos with beef ($4.79). And finally, *Fishbone Grille* (☎ 530-1915) at No 650, with fresh fish daily either grilled, blackened, sautéed, baked, Française or Oriental. Prices change according to what's on the chalk board. They have a very decent seafood gumbo ($3.95 to 4.95), and some interesting pizzas from $7.95 to 9.95.

East Coast Fisheries (☎ 373-8493) is Miami's oldest fish restaurant. It's right on the Miami River at 360 W Flagler St, and has been renovated so you can now watch the boats while you eat. Entrees range from $8.50 to $19. It's very big with the lunch crowd and popular for dinner.

Joe's Seafood Restaurant (☎ 374-5637), also on the Miami River, has a deck where you can sit outside. It's at 200 NW North River Drive.

Little Havana *Las Palmas* (☎ 854-9549) at 1128 Calle Ocho gets top billing for price and the fact that they're open 24 hours. *Carne con papa* is $1.99, Cuban sandwiches are $2.50. *El Pescador* (☎ 649-8222) at 1543 Calle Ocho has very friendly service and excellent Cuban dishes for about $2.50 including rice, potatoes and bread.

We liked the *Calle Ocho Marketplace* (☎ 858-1828), a combination lunch-counter (pan con bistec/Cubano/media noche sandwiches $2.50/2.50/1.75); coffee stand (guarapo $1.75, zoom juice 30¢, café con leche 60¢) coin laundry and food market at 1390 Calle Ocho.

El Rey de las Fritas (☎ 858-4223) at 1177 Calle Ocho has grumpier service but decent food; fritas with cheese for $2, Cuban fries for $1.75 and a steak sandwich for $3.25.

We really like the *Exquisito Restaurant* (☎ 643-0227) at 1510 Calle Ocho, for cheap coffee, great atmosphere and excellent food; most dishes are less than $5.

El Palacio Luna (☎ 285-9088) is a neat Cuban-Chinese place with chow mein for $4.50, curry chicken at $5.95 and honey garlic chicken at $6. It's at 1444 Calle Ocho.

We've heard great things from everyone about *Hy Vong Vietnamese Restaurant* (☎ 446-3674) at 3458 Calle Ocho, but somehow never got the chance to go in. Enter former Lonely Planet scourge Beth 'Not Without An Invoice, You Don't' Eilers, who's been there many times. She reports: 'It's just the best Vietnamese food I've ever had, and I love Vietnamese food. Get there early – it looks like a dive but the food is cheap and great, so it fills up fast.'

Don't expect the food at the very famous *Versailles* (☎ 444-0240, 445-7614) to match the gaudiness of the decor: that decor and the atmosphere are why you're here. The cavernous and unbelievably glitzy restaurant is a Little Havana Cuban landmark, and you really should go out of your way to do a meal here during your trip. Service is fine but the food pushes hard at the average barrier. Live with it: ropa vieja ($6.85), palomilla (Cuban steak) with fries or plantains ($7.50) or with white rice, black beans and plantains ($8.50); or *vaca frita*, shredded beef grilled with onions ($7.50). It's at 3555 Calle Ocho.

Many Cubans say that the food at *Islas*

Canarias (☎ 649-0440) is the best in Miami; at any rate it's about the same price and much better for food than the Versailles. It's at 285 NW 27th Ave. There are several others that have been recommended to us on Calle Ocho: try *La Carreta* (☎ 444-7501) at No 3632, a lot like the Versailles but a little less glaring and in your face. *Guayacan* (☎ 649-2015) at No 1933 is about the same price as all the others, and a Nicaraguan version of the Versailles: lots of glitz and flash.

Coral Gables Numero Uno on our list of places to eat in Coral Gables is *Daily Bread* (☎ 856-0363), which does superb falafel and gyro sandwiches ($3.50) in addition to being a Middle Eastern mini-supermarket that sells baklava, olives, tahini and halvah, along with their own excellent brand of pita bread – $1.10 for a bag of five. It's at 2486 SW 17th Ave (they've got another location at 12131 S Dixie Hwy), open Monday to Saturday from 9 am to 7 pm, but no falafel after 6 pm, closed Sunday.

Monte's (☎ 445-0996) at 2330 Salzedo Ave is an interesting place: run by Indians, it specializes in French dishes at dinner time, and very few Indian ones. No matter; it's a great place for lunch. Try the breaded steak ($5.25), lasagna ($4.35) or beer batter fish ($5.75), or sandwiches from $1.70 to 5. At dinner the prices go up: appetizers run from $2 to 4, main courses from $7 to 11.50 and it's BYO alcohol if you'll be wanting any.

Sho Bu (☎ 441-1217) is worth it if you're a) a sushi fanatic and b) able to eat a *lot* of sushi: this place offers all-you-can-eat sushi for $9.99 at lunch, $11.99 at dinner. The stuff is small but good. There are several *caveats*: 15-piece limit on eel, 20 on shrimp tempura, there's a 90-minute maximum sitting time on Friday and Saturday, and you always have to pay for each *un*-eaten piece, especially uneaten rice – and you can't take it out in a doggy bag. Still up for it? It's at 265 Aragon Ave. No smoking during dinner Friday to Sunday.

Everyone tells us that *Tropical Chinese Restaurant* (☎ 262-7576) at 7991 SW 57th Ave is *the* best place in Miami for dim sum: the *New Times* gives it a Very Good, and four people who called us to recommend it during our research.

There's a newly established and moderately priced 'restaurant row' on Giralda Ave between Ponce de León Blvd and Miller Ave with about a dozen places serving all kinds of food from Italian to French bistro. *Las Puertas* (442-0708) at 148 Giralda Ave is said to be a fine gourmet Mexican place. A real treat for those looking for fresh seafood, inventive presentation and just good salsa.

Coconut Grove There are a couple of little places in CocoWalk shopping center; we like *The Cheesecake Factory* (☎ 447-9898) which does about 25 kinds of cheesecake from $4.75 to 5.30 a slice, but they also have burgers from $6.95 to $7.50; and a mean Sunday Brunch including eggs Benedict and spicy Cajun Benedict ($8.50), and Mike's Breakfast Pasta (spaghetti, scrambled eggs, bacon, garlic and onions) for $9.50.

Johnny Rockets (☎ 444-1000) at 3036 Grand Ave, right across the street from CocoWalk is an excellent 1950s-style hamburger joint – they even use the old-fashioned Coca Cola glasses. Burgers are $3.55, a No 12 cheeseburger (with red sauce, pickles, lettuce and tomato) is $3.80. It's open until 2 am on Friday and Saturday, and delivers in the Grove.

Planet Hollywood Miami (☎ 445-7277), owned by a gaggle of action figures like Sylvester Stallone, Arnold Schwarzenegger, Bruce Willis and Demi Moore, spends boatloads of cash on promotions, but we don't take advertising so we're not even going to describe the place. But the food prices are a lot more reasonable than one would think, from penne with fresh broccoli, cauliflower, zucchini, squash and peppers, carrots and onions in a pesto cream sauce at $9.95 to Thai shrimp at $11.95, and generous portions of chicken or beef fajitas for $10.95. It's at 3390 Mary St. Reservations are recommended on weekends.

On the day before we went to press, a friend called in a panic and said we *had* to include *Le Bouchon du Grove* (☎ 448-6060) a bistro that South Florida Magazine called as 'French as DeGaulle'. Very friendly, if heavily accented, staff, in a very relaxed atmosphere. But it's pricey: count on a three-course dinner for two without drinks to run at least $55 to 60. Specials when we called were, appropriately, frog legs with garlic butter, and some sort of 'whaht feesh' wrapped in a cabbage leaf, both at $14.95. Locals go there to hide from the tourist chaos. It's at 3430 Main Hwy.

Northeast Step back into the past at the *S&S Restaurant* (☎ 373-4291), a classic '40s-style diner with downright sassy service ('Keep yer shirt on, hon!'), great food (except for the crab cakes, which are execrable) like humongous burgers ($2.75), baked macaroni & cheese ($4.75) and more adventurous entries like shrimp Creole with two veggies and bread ($5.50). It's a small horseshoe-shaped lunch counter that's always very crowded and there's usually a wait of a few minutes for a seat. Lots of cops. It's at 1757 NE 2nd Ave.

Another Miami tradition is the *Rascal House* (☎ 947-4581). While service here is just as snappy, and the atmosphere equally diner-ish (though this place is much, much bigger than S&S), the Jewish food is uniformly great. Our favorite is the Lake Erie whitefish salad ($11.30), but just get anything: we've been here several times and never had a bad or even a not-great meal. Expect to wait in line when you come; the line for the counter is usually shorter than that for proper tables. Sandwiches, like corned beef, tongue (yech!) or roast beef are $5.95, but some, like liverwurst or salami are $4.65. Don't miss the grilled salmon for $12.75. The restaurant is at 17190 Collins Ave (at 172nd St) in North Miami Beach.

Design District Drop by *Piccadilly Garden Lounge* (☎ 573-8221) at 35 NE 40th St for coffee and light meals in their lush little courtyard. They do a very nice

What's Happening & Where to Get Tickets

The best places to check for what's on during your stay is in the papers: the best of those are *Wire*, the Friday Weekend section of the *Miami Herald*, or the *New Times*.

On the internet, a very useful source is the Single Source (see the Online Services appendix) which gives a daily listing of special events around the area.

Tickets to specific events can always be bought at the venues themselves, and usually through Ticketmaster of Florida (☎ 358-5885).

There are also several telephone numbers you can call in Miami for pre-recorded information on upcoming events:

- Cosmic (and Comet) Hotline from Miami Planetarium ☎ 854-2222
- Jazz Hotline ☎ 382-3938
- Moviephone ☎ 888-3456
- WLVE Entertainment Line ☎ 800-237-0939
- WLYF Information Line ☎ 651-5050, option 2
- ZETA link ☎ 800-749-9490 ∎

caesar salad (for two) for $7, and beef dishes from $13.95 to $26.

We've had a couple of recommendations for *Charcuterie Restaurant* (☎ 576-7877) as a lunch spot. It's at 3612 NE 2nd Ave, open Monday to Friday from 11.30 am to 3 pm.

ENTERTAINMENT

To call Miami Beach a trendy nightspot would be a little like calling New York a fairly large city: this is one of the most totally fashionable places in the country right now for clubs and nightspots. But nightlife around here is far more than clubs: the New World Symphony is a totally unexpected treat, and legitimate theater is very active in the area. There's an art scene here that's evolved from a couple of grungy studio-galleries into a driving force in the American art world.

Theater

Area Stage (☎ 673-8002) presents cutting-edge original works with a strong emphasis on local talent. Ticket prices are $17 for adults, $8 for students under 25 with ISIC, based on availability. The theater's at 645 Lincoln Road.

The *Edge Theater* (☎ 531-6083) is another cutting-edge house at 405 Española Way on the 2nd floor above Java Junkies.

The *Florida Shakespeare Theatre* (☎ 446-1116, see the Online Services appendix) performs at their new mainstage at the Biltmore Hotel, 1200 Anastasia Ave in Coral Gables. The name is misleading: the company, which performs year round on mainstage and on tour, handles Shakespearean works as well as classic and contemporary works. Tickets to the performances cost $25 for adults, $15 for seniors, children and students; opening nights costs $30/20.

The *Jerry Herman Ring Theatre* (☎ 284-3355, see the Online Services appendix) stages contemporary plays at the University of Miami's Coral Gables campus recently celebrated its 50th anniversary.

The *Jackie Gleason Theater for the Performing Arts* (☎ 673-7300) at 1700 Washington Ave is the Beach's premiere showcase for Broadway shows, the Florida Philharmonic, the Miami City Ballet, the Concert Association of Florida and other big productions. Originally built in 1951, the place was actually the home of the Jackie Gleason television show. Ticket prices change by performance, but hover in the $30 to $50 range for Broadway shows and concerts.

The *Gusman Center for the Performing Arts* (☎ 374-2444) at 174 E Flagler St is a renovated 1920s movie palace now home to a huge variety of performing arts – including the New World Symphony and the Florida Philharmonic – and the annual Miami Film Festival. Ticket prices change for each performance.

The lovely *Coconut Grove Playhouse* (☎ 442-4000) celebrated its 40th anniversary in 1996, but the facility has been here for 70 years and constantly swaps shows with Broadway in New York – it sends some, and some of the more popular Broadway road shows stop here. There are two stages, the main Playhouse stage and the smaller Encore Room.

Tickets to the Playhouse cost $30 from Sunday to Thursday, $35 on Friday and Saturday, some student discounts apply. In the Encore Room, tickets are $22 Sunday to Thursday and $27 on Friday and Saturday. The facility is at 3500 Main Hwy, at the corner of Charles Ave, two blocks south of the CocoWalk shopping center.

The *African-Caribbean-American Performing Artists* (☎ 758-3534) stage performances at various venues around the city.

Spanish-Language Theater For Spanish language theater, check in the Spanish press, or contact *Teatro Las Mascaras* (☎ 642-0358), *Teatro de Bellas Artes* (☎ 325-0515), *Teatro Martí* (☎ 545-7866) or the *Manuel Artime Performing Arts Center* (☎ 525-5057).

Classical Music

There are classical concerts by the Florida Philharmonic and visiting orchestras throughout the year at venues like the Jackie Gleason Theater for the Performing Arts, the Gusman Center for the Performing Arts, and Dade County Auditorium, see their listings above and below for more information. For information about concerts throughout the city and state, contact the excellent Florida Concert Association (☎ 532-3491), at 555 17th St.

See the Music & Theater section in the Facts about Florida chapter for background on the wonderful *New World Symphony* (NWS; ☎ 673-3331), which performs in a season that runs from late October to Late April in both the Lincoln Theatre in Miami Beach or the Gusman Center for the Performing Arts downtown. About 30% of the performances are free, and in September there are a host of pre-season free concerts as well. Ticket prices for the remainder of the concerts cost from $18 to 43, depending on performance and seating. Tickets can be bought from the box office at the Lincoln Theatre, or through Ticketmaster offices.

The Beach's theatrical jewel, the beautiful *Lincoln Theatre* is host to more than just the New World Symphony: they hold a wide variety of performances including South

Beat Concerts, 'An Evening with Four Poets Laureate', free Musicians' Forum concerts and performances by visiting artists. Stop in when you're here or call the Lincoln Road Partnership at ☎ 531-3442 for specifics.

Besides being home to the Florida Grand Opera, the *Dade County Auditorium* (☎ 547-5414), 2901 W Flagler St, also sees classical music concerts held by the Concert Association of Florida, the Miami Symphony Orchestra (in 1996 also accompanied by the Boys Choir of Harlem) and the San Francisco Symphony. To get to the auditorium, go west on Hwy 836 to the 27th Ave exit, south on 27th Ave to Flagler St (the third light), turn right and the auditorium is on the right.

Opera

The *Florida Grand Opera* and the *Greater Miami Opera Association* (☎ 854-1643), which runs a program of visiting artists, perform at the Dade County Auditorium in Miami (see above). Past performances include *Un ballo in maschera* (A Masked Ball), *Werther* and *La Pasion de Cristo*.

Dance

There are performances by dozens of nonprofit dance organizations all over the area and the State of Florida; the best resource for information on what's happening when you're in town is the Florida Dance Association (☎ 237-3413) at the Miami-Dade Community College Wolfson Campus, 300 NE 2nd Ave, Miami, FL 33132. If you call or write them and let then know where you'll be and when you'll be there they'll send off a schedule of performances and events.

At 905 Lincoln Road, the *Miami City Ballet* (☎ 532-7713) regularly performs at the Jackie Gleason Theater, the Bailey Concert Hall in Davie, the Broward Center for the Performing Arts in Fort Lauderdale and the Raymond Kravis Center for the Performing Arts in West Palm Beach. They also give holiday performances of *The Nutcracker* at several venues: it's at the Jackie Gleason from December 18 to 23. Finally, the company goes on the road around the US and internationally.

Part of the Performing Arts Network (PAN), the *Ballet Flamenco La Rosa* (☎ 672-0552) is a professional Flamenco dance company that performs Flamenco with live music. They also perform at local festivals and special events and hold classes every day for children and adults ($10) in all forms of dance – jazz, modern, creative movement, Flamenco, ballet, Latin dancing, yoga ... They're all in the purple and yellow building at 555 17th St just behind the Jackie Gleason Theater.

Free (or Cheap) & Outdoors

Bayfront Park After Dark (☎ 358-7550) is a series of free concerts at Bayfront Park's South End Amphitheatre from February to May on Thursday nights at 6.30 pm.

But Bayfront Park's most famous for its *American Birthday Bash* Fourth of July celebrations at both the South End and the much larger AT&T Amphitheatres: this is South Florida's largest Fourth of July event. The event features music, kids' rides, watermelon-eating contests and a fireworks celebration.

There are frequent free concerts on Lincoln Road. There's free jazz every night in the 2nd-floor lounge at the Van Dyke Hotel (☎ 534-3600) at 846 Lincoln Road. On Friday and Saturday, Toni Bishop and her band play from 10 pm to 2 am, and Sunday to Thursday there are trios playing from 8 pm to midnight.

From May to December *SunTrust Twilight Music Series* on the third Saturday of each month features jazz-oriented (but not exclusive) concerts on Lincoln Road. From February to April the Lively Lunchtime concert series is held every Thursday from noon to 2 pm. At the *Full Moon Concerts* outside World Resources Café (☎ 534-9095) at 719 Lincoln Road, everyone gathers on the night of a full moon to hear live music ranging from African drumming to jazz to folk to dijeridu concertos. They also do regular World Beat performances on Friday nights from 8 to 10 pm.

The New World Symphony holds outdoor concerts as well, and on the Fourth of July does a performance at North Beach

Open Space Park, on the beach between 72nd and 82nd Sts.

Concert Venues

Big concerts are held at venues below like the AT&T Amphitheatre, Gusman Center, Miami Arena, Jackie Gleason Theater and Lincoln Theatre, but when people like Madonna come to town they're out at places like Joe Robbie Stadium and the Orange Bowl. See the Spectator Sports section below for more information on those venues.

Film

There are standard, multi-theater cinemas in most shopping malls, and none on the Beach yet. The film series at the Wolfsonian Foundation is often co-sponsored by the Miami Beach Film Society (MBFS; ☎ 673-4567), a fascinating organization which also runs series independent of the Wolfsonian like Inflatable Rubber Raft Drive-In at the Raleigh Pool for a screening of *Skirts Ahoy* to the annual *Food in Film: Movies to Dine for* series, which began in early 1996.

The Alliance Cinema (☎ 531-8504, 534-7171), tucked into the recess just east of Books & Books at 927 Lincoln Road, features independent films by lower-budget filmmakers that ordinarily wouldn't make it to Miami.

The Colony (☎ 674-1026) is a 465-seat venue with great acoustics which hosts some concerts (Melba Moore was here when we visited), theater and also shows independent and gay- and lesbian-oriented films. It's at 1040 Lincoln Road.

Bars

There are perhaps more bars than street corners in Miami Beach, so we're listing ones that we or our friends recommend. Remember to bring photo identification like a driver's license, passport or national identity card because if you look under 30 you will be asked for ID.

Watering Holes *Mac's Club Deuce Bar* (☎ 673-9537) at 222 14th St is the oldest bar in Miami Beach, established in 1926. It's definitely a prime local hangout, and it's easy to see why: there's no trendiness here, just a dark but friendly and welcoming room with a pool table and juke box, and no-nonsense service. It's open daily from 8 to 5 am, bottled beers are $2.25 to 3.25, well drinks are $2.50 – what more could you want?

Over on Alton Rd, the *Irish House Bar & Grill* (☎ 534-5667) at No 1430 is another local spot with a happy hour of varying specials Monday to Friday from 5 to 6.30 pm, two pool tables, some video games and a jukebox. Comfy bar; pitchers (depending on the brew) are from $8 to 12.

Ted's Hideaway (☎ 532-9869) at 124 2nd St is a pretty classic hole-in-the-wall open 24 hours. They have, surprisingly, a pretty good beer selection with things like Weissbier for $3.25, Red Stripe, Corona, Fosters and Caribe for $3, and a two-for-one happy hour from 4 to 6 pm and 2 to 4 am. They also have three pool tables.

Nearby, *Rolo's Bar* (☎ 532-2662) at 38 Ocean Drive looks like a café (the food is expensive and the service unbelievably slow) but we're listing it for its selection of beers, by far the best on the beach. They have a couple of hundred types of beer from Louisiana Abita Turbo Dog ($2.95) to Aussie Razor Edge ($3.50) to Polish Zywiec ($3.50) to orgasmic Belgian beers at $6.95.

The Palace Bar & Grill (☎ 531-9077) is *the* gay bar and restaurant; very popular on weekends and before the beach and Tea Dances. It's at 1200 Ocean Drive.

Brandt & Break (☎ 672-9958) is politely described by a friend as a 'redneck pool hall that's a great place to hang out' at 653 Washington Ave.

West End (☎ 538-9378) at 942 Lincoln Road is a primarily gay but all-welcome place that has a great happy hour from 8 am to 3 pm daily, and on Thursday and Sunday from 8 to 5 am, it's *three*-for-one drinks (!). They have three pool tables and are open daily from 8 to 5 am – check in *Wire* for their semi-regular drag shows with singers, drag magicians and dancers.

821 (☎ 534-0887) at 821 Lincoln Road is

a great local hangout; there's live music on many nights and lesbian night on Thursdays (See Comedy & Cabaret and Gay & Lesbian sections below).

Jam's Taverna & Grill (☎ 532-6700), 1331 Washington Ave, is open Monday to Friday from 11.30 to 5 am, Saturday and Sunday from noon to 5 am, with happy hour from 5 to 8 pm (two for one). They have three pool tables, large-screen TVs where they show sporting events, the music is usually fairly loud and they serve bar food like burgers and sandwiches for $2 to 8.

South Beach Pub (☎ 532-7821) is a friendly local hangout, with open-mic nights Sundays. It's at 717 Washington Ave.

The *Cosmic Cafe* (☎ 532-6680) adjacent to the Clay Hotel & International Hostel, 410 Española Way, was undergoing a change of management when we visited, but it's a very nice setting – low lighting, a nice curved bar and decent drinks. It was open from 9 to 2 am daily under the old management and did drinks and bar food.

Microbreweries *South Pointe Seafood House & Brewing Company* (☎ 673-1708) at 1 Washington Ave on Government Cut in South Pointe Park is a really fun place to sit and drink some excellent microbrewed beer – for $2 you can get a sampler with one small cup of each of their beers, and regular servings range from $4 to 4.50.

Abbey Brewery (☎ 538-8110) opened just as we went to press, so dammit we didn't get to taste any of their offerings, which are the Abbey Brown, Oatmeal Stout, Porter Christmas and Indian Pale Ale ($3.75 a pint). They also have about 13 other beers on tap from $3 to 4.25. Happy hour is Monday to Friday from 4 to 7 pm, $1 off all drafts. They have a small range of appetizers and bar food, and they're open every day from 1 pm to 5 am, 1115 16th St at Alton Rd.

Theme Bars At *Virtua Cafe* (☎ 532-0234, see the Online Services appendix) virtual-reality games (which change daily) are $5 for five minutes, but if you like to watch there are monitors which allow you to see the game from the point of view of the person playing. They also have two flight simulators, and for $1 you can sit at the bar and join in on a nationwide interactive computer trivia game for the whole night. There's also a pool table and some dancing. Bar food (pizza, burgers or sandwiches) is $3 to 7. It's worth checking out; Fridays there's unlimited virtual reality for $10. They're at 1309 Washington Ave.

Tap Tap (☎ 672-2898) at 819 5th St is a Haitian restaurant and bar that also does art shows, is home to community meetings and is generally a cool and colorful place to hang out drinking Haitian Babencourt rum ($4.60) or African Ngoma beer for $4. It's open Sunday to Thursday from 11.30 am to 11 pm, Friday and Saturday from 11.30 am to midnight.

If you've been to Berlin and liked it, you'll probably like *The Berlin Bar* (☎ 674-9300) at 661 Washington Ave: people in black, slick atmosphere, you'll get the idea if you've been to New York's Cafe Luxembourg. They do some live music and entertainment from 5 pm to 2 am daily.

Chili Pepper (☎ 531-9661) at 621 Washington Ave is a bar and concert space with live music on Sundays. There's never a cover charge and they've got specials throughout the week. Tuesday is Brit Night with $7 pitchers and $1 drafts of English beer; Mondays from 8 to 10 pm there's free pool (other times the pool tables cost $10.50 to 12.50 an hour with a one-hour minimum). It's open Sunday to Thursday from 9 pm to 3 am, Friday and Saturday from 9 pm to 5 am.

Dab Haus (☎ 534-9557) at 832 Alton Rd has the best selection of German beers, wines and schnapps in the area; they have Dortmunder pils and Alt Tucher hefe weizen, dark hefe weizen and Kristall weizen, Königs pils and Hacker-Pschorr all from $2.50 to 4, and wines by the glass from $3 to 4. They're also a darn serviceable German restaurant – see Places to Eat.

Live Music The best jazz club in the area is the *MoJazz Bar & Lazy Lizard Grill* (☎ 865-2636) at 928 71st St. They're closed

Monday, and have live jazz Sunday and Tuesday to Thursday from 8.30 pm to 12.30 am, Friday and Saturday from 9.30 pm to 2.30 am. There are no age restrictions and cover prices range from nothing to $10 depending on who's playing and where you're sitting. There's half-price cover on weekends before 8 pm or after midnight.

Rose's Bar (☎ 532-0228) is one of the only places around where you can hear live local bands like Manchild, The Goods, Day by the River and Darwin's Waiting Room. It's at 754 Washington Ave. The *Lizard Lounge* (☎ 674-8855) in the Century Hotel at 140 Ocean Drive is a quiet, often deserted

place to have a coupla beers, with a very nice outside garden. They do an excellent Sunday brunch for about $20 outside in their front courtyard.

Respectable Street Cafe (☎ 672-1707) at 218 Española Way is a nightclub that has a couple of live bands a week; other standard nightclub specials include Tuesday G Spot ladies night (no cover for ladies, the cheap skates). Call for show dates, which vary.

The *Cameo Theater* (☎ 673-9787, 531-4993) at 1445 Washington Ave also has live bands occasionally; see the Nightclubs section.

In Little Haiti, *Churchill's* (☎ 757-1807)

Don't you *know* who I am?!?

For reasons best left to psychology, the more offensively, awfully, breath-takingly rude a doorman; the more ruthlessly exclusive a club, the larger the clamoring hordes of short-skirted women and big-tipping men trying to gain entry.

'If you're not dressed to the nines and walking with an attitude that says you totally fuckin' belong here, forget it, baby,' counsels Melanie Morningstar, who writes the Nights Out with Morningstar column at *Wire*. Morningstar helpfully added that she's seen people successfully get in by offering bribes of up to $100 and even sexual favors to doormen at nightclubs.

Why anyone would pay $100 (the average nightclub cover charge on the beach is about $10) or risk death by anonymous sex to some lanky little thug to get into a place where drinks cost $8 a pop is beyond us, but there it is. But clearly, to get into some of the more popular clubs, all you can do is try one or more of the following strategies:

- **Be Polite** Don't be meek, but don't act as if you're Sean Penn (unless you happen to be Mr Penn, in which case . . . Hey look! A photographer!).
- **Attitude is Everything** You're a lean, mean, partying machine, and don't let no one mess with you. Oh yeah, you're gorgeous, too.
- **You're Cool** When the competition is as fierce as it is here (it's about equivalent to the atmosphere in a department store three days before Christmas), a second's hesitation is enough to keep you milling about on a crowded sidewalk filled with wanna-be's.
- **You're Dressed Properly** Standard nightclub garb here is as it is in New York, Paris or anywhere else: look expensive. Or at least interesting – drag queens, Star Trek characters and other Fabulously, outlandishly or outrageously dressed people get in as well.
- **You Know Someone** and/or
- **You Are Famous** ■

has been around for 50 years. It's an English pub with satellite TV broadcasts of English football and rugby, eight draft beers, about 50 bottled beers and live rock music on most nights. It's at 5501 NE 2nd Ave, open Monday to Saturday from 11 to 3 am, Sunday from noon to 3 am.

Little Havana

One of the best spots in Little Havana is *Cafe Nostalgia* (☎ 541-2631), with real Cuban music in a totally great atmosphere of Cuban memorabilia and a small dance floor. It's open Thursday to Sunday from 9 pm to 3 am. The house band is complimented with musicians who stop in to jam, like those in androgynous singer Albita's band across the street at *Centro Vasco* (☎ 643-9606), where she's been performing forever. The club, at 2235 Calle Ocho is a frequent haunt of Emilio and Gloria Estefan.

Nightclubs

Clubs here rise meteorically and fall like the 1987 stock market: the information in this section is among the most volatile in the book.

Nightclubs on South Beach are generally a healthy mix of gay, lesbian and straight, though several are more exclusively gay. In this chapter we've listed the ones that are mixed with the ones that are straight, as the lines are very blurry. If a place is predominantly gay, they'll probably put up a polite sign: 'Welcome to the Warsaw Ballroom. This is a gay nightclub'.

There's something happening every night at South Beach nightclubs, bars and lounges, and the players and the highlights change all the time, so check the *Wire* Calendar section, *The New Times* or just ask around for current information.

Straight & Mixed *Amnesia* (☎ 531-8858) is the home of South Beach's most famous Sunday Tea Dance (post-beach, pre-club), but Amnesia's not exclusively gay: many nights are mixed. There's also a dance floor out in the courtyard – dance under the stars – at 136 Collins Ave.

Bash (☎ 538-2274) at 655 Washington Ave is pretty much the hottest predominantly straight nightclub on the beach. Cool, good dance floor inside and another one in the courtyard outside.

Cameo Theatre (☎ 673-9787, 531-4993) is a predominantly straight dance club in a renovated theater at 1445 Washington Ave, which sometimes has really good cutting-edge music acts – check in *Wire* for what's up.

Club Cabana (☎ 534-1665) in the Club Cabana Hotel, 161 Ocean Drive opposite the Lizard Lounge has a gorgeous back yard on the beach where you can dance under the stars.

Glam Slam (☎ 672-4858) was closed when we went to press, but was one of the most popular clubs on the beach for years, and it is expected to reopen. It's at 1235 Washington Ave.

On Thursday, Friday and Saturday, *Groovejet* (☎ 532-2002) is *the* after-hours spot in town. Don't even think of showing up until at least 2 am. It's at 323 23rd St.

Les Bains (☎ 532-8768) at 753 Washington Ave, the sister club to one in Paris, has a surplus of modeling types and big-haired, yellow-suited men with lots of gold chains.

Liquid (☎ 532-9154) is an impossibly exclusive place that people are clamoring to get into – and unless you're dressed pretty Fabulously, don't even think about it (though they do host a come-as-you-are night, see Calendar below). It's at 1439 Washington Ave.

Twist (☎ 538-9478) at 1057 Washington Ave is a darkish (a coupla small lamps spread a dim light) place with music videos and a very nice wooden bar. Bartender and their press say it's for everyone ('never a cover, always a groove') but it's a predominantly gay crowd.

Dig the floating toys in the bar-moat at *Swirl* (☎ 534-2060); in the back garden the tables have sandboxes and toys – more funky than South Beach slick – they do Afro tea parties where guests are given Afro wigs. There are couches in the outdoor patio. Fabulous, with lots of cheery locals. It's at 1409 Washington Ave.

Gay & Lesbian The gay night scene at South Beach, according to a famous local quip, can be summed up as men that 'look like Tarzan, walk like Jane and talk like Cheetah'.

Hombre (☎ 538-7883) at 925 Washington Ave is totally gay, somewhat sleazy but fun all the same; they've got an outdoor bar as well that is said to be very cruisy and touchy.

Mary D's Ladies Night at *821* (☎ 534-0887) is the best known and most crowded lesbian night on the beach, with the Cabaret for Women every Thursday. Performances start at 9.30 pm, two-for-one drinks from 6 to 9 pm. 821 is at 821 Lincoln Road.

The Kremlin (☎ 673-3150) is a pretty exclusively gay disco (but on Fridays it's very welcoming to all) that does salsa and hot Latin nights during the week, and lesbian nights on Saturday. Check in *Wire* for theme nights, which change all the time. It's at 727 Lincoln Road.

Warsaw Ballroom (☎ 531-4499) is the longest lasting (it's been around for at least five years) and hottest gay nightclub on the beach; it's one floor plus a balcony. There are amateur strip nights on Wednesdays and After Tea on Sunday. It's at 1450 Collins Ave.

Loading Zone (☎ 531-5623) may be the answer to trendy South Beach-brand gay bars (where leather more often tends to mean shoes), with dark corners and less attitude – trendy attitude that is. It's in the alley between West Ave and Alton Rd at 14th St.

Comedy & Cabaret

People in South Beach aren't here to laugh, they're here to look good, and the paucity of cabaret acts around town shows it; see Mary D's Ladies Night at *821* under Gay & Lesbian clubs above for information on the Thursday Cabaret for Women.

The *Comedy Zone* (☎ 672-4788) at 1121 Washington Ave spotlights national comedy headliners Thursday to Sunday. Tickets cost $10 on Thursday and Sunday and $12.50 on Friday and Saturday. The rest of the week admission varies; there's gay comedy Tuesday and amateur night on Wednesday with free admission.

Gallery Walk

There are Gallery Walks on the second Saturday of the month (except in August) along Lincoln Road Mall. These have evolved into more than just popping into the galleries, which hold openings during the Walks, and now most locals who attend make an entire evening of it, with dinner before and some clubbing afterwards. There's no set way to go about it, you just show up and pop in to what's open.

Also of interest is Opening Night in the Design District, a gallery walk held the second Friday of the month. On these nights the Florida Museum of Hispanic & Latin American Art gives away free cocktails from 6 to 10 pm.

SPECTATOR SPORTS

Sports fans can go nuts in a city that has professional football, baseball, basketball and hockey franchises, Jai Alai, NASCAR racing, horse racing and respectable college teams.

The *Miami Dolphins* (☎ 620-2578), a successful NFL **football** team, play at least two home games a month during the season from September to January at Joe Robbie Stadium, a mile south of the Dade-Broward county line at 2269 NW 199th St. On game days there's bus service between downtown Miami and the stadium.

The *Florida Marlins* (☎ 626-7400) are a relatively new National League **baseball** team that lose quite often over at Joe Robbie Stadium during the season from May to September.

The *Miami Heat* play NBA **basketball** games at the Miami Arena (☎ 530-4444) between November and April. and the surprisingly good *Florida Panthers* play NHL **hockey** games at the Miami Arena (☎ 530-4444). Panther Pack tickets, sold from 10 am on the day of a game (noon on Sunday games) are $9; reserved seats are $20, 24 and 30.

Other Sports The Metro-Dade Homestead Motorsports Complex (☎ 230-5200) is a brand new $50 million **auto racing** center that debuted in November 1995 with two

NASCAR races. It holds five major race weekends a year, and if Formula One racing comes here as well, there could be many more. The complex is on the east side of the City of Homestead, at 1 Speedway Blvd.

For **horse racing** there's *Hialeah Park* (☎ 885-8000) at 2200 E 4th Ave in Hialeah (Metrorail stops right there), with its French-Mediterranean-style clubhouse that was built in 1925. Races are from March to May, though you can always come in to get a look at the park's grounds and flamingoes (they raise them). Admission is $1 to the grandstand and $2 to the clubhouse.

Calder Race Course (☎ 625-1311) is an indoor raceway with horse racing from late May to mid-January, and the Festival of the Sun Tropical Park Derby from November to January. They're way north at 21001 NW 27th Ave.

Jai alai can be seen (and bet on) at *Miami Jai Alai* (☎ 633-6400); admission is $1, $2 for reserved seats and $5 for Courtview Club seats. Matinees are on Monday, Friday and Saturday from 1 to 5 pm, evening games from 7 pm to midnight. The arena is at 3500 NW 37th Ave, near MIA; from Omni International Mall take Bus No 36, which stops right in front.

The annual Lipton Championships (☎ 442-3367) are a 10-day **tennis** tournament played at the Tennis Center at Crandon Park, on Key Biscayne. There are two tennis tournaments associated with the FedEx Orange Bowl Football Classic: the Rolex-Orange Bowl Tennis Tournament and the International Tournament for players under 14.

College Sports The University of Miami dominates college sports in the area, and the *Hurricanes*, or Canes, football team dominates UM sports. There's a devotion on the part of fans around here that takes on Spanish Inquisition proportions. You can see the Canes play football at Orange Bowl Stadium. Ticket prices are $16 for general admission, $23 for reserved seats.

The Hurricanes play college baseball at Mark Light Stadium. Tickets cost $5 for adults, $3 for children under 17 and senior

citizens; the Florida and Florida State series are $6/4.

Hurricane basketball is played at the Miami Arena. Tickets cost $13 for side-court seats; in the endcourt they're $9 for adults and $2 for children under 17.

THINGS TO BUY

Shopping malls dominate the scene so totally that there's really nothing left of a local shopping scene anywhere in South Beach. While Lincoln Road, Washington Ave and Alton Rd are lined with galleries and little knickknack shops, if you want to buy something big, you're probably going to end up in a mall.

Aventura Mall
  19501 Biscayne Blvd in Aventura, with a Macy's, Lord & Taylor and some funky security stuff (☎ 935-1110)
Bal Harbour Shops
  9700 Collins Ave in Bal Harbour, with really expensive stuff from people like Chanel, Tiffany, Louis Vuitton, Hermés, Zhiguli and others
CocoWalk
  3015 Grand Ave in Coconut Grove in the heart of a formerly charming neighborhood, cafés, Gap, Victoria's Secret, a cinema and one redeeming feature, The Cheesecake Factory (☎ 444-0777)
Dadeland Mall
  7535 N Kendall Drive in Kendall with Florida's largest Burdines department stores and over 150 other shops (☎ 665-6226)
Loehman's Plaza
  2855 NE 187th St at Biscayne Blvd; also in Aventura, with smaller chain shops (☎ 932-0520)
Miracle Center
  3301 Coral Way in Coral Gables with The Limited, Gap, Victoria's Secret and others (☎ 444-8890)
Omni International Mall
  1601 Biscayne Blvd, in downtown Miami with Gap, an AMC cinema (with a good deal on matinees), a photo shop and a software shop (☎ 374-6664)

Fashion

The casting directors of *Beverly Hills Cop* must have drafted the guy who played Serge from the staff at Versace Jeans

Couture (☎ 532-5993), at 755 Washington Ave, where discerning fashionplates can purchase Fabulous things like a $365 bathrobe. Those with more meager budgets might be able to walk away in a pair of blue jeans for the bargain price of $145. Frighteningly friendly staff may offer you an 'issprayso widda leetle laymon tweest, you'll lahk it, Ah make it mahself.'

Not to be outdone, Armani has his own A-X Armani Exchange (☎ 531-5900) at 760 Collins Ave, with similarly priced merchandise.

Betsey Johnson has two shops in the area; one at 805 Washington Ave (☎ 673-0023) and another at 3117 Commodore Plaza in Coconut Grove, that sell hugely popular womens clothing – some pieces are so revealing that they may as well be ribbons with pockets.

New & Used Clothing

The Beach is a great place to buy cheap used clothing. Try one of the two Recycled Blues locations at 1507 Washington Ave (☎ 538-0656) and 945 Lincoln Road (☎ 531-0349), which have used Levi's jeans for $12.

South Beach USA (☎ 674-0075) at 923 Lincoln Road sells really comfortable and soft cotton shirts, plus T-shirts and other really nice stuff. Miami Surf Style II (☎ 532-6928) at 421 Lincoln Road is great for cheap jeans, hats and T-shirts.

If you're female, Meet Me In Miami (☎ 538-8780) at 233 12th St is *the* place to get that ultimate SoBe outfit: glitzy plastic, piggy pink and polyester – they've got it all.

Mars (☎ 673-8040) at 1035 Washington Ave sells contemporary American clothing – Corinna really likes their colorful dresses ($40 to 140); men's shirts are around $60 and they also have sunglasses, backpacks and watches.

Motor Oil (☎ 673-1968) at 530 Lincoln Road does Calvin Klein Jeans for $38, and a lot of other colorful but not totally unique new clothing. And Deco Denim (☎ 532-6986) 645 Collins Ave has Levi's from $20, Ray Bans for about $60.

Flowers

Flora Flora (☎ 672-5075), an outdoor stand run by a very friendly English guy, has reasonably priced large plants, flowers and pots. It's at 1520 Lenox Ave (behind Blockbuster Video), open Tuesday to Saturday from 10 am to 6 pm.

Designs by Rodney (☎ 673-4233, 800-754-9598) at 1623 Michigan Ave has natural flower baskets and they even do edible flower arrangements. Open Monday to Thursday 10 am to 9.30 pm, Friday, Saturday and Sunday 10 am to 11 pm.

Flowers & Flowers (☎ 534-1633) at 925 Lincoln Road has hands down the best selection of exotic flowers, and does the best arrangements, on the beach. But, uh, they're also by far the most expensive. But this is the place to come to get an arrangement that will impress a date, and it's always nice to walk in here and look, even if you're not buying.

Gifts, Stuff & Knickknacks

Fabulous (☎ 532-1856) at 1251 Washington Ave has postcards, gifts, wrapping paper, picture frames and balloons; it's a nice place if the service doesn't get snooty.

Beachwear (☎ 538-3310) at 1602 Washington Ave has recycled Levi's, army surplus stuff and, for a neat gift idea, US license plates for $10.99. Details (☎ 672-0175), 1149 Washington Ave, is a knickknack store with somewhat eclectic stuff (jewelry, gifts, furniture, scent oils, etc) and free gift wrapping. They have another location at 1031 Lincoln Road (☎ 531-1325) with more furniture.

Studio Russo (☎ 534-3711) at 417 Española Way is one of our favorite shops on the Beach – actually it's an art gallery. Michael Russo is an artist who works with recycled rubbish, turning it into really creative works like scary faces in paper bags and a tremendous sculpture in the window that's just got to be seen to be believed. Russo sells most of the works in his place, and you can get something for under $20.

Ba-BaLú! (☎ 538-0679) at 432 Española Way, has a very eclectic collection of Cuban mementos, including postcards showing air routes between Miami and Havana, cigar box labels, concert posters, and a limited collection of music CDs.

Sunglass Hut (☎ 674-9977) at 948 Ocean Drive has a great selection of high quality sunglasses (all name brand) at very good prices, even for the States.

Music

Y & T Music (☎ 534-8704), 1614 Alton Rd, has records, tapes and CDs. Used CDs are $7.99, and music magazines are also available. Used CDs and Records (☎ 673-3293) at 1622 Alton Rd is smaller but friendlier, also with used CDs for $7.99 or less.

Boom Records (☎ 531-2666) at 1205

Adults Only

While Condomania of South Beach (☎ 531-7872), 758 Washington Ave, has many sex-related items like funky and functional condoms (glow in the dark, ribbed, spiraled, tickler-ed, extra large or just something so you'll have a different color every day); it's not a sex shop in that they don't sell any sex toys (other than a few vibrators) per se.

Given the amount of outrageous sexual openness and lewd behavior you'll witness on South Beach even when, say, walking to the store, it's surprising that real sex shops are very hard to come by in this neck of the woods. There's one on 15th St, just west of Washington Ave, but in the year we lived on the beach we never saw it open even once. We saw another one way up past the Aventura Mall, opposite the Circuit City that's at 20669 Biscayne Blvd. It sells videos and adult toys. For gay and lesbian videos, check out the Gay Emporium in Gay & Lesbian Bookstores, above, or New Concept Video (☎ 674-1111) at 749 Lincoln Road, which has gay, foreign, Japanese animation and XXX movies as well. And if you didn't come prepared, they'll even rent you a video player for $9 a night with a $150 deposit. ■

Washington Ave has a very good selection of new and used CDs and knowledgeable staff.

Spec's Music (☎ 592-7288) has almost 20 record supershops around Miami and the beach with a good selection of CDs and a smaller one of cassettes.

Power Records has two locations, 1419 Calle Ocho (☎ 285-2212) in Little Havana, and 1549 Washington Ave (☎ 531-1138) in South Beach. Both have great selections of Latin, salsa, rhumba, Cuban and South American music at decent prices.

Piercing & Tattoos

Everyone and their dog in Miami Beach seems to have a tattoo, and while piercing isn't as popular here as it is in some other large cities, Beach piercers can put a pin through it with the best of them.

Tattoos by Lou (☎ 532-7300) at 231 14th St is probably the most famous place on the beach for tattooing, and it's been here the longest. You have to be at least 18 years old (bring your ID). Art Attack (☎ 531-4556) at 1344 Washington Ave does tattoos and body piercing ($50 minimum). They're very friendly, seem to have experience (one rather dreads the word 'oops' during a clitoral piercing) and definitely have clean equipment.

GETTING THERE & AWAY
Air

Miami is served by two main airports: Miami International Airport (MIA) and the Fort Lauderdale/Hollywood International Airport (FLL). See Getting Around for information about getting from the airports to downtown and the Beach.

Miami International Airport MIA (☎ 876-7000, flight information 876-7770), is now the USA's busiest international airport in terms of aircraft, and the second busiest in terms of passengers. It is also one of the most poorly laid out and badly signed airports in the country. Parking lots are a good hike from the terminals, which are spread out in an open horseshoe design that makes all areas inconvenient. The main airport terminal building is in Concourse E. Concourses D, C and B are to the north of it, and F, G and H to the south.

Sample one-way fares between Miami and other Florida cities are: Tampa $39 to $44, Orlando $39, Jacksonville $40 and Tallahassee $70.

Fort Lauderdale/Hollywood International Airport
FLL (☎ 359-1200) is about 30 miles north of Miami, just off I-95. It's a much smaller and friendlier airport than MIA, but obviously there are fewer services. International flights arrive at Terminal 3.

Bus
Greyhound (☎ 800-231-2222) has three main terminals in Miami. The sleazy main downtown terminal is Bayside Station (☎ 379-7403) at 700 Biscayne Blvd. Greyhound's Airport Station (☎ 871-1810) is at 4111 NW 27th St, about a $5 cab or $1.25 bus ride away from the airport terminals; see the Getting Around section for specific information. The last is the North Miami Station (☎ 945-0801) at 16560 NE 6th Ave.

See the Getting Around chapter for Greyhound fares between Miami and other Florida destinations.

Train
The southern terminus of Tri-Rail (☎ 800-874-7245, TDD 800-273-7545), the commuter rail system that runs between Dade, Broward and Palm Beach counties, is in Miami. See the Getting Around Florida chapter for more information.

Amtrak (☎ 800-872-7245) connects the Miami Terminal (☎ 835-1222) at 8303 NW 37th Ave with cities all over the continental USA and Canada. It's totally inconvenient and expensive to use Amtrak within Florida.

Car
Miami is at or near the terminus of several major roads: Florida's Turnpike, I-95, I-75 and the Tamiami Trail (US Hwy 41). From Miami it's:

22 miles to Fort Lauderdale
39 miles to Boca Raton
64 miles to the Palm Beaches
141 miles to Fort Myers
155 miles to Key West
228 miles to Orlando
245 miles to Tampa
251 miles to Daytona Beach
302 miles to St Augustine
331 miles to Gainesville
649 miles to Pensacola

GETTING AROUND
To/From the Airports
MIA MIA is about 12 miles west of downtown, sandwiched between the Airport Expressway (Hwy 112) and the Dolphin Expressway (Hwy 836). Before you decide between a taxi or a shuttle, consider that one of the most civilized and cheapest methods of getting out of MIA is through Value Rent-A-Car's hourly rentals – see below.

Bus We, along with other backpackers, have waited and waited on several occasions, and in the end always opted for a taxi or the SuperShuttle, but your luck may be better than ours: take Metrobus No 7 to Government Center (where you can catch a connecting bus to your final destination). It leaves from the lower level of Concourse E, ostensibly every 40 minutes and costs $1.25 and runs from 5.25 am to 9.06 pm. The J bus leaves from the same place supposedly every 30 minutes and takes a circuitous route ending up in Miami Beach about an hour and some later, with service starting and ending about the same time.

Shuttle It is sometimes cheaper for two people (and always cheaper for three) to take a taxi from MIA to Miami and Miami Beach. From MIA, blue SuperShuttle (☎ 871-2000) vans prowl the lower level outside the baggage claim area frequently – just wave one down. Costs vary depending on destination, calculated by the zip code of where you're going: the cost from the airport to the Clay Hotel & International Hostel is $10 per person, to other areas it can be as much as $14.

Car If you have your own liability and collision damage waiver insurance, are over 25 and have a major credit card, the cheapest way to get from MIA to Miami Beach (South or Northern), Coral Gables or the Port of Miami is to drive in a car from Value Rent-A-Car, which offers an hourly rate on its cars with no minimum charges. So a one-hour rental of a full-size car including Florida road charges ($2.05) and sales tax (6.5%) would clock in at a whopping $4.30. That's right, $4.30.

All the major car rental companies, as well as some little ones, have offices at MIA as well. The most direct route from MIA to Miami is to take Hwy 112 to I-95 south (25¢ toll) and follow the signs for downtown. To South Beach, take 37th Ave to Hwy 836 east to I-395, which leads into the MacArthur Causeway. For Northern Miami Beach, take Hwy 112 to I-195, the Julia Tuttle Causeway. There's always a traffic jam in front of the terminals.

Taxi There is a flat fee scheme in place between MIA and five zones: generally the flat fee to anywhere on Miami Beach between Government Cut and 63rd St (zone 4, which includes all of South Beach) from MIA is $22. There's also a flat rate between MIA and the Port of Miami of $15.75. These rates are per carload, not per person. Taxis swarm the lower level roadway.

FLL Many deeply discounted tickets from the USA and Europe plop you down in Fort Lauderdale's shimmering new terminal. About 30 miles north of Miami, it's a great airport: fewer crowds, a slower pace and newer, cleaner and easier-to-use terminals speed you through.

Bus & Train Tri-Rail (☎ 800-874-7245) has a shuttle bus from the airport to the Fort Lauderdale Airport Tri-Rail station (you can also take Broward County Transit (BCt) bus Nos 3 or 6), with trains heading down to the Tri-Rail/Metrorail Transfer Station ($3) about once an hour at rush hours, once every two hours in midday, starting at about

5.50 am to 11.30 pm on weekdays and less frequent service on weekends. From the Transfer Station, take Metrorail to Government Center, where you can change for a bus to your destination. To Miami Beach, this journey will take about two to 2½ hours, and cost about $4.25.

Shuttle Gray Line (☎ 954-561-8886) runs private limos and shuttles. A shared shuttle bus from the airport to South Beach is $12 per person. A private limo (more of a car, really) is $48. Catch the shuttle outside the terminal baggage area. They run from 8 am to 2 am.

SuperShuttle can take you to, but not from, Fort Lauderdale. From the Clay Hotel the cost is $21; from a residence anywhere in the 33139 and 33141 zip codes it's $28.

Car Value has a rental car office in Fort Lauderdale, and hourly rentals are available for the price of $1.99 per hour or less, with no minimum; a one-hour rental (long enough to hustle to South Beach) is $7.26.

There are almost as many car rental companies here as there are in Miami. Driving is really straightforward: I-95 south (there's an airport on-ramp) to I-195 east for Northern Miami Beach; I-395 for South Beach; and straight through to downtown Miami.

Taxi Yellow Cab Company (☎ 954-565-5400, 954-565-8400) is the official airport taxi in Fort Lauderdale; a trip from FLL to South Beach would run about $40 to 45.

Metrobus

Metro-Dade Transit's buses cover a healthy amount of the city; call ☎ 638-6700, TDD 638-7456 Monday to Friday from 6 am to 10 pm, Saturday and Sunday 9 am to 5 pm for specific route information, or for travel planning assistance. Bus fare is $1.25, transfers are 25¢.

Disabled travelers should contact Metro-Dade at least two weeks before a trip for Special Transportation Services (STS) information. For lost & found, call ☎ 375-3366 Monday to Friday from 8.30 am to 4.30 pm.

Transit Booths & Routes Transit booths, where you can get maps, scheduling information and tokens, are at Government Center (☎ 375-5771), NW 1st St between NW 1st and 2nd Aves; a second booth is at the corner of E Flagler and E 1st Aves (no ☎), and a third at the Omni Metromover Terminal (no ☎) at the Omni Mall at Biscayne Blvd just south of NE 15th St.

The Omni Metromover and Government Center Terminals are main junction points for buses downtown.

Some major routes are:

C, K   Between Miami Beach and Government Center

S, M   Between Miami Beach and Omni Mall

S   From the Omni Mall, to South Beach, north on Alton Rd then east on 17th St and north on Collins Ave past the South Beach Library and Bass Museum, and up to the Aventura Mall

8   Between the downtown transit booth and Calle Ocho

6,17,   Between Government Center and
22   Vizcaya/Museum of Science & Space Transit Planetarium and Coconut Grove

B   Between the downtown transit booth and Seaquarium and Key Biscayne on the Rickenbacker Causeway.

24   Between the downtown transit booth and Miracle Mile, Coral Gables

Metromover

Metromover is a neat solution to downtown congestion: it's made up of one- to two-car, rubber-wheeled, computer-controlled vehicles (there's usually no driver on board), running on an elevated track. It's also a great way to get a cheap orientation tour of the entire downtown area.

There are three lines on two 'loops'. The Outer Loop's two lines, the Omni and Brickell Loops, run between the School Board Station west of the Omni Mall, and the Brickell Financial Center Station at SE 14th St and Brickell Ave. The Omni Loop starts at School Board Station, through the Omni, around downtown and Government Center

then back north. The Brickell Loop starts at the Brickell Financial Center Station, north to Government Center and around downtown then back south. The Outer Loop runs from about 5 am to 10.30 pm, and shuttle buses run on the Brickell Loop between 10.30 pm and midnight.

The fare is 25¢. You can change between Metrorail and Metromover at Government Center. Metromover information is available at the transit booths or on the telephone numbers above for Metrobus information.

Metrorail

This is a 21-mile-long heavy rail system with one line, running from Hialeah, through downtown Miami and then south to Kendall, connecting with Tri-Rail at the Tri-Rail/Metrorail Transfer Center at 2567 E 11th Ave, Hialeah, and with Metromover and Metrobus at Government Center).

The fare is $1.25, or $1 with a Metromover transfer. Metrorail or Tri-Rail to Metromover transfer is free. The trains run every day from 6 am to midnight.

Water Taxi

The Water Taxi (☎ 467-6677) is a fleet of cute little boats that tootle around the local waterways. They have two major routes, both of which run from 10 am to about 11 pm every day. The first, between Bayside Marketplace and the 5th St Marina at the southwestern end of South Beach or the western end of Lincoln Road (you need to phone in advance to be picked up) costs $7 one way, $12 roundtrip and $15 for an all-day pass.

The second line is a downtown water shuttle service between Bayside Marketplace and the following locations: Biscayne Marriot, Crown Plaza, Plaza Venetian, Omni, Watson Island (Chalk's Airlines), Port of Miami, Hard Rock Cafe, Hotel InterContinental, DuPont Plaza, Sheraton Biscayne, Barnett Plaza, Brickell Key, Hyatt Regency, Holiday Inn Downtown, José Martí Park, East Coast Fisheries, Fisher Island (with resident or guest ID).

The cost is $3.50 one way, $6 roundtrip and $7 all day. They ask that you tip the driver; if they're nice, $1 for the shuttle or $2 for the Beach/Bayside trip is plenty, and if they're not, nothing is perfectly appropriate. Water Taxi also operates a much more comprehensive network of routes in Fort Lauderdale.

Car & Motorcycle
The sprawl of the Miami area is such that most visitors will end up doing some driving. Miami drivers are generally civil, though see the Dangers & Annoyances section in the Facts for the Visitor chapter under Crime for tips on when they are not.

To/From Miami Beach Miami Beach is connected to the mainland by four causeways built on Biscayne Bay. They are, from south to north the MacArthur (which is also the extension of Hwys 41 and A1A), Venetian (50¢ toll), Julia Tuttle and John F Kennedy Causeways.

North-South The most important highway in the area is I-95, which runs almost straight north-south until it ends at US Hwy 1 south of downtown. US Hwy 1, which runs from Key West all the way north to Maine, hugs the coastline and is called Dixie Hwy south of downtown and Biscayne Blvd from there north to (and somewhat past) the city limits. Hwy A1A is mainly Collins Ave on Miami Beach.

East-West Besides the causeways to Miami Beach, the major east roads are Calle Ocho, Hwy 112 (the Airport Expressway) and Hwy 836, which connects to I-395, both called the Dolphin Expressway, which runs from the Homestead Extension through northern downtown and connects to the MacArthur Causeway.

Parking Except in Coral Gables, South Beach and downtown, parking is pretty straightforward: regulations are well-signed and meters usually tell when you need to use them.

Parking in downtown can be a nightmare, or at least expensive. A good way to do it is to park in the Cultural Center Garage at 50 NW 2nd Ave, just west of the Metro-Dade Cultural Center. If you visit one of the museums in that complex, or take a book out of the library, you can have your parking ticket validated and parking is $2. Otherwise, you're at the mercy of private lots or undiscounted public ones.

On Miami Beach, there is municipal parking at 13th St and Collins Ave, 12th St between Collins Ave and Ocean Drive, on the corners of Washington Ave below 10th St, and just north of Lincoln Road Mall.

Parking fines are generally less than $20, but a tow could cost you up to $75. If you find your car gone, your first call should be to Beach Towing (☎ 534-2128) to ask them if they have it. They'll either tell you that they have it, the number of another company that may have taken it, or to call the police.

If Miami Beach is tough on enforcement, Coral Gables is positively Orwellian: meter parking is everywhere that valet parking is not, and if you're a second late the meter-watcher's there and you're hit with varyingly outrageous fines – we got hit with three tickets in two days, once because we were two hours late (and they put the second ticket right on top of the first one!).

Car Rental All the big rent-a-car operators can be found in the Miami Area, particularly at the airports, along with a host of smaller or local operators. See the yellow pages for local numbers.

Motorcycle Rental Rolling Thunder (☎ 668-4600, 800-851-7420, fax 441-0519) at 4537 Ponce de León Blvd in Coral Gables rents late model Harley Davidson motorcycles including Low Riders, Heritage Softtails and a Fat Boy. The cost is $135 for a full day and $850 a week including 100 free miles (20¢ each additional mile or an extra $25 charge for unlimited mileage) and two helmets, rain suits and night glasses. You need a motorcycle license (from any state or country) and must be 25 or older. You'll need to put down a cash deposit or a credit card draft (which they don't put through) for a $1500 damage and theft deposit.

Taxi

Meter rates are $1.25 flagfall, $1.75 a mile. Taxis here are in generally bad shape, but they'll get you where you're going. If you have a bad experience, make sure you get the driver's chauffeur license number, his name and, if you can, the car's license plate number and contact the Taxi Complaints Line at ☎ 375-2460. These folks really do chase down offensive drivers.

There are taxi stands here and there, but the usual way of catching one – outside MIA and the Port of Miami – is to phone. Companies include AAA Cab (☎ 999-9990), All Dade Cab (☎ 638-4444), Central Cab (☎ 532-5555), Eights Cab (☎ 888-8888) and Sunshine Cab Co (☎ 445-3333).

Bicycle

Miami is as flat as a pancake and smooth as a baby's butt, so biking around the Beach makes a lot of sense. In fact it makes so much sense that people who don't have bikes will try to steal yours so they, too, can enjoy it. Bring along a sturdy, U-type bike lock, or, better, two. Chains and padlocks do not deter people in Miami Beach, where bike theft rates rival those of Amsterdam. Everyone we know in Miami Beach has had a bike stolen, so be careful.

Bicycles are not allowed on buses, Metrorail or Tri-Rail, but you can bike across the causeways.

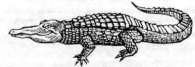

The Everglades

HIGHLIGHTS

- The alligators – look, but DON'T FEED!
- Explore the 10,000 Islands by kayak and camp (free) on secluded island 'chickees'
- Canoe and hike in Collier Seminole State Park
- Watch for egrets, herons, spoonbills, ospreys, anhingas, eagles, and other birds
- Hike or bike the 17-mile trail to the Shark Valley Observation Tower for a 50-foot-high overview of the prairie – or kick back and take the tram instead
- Send a postcard from the nation's smallest post office in Ochopee

The second-largest US national park (after Yellowstone) and largest subtropical wilderness in the continental USA, the Everglades is a unique and delicate ecosystem made up of swamps and marshes at the southern tip of the Florida peninsula.

It's also one of the most well known and poorly understood areas of the USA. Visitors to South Florida hear about tours and the Shark Valley tram ride, and of the ecological threat the area is faced with, but many aren't able to take the time to find out more, or are scared off by tales of renegade alligators and poisonous snakes that lurk in the muck, waiting for innocent tourists to happen by.

While vast tracts of the Everglades are inaccessible to the public, the remainder is one of the most accessible wilderness areas in the state, with developed canoe, kayak, hiking and biking trails, and a very good information infrastructure.

Though the threat to the Everglades is very real, it is an absolutely spectacular place to get into the real nature of South Florida. In the park you'll see an amazing variety of flora and fauna. From the brackish waters of the mangrove and cypress swamps, to the hardwood hammocks, sawgrass flats, Dade County pinelands and marshes, to fascinating creatures like crocodiles and alligators, bottle-nosed dolphins, manatees, snowy egrets, bald eagles and ospreys, there is simply no place in the entire world like the Everglades.

Whether you just visit for an afternoon at the Main Visitor Center west of Florida City, take the Shark Valley Tram Tour or get full into the canoeing and free camping possibilities in the 10,000 Islands and along the Wilderness Waterway, we can't urge you enough to come here.

Also in the area is the Big Cypress National Preserve, a protected area at the northern end of the Everglades that is also accessible to hikers and even by car tour.

The Tamiami Trail (US Hwy 41) is the main artery running between Miami and the southwest Florida coast, and is the best place to access the parks.

High Season & Aaaahh! Season
The Everglades' seasons can be described as the dry season (roughly November to May), and the mosquito and no-see-um (so called because of their disturbing tininess in size but hugeness in biting power) season, which is the rest of the time. While the park is open year round, the best time to visit is in the dry season. ■

At the western end of the 'Glades, Everglades City is a good base for trips out to the 10,000 Islands, and even to the fabulous beaches on the only inhabited one of those, Marco Island, a wealthy enclave off the state's southwestern coast.

Everglades National Park

☎ 941 west of Shark Valley
☎ 305 Shark Valley and east

History & Ecology

The Calusa Indians called the area Pa-hay-okee, or grassy water. Marjory Stoneman Douglas called it the River of Grass, but says in her book *The Everglades: River of Grass* that Gerard de Brahm, a surveyor, named them River Glades, which on later English maps became Ever Glades.

The Everglades is part of a 'sheet-flow ecosystem', beginning at the Kissimmee River, which empties into Lake Okeechobee at the south-center of the state, which, before humankind's meddling, overflowed

Marjory Stoneman Douglas, Everglades activist and author of *Everglades: River of Grass,* 106 years old and going strong

and sent sheets of water through the Everglades and finally into the Gulf of Mexico. The resulting ecosystem was home to thousands of species of flora, and wildlife flourished, including wading birds, amphibians, reptiles and mammals.

Enter business. Sugar growers, attracted by muck as they are, swarmed into the area and pressured the government to make the land available to them. In 1905, Florida Governor Napoleon Bonaparte Broward personally dug the first shovelful of dirt out of what would become one of the largest and most singularly destructive diversions of water in the world. The Caloosahatchee River was diverted and connected to Lake Okeechobee; hundreds of canals were dug directly through the Everglades to the coastline in order to 'reclaim' land. The flow of water from the lake had been restricted by a series of dikes, and farmland began to sprout up in previously uninhabited areas.

Efforts to save the Everglades were begun as early as the late 1920s, but they were put on the back burner by the Depression. In 1926 and 1928, two major hurricanes allowed Okeechobee to break free and the resulting floods killed hundreds, so the Army Corps of Engineers came in and did a *really* good job of damming the lake – the Hoover Dike was constructed.

What the farming was doing was a) diverting the fresh water desperately needed by nature in the Everglades, and b) producing fertilizer-rich waste water which created explosions in growth of foliage, which clogs waterways and further complicates matters. And with all the chemicals and other crud we're pouring into the 'Glades and local waters, the Florida Aquifer, the source of Florida's fresh water supply, is in great danger of being contaminated. Autopsies of local animals, including Florida panthers, have shown that mercury levels are extremely high.

Through the efforts of conservationists and prominent citizens, notably Douglas, the Everglades was declared a national park in 1947, but the threat to the Everglades is far from over. Pollution running into the area from industry and farming in the north is killing foliage and because of the diversion of the area's water, salt water from the Gulf of Mexico is flowing deeper into the park than ever before. There are 16 endangered and five threatened species of animals within the park.

Restoration In 1995, Congress voted to cut subsidies to Florida sugar growers by a penny a pound, and to use the savings to buy 126,000 acres of land to restore a natural flow of water through South Florida. Eventually, about one-fifth of Florida land now in sugar production would be purchased and allowed to revert to marshland.

Additionally, the federal and state governments will spend $100 million to reroute and reconstruct South Florida's dikes, dams and levees.

As Florida was expected to be a major player in the 1996 US presidential elections, the project was given the full backing of the Clinton Administration. It remains to be seen whether implementation will bring restoration.

Information
The main points of entry to the park all have visitors centers where you can get maps, camping permits and information from rangers.

The Main Visitor Center (☎ 305-242-7700) and the Royal Palm Visitor Center (same ☎) are both off Hwy 9336 just inside the eastern border of the park, about 20 miles from Florida City. For advance tourist information, write them at Information, Everglades National Park, 40001 State Rd 9336, Homestead, FL 33034-6733.

The Gulf Coast Visitor Center (☎ 941-695-3311), on Hwy 29 in Everglades City (see Around the Everglades, below), is the northwesternmost ranger station, and provides access to the 10,000 Islands area.

The Shark Valley Visitor Center (☎ 305-221-8455) is just off the Tamiami Trail (US Hwy 41).

The Flamingo Visitor Center (☎ 941-695-3094) is in Flamingo, at the park's southern coast.

Planning
See the Outdoor Activities chapter for gear and packing tips. For all trips, you can work out specific itineraries with the assistance of the rangers, and the *Backcountry Trip Planner* guide to the park published by the NPS. Dennis Kalma's *Boat & Canoe Camping in the Everglades Backcountry and Ten Thousand Island Region* (Florida Flair Books, Miami) is an excellent guide to trails.

For nature information and identification, the rangers themselves use *Florida's Fabulous Birds* by W Williams, *Florida's Fabulous Reptiles & Amphibians*, the National Geographic's *Field Guide to Birds of North America*, and *Peterson Field Guide to the Birds* by Roger Tory Peterson.

The Gulf Coast Ranger Station sells the charts you'll need while canoeing in the 10,000 Islands (National Oceanic & Atmospheric Administration's *Coast & Geodetic Survey*). Paper charts are $14.86, waterproof (we recommend this) $16.91 including tax. You're looking for Charts No 11430, 11432 and 11433. You can also order these charts directly from the Distribution Division N/CG33, National Ocean Service, 6501 Lafayette Ave, Riverdale, MD 30737.

Regulations
All the resources in the park are protected, including the plants, shells, artifacts and buildings. You can fish, but only with a state fishing license; check with the ranger stations for more information. Free permits, available at the ranger stations, are required for all overnight stays. In areas that do not have toilets, you'll need to dig a hole at least six inches deep to bury waste. Campfires are prohibited except at several beach sites: use dead and down wood only, and build below the high-tide line. Remove all your garbage from the park when you leave.

Dangers & Annoyances
The main dangers you'll encounter will be weather and insects, though bad tides can be a real pain in the butt, not to mention in the blistered hands and sunburned face. See Tide Charts below for information and be

certain you understand how to predict and use the tides to help you.

Weather Thunderstorms and lightning are more common in the summer – but in summer the insects are so bad you won't want to be out here anyway. In emergency weather, rangers will come looking for registered campers. But note that under ordinary circumstances, unless rangers receive a call from someone saying you're missing, they will not search for campers. If you're camping, have a friend or family member ready to contact rangers if you do not report back by a certain day.

Biting Insects Mosquitoes are about half of the insect problem – and in summer the Everglades would appear to be the world's central mosquito-manufacturing facility. The other half is made up handily at dawn and dusk by the insidious no-see-ums: tiny (almost invisible) yet ferocious and really god-awful biting insects. Avon Skin So Soft or REI Jungle Juice are key equipment. But note that the insect problem in the dry season isn't so bad. Information on mosquito levels during the summer is available at ☎ 305-242-7700.

Alligators & Crocodiles While alligators are common in the park, they're not very common in the area of the 10,000 Islands, as they tend to avoid salt water. If you do see an alligator, it probably won't bother you, unless you do something overtly threatening or try and angle your boat between it and its young. If you hear an alligator making a loud hissing sound, get the hell out of Dodge – that's a call to other alligators when a young gator is in danger. Finally, never, ever, *ever* feed an alligator – it's stupid, selfish and illegal. See the Flora & Fauna section in the Facts about Florida chapter for more information.

Snakes There are four types of poisonous snakes in the Everglades: diamondback rattlesnake *(Crotalus adamanteus)*, pigmy rattlesnake *(Sistrurus miliarius)*, cottonmouth or water moccasin *(Agkistrodon*

piscivorus conanti) which swim along the surface of water, and the hugely colorful coral snake *(Micrurus fulvius)*. Wear long, thick socks and lace up boots and keep the hell away from them.

Critters Less dangerous but very annoying are raccoons and rats who will tear through anything less than a solid and sealed plastic cooler to get to your food. Keep your food and food garbage inside the sealed cooler, and your water bottles sealed and inside your tent (open water can be smelled through your tent and the last thing you want at 4 am is a raccoon slashing through your sleeping bag in search of a sip).

Canoeing & Kayaking

Rental There are rental outfits at Everglades City and Flamingo. In Everglades City, we highly recommend North American Canoe Tours (NACT; 941-695-3299) at the Ivey House Hotel, 107 Camilla St (see Everglades City, below), which rents out first-rate canoes for $20 for the first day, $18 each additional day or $16 for eight hours. Sea Lion kayaks are $35 a day; Sea Lions with rudders and upgraded paddles (which make going against the current a whole lot easier) are $45 a day.

NACT has a representative office at Glades Haven Recreational Resort, 800 SE Copeland Ave, right across the street from the Gulf Coast Ranger Station. Note that NACT and the Ivey House close from May 1 to October 31, during which time that may be reached at their Connecticut office, ☎ 860-739-0791.

A good deal they have is a shuttle service for those willing to make the five-day trip between the Gulf Coast and Flamingo Ranger Stations: for a $140 fee NACT will drive your car to Flamingo; when you arrive, turn in the canoe or kayak to the dockmaster, who will give you the keys to your car, and you can drive away. It is possible to work out a shuttle schedule for a Flamingo to Everglades City trip, but you'll need to negotiate that with NACT.

Just south of Glades Haven, Huron Kayak Adventures (☎ 941-695-3666) rents canoes for $15 for eight hours or $20 for 24-hours, and sea kayaks for $20 for eight hours, $35 for the day.

Everglades National Park Boat Tours (☎ 941-695-2591) in the Gulf Coast Visitor Center, is the most expensive for overnight canoe rentals: it's $18 from 8.30 am to 5 pm or $36 for an overnight rental. They'll take your car to Flamingo for $150.

At the Flamingo Lodge Marina & Outpost Resort (☎ 941-695-3101, 800-600-3813) TW Recreational Services rents canoes for $22/27/30 for four hours/eight hours/overnight. Bicycles rent for $2.75 an hour, and $7.75/13/16. They also rent kayaks – a single is $25 for four hours, $40 for eight; a double is $35/50, no overnights on kayaks.

Tide Charts Tide charts are as important to your journey as your ability to paddle – or lack thereof. They can be the difference between a fun trip and a nightmare of cross-country-in-the-station-wagon-with-the-family proportions. Get National Oceanic & Atmospheric Administration (NOAA) charts from the ranger stations, at marinas, or in local newspapers.

Tide charts list the date, the time and the height of low and high tide, but you'll need to calculate the correct tides for your location, as tide charts are set to a fixed point, such as Everglades City: for the most obvious example (the ones printed on the ranger station charts), when it's high tide at Everglades City, you'll need to:

add ½-hour at Sweetwater and Sunday Bay
add 1½ hours at Plate Creek
subtract one hour at the Watson Place
subtract 1½ Hours at Tiger and Pavilion Keys
subtract two hours at South Lostman's

Camping

Three types of campsites are available at no cost with a reservation from the Gulf Coast Ranger Station (☎ 941-695-3311): **beach sites**, on coastal shell beaches and in the 10,000 Islands; **ground sites**, along the interior bays and rivers, which are basically mounds of dirt built up above the mangroves; and **chickees**, wooden platforms built above water on which you can pitch a free-standing (no spikes) tent.

Chickees, which have toilets, are the most civilized of the three, and certainly are unique: there's such serenity inherent in sleeping on what feels like a raft levitating above the water in the middle of a natural wonder. We found the beach sites to be most comfortable, though in all three biting insects like mosquitoes and no-see-ums are rife in summer, though less so in winter. The ground sites tend to be the most bug-infested of all.

There is an additional Everglades campsite at Chekika, at the western end of Richmond Drive (SW 168th St), accessed through Krome Ave about 20 miles south of the Tamiami Trail.

There are campsites along the Tamiami Trail (US Hwy 41); see Big Cypress National Preserve, later in this chapter, which manages those sites, for more information.

10,000 ISLANDS

We think that the finest way to experience the serenity and unique beauty – which is somehow desolate yet lush, tropical yet foreboding – of the Everglades is by canoeing or kayaking through the excellent network of waterways that skirt the northwest portion of the park.

The 10,000 Islands are made up of a lot (but not really 10,000) of tiny islands and mangrove swamp that hug the point of the southwesternmost border of Florida's peninsula. On the habitable islands, the NPS allows free camping. These islands offer some amazing opportunities to enjoy the Everglades on an intimate basis.

Most of the islands are fringed by narrow beaches with sugar-white sand, though note that in most of the area, the water is brackish, not clear, and very shallow. It's not Tahiti, but it is a fascinating area. The best part is that you can get your own island for up to a week for nothing. That's right, free.

The **Wilderness Waterway**, a 99-mile path between Everglades City and Flamingo, is the longest canoe trail in the area; there are shorter canoe trails near Flamingo.

Near Everglades City at the park's northwest corner, you can take a downstream trip on the **Turner River** alone or with a group, and make it either an easy with-the-current drift to Chokoloskee Island, or add a bit of a challenge at the end and go upstream in the boating canal to the Gulf Coast Ranger Station. You can also canoe around the 10,000 Islands for any period of time you wish, and we highly recommend it!

Canoe & Kayak Itineraries

Note that despite what it says on Everglades National Park maps, Comer Key is permanently closed – it washed away in 1995. Getting around in the 10,000 Islands is pretty straightforward if you religiously adhere to NOAA tide charts, and rangers will help you develop an itinerary based on what you'd most like to see. For all these journeys, it is absolutely imperative that you have a nautical chart and a tide chart. Going against the tides is the fastest way to make it a miserable trip.

For an easy day of paddling around the islands, just get a boat and cross the bay from the Gulf Coast Ranger Station and paddle out and around the mangroves, to Sandfly Island or on the Chokoloskee Bay Loop.

For an easy overnight, or two-night trip, you'll be wanting the islands closest in to the ranger station: Tiger, Picnic, Rabbit, New Turkey, Turkey and Hog Keys, all with beach campsites.

For a nice few days (three to four) of canoeing, head south from the Gulf Coast Ranger Station, past Chokoloskee and up the Lopez River, north near Sunday Bay, then southeast to Sweetwater Bay, where you spend the night at the chickee there; the next morning head out towards the Watson Place and southwest to Pavilion Key for a second overnight at the beach campsite; then north to Rabbit Key for a final night on the beach; in the morning, head back north to the Gulf Coast Ranger Station.

There are hundreds of other combinations; see the rangers for more recommendations.

Organized Tours

Rangers lead free 5½-hour **canoe trips** through the overhanging mangrove tunnels along the Turner River on many Saturdays during the dry season. They leave the Gulf Coast Ranger Station at 9 am. David Har-

raden's NACT (see Canoe Rentals above) is the best outfit in the whole park for regular guided tours. For $40 per person, you can get a guided canoe trip down the Turner River, including an excellent lunch. The tours start daily at 9 am and return at 3 pm. You can also get day tours from NACT within the 10,000 Islands for about the same price.

For longer trips, though, it gets expensive: a four-day, three-night camping journey through the islands is $450 per person.

The simplest of all are **boat tours** from Everglades National Park Boat Tours (☎ 813-695-2591, 800-445-7724). Tours on the large pleasure boats leave from the dock in front of the Gulf Coast Ranger Station at Everglades City from December 20 to April 15 aboard the *Panther I* (at 9 and 11 am and 1 and 3 pm); *Panther II* (10 am, noon, 1.30 and 3.30 pm); *Manatee I* (9.30 and 11.30 am and 1.30 and 3.30 pm) and *Manatee II* (10.30 am, 12.30 and 2.30 pm, and a special two-hour sunset tour at 5 pm in December and early January). From April 15 to December 20, boats leave the dock every half hour between 9.30 am and 5 pm. All tours (except the special sunset tour) are 1¾ hours through the 10,000 Islands. The cost for all tours is $11.66 for adults, $5.83 for children aged six to 12 including tax. Their slightly longer Mangrove Wilderness tour costs $14.84/7.42.

10,000 Islands Aero Tours (☎ 941-695-3296) in Everglades City runs **air tours** of the entire area from the tiny Everglades Airport, just west of Hwy 29, south of the traffic circle at the end of Airport Rd in Everglades City, but they weren't there when we visited and we haven't been able to contact them by phone. We know they're there: we saw the office and a plane. Try your luck when you're here.

Getting There & Away

From the Tamiami Trail, turn south on Hwy 29; go until you're forced to turn right, which will bring you to the traffic circle. Turn left and follow the road and it will bring you straight to the Gulf Coast Ranger Station. The whole trip from Miami takes a little less than two hours on the Tamiami Trail, 3½ to four if you add a side trip on Loop Rd.

Flora & Fauna of the Everglades

CHEYENNE ROUSE

Baldcypress Tree

FLORIDA DEPT OF COMMERCE

Sawgrass can grow up to 10 feet tall.

JAN BUTCHOFSKY-HOUSER

Airboat excursion

FLORIDA DEPT OF COMMERCE

The Everglades' 'river of grass' grows over the largest deposit of organic soil on the planet.

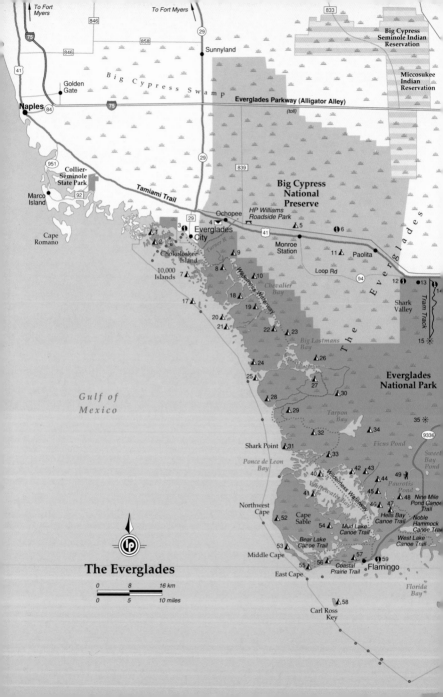

The Everglades

0   8   16 km

0   5   10 miles

Bouys •
Park Boundary —

CAMPGROUNDS
1 Tiger Key
2 Picnic Key
5 Monument Lake
7 Rabbit Key
8 Lopez River
9 Sunday Bay Chickee
10 Sweetwater Bay Chickee
11 Midway
16 Chekika
17 Pavilion Key
18 The Watson Place
19 Darwin's Place
20 Mormon Key
21 New Turkey Key
   & Turkey Key
22 Plate Creek Bay Chickee
23 Lostmans Five Bay
24 Hog Key
25 South Lostmans
26 Willy Willy
27 Roger's River Bay Chickee
28 Highland Beach
29 Broad River
30 Camp Lonesome
31 Graveyard Creek
32 Harney River Chickee
33 Shark River Chickee
34 Cane Patch
38 Long Pine Key
40 Oyster Bay Chickee
41 Joe River Chickee
42 Watson River Chickee
43 North River Chickee
44 Robert's River Chickee
45 Lane Bay Chickee
46 Hells Bay Chickee
47 Lard Can
48 Pearl Bay Chickee
50 Old Ingraham
51 Ernest Coe
52 Northwest Cape
53 Middle Cape
54 South Joe River Chickee
55 East Cape
56 Clubhouse Beach
57 Eco Pond
58 Carl Ross Key
60 Little Rabbit Key
61 North Nest Key

OTHER
3 Gulf Coast Visitor Center
4 Ochopee Post Office
6 Big Cypress National
   Preserve Visitor Center
12 Tamiami Ranger Station
13 Miccosukee Cultural Center
14 Shark Valley Visitor Center
   & Trails
15 Shark Valley
   Observation Tower
35 Pay-hay-okee Overlook
36 Pinelands Trailhead
37 Main Visitor Center
39 Royal Palm Visitor Center
49 Mahogony Hammock
   Trailhead
59 Flamingo Visitor Center

Roseate spoonbills

Pelican

Wood stork

Wood stork

Anhinga

Immature white ibis

Blue heron

Wading birds such as herons, egrets, ibis (above) and wood storks have long legs and necks and uniquely adapted bills for plucking fish and crustaceans out of the water. Anhingas (above left), which are not waders, frequently swim with just their head and neck out of the water.

Visitors to the Everglades often confuse alligators and crocodiles. If you must know for sure, get close enough to check for a fourth exposed tooth (crocodiles only).

Look but don't feed.

Baby alligators clambering on a turtle shell

Alligator

Crocodile

NATIONAL PARK SERVICE/HB MULLER

Mangrove water snake

NATIONAL PARK SERVICE

Water moccasin, also called a cottonmouth

NATIONAL PARK SERVICE/TAYLOR

Five-line skink

NATIONAL PARK SERVICE

The rat snake (above) poses no threat, but four types of venomous snakes haunt the Everglades: the diamondback rattlesnake, pygmy rattlesnake, water moccasin and the coral snake.

Black mangrove

Strangler fig

The red mangroves (above) are the advance armies in the life cycle of a mangrove hammock: their sturdy, salt-filtering roots catch sediment in the flowing water and cause it to build up into banks of soil suitable to less hearty trees, like the black mangrove (above left).

SHARK VALLEY

At the northern border of the park, accessed just off the Tamiami Trail (US Hwy 41), the Shark Valley Visitor Center (☎ 305-221-8455) is a very popular way to get yourself easily and painlessly immersed in the middle of the Everglades prairie. You can walk or bike the 17-mile trail between the entrance and the 50-foot-high Shark Valley Observation Tower, which gives a pretty spectacular overview of the park. You will see a lot of flora and fauna – the last time we went, there was a 10-foot alligator in the main parking lot, lazily sunning himself with his mouth wide open. We gave him a wide berth.

Bicycle rentals (they're one-speeds but the ground is pretty flat) are available from the cash desk in the entrance to the park; the cost is $3.25 per hour per bike including tax, or you can take the Shark Valley Tram Tour, led by rangers or 'experienced tram drivers' – whatever they are – which make the journey over the paved 15-mile tram road in two hours. The cost is $8 for adults, $7.20 for seniors over 62 and $4 for children under 12. There's also a park entry fee of $4 per carload or $2 for pedestrians.

The trams leave every hour on the hour between 9 am and 4 pm in high season, and at 9.30 and 11 am and 1 and 3 pm in low season. Reservations are recommended in high season.

Getting There & Away

There's no public transportation to this point. Driving, it's about 18 miles from the western border of the city of Miami, on the south side of the Tamiami Trail.

MAIN VISITOR CENTER

The Main Visitor Center (☎ 305-242-7700) for Everglades National Park is just southwest of Homestead, a 30-minute drive from downtown Miami. This is the fastest and easiest way to see the Everglades, or at least some of it, and the visitors center is packed with excellent information on everything in the park.

Very close to the entrance, the Royal Palm Visitor Center (same ☎) is the entry-way to the three-quarter-mile **Gumbo-Limbo Trail** with gumbo-limbo and royal palm trees, orchids and lush vegetation, and the **Anhinga Trail** named for the odd anhinga birds (also called the snake bird, for the way it swims with its long neck and head above water), a half-mile route on which you'll probably run into alligators, turtles, waterfowl, lizards, snakes and, well, be prepared for anything.

You can drive the 30-odd-mile main road that runs between the entrance and Flamingo; along the way are walking trails including: the Pinelands, a half-mile trail through Dade County pine forest – look for exposed limestone bedrock; **Pa-hay-okee Overlook**, a very short (quarter-mile) boardwalk trail with an observation tower; Mahogany Hammock, a half-mile boardwalk that leads into totally lush and overgrown vegetation; and West Lake Trail, a half mile through red, white, buttonwood and black mangroves. The longest series of trails is at Long Pine Key, the starting point of a 15-mile series of walking trails where you may see many species indigenous to the Everglades. You may even get a chance, if you're very quiet and patient, to see a Florida panther.

The official mammal of Florida, Florida panthers are one of the most threatened species in the country.

Admission to the park at this entrance is $5 per carload, or $3 for pedestrians. The main gate is open 24 hours, the Main Visitor Center from 8 am to 4.30 pm daily, Royal Palm Visitor Center from 8 am to 4.15 pm daily. Camping is $8 for tent sites and $10 for RVs and camper vans.

Getting There & Away

The only way to do this by public transport is idiotic: you can take Metrorail from Miami to Dadeland North ($1.25), then Bus No 1 to the Cutler Ridge Mall ($1.25) and then No 35 or No 70 to Florida City (25¢ transfer). The last public bus from Florida City that will allow you to make your connection at Cutler Ridge Mall is No 35 at 9.45 pm; the last No 1 is at 10.40 pm; Metrorail runs until midnight.

Greyhound serves Florida City three times a day (1½ hours), tickets are $8/16. The last Greyhound out of Florida City leaves at 8.25 pm. But once you're in Florida City, you still have to get a taxi to the park, for at least $10 but up to as much as $20.

By car, which, face it, is how you have to get here, take Florida's Turnpike Extension (toll) or US Hwy 1 to Florida City and take Hwy 9336 to the entrance of the park.

FLAMINGO

Flamingo, at the southernmost tip of the mainland of Everglades National Park is more developed than the 10,000 Islands, and the least authentic Everglades experience you can get; it's really geared to holidaymakers, with sightseeing and bay cruises. There are nature and bike paths, picnic tables, a bar, tourist trap . . . er . . . gift shops, tram tours, etc, as well as short canoe trails, which include West Lake, a one-way 7½-mile path; Nine Mile Pond, a 5½-mile circuit; Hells Bay, also a 5½-mile circuit; Mud Lake, a 5.8-mile loop and Bear Lake, two miles one way. Entry to Flamingo is through the Main Visitor Center road, Hwy 9336.

And in Flamingo, everything's more expensive, including canoe rentals (see Canoeing & Kayaking, above).

Places to Stay

You can stay in the *Flamingo Lodge* (☎ 941-695-3094, 800-600-3813) at the southernmost point in Flamingo for $72 in low season (May to October), $82 in fringe seasons (October to December and April to May) and $97 in high season. Rooms are all identical, and have two double beds, TV and air-conditioning. You can camp at the campground here, run by the Flamingo Visitor Center (☎ 941-695-3101,); sites with no hookups are $8 for tents, $10 for RVs.

Houseboats Flamingo Lodge rents two types of houseboats which, if you're with five other people, can work out to be cheaper than you'd think: even with the top luxury model, it would work out to $47 per person per night. The boats, luxury 37-foot Gibson Sport Series and the less luxurious and boxy, but somewhat larger, 40-foot pontoon boats, all include a refrigerator/freezer, stoves and ovens, bathrooms with showers, propane, linen, pots and pans and flatware, life-vests and charts. The Gibsons are air-conditioned and have diesel electric generators; the pontoon boats do not.

The pontoon boats, which sleep six comfortably and eight not so comfortably, cost $295.63 for one night and $365.50 for two nights in summer; in winter there is a two-night minimum, and it costs $510.62.

The Gibsons have a two-night minimum year round, and cost $564.38 in summer, $618.13 in winter. Expect to pay an extra $40 a day in fuel, and there's a $500 damage/fuel deposit required for all boats (cash or credit card). You don't need a special license; if you've never driven a boat before, cap'n, they'll give you a half-hour orientation course and set you free on the high seas with a $270,000 piece of maritime transport.

Getting There & Away

From the Main Visitor Center, follow Hwy 9336 to the bitter end: welcome to Flamingo.

Around the Everglades

ALONG THE TAMIAMI TRAIL

The Tamiami Trail, which blazes the way between Miami and Tampa, is for the most part straight as a die through monotonous swampland. But there are several points of interest along the way.

Miccosukee Cultural Center

This is a collection of tourist shops and pointless, inhumane alligator wrestling displays ($5) tended by morose and insolent staff. Expensive gasoline at the filling station, and the gentleman running the restaurant – its air redolent with the scent of elderly frying oil – wouldn't let us write down prices in our notebooks: 'You want to buy something, fine, otherwise get out,' he said from behind his sunglasses. Nothing like that down home Southern hospitality to gear up the ol' taste buds for deep fried 'gator' nuggets, eh? Our advice: fill up the tank and grab a bite before you get here.

Picnic Areas

There are three rest stops with picnic areas along the Trail; at the Oasis Visitor Center (see Big Cypress National Preserve, below), Kirby Sorter Roadside Park, with tables, grills and a small interpretive trail; and HP Williams Roadside Park, with picnic tables, just east of the entrance to the Turner River Rd.

Ochopee

Driving through the tiny hamlet of Ochopee (population about 115)...no...wait... turn around, you've missed it. That's right, kids, break out the cameras: Ochopee's claim to fame is the USA's smallest official post office! In a former tool shed, a charming and friendly female postal worker patiently poses for snapshots and for the cost of a stamp, you can send a postcard or letter from here, though be certain that she cancels the stamp nicely – some of ours were as smudged as a Russian visa stamp. The office is in the little shack on the south side of the Tamiami Trail.

BIG CYPRESS NATIONAL PRESERVE

Big Cypress is a 1139-sq-mile federally protected area that came about as a compromise between environmentalists, cattle ranchers and oil and gas explorers as a method of protecting the land while allowing pre-existing development to proceed to a certain extent. The area is a major player in the Everglades' ecosystem; the rains which flood the prairies and wetlands here slowly filter down through the 'Glades.

The preserve comprises about 45% of the total area of the cypress swamp which, by the way, is not a swamp at all but a group of mangrove islands, hardwood hammocks, islands of slash pine, prairie and marshes. It is not pristine – there is rutting, growth of new and abnormal vegetation and shifts in elevation.

The preserve's name comes from the sheer acreage – not the height – of the dwarf pond cypress trees that fill the area. The great bald cypress trees are nearly gone from the area, after lumber and other industry took its toll before the preserve's establishment. Animals in the preserve include alligators, snakes, wading birds including white ibis, wood stork, tri-color heron and several types of egret, and a variety of other animals including the Florida panther (rarely), wild turkey and red cockaded woodpecker.

Under the park's charter, the retention of ownership of private lands bought before the preserve's establishment was permitted, as are off-road-vehicle activity, hunting and fishing, oil and gas exploration and cattle grazing. The trick of it all is to maintain a threshold of activity low enough to protect the region's flora and fauna yet high enough to accommodate the nature-bashing yahoos with their guns and swamp buggies.

The preserve is also the southern terminus of the Florida National Scenic Trail (FNST, see the Outdoor Activities chapter).

THE EVERGLADES

Information

The main visitors center is the Oasis Visitor Center (☎ 941-695-4111) about 19 miles west of Shark Valley along the Tamiami Trail. The Big Cypress National Preserve Headquarters (☎ 941-695-2000) – which is not the same thing as the visitor center – is just east of Ochopee. Write for advance information to Big Cypress National Preserve, HCR 61, Box 11, Ochopee, FL 33943.

Hiking

There are 31 miles of the FNST, maintained by the Florida Trail Association within the Big Cypress National Preserve. The southern terminus is just north of Loop Rd, accessed by car from either the Monroe or Tamiami Ranger Stations. The trail runs 8.3 miles north to the Tamiami Trail, passing right by the Oasis Visitor Center before continuing north. There are two primitive campsites, with wells but nothing else, along the trail. Note that off-road vehicles are permitted to cross, but not operate on, the FNST – use caution. See the Outdoor Activities chapter for more information on the FNST.

For the less adventurous, there's the short Tree Snail Hammock Nature Trail, opposite Loop Road Environmental Education Center (which is closed to the public) off Loop Rd.

But for the totally rad, those who relish the thought of slogging through snake- and alligator-infested total backwater areas, you'll need permission from the Cypress Chief Ranger's office (☎ 941-242-7730). You'll need to go in for an interview, and if the ranger decides you know what's what and where not to put your foot, you'll get a backcountry permit.

Driving

The two main trails for on-road vehicles are Loop Rd, a potholed dirt road that runs between the Monroe and Tamiami Ranger Stations, and Turner River Rd, which shoots straight as an arrow north from the Tamiami Trail just west of the HP Williams Roadside Park. There are excellent wildlife viewing opportunities along the entire stretch of the road, especially in the Turner River Canal that runs along the east side of it. This leads to the northern area of the preserve where off-road vehicles are permitted to rut and root their way through the land.

Camping

Aside from the two sites on the FNST, there are a total of seven campgrounds on the preserve. With the exception of Dona Drive Campsite at the western end of the preserve, the campsites are totally primitive: bring your own water and food. See the camping section in the Everglades section above for how to pack food and water. Dona Drive has a dump station with drinking water, picnic tables and grills and, at holiday times, chemical toilets (how festive). Dona Drive costs $4 a night; other campsites in the preserve – Bear Island, Midway, Monument Lake, Loop Rd, Mitchell's Landing and Pinecrest are

---

Air Boats & Swamp Buggies

Air boats are flat-bottomed boats that use powerful fans to propel themselves in the water. While they are capable of traveling in very shallow water, they are very loud, and their environmental impact has not been determined. One thing is clear: while air boats in the hands of responsible operators, like naturalists and geologists, have little impact, irresponsible operators can cause lots of direct and collateral damage to the surrounding wildlife.

Swamp buggies are enormous balloon-tired vehicles that can go through swamps. They definitely cause rutting and damage wildlife.

You'll be offered air boat and swamp buggy rides at stands all along US Hwy 41. Please assess the motive behind the operator's existence before just getting on a 'nature' tour: you may be helping to disturb the Everglades' delicate balance. ■

free, and you needn't register. Note that Mitchell's Landing, Loop Rd and Pinecrest only accommodate tents, not RVs.

Getting There & Away

Again, there's no public transport to speak of. By car from either the east or the west, take the Tamiami Trail (Hwy 41); the Oasis Visitor Center is about halfway between Everglades City and Shark Valley.

EVERGLADES CITY

• *pop 400 in summer, 1500 in winter*
☎ *941*

Everglades City is a tiny little town that survives from the trade of fishermen who pull into the marina and live in RVs at the campground, and people coming through to visit the Everglades. It's a perfectly pleasant little town, in a fisherman's paradise kind of way; it's a sensible place to spend a night to get an early start on canoe trips in the 10,000 Islands. The Gulf Coast Ranger Station is at the southern end of town.

Orientation & Information

Hwy 29 runs south and through the city. At the intersection of the Tamiami Trail and Hwy 29 there's the Carnestown Welcome Station, a source of pamphlets and brochures, and at the traffic circle in downtown Everglades City, in the beautiful little City Hall Building is the Everglades City Chamber of Commerce (☎ 695-3941), which has very primitive maps of the city. The Gulf Coast Ranger Station (☎ 695-3311) has stacks and piles of information on the 10,000 Islands and the Everglades. Also in the city hall building is the city library.

Wash clothes at the coin laundry across the street from City Hall next to the Right Choice (only choice, actually) Supermarket.

Places to Stay & Eat

Glades Haven (☎ 695-3954), the commercial campground at 800 SE Copeland Ave (Hwy 29) across the street from the Gulf Coast Ranger Station, is geared more to RVs than to tents but tents are welcome. Tent sites are $12.50 in summer, $15 in winter, RV sites are $15/22, all including

water, sewer and electric. There are hot showers in the bathrooms.

The Ivey House (☎ 695-3299, fax 941-695-4155) at 107 Camellia St at the northern end of town, behind the Circle K convenience store and the post office, is a lovely, if a bit institutional-feeling, place to stay for the service and the food. Formerly a recreation hall for laborers working on the Tamiami Trail, the family-run place offers good meals (there's not a deep fryer in sight) and the rooms, while simple (no TV or telephone, shared bathrooms) are comfortable and clean and cost $40 from November 1 to December 14 and from March 16 to April 30, $50 from December 15 to March 15, including breakfast and use of the bicycles on a first-come, first-served basis. (They rent bikes for $3 a day to non-guests.) Dinner – for guests and non-guests – is $10. These folks also run NACT, which operates some of the best nature trips around; see The Everglades' 10,000 Islands section above for more information. The hotel and NACT are closed from May 1 to October 31.

The *Rod & Gun Club Lodge* (☎ 695-2101) at 200 Riverside Drive, west of Hwy 29, is a swank place, built as a hunting lodge by Barron Collier (See Collier Seminole State Park, below) in the 1920s as a place to relax after watching people dig his Tamiami Trail. It's open as a guesthouse now, with rooms at $50 in summer, $65 to 80 in winter. Their restaurant has seafood averages $8 at lunch, $15 at dinner, steaks and other meat dishes average $17 to 18.

The *Captain's Table* (☎ 9695-4211, 800-741-6430) at the right jig in Hwy 29 east of the downtown traffic circle has surprisingly clean and cheerful rooms and very nice staff; rooms run from $39.50 to 55 in summer, $70 to 90 in winter, and include a 10% off coupon to the *Captain's Table Restaurant* (☎ 695-2727), no relation to the hotel, a very Social-Realist-looking restaurant next door that does good, but expensive, seafood dishes. At lunch, from 11 am to 5 pm, sandwiches run from $4.75 to 7.95 and fried seafood baskets from $5.95 to 8.95; at dinner, broiled, blackened, grilled or fried seafood dishes run from shrimp scampi at $13.95 to bay scallops, Everglades alligator or snapper for $14.95, and their Captain's platter of fried shrimp, scallops, oysters, clam, grouper, conch fritters, crab cake and alligator is $22.95.

Cheaper fare can be had at *Burger Express* (☎ 695-4210) on Hwy 29 next to the BP gas station with burgers from $1.39 to $3.39, fish and barbecue pork sandwiches and other offerings for a little more. They do fried chicken and country fried steak at night for $4.95, with mashed potatoes and gravy, veggies and a roll.

At *Cheryl's Deli* (☎ 695-2746) at Glades Haven they make good sandwiches for $3.79, including lots o' toppings, but it's an extra 30¢ for cheese or hot peppers. If you ask for a sandwich at breakfast time it takes forever: 'You ordered an unorthodox breakfast,' we were chided.

Almost everything on the menu at *Susie's Station* (☎ 695-2002) is fried: chicken strips are $5.95, fried shrimp with French fries is $8.95, but the atmosphere is pleasant enough. It's on the west side of the traffic circle. And speaking of fried, maybe it was a bad night, but we had one of the worst meals we've ever had in the state at the *Oar House*.

For groceries – especially if you're going camping for more than a day and need supplies – it's best to stock up before you come, as the Right Choice Supermarket just east of the traffic circle has some stuff, but it's about 25% more expensive than any Publix.

Getting There & Away

From the Tamiami Trail, turn south on Hwy 29; go until you're forced to turn right (you'll see the Captain's Table Hotel and Restaurant in front of you), which will bring you to the traffic circle. From there, turn left and follow the road and it will bring you straight to the Gulf Coast Ranger Station. The whole trip from Miami takes a little less than two hours on the Tamiami Trail, 3½ to four if you add a side trip on Loop Rd.

COLLIER SEMINOLE STATE PARK

Perhaps the only memorial that celebrates man's conquering of the Everglades outside a sugar plant's offices, this state park and wilderness preserve (☎ 941-394-3397) is named after Barron Gift Collier, one of the main developers of the Tamiami Trail. You can see the Bay City Walking Dredge that was used to dig the muck away from the limestone base of the highway in the 1920s on permanent display just past the entrance on the right hand side of the road.

The preserve is a 4070-acre section of the park where fresh and salt water meet, and the area is made up of red, black and white mangrove and buttonwood. Inside the reserve, you'll see manatee (especially in winter), white ibis, snowy egrets, alligators, over 40 species of trees, three species of lizard – the five-lined skink, the brown anole and the chameleon-like Carolina anole.

There's a 13-mile canoe trail along the Blackwater River; rent canoes from the concession stand at the marina, just south of the entrance station: they cost $3 an hour, or $15.90 for 24 hours. There are ranger-led canoe trips at 9 am on Sundays. You can also canoe, with reservations, down to the primitive campsites at Grocery Place (free) or pay for developed camping in one of two sites, both with full bathrooms and water and electric hookups within the state park (not the preserve) section. The cost is $14.17/8.72 with/without electricity in the summer, $16.29/ 10.84 in the winter.

There's a 6½-mile hiking trail through the reserve that winds through pine flatwood and cypress swamp, and an interpretive center near the main campsites. There are campfire programs on Saturday nights at the campfire ring at the west end of the campsite.

Check the rangers' Mosquito Chart at the entrance.

Admission to the park and preserve is $3.25 per carload or $1 for pedestrians and cyclists. They're open every day of the year from 8 am to sunset. The park entrance is about 15 miles northwest of the intersection of Hwy 29 and the Tamiami Trail.

MARCO ISLAND

- *pop 12,500 in summer, 35,000 in winter*
☎ *941*

The only inhabited island in the 10,000 Islands, Marco Island has a gorgeous Gulf coast beach, but it's highly developed by resorts, and not really a budget traveler's destination. Nonetheless, it's becoming hugely popular with overseas visitors – especially English and Germans, and if you have the dosh and like resort life it's a pretty awesome place to kick back on a dazzling white sand beach and have a nice rest.

Orientation & Information

The island is at the very southwestern end of the state. San Marco Drive cuts straight west to Collier Blvd, which shoots up the Gulf Coast and becomes Hwy 951, crossing East Marco Bay and reconnecting with the Tamiami Trail. The main resorts – the Hilton, Radisson and Marriott – are at the southwestern end of the island on S Collier Blvd.

Get tourist information and excellent free maps at the Marco Island Convention & Visitors Bureau/Chamber of Commerce (☎ 394-7549, 800-788-6272) at 1102 N Collier Blvd. Wash clothes at Cathy's Laundry of Marco (☎ 642-6635) at 277 N Collier Blvd.

Beaches

There are two official public beaches, Marco South, at the southern end of S Collier Blvd before it cuts east, and Tigertail Beach, the more developed of the two. At Tigertail, about three-quarters of the way up the western side of the island, there are public toilets and showers and a snack bar.

Organized Tours

The Marco Island Trolley (☎ 394-1600) tootles around the island on several loops from 10 am to 5 pm every day of the year. The fare is $10 and you can get on and off as often as you'd like. To use it as an orientation tour, just stay on for one complete loop, about 1½ hours, with narration.

Places to Stay

There's one place to camp, and that's with the friendly folks at *Mar-Good RV Park* (☎ 394-6383), where tent sites are $15 in summer and $20 in winter. The site has bathrooms with hot showers, a convenience store and a tiki bar. It's at 321 Pear Tree Ave in Goodland; take San Marco Drive to Goodland Drive, a right turn just before the Goodland Bridge back to the Tamiami Trail, down to Goodland Drive West, and left on Pear Tree Ave.

The other options are resorts, of which we'll cover the big three, and condo rentals, which we'll leave in the capable hands of the chamber of commerce. They will send you a brochure entitled *Marco Island & the Everglades*, with listings of 32 (count 'em!) realtors, all of whom we're just certain would be happy to help.

The three resorts are all enormous places that are complete holiday destinations in and of themselves, with health clubs, swimming pools, great beach access with cabanas and of course, equipment, wave runner, bicycle and other sports rentals, kids' activities, nightclubs and restaurants – from top end to Pizza Hut and convenience stores. As with any resort, note that these prices are the standard rack rates for those who question nothing except, 'Where do I sign?' – you can always get better deals through a travel agent.

The *Radisson Suites Beach Resort* (☎ 394-4100, 800-333-3333) at 600 S Collier Blvd, the southernmost of the big three, has the best prices and very good services. Though it's not as blow-out swank as the Hilton or the Marriott it's awfully respectable, with friendly and attentive staff, an enormous pool and beach that's every bit as good as the more expensive neighbors to the near north. They run a year-round supersaver deal for $79 a room without breakfast, though this could change at any second and isn't always available; room rates run from $99 in summer, $199 in winter, suites run from $129 to 299 in summer, $199 to 649 in winter. They have several seasons, and many special offers.

Marriott Marco Island Resort (☎ 394-2511, 800-438-4373) at 400 S Collier Blvd has 735 rooms, 16 tennis courts and four swimming pools; room rates range from $119 to 184 in summer, $269 to 365 in winter, suites from $325 to 375 in summer, $550 to 620 in winter, tower suites $360 to 550 in summer, $580 to 840 in winter.

The *Marco Island Hilton Beach Resort* (☎ 394-5000, 800-443-4550) at 560 S Collier Ave is certainly the most expensive, with rooms running from $99 to 199 in summer, $199 to 339 in winter, and suites from $249 to 800 in summer and $339 to 1400 in winter.

Places to Eat

For quick snacks, hit the *Empire Bagel Factory* (☎ 642-4141) at 277 N Collier Ave, next to the laundry, with good bagels and sandwiches.

We were thrilled with the cheap and good food and service at *Taste of Chicago* (☎ 394-1368), a family-run place with great breakfasts. Also, pasta dishes are priced from $6.50 to 8.95, chili is $2.95 (with cheddar cheese and a side of spaghetti $4.95), and on Wednesdays from 11 am to close, beer-batter fish fry, with either grouper or shrimp is served for $8.95 and a combination platter for $10.95 with salad, fries and bread. They're at 297 S Collier Ave.

A good deal is the Sunday brunch at Marriott's *Voyager Restaurant*, from 10 am to 2 pm, with all-you-can-eat everything –

omelets to seafood chowder to pancakes to an ice cream and dessert bar – for $16.95, or $20.95 with champagne.

Vito's Ristorante (☎ 394-7722) at 1079 Bald Eagle Drive is a pricey but well-regarded Italian place with fish dishes from 16.95 to 19.95 and pasta from $10.95 to 14.95.

The *Olde Marco Inn* (☎ 394-3131), 100 Palm St, built as the home for the family of Captain William D Collier (not Barron Gift Collier) was the island's first hotel. It's now open as a restaurant, and every visitor to the island comes here at least once. Appetizers range from gulf shrimp or clams casino at $7.95 to Marco Island stone crab claws or escargot at $8.95. Main courses specialize in seafood: sautéed snapper or grouper is $18.95, and a baked seafood combination of scallops, lobster, shrimp and fish is $22.95. Meat dishes include roast prime rib for $18.95 and filet mignon au poivre verte at $20.95. They also have a huge selection of boozy coffees – Irish to Swiss to Mexican.

Also, the resorts all have at least one restaurant.

Getting There & Away

There's no public transport, so you'll have to drive. It's about 30 miles west of Everglades City, via Hwy 92 off the Tamiami Trail, across the Goodland Bridge over Goodland Bay and up to San Marco Drive. From I-75, take the last Naples exit, then Hwy 951 west to the island.

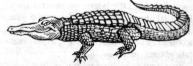

Florida Keys

• *pop Keys: 78,000, Key West: 25,000*
☎ *305*

The string of islands to the south of Miami have held a fascination to visitors since the original Spanish landings in the early 16th century. But what most people head to is Key West. About 90 miles north of Havana, Cuba, Key West is the legendary land of Hemingway, sunset celebrations, Jimmy Buffet's *Margaritaville* and Key lime pie.

While divers will have a good time here, and visitors won't regret the trip to Key West, the Florida Keys' reputation as a romantic, untouched, steamy paradise is quite simply slanderous and libelous bilge.

After Juan Ponce de León first sailed around the Keys in 1513 ('key' is the Anglicized version of the Spanish *cayo*, or island), he was attacked by fierce Calusa Indians at the southwest corner of the state. Today, tourists making their way down the Keys will be attacked with as much vim and vigor by hawkers of everything from T-shirts to sponges, seashells to wind chimes, dive trips to crap of the 'someone-went-to-blank-and-all-I-got-was-this-lousy-blank' caliber. Keys residents are cynical and weary from watching over 5 million tourists a year drive too fast, wreck the coral

and litter. Outside Key West there's not a lot of concentrated 'attractions', and you may have to drive many miles between places of interest. Mostly you'll see billboards and innumerable islands.

But if you gear your expectations realistically, and take the time to unearth what you're after, finding the romantic, quirky and, yes, even sultry side of the Keys is very possible. Key lime pie *is* awesome; Jimmy Buffet *does* serve up a mean margarita; Ernest Hemingway *did* live, work and drink here; and while it's under duress, the coral reef off the Keys is some of the most beautiful and ecologically diverse in the world.

Nowhere else in the world can you wake up in an underwater hotel, snorkel along spectacular reef, see the adorable but endangered Key deer, watch the juggling and acrobatic nonsense at that sunset celebration and finish off the evening with a Hemingway Hammer at Sloppy Joe's Bar. And while conchs – native Key West residents – can be cynical, they're also some of the most fun-loving, quirky, radical reactionary, friendly and downright interesting people you'll come across. Even if they are wearing Naugahyde sandals.

Early settlers in the Keys farmed limes, tamarind and breadfruit. The lower Keys

Key Deer

The tiny Key deer live primarily on Big Pine and No Name Keys. An endangered species, Key deer are classified as a subspecies of white tail deer. Once mainland-dwelling animals, the formation of the Keys stranded them on the islands, and evolutionary changes have resulted in a reduction in their overall size – since winter temperatures are higher here than on the mainland, they no longer require as much body mass to carry them through. Another major evolutionary change has been a reduction in the size of litters, from multiple to single births, to compensate for reduced grazing lands and scarce fresh water.

The biggest threat to the Key deer has been humans, who can't seem to stop feeding them. This has caused Key deer to fearlessly approach humans and, unfortunately, their vehicles. Key deer also have begun to change their natural behavior and travel in herds, which is against their solitary nature, in pursuit of handouts from people.

This lack of fear has lead to massive vehicular deaths – about 65% of which occur along US Hwy 1. In 1995, there were 94 Key deer deaths, of which 66 were positively confirmed to have been caused by deer getting hit by cars. Of the remaining 28 deaths, 15 to 18 are suspected to have been caused by vehicles.

Key deer are generally light to 'dead-leaf' brown with black tails and a white rump. Fawns have white spots on their back and rib area for about the first month, after which they lose the spots. Some full-grown deer have a dark black mask over the eyes and the forehead.

Full grown bucks normally weigh about 75 to 80 pounds, does about 65 pounds. Bucks are from 28 to 32 inches high at the shoulders, does from 24 to 26 inches, and fawns weigh from two to 3½ pounds at birth.

The rut, or mating season, is from September to December and the Key deer's gestation period is 204 days (fawning occurs in April and May).

Slow Down Speed limits are strictly enforced, and while there is no penalty for hitting a Key deer inadvertently, if you're speeding or intentionally trying to hit one, you're in violation of state and federal laws. If you are speeding, fines vary depending on the agency that catches you: state fines begin at $540 (reported to be dropping to $230) and federal fines at $230.

And Don't Feed Them Feeding Key deer is absolutely illegal, and if you're caught, fines can reach $25,000. ■

saw pineapple farming, and over on Big Pine Key locals caught and skinned sharks, salted the hides and prepared them for processing into shagreen leather.

In Key West and Islamorada, the non-farming population found a rather unique way of supporting themselves: they became 'wreckers', salvaging goods from sinking or sunken ships. But these guys weren't pirates – they were federally licensed workers who would scavenge wrecks, bringing the cargo into Key West for auction.

Key West also saw sponging, or diving for natural sponges. Today you can still buy them in Mallory Square for a lot of money, but the main sponging industry moved north to Tarpon Springs, now a horrendous tourist trap in its own right about half an hour north of Clearwater Beach (see the Southwest Florida chapter). But tourism – especially after Flagler extended his FEC Railroad to Key West in the late-19th century (see the History section in the Facts about Florida chapter) – became the Keys' main money-maker and remains such to this day.

ORIENTATION

The keys sprawl from the northeast to the southwest, beginning in the north with Key Largo. They're connected by US Hwy 1, the Overseas Hwy – a combination of highway and causeways built on the foundations and pilings of the FEC Railroad, which was destroyed in 1935. US Hwy 1 is the main road through the Keys, and in many areas the only road.

The keys are made up of hundreds of tiny islands, of which only about 45 are populated. From north to south, populated keys include Key Largo, Plantation Key, Upper Matecumbe Key, Fiesta Key, Long Key, Conch Key, Duck Key, Grassy Key, Key Vaca, Bahia Honda Key, Big Pine Key, No Name Key, Summerland Key, Sugarloaf Key, Boca Chica Key and Key West.

Addresses in the Keys work on a system of mile markers (MM), which are located along the Overseas Hwy: mile 0 is in Key West at the corner of Fleming and White-head Sts, and the final marker, MM 126, is one mile south of Florida City. The markers are small green signs at the side of the road, and sometimes addresses are further pinpointed by a 'bayside' (north) or 'oceanside' (south) appendix. While some businesses will give an exact address (a product of a local street number or Over-seas Hwy address, as in many other Florida cities), most everyone just quotes and refers to an MM.

DIVING

The diving and snorkeling opportunities along the Keys are amazing, ranging from the fantastically colorful fish and coral on the Florida reef to artificial reefs – sunken boats and planes that have been placed off the Florida reef to attract sea life – to actual wrecked ships on the ocean floor. The delicate Florida reef can be damaged

by even touching it; see the Flora & Fauna section in Facts about Florida for more information.

There are dive shops on every Key; we list some that have been recommended to us, but there is such a high level of competition for diving business that you'll have no problem finding out your options once you arrive. The reefs are all about five miles offshore. In general, you can count on an average $50 for a two-tank dive including tanks and weights; expect an extra $20 for BC and regulator. Tank rentals themselves cost about $6 to 7 each. Dive shops will negotiate for lower prices in off-seasons, but it's a seller's market at peak times.

Wrecks & Ships

There are a number of popular shipwrecks and boats sunk as part of an artificial reef program. See the Key West diving section later for what's around that neighborhood. Some of the ships sunk were confiscated drug boats, others include obsolete Coast Guard cutters and commercial vessels. And some of the wrecks include Spanish galleons or their remains. In all cases, any loot that may have been inside has long since been picked clean; doubloons and bags of dope are best sought on dry land.

From south to north, wrecks and ships include the *Thunderbolt* (1986, 115 feet) off Grassy Key; portions of the remains of a Spanish galleon (1733) off Indian Key; the enormous four-decked *Eagle* (1985, 110 feet) on Alligator Reef off Islamorada; and the US Coast Guard cutters *Duane* and *Bibb* (1987, 100 feet and 90 feet – the *Duane* stands upright, the *Bibb* on its side) and the remains of the *Bentwood*, sunk during WWII, all off Key Largo.

NATIONAL MARINE SANCTUARIES

The Key Largo and Looe Key National Marine Sanctuaries were established in 1971 and 1981 to protect sensitive areas within the Keys, but they are actually a compromise between commercial activities and environmental protection. Activities that are permitted within the sanctuaries

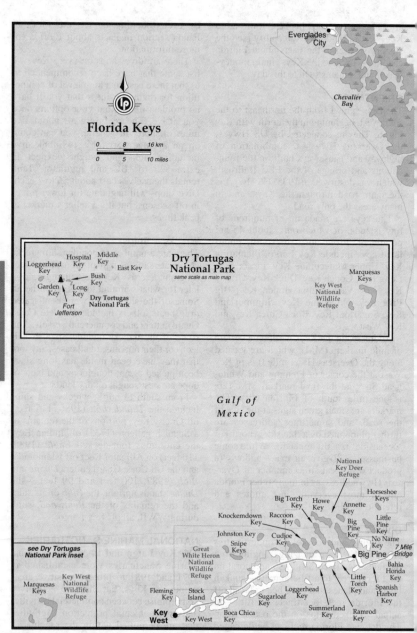

Florida Keys

| 0 | 8 | 16 km |
| 0 | 5 | 10 miles |

Everglades City

Chevalier Bay

Loggerhead Key

Hospital Key

Middle Key

East Key

Garden Key

Bush Key

Long Key

Fort Jefferson

Dry Tortugas National Park

Dry Tortugas National Park
same scale as main map

Key West National Wildlife Refuge

Marquesas Keys

Gulf of Mexico

National Key Deer Refuge

Big Torch Key

Howe Key

Annette Key

Horseshoe Keys

Knockemdown Key

Raccoon Key

Big Pine Key

Little Pine Key

Johnston Key

Cudjoe Key

No Name Key

7 Mile Bridge

Snipe Keys

Great White Heron National Wildlife Refuge

Big Pine

Bahia Honda Key

Little Torch Key

Spanish Harbor Key

see Dry Tortugas National Park inset

Marquesas Keys

Key West National Wildlife Refuge

Fleming Key

Stock Island

Sugarloaf Key

Loggerhead Key

Summerland Key

Ramrod Key

Key West

Key West

Boca Chica Key

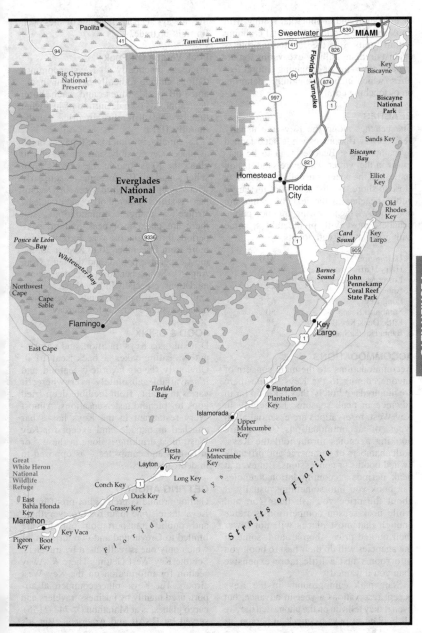

include sport and commercial fishing with hook and line and lobstering and crabbing within limits. But the sanctuary protects against dredging, filling, excavating, building and removing or damaging natural features (which includes standing, anchoring on or touching coral).

BEACHES

The beaches along the Keys are usually very narrow ribbons of white sand lapped by calm waters. Beaches tend to be narrower in the winter. There are sandflies on some, and the water is usually very shallow close to shore. We list several of the larger public beaches in the text, but some are noteworthy – the following are good public beaches, most with picnic tables, some with grills and all with toilets:

Destination	MM
Harry Harris County Park	92.5
Lower Matecumbe Beach	73.5
Anne's Beach	73
Long Key	67.5
Sombrero Beach	50
Little Duck Key Beach	38
Bahia Honda State Park	37

ACCOMMODATIONS

Accommodations are the main concern of anyone coming to the Keys; while there are hundreds of hotels, they book up far in advance in peak seasons. Especially in Key West, reservations are essential at all types of accommodations. There are booking agencies throughout the Keys, both chambers of commerce and privately owned booths or concessions. But even at peak periods, accommodation agencies can book you into something, usually at about the price you ask them for, and while peak-season competition is fierce enough that most places will not lower their quoted price, shop around; some of the agencies will do their best to book you into rooms just a little more expensive than you'd wanted.

State park campgrounds in the Keys accept reservations a year in advance, but even if they tell you on the phone that they're all booked, it pays to check in person, as they always keep a percentage of sites open for walk-up trade.

Peak Versus Off-Peak

Prices at practically all Keys accommodations change radically between 'peak' and 'off-peak' times, and each hotel determines its own definition of just what that is. The difference in price can be literally 100%.

Essentially, in winter you'll pay as much as places can possibly squeeze out of you along the Keys, one of the world's great seller's markets. But for some reason, early winter – up to the third week in December – is still considered off-peak, or at least 'fringe', at many accommodations. And there are pockets of peak and off-peak periods throughout the year. Expect to pay more from December 20 to March 30, the most expensive period, and the least from August to September. Also, weekday accommodations, especially in Key West, are generally cheaper than weekends. 'Weekends' in the Keys are Thursday to Saturday.

FOOD & DRINK

Drinking is a Keys tradition, and unfortunately, eating takes a back seat to it. Obviously, the big favorite is seafood, and it's available absolutely everywhere; it varies in quality from inedible deep-fried gook to splendid taste sensations. Almost every restaurant in the Keys has a bar attached or outside, and except for Key West, most drinking is done in these – or at resorts and campsites – as opposed to in dedicated bars.

GETTING AROUND

Getting around is pretty idiot-proof in the Keys: there's one main road to everything and public transportation options are limited to Greyhound and two airports, of which only one is really used by travelers. See the Key West Getting There & Away section for information on the Key West airport. The Keys' other commercial airport, used mainly by business travelers and cargo planes, is at Marathon (☎ 743-2155), served by USAir and American. But it's expensive to fly to Marathon, which is about a two-hour drive from Miami, so most people drive.

Unless you're staying in one place the entire time you're here, you'll need a car or motorcycle to get around the Keys. Greyhound runs the entire length of US Hwy 1 from Key West to Key Largo three times a day, but outside that and the local Key West city buses, there's no public transport, and distances are too far to make bicycling a real option for anyone except experienced riders. You can rent bicycles in most larger Keys, and bicycles and scooters in Key West.

Most major rental companies have offices in Key West, Marathon and Key Largo; see the Getting Around chapter for more information.

To/From Miami

See the Key West Getting There & Away section for specific Greyhound bus, shuttle service and air service to/from Key West and the Keys. By car, there are two options; from Miami take I-95 south to US Hwy 1 and follow that until you can't go any farther – that'd be Key West. A shorter route is to take Florida's Turnpike Extension (toll) south and then pick up US Hwy 1 south at Florida City.

The Conch Republic

Conchs are people who were born and raised in Key West. It's a difficult title to earn; even after seven years of living here you only rise to the rank of 'freshwater conch'. And by the way, it's pronounced 'conk' as in 'bonk', not 'contsh' as in 'paunch'.

You will no doubt hear (and see the flag) of the Conch Republic, and therein lies an interesting tale.

In 1982, the US Border Patrol and US Customs came up with a terrific, they thought, way of catching

The official flag of the Conch Republic

drug smugglers, illegal aliens and other riff-raff. They erected a roadblock at Key Largo. As traffic jams and anger mounted, many tourists decided they'd just as soon take the Shark Valley Tram in the Everglades, thanks very much, and disappeared.

Enter a bunch of outraged conchs, who came up with the brilliant idea of seceding from the USA. They formed the nation of the Conch Republic, whose first act was to secede from the USA, whose second act was to declare war on the USA and whose third act was to surrender and request $1 million in foreign aid.

Every February, Conchs celebrate the anniversary of those heady days with non-stop parties.

The Conch party went on to receive national attention in the 1984 and 1988 presidential elections, when Conch representatives clad in aloha shirts and wielding starfish and plastic cups of Margaritas stormed by force the Republican and Democratic national conventions. The Conch's boycotts of goods produced in the northern areas of the USA have lead to what insiders refer to as the Islamorada Wall. Presidents Reagan, Bush and Clinton have spoken in front of the wall and demanded, 'Mr Buffet, I challenge you . . . tear down this wall.' ■

KEY WEST
• *pop 25,000* ☎ *305*

The capital of the Conch Republic, Key West has a well-earned reputation as a tropical paradise with gorgeous sunsets and sultry nightlife. It's gotten overrun by tourists and its conchs have become cynical over the years, but if you look carefully, you'll find fleeting images of the Key West of the past: walking through the narrow side streets away from the action along Truman or Duval, you'll see lovely Keys architecture and get a sense of how the locals live, those who aren't there to sell you a T-shirt or book you on a glass-bottom boat ride.

History
The first European settlers in the area were the Spanish, who upon finding the bones unearthed from Indian burial sites named the place *Caya Hueso* (kah-ya WAY-so) – Bone Island, a name that was later Anglicized into Key West. Bought from a Spaniard by John Simonton in 1821, Key West first saw development as a naval base in 1822, and it was the base for David Porter's Anti-Pirate Squadron, which by 1826 had substantially reduced pirate activity in the region. From then on, Key West's times of boom and bust were closely tied to the military presence here.

The construction of forts at Key West and on the Dry Tortugas brought in men and money, and the island's proximity to the busy and treacherous shipping lanes that had attracted the pirates in the first place created an industry in wrecking – salvaging goods from downed ships.

In the late 1800s, the area became the focus of mass immigration and political activity for Cubans, who were fleeing oppressive conditions under Spanish rule and trying to raise the money and men to form a revolutionary army. Along with them came cigar manufacturers, who turned Key West into the USA's cigar manufacturing center. That would end when workers' demands in Key West became enough to convince several large

manufacturers, notably Vicénte Martínez Ybor and Ignacio Haya, to move their operations up to Tampa, in southwest Florida (see the Tampa chapter for a more complete history).

During the Spanish-American War, Key West may have been the most important staging point for US troops, and the military buildup lasted through WWI. And all of the Keys began to boom when Henry Flagler's Overland Railroad – a railway running over a series of causeways from the mainland to Key West – underwent construction.

In the late 1910s, Key West became a bootlegging center, as people stocked up on booze for the rainy day that Prohibition was to bring.

While the Depression, which bankrupted the city, and a hurricane in 1935 ended most people's enthusiasm about Key West (though writer Ernest Hemingway lived here from 1931 to 1940), WWII breathed new life into the place when the naval base once again became an important staging area. And everyone in Washington was happy about that when the Bay of Pigs crisis happened in 1962 (see the History section in the Facts about Florida chapter).

Key West has always been a place where people buck trends. A large society of artists and craftspeople were drawn to the area at the end of the Depression by cheap real estate, and that community continues to grow. Gay men have long been welcomed – but the gay community in Key West began to pick up in earnest in the 1970s. Today it's one of the most famous in the country, and if not the largest, it's certainly one of the best organized.

But while it's home to dozens of hotels and hundreds of restaurants and bars geared to all sexual desires and tastes, Key West isn't a resort, and it isn't a 'gay' destination any more than Miami is. 'All welcome' here means just that, and despite cynicism and tourist price gouging, visitors from all walks of life find a stay in Key West to be almost as good as they'd imagined.

Orientation

The island of Key West is roughly oval shaped, with most of the action taking place in the west end. The main drags are Duval St and Truman Ave (US Hwy 1). In the downtown area there's a grid street structure, with street numbers (which are usually painted on lampposts) in a hundred-block format counting upward from Front St (100) down to Truman Ave (900) and so on. Mallory Square, at the far northwestern tip, is the site of the nightly sunset celebrations. The Greyhound Station (☎ 293-0410) is in the alley behind 615½ Duval St, between Angela and Southard Sts.

Maps There are free tourist maps everywhere; the best is published by the Key West Business Guild (see below), a gay-and-lesbian-oriented business association that has excellent information on gay/lesbian/bi-owned and -friendly businesses.

Information

Tourist Offices The Greater Key West Chamber of Commerce (☎ 294-2587, 800-527-8539) at 402 Wall St in Old Mallory Square is an excellent source of information, brochures, maps and advice. They're open daily from 8.30 am to 5 pm. The Florida Keys & Key West Visitor's Bureau (☎ 296-1552) runs an excellent website (see the Online Services appendix); it's packed with information on everything the Keys have to offer. On the way into town on US Hwy 1, you simply can't miss the Key West Welcome Center (☎ 296-4444, 800-284-4482), 3840 N Roosevelt Blvd, which has a discount ticket booth that gives 25 to 50¢ off admissions to museums and attractions. Other Key West information booths include: 1029 Truman Ave (☎ 296-0379); 500 Truman Ave (☎ 292-0300); 3340 N Roosevelt Blvd (☎ 296-6002).

Hospitality House (☎ 294-9501) is a volunteer organization in the old steamship ticket house behind Mallory Square that gives out maps and pamphlets. They offer house and garden tours throughout the city

at various times and various prices; call or stop by if you're interested.

Telephone Information Lines Key West Hotline (☎ 295-0079) is a touch-tone menu-driven information service that eventually gives you general information about a huge array of subjects, from accommodations to medical advice. The Key West Welcome Center (☎ 296-4444) gives information on accommodations and restaurants.

Money Barnett Bank's main office (☎ 296-7845) is at 1010 Kennedy Drive; there's an Old Town office (☎ 296-7845) at 510 Southard St: dig the trippy decor. American Express (☎ 294-3711) is represented by Boulevard Travel at 811 Peacock Plaza. The Depot of Key West (☎ 293-0410), 615½ Duval (in the alley next to the Greyhound Station), has a Western Union office as well as lockers for $1 a day. They're open daily from 7.30 am to 7.30 pm. Private exchange offices abound, at hotels, motels and attractions.

Post & Communications The Key West post office (☎ 294-2557) is at 400 Whitehead St. You can buy prepaid telephone cards in dozens of shops and hotels, including the Key West International Hostel.

Bookstores & Libraries Blue Heron Books (☎ 296-3508), 538 Truman Ave, has a small travel section (not enough but some LP), a gay studies section and a decent nature section, and they carry the Sunday *New York Times*.

L Valladores and Son (☎ 296-5032), 1200 Duval St, has paperbacks, a diverse foreign press and magazine section and a good Key West book section. They're open daily from 8 am to 9 pm.

Bargain Books (☎ 294-7446), 1028 Truman Ave, is stocked from floor to ceiling with good used travel, gay, erotica, tons of fiction, some pornography and magazines.

South Florida's first public library (☎ 292-3595), 700 Fleming St, was founded here in 1892; it's a pretty well-stocked place.

FLORIDA KEYS

PLACES TO STAY
16 Colours Key West
19 Big Ruby's Guesthouse
20 Jabour's Trailer Court
25 Eaton Square
26 Coconut Grove
30 Pegasus Hotel
33 Mangrove House
35 Curry House
36 Francis St Bottle Inn
42 Tilton Hilton
51 Gardens Motel
53 Mahogany House
54 Merlin Guesthouse
58 Andrew's Guesthouse
59 Key Lodge Motel
60 Duval Gardens
61 Wicker Guesthouse
68 Conch House Heritage Inn
69 Chelsea House
70 Red Rooster
71 Key Lime Village
73 Sea Isle Resort
74 El Rancho Motel
78 White St Inn
85 The Rainbow House
86 Spenddrift Motel
87 Southernmost Guesthouse
89 Southwinds
90 Atlantic Shores Resort
91 Santa Maria Hotel
92 Tamarind Motel
93 Banana Cabana
95 Seashell Motel & Key West
      International Hostel
96 Marriott Casa Marina

PLACES TO EAT
3 The Place
4 La Crêperie
18 Margaritaville Café
24 Pepe's
28 Barefoot Bob's
31 Alexander's Café
32 Island Wellness
37 Donnie's
39 Dim Sum
41 The Lunch Box
46 5 Brothers Grocery
47 Yo Saké
49 Camille's
55 Siam House
65 The Deli
75 Kyushu Japanese
      Restaurant
76 Breakfast Anytime
79 Mo's Restaurant
82 Banana Café
83 El Meson de Pepe
94 Louie's Backyard

OTHER
1 Chamber of Commerce
2 Billie's Bar
5 Key West Aquarium
6 Mel Fisher Museum
7 Audubon House
8 Captain Tony's Saloon
9 Rick's, Durty Harry's
10 Sloppy Joe's Bar
11 Curry Mansion
12 Jessie Porter's Heritage
      House Museum
13 Wreckers' Museum

14 Red Barn Theater
15 Post Office
17 Key West Business Guild
21 Schooner Wharf
22 Reef Relief &
      Waterfront Market
23 Caroline St Books
27 Kokomo Cabs
29 Ripley's Believe It or Not
34 Public Library
38 Piano Bar
40 The Copa
43 The Depot
44 Greyhound Bus Station
45 Barnett Bank
48 Bourbon St Pub
50 Smokin' Edna's
52 801
56 Lighthouse
57 Hemingway House
62 Elite Launderette
63 Keys Moped & Scooter
64 The Club International
66 Blue Heron Books
67 Moped Hospital
72 St Mary's Church
77 Bargain Books
80 Treetop Bar at La Te Da
81 L Valladores & Son
84 Sand Castles by the Sea
88 Southernmost Motel
      Scooter Rentals
97 Southernmost Point

Curry's
Dock

Gulf
Dock

Mallory
Square

Front St
Ann St
Simonton St
Greene St
Duval St
Wall St
New St
St Charles St
Caroline St
Dey St

Pier A

Pier B

Whitehead St
Eaton St

Truman
Annex

ATLANTIC
OCEAN

Submarine
Basin

Thomas St

Ermina St

Fort St

Geraldine St
Covington Ave
Detalbs Ave

Fort Zachary Taylor
State Historic Site

Harry S Truman
US Naval
Reservation

Whitehead
Spit

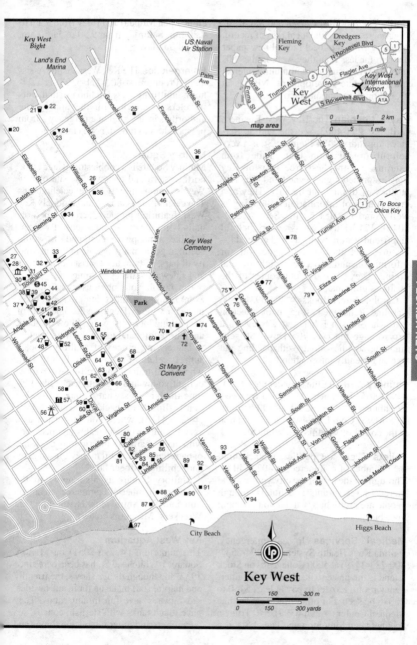

Key West

Media The *Key West Citizen* and *Key West: The Newspaper* are the local rags of record. *Solares Hill* is the local radical newspaper (though far less than they were in the '60s and '70s), focusing on community interest and real estate development. NPR is at 91.3, though reception is terrible.

Gay & Lesbian The Key West Business Guild (☎ 294-4603, see the Online Services appendix), 424 Fleming St, is a very helpful organization that, aside from handing out the best free map of Key West, represents gay-owned and -friendly businesses throughout the city. They're a great source of information on lodging as well. Sand Castles by the Sea (☎ 292-3048), 1219 Duval St, is a very helpful and friendly store with gay and general literature, and they're really helpful for information and advice on nightlife and dining. They also give out copies of the business guild map.

Caroline Street Books (☎ 294-3931), 800 Caroline St, has the best gay book selection in town. Smok'n Edna's (☎ 294-5995), a very orange place at 705 Duval St, sells smoking supplies along with handing out free and friendly information.

Laundry We used Elite Launderette (☎ 294-4493) at 517 Truman Ave. Also try Lee's Washhouse (☎ 294-3258) at 400 Truman Ave. M&M Coin Laundry is another option at the corner of Virginia and White St.

Toilets There are public toilets behind the chamber of commerce, at 402 Wall St. Throughout the rest of the city you're at the mercy of restaurants and hotels, though people are pretty happy to let you go about your business.

Medical Services In an emergency, Florida Keys Health Systems (☎ 294-5531, 800-233-3119) at 5900 College Rd on Stock Island is the place to head, a 24-hour emergency room. Expect to pay at least $150 to 200 to be seen. For other illnesses, Truman Medical Center (☎ 296-4399), 540 Truman Ave between Simonton and Duval Sts, is a clinic open Monday to Friday from 9 am to 4.30 pm, Saturday from 9.30 to 11.30 am, closed Sunday.

Emergencies The Key West Visitor Assistance Program (☎ 800-771-5397) is a 24-hour, multilingual switchboard that puts travelers in touch with the appropriate authorities in any kind of emergency – from passport loss to rape to hotel complaints.

Mallory Square

Mallory Square is a cobblestoned area at the northwestern end of town, the site of Key West's famous nightly sunset celebrations. The celebration is unique and uniquely Key West, featuring jugglers, acrobats, bed-of-nails-lying-downers, and a generally carnival-like atmosphere designed, it would seem, to get as many people in the proximity of bars, restaurants, tourist trinket shops and sidewalk stalls as possible.

But despite our obvious cynicism, the event *is* a fascinating thing – once. It takes place on Mallory Dock, on the other side of the parking lot by the water. Show up about an hour beforehand to get the full effect.

The saving graces of Mallory Dock's sunset celebration include Parrot Bill, whose well-trained and well-treated parrots delight young and old with tricks like flipping the bird (it's what it sounds like, but don't flip them back), and Pat's Pots (☎ 296-4158), where you can watch as a very friendly woman creates jars inscribed with such charming inscriptions as 'ashes of bad clients', 'face lift money', 'used gum' and, chillingly, 'beer farts'.

Mallory Square is also home to the excellent chamber of commerce, an aquarium and the Shipwreck Historeum (see Wreckers' Museums below).

Key West Aquarium

This aquarium (☎ 296-2051) on Mallory Square, 1 Whitehead St, has been here since 1932, and though its age shows, the friendly and helpful staff make up for it, and besides, kids always have fun in aquariums. They have touch tanks with starfish, conchs, sea cucumbers and other interesting things and lots of fish tanks filled with catfish, doctor-fish, snappers, angelfish and many more. Outside are the tanks for barracudas, sharks and sawfish; there are also turtles. Staff sometimes bring around live sharks for visitors to touch as part of their 'Pet a Shark' program. Signs are well done and the staff are happy to answer your questions. It's open daily from 10 am to 6 pm, and there are tours at 11 am and 1, 3 and 4.30 pm. Tours take about 40 minutes and are included in the admission price, which is $6.50 for adults, $3.50 for kids eight to 15. Tickets are valid for two days.

Hemingway House

This is, to us, one of Key West's great attractions. From 1931 to 1940, Hemingway lived in this lovely Spanish-Colonial house (☎ 294-1575) at 907 Whitehead St. It was here that he wrote 'The Short Happy Life of Francis Macomber', *A Farewell to Arms*, *Death in the Afternoon* and *To Have and Have Not*, and where he began *For Whom the Bell Tolls*. It was here, in the garden, that Hemingway installed Key West's first saltwater swimming pool: a construction that set him back so much that he pressed 'my last penny' into the cement on the pool's deck. It's still there today.

Also note the Hemingway cats who rule the house and grounds – the brood features six toes.

Hemingway kept ownership of the house until his death in 1961. The house is open daily from 9 am to 5 pm. Tours depart every 15 minutes and last about 30 minutes. Admission is $6.50 for adults, $4 for children, $5.50 for students.

Key West Cemetery

This is one of the more enjoyable cemeteries in the country for the odd characters buried here – tombstone epitaphs include 'I told you I was sick' and 'At least I know where he is sleeping tonight'. Guided tours are available on Saturday and Sunday at 10 am and 4 pm at the Margaret St entrance (☎ 292-6829) at the sexton's office (☎ 292-6829) at the Margaret St entrance (see the Key West map); the cost of the tour is $5 for adults, $1 for children.

Ernest Hemingway is remembered in Key West for his marlin fishing, heavy drinking and, of course, for writing some of his most famous novels.

Curry Mansion

This hundred-year-old Victorian mansion (☎ 294-5349), 511 Caroline St, was built by Milton Curry, one of Florida's first millionaires; it now functions as a guesthouse. On most days you can take a self-guided tour of the antique-packed rooms for $5 for adults, $1 for children. If you're impressed enough by what you see to want to stay, rooms range from $125 to 170 a night in low season, $160 to 210 in high season. Note that the Curry Mansion is not the Curry House, Key West's oldest exclusively gay male guesthouse (see Places to Stay, below).

Wreckers' Museums

There are two museums dedicated to study of the wreckers. The **Wreckers' Museum/the Oldest House** (☎ 294-9502), 322 Duval St, was the home of Francis B Watlington. It's filled with period antiques and has friendly, volunteer-led tours. It's open daily from 10 am to 4 pm; admission is $4 for adults, 50¢ for children.

More expensive and more interesting is

the **Key West Shipwreck Historeum**
(☎ 292-8990), 1 Whitehead St, which has a
narrated film showing the lives and times of
the wreckers. Knowledgeable volunteers
explain how Key West developed as a port.
It's open daily from 9.45 am to 4.45 pm;
admission is $7 for adults, $3.50 for kids
four to 12.

Ripley's Believe It or Not
Ripley's Believe It or Not is a chain of
museums that has a good branch in Key
West (☎ 293-9694), 527 Duval St. See the
St Augustine section of the Northeast
Florida chapter for a full description of
Ripley's and Ripley himself. The 'believe it
or not' part is up to you. Even if the
answer's 'not', it still may be worth the
admission price, and you can easily spend
an hour here. This one has a cool exhibit
where you can see an actress' bum – we
argued over whether it was Monroe or
Mansfield. They totally do the place up to
the nines during the month of October for
Halloween. It's open Sunday to Thursday
from 10 am to 11 pm, Friday and Saturday
10 am to midnight; admission is $9.95 for
adults, $6.95 for seniors and children five
to 12 (under five are free).

Southernmost Point
This is, after all, the southernmost point in
the continental USA, and there's a marker
here at the corner of South and Whitehead
Sts, along with some street performers and
many photo-seeking tourists. There's a
shell salesman who sets up shop here.

Heritage House Museum
A Caribbean-Colonial house, Jessie Porter's
Heritage House Museum & Robert Frost
Cottage (☎ 296-3573), 410 Caroline St, has
the original furnishings and antiques of a
Key West family who lived here. In the
flower garden they play spoken word
recordings of Robert Frost's poetry. There
are guided tours Monday to Saturday from
10 am to 5 pm, Sunday from 1 to 5 pm.
Admission is $6 for adults, $5 for seniors,
children are free.

Key West Lighthouse
The Key West Lighthouse (☎ 294-0012) is
a still-functioning lighthouse at 938 Whitehead St. Whitehead St? Yes. It may be
farther inland than people might expect, but
there are a couple of reasons for that. First,
the navy filled in about two thousand yards
between here and Fort Taylor. Second, the
placement of the lighthouse isn't all that
important when you consider that it's at the
high point (10 feet above sea level) on a flat
island in the middle of the ocean. Lighthouses are designed so that boats know that
if they're lined up with the lighthouse's red
lens, they're in trouble, so sometimes lighthouses end up in what may appear to be
strange places.

The lighthouse has a third-order lens, but
they also have a first-order lens that you can
walk into (for an explanation of lighthouse
lenses, see the Cape Florida Lighthouse in
the Miami chapter), and you can also climb
the 88 steps to the top. Next door is the
interesting lighthouse keeper's house. It's
open daily 9.30 am to 4.30 pm; admission
is $5 for adults, $1 for kids over seven.

Audubon House
This lovely house (☎ 294-2116), 205 Whitehead St, was built in the early 19th century
by ship's carpenters for the Captain John H
Geiger family, who lived here for about 120
years. In 1958 Colonel Mitchell Wolfson
bought it and had it restored as a public
museum (this was the first building to be
restored in Key West). It was named after
John James Audubon, who visited the house
in 1832. You can wander through the house
by yourself or, if you ask for it, get a free
half-hour guided tour through the different
rooms, which are filled with authentic 19th-
century Key West furniture and many of
Audubon's lithographs. The tropical gardens
are especially nice, filled with many different kinds of beautiful flowers and other lush
vegetation, like birds of paradise, star fruit
trees, fishtail fern and palms, hibiscus and
jasmine (the list could go on and on). It's
open daily from 9.30 am to 5 pm; admission
is $7.50 for adults, $2 for kids.

Mel Fisher Museum

The Mel Fisher Maritime Heritage Society Museum (☎ 294-2633), 200 Greene St, exhibits the galleon treasures of the Santa Margarita and the Atocha, discovered by Mel Fisher in 1980-85 (he started the search for these galleons in 1969). The various jewels, tools, coins and navigational pieces are displayed on the ground floor, along with a world map showing the routes of those ships and some hands-on stuff (like touch an item that you can't see and figure out what it is). On the 2nd floor you'll find displays of modern diving techniques, an electrolysis tank and the like. Mel, whose motto is 'Today's the day', can often be seen wandering through the museum – look for a guy with massive gold chains and coins hanging from round his neck, and you've got your man. It's open Tuesday from 9 am to 5 pm and Wednesday to Monday from 9.30 am to 5 pm; admission is $6 for adults, $4 for students and $2 for kids aged six to 12.

Little White House

This museum (☎ 294-9911) used to be the vacation house of President Harry S Truman. Visitors can only go through and look at it on a half-guided tour, not by yourself. You'll see Truman's piano, a lot of original furnishings and a 15-minute video about Truman's life. It's located in the Harry S Truman Annex (in which you can wonder around yourself) at 111 Front St, and it's open daily from 9 am to 5 pm. Admission is $7 for adults, $3.50 for children.

East Martello Museum

The East Tower (☎ 296-3913), 3501 S Roosevelt Blvd (across from Key West airport), houses an art gallery and an interesting museum of Key West history. You can climb the citadel in the central tower (48 steps) to a watch tower that affords a horrible view of the airport and a totally unimpressive view of the beach. But inside the tower are insane metal sculptures, which were stored here originally for lack of space elsewhere, that have turned into an attraction in and of themselves. Sure are

better than the view. It's open daily except Christmas from 9.30 am to 5 pm. Admission is $5 for adults, $1 for kids.

West Martello Tower

The West Martello tower on Higgs Beach is now said to be home to the Key West Garden Club, but it was never open when we visited.

Fort Zachary Taylor State Historic Site

Fort Zachary Taylor (☎ 292-6713), at the southwestern end of the island, was in operation from 1845 to 1866, and it guarded blockade-running Union ships during the Civil War. Today it's open as a state historic site and park, with showers and picnic tables and a beach – the deepest, clearest water on the island – great for swimming. It's open daily from 9 am to 5 pm, with ranger-led tours at noon and 2 pm. Admission is $3.75 per vehicle, $1.50 for pedestrians.

Key West Cigar Factory

This small cigar factory (☎ 294-3470), at 3 Pirates Alley off Front St, has been producing cigars for 40 years. It's very old and charming; if you come during the week from 9 am to 4 pm, you can watch cigars being rolled, and, if you're so inclined, buy some. And they have two very friendly cats.

Beaches

There are three city beaches on the southern side of the island, all of them narrow, and the water is very calm and clear. **City Beach** is at the end of South and Duval Sts. **Higgs Beach**, at the end of Reynolds St and Casa Marina Court, has barbecue grills and picnic tables, and **Smathers Beach**, farther east off S Roosevelt Blvd, is more popular with the vroom crowd of jet skiers and parasailers. There is also an excellent beach at Fort Zachary Taylor State Historic Site (see above).

Diving & Snorkeling

The dive opportunities in Key West aren't as plentiful as in some of the more northern

FLORIDA KEYS

Keys, but they are definitely here. Because of pollution and activity, there's no snorkeling to speak of on Key West's beaches. Most of the Key West dive companies take you west, to sites including Cottrell, Barracuda, Boca Grande, Woman, Sand, Rock and Marquesas Keys. Southwest of Key West, Joe's Tug, a submerged tugboat, is at a depth of about 65 feet. In some of the dive sites – especially around the Marquesas – non-divers can go along and snorkel. Don't touch the coral.

Reef Relief Reef Relief (☎ 294-3100), at the end of William St in the same building as the Waterfront Market (see Places to Eat below), is a nonprofit organization that maintains a network of anchoring buoys along the Keys. The idea is that if boaters have an alternate anchoring spot, they won't lower their anchors onto the coral, damaging it. The buoys are free to all. Experienced divers who are interested in volunteering to clean the buoys, which is frequently necessary, should contact Reef Relief. If you're qualified, they'll provide all the equipment you'll need and take you out to the buoys free.

Inside Reef Relief's headquarters, you can see free exhibits on coral, the Florida reef system, and get detailed ecological information from the volunteers and staff.

Dive Companies Dive companies set up at kiosks around Mallory Square and in other places in town, notably the corner of Truman and Duval Sts, to hawk to customers. Shop around carefully as prices vary greatly.

A diver friend recommended Captain Billy Dean's Diving (☎ 294-7177, 800-873-4837) at MM 4.5. He's said to be the high-tech diving guru around here. Some other dive shops include:

Bonsai Diving
310 Duval St (☎ 294-2921)

Capt David Hart's
631 Greene St (☎ 296-0606)

Dive Masters of the Keys
Key Haven Rd (☎ 292-9110)

Key West Pro Dive
1605 Roosevelt Blvd (☎ 296-3823)

Organized Tours

Old Town Trolley Tours (☎ 296-6688) narrated tram tours leave from Mallory Square and make a large, lazy circle around the city with stops including Key West Handprint Fabrics, Angela St Depot, Trolley Barn, Key West Welcome Center, East Martello Fort/Museum and the Southernmost Point. The cost is $15 for adults, $6 for children for one full circle from any point on the route (you can get off and back on in the same direction for one rotation only), and it includes $1 off on admission to the Hemingway House. The trolleys depart every half hour between 9.30 am and 6 pm.

The Conch Train Tour (☎ 294-5161) is pretty much the same thing, run by the same parent company as the Old Town Trolley Tours. Trams leave every 20 minutes in high season, every half hour in low season, between 9 am and 4.30 pm. The cost is $14 for adult, $6 for kids.

Kokomo Cabs (☎ 745-5652), 519 Duval St, offers a half-hour tour in a bicycle-powered rickshaw for $25.

The friendly people at Mosquito Coast Island Outfitters & Kayak Guides (☎ 294-7178), 1107 Duval St, offer four- to five-hour near-shore natural history tours to Geiger and Sugarloaf Keys. You show up at their office at 8.45 am and they drive you to either Geiger or Sugarloaf, where you paddle. The $45 cost includes snorkel equipment, snacks, bottled water and the guide – nice friendly people.

Liberty Cruises (☎ 292-0332) does sailing tours every day from the Hilton Resort Marina at the corner of Front and Green Sts. Two-hour lunch sails are $25 for adults, $12.50 for children; two-hour sunset tours with champagne and hors d'oeuvres are $32.

The *MV Discovery* (☎ 293-0099) is a glass-bottom boat that does tours at 9.30 am, noon, 2.30 pm and sunset in summer, and at 10.30 am, 1.30 pm and sunset in winter. They're at the Land's End Marina at the end of Margaret St. Call for prices.

Miss Sunshine (☎ 296-4608) is a gay cruise with male strippers, wine, beer and hors d'oeuvres for $30. They also run a day snorkeling trip at 11 am, including lunch, for $45 a person. Call for departure times and more details.

Places to Stay

Key West is packed with rooms of all sorts, and picking one can take a bit of planning. The basic categories are motels and hotels, B&B/guesthouses, gay/lesbian guesthouses and one newly admitted to HI Key West hostel. There is one (very expensive) campground in Key West itself. If you want the more authentic Key West experience, book a room in one of the city's dozens of B&Bs.

There are a number of exclusively gay and lesbian guesthouses, but traditionally all of the city's guesthouses are very welcoming to gay and lesbian couples – hey, it's Key West.

Except for the hostel, count on spending a rock bottom of $45 in low season and $60 in high season, despite what rack rates may be listed here. The room rates in all non-hostel accommodations are totally negotiable, and as changeable as the crowds on the day you arrive. One hotel booker told us that he pushes the price to the absolute limit of what the market will bear – a hotel room that rents for $120 on Saturday may be blown out for as low as $50 on Sunday. And as a rule, prices dip by at least 40% in summer.

Accommodation Agencies In downtown Key West at the chamber of commerce (as well as in some chambers on other Keys) is a booking desk. The ones in the chambers are as honest as the day is long – though don't expect them to go out of their way to find hotels that are not chamber members. The chamber will try to book a room in your price range, but if you've ever told a real estate agent that you're absolute limit is X, you know how quickly X can become Y.

Agencies in booths on street corners advertise great bargains that may or may not exist. As in any city, when dealing with an agency, try not to pay until you've seen the room.

Camping Just outside Key West, *Boyd's Key West Campground* (☎ 294-1465) on Stock Island at 6401 Maloney Ave (turn south at MM 5) has tent sites for $26, plus an additional $5 for electricity and water; waterfront sites are $37. There's a bus stop right there.

Just past Boca Chica Key and accessible by bus is the *Geiger Key Marina* with sites for $30 in winter, 'less' in summer. It's at MM 10.5 and finding it is a little tricky: turn east past the Circle K onto Hwy 941 and left onto Geiger Rd.

Jabour's Trailer Court (☎ 294-5723), 223 Elizabeth St, just east of the Key West Bight at the northern end of Elizabeth St, is the only campground actually in Key West; they have tent sites in summer/winter from $30 to 38/38 to 45. They also rent rooms, with TV and air-conditioning but no telephones, and some with shared bathrooms, in summer/winter for $60 to 70/85 to 95; on-site travel trailers for $65/85; and on-site mobile homes that sleep four to six people for $90 to 125/125 to 175.

Youth Hostel In 1996, the *Seashell Motel & Key West International Hostel* (☎ 296-5719, 800-514-6783), 718 South St, joined HI, and it's a friendly hostel with helpful staff. We met a lot of travelers here. There had been some complaints about cleanliness and safety before, but when we visited things were definitely heading in the right direction. Beds in the dorm rooms are $17 for members, $20 for nonmembers; motel rooms with TV and telephone are $40 to 50 in low season, $75 in midseason and $100 from late-February through March. They serve dinner for $1 at 5 pm – 'Don't be late and wash your plate.' Alcohol is prohibited. A taxi between here and the Greyhound station is $3 to 4.

Motels & Hotels Chain hotels are represented by Ramada (☎ 294-5541), Best Western's two places (☎ 294-3763 and 296-3500), Days Inn (☎ 294-3742), Marriott's two places (☎ 296-5700 and the resort, see below), EconoLodge (☎ 294-5511), Holiday Inn (☎ 296-2991) and Howard Johnson (☎ 296-6595).

Key Lime Village (☎ 294-6222, 800-201-

6222), 727 Truman Ave, has friendly management and nice little cottages with shared baths in summer/winter for $32/60. Cottages with private baths are $48 to 75/90 to 120. Bike rentals are available for $5 a day; there is free coffee and a beer and wine bar.

The Tilton Hilton (☎ 294-8697), 511 Angela St close to the Greyhound station, has rooms on the small, simple side, and most have ceiling fans (not air-conditioning), shared baths and TVs; some also have a small fridge. Room rates range from $40 (lower in slow periods) to 75; weekly rentals are $180. One of the rooms does have a private bath at no extra cost, but you need to reserve it specifically. A washer ($1.50) and dryer (50¢) are on the premises, and they have a barbecue grill and free off-street parking.

Eaton Square (☎ 294-3333, 800-403-2866), located at 1031 Eaton St at Frances, has friendly management and typical clean motel rooms that include a small fridge, TV, air-conditioning, private bath and telephone for $49/69 in summer/winter.

The perfectly located and clean and friendly *Pegasus Hotel* (☎ 294-9323, 800-397-8148) 501 Southard St, has rooms in summer/winter for $59 to 99/99 to 199; most rooms have only showers. It looks pretty good: when we visited they were installing a new heated pool and Jacuzzi.

The Spendrift Motel (☎ 296-3432), 212 Simonton St, is a perfectly average motel with rooms in summer/winter from $59 to 89/89 to 119. *Southwinds* (☎ 296-2215), 1321 Simonton St, has clean rooms with queen-size beds from $59/99, rooms with two doubles from $69/109 and efficiencies from $75/120. There is a pool and a washer/dryer ($1/50¢).

El Rancho Motel (☎ 294-8700, 800-294-8783), 830 Truman Ave, is a pleasant enough place, with a pool and clean rooms if not overly chipper management; no pets. Rooms in summer/winter are $59 to 175/75 to 299.

The *Tamarind Motel* (☎ 296-2829), 625 South St, has no pool but a nice, lush yard. It's a pleasant place, family run, clean and pretty quiet. Rooms are carpeted and, depending on size and season, cost from

$60 to 200. Note though that the property, which was formerly called the Lord's Motel, is under new management and prices may change significantly.

The mongo *Santa Maria Motel* (☎ 296-5678, 800-821-5397), 1401 Simonton St at South St, has clean rooms and a nice swimming pool with an astounding array of pricing, which boils down to $59 to 69 in low and fringe seasons and $135 to 155 in winter – but they change often and always seem to go up when *you* want to stay there.

The *Key Lodge Motel* (☎ 296-9915, 800-458-1296), 1004-t Duval St, has large clean rooms, all with fridges, some with kitchens. In low season, they're from $75 to 93 on weekdays, $85 to 103 on weekends; in high season, they're $145 to 168 every day. There's a heated pool and free off-street parking. Coffee is served in the morning but not breakfast.

Marriott Casa Marina (☎ 296-3535, 800-626-0777), 1500 Reynolds St next to Higgs Beach, is a resort with the largest private beach on the island, which means they feel they can gouge you for room rates: non-ocean view standard rooms *start* at $162 in summer, $180 in fringe seasons and $290 in winter. The place has two pools, Jacuzzi, sauna, health club, full-service water sports department, three lighted tennis courts and two restaurants. You can find supersaver room rates that can get as low as $125 a night at different times during the year, but it's easier to get that rate in summer.

The Gardens Hotel (☎ 294-2661, 800-526-2664), 526 Angela St, is a pretty spectacular place: the house was formerly Key West's largest private residence – and the walls around the hotel take up almost an entire city block in the historic district. The gardens are unbelievably lush, there's a kidney-shaped pool and they have rooms and cottages. In summer/winter, rooms run from $200 to 265/225 to 315, cottages from $385 to 575/435.

B&Bs The *Merlin Guesthouse* (☎ 296-3336), 811 Simonton St, is set in a beautiful green, secluded garden with a pool and wooden, slightly elevated walkways. The rooms are very airy, light and clean; everything is made from bamboo, rattan and wood. Breakfast includes quiche, muffins, cake, fruit, coffee, tea and juice, and in season between 6 and 7 pm they serve rum punch, crackers, dips, salsa and cheese. Their cheapest room has no air-conditioning or TV, but it's $36/50 in summer/winter – it's usually booked so call ahead. Other rooms are $70/100, apartments are $100/135 and the tree house (which isn't really in a tree, but is pretty high up) and the wheelchair-accessible tea house are $115/150.

Southernmost Point Guesthouse (☎ 294-0715), 1327 Duval St (opposite the blah Southernmost Motel), is a gorgeous Victorian house with a nice garden and porch area. Standard rooms are $55/110 in summer/winter, efficiencies are $75/125 and suites $95/150; continental breakfast is included.

The *Mahogany House* (☎ 293-9464, 800-336-0625), 812 Simonton St, is a guesthouse with an efficiency apartment at $69/129 in summer/winter and a one-bedroom apartment with a loft and two futon mattresses (it's large enough to sleep six) for $175/250. Both come with full kitchens, it's clean and comfortable and there is a Jacuzzi and a free washer and dryer on the property. They also rent out simple but clean cottages with fridges and microwaves in private homes for $49 to 59/59 to 69 (prices are negotiable).

The *Wicker Guesthouse* (☎ 296-4275, 800-880-4275), 913 Duval St, is a lovely place – despite its location – with an excellent pool and secluded garden. They have rooms with shared bathrooms for $63/75 in summer/winter, and rooms with private baths are $79/125; they also have suites that sleep four for $125/155. As the name implies, they have tons of wicker and wood furniture. The continental breakfast – a big one – is served buffet style out in the garden. There's a shared kitchen, and hey, don't stand under the palms when the wind's blowing, okay?

The *Conch House Heritage Inn* (☎ 293-0020), 625 Truman Ave, was built in 1875 and has been family owned since 1889. The place is very clean and the people are nice, and while it's gay and lesbian friendly, kids under 12 are a bit iffy. There's a small pool, a nice dining room, and continental breakfast is included. They rent three cottages and five rooms in the main house for $68/98 in summer/winter, cabanas are $78/118, deluxe rooms are $88/128, master rooms $98/138 and suites $118/168.

We really liked the *Frances St Bottle Inn* (☎ 294-8530, 800-294-8530) at 535 Frances St. It is gay friendly and staff make you feel at home. Rooms are $70 to 85/90 to 110 in summer/winter, and they are very comfortable. The cheap rooms have the bath across the hall, and the private baths have shower only (no tub). There are antique bottles in every room (hence the place's name), and there is a huge porch. They do a continental breakfast and have a very nice cat, Calvin.

These next two defy categorization as either 'gay' or 'straight', since the majority of guests may be gay or straight on any given day. Both are charming places, though the *Chelsea House* (☎ 296-2211, 800-845-8859), 707 Truman Ave, is the nicer of the two; it was built in 1870. Rooms, with TV, air-conditioning, fridge and bath, cost $75 to 165 in summer, $95 to 200 in fringe seasons and $115 to 270 in winter. Breakfast includes fruit, cereal, muffins, bread and oranges (squeeze your own juice). The atmosphere is sort of like a college dorm in a Victorian mansion; there's lots of free parking, and cute brick paths lead to the small pool out back. It's an all-welcome place, with a clothing-optional sun deck, and Professor, the cat, reigns over the paperback book library. Next door, the *Red Rooster* (☎ 296-6558, 800-845-0825), 709 Truman Ave, is a gay-staffed place with a very nice coffee bar downstairs and classical music piped throughout. It was more famous in its last incarnation – a notorious brothel whose wanton activities forced the nuns at St Mary's Church, across the street, to shade the windows to prevent students from peering across. It's been renovated and cleaned up, though a little of the former atmosphere remains. Staff are very friendly, and they have a really nice side garden. Rooms are $59 to 109/89 to 169 in summer/winter.

Duval Gardens (☎ 292-3379, 800-867-1234), 1012 Duval St, has rooms with queen-size beds for $85/115 in summer/winter, efficiencies or a junior suite with living room and French doors for $99/135 and one-bedroom suites for $115/175. They have wicker and rattan furniture, a Jacuzzi and a sun deck, but no pool. It's run by a very helpful couple, and breakfast is quite elaborate: they start out with a buffet of pastries, fruit, coffee and juices and then start serving different hot dishes, like banana and syrup pancakes or toasted English muffins topped with tomato, bacon, egg and Hollandaise sauce. Parking is available, and there is a free cocktail hour around sunset.

White St Inn (☎ 295-9599, 800-207-9767), 905-907 White St, has beautiful gardens and a pool; rooms range from $85 to 120/130 to 200 in summer/winter. Continental breakfast is included. Try for a room not facing White St.

Banana Cabana (☎ 294-3662, see the Online Services appendix), 719 South St, is a very colorful Caribbean-style place with beautiful attention to detail; all rooms have full kitchens, tiled floors and wicker furniture. Prices are $90/135 (this is negotiable in the off-season); continental breakfast and bicycles are included. They also have a 'holiday package' for $185, which includes your choice of a snorkel or sailing trip. They do barbecues on Sundays and Wednesdays and a daily happy hour with beer and wine from 5 to 7 pm. They don't have a pool, but they do have a Jacuzzi, and the place is lush and homey.

Andrew's Guesthouse (☎ 294-7730), Zero Walton Lane, is another place with a beautiful backyard, a pool and a delightful tropical feel. Rooms with a queen-size bed are $98/148 in summer/winter; king-size beds are $108/158. Most rooms have a private deck (where clothing is optional), but around the pool clothes are required. Basically each room has its own cat that hangs out, and a full hot breakfast is included – as is the full, open liquor bar.

Gay Lodging You will notice a dearth of lesbian-only places – though there's a good one in the Rainbow House – but don't despair: many of the smaller gay guesthouses are lesbian friendly. Contact the Business Guild (☎ 294-4603) to see if any more have opened when you arrive.

Coconut Grove (☎ 296-5107, 800-262-6055), 817 Fleming St, is a friendly gay place with rooms in summer/winter from $55 to 120/85 to 220. They have a rooftop sun deck – kinda unique – and a clothing-optional pool and Jacuzzi. All the rooms have fridges, and breakfast is a light continental affair – mainly cereal, fruit and coffee cake.

The very clean and Art Deco-ish *Atlantic Shores Resort* (☎ 296-2491, 800-526-3559, see the Online Services appendix), 510 South St, defies categorization: all are welcome, but it's very popular with gay men, lesbians and Europeans because of its clothing-optional pool. They have a lot of different seasons here, and rooms range from $63 to 220, efficiencies from $73 to 240. Apparently, gay women like it here a lot.

The suspicious folks at the *Mangrove House* (☎ 294-1866, 800-294-1866), 623 Southard St, are protecting an okay place with rooms for $65/95 in summer/winter and apartments for $110/150. There are weekly discounts, and a nice, if small, clothing-optional pool out back. If you're looking for seclusion, this is it.

The Rainbow House (☎ 292-1450, 800-749-6696), 525 United St, is exclusively for women – gay or straight. It's a very nice place with excellent and helpful staff, bleached wood furniture and two sun decks – one with a heated pool, the other with a hot tub. Rooms, including a continental breakfast, are $69 to 139/99 to 189.

Key West's oldest exclusively gay male guesthouse, *Curry House Mansion* (☎ 294-6777, 800-633-7439), 806 Fleming St (not to be confused with the Curry Mansion, see above), is in a hundred-year-old, Victorian-style three-story mansion. Rooms in summer/winter are $78 to 95/130 to 160; some have shared baths. They do a full hot breakfast and have a happy hour daily from 4 to 6 pm except Sunday; there's a clothing-optional pool and Jacuzzi.

Big Ruby's Guesthouse (☎ 296-2323), 409 Appelrouth Lane (just off Duval between Southard and Fleming), is a clean and slick place in an *Architectural Digest* sort of way; they have a nice and very tropical pool area and four dachshunds yipping around. Rooms are 'always under $3000' – okay, they're $78 to 128 in summer, $125 to 210 in winter, $97 to 164 in fringe.

Colours Key West (☎ 294-6977, 800-277-4825), 410 Fleming St, is an interesting place: it's in the (possibly haunted) mansion formerly owned by a cigar manufacturer. Some of the rooms are very large (if a little old) and some have kitchens; they range from $80 to 135/115 to 185 in summer/winter.

The *Sea Isle Resort* (☎ 294-5188, 800-995-4786), 915 Windsor Lane, is very clean and pleasant, with split rattan furniture, tiled floors and small fridges. Most of the rooms have showers only (three have bathtubs), and they always put a flower on your pillow in the evening. Rooms with queen-size beds are $85/120 in summer/winter, king rooms are $95/130, two queens (no pun intended) $100/140, poolside suites with kitchen $115/150; all rooms include continental breakfast. The entire place is clothing optional (a wood fence gives privacy), though you're asked to wear something at breakfast. An elevated wood deck overlooks the pool. Though it's 98% gay, it's not exclusively so.

Places to Eat

The cuisine of Key West has a good reputation that's undeserved – food has always taken a back seat to drink here, and there are only a few amazing culinary delights to be had without spending an awfully large sum of money. But most of the restaurants here offer reliably good food, fresh seafood and decent portions. It's not the best, but it's certainly not bad, either. And it's interesting to note that a good percentage of the seafood comes from somewhere other than

the Keys – that 'local' catch may be from the clear blue waters off Brooklyn.

Breakfast is an important meal here – probably as a hangover helper – and portions are large and full of grease. Lunch is an afterthought.

The problem, of course, is that many places cater to tourists, who can't really complain. The idea, therefore, is to find the few places left that cater to Conchs. It is in these places that Key West's charm, and that elusive Key West cuisine – spicy seafood, Italian- and Spanish-influenced cooking and tropical-theme side dishes and desserts – comes through loud and clear.

Don't miss Key lime pie, a sort of lime meringue made with Key limes, which are more lemony than standard-issue limes. There's such controversy over where the 'best' Key lime pie and conch chowder is to be found that we're copping out of it entirely: we have our favorites, but committing an opinion to paper about these sacred Conch subjects is dangerous – and we want to be alive to work on the next edition. Okay, our favorite pie is at The Deli (see below), but that's all we're saying.

Breakfast *Breakfast Anytime* (☎ 292-2023), 934 Truman Ave, is a classic Key West find, and they take their grease seriously: try the triple-bypass omelet (three cheeses and bacon) for $5.75, or lighten up (a bit) and get eggs, home fries or grits and toast for $2; lunch sees burgers from $2.50 to 3.75 and sandwiches from $2.75 to 5.75. It's open daily from 7 am to 3 pm year round.

Waterfront Market (☎ 296-0778), 201 William St next to Schooner Wharf, isn't just a breakfast place – it's open most of the day and night – but it's a good spot for a bagel and coffee. It's great for sandwiches, organic produce and health foods. They've got a juice bar and sell wine and beer. Outside the market is the Wyland Wall, a poor undersea mural.

Camille's (☎ 296-4811), at 703 Duval St, is an islander favorite that's been around forever; it does breakfasts (eggs $2 to 6.50, omelets $3.75 to 5.95), lunch (specials from \$5.95 to 7.95) and daily dinner specials that run the gamut from \$7.95 to 15.95. There's good, friendly service.

Banana Café (☎ 294-7227), 1211 Duval St, seems to know what it's doing: for breakfast, three scrambled eggs with vegetables, cheese and toast is \$6.50; see Lunch and Dinner – middle & top below for the good stuff they do at those meals as well!

Lunch & Snacks *5 Brothers Grocery and Sandwich Shop* (☎ 296-5205), 930 Southard St, is local favorite; a Cuban market that does great sandwiches like the 'midnite' (\$2.55), Cuban (\$2.80) and pork (3.35). Hamburgers/cheeseburgers are \$1.80/2.05, a large café con leche is \$1.75, and on Fridays they have conch chowder (\$2.75).

If you can get past the criminally negligent service, *Baby's Place* (☎ 296-3739), 1111 Duval St, has lots of varieties of great premises-brewed coffee (\$1.25), espresso and cappuccino (\$2.25 to 2.75). They also have pastries and bagels and stuff, but we stormed out before getting the prices.

The Lunch Box (☎ 294-5667), 629 Duval St near Angela St, is a sandwich stand with veggie chili for \$2.25, 'very veggie' sandwiches for \$3.25 and burgers for \$3.95.

For friendly Middle Eastern folks and food come to *The Place* (☎ 292-1422), tucked back in the recess at 111 Duval St. Hummus sandwiches are \$3.50, falafel sandwiches are \$4 and chicken shish kebab are \$5.25. It's open late.

Banana Café (☎ 294-7227), 1211 Duval St, is great for lunch, when crêpes range from \$4 to 7.

Vegetarians will appreciate *Island Wellness* (☎ 296-7353), 530 Simonton St, a kind of juice-bar-veggie-food-holistic-massage-aromatherapy-trapeze kind of place – *you* know. Anyway, they serve very good veggie and tofu-burger platters for \$4.25 to 4.75, hummus platters for \$4.50, steamed veggie platters for \$5.95 and black beans and brown rice for \$4.50.

Alexander's Café (☎ 294-5777), 509 Southard St, is a very comfortable place with friendly service and reasonable prices. Their fresh fish sandwich is a bomb of a

meal – huge and served with veggies and fries for \$5.95. They've also got a good range of Italian food including pizza (\$2 a slice or \$10 for a 16-inch pie), spaghetti and meatballs (\$7.95) and fettuccine Alfredo (\$8.95).

Dinner – bottom end We followed our noses back through the tiny alleyway into *La Crêperie* (☎ 292-0099), 117 Duval St, where we found pretty cheap lunch crêpe specials like cheese (\$3.25), spinach au gratin (\$5) and crab in sherry sauce (\$6.25). At dinner prices go up, but not so much: chicken curry is \$9.50, but watch out for that \$15 catch of the day . . . in a crêpe.

That fabled real local hangout with good food and not so many tourists is *Mo's Restaurant* (☎ 296-8955), 1116 White St, where inexpensive and great meals abound. Nothing but well-prepared, great food and good service. It's a little small (let's call it intimate) and you may have to wait a while for a table on weekends.

And speaking of excellent local hangouts, you gotta love *The Deli* (☎ 294-1464), 926 Simonton St. Run by the same family since 1950, it's got really friendly service and extremely well-prepared food. Vegetarians can pile on side dishes like mashed potatoes, rice and beans, zucchini, carrots and other veggies for \$1.20 each, and others can hit the meaty dinner specials (\$6.50 to 9.15, steak \$12.95 and half a rack of ribs \$4.75) or fish and chips (\$5.95). Sandwiches are from \$1.50 to 5.95. No alcohol is sold, and it's closed Wednesday.

Dinner – middle & top end We were on the verge of deciding that the *Siam House* (☎ 292-0302) wasn't worth a try when a customer told us it was a mistake to leave. He was right – and he didn't even mention the excellent and friendly service. Awesome Thai food, good spring rolls (\$2.95), excellent fried rice and ginger vegetables (\$8.95), as well as shrimp dishes (\$14.50) that set diners' mouths watering when they were carried out to some lucky patron's table. Only problem was the doughy tempura. They're open

Recipe for Key Lime Pie,
or How to Start an Argument in the Conch Republic

No person who considers him- or herself a true Conch (Key West native) would ever give out their secret recipe for Key lime pie, but Kim Dyer went to an awful lot of trouble to compile *all* the recipes she could find and publish them (believe it or not) in a FAQ on an internet newsgroup for Jimmy Buffet fans (alt.fan.jimmy-buffett). Thanks, Kim!

For Lonely Planet's first foray into the cookbook world, we've decided to use the simple, basic 'Key Lime Pie: Variant No 1'.

9-inch pie crust:
  1 cup flour (Wondra if possible)
  ½ tsp salt
  ⅓ cup and 1 tbsp shortening
  3 tbsp cold water
Combine flour, salt and shortening together, then while still mixing, add water. Roll out dough onto a floured board, bake in pie pan in preheated 375°F oven for 10 minutes, or until lightly brown.

Filling:
  1½ cups sugar
  Juice from 1½ Key limes*
  Grated skin of one lime
  3 eggs
  2 tbsp corn starch
  2 tbsp flour
  2 cups milk (yes, milk)
  1 tbsp butter
Combine all this and then cook in a double boiler – not on direct heat or it will burn – and stir until thickened, about 20 to 25 minutes.

Meringue:
  5 tbsp sugar
  1 tbsp corn starch
  ½ cup water
  3 egg whites
  ½ tsp cream of tartar
Combine 2 tbsp sugar, corn starch and water. Cook on direct heat until it thickens and becomes clear. Set aside. Combine the egg whites with the 3 tbsp sugar and ½ tsp cream of tartar and mix with an electric beater on high until smooth. Add the cooked sugar, water and corn starch and beat the entire mixture until fluffy.

Add filling to the pie crust, then pile on the meringue. Bake at 300°F for 10 minutes, then at 350° until the meringue browns. Cool and serve.

*If you can't get Key limes, the next best option is to buy some Key lime juice through a company like Key West Aloe (☎ 294-5592) – 16-ounce bottle costs $4.20 and two are $7.95 (add $5.95 shipping). Failing that, use a mixture that's half lemon juice and half lime juice. ∎

every day for dinner; they also do an all-you-can-eat buffet lunch ($6.95) Monday to Saturday from 11 am to 3 pm; they're open every day, other menu items are in the $8 to 10 range.

Another great backyard place is *Donnie's*

(☎ 294-5620), behind 618 Duval St. It's got two large bars and live entertainment every night in addition to the restaurant, which is open 24 hours (!). Breakfasts run $3.50 to $5.95; at lunch, salads are $3 to 6.95, sandwiches are $3.25 to 6.95, and hot dishes, like shrimp and veggies over pasta or rice, are $12.95. Dinners can go as cheap as $9.95, but they average $12.95.

El Meson de Pepe (☎ 296-6922), 1215 Duval St, is rustic, simple and Spanish-feeling, and is said to be excellent: they have a $7 chicken plate or grilled steak for $9.90 and shrimp Creole for $12.50. Open for lunch and dinner.

The pan-Asian food at *Dim Sum* (☎ 294-6230), 613½ Duval St, down the tiny alley that runs straight back to the Greyhound station, is fantastic, as is the atmosphere – very slick Japanese design, dark and intimate. It's very popular, very small and open only for dinner, so reserve. Try the Indonesian beef rendang ($16.95), veggie dishes ($12.95 to 13.95), chicken and shrimp in Thai green curry sauce ($17.95) and Indian chicken curry ($15.95).

Yo Saké (☎ 294-2288), 722 Duval St, is our favorite Key West sushi place for its great service and better sushi – though it's on the pricey side (by the piece it's $3.50 to 4.50, rolls from $4.50). Dinners include vegetable and seafood tempura for $12.75 and beef Yakiniko (steak marinated in garlic, mushroom and soy sauce) for $16.75. The sushi bar seats are pretty uncomfortable, and we prefer the traditional Japanese seating outside, off the romantic garden.

We suggest poking your head inside the sushi bar at *Kyushu Japanese Restaurant* (☎ 294-2995), 921 Truman Ave, to see if things smell fresher than when we visited – we went at an off hour, and the place looks so funky and friendly it would be a shame not to give it a chance. Sushi dinners are $15.95, chicken teriyaki is $13.95 and steak teriyaki is $17.95. Lunch specials are $8.95.

Antonia's Restaurant (☎ 294-6565), 744 Windsor Lane, was recently gutted by fire, but they plan to reopen. Said to be an excellent restaurant treasured by the locals for birthday parties and other special events, it's a little expensive at about $20 an entree. Check when you're here.

Pepe's (☎ 294-7192), 806 Caroline St, looks shabby from the outside but the inside is clean and simple. Breakfast specials run $1.75 to 5, main courses at lunch and dinner include broiled fish at $13, and the house special, steak smothered in onions and pork chops for two with side dishes, is $29.70. It's supposed to be huge and great.

Louie's Backyard (☎ 294-1061), 700 Waddell Ave, was started by a Conch in his house and has grown into one of Key West's most popular – if expensive – places. It's a great place for drinks on the deck, and the classic Key West food's not bad either, if you can afford it.

Banana Café (☎ 294-7227), 1211 Duval St, seems to know what it's doing. For breakfast and lunch, see those headings. Their set dinner menu is $25, including soup, salad, entree and dessert. Other entrees include sautéed salmon at $18 and filet mignon at $21. It's a very pleasant place with a few outside tables, and there's live jazz on Tuesday nights.

Entertainment
Theater The *Red Barn Theatre* (☎ 296-9911), 319 Duval St, is a tiny little playhouse that's been putting on a variety of plays for the past 16 years or so. The last season featured well-known and original shows, including *Jeffrey*, *Dames at Sea*, *El•ee•mos•y•nary* and *Keely & Du*.

The *Key West Players* (☎ 292-3725) at the Waterfront Playhouse at Mallory Docks is the community theater, putting on plays and musicals for adults and children.

Bars & Live Music More than a couple of people have been known to tip back a few in Key West – in fact, drinking is a Key West institution with a long and illustrious history of lushes from rumrunners (the people, not the drink) to Hemingway. And it's immortalized in Jimmy Buffet's song *Margaritaville*.

Most bars in town have some sort of live music on most nights, and happy hours and drink specials happen all the time. Bars stay open until most people leave, at least until 2 am and sometimes later. The Pub Crawl is another institution here, and bars freaked out when police began enforcing open-container laws that hindered customers from walking between bars carrying their drinks. Enforcement isn't as gung-ho now, but note that it is illegal to walk with an open container holding an alcoholic drink – even if it's in a plastic cup.

For watering holes, most people head for one of a couple of places: *Sloppy Joe's Bar* (☎ 294-5717), 201 Duval St, is the Hemingway Hangout of Record, with live entertainment every night; their Hemingway Hammer ($6.50) is made from 151-proof rum, banana and strawberry liqueur, blackberry brandy and a dash of white rum. Drinks and a 'cheeseburger in paradise' can be had at Jimmy Buffet's *Margaritaville Café* (☎ 292-1435), 500 Duval St. *Schooner Wharf* (☎ 292-9520), 202 Williams St, is a pretty authentic-feeling sailor's bar and a real Conch hangout. It's on the water and a great place for drinks while watching the sunset or grabbing a cruise. Local musicians – from banjos to reggae – and local entertainers perform nightly.

Rick's (☎ 296-4890) – what a meat market! But people seem to really like it, and not just for their Wednesday and Thursday night specials: for $5 (low season) or $7 (high season) you get a wrist band allowing you to drink all you can from 9 to 11.30 pm (bring your ID). Then, if you can maneuver the stairs, Upstairs at Rick's is a dance club. It all happens at (*hic!*) 202-208 Duval St.

Billie's Bar (☎ 294-9292), 407 Front St, has two bars, both open until 4 am. Their sunset happy hour has draft and domestic beers ($1 to1.50) and $2 well drinks; they also serve sandwiches for $3.75 to 7 and entrees for $10 to 20.

Barefoot Bob's (☎ 296-5858), 525 Duval St, has an outdoor garden; inside, it's sort of hippie-ish, but not in an annoying kind of way.

Captain Tony's Saloon (☎ 294-1838), 428 Greene St, has live music almost every night, and the *Piano Bar* (☎ 296-6625), 611 Duval St, is just that, with specials on frozen and sweet drinks.

Durty Harry's (☎ 296-4890), 208 Duval St, has five bars with live music every day.

Literally the day we went to press, Hard Rock Cafe announced that they were constructing an 11,000-sq-foot bar and restaurant in Key West at 313 Duval St near Caroline. It will, of course, have an attached shop. Both should be open by the time you read this.

Gay & Lesbian Bars Note that the 'straight' section of town begins from Mallory Square and continues to about the 500 block of Duval St. From that point on it's a healthy Key West mix of straight and gay.

Gay and lesbian bars change as often as they do in Miami Beach, so beware and check when you're here: publications like *Key West Columbia Fun Map* or *Crooz Control* are available at gay-owned and -friendly businesses throughout the city.

Atlantic Shores (☎ 296-2491), 510 South St, is a very popular local poolside spot for all-over sunning; there's a small snack bar and grill, the pool and, on Sunday, Tea by the Sea, the largest tea dance in Key West.

The Club International (☎ 296-9230), 900 Simonton St, is the only real lesbian club in town.

Bourbon St Pub (☎ 296-1992) at 730 Duval St has a happy hour from noon to 8 pm every day – the longest on island – and all-you-can-drink beer from 6 to 10 pm on Sunday. They do shows from jazz sax to drag throughout the week. It's a locals' hangout.

The beautifully named *Treetop Bar at La Te Da* (☎ 296-6706) at 1125 Duval St also does lots of shows, and lots of locals show up for the happy hour. There are drag shows at midnight a couple of nights a week and live entertainment on weekends.

The Copa (☎ 296-8521), 623 Duval St, was *the* heart of gay Key West before it burned in August 1995; it will be reopened by the time you read this, and totally reconstructed.

801 (☎ 294-4737), 801 Duval St, has two bars downstairs and one upstairs; down-

FLORIDA KEYS

stairs in back are gay porn and leather parties, especially on weekends. Upstairs there are drag shows two or three times a week, and on Sunday, it's Sunday Afternoon Benefit Bingo – participatory bingo that benefits AIDS Help Inc of Monroe County. (Every number elicits a response from the crowd: 'B-10'=Black and *Blue!* And when 'O-69' is called the place is total pandemonium.)

Things to Buy
The first order of business is to get yourself a pair of Kino Sandals, the classic Key West footwear: Naugahyde sandals that are slippery when wet but cheap – expect to spend about $8 for a pair. There are many styles and colors, and they come in leather as well – and if they ever break, bring them in and they'll be repaired.

There are so many opportunities to buy tourist stuff that you won't be able to avoid it. For a nice taste treat, look for Nelly & Joe's Key West Lime Juice salad dressings.

Getting There & Away
Air At the time of writing – and prices change drastically – one could count on spending from $150 to 180 for a roundtrip flight between Miami and Key West. A direct flight between New York City and Key West can be as low as $284. American Airlines (☎ 800-433-7300), Chalk's International Air (☎ 800-424-2557), Gulfstream Air (☎ 871-1200, 800-992-8532) and USAir (☎ 800-428-4322) all have several flights a day (American has the most). Gulfstream, though, consistently has a better range of cheaper tickets than the others.

Key West International Airport is off S Roosevelt Blvd on the west side of the island.

Bus The Greyhound station (☎ 293-0410) is in the alley behind 615½ Duval St, between Angela and Southard Sts. Greyhound has three buses to/from Miami daily; they cost $26/50 one-way/roundtrip on weekdays, $27/52 on weekends. Buses leave Miami's Bayside Station for the 4¾-hour trip at 7.10 am, 11.45 am and 6.15 pm.

You can take the bus from Key West or Miami to any destination along US Hwy 1 in the Florida Keys; there are official stops, but just tell the driver where you want to get off and they'll stop.

Fares and *approximate* travel times to other keys from Key West include the following (add $1 to all these prices on weekends):

Destination	Price	Duration
Boca Chica	$5	15 minutes
Big Pine	$8	40 minutes
Marathon	$11	1 hour
Islamorada	$17	1 hour 50 minutes
Key Largo	$21	2 ½ hours

If you're trying to get back to Miami from somewhere in the Keys, note that buses leave Key West at 8 am, 12.30 and 5.15 pm. Stand anywhere on US Hwy 1, and when you see the bus in the distance, signal – firmly and visibly, using all methods at your disposal up to and perhaps including a flare gun – and the bus will stop and pick you up. *If* the driver sees you.

Shuttle Check with the Clay Hotel and International Hostel (see the Miami Beach section) for information on the plethora of shuttle services that pop down to the Keys. Paradise Transport in Miami (☎ 305-293-3010) offers 15-passenger van service for $295 each way – which works out to about $20 per person each way if you fill the thing (putting a sign up on the bulletin board at the Clay is the best bet). For the flush (or flash), they also offer limo service for a mere $320 each way.

Car It's about 160 miles from Miami to Key West along US Hwy 1. Take Florida's Turnpike Extension (toll) south and then pick up US Hwy 1 south at Florida City. Don't be in a hurry; enjoy the view. There are keenly enforced speed limits at various places along the route, speeding fines are high, you'll probably get caught, and should you hit a Key deer while speeding, penalties are stiff. Slow down.

Getting Around

Bus The Conch Loop (☎ 292-8200), not to be confused with the Conch Train tours, is a city-run bus service with two buses that ply the same route. Outbound buses run from Mallory Square to Stock Island, inbound runs the reverse route.

Outbound route: begins at the corner of Duval and Eaton Sts, up to Truman, left to Simonton, to South St, to Reynolds, to Flagler Ave, to Kennedy Drive, to Northside Drive, left to Key Plaza Shopping Center, back on Northside Drive, to 20th St, about 3 blocks to Duck Ave, to S Roosevelt Blvd (US Hwy A1A) out to US Hwy 1 and Stock Island.

Buses run every 15 minutes or so, beginning at 6.05 am, continuing until 10.30 pm. Get printed schedules right on the bus. Fare is 75¢ for adults, 35¢ for seniors and students, but they need a reduced fare card ($1.50) from the Transportation Department office at 627 Palm Ave.

Car The best thing to do with a car in Key West is to sell it: parking is murder, parking tickets cost $10, they're quick to tow and traffic is restricted. The city is constructing a public parking lot on Caroline St, but until that's done you're at the mercy of private lots or hotel parking.

Moped, Bike & Scooter Rentals You can rent mopeds or scooters at several places on the island, and you don't need a motorcycle license; prices average $15 a day (from 8 am to 6 pm) or $25 for 24 hours. Try Keys Moped & Scooter (☎ 294-0399) at 523 Truman Ave; Scooter Rentals in the Southernmost Motel, 1319 Duval St; and Moped Hospital (☎ 296-3344) at 601 Truman Ave. The Key West International Hostel rents bicycles for $4 a day, $6 for 24 hours. Bicycle rentals are also available in lots of places; prices average $7 to 10 a day.

AROUND KEY WEST
Dry Tortugas

The Dry Tortugas (tor-TOO-guzz), a tiny archipelago of seven islands about 69 miles southwest of Key West, was first 'developed' 300 years after its discovery by Juan Ponce de León. Today it's open as a national park, under the control of the Everglades National Park office (☎ 305-242-7700), and you can only get there by boat or plane.

Ponce de León named the area *Las Tortugas* – 'The Turtles' – for the hawksbill, green, leatherback and loggerhead turtles that roam around the islands, and sailors later changed that to Dry Tortugas for the obvious reason that there's no fresh water here.

The first development consisted of a lighthouse on Garden Key, to warn ships of the rocky shoals around the islands. In 1846, construction began on Fort Jefferson: the USA saw the wisdom in a fortification there to protect and control traffic into the Gulf of Mexico.

A federal garrison during the Civil War, Fort Jefferson was also a prison for Union deserters and for at least four people, among them Dr Samuel Mudd, arrested for complicity in the assassination of Abraham Lincoln.

In 1867, a yellow fever outbreak killed 38 people, and after a hurricane in 1873, the fort was abandoned. It was reopened in 1886 as a quarantine station for those with smallpox and cholera.

The fort was established as a national monument in 1935 by President Roosevelt, and in 1992, George Bush showed great character by signing legislation that changed the name from Fort Jefferson National Monument to Dry Tortugas National Park.

Though still very rare, the loggerhead is the most commonly spotted of Florida's sea turtles.

FLORIDA KEYS

1/1 Hst Frt w/Grt Vws, Trtls, Exc Snrkl & Dvg, No Wtr

How'dya like to live in a historic fort on a deserted island? Members of the NPS do. The nine full-time residents of Fort Jefferson live in apartments within the fort, using the ancient fort's catchment system (yeah, we believe that) and modern desalination devices to make fresh water; diesel-powered generators provide electricity for appliances, satellite dishes, TV/VCRs and stereos. It's a little like working in a far-off embassy to a country we're somewhat on the outs with except for one thing: it's *here*, in a tropical paradise where work is snorkeling and telling other people how to.

Competition for the positions – which usually last about two years – is fierce. So fierce, in fact, that the NPS actually gets away with charging the rangers rent to live out here.

The residents get four days shore leave for every four weeks worked, and they travel to and from the civilization of Key West aboard the *Activa*, an NPS boat. ∎

Today the park is open for day trips or overnight camping. On Garden Key you'll see Fort Jefferson, the site of the park's visitor center. There you can pick up information on the entire park, as well as walk around the seawall: information plaques on the seawall describe the wildlife you're likely to encounter both in the moat and in the water around the islands.

The fort's a fascinating place, and the sparkling water offers excellent snorkeling and diving opportunities. And sleeping over is a unique experience: so close to the hubbub of Key West, but blissfully peaceful.

The Islands The park is made up of seven islands: Garden Key, on which the fort located, is the only place you can stay overnight. Bush Key is closed to the public from March to September – it's reserved for nesting terns. The remaining keys – East, Middle, Hospital, Long and Loggerhead – are all closed from sunset to sunrise from May to September to protect nesting turtles.

Camping There are 10 free campsites on Garden Key, given out on a first-come, first-served basis, so reserve early by calling the Everglades National Park office (☎ 305-242-7700). Your stay is limited to 30 days per year and no more than 14 days per stay. There are toilets but no freshwater showers or drinking water; bring everything you'll need (see the Everglades section for some packing suggestions).

Getting There & Away If you have your own boat, the Dry Tortugas are covered under National Ocean Survey Chart No 11438.

The *Yankee Freedom* (☎ 294-7009) is a ferry that runs between Garden Key and Land's End Marina at the foot of Margaret St in Key West. The roundtrip fare is $75 for adults, $65 for students, seniors and military, and $45 for children under 16. They'll leave you out there overnight for $90 per person, including you and transport of 100 pounds of your gear (you need your own – they don't rent the gear itself). The journey takes about 3½ hours. Board on Monday, Wednesday, Friday and Saturday at the marina at 7.30 am and leave at 8 am, get back at 7.30 pm. Reservations are necessary. Breakfast – eggs, sausage and toast – and box lunches are included in the fares.

By plane, Key West Seaplane Service (☎ 294-6978) will take you and up to five passengers (flight time 40 minutes each way): a four-hour trip is $159, an eight-hour trip is $275. They'll fly you out there to camp for $299 per person, including snorkeling equipment. They'll pick you up at the beach in Key West; reserve a week in advance. Prices dip in the summer.

THE LOWER KEYS

The main attraction in the Lower Keys is the National Key Deer Refuge, but there's skydiving and, of course, great diving and snorkeling as well, especially at Looe Key and Bahia Honda State Park. You can also arrange some wonderful kayak trips among the mangroves of the Great White Heron National Wildlife Refuge.

Orientation & Information
The Lower Keys stretch from Boca Chica to the Seven Mile Bridge just northeast of Bahia Honda Key. Get tourist information, accommodations and snorkel or dive information at the very helpful Lower Keys Chamber of Commerce (☎ 872-3580, 800-872-3722, 800-352-5397) at MM 31 on Big Pine Key. Get information on the National Key Deer Refuge and local flora and fauna at the refuge headquarters (☎ 872-2239) in the Big Pine Shopping Center, MM 30; the headquarters are open Monday to Friday from 8 am to 5 pm.

Dive shops include Looe Key Reef Resort & Dive Center (☎ 872-2215, 800-446-5663), MM 27, and Reef Runner Dive Shop (☎ 745-1549), MM 25.

Change money at the Barnett Bank (☎ 872-0619) at MM 30.5. There's a coin laundry off Key Deer Blvd in Big Pine Key. A stop at the Big Pine Shopping Center, MM 30.5 (turn north on Key Deer Blvd, and it's on the right), will take care of a lot of needs: it has a Winn Dixie, the biggest food market in the area; Edie's Hallmark Shop, which has a small selection of books, mainly best-selling paperbacks; the Big Pine Key public library (☎ 289-6303); and the Big Pine Medical Complex (☎ 872-3735), a walk-in clinic.

Another Lower Keys walk-in clinic is the Big Pine Medical and Minor Emergency Clinic (☎ 872-3321) at MM 30 oceanside. For major emergencies, the closest hospital is Florida Keys Health Systems (☎ 294-5531, 800-233-3119), 5900 College Rd on Stock Island, a 24-hour emergency room.

Great White Heron National Wildlife Refuge
The Great White Heron National Wildlife Refuge (☎ 872-2239) is comprised of two large but little-visited wading bird nesting areas, where you can see herons, ibis, egrets, ospreys, hawks and even eagles, as well as fish, crabs, sponges, coral and mangroves.

Kayaks and canoes are permitted within the preserve, since much of it is inaccessible except by boat, but there are no services. For more information contact the National Key Deer Refuge headquarters in the Big Pine Shopping Center (see below). See Kayak Nature Tours below for organized trips to the refuge.

Kayak Nature Tours
Nature photographer Bill Keogh at Lost World Adventures (☎ 872-8950) offers guided kayak journeys into both the Great White Heron and Key Deer Refuges. The trips are usually three to four hours and leave regularly in the morning and the afternoons, though special-occasion sunset and sunrise journeys can be arranged. You'll paddle along the red mangrove coastlines through the shallow habitat and check out what's what; the cost is $45 per person, and he usually takes no more than six people per guide to ensure that it's peaceful enough for all. Keogh also rents one-person kayaks for $25 for a half day (four to five hours), $30 for a full day (eight hours), and $45 for 24 hours. Doubles are $40/55/65.

Rentals and tours leave from Jig's Fishing and Snorkeling Center MM 30.2 bayside on Big Pine Key.

For the same prices as Lost World, Reflections Kayak Nature Tours (☎ 872-2896) will take you out on guided tours as well; they also offer similarly priced kayak rentals. Tours leave from Palmer's Place Guesthouse (see Hotels & Motels below), which is on Barry Ave off MM 28.5 on Little Torch Key (which is one mile west of Big Pine Key). They'll deliver and pick up a kayak anywhere between Marathon to Sugarloaf Key for $20.

See Looe Key for information on snorkeling and kayaking there.

National Key Deer Refuge
The National Key Deer Refuge (☎ 872-2239) is on large tracts of property that sprawl over several Keys, but the sections that are open to the public – such as Blue Hole, Watson's Hammock and Watson's

Nature Trail – are on Big Pine and No Name Keys. Stop in at the Refuge Headquarters in the Big Pine Shopping Plaza, off MM 30, for lots of information; it's open Monday to Friday from 8 am to 5 pm.

The best times to see Key deer are in the early morning and late afternoon; ask at the headquarters where the best places to see them are on the day you come. Admission to the entire refuge is free. There are three established refuge areas but all areas in the refuge marked with signs that say 'US Fish & Wildlife Service – Unauthorized Entry Prohibited' are open to the public from a half hour before sunrise to a half hour after sunset. Areas with a sign saying 'Closed Beyond This Point' are off-limits.

From MM 30.5, take Key Deer Blvd for 3½ miles. The first place you'll reach is Blue Hole; the Watson's Nature Trail and Watson's Hammock are about a quarter mile farther on the same road.

Blue Hole Blue Hole, the largest body of freshwater in the Keys, is in an old quarry, where you'll see very large alligators, turtles and fish along with a huge variety of wading birds. Please don't ignore the signs imploring you not to feed the wildlife – many tourists go right ahead and feed anything that wiggles, which is illegal.

Watson's Nature Trail This is a two-thirds mile self-guided walk through the Key deer's natural habitat. Guided walks are available to groups and individuals. On weekends from December to March there are ranger-led three-hour guided walks of Watson's Hammock, a prime Key deer fawning area, but the hammock is closed completely to the public in April and May. Guided walks begin behind Blue Hole, but check with the rangers at the headquarters.

No Name Key No Name Key is a very good place to see Key deer in the early morning and late afternoon, and there are fewer visitors here than in the Blue Hole or Watson's Nature Trail. Take Key Deer Blvd to Watson Blvd, turn right, go about 1½ miles to Wilder Blvd, turn left, follow it for

---

Underwater Camera Rentals

Tropic Isle Photo (☎ 289-0303) at MM 52.9 in Marathon rents Nikonos underwater cameras, which range in cost from $25 to 45 per day based on how much stuff you get. They also rent Sony underwater VHS and Hi-8 video cameras for $60 and 85 a day, respectively. You'll need to give them a credit card or cash deposit for the full value of the equipment – the Hi-8 and housing, the most expensive piece of gear they have, is worth $180. ■

---

two miles to Bogie Bridge, cross it and you'll be on No Name.

SeaCamp

The Newfound Harbor Marine Institute (☎ 872-2331, see the Online Services appendix), Newfound Harbor Rd on Big Pine Key, is a nonprofit environmental education center that runs an educational camp. Between seven and eight thousand people a year take part in SeaCamp programs, which run from three to 30 days, and while many are geared to children, there are some expanding adult programs as well.

In summer it's a full-blown coed summer camp with three 18-day sessions for campers 12 to 17 years old. The season runs from June 1 to August 26, and the cost is $2195 (about $120 a day), including housing, meals and programs. There's scuba, photography, arts & crafts and, of course, lots of time in the water learning about the environment. Residential adult programs run from September to May and cost an average of $110 a day.

For more information, write to Sea-Camp, 1300 Big Pine Ave, Big Pine Key, FL 33043.

Looe Key

Pronounced 'Loo', this isn't a Key at all but a grove reef off Ramrod Key. Proclaimed a national marine sanctuary in 1981, it's named for an English frigate that sank in the area in 1744.

Within the sanctuary, snorkeling and

diving is permitted, and thousands of varieties of hugely colorful tropical fish, coral and sea life abound. There are snorkeling trips to Looe Key on the *HMS Looe* (☎ 872-2685, 800-553-0308) at the Dolphin Marina, behind Little Palm Island at MM 28.5. The trips go every morning at 10 am and on Thursday and Saturday to Tuesday afternoons at 2.30 pm. The four-hour trips cost $19.99 per person plus $5 for equipment rental.

Island Excursions with Strike Zone Charters (☎ 872-9863, 800-654-9560) at MM 29.5 also does four-hour Looe Key snorkeling and diving trips at 9.30 am and 1.30 pm for $25 per person and $5 for equipment for snorkeling, $40 plus $25 for equipment for divers.

Blue Water Tours (☎ 872-2896, 800-822-1386) has guided three-hour sea kayak tours and rentals as well.

The Looe Key Reef Resort (☎ 872-2215), MM 27.5 (see Hotels & Motels below), runs snorkel or diving trips for $25/40 without the equipment; if you need to rent the gear, add $5 for snorkeling, $25 for diving. The trips last about four hours and hit two different locations.

Nature photographer Bill Keogh at Lost World Adventures (☎ 872-8950) does snorkeling trips in the summer to Looe Key with kayaks, or you can charter his 27-foot catamaran. The cat takes up to six people, and the cost is $160 for four hours.

Bat Tower
The Bat Tower, on the National Register of Historic Places, is a wooden tower built in 1929 by Righter Clyde Perky. The idea was that the tower would attract bats, who would then eat the swarming masses of mosquitoes and make the Keys a wonderful place. The bats didn't come. The tower is off MM 17 on Lower Sugerloaf Key; if you're headed away from Key West, turn left, then go left on the little road off the parking lot.

Skydiving & Air Tours
The strangely named Instant Downplane Productions (☎ 745-4386), right near the Bat Tower off MM 17, does tandem sky-

dives for $219 (if you weigh over 200 pounds, they charge $1 a pound more for each pound over 200), or $199 if you pay cash. Solo jumps (license and 300 jumps required) are $35, and you can save the whole thing for posterity on videotape for $99. At the same location, Fantasy Dan's (☎ 745-2217) does airplane tours from $20 to 50, depending on time in the air.

Bahia Honda State Park
One of the Keys' best beaches, Bahia Honda State Park (☎ 872-2353) at MM 36.5 – at the foot of the Seven Mile Bridge – is a 524-acre park, including one small off-shore island. The beaches are sparkling white sand and very pretty, but in summer sandflies are rife. It's a very popular place – the 2½-mile expanse and the shape of the beach allow you to secrete yourself in little nooks and crannies for privacy, but despite listings in naturalist magazines, note that topless (women) or nude bathing is prohibited. Rangers will tell you to put on clothes once, after which you could be fined and ejected from the park.

The park concession (☎ 872-3210) rents snorkeling equipment ($5) and offers snorkel excursions every day at 9 am, noon and 3 pm; the cost is $22 for adults and $18 for anyone under 16. In high season, reservations are a good idea; call and they'll put your name on the list. The concession also rents kayaks (singles/doubles are $10/20 an hour), and there's a restaurant and grocery store.

Bahia Honda is the southernmost Key with exposed limestone, and along its nature trails you'll find silver palms, yellow satinwood and lily thorn (endangered). Admission is $3.75 per car, $1 for pedestrians or bicyclists, and tent sites and cabins are available (see Camping below).

Places to Stay
Camping *Big Pine Key Fishing Lodge* (☎ 872-2351) at MM 33 has tent sites for $22.50 and full hookup sites for $26 all year. They have an artificial beach, and while swimming in the ocean is not so great here, there is a pool. They also have

FLORIDA KEYS

motel efficiencies for $68 per night all year; there is a three-night minimum stay.

Sunshine Key Camping Resort & Marina (☎ 872-2217) is a campground with very friendly and helpful staff at 38801 Overseas Hwy (MM 39). They have tent sites without hookups in summer/winter for $21.95/29.95; with water and electric it's $25/41; and waterfront sites with water and electric are $39/51.

There's camping at *Bahia Honda State Park* (☎ 872-2353), MM 37; sites are $23.69 without electricity and $25.73 with. Waterfront sites (reserve far in advance or forget it) are an additional $2.30. Cabins are $96.85 from September 15 to December 14 and $124.60 the rest of the year.

Hotels & Motels *Palmer's Place Guesthouse* (☎ 872-2157) on Little Torch Key is a resort based around nature excursions run by its in-house nature tour company, Reflections Kayak Nature Tours (☎ 872-2896). Motel rooms range from $66 to 70; larger motel rooms are from $65 to 85. There are also efficiencies and cottages available; all prices include continental breakfast. Trips are additional (see Kayak Nature Tours above). They're on Barry Ave off MM 28.5 on Little Torch Key; call for directions.

Sugarloaf Lodge (☎ 745-3211) is something of a resort – not so huge, but not just a hotel – at MM 17 in Lower Sugarloaf Key. All waterfront rooms are from $55 to 65 and efficiencies are $70 from September 1 to December 18; $65 to 80/85 from May 1 to August 31; and $105 to 115/120 from December 19 to April 30.

Looe Key Reef Resort (☎ 872-2215) at MM 27.5 has motel rooms with two double beds, TV and phone for $60 to 110, depending on the season. They also rent snorkel equipment ($5) and diving equipment ($25) and run snorkel/dive trips (see Looe Key above).

B&Bs There are three B&Bs on Big Pine Key, all oceanside: *Casa Grande* (☎ 872-2878) on the ocean at MM 33 has rooms for two with breakfast for $75 in summer,

$95 in winter. Their Jacuzzi is hot in winter and cold in summer. *The Barnacle* (☎ 872-3298) at Long Beach Drive off MM 33 is another choice, with rates from $75 to 110, and *Deer Run B&B* (☎ 872-2015), also on Long Beach Drive, has rates from $85 to 110.

Places to Eat

Pizza Works (☎ 872-1119) at the Big Pine Shopping Center, MM 30.5, has good slices from $1 to 2.50, sandwiches from $4 to 5 and pizzas at around $10. In the same shopping center is *Coco's* (☎ 872-4495), which is open Monday to Saturday 7 am to 7.30 pm. They have a good stuffed crab, bean, onion and cheese burrito for $1.25, veggie rice is $2.50 and spare ribs with yellow rice is $5. They also have good sandwiches and are very friendly.

Good Food Conspiracy (☎ 872-3945) at MM 30 is a killer health food place with prepared foods as well as a juice bar, vitamins and the like.

Right next to the Big Pine Post Office at MM 30, the *Big Pine Coffee Shop and Restaurant* (☎ 872-2790) is a trip into the past with breakfast specials from $2 to 3.50, a lunch-special cheeseburger with fixin's and fries for $5.15 and sandwiches from $3.85 to 4.95.

Island Reef Restaurant (☎ 872-2170), MM 31.5, serves sandwiches for $4.95, burgers for $4.50 to 5.95 and seafood salad for $7.95. Entrees like meatloaf are $5.95, and fish and chips are $7.95. They are closed on Sunday.

Dip 'N' Deli (☎ 872-3030), MM 31, has lots of subs and sandwiches for $2.75 to 4.60; their garden burger is $4.50. At dinner entrees range from $7.95 to 10.95, including steak, barbecue chicken, pork or ribs, fried chicken and meatloaf.

Mangrove Mama's (☎ 745-3030) at MM 20 is a very hip place, with live music (no cover charge) in their great bar on weekends and reggae on Sunday from 7 to 11.30 pm. They do mainly Caribbean-inspired dishes and seafood; starters like conch fritters and vegetable tempura are $4.25 to 7.50, salads $3 to 8, lunches (like fried fish) $6.75 and burgers start at $5.75. Fish chowder is $1.95 to 2.50. Dinner is more expensive, like catch of the day for $15 or coconut shrimp for $15.95; a surf-and-turf dinner is $21.95.

MARATHON KEY
• *pop 9000* ☎ *305*

People come to Marathon to fish. That's not to say that nonfishers will be completely bored out of their minds; it's just that the area is really geared to fishing. But Marathon is also home to the Dolphin Research Center, where you – yes, you – can swim with dolphins in supervised programs.

The area is also home to Pigeon Key, in the middle of the Old Seven Mile Bridge, and a trip to this island is a very interesting look at the building of the very lifeline of the Florida Keys – the Overseas Hwy.

Orientation & Information
The Marathon area runs from the northeast end of the Seven Mile Bridge up through the Conch Keys. Get a motherlode of information at the Marathon Visitors Center/Chamber of Commerce (☎ 743-5417, 800-262-7284, see Online Services appendix) at MM 53.5. The chamber also sells Greyhound tickets; the Greyhound station in Marathon Key is between the FedEx building and the fire station between MMs 51.5 and 52. The Marathon Airport is at MM 52.

Change money at the Barnett Bank (☎ 743-5002), 6090 Overseas Hwy, MM 50.5. Fisherman's Hospital (☎ 743-5533), MM 48.7, has a major emergency room.

Marathon Book Exchange (☎ 743-2284), MM 48.5, buys and sells used books, and Food for Thought (☎ 743-3297) at the Gulfside Village Shopping Center, MM 51 bayside, is a combination bookstore and health food shop – it carries newspapers, such as the *New York Times* and *Wall Street Journal*, some LP titles and other guidebooks, general fiction and literature, as well as vitamins, bulk products and frozen foods (but no juice bar).

Do laundry at the Maytag Coin Laundry (☎ 743-3448), at about MM 53.5, for $7.25 per load; it's open Monday to Friday from

7 am to 9 pm, Saturday and Sunday from 7 am to 7 pm. Marathon Cleaners (☎ 743-5142) is at MM 51.5.

Tropic Isle Photo (☎ 289-0303), MM 52.9 oceanside, does one-hour photo developing starting at a little over $10.

Pigeon Key Museum
Pigeon Key is a five-acre island about two miles west of Marathon over the Old Seven Mile Bridge. As Henry Flagler's FEC railroad progressed southward, the construction of the Seven Mile Bridge between Marathon and Bahia Honda Keys (actually Little Duck Key) became an immense project. Pigeon Key was home, between 1908 and 1912, to about 400 workers.

After the completion of the bridge, Pigeon Key became home to maintenance workers. But after the hurricane that wiped out Flagler's railroad in 1935, the key once again became home to workers, this time converting the railroad to automobile bridges.

After a brief stint in the 1970s as a research facility leased by the University of Miami, the Pigeon Key Foundation formed to preserve the island's buildings and to tell the story of the railroad and its workers.

Today the museum is open to the public, and you can see the old city, including the 'honeymoon cottage', assistant bridge tender and bridge tender's houses, the section gang's quarters and several other buildings, including the 'negro quarters'.

Tours of the museum (☎ 289-0025, see Online Services appendix) run daily, and are $5. You park at Knight Key, the western end of Marathon (MM 47), and pick up a shuttle out to the island. Shuttles leave hourly from 10 am to 4 pm; the last shuttle returns to Knight Key at 5 pm. You can ride or walk across the bridge – if you do admission's $2.

Fishing Bridge
The Old Seven Mile Bridge is open as 'the World's Longest Fishing Bridge'; entry is free and it's right at the parking lot at the eastern foot of the bridge. If you've seen the movie *True Lies*, you'll recognize the

Swimming with Dolphins

The idea of swimming with a dolphin is so romantic and mystical that some tourists don't stop to consider the effect it might have on the animals or themselves. The idea of just jumping in the water and swimming with wild dolphins is not altogether a good one – if you don't scare them away, they may just go ahead and treat you like a dolphin – and dolphins playing among themselves have a grand time body-slamming and biting each other.

Experts say that 'structured' programs – in which staff accompany swimmers in controlled areas for swims with dolphins that are accustomed to human contact – are safer and more humane than 'unstructured' ones.

There are three swim with dolphins programs on the Keys; two – the Dolphin Research Center and the Theater of the Sea – offer all structured programs: swims are choreographed by staff who are there with you. The third, Dolphins Plus, offers an unstructured program for those who are 'comfortable' in the water. While Dolphins Plus offers classroom training and orientation, unstructured programs may be riskier than structured ones. Dolphins Plus also offers a structured program on weekends and some holiday periods. See the Marathon, Islamorada and Key Largo sections for full descriptions and prices. ■

parking lot as the spot where the jarhead lost his Harrier.

Dolphin Research Center

The Dolphin Research Center (☎ 289-1121), MM 59 bayside on Grassy Key, is a nonprofit educational center in an open lagoon dedicated to spreading understanding about dolphins. In addition to programs that introduce dolphins to the mentally handicapped and use dolphins for physical therapy, they run half-day 'Dolphin*insight*' programs three times a week, which include a guided tour of the facility and a workshop that explains dolphin physiology, training and conservation. The cost is $75. Not hands-on enough? You can join a full-day Dolphin Encounter program, in which you'll learn about and then swim with their dolphins for $90.

They also run educational walks at 10 and 11 am and 12.30, 2 and 3.30 pm; the charge is $9.50 for adults, $7.50 for seniors, $6 for kids four to 12. They're open Wednesday to Sunday from 9 am to 4 pm.

Museum of Natural History

This 63-acre museum (☎ 743-9100), MM 50 bayside, across from K-Mart, is a fun place to stop. They have a geological and geographical history of the Keys, exhibits on pirates and wrecking, and a coral reef

tunnel – which you can walk through – featuring underwater sounds. Also shown are tropical plants, mangroves and, best of all, a showcase with a cut-away sea turtle nest, allowing a rare glimpse. There are short but nice walking trails through the hammock, and the staff are very helpful and friendly. It's open Monday to Saturday from 9 am to 5 pm, Sunday from noon to 5 pm. Admission is $7.50 for adults, $6 for seniors, $4 for students and kids under six are free.

Beaches & Wrecks

There is a public beach at the end of Sombrero Beach Rd, about two miles from US Hwy 1 MM 50. There is a picnic area, barbecue grills, public bathrooms, a little playground and volleyball nets.

The wreck of the slave ship *Ivory Coast* (1853) is at Sombrero Reef; it's marked by a light tower, and there's an artificial reef built by Flagler to support the Overseas Railroad.

Other Activities

Rent bicycles at the Blue Waters Motel, MM 48.5 (see Places to Stay below), or at Tilden's Pro Dive Shop (☎ 743-5422, 800-223-4563), MM 49.5, for $2.50 for an hour, $5 a half day, $8 a day. Tilden's rents scuba equipment for $36 a day; half-day snorkel/dive trips are $25/30. They'll they go to 53 different locations of various depth; to get a full open-water certification is $275 for five days.

The Flight Department (☎ 743-4222), MM 55 bayside, does half-hour sightseeing flights for $75 (for up to three people), or if you're lucky enough to have a pilot's license, you can rent private planes here (call for specific prices).

Places to Stay

Camping Some of the best camping is at Bahia Honda State Park, just on the other side of the Seven Mile Bridge (see above).

Jolly Rogers Trailer Park (☎ 289-0404, 800-995-1525), MM 59.5 bayside, has tent sites in summer for $20, in late summer for $22 to 25, in fall for $20 again, and in peak seasons and times for $25 to 30. Sites with and without electricity are the same price, but the ones without water and electric are on the waterfront.

There's tent camping at the very friendly *Knight Key Campground* (☎ 743-4343, 800-348-2267), MM 47 oceanside (the last exit before the Seven Mile Bridge). Sites without electricity or water are $22.24, sites with tent and table (water and electricity) are $27.82, inland sites with water and electric are $33.89, shoreline sites $38.97 and marina sites $46.77. In off-peak times it's three days for the price of two.

Motels & Hotels Here's a neat one: *Sea Cove* (☎ 289-0800, 800-653-0800), MM 54, is a family-owned place with houseboat accommodations. The boats are chained in, so it's not as if you can go tootling off, but it's nice to sleep on the water. Single double-bed rooms in their enormous 12-room floating hotel run $39 to 69, two double beds are $49 to 79, and the seventh night is always free. They also have three small apartment houseboats, which go from $79 to 125 (sleeps up to four people, but you can bring air mattresses for more), and a 'baby boat' that sleeps two people is $59 to 79. On land, efficiencies (half cottages that sleep up to six in one large room) are $59 to 99. The

people here are very friendly; off-season prices are very negotiable. All rooms – on land or sea – have air-conditioning, color cable TV and local calls are free.

The startlingly clean *Siesta Motel* (☎ 743-5671), 7425 US Hwy 1, has been here for 36 years and provides great service. Singles/doubles are $40 in summer/48 in winter; efficiencies are $55 all year.

The *Royal Hawaiian Motel Botel* (☎ 743-7500), MM 53, is a clean place with rooms that sleep four. In low/peak season they're $40/85; all have a fridge and coffeemaker. They also have efficiencies that sleep five and cost $50/95; there's a boatdock/ramp and a pool.

Kingsail Motel (☎ 743-5246, 800-423-7474), MM 50.5, smelled very clean, but the furniture and carpet aren't shockingly new; no pets. Rates are complicated (location, size, view, month, earth rotation, mood). For motel rooms, prices range from $51 to 83, efficiencies $64 to 163, and they also have apartments and suites.

Banana Bay Resort (☎ 743-3500, 800-226-2621), MM 49.5 bayside, is a fine option for the money, with very friendly and helpful staff and a really lush tropical setting. Depending on view, rates are $75 to 125 in summer, $85 to 175 in winter and $95 to 195 in peak times. A good breakfast buffet (coffee, juice, bagels, pastries, fruit) is included, and there is a nice pool. They also offer snorkel and diving packages. No pets.

Seahorse Motel (☎ 743-6571, 800-874-1115), 7196 Overseas Hwy, has medium everything – rooms in summer/winter are $40/54; efficiencies are $65/80.

The *Blue Waters Motel* (☎ 743-4832, 800-222-4832), MM 48.5, is a very friendly and nice place. Rooms have very large bathrooms and cost $50 to 80. There is a pool, docks and a boat ramp (no charge), and you can fish here; local calls are free and they rent bicycles for $5 per day.

Places to Eat

All of the following also have bars that get packed at night. The *Banana Cabana Restaurant* (☎ 289-1232), MM 49.5, at the

Banana Bay Resort (see above) does good cheap lunches; burgers and sandwiches are $5.25, salads are $5.95 to 7.95. The dinner menu changes daily (served from 6 to 10 pm) and offers dishes like linguini in lobster sauce for $13.95 (delicious and huge) or a popular roasted duck for $12.95. The setting is quite tropical.

Shucker's (743-8686), 725 11th St, has sandwiches for $4.95 to 6.50 and Cajun chicken salad for $6.95. After 5 pm, grouper or shrimp (various preparations) is $16.95, filet mignon $19.95, and all entrees include salad, bread, potato or linguini or rice or fries. It's open daily from 11.30 am to 10 pm.

Herbie's (☎ 743-6373), MM 50.5, is a very popular local place; burgers are $3.25, fried fish sandwiches $4.25. Platters include fries, slaw and sauce and are $4.95 to 8.95, and their seafood combo platter is $11.95.

The *7 Mile Grill* (☎ 743-4481), 1240 Overseas Hwy, is a very popular outdoor place, roofed with table and bar service. Shrimp bisque is $2.75, fish sandwiches are $4.75, a fish plate $8.95 and crab cakes $7.95. They are open for breakfast from 7 to 11 am, lunch and dinner are served from 11.30 am to 8.30 pm. They are closed Wednesday (in the summer also on Thursday).

Hurricane (☎ 743-57550), MM 49.5, does live music on Thursday, Friday and Saturday nights – no cover.

ISLAMORADA
• *pop 1220* ☎ *305*

Home to some significant state historic sites, as well as to the cheesy-looking but fun Theater of the Sea, Islamorada (Eye-luh-murr-ahda) is probably worth a stop on the way through, even if you don't stay over.

Orientation & Information
The Islamorada area spans from Layton to Plantation Key. The Islamorada Chamber of Commerce (☎ 664-4503, 800-322-5397) is in an old caboose at MM 82.5 bayside. The main Greyhound station is at the Burger King at MM 82.5.

Change money at the Barnett Bank

(☎ 453-0704) at MM 81.5. Islamorada Coin Laundry (☎ 664-4141) is at MM 82.2; it's open Monday to Saturday from 8 am to 8 pm, Sunday 9 am to 5 pm. It's $1 per pound, $10 minimum; self-service is $2 for 20 pounds; and dryers are $1.

The Islamorada Medical Clinic (☎ 664-9731) is at 82685 US Hwy 1, and the Mariners Hospital (☎ 852-4418) is on Plantation Key at MM 88.5.

Dive shops in the area include Cheeca Divers (☎ 664-2777, 800-934-8377) at the Cheeca Lodge (see Places to Stay below), Holiday Isle Dive Center (☎ 664-4145, 800-327-7070), MM 84.5, and the Reef Shop (☎ 664-4385), 84771 US Hwy 1.

Indian Key State Historic Site
This historic site (☎ 664-4815) is a little island of only about 10 acres, but it has quite an interesting history. In 1831, renegade wrecker Jacob Housman bought the island after a falling out with wreckers in Key West, and he opened his own wrecker station on it. About 40 to 50 people lived permanently on the island, which Housman built up into a thriving little city, complete with warehouse, docks, streets and a hotel.

By 1836 Indian Key was the seat of Dade County. But Housman eventually lost his wrecker's license and the Second Seminole War was adding to his difficulties: in 1840 Housman lost the entire island after an Indian attack.

Today there's not much here, just the remains of the foundations of the original structures and some cisterns, Housman's grave and lots of plant life. But there is an observation tower and trails, and the free 1½- to 2-hour ranger-led tours (from Thursday to Monday at 9 am and 1 pm) give a great history, not just of the wrecking operation but of the geological and natural history of the island. There's a catch, though: you need to have a boat or take a $15 per person shuttle on the 10-minute ride from Robbie's Marina (see below). The shuttles leave starting about an hour before the tours begin – it pays to show up early as the boat only has room for six people. If you've got your own boat, the island's open all the time, admission is free, but camping is not permitted. There's another privately led tour from Papa Joe's Marina (see Organized Tours below).

Lignumvitae Key
Lignumvitae Key State Botanical Site (☎ 664-4815, pronounced lignum-VITE-ee) is a 280-acre island of virgin tropical forest. The main attraction here is the Matheson House (1919), its windmill and cistern.

The forest here includes strangler fig, mastic, gumbo-limbo and poisonwood trees, as well as the native lignumvitae tree, known for its extremely hard wood. Bring mosquito repellent.

On the island, 1¼- to 1½-hour ranger-guided walking tours are available Thursday to Monday at 10 am and 2 pm, but again, as with Indian Key, you can only get here by boat. From Robbie's Marina, tour boats leave on the 15-minute trip about a half hour before each tour – reservations highly recommended. The cost is $15 per person. Papa Joe's Marina also gives their own guided tour (see Organized Tours below).

Robbie's Marina
Robbie's (☎ 664-9814), MM 77.5 bayside, rents boats; rates start at $50 for half a day and, depending on boat size and number of people, rise quite briskly from there. Robbie's pier is open from 8 am to 6 pm.

Theater of the Sea
It looks very much like the cheesiest tourist attraction around, but the Theater of the Sea (☎ 664-2431), MM 84.5 bayside, has been here since 1946 and actually runs some very nice programs, including a structured dolphin swim. Their sea shows, which run continuously from 9.30 am to 4 pm, include dolphins and sea lions; a marine exhibit has sharks, sting rays and tropical fish. Trainers feed the animals while describing their behavior and habitat. There's also a living shell exhibit, and a five-minute boat ride into their dolphin

lagoon. Admission to the shows is $14.25 for adults, $7.95 for children three to 12. It's open daily.

Their structured dolphin swims include a half hour of instruction and a half hour of supervised swim; the cost is $80 for swimmers and $15.25 for adult observers, $8.75 for children observers. They're by reservation only; reservation times are at 9.30 am, noon and 2 pm.

Somewhere in Time
Somewhere in Time, the Museum of Spanish Shipwreck Treasures (☎ 664-8010), MM 82.8 oceanside, is a collection of artifacts salvaged from shipwrecks along the Keys over many years that were bought by owner Dick Holt. There are religious artifacts, bottles and coins on display. Holt, a jeweler, mounts coins and sells them as earrings, pendants, necklaces and so on. The museum is open daily from 9 am to 5 pm; admission is free.

Long Key
Long Key State Recreation Area (☎ 664-4815), MM 68, is a 965-acre park that opened in 1969. Inside, you'll see gumbo-limbo trees, crabwood, poisonwood, and *lots* of wading birds in the mangroves (especially in winter). The park has sections on both the gulf and ocean, and their beach is small at low tide and gone at high tide.

The two nature trails, the 1¼-mile Golden Orb and half-mile Layton Trail, head through several distinct plant communities.

In winter there are ranger-led programs Wednesday to Friday; on Wednesday mornings there are two-hour guided walks on the nature trails. On Thursday it's 'ranger's choice' day – what you'll see depends on who's on duty and their mood; talks could be on Indians, mangrove walks, bird watching and more. On Friday evenings they run campfire programs for the campers here.

The park also has a 1½-mile canoe trail through a salt-water tidal lagoon. Canoes cost $4 an hour or $10 per day.

Admission to the park is $3.25 per car, 50¢ per person, and there's camping here as well, see below.

Organized Tours

At Robbie's Marina (☎ 664-9814), MM 77.5 bayside, you can feed tarpon aboard a diesel-powered fiberglass motorboat; admission is $1 per person and a bucket of fish is $2. The best time to show up for tarpon feeding is midmorning.

Papa Joe's Marina (☎ 664-5005), MM 79.7 bayside, does guided tours to Indian Key from Thursday to Monday at 9.15 am, 1.15 pm and, in summer, an additional run at 3.15 pm. Guided tours to Lignumvitae Key include the Matheson House and the gardens as well as the ranger-led tours that are given Thursday to Monday at 10 am and 2 pm. There is also a two-hour scenic sunset cruise out onto Florida Bay. All their cruises are $24 for adults, $14 for children.

Places to Stay

Camping The *Long Key State Recreation Area* (☎ 664-4815), MM 68, has ocean-front campsites for $23.69 (no electricity or water, but there is a communal water faucet at every fifth site). Sites with electricity and water are $25.84, and there is a free dump station, though no sewer hookups.

KOA (☎ 664-4922), MM 70 on Fiesta Key, has sites with no hookups for $24.95, sites with water for $27.95 and with water and electricity for $29.95. On holidays these sites are $32.95/36.95/39.95. Full hookup sites are $44.95 inland and $54.95 waterfront; on holidays $54.95/67.95.

Motels & Hotels The simple rooms at the *Key Lantern* (☎ 664-4572), MM 82, aren't oceanfront, but staff are friendly. Rooms include TV and fridge, but there's no pool. In the off-season, rooms are $35 from Sunday to Thursday; on weekends rooms with one double bed are $45, with two double beds $50; and efficiencies are $53 to 58. At peak times these weekend prices run through the week.

The *Drop Anchor Motel* (☎ 664-4863), MM 85, has motel rooms with refrigerators and coffeemakers; there are no phones in the rooms, but there is a pay phone. They have a pool and barbecue grills. From September to December, rooms run $50 to 125;

from April to September, they're $55 to 135; and December to April $70 to 165.

The *Holiday Isle Resort* (☎ 664-2321, 800-327-7070), MM 84 oceanside, is a city of hotels and restaurants, including the *Holiday Isle, Harbor Lights* and *El Capitan Motel* and *Howard Johnson Resort*. There's also a Subway sandwich shop, a shopping mall, Jaws Raw Bar, a stage, a Tiki Bar and Rum Runner's, and Jose Cuervo Cantina and BBQ. They also have playgrounds, jungle-gyms, volleyball and basketball and, on the weekend, live Polynesian and reggae bands. The activities are endless and based around partying, fishing, diving and para-sailing; sort of a 'little Acapulco' (the atmosphere's the same, too).

Room rates at these hotels are fantasti-cally complex; suffice it to say that these base prices are the least you can expect to pay, but you can always spend a whole lot more: Harbor Lights has off-peak/peak rooms from $65 to 75/85 to 100. Holiday Isle runs from $75 to 110/95 to 145; El Capitan rooms are $90/120; and the Howard Johnson Resort costs $100 to 110/130 to 145. Guests at any of the above have the run of the resort.

The fabulously luxurious *Cheeca Lodge* (☎ 664-4651, 800-327-2888), MM 82 oceanside, is a beaut of a resort if you like things like angling, croquet, golf and tennis – though of course, they have most everything else you've ever desired as well. Their dive shop can arrange trips out to Alligator Reef and to see *The Eagle* as well as to other destinations, or you can just walk on the lodge's own nature trails or sit by their pool or in the spa. Their Cheeca Van provides transport between the lodge and MIA ($150 for up to six people). Room rates range from $155 to 475 in off-peak seasons, $240 to 585 in peak seasons; suites are from $255 to 775/315 to 1000.

Places to Eat

Manny & Isa's Kitchen (☎ 664-5019), MM 81.6, is a Spanish/American place with sandwiches from $2.50 to 4.50. 'Chopped sirloin' steak with grilled onions (which sounds suspiciously like a hamburger) is $7.95, pork chops are $8.90 and broiled lamb chops $13.50. They have daily changing specials for about $7.95, and seafood dishes are $14 to 17.

There are about six restaurants at the Holiday Isle Resort (see above), including the *Horizon Restaurant* (☎ 664-2321 ext 600), MM 84, which does salads for $3.95 to 7.95, sandwiches for $4.25 to 7.95 and a soup-and-sandwich combination for $5.50. At dinner, vegetable lasagna is $12.50, catch of the day $16 and baked stuffed shrimp $18.

Whale Harbor (☎ 664-4959), MM 84, does an all-you-can-eat seafood buffet; adults pay $19.95, kids $9.95 and children five and under $4. It's open Monday to Saturday from 4 to 9 pm and Sunday from noon to 9 pm.

Atlantic's Edge (☎ 664-4651), MM 82, is the *Cheeca Lodge*'s restaurant. They prepare the catch of the day any way you like; it comes with vegetables, mixed grains and steamed creamer potatoes for $15.50 per person (or $19.50 if it's their catch). Other entrees include their vegetarian medley for $15, baked mahi-mahi $20 or rack of lamb $36.

KEY LARGO
• *pop 11,500* ☎ 305

Key Largo leapt to the public eye after the 1948 film of that name starring Bogart and Bacall, shot almost entirely on Hollywood, California, sound stages. Sensing that they'd better get their act together to capitalize on this but quick, the town, which had been known to that point as Rock Harbor, swiftly changed its name to Key Largo. Despite the presence of *The African Queen* in town, from the Bogart movie of *that* name, Bogie himself never came here to shoot anything; the boat was brought in as a tourist attraction.

Key Largo's biggest attraction is justifiably the underwater John Pennekamp Coral Reef State Park, the most accessible way to see the Florida reef, and divers looking for a unique experience will love Jules' Undersea Lodge, an underwater hotel.

Orientation & Information
The Key Largo area stretches from the northernmost section of the Keys down to Plantation Key. The very helpful Key Largo Chamber of Commerce (☎ 451-1414, 800-822-1088, see the Online Services appendix), MM 106 bayside, has tons of information on Key Largo and the rest of the Keys. The Key Largo Greyhound stop is at MM 102.

The Book Nook (☎ 451-1468), in the Waldorf Plaza shopping center at MM 99.5, sells tons of nature and travel books (including Lonely Planet) along with magazines, fiction and music; they have a big Florida book section and have been here over 25 years. Cover to Cover Books (☎ 852-1415), in Tavernier at MM 90 oceanside, is another large general bookshop with a good Florida and travel section, as well as children's books, and they also have a coffee bar where you can sit and read their out-of-town and foreign newspapers. The Key Largo branch of the public library (☎ 451-2396) is in the Tradewinds Plaza shopping center at MM 101.5 – where there's also a Publix and K-Mart.

Change money at the Barnett Bank (☎ 453-0704) and wash clothes at the Waldorf Plaza Laundry (☎ 451-4575) in the Waldorf Plaza shopping center at MM 99.5. The biggest hospital in the area is Mariners Hospital (☎ 852-9222) at MM 88.5 on Plantation Key.

John Pennekamp
Coral Reef State Park
The first underwater park in the USA, John Pennekamp Coral Reef State Park (☎ 451-1202) has a public area of 75 sq miles of ocean, containing living coral reef, and 170 acres of land. It is by far the most user-friendly way to get out onto the Florida reef, with excellent ranger-led programs in winter, good information at the visitor center and a concession (☎ 451-1621) that rents anything you might need to get snorkeling or diving; it runs glass-bottom boat, snorkeling and diving trips every day. The park also has walking trails and a three-mile network of canoe trails.

FLORIDA KEYS

The Wild Tamarind Nature Trail is home to air plants, gumbo-limbo, wild bamboo, Jamaica dogwood, crabwood and, of course, wild tamarind. Other plantlife along the trails includes white stopper bush (the skunky one), West Indian mahogany and strangler fig.

For snorkeling and diving, the best way to see the reef, you'll need transportation of some sort; you can rent sailboats, canoes, kayaks and motorboats, or hook up with organized snorkel and dive trips.

The entrance to Pennekamp is at MM 102.5, and the park is open every day from 8 am to sunset. Admission is $2.50 for a car and driver. For more than one person in a car the cost is $5 plus 50¢ per person over age five. Pedestrians and cyclists are $1.50 per person.

Visitors Center The Pennekamp visitors center is billed as 'the reef you can walk out to' – in case you don't have the time or inclination to don a bathing suit and jump in the water. The main feature in the center is their 30,000-gallon aquarium (along with several smaller ones) that showcases living coral and tropical fish and plant life. There's also a theater, where nature videos are shown continuously throughout the day.

Organized Tours In winter the park holds a wide variety of ranger-led programs that change regularly, including guided canoe trips, nature walks through the mangrove and hardwood hammocks, a campfire program, and a lecture series, usually held in January and February, with rangers and guest speakers holding talks on a range of environmentally related subjects, such as crocodiles, raising bananas, native versus non-native vegetation, area birds and wildlife. There are also sometimes special ranger-led snorkeling tours as well.

Diving You can rent a full scuba outfit – mask, two tanks, regulator, BC and weight belt – for $29 a day. Four-hour, two-dive trips leave at 9.30 am and 1.30 pm and cost $37; show up 45 minutes in advance.

Snorkeling The concession rents snorkel equipment for $10 a day, with a $35 deposit. They also operate 2½-hour snorkel tours at 9 am, noon and 3 pm; adults/children under 18 are $23.95/18.95, including equipment. A four-hour sailboat snorkel trip leaves at 9 am and 1.30 pm for $28.95/23.95.

Boating The park's three miles of canoe trails begin at the park marina; they are well-marked, easy trails through the mangroves. Paddleboats, canoes, kayaks and Hobie One sailboats and powerboats are available from the park concession. Canoes and kayaks cost $8 an hour, $28 for four hours, $48 for the day; paddleboats are $10 an hour; 12-foot Hobie One sailboats are $16/48.

Powerboat rentals are available for divers and snorkelers as well; show up between 8 and 8.30 am to get one. A 19-foot boat (the smallest) costs $25 an hour, $80 for four hours, $150 for eight hours; 22-footers cost $35/110/200. A 24-foot boat is $40 an hour, $275 for eight hours; 28-footers $45/325 – no half-day rentals on the 24- and 28-footers. These prices don't include tax or fuel.

Reefs & Attractions Administratively speaking, diving and snorkeling along the reef isn't in the state park at all; it's out past the three-mile limit in the federally managed Key Largo National Marine Sanctuary (☎ 451-1644), which extends for about 20 miles southwest along a line three miles off the Keys' Atlantic shore beginning at Broad Creek. The areas are covered by NOAA Nautical Charts 11462 and 11451, available at dive shops along the Keys but not at Pennekamp.

Rangers and the concession are very helpful; ask about planning specific trips. The main snorkeling and diving areas within the sanctuary are, from north to south, Carysfort Reef, where you'll also find the 100-foot Carysfort Lighthouse (1852, now under renovation). Just south of the lighthouse is Carysfort South, the biggest shallow reef in the area, whose calm waters are perfect for snorkeling.

Elbow Reef, with three major wrecks, is a very popular dive site, but the most famous snorkel and dive site in the park is at Key Largo Dry Rocks: the Christ of the Deep Statue. It's a nine-foot-high, 4000-pound, algae-covered bronze statue of Christ built in Italy by Guido Galletti, installed as an underwater shrine to sailors and those who have lost loved ones to the sea.

Just southwest of the sanctuary are the sunken USCG cutters *Duane* and *Bibb*; see Wrecks & Ships under the Keys' introduction.

Glass-Bottom Boat Tours The 2½-hour glass-bottom boat tour (☎ 451-1621) goes out to Molasses Reef, at the southern end of the sanctuary, aboard the *San Jose*. Molasses Reef is part of a reef tract that extends from Fort Lauderdale through the Keys and on through the Dry Tortugas; it's named for a wrecked Jamaican ship that was carrying sugar cane molasses.

If this is the only chance you'll have to see the reef, you'll still come away amazed at the brilliant colors, the abundance of soft and hard coral and the tropical fish, sting rays, turtles, barracuda, angel fish, parrot fish, Jewfish, grunts, grouper and snapper. The glass-bottom boat does not visit the Christ statue (see above). It leaves daily at 9.15 am, 12.15 and 3 pm, and costs $13 for adults, $8.50 for children under 12.

The *Key Largo Princess* is another glass-bottom boat tour of the area, leaving from the Holiday Inn Key Largo Resort & Marina (☎ 451-4655, see below). They leave at 10 am and 1 and 4 pm; the cost is $14 for adults, $7 for children, and you cruise for about two hours.

Key Largo Undersea Park
This place is a trip. Key Largo Undersea Park (☎ 451-2353) is a sheltered natural mangrove lagoon area that's home to Jules' Undersea Lodge, an underwater hotel (see Places to Stay below), which is reached only by diving. The 50-by-20-foot, steel-and-acrylic structure is permanently anchored 30 feet beneath the surface of the lagoon.

Originally, it was La Chalupa Labora-

tory, a research lab 110 feet underwater off the coast of Puerto Rico. The lab was home to aquanauts doing saturation dives to explore the continental shelf.

You can stay at the hotel or just visit it during the day. Divers can dive around the hotel with their own tanks (or rent equipment here; a one-tank dive is $25). If you want to actually enter the hotel, you can sign up for their three-hour mini-adventures ($90), which give you access to the hotel and use of its facilities as well as their three breathing hookahs – 120-foot-long air hoses that allow tankless diving.

Snorkelers can use the area as well for $10 including gear. It's not in a coral reef, but you will see some reef fish – like angelfish, parrot fish, French angel fish and the like, lots of invertebrate growth and juvenile fish like baby barracuda. You may get lucky and see some of their local snorkeling Elvises.

The entrance to the park is at MM 103.2; their office is open daily from 9 am to 3 pm.

African Queen
At the Holiday Inn Key Largo Resort & Marina (☎ 451-2121, 800-843-5397), MM 100, you can take a ride on the *African Queen* – the one used in the movie with Hepburn and Bogart – when it's in port. It's an antique steam-engined vessel that can carry up to 15 people. Rides are $15 per person (at least two passengers), and you cruise the Port Largo Canal for about an hour. Reservations are a very good idea.

Dolphins Plus
Dolphins Plus (☎ 451-1993, see the Online Services appendix) is a dolphin education center off MM 99.5 bayside (but it's tricky to find, call for specific directions). It specializes in swims with dolphins in recreational, educational and therapeutic programs. Their unstructured swims with dolphins (see Swimming with Dolphins sidebar), which require a good deal of knowledge before embarking upon, are held twice daily, at 9 am and 1.30 pm. It includes a classroom session and an hour in the water for $80. Longer swims

are available as well. Their structured swims, which also include a classroom session, are only offered on some weekends and holidays (call for availability) and cost $90. If you're not swimming, admission is $7.50 for adults, $5 for students and children. Call for information on their in-water therapy sessions for special needs children and adults.

Maritime Museum
The Maritime Museum of the Florida Keys (☎ 451-6444), MM 102.6, is a small but interesting museum. It is inside, of all places, a castle, and artifacts, treasures and other items from different fleets that sailed from the 1600s to 1700s are on display. They also show a 25-minute video on the Spanish Fleet of 1715. Admission is $5 for adults and $3 for children six to 12 (under six free) and seniors get a 10% discount. It's open daily from 10 am to 5 pm.

Wild Bird Center
The Florida Keys Wild Bird Rehabilitation Center (☎ 852-4486), MM 93.6 bayside, is a nature center with a boardwalk and nature trail, and a bird rescue program – if you should spot an injured bird, call here. You can learn about the birds in their tiki hut educational center, which also, of course, sells T-shirts and such. There are sometimes guided tours, but usually it's a self-guided walk through the facility – bird habitats are well-signed. Expect to spend about 30 minutes to see their birds, which include herons, pelicans, hawks and ospreys. The center is open daily from 8.30 am to 5.30 pm; admission is free (though they do depend on donations).

Diving
Most dive shops are in the Pennekamp Park, and two others come recommended – Capt Slade's Atlantis Dive Center (☎ 451-3020, 800-331-3483), MM 106.5, and Amy Slate's Amoray (☎ 451-3595), MM 104.2.

Organized Tours
Florida Bay Outfitters (☎ 451-3018), 104050 Overseas Hwy, rents kayaks for $10 to 20 an hour, $20 to 40 for four hours and $35 to 60 for eight hours. They also have canoes for $10/20 to 25/30 to 35 (depending on size and rental time), and snorkel, camping and boating equipment are also available. From November to April (only in winter, simply because in summer there are too many bugs) they do half-day backcountry tours to seven-day wilderness trips into the Everglades National Park or two-day tours to Lignumvitae Key and Indian Key Historic Site (see Islamorada above).

Places to Stay
Camping Non-waterfront camping is available at *John Pennekamp Coral Reef State Park* (☎ 451-1202). Campsites are $23 without electricity and $25 with; all sites have water hookups. There's a central dump station for RVs. If you've come by boat, there's overnight camping on the water within the park (you moor to the buoys) for $11, which includes use of the dump station and showers. You can reserve up to 60 days in advance.

All tent sites at the *Calusa Camp Resort* (☎ 451-0232), MM 101.5 bayside at the shopping center, have water and electricity; they cost $27.88 for one or two people (extra person $3); full hookup sites (with sewer) are $31.22. They're not on the beach, but they do have a pool. While there are no grills provided and no open fires permitted, you can bring your own grill; no pets.

The friendly people at *America Outdoors Campground* (☎ 852-8054), MM 97.5 bayside, charge $33 for sites with water, electricity and cable; $38 for sites with sewer hookups; and $45 for waterfront sites. There are no grills, but you can bring your own. Pets (on a leash) are allowed in the campsites but not on the beach.

Hotels & Resorts Rooms at the clean *Bay Harbor Lodge* (☎ 852-5695), MM 97.7, are $50 for single or double, $65 for efficiencies and $75 for cottages. Other Key Largo options are not very cheap and are mainly resorts. The *Holiday Inn Key Largo Resort & Marina* (☎ 451-2121, 800-843-5397),

MM 100, is the largest in the Keys, and it's a city in and of itself, with restaurants, activities and, from the marina, casino cruises. Once again, rates vary wildly depending on the season; we were only quoted rates for June, which run about $99 on Sunday to Thursday and $109 on Friday and Saturday. In September they are $89/99, but prices during December at peak seasons are 'higher'.

The *Sheraton Key Largo Resort* (☎ 852-5553, 800-826-1006), MM 97, is another large resort. The prices here vary mainly on the view: 'nature trail' view rooms are $200, island views $220 and bayviews $250. Jacuzzi suites are $340. All rooms have a balcony, and there is a pool, restaurants, bars, a hair salon and more.

Underwater *Jules' Undersea Lodge* (☎ 451-2353) is an underwater hotel that can accommodate up to six people; it's permanently anchored 30 feet beneath the water's surface. The entrance is at Key Largo Undersea Park, MM 103.2 (see above).

The first question everyone asks is whether it's safe. Well, consider that the safety systems here were designed for scientists living onboard for long periods of time. Even if all the backup generators and systems failed, there would still be about 12 hours of breathing time inside the hotel. During Hurricane Andrew, it remained completely on-line – when people on the surface were without power, the air-conditioning still worked down here!

Your luggage is sent down separately. The rooms themselves are quite luxurious, complete with TV, VCR, showers, and in the living room there's a microwave oven for popcorn. There are, of course, telephones and an intercom to the surface. You can even call for room service – there are staff members on duty 24 hours when guests are in the place.

If you're not a certified diver you can still stay here; they'll get you a quick limited certificate for $85. There are several accommodation packages; the cheapest, the 'European-style' package, costs $195 per person, check-in at 5 pm, check-out at 9 am. The 'luxury aquanaut' package is $295 per person (if at least four people go, the price goes down to $250 per person). This package includes an aquanaut certificate, dinner and breakfast, and check-in is 1 pm, check-out 11 am. And the 'ultimate romantic getaway' package is $1000 for two people per night – you get the place all to yourselves with flowers and caviar and other little extras. Reservations are required for all stays.

Advanced divers can also get an optional ($100) specialty 'underwater habitat' certificate, which includes learning how to transfer luggage and goods to the hotel without getting them wet and study of the history of underwater exploration – basically, it's something you can lord over your friends for the rest of your life. To stay here you must be at least 12 years old, and no alcohol, smoking or pets are permitted.

Places to Eat

Outside the resorts and the restaurant at Pennekamp park, try the *Crack'd Conch* (☎ 451-0732), MM 105, which is a fun seafood restaurant. Sandwiches (lunch only) are $5 to 6, dinners average $13, and steamed shrimp with salad and sides are $11.95. The most expensive thing on the menu is a platter with 'lots of different seafood' for $17.95.

Señor Frijoles (☎ 451-1592), MM 104, is, believe it or not, a Mexican place. Their Mexican burger is $6.50, the burrito supreme is $7.95 and camarones ranchero are $12.95. But tequila takes center stage.

Sundowners (☎ 451-4502), MM 104, next to Señor Frijoles, has an outside verandah and a glass-walled dining room. They do a marinated chicken breast for $11.95, seafood and steak kabobs are $13.95 and their surf and turf is $21.95.

Snapper's Waterfront Saloon & Raw Bar (☎ 852-5956), MM 94.5, has peel and eat shrimp for $8.95, pasta primavera for $9.95 and fried jumbo shrimp for $16.95.

Southeast Florida

HIGHLIGHTS

- Kayak among the mangroves in Hobe Sound
- Sign on board a yacht in Fort Lauderdale and sail away . . .
- Check out the latest in 3-D movie technology on a five-story screen at Fort Lauderdale's IMAX theater
- Attend a tea ceremony at the Morikami Gardens in Delray Beach
- Marvel at the Norton Museum of Art's fine collection of Impressionist and Post-Impressionist paintings
- Watch the sea turtles nest at John D MacArthur State Park
- Camp, hike and canoe at Jonathan Dickinson State Park

Between the hubbub of Miami and the Right Stuff on the Space Coast sit some of Florida's most famous – and infamous – beaches. In most of the places along this section of the Florida coast you'll run into opulence. From what is arguably the USA's yachting capital in Fort Lauderdale to the staggering (even swaggering) mansions at Palm Beach, this is a moneyed area.

But it's also very accessible. Even the most exclusive places are at least polite to travelers, and you can find ways to see the glamour without paying through the nose. For example, you can have a great time window-shopping on Palm Beach's Worth Ave (looking at $600 pants!) and still manage to find a motel room for $25 to 35 in southern West Palm Beach or Lake Worth. You can get great Thai food for under $4 in West Palm Beach and loll on Fort Lauderdale's newly renovated beaches while spending no more that $11 (including tax) for a bed.

But the natural gem of the southeast coast is the area between Stuart and North Palm Beach, where pristine wilderness awaits in state parks and the Hobe Sound National Wildlife Refuge. The area is wide open for exploration and a wonderful way to get away from the golf courses, the developments and the highways. You can kayak around St Lucie Inlet Park, canoe along the Loxahatchee River and camp in Jonathan

Dickinson State Park, in either developed or totally primitive campsites.

And finally, Florida's southeast coast has a prize of such value, such eminence . . . well, it's obvious what we're saying is that on your way through you simply *must* snap a photograph of the world headquarters of the *National Enquirer* in Lantana. Tell 'em Liz sent ya.

FORT LAUDERDALE
• *pop 150,000 ☎ 954*

As recently as the late 1980s the sand in Fort Lauderdale was sticky from beer. The reason? The streets were full of college students storming about drinking cheap drafts till they passed out, celebrating that American university rite of passage, Spring Break.

Each spring, locals would watch in horror as their city was taken over by these yahoos, and they finally decided to do something about it. Over the last few years,

---

Reach Out & Confuse Someone
The area codes for the entire southeast of Florida have changed. Many business cards, pamphlets, coupons or tourist magazines will still list the old ones for the next couple of years. The Fort Lauderdale area has changed from ☎ 305 to ☎ 954, and all of Palm Beach County has changed from ☎ 407 to ☎ 561. ∎

the town has managed to divest itself completely of even fleeting images of the spring break scene. They've renovated, groomed and trimmed the whole place, and done an exceedingly good job of it.

Today Fort Lauderdale is known more as an international yachting center than as a party spot. That's not to say it's not a partying town: it decidedly is. These days you can party at dozens and dozens of clubs, bars, pubs and beach nightspots, as long as you dress respectably (meaning in clothes of some sort) and behave yourself. You can still party till you puke – if you like – but you'll puke in a sophisticated nightclub, in a toilet, and not out on the beach. Thank you very much.

For a beach town, Fort Lauderdale has a surprising number of cultural and historical sites, as well as some lovely areas to walk through – notably the shopping district along E Las Olas Blvd and Riverwalk. Don't miss the peaceful Hugh Taylor Birch State Recreation Area, and definitely get a water taxi ride or river cruise through Millionaire's Row – Fort Lauderdale by water is a unique look at an otherwise unseen display of the good life.

Orientation

The city is set in a grid wherever physically possible (it's hard with all the water), and it's divided into three distinct sections: the beach, on the east side of the Intracoastal Waterway; downtown, which is on the mainland; and Port Everglades, the cruise port at the south of the city.

US Hwy 1, here called Federal Hwy, cuts through the downtown, swooping under E Las Olas Blvd via the New River Tunnel. Hwy A1A runs along the ocean and is therefore appropriately named Atlantic Blvd south of Sunrise Blvd, and north of Sunrise Blvd it's called Ocean Blvd. Seabreeze Blvd begins at the Swimming Hall of Fame just south of Las Olas Blvd and continues south until the curve where it becomes 17th St. The whole stretch is Hwy A1A.

Broward Blvd is the north-south dividing line; Andrews Ave, just west of Federal Hwy, is the east-west line. As in Miami, streets and

Southeast Florida

SOUTHEAST

addresses are oriented by cross street and relation to Broward Blvd and Andrews Ave – N, S, E and W.

The main arteries between downtown and the beach are Sunrise Blvd to the north (which runs from the beach at the east to the massive Sawgrass Mills Outlet Center to the far west), E Las Olas Blvd in the center and 17th St to the south, which connects the beach to the Port Everglades.

Between the beach and the mainland are almost two dozen small finger islands. Here, there's a mooring at every house and what seems like a boat and a half at every mooring – this is yacht country, maybe the yacht capital of North America. And along with yachts, of course, come the millionaires that putter around on them. If you're waterborne, you can cruise by Millionaire's Row on the New River, just west of the Intracoastal Waterway – that's south of E Las Olas Blvd, west of Las Olas Isles and east of downtown.

Maps Of the two main free handout maps, the one published by the Las Olas Merchant Association is better on the whole than the one from the CVB, which resembles a Where's Waldo comic. Ask at a Barnett Bank branch if they happen to have any copies of the *Barnett Bank Map of Broward County*, which is a freebie version of the Dolph Map Company's *Map of Metropolitan Broward County* – the latter has no advertising, the former does but the base map is the same.

Information
Tourist Offices The Greater Fort Lauderdale Convention & Visitor's Bureau (CVB; ☎ 765-4466, 800-227-8669, see Online Services appendix) is a bottomless source of practical information and assistance. Their new offices are in Port Everglades at 1850 Eller Drive, Suite 303; from 17th St, Eisenhower Blvd winds south through the Port. Turn right on Eller Drive, and it's the first large building on the left. There's a very helpful activity line (with information on restaurants, nightlife, African-American and Caribbean culture) and travel directions service (☎ 527-5600)

where actual human beings tell you the fastest way between A and B after you push a lot of buttons on your phone. The City of Fort Lauderdale also runs an internet website (see the Online Services appendix) that has a ton of historical information and photos of the city, links to other sites and some really boring 'don't run with scissors'-type advice from the fire marshal. The HI Fort Lauderdale Hostel and Floyd's Crew House are great sources of local information as well (see Place to Stay below). There's a small tourist information booth on the beach side, on Atlantic just south of 5th St.

Money Barnett Bank has branches at 1 E Broward Blvd (☎ 765-1510) and 2404B E Sunrise Blvd (☎ 563-6500). American Express (☎ 565-9481) has an office at 3312-14 NE 32nd St.

Post The main post office (☎ 527-2077) is at 1900 W Oakland Park Blvd; there's another at 330 SW 2nd St, and a smaller one at 1404 E Las Olas Blvd.

Travel Agencies We met two travelers in Travel Etc (☎ 522-6111), 908 E Las Olas Blvd, who said the service is very flexible and helpful. It's open Monday to Thursday from 10 am to 7 pm, Friday from 10 am to 8 pm and Saturday from noon to 8 pm.

Bookstores Clark's Out of Town News (☎ 467-1543), 303 S Andrews Ave at Las Olas Blvd, is an excellent source for out-of-town and foreign newspapers, travel books (though not enough Lonely Planet stuff) and local news.

MacCarthy's (☎ 467-7410), 1400 E Las Olas Blvd, has some international (German, British, Spanish) newspapers and magazines. It's open Monday to Saturday from 8 am to 5 pm, Sunday from 8 am to 3 pm.

Library Fort Lauderdale's main public library (☎ 357-7444) is at 100 S Andrews Ave.

Media There are two competing dailies, the *Sun Sentinel* and the *Miami Herald*. *XS* is a

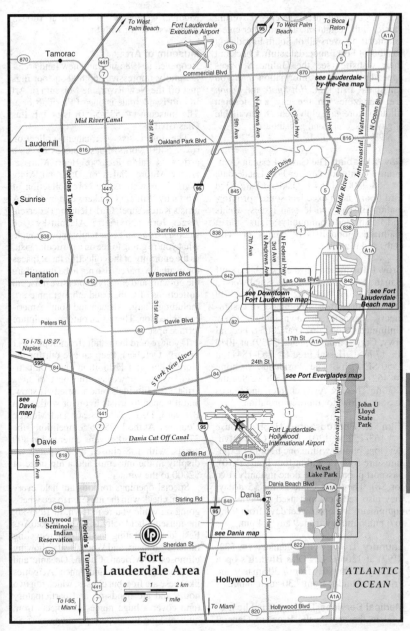

To West Palm Beach

Fort Lauderdale Executive Airport

To West Palm Beach

To Boca Raton

Tamorac

Commercial Blvd

see Lauderdale-by-the-Sea map

Mid River Canal

Lauderhill

Oakland Park Blvd

Wilton Drive

Sunrise

Middle River

Intracoastal Waterway

N Ocean Blvd

Floridas Turnpike

Sunrise Blvd

Plantation

W Broward Blvd

Las Olas Blvd

see Downtown Fort Lauderdale map

see Fort Lauderdale Beach map

Peters Rd

Davie Blvd

17th St

To I-75, US 27, Naples

S Fork New River

24th St

see Port Everglades map

see Davie map

John U Lloyd State Park

Davie

64th Ave

Dania Cut Off Canal

Fort Lauderdale-Hollywood International Airport

Griffin Rd

West Lake Park

Hollywood Seminole Indian Reservation

Dania Beach Blvd

Stirling Rd

Dania

S Federal Hwy

Ocean Drive

see Dania map

Sheridan St

Fort Lauderdale Area

Hollywood

ATLANTIC OCEAN

To I-95, Miami

To Miami

Hollywood Blvd

0   1   2 km
0   .5   1 mile

31st Ave
9th Ave
N Andrews Ave
N Dixie Hwy
N Federal Hwy
7th Ave
3rd Ave
N Andrews Ave
N Federal Hwy
31st Ave

very well done local weekly covering music, club, restaurant, art and other entertainment; it covers all of South Florida but has lots of Fort Lauderdale stuff. Check out their website (see the Online Services appendix) for more information than you can shake a stick at. *Hot Spots* and *Scoop* are magazines on the gay and lesbian (though more gay) club scene; it's available at gay bars, clubs and guesthouses.

NPR is at 91.3 FM.

Gay & Lesbian The Gay & Lesbian Community Center of Greater Fort Lauderdale (☎ 563-9500), 1164 E Oakland Park Blvd (3rd floor), is an excellent source of information on gay and lesbian issues, events and health and community affairs, and it maintains good lists of what's on with clubs and nightlife.

Crew Information Most crew-related stuff is in the Port Everglades area. Smallwood's Uniform Shop (☎ 523-2282), 1001 SE 17th St maintains a three-ring binder of assignments. Agencies in town include Crew Unlimited (☎ 462-4624) at 2065 S Federal Hwy, Crew Finders (☎ 522-2739) at 4040 SE 17th St, Hassel Free (☎ 763-1841) at 1550 SE 17th St and Worldwide Yachting (☎ 462-3705) at 1053 SE 17th St. See the Getting There & Away chapter, and Places to Stay, below, for more information.

Film & Photography Hobby House (☎ 463-1522), 1201 E Las Olas Blvd, develops photos within one hour (24 exposures are $12) or within four hours ($10); passport photos can be done instantly (two for $8). They rent cameras for $5 a day; they also sell new and used cameras and equipment. It's open weekdays from 9 am to 6 pm, Saturday from 9 am to 4 pm.

Laundry Try Las Olas Laundry (☎ 522-8197) at 1206 E Las Olas Blvd. It's open Monday to Thursday from 7.30 am to 9 pm, Friday to Sunday from 7.30 am to 8 pm.

Medical Services The largest public hospital in the area is the Broward General

Medical Center (☎ 355-4400) at 1600 S Andrews Ave (at 15th St).

Museum of Art

Reopened in 1985 in brand new (and architecturally impressive) 63,800-sq-foot digs just off the New River, the Museum of Art in Fort Lauderdale is one of Florida's best. The museum (☎ 525-5550) is at 1 E Las Olas Blvd.

The impressive permanent collection (over 5400 works) boasts pieces by such artists as Pablo Picasso, Henri Matisse, Henry Moore, Salvador Dali and Andy Warhol, as well as the core collection of works by William Glackens and by CoBrA artists Karel Appel, Carl-Henning Pedersen, Asger Jorn and Pierre Alechinsky (see sidebar). You can't ever really know, though, what you're going to see on a particular visit, as the enormity of the collection far outpaces the available space. Also not to be missed are the growing and equally impressive museum collections of Cuban and ethnographic art, including a large African and South American collection. There's an outdoor sculpture terrace upstairs.

If you're here in the fall (from September to early October), keep an eye out for the Hortt Memorial Exhibition and Competition, which showcases the best of area artists. It's Florida's oldest juried art show, and it's open to artists living or working in Broward, Dade, Palm Beach and Monroe Counties. At the 1995-96 competition – the 37th – 1437 works were entered by 800 artists, with 108 chosen by the panel for display in the museum, and a top prize of $2000 to the winner.

Special openings for kids are held every month; check with the museum to see what's going on while you're in town. In 1995-96, the museum held activities like the EcoArts Fest, demonstrating methods of recycling materials into art, and World Beats, showing glimpses of African, Cuban, Oceanic and Caribbean art, music and dance. Activities like these are free, but classes, which run two hours and are hands-on and participatory (and cover a huge range of subjects from quilt making to tempera painting), cost $8

Highlights of the Museum of Art

CoBrA The museum's CoBrA collection – CoBrA is an acronym for COpenhagen, BRussels and Amsterdam – is the largest in the US, and it was donated by Meyer and Golda Marks, who fell in love with the work in the 1960s and began buying up all they could. The movement emerged just after WWII. Led by Karel Appel, Asger Jorn and Cornelis Van Beverloo (Cornielle), this group of artists, disenchanted with the what they felt to be the restrictive art schools of the day – mainly Cubism, Mondrian and other geometric abstraction – developed a fresh new style that broke all the rules – no squares allowed. What emerged was playful and childlike, colorful and violent.

Works you hope are up when you visit include Christian Dotremont's calligraphic *Quelque Fois . . . Rien*; Reinhoud D'Haese's really wacky copper statue *Don't Be So Shy*; Pierre Alechinsky's weird and tiny occupational study *Les Métiers*, including *The Auto Mechanic*, *The Priest* and *The Fireman*; and Karel Appel's brilliant but *Untitled* ceramic, well, plates, as well as his *Singing Boys II* and just about anything else by Appel.

Glackens The works of William Glackens (1870-1938) are the jewels in the museum's crown, many pieces donated by the artist's son, Ira. The collection is made up mainly of Glackens' turn-of-the-century works, including *Outside the Guttenburg Race Track*, *Back of Nude*, the lovely *Artist's Daughter in Chinese Costume* and *Dancer in Blue*. Other works included in the bequest are by artists associated with Glackens, especially John Sloan, Ernest Lawson, Maurice Prendergast and George Luks.

African Art The theme of the African art collection is harmony, and many of the pieces are religious, ceremonial or spiritual. The mask collection – including *ancestor figure*, *Idan mask*, *Dance mask for Mukhanda Rite*, and the neato *Mgbedike* (or 'time of the brave') mask – is fascinating. The detailed explanations of the pieces are very good as well. ■

for nonmembers (members $6), and advance registration is required.

Parking is available at meters all over the place, but it's a better bet to use the small lot just west of S Andrews Ave, which charges $1 an hour. Buses serve the area constantly – it's in the heart of downtown. Prerecorded information on exhibitions, educational programs and special events is available 24 hours a day at ☎ 763-6464. The museum is open Tuesday from 11 am to 9 pm, Wednesday to Saturday from 10 am to 5 pm and Sunday from noon to 5 pm; it's closed Monday and federal holidays. Admission is $5 for adults, $4 for seniors (with ID), $2 for students (with ID) and free for children 12 and under.

Museum of Discovery & Science

Fronted by the 52-foot-tall Great Gravity Clock, Florida's largest kinetic energy sculpture, the Museum of Discovery & Science (MODS; ☎ 467-6637), 401 SW 2nd St, is absolutely excellent and worth a visit by children and adults alike. The environmentally oriented museum is very visual and hands-on, and the staff is friendly and helpful. In addition, MODS recently added an IMAX theater. Though some kids (and kids at heart), could spend all day in a place like this, you can do all the rides, play all the games and talk to all the robots in about 2½ totally fun hours.

There are permanent exhibits on space, health, computers, ecology, energy, sound and conservation, as well as rotating exhibits. In 'Florida Ecoscapes', you are introduced to Florida's 10 different ecosystems: you pass through a series of forests, swamps and sloughs – petting friendly sting rays, observing a fascinating synthetic beehive – all the while surrounded by appropriate animal noises. The museum raises many endangered species, and several times a day the hatchlings – like adorable baby crocodiles and sea turtles – are brought out for inspection.

The 'Voyage to the Moon' flight simulator ride is a bit lame, but the Manned Maneuvering Unit is a pip. It simulates weightlessness; you sit in a high-tech NASA chair and use air jets to launch up to a satellite and position it correctly at earth – and then get scored in how you do for all to see. Scales show your weight on different planets. A visit to 'Gizmo City' is a must: experiment with virtual reality,

computer games and the 'Human Hurricane', which spins you like a figure skater to demonstrate angular momentum (barf). If you fail to speak with Gizmo, the caustic robot, he'll insult you and how you're dressed.

More educational but equally interesting is the electric car, the damning exhibit on fossil fuel use and abuse, the trippy 'Kaleidovision', the cutaway human body (ewww gross!) and the other health exhibits on AIDS, pregnancy, the brain, nutrition and aging.

The museum is open Monday to Saturday

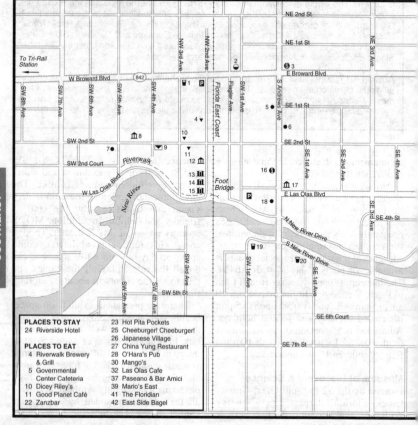

PLACES TO STAY
24 Riverside Hotel

PLACES TO EAT
4 Riverwalk Brewery & Grill
5 Governmental Center Cafeteria
10 Dicey Riley's
11 Good Planet Café
22 Zanzbar
23 Hot Pita Pockets
25 Cheeburger! Cheeburger!
26 Japanese Village
27 China Yung Restaurant
28 O'Hara's Pub
30 Mango's
32 Las Olas Cafe
37 Paseano & Bar Amici
39 Mario's East
41 The Floridian
42 East Side Bagel

from 10 am to 5 pm, Sunday from noon to 5 pm. Admission to the museum is $6 for adults, $5 for children three to 12 and seniors over 65; IMAX is $5 for adults, $4 for children and seniors. A combination museum/one film ticket is $8.50 for adults and $7.50 for children and seniors.

Blockbuster IMAX 3-D In October 1996, MODS became the fourth theater in the world to offer IMAX 3-D films with their way cool magic helmet. The helmet, which looks like a virtual reality gizmo, includes several speakers for totally rad sound place-

ment, as well as high-tech 3-D goggles (no more plastic glasses). IMAX screens are five stories high adding to the total experience.

Fort Lauderdale Historical Society

The Fort Lauderdale Historical Society (☎ 463-4431) maintains a museum and a collection of historic buildings at 219 SW 2nd Ave, west of the railroad tracks, just near the start of Riverwalk. The buildings are the former New River Inn (1905), the King-Cromartie House (1907) and the Philemon Bryan House (1905). The museum holds exhibits on the history of

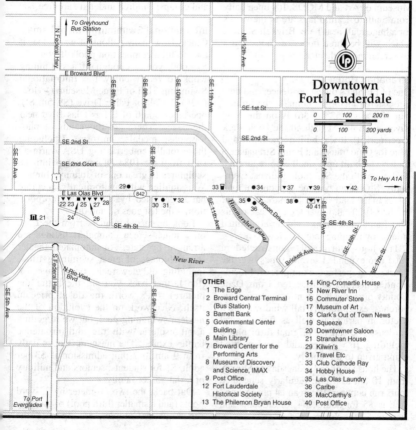

Downtown Fort Lauderdale

To Greyhound Bus Station

N Federal Hwy
NE 7th Ave
E Broward Blvd
NE 12th Ave
SE 8th Ave
SE 9th Ave
SE 10th Ave
SE 11th Ave
SE 1st St
SE 2nd St
SE 2nd St
SE 2nd Court
SE 5th Ave
SE 9th Ave
SE 13th Ave
SE 15th Ave
SE 16th Ave
To Hwy A1A
E Las Olas Blvd
842
Himmarshee Canal
Tarpon Drive
SE 15th St
SE 16th St
SE 4th St
SE 4th St
SE 17th St
Brickell Ave
New River
S Federal Hwy
N Rio Vista Blvd
SE 5th Ave
SE 9th Ave
To Port Everglades

29 33 34 37 39 42
22 23 25 27 28 30 31 32 35 36 38 40 41
24 26
21

OTHER
1 The Edge
2 Broward Central Terminal (Bus Station)
3 Barnett Bank
5 Governmental Center Building
6 Main Library
7 Broward Center for the Performing Arts
8 Museum of Discovery and Science, IMAX
9 Post Office
12 Fort Lauderdale Historical Society
13 The Philemon Bryan House
14 King-Cromartie House
15 New River Inn
16 Commuter Store
17 Museum of Art
18 Clark's Out of Town News
19 Squeeze
20 Downtowner Saloon
21 Stranahan House
29 Kilwin's
31 Travel Etc
33 Club Cathode Ray
34 Hobby House
35 Las Olas Laundry
36 Caribe
38 MacCarthy's
40 Post Office

To Port Everglades

SOUTHEAST

Fort Lauderdale and Broward County, Seminole folk art and baseball history. They also hold walking tours around the houses by arrangement. In mid-1998, they plan to open Old Fort Lauderdale, which will be a pedestrian plaza connecting those buildings. The museum is open Tuesday to Friday from 10 am to 4 pm; tours are $2 for adults, $1 for students, and free for children aged six and younger.

Riverwalk

A strip along the New River running west from the FEC railroad tracks to SW 5th Ave, Riverwalk is just a very pleasant bit of green and a lovely way to walk between the Museum of Art and MODS. It's open daily from 5 am to 1 am. Plans are in the works for a huge mall near here, Brickell Station, which will be three floors of shops and a 24-screen movie theater.

Stranahan House

One of Florida's oldest residences and now a registered historic landmark, the Stranahan House (☎ 524-4736) is on the New River at SE 4th St (behind the Hyde Park supermarket). It was built as the home and store for Ohio transplant Frank Stranahan, a trader who built up a small empire through dealings with the Seminole Indians. Eventually, Stranahan became despondent over losses in the land and stock market busts of the late 1920s and over the collapse of his Fort Lauderdale Bank, and he committed suicide by jumping into the New River.

The house, originally constructed in 1901 and expanded several times over the years, is a perfect example of Florida frontier design. Constructed from Dade County pine, the house now features wide porches, exceptionally tall windows and a Victorian parlor, as well as fine tropical gardens. You can see original furnishings, including fish dishes and hand-painted china given to the family.

The house is open Wednesday to Sunday from 10 am to 5 pm; regularly scheduled tours run between 10 am and 4 pm. Admission is $5 for adults, $4 for students and seniors, $2 for children.

Bonnet House

The Bonnet House (☎ 563-5393) is a beautiful estate at 900 N Birch Rd (near the beach; enter through the west gate). The property's 35 acres are filled with native southern Florida and imported tropical plants, including an extensive orchid collection. However, you have to be on a tour to see the house and grounds, so you can't wander or bring a picnic. The tours, which last a little over an hour, leave at 10 am and 1 pm on Wednesday to Friday and at 1 and 2 pm on Saturday and Sunday (they suggest you show up 15 minutes prior to tour time). Admission is $7 for adults, $6 for senior citizens and $5 for students under 18 and groups; children under six are free.

International Swimming Hall of Fame

Quick: How many gallons of water does it take to fill a competition pool? If you said 573,000, you're enough of a swimming wonk to *really* enjoy the International Swimming Hall of Fame Museum (☎ 462-6536), 1 Hall of Fame Drive (SE 5th St), one block south of E Las Olas Blvd near the beach. There are thousands of photographs, medals, uniforms (including those totally embarrassing USA warm-up suits from the 1984 Olympics), paintings, sculptures (a great one of Johnny 'Tarzan' Weissmuller with anatomically accurate hands designed by a prosthetic corporation) – the list goes on and on.

Look up medal winners from the USA on a touch-screen computer; listings are arranged by state. An automated theater shows footage of great swimming films, including old newsreels, on a huge TV (the farther back you sit, the better the picture) – it's worth the ticket price in itself. Nice work on the evolution of the modern swimming pool, but we're getting a bit esoteric with the anti-turbulence baffles exhibit. The museum is open daily from 9 am to 7 pm; admission is $3 per adult, $1 for students, seniors and military or a flat $5 per family.

Out back, the two 50-meter-by-25-yard pools (and a smaller third pool) of the city-run Aquatic Complex are open to the

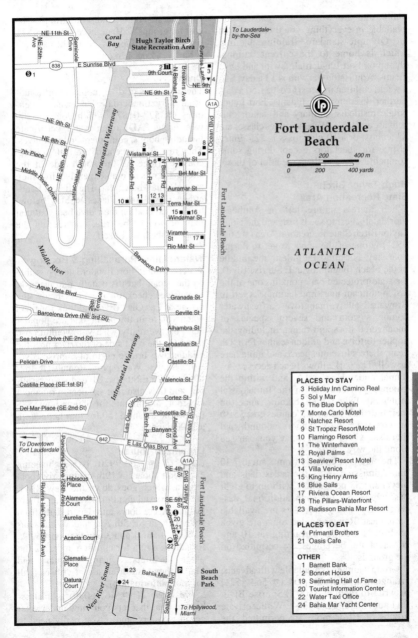

Fort Lauderdale Beach

0   200   400 m
0   200   400 yards

ATLANTIC OCEAN

PLACES TO STAY
3 Holiday Inn Camino Real
5 Sol y Mar
6 The Blue Dolphin
7 Monte Carlo Motel
8 Natchez Resort
9 St Tropez Resort/Motel
10 Flamingo Resort
11 The Winterhaven
12 Royal Palms
13 Seaview Resort Motel
14 Villa Venice
15 King Henry Arms
16 Blue Sails
17 Riviera Ocean Resort
18 The Pillars-Waterfront
23 Radisson Bahia Mar Resort

PLACES TO EAT
4 Primanti Brothers
21 Oasis Cafe

OTHER
1 Barnett Bank
2 Bonnet House
19 Swimming Hall of Fame
20 Tourist Information Center
22 Water Taxi Office
24 Bahia Mar Yacht Center

SOUTHEAST

public and are world class. Classes are available in everything you'd expect from an Olympic-standard training facility, which is home to the current national champion Fort Lauderdale Swim and Dive Teams. Admission to swim is $3 a day, $16 a week; children under six cost $1.50 a day. Further discounts for students, Fort Lauderdale residents, military and senior citizens are available. Water aerobics classes are $3 a class, or a 10-class pass is $25. Entry is free for spectators except during some competitions – and there are a lot of those.

Hugh Taylor Birch
State Recreation Area

When there's nature left in southeast Florida, it's best to see it fast, and the Hugh Taylor Birch State Recreation Area (☎ 564-4521) is one of the spots to get to during your stay. For almost a mile in the middle of the beach (beginning at E Sunrise Blvd), the state-protected park contains one of the last significant maritime hammocks left in Broward County, mangroves, a freshwater lagoon system and several species of endangered flora and fauna, including the gopher tortoise and golden leather fern. Oh yeah, there's luscious peace and quite here as well. The park allows beach access via a tunnel under Hwy A1A, and within the grounds you can fish in the Intracoastal Waterway, picnic, hike, bike or canoe (on their little half-mile trail; canoes cost $5.30 an hour). Friendly rangers abound, and there's a video about what you can see along the way.

The park is open daily from 8 am to 7.30 pm. Admission is $1 for pedestrians and bicyclists, $3 per vehicle with up to eight passengers, $1 for each additional passenger. Bus and group rates are available on request. Ranger-guided tours are given on Friday, weather permitting, at 10 am. No alcoholic beverages are permitted on the grounds.

Group camping is available with advance arrangement; call the park (☎ 564-4521) or write to them at 3109 E Sunrise Blvd, Ft Lauderdale, FL 33304. While private groups of 10 or more are permitted, the park prefers church and scout groups. The cost for groups of 10 or more in tents is $11 per person; groups of 30 to 72 can rent cabins at $4 per person.

Diving

There are tons of dive shops in Fort Lauderdale; try Lauderdale Undersea Adventures (☎ 527-0187), which does a $200 week-long PADI open water certificate including books, equipment and four dives. They're at the east end of the 17th St Intracoastal bridge on the south side of the street. There's also an expensive dive shop at the Bahia Mar center. The HI Fort Lauderdale Hostel (see Places to Stay below) had a good deal on their dive boat, but that may no longer be true, considering the shape of the hostel itself.

Water-skiing, Parasailing & Boating

Water-skiing in Fort Lauderdale is possible on the ocean, but it's usually outrageously expensive; check on the piers below the bridge at Las Olas Blvd and look for fliers when you're in town. Jet skis are popular here, but we really wish you wouldn't use them. On the west side of the river near the middle river bridge north of Sunrise Blvd, Bill's Sunrise Watersports Rentals (☎ 462-8962), 2025 E Sunrise Blvd, does parasailing, and they also rent six-person runabout (18-foot) motorboats for $50 an hour, $85 for two hours and $150 for four hours with a $200 deposit.

Organized Tours

Carrie B (☎ 768-9920) is a sightseeing excursion aboard a 19th-century riverboat replica, which goes down the New River, the Intracoastal and Port Everglades. Tours last about 1½ hours and depart daily from Riverwalk at SE 5th Ave and W Las Olas Blvd at 11 am, 1 and 3 pm; they cost $9.95 for adults, $4.95 for children under 12 (no other discounts). During February and March they also offer sunset cruises (call for more information).

Pro Diver II (☎ 467-6030) is a glass-bottom boat that lets you view underwater ocean wonders, and if you really need to

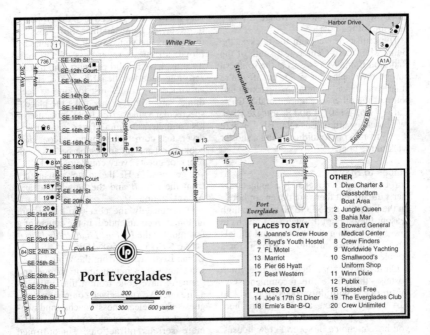

Map labels:
Harbor Drive
White Pier
Stranahan River
SE 12th St
SE 12th Court
SE 13th St
SE 14th St
SE 14th Court
SE 15th St
SE 16th St
SE 16th Ct
SE 17th St
SE 18th St
SE 18th Court
SE 19th St
SE 20th St
SE 21st St
SE 22nd St
SE 23rd St
SE 24th St
SE 25th St
SE 26th St
SE 27th St
SE 28th St
3rd Ave
4th Ave
4th Ave
S Federal Hwy
Miami Rd
S Andrews Ave
Cordova Rd
Eisenhower Blvd
Seabreeze Blvd
23rd Ave
Port Rd
Port Everglades
Port Everglades

OTHER
1   Dive Charter &
     Glassbottom
     Boat Area
2   Jungle Queen
3   Bahia Mar
5   Broward General
     Medical Center
8   Crew Finders
9   Worldwide Yachting
10 Smallwood's
     Uniform Shop
11 Winn Dixie
12 Publix
15 Hassel Free
19 The Everglades Club
20 Crew Unlimited

PLACES TO STAY
4   Joanne's Crew House
6   Floyd's Youth Hostel
7   FL Motel
13 Marriot
16 Pier 66 Hyatt
17 Best Western

PLACES TO EAT
14 Joe's 17th St Diner
18 Ernie's Bar-B-Q

0   300   600 m
0   300   600 yards

get closer, they have full snorkeling equipment for $5 extra. The cost is $15 for adults, $10 for children under 12, and one child under five can get in free with one adult. Departures are Tuesday to Saturday at 9.30 am and Sunday at 2 pm from the Bahia Mar Yacht Center (next to the *Jungle Queen* on the Port Everglades map).

Jungle Queen Dinner Cruise It's either a wondrous journey to a tropical island, a great meal and a funny vaudeville show, or the kitschiest, cheesiest romp into Borscht-belt glitz around, but you can't ignore the *Jungle Queen* BBQ & Shrimp Dinner Cruise (☎ 947-6597). A Fort Lauderdale tradition, the *Jungle Queen* sails for a three-hour tour in the afternoon or a four-hour dinner tour leaving at 7 pm, which includes a barbecue dinner and a show. The cruise itself is quite entertaining, with the narrator giving you all the dirt on the rich folks who own houses on Millionaire's Row, group participation in waving to several Misters

Johnson, the drawbridge attendants, and trivia and local lore along the way to the 'tropical' island on which you dine.

The barbecue dinner includes chicken (fine), ribs (good) and shrimp, which they make you peel – something they are not ashamed to tell you is done in order to slow you down. But you'll get full, for sure. Great beans and steak fries, too. Water, coffee and tea are included; soft drinks, beer and frozen drinks are extra ($2.50 to 3.95). After dinner, you're ushered out to the theater, where you'll see a great Swedish juggler (did the Carson show), a 'singer', and a comedian who's trapped in time ('Lady, I was *talking* to the duck!'). Your MC tells of vaudeville greats and glories, and sings ('You've gone for a cruise on a river/You've eaten a barbecue dinner . . . '). The audience seemed to love it. On the way back there's a sing-along, culminating in, of course, *God Bless America* as you return to port. For a good laugh, go on a Wednesday night, when patrons of

SOUTHEAST

the Downtowner Saloon arrange a group mooning of the boat.

The cruises leave from the dock at the Bahia Mar Yacht Center, just south of the Radisson Bahia Mar Resort at the southern end of town; parking is $5, but if you're smart you'll head to municipal parking just south of the otherwise unmemorable Oasis Cafe (☎ 463-3130) at 600 Seabreeze Blvd, two blocks south of Las Olas Blvd, where it's $3 from 6 pm to midnight and a shorter walk to the boat.

Places to Stay

Fort Lauderdale's not exactly a budget traveler's dream, but there are dozens of hotels on the beach in the $35 to 50 range in high season; they are a bit lower (not much) in low season when the bottom-end motels have specials for around $25 to 30 for a double room.

On the lower end, there are three youth hostels – though we only recommend staying in one – with dorm beds from $11 to $14 including tax, and if you're here looking for work on a foreign-flag vessel, you have a choice of several crew houses, all at around $100 per week.

The highest concentration of hotels, motels and B&Bs is on the beach, in the '-mars' area – from Rio Mar St at the south to Vistamar St at the north, and from Hwy A1A at the east to Bayshore Drive. Wherever you go in town, be very careful about advertised rates – many are for singles, with huge jumps for additional people. If you've been ripped off, or have complaints about a hotel, contact the Division of Hotels and Restaurants (☎ 958-5520). On the flip side, hotels listed with the city's Superior Small Lodgings (SSL) association are generally of high standards all around.

Youth Hostels The best deal on a cheap bed in town is at *Floyd's Youth Hostel and Crew House* (☎ 462-0631, see Online Services appendix), with clean dorm beds at $11 including tax. It's tucked away in the Port Everglades section of town, close to most of the crew placement agencies, and a short bus ride to the beach. The staff are

very friendly and protective of the property, those staying there and their stuff. Prospective guests are vetted on the telephone by Floyd: all guests regardless of nationality must have a valid passport, and there's zero tolerance for illegal drug use. He's a very nice guy – he's just looking to keep things safe. Many extras make the place a spectacular value – free local calls, use of his computer, incoming faxes, washer and dryer, tea, corn flakes, pasta, cocoa, rice, cooking oil and sugar, free barbecues (with beer) for guests every couple of weeks . . . you get the idea. He'll also pick you up free from the airport and the Greyhound and Amtrak stations.

Unfortunately, the next two hostels are no longer recommended. In the course of a few months the *HI Fort Lauderdale Hostel* (☎ 568-1615, fax 568-1595) at 3811 N Ocean Blvd (across from the Winn Dixie), went through a management change and seems to have gone from a fine option to a dire one. We've received complaints from guests about cleanliness, roaches and nonstop parties, an unusable pool and other more serious infractions. Unconfirmed reports say that HI itself is unhappy with the situation. At the very least, you should look at the rooms and speak to other guests before committing. A major complaint we've heard is that, after encouraging guests to pay in advance the cheaper weekly rate, management refused on at least two occasions we know of to give refunds to unsatisfied customers – even when HI headquarters was called. *Caveat emptor*. Beds here cost $13.08 for HI members, $16.35 for nonmembers.

And the third hostel, *Sol y Mar* (☎ 565-1419), 2839 Vistamar St, is no longer an HI or AYH member, and there have been allegations (we've seen one in writing and heard of others) by several female guests of a very disturbing nature. It has beds at $12 including tax.

Crew Houses These are not for the average backpacker, but rather for those seeking employment aboard yachts and ships moored nearby (see the Getting There

& Away chapter). Generally these are the best places to pick up information on boat jobs, and all have listings of all the agencies in town. The first two places are near Port Everglades. In most cases backpackers will not be admitted, so call first and make sure before showing up.

The exception to the no-backpackers rule is Floyd's Youth Hostel (see above), which is also a full-fledged crew house.

Joanne's Crew House (☎ 527-1636), 916 SE 12th St, is the best established in town and it's a beauty. In a sprawling and spotlessly clean ranch-style house, 20 people can await employment in true style. This one-acre property has an enormous screened-in backyard complete with pool and barbecue area. Everything – the kitchen, the rooms, the house – is huge, and the price is $100/week.

For the same price, the much smaller *Lynn Hawkin's Crew House* (☎ 779-7213), 1208 SE 6th St, has very nice and comfortable rooms, though it's a bit awkwardly located (far from port).

Camille's Crew House (☎ 676-3569, 527-4653) has several apartments (which hold four to eight people); weekly rentals are $100, which includes use of the washer and dryer and cable TV. Call for their address, which they don't print.

Motels & Hotels *Natchez Resort* (☎ 564-6233), 735 N Atlantic Blvd, claims to be the oldest building on the beach. They keep it clean enough, but it's a little worn (old carpets, sinks and bathtubs). Rates are tricky – they prefer to rent by the week, but they say you can get rooms in the low season from $25 ($165 per week) and in high season from $35 ($200 per week). They have far more expensive rooms as well. The rooms along the side are quieter.

Flamingo Resort (☎ 561-4658, 800-283-4786, fax 568-2688) 2727 Terra Mar St, is listed with SSL and is a nice, gay-friendly (though they cater to everyone) option set in a calm garden with friendly staff and satisfied guests. We liked the hosts, rooms were clean and kitchen appliances very new. Room rates start at $28 ($171 per

week) in low season and are from $50 to 58 ($340 to 395 per week) in high season.

The more modern *Villa Venice* (☎ 564-7855), 2900 Terra Mar St, is a good deal, with clean, modern rooms that are larger than average. They've got a nice wooden swing by the pool and a parrot. In low season, regular rooms/efficiencies are $29/39; in high season, this rises to $59/69.

The Winterhaven (☎ 564-5614, 800-888-2639, fax 565-5790), 2801 Terra Mar St, is run by the president of the Superior Small Lodgings association (which says something about the cleanliness), who's *really* into palm trees (he has dozens of species of palms planted all over his property and will gladly tell you anything about them). They have two pools, one out front, the other in the back garden, and they care about their guests, though furniture is of the large variety. Room rates by the day/week start at $35/225 in low season and go to $50 to 60/340 to 400 in high season.

Rooms at the *Monte Carlo Motel* (☎ 564-0436, fax 563-0436), 717 Breakers Ave (at Vistamar St), have a good feel to them, with tiled floors (which makes it feel cooler) and very clean, nice kitchens. Room rates start at $35 in low season, $55 in high season. There is a $25 phone deposit if you're not paying with a credit card.

Blue Sails (☎ 566-8606), 3117 Viramar St, is quiet and clean and management is very nice, but there's a little less of everything here than in other places: rooms have showers only (no tubs), no phones (there's a pay phone just outside) and no pool. Room rates start at $35 in low season, $68 in high season.

St Tropez Resort (☎ 564-8468), 725 N Atlantic Blvd, has very clean rooms and large bathrooms. It's a good deal in low season when, despite printed rates of $43 to 69, you can usually get a room for $35; prices rise to $80 to 105 in high season.

Sea View Resort Motel (☎ 564-3151, 800-356-2326), 550 N Birch Road at Windamar St, is an SSL member, which says it all about the rooms; rates range from $41 to 75 in low season to $72 to 129 in high season with a couple of midrange seasons as well.

Riviera Ocean Resort (☎ 565-4443, 800-457-7770, fax 568-9118), 505 N Atlantic Blvd, is another totally reasonable option, with clean, tiled rooms and a nice pool area, a pool bar and tennis courts. For the price, it's not bad. Room rates start at $45 to 70 in low season, $75 to 95 in high season.

The serene *The Pillars – Waterfront* (☎ 467-9639, 800-800-7666, fax 763-2845), 111 N Birch Rd, is a very lovely and quiet resort tucked away at the end of Sebastian St – two blocks from the beach on the Intracoastal Waterway. An SSL member hotel, they have very large and well-renovated rooms, efficiencies and suites, several with water views, a pool, barbecue area and tables lining their private pier. Staff is unbelievably helpful with directions to local attractions, sights, bars, clubs – and even to other hotels in the area that are cheaper if that's what you're looking for. If you're going to spend $49 to 110 in summer, $59 to 130 in fall and spring, and $99 to 159 in high season, this is the place to spend it. Above are advance reservation rates, posted rack rates are about $5 higher. They give senior citizen discounts.

The grand *Riverside Hotel* (☎ 467-0671, 800-325-3280), 620 E Las Olas Blvd, downtown near Federal Hwy, is the oldest hotel in Fort Lauderdale, though it's a bit swish for our taste. Rooms are large, with fluffy carpets, furnished with Jacobian oak (homey, if that's the sort of thing you like). It's very clean, elegant and luxurious, and there's a heated pool and all the amenities you'd expect. Room rates are fairly complicated but are basically as follows: April to September $74 to 134, October to December $84 to 139, December to April $109 to 199.

Radisson Bahia Mar Resort (☎ 764-2233), 801 Seabreeze Blvd, is a standard top-end place with perfectly comfortable rooms. It's also got a very private pool and tennis courts, and they're building a health club. They have around six seasonal rate changes; in the lowest (late April to late May) rooms range from $119 to 129 courtyard, $139 to 149 oceanfront, and in the highest (mid-December) it's $149 to 159 courtyard, $169 to 179 oceanfront. If you're up to spending this much, take a marina-view room for about $135, which has better views than the courtyard rooms and still offers a fair amount of ocean view as well. They have pay-per-view movies ($8.43 for the first, $5.25 for the next on the same day), and there's a decent bar and deli as well.

Gay & Lesbian Guesthouses Several charming gay men-only guesthouses can be found in the -mars area. There's only one lesbian guesthouse that we found, though more are expected to open this year.

The *King Henry Arms* (☎ 561-0039), 543 Breakers Ave, has no sign but is the cheapest gay guesthouse on the beach, with single/double rooms for $33/43 in low season, $47/57 in high season. Rooms are all large and clean, with room safes and small kitchens. There's a nice pool. It's predominantly gay, but management says that 'open-minded people of all orientations are always welcome.'

The Blue Dolphin (☎ 565-8437, 800-893-2583, fax 565-6015), 725 N Birch Rd, is a small, clean, slightly rundown but very comfortable men-only place. The house cat, Nessy, seems to enjoy the clothing-optional pool, and breakfast is served until 10 or 11 am. Rooms all have coffee service; there's free parking. Rates are $60 to 95 low season, $75 to 110 high season. Wheelchair accessible accommodations are available on advance notice. The staff speak fluent German and French.

The Inn (☎ 568-5770, 800-881-4814), 1520 NE 26th Ave, is Fort Lauderdale's sole lesbian-only guesthouse. It has three apartments, a large garden and a pool. You'll immediately become friendly with the host of exotic birds, cats and dogs. Rooms range from $60 to 100 per night in low season, $80 to 125 in high season.

The premiere gay guesthouse on the beach is the lovely *Royal Palms* (☎ 564-6444, 800-237-7256, fax 564-6443), 2901 Terra Mar St. This exquisitely done place has spotless, large airy rooms complete with CD/TV/VCR and library, a lush and constantly changing tropical garden, a very nice pool (they're planning a waterfall) and lots of perks and extras. It's very isolated and serene, and if they didn't discriminate against women and heterosexuals, we'd recommend it as possibly the beach's finest place. Rooms are $85 to 135 in low season, $125 to 175 in high, with free parking and breakfast included. Clothing optional. Dig the towel sculptures on the beds.

Places to Eat

Downtown & Mainland Who says fat-cat bureaucrats are unapproachable? If you're in the area and want to save a bit, why, pull up a bench and rub elbows with the best of them at the open-to-the-public *Governmental Center Cafeteria* (☎ 462-8368) in room 308 of the Governmental Center Building at 115 S Andrews Ave. Here you'll find the finest in administrative cuisine at taxpayer-subsidized prices: daily specials run about $3.50 to 4 for a whole meal, like lasagna, salad and a roll or chicken Caesar. They also have sandwiches ($2 to 2.25) and a breakfast special from 7 to 10 am with two eggs, toast, bacon and coffee for $1.85. It's open Monday to Friday from 7 am to 3 pm. You'll need to sign in with the security desk and get a pass to go upstairs.

The laid-back folks over at the *Good Planet Café* (☎ 527-4663), 214 SW 2nd St, ask that if you want service today, you should request it with your order. It has a hippy-dippy atmosphere (cacti on the tables) and health-oriented American cuisine: veggie melts ($4.75), burgers (about $5.95) and chicken breast platters ($6.95) are the mainstays. Try the interesting Posole del Buen Planeta, a hodge-podge of chick peas, onions, garlic and a bunch of other stuff ($2.75 a cup, 4.50 a bowl, $5.25 with a half sandwich). Excellent homemade bread. Staff are alternately anxious and slow to serve, but that's the idea of the place – relax, will ya? It's open daily from 11.30 am to about midnight.

There's a lot of Irish going on at *Dicey Riley's Irish Restaurant & Lounge* (☎ 522-2202, fax 522-7176), 217 SW 2nd St. It's

as close to an Irish pub as you'll get – draft Guinness, Bass and others. The traditional Irish menu (enforced by a traditional Irishman) has allowed some foreign stuff to creep in, like fettuccine, but there's always the Sunday Carvery Smorgasbord – $8.95 gets roast beef or turkey with stuffing, vegetables, Yorkshire pudding, gravy, potato, cranberry sauce and house salad. Buduhbing. They also have a decent brunch menu from $3.95 to $5.95. Oh, yeah, it's also a full bar, packed on weekends. It's open Monday to Sunday from 11 am to 2 am, Saturday from 5 pm to 4 am; Pat O'Carroll and the Big Shillelaghs play Irish traditional and contemporary tunes on Friday and Saturday.

Riverwalk Brewery & Grill (☎ 764-8448), 111 NW 2nd Ave, is a very nice restaurant/bar that also houses a micro-brewery, which makes about a dozen kinds of beer ($3 a pint, 50¢ off during happy hours). They'll let you sample all the beers free – they're on the bitter side, with a generally high alcohol content (from 3.8% to 7.5%). Most popular is their Riverwalk Red at 4.9%, which is full bodied and less bitter with a dark amber color, but there's also the very creamy Ramsay's Imperial Stout (7.5%), and if they've got raspberry beer when you visit (4%), you're in for a treat. Their Marlin's Light (3.8%) was a tad too bitter for us. Appetizers at lunch are around $5, salads from $4 to $7.50 and main dishes are $5.95 to $8.95. At dinner, the appetizers are the same but main courses include beef shish-kebab ($11.95) and fettuccine and penne ($10.95). It's open Tuesday to Thursday from 11 am to 11 pm, Friday and Saturday from 11 am to 1 am, Sunday from noon to midnight.

Along E Las Olas Blvd The cheapest place we found here is *Hot Pita Pockets* (☎ 832-0301), 604 E Las Olas Blvd, and happily it turned out to be excellent. They serve Middle Eastern pita sandwich's with a large vegetarian selection. We loved the vegetarian falafel ($3.75), hummus ($3.50) and Mujedra (lentils, rice, spices and salad), and the chicken borday ($4.50) looked great as well. Salads are from $2.75 to 5.95, and sandwich-salad combos are $5.95 to 7.95. All foods are prepared on the premises – definitely a good value. It's open Sunday to Thursday from 11 am to 9 pm, Friday and Saturday from 11 am to 11 pm, and they deliver.

Cheeburger! Cheeburger! (☎ 524-8824), 708 E Las Olas Blvd, is named for the *Saturday Night Live* sketches of a restaurant that served cheeseburgers but not hamburgers. They serve, what else, cheeseburgers (you won't find hamburgers on their menu, but you can order a cheeseburger without the cheese 'for no extra charge'). A quarter-pound sampler is $3.75, a grilled cheese sandwich $2.95, grilled chicken sandwich $4.75, and Ham's burgersteak dinner is $7.95. Free delivery.

East Side Bagel (☎ 728-8801), 1515 E Las Olas Blvd, is a bagel place that's open daily from 7 am to 3 pm.

Kilwin's (☎ 523-8338), 809 E Las Olas Blvd, is a delicious fudge, truffle, caramel, chocolate and ice cream place. They have been in business since 1949, and when you walk in, you'll know why: it smells overwhelmingly good and they make the fudge in front of you, $8 a pound (about two slices – and when you buy two slices, you get another one free).

Mango's (☎ 523-5001), 904 E Las Olas Blvd, serves the yuppie business lunch crowd. It's got ferns, snappy service and lunch specials (served till 5 pm) like chicken and veggies for $5.95 and pastas up to $7.95; dinner entrées are from $11.95 to $15.95. It's open Sunday to Friday from 7 am to 2 am, Saturday till 3 am.

The Floridian Restaurant (☎ 463-4041), 1410 E Las Olas Blvd, is an upscale 24-hour diner serving very good, if a bit pricey, diner food – but skip the coleslaw. Unique menu offerings, like their late-night 'Out too late, forgot to eat, I'm starving baby, can't make up my mind' special at $8.95, make the menu's fine print worth reading. Sandwiches are from $2.95 to 4.75, dinner specials from $6.25 to 7.95; no credit cards.

China Yung (☎ 761-3388), 720 E Las Olas Blvd, is a classic American Chinese restaurant, whose $4.95 to 5.50 lunch specials come with soup, egg roll and fried rice. Set dinners ($6.95 to 8.95) include ice cream. Entrées are cheap by Las Olas standards: vegetable dishes are $7.95, seafood $9.95 and black pepper steak is $12.95.

O'Hara's Pub (☎ 524-1764), 722 E Las Olas Blvd, features nightly jazz (info ☎ 524-2801) in a warm, comfortable atmosphere with wooden tables, high stools and exposed brick walls. During happy hour (Monday to Friday from 5.30 to 7.30 pm), drinks are $1 off, and they have a happy-hour buffet. But it's a nice place anytime; on the menu you'll find an antipasto plate ($5.75), crab nachos ($8), pizzas ($8 to 8.75), salads and sandwiches ($5.25 to 6.25). They have no draft beer, but that's no reason not to go. It's open Monday to Sunday from 11.30 am to 2 am; music begins around 9 pm (two-drink minimum).

Mario's East (☎ 523-4990), 1313 E Las Olas Blvd, is a modern Italian bistro. Lunch entrées include angel hair pasta ($6.25), spaghetti ($5.95) and chicken parmigiana ($7.95). Pastas at dinner are $6.25 to 8.95; veal, chicken and fish run $8.95 to 13.95.

Las Olas Café (☎ 524-4300), 922 E Las Olas Blvd, is a little hidden and makes for a truly romantic and lovely place. Sit outside on the green courtyard patio if you like. Appetizers are $2.95 to 9.95, walnut-crusted fresh fish is $15.95 and grilled swordfish with black beans, rice and fruit salsa is $16.95. It's open only for dinner Sunday to Thursday from 5.30 to 10 pm and Friday and Saturday from 5.30 to 11 pm.

Japanese Village (☎ 763-8163), 716 E Las Olas Blvd, is a crowded Japanese restaurant even though locals give it decidedly mixed reviews. It's also pricey: a spring roll is $5, a-la-carte sushi pieces run $1.25 to 3.50 and a sushi boat for three with soup, salad and rice is $48. Their teriyaki combo dinner entrée is $13.50. It's open for lunch Monday to Friday from noon to 2 pm and for dinner Monday to Saturday from 5.30 to 10.30 pm, Sunday from 5 to 10 pm.

Zanzbar (☎ 767-3377), 602 E Las Olas Blvd, is a coffeehouse and wine bar with African and 'nature' influences (note the paw prints in the cement outside). Their lunch and dinner menu consists mainly of quasi-exotic foods: appetizers are $4 to 9, cold entrées are $7 to 14, beef jerky is $10, ostrich filet (yes, ostrich) with mango passion fruit and wild mushroom rice is $26 and coconut and pistachio-crusted swordfish is $20. Mmmm. They carry a wide selection of South African wine.

Paesano & Bar Amici (☎ 467-3266), 1301 E Las Olas Blvd, is said to have great Italian food, but on the afternoon we were there the restaurant was closed (as it does every afternoon). The bar, which is open all day, serves sandwiches from $4.95 to 7.95 and entrées from $8.95 to 12.95. The main dining room serves lunch entrées from $7.95 to 13.95 and dinner entrées from $13.95 to 25.95. The dining room is open weekdays for lunch from 11.30 to 2.30 pm and for dinner from 6 to 10.30 pm.

On the Beach There's not a whole lot on the beach that's worth jumping up and down about. A great new offering is the *Primanti Brothers* (☎ 565-0605, fax 537-4882), 901 N Atlantic Blvd which does great New York-style pizza (scientifically proven to be the best style of pizza available in the free world) in both Neapolitan ($1.75 a slice) and Sicilian ($2 a slice). Large whole pies are $9.99, and $14.99 with everything. They also do . . . um . . . interesting sandwiches, like cheese, coleslaw and French fries on Italian bread for about $3.50.

Thai to Go (☎ 537-5375, fax 537-9001), 3414D N Ocean Blvd (Hwy A1A), has decent Thai to go – there are no seats in the restaurant except for waiting (smokers on the left, nonsmokers on the right). Lunch items start at $4.95; dinners start at $6.95. They have a few more expensive specials. There's free delivery within three miles, and they're very close to the HI Fort Lauderdale Hostel.

Port Everglades Crew-house dwellers will appreciate the large Publix and Winn Dixie markets on the north side of 17th St just west of the Marriott; there're also convenience stores along SE 17th St and on Federal Hwy.

It's worth the five-minute drive from E Las Olas Blvd to get to *Ernie's Bar-B-Q* (☎ 523-8636), 1843 S Federal Hwy (at SE 18th Court), a restaurant as famous for its squalor and good, cheap food as for the antigovernment and anti-finance rantings that grace its walls ('Eliminate the International Banker – Eliminate War'). It's a 38-year-old early-boom restaurant serving up enormous portions of conch chowder ($2 for a cup, $2.60 for a bowl) that comes with Bimini bread – basically challah with a sugary top. The soup itself can make a meal. Heartier appetites can go for the blackened chicken – juicy and perfectly cooked – at $5.75, or a barbecue chicken, beef or pork dinner, served with corn on the cob, cole slaw and Bimini bread, for $5.75 to 6.50. There's a rooftop dining area as well, and the staff are incredibly friendly. It's open daily from 11 am to 11 pm or midnight.

Joe's 17th St Diner (☎ 527-5637), 1717 Eisenhower Blvd at SE 17th St (the huge sign outside says *Joe Bel Airs Diner*) opposite Port Everglades and the Convention Center, has way-cheap specials (breakfast $1.75, lunch $2.75, dinner $4.95) and moderately priced diner food (dinners are $5.45 to 6.25), as well as a full bar. It's open 24 hours.

Entertainment
Performing Arts The Broward Center for the Performing Arts (☎ 462-0222), 201 SW 5th Ave (diagonally opposite the MODS), is one of the state's largest and most important. There are two venues here, the 2688-seat Au-Rene Theater and the 588-seat Amaturro. Regular performances are held here by the Florida Grand Opera, Florida Philharmonic and the Miami City Ballet, and the center is also host to the PTG Broadway Series, including shows like *Sunset Blvd*, *Les Miserables* and *A Chorus Line*. Tickets vary wildly, from $5 performances to the top-of-the-line seats for

Sunset Blvd, which clocked in at a New York-esque $66.50.

Their Family Fun Series, which runs from October through April, features shows like *Sorcerer's Apprentice* and *Swiss Family Robinson*, and performances by the Manhattan Tap Dance Co and the Lula Washington Dance Theater. Tickets for these shows range from $8 to 12.

The box office is open Monday to Saturday from 10 am to 6 pm, Sunday from noon to 6 pm.

Parker Playhouse (☎ 763-8813), 707 NE 8th St, does productions for children during the summer months (July and August) in their Story Theatre program. From April to August, the Fort Lauderdale Children's Theater (☎ 763-6882), 640 N Andrews Ave, does a wide range of performances for children.

Nightclubs This is, if you hadn't noticed, a party town, and there are literally thousands of options available to suit a variety of tastes, persuasions, nuttiness and libidos. Cover charges vary incredibly and constantly, and coupons abound. Check in *XS* for listings when you get to town, or check out the listings on their website (see the Online Services appendix). These are but a few of the available options.

Baja Beach Club (☎ 561-2432), 3200 N Federal Hwy, looks like an orgy at King Neptune's place and features dance music in their enormous multilevel place. It has spring-break parties, a Retro ('80s) Party on Thursday and dance parties on Saturday. Wednesday nights are ladies nights (18 and over, men 21 and over). It's in the Coral Ridge Mall behind Who Song And Larry's Mexican Restaurant at the northeast corner of Oakland Park Blvd and Federal Hwy.

Club Soda (☎ 486-4010), 5460 N State Rd 7, features dancing for clean and sober folks (no alcohol). Fridays it's adults only; Saturdays all ages are welcome. Head west on Commercial Blvd, turn right on Hwy 441 (State Road 7) and go half a mile north and you're there.

Nemesis (☎ 768-9228), 627 N Federal Hwy, is an alternative music club located in what was formerly a funeral home (now *that's* alternative), and it is naturally very popular with the People In Black. *Crash Club* (☎ 772-3611), 4915 NE 12th Ave (near Commercial Blvd and N Dixie Hwy), is another alternative place that does theme nights; some, like the painted lady and tattoo contests, are quite weird. *The Edge* (☎ 525-9333), 200 W Broward Blvd, is a staggeringly huge and pretty minimalistic dance warehouse with seven bars and outside patio and balcony areas (both with bars). There's often live music, featuring local and national bands. *Squeeze* (☎ 522-2151), 2 S New River Drive, is a progressive place with local bands on Wednesday and Friday.

For live blues music, head to *Cheers* (☎ 771-6337), 941 E Cypress Creek Rd. On Friday and Saturday, men must wear shirts with sleeves. *Dr Feelgoode's Boogie Woogie Emporium* (☎ 491-7440), 2471 E Commercial Blvd (Hwy 870), has live music Wednesday through Sunday. *Downtowner Saloon* (☎ 463-9800), 10 S New River Drive (near Squeeze), has live blues Thursday through Saturday in the blues room. The best time to go is Wednesday evenings at 10.30 pm, when everyone heads out back to moon the *Jungle Queen* cruise (then buy a $12 T-shirt to commemorate the event: 'I've been to the Moon at Downtowner Saloon'.

Gay Clubs There are at least 20 gay bars and clubs in Fort Lauderdale, though they're like rock groups in the early '60s: popular for five minutes, and then they've suddenly reworked their entire image – either out of business or sometimes even turning straight! Check in *Scoop* and *Hot Spots*, or ask around.

The Copa (☎ 463-1507), 2800 S Federal Hwy, has been around forever: it's a huge disco with an outdoor deck. Drag shows happen several times a week. *Club Electra* (☎ 764-8447), 1600 SE 15th Ave, is a high-energy dance club with nights for men during the week and women on Friday to Sunday. It's off 17th St four blocks east of Federal Hwy; turn right (south) on 15th Ave and it's behind the Arby's. *Club Cathode Ray* (☎ 462-8611), 1105 E Las Olas Blvd, is kind of a Guppie hangout. Happy hour (two for one) is every day from 2 to 9 pm; the place is open Sunday to Friday from 2 pm to 2 am, and Saturday from 2 pm to 3 am. *Club Caribbean* (☎ 565-0402), 2851 N Federal Hwy, 2 blocks north of 26th St on the west side of the street, and *The Everglades* (☎ 462-9165), 1931 S Federal Hwy, both do **tea dances** on Sunday evenings. Call them for more information. *The Other Side* (☎ 565-5538), 2283 Wilton Drive at

NE 6th Ave, is a lesbian club that's also been around forever; it features a separate dance area and the bar has pool tables.

Spectator Sports

There are no major league teams in Fort Lauderdale (yet), but it's close enough to Miami to be able to boast that city's pro teams. (See the Miami Spectator Sports section.) You can watch the Baltimore Orioles spring training games at their new home at Fort Lauderdale Stadium (☎ 938-4980), 5301 NW 12th Ave.

---

19 Million People Can't Be Wrong

The biggest news in town is the largest factory outlet mall in the USA – the unbelievably enormous, alligator-shaped Sawgrass Mills Factory Outlet Mall (☎ 846-2350). We're talkin' big: 19 *million* people came to this 2.35-million-sq-foot mall last year, making this a more popular draw than, say, Busch Gardens in Tampa. The prices, by the way, are the reason those millions of people came here: some are as much as 80% off retail. Clothes and stuff are incredibly cheap, since they are often discontinued lines or slightly damaged or 'imperfect'.

'Only in America could a shopping mall become a tourist attraction,' many Europeans might think at this point. Well, Klaus and Juliette, consider that about 80% of those 19 million people were foreigners. (And while we're on the subject – McDonald's restaurants were not placed in Europe by the US State Department's cultural wing. There'd be fewer if people didn't clamor for them.)

In the mall, there are three food courts, two sit-down restaurants, daily entertainment programs, a 900-member indoor fitness club with a 1½-mile (yes, a mile and a half) indoor walking and running course, and a themed area that sounds spookily Disneyan in its description:

. . . Cabana Court, which includes a beach scene and blue lagoon that houses a delightful animated alligator family and their singing flamingo and seagull friends.

The mall's main attraction (it's over two miles around the ring road) is the 275-some-odd stores, including outlet stores of Saks Fifth Avenue, Neiman Marcus, Barney's New York, JC Penney, Spiegel (Chicago, 60609), Loehmann's, Mondi, Bernini, Levi's, Nine West, Kenneth Cole, MCM, Ann Taylor, Emanuel-Emanuel Ungaro, Ike Behar and Jones New York. Whoo.

There are two staffed information booths (that give out good maps of the mall – you'll need one), a foreign currency exchange center (bah), three ATM machine areas *and* an 18-screen Cobb movie theater. Wheelchairs are available at the information booths and 'smart carts' are at each entrance. There are 11,000 parking spaces.

The mall is at 12801 W Sunrise Blvd in the city of Sunrise, nine miles west of Fort Lauderdale. By car, take the Sawgrass Expressway right to it (or take Sunrise Blvd, Hwy 838). Shuttle buses run between the mall and Miami Beach (but not Fort Lauderdale) from Monday to Saturday from several Miami Beach and Miami hotels; roundtrip fare is $5. The bus leaves from the DeLido Hotel at 17th St and Collins Ave at 8.55, 10.25 am and 12.15 pm, and it returns at 3 and 6.30 pm.

The mall is open Monday to Saturday from 10 am to 9.30 pm, Sunday from 11 am to 8 pm. ∎

Things to Buy

The *Swap Shop* (☎ 791-7927), 3291 W Sunrise Blvd about a mile east of Sawgrass Mills, is an enormous circus-like flea market. We mean it – there's a real *circus* there every day in addition to movies, a tiny amusement park and lots of stuff to buy.

Getting There & Away

Air Fort Lauderdale/Hollywood International Airport (FLL; ☎ 359-1200) is home to over 35 airlines, including some with nonstop flights from Europe. See the Getting There & Away chapter for more information.

Bus The Greyhound station (☎ 764-6551) is at 515 NE 3rd St at Federal Hwy, about 4½ blocks from Broward Central Terminal (see below), the central transfer point for buses in the Fort Lauderdale area. There are frequent buses to Miami ($5, about half an hour to an hour).

Train Tri-Rail runs between Miami and Palm Beach with stops in Fort Lauderdale. They also provide transportation to the Miami Arena for basketball and hockey games, to Joe Robbie Stadium (for Miami Dolphins and Florida Marlins games) and to several other tourist attractions. Daily tickets are $5. A wheelchair-access van service is available, as well as a feeder system of buses at no extra charge. Free parking is provided at most stations. Call ☎ 800-874-7245 or 728-8445 for Tri-Rail ticket and scheduling information. Amtrak (☎ 800-872-7245) passenger trains run on the same tracks as Tri-Rail.

The Fort Lauderdale station is at 200 SW 21st Terrace, just south of Broward Blvd, just west of I-95.

Car Florida's Turnpike, the state's main toll road, runs north and south from Miami to Longwood. I-595, the major east-west artery, connects the western suburbs with Port Everglades, the airport and downtown Fort Lauderdale. It also connects with I-95, Florida's Turnpike and the Sawgrass Expressway. The Sawgrass Expressway, a north-south toll expressway, links western suburbs and ties into I-95, the Turnpike and I-75. I-75 runs to Florida's west coast.

All major car rental companies have offices at FLL.

Boat Port Everglades Authority (☎ 523-3404) runs this enormous cruise port (second busiest in the world after Miami). From the port, walk to SE 17th St and take bus No 40 to the beach or to Broward Central Terminal. If you're coming here in your own boat (not unlikely here), head for Bahia Mar Yachting Center (☎ 764-2233). (Travis McGee fans please note: Slip F-18 doesn't exist – Bahia Mar slips have a letter and three numbers. Too bad.)

Getting Around

To/From the Airport The Fort Lauderdale/Hollywood International Airport (FLL) is about a 20-minute drive from E Las Olas Blvd. BCt Bus No 1 goes from the airport to Broward Central Terminal. Tri-Rail has a shuttle connecting it to the Fort Lauderdale Airport station (you can also take BCt bus Nos 3 or 6), with trains heading up to the Fort Lauderdale station ($3) about once an hour at rush hours, once every two hours in midday; trains run from about 5.50 am to 11.30 pm on weekdays, with less frequent service and more restricted hours on weekends. The official airport taxi is Yellow Cab Co (☎ 565-5400, 565-8400, see Taxi below). Gray Line (☎ 561-8886) runs private limos and shuttles. A private limo (more of a car, really) to/from the airport/Fort Lauderdale is $24; a shared shuttle bus is $8. You need to reserve 24-hours in advance on the shuttle from Fort Lauderdale to the airport. For information on getting from FLL to Miami, see the Getting Around section in the Miami chapter.

Bus It's not a breeze, but getting around can be done without a car here; frequent Broward County Transit (BCt) bus service runs between downtown and the beach, Port Everglades and surrounding towns and beaches. The Broward Central Terminal is the central terminal for buses in the area; it's at 200 W Broward Ave, two blocks west of S Andrews Blvd on the north side of the street.

You can call BCt for information on specific routes at ☎ 357-8400, TTY 357-8302. One-way fares are $1; seniors, disabled or youth fares are 50¢; transfers are 15¢. Fare boxes on board accept dollar bills.

From Broward Central Terminal take bus No 11 to upper Fort Lauderdale Beach, bus No 1 to Floyd's Hostel, Joanne's Crew House and the Port Everglades area, bus No 40 to 17th St and Federal Hwy and bus Nos 40, 11 and 20 to lower Fort Lauderdale Beach. From the Cyprus Creek Tri-Rail Station to HI Fort Lauderdale Hostel, take bus No 62; and from Oakland Park Blvd to Sawgrass Mills Mall, take bus No 72.

The Commuter Store (☎ 761-3543), 213 S Andrews Ave, is a one-stop shopping spot for anything transit related in the greater Fort Lauderdale area open weekdays 9 am to 5 pm. They sell bus tickets for $8 a week, or $30 a month for adults, $15 for those under 18, seniors, disabled or those on Medicare. Ride Share matching, sort of the American *Mitfahrzentrale* (a service pairing up passengers with drivers), is available from the Gold Coast Commuter Service (☎ 800-234-7433 in Broward County). The city is planning to install bicycle lockers downtown; call the Commuter Store for more information.

Trolley BCt's free Downtown Trolley (☎ 761-3543) loops through downtown. The Wave Trolley Company (☎ 429-3100) runs a $1 trolley service that loops through downtown, Port Everglades and the beach. South Florida Trolley (☎ 429-3100) runs a sightseeing loop between Sunrise Blvd and the SE 17th St causeway from the ocean to the Museum of Discovery and Science; you can get off and on as often as you like. Their all-day adult pass is $12, children under 12 are free. This may not be a time or money saver, as all these destinations are happily and conveniently served by bus, but the trolley's kind of pretty and includes narration.

Car Having a car is the easiest way to go, though parking is especially tight in high season, and you usually have to pay for it. Pay lots are located north and south of Las Olas Blvd ($1 per hour) and all-day parking at the beach can be had for $5 ($3 at night) at the municipal parking lot on Hwy A1A just south of SE 5th St, near the International Swimming Hall of Fame. Speed limits are enforced to such an extent that you may wonder if the cops get a commission – watch especially for flashing lights indicating school zones, in which speed limits are 15 mph. Generally speaking, the speed limit is 30 or 35 mph, but there are a lot of 20s out there, too, so be careful. Remove all valuables from your car when parking.

Taxi Meter rates are $2.45 flagfall, plus $1.75 per mile. Try Yellow Cab Company (☎ 565-5400, 565-8400).

Bicycle Fort Lauderdale's flatness makes it a great place to get around by bike. Floyd's Youth Hostel (see Places to Stay above) rents bicycles to its guests for $3 a day. The St Tropez Resort (☎ 564-8468), 725 N Atlantic Blvd, rents bicycles for $4 an hour, $10 a day (from 8.30 am to 8 pm), $15 for 24 hours or $40 a week with a $50 deposit.

Water Taxi The Water Taxi (☎ 467-6677), 651 Seabreeze Blvd, is a full-fledged transportation option in the canals and waterways of Fort Lauderdale. A $14 daily pass lets you ride as much as you'd like, though you're asked (or, rather, implored) to tip the driver each time. We say tip only if they're nice or helpful. Call from any commercial location downtown on the New River, or along the Intracoastal Waterway (anyplace with a dock) and they'll swing by and pick you up. They also offer sightseeing tours and an 'Eco Float' tour, though 'eco' should be taken with a grain of salt given some of the management's views toward the manatees ('they destroy property values'). The water taxi covers an area that is bordered by 17th St to the south, Atlantic

Blvd/Pompano Beach to the north, down the New River to the west and the Atlantic Ocean east.

AROUND FORT LAUDERDALE

The greater Fort Lauderdale area's division lines have been deliberately blurred by the CVB, which seeks to market the area's attractions as a package to entice more visitors. For this reason, many guidebooks and hand-out pamphlets list hotels, attractions and events in the entire region in a Fort Lauderdale context – for example, the Lauderdale-by-the-Sea chamber of commerce bills the Stranahan House as one if its attractions.

We've listed these towns and cities separately because they are indeed separate entities, but it should be noted that all are within a 20-minute drive of the others. All these towns are accessible by bus, and Tri-Rail serves Deerfield Beach, Pompano Beach and Hollywood. And many can be accessed via the Intracoastal Waterway.

Dania

• *pop 17,000* ☎ *954*

Just south of Fort Lauderdale is the city of Dania (pronounced 'DANE-ya'), which, among other things, has some of the loveliest stretches of beach in the state, a fledgling antique district, a peaceful state recreation area and the state's finest archaeological museum and collection. It's about a 10-minute drive or 15-minute bus ride from Broward Central Terminal to the Graves Museum (for more transit information see each listing). It's also home to the immense West Lake Park, best seen through the Ann Kolb Nature Center (see Hollywood).

Orientation & Information Dania is about five miles south of downtown Fort Lauderdale on US Hwy 1. It's covered in most handouts, tourist maps and area maps, as well as in the CVB visitor guide. The antique district is along S Federal Hwy (US Hwy 1) stretching two blocks north and south of Dania Beach Blvd. Dania Beach Blvd runs between the beach and fishing pier to S Federal Hwy. Change money at the Barnett Bank at 1991 Stirling Rd. A good landmark is the enormous Dania Jai Alai (☎ 426-433) at 301 E Dania Beach Blvd, with live action most days. There's a Barnett Bank with an ATM at 1991 Stirling Rd. The Dania Library (☎ 926-2420) is at 485 S Federal Hwy.

Graves Museum The wonderful nonprofit Graves Museum of Archaeology & Natural History (☎ 925-7770), 481 S Federal Hwy, between Sheridan St and Sterling Rd, is staffed and run by volunteer members of the Broward County Archaeological Society, who contribute time, knowledge, money and artifacts to the outstanding collection. The museum, easily identified by its huge skull relief on the façade fronting S Federal Hwy, has an extensive geology and paleontology collection, and very extensive pre-Columbian pottery and unique pre-Columbian miniatures collection, as well as museum-quality reproductions of objects discovered in the tomb of Tutankhamen. Its very reasonably priced gift shop is splendid, with many artifacts brought back by staff from their travels and field trips to sites around the world. It is truly worth a visit, and kids will love it as well.

Tours are available by appointment at no extra cost, and they can be tailored to your needs – students can spend a great deal of time here. Casual visitors, however, can do the place in about an hour and a half. All the exhibits (see sidebar) show the amount of love and care that has gone into them. Little details like the red-eyed tree frogs sitting on leaves in the jaguar showcase are very nice touches. The place is desperately struggling to pay its upkeep (like the $3000 per month air-conditioning bill), and donations (over and above the admission price) are appreciated.

Activities are available for kids on Saturday, and adult and children's classes are available year round. Call the museum for more information. Bus No 1 to/from Fort Lauderdale's Broward Central Terminal stops very close by.

It's open Tuesday to Saturday from 10 am

Highlights of the Graves Museum

Geology Gallery There are exhibits on South Florida geology and sea levels, including very colorful and huge crystals like quartz, amethyst, dolomite and malachite. The paleontology exhibit's main attraction is the ongoing reconstruction of a 66 million-year-old triceratops; it also has manatee ribs and the imposing jaws of *Titanothere Brontotherium*.

Homonid Development They have human skulls at various stages of evolution and reconstructive sculptures, as well as exhibits on the development of stone tool technology. Dioramas illustrate the prehistory of southern Florida through paleo-hunter, archaic villager and glades 'city dwellers' periods, as well as of Tequesta Indian and Caribbean cultures.

Maritime & Marine Gallery The museum is currently at work reconstructing an actual wrecked ship, and the Maritime Gallery features niceties like a compass binnacle from the *SS Priscilla*, a turn-of-the-century ship.

Central & Meso America This is the museum's most impressive section, with an unbelievable number of pre-Columbian pottery and miniature specimens, along with painted and decorated ceramic, stone and jade. They trace the development of the writing system and beliefs of the ancient Mayans.

Other Exhibits The ancient Egypt gallery has reproductions of the Rosetta stone, relics from King Tutankhamen's tomb and a mummy (along with instructions on mummification: 'brains removed through nostril with a hook'). There's a South America exhibit and an impressive collection of products made from endangered species that have been confiscated by the US Department of Fish and Wildlife. ■

to 4 pm, Sunday from 1 to 5 pm, closed Monday. Admission is $5 for adults, $3 for children four to 12. Tuesday is Senior Citizen Day, with a $4 admission for seniors.

Dania Beach This lovely stretch of coastline, whose action is centered around the Dania Fishing Pier, has white sand, fewer people than most South Florida beaches and, happily, several inexpensive places to grab something to eat during the day. The Seafair complex, a mall building opposite the beach on the Intracoastal Waterway houses Captured Image (☎ 922-8523), a kind of head shop and Deadhead fashion boutique with some great stuff at decent prices. Smoking paraphernalia is a bit expensive here, though magic lanterns, incense and other trippy stuff is better priced.

Fishing Pier This almost 900-foot stretch of pier is a must for fishers – we saw a nine-year-old boy walk off with a two-foot barracuda! The pier and tackle shop is open 24

hours a day. Admission is $3 per person, spectators $1; fishing rod rental is $6 with a $30 deposit, bait runs $1.75 to 2.50. There are aerated saltwater tanks along the pier to keep your catch swimming while you hunt down their friends.

Antique District 'District' is a bit of an overstatement. Tourist handouts hail this as the hottest antique market around, though that's not saying much. If you're looking, the bulk of shops are along S Federal Hwy (Hwy 1), stretching two blocks north and south of E Dania Beach Blvd.

Places to Stay The beach is easy to reach from Fort Lauderdale, where cheaper accommodations are available, so you may want to consider day trips to Dania. If not, there are a few local options.

The cheapest room on a daily basis is in the down-at-the-heels *Dania Beach Hotel* (☎ 927-8303), 180 E Dania Beach Blvd (a five-minute bus ride from the beach just off

SOUTHEAST

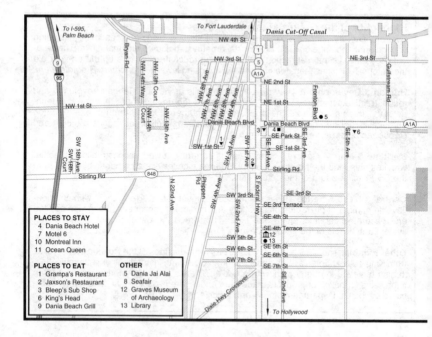

PLACES TO STAY
4 Dania Beach Hotel
7 Motel 6
10 Montreal Inn
11 Ocean Queen

PLACES TO EAT
1 Grampa's Restaurant
2 Jaxson's Restaurant
3 Bleep's Sub Shop
6 King's Head
9 Dania Beach Grill

OTHER
5 Dania Jai Alai
8 Seafair
12 Graves Museum of Archaeology
13 Library

S Federal Hwy). Built in 1926, this once-grand dame now has reasonably clean but small rooms, and a rather tough looking bar on the premises (we'd err on the side of caution).The place has singles/doubles for $28/30 including tax, or $119/135 a week in low season. Call the office (☎ 922-2226) for high-season rates, which change.

Right on the beach, the *Montreal Inn* (☎ 925-4443), 324-36 Balboa St, is a very nice family-run place smack on the dividing line between Dania and Hollywood, where most of the beachfront inns are located. The sprawling, cabana-style place has friendly staff, and rooms are clean and all have kitchens, cable TV and in-room safes (additional $2 per day). Doubles are from $34.50 ($189 per week) in low season, $49.50 ($389.50 per week) in high season – there are a couple of other seasons for pricing, but the highest season for these guys is February, which books out early. Prices are somewhat negotiable. They rent bikes by the hour/day for $5/18.50.

About halfway between the beach and S Federal Hwy is a clean-as-usual *Motel 6*, 825 E Dania Beach Blvd (bus No 7 stops directly in front), with standard rooms at $34.87/39.23 including tax; kids under 17 are free. AARP members pay $28.79/31.38.

For longer term – monthly – rentals, the best deal on the beach is *Paulie's Place* (☎ 927-2010), 5611 N Ocean Blvd, which has spotless one-bedroom apartments complete with kitchens and dining rooms for $200 a week – negotiable in high season, when prices tend to edge up another $25 a week. Very nice management.

The charming *Ocean Queen* (☎ 920-7149), 5600 N Surf Rd, right on the sand, has a friendly staff and nice rooms (with microwaves and coffeemakers) that get cheaper the longer you stay – $55 a day for a minimum three-night stay, $50 a day for seven days and $35 a day for a one-month stay. In low season, rooms go down to $35; efficiencies in low/high season are $60/65.

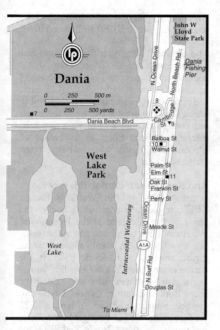

Dania

John W Lloyd State Park

N Ocean Drive

North Beach Rd

Dania Fishing Pier

0   250   500 m
0   250   500 yards

■7

8

Cambridge St ▼9

Dania Beach Blvd

Balboa St
Walnut St

West Lake Park

Palm St
Elm St ■11
Oak St
Franklin St
Perry St

Ocean Drive

Meade St

A1A

West Lake

N Surf Rd

Douglas St

Intracoastal Waterway

To Miami

Places to Eat You can barbecue your own food and dine al fresco in one of the chickee huts near the Dania Beach Grill – there are grills available right there.

For quick and cheap grindage on the beach, look to the *Dania Beach Grill* in the center of the main parking lot, near the pier, serving burgers, hot dogs and sandwiches. Nothing's over $4, draft beer is $1.25 to 2. On the fishing pier, the *Patio Bar* has tiny pizzas ($2), hot dogs ($1.50) and burritos ($2), along with soft drinks and frozen cocktails. It's open Wednesday to Friday from 6 am to 11 pm, Saturday from noon to midnight, Sunday from noon to 11 pm, closed Monday and Tuesday. Over at the Seafair, there's the meat-market-ish *Bloody Mary's*, with burgers and bar food for around $6 to 11 and lots of drink specials and beer.

We thought that the *Penn-Dutch Restaurant* (☎ 929-9220) at 218 E Dania Beach Blvd looked worth trying, but it was closed when we visited. Pennsylvania-

Dutch specialties like scrapple is on the menu and, if it's authentic, they'll probably have huge portions at breakfast for not a lot of money.

Bleep's Sub Shop (☎ 922-9522), 50 E Dania Beach Blvd, is a real '50s type lunch counter serving up good 10-inch submarine-style sandwiches for cheap – cheese or veggies $1.99, ham or salami and cheese $3.15 and meatball or eggplant $3.99.

Just shy of being a real British pub (they don't overboil the vegetables or undercook the bacon), the *King's Head Pub* (☎ 922-5722), 500 E Dania Beach Blvd (look for the original British phone box outside), does very nice shepherds pie ($7.95) and bangers & mash ($6.95), along with more upmarket entries at a slightly higher price. In the intimate bar section, complete with tube and BritRail station signs, 'Guinness Makes You Strong' posters and cheapo one-sixth gill measurements of Martini, you can get draught Guinness and Bass, several types of cider and other Britty things like (yuk) Pernod and black. It's a fun place with great friendly service and several regular expats, who keep their personal beer mugs hanging around.

Bring the kids to *Jaxson's Restaurant* (☎ 923-4445), 128 S Federal Hwy, for a few minutes, but any longer gets expensive. The 40-year-old ice cream emporium is a wonderfully designed place – stuff hanging from the ceilings, license plates on the walls – and the ice cream is great. Banana splits are $4.25/6 take-out/eat-in; hot fudge sundaes $4.50/8.

Grampa's Bakery & Restaurant, 17 SW 1st St, is worth a look, though we *hated* the prune Danish – breakfast specials like pancakes or waffles with fresh fruit and whipped cream are $2.25 to 3.99, sandwiches/subs $3.25 to 5.75, and burgers, chicken and fish dishes run from $3.95 to 7.95. It's open Monday to Saturday from 6.30 am to 9 pm, Sunday from 8 am to 2 pm.

Getting There & Away To downtown Dania, take BCt bus No 1 from Broward Central Station to Dania Beach Blvd. For

SOUTHEAST

Charter fishing is a Florida obsession.

the beach, transfer there for an eastbound No 7, which goes right to the beach and runs every 20 minutes on weekdays, every half hour to 40 minutes on weekends. If you're driving, turn east down Dania Beach Blvd and follow it to the end. Metered parking is available right at the beach for $1 per hour, quarters only. Unmetered spaces are for local residents only, and the tow trucks are on the prowl.

Hollywood
• *pop 125,000* ☎ *954*

Hollywood is directly below Dania, but the only reasons to travel this far south are the beach, the three-mile boardwalk that lines it – swarming with in-line skaters and cute hunks of all nationalities – and the Anne Kolb Nature Center in West Lake Park. It's worth a day trip.

Orientation & Information The city is just north of the Dade County line and the Aventura Mall. Hollywood Blvd runs between the beach and the center of town, which are about two miles apart. Get tourist information at the Hollywood Chamber of Commerce (☎ 923-4000), 330 S Federal Hwy.

Barnett Bank has a branch at 1900 Tyler St and on the beach at 3509 N Ocean Drive.

American Express (☎ 925-0500) has a representative office at 2025B Hollywood Blvd.

The Beach With rollerblading cops and a 'boardwalk' made of concrete that's packed with skaters and bikes, Hollywood beach is a scene. It's lined with snack bars, souvenir shops and junky tourist trinket touts. The sand itself is okay, and the beach has enough character to make a day here interesting. Rent bikes at a number of places, including the Montreal Hotel (see Dania above).

Ann Kolb Nature Center This new nature center (☎ 926-2481) in West Lake Park, a 1400-acre coastal mangrove wetland on the coast of the mainland at the Intracoastal Waterway, has a brand new 65-foot observation tower, a lagoon, boardwalks and canoe, kayak, rowboat and bicycle trails. In the nature center, there's a 4000-gallon aquarium and two staff naturalists who explain the local flora and fauna. Canoe, kayak and rowboat rentals are $6.25 an hour, $13.25 for four hours and $25 for eight hours. There are four trails: the 1.2-mile Red Trail, the one-mile White and Green Trails and the very short Blue Trail, all through the mangrove islands – not in the Intracoastal.

Admission to the nature center is free; the exhibit area is $3 for adults and $1.50 for children. They offer a 40-minute boat tour through West Lake every hour on the hour; the cost is $8 for adults and $4 for children.

The park is open weekdays from 9 am to sunset, Saturday and Sunday from 8 am to sunset. To get there, take Federal Hwy (US Hwy 1) to Sheridan St, go east for about 1½ miles and the marina is on the south side, the nature center on the north.

Places to Eat The *Now Art Gallery Café* (☎ 922-0506), 1820 Hollywood Blvd, home of Theatre With Your Coffee on the second and fourth Friday of the month, is a New Age (nonsmoking) coffee/snack bar with a wide range of performances: live acoustic guitar on Wednesday and Saturday, various musicians on Thursday, classical guitar on Friday.

Try My Thai (☎ 926-5585), 2003 Harrison St, has excellent Thai food with soups from $1.95 to $2.50, appetizers from $5.95 to $6.95 and entrées $7.95 to $14.95. It's open for dinner daily, for lunch from Tuesday through Friday.

We've heard good things about *Sugar Reef* (☎ 922-1119), 600 N Surf Rd on the boardwalk; they do French-Caribbean food with appetizers like Portobello mushrooms in red wine and pesto from $4.75 to $6, and main courses like grilled fish and steak from $6 to $15.

Club M (☎ 925-8396), 2037 Hollywood Blvd, is totally packed on weekends when it's a disco, but jazz and blues play on most other days.

Getting There & Away Hollywood has two bus terminals: at Young Circle at US Hwy 1, and on Hollywood Blvd, further west at the center of the city. From Broward Central Terminal take BCt bus No 1 or 9 to Young Circle, where you can change for No 17 or 28 to Hollywood or to Hollywood beach. The Greyhound station is at 17-7 Tyler St, just off Hwy 1 and Young Circle; there are about seven buses a day from Miami. By car, take US Hwy 1, Hwy A1A or I-95.

Davie
• *pop 50,000* ☎ *954*

If you've ever been to Dubbo, Australia, you'll get a familiar flash when you cross the Davie line. A sprawling, sparsely populated town that's slowly making the conversion from farmland to bedroom community, Davie's not a whole bunch of laughs – yeah, there are a lot of people on horseback, but that only takes you so far. The classic piece of tourist information is that the McDonald's (☎ 791-6657) at 4101 SW 64th Ave has a corral and hitching post. Whee.

But there is a rodeo that hosts national shows, and the Buehler Planetarium is interesting. Don't plan on spending a night here.

Orientation & Information Davie is southwest of downtown Fort Lauderdale. The downtown – don't blink – is a short strip of Davie Rd between Griffin Rd and

PLACES TO EAT
2 McDonald's
6 Hitching Post Restaurant

OTHER
1 Buehler Planetarium
3 Army Navy Outdoors
4 Davie Rodeo Arena
5 Chamber of Commerce
7 Davie Junction

Davie

0   150   300 m
0   150   300 yards

about SW 39th St. There's a tourist information booth at the Chamber of Commerce on Davie Rd at 42nd St, and a Barnett Bank at 6300 Stirling Rd. The folks at Army Navy Outdoors (☎ 584-7227), 4130 SW 64th Ave, opposite the McDonald's are helpful and friendly if you need to know anything about rodeos coming to town. We used the toilets at the Hitching Post Restaurant (☎ 587-1400), 4483 SW 64th Ave; sort of a diner kind of thing happening there.

Buehler Planetarium On Broward Community College's central campus, Buehler Planetarium, 2501 Davie Rd, is a cool place to spend an hour or two. Using their very small Zeiss star machine, the college's astronomers project fascinating night sky displays while you sit in chairs that are so comfortable you may not want to leave. See constellations only visible from the North and South Poles, as well as perfect views of stars in your own hemisphere you may never have seen before due to 'light pollution' – this place dims down to total darkness. Show times and costs change, so call the hotline at ☎ 475-6680 for information.

On Friday and Saturday (at 8.15, 9.30, 10.45 pm and midnight; $6 admission), these sky-wonks let their hair down and produce intense laser shows against the backdrop of the moving night sky set to music from Pearl Jam, Nine Inch Nails and lots of others. You can also catch a show of Pink Floyd's *Dark Side of the Moon*. For laser show information call ☎ 423 6417.

Matinees of *The Light-Hearted Astronomer* show are a bit tamer, but much more educational, and are held on Friday at 7 pm, Saturday at 3 and 7 pm and Sunday at 3 pm. Call for their prerecorded show information hotline (☎ 475-6680) for costs (which change) and for other shows that may be on when you visit.

Davie Rodeo Arena One block west of Davie Rd just north of the canal, at the corner of SW 42nd St and 66th Ave, the Davie Rodeo Arena (☎ 581-0790) is the place to see rodeos and the occasional folk or crafts show. The arena features monthly, national five-star pro rodeo events, and annually in early February, their huge 10-day 'Florida Westfair' western festival. No coolers, bottles, fireworks or firearms allowed inside. Darn.

Places to Eat *The Coffee Table* (☎ 424-3177), 7711 Nova Drive, does gourmet coffees and excellent desserts like cheesecakes and pies for about $2.50 to $5. All the art on the walls is by local artists, and there's an open-mike night Thursday at 8 pm; poetry reading on the fourth Friday of the month at 7.30 pm, and live music on

Thursday and Sunday nights. The *McDonald's* is in the 'heart' of 'downtown Davie' at Davie Rd just south of SW 41st St. Stick around long enough and you may see someone riding through the drive-thru on horseback. Or not.

If being here in the suburban east has you yearning for that country western thing, head for *Davie Junction* (☎ 581-1132), 6311 SW 45th St, where they don't exactly have a mechanical bull but they do have two-stepping rowdies and a couple of pool tables (if you're rusty, they offer lessons on Sunday nights).

Getting There & Away BCt bus No 9 runs between Broward Central Terminal and Davie Rd. By car, take I-95 S to Hwy 595 west, to exit 7. Turn south and you'll run into downtown.

Lauderdale-by-the-Sea
• *pop 3000* ☎ *954*
Just north of Fort Lauderdale, this condo-clustered village is struggling to attract tourists but without enough bait. The only bona fide attraction here is their fishing pier, where you can fish your heart out for a day (adults/kids under 12 cost $3/2). Rod rentals and bait are available here, too, but we think the Dania pier is better. That said, this is a pleasant place to spend a morning or watch a sunset, and brunch at Murphy's Beach House is a nice experience.

Orientation & Information You can easily walk all of downtown. E Commercial Blvd is the town's main east-west artery, and Ocean Drive (Hwy A1A) is the main north-south route. The pier is at the end of Commercial Blvd at El Mar Drive, one block east of Ocean Drive. This is also the spot for most of the restaurants and touristy stuff. Get tourist information at the Chamber of Commerce (☎ 776-1000, 800-699-6764), in the middle of the triangle formed by the intersection of Ocean and Bougainvillea Drives. They publish *The Seaside Village of Lauderdale-by-the-Sea*, an advertiser-driven tourist information magazine with a good map of the city.

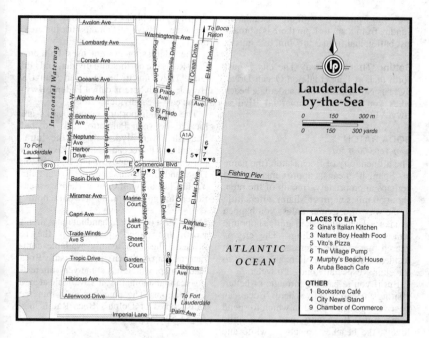

Lauderdale-by-the-Sea

PLACES TO EAT
2 Gina's Italian Kitchen
3 Nature Boy Health Food
5 Vito's Pizza
6 The Village Pump
7 Murphy's Beach House
8 Aruba Beach Cafe

OTHER
1 Bookstore Café
4 City News Stand
9 Chamber of Commerce

The Bookstore Café (☎ 772-0023), 4405 W Trade Winds Ave, on the east side of the Intracoastal Waterway, sells a huge range of LP books and are generally very friendly and helpful. There's a café upstairs. The City News Stand, 4400 Bougainvillea Drive, has out-of-town and foreign newspapers.

Places to Stay & Eat There's absolutely no advantage to staying here as opposed to in Fort Lauderdale. Prices for motels, hotels and apartments tend to be higher because the place is geared more to vacationing time-share and condo owners than to backpackers or travelers.

You can get a double room in the *Lauderdale by the Sea Motel* (☎ 776-1391), 4229 N Ocean Drive for $40, even in high season, though they post rates of $65 in winter and $40 in summer.

Vito's Pizza (☎ 351-0016), 4403 El Mar Drive has excellent New York-style pizza for $1.50 a slice, $9 for a large pie – stop here for a large garlic pie before getting

on the *Jungle Queen* and talking real close to everyone.

Nature Boy Health Food (☎ 776-4696), 220 E Commercial Blvd, sells healthful salads and stuff starting at around $3.59 to $4.85. Just down the street is *Gina's Italian Kitchen* (☎ 491-2340) 226 E Commercial Blvd, which does pizzas and lasagna-type dishes that looked and smelled great.

Murphy's Beach House (☎ 776-6708), 4400 El Mar Drive, does a great Sunday brunch for $6.95 to 8.95, and dinner specials like veal parmigiana or grilled chicken go for $7.95. At their take-out window you can get burgers ($3.50 to 4.25) and other fast food. Get sloshed next door at the *Village Pump* (☎ 491-9407), 4404 El Mar Drive, a fun and divey local bar and grill.

Aruba Beach Café (☎ 776-0001), 1 E Commercial Blvd, is a party place, sort of a Caribbean beach atmosphere. It's pretty big and pretty loud, and everyone we spoke to liked it. There's a large window overlooking the ocean. Happy hour is weekdays

SOUTHEAST

from 4 to 7 pm with $1 off all cocktails; on Sunday from 8 am to 1 pm there is a breakfast buffet, and from 3 to 7 pm, live music.

Getting There & Away The city is just north of Fort Lauderdale on Ocean Drive. BCt bus No 11 from Fort Lauderdale beach takes you right to Commercial Blvd at Hwy A1A.

BOCA RATON
• *pop 160,000* ☎ *561*

The affluent city of Boca Raton (the name in Spanish means, approximately and perhaps appropriately, 'mouth of the rat'), about 50 miles north of Miami, offers little in the way of activities unless you happen to take a keen interest in golf, shopping, tennis and pink buildings. The city is geared more to the interests of long-term residents or big shot golfers as opposed to travelers – especially budget travelers.

But if you're passing through, or better, visiting a friend who lives here, 'Boca' can be a very pleasant place in which to spend some time. Its county parks are quite lovely, the beaches are clean, white and safe, and if you're up for some house-gawking, you've come to a city with ample opportunities.

Orientation
As with many of the Gold Coast cities, Boca is divided by the Intracoastal Waterway, with the majority of the city on the mainland. The town is a sprawler, with residential neighborhoods stretching far west of I-95 and the Florida Turnpike.

The main action, such as it is, is in the quadrant north of Camino Real Blvd, south of Spanish River Blvd (actually, while this is a convenient dividing point, you'll rarely need to go north of, say, 28th St), and east of NW 9th Ave. As a constant reminder of the city's beginnings, the name Mizner (pronounced 'MIZE-ner'; see Florida History) is given to as many things as possible: Mizner Blvd meanders through downtown in a roughly north-south direction, and Mizner Park, on N Federal Hwy near NE 2nd St, is a faux-village filled with chi-chi

shops, a great bookstore and some surprisingly inexpensive restaurants (for the area, that is).

The addressing system uses Palmetto Park Rd as the north-south divider, and Old Dixie Hwy (not to be confused with US Hwy 1, which here is called Federal Hwy) as the east-west divider.

The most important county parks are located between Palmetto Park Rd and Spanish River Blvd, between the Intracoastal and the ocean. Camino Real splits the enormous grounds of the Boca Raton Hotel and Golf Course and the Royal Palm Yacht Club and Golf Course. Have we mentioned that golf is a major area attraction?

Maps Most of the free handout maps aren't worth the paper upon which they're printed. The most readily available commercial map of the city is Universal's Boca Raton map, which has some very interesting scalar anomalies; it's available at area gas stations. The chamber of commerce sells copies of Dolph's Boca Raton map for $1.50.

Information
Tourist Offices Here's a toughie. The best starting point is in your hands; Boca has no tourist information offices as such, though every hotel and many restaurants give away handouts to area attractions and disappointing maps. There is a marginally helpful chamber of commerce (☎ 395-4433), 1800 Old Dixie Hwy, which hands out pamphlets and the like. For information on Palm Beach County itself, contact the Palm Beach County CVB (☎ 561-471-3995) at 1555 Palm Beach Lakes Blvd, suite 204, West Palm Beach, FL 33401.

Money Barnett Bank has several offices in town, including 4000 N Federal Hwy, 2301 Glades Rd and 1000 N Federal Hwy. American Express has a representative office in Adventure Travels of Boca Raton (☎ 395-5722), 30 SE 7th St.

Post The main post office is at Mizner Blvd at NE 2nd St.

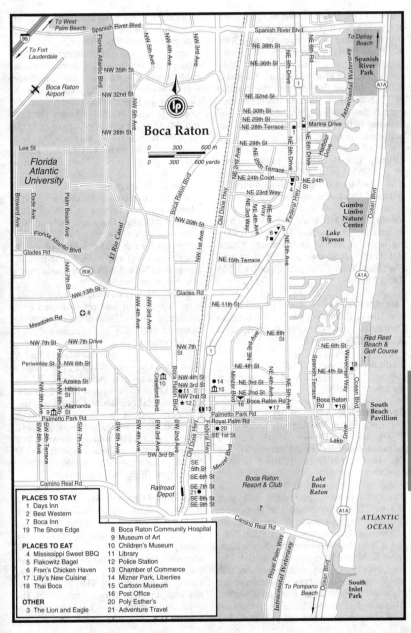

Boca Raton

0   300   600 m
0   300   600 yards

PLACES TO STAY
1 Days Inn
2 Best Western
7 Boca Inn
19 The Shore Edge

PLACES TO EAT
4 Mississippi Sweet BBQ
5 Flakowitz Bagel
6 Fran's Chicken Haven
17 Lilly's New Cuisine
18 Thai Boca

OTHER
3 The Lion and Eagle

8 Boca Raton Community Hospital
9 Museum of Art
10 Children's Museum
11 Library
12 Police Station
13 Chamber of Commerce
14 Mizner Park, Liberties
15 Cartoon Museum
16 Post Office
20 Poly Esther's
21 Adventure Travel

SOUTHEAST

Bookstores Hands down best in town, despite the fact that they let Newt Gingrich sign books here, is Liberties (☎ 368-1300), 309 Plaza Real (Mizner Park). They have a huge selection of LP and other travel books and a fantastic Florida section. They also have a café, and they're open late: Sunday to Thursday from 9 am to midnight (café open 8 am to midnight), and Friday and Saturday both are open until 1 am. You can mill about for hours.

Library The Boca Raton public library (☎ 393-7852) is at 200 NW Boca Raton Blvd, one block north of Palmetto Park Rd and two blocks west of Dixie Hwy.

Media *The Boca News* is a locally produced daily, and the *Sun Sentinel* is readily available, as are the big nationals. Check at Liberties (see above). NPR is at 90.7 FM (from West Palm Beach) or 91.3 FM (from Miami).

Laundry Boca Coin Laundry (☎ 368-7322) is at 101 W Palmetto Park Rd, and Camino Coin Laundry and Cleaners (☎ 395-4748) is at 261 W Camino Real.

Medical Services Boca Raton Community Hospital (395-7100), 800 Meadows Rd, is the largest nearby.

Boca Raton Museum of Art

The Boca Raton Museum of Art (☎ 392-2500), 801 W Palmetto Park Rd (the entrance faces lovely Alamanda St; see Old Floresta Historic District below), overcomes its tiny exhibition space by filling it with an impressive and well-balanced mix of its permanent collection and traveling exhibitions. The permanent collection begins outside the museum with outdoor sculptures, including Alan Sonfest's *Time Enclosures of the South East*: cubes fashioned from various materials like steel, copper, stainless steel and bronze that are designed to decompose and release the plant and flower seeds contained within. Also outside, Paul Waldman's *International Bird Museum* (atop the tall blue post) has interior walls that boast miniature works of art intended for the enjoyment of birds who may stop in from time to time.

Inside, the permanent collection features modern and contemporary works, such as Pablo Picasso's *Beach Scene* and *Nude Figures on the Beach* and Henri Matisse's *Girl Playing Violin at the Piano*; there are works by Andy Warhol, Charles Demuth and Maurice Brazil Prendergast. Sculptures include Henry Laurens' *The Two Sisters* as well as works by Etienne Hajdu and Georgio de Chirico. The museum also has collections of photography, African and pre-Columbian art.

Traveling exhibitions are very well done; when we visited they were running photographs by Robert Doisneau, including the famous *Kiss by the Hotel deVille* (also known as *French Kiss* – a print of which has graced all of our walls at one time or another). Other exhibits cover a huge range of subjects and media.

During the school year, Saturday is children's day, and it features tours and arts-and-crafts classes. Tours of the museum are available every day and specialized tours can be arranged free.

The museum's open Monday to Friday from 10 am to 4 pm, Saturday and Sunday from noon to 4 pm. Admission is $3 for adults, $2 for seniors (over 65), $1 for students and children under 12 are free. Surprisingly, there's no convenient public transport, so if you're not driving, you'll have to either walk from downtown or hop a trolley from the Boca Raton Historical Society, which should be running regularly by the time this book goes to print.

Museum of Cartoon Art

After many delays, the International Museum of Cartoon Art (☎ 391-2200), 201 Plaza Real in Mizner Park, finally opened temporary 1st-floor galleries in 1996. The museum, the brainchild of Beetle Bailey creator Mort Walker, has lived in previous incarnations in Greenwich, Connecticut, and Rye Brook, New York. The collection is made up of works by cartoonists from around the world, and it's the largest collection of its kind anywhere: over 160,000 works on paper, 10,000 books and thousands of hours of animated films. You'll see works by artists including Walker, Charles Schultz, Charles Addams, Jim Davis, Richard Outcault, Walt Disney, Winsor McCay, Franz Frazetta, Hérge, Dik Browne, Walt Kelly and Chic Young. Wait a second . . . let's get this straight: yes Jim Davis' *Garfield* but no Bill Watterson's *Calvin & Hobbes*? *Eine Schande*.

The museum is open Tuesday to Saturday from 11 am to 5 pm, Sunday from noon to 5 pm, closed Monday. Admission is $6 for adults, $5 for seniors, $4 for students and $3 for kids three to 12.

Schmidt Center Gallery

At Florida Atlantic University (FAU), the Schmidt Center Gallery (☎ 367-2966), 777 Glades Rd in the Schmidt Performing Arts Center, is a commercial and academic exhibition space with a diverse range of rotating shows by students, faculty and visiting artists. The art is mostly contemporary, in a variety of styles and media; when we visited they were running *Rocks-Bicycles-Dreams* by George Dombeck, a brilliant exhibition of paintings as well as bicycles that the artist has fashioned from twigs and branches. Other recent exhibitions included the second annual FAU Faculty Exhibition and original prints by French artist Françoise Gilot. Admission is always free and open to the public. The gallery is open Tuesday to Friday from 11 am to 4 pm, Saturday from noon to 4 pm, closed Sunday, Monday and holidays. Use parking lot 1 (visitors must use metered spaces), walk toward the enormous theater and turn left; the gallery is down the hallway on the building's 'arm'.

Ritter Art Gallery

Also at FAU, the Ritter Art Gallery (☎ 367-2660), on the 2nd floor above the 'breezeway', is a teaching gallery whose shows also feature contemporary art – though more in the lines of public art, BFA candidate exhibits and some foreign student shows. The exhibitions tend to last about four to six weeks and place a strong emphasis on large-scale sculpture and graphic design. The Ritter is free and open Tuesday to Friday from 10 am to 3.30 pm, Saturday from 11 am to 4 pm, closed Sunday, Monday and holidays. Also use parking lot 1 (visitors must use metered spaces), walk toward the enormous theater and turn right, go around the building and toward the outdoor tables of the Breezeway Café, enter the breezeway (ask anyone if you can't find it) and walk up the staircase in the middle of the corridor.

Mizner Park

Billed as a village within a city, this is an upscale shopping mall with free valet parking and plenty of chi-chi shops. Don't be put off: you'll also find a great bookstore, Liberties (see Bookstores), some good deals on dinner, a Steve's Ice Cream shop, a high-tech AMC cinema and many other interesting little stores. It's just north of NE 2nd St on the east side of N Federal Hwy.

Children's Museum of Boca Raton

In a lovely little house that very much resembles a country kindergarten (it's one of the oldest houses in Florida), the Children's Museum (☎ 368-6875), 498 Crawford Blvd, features such wonders as an insect room and a child-size supermarket. The staff is said to be lovely and the place very entertaining for smaller children; sadly, it was closed for a month when we visited. The museum's open daily from noon to 5 pm, closed holidays and the month of September. Admission is $1, children under two enter for free.

Boca Raton Historical Society

Come to the Boca Raton Historical Society (☎ 395-6766), 71 N Federal Hwy, even if only to see the building the society's in, the Boca Raton Town Hall (1927). Mizner had planned to build this gold-domed, Mediterranean-Revival building earlier, but the land bust intervened and architect William Alsmeyer scaled down the plans for the final building. It's nice to look at, especially its gold dome, hardwood and tile

SOUTHEAST

floors, and tall windows. The building was declared a historical landmark and turned over to the society in 1983.

The society gives lectures, city historical tours, slide shows and some classes, and also maintains and runs the Florida East Coast Railway Depot. They are planning to extend their tour schedule, using the Royal Palm Plaza trolley beginning in 1996. Admission is free.

Florida East Coast Railway Depot

Built in the 1930s as a station serving the Boca Raton Club, this lovely Mediterranean Revival-style train station on the west side of Old Dixie Hwy between SE 8th and 7th Sts has been restored (its official name is the Count deHoernle Pavilion) and now is used for meetings and conferences. Train buffs will probably be disappointed, as there's not much on display. On the north side of the depot is a somewhat dilapidated 1930 Baldwin steam locomotive and a 1964 Seaboard caboose, and on the south side are 1950s-era stainless-steel passenger cars, a dining car and a lounge, awaiting restoration.

It's open by appointment only; admission is free. Contact the Boca Raton Historical Society for details.

Old Floresta Historic District

Just north of the Boca Museum of Art, the Old Floresta Historic District is one of the town's loveliest areas. It's a nice place for a stroll before or after the museum; don't skip walking through Cardinal Ave between Periwinkle and Azalea Sts, canopied by trees and with little houses tucked on either side, almost totally overgrown by foliage.

Some high points are the following:

131 Hibiscus St – A very secluded pastel yellow corner house in a wild garden

801 Hibiscus St – China-colored medium-size house with arched windows and a lovely walled-in garden

800 Hibiscus St – Shaded by traveler palms, and a royal Poinciana tree overflowing with red flowers, this house has a gorgeous main entry door

Alamanda St, just behind the museum – A beautiful Spanish-style cottage almost completely overgrown by tropical plants, and 30 feet west, a similar house

875 Alamanda St – A storybook, pastel yellow Spanish Colonial-style house with a grapefruit tree out front, charming ceramic tiles on its pillars and a Japanese-style garden fence

Gumbo Limbo Nature Center

It's not clear what's most miraculous about the Gumbo Limbo Nature Center (☎ 338-1473) – the wonderful nature, the friendly and extremely knowledgeable staff or the simple fact that it's here. Whatever. It's a lovely, serene 27-acre nature reserve that holds classes, shows instructional videos, gives tours and lectures and more. Mainly it's a wonderful place to walk and take in the undeveloped splendor of it all: the relatively undisturbed coastal hammock contains native and imported trees, raccoons, egrets and other waterfowl. The microclimate between the ocean and lagoon is responsible for the presence of plant species ordinarily native only to tropical regions.

To see just how close, yet so far, you are from civilization, climb the 66 steps to the top of the 39-foot observatory and gaze out over the trees to the ocean and, turning north, to the high-rise condos.

The park also features four saltwater tanks in which they raise and care for endangered sea turtles – center volunteers also patrol beaches during spawning seasons to protect loggerhead sea-turtle eggs as they wait to hatch. Inside, see snakes, taxidermy of endangered species (either road kills or confiscations by the Department of Fish and Wildlife) and other educational displays.

The nature center is at 1801 N Ocean Blvd (Hwy A1A). It's easy to miss, as the entrance is tucked away in foliage. It's open year-round, Monday to Saturday from 9 am to 4 pm, Sunday from noon to 4 pm. Admission and parking are free, so please leave a donation.

Red Reef & South Beach Parks

Red Reef and South Beach Parks (☎ 338-1473) both take up 60-some acres just north and south of Palmetto Park Rd at the ocean. There's a small golf course, an artificial reef with snorkeling and lots of beach access. They offer nature walks in conjunction with Gumbo Limbo Nature Center and night excursions during sea-turtle mating seasons to watch females lay eggs in the sand. Fishing is allowed outside marked swimming areas. There are picnic areas with barbecue grills and tables. No pets or alcoholic beverages allowed. The parks are open 8 am to 10 pm year-round; parking is $8 on weekdays, $10 on weekends and holidays – no camping, camper vans or trailers allowed.

Spanish River Park

Spanish River Park (☎ 393-7815), between the ocean and the Intracoastal just south of Spanish River Blvd, is the city's most landscaped. It's a great place to walk through the wilds, though they don't have as much in the way of instruction or guided tours as Gumbo Limbo to the south. But this is the only park with camping facilities, though camping is limited to groups only (see Places to Stay below). The park is open no later than 8 am and closes at sundown year-round. Parking is $8 on weekdays, $10 on weekends and holidays.

Organized Tours

The Boca Raton Historical Society (☎ 395-6766) gives a weekly city historical tour on Thursday at 9.30 am, leaving from Old Town Hall, at the northwest corner of Federal Hwy and Palmetto Park Rd. The cost is $10 per person. At the time of writing they were planning to expand this schedule, but no details were available.

Places to Stay

It seems as if we're prefacing a lot of this chapter with warnings, and this section is no different; this is not a budget location. Count on a rock bottom of $35 a day or $150 a week for a double in low season and $65 a day or $450 a week in high season, which stretches out longer here than in most Florida cities. It may be well worth your while to stay outside Boca, like in,

say, Delray or Fort Lauderdale, where prices are somewhat cheaper.

Camping The only place to camp is at Spanish River Park, and camping here is limited to groups. The groups must be of 15 or more from an accredited organization (like the Boy or Girl Scouts, religious groups or others that pass the vigilant eyes of the rangers). Camping must be arranged in advance by writing to Parks and Recreation Director, Boca Raton Parks and Recreation Department, 201 W Palmetto Park Rd, Boca Raton, FL 33432. Camping costs vary with size of group.

Motels & Hotels The very friendly folks at the *Boca Inn/Boca Raton Motel* (☎ 395-7500, fax 391-0287), 1801 N Federal Hwy, have large and clean-enough doubles for $35 a day ($175 a week) in low season, $65 a day ($450 a week) in high season. This is probably the best deal in town in low season because of the size of the rooms and the cleanliness.

The *Shore Edge* motel (☎ 395-4491), 425 N Ocean Blvd, has perfectly nice rooms for the day/week for $45/2750. Efficiencies are $55/350 in low season and $75/475 in high season. There's a mid-season as well.

The *Days Inn* (☎ 395-7172, 325-2525), 2899 N Federal Hwy, has singles/doubles for $39/45 in low season, $79/89 high season. There's a 10% AAA and AARP discount.

Diagonally across the street is the *Best Western University Inn* (☎ 395-5225, fax 338-9180), 2700 N Federal Hwy, with doubles for $42 a day ($39 a day by the week) in low season, $99/79 in high season. Price includes continental breakfast and a free shuttle to beaches, malls, Florida Atlantic University and West Palm or Fort Lauderdale airports.

If you're really into treating yourself right, head for the enormous Spanish Mediterranean *Boca Raton Resort & Club* (☎ 395-3000, 800-448-8355), 501 E Camino Real, a 963-room, 37-suite resort built by Flagler and Mizner that opened in 1926.

Prices are simpler in summer: room rates range from $130 to 190 depending on view and placement; suites are from $175 to 385. In high season, from January to April, standard rooms are $240, deluxe rooms $280. In the concierge level Palm Court, open only in winter, rooms are $340, suites $575. Tower rooms are $350, junior suites $405, villa rooms $240, apartments $430, ocean-view rooms $390, water-view rooms $340, and suites from $495 to 515.

Places to Eat

Boca Raton's saving grace is its restaurants. For some reason, this town has gone Italian happy – dozens of Italian places dot the streets, and though we've only named a couple here, there are plenty more. Other goodies include bagels, seafood, Thai, Chinese and, of course, steak houses and French. Once again, prices get stellar quickly. But you can get good eats cheap in several places, and there are some unexpected – this means cheap – surprises. Fast-food and quasi-fast-food places abound as well, if you're so disposed.

We vote *Mississippi Sweet BBQ* (☎ 394-6779), 2399 N Federal Hwy, one of the top two reasons to visit Boca (the other is Gumbo Limbo Park). This little place has cheerful and friendly management, great service and killer barbecue. Try the hot Dixie wings ($3.95 to 5.95), ribs and wings basket ($4.95, or platter $8.95) and under-spiced Choctaw Catfish ($7.95). All platters come with choice of sides, including the best deep-fried sweet potato slices we've ever had in the States, homemade apple-sauce, criss-cut fries or coleslaw. They also serve an excellent chicken soup ($1.75 cup, $2.95 bowl). A good selection of hot sauces from all over is available- try the Inner Beauty. They deliver to most anywhere in a three-mile radius (minimum $8 order).

If your doctor has told you that you need to raise your cholesterol level, *Fran's Chicken Haven* (☎ 395-7898), 1925 N Federal Hwy, offers deep-fried everything (in 'cholesterol-free 100% vegetable oil') – like four pieces of fried chicken ($4.25) or eight ($8.10), and a chicken dinner for

$5.65. Your bill will be out of the fry-o-lator momentarily.

Lilly's New Cuisine (☎ 362-0208, 362-0216), 451 E Palmetto Park Rd, is also our kind of place – you can feel the garlic as you walk in. This Italian place has great pastas ($5.50 to 5.95 at lunch, $6.95 to 7.95 at dinner), chicken and fish dishes ($8.95) and daily specials like penne in vodka-cream sauce ($6.95). There's excellent garlic bread and friendly service, but they serve on those damn Styrofoam plates. It's open Monday to Saturday from 11 am to 10 pm, closed Sunday; cash only.

An old Boca standard is *Flakowitz Bagel Inn* (☎ 368-0666), 1999 N Federal Hwy. It's only open for breakfast and lunch, but whatta deal! A variety of specials, good veggie, lox and other flavored cream cheeses, and bagels by the dozen (baker's dozen – 13), can be had for $4.95 to 5.95. Try their 'everything' bagels, or if you're a bit upmarket, the sun-dried tomato bagels. It's open daily from 7 am to 3 pm; lines form outside for the take-away window or you can sit inside and let the waitresses call you 'sweetie' – no matter what your gender.

We were pleasantly surprised by the food, service and especially prices at *Seafood Connection* (☎ 997-5562), 6998 N Federal Hwy, where it can get a little pricey except during their early dinner specials, served daily 3.30 to 5 pm: a $4.95 full dinner gets you entrées like baked stuffed scrod or grilled mahi-mahi (steer clear of the oriental stir-fry), and $5.95 sees chicken cordon bleu or Alaskan salmon. There's happy hour at that time as well, and the bar fills up with golfers chugging $1 draft beers and $1.75 highballs. Prices during dinner hours average $9.95 per entrée.

Thai Boca (☎ 367-0500), 887 E Palmetto Park Rd, has some of the most generous portions of Thai food we've seen in Florida, and the prices are pretty reasonable as well. Lunch combos for $5.50 include soup, spring roll and fried rice! And their $8.95 to 9.95 early-bird dinner (5 to 6.30 pm, cash only) includes soup, appetizer, main course and dessert. Regular dinner entrées run from $7.95 (pad thai) to $11.95 (excellent

Panang duckling in a coconut curry sauce). Tables have photos (under the glass) of decorative food art carved from fruits and veggies by the chef. It's a nice place.

For Italian, another fine member of the *Mozzarella's* chain is in Mizner Park on the west side featuring friendly and well-trained service. Its lunches are a great deal for $3.99 (bottomless salad), $4.99 (veggies, beans and rice) and $5.49 (quiche). Regular main courses include pasta ($6.49 to 9.99), pizza ($5.99 to 8.49), grilled chicken breast ($7.99) and catch of the day ($10.99).

Entertainment

Theater The city's most concerted effort at bringing in legitimate theater is the Caldwell Theatre Co (☎ 241-7432, 930-6400), whose fare in 1995-96 included Arthur Miller's *An Enemy of the People*, Agatha Christie's *The Unexpected Guest* and Terrence McNally's *Love! Valour! Compassion!*. Tickets are $26 for side or rear seats, $29 for central seats (and for the first four days of new productions) and $37.50 for orchestra seats. Students (those with a valid ID, ISIC card or who can convincingly pull it off) are entitled to tickets to any performance for $5 – if available in the half hour before curtain. Performances are Tuesday to Saturday at 8 pm, Sunday at 7 pm, with matinee performances Wednesday and Sunday at 2 pm as well as certain Saturdays throughout the year. The theater's located at 7873 N Federal Hwy (Levitz Plaza), about a half mile south of the Boca/Delray county line.

If you like dinner theater (and you know who you are), the Royal Palm Dinner Theater (☎ 392-3755, 800-841-6765), 303 Mizner Blvd, has good shows. Or at least, ticket buyers seemed happy with the performances (it's not our cup of tea). Tickets are quite expensive: dinner and a performance Tuesday to Saturday are $45, Sunday they are $47. Tuesday to Saturday, dinner is at 6 pm, the show is at 8 pm; Sunday, dinner is at 4 pm, show at 6 pm. There are slightly cheaper ($39) matinee performances on Saturday and Wednesday,

with lunch at noon, show at 2 pm. There are special prices for kids – call the box office. Also in the possibly amusing category is the Friday night *Comedy Sportz*, which begins at (are you ready?) 8.31 pm. (Yeah, we didn't split our sides either, but at least you know what you're in for.) Shows cost $8 for adults, $6 for students and seniors.

Little Palm Theater for Young People is a nonprofit regional theater that produces classic children's stories and fairy tales on Saturday mornings at 9.30 am at the Royal Palm Dinner Theater, as well as at its home in Boynton Beach, north of Boca, at the Florida Academy of Dramatic Arts.

Symphony The Boca Symphonic Pops (☎ 393-7677) are a 75-member orchestra (including the 18-piece Boca Pops Big Band) in their 46th season, and they rank among the top in the USA. They play in the Florida Atlantic University Center Auditorium, but also in the Boca Raton Resort & Club, the Olympic Height high school and at other venues. Tickets range from $20 to 38.

Nightclubs Put those dance shoes away, for this is not a toddlin' town. If you want to boogie, you're much better off heading up to Delray or down to Fort Lauderdale. If you're determined, try *Poly Esther's* (☎ 447-8955), 99 SE 1st St, which is currently 'a popular place with the kids' lamented a local. It plays retro ('70s) music with lots of contests, promotions, games of Twister, costume nights and so on.

Bars There are at least two British pubs in town, both run by Brits and relatively authentic (in both places you're likely to run into some raunchy but fun-loving journos from the nearby offices of the *National Enquirer*). The *Lion and Eagle* (☎ 394-3190), 2401 N Federal Hwy, seems the more cozy and, well, British of the two. On one night we heard several instances of such phrases as 'there goes my bleeper', 'filthy sod', 'bollocks' and 'bleedin' 'ell'. Pints of draft Guinness, Fullers ESB, Bass and Harp, though, are quite dear – $4, in fact. It has live entertainment on some nights, and pub food like excellent chicken curry and chips, ploughman's lunch platters ($5.25) and other main courses from $6.50 to 10.25.

Up the road a bit at the *Ugly Duckling* (☎ 997-5929), 5903 N Federal Hwy, the staff is livelier and the atmosphere more upscale. It has a more extensive menu as well, with Cornish pastry ($6.50), chicken and chips ($6.95), toad-in-the-hole ($7.95) and other main courses from $6.50 to 9.95. It also does a Sunday morning roast – of beef, lamb or chicken – for $9.95. It has live entertainment, some disco nights and Sunday karaoke from 8 pm to midnight.

Getting There & Away

Air The closest international service is the municipal Palm Beach International Airport (PBI, ☎ 471-7420), about a half-hour drive to the north on I-95, three miles west of West Palm Beach on either Southern Blvd or Belvedere Rd. See Getting Around below for information on getting from PBI to Boca Raton. Ground transportation is downstairs at level 1. Ignore the 'helpful' volunteers at the information counters.

Bus The Greyhound stop (they couldn't actually put one of those ugly *station* things here) is at the corner of N Federal Hwy at NE 20th St at the city bus stop (across from McDonald's). See the Getting Around chapter for service details.

Train The Tri-Rail station is at 601 NW 53rd St (the Yamato exit from I-95). Amtrak stops at Deerfield Beach, five miles south.

Car Boca Raton is between I-95 and US Hwys 1 and A1A. It's about a 40-minute drive from Miami, or a 25-minute drive from Fort Lauderdale.

Getting Around

To/From the Airport To PBI by bus, take Palm Tran (☎ 233-1111) bus No 1S from downtown Boca Raton to the downtown West Palm Beach terminal ($1), and transfer (20¢) to bus No 4S to PBI.

Tri-Rail (☎ 800-874-7245) has service

between PBI and Boca Raton; the tickets are $4 one way, $6.25 roundtrip. From PBI, get a shuttle from the airport to the West Palm Beach Tri-Rail station, and another shuttle in Boca between the Tri-Rail station and the Boca Raton police station, 100 NE 2nd St. From the airport, shuttle service begins at 5.34 am weekdays with service about once an hour until 11.48 am, and then hourly from 2 to 10.21 pm. From Boca to PBI, the shuttle runs from the police station to the Boca Raton Tri-Rail station on approximately the same schedule, though the last one goes out at 8.02 pm.

A taxi from PBI to Boca Raton will cost about $25.

Bus Palm Tran (☎ 233-1111) runs buses all over the county. Bus fare is $1, seniors, students and people with physical disabilities pay 50¢; transfers are 20¢. Bus No 1S goes from Mizner Park to the beach, the Museum of Art and Spanish River Park (at Federal Hwy). Bus No 8 goes out to the Morikami Gardens in Delray Beach.

Car Free parking is everywhere, and there's really nothing special to be aware of except that the entire city is one giant speed trap – obey every sign and nobody'll get hurt (or ticketed).

Taxi Taxi rates are $1.25 flagfall, and each additional mile is $1.75. The biggest taxi company in the area is Yellow Cab (☎ 395-3221).

DELRAY BEACH

• *pop 49,000* ☎ 561

Delray Beach is a lively town with an interesting history that's far more welcoming than its neighbor to the south, and more affordable, too. In fact, we'd recommend staying here and going back into Boca only if you have to.

Originally populated by Seminole Indians, the land on which the town sits was bought in 1868 from the government by Captain George Gleason for $1.25 an acre (Gleason was the son of William

Gleason, the Lieutenant Governor from 1868 to 1873). The area was first settled by folks from Michigan (the land was bought by William S Linton, the postmaster of Saginaw, Michigan, who brought friends – Delray is named after a suburb of Detroit) and blacks from the Florida Panhandle. Flagler got hold of the land when it went into receivership: Linton went bust after the freeze of 1895.

Flagler's company began extending the FEC railway south, but it also brought in about a hundred Japanese farmers from the city of Miyazu, Japan, to work farms in a settlement southwest of the city called Yamato. The Japanese workers planted a number of crops, but chiefly they were here to farm pineapples. The settlement never amounted to much, the pineapple failed to reach expectation and, with added competition from Cuban fruit companies, pineapple farming in the entire area dried up.

But the FEC railroad was coming through regularly, and businesses sprung up to support the traffic it produced.

Today Delray Beach is a small but very pleasant resort town – energetic but not full of itself – with pleasant restaurants, beaches and museums, including one dedicated to the lives of the Japanese settlers at Yamato – the Morikami Gardens, a lovely and serene place where we highly recommend you spend a couple of hours, if only for the café.

Orientation & Information
The main drag of downtown is Atlantic Ave, which runs east-west between I-95 and the Atlantic Ocean. US Hwy 1 is split through downtown: 6th Ave is US Hwy 1 north, 5th Ave is US Hwy 1 south. Most of the hotels are on the east side of the Intracoastal Waterway.

The helpful chamber of commerce (☎ 278-0424), 64 SE 5th Ave, hands out maps of the city and discount coupons.

The Delray News Stand (☎ 278-3399), 429 E Atlantic Ave, has local, US and international papers. The library (☎ 276-6462) is at 29 SE 4th Ave.

There are toilets along the public beach.

Morikami Gardens
George Morikami was one of the settlers brought over to work in the Yamato settlement, and when everyone else left, he stayed on in South Florida and eventually struck it rich enough to buy several hundred acres of land in the area. He bequeathed 200 of them to the State of Florida to build a museum in memory of the settlement, and the Morikami Gardens (☎ 495-0233) is it. Located southwest of downtown Delray Beach, the Morikami is a splendid little piece of Japan, with a theater, several galleries, an authentic Seishin-An tea house, a wonderful nature trail and a somewhat disappointing bonsai garden.

Exhibit Galleries Tea ceremonies are held in the tea house from October to June on the third Saturday of each month at noon, 1, 2 and 3 pm. The two gallery areas inside the exhibition hall mainly house pieces from the museum's permanent collection, including stoneware, a ritual Buddhist prayer bell (that, believe it or not, was once owned by Mr Ripley himself), folk crafts, *kogo* incense holders for tea ceremonies and a Shinto shrine. There are also two 2½-meter-tall vases, donated to the museum by John D McArthur from one of his hotels on Singer Island (apparently it was not fun finding out what had been placed in the vases during the years they were in the hotel's lobby).

Rotating exhibitions from private collections and the museum's permanent one fill the second gallery, and when we visited they were running exhibitions of Japanese postcards from the end of the Russo-Japanese War to the 1930s, which was on exhibit for the first time outside Japan, and *The Name Above the Door* – an absolutely fascinating collection of Japanese shop signs, including those of sake-brewers, armorers, wig-makers and tea houses.

Yamato-kan Across the lake from the exhibit galleries is the original Morikami building, designed as a Japanese villa. Inside (remove your shoes) you can see a Japanese home, with exhibitions on the workings of Japanese businesses (tobacco

SOUTHEAST

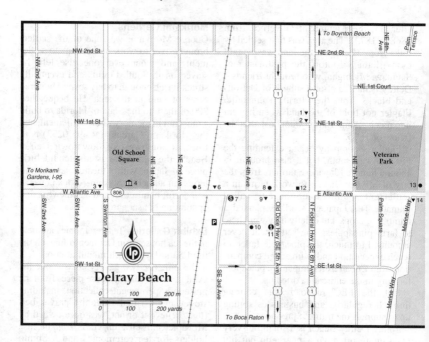

and kite shops, sushi bars, sake and noodle factories), a history of the settlement at Yamato and a 5th-grade Japanese boy's bedroom – note the Asia-centric map on the wall. There are guided tours for groups, or just walk on through.

Bonsai & Nature Gardens The nature trail, goldfish pond and Bonsai Gardens are near here. The bonsai when we visited were looking a tad peaked, but to be fair it was in the middle of summer. We really enjoyed walking around and looking at the little waterfall.

Café Back in the main building, on the patio, the museum's Cornell Café serves darn good home-style Japanese food like cold soba noodles and teriyaki chicken ($5.95), sushi rolls ($4) and sesame noodles ($4.95).

Classes In addition to a totally high-tech interactive computer area for kids, the Morikami offers classes in a wide variety of subjects, from Nihongo Japanese I to Sumi-e Ink Painting – Floral, to Haiku Japanese Poetry and two cooking workshops. Most classes are held during the winter months only.

Hours & Admission The museum is open Tuesday to Sunday from 10 am to 5 pm; closed Monday. Admission is $4.25 for adults, $3.75 for seniors over 65, $2 for kids aged six to 18.

Getting There & Away The museum is four miles east of I-95. From Delray Beach, take Atlantic Ave west to Carter Rd and turn south; the museum drive will be about three quarters of a mile on the right-hand side of the road. From Boca Raton, take Yamato or Glades Rds west to Jog Rd, turn right and the museum is about 1½ to 2¼ miles on the left.

Cornell Museum

The Cornell Museum of Art & History

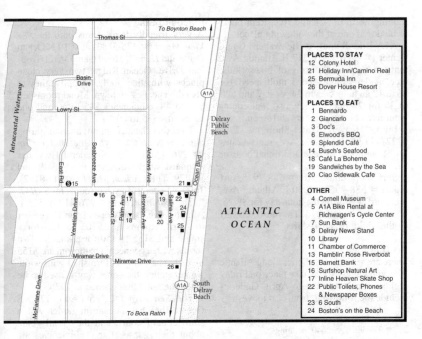

To Boynton Beach

Thomas St

Basin
Drive

Lowry St

Intracoastal Waterway

Seabreeze Ave

East Rd

15

16

Venetian Drive

Gleason St

Palm Ave

Bronson Ave

Andrews Ave

17

18

19

20

Salina Ave

22 23

24

25

26

Miramar Drive

McFarlane Drive

To Boca Raton

A1A

Delray
Public
Beach

Ocean Blvd

21

ATLANTIC
OCEAN

A1A

South
Delray
Beach

PLACES TO STAY
12 Colony Hotel
21 Holiday Inn/Camino Real
25 Bermuda Inn
26 Dover House Resort

PLACES TO EAT
1 Bennardo
2 Giancarlo
3 Doc's
6 Elwood's BBQ
9 Splendid Café
14 Busch's Seafood
18 Café La Boheme
19 Sandwiches by the Sea
20 Ciao Sidewalk Cafe

OTHER
4 Cornell Museum
5 A1A Bike Rental at
    Richwagen's Cycle Center
7 Sun Bank
8 Delray News Stand
10 Library
11 Chamber of Commerce
13 Ramblin' Rose Riverboat
15 Barnett Bank
16 Surfshop Natural Art
17 Inline Heaven Skate Shop
22 Public Toilets, Phones
    & Newspaper Boxes
23 6 South
24 Boston's on the Beach

(☎ 243-7922), 51 N Swinton Ave in Old
School Square (upstairs in the old elementary school), has got to have the largest military miniature exhibit there is. It covers
about two thousand years of history from
the Age of Knighthood to Napoleon, the
American Revolution, the Civil War, the
two World Wars and Vietnam. The owner
of the collection, Edward Reynolds, does
half-hour tours, but it's best to arrange it at
least a day before. Downstairs, the Delray
Beach Historical Society holds traveling
exhibits that change about every six
weeks – they had a fun cartoon exhibit
when we went.

Cason Cottage
Cason Cottage (☎ 274-9578, 243-0223), 5
NE 1st Ave (across the street from Old
School Square), was the home of Dr John
Robert Cason, Delray Beach's first doctor.
His brother-in-law, Luther Love, moved to
the area at Cason's request and became the
town's first pharmacist, and eventually the

mayor. The cottage (c 1920) is built in Vernacular Frame Florida-style and is the last
remaining of four buildings in the family
compound (the others were demolished).
The cottage was under renovation when
we visited and will be opened as a museum
by the Delray Beach Historical Society
when finished.

Sundy House
The Sundy House (☎ 278-2163), 106 S
Swinton Ave, is a Victorian house (1902)
on the south end of town that's packed with
antique Victorian furniture. There's a patio
out back, surrounded by a lush garden, and
a dining room where tea, lunch and some
dinners are served; admission is free. We
didn't eat, but thought it was worth stopping in (for a second).

Beaches & Rentals
There are two public beaches spanning 1½
miles north and south of Atlantic Ave, and
a paved boardwalk on N Ocean Blvd

SOUTHEAST

running north of Atlantic Ave. Rent bikes or blades at one of the following places.

A1A Bike Rental At Richwagens Cycle Center (☎ 243-2453), 217 E Atlantic Ave, rents an impossible array of bikes (kids, race, tandem, single-speed, multispeed) for $6 to 12 an hour, $15 to 24 per day and $20 to 35 for 24 hours. They also rent equipment like helmets, baskets and so on.

Inline Heaven Skate Shop (☎ 279-0222), 1122 E Atlantic Ave, rents skates for $8 an hour, $3 each additional hour or $25 for 24 hours.

Surf Shop Natural Art (☎ 588-7925, surf report ☎ 588-7953), 1030 E Atlantic Ave, rents surf boards by the hour/day for $8/25, boogieboards are $5/15. They also sell surf clothes, bikinis and T-shirts.

Art Galleries

There are several art galleries along Atlantic Ave, and gallery walks take place on Friday nights from November to April. Galleries include the following, from east to west:

Artcetera Fine Art
  ☎ 279-9939, No 640, paintings, sculpture, jewelry
Shared Visions Gallery
  ☎ 272-4495, No 504, Native American and Western
Lyons Gallery
  ☎ 278-9907, No 445, contemporary
Forms . . .
  ☎ 274-3673, No 415, Southwestern paintings
Carlynn Gallery
  ☎ 274-9286, No 413, contemporary
Cornell Museum of Art & History
  ☎ 243-7922, 51 N Swinton Ave

Water Tours

Narrated sightseeing and millionaire-row-gawking tours are available aboard the *Ramblin' Rose Riverboat* (☎ 243-0686). Prices depend on the tour and the day, so call for specifics; for an idea, a 3½-hour Saturday sightseeing day tour is $13.95 for adults and $4.25 for children, and Saturday dinner cruises (three hours) are $24.95. The ticket office is just west of the bridge at 801 E Atlantic Ave.

Places to Stay

A very friendly family runs both the *Sea View Motel* (☎ 276-5182) at 5019 N Ocean Drive and *Henri's Motel* (same ☎), 1 Tropical Drive, Ocean Ridge: two very clean places with nice pools. Happily, they're also the cheapest in town. Motel rooms are $30 to 48, efficiencies $35 to 60 and one bedrooms $35 to 70.

The other cheaper options are uninspiring but they won't kill ya': the *Budget Inn* (☎ 276-8961), 2500 N Federal Hwy, has standard singles/doubles for $35/49 and $69/79. The *Carlson Motel* (☎ 243-0182), 1600 N Federal Hwy, has rooms for $37/47.

The *Colony Hotel* (☎ 276-4123), 525 E Atlantic Ave, is only open from December to April. Rooms are $105 to 120 for a single and $135 to 150 for a double. Two rooms with a connected bathroom are $155 to 170. The lobby is furnished with white wicker, much the same way it used to be when the hotel first opened in 1926.

The *Sea Aire* (☎ 276-7491), 1715 S Ocean Blvd, has a beautiful garden with a shuffleboard court, and they really care about their guests. Large efficiencies are $55 to 68 (in summer) and $140 to 170. They have beach access, barbecue grills and a library for guests.

The *Bermuda Inn* (☎ 276-5288), 64 S Ocean Blvd, has clean rooms and nice service. From May to November rooms are $55, efficiencies $69 and one bedrooms $89; from December to April the rates are $85 to 89/98/100.

The *Dover House Resort* (☎ 276-0309), 110 S Ocean Blvd, has a garden with fountains and rents one-bedroom apartments, which are nice and clean and have tiled floors, for $80 to 150.

The *Holiday Inn Camino Real* (☎ 278-0882, 800-234-6835), 1229 E Atlantic Ave, has oceanfront rooms for $89 to 125 in off-season and $119 to 159 during the season. They have those cool glass elevators – it's a beautiful atmosphere and if you don't need or want a kitchen, it's definitely a nice place.

Places to Eat

Green Owl (☎ 272-7766), 330 E Atlantic

Ave, is a simple-looking breakfast and lunch place; young and old alike seem to enjoy coming here. Breakfast omelets are $2.70 to 4.45; two eggs, home fries or grits, toast and jelly is $2.35; sandwiches and burgers are $2.50 to 4.95 and a grilled chicken breast platter with cottage cheese, lettuce, tomato and cucumber is $4.95. It's open Monday to Friday from 7 am to 3 pm, Saturday from 7 am to 1 pm and Sunday from 8 am to noon.

Doc's (☎ 278-3627), 10 N Swinton Ave, is a classic American outdoor diner that's been here since 1951, and we definitely recommend it. The portions are enormous and delicious. Their burger combo comes with (terrific) fries and a drink for $3.30, a cheese vegetable sub is $2.79 and salads range from $2.99 to 4.65.

Sandwiches by the Sea (☎ 272-2212), 1214 E Atlantic Ave, has very large and good sandwiches from $3.75 to 4.95. It's more of a take-out place (there are no tables inside), but they do have tables around the corner in the back in a small, pretty courtyard.

Ellie's '50's Diner (☎ 276-1570), 2410 N Federal Hwy, is fun, with its '50s decor and tableside jukeboxes, and you can get a pretty good meal as well. Breakfast runs between $3 to 6, sandwiches are $4 to 7 and their very nice veggie melt is $6.

We loved *Café La Boheme* (☎ 278-4899), up the alley behind 1118 E Atlantic Ave. Their falafel is excellent ($4.95), as is the hummus ($4.95); they have sandwiches for $4.75 to 6.95, and crab cakes, chicken breast or pizza dishes are $5.95 to 9.95.

Giancarlo (☎ 274-2012), 102 N Federal Hwy, is in a lovely old building from 1932. It's very cozy inside, since it's not one big dining area but several separate rooms with three to five tables each. For lunch they have a vegetarian buffet for $7. The dinner buffet offers soups, meats, fish, pasta, veggies and salads for $13; pizzas are made in a brick oven ($6.95 to 7.95). It's closed Sunday.

Elwood's BBQ (☎ 272-7427), 301 E Atlantic Ave, is a very cool barbecue place in a converted filling station; there are old gas pumps and lots of paraphernalia –

and the bar in their patio dining area is an old hydraulic truck lift. Appetizers are $3 to 6, entrées $9 to 11, and it's cash only. On Sunday they have live music. They serve food till 11 pm, and the bar stays open till 1 am.

The *Splendid Café* (☎ 265-0135), 432 E Atlantic Ave, has lunch pastas for $7.95, sandwiches are $6.95 to 8.95, dinner pastas with a house salad are from $9.95 to 12.95, and main courses, like grilled tuna with sautéed mushrooms and garlic, are around $16.95.

Ciao Sidewalk Café (☎ 278-4520), off 1208 E Atlantic Ave in a green courtyard, has Middle Eastern and chi-chi food: quiche is 3.95, Syrian pizza $4.95 and sandwiches $4.95 to 6.95. It's open for lunch only, but if you call ahead, they'll deliver dinner to your hotel for $12.95.

Busch's Seafood (☎ 278-7600, 278-7609), 840 E Atlantic Ave (just west of the Intracoastal), is a Delray Beach tradition (in town since 1942). It serves great seafood dishes for $12.95 from 4.30 to 6 pm, which cost more (much more!) later. There is a lovely patio with a walkway/dock on the Intracoastal behind the restaurant.

Bennardo (☎ 274-0051) is in the historical Falcon House (1925) at 116 N Federal Hwy. It's a top-end place with an elegant atmosphere and several separate dining rooms – which keep space between you and that cigar guy who just sat down. Each room is named after a different family member – this restaurant is run by the same family that runs Giancarlo (above). Appetizers, like smoked salmon with pancakes, sour cream and caviar, average $8, and main courses include risotto primavera ($16) and seafood stuffed shells ($18). There's a patio – with a bocci lane – between Bennardo and Giancarlo.

Entertainment

Theater The *Quest Theater Company*, (☎ 832-9328), an African-American theater group at 444 24th St in West Palm Beach, holds performances in the Crest Theater, as well as in West Palm Beach at West Palm Beach Community College's

Duncan Theatre Stage West. Contact the company for performance and venue information.

Bars For live entertainment, try *Boston's on the Beach* (☎ 278-3364), 40 S Ocean Blvd, a mellow, dark wood and down-and-dirty watering hole. Monday is reggae night; happy hour is Monday to Friday from 4 to 7 pm. The slicker and more energetic *6 South* (☎ 278-7878), 6 S Ocean Blvd, doesn't have a happy hour, but it does have a Sunday brunch for $8.95 from 11 am to 5 pm (that right there should tell you what the difference between the two places is).

Getting There & Away
Bus The Greyhound station (☎ 272-6447, 800-231-2222) is at 402 N Federal Hwy. Buses to/from Miami ($11) go twice a day, to/from Tampa once a day and to Orlando three times a day and from Orlando twice.

Train Tri-Rail stops here; the station is at 345 S Congress Ave (which is west of I-95, off Atlantic Ave). See Getting Around for service details.

Car Delray Beach is just north of Boca Raton on I-95, US Hwy 1 and Hwy A1A. Watch out – there are speed traps on N Ocean Blvd between about 15th and 20th Sts.

LAKE WORTH
• *pop 27,000* ☎ *561*

Lake Worth is a charming little town that's cheaper than its nearby northern, southern and eastern neighbors and for some reason full of Polish and Finnish tourists. Well, *dzien dobry* and *huomenta, kiitos*. It was established in 1913, and for a while in the Roaring '20s it was quite the suave place to be seen – the Lake Worth Casino was a rollicking joint, and people came from miles around to frolic in the casino's enormous saltwater swimming pool. But the town never quite recovered its glamour after the 1928 hurricane wreaked havoc on the area.

Today Lake Worth is a sleepy place with not a whole lot to do except sit on the beach, but it's a good base for seeing the sights of Palm Beach and West Palm Beach, if only for a day or so.

In a Kaliningrad-esque freak of geopolitical divisions, Lake Worth's beach actually cuts across the southern portion of Palm Beach – a fact that enrages property owners in the latter, though they'd never admit it.

Psychics, Blind Baton Twirlers & Miracle Diets: Visiting the *National Enquirer*

If you're driving past the town of Lantana, a pilgrimmage to the headquarters of *National Enquirer* (☎ 586-1111) is almost a must – though, sad to say, there are no tours per se. The Enquirer's tasteless but (the industry grudgingly admits) accurate airing, er, reporting of the dirty laundry of celebrities – and their heroic tales of blind jugglers and miracle diets – have given it the largest circulation of any newspaper in the USA. The headquarters are at 600 SE Coast Ave in Lantana, but if you're traveling on US Hwy 1, you can't miss the enormous *National Enquirer* sign on the west side of the railroad tracks. If you call and ask for the marketing department and sound awfully convincing (we couldn't pull it off and we're *very* convincing when we try) they'll bring you through on a VIP tour – maybe you'll get to see the OJ War Room. ■

NICK SELBY

KENNETH DREYFUSS

Signs at Cypress Lane Museum near Palmdale

Shopping for art in St Augustine

The illustrious Gomek

Yellow hibiscus

Pelicans at the Florida Keys Wild Bird Center

You can see the big guy feed at St Augustine's Alligator Farm.

Orientation

Downtown Lake Worth is on the mainland just south of the city of West Palm Beach and north of Lantana, and Lake Worth beach is on the barrier island east of the Intracoastal Waterway separating Palm Beach's southernmost section from the city of South Palm Beach.

The main drags in downtown are both one way: Lake Ave, running west to east, and Lucerne Ave, running east to west. These two roads combine to the west of downtown and become Lake Worth Rd, and to the east of downtown they become the Lake Worth Bridge leading to the beach.

US Hwy 1 is Dixie Hwy here, and north-south running streets in Lake Worth are lettered from west to east (Dixie Hwy was formerly called I St).

Information

There aren't any tourist offices as such, but you can get area information at the public library or the Lake Worth Historical Museum (see below). The Polish-American Cultural Society of the Palm Beaches (☎ 640-2982) organizes Polish-American events and art shows.

Change money at the Barnett Bank at 14 N Federal Hwy.

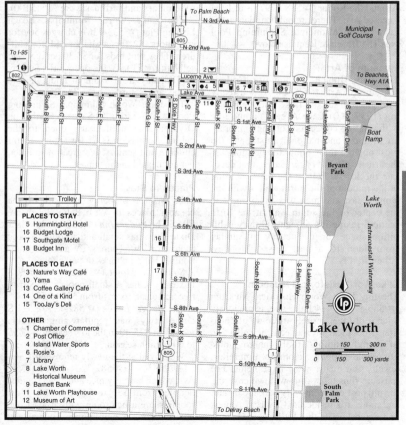

Lake Worth

0   150   300 m
0   150   300 yards

PLACES TO STAY
5 Hummingbird Hotel
16 Budget Lodge
17 Southgate Motel
18 Budget Inn

PLACES TO EAT
3 Nature's Way Café
10 Yama
13 Coffee Gallery Café
14 One of a Kind
15 TooJay's Deli

OTHER
1 Chamber of Commerce
2 Post Office
4 Island Water Sports
6 Rosie's
7 Library
8 Lake Worth
   Historical Museum
9 Barnett Bank
11 Lake Worth Playhouse
12 Museum of Art

SOUTHEAST

The main post office (☎ 964-1102) is at 4151 Lake Worth Rd.

Amoroso (☎ 533-5272), 205 N Federal Hwy, is a gay bookstore that's open Monday to Saturday from 10 am to 10 pm, Sunday from 10 am to 6 pm. They also sell gifts, crystals and art. Main Street News (☎ 586-4356), 608 Lake Ave, has lots of international and US newspapers.

The public library (☎ 533-7354) is at 15 N M St. It's open Tuesday to Thursday from 9.30 am to 8 pm, Friday and Saturday from 9.30 to 5 pm, closed Sunday and Monday.

Palm Beach Coin Laundry Inc (☎ 582-6123) is at 1904 Lake Worth Rd, and Ring Around the Kollar (☎ 588-6797) is at 1404 Lucerne Ave. There are public toilets at the Lake Worth Municipal Swimming Pool (see The Beach & Rentals below).

Museum of Art
The Palm Beach Community College Museum of Art (☎ 582-0006) is a really cool place in the old Lake Theatre Building (1939), 601 Lake Ave. It's a museum with rotating collections of contemporary art by local and national artists, and the most notable thing about the building are the friezes, *Battle of the Sexes*, that decorate the lobby. Follow the battle starting in the middle of the north wall – with the women east and men west; they meet in the center of the south wall at the Birth section. Inside it's a beautiful, airy exhibition space, open Tuesday to Sunday from noon to 5 pm, closed Monday. Admission is $2.

Lake Worth Historical Museum
The tiny Lake Worth Historical Museum (☎ 586-1700), 414 Lake Ave, is obviously a labor of love, entirely made up of donations from locals. It's an eclectic collection of period clothing, tools, photographs, household supplies, clothing, umbrellas, jewelry and many, many more items. The museum runs tours of downtown covering the old post office, the city hall, the theater and more. It's inside the City Hall Annex, and downstairs is the Art League Gallery,

where local artists show their works. It's open Tuesday to Friday 10 am to 2 pm or by appointment. Admission is free.

The Beach & Rentals
The beach here is every bit as nice as the one along Palm Beach to the north and Boca Raton to the south, but it's more fun. The pool is a classic, and great for the price.

The best part of the beach for surfing, boogieboarding, skimboarding and body surfing is on the south side of the pier; for swimming, stay on the north side. Island Water Sports (☎ 588-1728), 728 Lake Ave, rents skim boards for $5 a day with a $20 deposit, boogieboards are $10 ($50) and rollerblades and surfboards are $15 ($100).

The Lake Worth Municipal Beach Fishing Pier (☎ 533-7367) charges 50¢ for spectators, $2 for adults and $1 for children. They rent rods for $5.30 per day, and sell bait for $1 to 3. It's open daily, Sunday to Thursday from 7 am to midnight and Friday and Saturday from 7 to 2 am.

The Lake Worth Municipal Swimming Pool (☎ 533-7367), 10 S Ocean Blvd, is an Olympic-size pool that's open to the public. Admission is $2 for adults, $1 for children and seniors. It's great in summer, but not heated in the winter.

Places to Stay
Lake Worth is probably the best bet if the cheaper places in West Palm Beach are filled. The *Budget Inn* (☎ 582-1864), 828 S Dixie Hwy, has small and absolutely basic rooms for $30. There's TV and air conditioning, but no phones or pay phones.

Southgate Motel (☎ 582-1544), 709 S Dixie Hwy, has a small pool, a grapefruit tree and clean rooms from $32 to 53.

The *Budget Lodge* (☎ 582-1379), 521 S Dixie Hwy, has regular single/double rooms for $35/40 in the low season, $45/55 to 60 in high season.

We stayed at the newly renovated *Hummingbird Hotel* (☎ 582-3224), 631 Lucerne Ave, which has very nice and clean singles/doubles from $35 to 55/45 to 65. Most rooms share a bathroom with at least one other; there's a community kitchen and laundry facilities. All are welcome, and it's gay-friendly. It's a good deal with (cook it yourself) breakfast included and the feel (if not the service) of a B&B. You can negotiate a weekly rate that brings the price down to less than $30.

Places to Eat

One of a Kind (☎ 533-0874), 509 Lake Ave, is a little café and ice cream kind of place. They have a cottage cheese fruit platter for $3, a ham and cheese sandwich is $3.50 and a meatball parmesan sub with fries is $4. They serve ice cream and frozen yogurt as well.

The *Coffee Gallery Café* (☎ 585-5911), 517 Lake Ave, has lunch specials like quiche, salad, a soft drink and a cookie for $4.95, a burrito is $4.95 and lasagna or curry is $5.95. It's open daily from 11 am to 11 pm.

TooJay's Original Gourmet Deli (☎ 582-8684), 419 Lake Ave, is a mediocre diner with a very large sandwich selection for $5 to 7.50; sautéed chicken liver dinner is $6.99, the vegetable stir-fry is $7.99. They have other locations in the area, including one at 313 Royal Poinciana Plaza in Palm Beach.

Nature's Way Café (☎ 588-7004), 800 Lake Ave, is definitely worth a try, if only for their fruit juices ($1.35 to 3.25). Sandwiches are served on whole wheat pita bread with lots of vegetables, and, well, whatever else you want with it. The sandwiches are $3.25 to 4.95, veggie pasta is $3.50/4.95.

Yama (☎ 582-8294), 809 Lake Ave, does sushi (six pieces and one roll) for $11.95; teriyaki dishes run from $8.95 to 14.95.

Benny's on the Beach is a snack bar at the fishing pier; they serve cheap burgers and cheap beer.

Audrey's Cookie Boutique & Cheesecake Company (☎ 586-0424), 7 N L St, is said to make very good cheesecake.

Entertainment

The *Lake Worth Playhouse* (☎ 586-6410), 713 Lake Ave, seats about 300 people; tickets are about $15. The box office is open Tuesday to Friday from 9 am to 1 pm and 1.30 to 4.30 pm, Saturday from 10 am to 2 pm and one hour before the show. Right next door is the *Black Box Theater* (☎ 586-6410), which puts on children's shows and stages avant garde performances; tickets are about $10.

For ballroom dancing, head to the Polish American Club (☎ 976-1116), 4725 Lake Worth Rd (just west of Military Trail). On Tuesday they have a dinner dance with '40s and '50s Big Band music for $8. The menu varies, but usually you can expect roast pork, chicken, ham and the like.

Rosie's (☎ 582-4330), 612 Lake Ave, is a very cool and genial neighborhood bar with many different specials.

Getting There & Away

Greyhound has a flag stop on US Hwy 1.

Lake Worth is south of Palm Beach on Hwy A1A, north of Boca Raton, Delray Beach and Lantana and south of West Palm Beach on US 1.

Getting Around

There are three little trolley lines within Lake Worth, originating from a trolley depot at the corner of Lake Ave and H St: the Red Trolley goes out to (among other places) a Finnish-American Rest Home, the Lantana Shopping Center and the Publix Town & Country Shopping Center; the Yellow Trolley runs directly to Lake Worth Beach; and the Blue Trolley heads to the northern end of the city and very indirectly to the beach. Trolleys run Monday to Saturday from 9 am to 5 pm, Sunday until 3, 4 and 5 pm for red, yellow and blue, respectively. Fare is $1 for adults, 50¢ for those under 18, over 60 or handicapped.

WEST PALM BEACH
• *pop 760,000* ☎ *407*

A city of contrasts and a city between extremes, West Palm Beach is not a budget traveler's dream. It's the somewhat poorer cousin of its island-neighbor across the Intracoastal – Palm Beach, the famed land of moneyed excess. To the north, the dangerous Riviera Beach neighborhood lurks

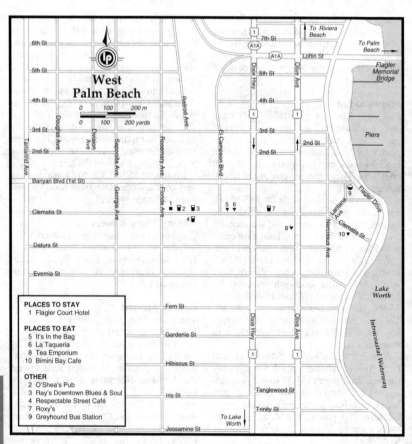

West Palm Beach

PLACES TO STAY
1 Flagler Court Hotel

PLACES TO EAT
5 It's In the Bag
6 La Taqueria
8 Tea Emporium
10 Bimini Bay Cafe

OTHER
2 O'Shea's Pub
3 Ray's Downtown Blues & Soul
4 Respectable Street Café
7 Roxy's
9 Greyhound Bus Station

like a lit cigarette smoldering in West Palm's couch after a party.

In fact, West Palm Beach seems to have many of the problems of a large modern city with few of the advantages. But that said, the advantages it does have positively shine: West Palm is home to the Norton Museum of Art, perhaps the finest art museum in the southeast, and the Kravis Center, one of the state's best performing arts centers. The city has been making great strides at revitalizing its downtown. Clematis St, the main strip there, is turning into a pleasant place to stroll (as long as you don't wander too far west).

Orientation

Note that many of the sights and attractions in West Palm Beach are far out of the city center. See the Palm Beach chapter for more museums, sights and attractions in the area.

West Palm Beach is on the west side of Lake Worth, the Intracoastal Waterway, which separates West Palm Beach from its better-known cousin, Palm Beach. With the exception of some winding, faux-British-named streets in the south (Marlborough, Argyle and Rugby, for example), the city is a straightforward grid with its unofficial borders as Flagler Drive at the east, Palm Beach Lakes Blvd to the north, Southern

Blvd to the south and Australian Ave to the west. Three main bridges connect West Palm Beach to Palm Beach: the Southern Blvd Bridge, the Royal Park Bridge (which connects Okeechobee Blvd with Royal Palm Way) and the Flagler Memorial Bridge (closed for renovation when we visited), which connects Flagler Drive with Royal Poinciana Way.

Downtown is pretty much centered around the stretch of Clematis St between Olive and Tamarind Aves, with rough north and south borders of 3rd St and Okeechobee Blvd, respectively. Note that 1st St is also and more often referred to as Banyan Blvd.

Maps It's difficult finding accurate and user-friendly free maps; the Convention & Visitors Bureau *Palm Beach County Map* is distorted – Palm Tran's (see Getting Around) system map actually tells you more about local streets. Dolph does a good area map.

Information

Tourist Offices The Palm Beach County Convention & Visitors Bureau (☎ 471-3995, 800-833-5733, see the Online Services appendix), 1555 Palm Beach Lakes Blvd, Suite 204, hands out helpful pamphlets and worthless '$500 coupon booklets' to anyone who asks. If you're looking on the internet, there are two websites, both of which offer general information about the city and county, attractions, hotels and some lame-o links.

Far more amusing is the Palm Beach Police Department's home page (see Online Services appendix), developed and maintained by Officer James Dean (this is the truth), which answers pressing questions like 'Why should I register my bicycle with the police department?' and 'My employer/job application requests that I have my fingerprints taken.'

AAA (☎ 694-9090) has an office at 9123 N Military Trail, No 110.

Money Barnett Bank has two branches in town. The Barnett Center Office is at 625 N

Flagler Drive. American Express has a representative office in North Palm Beach (☎ 845-8701) at Adventure Travels of the Palm Beaches, 630 US Hwy 1, Suite 101.

Post The main post office (☎ 697-2027) for West Palm Beach is at 3200 Summit Blvd. The downtown station (☎ 659-6114) is at 640 Clematis St.

Libraries The main library (☎ 659-8010) is at 100 Clematis St.

Media The *Palm Beach Post* is the local daily of record. NPR is at 90.7 FM.

Laundry Try the friendly folks at Rub-A-Dub (☎ 655-7833), 526 Belvedere Rd, or Wash Rite (☎ 832-3015), 2601 Poinsettia Ave.

Medical Services There are three major hospitals in the city: Columbia Hospital (☎ 842-6141) at 2201 45th St; St Mary's Hospital (☎ 844-6300) at 901 45th St, and Palm Beach Regional (☎ 967-7800) at 2829 10th Ave N. See also Good Samaritan Medical Center under Palm Beach.

Norton Museum of Art

Perhaps the best fine arts museum in the southeastern USA, the Norton Museum of Art (☎ 832-5196), 1451 S Olive Ave, reopened in newly expanded quarters in late 1995. The museum, founded in 1941 by steel industrialist Ralph Hubbard Norton (1875-1953), has a permanent collection of over 4500 works concentrated in three main fields: French Impressionist and Post-Impressionist paintings, American art from 1900 and Chinese collections.

The museum's holdings include important works by de Chirico, Brancusi, Chagall, Cezanne, Matisse, Renoir, Gauguin, Braque, Degas, Stuart Davis, Hopper, Marin, O'Keeffe, Warhol and Duane Hanson, and the Chinese collection contains archaic bronzes, jades, ceramics and monumental Buddhist sculptures. There are two main buildings, the museum and the south wing. Upon completion in January 1997,

SOUTHEAST

there will be a total of 19 galleries. The Norton also hosts regular traveling exhibitions, and the caliber is usually stunning.

The museum is open Tuesday to Saturday from 10 am to 5 pm, Sunday from 1 to 5 pm, closed Monday and holidays. Admission is a suggested donation of $5 for adults, $3 for students.

Mounts Botanical Gardens

This is a pleasant, 15-acre botanical garden (☎ 233-1749) with tropical and subtropical plants, a tiny rain forest, hibiscus and rose gardens and an herb garden. It's open Monday to Saturday from 8.30 am to 5 pm, Sunday from 1 to 5 pm, closed holidays. You can walk through on your own or grab a guided tour, given Saturday at 11 am and Sunday at 2.30 pm. Weekday tours are by appointment and with groups only. Admission is free. It's at 531 N Military Trail, between Southern Blvd and Belvedere.

South Florida
Science Museum & Planetarium

This is a fine science museum (☎ 832-1988), 4801 Dreher Trail N, just down the road from the Dreher Park Zoo (see zoo entry below for directions), and it's a must-do if you're here with kids.

The whole place is very hands-on, and there are exhibitions on sight (freeze your shadow against a wall, star in a psychedelic light show), sound (sound waves through water, a 75-foot echo tube) and holograms and weather (there's a great tornado display). Also see Suzie, a reconstructed 'imperial mammal', and the jaws and rib of a sperm whale. There's a good electricity demonstration with a Jacob's ladder, as well as resistance and capacitance demos and more. Skip the small aquarium exhibit. In October, the museum does a great Haunted House exhibit – with live snakes yet! The museum's open Saturday to Thursday from 10 am to 5 pm, Friday from 10 am to 10 pm. Admission is $5 for adults, $4.50 for seniors (over 62), $3 for students (13 to 21) and $2 for kids aged four to 12.

The planetarium shows are held upstairs on weekdays at 2 pm, Friday at 7 and 8 pm and Saturday and Sunday at noon and 2 pm ($1.75 in addition to admission). Laser light shows are held Friday at 9 and 11 pm; the 9 pm show is $2, the 11 pm $4.

Dreher Park Zoo

The Dreher Park Zoo (☎ 533-0887), 1301 Summit Blvd, is an interesting little zoo, but even if you're not a zoo person, you should grab the opportunity to see the Florida panthers – North America's rarest animal. The awfully sweet-looking George, Tayki and baby Colin are all very friendly and a treat to see.

There's lots of shade here, and it's very well signed and user-friendly (though the cages are a bit on the small side); you can do the whole zoo in about an hour. Among the highlights are the American and bald eagles, rabbits, llamas and sheep, as well as the fire ants, waterfowl, reptiles and plants. There's a small lake, but skip the boat ride. We only saw two butterflies in the butterfly garden.

The zoo is open daily from 9 am to 5 pm. Admission is $6, $5 for seniors, $4 for children three to 12. Holiday Nights are is $4 for adults, $2 for children. Stroller rentals are available for $3, wagons and double strollers for $4; a zoo map is 25¢ (skip it). The easiest way to get there from anywhere is to take I-95 to the Southern Blvd exit, go east to Parker Ave, turn right on Parker and continue to Summit Blvd, turn right, and the zoo and science museum will be on the right-hand side.

Lion Country Safari

It may feel like a long way to drive, but this is definitely worth the trip. Established in 1967 as one of the first 'natural habitat' zoos, Lion Country Safari (☎ 793-1084) accomplishes neatly what other parks, notably Busch Gardens, fail to do: bringing you very close to some exotic and dangerous animals. And it's the cheapest theme park of the sort – we had a blast here.

You tour the safari section in your car (and with, as about 400 signs admonish, your windows closed). No pedestrians are permitted (see *Jurassic Park* for more information). The safari section is broken into five sections that roughly approximate regions of Africa from where the animals originate.

As you enter you'll pass bison and, just past them and staring longingly, a pride of lions. Ignore the totally cheesy 'dinosaurs', but do watch for African elephants, lots of zebra, a rhino or two, some giraffes and chimps, water buffalo, Watusi, weirdly horned blackbucks and lots of others. The theme park section is harmless enough, and there are no bang-'em-over-the-head attempts at sales of kitsch, though there is a gift shop. Bring a picnic and some insect repellent. If you want to ride through the safari a second time, go for it – a second spin through is included in the price.

The park is open every day from 9.30 am to 5.30 pm; the last vehicle is let in at 4.30 pm. Admission is $13.95 for adults, $9.95 for children up to 16, and there are senior discounts that vary, so ask.

To get there take Southern Blvd (US Hwy 98) due west until you run out of gas, or about 17 miles west of I-95. Turn right at the sign (it is clearly visible; you didn't miss it) and drive about another two miles. The KOA camping entrance (see Places to Stay below) is right before the park entrance. The trip from West Palm Beach feels longer than it is – just remember that past Hwy 7 it's another eight miles to the park turn-off.

Ann Norton Sculpture Garden

Not connected in any way with the Norton Gallery of Art, the Ann Norton Sculpture Garden (☎ 832-5328), 253 Barcelona Rd at the western edge of Lake Worth, contains brick sculptures that are . . . unique, anyway, and set in a lovely garden. It's probably enough to hitch yourself over the brick wall and gaze. Unless you're some kind of Ann Norton buff, it's probably not worth the price of admission. It's open Tuesday to Saturday from 10 am to 4 pm.

Places to Stay

Staying in West Palm Beach is not all that much cheaper than staying in Palm Beach, though you have a lot more choice for doubles down in the $30 to 40 range in low season, $40 to 50 range in high season.

The best area we found for cheap lodging was at the southern end of town just north of the Lake Worth line, where several family-run mom-and-pop motels line S Dixie Hwy. But prices get even a bit better if you keep on going farther, into Lake Worth proper (see Lake Worth chapter).

Camping *KOA* (☎ 793-9797) has a campsite at Lion Country Safari (see above for directions), where tent sites for two people are $21, including electric and water hookup; each additional person is $3. RV sites are $24, including electric, water and sewer.

Motels For the cheapest places, head to the south end of town along S Dixie Hwy, where among the offerings is the fastidiously scrubbed *Apollo Motor Lodge* (☎ 833-1222), 4201 S Dixie Hwy, one block south of Southern Blvd. Here you'll find large singles/doubles with TV, telephone and bright, yellow doors for $27/30 ($35 for two double beds and a small fridge) in summer, $35/40/45 in winter. Weekly rates are negotiable.

Vali Motel (☎ 585-2633), 5515 S Dixie Hwy, has adequate, clean and basic singles/doubles (no telephones but basic cable) for $27.50/32 year round. It's half a block south of Bunker Rd; look for the red and white striped chairs and palm trees in front of each room.

The *Aqua Motel* (☎ 582-7506), 7800 S Dixie Hwy, has clean and fine rooms (single or double) for the day/week at $28/150 in summer, $32/180 in winter. There is friendly management (despite the scowls you may get at first, which almost made us walk out) and a small but nice pool outside. No phones in the rooms, but there's a pay phone in front of the office.

Just north at 7000 S Dixie Hwy, the *Royal Palm Motor Lodge* (☎ 582-2501/2/3) has spotlessly clean rooms, all with fridges and phones. There are two sections; the one along S Dixie is cheaper, with doubles starting at $33 ($38.50 with two double beds) a day, or $165 a week, in summer; $40/45/250 in winter.

The cheerful *Mt Vernon Motor Lodge* (☎ 832-0094), 310 Belvedere Rd, east of S Dixie Hwy, would be higher up on this list if we went by weekly prices, and if you're staying that long this is a good deal: clean and standard singles/doubles are $29/35 a day, $145/159 a week in summer; $39/49 a day, $175/199 a week in winter. There's a pool. Book early, as it fills up with package snowbirds.

An extra $20 or so could get you into one of the expensive chain hotels near the highways, but if you're willing to part with $44 to 55 in low season, $69 to 84 in high season, you may as well give your money to a nice, high-end family-run motel like the *Parkview Motor Lodge* (☎ 833-4644, 800-523-8978), 4710 S Dixie Hwy. Very friendly management gives out little guidebooks and pamphlets on local sights and attractions, and there are lots of other small extras. Rooms are comfortable and very clean. They offer a 10% discount for AAA and AARP members, and they are a AAA-listed hotel with lots of repeat business – reserve as soon as you can.

Guesthouses We're not sure that recommending the city's cheapest option is a good idea, especially for women traveling alone, but the cheapest it is: the *Flagler Court Hotel* (☎ 655-3336) is at 535 Clematis St, just west of the railway tracks; enter through the tiny doorway (the buzzer's there but hard to see) and up the steep staircase. It has comfortable enough singles/doubles for $22/34 a day, $70/84 week, plus $10/week for air conditioning, if you'll be wanting any. You can probably negotiate for a lower daily rate. There are separate and reasonably clean toilets and showers down the hallway, and a common area (take this literally) with a TV ('Fifteen years old and still works great!') near the staircase. Management seemed friendly, though the sign on the door saying it's a hostel is a lie.

Places to Eat

Good news: West Palm Beach has several cheap and even good eateries, and decent midrange choices abound. And as with places to stay, the main area to head for is the southern section of town. There are a growing number of restaurants on Clematis St, which is experiencing something of a rebirth.

Along S Dixie Hwy For quick snacks, *Nicky's Donuts* (☎ 582-4565), in the 1950s-era building at 7116 S Dixie Hwy, is very cheap for breakfast (99¢ for one egg, one slice of bacon and toast; $3.99 for two eggs, bacon, grits or home fries and toast) and has some quick-and-dirty lunch offerings like burgers ($2.39), grilled cheese ($2.50) and turkey sandwiches ($2.80), as well as donuts and coffee all day.

Perhaps the best Thai food we've had outside Thailand was at *Oriental Food Market & Takeout* (☎ 588-4626, 588-4699), 4919 S Dixie Hwy, in Raintree Plaza, a tiny shopping mall, where humongous, steaming-hot portions of pad thai with mixed vegetables cost an unbelievable $3.75. Excellent garlicky vegetable soup is $1.60, and sumptuous red curry Panang (veggies, bell peppers and peanuts in a coconut-curry sauce) is $3.75 (or $4.75 with meat). Skip the spring rolls, though – they were disappointing and served with maple syrup. Specify degree of spiciness when ordering, and though you can eat there, it's really a take-out place. The only drawback is the Styrofoam plates. The place is also a first-rate Asian food and spice market. It's open Monday to Saturday from 11 am to 8.30 pm (last order 8 pm).

Up the road a bit, at 6801 S Dixie Hwy (with another location at 330 Clematis St), is *Havana* (☎ 547-9799), a basic, decently priced Cuban place with a 24-hour take-out window. A Cuban sandwich is $3.79; other sandwiches are $1.99 to 4.59. Daily lunch specials are $4.99 to 5.99. The restaurant is open Sunday to Thursday from 11 am to 11 pm, Friday and Saturday from 11 to 1 am.

There are mega-cheap lunch deals and early bird dinner specials at *Don Ramone*

(☎ 547-8704), 7101 S Dixie Hwy. Cuban main courses like bistec de pollo, lechon asado or ropa vieja, salad, white or yellow rice, black beans and sweet plantains are $4.95 between 4 and 6 pm. Lunch specials get as cheap as $3.25 on Wednesday (chicken salad, two croquettes and French fries) and average $4 to 5; lunch is served till about 2.30 pm with several choices every day. As one might suspect, this place gets very crowded at lunchtime. At other times, beef dishes are about $9, chicken about $8 and seafood about $12. It's open till 10 pm.

Down at the *Royal Greek Restaurant* (☎ 585-7292), 7100 S Dixie Hwy, you can watch belly dancing on Saturday evenings at 7.30 pm. They have very cheap Greek and Mediterranean specialties like lamb shish-kebab over rice pilaf ($5.95), gyro ($3.50) and an early bird special dinner that's $14 for two people. It's a main course, potato, soup, Greek salad, coffee and dessert, served Monday to Saturday from 3 to 8 pm, Sunday from noon to 8 pm.

Howley's Restaurant (☎ 833-5691), 4700 S Dixie Hwy, does very cheap lunch specials ($3.65 to 5 from 11 am to 2 pm) and early bird dinners ($4.65 to 7.95 from 5 to 7 pm), in addition to big burgers ($1.95 to 3.65) and sandwiches ($1.95 to 4.95). It's open daily from 7 am to 10 pm year round.

Ranch's Family Restaurant (☎ 820-8886, fax 820-8939), 3800 S Dixie Hwy, is a very clean place doing breakfast and lunch only. Most aren't up for the Pigout Breakfast (three eggs, two bacon, two sausage, ham, potatoes *and* two pancakes) at $5.89, but there are lighter offerings from $1.95 to 3.99. They do office business delivering sandwiches at lunchtime (call or fax your order); large sandwiches with chips and pickles are $2.99 to 5.50. Free salad and soup come with eat-in lunch entrées. It's open Monday to Saturday from 7 am to 2 pm.

Down Dixie Roadside Grille (☎ 832-4959), 3815 S Dixie Hwy, does Southern-style lunch specials from $3 to 7, and dinner specials like Cajun grilled chicken for $8.95. It's a nice, relaxed place.

A strange entry, and one that is a bit out of the loop location-wise, is the *391st Bomb Group Headquarters* (☎ 683-3919), adjacent to the airport at 3989 Southern Blvd. You walk into what appears to be a WWII US Army Air Force base in France or England – the front yard is filled with Willys, Jeeps, sandbags and artillery; you get the idea. Inside service is very good and it's a nice place for a steak ($16.95 to 21.95). Pasta is too expensive, though, at $14.95 to 18.95. Prices go down substantially at lunch (weekdays from 11.30 am to 3.30 pm) with specials from $5.95 to 9.95, and entrées like shrimp and scallops with penne at $10.95. There's a two-for-one happy hour in their comfortable bar on weekdays from 4 to 7 pm. There are headphones in all the booths (not at all the tables though) on which you can listen to PBI Air Traffic Control. Could be fun.

Along Clematis St *La Taqueria* (☎ 655 5450), 419 Clematis St, looked very promising, and it has burritos for $2.75, taco salads for $4, nachos for $2.50 and tacos for $1.75. *In the Bag* (☎ 655-4505), 423 Clematis St, does take-away sandwiches from $2.99 to 5.75.

Roxy's (the sign on the door also says 'Comeau Bar & Grille', but everyone ignores that; ☎ 832-2402, 833-1003), 319-23 Clematis St, is a favorite of Palm Beach and West Palm Beach residents of all income brackets and walks of life – their burgers ($3.35 to 4.75) are the reason. It's a neighborhood, *Cheers*-y kind of place that also does more expensive fare – like seafood dinners for $12.95 – but people we spoke with stuck to the basics. Roxy McMuffins, by the way, are $2.25. It's open every day from 7.30 am – the kitchen takes a break between meals – and the lounge stays open till 3 am. Brunch on Sunday is from 11 am to 3 pm.

The *Bimini Beach Café* (☎ 833-9554), 104 Clematis St, has a nice location at the eastern end of block, near the Greyhound station and overlooking the lake. But the main reason we'd stop here is for the free buffet at happy hour (Monday to Friday from 5 to 7 pm), with two-for-one drink specials at the bar and lasagna and veggie dishes at the steam tables. If you stay (the patio is nice enough), sandwiches and burgers are $5.95 to 7.95, soups $3.50 to 4.50. At lunchtime, pasta dishes are $5.95 to 7.95; at dinner $11.95 to 14.95.

Entertainment
Supremely useful is the Palm Beach County Cultural Council, which operates a 24-hour information service (ArtsLine) on cultural events within the entire county. Call them at ☎ 800-882-2787 – you'll get a recording at night but live humans during the day.

Theater For more on legitimate theater in the area, see the Palm Beach section.

The *Raymond F Kravis Center for the Performing Arts* (☎ 833-8300) at 701 Okeechobee Blvd is an example of something *obviously* gone wrong with a public-private sector cooperative effort: it is beautiful and acoustically pleasing, architecturally cunning and blessed with enough bang for the PR buck to attract top-notch shows. There are three venues, the Alexander Dreyfoos Concert Hall (that's the one with the neato Art-Deco-meets-European-opera-house architecture), the black box Marshall Rinker Playhouse and the outdoor Gosman Amphitheatre.

You never know who you may see; in 1995 and 1996 they had such diverse acts as Spyro Gyra and the Central Ballet of China, the Magic (pah!) of David Copperfield and the excellent regional arts series with classical symphony orchestras and recitalists.

Prices change by performance and performer; classical concert tickets generally range from $15 (balcony) to $65 (orchestra) – Copperfield conjured $35 to 47, and Roy 'Hee Haw' Clark wheezed out $15 to 35.

The *Quest Theater Company* (☎ 832-9328), an African-American theater group, holds performances in West Palm Beach at West Palm Beach Community College's Duncan Theatre Stage West, as well as at the Quest Theater in Delray Beach (see that section above). Call for show dates, prices and venues.

Bars & Nightclubs Clematis St is the best option, with the most famous offering being *Roxy's* (see Places to Eat above). The *Bimini Bay Café* has a great happy hour and huge outdoor patio overlooking Lake Worth (see Places to Eat above).

For live music, *O'Shea's Pub* (☎ 833-3865), 531 Clematis St, is about as traditional Irish as you can find here. It's a great late-night drinking spot with live music Wednesday to Sunday at around 10 pm, and no cover charge. *Ray's Downtown Blues & Soul* (☎ 835-1577), 519 Clematis St, is a bar and nightclub with live blues and soul, Wednesday through Sunday, that also looked worth a try, as did *Respectable Street Café* (☎ 832-9999), across the street at 518 Clematis St. They have theme nights – Tuesday is British, Wednesday retro/ladies' night, Thursday rave and Friday and Saturday techno, when it stays open until 4 am. It opens at 9 pm.

Gambling If there's any action when you visit at Palm Beach Jai Alai (☎ 840-1386), 1415 W 45th St, it will probably be television simulcasts: the management says that they weren't making any money on the live thing and are, at least for the 1996 season, going with an inter-track wagering system for horse racing, jai alai and dog races. Admission is 50¢. If you're really set on gambling and you've just gone all the way up to the jai alai building and now you're stuck, head across the street, where a bingo hall runs games from 4 pm daily. Lightning rounds start at 10.45 pm and finish when the last person quits – it can go till 2 or 3 am. A set of cards is $10.

Spectator Sports
Baseball West Palm Beach is the winter home of the Atlanta Braves and the Montreal Expos, at the stadium on Palm Beach Lakes Blvd, where the teams rotate use of the field and take on other major league teams in exhibition season games.

Games are generally held during March; call ☎ 683-6100 for a schedule. Box seats are $7, grandstand $6, bleachers $4.

Polo The Palm Beach Polo & Country Club (☎ 793-1440), 13240 S Shore Blvd, holds polo matches that are open to the public, and who knows, you may even get to see the Prince of Wales fall on his royal bum. The season runs from January 7 to April 14, and matches are held on Sunday at 3 pm. The box office is open Monday to Friday and on some Saturdays from 9 am to 5.30 pm. Admission is $8 general, $20 to 26 for box seats. From downtown West Palm, take I-95 north to the Forest Hill Blvd exit and go 12 miles west.

Getting There & Away
Air Palm Beach International Airport (PBI, ☎ 471-7420) is about three miles west of I-95 on either Southern Blvd or Belvedere Rd. PBI is served by major airlines including American, Continental, Delta, Northwest and United.

See Getting Around, below, for info on getting from PBI to downtown. Ground transportation is downstairs at level 1.

Bus The Greyhound station (☎ 833-9636) is at 100 E Banyan Blvd. You can take Palm Tran (formerly Co Tran) buses (☎ 233-4287, option 4 for route information) from as far north as Tequesta and as far south as Boca Raton. From Boca Raton, take bus No 1S from Mizner Park to downtown West Palm Beach. From Tequesta City Hall, take bus No 22 to Gardens Mall, then to bus No 1C.

Train There are two Tri-Rail stations in town. The downtown station (which is also the Amtrak station) is at 201 S Tamarind Ave just north of Okeechobee Blvd, and the airport station is at 2600 Mercer Ave near Belvedere Rd.

Getting Around
To/From the Airport Between the airport and downtown, it's a grim scene for direct service. Bus No 4S runs only every two hours between the airport terminal and the corner of Banyan Blvd and Olive Ave. From the airport, service runs from 7.35 am to 5.35 pm; from downtown it's from 8.05 am to 6.05 pm. A more frequent, though by no means easier, route is to take the Tri-Rail shuttle from the airport to the Tri-Rail airport station, then take Tri-Rail shuttle No 4 to Palm Beach Mall, then Palm Tran bus No 4C (every 30 minutes at 25 and 55 minutes past the hour) to the downtown station (the Quadrille).

Palm Tran bus No 4C runs from Drexel Plaza shopping center at the west, down Okeechobee Blvd through downtown West Palm Beach, over the Royal Park Bridge, through most of the main downtown sights on the island of Palm Beach and back west over the Flagler Bridge. It will cost about $12 to get to downtown West Palm in a taxi, $18 to Palm Beach.

Bus Palm Tran serves the entire county. Buses cost $1, and 20¢ for transfers.

Car Parking is a snap, with unmetered parking almost everywhere.

Bicycle The city is pretty bicycle friendly, and streets are expensively smooth and easy to ride. See the Palm Beach chapter, below, for bike rental information.

Taxi Meter rates are $1.25 flagfall and $1.75 a mile. The biggest companies are Yellow Cab (☎ 689-2222) and Checker Cab (☎ 820-8121).

PALM BEACH
• *pop 9500 in summer, 25,000 in winter*
☎ 407

Few playgrounds of the rich and famous in this country attract as much attention as Palm Beach, known primarily for its stunning mansions, society events ('Which disease is it tonight, dear?') and exclusivity. This is one of the most elite and strangest enclaves in America. It's populated during the winter 'social season' (which everyone calls simply 'the Season') by a veritable *Who's Who* from a 1986 Jay MacInerney novel: people like Ron Pearlman and Rod 'I won't retire – I *won't*' Stewart, F Lee Bailey, Mary Lou Whitney, Celia Farris, Jimmy Buffett, the Kravises and Du Ponts, Jack Nicklaus and, at

SOUTHEAST

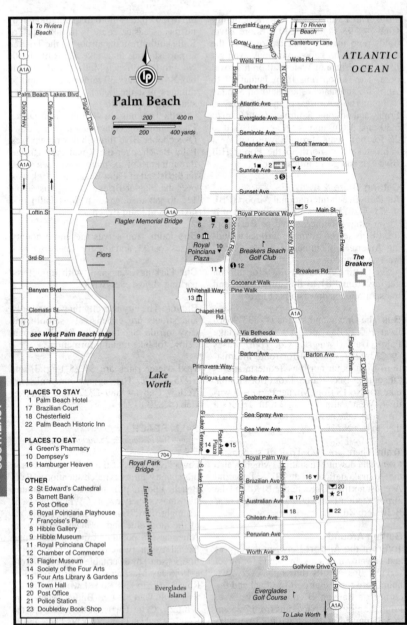

Palm Beach

ATLANTIC OCEAN

To Riviera Beach

Emerald Lane
Coral Lane
Canterbury Lane
Wells Rd
Wells Rd
Dunbar Rd
Atlantic Ave
Everglade Ave
Seminole Ave
Oleander Ave
Root Terrace
Park Ave
Grace Terrace
Sunrise Ave
Sunset Ave
Royal Poinciana Way
Main St
Breakers Row

Palm Beach Lakes Blvd
Dixie Hwy
Olive Ave
Flagler Drive
Bradley Place
Crescent Drive
N County Rd
S County Rd

Loftin St
Flagler Memorial Bridge
Royal Poinciana Plaza
Breakers Beach Golf Club
Breakers Rd
The Breakers

3rd St
Piers
Cocoanut Row
Cocoanut Walk
Pine Walk

Banyan Blvd
Clematis St
Whitehall Way
Chapel Hill Rd

see West Palm Beach map

Evernia St
Via Bethesda
Pendleton Ave
Pendleton Lane
Barton Ave
Barton Ave
Primavera Way
Antigua Lane
Clarke Ave
Flagler Drive

Lake Worth
Seabreeze Ave
Sea Spray Ave
Sea View Ave

Royal Palm Way
S Lake Terrace
Fourth Plaza
Cocoanut Row
Brazilian Ave
Hibiscus Ave
S Ocean Blvd

Australian Ave
Chilean Ave
Peruvian Ave

Royal Park Bridge
S Lake Drive
Worth Ave
Golfview Drive

Intracoastal Waterway

Everglades Island
Everglades Golf Course
To Lake Worth

PLACES TO STAY
1   Palm Beach Hotel
17 Brazilian Court
18 Chesterfield
22 Palm Beach Historic Inn

PLACES TO EAT
4   Green's Pharmacy
10 Dempsey's
16 Hamburger Heaven

OTHER
2   St Edward's Cathedral
3   Barnett Bank
5   Post Office
6   Royal Poinciana Playhouse
7   Françoise's Place
8   Hibble Gallery
9   Hibble Museum
11 Royal Poinciana Chapel
12 Chamber of Commerce
13 Flagler Museum
14 Society of the Four Arts
15 Four Arts Library & Gardens
19 Town Hall
20 Post Office
21 Police Station
23 Doubleday Book Shop

SOUTHEAST

the time of writing, even OJ Simpson was sniffing around nearby properties while not doggedly pursuing the real killers.

Except for OJ, all these people, and many many more, have lollipop- and Candyland-colored houses on or near Ocean Blvd, on which you can drive and be dazzled.

But surprisingly, the exclusivity doesn't quite slam down upon you like a fortress gate, and visits by backpackers will be tolerated in an amused sort of way. Unless you're looking to spend a whole bunch of money, it's best to make it a day trip (and pack a lunch).

Orientation

The long and narrow island of Palm Beach sits between Lake Worth (the Intracoastal Waterway) to the west, the Atlantic Ocean to the east and north, and the town of Lake Worth to the south – with a tiny piece of South Palm Beach just below Lake Worth. There's a grid system in place even here, with County Rd as the main north-south artery and running approximately through the center of the island.

Downtown is concentrated in the area between Royal Palm Way to the south, Royal Poinciana Way at the north, S County Rd at the east and Lake Worth, though it could be argued that downtown really consists of the entire area between Worth Ave at the south and Seminole Ave at the north.

In the downtown area, another important north-south road is Cocoanut Row, not to be confused with the east-west running Cocoanut Walk, which connects Cocoanut Row with S County Rd and the southern end of the Breakers hotel property.

While Worth Ave (see below) grabs most of the fame and the glamour, don't miss Ocean Blvd (Hwy A1A), on which sit some of the most grandiose and luxurious houses in the USA. Farther north, you won't see much more than a long stone wall at the Kennedy Compound, the family estate of the Kennedy clan that hit its height of notoriety in 1991 – when a visiting lesser Kennedy relative was arrested here, charged with rape and – prepare for a shocker – acquitted.

Maps The best street map available also happens to be free; it's the chamber of commerce's *Indexed Street Map of Palm Beach*, available at the chamber (see below). Also see the West Palm Beach section above for other area maps.

Information

Tourist Offices The Palm Beach Chamber of Commerce (☎ 655-3282) was more helpful than we would have expected, and it provides heaps and loads of pamphlets, coupons and even friendly local pointers. With luck you'll be able to snare a copy of their annual but somewhat rare *Official Guide to Palm Beach*, a free (if you pick it up at the office, otherwise it's $3 including postage) and advertiser-driven but extremely helpful paperback book crammed with ads, listings of accommodations, restaurants, museums and theaters, and some unforgivably puffy articles. The chamber is at 45 Cocoanut Row, opposite the Royal Poinciana Chapel. Squint: It's tucked slightly beneath road level on the east side of the street.

Money Barnett Bank has an office at 140 N County Rd. There's no American Express office.

Post The main post office is just north of Main St on S County Rd (you can't miss it).

Bookstores The friendliest bookstore we found, and one that also happens to carry a bunch of LP titles, was Doubleday Book Shop (☎ 655-0736), 228 Worth Ave.

Libraries The only public library is at the Society for the Four Arts (see Entertainment below).

Laundry If there's a coin laundry here, we didn't find it.

Toilets Many businesses are quite friendly about letting you use their facilities. Your best bets are the larger hotels (we used the Breakers). There are public toilets with showers in Phipps Park, at the north and the south ends, open sunrise to sunset.

Medical Services There are no hospitals on the island; Good Samaritan Medical Center (☎ 655-5511), 1300 N Flagler Drive, is the nearest.

Worth Ave

The Rodeo Drive of the East Coast (we can hear the cries against that description already), Worth Ave is a little (and little) more than a quarter-mile of fantastically expensive boutiques and shops (we counted 15 jewelers before giving up), including Cartier, Daniel Foxx, Gallery Versailles, Georgio Armani, Gucci, Chanel, Brooks Brothers and Frances Brewster. On the northern side of the western end, three alleys connect Worth Ave with Peruvian Ave via lovely little courtyards – from east to west, Via Demario, Via Mizner and Via Parigi. All are worth ducking into for their smaller art galleries, cafés and generally lovely architecture. On the south side of the street are similar – though less charming – courtyards containing similar fare. One crafty local suggested that one can pop into art gallery openings when one stumbles across them for free white wine, champagne or, more rarely, full bars. But dress well – if you look as if you can't afford a free drink, they'll politely kick your ass back out on the street.

Ocean Blvd

One must see for oneself the profusion of staggeringly spectacular – nay, overwhelmingly ostentatious (extravagantly magnificent?) – palatial homes that line this most exclusive of thoroughfares. You can't help but notice Donald Trump's Mar-A-Largo at the southern end, just around the bend from the Southern Ave Bridge. The coral- and sand-colored palace is surrounded by a 15-foot-high stone fence, and guarded by statues of overburdened jokers in court jester hats, painted in such vivid colors you can almost hear them groaning under the weight of the golden gas lamps that illuminate the wrought-iron entry-fence. Note, too, the light tower, said to be illuminated only when the squishy high-roller is in residence.

A drive along here reveals mansion after mansion, and as people in the chamber of commerce weren't exactly falling over each other to tell us who owns what, you'll just have to gaze in wonder as to who lives where.

Most of the beach beneath the sea wall has been eroded, and some may take satisfaction in the fact that these people paid all that money for beachfront property in an area where no beach now exists.

Oh, and obey all the speed limit signs.

Phipps Ocean Park

This is one of the two public beaches on the island (the other is Midtown Beach, or the Palm Beach Municipal Beach, which has just undergone renovation), located almost halfway between Sloan's Curve (south of Southern Blvd) and the Lake Worth Bridge, just opposite the southern fire station and Ibis Way. It's about a quarter mile of sand, and it's well patrolled by beach rescue. Metered parking is 25¢ for 20 minutes. Public showers and toilets are at the northern and southern ends of the park.

Bike Rentals There are bike paths at both Phipps Ocean Park and Midtown Beach, and in other places on the island. Palm Beach Bicycle Trail Shop (☎ 659-4583), 223 Sunrise Ave, rents bikes for $7 an hour, $18 from 9 am to 5 pm and $24 for 24 hours.

Flagler Museum

In 1901, Henry Morrison Flagler, the industrialist who is almost single-handedly responsible for the creation of South Florida for the rich, gave Whitehall mansion to his bride, Mary Lily Kenan. Designed to be every bit as ostentatious as any mansion in Newport, Rhode Island, it succeeded – and how.

The house, which cost $2.5 million to build and $1.5 million to furnish (and them's 1901 dollars) was in danger of being razed before Flagler's granddaughter, Jean Flagler Matthews, took the place over in 1959 and began raising money for its restoration.

Today, it's open as a museum (☎ 655-2833), at Cocoanut Row and Whitehall

Way (just south of Royal Poinciana Plaza), and its very pink ballroom is host to several balls, celebrations and school proms throughout the year.

And with all that said, there's not much reason to pay the admission fee. The knowledgeable staff is appropriately reverent as they guide frequent tours throughout the palace, though some of the stories they tell simply reinforce a notion of a family of greedheads. Downstairs, the Swiss billiards room is nice, and the kitchen area houses a somewhat interesting silver collection and a surprisingly good gift shop. You can also gawk at the dining rooms, courtyard and lake rooms. Upstairs, you can trace the Flagler family tree and see a series of thematic guest bedrooms. There's also an exhibit gallery, with constantly rotating exhibitions – they had flapper dresses and other Roaring '20s paraphernalia when we went. Outside, you can look at Flagler's private railway car, the FEC Railway *Rambler*. The museum's open Tuesday to Saturday from 10 am to 5 pm, Sunday from noon to 5 pm, closed Monday. Admission is $7 for adults, $3 for children six to 12.

Hibel Museum of Art
A visit to this museum (☎ 833-6870), 150 Royal Poinciana Plaza, is one of Palm Beach's loveliest experiences. Dedicated entirely to the art of Edna Hibel (pronounced HIBB-ull), who at the time of writing was 78 years old and living on Singer Island (just north of Palm Beach), the museum came about through a grant by her foremost benefactors, Ethelbelle and Cayton Craig. Hibel's art – she works in many media, including rice paper, silk, shells, plaster, butcher paper and wood – can't really be nailed down into a single classification. The staff is frighteningly dedicated, and Edna herself stops in once a year to sign her works, which she feels is anything she may have been involved with, including the calendars the museum gives out with a $20 membership. There's a Hibel Gallery in separate quarters in the plaza as well.

Follow her time in Mexico, beginning with *Mexican Beggar*. The model for this painting appears in many of her Mexican works, and he ends up a rich man in the last picture of the series. Also of note are her Breton series, especially *Breton Boy, Head*, and *Breton Woman*; her portraits of family, especially including her Russian *Grandmother* on aluminum; and paintings of her children at various stages of their lives. Perhaps most moving is the story behind the portrait of art school friend Winnie Chung, whom Hibel credits with introducing her to life in Boston's Chinatown and to Asian painting techniques.

Chung, who moved back to China, was arrested with her husband in 1966 as 'American Spies'. They were released in 1970, after torture led to illness. Chung died in 1978, but Hibel tracked down the family during an exhibition in Beijing, and met with her grandson, whom she sketched.

The museum is open Tuesday to Saturday from 10 am to 5 pm, Sunday from 1 to 5 pm, closed Monday. Admission is free.

Episcopal Church of Bethesda-by-the-Sea
This historic landmark Gothic-style cathedral, 141 S County Rd, was built in 1926 to replace the city's original church (1889). It features somewhat impressive stained glass and the small but lovely Cluett Memorial Gardens out back. Sit by the lily pads. It also has good acoustics to complement its *Music at Bethesda* series of choral works (☎ 655-4554), which are usually on the first Sunday of the month with additional performances throughout the year. Services are Sunday (Holy communion) 8 am, (family service) 9 am, (worship and sermon) 11 am; Tuesday 8 am; and Wednesday and Friday 12.05 pm.

St Edwards Cathedral
The very crowded Catholic church holds Sunday Mass at 7, 9 and 10.30 am and at noon; on weekdays, services are Monday to Saturday at 7.30 and 8.30 am.

SOUTHEAST

The Breakers

The Breakers (☎ 655-6611) at 1 S County Rd is an extremely elegant hotel offering the best of everything. It began as an addition to Flagler's Royal Poinciana Hotel, which was so large that bellhops sometimes delivered messages by bicycle. In 1896 he had the Palm Beach Inn added to the property's beachfront: a smaller, quieter version of the same elegance. Guests began to request rooms 'over by the breakers', which soon became the hotel's name.

In June 1903, the hotel burned down, but it reopened nine months later. What building material do you suppose they used right after a disastrous fire? In 1925, the newly built wood place burned again.

The hotel was rebuilt yet again in 1926. This Italian Renaissance version of the Breakers is what stands today.

The exterior of the hotel, modeled after the Villa Medici in Rome, has a 200-foot-long lobby with high arched ceilings. It's so vast Corinna almost couldn't find the bathroom. The hotel offers, of course, golf, tennis, a fitness center, great children's programs, jogging trails and every other conceivable comfort (see Places to Stay below for prices).

There is a free, one-hour guided tour that runs through the public areas of the hotel on Wednesday at 3 pm, and the best part is the banter from Mr Ponce, the hotel historian for the past 42 years. The tour leaves from the south Logue, and you'll hear local and hotel history and stories about the various rooms you'll pass – like the Florentine dining room and the private dining rooms, site of drinking and smoking parties during Prohibition, and the social status-based seating arrangements of parties and get-togethers. Contact the hotel for more information on tours.

Royal Poinciana Chapel

This charming wood chapel (1895, established 1894), opposite the chamber of commerce on Cocoanut Row just south of Royal Poinciana Plaza, with vaulted ceilings and large, bright windows, holds interdenominational services on Sunday at 10.30 am.

Places to Stay

As you may have surmised, this is a fantastically expensive city in which to sleep. Unless you're completely committed to making the scene during 'the Season', we'd suggest heading to one of the more inexpensive hotels or motels in nearby West Palm Beach or, even cheaper, Lake Worth.

Hotels The *Heart of Palm Beach Hotel* (☎ 655-5600, 800-523-5377), 160 Royal Palm Way, truly is in the heart of the city. Room rates for the large rooms (all with fridges and either a terrace or a balcony) are $69 to 129 in low season, $129 to 199 in high season, though ask about discounts, because there seem to be a lot of ways to get them.

The Palm Beach Hotel (☎ 633-4580, 800-232-7256), 235 Sunrise Ave, has seen better days; while it's glorious outside and rooms are perfectly pleasant and clean, the halls are a tad shabby and the furnishings a little old. Location's pretty great, though, and prices relatively low – room rates range from $70 to 100 in low season, $99 to 170 in high season, and weekly and monthly rates are available and can be a good deal, like $89 per day in high season for a basic room on a weekly rate.

The *Brazilian Court* (☎ 655-7740, 800-552-0335), 301 Australian Ave, is bright and cheerful and has friendly staff; there are two large courtyards, and rooms have enormous closets and lots of extras, though there are no elevators and lots of stairs. Rooms/suites range from $95 to 150/250 to 400 in low season, and $195 to 315/525 to 850 in high season.

The Chesterfield (☎ 659-5800, 800-243-7871), 363 Cocoanut Row, does its best to achieve that chummy, old-boy, 'Tally-HO! chaps, Back to Blighty, what?' look, with a wood-paneled card and game room and traditional English tea served (by a traditional Nicaraguan) in the afternoons. Okay, enough fun – the rooms are swell, immaculate and very luxurious indeed, with tons of amenities. Service is excellent, and staff is very friendly. Amenities include free newspapers in the lobby, and free London taxi service to Worth Ave (please – it's 300 yards south) and downtown West Palm Beach (now yer talkin'). In low season, room rates range from $75 to 175, suites from $195 to 300 and the penthouse is $450, and in high season it's $185 to 280 for rooms, $375 to 650 for suites and $800 for the penthouse.

Rooms at *The Breakers* (☎ 655-6611) at 1 S County Rd carry a grand price tag to match the opulence of the place: they have four different seasons and prices range widely. A traditional guestroom is, depending on the season and the view, $135 to 295, the deluxe rooms are $165 to 365, oceanfront rooms $245 to 470. Suites are $300 to 495, oceanfront suites $550 to 850 and imperial suites $1150 to 2000.

B&Bs The *Palm Beach Historic Inn* (☎ 832-4009), 365 S County Rd, is a charming, antique-filled Victorian-style house with spotless rooms, fluffy carpets, lots of flowers and lace – it's very romantic. It's also perfectly located just across the street from Town Hall, and a couple of minutes from the beach and Worth Ave. Breakfast (slightly more than continental but less than a full one) is served in your room from 8 to 9.30 am. Room rates are low enough – if you're already in this bracket – to be considered reasonable, and rooms/suites range from $75 to 95/125 to 225 in low season, and $125 to 150/175 to 225 in high season. Reserve early, as it's a popular place.

Places to Eat

Mizner's Moveable Feast (☎ 655-9100) is a sandwich place tucked away at 8 Via Mizner that was better and cheaper than we thought. Decent and filling sandwiches range from $3 to 6.

Green's Pharmacy (☎ 832-0304), 151 N County Rd, is a pretty classic pharmacy and lunch counter. Service is really rough around the edges unless they really know you – but we've spoken with 25-year residents who say that *they* aren't known here yet. Breakfast runs till 11.30 am and is $2.55 to 3.55. Burgers are $4.25 to 5.95, sand-

wiches $3.95 to 5.35, chili $1.95 to 2.50 and a fruit platter with cottage cheese $5.50.

And then there's *Hamburger Heaven* (☎ 655-5277), 314 S County Rd, the slumming-it-but-gently standby for Palm Beachers with simple fare served (when we visited) by a woman who had to be the voice of Natasha in *Rocky & Bullwinkle*. Dependably good burgers are $4.75, cheeseburgers are $5.25, and sandwiches range from 3.50 to 6.50.

Dempsey's (☎ 835-0400), 50 Cocoanut Row (near the Hibel Museum), is a New York Irish pub kind of place; lunch specials are $8, sandwiches from $5 to 7 and chicken hash is $6.95. At dinner, burgers are $9, veal or chicken dishes from $13 to 18 and nightly specials from $16 to 20. They do a Sunday brunch (make reservations) with eggs, bacon, toast and coffee for $7.25, omelets are $7.95.

Slick *Chuck & Harold's* (☎ 659-1440), 207 Royal Poinciana Way, does lunch with lighter food – tropical fruit salad ($7.50), smoked chicken quesadilla ($7.75) and pastas ($10.50 to 14). They serve nightly specials like giant eggplant ravioli at $16.75 or pan-fried rainbow trout for $18.25; regular entrées include pasta from $14 to 26 and New York strip steak at $23.50.

ER Bradley's (☎ 833-3520), 111 Bradley Place at Royal Poinciana Way, is another Irish pub kind of place, not too shabby and not too expensive. It's probably more famous for its hangover brunches – favorites like steak and eggs for $8.50, corned beef hash and eggs for $6.95 and Bradley's Benedict at $6.95. Dinners feature things like New York strip steak at $16.95, jumbo fried shrimp at $13.95 and grilled swordfish for $14.95.

There's good homemade pasta at *Amici Bar & Ristorante* (☎ 832-0201), 288 S County Rd. Appetizers run from $5 to 12, and the pasta includes tortellini stuffed with homemade cheese in a roasted pepper sauce ($16.50) or fettuccine with chicken, string beans, snow peas, leeks and sundried tomatoes ($17.50). Pizzas run from $12 to 15.50, and meat and fish main courses range from $19.50 to 28.

SOUTHEAST

The Florentine Dining Room (☎ 655-6611) at The Breakers isn't as expensive as you'd expect, but it's still right up there: appetizers, like saffron angel hair pasta or jumbo lump crabcakes range from $9.50 to 13. Entrées start at roast chicken breast with tomato fennel and garlic polenta for a cool $25 and include seafood linguine for $27 and herb-crusted grilled lamb chops for $32.

Entertainment

Theater The Royal Poinciana Playhouse (☎ 659-3310), 70A Royal Poinciana Plaza, is a legitimate stop-off for Broadway shows and productions despite its relatively small size (about 900 seats) – a recent season had Neil Simon's *Laughter on the 23rd Floor* (directed by Jerry Zaks) and *STOMP*.

Admission to all performances is $45 – except for opening nights, which are $50.

Society of the Four Arts A lovely exception to the exclusivity of Palm Beach life, the Society of the Four Arts (☎ 655-2776) at 2 Four Arts Plaza at the western end of Royal Palm Way (just east of the Royal Park Bridge) throws its arms open to the public with concerts, films, lectures, recitals and documentaries through The Season and some of the summer. There is a sculpture garden, library, garden and auditorium.

The film series is every Friday during The Season at 3 and 8 pm, and admission is $3. On Sunday there are free films, usually documentaries or historical films that are tied to exhibitions – like the special on tsarist life during their Russian porcelain exhibit. There's no charge for exhibitions either, though a $3 donation is requested.

During The Season there are monthly concerts, usually on a Sunday at 3 pm. In 1995-96 they ran a series of twice monthly concerts working their way through all of Beethoven's string quartets. Concerts are usually about $10.

On Tuesday during The Season there are lectures at 3 pm ($15). In 1995-96, the lecturing luminaries included John Updike and Sir David Frost.

The library is open for research year-round; only members ($35 a year for non-Palm Beach residents, $25 a year for residents) are permitted to sign out books. Unfortunately, the library volunteers can get a tad snooty.

Behind the library is the Philip Hulitar Sculpture Garden, in the Four Arts Gardens, which are open year-round and maintained by the Garden Club of Palm Beach.

Bars Of course, the leagues of *National Enquirer* readers are here for just one thing: Au Bar, which, we're sorry to say, does not exist as such anymore. The Au Bar people sold out to *Françoise's Place* (☎ 832-4800), 336 Royal Poinciana Way in the Royal Poinciana Plaza, and they're running the same kind of super classy place as the previous owners, who encouraged members of Palm Beach society to drink, stagger and swagger until the wee hours of the morning. After which some would then call their attorneys. It's open every day (except Monday) from 5.30 pm to 3 am during the Season, and it's closed Sunday, Monday and Tuesday in summer. In Season there's a $10 cover charge on weekends.

Getting There & Away

There is no direct plane, train or Greyhound bus service to Palm Beach. If you're not driving, get to West Palm Beach and take Palm Tran bus No 4C. If you are driving, from the city of Lake Worth take the Lake Worth Bridge to Hwy A1A and turn north.

Getting Around

Palm Tran bus No 4C runs from Drexel Plaza shopping center at the west, down Okeechobee Blvd through downtown West Palm Beach, over the Royal Park Bridge, through most of the main downtown sights on the island of Palm Beach and back west over the Flagler Bridge.

There's free one-hour parking available (it goes fast in high season, so be prepared to drive around the block a few times) along Worth Ave, and lots to the north.

MacArthur State Park to Stuart

☎ 561

By the time many travelers get to this neck of the woods, they've probably driven along I-95 and seen nothing but highway, development, cities and signs for golf condos. But the area between North Palm Beach and Stuart offers the greatest opportunities along the southeast coast to get out into Florida nature. North of the urban and suburban sprawl of the southern cities, the areas here along the barrier islands and the Intracoastal Waterway are largely undeveloped and protected.

The attractions of the nearby cities simply don't stand up to moonlight kayak paddles through St Lucie Inlet State Park, turtle watching at the Hobe Sound National Wildlife Refuge or camping at Jonathan Dickinson State Park. John D MacArthur State Park has an excellent nature center, with ranger-led snorkeling trips. If the windswept sand dunes of these beaches aren't quite as dazzling as the beaches of the southwest coast, the peace and quiet here more than make up for it. And even if you're just driving through, stopping for a few hours will be a memorable rest.

ORIENTATION & INFORMATION
The area described in this section is mainly confined to the stretch of Intracoastal Waterway from north of Palm Beach to the town of Stuart. For much of the way, US Hwy 1 and Hwy A1A are the same road, until just north of the Jonathan Dickinson State Park, when Hwy A1A splits off and becomes Dixie Hwy, and US Hwy 1 becomes Federal Hwy. Hwy A1A and US 1 meet again in downtown Stuart.

Note that Greyhound only provides service to Stuart; otherwise public transportation into this region is extremely inconvenient.

For tourist information, contact the parks listed below, the Stuart Chamber of Commerce (see Stuart) or the helpful people at Cove Kayak (see St Lucie Inlet below).

JOHN D MACARTHUR STATE PARK
While this state park (☎ 624-6950) is one of the smallest in the region, it runs excellent ranger-led interpretive walks and has one of the best turtle-watching programs around. Loggerhead, green and leatherback turtles nest along the beach here from May to August. The beach is across the 1600-foot boardwalk between the nature center across Lake Worth Cove to the beach, where there are dune crossovers leading out to the shore.

There's no camping, and there's no canoeing here (there are no boat launches). But if you've got a light kayak (there are no concessions in the park), you can bring it and paddle through Lake Worth Cove.

Interpretive Programs
The interpretive and nature center (☎ 624-6952) is just south of the main parking lot, where there's an exhibit on baby sea turtles, several aquariums, snakes and other exhibits on animals you may run into within the park. They also show a 15-minute video on the park's wildlife.

Ranger-led turtle-watching trips to observe nesting turtles run on Monday and Thursday evenings during June and July – but you'll need to reserve. Contact the nature center at least a month in advance to ensure a spot – groups are limited.

In summer, there are ranger-led snorkeling trips on the first and third Saturday of the month for advanced snorkelers with their own equipment. You'll see a 15-minute slide show of the area's sea life, then you're out to the reef alongside the beach.

And on weekends at 10 am there are nature walks through all the park habitats, with rangers pointing out the flora and fauna.

The nature center is open from 8 am to sunset, and closed Tuesday. The park is open every day from 8 am to sunset. Admission is $3.25 per carload, $1 for pedestrians and bicyclists.

SOUTHEAST

Getting There & Away

The park is at the northern end of Singer Island. From the north, take PGA Blvd straight east to Hwy A1A; from the south, take Blue Heron Blvd to Hwy A1A. The entrance is just past the Blue Heron Bridge.

JONATHAN DICKINSON STATE PARK

Made up of almost 11,500 acres, this excellent state park (☎ 546-2771), between US Hwy 1 and the Loxahatchee River (just north of Tequesta), is a great stop – either for a day, overnight or longer. Hikers will love the East Loop and Kitching Creek hiking trails, and there's great canoeing along the river. Primitive and developed campsites and cabins offer a variety of overnight options, and for day-trippers looking for a lazy afternoon, a river cruise down to the Trapper Nelson Interpretive Site to see the former home of the Wild Man of Loxahatchee is nice.

There's no ocean access within the park, which from 1942 to 1944 was Camp Murphy, a US Army Radar Instruction Facility. The park's attraction lies in its several habitats: pine flatwood, cypress stands, swamp and the 20% of it that is made up of 'globally imperiled' coastal sand pine scrub.

The park, open daily from 8 am to sunset, is named for Jonathan Dickinson, a Quaker merchant who shipwrecked at Hobe Sound in 1696 on a journey from Jamaica to Philadelphia and was captured by Jobes Indians (see Books in the Facts for the Visitor chapter *Jonathan Dickinson's Journal*). Admission is $3.25 per carload, $1 for pedestrians and bicyclists.

Observation Tower

You can drive out to the Hobe Mountain Observation Tower (Hobe 'Mountain' is a little hill) for an overview of the park. At the first stop sign after the park entrance, turn right and go about half a mile, turn right again and go about a quarter mile. There's a billboard telling you what's what. The tower is about 40 feet high, but 86 feet above sea level. There's no wheelchair access to the tower.

Canoeing

Rent canoes from the concession stand at the boat launch (☎ 800-746-1466) on the Loxahatchee River; the cost is $6 per hour, $10 for two hours, $15 for four and $22 for eight. The concession is open daily from 9 am to 5 pm.

Southern Exposure Sea Kayaks (☎ 575-4530) rents kayaks and does tours of the area as well; call for prices.

Hiking & Biking

There are several short-loop hiking and bicycle trails in the park, the most popular of which is the Kitching Creek Nature Trail (not to be confused with the Kitching Creek Hiking Trail, see below), just north of the boat landing, which can be walked in about 1½ hours.

There is about a two-mile bicycle trail leaving from very close to the entrance to the park to the main park road.

For more advanced hikers and backpackers there's an excellent network of hiking trails, maintained by the Florida Trail Association, which lead to two primitive campsites.

From the ranger station, pick up the East Loop of the white-blazed Florida Trail, which leads to the Scrub Jay campsite, 5.6 miles from the ranger station. From about there, you can pick up the Kitching Creek Hiking Trail, which continues west-southwest toward the Kitching Creek campsite, 9.3 miles from the ranger station. The Kitching Creek campsite is 0.6 of a mile south of the Kitching Creek Return Trail, which heads back to the East Loop. See Camping below for more information.

The trail snakes its way in several directions, but it's well marked and blazed, and there aren't any major physical challenges along the way. Mosquitoes are rife and there is flooding and mud in summer. Get maps and instructions from the ranger station.

River Cruise

You can go on two-hour boat trip aboard the *Loxahatchee Queen II* down the river to the Trapper Nelson Interpretive Site. Nelson, the son of Polish immigrants, lived in the area for 38 years from the 1930s and created a zoo and nature sanctuary. While the buildings are still standing, there are no animals, but the narrated tour gives a good idea of the history. Boats leave four times a day on the two-hour cruise (45 minutes down the river, half an hour at the site and then back), and the cost is $10 for adults and $5 for children.

Interpretive Programs
The main interpretive program is the river cruise, but there are ranger-led nature walks every Sunday morning at 9 am and campfire programs every Saturday night at 7 or 8 pm, depending on daylight saving time.

Camping
The park has three developed campgrounds – one for youth groups only – two primitive campsites along the East Loop and Kitching Creek Hiking Trail and, for the tentaphobic, cabins.

Primitive Camping The Scrub Jay campsite is at about the halfway point of the East Loop, and the Kitching Creek backpack campsite is about the halfway point on the Kitching Creek Hiking Trail. Both are totally primitive sites, but there are water pumps at each. This water – which you shouldn't depend on even working – must be chemically treated or, preferably, boiled. Bring along water, and make sure to seal the bottle and bring it inside your tent at night to protect it from raccoons. The cost for the primitive sites is $3 for adults and $2 for anyone under 18.

Full-Service Camping Tent or RV/van sites are $14 without electricity, $16 with electricity; both include up to four people (second vehicle is $3). There's no sewer hook-up, but there is a dump station.

There are grills on the sites, and you can make campfires if you bring your own wood (no gathering in the park, though you can buy wood from the rangers for $7 a bundle). There are hot showers in the park.

Cabins The fully equipped cabins cost $65

per night (a two-night minimum stay is required on weekends) or $355 for six nights/seven days.

HOBE SOUND NATIONAL WILDLIFE REFUGE
Hobe Sound National Wildlife Refuge (☎ 546-6141) is a 968-acre federally protected nature sanctuary with two sections: a small slice on the mainland between Hobe Sound and US Hwy 1, opposite the Jonathan Dickinson State Park, and the main refuge grounds at the north end of Jupiter Island, accessed at the northern end of N Beach Rd.

The Jupiter Island section has 3½ miles of beach (it's a favorite sea turtle nesting ground), mangroves and sand dunes, and the mainland section is a pine scrub forest. In June and July, sea turtle walks take place on Tuesday and Thursday evenings (reservations are necessary), and birding trips can also be arranged through the Hobe Sound Nature Center.

The refuge is open to the public from 8 am to sundown every day, and it can get crowded in the winter. Admission is free, but donations are greatly appreciated. Vehicles (and this includes bicycles) are only allowed on the paved section of N Beach Rd, which extends as far into the park as the beach parking lot (there's wheelchair access to the beach from here).

Jupiter Island
The beach here is windswept dunes and is excellent for walking and swimming. There are no toilets or showers. Among the flora you may encounter here are hand fern, milkweed and golden polypody, and fauna might include tortoises, snakes and bobcats as well as brown pelicans, osprey, scrub jays and other songbirds.

There's a campground on the island, but only Boy Scouts can camp there.

Blowing Rocks Preserve This preserve is a mile-long anastasia limestone formation outcropping that's riddled with holes, cracks and fissures that cause, in heavy seas, water to spew forth as if from a geyser. It's about four miles south of the Hwy 707 bridge on Jupiter Island.

But while it's famous for its spewing water, it's also an area of four distinct plant communities: shifting dune, coastal strand, interior mangrove wetlands and tropical coastal hammock.

Hobe Sound Nature Center

The nature center (same hours as the park), on the mainland strip just north of the entrance to Jonathan Dickinson State Park on the east side of US Hwy 1, has classrooms and a small area where incredibly friendly and knowledgeable rangers and volunteers will give you an up-close look at baby alligators, snakes and Terra – their Chilean rosehair tarantula.

They'll also explain how the sand pine scrub forest is a fire-tolerant plant community: rangers manage the plant life through controlled burning of the forest, the heat causing the sand pine cones to release their seeds.

Getting There & Away

For the nature center, take US Hwy 1 to just north of the Jonathan Dickinson State Park, the driveway is on the right. To the Jupiter Island section, continue north on US Hwy 1 until it forks, then bear right on Hwy A1A. Take that to Hwy 707 (Hwy 708) east, across the bridge to Jupiter Island, and turn left (north) on N Beach Rd.

ST LUCIE INLET STATE PARK

St Lucie Inlet State Park (☎ 744-7603) protects six sq miles of submerged anastasia limestone formation rock reef that's accessible only by boat in the Atlantic Ocean just off Jupiter Island. There are 12 species of hard and soft coral on the reef, so you're urged to anchor only on sandy bottom.

Snorkeling and diving is permitted (and there are sometimes snorkeling excursions through the Hobe Sound Nature Center, see above).

The St Lucie State Park borders also cover the northern tip of Jupiter Island, north of the Hobe Sound National Wildlife Refuge. There are excellent beaches all along the tip, and there are toilets and running water, as well as piers, canoe trails and hiking trails. From the mainland at the eastern end of Cove Rd, there's a boardwalk running from the dock opposite County Park to the beach.

Cove Kayak Center

This kayak rental and tour center (☎ 220-4079) is run by really friendly and helpful people who offer several guided and unguided kayak trips, and they're definitely into helping people understand exactly what the area has to offer.

Their territory is in the St Lucie Inlet State Park, and they rent entry-level one-person, advanced one-person and two-person kayaks for $25/30/60 a day, from 10 am to 4 pm. They'll bring the kayaks out to County Park, at the eastern end of Cove Rd, across the Intracoastal from St Lucie Inlet Park's Jupiter Island section, and pick them up when you're done. The price includes an orientation, a laminated trail map and instructions on how to see what's best for you – it's a fairly easy-going network of kayak trails, and you can get out and hang on the beach or picnic.

They offer three main guided tours for $35 per person in one-person kayaks, $30 per person in tandem kayaks. The tours are three to 3½ hours and head either into St Lucie Inlet, down the south fork of the St Lucie River, or to the Spoil Islands and Indian Lagoon.

Friday evenings from 6.30 to 10 pm they do their full moon and sunset paddles; it's $25 per person, but free to the physically or environmentally disabled – Rob, one of the partners in the outfit, spent eight years in a wheelchair. You paddle out, watch the sunset, have some wine and paddle back.

You can call and arrange to have them meet you, or stop into their office, which is in Stuart at 4595 SE Dixie Hwy (Hwy A1A), at the corner of Barcelona St, just south of St Lucie Blvd. Say hi to their incredibly sweet (but very shy) coyote (named Sundancer) and their not as charming but certainly friendly Vietnamese pot-bellied pig (named Albert). It's open every day from 10 am to 6 pm.

STUART
• *pop 12,000* ☎ *407*

The old town of Stuart may not be the most exciting place in the world, but it's a very pleasant Florida pioneer town, established around 1880 by would-be pineapple growers. The pineapples never made anyone rich, but the crowds kept coming for the fishing along the St Lucie and sailors who washed ashore here had a grand old time at Gilbert's Bar House of Refuge, a safe haven for shipwrecked sailors.

Orientation
Downtown Stuart is on a delta of the St Lucie River, where it branches off into the Atlantic and to the southwest, eventually to Lake Okeechobee along the St Lucie Canal.

Downtown Stuart is bounded by Dixie Hwy (Hwy A1A), which slashes through the city from southeast to northwest; its main drags, Flagler Ave and Osceola St, are parallel to Dixie Hwy. E Ocean Blvd runs along the south of downtown, and Colorado Ave runs along the east. Colorado Ave becomes Kanner Hwy when it crosses US Hwy 1 south of downtown. By the way, in downtown, no matter what you do, you will get confused at the convergence of Colorado Ave, Flagler Ave, Dixie Hwy and E and W Ocean Blvd. Nothing you can do about it. Locals call it Confusion Corner; we called it 'driving around the block 10 times'.

E Ocean Blvd connects downtown to Stuart Beach, on Hutchinson Island, a barrier island east of the Intracoastal Waterway. Sewall's Point is a spit of land between Stuart and Hutchinson Island, separating the St Lucie River from the Intracoastal.

Maps We couldn't find any accurate maps of the downtown area, but the chamber of commerce hands out an *Historic Walking Tour* pamphlet with a street plan that's good enough for getting around.

Information
The chamber of commerce (☎ 387-1088) is at 1650 S Kanner Hwy, about three quarters of a mile south of downtown; take Colorado Ave south and it's on the right-hand side of the road after you pass US Hwy 1.

Change money at the Barnett Bank at 900 S Federal Hwy, or at 3727 E Ocean Blvd on Sewall's Point. Island Hobby, 2401 SE Ocean Blvd, has out-of-town newspapers, including the *New York Times*, the *Times* of London, the *Daily Telegraph* and the *Village Voice* and *Miami Herald*.

Hutchinson Island
Stuart's **beaches** are first rate for walking, swimming and even some snorkeling.

We really liked the **Elliott Museum** (☎ 225-1961), 825 NE Ocean Blvd on Hutchinson Island. It's dedicated to inventor Harmon Elliott but contains an eclectic collection of exhibits, including a fabulous miniature circus and recreations of turn-of-the-century shops, such as an apothecary, barber shop and ice cream parlor. As you move through you'll also pass a Victorian parlor, a 1925 dining room and a typical 18th-century girl's bedroom. There is also a display of a hundred of Elliot's 118 patent certificates.

There seems to be no rhyme or reason for the selection of the displays, but they're fun all the same: baseball cards of Gaylord Perry, Lloyd Waner and Ralph Kiner, a music room, a toy collection and, in the back, an impressive collection of antique cars – including an 1879 fire truck, a 1926 Rolls Royce Phantom I, a 1921 Martin County Fire Department rescue vehicle, a 1902 Stanley Steamer . . . *and* all becomes clear when you see the 1886 Sterling Elliott Quadricycle and a 1903 Cadillac.

It's open daily from 11 am to 5 pm; admission is $4 for adults, 50¢ for children under 14.

Directly across the street, the Florida Oceanographic Society's **Coastal Science Center** (☎ 225-0505), 890 NE Ocean Blvd, is absolutely great for kids, who spend more time in this tiny place than you'd think possible. The incredibly enthusiastic staff run guided nature walks on Wednesday and Saturday at 10 am (and a boardwalk for self-guided tours was under construction when we visited).

Inside, they have four 300-gallon aquariums filled with tropical fish, an exhibit of a worm reef, and there are touch tanks with crabs, sea cucumber, starfish and other small yicky stuff.

The Frances Langford fish collection is an entire wall of mounted fish, and you can play a computer game to see if you can guess which fish are which. They also have a really cool computer program called Oceans Below, which simulates a scuba dive in any ocean in the world. It's small, but fun.

It's open Monday to Saturday from 10 am to 5 pm; admission is $3 for adults, $1.50 for children six to 12.

South, along the beach at 301 SE Mac-Arthur Blvd, is **Gilbert's Bar House of Refuge** (☎ 225-1875), located in the oldest house in Martin County (built in 1875). In more adventurous days it was one of 10 houses that the US Life-Saving Service established as a safe haven for shipwrecked sailors, who would find food and shelter here if they washed ashore. Inside there are exhibits of model ships and two aquariums, and out back, the boat house has maritime exhibits and samples of turn-of-the-century lifesaving gear. Brr.

Downtown Stuart

The primary attraction downtown is the **Heritage Museum** (☎ 220-4600), which is in the former George W Parks General Store at 161 Flagler Ave. If you've been out to the Elliott Museum on Hutchinson Island, this isn't really worth the effort, as it's pretty much the same stuff: turn-of-the-century antiques and way-of-life exhibits. But the building, a 19th-century wood-frame vernacular, is very nice. It's open Tuesday to Saturday from 11 am to 3 pm.

There's also an egregiously under-publicized art gallery at the **Courthouse Cultural Center** (☎ 287-6676), inside the 1937 WPA-built Martin County Courthouse. It's open Monday to Friday from 9 am to 5 pm; admission is free. Their gallery has rotating six- to eight-week exhibitions of works by local and regional artists.

Places to Stay

Motels *The Southwind Motel* (☎ 287-0773), 603 S Federal Hwy, is a clean place with nice management. In summer, singles/doubles are $26/32, efficiencies are $45 and cottages $65; in winter, singles/doubles $40/48, efficiencies $65, cottages $85. On weekends they have free barbecues.

The *Royal Palms Motel* (☎ 283-7608), 628 S Federal Hwy, has small but clean rooms, some with kitchens, and there's a pool; rooms are $38 to 42 in summer, $45 to 55 in winter.

The *Holiday Inn-Downtown* (☎ 287-6200), 1209 S Federal Hwy, has rooms for $65 in summer, and about $95 in winter.

Howard Johnson Lodge (☎ 287-3171), 950 S Federal Hwy, has rooms for $58 in summer, $85 in winter.

B&Bs *The Homeplace* (☎ 220-9148), 501 Akron Ave (in the historic district), is a romantic, antique-filled place with four bedrooms, all with private bath. Rooms are $75 from Sunday to Thursday and $95 on Friday and Saturday and include a full hot breakfast that changes daily – coffee, juice, fruit, homemade muffins or biscuits, cereal, an egg dish and a main dish like quiche or casserole. In the evenings they serve wine and snacks; they have a pool and a hot tub.

At the *Harbor Front B&B* (☎ 288-7289), 310 Atlanta Ave, a Florida cracker-style home on two acres of land, rates range from $65 to 155, including a full hot breakfast with a wide variety of good food.

Places to Eat

We liked *Alice's Family Restaurant* (☎ 286-9528), 2781 E Ocean Blvd (in the same shopping plaza as the Golden Peacock below). Food and service were good: breakfast is $2.45 to 4.25, steak and eggs are $6.45, sandwiches and burgers $3.25 to 4.95. Dinner specials (served Monday to Saturday from 3 to 8 pm) include two side dishes and are $4.25 to 5.50.

Nature's Way Café (☎ 220-7306), 25 SW Osceola St, has excellent fruit juices ($1.35 to 3.25). Sandwiches, on whole wheat pita bread with lots of vegetables, are $3.25 to

4.95; veggie pasta is $3.50 to 4.95. They have another location in Lake Worth.

Osceola St Herbs Juice Bar (☎ 221-1679), 26 SW Osceola St, is totally vegetarian: salads are $2.50 to 4.95, sandwiches are $2.75 to 4.25, the veggie burger platter is $4 and smoothies are from $2 to 4.

Edelweiss Deli, 40 SE Ocean Blvd (next to Groovy Movies a Go Go, see below) has good subs and German beer. *Michelle's Kitchen/The Sweetbrier Café* (☎ 286-4712), 2571 E Ocean Blvd, has great sandwiches from $3.25 to 4.95, awesome ratatouille for $5.95 and spinach lasagna is $6.25.

We were highly suspicious of the looks of the *Golden Peacock Chinese Restaurant* (☎ 286-1661), 2389 SE Ocean Blvd, but the food proved good enough that we dragged one of their damn fridge magnets around the state with us because they didn't have any business cards. They're very friendly, and they do cashew chicken for $7.95, beef chow mein for $6.95, great vegetable dishes from $4 to 6 and seafood dishes from $7.95 to 9.25. Recommended, despite the fact that it looks as if it came from central set design for a 1950s kung fu movie.

The *Black Marlin* (☎ 286-3126), 53 SW Osceola St, is a very friendly, *Cheers*-y kind of place, with pasta dishes from $8.95 to 11.95, pizza from $6.95 to 9.95 and sandwiches from $5.95 to 7.95. Appetizers like lobster ravioli with sundried tomatoes run $4.95, and dinner specials like Caribbean chicken are $10.95. Smoking's permitted.

The *Ashley Restaurant* (☎ 221-9476), 61 SW Osceola St, is a nouveau Bohemian hangout. Lunch crepes are $6.95, salads are $5.95 to 8.95 and, for dinner, coco mango chicken is $13.95, New York strip steak $15.95 and poppy seed grilled salmon $16.95.

Mainstreet Bar & Grill (☎ 221-3333), 10 SW Osceola St (with another entrance at 7 SW Flagler Ave; see also below), has sandwiches for $5.95, mussels marinara for $7.95 and chicken and sundried tomato scampi for $12.95.

The *Riverwalk Café* (☎ 221-1511), 201 SW St Lucie Ave, is a very nice place, with exposed brick walls and a relaxed atmosphere; main courses range from $12.95 to $15.95. For instance, grilled Beijing tuna with oriental vegetables is $12.95, and orange-glazed duck with braised red cabbage is $13.95. Small tables, no smoking.

Entertainment

The *Lyric Theatre* (☎ 220-1942), 59 SW Flagler Ave, a historic landmark theater built in 1926 and recently renovated, puts on a variety of shows, from performance art to classical concerts to rock concerts to opera. It's home to the Discovery Series, with daytime performances for schools and children. Call for information when you're in town.

The *Barn Theater* (☎ 287-4884) does mainly musicals; showtime's at 8 pm (the doors open at 7.30 pm). It's way out at 2400 SE Ocean Blvd, between the shopping mall and the Chevron station, next to the Lutheran church. Tickets are $13 to 16.

Groovy Movies A Go Go (☎ 221-0400), on the south side of Confusion Corner at 28 SE Ocean Blvd, is trying to start up a coffee-bar-video-screening place, showing foreign, independent, 'weird' and hard-to-find videos. We hope they make it; they're nice people and they mean well.

The *Mainstreet Bar & Grill*, 7 SW Flagler Ave, does live blues and jazz on Friday and Saturday nights, and they have about 70 different kinds of beer. (They have another entrance at 10 W Osceola, see Places to Eat above.)

Getting There & Away

The Greyhound station (☎ 287-7777) is at 6545 SE Kanner Hwy. The closest Amtrak station to Stuart is in West Palm Beach. Avis, Dollar and Hertz have car rental offices in Stuart; see the Getting Around chapter for more information. Unfortunately, there's no public transportation within or around the Stuart area, so you'll need to have a car to get around.

Central Florida

From Disney World and the theme park madness of Orlando to the spiritualist outpost at Cassadaga; from canoeing in Ocala National Forest and De Leon Springs to horseback riding and bicycling in Paynes Prairie; from the fern capital of Pierson to the student nightlife in Gainesville, central Florida is a fascinating area. Though its reputation is built on costly, glitzy amusements (it has the densest concentration of theme parks in the world), there's much beyond the immediate Orlando area to tempt you away from the water slides, movie studios, roller coasters, fairy tale palaces and costumed characters.

There's exceptional diving in the natural springs that pop up here and there – don't miss Devil's Den, a spectacular underground spring just southwest of Gainesville, and you haven't really lived until you've seen the manatees gathering at Blue Spring State Park, an oasis less than half an hour from downtown Orlando. Innertubing the Ichetucknee River, climbing down into some huge sinkholes and sleeping in a famous bordello are just a few of the cool draws of central Florida.

You'll need a car or a good bicycle to get anywhere off the beaten path, as public transport only works in the major cities and shuttle services are expensive.

Orlando

• pop 171,000 ☎ 407

If you're looking for Walt Disney World and you've opened to this section, think again: it's in its own section, where it belongs, as it's in the entirely separate city of Lake Buena Vista. Orlando is, believe it or not, a city in its own right whose locals would feel just fine, thank you very much, if all those ear-wearing yahoos would just get back in their cars and keep moving (except, of course, when they spend their money here).

HISTORY

At the end of the Second Seminole War, settlers and traders followed soldiers into the area. Originally named Jernigan (after settler Aaron Jernigan), the settlement grew up around Fort Gatlin, and became the Orange County seat in 1856. In 1857, the city was named Orlando, for Orlando Reeves, a soldier killed by Indians at Lake Eola.

The city boomed several times; a railroad boom (which fueled a population boom), a real-estate boom and a citrus boom. The late '50s brought a boom that was to last: the beginnings of the Space Age. The Glenn

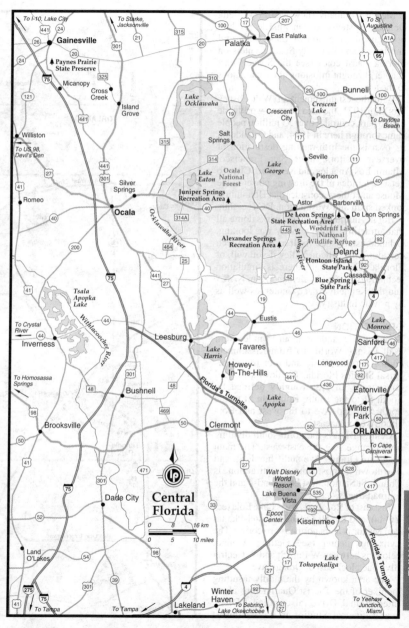

L Martin Company (now Martin Marietta Defense Systems) began missile production, and the creation of Cape Canaveral and later Cape Kennedy Space Centers on Florida's east coast (see the Space Coast chapter) brought infusions of cash and jobs to the area.

With the establishment of Walt Disney World in 1971, the area became worldwide theme park central – over 33 million people came through here in 1994, and Orlando on its own is the fifth-ranking destination of overseas visitors, after San Francisco, Miami, Los Angeles and New York City. To get a better idea of the drawing power of the Mouse and others, consider that Honolulu is ranked sixth and Washington, DC is eighth.

But it's not just the theme parks doing all that attracting: while nobody was looking, Orlando established itself as the high-tech corridor – the Silicon Valley if you will, of Florida. The specialty here is simulation technology, fueled by demand from NASA and the Kennedy Space Center, as well as by private industry.

ORIENTATION

Downtown Orlando is about 15 miles from Walt Disney World, 10 from Kissimmee, eight from Sea World and four from Universal Studios Florida. The downtown grid consists of an area roughly defined by South St to the south, Robinson St to the north, Garland Ave to the west and Rosalind Ave to the east.

Central Blvd is the north-south dividing line; Orange Ave the east-west. The main drags are Orange Ave and Church St, and downtown's most famous attraction is Church St Station, just between I-4 and the railroad tracks.

Just east of Rosalind Ave is Lake Eola (ee-YO-la), and the HI Orlando Hostel-Plantation Manor is at its northeastern corner. The Lynx bus center (see Getting Around, below) is between W Pine St and W Central Blvd one block east of Orange Ave.

The area known by the mildly insulting moniker of the Tourist Quarter runs along International Drive, also called I-Drive, near Universal Studios in the southwest

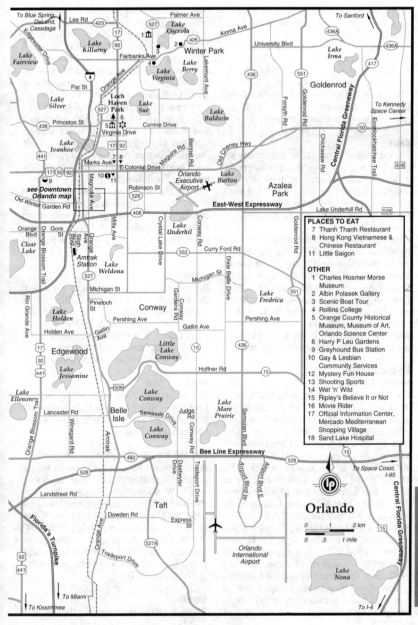

PLACES TO EAT
7   Thanh Thanh Restaurant
8   Hong Kong Vietnamese &
    Chinese Restaurant
11 Little Saigon

OTHER
1   Charles Hosmer Morse
    Museum
2   Albin Polasek Gallery
3   Scenic Boat Tour
4   Rollins College
5   Orange County Historical
    Museum, Museum of Art,
    Orlando Science Center
6   Harry P Leu Gardens
9   Greyhound Bus Station
10 Gay & Lesbian
    Community Services
12 Mystery Fun House
13 Shooting Sports
14 Wet 'n' Wild
16 Ripley's Believe It or Not
16 Movie Rider
17 Official Information Center,
    Mercado Mediterranean
    Shopping Village
18 Sand Lake Hospital

CENTRAL

part of the city. This is served by regular Lynx bus service as well as the I-Ride system (see below).

Universal Studios Theme Park is near the intersection of I-4 and Florida's Turnpike; the main entrance is about a half-mile north of I-4 on Kirkman Rd (Hwy 435).

Sea World is at the intersection of the Bee Line Expressway and I-4, about 10 miles south of downtown Orlando.

Maps

A good map is essential as the area is so sprawled out, and you'll have to spend some money to get anything with any sort of detail of the entire area. The CVB puts out a decent free *International Area Guide*, a guide to the whole city in a variety of languages.

For the most detailed free map of the area, the airport and some of downtown, contact the Orlando/Orange County Expressway Authority (☎ 825-8606) for their useful *Central Florida Express Map*. If you're going to pay, the cheapest, most readily available commercial map is Universal Map's *Greater Orlando, Orange County & Seminole County* for $2.50. Rand McNally and Dolph also publish maps to the area.

INFORMATION
Tourist Offices

The Official Tourist Information Center (☎ 363-5871, 800-551-0181) for the city is in the Mercado Mediterranean Shopping Village, 8445 International Drive, Suite 152; it's open daily except Christmas from 8 am to 8 pm. There's also an Official Information Center at the Airport (☎ 825-2352, TDD 825-4687), open daily from 7 am to 11 pm. For the mother lode of information, contact the Orlando/Orange County Convention & Visitors Bureau (CVB; ☎ 363-5800) at 6700 Forum Drive. They publish a reasonably informative *Official Visitors Guide* complete with coupons to and descriptions of jillions of attractions; it's available at the official information centers.

The city of Orlando runs a helpful website (see the Online Services appendix) which, though it isn't flashy, is a great source of practical information, phone numbers, parking information and lots more.

The AAA has two offices in the area. The Orlando office (☎ 894-3333) is at 4300 E Colonial Drive, and the main headquarters for Florida, Louisiana and Mississippi (☎ 444-4300, 800-596-2228) is nearby at 1000 AAA Drive, Heathrow, FL 32746.

Private information centers are practically everywhere, and usually associated with the infamous discount ticket brokers (see the Getting Tickets sidebar for an important *caveat* on these folks). Almost every hotel has a pamphlet rack with leaflets from the usual suspects.

For a 25¢ surcharge you can get recorded information on attractions, theme parks and even some other garbage (like soap opera updates) by dialing ☎ 211 from a private phone (not from a pay phone) and pushing lots of buttons. Bah.

Money

Barnett Bank's main branch in town is at the Barnett Tower (☎ 420-2700), 390 N Orange Ave. American Express has a full-service office (☎ 843-0004) at the Sun Bank Center, 2 W Church St, Suite 1. Most of the theme parks and attractions have cash machines and foreign exchange desks.

Post

The main post office is on Magnolia Ave, between E Robinson and E Jefferson Sts. It's mailing address is 46 E Robinson St, Orlando, FL 32802.

Bookstores & Libraries

All the chains have shops in malls around the area: B Dalton (☎ 839-5809) has a shop at 55 W Church St; Barnes & Noble (☎ 856-7200) has a superstore with a café at 8358 S Orange Blossom Trail. In Winter Haven, The Booktraders (☎ 941-299-4904), 301 W Central Ave, has an enormous collection of used books, records and magazines. The main downtown library branch is at 100 E Central Blvd.

Media

The main daily newspaper is the excellent

Getting Tickets
Discount tickets for most attractions, with the notable exception of tickets to Walt Disney World, are available at ticket outlets throughout the city. While many of these are legitimate outlets, many more are decidedly not – they're scams, shams and shiests. The Orlando Police Department is unable to effectively control these outlets because they are so widespread and portable – many are in booths that can be moved if a complaint is ever lodged.

Another common ploy is to offer free or deeply discounted tickets in exchange for your time and/or a commitment to buy something. The most common of this sort is run by time-share condominium or other property 'opportunities'. These can be fine if you're willing to give up a significant portion of your time listening to some salesperson extolling the benefits of the good life at Squeezy Acres, but before you do that be totally certain that you'll be under no obligation to buy or to commit to buy *anything* in exchange for the tickets – that all you have to do is listen to the pitch and the tickets are yours. If you don't see it in writing, move on. Also, if you're going to be driving to a place to listen to a sales pitch, find out if you can be reimbursed for your gas, as well.

The best bet is to buy discounted tickets at the official ticket outlets run by the CVB, whose main outlet is at the Official Tourist Information Center (☎ 363-5872) at the Mercado Mediterranean Shopping Village – the ticket desk is in the visitor information center and *not* at the booth outside, which deals in time-share condos – at 8445 International Drive, open daily from 8 am to 7 pm.

Disney does not sell discounted tickets, and will not honor tickets that were not officially purchased. Any discounted Disney tickets you will be offered are therefore either false, dated, stolen or partially used, and invalid, worthless junk. ■

Orlando Sentinal. Weekend pullout sections include special event and calendar listings. There are a few informative free handout papers with more timely information on bars, clubs, concerts, theater, comedy, etc. Try *Downtown Orlando Monthly*, *Axis Orlando* or *UR – The University Reporter*, all available at bars, restaurants and street boxes. *Orlando* magazine is an upscale read, with expensive restaurant listings and information on cultural happenings.

NPR has two stations here, at 90.7 and 89.9 FM.

Gay & Lesbian
The excellent and helpful Gay & Lesbian Community Services office (☎ 425-4527, see the Online Services appendix) at 712 E Colonial Drive (Hwy 50), has a library, a resource center and database including gay-owned and -friendly businesses, bars, restaurants and bookshops, and offers free HIV testing, flu shots and other community services. Out & About Books (☎ 896-0204) at 930 N Mills Ave sells a wide range

of g/l/b literature and fiction and sells and rents videos.

Laundry
There are coin laundries scattered throughout town, and the hostel has laundry service available (though that can get expensive). We heard good things about Lake Eola Coin Laundry (☎ 841-2852) at 807 E Washington Ave.

Curfew
There is a curfew in effect from midnight to 6 am in downtown Orlando for anyone under 18 years old. Offenders will be detained and, perhaps worse, their parents will be summoned to fetch them. It's not a joke – over 1700 presumably insomniac youths have been arrested since the curfew's institution on June 1, 1993.

Medical Services
All of the larger theme parks have first aid stations. MediClinic (☎ 396-1195, 239-1195) operates two walk-in clinics in the area: at 14421 International Drive, and

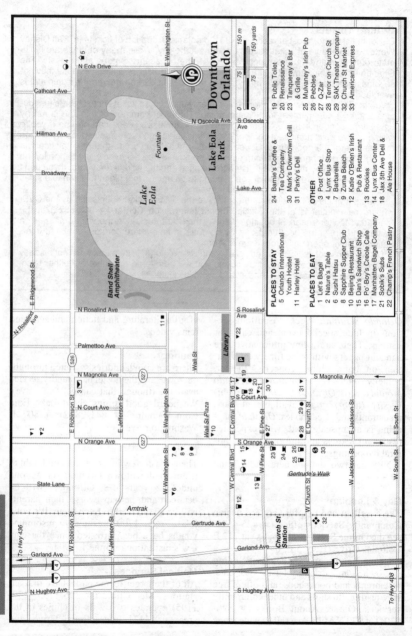

Downtown Orlando

Lake Eola Park

Lake Eola

Fountain

Band Shell Amphitheater

Library

Church St Station

Amtrak

Gertrude's Walk

0   75   150 m
0   75   150 yards

PLACES TO STAY
5   Orlando International Youth Hostel
11 Harley Hotel

PLACES TO EAT
1   Let's Bagel
2   Nature's Table
6   Sushi Hatsu
8   Sapphire Supper Club
10 Beijing Restaurant
15 Dan's Sandwich Shop
16 Po' Boy's Creole Cafe
17 Manhatten Bagel Company
21 Sobik's Subs
22 Champ's French Pastry
24 Barnie's Coffee & Tea Company
30 Mark's Downtown Grill
31 Parky's Deli

OTHER
3   Post Office
4   Lynx Bus Stop
7   Barbarella
9   Zuma Beach
12 Katie O'Brien's Irish Pub & Restaurant
13 Rookies
14 Lynx Bus Center
18 Jax 5th Ave Deli & Ale House
19 Public Toilet
20 Renaissance
23 Tanqueray's Bar & Grille
25 Mulvaney's Irish Pub
26 Pebbles
27 Q-Zar
28 Terror on Church St
29 SAK Theater Company
32 Church St Market
33 American Express

Saturn V rocket, Kennedy Space Center

Daytona International Speedway

In square miles, Jacksonville tops the list of US cities.

St Peter's Parish, St Augustine

Home of the state's most beautiful beaches

Daytona Beach's drive-in church

Ma Vynee Betch, the unofficial mayor of American Beach

2901 Parkway Blvd, Suite A-3, in Kissimmee, open from 8 am to 8 or 9 pm daily. A visit to the clinic is $67, and you have to pay up front. They also offer a 24-hour house-call service that sends doctors to most hotels in the area; the cost is $98 from 8 am to 10 pm and $128 from 10 pm to 8 am, plus medications.

The largest hospital in the area is Sand Lake Hospital (☎ 351-8550) at 9400 Turkey Lake Rd. Check in the telephone book under Pharmacies for listings of the several 24-hour pharmacies in the area.

HARRY P LEU GARDENS

This beautiful 50-acre estate (☎ 246-2620, see the Online Services appendix) is justifiably famous for its large camellia (over 2000 varieties) and rose collections. Harry P and Mary Jane Leu traveled the world collecting exotic seeds; they had planned to grow tea here on their estate, but it didn't work out. The land was donated to the city in 1961 to be used as a botanical garden.

Highlights include the Ravine Garden, the tropical plant area, and the North and South Woods with oaks, pines and camellias (which have an absolutely lovely smell – the best time to experience it is from December to March).

In the Conservatory you'll find orchids, and the Rose Garden has over 1000 rose displays; one of our favorites is the floral clock, an enormous clock whose face is formed by delicate flower arrangements (it no longer tells the time, because kids had climbed on the hands and tried to ride them, thus stripping the gears).

There are hundreds of other plants (all of which are well labeled), and it's perfect for an afternoon picnic or just a pleasant stroll.

Twenty-minute tours of the **Leu House**, an 18th-century mansion listed on the National Register of Historic Places, are available every half hour until 3.30 pm.

The graves of the house's original owners, David and Angela Mizell, can be seen at the Mizell Cemetery – this is the only botanical garden in Florida with a cemetery.

The gardens are at 1920 N Forest Ave.

From I-4, take exit 43 to Princeton St, follow that to Mills Ave (Hwy 17-92). Turn right, go to the second traffic light (Virginia Drive); go left onto Virginia for about one mile, following the curve to the left. The gardens are on the left side of the street.

Admission is $3 for adults and $1 for children aged six to 16. The gardens are open 9 am to 5 pm daily, the house/museum Tuesday to Saturday from 10 am to 4 pm and Sunday and Monday from 1 to 4 pm.

LOCH HAVEN PARK & MUSEUMS

North of downtown off Mills Ave, Loch Haven Park is home to Orlando's three major museums: the Science Center, Historical Museum and Art Museum.

Orlando Science Center

Kids love this science museum (☎ 896-7151), 810 E Rollins St, with its excellent exhibits on nature, including a gator hole. During 'touch times', kids (well, everyone, actually) have the opportunity to pet different animals. There's physics stuff – electricity, sound, optics, weather, etc – in the Tunnel of Discovery; Waterworks is a play area for smaller kids. There are rotating traveling exhibits as well.

A very neat idea to get some space for yourself and some fun for the kids is to send them to one of the museum's **overnight camp-ins** on Friday and Saturday nights. Designed for kids aged six to 13, the cost is $20 and includes a planetarium show, dinner and breakfast, excellent and fun workshop activities, and a space on the museum's floor (you provide the sleeping bag).

It's open Monday to Thursday and Saturday from 9 am to 5 pm, Friday 9 am to 9 pm, Sunday noon to 5 pm, closed Thanksgiving and Christmas. Admission is $6.50 for adults, $5.50 for children. The planetarium show is included in the price.

Orange County Historical Museum

The county's historical museum (☎ 897-6350), 812 E Rollins St, has a permanent exhibition of prehistoric Florida, a newspaper pressroom, Orange County buildings and an exhibit on citrus production, along

CENTRAL

with rotating exhibitions. They also show a video of the history of Orange County in the 2nd-floor Grand Theater. Adjacent is the Orange County Museum of Firefighting (see below).

It's open Monday to Saturday from 9 am to 5 pm, Sunday from noon to 5 pm. Bus No 39 stops right in front. Admission is $2 for adults, $1.50 for seniors and $1 for children aged six to 12; free guided tours leave every day at 11 am and 2 pm.

Fire Station No 3 Boys especially love Fire Station No 3 (☎ 897-6350), accessed through (and part of the admission to) the Orange County Historical Museum. In the oldest standing firehouse in Orange County, you'll see late-19th- and early-20th-century firefighting equipment, including a 1911 American LaFrance *Metropolitan* horse-drawn steam pumper and the city's first motorized fire truck. Admission and hours are as in the historical museum above.

Orlando Museum of Art

Founded in 1924, this museum's (☎ 896-4231) permanent collection consists of 19th- and 20th-century American, Pre-Colombian and African art. Exhibits include Mayan archaeological finds from Caracol, Belize and African art from the Tishman Collection, all on long-term loan to the museum.

The museum is at 2416 N Mills Ave, open Tuesday to Saturday from 9 am to 5 pm, Sunday from noon to 5 pm, closed Monday and most major holidays. Admission is $4 for adults, $2 for children aged four to 11.

UNIVERSAL STUDIOS FLORIDA

Like the hugely successful Universal Studios tour in Hollywood, this is a combination working movie studio and theme park that's a very entertaining way to spend a day. In fact (and we're treading lightly with this next sentence, so read the whole thing before reacting), if you can do only one single theme park during your stay, we'd say to choose Universal over any *single* Disney park (though the *overall* Disney experience outshines all its competition).

The rides here are not as gee-whiz roller-coastery or plunge-to-earthy as they are in Busch Gardens or even MGM-Disney, but they are a great deal of fun and can be scary. Waiting times are generally less than at Disney, though they can get up there. We've listed the approximate maximum wait time in parenthesis at the end of each listing when applicable.

Orientation

Universal Studios Florida is near the intersection of I-4 and Florida's Turnpike; the main entrance is about a half-mile north of Exit 3B of I-4 on Kirkman Rd (Hwy 435). There's a second entrance on Turkey Lake Rd. The park sprawls on a northeast slant from the main entrance and is divided into six distinct areas: the Front Lot, Production Central, Hollywood, New York, Expo Center and San Francisco/Amity. New York, San Francisco and Amity are all cunningly realistic recreations of those cities, and they are sometimes used as backdrops for films.

Hollywood is mostly shops and a couple of demos (like the Gory Gruesome & Grotesque Horror Makeup Show); New York is home to Kongfrontation and Ghostbusters; San Francisco/Amity has most of the exciting action stuff, like Jaws, Earthquake, the Dynamite Nights show and the Wild, Wild, Wild West Stunt Show; Expo Center has the awesome Back to the Future, ET Adventure and a Hard Rock Cafe as well as the Purple Plagiarist (Barney, the purple dinosaur, was busted for stealing the music to 'This Old Man' for his 'I Love You, You Love Me' song. A court order said that the Purple Plagiarist couldn't use the song unless he paid royalties.) and Fievel's Playland.

Production Central is the film lot and the home of Nickelodeon Studios and its famous Slime Geyser. At the time of writing, the only non-Nick television series being shot here was Sea Quest DSV, and when we visited they weren't even shooting that. Production Central is also home to the FUNtastic World of Hanna-Barbera, the Murder She Wrote demonstration and

Value Pass
In early 1996, Universal, Sea World and Wet 'n' Wild got together and threw a major curve ball at Disney: a five-day pass, good for unlimited visits to all three parks, at $89.95 for adults, $72.95 for children. The partnership is going further, in some very cool ways, but full details were not available at press time. It is expected to include other promotions, like agreements with local hotels and motels to provide rooms as part of a ticket package; free shuttle transportation between participating hotels and attractions; and an early park admission to special ticket holders.

If the Value Pass is still around when you come, it's the best theme park deal around. ■

Alfred Hitchcock's 3-D Theater and is the starting point for the studio tram tour, an interesting way to get your bearings around the park.

The most strollable areas in the park are New York and San Francisco, and you should take a half hour or so to explore the nooks and crannies and find storefronts and walls from movies. In New York, note Genco Imports *(The Godfather)* and Nazarman Pawn Broker *(The Pawnbroker)*. In San Francisco, the Fisherman's Wharf set would be much more realistic if the water it fronts were a bit colder, grayer and choppier, but that's nitpicking, isn't it? Hollywood is also worth spending some time in.

Information

This section provides a highlights description. There's just so much to see and do here, so write or call before you go for an *Official Studio Guide* map and information packet: Universal Studios Florida (☎ 363-8000), 1000 Universal Studios Plaza, Orlando, FL 32819. Their website is excellent (see the Online Services appendix), and another excellent source of information is Tom Tipton's *Unofficial Guide to Universal Studios Florida*, a guidebook written by a former employee. Updates of the book are posted on the internet; see the Online Services appendix.

Get maps to the park at the gate. Guest Services, which is also the lost and found and lost-kids area (families are usually reunited within 30 minutes of a park-wide alert, which you can order through any staff member), is to the right after you enter the gates, or in the window to the right before you enter. The park is open every day of the

year. **Opening hours** vary seasonally and on special events, but generally the park is open between the hours of 9 am and 6 pm year round.

At the time of writing, **admissions** at the gate (including tax) were, for a one-day ticket, $39.22 for ages 10 and up, $31.80 for children aged three to nine; for a two-day ticket, $58.30/46.64 and for an annual pass, $92.75/74.20. Discount tickets at the Official Information Center were $37/30 for one-day passes only. There are, from time to time, discounts and specials like second-day-free programs, but ask, because no one will tell you. Parking is $5 for cars and motorcycles, $7 for RVs and campers.

Studio Tours (☎ 363-8182), which have the added benefit of getting you into the rides and shows without waiting in line, cost $90 per person or $900 for groups of up to 15 people.

You can change **money** at the First Union Bank just inside the main entrance; there's an ATM inside the park, near Guest Services, and also an ATM outside, also near Guest Services.

Most rides are wheelchair accessible. You can rent **wheelchairs** ($6) and electric wheelchairs ($30 plus deposit) at Guest Services. You can rent single and double **strollers** ($6/12) there as well.

For $5 you can place your animal in either indoor or outdoor **kennels**. Water is provided but food is not, though you can return during the day to walk and feed your pet.

Rides & Attractions

Terminator 2: 3-D The newest ride at Universal was not yet open at press time, so all we can do is tell you what Universal and

Tom Tipton have said about it: it will be housed in the CyberDyne headquarters building along Hollywood Blvd, and will be a three-screen, 3-D, surround-sound and simulator experience. It's cracked up to be spectacular: the first of a new generation of rides. The film will star principals from the movie, including Arnold Schwarzenegger, Linda Hamilton and Robert Patrick (and yeah, the kid will be in it too).

Tipton recommends that, as the thing is close to the park entrance and crowds will form early, wait until the latter half of the day to try and get in to cut down waiting time.

Back to the Future This is hands-down the best flight simulator ride in the state, maybe even in the country (outside, of course, Boeing's Seattle training center!). There are 24 DeLorean-shaped simulators that are stacked atop one another in a seven-story, 60-foot-high screening area that they fill with liquid nitrogen fog. You start the ride in the 1950s and then blast into prehistoric times: through jagged mountains, down precipitous crevasses, in and around volcanoes – the special effects are phenomenal, and we'll be surprised if you don't 'feel' the Texaco sign. The film is said to be, if you calculate by the minute, the most expensive ever made, clocking in at a Costner-esque $16 million for 4.5 minutes. (half-hour wait)

Earthquake – The Big One After being subjected to a film starring Charlton Heston which highlights the now dated and creaky but then spectacular special effects from the movie *Earthquake*, there's a brief and accurate demonstration of chroma-key and matte technology.

You then enter a really bitchin' replica of a San Francisco BART subway station and get into a pretty good BART subway train. Then the Big One (8.3 on the Richter scale) hits: the tracks buckle, the place crumbles, and you're nearly hit by an oncoming subway train and an 18-wheel truck that drops in . . . before, of course, the whole place catches on fire and floods. (20-minute wait)

ET Adventure This is billed as a sequel to the movie, and it's a charming ride you take in little bicycle-like contraptions with an ET in the front basket. You're rescuing ET, taking part in the last minutes of the movie – you start to fly and skim the roof of a police car, then up over the city and through the sky to ET's home planet. It's one of the most harmless rides, great for kids but we loved it, too. On the way, you see ET babies and other weird spacey stuff, and at the end of the ride ET says good-bye to you by name! (10-minute wait)

FUNtastic World of Hanna-Barbera This isn't really a ride, more of a ride-through-cartoon. It's a flight simulator of sorts (though there are also non-movable seats available), taking you through a computer-generated 3-D toonscape of a spaceship. Eh. You emerge into the very entertaining world of Bedrock, which includes interactive video games, incredibly fun looping, SFX and dialogue editors, and really cool digital samples of cartoon noises at Yogi's Silly Sounds booth. (10-minute wait for the ride, none for the rest)

Jaws It can get a little scary, but the kids we were with absolutely loved it. You board a tour boat in the town of Amity, and start a little tootle around a lake before suddenly! you're under attack by gigantic rubber sharks. The explosions are terrific and it even gets a tad warm as flames burst forth from every which way and, in the end, fry the pesky beasts. (half-hour wait)

Kongfrontation This takes place in an absolutely fantastic recreation of New York City's Roosevelt Island Tram, with surprising – even for here – set detail (down to the gum on the streets, authentic manhole covers and fire hydrants), and start a ride to the peaceful island of thin-walled condos when suddenly! you come under attack by the lady-lifter himself, King Kong. He grabs hold of your tram and shakes it (it's not too violent) and as he presses his rubbery Kong face against your tram you smell his Kong Breath (which smells like ... nah, we won't ruin it). You emerge – surprise surprise – into the Kong shop, where you can buy Kong stuff and, for $4.50, have your photo taken in the beast's hand. (half-hour wait)

Fievel's Playland Inspired by the cartoon *An American Tail* about a family of mice who immigrate from Russia, this really excellent area has giant-size sets which make you mouse-size, and a really fun waterslide. You wait about 15 minutes to board a little rubber raft, and spiral down (three big turns).

A Day in the Park with Barney If your kids like this popular purple dinosaur, then this is the place to take them – personally we recommend telling your kids that Barney died in a horrible chipper-shredder accident, but hey, they're *your* kids, right? Twenty-minute shows start frequently throughout the day. Outside, there's an excellent Playland with lots of very creative things for kids to bang on, push, climb and roll through and a very interesting whirlpool.

Shows
There's a range of stuff to be seen here, at a range of venues, and you probably won't be able to see everything in just one day unless you're a very good planner. Show times change frequently, but when you arrive you'll be handed a list of that day's shows, showtimes and venues.

Animal Actors Show Animals' rights activists may get upset with this one, but Nick thought it was fantastic. There's Babe the pig, Beethoven the dog, Mr Ed, Benji (who plays dead pretty hilariously), an alligator named Chompers, a sea lion, Holly the stunt chimp and even a skunk. Ace Ventura's pet bird stops in and does a bit of flying over the audience's head in search of money.

Dynamite Nights Stuntacular It's an explode-a-rama with cops in speedboats and on jet skis chasing robbers in speedboats through dangerous fire rings. It's

held every evening before closing on the main lake at the center of the park. If you love chase scenes you'll have a blast – or at least they will. Views are pretty good all around the lake, but they're probably best from the 2nd floor of Lombard's restaurant (though the 2nd floor isn't really open to the public, maybe you can sweet-talk your way upstairs – we did).

Ghostbusters Kids will love the slime. At a Ghostbusters seminar (sort of a live infomercial on how to open your own GB franchise), you learn the basics of ghost-busting before being treated to an actual haunting. Great special effects create the Spook Central tower from the movie, and some very energetic Ghostbusters fight off some very energetic spooks that seem quite three dimensional, thank you very much. Did we mention slime?

The Wild, Wild, Wild West Stunt Show We came with cynicism in our hearts and left converted: this is a fun stunt show starring a twinkly-eyed, fair-haired hero named Dusty or Randy or something, his dim-witted sidekick and a Ma Baker-inspired trio of bad guys that root, toot and shoot their way around the set for about 20 minutes. Some of the stunts are great – fist fights, trick shooting, explosions and a couple of from-the-rooftop and through-the-balcony falls, but the best part is staying around for a few minutes after the show and watching the set repair itself.

Murder She Wrote Jessica Fletcher has managed to haunt us from beyond the grave: despite merciful cancellation by CBS of the long-running series, this show lives on, at least it did as we went to press. It's a demonstration of production techniques that were used on show, which was about a writer/sleuth in a New England town in which everyone is murdered every week. You'll learn about how they cut the final scenes in several different ways, and discover the magnificent and totally under-appreciated world of Foley work – next time you watch a movie, pay attention to the creaking doors, the stabbing sounds and the footsteps, all of which are artfully added in post-production by Foley artists.

Gory Gruesome & Grotesque Horror Makeup Show

This delivers what it promises, though if you're really into horror make up it may be a little too short. (But, as the press-kit gushes, the show annually goes through '365 straight-edge razors, 14,600 blanks, 912 quarts of stage blood and 547 gallons of our special blood and guts mixture', so you won't feel cheated on gore!) It's a discussion and demonstration – with volunteers – of basic horror makeup. One volunteer gets slashed with a knife with predictably bloody results, and you'll see props and makeup from *The Exorcist*, *Beetlejuice* and *An American Werewolf in London*. The finale is the transformer machine from *The Fly*. You'll exit, of course, into the Hollywood Makeup & Masks Store.

Hitchcock 3-D Theatre

The Hitchcock 3-D Theatre is just what it sounds like: a tribute to the films and filmmaking techniques of the portly master of suspense, including scenes from his movies, some of which become 3-D.

Nickelodeon Studios

About 85% of the original programming on the Nickelodeon cable television network is shot here, along with material for MTV and other Viacom-owned networks. You can tour the studios and look in on sets, though they may not be taping when you come (you'll always get the tour, and if they're not taping a real show you'll get to participate in a mock-up). Nickelodeon is, during the day, a children-oriented network, with such blockbusting hits as *Gullah-Gullah*, *GUTS* and *Wienerville*. At night, Nick at Nite runs classic TV re-runs like *Taxi*, *Mary Tyler Moore* and *Bob Newhart*.

Nickelodeon runs a recorded taping schedule at ☎ 363-8586 so check before you come. You can speak to a human at ☎ 363-8500. (For information about taping and filming throughout central Florida, call the Central Florida Production Hotline (☎ 236-0001), which will give you locations and set coordinator contact numbers.)

Studio Tour

It's great fun, especially if you've never been in the magic world of TV. You'll see Stage 18 and, if you're lucky, whatever's being shot in it. If there's nothing taping on that day, you'll head for a second control room and watch a videotape describing the various jobs around the studio (carried out by members of the International Brotherhood of Guys Who Stand Around the Coffee Truck Talking Penalty Time Local 1212 – Q: How many Teamsters does it take to change a light bulb? A: 53, got somethin' to say about it?), and then move on to Stage 17, where you'll see either a game lab or just a mock-up of a game show complete with audience participation and, of course, GAK. You'll also pass through the classic TV memorabilia room, where you can see Jeannie's original bottle and other classic TV artifacts. (45-minute wait, but there's entertainment in the line)

Green Slime Geyser

Nickelodeon will be remembered for the perfection of slime into their GAK product – a slimy gelatin-like substance that, in thickened form, is fun at home and in thinned form is used to dump on and throw at contestants on Nickelodeon programs. The Green Slime Geyser in front of the studios erupts every few minutes (on a random schedule), spewing forth GAK and splashing those standing within the clearly marked SPLAT ZONE.

Places to Eat

Throughout the park stands sell quick snacks, but bring your own bottled water or drinks because who wants to spend $2.50 for a small bottle of water or $2 for a Pepsi? Vegetarian and kosher meals can be arranged through Guest Services one day in advance (☎ 354-6356). For quick sandwiches and salads, head for the *Boulangerie*, where 'health sandwiches' are $5.99, and a soup and salad combo is $4.99.

Schwab's Pharmacy is a pharmacy lunch counter with chili dogs for $3.86, hot dogs for $3.07 and ice cream for $2.19.

Mel's Drive-In is a '50s diner with a double burger and fries for $5.79, chicken sandwich for $6.49 and lots of vintage cars out front.

In New York, what looks like Louie's Restaurant, Giovanni's Fruit and Mamma Lugina's is all actually *Louie's Italian* which does cafeteria-style Italian food – underwhelming at that. Linguini and clam sauce is $6.29, lasagna $6.39.

On the pricier, sit-down side, there's *Finnegan's*, a New York-Irish-style bar and grill with sandwiches from $7.50 to 9.25 and main courses like Yorkshire Rib Eye for $12.95 and fish & chips for $9.60. From 5 to 7 pm there's a happy hour with half-price beer and wine.

The *Studio Star* has a buffet for $9.95 ($4.95 for kids aged nine and under) until 4 pm, after which it's $12.95 for adults, $6.95 for kids.

Lombards at Fisherman's Wharf has similar prices and 'San Francisco' food, and there's always the *Hard Rock Cafe* at the highest end: memorabilia notwithstanding, we just don't pay that much for a sandwich and coffee.

WET 'N' WILD

Wet 'n' Wild is one of Florida's first water parks, and it's a very good one. The star of the show is Der Stuka, a six-story speed slide.

Located right at the heart of International Drive, it's easy to get to, and lines for this are far shorter than those at Disney. It's well done, clean and safe, definitely family oriented and the rides are pretty cool, too. *Orlando Magazine* voted it the Place with the Scariest Thrill Rides in 1994 *(before Disney's Summit Plummet)*.

At the center of the park is a tide pool; to the left is Raging Rapids and Mach 5, to the right Der Stuka and Bomb Bay; straight ahead is the Wild One and Knee Ski. The park is surrounded by Lazy River, a swiftly flowing channel on which you can float aimlessly on a raft. Raging Rapids and Mach 5 are mat slides. On Mach 5 you're given a choice of routes: B is the shortest with the quickest turns, C is the longest and slowest (and if you're overweight they'll send you on this line). Bomb Bay and Der Stuka are speed slides; for Bomb Bay you step inside a capsule which is moved forward over the slide, at which point the floor drops out from under you.

Wet 'n' Wild (☎ 351-1800, 24-hour recorded information 351-9453, 800-992-9453) is at 6200 International Drive. Parking ($3 for cars, $5 for campers and buses) is across the street from the park. There's a Sunbank ATM at the entrance, and lockers are to the right as you enter. You can bring a picnic with you to save on food; there's a covered picnic area behind Bubble Up, the enormous climbable beach ball. In winter, the pools are heated to 85°F.

Admission is $22.95 for adults, $17.95 for kids aged three to nine, $11.50 for seniors (over 55). A second-day pass is $11.50. An annual family pass is $75. There's an extra $3 fee for the Wild One, where you're pulled around the lake on a bouncy tube by a jet ski. Inner tube rentals are $4 for adults, $3 for kids, with a $1 deposit; towels are $1 and life vests are free.

Hours are incredibly varied by season. They're open year round, but hours are longest from June 19 to August 11, when they're open from 9 am to 11 pm, and shortest from October 30 to April 9, when they're open from 10 am to 5 pm.

SEA WORLD

We visited Sea World on a day marred by torrential rains and still managed to have a good time, but we do think that the admission prices are more than a little out of line – it's $3 more than a Disney park! There are some mitigating factors: the Sea World Animal Rescue Team is one of the best in the country, and it's partially funded by the admissions, and if you're the sort of person who likes leaping dolphins, sliding sea lions and crashing whales, you're going to have an incredible time.

Orientation & Information

Sea World (☎ 351-3600, see the Online

Services appendix), at 7007 Sea World Drive, is near the intersection of I-4 and the Bee Line Expressway.

The park is oval-shaped, with the main entrance, Guest Services and the lost and found center at its northwest curve. All the attractions are in a rough semi-circle surrounding the lake, at about the center. Get maps as you pick up your ticket. The park is open year round, but they don't want their hours printed as they say they change too often. Suffice it to say it's open from around 9 am to around 7 pm, later in summer.

The **admission** cost is $39.95 for adults, $32.80 for children aged three to nine, Florida residents $27/22. Parking is $5 for cars, $7 for vans and buses. Admission to the utterly unexciting Sky Tower is an extra $3 plus tax. They accept Visa/MasterCard but do not accept American Express cards.

You can change **money** at an appalling rate at the Guest Relations window from 10 am to 3 pm. There's an ATM at the main gate and pay lockers ($1) near the main entrance. All the attractions in the park are wheelchair accessible. **Stroller and wheelchair rentals** are $5; double strollers are $10; electric wheelchairs are $25. Air-conditioned **kennel** service is $4 per day, BYOF (bring your own food).

Toilets are well-signed and clean. There are diaper changing areas outside all women's toilets, and outside the men's toilets near Shamu Emporium. There're unisex diaper changing areas near Wild Arctic and at the Hospitality Center. Nursing mothers have their own area (imagine the scandal . . . the dis*grace* . . . of actually nursing a human child in public!) near the women's toilet at the Friends of the Wild.

Attractions

Other than the new flagship area at Wild Arctic, the main attractions here are not rides but shows and displays. These highlights are listed roughly in counter-clockwise order (with a couple of jigs and jags) from the entrance at the ticket plaza.

Stingray Lagoon Rays, the docile animals related to sharks, glide through the water with a grace and beauty all their own. This section of the park features a whole lot of them, including the cownose, southern diamond, bat and shovel-nosed guitarfish (actually a skate). You can feed the flappy fellers with stingray food ($1) of smelt, shrimp, clam and squid available from the very friendly staff.

Whale & Dolphin Stadium This is the home of Sea World's excellent false-killer whale and dolphin shows, starring some of the 40 dolphins that have been born at the park. Atlantic bottle-nosed dolphins boogie to sampler-driven Caribbean music, performing synchronized leaps from the water as the foxy babe-vet rides on the backs of Cindy and Dolly, the stars of the show.

Manatees: the Last Generation? Endangered manatees, whose population took even more of a pounding in early 1996 as a result of a disease whose cause was still unknown at the time of writing, are the focus of this excellent exhibit. The Sea World Animal Rescue Team rescues manatees every year, and in 1996 was one of the major players in the race to discover what was killing the gentle mammals off the southwestern coast of Florida.

Outside you'll see alligators, crocodiles and turtles. Inside, to the sounds of crickets and frogs, you'll see a four-minute film about the life of manatees, and how human behavior is so devastating to this species that has no other natural enemies. See the Flora & Fauna section in the Facts about Florida chapter for more information about manatees and how they're threatened.

Penguin Encounter We had a blast here, as people movers carried us past penguin tanks with manufactured snow, the sounds of penguin calls barely audible over the hilarious and appropriate *oom-pah-pah* music. Dig the wild rockhopper penguins, which look very much like mid-1980s Rod Stewart.

There's a learning center here as well,

with a puffin exhibit, and touch-screen instructional videos on each type of bird included in the exhibit.

Sea Lion & Otter Stadium This is home to *Hotel Clyde & Seamore*, a 'funny' show starring sea lion, otter and walrus 'comedians'. As you enter, the Sea World mime will try to trick you in various ways – hitting him in the nose seems to be the only way to make him stop, though we can't recommend that. But this is an excellent show for kids, who do find it screamingly funny. It features the animals as maintenance staff, and it's always nice to see Clyde shove the detestable manager out of the way.

Terrors of the Deep With the exception of Wild Arctic, this is probably the most popular exhibit in the park (well, okay, after the itty-bitty glasses of free beer at the Anheuser Busch Hospitality Center). The sharks, rays, barracuda, lion fish and skates in this exhibition are swimming all around the Plexiglas tube that you're carried through on a conveyor belt. It's absolutely fascinating to be this close to the enormous sharks, and kids love it when rays and skates glide over the surface of the tube eating little pieces of algae . . . eeeeyoow!

Anheuser-Busch Hospitality Center Anheuser Busch, America's largest brewers (they made 1,219,264,500 cases of 20 varieties of beer in 1994, as well as a host of other products including those little roasted nut packs you get on airplanes – slick, huh?), owns Sea World. At their hospitality center you can taste free samples of their beers, meted out in little 10-ounce cups (two per person over 21). But it's actually a very interesting attraction without the beer: you can also learn a lot about recycling (A-B has its own recycling subsidiary), printing (yeah, they have a printing subsidiary, too) and other A-B endeavors. Out back, the **Clydesdale Hamlet** is home to a stable of Clydesdale horses, which are the trademark of Budweiser beer.

Shamu's Happy Harbor This is a wonderful kids' recreation area with probably the best climbing nets on earth (all ages), an air-bounce for kids up to 48 inches (122 cm), very cool water slides for kids under 42 inches (107 cm) and a great sandbox. There's also a small arcade and some neato but expensive radio-controlled boats and cars (it's an additional $1 for 2¼ minutes with the boats and $1 for 2 minutes with a truck).

Shamu Stadium Killer whales doing stunts, splashing the crowd. Some choreographed to rock music. Natural our ass.

Wild Arctic This is the park's flagship attraction, and it's a darn good one. It begins with an excellent flight simulator ride; you're traveling to an Arctic station with a bad storm front moving in (but they say they'll do their best to get you there safely) in an incredibly high-powered helicopter. It's being flown by a nature-loving pilot who brings you very close to some polar bears before setting down on thin ice. Of course, after hearing an awful rumbling sound, you fall through the ice and it's touch and go there for a while, but . . .

You can also ride this in a non-moving platform, for which lines are shorter.

Once you reach Base Station Wild Arctic, you'll see a fascinating Arctic exhibit featuring harbor seals, a beluga whale, polar bears, walruses and fish. There are touch-screen interactive displays and very helpful and informed staff. And you emerge from your Arctic adventure in . . . the Wild Arctic gift shop.

Atlantis Water Ski Stadium This stadium fronting the lake is home to the Baywatch at Sea World show, which, believe us, is every bit as exciting as the television series. Okay, it's got some great waterski and jet ski stunts, and stars the *voice* of David Hasselhoff, who plays Mitch on the TV show. He's referred to in press materials as an 'internationally renowned recording artist', and he sings *Fallin' in Love* as part of the show. You don't want to miss that.

Splash zones are rows one to 15. There are a couple of explosions during the show, so if you hate bangs, sit in the back.

RIPLEY'S BELIEVE IT OR NOT

See the St Augustine section of the Northeast Florida chapter for general information on Robert Ripley.

The Orlando Ripley's Believe It or Not (☎ 363-4418) is a) enormous and b) in a building that's cunningly designed to appear as if it were collapsing into a sinkhole. It's at 8201 International Drive, one block south of Sand Lake Rd; take I-4 to exit 29.

There are the usual Ripley draws: shrunken heads, double-pupilled wax figures and the holographic image of Robert Ripley, as well as interactive exhibits and films. It's fully wheelchair accessible.

It's open from 9 am to 11 pm daily. Admission is $9.95 for adults and $6.95 for children aged four to 12. A combination Ripley's/Movie Rider ticket (see below) is $14.95.

MOVIE RIDER

These theaters (one at 8815 International Drive (☎ 351-0999) and a second scheduled to open in Kissimmee at 5390 W Hwy 192, next to the Cracker Barrel Restaurant) are flight simulators, currently offering two films: supersonic flight and Dino Island. Admission (including both films) is $8.95 for adults and children, $1 off for seniors and active military, $2 off for AAA members. This is run by the same management company as Ripley's (see above).

TERROR ON CHURCH ST

This excellent spook show (☎ 649-3327) in the center of downtown Orlando is a walk through 23 different sets, all of them 'haunted' by actors in spooky costume, special effects, lights and sound. It's really fun to stand outside and watch the television monitors of victims walking through and getting the pants scared off them. If you're a horror movie or spook-house fan, you can't do much better around here. It's $10 per person; kids under 10 are not admitted without a parent or guardian. It's

at (BOO! Just kidding.) 135 S Orange Ave (northeast corner of Church St), open Tuesday to Thursday and Sunday from 7 pm to midnight, Friday and Saturday from 2 pm to 1 am.

MYSTERY FUN HOUSE

The Mystery Fun House (☎ 351-3355 for recorded information, 351-3359 for a human) is a 15-room maze inside a large house. It's dimly lit, and you have to navigate your way through the creepy twists and turns. It's not a horror show: nothing comes out and grabs you or says 'boo'.

Their other big draw is **Destination Starbase Omega**, a souped-up laser tag game. You're equipped with a vibrating shield and a laser gun, and you and other warriors enter a flight simulator which 'brings you' through an asteroid field and lands you on the starbase, where you proceed to leave the simulator and shoot the hell out of all the people who rode there with you.

Admission to the fun house (you can go through at your own pace) is $7.95 for all ages, the Starbase Omega bit (which lasts for a total of a half-hour, the shooting part itself only 10 minutes) is $6.95, and a combination ticket is $11.90. There's **mini-golf** outside. It's open from 10 am to 11 pm daily, and the box office closes at 9 pm. It's at 5767 Major Blvd, opposite the main gates of Universal Studios.

SHOOTING SPORTS

Foreigners will be aghast at the ease at which this shooting range (☎ 363-9000), approximately opposite Wet 'n' Wild at 6811-13 Visitors Circle, rents handguns, shotguns, automatic and semi-automatic weapons out to anyone – anyone over age 18 and able to behave in a non-insane manner. We're listing it because it's very popular and, okay, we did it, too. It works like this: you rent the piece (we chose a Glock 17) for $5 to 9, pay a range fee (Thursday to Tuesday $3, free on Wednesday) and buy your ammunition (prices vary based on caliber) and targets, and then head for the indoor range. If you don't know how to shoot, a lesson is included in the rental price. Someone rented an *Uzi* when we were there. We left soon after. Blammedy Blam Blam!

PLACES TO STAY

Most of the places to stay in the area are not in downtown Orlando, but along I-Drive, out by Disney and in Kissimmee, and most of the options are chain hotels that we won't bother describing. In the chains, package tours combining air fare, hotel, Disney ticket, etc are often the best way to go, and rates vary wildly from day to day. The greater Orlando area has the highest concentration of hotel rooms in the USA, so competition is fierce, rates are generally low and quality is acceptable.

It's usually cheaper to stay in Kissimmee (see Around Orlando, below), where multitudes of motels line Hwy 192 and rooms begin at $19.95 throughout the year. Note also that the HI Orlando Resort is actually located in Kissimmee.

For the I-Drive chains, quoted prices on the telephone are often deceptive: you can always negotiate.

Camping

The Orlando area is one of the few in the state in which camping is actually convenient and inexpensive. It's also relatively safe, though make sure to leave valuables with management when you're away from the site.

KOA has two campsites in the area in the city of Orlando proper (☎ 277-5075, 800-999-5267) and in Kissimmee (see Around Orlando, below). Both have tent sites for $17.95 and RV sites with full hookups for $28.95 and 29.95 respectively. The Orlando KOA is at the southeastern end of the city, on Hwy 15, five miles south off the Beeline (Hwy 528) or one mile south of the Greenway (Hwy 417) at 12343 Narcoossee Rd.

Yogi-Bear's Jellystone Park Camp Resort (☎ 800-776-9644), 9200 Turkey Lake Rd in Orlando, has tent sites for $18 year round. Sites with water and electricity are $23 in low season, $29 in high season and full hookup sites are $25/31. There's another location in Kissimmee (see Around Orlando, below); weekly and monthly

deals are available at both. As we went to press, one of these Jellystone locations (we're not sure which) was in the process of being sold, so call ahead.

Hostels

The *HI Orlando Hostel – Plantation Manor* (☎ 843-8888, reservations 800-444-6111), 227 N Eola Drive at the northeast corner of Lake Eola, is perfectly located for people who want to stay in the heart of downtown (there's a bus stop right across the street), but there are some problems.

It's been around forever, in a large old house that's convenient to public transport and within walking distance of the center of the city. But over the years, the hostel has become rundown, and with the opening of the HI Orlando Resort in Kissimmee (an HI-owned property as opposed to an HI affiliate), a mood of bitterness has settled on the place that many hostellers and travelers we spoke with – as well as both of us – had picked up on. When we visited things were very dire indeed, and service was bad – answers to simple questions were evasive and we got the feeling we were never getting a full story about anything.

HI reports that since we visited the place has been tented for insects, and that renovations are underway. We strongly hope that this place can get back on its feet, and you should check when you visit to see if it has. The cost is $11 per person in the dorms; private rooms for two are $28.60 including tax.

Hotels

Downtown The options here are not altogether the best; the *Harley Hotel* (☎ 841-3220) at 151 E Washington is well-located, but the rooms are somewhat aged and the whole thing is a little too expensive for what you get, with rooms starting at over $100. There's a *TraveLodge* (☎ 423-1671) at 409 N Magnolia Ave.

International Drive All of the motels and hotels along I-Drive are chain places, and they're all about the same: designed to accommodate package tourists from the

USA and Europe, they each have pools, lounges, restaurants and are all convenient to fast food places. They all offer shuttle services to the airport and to the theme parks for about the same price. It's always cheaper to book these places through a travel agent as some sort of package as opposed to coming in and asking for their rack rates. See the Accommodations section in Facts for the Visitor for more information on package tours and toll-free numbers for the larger chains.

Hotels along I-Drive include:

Best Western Plaza International (☎ 345-8195), No 8738; somewhat but not entirely swank
Comfort Suites Orlando (☎ 351-5050), No 5825; usually very comfortable indeed with lots of perks, including free breakfast
Continental Plaza Hotel (☎ 352-8211), 6825 Visitors Circle; a huge place with a pool opposite Wet 'n' Wild
Days Inn has two locations on I-Drive: No 7200 (☎ 351-1200), and No 9990 (☎ 352-8700)
Hampton Inn (☎ 345-1112), 7110 S Kirkman Rd; comfortable and reasonable
Holiday Inn International Drive Resort (☎ 351-3500), No 6515; one of the nicer entries. Other Holiday Inns on International Drive are the *Holiday Inn Castle Hotel* (☎ 345-1511) at No 8629 and a *Holiday Inn Express* (☎ 351-4430) at No 6323.
Howard Johnson (☎ 351-2900), No 6603; they have a nicer Resort Hotel (☎ 351-2100) at No 5905 and the Howard Johnson Universal Tower (☎ 351-2100) at No 5905.
Orlando Marriott (☎ 351-2420), No 8001
Quality Suites, with two locations on I-Drive, at No 7600 (☎ 351-1600) and No 9000 (☎ 345-8585); the same kind of perks as Comfort Suites but with large outdoor heated pools, though no breakfast
Radisson Barcelo Hotel Orlando (☎ 345-0505), No 8444; a flashy place
Ramada Hotel Resort Florida Center (☎ 351-4600), No 7400, even flashier

PLACES TO EAT

There are few outstanding restaurants in Orlando in terms of places to dress up for, but there's a never-ending supply of fast food, chain restaurants and some interesting international cuisine that's very inexpensive. You can't fire a pistol on I-Drive without hitting a restaurant of some sort, and all the steak houses and some of the other larger places have all-you-can-eat breakfast buffets, which we found to be both crowded and a rip-off. Theme dinner shows in Kissimmee provide entertainment while you eat: see Around Orlando.

The following restaurants are in downtown Orlando.

Restaurants & Cafés

Mark's Downtown Grill (☎ 872-1947), 68 E Pine St, is a simple, nothing fancy, quick in-and-out kind of place. Sandwiches are $3.75 to 4.50, lunch combos like soup or salad and a half sandwich are $3.75 and burgers run from $3 to 4. They are open Monday to Saturday from 11 am to midnight.

Parky's Deli (☎ 841-9878), 71 E Church St, serves healthy submarine sandwiches for $3.50 to 5; we've heard raves about their Italian cheese steak and Cajun chicken ($4.50). It's open Monday to Thursday from 10.30 am to 6.30 pm, Friday and Saturday till 4 pm.

Dan's Sandwich Shop (☎ 425-8881), 28 S Orange Ave, is breakfast central – for $1.70 you'll get two eggs, potatoes or grits and toast; omelets are $2.20 to 3.35. At lunch, a turkey melt platter with fries and cole slaw is $4.50 and a tuna melt platter with chips and pickles is $3.15. It's open from 7 am to 3 pm Monday to Friday, closed Sunday.

Barnie's Coffee & Tea Company (☎ 894-1416), 118 S Orange Ave, is a chi-chi chain – not as chi-chi as Starbucks but chi-chi nonetheless; they have a wide variety of different flavored coffees and teas, as well as bagels, pastries, Danish pastries and cakes. One of those with coffee is $1.75.

We loved the stuff at the tiny *Champ's French Pastry* (no ☎) at 132 E Central Blvd, where cookies are 50¢, brownies and croissants are $1 and cinnamon rolls $1.35. It's open Sunday to Monday from 7 am to 6 pm, Saturday from noon to 6 pm.

The very friendly folks at *Po' Boy's Creole Cafe* (☎ 839-5852), 50 E Central Blvd, do po' boys – sandwiches pressed in a grill like a Cuban – in six- and 12-inch lengths. They're pretty awesome, and this is a very popular lunch spot. Favorites include blackened chicken $4.25/5.80, veggie $2.50/3.50, crab meat omelet à la Creole $7.45 and eggs Benedict at $5.95.

Just next door to Po' Boy's, also at 50 E Central Ave, is the *Manhattan Bagel Co* (☎ 422-1987), perfect for quick snacks like their pizza bagels ($1.99, pepperoni $2.49). A dozen bagels is $4.99. They're open Monday to Friday from 6.30 am to 4 pm and Saturday and Sunday from 7.30 am to 2 pm.

Sobik's Subs (☎ 425-0164), 55 E Pine St, is a central Florida chain of sandwich places doing excellent healthy and large sandwiches. A chicken parmegian sub is $2.99/3.79, spaghetti with sausage is $2.89 and salads are $2 to 3.50.

Beijing Restaurant (☎ 423-2522), 19 N Orange Ave, is a decent Chinese place with lunch specials served with eggroll and rice, like beef or chicken stir fry for $4.25, veggie specials for $3.75. At dinner, prices for meat, chicken and fish dishes range from $7 to 11, vegetarian from $5 to 7.

Over on N Mills Ave, on the way out to the Leu Gardens, there are three very good Vietnamese restaurants that we highly recommend. We had a terrific meal at *Thanh Thanh Restaurant* (☎ 897-6070), 924 N Mills Ave. We were highly suspicious until the food came out: try the chicken coconut curry at $6.25, vegetable vermicelli at $4.50 and excellent spring rolls and wonton soup for $1.50 each. They do karaoke on some nights as well.

We looked in across the street at *Hong Kong Vietnamese & Chinese Restaurant* (☎ 898-8543), 921 N Mills Ave, which has lunch specials for $3.95 and the same sort of main courses from $4.25 to 6, but the bar seems to do more business than the restaurant and they have a huge karaoke that gets very loud. Still, locals said the food's good.

Little Saigon (☎ 423-8539), around the corner at 1106 E Colonial Drive, came highly recommended, and the service is excellent. They have a lot of items on their menu for $4.50 to 5.50, and daily lunch and dinner specials like shrimp paste on sugar cane, char-broiled beef and spring roll with rice vermicelli for $7.95 – definitely worth a try.

Several thumbs up for *Sushi Hatsu* (☎ 422-1551), 24 W Washington St, a Korean-Japanese (?) place that does excellent kim-chee (garlic and herb spicy marinated cabbage) for $3, great sushi by the piece from $1.75 to 3.50, and blow out lunch ($5 to 7) and dinner ($8 to 15) specials. We had a great meal here.

Nature's Table (☎ 872-7526) is a health-oriented sandwich shop, though it's open only during the week and for lunch, until 3 pm. Their very good and overstuffed tuna sandwiches are $3.89, vegetarian sandwiches $2.99 and taco salad $4.30. It's at 331 N Orange Ave, just north of Robinson St.

Let's Bagel (☎ 425-2972) is a perfectly serviceable bagel joint selling plain bagels for 45¢ or $4.99 for a bakers dozen (13); breakfast sandwiches, salads and pizza are $2 to 6. It's at 345 N Orange Ave between Robinson and Livingston Sts.

Markets

Orlando is one of the great melting pots of Florida, and if you're staying in a hostel, campsite or at a hotel with kitchen facilities you could do worse than stocking up on some interesting imported stuff. All the local Publix and Winn Dixies have expanded international food sections to accommodate the teeming hordes of foreign tourists; you won't find Vegemite, but chances are you will find Marmite and some other foods from Commonwealth countries there. There's a huge 24-hour Publix right across the street from the HI Orlando Resort in Kissimmee.

For more exotic offerings, Orlando has several markets specializing in Asian, English and gourmet foods; many of them also sell prepared foods, deserts and cheeses and cold meats. Some international markets are:

Apna Bazaar (Middle Eastern & Pakistani)
    9432 S Orange Blossom Trail, ☎ 856-0238
Bombay Bazaar (Indian)
    11301 S Orange Blossom Trail, ☎ 856-1780

D&M West Indian & American Grocery
   300 W Church St, ☎ 841-8933
Dong-A (Vietnamese/Asian)
   816 N Mills Ave, ☎ 898-9227
Pence & Pound House (British)
   630 S Maitland Ave, Winter Park,
   ☎ 628-4911
Trung My (Vietnamese)
   720 N Mills Ave, ☎ 894-4241

ENTERTAINMENT

Nightlife in the Orlando area is either described in breathless press releases from the major theme parks saying how great their nightspots are, or grumbles from visitors who say there's nothing to do. They're both wrong: there's a somewhat healthy nightlife scene in and around Orlando, and there is, despite what you'll read elsewhere, more to nightlife than Pleasure Island (see Entertainment in the Disney section) and Church St Station.

See Kissimmee, under Around Orlando, for the most popular of the dinner theater venues.

Church St Station

Highly popular Church St Station (☎ 422-2434) is a collection of bars and nightclubs in some beautifully renovated turn-of-the-century buildings on Church St between Garland Ave and the railroad tracks, just east of I-4. The complex, done up in an Old South/Grand Ole Opry theme takes up both sides of Church St.

On the north side of the street is *Lili Marlene's*, a steak house; *Phineas Fogg's*, a dance club filled with airplanes and balloons that serves really *really* cheap beer on Wednesday from 6.30 to 7.30 pm (5¢ a cup!); and *Rosie O'Grady's* where there are Dixieland bands and can-can girls. On the south side is the *Cheyenne Saloon*, with an enormous grizzly bear at the entrance, live music downstairs, a bar, steak house and barbecue restaurant on the 2nd floor and a pseudo-casino (blackjack, billiards and checkers for fun only). *Crackers* is a seafood restaurant with a beautiful downstairs wine cellar (okay, liquor store) which you can reserve for a private meal (it's really nice down there).

The complex is open from 11 am to 2 am every day; there's no admission price until 6 pm, after which tickets cost $15.95 for adults, $9.95 for children (no one under 21 admitted to Phineas Phogg's), which includes admission to all the shows (there are several a night) and the bars (which are not very cheap) and restaurants (ditto). The first shows start at 7.15 pm. One nice feature is that there's an (unsupervised) playground on the 3rd floor of the north side complex.

Note that while it may seem as fake as Disney, the buildings and especially the railroad are real: if you see the Railroad Crossing warning light up get out of the way or risk being flattened by a mile-long flatbed hauler!

Bars & Pubs

Tanqueray's Bar & Grille (☎ 649-8540), 100 S Orange Ave, has live music Friday and Saturday nights. Happy hour is Monday to Friday from 11 am to 7 pm, and they have lunch specials like chicken and rice with salad and soup for $3.95.

Mulvaney's Irish Pub (☎ 872-3296), 27 W Church St, has Guinness, Murphy's Irish Stout, Newcastle Brown Ale, Samuel Adams and Killian's Red on draft. During happy hour, Monday to Friday from 11 am to 7 pm, drafts are $2. It's open till 2 am.

Jax Fifth Ave (☎ 841-5322), 11 Court Ave, has a very comfy atmosphere, happy hour from 5 to 7 pm Monday to Friday, and food. Sandwiches are $3.75 to 5.75, a vegetable pita is $3.95 and drafts are $2.75 to 4.

Kate O'Brien's Irish Pub & Restaurant (☎ 649-7646), 42 W Central Blvd, has live music on Friday and Saturday from 9.30 pm to 1.30 am, Newcastle Brown Ale, Guinness, Killian's and Samuel Adams on tap, and a buffet at their late afternoon happy hour. Fish and chips are $6.95. There is no cover.

The following seems to be both a restaurant and a bar: *Rookies* (☎ 420-9003) at 17 W Pine St. Happy hour is from 4 to 8 pm with $1 drafts and $5 pitchers. Burgers are $3.95 to 5.95 and the apparently famous corned beef pastrami for $7.95. It is open 11 to 2 am.

Pebbles (☎ 839-0892) has happy hour from 4 to 7 pm. Margaritas, light pints and wine are $2.50 and well drinks are $1 off. It's at 17 W Church St.

Howl at the Moon (☎ 841-4695), 55 W Church St, is a comedy piano bar where everyone we saw was having a great time singing along to kitschy show tunes and dodging the waiters. Get this: bring your own *food*; you must be at least 21 to get in.

The *Sapphire Supper Club* (☎ 246-1419), 54 N Orange Ave, is a supper club with food and music, and sometimes live jazz or alternative music.

Nightclubs & Discos
Nightclub cover charges in Orlando range from $4 to 8. There's usually not much of a wait to get in, and they're certainly not as exclusive as those in Miami Beach or Fort Lauderdale, but they can be fun.

The Edge (☎ 426-9166) at 100 W Livingston St is *still* the most popular disco in town, with lights, smoke, boom-boom-boom and a huge outdoor dance area in the back that is sometimes home to live concerts.

Barbarella (☎ 839-0457) is very crowded on Monday and Thursday nights, which are disco nights; we hear it's great music and dancing, the male/female ratio is about equal and they have large-screen TV with music videos. It's at 68 N Orange Ave.

Zuma Beach (☎ 648-8727) is a meat market of epic proportions at 46 N Orange Ave. *Renaissance* (☎ 422-3595), 22 S Magnolia Ave, was a brand new disco when we visited, but we heard very good things about it from locals.

Gay & Lesbian
It's not Miami, but hey, at least there's something: the *Cactus Club* (☎ 894-3041) is a preppie hangout at 1300 N Mills Ave; *Southern Nights* (☎ 898-0424) attracts more of a mixed crowd at 375 Bennett Rd, just north of the Orlando Executive Airport.

The *Club at Firestone* (☎ 426-0005), 578 N Orange Ave, corner of Concord (also known as *Freakstone*), is mainly gay except on Thursdays. Sunday is reggae night – it's said to be a very wild crowd throughout the week.

More respectable than it should be given its location is *Uncle Walt's Backstage* (☎ 351-4866) at 5454 International Drive very close to Disney. Conversation bar with entertainment runs from Tuesday to Saturday; it's mixed men and women.

Parliament House (☎ 425-7571), 410 N Orange Blossom Trail, is actually a motel with a bunch of cruisey, sceney bars including Western, piano and poolside bars. There are drag shows and other live entertainment. Next door at No 500 is a leather/Levi's place called the *Full Moon Saloon* (☎ 648-8725).

There are two lesbian places we found: *Faces* (☎ 291-7571) at 4910 Edgewater Drive, north of downtown and on the west side of I-4; and *Ladies* (☎ 678 3043) at 7124 Aloma Ave in Winter Park. Ladies is in a room at the Phoenix Club, another gay men's bar, on Wednesday, Thursday and Saturday nights only.

Performing Arts
The two major performing arts centers in town are the *Carr Performing Arts Centre* (☎ 849-2020) at 401 W Livingston St, and the *Civic Theater of Central Florida* (☎ 896-7365) at 1001 E Princeton St, both of which are host to performances of opera, classical music and theater.

The *SAK Theater Company* (☎ 648-0001) is a comedy/improvisation group that's been around for about five years, and despite signs promising otherwise, there's no sushi available anywhere in the building. It's always full on weekends, so you'll have to make reservations. Tickets are $11, and during the week there is a discount for Florida residents, students, military and seniors, who pay $6. On weekends, Florida residents pay $9 and students, military and seniors $7. The theater is in the corner building at 45 E Church St.

Q-ZAR
More aggressive travelers might enjoy Q-ZAR (☎ 839-0002), a laser tag game in which you charge like a lunatic through various rooms shooting at opponents with a laser-pistol and trying to 'capture' their 'base'. One game is $7, three are $18. You

can get hit four times before you're 'out'; games last for 15 minutes or until everyone's dead. Hmmm. It's at 1010 S Orange Ave.

SPECTATOR SPORTS

The biggest news in town is the NBA Orlando Magic (☎ 896-2442), which plays home games at the Orlando Arena. In 1995-96, despite the injuries of their super-star Shaquille O'Neal, the Magic set a franchise record of 60 wins, and made it all the way to the Eastern Conference Finals before being defeated by Chicago. Though O'Neal is no longer playing here, the Magic is still the most popular team in the state. The Arena (also called the 'O-rena') is at 1 Magic Place (600 W Amelia Ave – take I-4 to the Amelia Ave exit).

THINGS TO BUY

All of the theme parks and museums have gift shops; the theme parks each have several (Disney has its own full-scale shopping mall in the Disney Village Marketplace), and there's no way you can miss them. And Orlando International Airport, in addition to its airporty duties, manages to be one of the city's biggest shopping malls as well: dozens of shops cater to last-minute souvenir purchases (the prices aren't bad at all), and there's a bitchin' video arcade to keep the kids happy.

The area has several very popular shopping malls; downtown at Church St Station is Church St Exchange (☎ 422-2434) at 124 W Pine St. I-Drive is home to two major malls; at the southern end is the Mercade Mediterranean Village (☎ 345-9337) at No 8445, and at the north the enormous Belz Factory Outlet Stores (☎ 352-7110) at No 4949 is so large it takes up football-field-sized buildings on both sides of the street. Out by Disney, the Crossroads Mall of Lake Buena Vista (☎ 827-7300) at 8510 Palm Parkway is a smaller affair than the others, but at night it's great fun to see the younger Disney staffers tearing loose and tossing back shot after shot at the Baja Beach Club there (the mall is very close to Disney staff housing).

GETTING THERE & AWAY

Air

Orlando International Airport (☎ 825-2001), in the far southeastern corner of the city, is the largest in central Florida. It's also one of the few airports outside Kentucky and Virginia to still permit smoking in designated areas.

It's served by almost all major airlines, as well as charters and discount airlines. There are more packages available to Orlando than to any other Florida city, as cross-marketing plans with the theme parks and hotels and various airlines lower prices.

It is almost always cheaper to fly here as part of a package; see the Getting There & Away chapter for more information on charters, travel agents, packages and discount airlines.

Typical one-way fares to/from other Florida cities are: Miami $39, Tampa $50, Jacksonville $80 and Pensacola $170.

Bus

The Greyhound station (☎ 292-3424) is at 555 N John Young Parkway (Hwy 423). Routes to/from other cities are listed below (there are between six and ten daily for each destination. Prices listed are one way/roundtrip.

Destination	Price	Duration
Miami	$35/69	5½ to 11 hours
Jacksonville	$26/52	2½ to 4¼ hours
Tampa	$18/36	1¾ to 3 hours
Gainesville	$22/44	2½ to 3½ hours
Tallahassee	$37/73	4½ to 8½ hours

Train

Amtrak (☎ 800-872-7245) has service to Orlando on the *SilverMeteor* and *SilverStar* trains, which run between New York City and Orlando. Travel time from New York to Orlando is 22 hours. The terminal (☎ 843-7611) is at 1400 Sligh Blvd about one mile south of the center of the city, three blocks west of Orange Ave. *Sunset Limited* runs between Los Angeles and Miami via Orlando. Fares depend on a wide variety of variables including day, month, passengers, whether you take a car or not, seating or cabins and for all we know how many socks the president of Amtrak has in the dryer when you call. See the Getting There & Away chapter for more Amtrak information and for a better idea of their complex pricing system.

Car

I-4 runs right through Orlando, and connects with Tampa to the southwest and near Daytona at the northeast. To/from anywhere north of Daytona on the East Coast and anywhere on the southwest coast I-4 is the best bet. From Miami, the fastest and most direct route available is on Florida's Turnpike (toll) right into Orlando. It's about a 4½-hour drive. To avoid the tolls at the cost of about an hour, take I-95 to Hwy 50 south of Titusville and go west to Winter Park and south to Orlando. You can also take I-95 to Hwy 528, the Bee Line Expressway, which speeds things up but involves another few bucks in toll. From the northwest, take I-75 south to Florida's Turnpike.

GETTING AROUND
To/From the Airport

There's bus service between the airport and the downtown Lynx Bus Center. During the week, bus No 11 picks up at the first level of the airport in terminal A, at 10 minutes after and 40 after the hour, beginning at 5.40 am and running through 7.40 pm; after that it's hourly between 8.40 and 11.40 pm. From the Lynx Bus Center to the airport, buses start running at 4.45 am at quarter after the hour and quarter to the hour until 6.45 pm, then hourly from 7.45 till 10.45 pm. Weekend service is slightly reduced. The fare is 75¢.

Bus

Orlando is blessed with a highly efficient and inexpensive public transportation system. The Lynx System (☎ 841-8240, TDD 423-0787) operates 47 numbered routes, a 'FreeBee Downtown Circuit' and the Laser Shuttle connecting the University of Central Florida to routes 13 and 32, which leave from the Lynx Bus Center.

Fares are 75¢ per ride, 25¢ for students

and seniors; a 10-ride pass is $7, a 20-ride pass is $12 and an unlimited monthly pass is $30. Bus stops are marked with a sign bearing a Lynx paw-print of sorts along with the number of the route/s that stop there.

Getting to/from downtown Orlando will bring you through the highly efficient **Lynx Bus Center**, in the alley between W Pine St and W Central Blvd one block east of Orange Ave. You can buy tickets and monthly passes and get system maps and specific route information from the information booth, which is open Monday to Friday from 6.30 am to 8.15 pm, Saturday from 7.30 am to 6.15 pm and Sunday from 8 am to 4.15 pm. You can also use the Lynx System to get to Winter Park (Nos 1 and 9, hourly), Kissimmee (Nos 4 and 18, hourly) and Walt Disney World (No 50, every two hours), though it's a long, long ride from the bus center.

Shuttle & Limo Services

The biggest in the area is Mears Transportation (☎ 423-5566), which does shuttle vans between most major hotels, the youth hostels, campsites and the major theme parks. Expect to pay between $8 and 12 roundtrip for shuttle service unless your hotel or hostel has a special deal – many do.

Taxi

Fares are $2.45 flagfall plus $1.45 for each additional mile. You need to call (as opposed to hailing on the street) a taxi. Some major taxi services include Ace Metro Cab Co (☎ 855-1111), City Cab (☎ 422-5151) and Checker & Yellow Cab Co (☎ 699-9999).

Car

The major rental car companies all have offices in and around Orlando, and at the airports. Several have desks at I-Drive hotels as well. See the Getting Around chapter for the 800 numbers of the big companies.

Downtown Orlando has an infuriating one-way system which would seem to have been taken right out of either Kafka or Boston. Much of the eastern end of Church St is pedestrian only, that which isn't

CENTRAL

mainly runs east only. Avoid the traffic circle around Lucerne Park to the south of Anderson St, where the southern area of downtown is crossed by the East-West Expressway; if you're not careful you can go several times around Lake Lucerne before you get way over to the right and back into downtown.

Parking All of downtown is controlled by highly accurate digital parking meters, with highly accurate and seemingly digital parking enforcement personnel waiting to pounce with $10 tickets at the first second after meter expiration.

Parking for Church St Station is in the large public lot beneath I-4. Here a central meter system is in use. Remember your spot number and find the nearest central meter (a big yellow machine under a green umbrella). On the touch tone key pad, enter your spot number, insert 75¢ per hour, then push the big button to the right for a receipt. Cops patrol constantly, and possess an evil secret code which tells the central meter to tattle on scofflaws.

The City Parking Bureau (☎ 246-2154) also runs Central Blvd Garage at 53 W Central Blvd between Orange and Garland Aves; Library Garage at 112 E Central Blvd, opposite the Orlando Public Library; and Market Garage at W Pine St, east of Church St Exchange (see Things to Buy, above); open 24 hours. Much more expensive private lots are also easily found.

AROUND ORLANDO
Winter Park
This pleasant college town just north of Orlando is a lovely place for a stroll or a boat ride (free on your birthday!), a cappuccino and some gallery and museum hopping. Park Ave is the main drag here, where you'll find lots of cafés and trendy shops – for some reason, it reminded us of a mix of Miami Beach and Palm Beach – fashionable yet accessible, chic but still not too expensive.

Get tourist information at the Winter Park Chamber of Commerce (☎ 644-8281) at 150 N New York Ave.

Cornell Fine Arts Museum This is a very respected museum (☎ 646-2526) and there is no charge to see their exhibits. Unfortunately, when we visited hardly any of their permanent collection was on display – though we did see the *Steel Quilt* and *Ancient Games* by Doris Leeper. There are different shows each summer, usually containing 60 to 70 pieces of their permanent collection, and usually a gallery devoted to the permanent collection as well as traveling exhibitions (mostly by Florida artists) in winter. Admission is free, and the museum is at 1000 Holt Ave, on the Rollins College campus.

Charles Hosmer Morse Museum of American Art This very pleasant and beautiful museum (☎ 645-5311), has a large Tiffany glass exhibit; we loved the exquisite *Magnolia Window* made from drapery glass (which is heated and then folded to give it a three-dimensional look) and the *Butterfly Window*, which was made for Tiffany's New York house. Also on view are paintings and designs by Tiffany; late-19th- and 20th-century paintings and American art pottery. The objects on display vary. The museum is at 445 Park Ave N; admission is $2.50 for adults, $1 for children and students.

Albin Polasek Galleries The works of the Czech sculptor Albin Polasek are shown here (☎ 674-6294) in the serene lakeside gardens and interior of his last residence, at 633 Osceola Ave. As you enter the front garden you'll see the very impressive *Man Carving His Own Destiny* or *The Sower*; inside the house is a showcase with Polasek's sculpting tools, and our favorite of his works, *Mother Crying Over World*. Enthusiastic and friendly volunteers will tell you more about the sculptor's life and works. Admission is free, the museum is open on Sunday from 1 to 4 pm and Wednesday to Saturday from 10 am to noon and 1 to 4 pm.

Arts Mall This is a 172,000-sq-foot studio space (☎ 647-3199) available to about 50 artists who hold rotating exhibits and shows.

Fiction & Folklore: Zora Neale Hurston

Zora Neale Hurston (1901-60) was born in Eatonville, the first black incorporated town in the US, about five miles from Orlando. Her family broke apart when she was young, and she supported herself from the age of 14, working odd jobs and finding her way in 1919 to Howard University in Washington, DC, an all-black institution. Following a sporadic education, she moved to Harlem, the cultural capital of black America, in 1925. She distinguished herself quickly as one of the bright young literary voices – along with poet Langston Hughes and others – in what came to be known as the Harlem Renaissance, a movement of celebration of the African American experience, and a flowering of black creative and intellectual achievement.

Hurston came from a background of storytelling. As a child she'd listened to the men gathered on the porch of Joe Clark's store tell their 'big ol lies' to entertain one another. Up in Harlem such storytelling made her the life of every party, and it also led her into the anthropology department of Barnard College, where she came into contact with Franz Boas, the father of modern American anthropology, and discovered the study of folklore.

Under Boas' guidance, Zora won a research fellowship from Columbia University, and she headed back to Florida to record the songs, tales, superstitions, games and traditions she'd grown up with. Throughout her travels, from Florida to New Orleans and eventually into the rich culture of the Caribbean, Eatonville was to remain at the center of her work, both folklore and fiction. Through her wild adventures – in the interest of folklore she posed as a runaway bootlegger's moll, lived in the shanty towns of migrant turpentine workers, and was poisoned nearly to death by a voodoo witch doctor in Haiti – it is Eatonville and the porch of Joe Clark's store that appear again and again.

Mules and Men was published in 1935, and is considered by many the greatest work on black American folklore ever written. In Southern vernacular it recounts tales of conjure men and hoodoo cures; Ol Massa and his favorite slave, John; Brer Rabbit and Brer Gator (like Disney has never seen them); and more. Before Hurston, white folklorists had portrayed blacks culture as the product of childish, silly and unsophisticated minds. Hurston instead revealed its wit, humor, imagination and complexity.

Her famous novel, *Their Eyes Were Watching God* was published in 1937. It is one of the earliest black feminist novels, telling the story of Janie Crawford, an independent black woman who loved who and how she wanted. The book was savaged by contemporaries like Richard Wright, author of *Black Boy* and *Native Son*, because it did not address race relations and black oppression, but rather black community and black folk.

Hurston died in a welfare home in 1960 and was buried in an unmarked grave in the Garden of Heavenly Rest, in Fort Pierce. In the '70s a few dedicated black writers and scholars began the 'Hurston Renaissance', her seven books were reissued, and Alice Walker made a pilgrimage to Fort Pierce in 1973 to place a memorial stone on her grave. It reads:

Zora Neale Hurston
'A Genius of the South'
Novelist/Folklorist/Anthropologist
1901-1960 ■

There are also ballet and theater performances here, and they offer classes and workshops for adults and children on lyrics, theater, etc. It's at 500 N Orlando Ave.

Scenic Boat Tour Hour-long tours (☎ 644-5056) through 12 miles of the canals and lakes of the area leave from the eastern end of Morse Blvd. Among other things you'll pass by Rollins College, its Azalea Gardens, the small 'Isle of Sicily', the Polasek Gallery and see the local mansions and many birds. They leave every hour on the hour between 10 am and 4 pm daily, except Christmas. Admission is $5.50 for adults, $2.75 for children aged two to 11. On your birthday you get to ride free, they also do canoe and rowboat rentals for $5 per hour, each additional hour is $1.

Getting There & Away It's a snap to get from the Lynx Bus Center to Winter Park; bus Nos 1 and 9 make the trip hourly. By car, head north on I-4 to exit 46, go west on Lee Rd and you'll hit downtown Winter Park.

Kissimmee

The area around Kissimmee (kih-SIH-mee) was once a peaceful landscape of swamps and green, but the extraordinary growth of theme parks has had a profound effect on the surroundings. Kissimmee's main strip, Hwy 192 (called Irlo Bronson Memorial Hwy and Vine Ave), is a horror of strip development; a soul-depressing, sprawling ribbon of endless concrete, motels, shopping malls, fast-food and chain restaurants, wanna-be attractions, theme restaurants, murderous traffic, blazing neon, tourist traps, oil-change joints and discount ticket stands of dubious reliability. It is also the area's cheapest place to put your head down on a pillow for the night.

There are, of course, some attractions, and HI opened its HI Orlando Resort here in 1995. For tourist information, contact the Kissimmee/St Cloud Convention & Visitors Bureau (☎ 847-5000, 800-327-9159) at 1925 W Hwy 192.

Splendid China This theme park (☎ 396-7111, 800-244-6226) does a tremendous job of simulating China's sights (in miniature form) down to the smallest detail: in fact, crowds are thick and jostle you, staff (when we visited) barely spoke English, were recalcitrant, heavily bureaucratic, loathe to part with specific details and generally uncooperative . . . almost exactly like being in Beijing without the spitting!

That said, it's a very interesting park with exquisite attention to detail, glorious landscaping (butterflies were everywhere when we visited) and if you follow the guides religiously you'll probably learn a lot about Chinese history. Exhibits are replicas of famous Chinese sights, like the Stone Forest, Great Wall, Temple of Confucius, Summer Palace, Imperial Palace/Forbidden City, and Dr Sun Yat Sen's Mausoleum.

We were fascinated by the **Terra Cotta Warriors** display, a replica of the tomb that Emperor Qinshijuang had built in order to have all his concubines, thousands of soldiers, his horses and vehicles buried with him (the original tomb was discovered in 1974).

To get information and background on a particular site, push the little button on the green box located at each site or simply read the sign (they are identical). There's a free tram that circles the park, hitting most sites, and guided tours ($5), which leave from Guest Services.

All kinds of performances (magicians, jugglers etc) are held at different locations throughout the park; schedules are available at the ticket window. There are five restaurants within the park serving various regional Chinese dishes.

Admission here is $22 for adults, $13 for children aged five to 12. They are at 3000 Splendid China Blvd, just off Hwy 192 west of I-4.

A World of Orchids A lush display of hundreds of varieties of orchids in an indoor tropical jungle, A World of Orchids (☎ 396-1887, 396-1881) is at 2501 Old Lake Wilson Rd.

The effect of walking from the stark,

concrete entry area through the giant metal doors that lead to the gardens is a lot like walking into Star Trek's Holodeck: you're suddenly immersed in a glorious land of windmill and areca palms, a beautiful fern called Florida ruffles; pineapple ginger and spider lilies.

The huge (and fat) goldfish in their pond are so used to being fed that if you hold your hand out over the water they'll scramble for food – whether you drop any or not.

Among the orchids on display you'll find the *Dendrobium*, *Phalaenopsis*, *Vanda* and *Onicidium*; we found the back right quadrant to be most fragrant when we visited. Most of the plants you see here can be bought as well. They say they're opening an outside walking trail in the near future. Admission is $8.95 per person, ages 16 and under are free; $7.95 for AAA members and seniors. Guided tours are available Monday to Friday 11 am and 3 pm and Saturday and Sunday 11 am and 1 and 3 pm.

Green Meadows Petting Farm This is a pretty cool place for kids, a sort of working farm/petting zoo (☎ 846-0770). Kids get to run amok touching and petting cows, goats, donkeys, geese, ducks and chickens; ride on horses and, if you take the tour, milk a cow! The cost is a little stiff at $13 per person, but Florida residents get a $2 discount and children under two are free.

Tours leave regularly between 9.30 am and 4 pm. You can bring a picnic and hang out amongst the creatures on the farm grounds. It's on Poinciana Blvd (there's no street address), about five miles south of Hwy 192.

Flying Tigers Warbird Air Museum This is a must for WWII nostalgia buffs: a museum (☎ 933-1942) that displays warbirds – WWII fighter planes – in various stages of restoration. Workers can take up to several years per plane, and some of the finished products can be seen for a fleeting period before they fly away to join air shows and air tour company fleets. The museum is at 231 N Hoagland Blvd, in Hangar No 5 at Kissimmee Regional Air-

port. From the HI Orlando Resort, go east on W Hwy 192 to the second light after Medieval Times dinner theater, turn right and the entrance to the airport is about three quarters of a mile down on the left hand side of the road. It's open Monday to Saturday from 9 am to 5.30 pm, Sunday from 9 am to 5 pm.

Places to Stay – camping The KOA Kissimmee campground (☎ 396-2400, 800-331-1453), 4771 W Hwy 192 just east of I-4, has tent sites for $17.95 and RV sites with full hookups for $28.95 and 29.95 respectively. There are weekly rates as well, depending on the season.

Yogi-Bear's Jellystone Park Camp Resort (☎ 800-776-9644) also has a Kissimmee location at 8555 W Hwy 192, very close to the HI Orlando Resort. Tent sites are $18 year round, sites with water and electricity are $23 in low season, $29 in high season, and full hook-up sites are $25/31. Weekly and monthly deals are available at both. It's possible that this campsite will have been sold out when you visit, so call in advance.

Places to Stay – hostels We stayed at the *HI Orlando Resort* (☎ 396-8282, reservations 800-444-6111, see the Online Services appendix), at 4840 W Hwy 192, twice and had fun both times. It looks more like a motel than a hostel, but there's a large common area and kitchen, a small swimming pool and a lake out back (though no swimming in the lake is allowed).

Rooms (dorms and motel-style private rooms, some with kitchenettes) are clean and comfortable, and there are activities like weekly barbecues, swamp walks, trips to spring-training baseball games and activities in the common room like Scrabble and Jinga.

We have heard complaints from travelers on two matters: that it's inconvenient without a car, and that it can cost more than a motel. It's not reachable by public transport, but only by private shuttle – the shuttle to Disney is $6.80 roundtrip per person. Other shuttle options include Orlando Airport ($12); Universal Studios,

CENTRAL

Wet 'n' Wild and Sea World ($8.50); Amtrak Orlando ($2, daily at 6.25 pm); and Greyhound Orlando ($2, daily at 6.20 pm).

To the matter of cost, we say this: you *can* find motels that will be cheaper than two dorm beds here (just, but it's possible). The hostel's advantages are that you know that the rooms are going to meet higher standards of cleanliness than the murderously cheap motels, the common area and activities offer a chance to meet up with other travelers and for women traveling alone it's the best option in town.

Dorm beds cost $13 for HI members, $16 for non-members; private rooms run: single (one to two people) $27/33, double (two to four) $30/36 and family (with kitchenette) $38/47.

Places to Stay – motels & hotels We went into dozens and dozens of the over 100 motels along Hwy 192, and found that with few exceptions they were identical: brownish carpets, reasonable cleanliness, reasonably friendly service, slightly run-down but perfectly acceptable rooms with cable TV.

Rates tend to stay very low: typically, the cheaper motels run from about $20/25 single/double most of the year, with bursts (they call them 'high season') during school holidays, when you should expect about a $15 to 20 increase. And at Christmas time the average double on the strip is between $44 and 50.

Of the cookie-cutter standard motels and hotels along the W Hwy 192 strip, these are as good at these as any:

The cleaner-than-average *Sun Motel* (☎ 396-2673), at No 5020, is a cool deal with singles/doubles at $19/24 for most of the year. Also cleaner than most, the *Park Inn International* (☎ 396-1376, 800-327-0072), No 4960, has doubles including breakfast for $25 in low season, $59 in high season (in high season AAA members pay $45).

The totally average *Key Motel* (☎ 396-6200), No 4810, has singles/doubles for $19/22 in low season, $30/45 in high season, and they boast that 'cold beer is available here'.

We liked the friendly service and cleanliness at the *Casa Rosa Motel* (☎ 396-2020, 800-432-0665), No 4600. In fall and spring, singles are $20, doubles $25, during the 'mid-season' – summer – it's $27/40, and on New Year's Eve all rooms are a whopping $79. It's at W Hwy 192.

The *Golden Link Motel* (☎ 396-0555) is an okay option at the junction of Hwy 535; doubles are $25 in low season, $39 in high season, higher at Christmas (around $44 to 50).

Right next to the HI Orlando Resort at No 4880, is the predictable *Super 8 Motel* (☎ 396-1144) with rooms including breakfast and HBO, for $26. Other little cheap motel chains along the strip are *Econo-Lodge* (☎ 396-4343, 800-228-2027) at No 4985, with singles or doubles $29, $25 for AAA members; and the *Ramada Limited* (☎ 424-2621) at No 9200 with singles/doubles for $22/24.

Buena Vista Motel (☎ 396-2100) at No 5200, is a motel with an attached cheesey liquor store, doubles are $26 (extra person $4).

The *Residence Inn by Marriott* (☎ 396-2056, 800-228-9290) at No 4786 is a very nice family-oriented place with more expensive but absolutely superior rooms and suites. Prices here *are* negotiable, despite appearances: in high season they list $99 for a studio (a suite with a queen-sized bed and fold-out couch) and $149 for their deluxe penthouses, but when we visited we were offered as low as $79 and $129 for the same rooms.

Places to Eat – restaurants Hwy 192 is lined with every conceivable fast food and upscale fast food place imaginable, including Red Lobster, Outback Steakhouse, Shoney's, KFC, McDonald's, Denny's, etc.

Taco Cabana (☎ 846-1633), 910 W Hwy 192, serves beans and cheese for 89¢ for breakfast, also bacon and eggs for 99¢ or a full breakfast for $2.99. Lots of combination plates are $3.50, the half-chicken platter with rice, beans, flour tortillas and lime is $5.29, a pitcher of frozen margaritas $7.99 and three tacos and a soft drink (Taco Taxi) $3.33.

The *Puerto Rico Café* (☎ 897-6399), 507 W Hwy 192, has meat dishes for $5 to 9 and seafood dishes for $10 to 15.

Havana's Cafe (☎ 846-6771) is at 3628 W Hwy 192. Lunch specials are $5 to 6, pepper steak $6.99, chicken filet skillet $8.95 and seafood dishes $12.95.

There's good French-influenced Thai food at *Basil's Restaurant* (☎ 846-1116), 1009 W Hwy 192, where appetizers range from $4.50 to 8, and main courses like lime-grilled chicken with honey butter are $9.95; others go up to about $15.

Places to Eat – dinner shows For some reason, Kissimmee is dinner theater central, with three major offerings for those who like to watch, say, jousting while dining. The prices listed below are at the door, undiscounted – *always* check in tourist rags and handout coupon books for discount tickets, which you'll always find and which could be significant.

Medieval Times (☎ 396-1518, 800-327-4024) offers 'dinner and tournament' – mainly jousting and sword fighting (this is appetizing?) – and a dinner of chicken and ribs, soup, a cocktail and two rounds of beer, wine or soda. The cost is $34.95 for adults, $22.95 for kids. Shows begin at 8 pm and last two hours. It's at 4510 W Hwy 192.

The gaudy neon at *Arabian Nights* (☎ 239-9223, 800-553-6116) promises a slew of performing horses, chariot races, etc. The two-hour dinner shows begin at 7.30 pm and dinner includes prime rib *or* veggie lasagna, salad, potatoes and lots of vegetables, dessert and unlimited Budweiser beer (this is appetizing?), soft drinks or wine. It's $36.95 for adults, $23.95 for children and is at 6225 W Hwy 192, just east of I-4.

Capone's Dinner & Show (☎ 397-2378) is certainly the funniest – a 'cabaret and speakeasy' set in Prohibition-era Chicago (though half the cast seems to have Long Island, New York, accents). The show is a gangland revue – 'mobsters, dames in hootchie kootchie outifts' – you get the drift. There's an unlimited buffet including lasagna, ziti, sausage and peppers, chicken,

ham, veggies and dessert. It's $29.50 for adults, $14.75 for kids including unlimited soft drinks and unlimited beer, sangria and rum runners. The two-hour shows start at 7.30 pm; it's at 4740 W Hwy 192, a mile east of Hwy 535.

Getting There & Away Kissimmee is about 25 miles southwest of downtown Orlando; you can take bus Nos 4 and 18 from the Lynx Bus Center to Kissimmee. It's about a half-hour drive on I-4 or take the Orange Blossom Trail to Hwy 192 and turn west.

Yeehaw Junction
• *pop about 100* ☎ *407*

There's not much going on at Yeehaw Junction, about 60 miles south of Orlando, but the town has two die-hard tourist attractions that pack 'em in as people make the journey from Miami to Orlando along Florida's Turnpike. One is pretty ho-hum, the Yeehaw Travel Center (☎ 436-1616), a discount ticket outlet that's open Sunday to Thursday from 7 am to 9 pm, Friday and Saturday from 7 am to 10 pm; but the second attraction has charm, character and the dignity of having been placed on the National Register of Historic Places. We speak, of course, of the Desert Inn, one of central Florida's famous bordellos operated to entertain workers on the Florida East Coast Railway and later I-95.

The Desert Inn Motel (☎ 436-1054) has been completely renovated by owner Beverly Zicheck, who has created what is probably Florida's first Bordello Museum. You can even stay here, and though room service isn't what it used to be, the food itself is pretty rockin'. The inn charges $33.30 a night per room, slightly less if you're a truck driver. The museum, in several of the rooms, shows the bedrooms as they looked during the place's heyday from 1889 to 1953, complete with red satin bedspreads, hardwood floors, red-lined swings and saddles. Admission to the museum is $1.

The restaurant downstairs serves up awesome chili and everything there is

CENTRAL

homemade. While people line up for the periodic roast beef dinners (Beverly starts with a 30-pound piece of meat) that cost $6.95 and come with dressing, real mashed potatoes, cole slaw, Texas toast and a vegetable, other more exotic offerings include turtle, gator or frog dinners at $9.95 or a turtle/gator/frog combo at $11.95 and gator burgers for $3.95. At breakfast (they open at 7 am) their special is hash browns with onions topped with bell pepper, ham and eggs for $4.50 and homemade pies, which are served all day ($2.25 for meringue types, $2 for standard apple, peach, cherry and blueberry).

From January 18 to 21 they hold the annual Bluegrass Festival and Chili Cook-off at the Desert Inn; contact Beverly for more information.

Getting There & Away From Florida's Turnpike, take the Yeehaw Junction exit and head west at the traffic light for about a half mile – look for the sign that says 'Desert Inn Good Food Bar' – it's at the intersection of US Hwy 441 and Hwy 60, at 5570 Skenansville Rd.

Walt Disney World

☎ 407

When southern California's Disneyland attraction took off in a huge way, the concept of theme parks changed dramatically and permanently. Disneyland quickly became the world standard for a family-oriented vacation resort, and parks everywhere found themselves scrambling to bring themselves up to the new scratch.

But something that especially caught Walt Disney's attention was that other hotels and concessions had begun building up around his property, in a manner that he (probably rightly) felt was entirely parasitic. So in the mid-1960s, under the *nom de guerre* Reedy Creek Development Company, Walt bought up thousands of acres of land in central Florida, with the revolutionary idea of creating an environment in which he would control every aspect of – and take all profits from – family vacations: Disney hotels, resorts, restaurants, cafes, parks, parking and transport. Disney's land grab was perhaps topped only by its negotiating techniques with the state of Florida, which granted the company, among a lot of other things, the right to self-govern the municipality.

Walt Disney died in 1966 and his brother Roy took over responsibilities for guiding the project through to completion. The park opened in 1971, and in its first year saw over 10 million visitors.

When Disney World celebrated its 25th anniversary in October 1996, the park – and its 35,000 staff members – had hosted over 500 million guests – about 23 million a year or 65,000 per *day*.

That should give you some idea of the staggering size of this operation. It's its own city, complete with an elaborate transportation system (featuring buses, trams, ferries, shuttles and a monorail) that is the envy of many US cities, full-fledged emergency services like a fire department, several medical centers, an efficient and incorruptible police force, an energy plant, a *florist*, and an entire building dedicated to something called 'DOT compliance, RCID Environmental Permitting & Planning, Resort Design and Resort Displays'. There's even a complex tunnel system beneath the Magic Kingdom park with *at least* 27 different entrances, which enables cast members to materialize as if by magic. All this is designed to make the theme park as isolated, self-sufficient and perfectly happy as it can be.

And, of course, to make as much money as possible from visitors, every penny you spend on anything goes to some Disney subsidiary or another. That's not to say it's unfair: it is not. While people can be shocked by the sticker price of a Disney vacation, we will say this: it is good value for the money, a truly family-oriented vacation spot that doesn't neglect the kids *or* the adults (it says a lot that over 1000 couples get married here every year), and a place with a great feeling of fun and safety.

CENTRAL

While there are no bargains to be had, neither are there any rip-offs. Entire departments exist to ensure that you are getting exactly what you pay for. And you do.

If it seems like we're kissing Mouse ass, you're wrong. We calls 'em like we sees 'em, and when we see a trap or something we don't like, we tell you about it. But we do say that if you're thinking about going, you'll probably have a great time. Now if we could just get all these screaming little kids out of here . . . .

There's no way to cover all that Disney has to offer in this kind of format, so what follows is a highlights tour.

WHEN TO GO

As far as accommodations go, the cheapest time of year to go is from the beginning of August to about December 18; it's very expensive around holidays. July and August are hot, as in *Africa hot*: temperatures average in the mid-90°s F, and humidity levels hover at what feels to be 150%. There are frequent downpours. Weather-wise, the best times to come are in the early autumn, but note that closing hours in autumn are earlier than at other times, and certain night events like fireworks and laser shows are seasonal – so if you have your heart set on seeing IllumiNations, check with Disney before going to make sure it will be on when you visit.

For reasons best left to sociologists, weekends tend to be less crowded than the beginning of the week.

WHAT TO BRING

Even when it's raining the temperatures are usually warm, so bring a lightweight rain poncho, comfortable clothing that you don't mind getting wet, a bathing suit, suntan lotion and sunglasses. Carry it all in a backpack compact enough to keep on your lap during rides. Bring a two-liter, solidly resealing bottle of drinking water per person (water refills are free at any Disney restaurant). Though you're not supposed to, we saw that many people brought sandwiches (note that food from outside is not permitted in the parks). You can bring along some mosquito

Not Without Seeing Minnie

Customer satisfaction is the name of the game at Walt Disney World, and the staff has been trained to withstand with a smile onslaughts of abuse that would level mere mortals.

Staff (they're called 'cast members', by the way) are empowered to go to heroic lengths to ensure that a visitor (you're called a 'guest') is happy about everything. This covers things like giving an extra cinnamon roll to the family that's too hot and tired to have any more fun, coordinating searches for missing kids, etc.

During our visit, we watched in amazement as an angry mother told a cast member that she'd come all the way down from New York City and her daughter hadn't seen Minnie Mouse once. There was no way, by god, that she was leaving before her daughter saw Minnie.

The cast member found out that there were no Minnies around (there are, of course, several), and after looking at the guest again and seeing the determination in her eyes, the cast member went ahead and called a Character Zoo (there are, of course, several) and arranged for a Minnie to get into costume and haul her tail out there pronto.

It's something we don't recommend you try at home: produce a French university student in an air-conditioned Muppet-fur suit in less than an hour. From angry start to Waving Minnie/Smiling Kid/Satisfied Mom finish, this transaction took seven minutes and 40 seconds.

That's cast dedication and a finely honed machine.

Have a nice day. ∎

repellent, but the grounds are sprayed and mosquitoes are generally not a problem – even in Fort Wilderness Campground, though there we'd play it safe. Speaking of spraying, a former Disney employee suggests bringing a spritzer bottle to shoot at the kids when it gets too hot in line.

ORIENTATION

Walt Disney World is on a formerly marshy area north of Hwy 192, roughly west of I-4

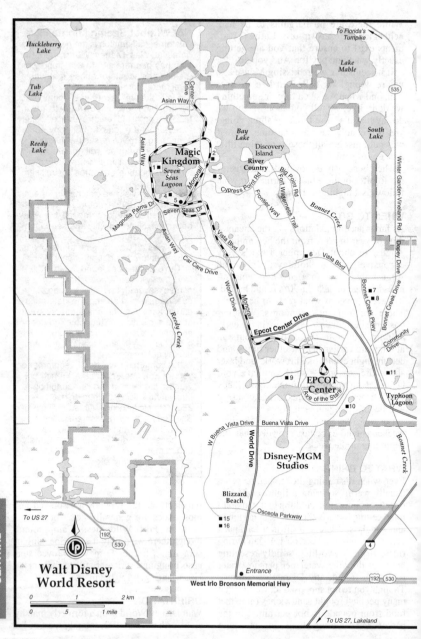

CENTRAL

Walt Disney World Resort

0   1   2 km

0   .5   1 mile

PLACES TO STAY
1 Disney's Grand Floridian Beach Resort
2 Disney's Contemporary Resort
3 Disney's Wilderness Lodge
4 Disney's Polynesian Resort
6 Fort Wilderness Resort & Campground
7 Disney's Dixie Landings Resort
8 Disney's Port Orleans Resort
9 Disney's Beach Club Resort
10 Disney's Caribbean Beach Resort
11 Disney's Vacation Club Resort
12 Disney's Village Resort
15 Disney's All-Star Music Resort
16 Disney's All-Star Sports Resort

OTHER
5 Tickets & Transportation Center
13 Pleasure Island
14 Disney Village Marketplace

and skirted on its east and some of the north by Hwy 535. It's about 20 miles southwest of the City of Orlando, and about four miles northwest of Kissimmee.

There are three main parks: Magic Kingdom Park, EPCOT Center and Disney-MGM Studios Theme Park; two main water parks: Blizzard Beach and Typhoon Lagoon; and several resorts and areas for other activities, like Disney Village Marketplace and Disney's All Star Sports and Music Resorts.

Magic Kingdom is the northernmost park. The main Ticket & Transportation Center (TTC) is off of Seven Seas Drive, as are the main bus station and parking lots for Magic Kingdom Park.

EPCOT Center is practically in the center of the Disney property, and very close to Disney-MGM Studios Theme Park to the southwest. In fact, you can see one park from the other in some areas, a fact which Disney staff tries to disguise with tricky paintwork. For example, the rear section of the Tower of Terror's Hollywood Hotel is painted with the background of a Moroccan palace because it can be seen from EPCOT's Morocco Pavilion.

Disney's answer to Orlando's Church St Station ('We have information that people are drinking elsewhere, sir') has the vaguely lewd name of Pleasure Island, and is at the eastern end of the property, just west of I-4.

Maps

The best handout map is the somewhat difficult-to-find *Walt Disney World Resort Map*, which has an overview of the park, breakdown maps of the three main parks, and a useful transportation network chart showing services between parks and resorts. In any event, you'll get free handout maps of each particular park, which are useful enough for navigating (there are signs everywhere, anyway). The idea is to make the place seem huge and magical, so don't let it upset you. Transportation maps are available at the TTC.

INFORMATION

Getting information about Disney is one

CENTRAL

area where we feel that things could be a little easier – or cheaper: Disney does not even have a toll-free information or reservations telephone number. But unless you're actually staying at a Disney resort – and you don't have to – you really don't have to call Disney for much beforehand, anyway.

For reservations at Disney resorts, information on a slew of Disney-related information, or for prices and hours call ☎ 934-7639 (that spells WDISNEY) weekdays from 8 am to 10 pm, and Saturday and Sunday from 8 am to 6 pm. There's a TDD number for hearing impaired guests as well at ☎ 939-7670. US military personnel and their families (who are given discounted admissions and hotel lodgings) should call Disney's Shades of Green Resort (☎ 824-3600) for information.

This thing about the no toll-free number can be annoying. At peak times, you can expect a wait of about five to 10 minutes just to get to speak to an operator, and then another 10 to 15 minutes on the phone discussing options and making the reserva-

tion. The best time to call is early in the morning, as close to 8 am as possible. If you have been on hold for a while, there's an option that allows you to enter your phone number and have Disney call you back. They promise to do so within two days; if you haven't heard from them by then, call back. Operators are, of course, preternaturally friendly.

For other information, call the main Disney operator at ☎ 824-4321. By mail, send requests for brochures or other information to Walt Disney Guest Communications, PO Box 10,000, Lake Buena Vista, FL 32830-1000.

See the Online Services appendix for Disney's official and unofficial websites.

Books

That there are several guides to Walt Disney World gives you some idea of its sheer size and draw. The importance of planning your daily itinerary within the parks is that it allows you to maximize time spent on rides as opposed to walking through the parks, getting sidetracked by shows and parades, 'ooh! they're selling cinnamon rolls', and other obstacles.

The most complete book to the resort is probably Birnbaum's *Walt Disney World*, which is billed as Disney's Official Guide – it's accurate to the point that Walt Disney public relations quoted it to answer several of our queries. With the exception of the binding, though, we preferred *Walt Disney World Made Simple* (see below) for general information. But when it comes to accommodation information, restaurant descriptions and pre-trip planning, the most up to date and complete information is definitely in Birnbaum's.

A zealously pro-Disney college student who's been to Disney at least eight times, Todd D McCartney began compiling his self-published *Walt Disney World Made Simple* guidebook for some friends in England. Released initially only on the internet, McCartney's book has now sold several thousand copies in print ($6.95) and should do very well indeed: it's good, and contains totally independent advice, though

Gay Day at Disney

Gay Day started in the early 1990s when a notice in a local gay computer bulletin board service saying, 'Hey, if you're into Disney let's show up.' Disney eventually put up disclaimers saying it was not an official event, but over the years it has grown into one of its biggest money-making days, and Disney (whose recent record of fair treatment to gays and lesbians has been exemplary, going so far as to extend its health-care benefits to same-sex partners of its employees) now not only tolerates but assists in planning of the event. It's still not an official Disney event, but in 1996 an estimated 40,000 gay and lesbian visitors descended on Cinderella's Castle on what is now a gay Florida tradition: Gay Day at Disney, the first weekend in June. For more information, get in touch with any gay travel agent, or Good Times Tours at ☎ 305-864-9431, or check out the Gay Day website (see the Online Services appendix). ■

we think he gushes a wee bit sometimes. It's available from McCartney by mail or e-mail (see the Online Services appendix); write to him at 18 Caroll Drive, Somerville, NJ 08876.

Post & Communications

There are mailboxes in all the Disney parks, and in all the hotels. Note that mail sent from here will be postmarked Lake Buena Vista, FL, and not Walt Disney World.

Within the Disney property, you can dial ☎ *88 for reservations at Disney restaurants or resorts.

Money

There are cash machines in every park. You can change money at the Sun Bank in every park, from 9 am to 4 pm, and at Guest Relations after 4 pm, but we recommend bringing US money as exchange rates are generally poor. All Disney concessions accept travellers cheques, American Express cards and Visa and MasterCard (but not Discover) credit cards.

The Disney Dollar (D$) is a coupon on a 1:1 exchange rate with the US dollar. Mickey is on the D$1, Goofy on the D$5 and Minnie on the D$10. While normal American money can be used anywhere in Disney, the powers that be would rather you use Disney Dollars, which are as good as cash in all Disney parks and concessions, and at Disney stores around the USA. The reason for this is obvious: how many people spend every Disney Dollar they exchange? The answer, of course, is none, and Disney pockets the difference (if you've ever traveled overseas, didn't you come home with a pocketful of foreign change and a couple of banknotes?). If you think they make a nice souvenir, you can buy Disney Dollars at various places around the park.

Admissions

Disney traditionally raises its prices every year, so these will probably be a little low when you go. It's best to buy your tickets before you get to the park – at a Disney

> ### Buy Tickets Early
> With the exception of one-day passes, which must be bought at the gate, it's always a better idea to buy tickets as far in advance as possible. Tickets should, if possible, be ordered three weeks in advance. If you're on the road, have them mailed to your hostel or hotel. Lines inside the park to buy tickets are long and slow, but if you must do it, show up *early* – at least an hour before opening. ∎

store, or through the mail, as lines to buy tickets can be very long.

Figuring out what type of ticket you need can get confusing, and you really need to pay attention to avoid the disappointment of being told that your ticket doesn't cover the attractions you want.

Children under three years are admitted free. Ticket prices given below (tax not included) are for ages 10 and up/ages three to nine.

One-Day One-Park
> It's just that: one park only. You *can't* dash between parks, so be absolutely certain that the park you're entering is the one you want. These tickets are only available at the Disney gate, and are only good on the day issued. $37/30.

Four-Day Park-Hopper Pass
> Unlimited admission to Magic Kingdom, EPCOT and Disney-MGM Studios Theme Park for four days. You can visit any combination of those parks on any of the four days, but note that this *does not* include the water parks or any other attractions. It never expires; you can come back and use unused days whenever you want. $137/109.

Four-Day Value Pass
> Good for four days following the *purchase*, this ticket allows one day at Magic Kingdom, one at EPCOT and one at Disney-MGM Studios Theme Park, and then a second day at any one of those parks. Only sold at the gate. $124/97.

Theme Park Annual Pass
> One year unlimited admission to Magic Kingdom, EPCOT and Disney-MGM Studios Theme Park. $236/205.

Five-Day World-Hopper Pass
This is a tricky one. It provides unlimited admission to Magic Kingdom, EPCOT and Disney-MGM Studios Theme Park on *any* five days. You can come back, say, on another trip – even a year later – and reuse the ticket. You can visit any combination of those parks on any of the five days. Now here's the tricky part: this ticket also includes admission to Blizzard Beach, Typhoon Lagoon, River Country, Discovery Island and Pleasure Island, but only for 'a period of seven days beginning with the first date stamped (first use).' So if you come back a year later you can still get into the theme parks, but you'll have to repurchase tickets to the water parks and Pleasure Island. Go figure. $186/148.

Premium Annual Pass
One year unlimited admission to Magic Kingdom, EPCOT, Disney-MGM Studios Theme Park, Blizzard Beach, Typhoon Lagoon, River Country, Discovery Island and Pleasure Island. $319/280.

Water Park Hopper
Either a one-day or annual pass for unlimited admission to Blizzard Beach, Typhoon Lagoon, River Country, Discovery Island and Pleasure Island. One-day $22.50/17, annual $99/79.

Pleasure Island
Either a one day or annual pass for unlimited admission to Pleasure Island. Note the price of an annual pass is just a tad higher than two single admissions, so if you're going to go at least three times, the annual pass is probably worth it. Now ask yourself if you really want *three* nights of frozen blue drinks to make the annual pass worth your while (drinks, of course, cost extra). One-day $16.95, annual $40.95, no one under 18 admitted.

Discovery Island Single Excursion $10/5.50.
River Country One-Day Pass $14.75/11.50.
River Country Annual $55.25 for everyone.

Discounts Florida residents (and you'll have to prove it) are occasionally given relatively hefty discounts on Disney admissions – there's no way to know when the specials are on without calling Disney and asking. During spring break periods students with an ISIC card can get a hefty discount: a friend of ours once got $13 off a One-Day One-Park pass just for showing his ISIC. Be sure to ask if you qualify for a discount before you buy your ticket, as no one's going to come out and tell you.

Other than for Floridians, students and US military, there are no discount tickets for Disney attractions anywhere (not even for seniors, usually), so anyone who offers you one also may have a bridge to sell you in the New York area.

Due to illicit trade in tickets, Disney's recently introduced a new ticket system. Now long-term tickets are magnetic-striped plastic cards. Spin doctors tell you that the new cards are 'colorful and collectible'. Whatever.

When you arrive at a turnstile, insert your pass into the slot at the front of the turnstile. The machine reads your card, decides whether you're worthy of admission and, if you are, unlocks the gate and gives you your ticket back.

Tours

There are currently nine tours available in the parks through the Disney tours department (☎ 939-8687). They range dramatically, from two-hour Saturday tours of the World Showcase's architecture, design and construction for $25; to the daily four-hour Keys to the Kingdom tour behind the scenes at the Magic Kingdom (which includes a look at the Production Center and the tunnel system) for $45; to the Monday and Wednesday to Friday seven-hour Grand Backstage Magic tour through all three parks for $160. American Express card members get significant discounts on all the tours: the three mentioned above respectively, would cost $20, 36 and 128 when charged to an American Express card.

Parking

There's a flat $5 per car, $6 per camper/trailer, $10 per bus fee at the Disney parking lots.

The parking lots make those at Superbowl football games look puny. They're enormous and go on forever. Pay close attention to the character and row number you're parked in. The main reference marker is a Disney character: Pluto 44 will be in the Pluto Lot, row 44. A section of your parking permit is detachable, and designed to have you write down your spot.

Trams come by frequently and tell you what we just did as soon as you get on. If you do lose your car, after calling yourself a bonehead, find a uniformed attendant, who will mournfully arrange for a car to take you around until you figure it all out.

Disabled Travelers

Ask Disney for their excellent *Guidebook for Guests with Disabilities* which has maps and information on everything from drinking fountains and counter-service dining to rides and parades.

Disney has been outstanding in ensuring accessibility to disabled guests. Most attractions, shows and restaurants are wheelchair accessible. In fact, visitors using wheelchairs often end up being whisked past the lines waiting for rides and brought right up front! All the signs for rides carry information for disabled guests as to turbulence. Motorized wheelchairs are available for rental, but you can't use them on many rides; you'll have to switch to a non-motorized wheelchair. There are also some rides for which you'll need to leave the chair entirely (staff will assist you if necessary).

Visitors with other disabilities will find assistance as well; Braille and pre-recorded tours are available; check with Guest Relations for more information.

Personal Translator Units are available at Guest Relations. They're narration devices for the hearing impaired that offer tours in certain areas of EPCOT in English, French, Spanish and German. The units cost $4 plus a $40 deposit that's refundable only if you return the unit on the same day.

Baby Centers & Sitters

There are baby centers in each park; see each park's handout map for specific locations, or check at Guest Relations. For private baby-sitting, call Kinder-Care (☎ 827-5444 for individuals, 827-5437 for groups).

First Aid

There are excellent nurse-staffed centers in each park that hand out bandages, treat sunburn and can cope with more serious injury as well.

Lockers

Each park has a set of lockers for visitors' use. The cost is $3 a day, with a $2 deposit. There's no additional fee if you change parks during the day: bring your key back to the first park, they'll give you a receipt. When you get to the second park, give them the receipt, they'll give you a new key. You get your $2 back if you return the final key before the park you're in closes for the day.

Kennels

There are kennels at the Magic Kingdom (☎ 824-6568), EPCOT Center (☎ 560-6229), Disney-MGM Studios (☎ 560-4282) and Fort Wilderness Resort & Campground (☎ 824-2735). All cost $6 per day and $11 overnight, though there are no attendants at night. The kennels accept all house pets, and all 'exotic house pets', provided that they're self-contained: if you want to bring your Boa constrictor, bring a good, strong cage as well. In some cases (such as when you bring your Boa along) Disney may send a supervisor down to decide whether it will take the thing: call first. There are no runs available, so you're encouraged to visit your pet as often as possible during the day to walk it.

RIDES

We were a bit surprised that the rides at Disney World are kind of . . . well, tame. If you're looking for mad, swooping roller coasters or really terrifying stuff, head for Busch Gardens in Tampa. There are exceptions: the Tower of Terror (Disney-MGM Studios) is amazing, and the final plunge at Splash Mountain (Magic Kingdom) is as heart-in-throat as you'll really want.

If you haven't ridden on a flight simulator before, it's an experience you've got to have: they're rooms that pivot, buck and rock in perfect time with a picture on a screen. The combined effect of movement, picture and sound effects makes it feel unbelievably real. So in Body Wars (EPCOT),

CENTRAL

when you're placed in a miniaturized pod and injected into the human body, get set for a wild ride. There are several simulator rides here, and we include Honey I Shrunk the Audience (EPCOT) in that category.

Lines

Crowds can get amazing, especially in high seasons. Disney makes them as painless as possible – providing in-line entertainment, ingeniously hiding the snake formation of a line so you can't tell how long it is, putting up signs that overestimate the actual waiting time to trick you into feeling like you got away with something – but at the end of the day, chances are you're going to stand in line for 45 minutes to an hour to go down Splash Mountain. It could be a charming 45 minutes, but 45 minutes it is.

Most of the rides and attractions have signs posting the approximate waiting time. And if you want to test Disney Security, try and cut in – we saw two people try on two occasions and both were nabbed by very polite, suited and burly gentlemen who appeared seemingly out of nowhere.

Lines are the main reason you'll need to bring sun block, and another good idea is a spritzer bottle of water to shoot at the kids when they start to complain.

The only strategy, unfortunately, is the same one everyone else will tell you: get there early and get in line for the most popular rides first. We found that in downpours – very common in the summer months – people tend to seek shelter, and that's always a good time to nip in to a line. And, if you or your kids are not absolutely devoted to the idea of a parade, you're in luck: lines empty considerably while they're on.

Autograph Books

These things are very popular with kids; you can buy them here or bring your own.

Why Don't We Do It in the Moat?

Disney Cast Members, as chipper as they may be, are a little like New York City cops: they've seen it all. But admirable company loyalty makes them uncomfortable when asked about anything that may be construed as being 'against' Disney.

So when we asked around about the most outrageous thing that's happened at Disney, there were lots of tight-lipped smiles and not too much else.

But then: paydirt. A former cast member (and we won't tell you their nationality or sex) laughingly mentioned one incident in which a young couple smoked marijuana and then stripped naked and tried to have sex under a bridge on the banks of the moat surrounding Cinderella's Castle in the Magic Kingdom.

Well, a couple of months later, we met a member of that very party and got more of the story.

It was a group of Floridians on holiday with their teenagers, and yes, the parents admit that their then 14-year-old son (let's call him 'James') met a teenage woman in the park, shared his marijuana with her and that, after a little discussion, the two agreed to have sex under the bridge.

They say that the teens were nabbed by undercover officers, posing as tourists, who popped up out of nowhere before any serious action had taken place, forced the naked teens to dress and then hauled them into custody. And as in Beverly Hills, the officers were forceful yet exceedingly polite. Disney won't really comment too much on its security forces, though it is generally believed that they have the power of arrest, and that they operate undercover agents who mingle with crowds watching for pickpockets and other miscreants – including, apparently, copulating couples.

As for James, he says that he was told by the Disney security that not only was he being ejected from the park – which is pretty much par for the course – but that he was also being declared *persona non grata* at all Disney property worldwide. Forever.

If this is true, Disney may have succeeded where several noteworthy American politicians have failed: deportation of troublemakers.

Don't mess with the Mouse. ■

They're used to collect character autographs. Do yourself and the characters a favor and bring a large, thick pen – it's hard to grab a skinny little ball point in a 50-pound rubber suit. Just be ready to run around the park seeking out the White Rabbit and other rare characters – kids use these things as status symbols.

Acronyms

Disney would seem to be more acronym-happy than even the United Nations. In the text, we try as often as possible to avoid using them, but there is at least one you'll absolutely have to get used to: AA=Audio Animatronics, which are 'robots' of sorts.

Todd McCartney's Disney pages on the internet (see the Online Services appendix) have a great deal of information, including a complete list of Disney acronyms.

MAGIC KINGDOM

When most people think of Disney World, they're thinking of the Magic Kingdom: its centerpiece is Cinderella's Castle, the most recognizable of Disney's logos. Note that the castle isn't really an attraction, it's just kinda there, though there's a really nice restaurant and some shops inside.

The Magic Kingdom is divided into seven sections. The following highlights are listed counter-clockwise beginning at the entrance with Main St USA proceeding to New Tomorrowland, Mickey's Starland, Fantasyland, Liberty Square, Adventureland and Frontierland. Guest Relations is at the south end of Main St at Town Square.

Cast members in this park are wonderful, and all are dressed in garb appropriate to the area; in New Tomorrowland, for example, they're space people. The effect is called 'streetmosphere'.

Walt Disney World Railroad, a steam-driven locomotive, circumnavigates the entire park, with stops at the main entrance, Frontierland and Mickey's Starland.

Main St USA

This is the first area of the park you'll see;

it's a quaint replica of a good ol' American town. You can ride on a horse-drawn trolley (it's great to see the doo-doo cleanup person following the cart) or spend money in all the shops that line this street (which stay open for up to an hour after the park officially closes).

New Tomorrowland

With space and spacey stuff, this is the area that most kids head for first – especially with the drawing power of its two flagship rides, ExtraTERRORestrial Alien Encounter and Space Mountain.

Tomorrowland Transit Authority This is a mini-monorail ride above and around New Tomorrowland – it's a good way to get an orientation tour of the section and you'll even pass through the Space Mountain ride, so anyone in your party who may be getting cold feet can get a preview. Another good thing is that there's no waiting for this train ride.

ExtraTERRORestrial Alien Encounter This can scare the daylights out of younger kids, who will then ask to do it again. When you enter, an electronic steel scientist (whose voice will be instantly recognizable to anyone who knows the words to *Time Warp*) demonstrates an exciting molecular transfer procedure in which a little alien is transported, Star Trek-style, from one tube to the next. You then take part in a similar experiment, something, of course, goes wrong, and a ferocious alien is transported into your ship instead. Brrrr. It's about a 20-minute thing from start to finish. The waits were about 45 minutes in August, 1¼ hours in March.

Space Mountain This is a very popular 3½-minute roller coaster ride through, what else, space. You coast by earth as it would be seen from outer space, past astronauts working on the moon and swirl around the star sprinkled galaxy. It's a fun little ride, but not as rough as we had expected and despite the promises of total darkness we could still see the tracks

CENTRAL

throughout the entire ride. Waiting time for this one is about 45 minutes in August, 1¼ hours in March (TV monitors entertain with the latest news from the galaxy and lots of FedEx ads).

Dreamflight On this sweet, relaxing ride for the whole family, just kick back and let yourself be swirled around in your seat through a very entertaining history of flying. Swinging tunes and colorful cartoons accompany you on your way and you even get to fly through the clouds. You'll experience short waiting times and lots of Delta Airlines plugs. The round-the-world images, with the Eiffel Tower and other landmarks, are excellent.

Grand Prix Raceway This is probably a must for kids, who can streak around a track that circumnavigates the section in gas-powered grand-prix style go carts.

Mickey's Starland
This is the area to head for with very small children. Most everything here is built to kid-size scale. Kids love to have their photos taken in front of the Daisy's Cafe, Duck County School and Duckburg News buildings.

Mickey's House The Mouse's house is excellent even though all the rooms are roped off; see Mickey's bedroom (where his striped pajamas are waiting for him), living room, office and kitchen (note the shopping list on the fridge). Walk through the backyard into **Mickey's Starland Show**, a stage show where you get to see Disney characters like Goofy, Minnie, etc; the show takes place every half hour from 11 am to 2 pm and 4 pm to 6 pm. If you're worried that your kid won't get to see Mickey before they leave, this is the sure-fire place to catch him.

Grandma Duck's Farm This vegetable garden grows everything Mickey and his friends like to eat, and has a great petting area with goats, sheep and ducks. They actu-ally use some of the vegetables growing here in some Disney restaurants (we're told).

Fantasyland
The name is pretty accurate for younger kids, who go wild on the very sweet and rel-atively harmless rides, like Cinderella's Golden Carousel, Dumbo the Flying Ele-phant, It's a Small World (from which you'll emerge with that song permanently embla-zoned upon your psyche), the ever-popular Mad Tea Party tea-cup ride, Mr Toad's Wild Ride and Snow White's Adventure.

Liberty Square
This is not the most exciting area of Disney World, but hey. Highlights include:

Haunted Mansion We loved this old-fashioned, ghostly ride/adventure, which is pretty much a glorified haunted house. A nice gimmick is the incredible expanding room as you enter – you can't tell if the ceiling's rising or you're sinking. Once in your cart, howling wolves and dogs pop in as you pass tombstones, hear lots of 'boo'-type sounds and see waltzing ghosts. Smaller kids may be scared by the 'ghost' that 'sits' in your cart on the way out. Eek.

Hall of Presidents Talk about ham-fisted propaganda! This is an AA show, starring every US president to date, narrated by Maya 'Raspy' Angelou and extolling the virtues of the American system of govern-ment, life and culture in a sickeningly superior and self-congratulatory tone. The only lighter moments are provided by unin-tentional ironies; like the fact that the Ronald Reagan AA is more animated than the real president was. There are some neat aspects, such as the presidents mumbling amongst themselves during speeches. When we visited, Bill Clinton's AA gave a speech which Clinton himself recorded specifically for the attraction.

Frontierland
This is the most action/adventure-oriented section of the Magic Kingdom, and lines for its rides are generally the longest during

the day. It may pay to begin here, as opposed to in New Tomorrowland, especially if you're trying to get in more than one run on Big Thunder.

Splash Mountain Our favorite ride at the Magic Kingdom – not just for the thrills and chills but also for the brilliantly creative (and very cute) sets and music. Even if you've ridden the one at Disneyland, you should head here, as this one is longer and more fun. The sets are based on the Disney movie *Song of the South*, and feature its characters.

There's sort of a 'story' going on here, in which you're allegedly taking part, involving an insidious plot by Brer Bear and Brer Fox to stop Brer Rabbit from getting on in his life. Anyway, you float through very amusing pathways and go down a couple of little drops (one in darkness) before the third one – the killer – sends you down a drop over 50 feet, at over 40 mph.

After the first two drops, you go through Brer Rabbit's laughing land (a welcome relaxation phase), which is filled with frogs, singing ducks and other happy creatures (we were especially delighted by the bees).

If you think you winced during the drop, you can find out: video cameras are strategically placed to catch your expression on the way over; monitors on the way out show these images, and you can get a color printout of your mug for $9.95. Waiting times for this ride can get long: in August we waited almost a full hour, in March it was just under 1½ hours. Kids have to be at least three years old and at least 44 inches tall to ride.

Big Thunder Mountain Railroad It's a toss-up whether this or Splash Mountain is the most popular ride in the park; both are very popular and the waiting times are about equal. The sets are also excellent, and the ride is pretty wild.

You're on a mine-cart heading through an old mine, and if you ever wondered what it was like to be in a mine shaft rail chase, this is the place to come.

. . . but this one takes the cake

Disney's Imagineers have come up with many compelling ways to separate you from your money. But with the Walk around the World project, they've reached the height of unmitigated gall.

The Walk is a project to build a walkway, made of bricks bearing the name of sponsors, around Magic Kingdom Park at Disney World. For $96, you, yes *you*, can immortalize your devotion to Disney by sponsoring the installation on the Walk of a 10-inch hexagonal brick tile embossed with your name and home state.

$100. For a brick.

And that $100 doesn't even *buy* you the brick! According to the Sponsorship Agreement,

Neither this agreement nor the installation of the brick entitles the Sponsor to any ownership interest in the brick . . . or free or discounted admission to the Magic Kingdom Park or any other part of Walt Disney World Resort.

And . . .

Sponsor shall have no control over the design, format, material, appearance, construction, manufacture, installation, maintenance, repair, admission, or access to, or operation of the brick or the walkway.

You not only don't own it, you're not even allowed to *operate* it! People, of course, are buying the things up as fast as they can.

So once again, Disney has convinced the visiting, *paying* public to not only cover their construction costs, but to turn the Walk into a profit center. We want to party with these guys. ∎

Tom Sawyer Island To get your wits back, and let the little ones burn off some of the energy they've stored up waiting in line and then freaking on the rides, take a short raft ride (it leaves from the little dock between Big Thunder and Splash Mountains) over to this little playground/island filled with rope bridges, caves and other fun things to climb in/on.

CENTRAL

Adventureland
This is a jungley, safari-ish kind of place with great streetmosphere. We liked:

Pirates of the Caribbean We loved this water cruise almost as much as the kids with us did. It's a larger version of the one at Disneyland in California. You're on a riverboat, seeing first-hand how pirates lived, partied, robbed and burned down towns, but it's all in a very happy setting with lots of pirate songs. Yo ho ho. There are a couple of little sections of rapids, but for the most part it's pretty relaxing. Lines weren't very long when we went (about 20 minutes in August, 45 minutes in March), but can get up there.

Jungle Cruise It's exactly what it sounds like; a cruise through the Jungles of the World. Lots of very cute animals, AA figures and waterfalls. We liked it, but lines can be intolerable – best to show up early or during a parade or show.

Swiss Family Tree House If you still have the energy, climb the long staircase here (no wheelchair access) and take in the view of Adventureland. The tree itself is pretty astounding.

DISNEY-MGM STUDIOS THEME PARK
This park's rides and attractions are absolutely first rate, but it's far less of a 'working studio' than they'd have you believe. And we were really disappointed with the alleged 'special effects' demonstration, which we thought was uninformative, patronizing and, worse, unimaginative. But there are great parades and shows here, and while the sets and street scenes may not be as impressive as those at Universal Studios Theme Park, it's absolutely worth coming, if only to fall down an elevator shaft.

Shows & Characters
These change often. When we went, the offerings included:

Mickey Mouse Autograph Sessions
    On Sunset Blvd all day

Toy Story Parade
    This is the biggie, with all the Toy Story characters in a huge parade that snakes around the circle and down Hollywood Blvd; it's about a 20-minute show at 11.30 am and 3.30 pm. Good time to get in line at the Tower of Terror
Disney Character Parades
    . 15-minute appearances at 11 am, noon, and 1, 2, 3, 4, 5 and 6 pm, Mickey Ave
Pocahontas: A Legend Comes to Life
    Behind-the-scenes of the film; continuous showings Thursday to Tuesday 9.30 am to 9.15 pm; Wednesday 10 am to 9.15 pm, Walt Disney Theater
The Spirit of Pocahontas
    25-minute stage show with performances at 3, 4.15, 6.15, 7.30 and 8.45 pm, Backlot Theater
Voyage of the Little Mermaid
    Multimedia show with live action, lasers and animation; 20-minute shows continuously from 9 am to park closing
Indiana Jones Epic Stunt Spectacular
    Booo. We went with open minds (we're *Indiana Jones* fans) but we were really disappointed in this 30-minute show – in which they stage bad stunts too slowly and use 'technical talk' that's dumb and just plain wrong (an actual quote: 'Let's shoot at 48 frames-per-second to give Cairo a really good look here, Bob.' Memo to writers: stationary objects like 'Cairo' don't look 'good' in slow motion, which is the result of shooting at 48 fps). Runs on a changing schedule. Hissss . . . .
Disco
    In summer, there's a nightly disco set up on Sunset Blvd (the street leading to the Tower of Terror) where you can boogie down with Chip & Dale

Rides & Attractions
Most of the 'rides' here are 3-D, participatory or simulator based, with the notable exception of our first entry:

Twilight Zone Tower of Terror This may be the best and most terrifying ride in all of Disney World, and judging by the screams and the lines, a lot of people agree with us on that one.

It's in the imposing Hollywood Tower Hotel, which 'closed in 1939'. It's a beast of a Deco building, and looks eerily gloomy even on sunny days, but what makes it really terrifying is that you can hear the muffled screams of riders from a quarter-mile away. AAAhhhhh!

The detail in the place is spectacular, and when you finally get to the entrance you'll see a video starring none other than Rod Serling, who tells the tale of the last guests to stay here before the place closed. You get into the elevator (sitting down and strapped in) and feel as if you're truly entering another dimension – it looks as if you're traveling in space, seeing stars and holograms float by. Though it only feels as if you've gone up a floor or two, in fact you've gone up 133 feet. The first falls are only a few feet each – the fall program is changed frequently, so yours may be different – but the big one is always 13 stories, which you descend in an astonishing 2.7 seconds: it's not a free-fall, but rather a forced fall, which is faster!

One guest wrote us,

My knees were shaking for about five minutes after this totally gruesome, stomach flipping ride – it's excellent fun, but I don't recommend bringing little kids on this one, it just feels too real.

Jim Henson's Muppet Vision 3D is beautifully made, extremely funny and the 3-D stuff is so real that the kids actually try to reach for the characters. The theater is pretty much a replica of the one on the *Muppet Show*. Some of the Muppets stars appear 'live' (AA) – watch for the hecklers, who are sitting just where they should be, and the projectionist – or should we say, Proyekshunuster – is none other than Swedish Chef. You'll come out laughing. Waits can get long, but once you're in the main waiting area, a brilliant multi-screen Muppet show awaits – no chance escaping knowledge that the show is sponsored by Kodak, as several characters will haul the logo out and hold it in front of you. Sam Eagle's safety instructions are a hoot, and Fozzy conducting the all-penguin orchestra is a treat. Before you enter, take note of the spectacular bronze statue/fountain of Miss Piggy as the Statue of Liberty, rotating on a shell pedestal and surrounded by Muppets. Too much. Even if your kids aren't Sesame

Street fans, haul them into this one and they'll love it.

Honey I Shrunk the Kids Movie Set Adventure Behind New York St, this is a fantastic playground area scaled to bring you down to sub-ant size. It's set in the backyard from the movie, with oversize weeds, gigantic insects, huge Lego pieces, an oversize, water sprinkling garden hose (oh, boy do kids like this one – there are triggers in the floor) and other enlarged items make you feel decidedly shrunken. It's mainly for small children.

Star Tours Thrill Ride It's a flight simulator ride, based on a *Star Wars* theme, and there are no surprises: you're on a routine journey, the pilots (R2D2 and C3PO) are idiots and make a terrible mistake, you're in mortal danger, you're saved. For a simulator ride it's about average, but if you haven't ever tried one before it's incredibly real as your ship ducks, weaves and dips through a terrifying course.

EPCOT CENTER

It stands, of course, for Experimental Prototype Community of Tomorrow. Its trademark silver geodesic dome is visible throughout the park. EPCOT is broken into two main sections: Future World and the World Showcase. While we went to the World Showcase with our Experienced World Traveler decoder rings held high, totally prepared to scoff, we were completely humbled by the extraordinary job Disney has done in recreating the very best of 11 countries. And while Future World is definitely advertiser-driven, we enjoyed it (especially the Honey I Shrunk the Audience experience!).

Future World

This area is a combination amusement and educational park. Most of the rides are journeys through some aspect of technology through history, with bold predictions about the future, and it can be very entertaining for older children and adults.

But while we did see a lot of people

really enjoying themselves, we were a bit let down by the fact that this once glisteningly futuristic section has fallen a bit behind in its predictions. It's no one's fault: the pace of technology has been extraordinary since the place was opened in 1982, but there were a couple of times that we looked at each other and felt that the thing was more than a little creaky. That said, EPCOT still has plenty to offer, and when you take both Future World and World Showcase into account, you'll get your money's worth.

Just as we went to press, Apple Computer installed a huge display of their computers here, allowing visitors to video-conference and manipulate way cool images on souped-up Macs that, unlike ours, were set up by people who actually understand Extensions installation and therefore don't crash at key moments of manuscript production.

It's broken up into sponsored pavilions, and there's no attempt to hide it: 'Major corporations have combined their creative thinking with Walt Disney Imagineers to explore projections about the future,' gushes the guide map. Okay, so in the future we'll drive Exxon gas-powered GM cars while eating Nestlé chocolate, taking photographs on Kodak film and making AT&T cell-phone calls – those are the major sponsors. What a far-fetched vision of the future!

Most of the rides in EPCOT have short or at least fast-moving lines, as they operate on a conveyor-belt principle: the cars are constantly moving, and the entry and exit platforms are usually rotating at the same speed as the rides, prompting endless staff 'Watch-your-steps!'

Here are some highlights, beginning in Spaceship Earth and proceeding clockwise:

Spaceship Earth If anything, this is relaxing, as you spiral slowly up and down within the geosphere past displays of communication technology through history (sponsored, of course, by AT&T). You'll see cavemen and hieroglyphics; displays on ancient Egypt, the development of paper and alphabets, ancient Greece, the Roman Empire, the Renaissance, on to the movable-type printing press into our wonderful modern world where communication is flawless, gapless and seamless as long as no one uses MCI. It's not heavy-hitting technology, but it is interesting and some of the displays are very good.

Wonders of Life This is an amusing area, based around exploring the human body. The main attraction is the flight simulator ride here, **Body Wars**, essentially based on the movie *Inner Space*, in which a ship (with you inside) is miniaturized and injected into a human body. Something, of course, goes horribly wrong and you're in danger of being sucked into the heart, which as we all know would mean total destruction for your ship and the human host. Brrr.

Other attractions here include the laudable **Making of Me**, which shows the reproductive process from fertilization to birth (unfortunately they don't show any pre-fertilization events, but, come on, this is Disney), and **Cranium Command**, a totally hilarious look at the command and control systems of a 12-year-old boy's brain and body. It's a film, not a ride, and has what must be the finest casting ever; to wit, Bob Goldthwait as the adrenal gland. That does say it all, but there are also great performances by a persnickety Charles Grodin as the brain and Hans and Franz as the heart) – very funny.

World of Motion We were highly suspicious when we read that it was a 'humorous' General Motors presentation, but it's a genuinely amusing romp through the history of transportation from feet to the development of the wheel, the steam engine and the automobile to today and beyond. We thought the best part was the simulated plane ride through the clouds. The ride ends with a spacey light show. In the lobby, there are prototype vehicles, and a car showroom with GM and, surprisingly, other manufacturers' cars that you can climb all over and sit in. Note that some time in 1997, GM and Disney plan to replace this attraction with a new pavilion featuring, the press release tells us, 'every aspect of automobile testing – acceleration, braking, hill climbs, curvy roads and long straight-aways. The turns and corners are anticipated to be especially thrilling for the guest.'

Journey into Imagination This is probably the best area of EPCOT, and certainly our favorite; it features the Journey into Imagination attraction as well as the magnificent Honey I Shrunk the Audience. Outside the buildings, smaller kids go absolutely wild with the jumping water fountains: they send little blups of water out of one hole, in an arc, down into another hole, and they're timed to make the water behave like a dolphin, swimming and jumping. Yay.

In Journey into Imagination – the ride – you sit in what looks like a huge recliner and, along with your large cuddly AA host and his purple AA dragon, travel through an Imagine-Scape that's a lot like flying through a dream. It's a magical, smokey-foggy journey, and all the while the dragon is telling kids to use their imagination to help them be successful at life. Corinna came out singing the song and hasn't stopped yet, dammit.

Upstairs there are tons of extremely neat techno toys, like touch-screen machines that take a video snapshot of your face and let you add mustaches, extra eyes, etc; Dreamfinders School, which lets you enter a storybook (by way of a blue matte projection screen); Magic Palette video paintbox, synthesizers and digital sampler instruments and even low-tech pin-tables: put your hand underneath and press up an impression in the pins.

To say that **Honey I Shrunk the Audience** is a 3-D film is a like saying that the Space Shuttle is a fancy airplane: it's a complete sensory experience, with a moving floor, audience-film character interaction and even dog-sneeze and mice. It's absolutely a don't-miss. It's based on the Disney films *Honey I Shrunk the Kids* and *Honey I*

Blew Up the Kids, and the original cast appears here.

The film begins with an awards ceremony at which Wayne Szalinski is receiving some sort of hokey award, and you're in the audience watching the smarmy ceremony. At the beginning of the film, the 3-D was a little blurry. But when Wayne accidentally fires his famous shrinking ray at the audience, the entire theater seems to come to life, everything gets clear and so help me it really *feels* as if you're shrinking! The floor rumbles and actually moves, and becomes essentially an enormous flight simulator ride.

We're not going to give the whole thing away, but suffice it to say that you're truly in contact with many small things (like the aforementioned mice and dog sneeze) and it's pretty hysterically funny, especially when people look in at the audience. Four thumbs up.

Living Seas We really enjoyed this look at underwater life. Not so much a ride as an attraction, but there are some ride elements involved, and you should catch it. It's not Sea World, but they try pretty hard with this pavilion: they have one of the world's largest aquariums.

World Showcase
When we do our research, we're always on the lookout for something to make a joke about, and we thought that coming here would be the mother lode. How disappointing it was for us, then, when we saw just how well this section was done. For those who remain cynical, consider that a) all the employees in a country's section are from that country; b) all the country sections were designed and built with the cooperation of their own national tourist boards; and c) the reproductions are astounding.

All the country pavilions exhibit the absolute best that the real country boasts, and we're happy to report that, while it may be a little kitschy to make all the France employees wear berets, this place is absolutely fantastic.

The countries represented are (clockwise

CENTRAL

from the main park entrance, that is, from east to west): Mexico, Norway, China, Germany, Italy, America, Japan, Morocco, France, United Kingdom and Canada.

One story we can't confirm was that when Disney was fielding countries to be represented here, the then Soviet Union demanded (as they tended to) more space than any other country. Would have been funny if they built a wall between themselves and Germany, but Disney, it's said, turned them down.

Each country has restaurants and snack bars, shops, and evening entertainment. See the Places to Eat section for more information on the restaurants, and the Entertainment section for information on the bars and evening entertainment.

All the countries are skirting the World Showcase Lagoon, in which the IllumiNations display is held, which features lasers, music and fireworks on certain nights – check with Disney to see if it's on when you visit.

You can get a World Showcase Passport from any shop and have them stamped by the different country pavilions – there's a space for comments and signatures. It's a nice touch for kids.

WATER PARKS

It's surprising, when you think about it, that Disney hadn't really persued the water park concept until very recently, except for the 'swimmin' hole' concept of River Country. With Blizzard Beach, Disney has one of the most exciting water playlands around; we went on a rainy day and had an absolute blast.

Admission for the water parks works like this: there's a pass good for all three *and* Discovery Island and Pleasure Island, either for one day ($22.50/17), or one year ($99/79). River Country alone is $14.75/ 11.50 for the day, $55.25 for everyone.

Blizzard Beach

This is the home of the world's tallest and fastest free-fall slide, Summit Plummet. Themed to look like a ski resort (and so much fun we'll forgive the execrable puns

like the 'Avalunch' restaurant), Blizzard Beach features ski-ish things like a ski-lift and snow-capped mountains, but mainly it's a slide and raft park that is a great way to spend at least a half-day.

Lockers are available; the keys are on rubber wrist straps. You can also rent life preservers.

Slides & Rides Disney's main water attraction is **Summit Plummet** – a 120-foot water slide on which riders reach speeds of 55 mph (!). Take it from us, you want your arms crossed on your chest, your eyes closed and either pinch your nostrils closed or bring along a pair of rubber nostril-pinchers, because water flying up your nose at 55 mph is as much fun as a dental cleaning. We had such a great time we blew off research for two hours just to do it three more times! You scootch off the top, pass through a tunnel (it's the one that looks like a ski-jump from the ground) and slide your buns off. It seems terrifying, but just go for it!

Slush Gusher is for those who don't feel quite up to the challenge of Summit Plummet – it's the same kind of slide – and you go pretty fast – but just not as intense and without the tunnel. You use mats for **Snow Stormers & Toboggan Racers**; the former is a very twisty slalom course, the latter straight down; both have sudden dips and are pretty fast. Follow the safety instructions or risk friction burns (Nick got one, but he *was* being an idiot at the time, and that's all he's got to say about that).

Teamboat Springs is a really fun family-oriented white-water raft ride; rafts hold six people and streak down a 1200-foot course. **Cross Country Creek** is the standard slow-flowing moat around the park in which you can lazily circumnavigate the area on a rubber inner-tube. You'll pass through a waterfall on your way out of the tunnel beneath. **Tike's Peak** is the kiddie area at the base of Mt Gushmore specifically designed for smaller children.

Typhoon Lagoon

This park has essentially the same slides

and raft rides (though less radical) as Blizzard Beach, with the major exceptions of Typhoon Lagoon, a bloody huge wave pool, and Shark Reef, a fish observatory. It's a place for relaxing at the 'beach'; you're allowed to bring coolers (but not alcoholic beverages or glass bottles).

You can't miss **Typhoon Lagoon**: it's the huge body of water as you enter that produces body-surfable waves every few minutes. It's pretty impressive, and those who don't like the waves can just hang out by shore. There are several slide rides from about the mid-point of Mt Mayday. Castaway Creek is pretty much the same as Blizzard Beach's Cross Country Creek.

River Country

Though aged, River Country is still a popular water park near Fort Wilderness. There are small water slides, ropes and tube rides, all built around an enormous swimming pool. It's a nice place for a picnic, but as a water park it doesn't hold a candle to the other two.

OTHER ATTRACTIONS

Disney opens new people-draws all the time, mainly geared towards keeping guests (and their wallets) on the compound – and away from the competition of shops in Orlando. But Discovery Island is a wonderful exception: a nature preserve in the middle of the Disney property.

Discovery Island

This 11½-acre zoological park in Bay Lake is home to trumpeter swans, Galápagos tortoises, brown pelicans, alligators, muntjack deer, lemurs and other exotic animals. Parents who are willing to pay for a little space for a few hours can buy their freedom at the reasonable figure of $32, for which Disney will take your kid (aged eight to 14) on a four-hour adventure they'll remember forever: the **Discovery Island Kidventure** (☎ 824-3784), which goes to Marshmallow Marsh (off Fort Wilderness) where they'll do some track casting and animal and plant identification, then over to Discovery Island for a guided tour of the zoo and a photo-op with one of the park's birds. The cost includes lunch and the photograph. Kidventure is available (with reservations) on Wednesday during the winter and on Wednesday and Sunday in summer. Pickup is at 8.30 am at the Contemporary Resort.

They also operate an animal hospital, and hold educational programs throughout the year for groups of school children.

From the TTC or Contemporary, regular boat service begins at 10 am every day, the last boat over is at 4.45 pm. Hours are extended slightly in summer.

Disney Institute

Created as an educational approach to holiday making, the Disney Institute (☎ 800-496-6337) offers a total of 80 classes and programs, hosted by artists-in-residence or experts of the particular field, in nine categories. They include Entertainment Arts, Sports & Fitness, Culinary Arts, Lifestyles, Design Arts, Environment, Story Arts, Performing Arts and Youth.

The idea is to bring experts from different fields together with resort guests in workshops and classes. But the experts – or superstars, as the case may be – aren't constrained to work in the field for which they are best known. Excellent examples are: Grammy-award winning clarinetist Richard Stoltzman leading a class on bread baking, Bill Walton in a classical piano concert, and the collaboration of actor Andy Garcia and Mambo King Israel Lopez on a Latin Music Festival.

Programs to choose from include animation, photography, rock climbing, canoeing, cooking, self-discovery, storytelling, interior and agricultural design, landscaping, Florida wilderness, as well as dance, theater arts, music or spoken word. You get the idea. There's about a 15:1 student-teacher ratio.

The resort is different in that it offers packages, lodging and programs in all the areas of interest. In the evening events like live performances by artists-in-residence take place. Designed like a quaint, turn-of-the-century town, you

CENTRAL

stay in either bungalows or townhouses (see the Disney Institute listing in Places to Stay, below).

Disney Village Marketplace
Disney Village Marketplace today is a quaint shopping mall, but in the near future Disney plans to expand the boundaries of Pleasure Island to include the Disney Village Marketplace area with an expanded movie theater and celebrity-owned restaurants (including one owned by Gloria and Emilio Estefan). See the Places to Eat section below for information on the existing restaurants.

PLACES TO STAY
The best source for full descriptions of all the Disney places to stay is Birnbaum's *Walt Disney World*, which lists each resort's features and services, which are varied and multitudinous.

Disney accommodations are designed with family stays in mind, so most of the rooms are large enough to accommodate groups of four or more. Suites are available in many of the resorts, and their price and capacity is very complicated, so call Disney for information.

The main advantages of staying at the resorts, as opposed to in Kissimmee or Orlando, are convenience, preferential treatment at all Disney-owned attractions, the opportunity to enter the parks 1½ hours before the general public are admitted, and the excellent transportation network. Oh, yeah, and free Disney Channel cable in the rooms.

The disadvantage is that you'll spend a whole lot more money here than you would staying at a hostel or motel in Kissimmee or Orlando.

Of course, non-smoking, wheelchair accessible and practically any other special needs rooms one could think of are available.

To make reservations and get rates for suites at any of the following places, call WDISNEY (☎ 934-7639), or, if you're calling on the day you want to stay, you can save yourself some hold time and contact the resort directly.

We list these prices for low season/high season.

Camping
There are several advantages of camping at *Fort Wilderness Resort & Campground* (☎ 824-2900). It's gorgeous and incredibly civilized; all 1192 tent and RV campsites have water and electricity ($35/44); some have sanitary disposal ($43/52) and some have all that plus a cable-TV hookup ($49/58). The hookups, of course, are secreted within Disney trees. There are also 408 air-conditioned cabins (RVs, actually) with full kitchens ($185/215). These sleep up to six.

There are no mosquitoes, snakes, bugs, creeps or bothers, and it's getting away to the great outdoors without all the fuss: roughing it, but very gently. You're treated, for all intents and purposes, as a Disney Resort guest, with all the privileges accorded to them, like early park entry and preferred restaurant reservations. And there are activities like nightly sing-a-longs at the campfire, movies, etc. You can rent bicycles and golf carts, and horseback riding is available.

All Star Resorts
The relatively new *All Star Sports Resort* (☎ 939-5000) and *All Star Music Resort* (☎ 939-6000) are Disney's cheapest fully equipped hotels, designed to appeal to young travelers and sports and music nuts. Both have 1920 rooms, and all are themed: baseball, football, tennis, basketball, surfing, Broadway, calypso, jazz, rock & roll and country. Rooms in both resorts are $69 to 79 all year, for up to four people.

Dixie Landings & Port Orleans
At *Dixie Landings* (☎ 934-6000) it's a rural South theme – actually, it's a lot like *Gone With the Wind*'s Tara. The 2084 rooms are $95 to 124/99 to 129, and sleep four.

Port Orleans (☎ 934-5000) does a fine job of reproducing the French Quarter in New Orleans (*avec* nightly Mardi Gras but *sans* filth and drunken creeps). It has 1008 rooms priced from $95 to 124 for doubles, $99 to 129 for quads depending on season.

Disney Institute

The Disney Institute opened on, and took over for, what was formerly referred to as the Disney Village Resort. But it is not just a bunch o' courses, it's an entire program as described above.

You can stay in the Disney Institute as part of a Disney Institute package, or just as a straight accommodation deal while visiting the Disney parks.

For accommodation only, the nightly cost is $195/215 for bungalows, $285/305 for one-bedroom townhouses, $320/340 for two-bedroom villas.

The treehouses, which sleep six, are $355/375; eight-person fairway villas are $375/400; and Grand Vista homes, which sleep six to eight, are $975 to 1150.

The Disney Institute Basic Plan includes accommodation, programs, baggage tips, and a one-day pass to any one theme park. The cost per person is: in a bungalow, $429 for a three-night (minimum) package; four nights $559 and seven nights $949; in a one-bedroom townhouse, $540/707/1208, or in a two-bedroom villas $584/765/1310. The Disney Institute Deluxe Plan includes all of the above plus all meals, non-alcoholic drinks and meal tips. In a bungalow the cost is $576/755/1291, in a one-bedroom townhouse $687/903/1550, or in a two-bedroom townhouse $730/961/1652.

Disney Vacation Club

Modeled after Key West, the houses here (☎ 827-7700) are available for rent *and* purchase – it's fantastically complicated, involving Disney's 'vacation ownership' (which the rest of us call 'timeshare condo'), so call for more information. A four-person studio here is $195/215; one-bedroom unit $265/290; eight-person two-bedroom unit $365/385; and 12-person grand villas are $780 year round. Wednesday and Sunday there are character breakfasts.

Magic Kingdom Resorts

The *Wilderness Lodge* (☎ 824-3200) has a Wild West atmosphere; rooms are $159 to 270/174 to 290. There are character breakfasts daily at Artist Point.

The slightly hokey but fun all the same *Polynesian Resort* (☎ 824-2000) has a lush and tropical setting; standard rooms are $200 to 285/215 to 305, 'concierge' rooms $305 to 360/325 to 380. Minnie's Menehune character breakfast is held daily in Ohana.

The *Grand Floridian Beach Resort* (☎ 824-3000) is a very posh Victorian-style place at the Seven Seas Lagoon. It's best to walk into the immense lobby, listen to the grand piano tinkling, gawk at the giant birdcages and, on the Fourth of July, to watch the fireworks at Magic Kingdom, and then stay in Fort Wilderness! Standard rooms are $265 to 340/290 to 375, 'concierge' rooms $465/470. A character breakfast and dinner is held daily at 1900 Park Fare.

The socialistic-1970s-vision-of-the-future-looking *Contemporary Resort* (☎ 824-1000) has over 1000 rooms; note that wheelchairs can't board the Monorail here. Garden wing rooms are $195 to 250/215 to 270, tower rooms $270/290, they all sleep up to five people. There are character breakfast buffets held daily in the Contemporary Cafe.

EPCOT Center Resorts

The *Caribbean Beach Resort* (☎ 934-3400) is made up of 'villages' modeled after Jamaica, Trinidad, Martinique, Barbados and Aruba. There are over 2000 rooms here, which sleep up to four people, priced from $95 to 124/99 to 129.

Boardwalk Villas (☎ 939-5100) has a turn of the century design. Studios, which sleep up to four, are $210 to 235/225 to 250; one-bedroom villas (which sleep four) are $285/310; two-bedroom villas (up to eight people) are $385/406 and grand villas (up to 12 people) are $780. The *BoardWalk Inn* (☎ 939-5100) has 532 cottages and 378 rooms. Standard rooms sleep up to five people and cost $225 to 285/240 to 305, 'concierge' rooms, which also sleep up to five people, cost $380 to 460/400 to 480.

Ahrr, matey: the New England-style

rooms at the *Yacht Club* (☎ 934-7000) cost $225 to 285/240 to 305; 'concierge' rooms $370 to 385/390 to 405.

Rooms at the *Beach Club Resort* (☎ 934-8000) cost $225 to 285/240 to 305. There's a daily character breakfast at the Cape May Café.

The two biggies here are the enormous *Swan* (☎ 934-3000, 800-248-7926), with its two gigantic (46-foot) swans on the roof. Rooms range from $245 to 270/275 to 305, 'concierge' rooms $335/350. There are character breakfasts held on Wednesday and Saturday mornings at 8 am, and character dinners on Monday, Thursday and Friday at 6 pm at the Garden Grove Cafe. The similarly enormous *Dolphin* (☎ 934-4000, 800-227-1500) has a tropical setting, and a 56-foot-high dolphin statue. Standard rooms are $220 to 289/255 to 335, 'concierge' rooms $310/365. Character brunch is held on Sunday at Harry's Safari Bar & Grille and at Juan & Only's Cantina.

PLACES TO EAT
Individual menus in the non-sit-down restaurants are about the same throughout the complex: burgers run from $3 to 6, hot dogs from $1.75 to 3. Pizza, Mexican and other fast food (excuse us, 'quick service') prices run basically between $4 and $8 per person.

Character Dining
Kids absolutely love these things, where Disney characters prance around your restaurant being generally charming while you eat. The schedule and variety of these is so complicated we're going to cop out and give you a couple of examples and then tell you to call Disney (☎ 939-3463) for more information and reservations. (Okay, we list a few more under Places to Stay, above, and restaurants, below).

If you're going to one inside a Disney park, you'll need a valid ticket for that park – you can't go in just for the meal (nice try).

You can usually make reservations up to 60 days in advance. Reservations are almost always required, and if they're not, it's a good idea to make them anyway.

Prices listed are for aged 12 and older/aged three to 11.

One good bet is Once Upon a Time, at King Stefan's Banquet Hall in Cinderella Castle, with Cinderella and others. It costs $14.95/7.95. The breakfasts are held daily; on Monday, Thursday and Saturday from 7.30 to 10 am, Tuesday, Wednesday, Friday and Sunday from 8 to 10 am.

There's a buffet breakfast in the Soundstage Restaurant (Disney-MGM Studios) with Pocahontas and Aladdin characters daily except Wednesday and Sunday from 8.30 to 10.30 am. On Wednesday and Sunday they have surprise character guests from 7.30 to 10.30 am. The cost is $12.95/7.95.

The Garden Grill Character Experience is open every day for breakfast, lunch and dinner with Mickey Mouse and his gang (check times when you go). Breakfast costs $14.95/7.95; lunch and dinner $16.95/9.95.

Magic Kingdom
Main St USA *Tony's Town Square Restaurant* serves Italian dishes for breakfast, lunch and dinner, and the *Plaza Restaurant* has sandwiches and light entrees for lunch and dinner and the largest ice cream sundaes in the Magic Kingdom. Outside is the park's only cappuccino cart.

The Crystal Palace, a Buffet with Character is a cafeteria with chicken, pasta and salad dishes; character visits take place here.

Casey's Corner is the place to grab a quick hot dog or fries, tables are available, but it's self service. There are bleacher seats, and lots of cartoons.

Both the *Main St Bake Shop* and *Plaza Ice Cream Parlor* are responsible for the overwhelmingly good smells that hit you as you enter the Magic Kingdom (baking exhaust is pumped out onto Main St).

Adventureland There are no full-service restaurants in here, but no worries: light snacks like tacos, nachos, tropical fruit and citrus yogurt (fitting to the theme) abound.

The best deal in the park is here, though, where gigantic, sumptuous smoked turkey drumsticks are $4 from the little cart – just

---

Turkey Legs

Disney's constantly tempting guests with food throughout the parks: note the heavy smells of freshly baking cinnamon buns as you walk down Main St USA, which are purposely pumped out onto the street. But one offering that proved irresistible to us – and we're for the most part vegetarian – was the smoked turkey legs. Smoked and then baked, the enormous legs (one's good enough for lunch) are simply good enough to make two vegetarians backslide. They're sold from the little stands near Frontierland and near Rockettower Plaza for $4 apiece. ∎

---

follow the happy customers to the line (if you time it right there's no wait at all, but at peak lunch hours there can be lines of up to 20 minutes for these babies – they're *that* good).

Pecos Bill Cafe has burgers, smoked chicken and the like and *Aunt Polly's Landing* does sandwiches, apple pie and cookies.

Vegetarians will kindly form a line at *Sleepy Hollow*, which serves awesome and hearty vegetarian chili in a bread bowl and pita sandwiches. It's not only good for you, but the outside patio has the best view of the castle.

Fantasyland Inside Cinderella's Castle is *King Stefan's Banquet Hall*, where they do morning character breakfasts – and since Cinderella is around for lunch and dinner as well we recommend you make reservations for those, as well, and *early*. It's big, beefy and Henry VIII-style drumstick fare, with entrees from $9 to $20.

For burgers, sandwiches and salads, try *Pinocchio's Village House*, which also serves up pseudo-German stuff like wieners and has an outside pretzel cart, and *Lumiere's Kitchen*, serving various fried nuggets and grilled cheese sandwiches. They're mainly for children, though there are some concessions to the grownups, too.

New Tomorrowland Here you'll find the very good *Cosmic Ray's Starlight Café* with meat and vegetarian burgers, salads, soups and sandwiches, and the *Plaza Pavilion*, which has pizza and subs. Both are cafeteria-style. And have we mentioned those awesome turkey legs? Well here is your second chance at Rockettower Plaza.

Liberty Square The *Columbia Harbor House* does fried fish and chicken baskets, but the big attraction here is the *Liberty Tree Tavern* (☎ 939-3463), a full service restaurant in Liberty Square with character dinners for $19.50 for adults, $9.95 for children; reservations are necessary. Dishes include fish, ribs, chicken, oysters and clam chowder. They're open for (character-less) lunch as well.

Disney-MGM Studios

There are four full-service restaurants in this park, the most expensive one is *Hollywood Brown Derby* for seafood, steak, chicken and Cobb salad (tossed and served tableside); *Mama Melrose's Ristorante Italiano* does their pizzas in a brick oven and serves, of course, all kinds of Italian food.

The *Sci-Fi Dine-In Theater* is a recreation of a 1950s drive-in movie theater: tables are in vintage cars and as you eat your burger, pasta or sandwich ($6 to 10), you watch cheesy 1950s science fiction movies.

Maybe we went to the *'50s Prime Time Café* on a bad day – we had a bad time, but everyone else we spoke with had a blast. They've got good old American cooking like meatloaf and pot roast.

The *Soundstage Restaurant* does an all-you-can-eat character breakfast for $12.95 for adults and $7.95 for children; for lunch and dinner they serve pizza, pasta and sandwiches in a setting that does a very good job of approaching eating in Toontown.

Other places to eat within this park, like *Backlot Express*, *Min & Bill's Dockside Diner* and *Hollywood & Vine*, serve salads, burgers, sandwiches and other fairly simple and light things.

EPCOT Center

While all the restaurants in Disney do a fine job, this is where they really shine. The international food is authentic, and while somewhat pricey, you definitely get your money's worth. Note that we're only listing the flagship or at least our favorite restaurants at each of these countries – they all have more than these to offer.

Reservations, which are an exceptionally good idea, are given on a Disney-resort guest priority basis. When you call WDW-DINE (☎ 939-3463), you're asked for your hotel and room number, but even if you're staying at one of the hundreds of anonymous campsites at Fort Wilderness you can still get resort guest reservation status.

Canada *Le Cellier* (no reservations are required) is probably the least expensive option in the area, with chicken and meatball stew or traditional pork pie for $9.95, or an eight-ounce prime rib for $15.95. They also have an excellent (we're told) cold smoked beef brisket sandwich, and daily special sandwiches, for $7.50. Children's offerings include that old Canadian favorite, macaroni and cheese, or chicken and meatball stew for $3.99 with a drink and a cookie. Good deal, eh?

China Four major regional cooking styles of China are served up at the *Nine Dragons* restaurant, including Cantonese sweet and sour pork ($11.25) and Jade Tree beef (stir fried with broccoli and oyster sauce); Szechwan *kang bao* (stir fried with peanuts and hot chili peppers) and the inevitable General Tso (or Chow or Tsau or Ting or . . .) chicken ($12.25 and 12.45); Mandarin Great Wall duck ($13.45) or Mu Shu Pork (stir-fried shredded pork with vegetables, served in paper thin pancakes with a rich, sweet brown sauce) and Kiangche, like saucy chicken ($11.25) and lemon chicken ($12.45).

United Kingdom The *Rose & Crown Pub & Dining Room* has, of course fish and chips for $11.50, Yorkshire pudding for $10.75 and traditional cottage pie at $11.75,

and bubble and squeak for . . . just kidding. Prices rise slightly between lunch and dinner, and they have a kids' menu from $4.95 to 5.95. And during IllumiNations, the porch behind the beautifully done English pub is probably the best place to watch – if you can get out there. They don't accept reservations for seats out there, so you just have to show up early and try your luck. Also at the pub, Alice's Tea Party takes place on certain days, which is a free character 'tea' party (actually apple juice) with cookies, hosted by Alice and the White Rabbit. Ask when you're here.

France The best fun here is the *Chefs du France*, with main courses from $9 to $15, very French (shall we say 'brisk') service and tuxedoed (albeit in polyester) waiters and maitres d' serving Bermuda shorted, flip-flop-shod tourists: 'Garkone . . . ah bay voo any more o' that kammenbare?'

The *Au Petit Café* comes up with creations like *le suprême de volaille en croûte sauce au porto* (herb-marinated chicken breast with julienne vegetables in puff pastry with port wine-cream sauce) for $13.50 or just a simple quiche Lorraine for $7.95.

Germany Walking into the *Biergarten* in Germany was almost scary for Corinna for it felt (and smelled) so real. The all-you-can-eat dinner buffet with roasted chicken, all kinds of sausages, sauerkraut, potatoes and more is $14.50.

Italy When you order the fettuccine Alfredo ($16.50) at *Alfredo* (also known as *L'Originale Alfredo di Roma Ristorante*), you'll get to see their solid-gold serving spoon and fork (and hear the story of why, which brings us back to 1927, when Mary Pickford and Douglas Fairbanks . . . Okay, okay, the somewhat interesting story is printed on the menu); other dishes here include linguine con calamari $14.25 or pollo alla parmigiana $19. Look through the window at the front where you can see pasta being made fresh.

Japan *Mitsukoshi Teppanyaki* is the sort

of place where quick-handed chefs chop, dice, slice and sizzle right at your tabletop things like *kaibashira*, scallops served with vegetables and rice, $11.50 at lunch, $19.50 at dinner. They also offer combinations for two at lunch, like *tonosama*, sirloin and chicken served with salad, vegetables and rice, $23.90, and at dinner the *san-kai*, with shrimp appetizer, salad, soup, beef tenderloin, lobster tail, vegetables with noodles, rice, dessert and tea) for $59.90. There's a trendy tempura bar here as well.

Mexico *San Angel Inn* is run by the same family that operates the one in Mexico City; try the *chilaquiles*, fried tortillas and shredded chicken with green tomatillo sauce, cheese, sour cream and onion served with rice and refried beans, $10.25; *huachinango a la Veracruzana*, red snapper filet poached in wine with onions, tomatoes, olives and peppers served with rice, $15.50; or *plato tarasco*, grilled tenderloin beef topped with ranchero sauce, chili pepper strips and cheese, with chicken enchilada, cheese *chili relleno*, refried beans, guacamole and rice, at $20.50.

Morocco The excellent *Marrakesh Restaurant* does couscous – steamed and rolled semolina – in three flavors: vegetable ($13.75), chicken ($17.95) and lamb ($18.95); shish kebab ($18.95) or *diffa* – elaborate set meals for two – for $49.95. Other dishes include tangine of grouper (baked grouper with tomatoes, green peppers and garlic on almond-raisin rice, $18.25), and, of course, the Casbah Special: meatballs with carrots and peas, tomato sauce and almond-raisin rice, plus Hairira soup and pastries, for $19.95. There's belly dancing (the dancer's, not yours) here in the evenings.

Norway *Akershus*, modeled after a medieval Norwegian fortress, offers a spectacular *koldtbord* buffet for lunch ($11.95 for adults, $4.75 for children) and dinner ($17.95 for adults, $7.50 for children) with

simply wonderful selections of salads, herrings and *lots* of other fish and seafood items, plus meatballs, lamb, vegetables and Norwegian-style breads.

Pleasure Island

Call ☎ 824-4321 for specific information when you come. Snacks can be had at the *Hill St Diner* and sweet stuff at *D-Zerts*. The *Portobello Yacht Club* serves Italian food like good pizzas (they've got a wood-burning pizza oven) and pasta dishes. There's a Mardi-Gras all-you-can-eat Sunday brunch at the *Pleasure Island Jazz Co*, and the $22 for adults includes re-admission in the evening (it's $12 for kids under 12, who can't come in at night).

According to media reports, the *Planet Hollywood* (see the Places to Eat section in the Miami chapter for a fuller description of this celebrity-owned chain) here is the highest-grossing restaurant in the *world*, raking in over $50 million a year. Yippie kayay. Co-owner Arnold Schwarzenegger attributes his impressive personal success and business prowess to a constant rethinking of the markets: 'Dee mooah I come in kuntekt wit peepull,' said the star, 'dee mooah I loouhn.'

ENTERTAINMENT
Pleasure Island

This is Disney's version of Church St Station, a theme-entertainment complex in downtown Orlando that was drawing guests away from the resorts. It's basically an adult theme park (it serves liquor) within the Disney grounds. They've tried to accommodate all tastes: comedy at the Comedy Warehouse; retro '70s tunes at 8traxx, the Rock 'n' Roll Beach Club, the Jazz Bar, pop dance hits at Mannequins Dance Palace, live country & western at the Neon Armadillo Music Saloon, jazz from the Pleasure Island Jazz Co, and a nightly New Year's Eve party at midnight.

There's an AMC cinema nearby, as well.

Dinner Shows

There are dinner shows at Fort Wilderness's *Pioneer Hall*, with an all-you-can-

Mouse, Shmouse . . .
Where can I get a drink?

Attention: there are no alcoholic beverages served in the Magic Kingdom. Period. If you're there and you feel the urge for a brew, head for the nearby Contemporary Resort's bar.

Beer is served at the fast-food (excuse us, 'quick-service') restaurants at Disney-MGM Studios, and it's always fun to watch a father with several screaming kids sucking down a Bud Light while waiting for the burgers to arrive.

But the place to go for good wine and beer or exotic liquor and liqueur is the World Showcase at EPCOT, where you can sample stuff from around the world. The Rose & Crown Pub in the United Kingdom is a favorite. ■

eat barbecue dinner and the Hoop-Dee-Doo musical revue ($36 for adults, $26.50 for kids 12 to 20, $18 for kids three to 11. Other dinner shows (at the same price or slightly less) include Mickey's Tropical Luau and the Polynesian Luau at the Polynesian Resort; and oom-pah-pah sounds at the *Biergarten*.

GETTING THERE & AWAY
Bus & Shuttle Service

It's either inconvenient or expensive to get to Disney by public transport or private shuttle services. From Orlando's Lynx Bus Center, in the alley between W Pine St and W Central Blvd one block east of Orange Ave, buses can be caught to Kissimmee (Nos 4 and 18, hourly) and the Disney Parks (No 50, every two hours), but it's a long, long ride.

Private shuttles from the HI hostels and area hotels are $8 to 10 per person, and run every 15 minutes or so all day.

Car

It's awful, but the whole place is designed to be accessed by car. From the Orlando Airport, take Hwy 417 to Hwy 536, which runs right through Disney. From downtown Orlando, take I-4 and the exits are very

clearly marked. From Kissimmee take Hwy 192 to Hwy 535 and go north.

North from Orlando

☎ 904

Following Hwy 17 north from the Orlando area brings you into an area that's lovely to drive through, and there are several notable towns that are easy day trips from major cities along Florida's east coast and Orlando.

This area is charming for its rurality: the highlights here include getting into nature, seeing the manatees at Blue Spring, getting a spiritual reading, watching ubiquitous bass fisherman and seeing other things to write home about, like America's fern and potato capitals.

If you go in the spring and summer, all the free flowers you can pick sprout up roadside in glorious carpets of purple, yellow and blue – they're part of a county beautification program. To be nice to the flowers, be careful not to remove the roots.

BLUE SPRING STATE PARK

Blue Spring State Park (☎ 775-3663) is simply the best place in the state to come and see manatees in their natural habitat. The best time to visit is between November and March, when the St John's River, to the north, gets cold enough to make the peaceful mammals seek the relative warmth of Blue Spring's 72°F spring run. During the peak season, there are an average of 25 to 50 manatees here daily, but during exceptionally cold seasons (like 1996) the number is higher – the record in that year was 88.

Rangers count the manatees every morning and post their numbers at the entry gate. The manatees head right for the crystal-clear spring run, not the park's lagoon, and there's no swimming when manatees are present.

The park's other main attraction is the **Thursby House**, a three-story frame house (built in 1872, the 3rd story was added by Thursby's son, John, in 1900), which is being restored to its 1875-87 period appearance. Since extensive renovation was under way on the house, at press time it was only open the last weekend in January.

Places to Stay
Camping here is a great idea; primitive sites are $3.33 for adults and $2.22 for anyone under 18; non-electric tent sites are $15.54; sites with electric hookups (which also accommodate RVs and vans) are $17.66; all prices here include tax. Reservations are a good idea, and they're accepted up to 60 days in advance.

There are fully equipped two-bedroom cabins here as well, for $55.50. Cabins have central heating and air-conditioning, bathrooms, fireplaces and full kitchens, but they're under very high demand – weekends are booked months in advance, and reservations are accepted up to one year in advance, so do it.

The park is off French Ave at the northern end of Orange City. Their five-foot by 10-foot sign is impossible to miss if you're looking. Park admission is $3.25 per car, $1 for pedestrians and bicyclists.

More camping opportunities exist at nearby **Hontoon Island State Park** (☎ 736-5309), northwest of Blue Spring. It's a lovely little island with an observation tower and playground. When you stand on the shores of the St John's River, at the edge of the parking lot, a ferry zips over and takes you on the one-minute ride to the island. The park is six miles southwest of DeLand, off of Hwy 44.

CASSADAGA
About 20 minutes north of Winter Park, this sleepy little town is home to the Cassadaga ('kassuh-DAY-guh') Spiritualist Camp, established in 1884 by George P Colby. Today it's a federally registered historic district. The camp consists of a group of about 25 spiritualist-mediums who live and work in privately owned houses on church-owned land. The church, the Southern Cassadaga Spiritualist Camp Meeting Association (SCSCMA; ☎ 228-2880), believes in infinite intelligence, everlasting life on many planes of existence and the precepts of prophecy and healing.

For what it's worth, we believe that these folks genuinely believe in what they are doing: we say they're not shucksters or charlatans in that their goal is to spread the word as opposed to lining their pockets. They don't practice witchcraft or black magic, and they don't call themselves psychics but rather mediums.

Orientation & Information
The camp is mainly south of County Rd 4139, bordered roughly by Horseshoe Park at the west, Lake St at the south, and Marion St at the east. The Cassadaga Grocery & Sunflower Deli is on the north side of County Rd 4139 at Stevens St, diagonally opposite the Andrew Jackson Davis Building.

If you're a believer and/or you are looking for a reading, note that while dozens of psychics, hypnotists, faith healers and others have put out shingles in and around the compound, only SCSCMA-certified mediums are affiliated with the organization, which by the way does not condone hypnotism or promise to tell you your future.

Contact the SCSCMA for a list of certified mediums. You can get more information in the Cassadaga Spiritualist Camp Bookstore & Information Center in the Andrew Jackson Davis Building, where there's free information, public toilets, a bulletin board announcing services, and a spiritual bookshop.

Readings & Healings
Church services and healings (laying-on-of-hands) are held at no cost at the **Caesar Formal Healing Center**, next to the **Colby Memorial Temple** at the intersection of Stevens and Marion Sts, Sunday at 10 am and Wednesday at 7 pm. Private sessions with mediums and healers vary in price from person to person, but generally speaking a one-hour reading costs in the neighborhood of $50.

Places to Stay & Eat
There's no camping allowed in the town. Of the two options, the more expensive is

the better. The cramped rooms at the shabby *Cassadaga Hotel* (☎ 228-2323) are not very clean (we found dirt in the closets and the place smelled very stale when we visited); most have just showers and it just wasn't worth the $50/60 single/double price. The hotel is not affiliated with the camp but does offer spiritual readings and has a small restaurant.

Just north of town, though, is *Clauser's B&B* (☎ 228-0310, 800-220-0310), an historic landmark building with spotless rooms, some with Jacuzzis and most with screened-in balconies. They also run *Sherlock's*, an English-style pub. Rooms, including breakfast, range from $65 to 110 from Sunday to Thursday, $75 to 120 on Friday, Saturday and holidays. They're at 201 E Kicklighter Rd in Lake Helen.

The best food in the area is at the *Sunflower Deli* (☎ 228-3797) on County Rd 4139 at Stevens St, with smoothies ($2.50 to 2.75) and healthy vegetarian fare, like a vegetable sandwich ($3), veggie burgers from $3 to 3.50 and their absolutely awesome Cactus Chili for $1.75 to 2.50.

Getting There & Away

There's no public transport to Cassadaga. By car, either take I-4 to exit 54, head to the light, turn east on County Rd 4101 for a quarter-mile, then right onto County Rd 4139.

DELAND & DE LEON SPRINGS

DeLand is a quiet Southern town, home to not much other than its star attraction, Stetson University – the alma mater of the most reprehensible shyster of a lawyer we've ever met, but overall, we're sure, a fine school. But just to the north of the town is a state recreation area and a national wildlife refuge that offer wonderful ways to spend a day – you should come here if only for the pancakes at the Old Spanish Sugar Mill!

Woodruff Lake National Wildlife Refuge

This 19,000-acre protected refuge is open to canoeists, fishermen and, unfortunately, primitive hunters (those who use bow and arrow, blowguns or blackpowder firearms, as if that's more humane than an AK-47). The majority of the park is made up of freshwater marshes, lakes and streams, and it's home to over 200 species of birds, 42 of mammals, 58 of reptiles and 68 of fish, including osprey, ring-necked and wood ducks, alligators, bald eagles, manatees, swallow-tailed kites and blue-winged teal. But stay away from the place in September and October, when they hold indefensible bow & arrow and blackpowder firearms deer and wild hog hunts through the 'refuge' – on the theory that it's okay to murder animals as long as you're 'sporting' about it.

Admission and parking are free. You can arrange group tours in writing through the office of the refuge manager, Woodruff Lake National Wildlife Refuge, PO Box 488, De Leon Springs, FL 32130. Camping is not permitted; neither are there picnic facilities here. To get here, take Hwy 17 to Retta St, go one block to Grand Ave and turn left. The office is about a quarter-mile down on the right. To reach the park, continue past the office to Mud Lake Rd, turn right, drive about one mile and the entrance is across the railroad tracks. Many of your co-nature-lovers will be teenage couples in large pickup trucks – an appropriate vehicle, as this is a famous Lover's Lane.

De Leon Springs State Recreation Area

While the natural springs here are a year-round 72°F, it's a shame that the pool that was constructed around them is so ghastly: a Soviet-looking construction job that encased the quasi-oval-shaped gathering pool (☎ 985-4212) in cement. But hey, it's still a nice, large pool and except on weekends, it's usually pretty free of people. The concrete monstrosity metes out spring water into a creek that feeds into the Woodruff Lake National Wildlife Refuge, and you can (and really should, if you have the chance) rent canoes and peddle-boats ($6.50 an hour, $13.50 for four hours and $19 for eight hours) or kayaks ($5 an hour) from the little stand opposite the Old Spanish Sugar Mill (see below). Do *not* attempt to load a canoe on the boat launch – it's slipperier than a truckload of banana peels, and Nick ended up butt down in the soup three times before he could get up, and cut the sole of his foot in the process, only to be laughed at by both Corinna and the park rangers, who later made a peace offering of an iodine applicator and a bandage.

Why go through it? It's peaceful and pleasant and the water in the pool is wonderful (it's said to be a fountain of youth). Canoeing or kayaking through the area is a great opportunity to see wildlife, and best of all, afterwards you can have a meal at the *Old Spanish Grill & Griddle House* (☎ 985-5644). In a beautiful millhouse, they've installed electric griddles into the center of sturdy wooden tables; for $3.25 per person you make yourself all-you-can-eat pancakes at the table in two flavors: regular white flour or the excellent five-grain, all served with honey, molasses or maple syrup. We did something truly slick: ordered one fruit and cheese plate ($4.50) and one order of pancakes. Pour two large pancakes, flip them and put cheese and fruit on top of one, make a sandwich and flip the entire thing then cut and serve . . . yummers. At breakfast you can also cook your own eggs, bacon and sausage at the table. It's great fun.

Admission to the recreation area is $3.25 per vehicle, $1 for pedestrians and bicycles. There are picnic facilities but no camping. The entrance is just off Hwy 17 and is very well signed.

PIERSON

The self-proclaimed 'Fern Capital of America', Pierson is home to astounding greenhouses of the fuzzy green plants. It's not a retail outlet, but it's very interesting to see the copious quantities of 18-wheel trucks that transport the ferns to the northeastern USA, where they're a staple of city dwellings.

SEVILLE

We didn't see any barber shops here in this little town, but on Hwy 17 at Bruce St, just north of the city, is a wonderful house whose yard is filled with fascinating whirligigs, wind-driven planes, sculptures and doodads that need to be seen to be believed. You can't go in (No Trespassing signs abound), but you can pull over and take a peek for as long as you'd like.

PALATKA

Palatka (puhl-AT-kuh) is a lovely little town about 30 miles from St Augustine (see the Northeast Florida chapter) with a heartbreaking history, a lovely state garden and the best onion rings in northern Florida.

At the turn of the century, Palatka was a major steamship town, but bad news – around here, anyway – came in *fours*: the local cypress mill closed, the boats stopped coming, the town caught fire *and* the freeze of the winter of 1895-6 hit it with a clenched fist. But the town managed to hold on to its status as something of a tourist destination until WWI, after which it faded in significance.

Today Palatka is struggling to fuel a resurgence. There's a lively art scene and B&Bs are making their first tentative moves into the city: the Azalea House was first, in 1996, and more are coming, though it will be an uphill struggle to draw visitors from the riches of nearby St Augustine.

But overall, it's worth a stop. The town's two historic districts (Northside and Southside) are filled with turn-of-the-century houses, and it's a pleasure to stroll the districts. The main drag is Hwy 17, in town called Reid St. Get tourist information at the chamber of commerce (☎ 328-1503), at 1100 Reid St, just next to the Amtrak station, which is on 11th St just north of Reid St.

David Browning Railroad Museum

This museum in the Amtrak station is run by the Palatka Railroad Preservation Society (☎ 325-7425; ask for Jerry Iser). Inside, you'll see railroad paraphernalia like schedules and maps of the railroads that came through Florida, but the star of the show is definitely the Railrodeo model train set. Built by a reporter from Pennsylvania, this was the largest HO-scale transportable model railroad. Highlights are the

CENTRAL

animated objects like lights, crossings, bridges, a little girl in a tire swing, kites, and machinery like cranes, and front end loaders, and the hand-made circus wagons. They're open the first Sunday of the month from 1 to 4 pm. Admission is free, donations accepted.

Ravine State Gardens

This state park (☎ 329-3721) at the southeastern end of town was officially created as a WPA project in 1933. But the ravine itself was created over millions of years by water flowing from the St John's River. The 182-acre park has a two-mile loop road and walking trails along the creek. In March and April, this is the home of the Palatka Azalea Festival.

The park is open from 8 am to sundown all year; the loop drive is open to cars from 9 am to 4 pm. Admission is $3.25 per carload or $1 for pedestrians and bicyclists. No pets are allowed. To get here from the Larimer Arts Center (see below), drive west on Reid St to 9th St, turn left, follow the bend, continue after it becomes Crill Ave; turn left at Moseley Ave, and left again at Twigg St. The park entrance will be on the right hand side of the road.

Other Attractions

In the third week of October, the Putnam County Tourist Development Council holds its annual tour of homes in the historic districts. But driving or walking through the districts on your own at any time of year is a pleasant way to spend an afternoon. You can get maps of the districts at the excellent **Larimer Arts Center** (☎ 328-8998), in the old library building at 260 Reid St. The center holds rotating exhibitions every month except July and August, and admission is free. When we visited they were showing photographs and paintings by local artists.

In the Northside Historic District, the 1884 **Bronson-Mulholland House** (☎ 329-0140), the former home of Judge Isaac Bronson, is open as a historic museum Tuesday, Thursday and Sunday from 2 to 5 pm. And **St Mark's Episcopal Church**

(☎ 328-1474), at 200 Main St, built in 1854, was the missionary center of the Episcopal Church in St John's Valley and a Federal troop barracks during the Civil War. It's open for services Sunday at 8 and 10.30 am.

In the Southside Historic District, the **Tilghman House** (1884-87) is open as the gallery of the Palatka Art League Thursday to Saturday from 11 am to 4 pm. Admission is free; the house is at 324 River St.

Places to Stay & Eat

On the way out of town, don't neglect to stop into *Angel's Dining Car* (☎ 325-3927), an aluminum diner that claims to be the oldest in Florida. Maybe yes, maybe no, but the fusty place (the air's redolent with old cigarette smoke) manages to serve up traditional diner food that we haven't seen anywhere else for a long time: cherry Coke ($1), delicious and enormous and hand-made from St Augustine sweet-onion onion rings (95¢ to $1.35), and Pusalow (PUSS-uh-loh), which is chocolate milk with a little vanilla syrup and some crushed ice ($1).

Other dishes include huge and excellent cheeseburgers for $1.45 and sandwiches from $1.85 to 4.15. They're at 209 Reid St, open Sunday to Thursday from 5 am to midnight, Friday and Saturday 24 hours.

OCALA NATIONAL FOREST
☎ 352

The Ocala National Forest is a 400,000-acre park located about 10 miles east of Ocala and about 30 miles west of Daytona. There are several springs and lakes in the park, and you can camp anywhere you please, though developed campsites are available as well. Ocala offers fantastic hiking, canoeing, camping, fishing and swimming opportunities, and though it's not reachable by public transportation, once you arrive the place is very accessible: good signs, helpful rangers and good facilities.

Orientation & Information

Hwy 19 runs north-south through the park and Hwy 40 east-west. The three major spring areas are Juniper Spring (basically right at the park's center), Salt Springs (in the northern area of the park) and Alexander Springs (in the southeast); all have camping facilities.

Other areas with campsites include Fore Lake (near the western border of the park, roughly where Hwy 40 connects with Hwy 314), Lake Eaton (around the center of 314), Clearwater Lake (at the southeastern border of the park) and Lake Dorr (in the south near Hwy 19).

There are three visitors centers in the park:

Hwy 40 Visitor Center (☎ 352-625-7470) at 10863 E Hwy 40 (where Hwy 314 connects with Hwy 40), in Silver Springs.
Salt Springs Visitor Center (☎ 352-685-3070) at 14100 N Hwy 19 (where Hwy 315 forks off Hwy 19 in Salt Springs).
Pittman Visitor Center (☎ 352-669-7495) at 45621 State Rd 19 (where Hwy 445 forks off Hwy 19).

Juniper Springs Recreation Area
This is one of the oldest and most popular sites in the forest. There are actually two incredibly clear and beautiful springs here: Juniper Springs (swimming permitted, $2.25 admission for non-campers) and Fern Hammock Springs (no swimming). Together they produce about 13 million gallons of water daily.

There are three different camping areas at Juniper Springs (no water or electricity hookups) – the Sandpine Loop (south) and the Tropical Loop (north) which cost $12.75, and the tent area, near Fern Hammock, which is $10.75. There are showers ($1 for non-campers) and a dump station ($2 per use). The maximum stay is 14 consecutive days within a 30-day period. For more information on camping here call ☎ 352-625-3147.

A three-quarter-mile self-guided interpretive nature trail runs parallel to Juniper Creek and a 66-mile section of the Florida National Scenic Trail runs right through this area.

You can canoe down Juniper Creek for about seven miles; canoe rental (☎ 352-625-2808) costs $21.25 for two people or $24.25 for four people (plus a $20 deposit).

The run takes about four to 4½ hours and the price includes pickup and return shuttle at the bottom of the trail.

There are several toilets at this recreation area, as well as picnic facilities, parking, telephones, a concession stand and an amphitheater. The park is open daily from 8 am to 8 pm.

Salt Springs Recreation Area
This area features a two-mile loop trail and leads through hardwood hammocks, pine flatwoods and cypress forest.

Campsites are $12 with water and $10 without. There are showers ($1 for non-campers) and a dump station ($2 per use), for more information call ☎ 352-685-2048. The campground is open to non-campers from 8 am to 8 pm.

Canoe and boat rentals (☎ 352-685-2255) are available for the five-mile Salt Springs Run down to Lake George and the St John's River; canoe rentals are $10 for four hours, $20 for eight and small power boats are $25/40.

Alexander Springs Recreation Area
There is a one-mile hiking trail looping through the forest here.

Campsites (besides one, which is $15) have no water or electricity hookups and are $10. There are showers and a dump station ($2.50 per use). The campground is open to non-campers from 8 am to 8 pm.

Canoe rentals are $10 for two hours, $14.50 for four hours and $19.75 for eight (plus a $20 deposit), including pickup and shuttle. For more information call ☎ 352-669-3522.

There is a $2.25 swimming charge and a $5 charge for scuba diving for day users.

Fore Lake Recreation Area
Camping is $5, there are no showers and no dump station. The area is open 8 am to 8 pm.

Lake Eaton & Lake Eaton Sinkhole
The Lake Eaton sinkhole, which is a little east of the campground here, is a huge one: 80 feet deep and about 450 feet in diameter. There is a 2.2-mile interpretive walking

trail, which leads past it, as well as a boardwalk and staircase leading down into the hole. Note how quickly the temperature changes as you descend, becoming even chilly at the bottom. There is also an observation deck, and a boardwalk around the hole.

The primitive campground here (no hookups, showers or dump station) cost $3 for one person, $5 for two.

Clearwater Lake & Lake Dorr Recreation Areas

Camping (showers and a dump station but no hookups) at both these areas is $7; Clearwater Lake is open to non-campers from 8 am to 8 pm, Lake Dorr from 6 am to 10 pm.

Gainesville

• *pop 93,000* ☎ *352*

Gainesville is a college town, where most of the action focuses around the sprawling campus of the University of Florida (UF). In the last 10 years, the downtown has been totally overhauled, and people have been relocating here in droves since the city was voted Best Small Place to Live in the USA by *Money Magazine* in 1994.

ORIENTATION

The city is laid out on a grid system. Note that here, avenues run east-west and streets run north-south. University Ave is the main drag as well as the north-south divider; its intersection with Main St, the east-west divider, is considered the center of town. Downtown Gainesville is roughly bordered by 13th St at the west; 2nd St at the east, 2nd Ave at the north and 4th Ave at the center. The university is southwest of the center. Archer Rd between 34th and 43rd Sts is fast-food headquarters, with about 36 restaurants.

Addresses and streets are given a N, S, E, W or NE, SE, NW, SW prefix dependent on their relation to the intersection of Main and University. It's confusing, even to locals, whose trick is the mnemonic device

APRIL (actually APRL) which means: Avenues, Places, Rds and Lanes run east-west while everything else runs north-south. Addresses denote cross streets – a No 7150 would be between 71st and 72nd.

Maps

The VCB gives out tourist maps and a map to the Gainesville Bikeway System (see Getting Around, below). They also sell copies of Rand McNally's *Gainesville City Map*. Most buildings at the university that are open to the public also hoard detailed campus maps, which they reluctantly part with on request.

INFORMATION
Tourist Offices

The Alachua County Visitors & Convention Bureau (VCB; ☎ 374-5231, see the Online Services appendix) is at 30 E University Ave, just east of Main St. They hand out the usual tourist information. The Civic Media Center (CMC; ☎ 373-0010, see the Online Services appendix) at 1021 W University Ave has heaps of information on local culture, history, gay and lesbian resources, music and nightlife. They also host evenings of open-mic poetry readings and guitar concerts Sundays from 8 to 10 pm. Admission is $3 to 5 on a sliding scale depending on your income.

The Hippodrome (☎ 375-4477), at 25 SE 2nd Place just west of S Main St, is called 'the Hipp' by everyone in town and is a focus of the city's cultural scene (see below) and they also have a fair amount of local information and are generally helpful folks. The AAA (☎ 373-7801) has an office at 1201 NW 13th St.

Money

Barnett Bank has branches at 1116 W University Ave and 1961 N Main St. There's an American Express representative office at House of Travel, 3415 W University Ave (☎ 378-1601).

Post

The downtown post office (☎ 371-6748) is at 401 SE 1st Ave. There's another one at

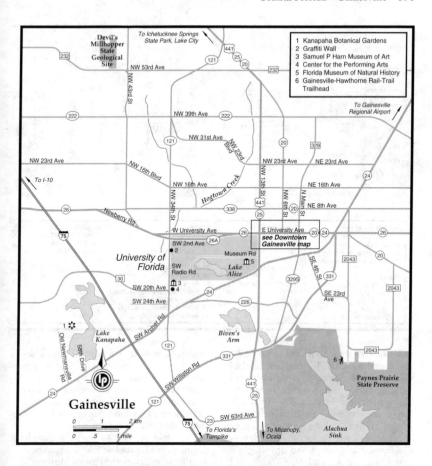

1 Kanapaha Botanical Gardens
2 Graffiti Wall
3 Samuel P Harn Museum of Art
4 Center for the Performing Arts
5 Florida Museum of Natural History
6 Gainesville-Hawthorne Rail-Trail Trailhead

1401 N Main St (☎ 375-5665) and yet another at 1630 NW 1st Ave (☎ 377-2993).

Bookstores & Libraries
UF has several bookshops: the main HUB (bookstore), the Collector's Shop at the Museum of Natural History and a Health Science Center bookstore. Downtown, several good used bookstores can be found: see the friendly folks at the chock-full-o'-Lonely Planet-guides Goerings' Book Center (☎ 378-0363), 1310 W University Ave; University Ave Bookshop (☎ 371-0062) at 804 University Ave; and Omni

Books (☎ 375-3755), a bit inconveniently located at the Westgate Publix Shopping Center at 99 SW 34th St (at University Ave). Iris Books (☎ 375-7477) sells feminist and women's studies books, as well as a good selection of gay and lesbian travel and fiction. It's at 802 W University Ave.

The downtown library (☎ 334-3977) is at 401 E University Ave at the corner of 3rd St, just east of the courthouse.

Media
The big daily is the *Gainesville Sun*. A free daily, the *Independent Florida Alligator* is

CENTRAL

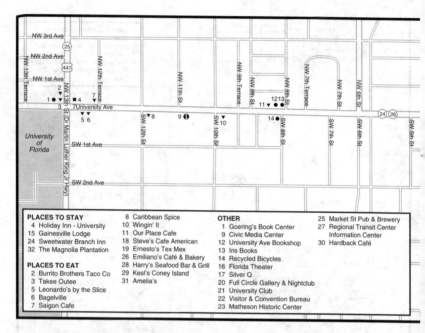

PLACES TO STAY
4 Holiday Inn - University
15 Gainesville Lodge
24 Sweetwater Branch Inn
32 The Magnolia Plantation

PLACES TO EAT
2 Burrito Brothers Taco Co
3 Takee Outee
5 Leonardo's by the Slice
6 Bagelville
7 Saigon Cafe

8 Caribbean Spice
10 Wingin' It
11 Our Place Cafe
18 Steve's Cafe American
19 Ernesto's Tex Mex
26 Emiliano's Café & Bakery
28 Harry's Seafood Bar & Grill
29 Kesl's Coney Island
31 Amelia's

OTHER
1 Goering's Book Center
9 Civic Media Center
12 University Ave Bookshop
13 Iris Books
14 Recycled Bicycles
16 Florida Theater
17 Silver Q
20 Full Circle Gallery & Nightclub
21 University Club
22 Visitor & Convention Bureau
23 Matheson Historic Center

25 Market St Pub & Brewery
27 Regional Transit Center
    Information Center
30 Hardback Café

published by students at, but not officially associated with, UF. It's free and available all around town. Other freebies available in vending boxes and at cafés, restaurants, clubs and bars include *UR* (University Reporter), a monthly entertainment guide; *Moon*, a biweekly that's heavier on arts and local news and politics. *Sleepless in Gainesville* is a down and dirty nightlife and music guide, and *Mea Culpa*, published by the CMC, is a monthly literary magazine.

NPR is at 89.1 FM.

Campuses

The star here is the University of Florida (☎ 392-3261). Florida's oldest university, established, as the East Florida Seminary in Ocala in 1853 and moved to Gainesville after the Civil War. It's a beast of a school sizewise, with almost 40,000 students, making it one of the 10 largest in the country. Its campus sprawls over 2000 acres, and has over 850 buildings, many of them historic

landmarks in their own right. There's a historical marker on the site of Native American burial mounds near the Holland Law Center building, and archaeologists have discovered artifacts from pre-Columbian settlements along Lake Alice, which is just east of the center of the campus.

The main reasons to visit the campus during your visit (unless you're a student or visiting scholar) are the Florida Museum of Natural History, the Harn Museum of Art, the Center for Performing Arts and, of course, Griffin Stadium (also called Florida Field), where the people who made it so difficult for you to get a hotel room will be watching the Gators football team. They're *nuts* about football here, and rooms are reserved as far as six months before a game. Free campus maps are available at all the campus museums.

Gay & Lesbian

For gay and lesbian information and resources, call the Gay Switchboard (☎ 332-

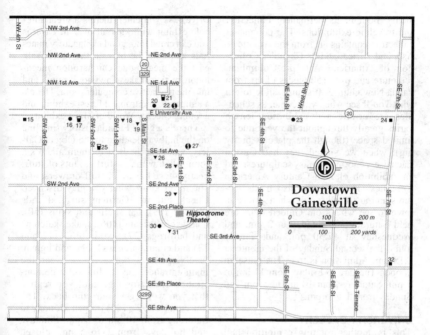

0700), or the LGB union at UF (☎ 392-1665 ext 310).

Laundry

Most of the coin laundries are a bit out of the center. The closest we liked was Coin Laundry, just before W 17th St on the north side of University Ave; also try the Washing Well, at the northwest corner of 34th St and University Ave. If you're staying in one of the dozens of motels on SW 13th St, head for A-Best Coin Laundry, 2411 SW 13th St.

Medical Services

The largest hospital in the area is Alachua General Hospital (☎ 372-4321), at 801 SW 2nd Ave.

GRAFFITI WALL

Also called the 34th St Wall, this is one of the city's finest examples of right, and liberal, thinking. The long cement wall that runs along the east side of 34th St just south of SW 2nd Ave is a graffiti-permitted zone, whose management has been effectively turned over to the students and graffiti artists that paint on it. The main focus is a well-maintained memorial to the five UF students who were murdered in August 1990 by a serial killer – an event that continues to haunt the city's and university's residents. With the exception of that memorial, the wall's an ever-changing exhibition of slogans, political manifestos, and thank you notes to parents for paying for students' education ('Thanks, Mom and Dad!'). While it's legal to tag here, it's considered bad form to paint over existing works or litter (there used to be garbage cans for used spray paint containers, but they frequently were knocked into the street, so they were removed).

SAMUEL P HARN MUSEUM OF ART

Another UF prize, the Harn (☎ 392-9826) holds rotating exhibits of fine art of all

CENTRAL

media, both in its permanent collection and traveling exhibitions. The permanent collection contains art from the Americas, Asia and Africa, and its Chandler Collection of American Art, pre-Columbian sculpture and over 150 pieces of art from Papua New Guinea. It's impossible to tell what you'll see when you come, as schedules are erratic and exhibition length varies greatly throughout the year due to limited space (though the place is pretty big); when we visited they had Gaston Lachaise's enormous brass sculptures, and an exhibition of 20th Century American Ceramics. The museum also holds lectures and artist talks; call when you're in town to see what's on. Guided tours are held Saturday and Sunday at 2 pm, and Wednesday at 12.30 pm, and 'family tours' the second Sunday of the month at 1.15 pm. Admission is free. The museum is open Tuesday to Friday from 11 am to 5 pm, Saturday from 10 am to 5 pm and Sunday from 1 to 5 pm.

UNIVERSITY GALLERY

This is another rotating exhibition hall (☎ 392-0201), dedicated to contemporary art by students and nationally known artists. In the spring, they hold exhibits of faculty and MFA candidate works; there are a total of six exhibits per year. It's in the Fine Arts Building complex on the campus, in Building B. It's open Tuesday from 10 am to 8 pm; Wednesday to Friday 10 am to 5 pm, Saturday 1 to 5 pm, closed Sunday and Monday.

OTHER GALLERIES

Public displays of locally produced art rotate through City Hall, the Gainesville Airport, the County Administration Building, and the Public Library. There's also usually art on display at Kesl's Coney Island restaurant (see Places to Eat, below).

FLORIDA MUSEUM
OF NATURAL HISTORY

We had a blast here, on the university campus on Museum Rd (park on the southeast corner of Museum Rd and Newell Drive). As you enter, there's a great sinkhole exhibit with kids all over it: caverns you can crawl into, good explanatory materials and note the bats on the roof. Walk past the mega-huge carcharodon megalodon, which makes Jaws look puny, and into the interactive computer room. There's a temperate and tropical forest exhibit, and a totally cheesey World of Maya exhibit.

There's a good Florida history timeline on the hallway leading to the Object Gallery, which is the best of them all. It's a room filled with . . . stuff . . . lots of stuff, neatly tucked away in stuff drawers, and you never know what you may discover. Check out the German surgical aids (drawer 199), bat skulls and skins (50), marine crustaceans (106), snake skeletons and bullfrogs (27), exotic birds (12 and 13) and common ones (1-11), and human (sadly, plastic) skulls (217). Near the main entrance, the satellite orbit demonstration is engrossing, until you realize that you won't get your coin back. The museum (☎ 392-1721) is open Monday to Saturday from 10 am to 5 pm, Sundays and holidays from 1 to 5 pm, closed Christmas. Admission is free.

HISTORICAL MUSEUMS

Don't go out of your way, but if you're in the neighborhood, the **Matheson Historic Center** (☎ 378-2280) is a pleasant enough museum filled with a very eclectic collection detailing the city's history – it's got a timeline, illustrations of the establishment of Gainesville, a very nice little store, and a lot of bottles. It's at 513 E University, admission is $2 for adults, $1 for students and 50¢ for children. It's open Tuesday to Friday from 9 am to 1 pm, Sunday 1 to 5 pm, closed Monday and Saturday.

The **Thomas Center** (☎ 334-2197) is another small historical museum; this one's at 302 NE 6th Ave. The building has been a private residence and a hotel, and is now owned by the city and houses city offices, a small history exhibition and art galleries with rotating exhibitions. Admission is free; it's open Monday to Friday from 9 am to 5 pm, Saturday and Sunday from 1 to 4 pm.

DEVIL'S MILLHOPPER STATE GEOLOGICAL SITE

Welcome to one of Florida's most famous holes in the ground. It works like this: limestone is susceptible to weak acids that are contained in formed when rainwater mixes with decomposing plant matter. As these acids eat away at the limestone, caverns are formed, and when there are enough, the whole thing collapses on itself, and presto! sinkhole. This one is over 120 feet deep and 500 feet across, and it's fascinating to walk down the 232-step wooden staircase, feeling the temperature decreasing with every step, and looking at what amounts to a cutaway section of Florida's geological formation.

Even if you're not up for the hole, the 63-acre park is pleasant enough to spend an afternoon in. There's an interpretive center without which I never could have written this paragraph; ranger-guided tours are held every Saturday morning at 10 am and orienteering classes on the fourth Saturday of the month at 9 am. The site (☎ 955-2008, 462-7905) is at 4732 Millhopper Rd, and is open 9 am to 5 pm daily. The admission of $2 per vehicle, $1 for pedestrians or bicyclists is paid on an honor system: take an envelope from the kiosk near the entrance, place your money in it, keep the stub on you or put it on your dashboard if you're driving (rangers check). To get to the park, take University Ave west to NW 39th Rd, which becomes NW 43rd St; follow that to its intersection with Hwy 232, which is Millhopper Rd. The entrance is on the right.

KANAPAHA BOTANICAL GARDENS

The most wonderful thing about these 62-acre gardens (☎ 372-4981), aside from the volunteers and Mr Gray, the cat, is its water garden: installed in 1994, the four waterfalls and the long babbling brook over newly landscaped hills and dales are courtesy of reclaimed waste water from the regional utilities board. Apparently, when they tried to just, well, shove the water back into the ground it wreaked havoc with the local pH balance, and the gardens and the utility came up with this ingenious, environmentally friendly and lovely method of reintroducing the stuff into the ground slowly and gently. This is a very serene place to take a stroll any time of year. They also feature a vinery, an herb garden and a butterfly garden – and there were still hummingbirds in the hummingbird garden when we visited in November! Admission is $2 for adults, $1 for children aged six to 13, under six free. To get there from downtown, take University Ave to 13th St, turn left, follow it to Archer Rd, follow that one mile past I-75, and the entrance is up the tiny dirt road on the right hand side (it's signed). The gardens are open Monday, Tuesday and Friday from 9 am to 5 pm, Wednesday, Saturday and Sunday from 9 am to dusk, closed Thursday.

PLACES TO STAY

Prices soar during special events, such as football games or graduation, when people book months in advance and come from as far as California to see their little darlings. Check in newspapers or with the VCB to see if any such special events are planned during your stay, and, if so, call *well* in advance for reservations!

Camping

There's not much. Rustic camping is available at *Paynes Prairie State Preserve* (☎ 904-466-3397), 10 miles south (see below, Around Gainesville).

Hotels & Motels

SW 13th St Most of the cheap motels are on the outskirts of town, either at the southern end of SW 13th St or on approach roads. SW 13th St is the best bet. The *Florida Motel* (☎ 376-3742), at 2603 SW 13th St, has shoddy but acceptable rooms for $23/25 single or double, $60 per double during special events; local calls are 35¢.

Just next to the excellent Bahn Thai restaurant (see below) at 2000 SW 13th St, the *Casa Loma Lodge* (☎ 372-3654) is a good deal, with clean rooms for $24, or $80 during special events. The rooms have

HBO, though that neon sign gets a bit loud – ask for a room away from it.

Over at the *Bambi Motel* (☎ 376-2622, 800-342-2624), 2119 SW 13th St, the rooms, which are $24/28 single/double, or $50/60 during special events, are nicer than the exterior would lead you to believe; large, with new TVs and HBO included; Beds were a bit soft for our taste, but hey.

Flashier is the *University Motel* (☎ 376-2222), 1901 SW 13th St, the one with the large pool and big back yard, where clean singles/doubles with new TVs are $25/30, or $75 per room during special events. Some of the rooms have refrigerators.

The nice *Cape Cod Inn* (☎ 371-2500) at 3820 SW 13th St has very clean rooms in a building that's a tad more romantic than the rest of its nearby competition, though it'll cost you: rooms are $41.95, $70 to 75 during special events, though a breakfast of muffins, juice and coffee is included.

Chains along SW 13th St include Radisson Inn, EconoLodge, Scottish Inn and Comfort Inn.

W University Ave Over on the main drag of W University Ave is the *Gainesville Lodge* (☎ 376-1224) at No 413, with singles and doubles for $30/35, or $60 to 100 during special events. Maybe it was us, but the service sure was surly: we weren't allowed to even *look* at a room. It could be a fine place, but proceed at your own peril.

There are two Holiday Inns in town, one near I-75, but the lax service and fusty rooms at the otherwise perfectly located *Holiday Inn – University* (☎ 376-1661) at 1250 W University Ave makes the standard rates of $82.50 per room and $98.50 per room in the pathetically under-appointed 'executive level' ($119.50 to 125 during special events) an absolute rip-off.

B&Bs
There are several B&Bs in town, usually east of Main St. Check with the VCB for a complete list. We liked *Sweetwater Branch Inn* (☎ 373-6760), at 625 E University Ave, with seven rooms and a carriage house, all with clawfoot tubs, some with fireplaces;

rooms range from $70 to 80 on weekdays, $80 to 100 on weekends, more during special events. We also liked *The Magnolia Plantation* (☎ 375-6653), 309 SE 7th St, for the free fridge filled with snacks and soft drinks, wine in the evening, and the pond out back. There's a VCR and TV in the parlor (no TV or telephones in the rooms), and the cats – Oliver, Whiner and Fievel. Rooms range from $70 to 95 a night, higher during special events.

Give the *Thomas Tourist Home*, 835 W University Ave, a big swerve, especially if you're German: 'I don't mind telling you,' said the owner to Corinna, a German national, 'that I don't think much of Germans.' Yeah? Well, we don't much care for you, broccoli nose.

PLACES TO EAT
This is fast-food heaven-college town, remember? Note that service in many places we list isn't what it could be; many servers have exams to cram for and, 'Hey, dude, we're puttin' the *band* back together!' attitudes and are therefore far too busy to bring you your tuna salad.

Budget
The corner of 13th St – both north and south – at University Ave is a great spot for cheap eats. We liked the veggie burritos at *Burrito Brothers Taco Co* (☎ 378-5948) so much that we bought one of their T-shirts for $13.50 – and later in our travels people all over the state (including a bellhop at the Sarasota Hyatt) recognized it and said, 'Yeah, those guys make *awesome* burritos!' These folks have been around for quite a while making kill-*ler* burritos ($1.90 to 2.40), tacos (90¢ to $1) and enchiladas ($1.75 to 1.90). None of the beans or tortillas contain animal fat, and they can prepare without dairy on request. Excellent guac and chips ($2) and primo salsa. Just do it! They're at 16 NW 13th St, open until 10 pm every day. Skip the Middle Eastern place two doors down, which microwaves their stuff and not very well.

Tantalizing smells emanated from the

Chinese place in the middle of those two, but the name – *Takee Outee* – struck even cynical us as being a tad on the politically incorrect side. They're at 14 NW 13th St (☎ 372-7907), and do take out only – entrées range from $2.75 (veggie deluxe) to $3.95 (General somebodyorother's chicken) and combos from $3.75 to 4.95; lunch specials are $2.65. *Café Saigon* (☎ 375-6612) at 101 SE 2nd St next to the Holiday Inn, has decent prices and is said to be good. There's no smoking inside, but they have outdoor tables as well.

Excellent pizza is cheap and hot on the south side of University Ave at 13th St, at *Leonardo's by the Slice* (☎ 375-2007), vending great slices from $1.50 to 1.95, and large 14-inch pies from $9 to 14. They're packed at lunchtime, and also do pastas like vegetable lasagna and spaghetti with meatballs ($4.99). Next door, a few feet east, *Bageland* serves up, eventually, hearty and filling sandwiches on bagels; cream cheese $1.19; tuna $1.99 and cream cheese and lox $4.25. They also do a breakfast special of bagel, orange juice and coffee for $2.29.

Caribbean Spice (☎ 377-2172) at 1121 W University Ave looks worth investigation – they were closed when we visited but promised Caribbean takeout lunch specials of beef or veggie patty and a soda for $2.35. *Wingin' It* (☎ 377-2473) at 923 W University Ave does 10 hot chicken wings for $3.95, and sandwiches from $3 to 4.50.

Up by the Hipp, *Kesl's Coney Island* (☎ 372-9288) at 210 SE 1st St does very healthy snacks and lunches in a great atmosphere of art and coffee. It's sort of new-age-Mex-California stuff, with hot dishes from $4.95 to 5.50, sandwiches from $3.25 to 5.50 and meatless burgers from $4.50 to 4.75.

Our Place Cafe (☎ 371-1172) is a little old (but in a comfortable way) and the people were quite friendly. The breakfast special (two eggs, toast or biscuit, home fries or grits) is $2.75, sandwiches are $3.95 to 4.50, quiche $3.45 and Greek salad $4.25. Smoking is not permitted, and it's at 808 W University Ave.

Middle & Top End
There's excellent Thai food at *Bahn Thai Restaurant* (☎ 335-1204), run by the second generation of the family that runs the one in Tallahassee; it's an exceptionally good deal at lunch time on weekdays, when they hold a 20-some-odd-entree buffet for $5.50 per person from 11 am to 2.30 pm. Dinner is pricier, with most entrees going for $8.95 and up, but the food is some of the best we've had in the state (and we like Thai food). It's at 1902 SW 13th St.

Ernesto's Tex-Mex Cafe (☎ 376-0750), 6 S Main St, has the best service we found in town, and food to match it: their chicken molé ($8.50) and veggie specials ($8.95 to 13.95) are definitely worth the price if you're going to splurge. They also have combo platters for $5.95 and some less expensive dishes.

Emiliano's Café & Bakery (☎ 375-7381) at 7 SE 1st Ave is a fine place to sit for lunch, either outside at a sidewalk table or inside (no smoking inside), with friendly but overworked service and a cheap tapas bar – fill up on finger food and get out for $10 for a couple, otherwise, lunch entrees are about $5.95 to 6.50, dinner twice that. Definitely try the cherry tomatoes and basil pesto ($2.95). Very friendly management.

Harry's Seafood Bar & Grill (☎ 372-1555),110 SE 1st St, in the old 1887 Opera House building, is another fine lunch place, with specials under $10. They also have a good happy hour, from 2 to 7 pm, with half-price well drinks and 75¢ off draft beer, and wings and oysters are half price. They hand you a beeper when you enter and page you when your table is ready.

Mr Hans (☎ 331-6400) is an excellent Chinese restaurant at 6944 NW 10th Place, just east of I-75 (exit 76). The fun thing is a formal attire requirement on some evenings for dinner, and the atmosphere is very authentic. They have great lunch specials like beef and chicken with Chinese vegetables in black bean sauce, or chicken and shrimp in orange sauce with hot and sour soup, egg roll and fried rice for $4.75. Dinner's more expensive; dishes like fried shrimp cake appetizers are $4.50, crab

CENTRAL

meat and sweet corn soup is $8 and main courses run from $7.50 (Hunan beef) to house special steak ($11.50).

For a flashy evening, *Amelia's* (☎ 373-1919) behind the Hipp is a romantic spot with good Italian food, mellow lighting and stellar bills. But for a date, it's not bad. Antipasti range from $5.95 to 8.25, fish from $13.95 to 15.95 and pastas from $8.95 to 11.95. Lunch is almost half price on everything. It's at 235 S Main St, and reservations are not a bad idea.

Friends in Gainesville say that *Leonardo's 706* (☎ 378-2001) at 706 W University Ave is considered to have the best food in town. It's fairly expensive ($10 to 20 for entrees), and is only open for dinner, but the Italian food here is said to be excellent, and served in enormous portions. It's got Nouveau setting, and lots of vegetarian dishes.

Steve's Cafe American (☎ 377-9337) is a little more elegant-looking (black and white tiles on the walls, fern-ish atmosphere), they do a Sunday brunch from 11 am to 3 pm for $12.50 for adults and $6 for children, including omelets, roast beef, toast, bacon, quiche, fruit, desserts and salads. On Thursday nights they have jazz. Lunch is served Monday to Friday from 11 am to 2.30 pm, sandwiches are $5.50 to 6.50, jambalaya $8.25. Dinner is served Monday to Saturday from 5 to 10 pm. Dishes on the menu are roasted, stuffed lamb rack with cilantro pesto $19, ricotta torte with herbed tomato coulis $12 or grilled salmon $15. It's at 12 W University Ave.

ENTERTAINMENT
Performing Arts
Formerly a federal building, later a post office, the *Hippodrome* building (1904-11) is one of Gainesville's most loved. Over the past 20 years, the Hipp (☎ 375-4477) has grown to be the city's cultural center, offering award-winning theatrical productions, a mega-cool experimental cinema series, educational programs, improvisational teen theater programs, kids' productions – this is a very cool place, and worth visiting. The cinema series concentrates on films not otherwise available in northern Florida, and the art galleries exhibit sculpture, painting, prints and photography by local, national and international artists, on rotating six-week schedules. Admissions vary. It's at 25 SE 2nd Place (you can't miss it). The little circular lane behind the Hipp is called Sun Center, a chi-chi shopping center.

UF's 1800-seat *Center for the Performing Arts* theater is home to concerts, theater and dance throughout the year. Tickets are available through the box office (☎ 392-2787) or through Ticketmaster. They average $30 for professional road show performances, and around $5 to 10 for local dance company performances, like those of Dance Alive!, a 30-year-old local dance troupe. There are almost always student discounts to performances, usually around $5, but sometimes (as with government-subsidized shows) admissions can be as low as 50¢. Downstairs, they have a smaller, 200-seat, 'black box' theater, home to UF Department of Theater (☎ 392-2038) productions, held usually once a semester. Call either venue and see what's on during your stay. The center is on the campus on Hull Rd, just next to the Harn Museum of Art.

Bars & Pubs
Have we mentioned that there are some college students here in town? As one would imagine, their raging hormones and tough (ha!) work schedules demand a few outlets. Check in *UR, Moon, Sleepless in Gainesville* and *Mea Culpa* for listings.

The *Market St Pub & Brewery* (☎ 377-2929) at 120 SW 1st Ave looks and smells English, they've got a huge beer list and serve up locally made concoctions but unfortunately (by the happy looks on customers' faces) we didn't get to sample them. Beers brewed on the premises include, on any given day, four or five of a list of seven, including Gainesville Gold, Hogtown Brown, Van Oakland Best Bitter and Der Honigweisse, all of which we would have loved to try. There's a happy hour, but they're cagey about just when it is – whenever, there are $2 pints. They also have live acoustic and jazz music on weekends.

Sports bars include *Silver Q*, at 225 W University Ave, which does happy hour Monday to Saturday from 4 to 8 pm and all day Sunday; there are 12 pool tables. An hour of pool is $5.75 including a pitcher of beer. Sports events are shown on their 20 TVs.

Gatormeisters (☎ 377-6444), 15 N Main St, and *The Swamp*, 1642 W University Ave, are two very popular drinking spots. Frat boys will please head for *Quarters*, upstairs at 1787 W University Ave.

Clubs & Live Music

The two most popular clubs are the *Covered Dish* (☎ 377-3334), at 210 SW 2nd Ave, which has original bands and a few cover-gigs (like the Thai Elvis! Cover charge ranges from $3 and 10, open Tuesday to Saturday); and *Richenbacher's* (☎ 375-5363) one of Gainesville's oldest, at 104 S Main St at the corner of 1st St, open Thursday to Saturday, with live local and other bands. Cover charge is usually $3. The *Florida Theatre* (☎ 375-7361) at 233 W University Ave, is a disco/club that also has live local bands every Wednesday night ($3). Tuesday and Thursday to Saturday they're a disco with different theme nights. On Friday and Saturday nights, their *High Note*, upstairs, does live jazz; 18 and over welcome. There's live local alternative music at the *Hardback Café* (☎ 372-6248) just opposite the Hipp – the doors open at 10 pm, $3 to 4 cover. They have punk and underground (some skinheads and dyke bands) music, at 232 SE 1st St.

Full Circle Gallery & Nightclub (☎ 377-8080) is an artsy, gay-friendly, all-welcome place at 6 E University Ave, that plays old wave, disco and acid jazz.

Gay & Lesbian

The *University Club* (☎ 378-6814) at 18 E University Ave (the entrance is around the back at NE 1st Ave and up or down the stairs), is predominantly gay, but it's open to everyone. Don't miss the Thursday night drag shows, and there's live music on Friday. On weekends the gay:straight ratio is probably 80:20. Tuesday nights are gay

dating games, and Wednesday there are strippers; 18 years and up are welcome, though under-21s wear armbands. Cover charge is $3 for those 21 and up, $5 for ages 18 to 20.

More decidedly gay is the *Melody Club & Ambush* (☎ 376-3772), a Western place that also does drag shows at 4130 NW 6th St.

In the middle of nowhere is *Oz* (☎ 332-2553), a lesbian bar with a whole lot of activities, from male dancers and lesbian bands to cookouts, way out at 7118 W University Ave, behind the Home Depot, two buildings down from the old Power Plant gym.

SPECTATOR SPORTS

Griffin Stadium (also called Florida Field, ☎ 375-4683, within Florida 800-344-2867), is the home of the UF Gators football team, which plays home games between September and December. Order tickets early – they go very, very, very quickly and cost about $21 for a single game. The Gators have men's baseball and men's and women's basketball teams as well; call the above number for ticket information to all Gators athletic events.

GETTING THERE & AWAY
Air
Gainesville Regional Airport (☎ 373-0249) is a mid-size airport about 10 miles northeast of downtown with regular service from Air South. Most non-business travelers don't usually fly to the area.

Bus
The Greyhound terminal (☎ 376-5252) is at 516 SW 4th Ave. Sample routes are listed below; prices are one way/roundtrip.

Destination	Price	Duration
Tallahassee	$33/65	3 hours, 10 minutes
Jacksonville	$15/29	1 hour, 40 minutes
Miami	$55/102	10¾ hours
Orlando	$23/45	3 hours

Train
The nearest Amtrak station serving the Gainesville area is in Waldo (☎ 468-1403),

13 miles northeast. A taxi from the station to the center of Gainesville costs about $25.

Car

Gainesville is in north central Florida, about three miles east of I-75, about 150 miles southeast of Tallahassee by way of I-75 to I-10, 108 miles northwest of Orlando; 62 miles southwest of Jacksonville, and 330 miles from Miami.

GETTING AROUND
To/From the Airport

There's no public transport to the airport. If you're slick you could jump a free hotel shuttle bus – we'd suggest the downtown Holiday Inn's if we were to ever suggest such a thing. Cabs (see below) charge about $10 to 12 for the ride.

Bus

Gainesville Regional Transit System (RTS; ☎ 334-2600, 334-2614) runs an excellent network of buses throughout the city. Fare is $1, transfers and the UF campus shuttle are 25¢. An unlimited ride weekly pass is $10, but sub-morons can spend the same $10 on a 10-ride pass as well. Bus Nos 1, 4, 5, 6, 7 and 10 cruise University Ave; Nos 1, 3, 4 and 7 cover SE 4th Ave and Nos 1 and 13 cover SW 13th St.

Taxi

The two big companies are Gator Cab (☎ 375-0313) and City Cab (☎ 375-8294). Taxi rates in Gainesville are $2.80 for the first mile, $1.30 for each additional mile.

Bicycle

Gainesville is an incredibly bike-friendly town, complete with a Bicycle & Pedestrian Program (☎ 334-2107) to answer questions about the city's 77 miles of bike-laned roads, 19 miles of curb-laned roads and many bike trails. In the city, bike lanes are marked with diamonds either painted on the street or on signs. In rural areas, bike trails or rail trails are signed. The largest of these is the 17-mile **Gainesville-Hawthorne Rail-Trail** which cuts across the northern end of Paynes Prairie State Preserve (see below), but note that it's crushed lime-rock and wide tires are recommended.

Recycled Bicycles (☎ 372-4890) at 805 University Ave doesn't really rent bikes, but you can buy a bike and sell it back to them the next day, they charge $10 per day (this is done for insurance). They are open Monday to Friday 9.30 am to 6 pm and Saturday 10 am to 5 pm.

AROUND GAINESVILLE
Ichetucknee Springs
☎ 904

Once a secret rendezvous for stoned UF students and cooler-toting locals, a day trip to the stunningly clear and blissfully refreshing waters of the now hugely and justifiably popular Ichetucknee River should be considered mandatory for any visitor to central Florida (unless you're here on a weekend, when it's so crowded it's just not worth the effort). It's simply one of the best paces in the state to effortlessly get out into nature, and generally a bitchin' good time is had by all, young and old alike.

The Ichetucknee (the name means 'beaver pond') River is fed by the Ichetucknee Spring group, which is made up of nine named springs (including Ichetucknee, Blue Hole, the three springs that make up Mission Springs, Grassy Hole Spring, Millpond Spring, Coffee Spring, and Devil's Eye) which together produce 233 *million* gallons of pure, sparkling clear water a day, which flow downstream at about 1¼ miles per hour and maintain a constant 73°F.

What all this means is that the river in this state park (☎ 904-497-2511 for a recording, 497-4690 for actual humans) is the finest place we know of to sit in an inner tube, rubber raft or canoe and lazily float downstream. The opportunities for spotting wildlife here are fantastic – as we put our tubes in on the last trip, two river otters lazily flopped around several feet from us, and the whole way down we saw turtles, all kinds of birds, spectacular flora and lots of fish. There are alligators here too, but we didn't see any.

While the spring has become so popular in recent years that the park now features regular trams bringing tubers to the river and shuttle services between the north and south entrances to the park, the Ichetucknee itself remains Florida's most pristine spring-fed river.

There's much more than just tubing and canoeing here; the park offers some splendid hiking trails, swimming, snorkeling and diving in some of the springs, and some ranger-led interpretive programs that are all worth the trip. While it is a stunningly diverse park, there's no camping on the grounds, though private campgrounds line the access roads leading to the entrances.

Park Rules Because of the huge numbers of people coming here and to protect the park's pristine conditions (as well as the sobriety of its guests), the park strictly forbids bringing in *any* alcohol, tobacco, disposable *any*thing, pets and bottles or cans. Rangers check bags as tubers board trams, and patrol occasionally; if you have any of the above you can be ejected from the park.

The park limits the number of tubers that can get on the river at the north entrance to 750 (technically) though on weekend days it's not uncommon to see a total of 3000 people along the entire river.

Tubing Tubing – sitting on a car tire's inner tube – is a wonderful occupation, and unfortunately it's not as comfortable as it looks. You use truck or very large car inner tubes, which you can buy at auto parts stores for about $10, or you can rent them from concessionaires along Hwys 238 and 47 for about $3 for inner tubes, $5/10 for one/two person rafts. If you rent the tubes, you needn't return them to the rental place but rather leave the tubes at the tube piles at the takeout point near the south entrance when you're finished – the vendors pick them up at the end of the day.

There are three options for tubing:

North Entrance The longest ride begins here, and is about a three- to 3½-hour-long trip depending on how much you clown around on the way down.

The north entrance is off the south side of Hwy 238. Drive in (admission for tubers for this run is $4.25 per person, kids under five free), and bring your party to the upper tube launch. Then the driver heads out of the park, and begins the seven-mile journey to the south entrance. Turn left on Hwy 238, and head to the stop sign. Turn left again and head to the next stop sign; turn left again and look for the south entrance sign on the left about a half-mile past the bridge over the Ichetucknee River. The whole route is very twisty and turny and you'll think you've made a wrong turn but you probably haven't.

At the south entrance, catch the van shuttles back up to the north entrance, where you join your party.

The north entrance is open for tubing from Memorial Day to Labor Day.

South Entrance There are two options at the south entrance: the Midpoint Tube Launch (about two hours to the bottom) or Dampier's Landing (about an hour). Park here (there are lockers, free with your own lock, or $1 for a lock at the concession) and either walk over to Dampier's or take the tram to Midpoint. Admission for tubers at the south entrance is $3.25 for adults, children under five free. The south entrance is open for tubing all year, though it's darn cold in winter.

Canoeing Canoes can be launched at the north entrance year round. They're available from private concessions around the park as well as from the park itself; at the park, rentals are $20 a day. There are ranger-led canoe trips at sunset and sunrise from October to March; call the rangers for more information on specific times. The trips, which last about two hours, cost $10 per person, with a minimum of two people per canoe. Admission for canoers is $4.25 per person.

Swimming There's great swimming and spectacular diving at the park's designated swimming areas at the north entrance at the Ichetucknee Head Spring or Blue Hole, natural pools with depths from one to 20 feet. Admission at the north entrance for swimmers is $3.25 per carload or $2 per carload if the honor system is in place. If it is, place your fee in the envelopes provided, slip them in the fee box and put the receipt in your car window.

Diving & Snorkeling There's snorkeling at the north entrance along the river from Memorial Day to Labor Day, as with tubing, and from the south entrance all year; admission prices are the same as for tubing. Certified cave divers are permitted to dive here from October 1 to March 31; the rangers hang onto your C-Card until you're finished with the dive. The cost is $5.35 per diver.

Hiking There are two small trails in the park, both well marked and featuring informational signs along the way, and both accessed through the north entrance; admission for hikers is $3.25 per carload, $2 when the honor system is in place. The Trestle Point Trail, the smaller of the two and the closest to the trailhead, is a three-quarter-mile trail with several stops along the way including Trestle Point, a river crossing for the phosphate cars that used to cross the river at this point, and an old phosphate mine pit.

The longer Pine Ridge Trail, on the east side of Old Rd, is a two-mile walk through hardwood hammock that goes by sinkholes, with a stop at another old phosphate mine pit.

Places to Stay & Eat The concession at the south entrance does hot dogs, pretzels, chips and soft drinks and, on weekends only for some reason, hamburgers. They're open the same hours as the park.

There are several campsites along Hwy 238, all offering essentially the same thing: campsites, a bar/restaurant and quick access to tubing. *Fort Ichetucknee* (☎ 497-1928), at the intersection of Hwys 47 and 238, seemed as nice as any, and the prices advertised were the same at all: $4 per person per night for sites with water and electric hookups.

Getting There & Away There's no public transportation available to or near the park, which is about 40 miles northwest of Gainesville. From downtown Gainesville, take NW 13th St straight north and pick up Hwy 441 (NW 13th becomes 441), take that straight up through High Springs, and take Hwy 27 to Hwy 47 north to Hwy 238 west to the park.

Paynes Prairie State Preserve

For world-class birding (there are tons of bald eagles, raptors and Florida wading birds and, in winter, sandhill cranes), spottings of really bizarre animals (they've got a herd each of wild horses and bison), mountain biking (over 34 trails including the 17-mile Gainesville-Hawthorne Rail-Trail), hiking and camping, it's very difficult to come up with a reason not to stop in this wonderful and eerie preserve (☎ 466-3397). Made up of wet prairie, swamp, hammock and pine flatwoods, the park is a very worthy day or overnight trip, and there's camping available within the park.

On weekends from November to April, free ranger-led tours of the prairie leave from the main visitor center at 8 am. On the first weekend of each month during that period, backpacking trips leave on overnight excursions. The only thing the park provides is an outhouse, a ranger guide and a great campfire, but you'll have a blast if you bring along insect repellent, a tent, food and marshmallows. The cost is an incredible $5.45 per person. It's good for all but the most avid hikers; you'll hike four miles the first day and two on the second, with lots of stops for beginners and less mobile travelers.

There are no canoe or mountain bike rentals, but you can bring your own. You can, however, rent **horses** through Oak View Riding Stable (☎ 237-8844) in Ocala for $45 per person (minimum six people). Once Oak View transports the horses to the preserve, a ranger will lead your group through on a two-to three-hour tour. There's a $5 gate fee in addition to the $45 rental/transport fee.

Gainesville-Hawthorne Rail-Trail The trails through the park are perfect for bicycling and the Gainesville-Hawthorne Rail-Trail is one of the hottest around. These types of trails, popular throughout central Florida, are built on the railbeds where railway tracks used to be. When the tracks are removed, hikers, bicyclists and equestrians have a perfect path.

Camping The park's camping options are family (drive in sites) or tent (walk in sites, but close to the parking lots). The cost per site is $13.02 with electric hookup, $10.90 without. You can reserve up to 60 days in advance, and because of football games in Gainesville, it's probably a good idea as the place gets booked out.

The preserve is between Gainesville and the city of Micanopy, on Hwy 441. Admission is $3.25 per car or $1 for pedestrians and bicyclists. It's open year round from 8 am to sunset.

Rawlings Estate

Marjory Kinnan Rawlings (1896-1953), was author of the Pulitzer-prize winning novel *The Yearling*, a coming-of-age story set in what is now the Ocala National Forest, and *Cross Creek*, a book about her life in this estate (☎ 466-3672), just north of Orange Lake off Hwy 325 between Island Grove and Micanopy.

Rawlings came to the area with her first husband in 1928, and she remained in the area after they divorced in 1933. She remarried in 1941, and continued to write at Cross Creek until her death.

The Cracker-style house is open for guided tours only ($1) Thursday to Sunday at 11 am and 1, 2, 3 and 4 pm, closed Monday to Wednesday and during August and September. Tour groups are limited to 10 people and are very popular, so expect a wait when you visit. The eight acres of grounds that are run by the historic site are open year round from 9 am to 5 pm. Admission is $3.25 per car or $1 for pedestrians and bicyclists.

Devil's Den

Devil's Den (☎ 528-3322) is an underground spring located just outside the

Marjorie Kinnan Rawlings

quaint town of Williston (known for its breeding of show horses; if you like horses, the area is nice to drive through just for a change of pace) about 18 miles southeast of Gainesville.

Divers simply do not want to miss this fantastic cave dive opportunity, though it's open to swimmers as well, and we thought it was one of the most spectacularly odd and beautiful places in the state. It's a fine spot for an overnight – there's camping at the site.

The spring bubbles up at a constant 72°F, so there's swimming year round, its eerie blue water illuminated by the sunlight that shines through an opening in the ground about 20 feet above the surface of the water. While divers used to lower themselves into the springs on rope ladders, there's now a staircase dug into the ground – it's a wonderful sensation to enter a hole in the ground, walk down through solid rock and emerge into something right out of the movie *The Abyss* (portions of which were actually filmed at nearby Silver Springs). Note that no pets are permitted in the park.

Diving Certified divers can dive here for $24 a day, and they have a full line of rental equipment if you've just brought yourself

CENTRAL

and your bathing suit. A basic package (not including flashlight, booties or hood) is $55 per day including admission to the park. The spring has a maximum depth of 56 feet, and there are numerous tunnels to explore. You'll see prehistoric fossils embedded in the walls and floor, and there are six species of fish in the spring.

The spring is open Monday to Thursday from 9 am to 5 pm, Friday to Sunday from 8 am to 5 pm; there are sunset dives on Saturday for an additional cost of $10 if you've been there all day, or $15 if you show up just for the sunset dive.

Swimming & Activities Swimming ($5 a day) is permitted unless there are too many divers in the water, and the park also has activities like volleyball and horseback riding (guided trail tours, $15 for a half-hour, $25 an hour).

Camping There is tent camping available at the park; if you've dived there it costs $5 per person, if you haven't it's $8.50 per person, children under six are a $1. Campfires are permitted, but they must be in a fire circle and you must have an extinguishing material (such as sand or a lot of people drinking beer). There are hot showers and barbecue grills available.

Cabins with kitchens are $75 a night and sleep up to four people. Buy food and supplies at the Winn-Dixie supermarket on the corner of 727 W Noble Ave at Hwy 27 in downtown Williston, where you'll also find a few little restaurants including the *Ivy House* (☎ 528-5410) at 106 NW Main St, that does lunch from Tuesday to Saturday with meals like chicken supreme with yellow rice and salad ($5.95) and desserts like pumpkin roll or chocolate fudge pie ($1.50). No smoking. They do turkey and prime rib dinners on the first Saturday of the month for $12.95.

Getting There & Away There's no public transport available. To get here by car, from Gainesville take I-75 to Hwy 121 south, for 15 miles to the junction of US Hwy 27, which will bring you into downtown Williston. Turn west on Hwy 27A (towards the town of Bronson) and the Den is on the right hand side of the road (look for the dive flag), up the dirt road past the fenced-off horse grazing fields; follow the signs. From Orlando, take Florida's Turnpike north to I-75 north, to exit 70, and take Hwy 27 north to Williston.

Silver Springs
☎ 904

One of the few saving graces of the otherwise debilitatingly boring city of Ocala is Silver Springs (☎ 236-2121, 800-234-7458), a theme park built around seven natural springs and the resultant stunningly clear Silver River. The park says that glass-bottomed boats were invented here in 1878 and if that's not enough of a claim try this one: *Tarzan* movies, and portions of *The Abyss* were shot here as well.

While there are a number of fascinating attractions here at the park, we're not certain that the admission prices of $26.95 for adults, $18.95 for children (10% discount for seniors, AAA members, active military and the disabled) are worth it. True, we didn't do *all* the attractions the park had to offer, but we did do a whole lot of them.

The glass-bottom boat ride is spectacular. As you slowly cruise over the eel grass, you'll pass over six small spring formations before the grand finale, a pass over Mammoth Spring, the world's largest artesian limestone spring.

Other attractions include our favorite, Doolittle Petting Area, where we met the sweetest camel on the planet: baby, you ain't lived till you been kissed by a camel. This one's got incredibly soft skin, smells clean and loves to be petted. But Corinna was in the middle of saying how cute he was when he reared back and *KABOOM!* – a concussive jolt and a shower of camel snot: a camel sneeze. *(Gesundheit)*. Other animals in the petting area are giraffes, goats, sheep, deer, buffalo, llamas and pigs.

Lost River Voyage is a boat ride through dense jungle, as is the Jungle Cruise, featuring animals from six continents including zebras, emus and giraffes; Jeep Safari is a trailer ride through a 35-acre jungle and a look at their alligator pit.

Shows include Reptiles of the World, with demonstrations using live reptiles like alligators, snakes and lizards; and Creature Feature, a live and video-taped presentation on creepy things like scorpions and other spiders, hissing cockroaches and bats.

Two must-sees are the new white alligator exhibit (it's one of only 17 in the world), which features a white skinned, blue-eyed gator, along with other leucistic and albino reptiles like pythons and mud turtles. And then you've got to see Sobek, who at 16 feet long and weighing literally a ton is said to be the world's largest captive American crocodile.

For area information, contact the Ocala/Marion County Chamber of Commerce (☎ 629-8051) at 110 E Silver Springs Blvd.

Places to Stay – camping
KOA Silver Springs/Ocala (☎ 237-2138) has tent sites for $16.95 in low season, $21.95 in high season; RV and van sites with water and electric hookups for $22.95/27.95 and with full hookups for $24.95/29.95; and Kamping Kabins for $29.95/39.95. They're at 3200 SW 38th Ave; from Silver Springs take Silver Springs Blvd west to I-75, and go south one exit, turn right onto Hwy 200, and 38th Ave is about a mile up the road. There are lots and lots of signs.

Places to Stay – motels & B&Bs
the chain hotels are clustered near I-75. We really liked what we saw at the Cloister Court (☎ 236-0799) at 5460 E Silver Springs Blvd, opposite Water Mania, a small water park. They have a pool and are very friendly; rooms are $25 or $35 year round for a king, suites $45 to 75. Most rooms have kitchenettes and the prices are negotiable.

Silver Springs Motel (☎ 236-4243) has rooms for $30/35 a single/double, during 'special events' about $5 more; weekly rooms are $120/140 in low season and $140/160 in high season, each additional person $20. Local phone calls are free,

they have a pool and cable TV, but the carpets were a bit worn, and we weren't overly impressed.

There's very friendly staff at the huge 1925 B&B Ritz Historic Inn (☎ 867-7700) at 1205 E Silver Springs Blvd, which charges $75 for standard suites (two rooms) and $85 for executive suites (one large room with an archway between the sleeping and living area). The building has been restored and it's rather beautiful, with hardwood floors and antique furnishings. All rooms have air-conditioning and ceiling fans, fridges, microwaves and coffeemakers. They do an elaborate continental breakfast of hot and cold cereal, bagels, croissants, muffins, pastries, donuts and coffee, tea or cocoa.

Places to Eat
The German Kitchen Restaurant (☎ 236-3055) smelled very good and authentic when we walked in. Liver and onions is $7.75, sauerbraten or goulash are $10.25, and schnitzel is $12.25. They have a variety of German beers from Spaten to Hofbrau to Warsteiner for $2.50 to 2.75; Maisl's Hefe Weisse is $4. It's at 5340 E Silver Springs Blvd.

B Healthy (☎ 867-8727) is a terrific health food shop and lunch bar at 2202 E Springs Blvd. Their juice bar/food counter has large salads from $2.25 to 3.55, sandwiches $3.25 to 3.95 and burritos $2.75 to 3.25. We had great vegetarian chili ($2.50) and they also make darn good smoothies and frozen yogurt. The health-food shop section sells the usual vitamins, dried fruits, nuts, berries, granola, curds and whey and whatever else those people eat and other healthful things.

Harry's Seafood Bar & Grill (☎ 840-0900) is a seafood bar and grill downtown; see the Gainesville Places to Eat section for more information – it's the same here as it is there. It's at 24 NE 1st Ave.

Andrew's Ocala Bakery & Sandwich Shop (☎ 622-7769) at 42 S Magnolia Ave, has big sandwiches for $3 to 3.50; soup with a grilled cheese sandwich for $3, cheeseburgers for $1.26 and chicken breast-on-a-bagel sandwiches for $2.25.

CENTRAL

Alfio's Pizza Restaurant (☎ 629-7228) has pizza by the slice for $1.40, sandwiches from $3.50 to 4, and pizzas from $7 to 12, at 103 SE 1st Ave.

Getting There & Away The Greyhound station (☎ 732-2677) is at 512 N Magnolia St at the corner of NW 5th St in Ocala. They have nine buses a day from Gainesville for $10 one way, $19 roundtrip, and the trip takes from 45 minutes to 1¼ hours.

There are eight a day to/from Orlando at $18 one way, $36 roundtrip, 1½ to 2½ hours duration.

By car, Ocala is 37 miles south of Gainesville and 72 miles northeast of Orlando. From Gainesville, take either I-75 or Hwy 301 south to Silver Springs Blvd (Hwy 40) and go east to get to Silver Springs. From Orlando, take Florida's Turnpike to I-75, and that to Silver Springs Blvd.

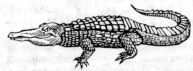

Space Coast

HIGHLIGHTS

- See a space shuttle launch at the Kennedy Space Center
- Watch birds and wildlife at Merritt Island NWR, home to more endangered and protected species than any other refuge in the country
- Attend Space Camp to learn rocket science and go on a simulated shuttle mission – or offload the kids for a week while you soak on the nearby beaches
- See the sea turtles lay their eggs at Canaveral National Seashore

☎ 904

The major attractions along the stretch of coast between Fort Pierce and Daytona Beach are the galactic activities at the Kennedy Space Center, and if you've ever read *The Right Stuff* and wondered about Tom Wolfe's description of Cocoa Beach, you'll be able to see for yourself just how dead-on accurate he was.

But the most surprising aspect of this region is that despite being the Western Hemisphere's only manned spaceport, its major distinction is its nature conservation and its protection of threatened and endangered species by the National Park Service (NPS) and US Fish & Wildlife Service (USFWS). Bird watchers have a field day at Merritt Island National Wildlife Refuge and Canaveral National Seashore, as do surfers, families and nature lovers. Whales have been spotted off Canaveral National Seashore, and some of the state's best sea turtle observation programs are run here. But you need to reserve early!

You'll definitely need your own transportation, as public transport is spotty and shuttles and taxis are expensive: they're more to service wealthy and ailing retirees from up north than anything else.

Despite the abundance of inexpensive and even free camping opportunities, for the most part the affordable lodging options are limited to motels that are packed to the rafters during launches and are generally on the rundown and sometimes spooky side. Unless you're camping, we highly recommend visiting the area from Orlando or somewhere inland as opposed to seeking shelter in the immediate vicinity.

KENNEDY SPACE CENTER

The Kennedy Space Center is among the most popular attractions in Florida, drawing over two million people a year. As the only site in the Western Hemisphere from which humans have been launched into space, the place is a fascinating excursion for the average visitor and the mother-lode to space junkies – and there are far more of those than you'd think. You can easily spend a full day here taking the two bus tours, watching the IMAX films and walking through the exhibits.

History

Early Rocket Science Modern rocketry dates to the turn of the 20th century, when Russian scientist Konstantin Tsiolkovsky proposed the use of multiple engines powered by liquid hydrogen and oxygen as opposed to the solid fuel – that'd be gunpowder – that had previously been used for

archives and large numbers of German scientists to boot.

The Making of NASA When the Soviets announced on October 4, 1957, that they had successfully launched the unmanned satellite *Sputnik*, the Americans found themselves beaten in a race they'd thought they had covered hands down. The USA launched its first unmanned satellite into Earth orbit in January 1958.

Fueled by propaganda campaigns and predictions of doom by American politicians, who envisioned Soviet flyboys over US airspace dropping atomic bombs at will, the National Aeronautics & Space Administration (NASA) established Project Mercury on October 7, 1958, and the race for manned space flight had begun. The central-eastern Florida coast was chosen for many reasons, chief among them the weather, its proximity to the ocean for splash landings and the huge and unpopulated tracts of land available to the government for testing.

Mercury Seven In recruiting the first seven astronauts (the word is derived from the Greek words *astro* – star, and *nautes* (naw-teez) – sailor, explorer), the government talent pool consisted of test and fighter pilots from the various branches of the military. The requirements called for a jet-qualified test-pilot-school graduate who had logged over 1500 hours of flight time in jets, held at least an undergraduate university degree, was a US citizen, and was less than 40 years old and under five feet, 11 inches tall (determined by the restrictive size of the capsule). There were 110 qualified applicants.

The testing and weeding-out procedure is well documented and in hindsight would seem to have been overkill in the extreme: applicants were subject to sleep, light and other sensory deprivation, and – in an effort to ensure a team of unshakable men – humiliation and psychological stress that bordered on cruelty. Odd physical challenges such as electric shocks and plunges into ice water were also endured, and in

rockets. The multi-stage rocket design is necessary to support the weight of the enormous amounts of fuel needed to propel an object free of the Earth's atmosphere. As each individually powered engine exhausts its fuel, it is jettisoned, allowing the remaining engines to boost the vehicle farther into space.

In 1926, American scientist Robert Goddard launched what is considered to be the first successful guided rocket. But rocketry didn't gain military significance until just before WWII, when German scientists led by Wernher von Braun began to experiment with rockets as a weapon delivery system. In 1942 the infamous V2 rockets were perfected, which could carry a payload of bombs at an altitude of 50 miles.

At the end of the war, American war spoils included von Braun (actually he defected) and about 100 V2s. For their part, the Soviets managed to clean out substantial sections of the German's bomb-making

one instance candidates were made to walk through a public hospital with their intestines filled to bursting with barium while holding the plug that prevented it from flushing out in an explosive rush. There were also routine donations of sperm, stool, blood, tissue, urine and anything else scientists could think of to test.

The US plan was to begin with a series of cannonball-like, sub-orbital 'lobs', in which the capsule is fired into outer space and falls directly back to Earth, and graduate to full orbital flight after systems had been tested in the environment of outer space.

When the Mercury astronauts – Gus Grissom, Deke Slayton, John Glenn, Wally Schirra, Alan Shephard, Scott Carpenter and Gordon Cooper – were introduced to the media in 1959, the USA treated them with nothing less than hero worship. And that worship continued despite the abject failure of one of the primary goals of the program: putting the first man in space.

First Humans in Space On April 12, 1961, the Soviet Union announced that the first manned spacecraft had been placed in Earth orbit. The cosmonaut who piloted the craft was announced to have been Yuri Gagarin, the first of 20 Soviet pilots that had been selected for the Soviet space program.

Secrecy has left many questions unanswered to this day and Gagarin's single Earth orbit may not have been the first. In his book *Heroes in Space: From Gagarin to Challenger*, Peter Bond says that there was speculation in the British press that Sergei Ilyushin had in fact completed three Earth orbits days before Gagarin's flight but had become ill.

But the Soviets beat the USA into manned orbital flight. The US had, after a series of almost comical and widely publicized mishaps during testing of launch vehicles, launched a chimpanzee into sub-orbital flight by this time. Stops were pulled and after multiple delays, on May 5, 1961, a Redstone rocket carried Alan Shephard into a 15-minute sub-orbital flight. There were a couple of amusing incidents during

the flight: a need for a human waste removal system became apparent after Shephard (who had been sitting in the capsule waiting to be launched for several hours) finally resorted to urinating in his spacesuit. Shephard had also forgotten to remove a gray filter from his cockpit periscope (the first Mercury capsule had no window), so the first American in space saw the world below in black & white.

On May 25, President John F Kennedy announced that the US intended to land a man on the moon by the end of the decade.

Titov & the Rest of Mercury Gus Grissom's Mercury flight, the second manned US sub-orbital mission (marred by the loss of the capsule after landing in the ocean) on July 21, 1961, came about a month before the biggest blow yet to the Americans: on August 6, 1961, the Soviets launched *Vostok 2*, piloted by cosmonaut German Titov who orbited the Earth 17 times in 25 hours.

While launches continued to leave from the Cape, Mission Control and the astronaut training program were moved to the Manned Space Flight Center (now the Johnson Space Center) near Houston, Texas. That's true to this day.

Four other Mercury launches took place (the seventh astronaut, Deke Slayton, had been grounded due to a heart condition and though he became Director of Astronaut Activities, he would not fly in space until 1975) before the end of the Mercury program, including John Glenn's, when he became the first American to orbit the Earth, and Gordon Cooper's. Cooper, the last of the Mercury Seven to fly, orbited the Earth 22½ times in 34 hours, and released the first satellite from a spacecraft. He was also the last American to fly alone in space.

Gemini The Soviets continued to beat the Americans in space firsts: first woman in space, first dual flight (two spacecraft in orbit together), first two- and three-person crew, and on. The US Gemini program, successor to the Mercury Project, was designed to work out the bugs and procedures for two-man crews, as well as for testing flight endurance and docking procedures which would be used for the Apollo missions to the moon.

The accomplishments of the Gemini crews were as astounding as they are unheralded. They involved true piloting of spacecraft in ways the Mercury astronauts never had, using the first on-board computers, space walks, spacedocking and over 1000 hours of space flight on ships that left Earth at a rate of two a month. But their accomplishments were, at least in the media, simply overshadowed by the more spectacular nature of the Apollo missions to the moon.

Apollo During training tests before the first Apollo flights, Gus Grissom, Edward White and Roger Chaffee were killed when fire swept through the capsule as it sat atop a Saturn V rocket at the cape. The Apollo capsules had been designed with an inward-opening hatch, (the ones on Mercury and Gemini opened outward), which required a minimum of 1½ minutes to open under optimal conditions.

Just after 1 pm on January 27, 1967, after a series of glitches during a flight test, Roger Chaffee said over the intercom, 'Fire . . . I smell fire.' As mission control watched helplessly on monitors, flames engulfed the oxygen-rich interior of the Apollo capsule; Grissom properly vented oxygen and Chaffee and White began the door opening procedure, but all were quickly overcome by smoke and fumes from the burning materials inside the craft.

After a minute and a half, ground crew – fully aware of the imminent danger of the entire service structure catching fire – reached the capsule and tried to open the door. According to accounts in *Moonport: A History of the Kennedy Space Center*, Donald Babbitt, James Gleaves, Jerry Hawkins, Steven Clemmons, LD Reece and Henry Rodgers managed, after five minutes, to open the hatch despite being driven back by smoke and heat.

The modifications to the door assembly delayed the first Apollo space flight until October 11, 1968. The deaths of the astro-

nauts were the last until the *Challenger* disaster in January 1986.

Apollo 7 through *10* were preliminary flights spent perfecting the procedures, including:

Apollo 8
the first manned spacecraft to leave Earth's orbit and orbit the moon; December 21 to 27, 1968

Apollo 9
the first space test of the lunar module and orbital rendezvous and docking techniques; March 3 to 13, 1969

Apollo 10
dress rehearsal for the lunar landing and survey of the landing site at the Sea of Tranquility; May 18 to 26, 1969

Apollo 11 left Earth on July 16, 1969. On July 20, *Eagle*, the landing module, landed on the surface of the moon. As the world watched on television, Neil Armstrong delivered two of the best lines ever said:

Houston, Tranquility Base here . . . Eagle has landed.

and

That's one small step for [a] man, one giant leap for mankind.

Six Apollo expeditions landed, and 12 human beings walked on the moon by the time the initial program was completed on December 19, 1972.

Skylab & Apollo-Soyuz With the moon behind it, NASA turned its attention to creating a space station: a space platform on which astronauts would live and work for weeks and months at a time. Skylab's initial deployment was marred when the meteorite shield/sunshade broke loose; astronauts repaired the glitch 10 days later and over the next nine months, three crews lived on board the station. After 513 man-days in orbit, Skylab was abandoned, and, on July 11, 1979, five years later, it fell through the atmosphere and disintegrated. National headlines screamed 'Skylab is Falling! Skylab is Falling!'

By 1975, politics had thawed enough to

allow the Soviets and the Americans to form a joint space venture: the Apollo-Soyuz Test Project, a link-up in space. The *Soyuz 19* and *Apollo* spacecraft launched on July 15; on July 17 they linked up and the world saw the first international handshake in space – the link up (not the handshake) lasted 44 minutes. Apollo-Soyuz also marked the first space voyage for Deke Slayton, who had been grounded during the Mercury program.

Shuttle Program The problem with all this high-fallutin' space flight was that it was awfully – nay, obscenely – expensive to send what amounted to disposable billion-dollar buggies into space. In 1972 NASA began a program to develop reusable spacecraft.

Part airplane, part spacecraft, the space shuttle changed the way man traveled to space after Apollo-Soyuz, and even the role of on-board personnel. Orbiters, NASA-ese for space shuttles, resemble chubby, short-winged airplanes: they're 122 feet long, 57 feet high and have wingspans of about 78 feet. They weigh, at lift-off, about 4.5 million pounds (of which 1.7 million is the external fuel tank), and their cargo bays, which are the whole point of the thing, really, are 60 feet long and 15 feet wide. The orbiters' heat shields are made up of thousands of heat-resistant tiles.

Shuttles carry everything from military and commercial satellites to scientific experiments, and are staffed by astronauts, scientists, technicians and specialists from many fields.

The orbiter is powered by three Space Shuttle Main Engines (SSMEs) that are fed a mixture of liquid hydrogen fuel and liquid oxygen oxidizer contained in an external fuel tank (which in turn is made up of several smaller tanks), and two solid

---

Close Calls

While there have only been a few major disasters in the US Space Program, it's had its share of close calls. The first came when the explosive bolt-driven escape hatch on *Liberty Bell 7*, Gus Grissom's Mercury craft, opened before the retrieval helicopter had hooked on to the capsule. Grissom jumped from the capsule, which filled with water and sank. Grissom's space suit also filled with water, and he nearly went under waiting to be rescued. There's debate to this day as to whether it was pilot error or technical malfunction.

John Glenn's *Friendship 7* Mercury craft sent back what turned out to be an erroneous message saying that his landing bag had deployed, making everyone on the ground panic that his heat shield had cracked – which would have led to his incineration upon re-entry. Glenn used up all his fuel trying to stop the capsule's bucking during re-entry but landed safely.

Scott Carpenter used up almost all his fuel doing what Tom Wolfe described as 'having a picnic', Jim Lovell called 'monkeying around' and Carpenter himself called an 'error in yaw'. What he was doing was swinging the capsule this way and that, taking photos and having a blast until he realized how low his fuel was. Carpenter misaligned his retro rockets and overshot the splash down target by 249 miles (402 km).

And then of course, the biggie: *Apollo 13*, in which Jim Lovell, Fred Haise and Jack Swigert experienced a hair-raising explosion and loss of power that required them to use their lunar module as a life raft to get home. The story's too well known now that the movie *Apollo 13* has been such a success, but if you haven't seen it or if you have and wonder how accurate it is on technical details, consider the words of a retired Mission Control technician we met: 'I hardly ever recommend movies, but *Apollo 13*'s different. Like it or not, that's what happened.'

Not quite. This is nit-picking, but here's one major difference: it was Swigert, not Lovell, who reported the problem, and despite the movie's posters and NASA paraphrasing, what he actually said was: 'Okay, Houston. Hey, we got a problem here.' ∎

booster packs which provide most of the thrust for liftoff. About two minutes into a flight, the spent solid rocket boosters are jettisoned and later recovered for re-use.

About eight minutes into the flight, the SSMEs are turned off, and the external tank jettisoned. The external tank disintegrates in re-entry to the Earth's atmosphere. During shuttle flights, the orbiter maintains attitude control with jets of hydrogen and oxygen. On re-entry, the orbiter is essentially a huge and exquisitely expensive (about $2.1 billion) glider.

Shuttles fly at an altitude of anywhere from 190 to 350 miles above sea level at speeds of about 17,500 mph.

By 1977 the space shuttle *Enterprise*, a non-orbiting prototype, had been launched four times from atop a modified 747 jet airplane. The first orbital shuttle flight was by the *Columbia* on April 12, 1981. Over the next few years, manned space flight became routine almost to the point that no one paid attention any more: there were 23 flights between the *Columbia* launch and the *Challenger* disaster, which meant that the shuttle was going up almost six times a year for four years. *Challenger* brought home the dangers of space exploration to the public for the first time since *Apollo 13*.

Challenger About 73 seconds into the flight of STS-51-L – the space shuttle *Challenger* – on January 28, 1986, a leak in one of the two solid rocket boosters ignited the external fuel tank and caused an explosion that killed all aboard. As the takeoff was televised, the event was telecast worldwide.

Before the incident, the *Challenger* flight was promoted by NASA as one highlighting its dedication to equal opportunities for minority crews. Lost were commander Dick Scobee, pilot Michael Smith, mission specialists Judith Resnik (one of the first female astronauts), Ronald McNair (one of NASA's first three black astronauts) and Ellison Onizuka (a Japanese-American). The two non-NASA personnel included Gregory Jarvis, a payload specialist for Hughes Aircraft, and most famous of all, Sharon Christa McAuliffe, a teacher at Concord High School in New Hampshire.

The press had gone wild over the telegenic and personable teacher when she was chosen from over 11,000 applicants in 1984 to be the first teacher in space: she simply exuded traditional American family values. The attention that was paid her throughout her year-long training period added to the impact of the disaster: while Americans hold all astronauts very dear to their hearts, Christa, as everyone called her, was familiar enough to make her loss seem like that of a personal friend.

The loss set the shuttle program back three years, as investigations into the cause of the explosion, and subsequent redesign of the solid fuel components and installation of new safety devices were carried out.

But the impact of the explosion is permanently etched on the minds of all who watched it. And as this final excerpt from the flight transcript reveals, it caught the crew as much by surprise as those on the ground:

T+1:05: Commander: 'Reading four eighty six on mine.'
T+1:07: Pilot: 'Yep, that's what I've got, too.'
T+1:10: Commander: 'Roger, go at throttle up.'
T+1:13: Pilot: 'Uh oh.'

Challenger's mission had been manifold: to launch a tracking data relay satellite; to fly a free-flying module designed to observe Halley's comet; to conduct a fluid dynamics experiment and three shuttle-student-involvement-program experiments; and to complete a set of lessons for the Teacher in Space Project.

International Links & the Space Station
From Skylab through the entire space shuttle program, links between NASA and other nations' space agencies have been consistently increasing. From the first flight carrying a non-US citizen (shuttle launch STS-9, November 28 to December 8, 1983) which carried West German physicist Ulf Merbold, to international cooperation in design of equipment and implementation of experiments, space exploration today is truly a global effort.

The NASA/International Space Station (ISS), officially under development since 1984, is a joint venture between six space agencies comprised of 13 nations: Belgium, Canada, Denmark, Germany, France, Italy, Japan, Netherlands, Norway, Russia, Spain, the UK and the USA.

The ISS will be an orbiting platform designed to accommodate astronauts and spacecraft. This 'spacedock' could be used in a number of ways, including orbital construction and launch of spacecraft.

Probably the biggest partner has been Russia, which has been sharing information and technology aboard Russia's Mir Space Station, which is now frequently visited by shuttle crews, and has been home to US astronauts along with Russian cosmonauts. The first stage of the ISS is expected to be put into operation around 2002.

Life on Mars In August 1996, NASA scientists announced the discovery of what appeared to be fossilized bacteria-like life forms in a chunk of a meteorite they say originated on Mars. The meteorite had been discovered in the early 1980s by scientists in Antarctica. Immediately before the NASA press conference that detailed the findings, President Clinton announced on national television the next two unmanned missions to Mars.

The findings of the NASA scientists are controversial, and will face scrutiny by the worldwide scientific community in the years to come. But the immediate excitement caused by the findings seemed to secure, and will probably result in increases in, NASA funding.

The Future of Space With the breakthroughs that have occurred since the Mercury and Sputnik/Vostok launches, and considering the way in which NASA has emerged from budget slashes, internal shakeups and disasters, it's no longer so snickerable that NASA is studying projects that include a lunar base in the next century and a manned mission to Mars. They're not planning them yet, but they have established an Office of Exploration to study

advances required to make those projects a reality. With seven to 10 shuttle missions a year, plus unmanned missions to Mars and Venus, NASA's got its hands quite full for the time being.

Orientation

The Kennedy Space Center (KSC) is on Merritt Island, on the east side of the Intracoastal Waterway (here called Indian River). The Banana River separates the main Kennedy Space Center complex from Cape Canaveral, the site of the first launches of the US Space Program. The Cape Canaveral Air Force Station is now the site of the Air Force Space Museum and facilities for unmanned launches that put commercial and government payloads into orbit atop Delta, Titan and Atlas/Centaur rockets.

The space shuttle launch facilities are at Launch Complex 39, pads A and B. B is northwest of A.

The KSC Visitor Center is at the eastern end of the NASA Causeway, which begins at the junction of Hwy 405 and US Hwy

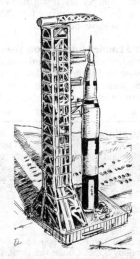

Viewing a rocket or shuttle launch at the only manned spaceport in the Western Hemisphere is an experience not to be missed.

1. You can also enter the facilities by taking Hwy 528 (the Bee Line Expressway) to the intersection of Kennedy Blvd, and turn north.

Maps The handout maps at the visitors center are colorful but useless, though for the purposes of visiting, they'll do just fine. For a much, much better idea of the lay of the land, get the Florida Official Transportation Map (see the Maps section in the Facts for the Visitor chapter).

Information
Tourist Offices The KSC Visitor Center (☎ 452-2121) is the best source of information on the facilities. It's closed during all launches; everything is shut during shuttle launches and Cape Canaveral is closed to visitors during Delta, Titan and Atlas/Centaur launches.

Information Central inside the visitor center complex has multilingual staff, and sign language and visual interpreters/guides are available on advance notice. Public TDD and free wheelchairs are also available. And get this: if you didn't bring a camera you can *borrow* one for nothing as long as you leave them an ID.

Shuttle Launch Information You can get recorded information on shuttle launches at ☎ 867-4636. During countdown, recorded launch status is available at ☎ 867-2314. On the internet, check out the Shuttle Home-

page for information on upcoming and past launches, and links to gezillions of other NASA sites (see sidebar).

Bus tours take visitors out to NASA's six-mile viewing site; they leave the visitors center three hours before the launch. Tickets ($7 for adults and $4 for children) go on sale seven days prior to a launch, and they're necessary. You can reserve by phone (☎ 452-2121, ask for group sales), but you must pick up your tickets five days before the launch or you will not be admitted on launch day.

If you've got a car, you can get a free car pass by mail to view a launch from within Kennedy Space Center. Send a postcard with your name and address and the mission number of the launch you'd like to see to Car Passes, PA-PASS, Kennedy Space Center, FL 32899. The pass will be mailed to you about a month before the launch; if you'll be on the road, leave an address in Florida (like your hotel) to which NASA can mail the pass.

Not as prime are locations around Brevard County like along the Indian River on Hwy 1 in Titusville; from Hwy 528 (the Bee Line Expressway), along the Banana River; and on Cocoa Beach.

Bookstores & Libraries The Gift Gantry at the visitors center sells quite a few books on subjects involving space travel and the center, but the NASA library unfortunately is closed to the public.

NASA Internet Addresses
NASA's got a huge presence on the World Wide Web, and you can easily get lost clicking through hyperlinks to ever more fascinating sub-sites including shuttle photography, movies and audio clips, launch schedules, flight transcripts, technical specifications, space station information, a searchable historical archive and Hubble telescope images – and that's just scratching the surface. To get started, check out:

NASA Homepage	http://www.nasa.gov
Shuttle Homepage	http://shuttle.nasa.gov
Mir Sightings	http:www.shuttle-mir.nasa.gov
Space Station Homepage	http://liftoff.msfc.nasa.gov/station/welcome.html
Kennedy Space Center Homepage	http://www.ksc.nasa.gov
KSC Visitors Center	http:///www.kscvisitor.com. ■

Books & Films The best known work on the Mercury program is, happily, the most readable, and it's so accurate that even NASA quotes and sites it in official publications: Tom Wolfe's *The Right Stuff*. The at times hilarious, no-holds-barred account of 1950s test piloting and the early days of NASA was later made into an Academy Award-winning film that, while far less technically and historically accurate, is always a great watch.

Jim Lovell and Jeffrey Kluger's *Lost Moon: The Perilous Voyage of Apollo 13*, recently re-released as simply *Apollo 13*, was the basis for the phenomenally successful film of the same name. The book is a great read (written in third person) and has as much *oomph!* as the film, with the bonus of details from Lovell's flight aboard *Apollo 8*, a glossary, index and a far more satisfying epilogue.

Peter Bond's *Heroes in Space: From Gagarin to Challenger* is a comprehensive history of space flight that includes excellent and highly engaging details of the Soviet space program and its cosmonauts: these men have all been heroes, overlooked by American readers and space fans due to political climate.

William R Pogue's *How Do You Go to the Bathroom in Space?* is far more clinical and humorless than its title would suggest but still an excellent question and answer format resource for kids, as are *A Day in Space* by Suzanne Lord and Julie Epstein based on interviews with shuttle astronaut Jeff Hoffman, and *My Life as an Astronaut* by Alan Bean, the fourth man to walk on the moon.

Man's Greatest Adventure is a coffee table book on the Apollo missions available at the KSC Gift Gantry, as are *Space Shuttle*, a technically detailed book on the development of the orbiter, and *Apollo to the Moon*, which describes each Apollo mission. Also available at the Gift Gantry are videos, including *America in Space, the First 25 Years* and William Shatner-narrated *The Universe*, both available in PAL and NTSC formats.

Air Force Space Museum

In Complex 26, from where the US's first satellite was launched in 1958, a group of highly dedicated volunteers staff a museum (☎ 853-3245) that, while it hasn't changed much since Barbara 'Jeannie' Eden visited in 1969, is an absolutely fascinating collection of equipment, mementos and space paraphernalia you won't find anywhere else.

What's great is that the knowledgeable staff volunteers show you equipment that they used personally as part of their jobs in the Space Program. Volunteers include the range safety officer and communications director from the Mercury project, the director of guidance systems from the Titan and Atlas launches and the director of development for Atlas tracking.

Inside you'll see a V2 rocket engine, portraits of pioneers of rocketry, a chart explaining the Patriot Air Defense System and a piece of a Scud missile one shot down. If you're looking for the source of the center's cafeteria food, it's in the display case behind the X-15. In the main building there are Sidewinder, Genie, Falcon and Mighty Mouse air to air missiles.

Firing Room A, probably the most interesting area of the museum, houses killer vintage equipment including countdown clocks and a Burroughs guidance computer.

The museum is open Monday to Friday from 10 am to 2 pm, Saturday and Sunday from 10 am to 4 pm; closed during launches. The Blue Bus Tour (see below) usually stops here as well. To get to the museum on your own, take Hwy 401 through the main Cape Canaveral Air Station gates.

There's parking in front of the museum, and the lot has Blue Scout, Rascal and Firebee Drone rockets around it. Surrounding the museum is a larger rocket (not rock) garden you'll drive through on the Blue Bus tour. It's virtually a history of modern rocketry with over 50 samples including Blue Scout, Navaho, Titan 1, Fire Bird, Rocket Sled, Polaris A-1 and A-3, and a Redstone and its gantry.

So You Wanna Be an Astronaut . . .

Think you've got the right stuff? NASA picks new astronauts about every two years, and US citizens have first priority. You'll need at the very least a degree in biology, physics or mathematics and three years of related progressively responsible professional experience. Pilot astronaut applicants must have logged at least 1000 hours of pilot-in-command time on jet aircraft and must be able to pass a NASA Class 1 space physical (mission specialists must pass a Class 2).

Wanna try? Write to the Astronaut Selection Office, Mail Code AHX, Johnson Space Center, 2102 NASA Rd One, Houston, TX 77058-3696. May the force be with you. ∎

KSC Visitor Center

Operated as an attraction by a NASA contractor, the KSC Visitor Center opened in 1966, then expanded to its present size in 1967. Admission to the center and parking is free; only the bus tours and IMAX films are extra.

Space Shuttle Plaza Hands down the coolest area of the visitors center, Shuttle Plaza features a full-size model of a space shuttle. You can walk through and see the cockpit and the cargo bay, but you can't really get close enough to touch anything.

Gallery of Spaceflight Packed with real spacecraft and scale models, the Gallery of Spaceflight's stars are the *Gemini 9* and Apollo-Soyuz spacecraft (the Apollo capsule is real, the Soyuz a full-scale model), with transparent plastic allowing you to peer inside and wonder just how they could stand being cooped up in those things for so long.

You can see a full-size model of the Lunar Rover, looking for all the world like a Tinker Toy, and cheesey 'walk through space' sections. There's also a collection of moon rocks, Apollo patches and a model of the Viking Mars lander.

Galaxy Center/IMAX Theater The five-story-high screens of the Galaxy Center's IMAX theater currently offer three films; ticket prices are $4 for adults, $2 for children aged three to 11.

Film schedules are subject to change, check when you arrive. *Destiny in Space* features exterior shots of the space shuttle in space and footage from the Hubble space telescope servicing mission. It's narrated by Leonard Nimoy.

Blue Planet is a fascinating look at Earth, with absolutely spectacular footage that should not be missed, but bring along a pair of earplugs: narration is inane ('We breathe air. Without it, we will die. We drink water . . . . ') and delivered in possibly the most offensively over-dramatized voice we've ever heard. But still, it's pretty glorious stuff; you'll see typhoons, earthquakes, volcanoes and Los Angeles.

The Dream is Alive, narrated by Walter Cronkite, is a compelling look at life aboard the space shuttle: our favorite bits were watching everyday housekeeping tasks and the astronauts asleep (they look as if they're surrendering).

The art gallery in the Galaxy Center includes some . . . let's say *interesting* works, like Lori McCay's *With the Spirit of Daedalus* – homo-rocket erotica – and upstairs, Jack Perlmutter's pop *Rollout.* Inside the Space Station Model you'll also see neat things like a salad machine, handwasher and space shower.

There is also a model of the Hubble space telescope and a full-size model of the flight deck of a space shuttle in the Gallery of Spaceflight.

Organized Tours

Double-decker, air-conditioned tour buses take groups around in two separate two-hour tours: the Red Bus, which concentrates on shuttle technology, and the Blue Bus, a ride into the history of the Space Program. Both tours cost $7 for adults and $4 for children aged three to 11. Tours start at 9.30 am and run every 15 minutes until two hours before dusk. The tours have recorded narration by astronaut Sally Ride, the first American woman in space, and drivers point out any wildlife – like alligators – you pass on the way. Nick's driver sounded exactly like newscaster Dan Rather.

As we went to press, there was a possible name change in the works for the bus tours (Red may become Kennedy Space Center, Blue may be Cape Canaveral), but routes will remain the same. Tours leave from the KSC Visitor Center.

Red Bus Tour You'll pass through some sections of the Merritt Island National Wildlife Refuge and a horrifically indus-

trial section of the center. The first stop is the new Apollo/Saturn V Center, where you can walk underneath a 363-foot-tall Saturn V rocket in a 100,000-sq-foot building dedicated to the Apollo era near the VIP launch-viewing site at Banana Creek.

You'll then circle the unbelievably enormous Vehicle Assembly Building (VAB), where . . . well, vehicles are assembled. There's a huge Saturn V rocket outside.

Next up are the two crawler-transporters: tank-treaded platforms with a maximum carrying capacity of 14½ million pounds that take six to eight hours to carry the

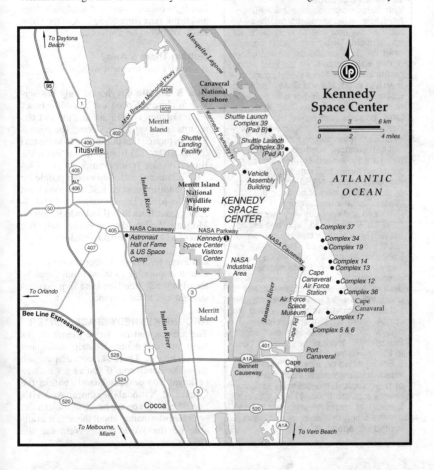

completed space shuttle stacks the 3½ miles from the VAB to the launch pad.

Blue Bus Tour The first stop on the Blue Bus tour, after you've seen about 50 buildings including communications and distribution centers, is the original Mission Control center from Alan Shephard's May 5, 1961, Mercury flight. It's fascinating to see the low-tech controls and analog

---

'Request Permission to Relieve Bladder'

With those words, astronaut Alan Shephard, forgive us, shepherded in the need for a whole new line of technology for space flight. Designers hadn't considered nature's calling on an astronaut during a 15-minute flight, but after sitting on the launch pad for several hours, the man had to go. Mission Control told him just to do it in his suit. For later flights, a sort of long condom was used, and even later, baggies and other 'containment devices' were used for solid waste, and overboard urine dumps for liquid.

That condom method would have been tricky indeed for female astronauts, so today, with extended flights on the space shuttle, NASA provides astronauts with the king of porto-potties: the Waste Containment System.

It looks and operates very much like a toilet on Earth would, with two exceptions. Thigh restraints keep the astronaut properly poised. But unlike on Earth, where gravity pulls waste matter away from the body, in the microgravity atmosphere of the orbiter an 'air flow system' much like a vacuum cleaner is used. When solid waste is present, the holding compartment is vented to space – the fecal matter remains on board, but the temperatures of space freeze dry it, and it is then brought back to Earth with the orbiter.

For liquid waste, a central hose is provided, and astronauts each have their own personal urine collector cup that attaches to the hose. The cup is customized for men and women (both can urinate sitting or standing) and urine is vented into space. ∎

---

display systems. You're shown a film on the Mercury and Gemini projects. Next you're off to the Air Force Space Museum and its rocket garden (see above) and back to the visitors center.

Places to Eat

Bring a picnic. The Lunch Pad (get it?!? *get* it?!? *lunch* pad?) and Orbit Cafeteria, in the visitors center, had a bad day when we visited, and we'll also say we were cranky and that everyone else said it was good.

That said, they both offer burgers, fries, a decent chicken sandwich and soft drinks. A fast-food balanced meal of sandwich, fries and drink runs from $3 to 5. And the Orbit food comes out on a silver conveyor.

Getting There & Away

It's totally inconvenient without a car.

Bus & Shuttle Greyhound only has service as close as Cocoa and Titusville; buses leave Orlando at 9.15 am and the last bus returns at 6.50 pm from Cocoa. The price is $13/26, though that doesn't include the taxi (about $10 to 12) from Cocoa to the KSC. Busy Traveler Transportation (☎ 800-496-7433) charters cars for up to four people for $65 roundtrip between KSC and downtown Orlando. Mears Transportation (☎ 407-423-5566), goes from the HI Orlando Resort on Monday, Wednesday and Friday only, at a cost of $14.45 per person roundtrip.

Car From I-95, Hwy A1A or US Hwy 1, it's almost impossible to miss. From Orlando, take Hwy 528 (the Bee Line Expressway) straight east to the entrance.

AROUND KENNEDY SPACE CENTER

The area around the Space Center ranges from pristine nature to strip malls and surfer beach. There's free camping on Klondike Beach and, if you've got a canoe or kayak, on several islands within the Canaveral National Seashore. And HI's newest hostel is on the beach at Indialantic.

Great information about the area is available on the World Wide Web; see the Online Services appendix.

Merritt Island National Wildlife Refuge

NASA uses only about 5% of its total land holdings for making things that go boom, and in 1963, it turned management of its unused land to the US Fish & Wildlife Service (USFWS), who established the Merritt Island National Wildlife Refuge (☎ 861-0667).

It is notable since it contains, in its mangrove swamps, marshes and hardwood hammocks, more endangered and threatened species than any other refuge in the continental USA. And along with Canaveral National Seashore (see below), the area is one of the best birding spots in the USA. Located right on the Atlantic Flyway, this is migratory bird central, as birds migrate between the northern USA and South America in September and October and back in the spring. Birders will be able to spot practically the table of contents of any ornithological guide: from bald eagles and the entire heron family to spoonbills, black neck stilts, terns and other sea birds and migratory birds.

Other species in the refuge include manatees, alligators, loggerhead and leatherback turtles, wild pigs, bobcats, gopher tortoises and deer.

Our first question was about the impact of the launches on the wildlife in the refuge, but rangers say that launches have but a short-term impact, mainly due to noise and commotion. Exhaust and its cumulative effects are monitored and the impact of a launch is surprisingly concentrated in a small area around the pads.

When to Go The best time to visit is from October to May, as that's the height of migratory bird season and the climate is most comfortable. In summer, the refuge is second only to the Everglades as a mosquito-manufacturing facility. Animal activity is highest between October and March, in the early morning and late afternoon.

Note that the refuge closes to the public two days before any launch, as NASA expands its security area. But if you're planning to visit right after a launch, be aware that more often than not launch dates are deferred due to technical problems or bad weather, and days can easily slip by with the refuge keeping its gates shut.

Visitors Center & Trails Admission to the refuge is free. To get to the main visitors center take Hwy 1 to Hwy 406, turn east into the refuge and bear right when the road forks (the left fork will take you to Black Point Wildlife Drive, see below). October to February, the center is open Monday to Friday from 8 am to 4.30 pm, Saturday and Sunday from 9 am to 5 pm. February to October it's closed Sunday. The center has excellent free information packages, including the main park brochure which offers a self-guided tour around the refuge's most popular and easily accessible attraction, the **Black Point Wildlife Drive**, a six-mile loop.

For a quick immersion into the area's nature, you can take a quick walk on the refuge's quarter-mile, universally accessible **Boardwalk Trail**, located directly behind the visitors center.

There are also three hiking trails in the refuge, about 1½ miles east (parking about a mile east) of the main visitors center: the half-mile **Oak Hammock Trail** and the two-mile **Palm Hammock Trail**, which winds through hardwood forest and has boardwalks above the open marsh.

At stop 8 along the Black Point Wildlife Drive is the entrance to the **Cruickshank Trail**, a five-mile trail surrounding a shallow marsh with a very small – about 12-foot-high – observation tower that gets you just high enough to have a better perspective of the marshes.

Canoeing & Kayaking You can canoe and kayak in certain areas here, notably in **Mosquito Lagoon**, through the open waters and in the marshes, but winds can get very strong, and the waters are shallow. See under Canaveral National Seashore for canoe and kayak rental information.

Canaveral National Seashore

Maintained by the NPS, the 25 miles of windswept and mainly pristine beach that make up the Canaveral National Seashore (☎ 267-1110 south, 428-3384 north) are a favorite haunt of surfers (at the southern end) vacationing families (at the north) and campers and nature lovers (on Klondike Beach, a 12-mile stretch in the center). There are unparalleled turtle-watching opportunities along the beach as well, but you'll need a guide and you need to sign up in advance – that's *months* in advance.

Visitors Centers At the northern end of the Seashore, actually in Volusia County, is historically significant Apollo Park, in which Tumucuan Indian remains have been found. You can get to the park through the city of New Smyrna Beach; to reach the visitors center and Apollo beach, take Hwy 44 east to Hwy A1A and then turn south – it runs right into the parking areas (there are five convenient to beach access). The north visitors center is about a quarter-mile past the lots; you can pick up free registration forms for camping here (see below).

The north visitors center (☎ 428-3384) offers activities every month, from beach walks to demonstrations of cast netting, studies of evidence of Timucuan Indian life in the area (like Turtle Mound Archaeological Site, a shell mound) and walking lectures on local fish and wildlife. All children attending park programs are eligible to become junior rangers. Activity schedules are printed monthly and are available at the visitors centers.

There's a small visitors center (☎ 267-1110) at the southern end of the Seashore near Playlinda Beach. Take Hwy 406 east across the causeway until the road peters out in the park entrance. Parking lots 6 and 7 are nearest to the best surfing.

Turtle Watching There are two crews of conservationists and rangers that patrol the beaches at night screening nests of loggerhead and leatherback turtles. About 4000 visitors a year take part in the **Turtle Watch Program**, governed by the Department of Environmental Protection. They lead small groups (a strict maximum of 20 people), along the beach between May and August

starting at about 10.30 to 11 pm. If you're lucky (and you usually are during nesting season) you'll find a female, watch her dig a hole, lay her eggs and return to the sea.

Demand is astounding: you'll have to call the north visitors center by January or February at the latest to sign up.

Beaches Apollo Beach, to the north, is favored by families because it has calmer surf and fewer jellyfish than beaches to the south, but note that there are riptides now and then; see the Dangers & Annoyances section in the Facts for the Visitor section for what to do if you're caught in one (as if you'll be thumbing through this book while being carried out to sea. 'Hmmm, Getting There & Away? No . . . Facts about Florida? glub glub').

Klondike Beach, the 12-mile coastal beach between Apollo and Playlinda Beaches, is as pristine as it can possibly be. Though there has been some dune erosion, there are no trails, and lots of native plants. It's great for walking and biking on the hard-packed sand. Klondike Beach has the only free-permit beach camping at the Seashore; see Camping, below.

Playlinda Beach, at the southern end, is the surfer headquarters with decent (for Florida) breaks and lots of guys named Dude.

Canoeing & Kayaking There's canoeing through Mosquito Lagoon (see Merritt Island National Wildlife Refuge, above) and you can camp on various islands here free (see Camping, below).

On Merritt Island, you can rent 16-foot canoes at Bob O'Connell's Rental Centre (☎ 453-2400) for $15 for 24 hours or $25 for the weekend. You can take these canoes into the refuge or the national seashore for overnight camping, but you'll need transportation to get the canoes out there (O'Connell's doesn't provide it). If you've got a rental car, flip the canoe upside down, cover the roof of your car with a towel and tie the sucker down. To get to O'Connell's, which is at 210 Borman Drive, take Hwy 520 east from Cocoa; on Merritt Island you'll see a K-Mart on the left and the

Merritt Square Mall on the right. Just east of the K-Mart is Borman Drive – turn left. It's open Monday to Friday from 7.30 am to 5.30 pm, Saturday from 7.30 am to 4.30 pm, closed Sunday.

Banana River Water Sports (☎ 452-5015) has only one one-person kayak, and you have to call a day in advance. It costs $45 for 24 hours. It's on Hwy 520 on the south side of the causeway (look for the Parasailing Watersport signs) at 1891 E Merritt Island Causeway (Hwy 520), open every day from 10 am to sundown.

Camping Camping is free at Canaveral National Seashore (☎ 428-3384) on Klondike Beach or on the islands that fill the north end of Mosquito Lagoon, including Orange, Shipyard, Headwinds, Government Cut, North Dredge, Middle Dredge, South Dredge and at Bissett Bay Islands. Note that you're locked in to the park at 6.30 pm. There are no showers, though there are toilets and sinks in all the parking lots.

In the nearby city of Cape Canaveral, the *Jetty Park Campground* (☎ 783-7111) has tent sites for $14.95 a night, tent and RV sites with full hookups are $18.43. It's at 400 E Jetty Rd.

Up in the town of Mims, just north of Titusville, is the *KOA Cape Kennedy Campground* (☎ 269-7361, 800-848-4562). Tent sites are $19 or $20 with electric and water; RV sites with full hookups are $20 and Kamping Kabins are $24 a night.

Cocoa Beach

Snuggled between Cape Canaveral and Patrick Air Force Base, the optimistically named city of Cocoa Beach, despite what you may have seen on *I Dream of Jeannie*, is a desolate place with a hard-packed sand beach filled with partiers and surfers. While the town's motels and the beach get swamped during shuttle launches, there's not much to see or do here unless you're one of the above – it's interesting to note that the PR agency in charge of the Space Coast lists Ron Jon Surf Shop (☎ 799-8888) as one of exactly two tourist attractions in the area. It's a surf shop that rents

boards and boogie boards and sells T-shirts, hoo-hahs, doodads and surfing accouterments. Interested? It's at the corner of Hwy 520 and US Hwy A1A at 4151 N Atlantic Ave. Look for the ridiculous building on the east side of the street.

Cocoa Beach Pier The other attraction, justifiably famous as a great spot from which to watch shuttle launches, is the Cocoa Beach Pier, an over-800-foot pier with some restaurants and bars. Parking is $3. There's free fishing from the pier on the first Tuesday of the month, the first week in November and on Veterans, Christmas and New Year's Days. At other times it's 50¢ for spectators, $3.50 for adults and $3 for children and seniors; you can rent a rod and reel for $9.50, and buy bait for $3.

And while you're out there on the pier, you may as well know what's in store for you. Tarot readings by Tina (☎ 784-6335) cost $15; she's open Monday to Saturday at unpredictable hours or call for an appointment.

There's a booth just west of the pier that does hourly rentals of bicycles ($3), volleyballs ($2), boogie boards, beach umbrellas and chairs (each $3 or $6 for four hours), or their Broiler Special: a day's worth of beach umbrella and two chairs for $14 in low season and $15 in high.

FLOP Members of FLOP (☎ 784-3235, ask for Frank), the Florida Land & Ocean Protectors (also known as Fat, Lazy, Overweight Paddlers) are generally over 40 years old, interested in kayaking or canoeing and, especially, surfing. Every Sunday morning at 8 am they hold a surf-in at 2nd St N on Cocoa Beach, where they get in about two good hours of surfing before the swimming crowds get to the beach. All are welcome, and for FLOPs, they're pretty energetic indeed.

Places to Stay The *Sand Dollar Oceanfront* (☎ 783-8628) has efficiency apartments with very interesting carpets from $55 to 75 a night (though there's a minimum stay required of five days), $300 to

400 a week and negotiable seasonal and monthly rates are available as well. It's at 1465 S Atlantic Ave.

The *Cocoa Beach Oceanside Inn* (☎ 799-0883, 800-874-7958) at 1 Hendry Ave, is a boxy modern place with large rooms that try for a resort feel; rooms are $59 to 99 for pool view, $69 to 109 on the top floors, and direct oceanview rooms for $79 to 119, higher in high season and during launches.

Talk about making lemonade from lemons: the *Silver Sands Motel* (☎ 783-2415) actually *boasts* that it's 'styled for an earlier decade and weathered by an ocean breeze . . . we don't have a swimming pool, luxurious furniture or a restaurant on site'. Okay, they do win when it comes to the clean rooms, the service is friendly and it's right on the beach. Motel rooms are $50 a night, $270 a week, and efficiencies are $59/325. It's at 225 N Atlantic Ave.

Places to Eat *The Pier* restaurant is open from 5 am to 10 pm, with cheapish breakfasts and seafood entrees from $12.95 to 19.95; downstairs at the base of the Pier is *Oh Shucks*, with happy hour Monday to Friday from 4 to 7 pm: $1 off drafts. At other times steamed shrimp is $5.95 a dozen, and clams and oysters are $3.95 for six.

Flaminia's Italian Kitchen (☎ 783-9908), at the southern end of town at 3210 S Atlantic Blvd, does pretty much standard Italian fare. Pasta dinners with bread sticks and salad range from $4.95 to 6.95; dinner specials include veal cutlet for $9.95 and eggplant/chicken Parmigiano at $6.95/7.95.

Cedar's of Lebanon (☎ 784-9005) at 110 N Brevard Ave, does Middle Eastern and Lebanese food. Appetizers like hummus and stuffed grape leaves are $2.95, baba ghanouj $3.95, and main courses like beef and chicken kebob and vegetarian Saba's Special (grape leaves, spinach pie and salad or tabouli) are $8.95.

Titusville

Known primarily as the main gateway to the Kennedy Space Center and the wildlife refuge, Titusville has only a few things to offer, though the town offers excellent vantage points from where you can watch a shuttle launch.

Space Walk of Fame Opened in May 1995, the US Space Walk of Fame fronts the western bank of the Indian River. The memorial to Project Mercury includes a 20-foot sculpture of the astronomical symbol of the planet Mercury, which was used as the Mercury logo.

The base of the monument bears the handprints of the five surviving Mercury astronauts: Glenn, Carpenter, Schirra, Cooper and Shephard.

Astronaut Hall of Fame The Astronaut Hall of Fame (☎ 269-6100) is dedicated to exhibitions of the minutiae of the astronaut's lives – they've got Buzz Aldrin's report card – along with films and way-cool exhibits like their shuttle landing simulator ride. They also have exhibits where you can get into a G-force trainer and a virtual reality weightlessness gizmo which puts your video image aboard the shuttle. It's open every day except Christmas from 9 am to 5 pm, later in summer, admission is $9.95 for adults, $5.95 for children.

The hall is at 6225 Vectorspace Blvd in Titusville, about seven miles west of the Space Center off Hwy 405.

US Space Camp The little darlings got you down enough to spend $100 a day to have freedom for almost a week? One of the most innovative ideas in a summer camp is the US Space Camp (☎ 267-3184, 800-637-7223) on the grounds of the Astronaut Hall of Fame. The idea for this was one of rocket genius Wernher von Braun, who envisioned a camp as a way of encouraging kids to study math and science. The original space camp opened in Huntsville, Alabama, in 1982, and this one opened in 1988. Since then, more than 30,000 kids have attended a program here.

The courses teach space science and rocket propulsion, have simulated shuttle missions and astronaut training simulators from different eras of the Space Program, and participants perform experiments in physics, chemistry and space science.

Corporate teams are also lining up to take part in the Space Camp corporate programs, which simulates launches and improves communications between departments by forcing them to be concise and clear and stay focused.

Programs include:

Space Camp
Five-day sleep-over program for kids aged nine to 12 every Sunday from February to December; cost is $550 to 650, including room, board and supplies.
Parent-Child Program
For parents and children aged seven to 10; $550 includes tuition, room, board and supplies for one adult and one child for three days.
Teachers Space Camp
Five-day program for teachers offered in conjunction with NASA and the Astronaut Memorial Foundation. Participating teachers may apply for continuing education credit through their individual school districts; $750.
Corporate Team Programs
Half-day, one and three-day programs, in which your team designs a space station and works on a simulated shuttle launch, from $50 to 300 per person, limited availability.

Warbird Air Museum In the TICO (TItusville-COcoa) Space Center Airport, this museum (☎ 268-1941) has exhibits of historic war aircraft from WWI, WWII, Korea and Vietnam including their flagship, a functioning C-47, built in October 1942, that's a veteran of the Normandy invasion, Operation Market Garden and the Battle of the Bulge. In 1995, the plane was used to ship 5000 pounds of toys to Cuban refugee children at Guantanamo Bay. Other highlights include a Korean War vintage C-45, an L-Bird (L-19), and a US Navy A-6 and an A-7, both Vietnam veterans, on loan.

Each year the museum holds an air show as a fund-raiser for itself and its aviation scholarship program; it's held in the third week of March, and over 100 warbirds take part.

Admission is $6 for adults, $4 for children under 12. The museum is open every day except Thanksgiving, Christmas and New Year's Day from 10 am to 6 pm. From I-95, take exit 79 to Hwy 405 east, the airport's on the right.

Places to Stay & Eat The *KSC Ramada Inn* (☎ 269-5510) has rooms for as low as $39 in low season, and fantastically complicated rates throughout the rest of the year, but it's a good option, with a pool, gym and sauna; it's at 3500 Cheney Hwy at exit 79 from I-95. For a flesh fest of epic proportions, hit *Fat Boy's Barbeque* (☎ 267-3468), where you can get stuff to go (baby back ribs $5 for half a pound, $9.25 for a pound; half/whole chicken $4/7.95). But eat-in may be the best deal: a large rib dinner is $10.95 with potato, garlic bread and cole slaw; chicken dinners are $7.95.

Getting There & Away Greyhound serves Titusville, but it's as inconvenient to get to the Space Center from here as it is from anywhere on the Space Coast. Game? The station's at 100 S Hopkins Ave (☎ 267-8760).

Manatee Hammock Park

Just south of Titusville at 7275 S US Hwy 1 in Bellwood, Manatee Hammock Park (☎ 264-5083) is a good camping option that will get you close enough to the hubbub of the Space Coast with a lot less noise and for a lot less money. Run by the Brevard County Parks & Recreation, this is a family-oriented campground; it has laundry facilities, a grill area, pool, recreation hall, and thrill-a-minute activities like croquet, billiards, horseshoes and shuffleboard. Get the inhaler, Mabel . . .

Dump, er . . . drop the kids off for organized swimming lessons at $2.50 a pop. There's also a nature trail running straight through the place.

Tent campsites here are $9.90 ('rustic': no water or electric), $16.23 ('semi-rustic', water and electric) and RV sites with full hookups are $16.75.

Cocoa

Mainly an inconvenient Greyhound gateway, not too many people stop here long enough to smell the flowers. But Cocoa has some claim to fame in its **Historic Cocoa Village**, a collection of 14 sites dating from between 1880 to 1925, along Brevard and Delannoy Aves between King and Church Sts. The Brevard Museum of History & Natural Science (see below) hands out walking tour maps of the historic area, whose highlights include the still functioning Cocoa Village Playhouse (1924), the Porcher Warehouse & Home (1883) and the Victor Theater (1924).

The **Brevard Museum of History & Natural Science** (☎ 632-1830) has a permanent collection of the town's history, archaeological items including Indian artifacts over 7000 years old, and exhibits on wildlife from the area. They also hold special exhibits, on subjects as diverse as arachnids, powder horns and turn-of-the-century weaponry. Regular admission is $3/1.50 for adults/children, special exhibits are $5/3. It's at 2201 Michigan Ave, open Tuesday to Saturday from 10 am to 4 pm, Sunday 1 to 4 pm, closed Monday.

Definitely worth a stop is the excellent **Astronaut Memorial Planetarium & Observatory** (☎ 632-1111, ext 63504), which houses Florida's largest public-access telescope – a 24-inch-diameter monster that's free to anyone who wants to view. They're open Tuesday, Thursday and Friday evenings, and about once a month there's a MIR Space Station window – when the Russian station is visible through the telescope.

Other activities include their excellent planetarium shows on the same days starting at 7 pm, which show off what's billed as the world's only tandem team of Digistar planetarium projectors and America's only Minolta Infinium star projector. Afterwards, there're films in their three-story-high IWERKS (it's like IMAX, but smaller) theater, at 8 pm. Admission to both is $7 for adults, $5 for seniors and students and $4 for children; admission to either single show is $4/3/2.

And as we went to press, they were gearing up for what they say will be the best

laser shows around, Thursday to Saturday at 8, 9 and 10 pm. Admission will be $5.

Places to Stay & Eat The *Dixie Motel* (☎ 632-1600), 301 Forest Ave, has clean rooms if curt service for $30 single, $34 double in low season, $40 to as high as 60 in winter, higher during launches. Another good bet is the *Econo Lodge* (☎ 632-4561) at 3220 N Cocoa Blvd (US Hwy 1), with absolutely standard chain motel rooms for $35/39 in low season, $44/54 during high season and launches.

The *Dutch Kitchen* (☎ 639-1270) at 1312 Dixon Blvd, does great breakfast specials like two eggs, toast, home fries and grits for $1.98, with bacon or sausage $2.50. They also serve Pennsylvania Dutch Scrapple, a sort melange of pork products in loaf form; a slice is 80¢. They have daily lunch specials like hot beef sandwiches, Philly cheesesteak, and rib eye with potato and vegetable from $3.25 to 4.25.

Paradise Alley Café (☎ 635-9032), also in the historic district at 234 Brevard Ave, does blackened fish sandwiches for about $5.75, and their specialty, during dinner, cassado – marinated steak, chicken or fish with sautéed veggies and rice for $6.95, and kebobs, with zucchini, yellow squash, mushrooms, peppers and either steak ($7.95) or chicken or shrimp ($6.95).

The slickest place to eat in town is *Café Margaux* (☎ 639-8343), in the Arcade, right in the center of the historic district at 222 Brevard Ave. It's a French place, naturally, and it's far cheaper at lunch than at dinner. At lunch there's a soup and Caesar salad or sandwich combination for $5.95, and a patty melt on pumpernickel rye bread or smoked ham, fresh spinach and Boursin cheese omelet ($4.95). While dinner can get expensive with items like braised Long Island duckling with mango ginger relish for $17.95, or seafood baked in puff pastry on steamed leeks with lobster creme for $19.95, you can get away for far less on pasta like shrimp fettuccine in roasted garlic Alfredo sauce, a relative steal at $9.95.

Getting There & Away The Greyhound station (☎ 636-6531) is at 302 Main St.

Melbourne

Most visitors don't stay too long in Melbourne, but if you're in the area there are a couple of interesting museums and a performance center with decent children's activities.

The new **King Performance Center** (☎ 242-2219, 632-1111) on the campus of Brevard Community College is home to some concerts (and we're talkin' greats here: Johnny Mathis, Gordon Lightfoot, Neil Sadaka . . . superstars all, and the list goes on) and performances by the Brevard Symphony Orchestra, the Brevard Community College Concert Choir's spring concert series and the Brevard Youth Orchestra & Community Chorus. It's also a good resource for children's performances in spring and fall, like *Where's Waldo*, *Goldilocks and the Three Bears* and *Charlotte's Web*. In summer, there are other performances, and a summer theater workshop (☎ 632-1111, ext 34280) for kids aged eight to 18. To get there, take I-95 south to exit 73, and Wickham Rd east for seven miles to Post Rd, east to the center at 3865 N Wickham Rd.

The **Brevard Zoo** (☎ 254-9453) focusing on Latin American jungles may be worth a stop to see their sloth, spider monkeys and jaguar; it's at 8225 N Wickham Rd, admission is $4 for adults, $3 for seniors over 60 and $2.50 for children aged two to 12.

Places to Stay HI's newest hostel is HI-Melbourne Beach (☎ 951-0004, 984-3505), 1135 N Hwy A1A, a 12-bed facility in a former apartment complex. The hostel is on the beach at Indialantic. Beds are $15.

Getting There & Away The Greyhound station (☎ 723-4329) is at 460 S Harbor City.

Northeast Florida

HIGHLIGHTS

- Get to the heart of Florida's history in lovely St Augustine, the USA's first settlement; take a tour of the country's alleged oldest house, drugstore, school, jail and more
- View the impressive collection at the Cummer Museum of Art in Jacksonville
- Check out the *really* fast cars in Daytona Beach
- Pick your own strawberries by the quart, at Tommy Howle's Vegetable Bin & Garden
- Visit American Beach, an important site on the Black Heritage Trail
- Indulge in an amazing Southern meal including ribs, collard greens, mashed potatoes and fried chicken at Fernandina Beach's Florida House Inn

Many people get their first impression of Florida while driving south and arriving in Jacksonville, and that's too bad. Because as they flee the urban horror there they might miss out on some of the lovely areas close by, notably Amelia Island and especially St Augustine, the oldest city in the USA.

St Augustine's charming cobblestone streets and old Spanish and English-built buildings (it's old not just by US standards but even by those of chilly damp countries in which people drive on the left side of the road: many buildings here date to the late 1700s) make it an irresistible stop for those plying the endless ribbon of concrete that is I-95, and with its cheap camping, youth hostel and relatively inexpensive motels there's just no reason why you shouldn't spend at least a day there, possibly more.

Northeast Florida is also home to the Birthplace of Speed, Daytona Beach, which at various times of the year is jammed with racing fans there to see the Daytona 500, swarming with motorcycle clubs during the madness of Bike Week, or seething with Spring Breakers, for whom Daytona is the last friendly port of call on the east coast of Florida.

DAYTONA BEACH
• pop 62,000 ☎ 904

What began with men and their very expensive and very fast cars racing along the hard-packed sand here in 1902 has culminated in an entire city dedicated to the pursuit of speed in cars, motorbikes, whatever.

Ransom Olds and Louis Chevrolet began the craze here, and were joined by wealthy wintering industrialists who either drove or financially backed race cars. By 1904, the event was called the Winter Speed Carnival, and over the next 30 years or so Daytona Beach was to drivers what Edwards Air Force Base was to test pilots in the '50s: the place where records were made and smashed. The record for speed on the beach, set in 1935, is almost 277 miles per hour.

Stock car racing became the new rush, and between 1935 and 1958 the beach was still the site of races. But in 1959, the Daytona Speedway opened, and made official what Daytona's tourist board had been claiming for years: Daytona Beach was the Birthplace of Speed.

Today Daytona Beach is a town that thrives on racing and party-based tourism: it has one of the last Atlantic coast Spring

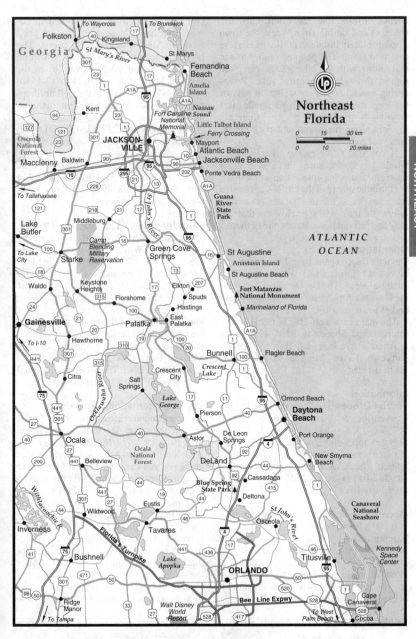

Breaks (arrests, hookers, drunk kids, fire engines) and during Bike Week, the town goes absolutely insane as hordes of Harleys roar into town. The people coming to see that, along with the other races, carry the region through the entire year. Prices during special events are stellar, to pay for the long months of relative solitude. But Daytona is never really empty – there are revelers along the beach and packing the bars year round.

If you don't like racing, there's not a whole lot to do: sure, there is a great museum and some interesting attractions, but the atmosphere of the city is so geared to 'race fans' – as the tour guides reverently refer to the masses of speed lovers – that you may feel left out if you're not one of them.

Orientation

Daytona Beach spans from I-95 all the way across the Intracoastal Waterway to the Atlantic Ocean. The Daytona Speedway and the Daytona Airport are both at the western end of town, near I-95.

The main east-west drag is US Hwy 92, International Speedway Blvd. Hwy A1A is Atlantic Ave here, US Hwy 1 is called Ridgewood Ave. Main St is the north-south divider.

Information

Tourist Offices The Daytona Beach Area Convention & Visitor's Bureau (CVB; ☎ 255-0415, 800-544-0415, see the Online Services appendix) is at 126 E Orange Ave. It's an exceptionally good source of information. The AAA Travel Assistance office (☎ 252-0531) is at 2525 International Speedway Blvd.

Money Barnett Bank's downtown branch is at 200 S Palmetto Ave. American Express is represented by Atlantic Travel Agency Inc (☎ 255-0070) at 2430 S Atlantic Ave.

Post The main post office (☎ 274-3500) is at 500 Bill France Blvd. The downtown office (☎ 253-5166) is at 220 N Beach St.

Bookstores & Libraries Mandala Books

(☎ 255-6728) at 204 W International Speedway Blvd has a huge selection and good women's studies and sci-fi sections. The biggest place in town is Books-A-Million (☎ 255-5588) at 90 N Nova Rd, in the Daytona Mall. Atlantic News (☎ 677-1510) at 2500 N Atlantic Ave in the Bellair Shopping Plaza, has national and international newspapers.

The library (☎ 239-6454) is at 1066 Ridgewood Ave.

Media The Daytona *News-Journal* is the biggie in town. NPR is at 90.7 and 89.9 FM from Orlando, and 89.9 FM from Jacksonville, if you can get it.

Laundry Volusia Laundraclean (☎ 255-3580) is at 1464 International Speedway Blvd. Snow White Laundromat & Dry Cleaners (☎ 677-8445) is at 2413 N Atlantic Ave. Diplomatic Center Laundry & Dry Cleaner (☎ 254-2971) is at 101 Seabreeze Blvd.

Medical Services There are two clinics, the Peninsula Medical Center (☎ 672-4161) at 264 S Atlantic Ave, and the Halifax Medical Center (☎ 254-4000) at 303 N Clyde Morris Blvd. The Memorial Hospital (☎ 676-6000) is at 875 Sterthaus Ave.

Daytona International Speedway

The most famous raceway in the USA after Indianapolis, the Daytona International Speedway (☎ 947-6782) is certainly big. And loud. And when there aren't races going on, you can take a tour of the entire complex that's worth the $5 if only to get a sense of the amazing scope of the place.

In the main entrance, ticket booths are to the left, and the enormous gift shop to the right (selling tasteful items like Daytona International Speedway placemats – makes a great Christmas gift for that special race fan in your life). Above the shop, on a cat-walk balcony is the Gallery of Legends, an interesting history of Daytona racing from Olds vs Winston in 1902 on.

On the tour, you'll take a tram ride

through the garage areas, and drive on Pit Rd, while the narrator tells of the incredible feats of pit crews that, in 20 seconds or so, can change four tires and jam 22 gallons of 110 octane racing fuel into a car, and perform chassis adjustments and other fussing during races. The speed limit during races on Pit Rd is a relatively quaint 65 mph. The tour continues on a loop of the 2½-mile track, with the narrator pointing out that on Turn 1, the monstrous 31° bank requires cars to travel at least 70 mph or slide off the road.

Back at the starting point, you can go into the stands and listen to a surround-sound demonstration of . . . well, loud cars screeching by.

The National Association for Stock Car Auto Racing (NASCAR) sanctions the Daytona 500 and Pepsi 400 at the Speedway (see below), as well as Goody's 300 Busch Grand National and the Daytona USA Motorsports Attraction 200, Goody's Dash Series event.

Races at Daytona include:

Speed Weeks
Sponsored races include things like the Busch Clash (a car race sponsored by a beer company called a 'clash'?) and Rolex 24 – the only round-the-clock endurance race in North America (an American LeMans so to speak) – culminating with the Daytona 500 NASCAR Winston Cup; February.
Bike Week
10 days of motorcycle racing, supercross, amateur motorcross, the Daytona 200 by Arai Motorcycle Classic and Vintage Motorcycle Racing; first week in March.
Classic Cars
Daytona Beach Classic Car Speedway Spectacular with antiques, classics, sports cars and vintage race cars; late May.
Independence Days
Pepsi 400 and RaceFest – meet NASCAR drivers and view show cars; 4th of July Weekend.
Daytona Turkey Run
Street rods and muscle cars, more of a car show than a race; Thanksgiving week.

Ticket prices to the Daytona 500 range from $60 to 150 depending on where you're sitting, and sell out several months in advance. Tickets to other events vary widely in price; call the box office at ☎ 253-7223 for pricing information.

Daytona USA

Daytona USA (☎ 947-6800, see Online Appendix) is the city's newest attraction, a racing theme park complex outside the Speedway that offers the chance to get more into racing than with the traditional Speedway tours. The facility, which opened after we researched, has a variety of passive and interactive attractions that make the whole thing very worthwhile to anyone interested in auto racing. Begin with racing exhibits: Sir Malcolm Campbell's original Bluebird V, a car which set the world land speed record in Daytona Beach in 1935, and a full-scale replica of the Daytona Beach gas station which 'Big Bill' France once owned, are part of the Goodyear Heritage of Daytona exhibit. There's a technology of speed exhibit, a trivia tower and a 14-minute film of the 1995 Daytona 500 (see below for information on the race itself).

The interactive displays let you announce a race, design and test a race car and try to take part in a pit stop maintenance session.

Daytona USA is outside the Speedway at 1801 W International Speedway Blvd. It's open daily from 9 am to 7 pm. Admission is $10 for adults, $8 for senior citizens, $5 for children.

Klassix Auto Museum

This museum (☎ 252-0940) is dedicated to classic cars, and has every Corvette model from 1953 to '94 (with an explanation of why there was no '83 'Vette) along with other cars and motorcycles including an excellent Harley Davidson collection, a 1932 Deusenberg, a '55 Messerschmidt, a '57 Chevy Black Widow, Richard Petty's '77 Monte Carlo, and Mello Yello, No 51 from the film *Days of Thunder*. Exit, of course, into the gift shop. The museum's at 2909 W International Speedway Blvd. Admission is $9 for adults, $5 for children aged seven to 12.

NORTHEAST

Museum of Arts & Science

The Museum of Arts and Science (☎ 255-0285) is an incredible surprise: with an excellent permanent collection of American, African and Cuban art, as well as rotating exhibitions, a planetarium and a nature and science center. About 20,000 school kids tromp through here each year.

The museum is in the process of expanding. In the **Dow Gallery of American Art**, you'll see items from their permanent collection including silver, glass, samplers and some great antique furniture.

Their **Africa: Life & Ritual** collection is impressive, featuring items like carved wood commemorative posts, spears, *Asen* iron staffs representing plants, humans and animals, a pair of *eshu* staffs, and a statue of the Yoruba god of mischief and chaos.

In the **Cuban museum**, the bulk of which was donated to the city by Fulgencio Batista (Batista lived in Daytona Beach after he was ousted from power in Cuba) features paintings by Cuban artists.

In the **science center**, the museum's prize display is the complete 13-foot-tall skeleton of a giant ground sloth, found three miles from the museum in South Daytona. While the bone condition was original, not mineralized, the head on the giant mammal is a reproduction (the real skull is in the case opposite the skeleton display, too delicate to be mounted on the larger exhibit).

There are a planetarium, science and history exhibits and free films every Saturday, courtesy of First Union Bank.

The museum is located at 1040 Museum Blvd off Nova Rd; admission is $4 for adults and $1 for students and children. Admission to the planetarium is $2, some astrological events are free.

Gamble Place

The 150-acre winter retreat of James Gamble (of Proctor & Gamble fame) at Spruce Creek Nature Preserve is open as a museum, and there are some very nice reasons to come down, not the least of which is the Snow White House. Built in 1938 by Gamble's son-in-law Alfred Nippert, it's an exact replica of the house in the Disney classic. You can also tour Gamble's turn-of-the-century Cracker home.

To arrange tours of the Gamble Place call the Museum of Arts & Sciences (☎ 255-0285), which runs the Gamble estate. From fall to spring, there are pontoon boat rides up Spruce Creek, which runs through the property, and there are canoe trips up the creek as well.

Admission to the museum is $5 for adults, $1 for students and children, canoe and pontoon boat trips are an additional $5/1. You must reserve through the museum for the special trips. It's closed in summer.

The estate is on County Rd, south of Daytona. Take I-95 south to Taylor Rd (Hwy 421), go west for about a mile and the entrance is on the left halfway through the sharp curve – look for five mailboxes and the small green 'Gamble Place' sign pointing the way down a narrow dirt road.

Beach

There are no surprises here: shops, mini-golf, arcades, cafés and fast-food places line the beach along the Boardwalk Amusement Area. During the day you can drive along the 18 miles of hard-packed sand on the beach; the cost is $5 in high season and during special events, otherwise it's free. Speed limit (strictly enforced) is 10 miles per hour. Enter the beach at one of almost a dozen clearly marked driveways.

At the eastern end of Main St at the ocean, the Daytona Beach Pier extends about a quarter mile.

Beach Rentals Maui Nix (☎ 253-1234) is a surf shop at 635 N Atlantic Ave. They rent boogie boards, surf boards and in-line skates for $8 for one hour, $15 for the day and $25 for the whole weekend. They require a credit card or $200 cash deposit. They're open 9 am to 10 pm.

Salty Dog Surfshop has three locations on the beach: at 2429 N Atlantic Ave (☎ 673-5277), 100 S Atlantic Ave (☎ 253-2755) and 700 E International Speedway Blvd

(☎ 258-0457) and if you want to rent a surfboard that's the one to go to. BZ boards (soft rubber boards with a slick finish) are $20 per day (10 am to 6 pm), boogie boards and the skimboard are $12 per day. They ask for a credit card imprint or your driver's license as a deposit.

Ponce Inlet Lighthouse
The Ponce de León Inlet Lighthouse Museum (☎ 761-1821), rebuilt in 1982, is an interesting place to spend an afternoon – and climbing the 203 steps to the top results in a splendid view of the entire area. (The lighthouse gets hit frequently by lightning so don't climb it in storms.) It no longer has a Fresnel lens, but now has a modern strobe.

On the porch in front of Building 2 you'll see Cuban rafts that were found on Ormond Beach on September 6, 1994. Also on display here are nautical navigation tools and photos of lighthouses from all over the USA. There is a glassed-off recreation of an 1890s lighthouse keeper's house. The newest edition to the museum is the lens exhibit building with first- to sixth-order lenses (see the Cape Florida Lighthouse in the Miami chapter for information on lens order), in various stages of restoration. The lenses are fascinating, and craftspeople are usually there to answer questions about them.

The museum is open from 10 am to 5 pm, last admission at 4 pm. Admission is $4 for adults, $1 for children under 11. It's at 4931 S Peninsula Drive, Ponce Inlet, about five miles south of Daytona.

Little Chapel by the Sea
One of our favorite area attractions, the Little Chapel by the Sea is a drive-in Christian church. That's right, you drive in and they put one of those things in your car window and you hear a sermon. Services are daily from 8.30 to 10 am. There's inside seating for Sunday morning services (see, no cynicism here) at 9.45 am. It's 3140 S Atlantic Ave, on the west side of the street, and worth a stop on your way to the Ponce

Inlet Lighthouse. Admission is free, though they have a donation box.

Jackie Robinson Ballpark
Off Beach St on City Island, diagonally opposite the CVB, Jackie Robinson Ballpark is the place where Robinson, the first black baseball player to play in the major leagues, played his first game. It's the home of the Class A Chicago Cubs farm team (☎ 257-3172).

Halifax Historical Museum
This museum (☎ 255-6976) exhibits Indian and Spanish artifacts, newspaper files dating back to 1883, a wood carved replica of the Ormond Hotel and memorabilia from earlier beach days. It's at 252 S Beach St.

Art League of Daytona Beach
The Art League (☎ 258-3856) has changing exhibits of state and national artists every three weeks between August and June. It's at 433 S Palmetto Ave.

Places to Stay
Motel and hotel prices in Daytona Beach are very low until a special event, the biggest of which are Bike Week and Speed Week, where prices at least quadruple, and rooms are booked out months in advance. The motels and hotels on Daytona Beach (there are about 400 of them) are absolutely alike – either small, semi-clean mom 'n' pop operations or big chains.

Hostel We thought that the *Daytona Hostel* (☎ 258-6937) at 140 S Atlantic Ave was one of the worst we've ever seen in any country; dirty rooms, old mattresses and a depressing atmosphere. Dorm beds (six to a room) are $13.35 per person or $70 a week, with a $5 key deposit. A private room usually is $22.50/99.90, but during Bike Week they're an unconscionable $110 per night. There are pool tables, steel lockers ($2 per day) and public showers outside for $5. We've heard tell of (but haven't seen) another hostel here, the *Camelia Motel* (☎ 252-9963) at 1055 N

Atlantic Ave; dorm room beds are said to cost $13.

Motels & Hotels The clean, sterile *Beachside Budget Inn* (☎ 258-6238), 1717 N Atlantic Ave, has rooms for $18/22; during Bike Week prices are $85 to 95 and during car races $75. The rooms have TVs.

Thunderbird Beach Motel (☎ 253-2562, 800-234-6543), 500 N Atlantic Ave, has large, very clean rooms with two double beds for $25 (single) and $27 to 32 (double, depending on the view) during August to January, and $35/45 to 55 from February to July. At special events those rooms are $80/90 to 105.

The *Royal Arms* (☎ 253-0558, 800-329-7316) has clean double rooms for $22/27 in low season, prices in high season seem to be hard to pinpoint, we got an estimate of $27/35, during Bike Week and special events they charge 'over $100'. It's at 801 S Atlantic Ave.

Esquire Beach Motel (☎ 255-3601) at 422 N Atlantic Ave, has rooms for $26 to 35 from September to February and $30 to 45 at other times. Rooms during Bike Week are $100.

Sun & Surf Motel (☎ 252-8412, 800-252-8411) at 726 N Atlantic Ave has free HBO, refrigerators and coffeemakers in the rooms and a heated pool. Rooms are $30 to 55, efficiencies $34 to 63 and one bedrooms $58 to 95.

The *Breakers Beach Motel* (☎ 252-0863, 800-441-8459) charges $35 to 65 for oceanfront rooms without a refrigerator, $40 to 70 for oceanfront rooms with fridge and $50 to 80 for efficiencies; during Bike Week or special events it's $100 to 110. It's at 27 S Ocean Ave.

The *Ocean Villa Motel* (☎ 252-4644, 800-225-3691), 828 N Atlantic Ave, has rooms for $41 to 118, efficiencies $47 to 118 and two bedrooms $72 to 184. They have two heated pools and a kiddie pool, a 60-foot waterslide, a game room and a shuffleboard court.

B&Bs The *Coquina Inn B&B* (☎ 254-4969) has four rooms from $69 to 105.

Some rooms have fireplaces, and there's a lush garden patio and a Jacuzzi. Bicycles are available. It's at 544 S Palmetto Ave.

The Villa (☎ 248-2020) at 801 N Peninsula Drive, is another B&B with four rooms, ranging from $65 to 145 in what they call the 'value season' and $90 to 170 in winter – call for special events prices which, we take it, are as high as the market will bear. It's in a Spanish-style mansion filled with antiques, there is a pool in the flower garden and continental breakfast is included.

Places to Eat
Fast food is pretty much the order of the day (or the Bike Week). *Steak & Shake* (☎ 253-5283) has double hamburgers for $2.50, a turkey club sandwich for $3.95, the fried chicken dinner is $4.95. At the time of writing they were located at 945 International Speedway Blvd, but they plan to move to No 1000. They're open 24 hours.

The Lighthouse Landing (☎ 761-9271), 4940 S Peninsula Drive, near the Ponce Inlet Lighthouse, is an excellent and fun place that does veggie burgers for $3.25, shark kebabs for $4.95, fish & chips for $8.95 and seafood for $9 to 12. It's open 11.30 am to 10 pm daily.

R Hot Dog (☎ 257-7766) does dogs for $1.35. Toppings (chili, cheese, sauerkraut, etc) are 25¢, a long dog is $2 (toppings 35¢) and a superdog (foot-long) is $3.25. It's at 425 N Atlantic Ave and open till 4 am.

Anna's Italian Trattoria (☎ 239-9624) is a very friendly place at 304 Seabreeze Blvd, at the corner of Peninsula Drive. Tortellini alla panna is $10, penne alla vodka $12, risotto $12 to 14 and early bird specials (served from 5 to 6.30 pm) run from $5 to 8.

Sophie Kay's Coffee Tree Family Restaurant (☎ 677-0300) has lots of different sandwiches for $3.25 to 4.75 and entrees like chicken Hawaii for $6.75 and roast turkey $7.95. It's at 100 S Atlantic Ave at Bosarvey Drive, in Ormond Beach. Sophie Kay also runs the *Waterfall Restaurant* (☎ 756-4444) at 3516 S Atlantic Ave. This is a dinner place only, and we recommend reservations: pastas are $9.95, veal Française is $14.95 and seafood dishes are $13.95 to 16.95.

Entertainment
Performing Arts The Ocean Center (☎ 254-4500) at 101 N Atlantic Ave is a multipurpose facility staging country and rock concerts, ice hockey matches, wrestling and art shows, etc.

The Seaside Music Theater (☎ 252-6200) stages professional musicals at 1200 W International Speedway Blvd at the Daytona Beach Community College.

The Peabody Auditorium (☎ 255-1314) at 600 Auditorium Blvd, holds mainly classical, but also pop concerts. Daytona Beach Civic Ballet performances are staged here and the London Symphony Orchestra performs here every other year (and has for 25 years).

There are constantly changing concerts at the Oceanfront Bandshell (☎ 800-881-2473) at 206 B Moore Ave. In May they host the Daytona Beach Music Festival.

The Daytona Playhouse (tel 255-2431) at 100 Jessamine Blvd, puts on local productions of musicals throughout the year. The box office hours are Monday to Friday from 1 to 3 pm.

Bars & Clubs You can't swing a cat without hitting some sort of bar in town. Most have happy hours, and all have them do during big events.

Razzles (☎ 257-6236) is a high-energy dance club at 611 Seabreeze Blvd.

Coliseum (☎ 257-9982), 176 N Beach St, is a top 40 and house and progressive dance club inside a historic movie theater building. It's in the North Beach Entertainment Complex, which has a couple of other bars (including *The Spot*, an enormous sports bar) and restaurants.

For reggae music try the *Green Turtle* (☎ 255-5411), 2301 S Atlantic Ave, or *Kokomos on the Beach* (☎ 254-8200) at 100 N Atlantic Ave.

The *Oyster Pub* (☎ 255-6348) is a sports bar with a happy hour from midnight till 3 am (closing) with 25¢ oysters. It's at 555 Seabreeze Blvd.

Things to Buy
A Farmer's Market is held every Saturday morning on City Island behind the Jackie Robinson Stadium.

Tobacco Exotica (☎ 255-3782) has everything tobacco: cigars, clove cigarettes, head-shop items, etc. It's at 749 International Speedway Blvd.

GI Jeff's (☎ 255-4000) sells new and used military clothing and equipment, leather and the like. It's at 936 International Speedway Blvd.

Getting There & Away
Air Daytona Beach International Airport (☎ 248-8030) is a 1st-class facility just east of the Speedway. It's served by many major airlines and some regional ones.

Bus The Greyhound Station (☎ 255-7076) is at 138 S Ridgewood Ave. Daytona is a major stop on Greyhound's east coast route and there are seven buses a day to/from Miami (6½ to 14 hours).

Train Amtrak (800-872-7245) does not go to Daytona, the nearest stop is DeLand, inland off US Hwy 92. There's connecting Amtrak bus service from the DeLand station, but it will cost about the same as a taxi: about $19.

Car Daytona is between I-95 and US Hwy 1 and Hwy A1A. It's about 53 miles from Daytona to Orlando (west) or St Augustine (north), about 139 to Tampa and 251 to Miami.

All major car rental companies have desks at the airport.

Getting Around
To/From the Airport From the airport there's no public transportation, a taxi from there to downtown will cost about $10 to 12, to the beach about $16, to Ormond or Ponce Inlet about $18 to 21.

Bus & Trolley Votran (☎ 761-7700) runs buses and trolleys in town. Bus and trolley fares are 75¢ for adults and 35¢ for children and seniors, under six years free, exact change is required. The trolley runs along Hwy A1A from Granada Ave in Ormond to Dunlawton Ave in Daytona Beach Shores from mid-January to Labor

Day, every day, every 45 minutes from noon to midnight.

Taxi Taxi rates in Daytona are $1.80 at flagfall, $1.20 a mile, $1 extra per person. The biggies are Yellow Cab Co (☎ 255-5555), Southern Comfort Taxi (☎ 253-9292) and A&A Cab Co (☎ 253-2522).

Car Parking is free and easy in most places, but in downtown watch out for meter maids – use store-provided lots when you can. Do not speed, especially if you're driving on the beach where the strictly enforced speed limit is 10 mph. During major events the speed limits in this speed capital are steady-as-she-goes or she-goes-to-jail.

ST AUGUSTINE
• *pop 14,600* ☎ *904*

The nation's oldest city, St Augustine was settled by Europeans in 1565. One of the earliest planned cities in the New World, St Augustine is a charming mix of narrow cobblestone streets, European architecture and a Spanish colonial flair that makes it an irresistible destination for at least a few days. (We liked it so much we moved here to complete this book!) There is simply a *lot* to do here.

Through the 144-block National Historic Landmark district clop horse-drawn carriages; throngs of pedestrians gawk at the architecture and fill sidewalks lined with crafts shops, cafés, restaurants and pubs.

It's Europe by Disney without the admission fees; it's an American city with, at least in the downtown area, more cobblestone than asphalt, more coquina than cement, and more time and patience for the pleasures of living than one runs across very often.

And the city government can be lauded for using its noodle and coming up with creative ways to save, as opposed to bulldozing, buildings by shrewdly recycling abandoned real estate. In that way, an abandoned hotel became a college, another a city administration office and yet another a courthouse. It all adds up to a living time capsule that's a pleasure to visit.

History

St Augustine was settled in 1565 by Spanish explorer Don Pedro Menéndez de Avilés, and by the time Florida was ceded to the US by Spain in 1821, St Augustine had been sacked, looted, burned and occupied by Spanish, British, Georgian and South Carolinian forces.

Menéndez arrived at Cape Canaveral (see Space Coast chapter) with about 1500 soldiers and settlers, who made their way north and established St Augustine on September 4, 1565 – named for the day on which they arrived on the Florida coast, August 28, the Feast Day of St Augustine, Bishop of Hippo.

Menéndez was here to battle French forces and Huguenot settlers that had established Fort Caroline, near present-day Jacksonville, but the French fleet did him the favor of getting caught in a hurricane; the few troops that survived it were butchered by Menéndez's men, giving the name to the bay near St Augustine: Matanzas, or slaughter.

The next attack came from the British, who occupied and burned the city in 1586 under the command of Sir Francis Drake. After another British attack in 1668, the Spanish decided that stone would suit their needs a bit better than wood, and they began work on the Castillo de San Marcos fort in 1672. Now the oldest masonry fort in North America, it has never fallen to attack, though it has been at various times under command of Spanish, British, US and Confederate troops.

In 1702, the British again burned the city; the fort held, unscathed. In 1740, British, Georgian and South Carolinian troops again attacked, this time from the south at Matanzas inlet. Though the city was set on fire during the retreat, the attack failed. But the attack showed the Spanish that the area to the south of the city was as inviting to invaders as a large welcome mat, so they constructed tiny Fort Matanzas in 1742.

Beaten finally by fighting elsewhere in the French & Indian War, the Spanish ceded Florida in 1763 to Great Britain in a swap for Cuba. The British would hold the fort through the American Revolution, though as part of the Treaty of Paris ending that war, the fort was ceded back to Spain in 1783.

The British had remained in town for 20 years, and left their mark in many ways. Under their rule, residents of the failed New Smyrna Colony came to settle in the area, and many of their descendants remain to this day. The colony, established in 1768 by London physician Andrew Turnbull, had brought about 1500 Greek, Italian and Minorcan workers to Florida to work an indigo plantation. For some reason, the term Minorcan has become the local classification for all workers of the colony; throughout the city you'll see references to 'Minorcan Greek settlers'.

The Spanish ceded Florida to the US in 1821. In the late 1880s, Henry Flagler brought his railroad through town, and created a boom in building, especially luxury hotels, gambling halls and restaurants. But as the railroad headed south, interest in the town by the rich northerners fell greatly, and the town was left in a condition similar to London's Docklands today: lots of very expensive, very luxurious and very empty buildings.

Today the city retains much of its European flair – in fact it reminds many of cities like Prague, Kraków and Regensburg. The coquina and tabby buildings (see Architecture, below) lend a faded, pastel but somewhat magical quality to the narrow streets, and the city's long and colorful history is palpable.

Architecture

The main building material used by the Spanish, and then everyone else, was coquina (in Spanish it means shellfish or

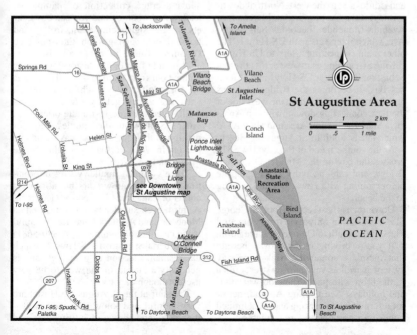

cockle): a mixture of broken shells, cement and sand; you'll also come across tabby, a mixture of oyster shells and cement, used in flooring. The buildings are mainly typical Spanish Colonial style, with fragments of British Colonial thrown in and sometimes added on to original Spanish structures. Of the churches in town, there is a hodge-podge of styles, from Venetian Renaissance to Greek Orthodox to Spanish Mission. There are also dozens of Victorian buildings fringing the heart of the downtown historic district.

Orientation

St Augustine is about 35 miles southeast of Jacksonville, served by both US Hwy 1, which runs through the city, and I-95, about 10 miles west. The Downtown Historic District is the area roughly bordered by Orange St and the Old City Gate to the north; Bridge St to the south; Avenida Menendez and Matanzas Bay to the east; and Cordova St to the west. North of downtown, past the Castillo de San Marcos fort, Avenida Menendez becomes San Marco Ave, which intersects with US Hwy 1. The other main connecting artery to US Hwy 1 is King St, running east-west across the San Sebastian River near US Hwy1 and Matanzas Bay. It becomes the Bridge of Lions and then Anastasia Blvd on the west side of the bay, connecting downtown with Anastasia State Recreation Area and Hwy A1A, which heads south to St Augustine Beach.

At the southern end of the city, Hwy 312 crosses the bay on the Mickler O'Connell Bridge, and runs near the KOA campsite before joining with Hwy A1A and heading to the beach.

Downtown is best seen on foot. St George St is a pedestrian-only zone from Cathedral Place at the south to Orange St at the north.

If you're driving in downtown, beware that there's a somewhat tricky one-way system as well as very narrow streets filled to the brim with pedestrians on weekends and holidays. See Getting Around, below for information on parking and what limited public transport options are available.

Maps Pick up decent downtown maps, along with ad rags like *Visitor's Guide to St Augustine & St John's County* and *Your Place in History*, published by the chamber of commerce; *See St Augustine*, published by See Magazines; and *Sightseeing Map of St Augustine & its Beaches*, from Atlantique Press, at the visitor information centers, chamber of commerce and many shops, motels and restaurants. Each has maps of varying decency. The best map of the area is the chamber's edition of the *Rand McNally* map of the city and beaches; the chamber sells them for $2.

Information

Tourist Offices This place has its act together as far as tourist information goes. The main Visitor Information Center (☎ 825-1000) is roughly opposite Ripley's at 10 Castillo Drive, at the corner of San Marco Ave, open 8.30 am 5.30 pm every day except Christmas. Here you'll find an above-average collection of pamphlets, leaflets and whatnot, and you can buy tickets for the sightseeing train, trolley and horse-drawn carriages on the spot (see Organized Tours, below). They also show a 52-minute film on the history of the city on the hour from 9 am to 4 pm. The cost is $3 for adults, $2 for children, though cheapskates can get by quite nicely as well – there's a free 16-minute orientation video. Still want the movie? Pay for parking in their lot – $3 per day – and one person in your carload gets the movie thrown in free. Wow.

There's a much smaller visitor information booth downtown at the northwest corner of Cathedral Place and St George St. A third, even smaller booth is at Avenida Menendez and Artillery Lane. Least helpful is the chamber of commerce (☎ 829-5681) at 1 Riberia St just off US Hwy 1, which has a small selection of pamphlets and is generally a bit out of the way to be very useful (though they try).

The staff at the St Augustine Hostel are very helpful and know the town well – they're a good source of information, and they also have a pretty good bulletin board and collection of pamphlets.

St Augustine has a home page on the World Wide Web (see the Online Services appendix), with virtual tours, information on local attractions and restaurants and, of course, advertising.

Money Barnett Bank has a branch at the corner of King and Cordova Sts.

Post & Communications The main post office (☎ 829-8716) is at 99 King St. Send and receive faxes across the street at St John's Printing & Office Supply (☎ 834-1496, fax 825-0994). Pre-paid phone cards can be bought at a number of places, including the information booth at St George St and Cathedral Place.

Bookstores & Libraries St Augustine is a haven for used-book lovers, with about a dozen used-book shops. The most well known are Avenue Books (☎ 829-9744) at 142 King St specializing in art books, and Wolf's Head Books (☎ 824-9357) at 48-50 San Marco Ave, specializing in antiquarian books, ephemera, searches, etc. There's a small but very friendly little place called Second Read Books (☎ 829-0334) at 51 Cordova St, which sells used general and children's fiction and has a good new and used selection of women's studies books.

For new books, try Booksmith (☎ 829-2975) at 8 Cathedral Place, opposite the Bridge of Lions, for general stuff including a small selection of LP stuff; and Dream Street (☎ 824-8536) at 64 Hypolita St, a gay-friendly bookshop with gay and lesbian resources, 'tools for planetary growth' and other hippie stuff. A huge Barnes & Noble should be open on US Hwy 1 near Hwy 312 by the time you read this.

The main St Augustine Branch of the St John's County Public Library System (☎ 823-2650) is at 1960 N Ponce de León Blvd (US Hwy 1), open Monday to Wednesday 10 am to 9 pm, Thursday and Friday 10 am to 6 pm, Saturday 10 am to 5 pm, closed Sunday.

A neat place if you're interested in the rich history of the area is the St Augustine Historical Society Research Library (☎ 825-2333), upstairs in the Sequì-Kirby Smith House at 6 Artillery Lane at the corner of Aviles St, open Tuesday to Friday from 9 am to 4.30 pm and some Saturday mornings (as posted) from 9 am to 12.30 pm. Here you'll find very dedicated historians and volunteers keeping watch over some incredible books, which you're welcome to read in house or photocopy (though that costs 50¢ per copy – it's how they support the library).

Media The paper of record is the *St Augustine Record*. The best what's-on guide is the excellent *Folio Weekly*, a free paper with club dates, restaurant reviews and listings, clubs, pubs and concert listings and good local scandals. See free paper listings under Maps, above. NPR is at 89.9 FM. The Flagler College radio station at 88.5 FM is hands-down the best in the state, with a terrific variety of new music, jazz and pop, and even good DJs. It's really great on weekends when they run world music programs. Check it out.

Campuses The students at Flagler College don't know how good they have it – in fact the tuition, including room and board, of only $8,668 per year made us consider enrolling! Voted third in Best Value and first in Most Efficient college categories by *US News & World Report*, the four-year liberal arts college's main building is the former Hotel Ponce de León. Once a getaway for the wealthy patrons of Flagler's railroad, the place has been restored: it looks like a palace but smells like a college. It's worth a look, and tours are available; see below.

Laundry Coin laundries are a bit inconveniently located; if you're staying at the hostel you can wash and dry for $3. Otherwise, the best bets are the St Augustine Laundromat (☎ 824-3487) at the corner of US Hwy 1 at 179 W King St, and the Laundry

NORTHEAST

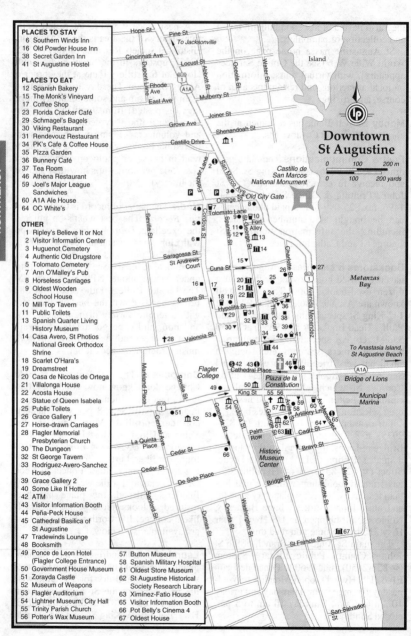

PLACES TO STAY
6 Southern Winds Inn
16 Old Powder House Inn
38 Secret Garden Inn
41 St Augustine Hostel

PLACES TO EAT
12 Spanish Bakery
15 The Monk's Vineyard
17 Coffee Shop
23 Florida Cracker Café
29 Schmagel's Bagels
30 Viking Restaurant
31 Rendevouz Restaurant
34 PK's Cafe & Coffee House
35 Pizza Garden
36 Bunnery Café
37 Tea Room
46 Athena Restaurant
59 Joel's Major League
    Sandwiches
60 A1A Ale House
64 OC White's

OTHER
1 Ripley's Believe It or Not
2 Visitor Information Center
3 Huguenot Cemetery
4 Authentic Old Drugstore
5 Tolomato Cemetery
7 Ann O'Malley's Pub
8 Horseless Carriages
9 Oldest Wooden
   School House
10 Mill Top Tavern
11 Public Toilets
13 Spanish Quarter Living
   History Museum
14 Casa Avero, St Photios
   National Greek Orthodox
   Shrine
18 Scarlet O'Hara's
19 Dreamstreet
20 Casa de Nicolas de Ortega
21 Villalonga House
22 Acosta House
24 Statue of Queen Isabela
25 Public Toilets
26 Grace Gallery 1
27 Horse-drawn Carriages
28 Flagler Memorial
   Presbyterian Church
30 The Dungeon
32 St George Tavern
33 Rodriguez-Avero-Sanchez
   House
39 Grace Gallery 2
40 Some Like It Hotter
42 ATM
43 Visitor Information Booth
44 Peña-Peck House
45 Cathedral Basilica of
   St Augustine
47 Tradewinds Lounge
48 Booksmith
49 Ponce de Leon Hotel
   (Flagler College Entrance)
50 Government House Museum
51 Zorayda Castle
52 Museum of Weapons
53 Flagler Auditorium
54 Lightner Museum, City Hall
55 Trinity Parish Church
56 Potter's Wax Museum

57 Button Museum
58 Spanish Military Hospital
61 Oldest Store Museum
62 St Augustine Historical
   Society Research Library
63 Ximínez-Fatio House
65 Visitor Information Booth
66 Pot Belly's Cinema 4
67 Oldest House

**Downtown
St Augustine**

0   100   200 m
0   100   200 yards

Hope St
Pine St
To Jacksonville
Cincinnati Ave
Locust St
Dupont Lane
Rhode Ave
East Ave
Mulberry St
Joiner St
Grove Ave
Shenandoah St
Castillo Drive
Island

Castillo de
San Marcos
National Monument

Old City Gate
Orange St
Tolomato Lane
Fort Alley
Spanish St
Saragossa St
St Andrews Court
Cuna St
Carrera St
Hypolita St
The Court
Treasury St
Cathedral Place
Plaza de la
Constitution
King St
Flagler
College
Seville St
Cordova St
Granada St
Palm Row
Artillery Lne
Cadiz St
Bravo St
Historic
Museum
Center
De Soto Place
Cedar St
Bridge St
La Quinta
Place
Central Ave
Markland Place
Sanford St
Dumas St
Oneida St
Washington St
St Francis St
San Salvador St
San Salvador
St

Matanzas
Bay

To Anastasia Island,
St Augustine Beach
Bridge of Lions
Municipal
Marina
Avenida Menendez
Charlotte St
Marine St
San Marco Ave
Fletcher Lane
Cordova St
Sevilla St
Valencia St
Saragossa St

Room (☎ 824-4262), about a mile east of the Bridge of Lions at 405 Anastasia Blvd.

Toilets There are clean and free public toilets in several locations: behind the Florida Cracker Café, behind A1A Ale House, in the Government House and at the main visitor center.

Medical Services Flagler Hospital has two large facilities in town; the Main Campus (☎ 829-5155) at 400 Health Park Blvd, opposite 1955 US Hwy 1 south of the city; and the West Campus (☎ 826-4700) across the street at 1955 US Hwy 1.

Museums & Historic Buildings
Spanish Quarter Living History Museum This museum (☎ 825-6830), at the northern end of St George St, is a re-creation of Spanish colonial St Augustine in the year 1740 – the year the British attacked and subsequently burned the city. Walled and fenced off from the street, once you've paid your admission you're free to wander through everything on your own except the de Mesa House, for which you'll need to be on a guided tour – they start every hour. The de Mesa House is probably the most interesting on the property, especially if you like antiques but if only to learn the origin of the term 'at loggerheads':

A loggerhead was a ping-pong-size ball of iron at the end of a staff that cowboys would use to heat drinks, by placing the ball in the fire, blowing off the ashes and then placing it in their drink. But the term comes from the drunken cowboys' tendency to brawl and try to crown each other with the devices.

Costumed employees go about the business of life in 1740 St Augustine – they're not re-enactors: they'll speak to you as a 20th century person explaining an 18th century procedure. And they're not, despite the pitiful state salaries they get, volunteers.

Many of the following sights are manned: the Gómez House (a store in a private home), de Hita House, de Burgo-Pellicer House, a tavern (*taberna*), and a working woodshop and blacksmith. Admission to the complex, which is open from 9 am to 4.30 daily, is $5 for adults, $3.75 for seniors (over 62), $2.50 for students aged six to 18 or $10 per family of four.

City Hall & Lightner Museum One of the grandest government office complexes you'll ever come across, St Augustine's City Hall at 75 King St, opposite Flagler College, is in the former Hotel Alcazar (1888), a resort which in its heyday featured the country's largest indoor swimming pool, a health club and oodles of luxury – in 1901 the *Tatler* wrote, 'the People of St Augustine are proud of the Ponce de León, but they love the Alcazar.'

Revamped, restored and currently home to a local government dedicated to raising already outrageous local water usage bills, the building is also home to the Lightner Museum (☎ 824-2874), primarily featuring 19th-century fine and decorative arts, early Americana and fine collections of European art including pieces from Tsarist Russian, decorative and applied art and loud classical music. It's worth a trip, and plan on spending between one and two hours here.

Take the elevator to the 3rd floor and work your way down. Among the 3rd floor exhibits are Victorian glass baskets, an alabaster model of the Taj Mahal, F Vichi's *Portrait Bust of a Young Girl*, a cradle from the 1860s and a colonial-style dollhouse. On the 2nd floor, we loved the story behind the Florentine painting *Cimon and Pera*, of a prisoner kept alive by his daughter's breast milk while his captors tried to starve him to death. There's also 19th-century glass vases and bowls, Tiffany, European, American and Bohemian glass, and German, French, Russian and English porcelain dated between 1700 and 1900. On the ground floor is the gift shop and two more display rooms featuring contents one would find in typical early American nautical, tobacco, clothing, camera, barber and toy shops. The museum's open from 9 am to 5 pm daily. Admission is $5 for adults, children over 12 and students $1, under 12 free.

NORTHEAST

There are great volunteers (perhaps a bit *too* enthusiastic), and a musical instrument demonstration daily at 11 am and 2 pm.

Government House Museum This is an unspectacular, though interesting, collection of the history of the settlement of the city, featuring exhibits on Spanish explorers including coins and artifacts from galleons; the British period; some archeological finds; early plans of the city; military architecture; and a neat historical timeline. The museum (☎ 825-5033) is at 48 King St, at the west end of Government House Square, open 10 am to 4 pm every day except Christmas. Admission is $2 for adults, $1 for students and children aged six to 18. There's a nice new Mediterranean-style sidewalk café out front.

Potter's Wax Museum The tone is this: Rambo and Whoopie are in the window, and as you enter, on your right you'll see Solomon, Moses and Abraham. If you're really into wax museums, or if you're with children, it may be worth it, but we were pretty underwhelmed. Check out Cleopatra (a hot one, with a snake), Julius Caesar, Marc Antony, Edward the Black Prince, and a concession to local history in the form of Juan Ponce de León, Pedro Menéndez de Avilés and Sir Francis Drake. If you're gonna go, you gotta see the tyrant room: Nixon, Hitler, Mussolini, Harry Truman (?) and others. Don't be afraid to miss the unintentionally hilarious slide show (they call it a movie) every 20 minutes. Great location, at 17 King St (☎ 829-9056, 800-584-4781), open daily 9 am to 5 pm, in winter, 9 am to 9 pm in summer, closed Thanksgiving and Christmas. Admission is $5 for adults, $4.25 for seniors (55 and older), $2.75 for children aged six to 12, under six free.

Oldest Wooden School House Billed as America's oldest wooden school house, built around 1750 or '60, this little house was bought by Juan Genoply who conducted classes here. Later the building would be used as a guardhouse and shelter

during Seminole Wars (1834-41). It has a very nice garden, and you'll learn a lot about 18th-century life and education – and a fair amount about carpentry; much of the wood used to build the building is driftwood from old ships, and that's an anchorchain surrounding the building. Admission goes for $2 for adults, $1.50 for seniors (over 55) and $1.50 for children aged six to 12. The museum (☎ 824-0192, 800-428-0222) is at 14 St George St, open from 9 am to 5 pm daily.

Spanish Military Hospital It's small, and it doesn't appear to be much, but the volunteers are wonderful: if you get a good one, plan on spending an hour hearing history, tales of Spanish explorers and perhaps the origin of the term 'sleep tight'. The building is a reconstruction of a military hospital that stood on the site during the second Spanish colonial period (1784-1821) – the Spanish had, er, liberated the building from an Englishman, William Watson, who had converted it from a stable to a residence. It's a fascinating, if small, collection of beds (note the length – the average height at the time was about five feet), medicines, medical equipment and an herbal apothecary. The hospital (☎ 825-6808) is at 3 Aviles St, open from 10 am to 4 pm daily; admission is free, but they request a donation of $1.

Button Museum While it may not deserve as much ink as we're giving it, we loved this place: 40 different displays of over 1200 buttons, kept in the family through five generations are here, with samples from the 1700s to the present. There's a button tree and a button garden, a spool of buttons and, of course, a button shop, where collector buttons (?!) are sold for between $2 and 25. Very friendly management runs the museum (☎ 825-0805) at 10 Aviles St; and unless you're some kind of a button nut it's probably not worth the admission of $1.75 for adults, $1.50 for children aged eight to 12 and seniors. Children aged seven and under are free.

González-Alvarez House Alleged to be the oldest house in America, it's said that continuous occupancy can be proven from the early 1600s to today. True or not (and there are some very persuasive arguments for its truthfulness, like the designated National Historic Landmark status and the fact that it's run by the St Augustine Historical Society), if you're going to visit just one 'oldest' site, the González-Alvarez House and grounds are perhaps the best of them, with some lovely gardens, and exhibits on the residents of the house, evolution of the house and of the British sacking of the city. There's a predictable museum store, and picnic tables. The house (☎ 824-2872) is at 14 St Francis St, and it's open daily from 9 am to 5 pm; free tours leave every 30 minutes. Admission is $5 for adults, $4.50 for seniors, $3 for students or $12 for a family of four. Price includes free parking.

Oldest Store Museum If you're in the neighborhood it *may* be worth stopping into this re-creation of a general store from the 1800s, complete with wood-burning stove, hats, shoes, grinders, a dentist's chair, cloth bolts, etc. It's $4 for adults, $1.50 for children. The store (☎ 829-9729) is at 4 Artillery Lane, open Monday to Saturday from 9 am to 5 pm, Sunday from noon to 5 pm.

Museum of Weapons Though it'd rather call itself a museum of American History from 1500 to 1900, it's just what the heading says it is: a room full of guns, though there are a few added attractions. Labeling is quite good, and our favorite was the 1⁵⁄₁₆-inch-long, 2 mm Pinfire Pistol from Austria. Made for ladies (though not, unfortunately, donated by Nancy Reagan), it fires teeny weeny lady-like bullets, designed to be fired into the ear canals of victims. You can also see a Bible that stopped a bullet during the Civil War – a period covered quite well indeed in terms of weaponry, equipment, Confederate money, etc – and hear the story of one Bible that did not stop the bullet.

There are also some interesting slavery and Confederate documents, a few Native American weapons and a good rifle collection. And finally, proof that the Confederates won both the Civil War and the current US Congress: a wartime coin design proposal with the motto *Owe Ever – Pay Never*. The museum (☎ 829-3727) is at 81-C King St, open from 9.30 am to 5 pm every day but Christmas. Admission is $3.50 for adults, $3 for seniors and AAA members, $1 for children aged six to 12, under six free.

Authentic Oldest Drugstore It's nice that something with 'oldest' in its name is free. This wooden house has an authentic pharmacy (complete with wax remote-controlled pharmacist and optometrist) and, what else, an overpriced gift shop. It's at 31 Orange St at the corner of Cordova St (☎ 824-2269, 800-332-9893), and is open from 9.30 am to 6 pm daily except Christmas, Thanksgiving and Easter.

Old Jail The former town prison and residence of the town's first sheriff, Charles Joseph 'the Terror' Perry (who stood 6 feet 6 inches tall, weighed over 300 pounds and was a shotgun, rifle and handgun marksman), is now open as a museum. Built in 1892, the simple (but strong) structure housed up to 64 of the riff-raff of the day. Upstairs, there's a firearms collection on the walls, and you can see some rather barbaric and cramped general population cells – complete with an Alcatraz-style main door opening system. Downstairs you'll see women's cells, solitary confinement and the kitchen. Narration makes it more interesting than it sounds, especially when they point out the picnic area out back beneath the 'bird cage', where locals used to picnic while harassing the unhappy occupant of the man-sized cage suspended above the lawn. Nice. Hear also of the hangings and, if you're lucky, the personal opinions of your tour guide regarding the death penalty. The museum (☎ 829-3800, 800-397-4071) is at 167 San Marco Ave. It's open daily from 8.30 am to 5 pm.

Admission is $4.25 for adults, $3.25 for children aged six to 12.

Tragedy in US History Museum We think this is a must-see, if only to irritate the chamber of commerce, which hates it. Owned by the family of LH 'Buddy' Hough (who died in 1996), this private collection of macabre and just weird artifacts from American history has been filling an old house across from the Old Jail to the brim for the last 30 years. All of the following attractions are alleged to be the original item, though we make no guarantee as to their authenticity (but it's nice to hope). See the ambulance in which Lee Harvey Oswald rode to Parkland Hospital after being shot by Jack Ruby; lots of the usual comparisons between Kennedy and Lincoln (number of letters in their names, etc), lots of photos of Oswald and James Dean; some racist letters; a rusting 'Spanish Jail'; Bonnie & Clyde's 'bullet-riddled getaway car as depicted from the movie *Bonnie & Clyde*' and the *pièce de resistance*, 'Jayne Mansfield Famous Movie Star Death Car'. Bring along some mosquito repellent. The museum (☎ 825-2389) is across the street from the Old Jail, at 7 Williams St, open daily from 9 am to dark. Admission is $3.50 for everyone.

St Augustine Lighthouse Three hundred yards northeast of its original location (it was rebuilt because the old one was being gradually washed away by the sea), the black and white striped St Augustine Lighthouse is a great place to bring kids over seven years and over four feet tall (none younger or shorter are allowed, which sounds age-ist and height-ist to us). Originally equipped with a 4th-order lens, it currently uses a beefy 1st, which can be seen for miles at night – look east while in downtown and you'll see it slashing through the night sky.

The lighthouse tower, after a lengthy renovation, has been opened to the public, and you can now climb the 219 steps to its top. The museum at the foot of the lighthouse contains things nautical. The lighthouse

(☎ 829-0745) is on Anastasia Island off Anastasia Blvd at the corner of Lighthouse Ave, sometimes called Old Beach Rd, and tiny Ocean Vista Ave. In the winter the museum's open from 9.30 am to 5 pm, and the lighthouse tower from 10 am to 4.30 pm. In the summer the museum's open from 9.30 am to 6 pm, the tower from 10 am to 5.30 pm. Admission for the tower and museum is $3.50 for adults, $2.75 for seniors (over 55), $1.75 for children aged seven to 11 (at least four feet tall). For the museum only, it's $2 for adults, $1.55 for seniors, kids are free.

Historic Museum Center The St Augustine Historic Museum Center is a collection of eight houses on a city block bounded by Palm Row at the north, St George on the east, Cordova on the west and Bridge St at the south. The highlight here is the **Prince Murat House** at 250 St George St and the corner of Bridge St. It's a pink coquina cottage, circa 1790, and named for Napoleon Bonaparte's nephew, Prince Achille Murat, who came to St Augustine in 1824 and lived in the house for only two months. Murat later moved to Tallahassee and married George Washington's grandniece, but on a return trip to St Augustine, he met Ralph Waldo Emerson, who later also lived in the house. The list of celebrities is long. In any of the houses on the route, or at the visitor centers, you can pick up a very detailed pamphlet entitled, not surprisingly, *St Augustine Historic Museum Center*, which has detailed histories of all the houses. The rest are:

Rose House	244 St George St
William Dean Howells House	246 St George St
Star General Store	149 Cordova St
Worcester House	145 Cordova St
Spear Carriage House	143 Cordova St
Dow House	42 Bridge St
Canova House	43 Bridge St

Peña-Peck House Built in the 1740s as the home of the Spanish royal treasurer, Juan Estaban de Peña, this was later the home of Dr Seth Peck, who renovated it, gutted a wing and set up his office here. The building remained in the Peck family until the 1930s, when it was given to the Women's Exchange, which operates it today. Of the 12 rooms, only nine are open to the public. Doting volunteers guide you through the antique-filled rooms for $2.50 for adults, $2 for seniors, $1.50 for children and students aged 12 to 18, under 12 free. The house (☎ 829-5064), a National Historic Landmark, is at 143 St George St.

Ximínez-Fatio House One of the few structures in the city remaining from the second Spanish period, this coquina block house was built in 1797 or '98 (different sources give different dates). This was the general store and home of Andres Ximínez (pronounced yah-MIN-is), a merchant from Ronda, Spain. Later the house was an Inn, owned by Louisa Fatio (pronounced FAY-shee-oh). Free guided tours are available between February 1 and August 31, Monday and Thursday to Saturday from 11 am to 4 pm, Sunday 1 to 4 pm, closed Tuesday and Wednesday. The house (☎ 829-3575) is at 20 Aviles St.

Along St George St Of all the historic buildings on St George St, several outside the Spanish Quarter Living History Museum are noteworthy. Though there are shops in them now, explanatory plaques outside the buildings give some further background. From north to south along St George they include:

Casa Avero
(built 1762) at No 41, now home to St Photios National Greek Shrine, memorializing the Greek workers at the New Smyrna Colony – see Churches & Shrines, below.

Rodríguez-Avero-Sánchez House
(built circa 1762) at No 52, home of Francis Xavier Sánchez.

Oliveros House
(built circa 1798) home of Corsican mariner Sebastian Oliveros and now home to Infiesta Cigars at No 59.

Acosta House
(built between 1803 and 1812, reconstructed 1976), at No 76, home of Corsican George Acosta (1764-1812).

Villalonga House
(built between 1815 and 1820, also reconstructed 1976) at No 72, home of another Corsican, Bartolomu Villalonga.

Casa de Nicholas de Ortega
(built circa 1740, reconstructed 1967), No 70, home of the gun-running Ortega family.

Hotel Ponce de León Henry Flagler was a visionary, but if he ever envisioned 175 college students chowing down on sloppy joes and fish sticks in his flagship luxury hotel's dining room – the one with all the Tiffany glass and the ornate 35-foot vaulted ceiling – he certainly never said so in his memoirs. The hotel, which was completed in May 1887, and saw its first official guests on January 12, 1888, quickly became the most exclusive winter resort in the USA. Flagler College, which took over the property and has extensively renovated it, offers free tours in the main building from May to August every hour on the hour between 10 am and 4 pm daily. The tours take about 15 to 20 minutes, and meet in the rotunda just inside the building's main entrance.

The main rotunda is open to the public; look up, and past the banners wishing happy birthday to students and announcing parties, to see if you can spot the astrologically themed designs. The best stained glass, surprisingly, is not within the awesome dining room itself but on the first landing of the staircases that rise to the left and right of the dining room entrance. Outside in the courtyard is the main turtles and frogs fountain and, in front of the gates, a statue of Flagler.

During the school year, you can arrange for a group tour with advance notice through the office of college relations (☎ 829-6481). Do try and see the Flagler Room, which makes the dining room look positively common – it's the site of some classes, concerts, poetry readings and the local community orchestra – check in *The Record* or *Folio Weekly* for ads of events here during your stay. Also check for concerts that may be going on across the street at the **Flagler Auditorium** (behind and to the west of the Lightner Museum; same telephone but ext 217), often home to classical music and jazz shows.

St John's County Courthouse Tucked into a recess at the corner of Cordova and King Sts, the St John's County Courthouse is housed in Flagler's former Cordova Hotel (circa 1880). The building was closed in the early 1930s, and re-opened as the courthouse in the 1960s. The lobby area is open to the public and filled with shops.

Historic Remains

Old City Gate The gate, built in 1739 to defend the northern St Augustine line from attacks by the British, the coquina pillars at the gate at the northern end of St George St were built in 1808. Today hardly anyone notices they're walking through something historic, and many people stuff litter into the small chambers inside the pillars.

Rosario Defense Wall Opposite the Tolomato Cemetery is a re-creation of a section of the Rosario Defense wall, an earth barrier constructed by the Spaniards in the early 1700s to fend off British attack. The wall, which today appears very small, stopped the Brits not just by making them climb a bit, but also with natural defenses on the top: hard and spiky yucca plants and prickly pear cacti.

British Slave Market In Plaza de la Constitution, opposite the Bridge of Lions in the heart of downtown, the remains of the old town market run by the British still stand. This was the central market for food and for slaves during the British reign in the city.

An interesting historical note on the market: when St Augustine was ruled by the Spanish, many slaves from Georgia and the Carolinas would escape to St Augustine, where treatment was far better than in British-run colonies: while the Spanish had slavery, they believed that even slaves had human rights – it was, for example, illegal when selling a slave to break up a family. To tweak the Brits further, the Spanish ruled that any slave escaping from a British

colony was granted freedom on arrival. When the British traded Cuba for Florida, many black slaves accompanied the Spanish there.

Attractions

Ripley's Believe it or Not! It's kitschy. It appeals to the base instincts. And we loved it. One of three of its kind in the state (others are in Orlando and in Key West), the offerings here are pretty much what you'll find in all of the Ripley's museums.

The Believe It or Not part is up to you. Even if the answer is 'not', it still may be worth the admission price of $7.50 for adults and students over 13, $5.50 for seniors, and $4.25 for children aged five to 12 (under five are free). Just past the entrance, note the genuine two-headed calf; at the stairs to the right, Ripley's original cartoon. Also see tallest, heaviest and skinniest men exhibits and the World's Greatest Fake (PT Barnum's mermaid). Upstairs, try your luck at twisting your tongue (many people can't). There's a mirror handy. And when you turn the corner, be sure and look through the little window. The museum (☎ 824-1606) is at 19 San Marco Ave, just up the street from the visitor center. It's open from 9 am to 10 pm daily.

Fountain of Youth It's a nice walk through a pretty park and gardens, and it does have some perfectly fine background on the area and the Timucuan Indians, a planetarium show and a model of a Spanish galleon, but to call this a Fountain of Youth is pushing the bounds of what even the most resolute tourist will believe. Okay, okay: allegedly, when Ponce de León was heading to Florida, he was searching for the fountain of youth, and it's said that he thought that this might have been it. It's a spring – granted, the water is high in calcium and iron and sulfur, but it's a spring. Admission to the park (☎ 829-3168) is $4.75 for adults, $1.50 for children and students, and it includes a sample of the magic water. Bottled water from the spring is $1.99 in the gift shop. It's at 11 Magnolia Ave, one block east of the Old Jail.

Robert Ripley

Many 'rad' travelers try to scoff at 'tourist attractions' but Ripley's museums are different. As a friend of ours (who spends about half his life in Asia as a buyer for his own business) says, 'Going into Ripley's gives you a sense of just what an amazing traveler and adventurer that guy was.'

That guy was Robert Ripley (1893-1949), a writer and traveler extraordinaire, who over 40 years traveled to 198 countries around the world in search of the strange, the amazing and the bizarre.

He began as a cartoonist for the *San Francisco Chronicle*, and eventually became a syndicated cartoonist with King Features. Later in his career, Ripley became a traveling broadcaster, and was the first man to do a live radio broadcast from Australia to New York. And he never stopped traveling until his death.

His taste certainly leaned to the weird: shrunken heads, six-legged and double-headed cows, pinhead sculpture (the Lord's Prayer, all 297 letters of it, etched into a pin head by a Sing Sing prisoner in the tank for forgery), miniature match-stick replicas, three-eyed men (he didn't actually *collect* that one) African human skin masks, and photographs and stories of a huge collection of freaks from around the world.

The St Augustine Ripley's Believe it or Not! was the first in a series. The building in which Ripley's now stands, Castle Warden, was built in 1887 by William Warden, a partner of Flagler and Rockefeller, and in 1941 it was turned into a hotel by none other than Norton Baskin and his wife Majorie Kinnan Rawlings, author of *Cross Creek* and *The Yearling* (see the Central Florida Chapter for information on Rawling's estate), and Ripley himself was a guest at the hotel several times.

Today the castle is open as the prototype Ripley's, and while some of the exhibits may seem hokey and contrived, others are the genuine article. Say what we will, Ripley simply was one of the trailblazers of modern travel information dissemination. Figuring out what's genuine and what's balderdash is simply a matter of whether you believe it or not. ■

Zorayda Castle Moor fans will love this one-tenth-scale replica of the Alhambra, a 12th-century Moorish palace in Granada, Spain. Franklin Smith, a man who some say had more money than sense, was so impressed with the palace on a trip to Spain that in 1883 he built an exact (though scaled down) replica of one of its wings. Filled with imported palatial appointments, it's a neat place, and kids will love it. Its claim to fame: portions of that fine motion picture, *Illegally Yours* starring pop-video and animated dancing sensation Rob Lowe, was filmed here.

There's a prayer room, and on the center of the ground floor a sultan's divan for lounging and entertaining, and silk rugs over 300 years old. Upstairs, the Sultan's Den features a gaming table and settee, inlaid with thousands of pieces of sandalwood, rosewood, satinwood, mother of pearl and ivory that took five men nine years to complete. You can also see the Tower Alcove, where, in the original, King Mohammed el Hazare placed his three daughters, lest men be able to see into their rooms (two escaped and eloped with Spaniards, while the third died in the tower as a spinster).

There's also an Egyptian room, with a 2300-year-old rug, woven from cat hair and said to be cursed. During Prohibition, the castle was turned into a speakeasy (the Zorayda Grill Club) for men. At the side end of the staircase on the ground floor is a pull-switch which could have been used to ring the alarm when the fuzz dropped in. The whole place, by the way, is riddled with secret passageways.

The castle (☎ 824-3097) is located at 83 King St, open from 9 am to 5 pm daily. Admission is $5 for adults, $4 for seniors (55 and older) and military, $1.50 for children aged six to 15.

Alligator Farm It's very fun and even educational, and unlike its nemesis in Kissimmee, this is not an alligator breeding farm but a legitimate zoological park. We recommend it highly; alligators are very misunderstood, and here's a great chance to learn a lot about them from the knowledgeable staff. There are pits teeming with the beasts – there are about 2500 of them, and cages for their gator zoo – see Siamese crocodile (extinct in the wild), and when we visited, a small Chinese alligator on loan from a New York Zoo.

There's a talk, starring a couple of baby beasties, and staff demonstrate how gators chomp down on objects that move into their mouths by reflex. The star of the show is not an alligator but a crocodile named Gomek, who's about a bejillion feet long and eats big things whole and crunchily – kids love it. Alligator shows are at the Reptile Theater at 11 am, 1, 3 and 5 pm.

The 3 pm show is followed by Gomek feeding, so hustle over and don't miss it.

Admission is $9.95 for adults, $3.95 for children aged three to 10. The farm (☎ 824-3337) is on Anastasia Blvd about a mile east of the bay. And hey: no pets, OK?

J&S Carousel This little trip to yesteryear is a lovely diversion, especially during Illuminations in December-January, when it's bordered by white lights and sports a waving Santa Claus. It's a small, old-fashioned carousel – complete with organ music – in Davenport Park, at the corner of San Marco Ave and May St (Hwy A1A) one block east of the library across the grass, which also has a small playground with picnic tables. Kids love it. It's open from around noon to around 9 pm, a bit later on weekends. Rides are $1. They signed a two-year contract which was up in 1996, but they say they'll stay on, perhaps permanently. Call ☎ 823-3388 to check if they're open when you visit.

Churches & Shrines
Cathedral Basilica of St Augustine This magnificent 1797 Spanish Mission-style Catholic cathedral (☎ 824-2806) at Plaza de la Constitution on the northeast corner of St George and King Sts is worth a look, whether to simply view the Rambusch stained glass or to take them up on their free guided tours, which run continuously Monday to Friday from 9 am to 4.30 pm, and on Saturday and Sunday from 1 to 5 pm. While most of the cathedral was destroyed by fire in 1887, many walls were left intact; the section south of the transepts is essentially original, while the roof and chancel wall were rebuilt. What stands today is an expansion and reconstruction, and the church was refurbished for the 400th anniversary of the city in 1965, when most of the dark wood-paneled ceiling was removed and the Chapel of the Blessed Sacrament added.

The courtyard is usually the site of some activity during city celebrations. Services are held Monday to Friday at 7, 9.30 and

11.30 am, Saturday at 5 pm, and Sunday at 7, 9.30 and 11.30 am and 6 pm.

Trinity Parish Church The stained glass at the Cathedral Basilica is thoroughly outshined by that at this building (1821), directly south across Plaza de la Constitution and home of the first Protestant church in Florida. The glass here was mainly designed and constructed either by Tiffany personally or his company; note the window in St Peter's Chapel, in the main building, signed by Tiffany himself. It's open from 9 am to 4 pm daily. Services are held on Sunday at 7.45, 9 and 11.15 am, and Wednesday at 10 am. Tours are available by volunteer guides, most every afternoon, though they don't adhere to a schedule, so call first. Groups are welcome on advance notice, and all tours are free.

Flagler Memorial Presbyterian Church This is our favorite in town. Built by Henry Flagler as a memorial to his daughter, Jennie, who died at birth, this spectacular Venetian Renaissance church (1889-1990), with its trademark dome (it's beautifully illuminated at night) is open for tours Monday to Friday from 9 am to 4.30 pm, Saturday from 9 am to 4 pm, and Sunday from noon to 4.30 pm; call ☎ 829-6431. It's worth seeing; each tile on the floors is imported Sienna marble; all the wood is Santo Domingo mahogany, and the 90-rank organ is the original, dating to 1890 and refurbished in 1970. The 105-foot-high dome contains a crown of thorns, which contains a triangle, which in turn contains three white dots, representing the Father, the Son and the Holy Spirit. The church is at 36 Sevilla St at the corner of Valencia St, on which you enter. To the left as you face the church is the entrance to the gardens, also open to the public though unspectacular. Services are held Sunday at 8.30 and 10.55 am.

St Photios National Greek Shrine In memory of the Greek workers who worked at an indigo plantation at New Smyrna Beach (there were also Minorcan and Italian workers, see History above), this shrine and museum (☎ 829-8205), in Casa Avero at 41 St George St, features a history of the development of the area, with old maps, mementos and diaries of settlers. And the shrine itself is in a lovely vaulted room that has piped-in chanting. You can light candles and make an offering in the shrine.

Back in the lobby you can watch an 18-minute video of the history of the colony. Admission is free, and it's important to remember that this is indeed a shrine, and not a standard museum: while shorts and T-shirts are allowed, food or drink are not, and you should ask permission to take photographs.

Our Lady of La Leche Shrine Built on the site of the first mass in St Augustine, at Mission of Nombre de Dios, the Shrine to Our Lady of Le Leche (☎ 824-2809) is a 208-foot-tall stainless steel cross, visible from many parts of downtown. Also on the grounds, the absolutely charming Prince of Peace Church holds services Monday to Friday at 8.30 am, Saturdays at 6 pm and Sunday at 8 am, and the Chapel of Our Lady of La Leche is open to the public as well. The mission is at the corner of San Marco Ave and Ocean St; it's hard to miss: look for the towering cross.

Cemeteries

Huguenot Cemetery During a yellow fever epidemic in 1821, half an acre of land was set aside as a public cemetery, now located just north of the Old City Gate. Owned since 1832 by the Presbyterian Church (see Churches, below), interments were discontinued in 1884. Many of the gravesites of Protestant pioneers buried here are not marked. You can walk through the cemetery when the gates are unlocked.

The most prestigious graves are at the southwest end of the cemetery, including those of the Dr Peck Family; directly behind the Burt family gravestones within the fence: Charles, Alice and Lucy Peck, antecedents of the owners of the Alligator

Farm, and, farther west of that, the center of the three crypts at the cemetery's western end is that of Ann Drysdale, notable in that on the top of the crypt her eulogy is engraved as spoken by an Episcopal minister. Leave a donation in the box within the right hand gate pillar on the way out. It's north of the city gate; there's no telephone.

Tolomato Cemetery On Cordova St between Orange and Saragossa Sts, this cemetery sits on the site of what was, prior to 1763, a Native American village. Among the luminaries buried here is the first bishop of St Augustine, Augustine Verot, buried in the mortuary chapel at the rear of the cemetery. The last burial was in 1892. Note the tree to the north of the cemetery, in front of No 6 Cordova St – it's a palm tree growing from the trunk of a live oak!

Parks & Monuments
Anastasia State Recreation Area The Anastasia State Recreation Area (☎ 461-2033) is a very nice state park with beach access at its eastern end, nature and hiking trails and a campground (see Places to Stay, below). Admission is $3.25 per carload, $1 for pedestrians and bicyclists. It's on Anastasia Island and the entrance is on Anastasia Blvd.

Castillo de San Marcos National Monument When the British had burned the city

Castillo de San Marcos, the oldest masonry fort in the USA

down around them one time too many, the Spanish began work on this coquina fort in 1672. It was completed 23 years later. Now the oldest masonry fort in the continental US and a national monument, the fort (☎ 829-6506) is now open to visitors from 8.45 am to 4.45 pm daily. You can explore the shot furnace, powder room, chapel and bastions. It's on the east site of San Marco opposite the Old City Gate. There is a second fort in the area, Fort Matanzas; see the Around St Augustine section, below, for more information.

Bridge of Lions One of the city's most distinctive features, the Bridge of Lions – with its trademark Mediterranean Revival-style towers – was built in 1926 to connect the city with Anastasia Island. The bridge is named for the two lion statues at its west end, sculpted by an Italian named Romanelli, which were donated to the city by Dr Andrew Anderson.

Queen Isabella At the northeast corner of Hypolita and St George St, in the little park, is a sweet little statue of Queen Isabella I, by Anna Hyatt Huntington. This is a very popular hang-out for Flagler students, hippies and other guitar-wielding people; a fun place to come.

Plaza de la Constitución This is the grassy area at the east end of King St between the Bridge of Lions and Government House. At the western end, two cannons point northwest and southwest. A monument to the Spanish Plaza de la Constitution is near the center, as is a gazebo. Another statue is just east of this, a memorial to Confederate soldiers who died in the Civil War. At the east end, a historical marker tells the story of this spot, where a British guardhouse and watchtower once stood, as well as the site of the town's central market (see British Slave Market, above).

Organized Tours
An orientation tour is not a bad idea here, and the locals who run these services are generally pretty knowledgeable and funny, in a hokey, touristy kind of way, if you go for that sort of thing.

Walking Tours The very friendly and knowledgeable Roland Loveless, bedecked in full early-1700s Spanish costume, runs 1½-hour walking tours through downtown daily for $7. Information and reservations should be made directly at ☎ 797-9733. He also arranges **ghost tours**, through another company called Tour St Augustine (☎ 471-9010) that walks through the town and the cemeteries telling stories and legends about ghosts and the supernatural in St Augustine for 1½ hours. The cost is $5.

Horse-Drawn & Bicycle Carriage Tours
For a more expensive trip around the district, you can use either of the two horse-drawn carriage tour firms in town – though animal lovers would rather you didn't as there are very few regulations in place in the city to protect the horses, which are often subjected to long working hours. There are Colee's Carriage Tours (☎ 829-2818) and Sightseeing Carriage Tours – Gamsey Carriage Co (☎ 829-2391); both leave from Avenida Menendez just south of the fort, both charge $10 for adults over 12, $5 for children aged five to 11 (under five free) or $35 minimum for a carriage. Both trips are about 2½ miles.

A far greener (and fresher smelling, if you use deodorant) option in good weather only is St Augustine Horseless Carriage Company (no ☎), which rents four-person bicycle-driven carriages for $10 per hour. It's at the lot at the corner of Orange and Castillo Sts, just south of the Old City Gate.

Train & Trolley Tours There's a nasty, cutthroat side of St Augustine life: the tourist choo-choo train market. There are two companies in the business here that loath each other, and they're not too happy about customers that patronize the competition, either.

The companies, in *alphabetical order* to avoid even a hint of favoritism on our part, are *St Augustine Historical Tours* (☎ 829-3800), and *St Augustine Sightseeing Trains* (☎ 829-6545). Both companies offer essentially identical product (though Sightseeing Trains has a few more stops on their route) for the same price: a narrated journey through the historic district aboard either a red-and-blue 'train' (Sightseeing Trains) or a green-and-white 'trolley' (Historical Tours).

Narration is as you'd expect, though you do get some good historical background and, if the narrator's not made of wood, some humor as well. Tickets for both, which are good for two days, are $12 for adults, $5 for children aged six to 12 and free for children under six. There is no senior citizen discount. You can get on and off your company's trolley as often as you'd like, but remember to wear your admission sticker (red for Sightseeing Trains, green for Historic Tours) at all times.

Sightseeing Trains offers free parking at 170 San Marco Ave or the Sugar Mill at the corner of Hwy 16 and San Marco Ave, north of downtown. Historical Tours has free parking at the lot in front of the Old Jail on San Marco Ave. Trolleys from both companies run about every 20 minutes; the first trolleys leave at around 8.30 am; the last trolley from Historic Tours is at 4.30 pm, Sightseeing Tours at 5 pm.

Boat Tours You can take a 1¼-hour cruise from Victory II Scenic Cruises (☎ 824-1806, 800-542-8316) for $8.50 for adults, $7.50 for AARP members, $5.50 for children aged 12 to 18 and $3 for children along the waterfront. The cruises leave from the Municipal Marina, just south of the Bridge of Lions at 11 am, 1, 2.45 and 4.30 pm daily. There are additional cruises at 6.15 pm from April 1 to May 21, and at 6.15 and 8.30 pm from May 22 to Labor Day. St Augustine Riverboat Co's *Anastasia* (☎ 824-3463), a paddleboat, does lunch, dinner, and Sunday brunch cruises. It, too, leaves from the Municipal Marina. Friday and Saturday dinner cruises ($36.95) cruise from 8 to 10.30 pm; Saturday lunch cruises ($21.95) from noon to 2 pm; Sunday champagne brunch cruises ($25.95) from 11 am to 1 pm and lunch Dixie Picnic cruises ($23.95) from 3 to 5 pm.

Air Tours Flights over the city and area are available in private planes from the small municipal airport (☎ 824-1995) at the northern end of the city on US Hwy 1. There are lots of options but a great one is with Florida Aviation Courier Training (☎ 824-9401), which has one-hour air tours for three passengers for $99 (total, not per person). You'll fly over downtown, and either down the coast to Marineland or north towards Jacksonville. For far, far more expensive trips, there are two specialty outfits in town: North American Top Gun (☎ 823-3505, 800-257-1636), which has flights in warbirds, and the Extra Experience (Jacksonville office ☎ 363-2608) with flights in an Extra 300 aerobatic stunt plane for $179 for half hour, $349 an hour – you can fly the plane at some point as well.

Places to Stay

St Augustine is not a totally cheap place, though you can definitely get a motel room for $25 to 30 for a double. There's a youth hostel, as well as a few camping possibilities, and the city is teeming with B&Bs.

Camping Camping is inconvenient without a car. Surprise, surprise. Camping at the *Anastasia State Recreation Area* (☎ 461-2033), is the cheapest in town in winter if you use their rustic sites, but never if you use sites with electricity, in which case you should see Indian Forest Campground, below, which we think is a better value if you're not set on sleeping in a state park. Tent sites at the park are $12 a night from October 1 to February 28, $15 from March 1 to September 30. Florida-resident senior citizens pay half price. Electricity is $2 a day. After the park closes at sundown, campers are given the combination to the gate to gain access at night.

The friendliest privately owned place in town for tent camping isn't really in town;

it's *Indian Forest Campground* (☎ 824-3574), about two miles east of I-95 (exit 94) at 1555 Hwy 207. Tent sites are $14 a day or $84 per week, and each has a fire ring and water and electric hookups. RV sites are $17/102, including electric, sewer and water and $19/112 with all that plus cable television.

KOA has two locations near town; the closest is at 525 W Pope Rd (☎ 471-3113, 800-992-5622), at the intersection of Hwy 3, just across the Mickler O'Connell Bridge on Anastasia Island. They're more expensive, but they run a handy daily shuttle between the campground and Plaza de la Constitution: it leaves KOA at 10 am and picks up at the Plaza at 4 pm. The cost is $4 per person roundtrip. Tent sites are $19.95 for two people including water and electric and a cooking grill. RV/van sites are $23 a night with water and electric or $25 with water, electric, sewer and cable TV. Kamping Kabins are $32 a night.

The second KOA (☎ 824-8309), 12 miles north of the city on Hwy 210 just off I-95 exit 96, is a bit cheaper than that but has no shuttle service: rustic (no services) campsites are $18 a night, tent sites with water and electricity are $21; RV/van sites are $24, Kamping Kabins $29 for one room, $33 for two rooms. All sites have the seventh night free.

Hostel The *St Augustine Hostel* (☎ 808-1999) couldn't be better located: two blocks north of King St at 32 Treasury St near the corner of Charlotte St. Rooms are very clean and comfortable, and cost $12 per person in a dorm, with private rooms for $28. There's a good kitchen, usually packed with travelers, a library/common room with books, board games and an organ (no television) and a large terrace on the 2nd floor with a barbecue grill. Smoking is prohibited inside the building, but allowed on the terrace. The hostel also rents bikes, is a great source of local information, and provides some lockers for valuables. There is only one telephone; local calls are free but use your calling card or call collect for long distance. Check in is from 8 to 10 am and 5 to 10 pm; no lock out, but there's a combination lock on the front door that's locked between 10 am and 5 pm and after 10 pm – you get the combo when you check in.

Motels There are plenty of choices in motels in town that run the gamut from as sleazy as you'd imagine to as nice as you'd want. The better ones are in the center, the cheaper ones along San Marco or Anastasia Blvd.

San Marco Ave Motels and chain hotels line this street, and the area near where it meets US Hwy 1; chains include *Knights Inn* (☎ 829-3321), 231 San Marco Ave, newly remodeled, very clean and very cheap at $20/23 single/double in winter, $30 a room in summer; *Scottish Inns* (☎ 824-2871), 110 San Marco Ave, very clean, $32 for a double in winter, $37 in summer on weekdays, $49 in summer on weekends; *Holiday Inn* (☎ 824-3383), 1300 Ponce de León Blvd, with rooms for $49 in winter, $66 on summer weekdays and $76 summer Fridays and Saturdays; *Comfort Inn Historic Area* (☎ 824-5554), 1111 Ponce de León Blvd, with rooms for $49.95 with breakfast in winter, $59 on summer weekdays and $69.95 on summer weekends.

The *Florida Motel* (☎ 824-2348), 253 San Marco Ave, is on the clean side and charges $23/25 for singles/doubles. If you can afford another $3 above the double price here, you should definitely spend it on the far cleaner *Keystone Motel* (☎ 829-8350), at 290 San Marco Ave, where motel rooms are $28, efficiencies $35 (three-day minimum) or $210 a week. HBO is included, staff is cheerful and there's a nice swimming pool.

The *Economy Inn* (☎ 824-4406) at 94 San Marco Ave, is a perfectly reasonable place; with singles/doubles $23/27 Monday to Thursday and $35/40 Friday to Sunday in winter, $40/45 and $55/65 in summer.

Anastasia Island Perhaps the nicest view in town is at the *Edgewater Inn* (☎ 825-2697), at 2 St Augustine Blvd, just off Anastasia Blvd at the eastern foot of the Bridge of Lions. There is very friendly service, spotless rooms, and some have large bay windows looking across the bay right at downtown. Rooms are $35 to 38 for a poolside view, and $39 to 42 for a water view in low season, $48 for the pool and $52 for the water in high season, and rooms with bay windows are always $5 extra. Some rooms have baths, some showers. Price includes basic cable, as well as juice, muffins and coffee in the morning. You can also dock at their private marina; 75¢ per foot, 15 foot minimum.

We were somewhat less impressed with the *Anchorage Motor Inn* across the street (☎ 829-9041) – rooms are nice and clean, and also have great views of the city, but service, when we visited, wasn't as happy (may be worth trying when you're here). Rooms are $36 in winter, $43 in summer, based on double; extra guests over 12 are $5 each.

B&Bs There are *at least* 25 B&Bs in the city, and we've yet to hear complaints about any, so just because we don't list one here, or if we list one higher up on the list than another it's really because it's a difficult field to narrow down and we had to just bite the bullet and pick just a few. If you're planning a lengthy stay in a B&B here, you should contact *Historic Inns of St Augustine*, PO Box 5268, St Augustine, FL 32084-5268 for their free pamphlet, which has descriptions of 23 B&Bs in town, their phone numbers, a good locator map but, alas, no prices. Be sure to find out about parking near the inn (it can be difficult), and ask if the price includes museum admissions or other perks (some do).

Our favorites in town – and again, this does not detract from the others – are:

At the *Victorian House* (☎ 824-5214), 11 Cadiz St, breakfast is usually homemade granola, pastries and breads, fruit, juice, tea and coffee; rooms range from $60 to 90. This is in one of the loveliest parts of town, to the south of King St. Some (not much) parking available.

The *Southern Wind* (☎ 825-3623) is actually two B&Bs, the first at 18 Cordova St, and the second at 34 Saragossa St. Rooms in both of these lovely properties range from $69 to 139, including free wine in the afternoons, and free champagne on honeymoons and anniversaries. Breakfast is usually granola, fruit, pastries, quiche, a toast bar, juices, coffee and tea.

The *Old Powder House Inn* (☎ 824-4149, 800-447-4149) is one of the best values in town – with a Jacuzzi, tandem bicycle, free coffee and tea all day, and free wine and hors d'oeuvres in the evening. Breakfast is a little elaborate, with more than 20 rotating entrees (like egg soufflé, baked apple and pecan pancakes, strawberry crepes), homemade granola, fruit, muffins, juice, yadda yadda yadda. Rooms range from $65 to 115 on weekends, $10 to 15 less Monday to Thursday. It's at 38 Cordova St, and free parking is available.

The *Secret Garden Inn* (☎ 829-3678), tucked way back at 56½ Charlotte St, is a very romantic place with only three suites. Breakfast is usually pastries and breads, fruit, juice, tea and coffee. Rooms range from $89 to 109 double (extra person $10). Parking is available.

Dat'l Do It

Be sure and try the fiery and flavorful locally grown datil (rhymes with that'll) peppers, available in mustard, vinegar (for splashing on collard greens) and sauces like Dat'l Do It and Dixie Datil (motto: ain't killed no one yet). All are available at *Some Like It Hotter* (☎ 829-2696), 34½ Treasury St right next to the hostel, which has a huge, though pricey, selection of pepper-related foods. Publix and some other local markets carry the Dat'l Do It brand for less. The advantage of Some Like It Hotter, though, is that you can taste an enormous variety of fiery sauces free. (Watch out for Dave's Insanity and Endorphin Rush, both made from pepper extract – the same ingredient used in self-defense pepper sprays!) ■

Places to Eat

There's plenty to keep you full, and cheaply. And cheap doesn't mean bad: case in point, excellent lunches at *Gypsy Cab Co*, a St Augustine gem.

Snacks, Pizza & Fast Food The bulk of the fast-food chains are on US Hwy 1, stretching a bit north, and a couple of miles south, of King St. There's a Pizza Hut downtown on King St, but otherwise it's old-fashioned small businesses. The most original snack spot is the *Spanish Bakery* (no ☎) at 47½ St George St, where the aroma of freshly baking empanadas ($2), mini-bread (50¢) and smoked sausage rolls begins wafting out onto the street with the first oven-load of the day at 11 am. The lunch special of soup, mini bread and a soft drink is $3. It's open daily from 9.30 am to 3 pm.

The best cinnamon rolls and pecan buns in the state are available at the *Bunnery Café* (☎ 829-6166) at 35 Hypolita St. The smells wafting out onto the street are nothing compared to sinking your teeth into one of these babies, which are $1.

We're arguing about the best pizza in town – it's between two. First, the *Pizza Garden* (☎ 825-4877) at 21 Hypolita St, which does pretty downright awesome slices ($1.50) and calzones ($4). Try the Stromboli with spinach, mushrooms, black olives and seasoning for $4.50, which is a meal. Beer and cappuccino are also served. It's open Sunday to Thursday from 11 am to 9 pm, Friday and Saturday from 11 am to 10 pm. The other contender loses lots of points for being inconvenient as hell to downtown but it's excellent: the *De León Pizzeria* (☎ 794-1917) at the Ponce de León mall, where succulent New York-style slices are $1.50

If you're at the Old Jail, the Fountain of Youth or the Tragedy in US History Museum, don't miss saying hello to Jim at *Jim's Lemonade & Fruit Shakes*, a tropical little place just across the street from the main entrance to the Fountain of Youth, at the corner of Magnolia and Williams Sts, with a ping-pong table and great fruit drinks for $1 to $3, and changing daily specials.

Schmagel's Bagels (☎ 824-4444) at 69 Hypolita St, turns out some very good stuff; hot pepper cream cheese on a bagel, or about a dozen other varieties of cream cheese, is $1.75; sandwiches are $3.50, veggie burgers $3.95. There are lovely courtyard tables.

The *Manatee Café* (☎ 826-0210), at 179A San Marco Ave at the corner of May St (across from the carousel), does excellent and healthful sandwiches (veggie burger $4.50, humus pita $3.95, veggie burrito $3.95 to 4.25) and absolutely astounding mixed veggie juice ($3.29 to 3.95). They serve killer veggie burgers and tabouli, but we skipped the chocolate tofu pie ($2.50).

Downtown, sub grindage is best at *Joel's Major League Sandwiches* (☎ 826-3322), 9B King St, which does big sandwiches cheap: turkey, ham, roast beef, three cheese or tuna salad subs are $3.25 small, $4.25 large; veggie cheese $2.95/3.95. They also have kids meals from 79¢ to $1.79, like the $1.79 sandwich, applesauce, fruit cocktail, potato salad or cole slaw and milk or juice and cookie.

Just because they have over 150 beers doesn't mean we can't list the *Rendezvous Restaurant* (☎ 824-1090) in this category – they also have a great sandwich selection, priced from $2.95 to 4.75. OK, they also have Franziskaner Hefe Weissbier for $3.50, but we're *really* recommending the sandwiches. And the Blackened Voodoo ($3). They're at 106 St George St (Belgian Cherry Lambic Ale in the cork-top bottle $7).

On US Hwy 1, *Ragin' Cajun* (☎ 829-1005) is a family-run little place doing respectable Louisiana food like jambalaya ($5.95 at lunch, $7.95 at dinner), chicken Creole ($6.95/8.95), shrimp Creole ($7.95/9.95) and shrimp baton ($6.95/8.95) as well as burgers and chicken wings. They are at 1574 US Hwy 1.

Restaurants & Cafés There's a good range of places in the under $10 category in town.

Budget to Middle Of the two British tea rooms in town, we only recommend this one: for a great treat and good value, one or two people can have afternoon tea at the *Tea Room* (☎ 808-8395), at 15 Hypolita St, for $6.95, which includes 'dainty' sandwiches (your choice of filling), homemade scones and shortbread and a pot of tea. Too bad the cream's whipped and not clotted Devonshire double, but hey.

The best tzatziki in the state can be found at the *Athena Restaurant* (☎ 823-9076), a classic Greek diner doing excellent breakfasts ($2.65 to 3.75), good burgers ($2.30 to 3.50), great salads (and only somewhat disappointing grilled fish when we visited). People line up outside for tables at dinnertime during special events and on some weekends. It's at 14 Cathedral Place.

PK's Cafe & Coffee House (☎ 825-4065) is a local favorite; a diner with a few tables spilling out onto St George St. Stuffed baked potatoes are $3.95, chili $3.25, lasagna $4.95, and there are some cheap breakfast specials. Newspaper machines outside sell out-of-town and local papers. Relax. It's at 135 St George St, at the corner of Treasury.

Out by the lighthouse in Lighthouse Park, the very comfortable and friendly *Lighthouse Park Restaurant* (☎ 826-4003) has lunch main courses from $4.95 to 6.25, burgers from $4.50 to 5.50, and dinners a bit higher from $9.95 to 10.95 – with entrees like coconut fried shrimp, south of the border chicken or chicken Creole.

For about 25 years, *The Monk's Vineyard* (☎ 824-5888), at 56 St George St, has been doing reliably good pub food; entrées average $8 to 10. They've got a huge wine list, a very pleasant (if narrow) front courtyard and good service.

Forget about service, though, at *OC White's* (☎ 824-0808), where the only reason to go is the pasta and some of the seafood entrées. The pastas – like seafood marinara and shrimp and scallop scampi, are very good ($12.95 to 14.95), and the fish dishes are fine, averaging $9.95 to $14.95. Skip the early bird dinners, which are skimpy. It's a really nice place to sit, either in their large courtyard or on one of their two floors (nonsmoking is upstairs). They're at 118 Avenida Menendez.

Riki Japanese Steak & Seafood (☎ 825-0520) in the Shoppes of Northtowne shopping mall at the northern end of town on the west side of US Hwy 1, is an excellent Japanese place with hibachi tables complete with food-acrobat-chefs who slice and dice as fast as any Ginsu knife ad. The sushi bar is a good one, with rolls at around $3 and sushi the piece from $1.50 to $2. Dinners average $8 to 10. It features friendly management, slow but earnest service.

The *Rosenhof Restaurant* (☎ 471-4340) at the intersection of Hwy A1A and Anastasia Blvd, is a very nice German place that has good food and service; German pancakes are $6.95, Hungarian goulash is $10.50, and their roast pork with bread dumpling and sauerkraut is $12.50.

We were shocked when we saw what we thought was a play on the joke from the movie *The Naked Gun* ('I know a little place downtown that does great Viking food') when we saw the *Viking Restaurant* (☎ 829-0906), next door to our house at 72 Spanish St. The place, run by Swedes, serves up Medieval portions of beef, lamb and chicken, served on their sizzling hot grillstones at the table: choose from beef ($12.97), lamb ($13.74), marinated shrimp ($12.11), duck ($12.84) and wild boar (market price – where's a boar market?). There's great atmosphere, nice staff and, of course, a huge bar. At lunch, they serve their Wild Viking Combination Platter ($18.93), which can easily feed two people interested in consuming buffalo, pheasant, elk and gator tail. Upstairs is The Dungeon, a popular nightclub.

Top End The *Gypsy Cab Co* (☎ 824-8244) is absolutely worth the trip to the east side of town at 828 Anastasia Blvd, for the excellent and cheap lunches, Monday and Wednesday to Saturday from 11 am to 3 pm. The lunch menu is about the same as the dinner menu with one big difference: you can get a full meal for $5.95 to $7.95. And the house dressing is superb. At dinner, entrées range from $11.99 to 16.99, including apricot chicken, stuffed pork chops with sour cream sauce or gypsy

---

Secret Dressing

One of the most highly guarded culinary secrets in St Augustine is the recipe for the house dressing at Gypsy Cab Co. Locals and visitors go nuts over it – a yeasty, garlicky taste sensation that defies description – to the extent that they buy up dozens of 10-ounce bottles of the stuff for $7 a piece. That's right, $7 (though it doesn't cost extra when you have it with the salad in the restaurant – ask for some extra dressing). Once you try it, you'll probably agree that taking a bottle home is worth the expense. We, of course, were lucky enough to snare a copy of the complex recipe: for yours, send $750 to Nick & Corinna, 78 Spanish St, St Augustine, FL 32084. Allow 16 to 26 weeks for delivery. ■

---

chicken at $11.99, and flounder almondine, baked snapper with mousseline, seafood New Orleans or veal Française for $15.99. Desserts are excellent as well, with offerings like raspberry cheesecake, tiramisu, coconut cream or Key Lime pie for $3.

The Raintree (☎ 824-7211) is a fine choice for a big night out, with excellent service and food that's cheaper than you'd expect. The atmosphere in the charming old yellow house is very relaxed, and entrées run from $8.95 to 20.95, including chicken breast and shitake mushrooms in clear champagne sauce for $12.95, brandy pepper steak at $18.50, shrimp and scallop moutarde for $14.50 and rack of lamb for $19.95. Early dinner specials, served from 5 to 6 pm, are from $8.95 to 10.95. It's at 102 San Marco Ave.

Entertainment

Theater Other than student productions at Flagler Auditorium, the biggest news in town is the annual production of *The Cross & Sword* (☎ 471-1965), the official Florida state play. It tells the highly romantic story, through Pocohantas-caliber rose-colored glasses, of the settlement of Florida, the befriending of the Indians and the various governments that led to the greatest . . .

well, you know. It runs from late June to early September every year at the St Augustine Amphitheatre (☎ 471-1965), about a half-mile east of the entrance to the Anastasia State Recreation Area on Anastasia Blvd. Admission is $12 for adults, $11 for seniors, $6 for children aged three to 12. There are other performances at the amphitheatre throughout the year that change annually, like performances of Rotagilla (see sidebar) and an annual Easter Passion Play in late March or early April. Call the amphitheatre for details of what's on when you're here.

Cinema This isn't a usual category, but this isn't a usual cinema: Pot Belly's Cinema 4 Plus (☎ 829-3101) shows first-run movies for $2.50 at all times. But wait – there's more: you watch these movies from the comfort and luxury of a recliner easy-chair, while waitresses bring you soft drinks, beer or wine, pizzas, sandwiches and other deli snacks and *smoking is allowed*. If you smoke, it's like watching a movie on a giant screen in your living room. Okay, it's not as flash as the big places (the film melted at the most crucial moment in *Apollo 13*, leaving all of us on the edge of our recliners while they spliced it back together), but hey, it's a great deal. It's at 31 Granada St. There's another, more modern and expensive, cinema, in the Ponce de León Mall, on US Hwy 1, south of the intersection of Hwy 301.

Bars, Music & Nightclubs The *Trade-Winds Lounge* (☎ 829-9336) at 124 Charlotte St, is the classic St Augustine local bar, under the same management for about 50 years. It's got live music every night by many local and regional musicians (though we're a little sick of the 'Chicken Shit' song) and their mainstay band, Matanzas, cheap drinks and a fun atmosphere. Great happy hours are in the evening.

The *Rendezvous Restaurant* (☎ 824-1090) has a huge beer selection and is a quiet little place that for some reason reminds us of an Eastern European beer room; see Places to Eat, above, for more information. It's at 106 St George St.

You can try to avoid it, but at the end of the day you'll end up at *Scarlett O'Hara's* (☎ 824-6535) at least once during your stay, and why not – it's a friendly neighborhood bar with great drinks (but poor food) and a good raw bar/liquor bar outside. Happy hour is from 4 to 7 pm Monday to Friday. It's at 70 Hypolita St.

The *St George Tavern* (☎ 824-4204) at 116 St George St, is a rowdy kind of local bar, with cheap drinks and a fun atmosphere – lots of Flagler students – they have daily $1.75 margarita specials and happy hours from 11 am to 1 pm and 4 to 7 pm,

NORTHEAST

Rotagilla

The best $14 we spent on our entire research trip was at the TradeWinds Lounge to see one of the rare performances of Rotagilla (pronounced rota-GEE-ya), a collection of guys from around the region (including a journalist and a member of the Orlando Symphony Orchestra) who say that they stopped doing drugs in the 1970s and are therefore no longer funny. They're wrong. They have a band made up of fiddle, mandolin, guitar, drums, whistles, washboard bass and banjo: if you've never heard of Galax, Virginia, this is the best bluegrass hybrid you'll come across.

They do spoofs on popular songs – *Swiss Mountain Breakdown*, *Volga Mountain Breakdown* – with drag hula dancers, and vying for the highlight: an a cappella version of the classic song, *Wipeout* and a series of songs concerning 'If the US Went Metric', including such classic hits as *805 Kilometers Away from Home*.

Half bar-band, half-play, Rotagilla is some of the very best of Southern American humor, but they never lose sight of the music, which is excellent. They play about once every three months; check at the TradeWinds when you're in town and don't miss it if you have the chance. ∎

sometimes three-for-one drinks. Just down the street, there's live acoustic folk and rock music at the *Mill Top Tavern* (☎ 829-2329) in the old millhouse at 10½ St George St, near the Old City Gate, which serves up its own micro-brewed Gristmill Amber Lager and Rosebud Pail Tail in a Weissbier glass for $3.25.

Ann O'Malley's Pub (☎ 825-4040) at 23 Orange St, a block west of the Old City Gate, is a nice little Irish pub run by a nice little Irish lass serving Guinness, Harp and Murphy's (and half-and-half Guinness and Harp) as well as a bunch of bottled domestic and imported stuff. No live music, but there's a jukebox.

The other microbrewery in town, *A1A Ale House* (☎ 829-2977) has seven varieties of their microbrewed stuff from $2.25 a pint to $4.50 for a taste of all of them. They do ragtime and other live music, and have an expensive restaurant upstairs. It's at 1 King St, on the south corner.

Upstairs at the Viking Restaurant (☎ 829-0906) is *The Dungeon*, a very popular disco that does music from the '70s to the '90s, and is packed Thursday to Saturday. On those nights, they have loud music in the courtyard outside, usually featuring a thoroughly ghastly female singer they refuse to fire. It's at 72 Spanish St.

There's also live music at OC Whites (see Places to Eat, above) every night.

About three miles north of the northern city boundary on the east side of US Hwy 1, the *King's Head Pub* (☎ 823-9787), 6460 US Hwy 1 N, is said to be an extremely authentic British pub – we've driven by but haven't gone in. Everyone we speak with says it's a hoot: look for the double-decker bus out front.

Things to Buy

This is an artsy town. Souvenirs are best found along St George St, and there are no surprises in availability. The wonderful people at Grace Gallery at 82 Charlotte St (☎ 826-1536) and 32 Charlotte St (☎ 826-1669) carry a great line of authentic Indonesian, Thai, Nepali, Guatemalan and Mexican handicrafts, as well as that

from local artists at really good prices – they do all their buying in the country it's from themselves, and they're great travelers, so it's a nice place to stop for conversation as well. More local art (look especially for sea-glass earrings by local artist Gaja) can be found at galleries like The Forest (☎ 824-4815) at 39 Cordova St, Moultrie Creek Pottery (☎ 829-2142) at 218 Charlotte St, and at the well-named Temple of Great Art – No Spitting (☎ 825-0837), at 82 San Marco Ave.

Antique shops are scattered all around the downtown area; for a list, contact the Antique Dealers Association of St Augustine, 60 Cuna St, St Augustine, FL 32084.

For discounted clothing, cookware and a bunch of other stuff, try the St Augustine Factory Outlet, at the intersection of Hwy 16 and I-95.

Getting There & Away

Air St Augustine's tiny municipal airport (☎ 824-1995) accommodates only private planes and charters, so the nearest commercial airport is Jacksonville International Airport about 50 miles from town and served by American, United and Air South. The St Augustine Hostel runs a shuttle service between the airport and the hostel for $40, though if you've got a lot of time you can Greyhound to Jacksonville for $10, and then try a taxi from downtown Jacksonville to the airport and it will work out cheaper.

Bus The Greyhound station (☎ 829-6401) is at 100 Malaga St, one block north of King St, just east of the bridge over the San Sebastian River. It's a quick walk down King St east, over to the heart of downtown, or you can use the hostel's shuttle ($1.50) by calling them in advance.

Train Amtrak, infuriatingly, does not serve St Augustine but rather the thoroughly inconvenient town of Palatka, 25 miles west (see the Central Florida chapter). Taxis from Palatka to St Augustine run about $25 to 30. The hostel runs a shuttle between it and the Amtrak station that costs $25 a person.

Car From the north, take I-95 south to exit 95 and turn left (east), past US Hwy 1 to San Marcos Ave; turn right and you'll end up at the Old City Gate, just past the fort. Alternately, you can take Hwy A1A along the beach, which intersects with San Marco Ave; or US Hwy 1 south from Jacksonville. From the south, take I-95 to exit 94, Hwy 207 east; make a left when it dead ends into US Hwy 1, and a right on King St to get to downtown. Exit 93, US Hwy 1, takes longer and is slower.

Getting Around

There's no public transport in town.

Taxi Rates are set by each company, though the first two of these are actually owned by the same parent company. They are: Ancient City Cabs (☎ 824-8161), $1.75 per person in downtown, $4.50 and up to St Augustine Beach, $49 per carload to Jacksonville International Airport; the same trips from the others cost: Baas LH Cab Co (☎ 829-3454), $1.50 a person downtown, $4 to St Augustine Beach and $1.50 each additional person, $65 per car to the airport; and probably the worst option (because of often unsavory drivers and rattly, broken down old Jalopies), Comfort Cab Co (☎ 824-8240), which charges $1.75 around downtown, $4.25 to St Augustine Beach, $1.50 each additional person, and $49 per carload to the airport.

Car For the downtown area, a car is a gorilla on your back – several pedestrian-only streets, a complex one-way system and parking from hell are a few reasons why. But for day trips, camping, shopping at a real supermarket or to head for Fort Matanzas or the beaches, a car is key. Most of downtown has a 25 mph speed limit, and you must stop at every corner, especially in the center. There's an Avis office at the St Augustine Airport, and Budget has an office at Jack Wilson Chevrolet, on US Hwy 1 south of the city (☎ 797-4567).

Parking Parking is metered almost everywhere, meters are in effect every day and spaces are scarce. Meter agents diligently comb the streets and alleys looking for scofflaw offenders, and have hearts of stone when it comes to ticketing. Fortunately, tickets only cost $7.50, but $7.50 here and $7.50 there can add up to some real money quite fast. You can park for $3 a day in front of the main visitor center, and in front of the Old Jail. On weekends only, head early to the lot on Treasury St between Cordova and Spanish Sts (adjacent to 78 Spanish St, the three-story pink Victorian that we used to live in), where free parking is available in the Barnett employee parking lot, but act fast. There's parking for hostel guests right out front (but it's limited, speak to the management).

Bicycle Rent bicycles at the St Augustine Hostel or at the Coffee Shop (☎ 824-5421), at 41 Cordova St. Both charge about $3 an hour, $10 for half day, or $15 per day.

AROUND ST AUGUSTINE

There are some lovely areas and little towns to the west of St Augustine, including Palatka and, farther south, Pierson, Blue Springs and Cassadaga; see the Central Florida chapter for information on those.

St Augustine Beach

The seven-mile stretch of St Augustine Beach is a nice, wide one, and other than a couple of barbecue places and surfer hangouts and the fishing pier there's not much to do but hang out for a while. Take Anastasia Blvd to Hwy A1A right out to the beach; there's a visitor information booth right at the foot of the pier.

Berry Picking

About 13 miles west of I-95 on Hwy 207, the town of Elkton offers peace and quiet and the opportunity to pick your own strawberries for $1 a quart at Tommy Howle's Vegetable Bin & Garden on the right-hand side of the road on the eastern end of the town. The farm and market, which also sell excellent fresh vegetables and fruits including Augustine (sweet) onions and they-pick-em strawberries for $1.50 a quart, is just east of the St John's County Fair Grounds, home to various festivals throughout the year like the annual Cracker Day (which is, *of course!*, celebrated on October).

Spuds

While potatoes are the primary crop (and 'thing to see & do') in this sleepy little farming village just west of Elkton, it's not the Potato Capital of Florida. That honor goes to Hastings – the next town to the west, where potato chip stands abound (well, abound in a rural Florida kind of way – there are maybe four). But we've included Spuds because we just really wanted to see the town's name in print. Spuds, Spuds, Spuds. There's a college out there as well: Bethune Cookman College – Spuds Campus (☎ 692-1001).

Fort Matanzas National Monument

The area's second fort, Fort Matanzas (☎ 471-0116) was built in 1742 to secure the city from naval blockades, which had occurred on several occasions: during one attack the early city was spared only by weather, which forced a British retreat that allowed Spanish supply ships to make their way back to the city from Cuba. But this tiny stone fort never saw action in a full-on war. Used until 1821, it's now a national monument. Admission and the short ferry ride aboard the *Matanzas Queen* from the entrance park on Anastasia Island, 14 miles south of the city, is free. There is unfortunately no public transport down to the park. By car, cross the Bridge of Lions and take Anastasia Ave to Hwy A1A south; the entrance to the park is on the right. The main park, which has about a half-mile nature trail, a movie on the history of the fort, and beaches, is a lovely place to have a picnic. The ferry runs daily except Christmas (and during turbulent waters) from 9 am to 4.30 pm.

Marineland

It's seen better days, but Marineland (☎ 471-1111, in state 800-824-4218, out of state 800-828-5151) was Florida's first aquatic theme park. It's its own city (population 15) – it incorporated in order to allow its cocktail lounge to stay open on Sundays and late at night.

It's a little sad, and conditions are far worse than at other parks like SeaWorld and Seaquarium, but it continues to be a major draw in the region.

There are dolphin shows (they've got 11 of them) and lots of kid activities – playports with rope ladders, air bounces, etc) and dolphin feedings, as well as animal shows and films during the day. The Oceanarium is on three levels – the bottom two featuring rather green and dark windows.

Admission is $14.95 for adults, $11.96 for seniors, $9.95 for teens aged 13 to 18 and $7.95 for kids aged three to 12.

It's on Hwy A1A south, about 20 miles south of St Augustine. Take Anastasia Blvd to Hwy A1A and continue south.

JACKSONVILLE

• *pop 980,000* ☎ 904

Jacksonville residents refer to their city by its airport code, JAX, and that should tip you off that Jacksonville has all the charm and welcoming atmosphere of a medium-size municipal airport. While its tourist brochures breathlessly describe it as a place 'overrun with sea oats and palm trees, not traffic and noise', Jacksonville – the largest city in America in terms of square mileage – probably has more square feet of concrete and asphalt than we've ever seen in one place. More? The Jacksonville Convention & Visitors Bureau *brags* that Jacksonville has/was/is the:

- first graded road built in Florida: Old King's Rd, 1763
- first building using skyscraper technology: 1901
- busiest military airport in the country: 1991 during the Gulf War
- birthplace of Pat Boone; residence of Slim Whitman

It's oppressive; it's built on Muscovian scale; it's got a dangerous downtown and you need a car to get anywhere (there's not

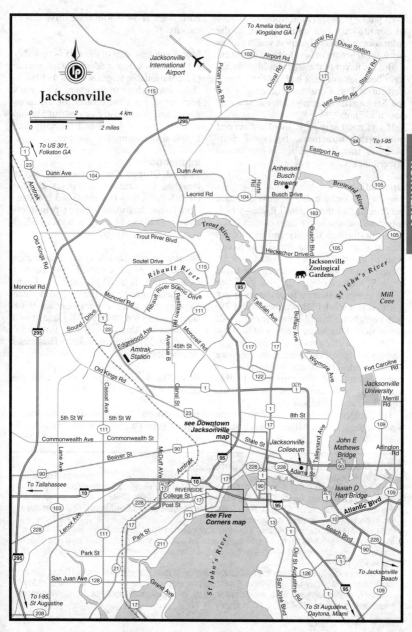

even public transportation from the *airport* to downtown!), and unless you're in the insurance or banking business you'll probably want to get out of here as fast as you can.

But the flavor of the area would probably have been far different had the French settlement at Fort Caroline succeeded – see the St Augustine section for the story of how it did not.

If you must stay here, there are several noteworthy attractions, but most non-business travelers end up saying *adios* rather quickly.

Orientation

The city of Jacksonville is tri-sected in a very rough T by the St John's River – which runs north-south, with a little east and then north jig, through the city and then banks almost due east – and the Trout River, which joins the St John's from the west. Downtown Jacksonville is on the west side of the St John's River on the little jig.

I-95 comes in straight from the north to a junction just south of downtown with I-10. I-295 breaks off from I-95 and forms a half circle around the western edges of the city.

One of the city's more charming neighborhoods is Riverside, home to the Cummer Museum of Art, at the intersection of Lomax, Park and Margaret Sts. In this section of town are several restaurants, nightclubs and coffeehouses.

The Jacksonville beaches – from Ponte Vedra at the south to Atlantic Beach at the north – are about a 40-minute drive east of the city.

Maps The best map of the area is probably HM Gousha's *Street Map of Jacksonville* ($2.25) available at gas stations and bookshops everywhere in the town. We say it's best because it's the clearest of the maps we looked at and also has a useful blowup of downtown. AAA, Rand McNally and Dolph also have maps to the area.

Information

Tourist Offices The Jacksonville & the Beaches Convention & Visitor Bureau (☎ 798-9148, 800-733-2668) at 3 Independent Drive, has useful tourist pamphlets and some discount coupon books and, if you ask very nicely, bus maps.

Money Barnett Bank has over 25 branches in the city of Jacksonville; the Barnett Center office is at 50 N Laura St, downtown near Jacksonville Landing. American Express has three offices; one at 9908 Baymeadows Rd (☎ 642-1701), and at two locations of Akra Travel: 841 Prudential Drive (☎ 391-7289) and 3216 Hendricks Ave (☎ 396-3388).

Post The downtown post office is at the corner of Julia and Duval Sts.

Bookstores & Libraries Five Points News Center (☎ 354-4470) has out of town,

---

'Oh, Mom, can't I go to see Dr Jeremiah?'

Feeling ill in Jacksonville can be more fun than in most places. Welcome to Arlington Acute Care Center (☎ 743-2466), 1021 Cesery Blvd just north of the Arlington Expressway, and Lakewood Acute Care Center (☎ 737-8686), 5978 Powers Ave, just west of Philips Hwy. Run by Dr Clifford Jeremiah, both these centers are full medical treatment facilities that also feature museums.

Museums?! Museums. Keeps the kids occupied, keeps the parents happy. At Arlington, there are exhibits of mammal fossils, and an ocean series of sea-displays and shark replicas, while Lakewood offers exhibits on the Cretaceous period: life-size dinosaurs. In the waiting room.

It's a cool idea and staff is very friendly. Arlington's open daily from 8 am to 10 pm, Lakewood's open Monday to Friday from 8 am to 8 pm, Saturday 8 am to 4 pm, closed Sunday.

Other, more conventional, medical facilities in Jacksonville include Saint Vincent's Medical Center (☎ 387-7300), 1800 Barrs St. ■

US, some UK and European newspapers and tons of magazines. It's at 1060 Park St. The main library (☎ 630-2665) downtown is at 122 N Ocean St.

Media The conservative *Florida Times-Union* (abbreviated 'Fla TU' – handy mnemonic device: you can't spell *flatulent* without Fla TU!) is the daily paper of record around here. *Folio Weekly* is an excellent weekly with politics, restaurant reviews and club listings; it's available free throughout the area. NPR is at 89.9 FM, but on the air they refer to themselves as Stereo 90.

Laundry Dunn Coin Laundry (☎ 751-0186) at 1403 Dunn Ave, is open every day from 7 am to 10 pm; other coin laundries in the area include Baymeadows Maytag (☎ 730-3610) at 5111 Baymeadows Rd, and Jean's Coin Laundry (☎ 389-8698) 1842 Blanding Blvd.

Cummer Museum of Art & Gardens

Northeast Florida's best collection of Western art is housed here, in a building that looks more like a bank than a museum. Galleries are named and numbered, and straddle the courtyard. The formal gardens are behind the main building.

From the entrance, the rooms progress in numerical order from 1 to 5 on the left hand side of the courtyard, and from 6 to 12 and the Tudor Room on the right.

Rooms include:

Room 1	Medieval to early Renaissance
Room 2	Renaissance works including Raphael's Colonna Madonna
Room 3	Late Renaissance
Room 4	Baroque – a vaulted gallery, featuring Rubens' The Entombment of Christ and French tapestry
Rooms 5 & 6	traveling exhibitions
Room 7	porcelain
Rooms 8 to 10	19th-century paintings including Thomas Sully's Portrait of a Young Lady, Gainsborough landscapes, Winslow Homer's Waiting for a Bite and Bouguereau's

	splendid Return from the Harvest
Room 11	Modern Impressionist
Concourse Gallery	A hodgepodge of antiquities – don't miss the unbelievably intricate Comic Mosaic Mask.

In the **Formal Gardens**, designed in the early 1900s and built in the 1920s, there's a spectacular live oak tree. The gardens are designed in the style of both English and Italian gardens. With your back to the museum, to the right is the English section, with ivy-covered benches, lovely shrubs and a view out over the St John's River, and, to the left, the Italian section, with Italian fountains, arches and pools.

In the **Art Education Center**, at the end of the Concourse Gallery, there are lots of hands-on art exhibits for kids, and lots of PCs running things like paintshop and less complicated drawing and illustration software.

The museum (☎ 353-1001) is at 829 Riverside Ave, just southwest of downtown, open Tuesday from 10 am to 9.30 pm (free admission from 4 to 9.30 pm), Wednesday to Friday from 10 am to 4 pm, Saturday from noon to 5 pm, Sunday from 2 to 5 pm. Admission is $3 for adults, $1 for children and students, $2 for seniors and military.

Museum of Science & History

We had a blast in this museum. Downstairs are all kinds of balance, weight, sound, flexibility, etc test machines, a good geology exhibit as well as exhibits on manatees and a 'Native Wildlife of St John's County' showcase (note the detail in the background painting, even the power plant is included).

Upstairs are traveling exhibits (changed about every three months). When we visited, we saw 'Criminology & Detectives', where kids could dust a crime scene for prints, examine (we swear) bloody gloves and feel like a real detective hot on the trail.

There are shows in their planetarium (we caught *Where in the Universe is Carmen*

NORTHEAST

NORTHEAST

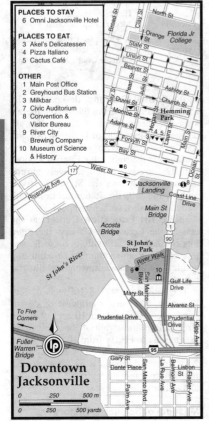

PLACES TO STAY
6 Omni Jacksonville Hotel

PLACES TO EAT
3 Akel's Delicatessen
4 Pizza Italiano
5 Cactus Café

OTHER
1 Main Post Office
2 Greyhound Bus Station
3 Milkbar
7 Civic Auditorium
8 Convention &
   Visitor Bureau
9 River City
   Brewing Company
10 Museum of Science
   & History

Downtown
Jacksonville

0   250   500 m
0   250   500 yards

Sandiego) Monday to Friday at 2 pm, Saturday and Sunday at 1.30 and 3.30 pm. The museum (☎ 396-7062) is at 1025 Museum Circle, across the river from Jacksonville Landing. Admission is $5 for adults, $3 for children, $4 for seniors and military. It's open Monday to Friday from 10 am to 5 pm, Saturday from 10 am to 6 pm, Sunday from 1 to 6 pm. Staff is very friendly.

Jacksonville Zoological Gardens

In the midst of an enormous renovation and expansion, the Jacksonville Zoological Gardens (☎ 757-3937) at 8605 Zoo Rd

(exit 124A from I-95), will be a wonderful place if it ever gets finished.

Northeast Florida's only major zoo, which opened in 1914 with a collection comprised of one deer, has kept several of its excellent exhibitions open during their $17 million expansion. Most famous for its two Florida panthers and three white rhinos, the exhibits open at the time of writing included the **Main Camp Safari Lodge**, a huge thatched-roof area with the nuts and bolts of the park: café, first aid, wheelchair and stroller rental stands, etc; **Okavango Village**, where boardwalks lead from the aviary to exhibits and petting areas including black-cheek love birds, a dwarf zebu, goats and miniature horses; and areas featuring Transvaal lions, naked mole rats, elephants, alligators, jaguars, cape buffalo, giraffes, zebras and leopards.

Shows include Radical Reptiles, daily at 10.30 am; Raptor Rap, Monday to Thursday at noon; Elephant Encounter, Monday to Friday at 11.30 am, Saturday and Sunday at noon and 2.30 pm; and alligator feedings, Saturday at 2 pm.

There's a train ride around the zoo's 73 acres as well. Admission is $6.50 for adults, $4.50 for seniors over 65, $4 for children aged three to 12. The train ride is an additional $3/2/1.50. Admission is free on Monday from 9 to 11 am. The zoo is open daily from 9 am to 5 pm, closed Thanksgiving, Christmas and New Year's Day.

Anheuser Busch Brewery

Very close to the zoo, the Anheuser Busch Brewery (☎ 751-8118) offers free tours and 10-ounce samples of their beers. See the SeaWorld listing in the Central Florida chapter for an idea of what to expect. They're open Monday to Saturday from 9 am to 4 pm; tours depart on the hour. It's at 111 Busch Drive; take I-95 north to the Busch Drive exit and follow the enormous billboards.

Brest Museum

The Alexander Brest Museum and Gallery (☎ 744-3950, ext 3371) in the Philips Fine Arts building on the campus of Jacksonville University has a small and interesting collection of decorative arts including collections of works by Steuben and Tiffany, Asian and European ivory from the 17th to 19th centuries, pre-Columbian artifacts from Mexico and Central America from 3000 BC to 1500 AD and Chinese porcelain and cloisonné from the 18th to 20th centuries. Admission to the museum is free; it's at 2800 University Blvd N, open Monday to Friday from 9 am to 4.30 pm, Saturday from noon to 5 pm. From downtown, take the Mathews Bridge east to Hwy 109 north, which becomes University Blvd.

Fort Caroline National Memorial

Part of the Timucuan Ecological & Historic Preserve, a federally run reserve of land making up most of the northeast section of Jacksonville up to and including the Kingsley Plantation (see Around Amelia Island, below), the Fort Caroline National Memorial (☎ 641-7155) is an approximately two-thirds scale model of the original fort founded here by French Huguenots in 1562. (See the St Augustine section to find out what happened to them.) Today the re-creation, made from earth and wood, is on the site where it is believed that the original fort stood. Admission is free.

The park also features several-hundred acres of pristine wilderness along the St John's River, and wildlife you'll likely run into include painted buntings (songbirds), woodstorks, red fox, raccoons, osprey, alligators, wading birds, and occasionally river otters, bald eagles and bobcats.

To get to the main visitor center from downtown, take the Mathews Bridge to the Atlantic Blvd Expressway (Hwy 10 east) and then turn left onto Monument Rd; follow that to Fort Caroline Rd and turn right. The entrance is about a half-mile ahead. From the north, take I-95 to Hwy 9A (essentially the eastern extension of I-295) and follow that to Merrill Rd (there are big signs all the way). Turn left on Merrill, which becomes Fort Caroline Rd. About a half-mile east of the main visitors center is a monument, on the bluff 75 feet

above the St John's River, that reproduces the original column left here by Jean Ribault, who first landed at the inlet.

Ranger-led programs have been drastically reduced thanks to Newt and his cronies in Congress, but the ones that are left are on Saturday: at 1 pm there's a half-hour guided walk to the fort, and at 2.30 pm a 1½-hour guided walk through the Preserve's Roosevelt area, a 550-acre section of nature walks and interpretive information on the area's shell mounds. The shell mounds themselves have created an alkaline condition that has produced some very interesting flora; ask the rangers how best to see it.

In the visitors center, 10- to 12-minute videos on the Fort Caroline story and the preserve run continually throughout the day.

The fort is at 12713 Fort Caroline Rd, open daily from 9 am to 5 pm. From downtown, take the Atlantic Blvd Expressway (Hwy 10 east) over the Mathews Bridge; turn left on Monument Rd, follow that to Fort Caroline Rd and turn right.

Museum of Contemporary Art

The Jacksonville Museum of Contemporary Art (☎ 398-8336) has contemporary arts and a smaller pre-Columbian exhibition from 600 AD on. There are constant rotating exhibitions, and the permanent collection features works from Joan Miró, Alexander Calder (the inventor of the mobile), Enzo Torcoletti, Tommy Mew and many more. The museum is at the rear of the Koger Business Center at 4160 Blvd Center Drive. From downtown take the Main St Bridge and follow signs to '90 – Beaches', take that to Beach Blvd, which becomes, in a mile, Blvd Center Drive, and the entrance to the Koger Business Center is on the left. Admission is $3 for adults, $2 for students and seniors. It's open Tuesday, Wednesday and Friday from 10 am to 4 pm, Thursday from 10 am to 10 pm, and Saturday and Sunday from 1 to 5 pm, closed Monday.

Jacksonville Landing

This is a shopping mall (☎ 353-1188) in the heart of downtown with a bunch of shops, a

NORTHEAST

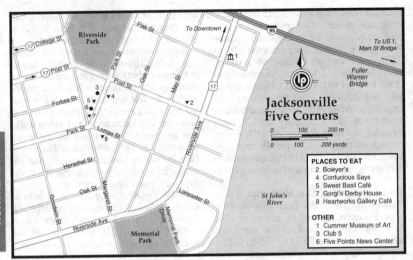

PLACES TO EAT
2 Bowyer's
4 Confucious Says
5 Sweet Basil Café
7 Gorgi's Derby House
8 Heartworks Gallery Café

OTHER
1 Cummer Museum of Art
3 Club 5
6 Five Points News Center

food court, restaurants and coffee bars, and live entertainment; call to see what's on during your visit. On weekends it becomes a yuppie watering hole. It's on the north side of the St John's River, at the northwestern foot of the Main St Bridge.

Riverwalk

This 1.2-mile boardwalk on the south side of the St John's River opposite downtown and Jacksonville Landing is a somewhat pleasant city park, and there's a water taxi (see Getting Around, below) between here and the landing.

Beaches

The beaches, about 15 miles west of downtown (but 40 minutes' drive due to Jacksonville's snarled traffic), are about 25 miles of white sand from Ponte Vedra at the south to Atlantic Beach at the north. There's not a whole lot to do out on the beaches except broil yourself, and prices at the beach resorts here are higher than you'd expect.

Organized Tours

Sideline Tours (☎ 278-9409) does personalized tours around the entire area; you can

get one for as low as $20 if you're with a group, or personal orientation tours for an afternoon for about $80.

You can take 15- to 20-mile chugs up the St John's aboard the *First Lady of Jacksonville* (☎ 398-0797) through Riverwalk Cruise Lines at 917 Dante Place, which runs lunch ($21.30) and dinner ($25.56) buffet cruises; children aged three to 11 are half price. The buffet includes roasted chicken, baked ham, two vegetables, salad, peach cobbler, rolls, tea and coffee. At lunch there is a saxophone player tooting in the background, at dinner a DJ.

Places to Stay

There are no hostels or camping in the immediate area; see the St Augustine and Around Amelia Island sections for information on nearby options for hostels, camping and more hotels. The KOA just *north* of the Georgia border, that calls itself the *Jacksonville North/Kingsland KOA* (☎ 729-3232, 800-562-5220), is just misleading: if Georgia is 'Jacksonville North' so is Raleigh, North Carolina.

Hotels & Motels Jacksonville's accommodation scene is pretty institutional: except for a couple of B&Bs it's all chains and all average in everything. Check along I-95 and I-10, where chains congregate. The chains include *Super 8 Motel* (☎ 751-3888, 800-800-8000) at 10901 Harts Rd; *Best Western* (☎ 751-5600, 800-528-1234) at 10888 Harts Rd; *Holiday Inn* (☎ 737-1700) at 9150 Baymeadows Rd; *Travelodge* (☎ 731-7317) at 8765 Baymeadows Rd; and *Quality Inn* (☎ 281-0900, 800-842-1348) at 4660 Salisbury Rd. Baymeadows Rd (Hwy 152) is about 30 miles south of downtown off I-95; Harts Rd is north, off Hwy 104 on the opposite side of I-95 from the Anheuser Busch Brewery.

Downtown One of the largest hotels downtown is the 320-room *Marina Hotel & Conference Center* (☎ 396-5100, 800-342-4605) at 1515 Prudential Drive. Rooms run from $59 to 109 and suites $149 to 199. The city's other biggie is the sparkling, 350-room *Omni Jacksonville Hotel* (☎ 355-6664) at 245 Water St, with rooms from $99 to 149.

Jacksonville Beach Out on Jacksonville Beach, staff at the *Hillsmoore Oceanfront Motel* (☎ 246-2837) are very helpful and friendly: that and their prices take the sting of not having a pool out of it (they do have a Jacuzzi): efficiencies, which sleep up to four, run from $25 to 79. They have a restaurant, gift shop, bar, etc so 'you don't have to leave' the place, at 982 1st St.

The *Surf Side Motel* (☎ 246-1583) has surly staff, but rooms, which are OK, are $39.99 to 49.99 during the week, $69.99 on weekends and $79.99 on holidays. It's at 1236 1st St and has a pool.

The *Atlantis Motel* (☎ 249-5006) has rooms for $53 to 68 for singles and $58 to 70 for doubles, depending on the season. It's at 731 1st St.

Comfort Inn Oceanfront (☎ 241-2311) has nice and large rooms from $69 to 109, pool view rooms from $79 to 119 and oceanfront rooms from $89 to 129. They have a huge pool with waterfalls, a tiki bar that's packed with partiers and the price

includes breakfast of cereal and muffins on Styrofoam plates. It's at 1515 N 1st St.

The *Seabreeze Motel* (☎ 249-9981) looks cool, it's in a '50s-style house next to the Beach Bakery.

B&Bs There are two B&Bs in the Riverside section of town; the *House on Cherry Street* (☎ 384-1999), 1844 Cherry St, is a B&B with rates from $75 to 85, including a full hot breakfast and wine in the evenings. Take Riverside Ave past St Vincent's Hospital, two streets beyond King St and make left on Cherry; it's the last house on the right.

Another B&B is the 1914 prairie-style *Cleary-Dickert House* (☎ 387-4762) with singles/doubles at $75/85, and their honeymoon suite for $95; all prices are year round. Free wine and snacks in the afternoon and a full hot breakfast in the morning are included. The owners are very friendly and Betty bakes all the bread and biscuits herself (she loves to cook). It's at 1804 Copeland St, just off the river. From downtown, take Riverside Ave past St Vincent's Hospital and turn left on Copeland; it's at the corner of St John's.

Places to Eat

Downtown *Akel's Delicatessen* (☎ 356-5628), 130 N Hogan St, is a very popular downtown lunch spot with very big sandwiches for $2.95, decent pasta salad, but repugnant knishes. Service is very friendly and we walked out with lunch and soft drinks for two for $5.30. They're open from 7 am to 4 pm, breakfast runs from $1 to 3.

Pizza Italiano (☎ 355-8181), 122 W Adams St, does small pizzas for $2.95 to 4.95, lunch specials are $4.95 and pasta $5 to 6. It's only open for lunch. *Cactus Café* (☎ 350-9070) is a great deal with a two-pound burrito for $4.95, a 'regular' one-pound burrito for $3.95, and other specials from $4.25 to 4.95. It's open Monday to Friday from 11 am to 2.30 pm at 126 W Adams St.

At Jacksonville Landing (☎ 353-1188) there are several choices, and most people in downtown Jacksonville end up heading here for lunch and dinner. Fast-food places include an *Arthur Treacher's Fish & Chips*, *Bains Deli*, *Boardwalk Fries*, a sort of chi-chi fry place, *Chinese Combo King* (guess), *Johnny Rockets*, a '50s hamburger stand, and a *Sbarro* overpriced pizza joint. There are several restaurants here as well, none notably noteworthy, including a *Fat Tuesday*, *L&N Seafood* and *Silver Spoon*.

On the south side of the St John's, *River City Brewing Company* (☎ 858-6700), at 837 Museum Circle, is a chic microbrewery that makes several kinds of beer – four are usually on hand at any time, with a fifth seasonal offering on tap as well. The restaurant certainly smells good enough: try their sausage sampler (beer, duck and Chinese smoked sausage) for $6.95; lunch dishes include sandwiches from $4.95 to 7.95, pasta from $6.25 to 6.95 and main courses like skewered grilled shrimp for $7.25. At dinner the pastas head north from $11.95 to 15.95 and more creative main courses, like nut crusted pork tenderloin, average $14.95. They have another location at 9810-3 Baymeadows Rd (☎ 642-6310).

Five Corners The best area we found for food was out of downtown in the Five Corners area: *Heartworks Gallery Café* (☎ 355-6210) is a very cool gallery/café with exhibits of works by local artists that change about every six weeks. Oh yeah, food: four cheese black bean burrito and rice is $1.50, black bean chili and chips is $3 and their pasta of the day is $5.50. It's at 820 Lomax St (at Five Corners).

Gorgi's Derby House (☎ 356-0227) has good breakfast specials for $1.99, sandwiches for $3 to 4 and burgers for $2 to 4. Dinner specials, which come with two sides and bread, are $4 to 5 and include baked chicken, meat loaf and Polish sausage. It's at 1068 Park St.

Confucius Says Chinese Restaurant & Mongolian BBQ (☎ 355-9333) at 1023 Park St, does an all-you-can-eat lunch buffet Monday to Friday from 11.30 am to 2.30 pm; it's $4.75 for adults and $2.40

for children. Regular dinners run from $4.25 to 9.50.

Sweet Basil Café (☎ 633-9001) looks like a Little Italy joint and is said to be very good. At lunch, pizza is $3.95 to 4.95, pasta $4.75 to 6.50; at dinner pastas run from $6.50 to 8.50 and more substantial dishes from $8.95 to 10.95. It's located at 1038 Park St.

Bowyer's (☎ 358-1813), only open at lunch (from 11 am to 2 pm), serve up great Creole and Cajun food. Cajun boudin (spicy sausage filled with rice, pork and Cajun spices) goes for $5.95, grilled chicken for $5.60 and a seafood combo for $6.95. The atmosphere is really friendly, and it's at 717 Post St.

Jacksonville Beach Out on Jacksonville Beach, the *Bread & Pasta Shop* (☎ 246-1905) was a lifesaver for their fresh and healthy offerings, like prepared prepackaged pastas and excellent sandwiches. It's at 1128 N 3rd St.

Entertainment

Performing Arts The Jacksonville Symphony Orchestra (☎ 354-5547), having played at a wide range of halls over the years, is looking forward to settling down into its new home at the Robert E Jacoby Symphony Hall in 1997. Currently they play at the Civic Auditorium, the Florida Theatre (see below), the Landing, and at other venues around the area and the region.

The Florida Theater (☎ 355-2787) (say thee-yator) is home to an eclectic mix of plays (from *Jesus Christ Superstar* to *Will Rogers' Follies*), music (from Seven Mary Three to the Jacksonville Symphony Orchestra to the WJCT Jacksonville Jazz Festival) and special events like the Budweiser Comedy Fest. It's at 1128 E Forsyth St.

The *Alhambra Dinner Theater* (☎ 641-1212, 800-688-7469) is something of a JAX institution: a buffet dinner and show. It's at 12000 Beach Blvd, about halfway between downtown and the beach. The cost for performances is $31.42 for Sunday to

Thursday shows, $33.55 on Friday and Saturday evenings, and $28.22 for on Saturday and Sunday matinees.

Bars & Clubs *Milkbar* (☎ 356-6455) at 128 W Adams St, has cheap drinks and lots of local and national bands throughout the week – it's a very popular place, if only for the music (there are DJs on nights when there are no concerts) and specials: every Monday is old wave night, with $1 beers, and Wednesday is ladies night, women get in and drink free.

Club Five (☎ 356-5555), in a former theater at 1028 Park St at Five Corners, does house, top 40 and hip-hop dance music; Thursday to Saturday there's a $5 cover. Thursday is ladies night, with free admission and drinks for women.

Einstein a Go Go (☎ 246 4073) has been out on Jacksonville Beach for a long time – over 10 years – surprising when you consider that it's an all-ages-welcome place. They play alternative and indi college rock and dance music; it's at 327 N 1st St.

The *Comedy Zone* (☎ 292-4242) at the Ramada Inn Mandarin, I-295 at San Jose Blvd (Hwy 13) south of the city, does shows on Tuesday to Thursday at 8.30 pm, Friday at 9 pm and Saturday at 8 and 10 pm. There's more weekend comedy at *Def Comedy Jam* at Club Carousel (☎ 725-2582) at 8550 Arlington Expressway.

Gay *Bo's Coral Reef* (☎ 246-9874) has been around for something like 30 years at 201 5th Ave at 2nd St. Thursday is amateur night – anything goes, no cover, and Saturday there are cabaret and drag shows.

Metro (☎ 388-8719, 800-380-8719), with four enormous bars, calls itself a gay entertainment complex, complete with disco, cruise bar, piano bar and leathery boiler room. For special events there are drag shows and cabaret. It's at 2929 Plum St.

Spectator Sports
The Jacksonville Jaguars (☎ 633-2000), a new NFL team that locals are positively deranged about backing, play at 73,000-seat Jacksonville Memorial Stadium during the pro football season from September to December – but get this: all season tickets are sold out and many individual tickets sell out as well, so plan ahead. The Jaguars are the area's only professional team, but the Jacksonville Lizard Kings (☎ 448-8800) are an East Coast Hockey League team and hope to be NHL soon; they play at the Reptilian Pavilion, formerly the Veterans Memorial Coliseum.

The Toyota Gator Bowl (☎ 396-1800) is a 50+year-old college football match with top-ranked teams from the Atlantic Coast Conference and Big East on New Year's Day in Jacksonville Memorial Stadium. Buy tickets well in advance; it's at the Gator Bowl, at the eastern end of Adams St.

Getting There & Away
Air Jacksonville International Airport (☎ 741-4902) is one of the city's best offerings: a sparkling new terminal that's sensibly laid out and served by several major and some regional airlines. Too bad there's no public transportation to the city! But all major rental car companies have offices here.

A one-way flight to/from Miami ranges from $40 to 80 depending on airline (American is the more expensive), to/from Orlando $80, to/from Pensacola $150 to 175 and to/from Tampa $60 to 70.

Bus The Greyhound station (☎ 356-5521) is at 10 Pearl St at the western end of downtown. Jacksonville is a major Greyhound hub, with service heading south down I-95 up to 10 times a day (see the Getting Around Chapter) and west out I-10 to Pensacola there are five buses a day, which take from 8¼ to 9½ hours and cost $49 one way, 98 roundtrip.

Train The Amtrak station (☎ 766-5110) is in the middle of nowhere, about five miles northwest of downtown at 3570 Clifford Lane. JTA bus No NS4 runs between here and downtown, or you can do a $10 taxi in a quarter of the time.

Car Jacksonville is about 36 miles south of the Georgia border, about 39 miles north of St Augustine and about 340 miles north of Miami, all right along I-95. Take I-10 east from anywhere in the Panhandle.

Getting Around

To/From the Airport There's no public transport to or from the airport. There are flat taxi fees to most destinations in town; the average fare is between $20 and 25, $30 to the beaches and $55 to St Augustine. The taxi stand is in the center island outside the main airport exit. Taxis at the airport are usually very clean and drivers know the area well.

Bus Jacksonville Transportation Authority (JTA; ☎ 630-3100) runs horribly inconvenient local bus service in town (bus fare is a base of 60¢) and to the beaches ($1.25). The main downtown transfer center is at 201 State St opposite the FCCJ main building. From the downtown transfer center take Northside bus No 10 – Panama to the Anheuser Busch Brewery and the Jacksonville Zoological Gardens, weekends only to both; Westside bus No 4 or 2 to the Cummer Museum of Art; and Beaches bus 1, 2 or 3 to the beach.

Monorail There is a monorail throughout downtown, the Automated Skyway Express. It makes a simple loop over downtown for 25¢. Whee. Pick it up at the main station at Myrtle Ave at Jefferson.

Car Face it: you're going to get lost at least once, probably trying to find Riverwalk. Traffic is frightful, drivers reptilian, especially during rush hours, which are always. Tune to NPR for rush hour traffic information during All Things Considered in the afternoon which usually features the sentence, 'We have a multi-car accident on the Mathews Bridge . . . ' Mathews Bridge, along with the Hart and Warren Bridges, are the main east-west connectors between downtown and the beach. The Hart Bridge leads, confusingly, to Beach Blvd (US Hwy 90), out to the

beach; the Warren Bridge, which is I-95, has an exit on J Turner Butler Blvd, also a hateful beach connector.

Parking is generally less of a problem than navigating.

Taxi Metered taxi rates in Jacksonville are $1.25 flagfall, $1.25 a mile. The biggest company is Yellow Cab (☎ 260-1111).

Water Taxi The water taxi runs between the Riverwalk and the Jacksonville Landing, fares are $2 one way and $3 roundtrip for adults, children and seniors pay $1/2.

OLUSTEE BATTLEFIELD

About half an hour's drive west of Jacksonville on I-10, the Olustee Battlefield Historic Site (☎ 904-758-0400) is a small interpretive center on the site of the Battle of Olustee, the largest Civil War battle to take place in Florida, on February 20, 1864. The battle, which involved about 10,000 troops, was significant as it denied Union troops the opportunity to cut off Confederate supply lines of food coming from Florida. But was very short – it lasted an afternoon, after which the Union troops retreated to Jacksonville.

Though it is very pleasant and the visitors center museum has some interesting exhibits on uniforms, money and the like, unless you're here during the annual February 20 re-enactment (when thousands of Civil War nuts gather in full battle gear to recreate the battle), the most interesting attractions in the area are the two enormous nearby correctional facilities (that's 'jail' to you): the shiny Baker Correctional Institution (☎ 752-9244) is a nice place to start, right across the street. You can arrange a tour of the facility if you're very persuasive, by contacting the secretary to the superintendent at extension 213. Also nearby is the Columbia Correctional Institution (☎ 758-8090) a bit farther away on US Hwy 90 East in Lake City.

The interpretive center at the battlefield is open Thursday to Monday from 8 am to 5 pm, the museum is open Thursday to Monday from 9 am to 5 pm, everything is closed on holidays from November to April. The site is off US Hwy 90 about five miles south of I-10's exit 45. Note that if you're coming from the east, there's an exit, but no entrance, to I-10 at exit 45, so you'll have to loop back east and then turn around if you want to continue heading west.

AMELIA ISLAND
• *pop 14,835* ☎ *904*

While Amelia Island doesn't exactly leap to the tongue of many travelers, this richly historic area is one of northern Florida's greatest destinations. Home to Fernandina Beach, a small city with a hugely intricate history, and American Beach, the first resort for blacks in Florida (a must-see on the Black Heritage Trail), two resorts and miles of shark-tooth filled coastline, we highly recommend a stop here, even if it's just for the day. Just to the south, on Little Talbot Island and Fort George Island, are two excellent state parks, and beyond those, the ferry to Mayport and Jacksonville.

History
The French first landed on an island off the coast of present-day South Carolina in 1562. Two years later, they moved south and established a settlement in the St John's River delta and began building Fort Caroline in Spanish-claimed territory. Upon arriving in St Augustine to defend the Spanish claim, Don Pedro Menéndez de Avilés launched two attacks against the French, and the second one led to the slaughter of 600 French settlers (see the St Augustine History section).

During the early years of the second Spanish period, Amelia Island's strategic location became key. In 1807, President Jefferson established his Embargo Act and, in 1808, a prohibition on slavery importation, and (to the delight of the chamber of commerce, which is thrilled to have something so scandalous in the area's past) Amelia Island became black market central: pirates, cut-throats and smugglers traded slaves and rum, and prostitutes roamed freely.

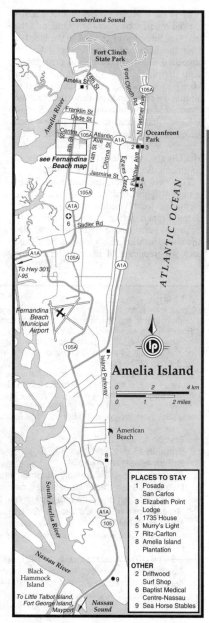

Amelia Island

PLACES TO STAY
1 Posada
  San Carlos
3 Elizabeth Point
  Lodge
4 1735 House
5 Murry's Light
7 Ritz-Carlton
8 Amelia Island
  Plantation

OTHER
2 Driftwood
  Surf Shop
6 Baptist Medical
  Centre-Nassau
9 Sea Horse Stables

In 1812, a group of US-financed and -backed rebels took over the island, and the next day turned over control to the US, but after the Spaniards hit the roof, the US conceded that they really had no right to keep the place. Then in 1817, Sir Gregor MacGregor, a Scottish mercenary with revolutionary experience in Venezuela and the financial support of businessmen in Savannah and Charleston, hired on a force which took over the island from the Spanish on June 29. When the money ran out, so did MacGregor, who left two lieutenants in command. But wait . . . there's more!

The two left holding the bag, Lieutenants Ruggles Hubbard and Jared Irwin, formed a joint venture with a Mexico-based French pirate named Louis Aury (who was permitted to fly the Mexican flag anywhere he wanted, so long as he kicked back a percentage of his plunders to the Mexican government), and these three managed to turn the place into an even *more* scandalous town – it's said that there were more bars than street corners, and even more brothels.

Perhaps using moral outrage as an excuse to nab some nifty real estate, US troops moved in and took over in December 1819. In a face-saving compromise, Spain officially turned Florida over to the US in 1821 in exchange for US promises to pay claims of Spanish subjects (none of which, by the way, were ever paid).

Confederates took over the town for one year during the Civil War, after which the US regained control.

In the mid-1850s, a keen US Senator David Yulee (the first Jewish member of the US Senate) began work on his Ralph Kramden-esque dream of a trans-Florida railroad, which he completed in March

---

10 Flags

Local lore holds that since the Europeans showed up Amelia Island has been ruled under eight flags. There are several problems with that, though, because of interrupted Spanish rule and the US Civil War. If you're going to count Spain twice in the beginning, as several tourist pamphlets do, then we say you should count the US twice in the end, as the US rule was indeed interrupted for a full year by the Confederates, who decidedly had a flag of their own.

And then there's argument about flags themselves – 'There's no documentation,' says James Perry, curator of the Amelia Island Museum of History, 'that the French ever even flew a flag.' And what is a flag, anyway – the Patriots flew one, while representing not a sovereign nation but a group of mercenaries and hot heads. To settle the argument, we say that there were eight different flags flown at 10 different times, and they are:

French 1562-1565
Spanish 1565-1763
British 1763-1783
Spanish 1783-1821, though with three interruptions:
Patriots US spy-backed rebels, who captured the island on March 17, 1812, gave it to the US the next day, who promptly gave it back to Spain.
Green Cross of Florida Gregor MacGregor's gang, 1817
Mexican Rebel Flag Also in 1817, Louis Aury and the boys. The US moved in and took over the island, holding it in trust for Spain, which finally ceded Florida to the US in 1821.
US The US took over officially in 1821, and happily ran things until the Civil War
Confederate The secessionist Confederate army took over in 1861. They managed to hold the island for a year, but on March 3, 1862, the US took over once again.
US The island has been under continuous US rule since 1862. ∎

1861. In the one month during which it operated, the railroad ran freight between the island and Cedar Key on the Gulf coast, with stops at Baldwin, Gainesville and Bronson. Confiscated at the beginning of the war, the railroad was dismantled and the rails were diverted by the Confederate government to run north into Georgia. After the war, the railroad was rebuilt, but Yulee was by that time in prison in the north for treason.

During the boom years after the Civil War, hotels popped up like mad, and resorts (separate ones for white and blacks) rose on the beach. In 1897, the island became a major staging area for the US forces in Cuba. But the boom was killed when Flagler's railroad started sucking more and more northern tourists directly to the resorts at St Augustine, Palm Beach and Miami – and it all happened so fast. In a Pompeii-like flash, the boom town was frozen in time, and much of what you'll see here today remains practically unchanged.

Orientation

Amelia Island is Florida's northernmost barrier island, located just south of the Georgia coast and 30 miles northeast of Jacksonville. It's about 13½ miles long. The main activity is centered around the Downtown Historic District, at the northern end of the island in the tiny city of Fernandina Beach. The historic district is laid out in a grid, with east-west streets given names and north-south street numbers. Centre St is the main street in this area, and is the north-south divider; it becomes Atlantic Ave east of 8th St.

The Ritz-Carlton Resort is just about in the center, and, farther south, Amelia Island Plantation. Nestled quite valuably between these opulent resorts is American Beach (population: about 30 families), featured on the African American Heritage Trail as the first (and only) African American beach community in Florida.

Maps Good free maps are hard to find; the best free map for downtown is actually part of the rate sheet for the Florida House Inn

(see below, Places to Stay), which shows the downtown historic district in good detail but no matter what they say, key No 9 was in the wrong place when we visited (we argued about it). The best map will cost you, and it's hard to find; it's a blue and white copy of *Nassau County* by Merchant Maps, showing excellent detail on the entire island. *Amelia Now* is a privately published, advertiser-driven free guide to the city that contains a somewhat helpful map (it's very broad and only main streets are shown), and a hodgepodge of features, ads, coupons, etc. It's available everywhere.

Information

Tourist Offices The surprisingly excellent Amelia Island/Fernandina Beach/Yulee Chamber of Commerce (☎ 261-3248, 800-226-3542), in the old Railroad Depot at the west end of Centre St in Fernandina Beach, hands out tons of documentation and the staff is helpful but, staggeringly, the place is closed on weekends. See the Online Services appendix for Amelia Island's website, packed with practical information, telephone numbers, photos and un-pushy propaganda. Each of the bejillion B&Bs in town offer local information and restaurant recommendations.

Money Barnett Bank has a branch at the corner of 5th and Centre Sts.

Post The main post office (☎ 261-4848) is at the corner of 4th and Centre Sts.

Bookstores & Libraries Our favorite bookshop, for both conversation and selection (though they could keep more Lonely Planet books on hand), was the Book Loft (☎ 261-8991) at 214 Centre St. The main library is at 25 N 4th St (☎ 277-7365).

Media The *Florida Times-Union* is the daily of note, though some shops do sell *The New York Times* and the *Miami Herald*. NPR is at 89.9 FM from Jacksonville.

Laundry We used the *Maytag Laundry* (☎ 277-3730) at 913 S 14th St on Hwy A1A.

Toilets Look for the spotless 'comfort stations' just behind the tourist information center in downtown Fernandina Beach, open daily from 9 am to 9 pm in summer, 9 am to 6 pm in winter.

Medical Services The island's hospital is the Baptist Medical Center – Nassau (☎ 261-3627) at 1250 S 18th St at Lime St. There's a medical clinic in the Wal Mart plaza at the corner of US Hwy A1A and Sadler as well.

Fort Clinch State Park
The US Government began construction of Fort Clinch in 1847. It has never been completed, and rangers can point out where different construction phases are visible in the masonry. It was occupied by both sides during the Civil War, but never saw any real fighting. Today the fort is open as a state park (☎ 277-7274), and re-enactors (whom most call authentic and others call nuts) hold open-house garrison weekends, candlelight viewings and candlelight tours at least once and often more times a month, featuring demonstrations of the weaponry (the cannons are loud!), fireplace cooking, the fully equipped Civil War infirmary (Why, we asked, is it up a flight of stairs? No one knew.) and jail. The fort by candlelight is beautiful, and the re-enactors – who sleep in the fort during the garrison weekends to help stay in character – are a treat, whether they're playing Union or Confederate troops (they do both).

Fort Clinch Rd is just west of the beach off Atlantic Ave, but if you're bicycling or walking to the fort from downtown, there's a quicker way: take Centre St to 14th St, go left to the end of the road and over the bridge; there you'll see a fence; you can slip your bike through and hop over. This is a time-saver only: slipping through the fence is not exactly a kosher move, and you still must pay the $1 admission fee for pedestrians and bicyclists at the Ranger's office. Admission for cars is $3.25.

Fernandina Beach
Most of the action on the island takes place in this small city that's just crawling with characters – stop by the Ship's Lantern and say hello to Bob Lannon, self-proclaimed Town Genius, who laments in a long, south Georgian drawl to Northerners who stop in about the mosquitoes that 'wuhnt heah buhfaw you Yankees came down.' (Mr Lannon, it is believed, is from New Jersey.)

Fernandina Beach residents, who refer to the rest of the world as being 'off-island,' eat well in several very good restaurants (the Florida House Inn's restaurant is one of the best deals in the entire state), live well in lovely Victorian houses, and guests stay well in one of many spectacular B&Bs (don't panic – there's camping and a couple of motels as well). The only drawbacks are the paper mills just upwind of the city, which occasionally send whiffs of production aroma townward. This is offset, we guess, by the smell of the fresh timber when it's railed in on boxcars right through the center of the city.

Walking Tours The Amelia Island Museum of History (see below) conducts two-hour walking tours of the Downtown Historic District by appointment for $10 for adults, $5 for students. On Thursday and Friday at 3 pm, they also hold a Centre St Stroll for $5 for adults, $2.50 for students. Call ☎ 261-8883.

Amelia Island Museum of History Florida's only oral history museum (☎ 261-8883), this very well thought out and maintained collection, located in the former city jail (1879-1975), is open for docent-led tours Monday to Saturday at 11 am and 2 pm. The 2nd-floor research library is open Monday to Friday from 10 am to 5 pm. The exhibits in this museum, while fascinating in and of themselves, are secondary to the oral history from the volunteers. Don't miss the Galleon Room, dedicated to Spanish explorers and gold ships, with not much treasure but heaps of artifacts. Upstairs, wander freely and look at the old drugstore soda fountain. The museum is at 233 S 3rd St. Admission is $2.50 for adults, $1 for students.

PLACES TO STAY
12 Florida House Inn
17 Hoyt House

PLACES TO EAT
1 Eight Flags Antique
   Warehouse & Cafe
2 Maggie's Diner
3 Marina Restaurant
11 Shakespeare's Kitchen,
   As You Like It
13 O'Kane's Irish
   Pub & Eatery
20 Beech St Grill

OTHER
4 Main Library
5 Main Post Office
6 St Peter's Parish
7 Chamber of Commerce
8 Public Toilets
9 Ship's Lantern
10 Book Loft
14 Nassau City Health Center
15 Barnett Bank
16 Fernandina Beach Bike
   & Fitness
18 Tennis Courts
19 Police
21 Amelia Island Museum
   of History

St Peter's Parish This beautiful neo-Gothic Episcopal church (☎ 261-4293), built between 1881 and '84, features impressive stained-glass windows and a magnificent Harrison organ. Services are held Sunday at 7.30, 9 and 11 am and Tuesday at 7 pm. It's at the corner of 8th St and Atlantic Ave. Great sign outside in no parking zone: Thou Shalt Not Park.

Beaches The main beaches are accessible by heading straight east on Atlantic Ave to the ocean. There are some limited fast food options available, as well as some accommodation options (see Places to Stay). Two

hours before and after a tide, run to the shore and look for the shark's teeth and fossils that are washed in.

Tennis There are free (unlit) municipal tennis courts at the corner of Centre and 13th Sts. In the unlikely event that it's locked, get the key ($5 deposit) at the Atlantic Ave Recreation Center, 2500 Atlantic Ave, open Monday to Friday from 8 am to 8 pm, Saturday from noon to 8 pm, and Sunday from 2 to 4.30 pm.

Horseback Riding Sea Horse Stables (☎ 261-4878), down the earth path that's the last left turn at the southern tip of the island before you reach the bridge over Nassau Sound, runs five-mile, 1¼-hour horseback tours along the beach – at a walk only – every day. In summer, rides leave at 10 am and 2 and 4 pm, in winter they leave at 11 am and 3 pm. There's a 200-pound weight limit and you must be at least 4 feet 10 inches tall. The cost is $35 per person including tax. Reservations are recommended on weekends and holidays.

Surfing It's not, like, tubular, but it's surfable – in fact, they held the first annual Surf Dog Championships in 1995, and it may become an annual event. No surf rentals are available because of liability, but you can buy a board and then sell it back later (for about $10 to 15 less than you bought it for, get it?) from Driftwood Surf Shop (☎ 321-2188), 31 S Fletcher Ave.

American Beach
In 1901, A L Lewis (1865-1947) opened Florida's first insurance company, and it catered to black people. The Jacksonville company became very successful, and in 1935 Lewis, who was black, bought up land on Amelia Island and founded American Beach: the first black beach along Florida's segregated shores.

At its heyday, American Beach catered to throngs of Northern blacks, who boarded buses that would arrive 40 and 50 at a time, disgorging the masses into a resort owned and operated by black businesspeople. Blacks owned the motel, the restaurants, the nightclubs. Black entertainers who performed at clubs in Jacksonville like the Two Spot would head up to American Beach after their sets and play the rest of the night at the Ocean Rendezvous, then the resort's largest nightclub. That club also saw concerts by Ray Charles, Count Basie, Duke Ellington and a host of stars of the day.

After desegregation the beach became less attractive than beaches closer to home, and the business dried out. Today, while the resort is still open, it is a ghost of its former glory. And surrounded by big business in the form of the Amelia Island Plantation, a multi-million dollar resort complex, local residents worry that some of the 35 families that call American Beach home will sell out to golf course developers, who plan to build a five-hole, 36-acre course and between 50 to 60 single family houses on the area between Ocean St and Hwy A1A, from Burney Blvd to south of Lewis St.

Local resident, great-granddaughter of Lewis and 'unofficial mayor' MaVynee Betsch (pronounced may-VEEN BECH) has been leading the fight to get the beach listed on the National Register of Historic Places to protect it from further development, and despite increasing media attention, at the time of writing things were looking bleak – there's a plot of about 40 acres just to the south, slotted for a golf course and some luxury housing.

Today American Beach still operates as a summer resort, primarily for blacks but people of all races are welcome, and you can visit for a tour anytime. Ms Betsch is always happy to guide tours personally, and she operates the **American Beach Museum** out of a small mobile home parked at the corner of Gregg and Lewis Sts.

On your own, the main sight other than the beach itself, with its long boardwalk, is **Nana**, a 55-foot sand dune – the tallest on the island, just south of the corner of Lewis and Ocean Sts. A tour is a far better idea, because it will cover aspects of the city and the resort that you'd never find out on your own. For tour or any other information, contact MaVynee (☎ 277-2404) or write her at 5466 Gregg St, American Beach, FL 32034.

Places to Stay
Most places to stay are in Fernandina Beach. If you want to stay in American Beach, the oldest black-owned oceanfront motel in America is *American Beach Villas* (☎ 261-0840), open only from Easter to Labor Day. Also, several homes can be rented out by the day, week or month. For information on rentals, contact MaVynee Betsch (☎ 277-2404).

Camping Tent camping is free on American Beach, but you're only allowed to do it on weekends. Primitive and improved (but not full-hookup) campsites are available at *Fort Clinch State Park* (☎ 277-7274). The primitive sites (no water or nothin') are $3 per adult, $2 per child, per night year round. Improved sites (with water, optional electricity and a grill and table) are $12 from October 1 to February 28, and $17 from March 1 and September 30. There are sites along the river or at the beach behind the dune system; fires are in grills only, and you'll need to bring your own firewood as gathering it in the park is *verboten*; many Publix and Winn-Dixie supermarkets sell bundles at outrageous prices. No pets allowed. There's a dump station and a bath house.

There's other camping nearby, at Little Talbot Island State Park – see Around Amelia Island, below.

Motels Most of the motels are on the beach side of town. The calm and friendly staff at the *Golden Isle Motel* (☎ 261-6795), 2811 Atlantic Ave, has clean-looking singles and doubles with kitchen for $30, or $100 during special events.

The *Ocean View Inn* (☎ 261-0193) at 2801 Atlantic Ave, makes life difficult with their complex pricing system of $40 for a room with a queen-size bed, $45 for two doubles, rising to $50/60 between March 15 and September 3; you can upgrade to a room with a small living room area for $5 extra, weekly rates begin at $210. Coffee and juice are available.

The friendly and polite people at the *Beachside Motel Inn* (☎ 261-4236) at 3172 S Fletcher Ave, have similarly convoluted rates which take up an entire page of our notes – suffice it to say that double rooms range from $64 to 84 in low season, $86 to 123 in high season and that there are five (count 'em) seasons. No pets. For that, we'd take a B&B.

Hotels & Inns *1735 House* (☎ 261-5878, 800-872-8531) is a very cozy suite-only hotel on the ocean that looks as if it belongs

in Cape Cod. All the very homey, nautically decorated suites have a fridge and microwave, but no telephone, and the price of $100/120 in winter, $110/130 in summer includes a continental breakfast. They also rent out *Murry's Light*, a lighthouse next door that has double accommodations for $165 in winter, $185 in summer. They have one contemporary room with all the charm of a college junior's dormitory room. The 1735 House is at 584 S Fletcher Ave.

The *Elizabeth Point Lodge* is a flashy, frilly kind of place, designed to look a lot older than it is (it's actually just a couple of years old!) and service is good enough to make it seem like a B&B even though it's more of a hotel (but the price does include a hot breakfast). Rooms have great ocean views, all have large tubs and nine have Jacuzzis; the decor is also très nautical. Prices range from $115 to 125. It's at 98 S Fletcher Ave.

B&Bs As in a couple of other towns, selecting a specific B&B from all those available in town is a daunting task, best left to individual tastes. We went into all of them, and with the exception of one place we were charmed and delighted by all the offerings. In the interest of space, we've had to leave some out, and listed only our favorites. If you're lucky, you'll show up in time for the annual Christmas tour of the B&Bs, the first weekend in December – contact the chamber of commerce for a complete list, or check the island's website (see the Online Services appendix) for more information. The others are easy to find – their pamphlets are in racks at the chamber of commerce and in some restaurants.

The *Florida House Inn* (☎ 261-3300, 800-258-3301) is Florida's oldest hotel (1857), and in its heyday was host to luminaries including Ulysses S. Grant, Cuban freedom-fighter José Martí and Rockefellers and Carnegies. It had a pretty rough patch this century, when it devolved into a flophouse. Enter Bob and Karen Warner, who came through like a white tornado and restored the place to what may be a better than original condition; the renovation is nothing short of spectacular. Many of the rooms have fireplaces, all are beautiful and decorated with obviously loving touches. Some have showers, others claw-foot tubs, two have Jacuzzis and all have telephone, air-conditioning and TV. Breakfast includes homemade granola and varying hot entrées. The huge porches (upstairs and downstairs, front and rear) and garden area are wonderful (say hello to Halfway, Tatty and Libby the cats, and Shelby the dog). There's a very friendly pub downstairs, and their restaurant serves up remarkably good Southern cooking (see Places to Eat). The hotel is at 20 and 22 S 3rd St. Prices range from $70 to 130 double and reservations are a very good idea.

The irresistible warmth of the *Hoyt House* (☎ 277-4300, 800-432-2085) – its owners, Rita and John, and their warm and welcoming kitchen – drew us back again and again during our visit. Another fabulously renovated house, this one Victorian (1905), the Hoyt House opened in 1993 with nine rooms, all with telephone, air conditioning and TV. Each room is unique. There are little touches from Rita and John throughout the day, like homemade cookies, scones and biscuits, free wine in the afternoons, and lots of good food. Breakfast is a little elaborate, with fresh everything and lots of it. Stop in the kitchen and say hello, or on the porch, say hi to Ivy the cat. Rooms range from $80 to 135 (specify whether you want contemporary or Victorian decor), though you can bargain away at that a bit during the week. In January and February rooms are three nights for the price of two. It's at the corner of Atlantic Ave and 8th St.

If *Posada San Carlos* (☎ 277-8744) at 212 Estrada St, looks familiar to you, think Pippi Longstocking – it was filmed here. Don't load those kids into the wagon quite yet – they don't allow guests under 12. But the management is very friendly, and the two rooms have a nightly turndown service with nice touches like chocolate and, nicer, port wine. It's $100 for a double, breakfast is another elaborate affair, and that big but

friendly Rottweiler is named Angus. It's out of the center, at Plaza San Carlos.

Resorts The *Ritz-Carlton* (☎ 277-1100, 800-241-3333) has the immaculate service one would expect from a Ritz anywhere, and holds very creative special programs, from cooking classes to skydivers arriving with the Beaujolais Nouveau. The resort has 449 rooms, 43 suites and two presidential suites. All rooms have balconies, and twice-daily maid service. There's 24-hour room service, marble bathrooms with plush robes and countless other amenities.

The Club Level is extra exclusivity in exchange for more than a little extra money, though it does have its perks: keyed entry in the elevators, evening cocktails, and *great* chocolate chip cookies.

The hotel is on about 13 acres of awesome beachfront; there is (of course) an 18-hole golf course, tennis courts, a spa and an indoor and outdoor pool. Rates begin with standard category rooms ranging from $123 to 195, deluxe oceanview rooms $173 to 245, club suites from $323 to 395, and club level rooms $248 to 320. It's at 4750 Amelia Island Parkway.

Matthew Medure, the 26-year-old chef at the hotel's AAA five-diamond *The Grill* restaurant, is charming and one of the best chefs around, and *everyone* tells him so. He's the youngest chef ever in a Ritz Grill restaurant, the company's flagship restaurants. If you're not sure what you want, he may just say 'Tell me what you don't like,' and then whip something up. Dangerous guy. You mix and match from the menu's offerings: $48 for three courses, $58 for four or $65 for five. Appetizers include baked camembert in phyllo with lettuce and citrus, spring salmon on fennel cucumber salad and caviar and pea soup with corn ginger relish; second courses include roast spaghetti squash with wild flower honey and lobster, porcini mushrooms and proscuitto and charred foie gras; and main courses include sautéed striped bass, artichoke risotto and oven-dried tomatoes, barbecued rack of lamb with shitake mushrooms and spring onion, and duck breast with confit, date purée and preserved onions. There are cheeses and dozens of dessert offerings – it's pretty awesome, and if you're looking to splurge, this is the place to do it.

Also on the premises is *The Café*. Breakfast specials run from $9.75 to 13 though eggs, toast and potatoes is only $5.25. At lunch time starters run $4.50 to 8.75, main courses $5.50 to 13.75 and pizzas from $8.25 to 9.25 with awesome toppings like caramelized onion, barbecued chicken, smoked shrimp. At dinnertime expect to pay $6.50 for starters like Italian cheese quesadilla, $7.75 for chilled Atlantic salmon with fennel yogurt and salad; main courses like pan-seared salmon with sun-dried tomato broth are around $13.50 to 17.75. Macrobiotic foods are also available. The *Ocean Bar & Grill* serves lighter fare outside.

Amelia Island Plantation (☎ 261-6161, 800-874-6878) is a 550-room resort primarily based around their two gonzo golf courses: the Amelia Links (designed by Pete Dye) and Long Point (designed by Tom Fazio). Now, we don't know what that means, but they seem very proud of it. They also have 21 swimming pools, lots of tennis courts, a sports bar, the Ocean View Amelia Inn Restaurant and Lounge, Golf Shop Restaurant, and more. Room rates in low season (winter) are $158 for rooms, $194 for one-bedroom suites; in high season it's $224/292. It's on Amelia Island Parkway south of American Beach – follow the signs.

Places to Eat

For snacks and an upscale jolt of caffeine, hit the *Amelia Island Gourmet Coffee Co*, on 4th St opposite the post office, where the local yuppies and politicos hand out drinking good coffee (about $1 to 3 a cup) and great pastries, like Plantation pecan pie ($3.75) and fruit of the forest pie ($3.25).

KP Bola's (☎ 261-6251) at the Sadler Square shopping center, 2124 Sadler Rd, is a local favorite, and the closest you'll come to a vegetarian place in town. Great food, great prices and very popular.

Maggie's Diner (☎ 261-9976), at 18 N 2nd St, won't blow you away with their cooking but if you stay simple it's fine. Omelets are $3.75 to 5.25, salad bar with grilled chicken breast or soup is $4.95, burgers and sandwiches are $3.95 to 5.95, and moon pies are 50¢. The back room is nonsmoking.

Eight Flags Antique Warehouse & Cafe (☎ 277-7006) at 21 N 2nd St, wasn't open when we visited but planned to do sandwiches and soup for $3 to 5, and coffee and desserts. They're going to be open Monday to Saturday from 10 am to 5 pm, Sunday from noon to 5 pm.

At *Shakespeare's Kitchen* (☎ 277-2076), 316 Centre St (upstairs, 2nd floor), it feels as if you're walking into someone's house; they serve generous portions of healthy, light sandwiches: blackened chicken and avocado $5.25 and veggie $4.95, and a ploughman's special (fruit with mixed cheeses, fresh greens and bread) is $6.95. Weekdays they're only open for lunch, but on Friday and Saturday they also serve dinner from 6.30 to 11 pm; there may even be live guitar music out on the beautiful rooftop terrace. Downstairs, you'll find *As You Like It* (☎ 277-2005), open Monday to Saturday from 10 am to 6 pm. This small place smells fantastic when you walk in – they sell gourmet cheeses and cold cuts, wines, fresh-baked bread and they make goodies like blue cheese biscuits. About once a month they have a wine tasting.

Cooking at the Ritz

Matthew Medure runs a cooking school at the Ritz that's getting more and more famous – and crowded – as we speak. The classes take place on Tuesday and Wednesday and will have you dicing and slicing with the best of them. Classes are themed on a particular style of cuisine, and the members cook all day and then eat the fruits of their labor family-style. The cost is $695 per couple including classes, supplies and accommodations. ■

The *Marina Restaurant* (☎ 261-5310), 101 Centre St, is quite popular. Locals and visitors alike line up for lunch specials like chicken croquettes, pepper steak or breaded veal, all with three vegetables, for $5.50. Prices double at dinner.

Elizabeth Pointe Lodge (☎ 277-4851) at 98 S Fletcher Ave, at the hotel of the same name, is a nice place for lunch. A ham and cheese melt, or soup with salad and bread are $5.95; club sandwich and soup goes for $7.90.

O'Kane's Irish Pub & Eatery (☎ 261-1000), at 318 Centre St, does serviceable Irish specialties but stay away from anything creative or vaguely Continental, which they're not as good at. Service is friendly. At lunch, try the chicken stew pie for $5.25 or quiche for $5.95, and at dinner definitely do the Irish Stew ($8.50) and any Irish specials ($12.95 to 15.95). The portions are very large, but what we had was a little oily (though it would make a good base for drinking, and there's plenty of that in the attached Irish pub). Happy hour is Monday to Friday from 4 to 7 pm and all day Sunday. It's open Monday to Thursday from 11.30 am to 11 pm, Friday and Saturday from 11.30 am to midnight, Sunday from noon to 10 pm.

The *Beech St Grill* (☎ 277-3662), 801 Beech St, is excellent, and well spoken of locally for their exquisite seafood. While they are *not* cheap, you get what you pay for: grilled New York strip for $18.95, veal picatta for $17.95, roasted duck or roasted salmon filet for $16.95, daily fresh seafood specials for about the same price (some a bit cheaper) and fine service. (They were even polite when our credit card came up tilt on our splurge evening out – dinner for the two of us, with a bottle of wine and dessert, was $60.) All entrées come with vegetables. Reservations are recommended, and they are open for dinner from 6 to 10 pm daily.

Lots of locals swear by the *Down Under Marina Restaurant* (☎ 261-1001), on the west side of the Intracoastal Waterway at Hwy A1A, under the bridge. Their main courses range from $12.95 for boiled shrimp to $16.95 for grouper Monterey or a seafood platter, and rib-eye steaks for $15.95.

If you're looking for the absolute finest, and price is no object, see The Grill at the Ritz-Carlton, in Resorts, above.

Entertainment

It's not exactly a swingin' town, but there are some nice options for a drink or six. The pub downstairs at the Florida House Inn is a wonderful place with great service, a hundred or so types of beer and a great old-fashioned bar.

The most jumping place in town is the landmark *Palace Saloon* (☎ 261-6320) at 113-117 Centre St, where the atmosphere is gun-running free-spiritedness – perhaps because of the quantities of their trademark Pirate's Punch (it's a mix of red wine and what seems like the bottom nine rows of the bar – packs a wallop) being imbibed. It's a scene.

Florida House Inn – Best Dining Value

The *Florida House Inn* (☎ 261-3300) is, for food, service, atmosphere and price, perhaps Florida's best dining value. It's a boarding house-style restaurant (all the food is brought out in big bowls and everyone helps themselves), with brilliantly-cooked traditional Southern dishes: delicious collard greens, great mashed potatoes and assorted other vegetables, awesome crabcakes, ribs, roast beef and real Southern-fried chicken, as much as you can eat (we took that to be a personal challenge) for $5.95 at lunch (!!!), $9.95 at dinner. Lunch is Monday to Saturday from 11.30 am to 2.30 pm, and dinner Tuesday to Saturday from 5.30 to 8.30 pm. Sunday brunch is $7.95. And don't forget to take up your dirty dishes when you're done (really). The boarding-house theme, which is a restoration of the original inn's dining room, is a really nice way to meet fellow travelers and locals – we had a great time and highly recommend it. It's at 20 and 22 S 3rd St. ∎

The Amelia Community Theatre (☎ 261-6749), 209 Cedar St, is a lovely little community theater now in its 16th season. On average, they perform eight plays a year, sometimes with dinner theater productions, and tickets start as low as $3; call when you're in town to see if anything's on.

Getting There & Away
There's no public transportation between the mainland and the island, so you'll need a car, bicycle or a very expensive taxi.

Air Jacksonville International Airport (JAX) is the closest. If you've got a private plane, you obviously don't need this book, but you can land at Fernandina Beach Municipal Airport (☎ 261-7890), just about in the center of the west side of the island.

Car Take exit 129 from I-95 to Hwy A1A east; follow this straight out to the island, about 15 miles. If coming from the west, take I-10 to the Baldwin exit, stay on Hwy 301 through Baldwin to Callahan, and Hwy A1A for about 40 miles.

Ferry From the south, take Hwy A1A north to the little town of Mayport, where you can catch the **St John's River Ferry** (AKA the Mayport Ferry, ☎ 251-3331) which runs between the northern end of Mayport (follow the signs – it's unmissable) to Ft George Island, leaving daily every half hour from about 6 am to about 10.15 pm. You can drive, motorbike, bike or walk on; cars, motorcycles and scooters are $2.50, pedestrians and bicycles are 50¢. Pee first – there are no toilets on board. The ferry drops you on Fort George Island about a quarter-mile south of the turnoff for the Kingsley Plantation (see Around Amelia Island). To Amelia Island, continue up Hwy A1A – there's no public transportation; you'll have to drive.

Getting Around
Car For Fernandina Beach, walking is the best bet, but cars are necessary to get around the greater island. Parking is a snap, and it's free.

Bicycle It's a great biking town and island – very flat and no major distances. Rent bikes at Fernandina Beach Bike & Fitness (☎ 277-3227), 115 8th St just behind the BP station, for $2.50 an hour, $10 a day or $40 a week, closed Tuesday and Sunday. Reserve early. Bikes should also be available at Driftwood Surf Shop (☎ 321-2188), 31 S Fletcher Ave, Fernandina Beach, for $10 per day and $40 per week.

AROUND AMELIA ISLAND
Just to the south of the island are two very interesting state parks.

Little Talbot Island State Park
This treasure of an island (☎ 251-2320), about nine miles south of American Beach across Nassau Sound, is a 2500-acre park with fishing, nature and hiking trails, five miles of beaches, canoeing ($3 an hour, $12 a day), camping and a picnic area. The maritime forest is made of Southern magnolia, live oak and American holly; Spanish moss is everywhere. Canoeing permission is granted depending on the tides.

There's **camping** here; it costs $15.75 year round for sites without electricity, $17.88 with electric hookups. All sites have water hookups.

The park entrance is on the east side of Hwy A1A; admission is $3.25 per car, $1 per bicycle or pedestrian; the park is open 8 am to sundown every day. See St John's River Ferry, above.

Kingsley Plantation
Zephaniah Kingsley and his Senegalese wife (whom Kingsley had originally bought as a slave) established a cotton, sugar cane, corn and citrus plantation here on Fort George Island in 1814. Today the plantation (☎ 251-3537), kitchen house, garden, barn and the remains of the 23 slave cabins are open as part of the Timucuan Ecological & Historic Preserve, and are a wonderful place to spend an afternoon

with or without a picnic. The cabins are chilling, for their tiny size and their jail-like arrangement. There's printed information on the lives of the slaves, their task system and the slave community, but the rangers' oral history is far more compelling.

In the small garden, you can see Sea Island cotton growing – with beautiful yellow flowers. Ranger-guided talks are given at 1 pm daily; the park is open Monday to Friday from 9 am to 5 pm, Saturday and Sunday from 1 to 3 pm. Admission is free; donations are appreciated. There's drinking water in the bathrooms.

Getting There & Away From Fernandina Beach, take Hwy A1A straight south to Fort George Island. The access road is on the west side of Hwy A1A; at the fork in the road, the left route is more direct; the right, through gorgeous canopied forest, is longer (about three miles) but far prettier. On either fork, watch out for pot holes the size of hall closets.

From the south, take the St John's River Ferry (see Amelia Island, above) across to Fort George Island; it drops you off about a quarter-mile south of the turnoff for the Kingsley Plantation.

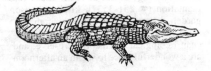
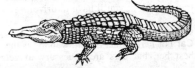

Southwest Florida

With the warm, calm waters of the Gulf of Mexico lapping its white sand beaches, southwest Florida is one of the state's most beautiful regions. It offers some of the best opportunities for getting out into nature in the state.

The area was developed just before the turn of the century, when Henry B Plant, Florida's west coast version of Henry Flagler, built a railroad line connecting the area with the northeast and ran a steamship line between Tampa and Havana, which brought in the tobacco that made Tampa America's cigar-making capital.

Henry Ford, Thomas Edison, John Ringling (who was as serious about art as he was about circuses) and a fascinating religious commune set down roots here, and the region is rich with cultural attractions. You can tour Edison's rubber laboratories and winter home (along with Ford's winter home) and gawk at the fantastic collections of European, American, Asian and pre-Columbian art at the St Petersburg Museum of Fine Arts, maybe the state's best. And you can still watch cigars being hand rolled in Tampa's historic Ybor City district.

For getting out into nature, there are the splendors of the Gulf barrier islands, from Fort Myers to Clearwater Beaches, where swimming, canoeing, kayaking, hiking and biking opportunities abound. The Lee County Parks Department, around Fort Myers, runs some of the best programs around, and even in a place as developed as Fort Myers Beach, you're never more than a half hour from total immersion in wilderness. Some of the best souvenirs and sightseeing are found right along the coast: from the mounds of shark's teeth that wash up on Venice Beach to the unparalleled shelling at Sanibel and Captiva Islands and the area near Clearwater Beach.

But the area's two theme parks are also definitely worth a visit: Busch Gardens has the best roller coasters in the southeastern USA, and Weeki Wachee Springs is famous for its weirdly campy underwater mermaid shows.

Hotels and motels in the region are priced a little higher than in other areas of the state, but there's inexpensive camping in several state parks and historic sites (best on some of the barrier islands west of Fort Myers) and there are youth hostels in Clearwater Beach and St Petersburg.

But the best part is that there's less development here than on the east coast. Much

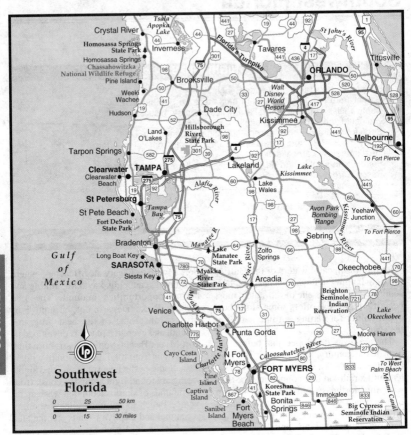

Southwest Florida

```
0       25        50 km
0       15        30 miles
```

of the coastline is protected, and the residents on the barrier islands and beach communities are quite content to leave the screaming hordes of Spring Breakers and the gaggles of fashionplates where they are, about 150 miles east of their serene coastline.

FORT MYERS

• pop 324,500 ☎ 941

Dubbed the City of Palms for the two thousand royal palm trees that line McGregor Blvd, Fort Myers was a sleepy resort town

in 1885 when Thomas A Edison decided to build a winter home and laboratory here.

It was Edison who began planting the palms: he made a deal with the city that he would plant them if the city agreed to maintain them after his death. He planted 543 as seedlings, and he imported a further 270 from the Everglades, which lined the first mile of the avenue. Today McGregor is lined with palms for 14 miles.

Edison moved to the area in 1886 and expanded his estate over the years. In 1914, Henry Ford visited Edison here and liked the place so much that he bought the house next door.

Today both houses are open as museums, yet Fort Myers is known more for its beach life and excellent county and state parks than for its grand experiments.

Orientation

The sprawling greater Fort Myers area is at the southwest corner of Florida, just northwest of the Everglades and the 10,000 Islands. The city of Fort Myers sits on the southern banks of the Caloosahatchee River; on the north bank is North Fort Myers and Cape Coral is to the west. To the southwest are San Carlos and Estero Islands; the City of Fort Myers Beach is on the latter.

The downtown area is broken up by two intersecting grid sections. The core of the downtown historic district is comprised of a network of streets that are at a 45° angle to the standard north-south, east-west grid system that makes up the rest of the city. The 45° section is bounded on the south by ML King Jr Blvd, on the east by Evans Ave, and on the west by Cleveland Ave (US Hwy 41, the Tamiami Trail), which runs into the Caloosahatchee Bridge and on to North Fort Myers.

There's not really a main drag in downtown, but what action there is (which is to say not much) is concentrated in the area bounded by Edwards Drive at the north, Fowler St at the east, ML King Jr Blvd at the south and Monroe Ave at the west. A little mall called Patio de León is bounded by Main, 1st and Hendry Sts and Broadway.

Maps The best downtown map is right in this book, but you can find copies of downtown maps in *Downtown & Around Town Fort Myers Digest* (see Information below) and sometimes on the tram tour (see Organized Tours below). Dolph Map Co's *Map of Fort Myers and Vicinity* is probably the best commercially produced map, with a good insert blowup of downtown; the Fort Myers Chamber of Commerce sells an imprinted edition of this map for $1. AAA's *Map of Fort Myers* is pretty good, though the scale could do with some enlargement,

and for the beach, their *Map of Cape Coral* features a similarly scaled inset of Fort Myers Beach and other areas, including Sanibel, Captiva and Pine Islands.

Information

Tourist Offices The Lee County Visitors & Convention Bureau (☎ 338-3500, 800-533-4753, ext. 200), 2180 W 1st St, Suite 100, has some very helpful planners and information kits. Among them, *Lee Island Coast – Vacationer's Guide*, an all-round orientation and information pamphlet; *A Nature Guide to the Lee Island Coast*, which is just that; and the excellent *Access Ability Guide* for handicapped visitors, listing ADA information on most major sights in the county.

Right downtown, the Greater Fort Myers Chamber of Commerce (☎ 332-3624), at the corner of Lee St and Edwards Drive, has the usual array of pamphlets and tourist brochures and the *Downtown & Around Town Fort Myers Digest*.

The enormous local AAA office (☎ 939-6500) is at 2516 Colonial Blvd. Colonial, a major connector, is reached by taking Cleveland Ave (US Hwy 41) south.

How Far?

Distances in the Fort Myers area are incredible: the Lee County Parks Department told us that the new Lee County Manatee Park, which is eight miles northeast of downtown, was 'Pretty much downtown Fort Myers.' Anywhere you'll want to go outside of your immediate vicinity is bound to be at least 40 minutes away by car. And traffic, by the way, is murderous. So take that into account when you're planning a trip: to stay at Fort Myers Beach is great if you're after sun and surf, but if you're looking to canoe around the Matlacha Pass Aquatic Preserve (see Pine Island & Matlacha Pass below) or hit the Edison and Ford Estates, you're in for a long drive. ∎

SOUTHWEST

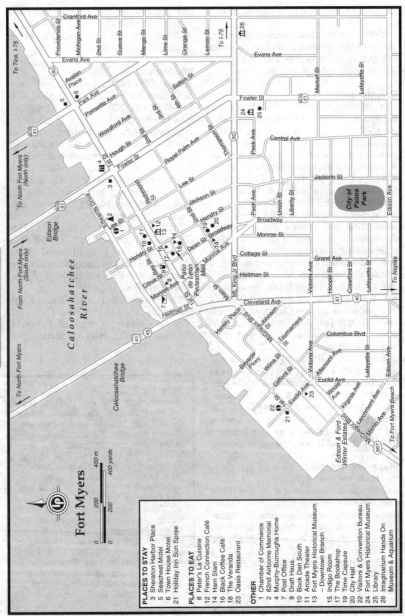

Fort Myers

PLACES TO STAY
3   Sheraton Harbor Place
5   Seachest Motel
6   Town House Motel
21 Holiday Inn Sun Spree

PLACES TO EAT
8   Peter's La Cuisine
12 French Connection Café
14 Ham Slam
16 Black Coffee Café
18 The Veranda
23 Oasis Restaurant

OTHER
1   Chamber of Commerce
2   82nd Airborne Memorial
4   Murphy-Burroughs Home
7   Post Office
9   Draft Haus
10 Book Den South
11 Arcade Theater
13 Fort Myers Historical Museum
    – Downtown Branch
15 Indigo Room
17 The Bookshop
19 Time Capsule
20 City Hall
22 Visitors & Convention Bureau
24 Fort Myers Historical Museum
25 Library
26 Imaginarium Hands On
    Museum & Aquarium

Money Barnett Bank's main office downtown is at Barnett Centre, 2000 Main St. American Express has two representative offices; at the Travel Chest (☎ 275-6261), 7290 College Parkway; and Ship 'n' Shore Cruises (☎ 433-0013), 15250 S US Hwy 41.

Post & Communications The main downtown post office is at the corner of Bay St and Monroe Ave. The area code for Fort Myers and around changed from ☎ 813 to ☎ 941 in May 1995. The old area code should be entirely phased out by the time you read this, but many businesses still list 813 on pamphlets – dial 941.

Bookstores The biggest bookshop in town is the Books a Million (☎ 936-8871), 4125 Cleveland Ave in the Edison Mall shopping center. Downtown, the Book Den South (☎ 332-2333), 2249 1st St, has high-quality used books, paperbacks and a travel section that's more literature than guides (with no LP offerings). Close by, the Bookshop (☎ 334-0141) in Patio de León has more paperbacks and a book search service.

Libraries The main library (☎ 338-3155), 2050 Lee St, is next to the Fort Myers Historical Museum.

Media The main daily newspaper is the *News-Press*, a Gannett paper (which according to some hot-headed local critics has an editorial policy somewhere to the left of *Pravda*, but we think the thing's just fine). For freebies, get the very good *Downtown & Around Town Fort Myers Digest*, which has a monthly events calendar, a pretty helpful downtown classified section and a good downtown map. NPR is at 90.1 FM; astronomical (not astrological) forecasts are broadcast Monday morning at 7.58 am.

Toilets There are public toilets outside the entrance to the Edison Estate & Laboratory.

Laundry We used the U-Turn Laundromat (☎ 334-7111), 2412 Cortez Blvd, near the Edison Estate.

Thomas Alva Edison

Thomas Edison (1847-1931) was a tireless and entirely commercially minded inventor who has a total of 1093 patents to his name (17 of these were co-patents with another inventor).

In Robert Conot's *A Streak of Luck*, Edison is quoted as having said, 'Anything that won't sell I don't want to invent. Its sale is proof of utility, and utility is success.'

And utilitarian Edison most certainly was: his patents include 389 under the category of 'Electric Light and Power', 195 for phonographs, 150 for the telegraph, 141 for batteries, 62 for ore separators, 40 for cement, 34 for railroads, nine for motion pictures, eight for automobiles, five for 'electric pen' and mimeograph, three for typewriters, one for vacuum preservation, three for chemicals, an auto-giro (described as a cross between a helicopter and an airplane), three for military projectiles, two for radio and one for rubber.

To get an idea of his energy, consider that he patented at least one gizmo a year for 65 consecutive years: he was issued 34 in 1872, 75 in 1882, 23 in 1907 and in 1931, the year of his death, he was issued two. But even death was not enough to completely sap his relentless pursuit: four patents were issued to him posthumously.

Source: Historical Division, Edison & Ford Winter Estates ■

Medical Services The largest public hospital in the area is Lee Memorial Hospital (☎ 332-1111), 2776 Cleveland Ave.

Edison & Ford Winter Estates

The town's main tourist attraction, the Edison Estate & Laboratory (☎ 334-7419) was the winter home of Thomas Alva Edison, one of America's most prolific inventors. The grounds are absolutely lovely – Edison was an avid botanist – with over 600 varieties of plants. We liked the Dynamite Tree, which spreads its seeds through pods that, well, explode! The other

Edison estate landmark is the unbelievably enormous banyan tree just outside the entrance. Remember to stay on the paths as you walk through – the grass is infested with fire ants.

Edison's laboratory here was devoted to his attempts to cross-breed an American rubber tree at the behest of car and tire makers Ford and Firestone, who wanted to establish a reliable domestic supply. After experimenting with thousands of plants, Edison successfully created a hybrid goldenrod plant that grew to a height of almost 12 feet in a season and contained 12% rubber – an unprecedented quantity. But the production process was too expensive and nothing commercial came of it.

The laboratory is a remarkable place, and it's been kept pretty much as Edison left it – the array of hoo-has and gizmos is amazing. Note the Hayfever Room at the far right-hand corner where goldenrod was thrashed and cut by unfortunate employees.

Adjacent to the laboratory is the Edison Museum, a fascinating collection of hundreds of Edison's inventions and possessions, like his 1908 four-cylinder Cadillac coupe, tons of office equipment, movie projectors and kinescopes, Edison light bulbs, phonographs and the first three-wire generator system behind a very Stalinesque bust.

There are guided tours through the estate, which include a visit to the adjacent **Henry Ford's winter home**, the automaker/sometime philanderer. There are more specialized tours as well: on Monday, Wednesday and Saturday at 10 am and 2 pm there are in-depth historical tours ($15 for adults and $7.50 for students and seniors) and on Tuesday and Saturday at the same times are botanical tours of the grounds ($16/8).

The museum and estate are open Monday to Saturday from 9 am to 4 pm, Sunday from noon to 4 pm. The cost is $10 for adults, $5 for children.

The estate straddles McGregor Blvd at Larchmond, south of downtown: the main entrance for both homes, the ticket office, Edison Museum and Laboratory and parking lots are on the east side of the street; the Ford home and garage, Edison home and guesthouse, memory garden and swimming pool are on the west.

Fort Myers Historical Museum

The Fort Myers Historical Museum (☎ 332-5955), 2300 Peck St (with a smaller branch on 1st St between Hendry and Jackson), is a hit with kids if only to tour the *Esperanza*, a private railroad car. A series of permanent exhibits tell the story of the city's history and include Calusa and Seminole artifacts, models of the local military bases and a display on Colonel Myers – the man for whom the city's named. (Though he never actually visited his namesake fort, just as General Robert E Lee never set foot in his namesake county!) Other exhibits include a Spanish cannon, a complete saber-toothed cat (*Smilodon*) skeleton and an exhibit on Fort Myers' two WWII training bases, which trained British, American, Canadian, Russian and Yugoslavian pilots and gunners.

There are always traveling exhibits as well: when we visited it was Cooper glass, dime store soldiers and war games. The museum's open Tuesday to Friday from 9 am to 4 pm, Saturday from 10 am to 4 pm, closed Sunday and Monday. Admission is $2.50 for adults and $1 for children.

Imaginarium Hands On Museum & Aquarium

The Imaginarium (☎ 337-3332), 2000 Cranford Ave off ML King Jr Blvd just past the *Post-News* and *USA Today* plant – look for the big water tower, is a hands-on science museum that kids will go crazy over. We loved the hot-air balloon exhibition and the golf-ball-driven model of the human digestive system. Take a spin in the chemical-abuse simulator jeep on the electronic obstacle course to test your reflexes after a couple of virtual snoots.

In the Tiny Town area downstairs there's a really cool bubble gadget – kids stand in the center of a circle and pull a string, which raises a hula hoop from a tray of soapy water at their feet and surrounds them with an enormous, cylindrical bubble.

Upstairs, a television station exhibit called WIMG puts your kid against a matte and in front of a TV camera; through weatherman technology, kids can then see themselves in the center of a hurricane video. There are also excellent exhibits on ozone depletion and weather – touch a cloud is neat – and a tornado machine. If their computer hasn't crashed, you can surf the internet and play interactive CD-ROM games.

Outside, there's a touch tank with a stingray (he was sick when we visited) and crabs, horseshoe crabs, living shells, starfish and more. The new freshwater lagoon will have (according to a press release that sounds more like a fishmonger than an aquarium) '1200 pounds of freshwater fish' and Florida aquaculture.

There's a 3-D theater downstairs that does different shows every half hour or so.

The museum is open Monday to Saturday from 10 am to 5 pm, and Sunday from noon to 5 pm, closed Christmas and Thanksgiving. Admission is $6 for adults, $3 for children three to 12. There's no senior discount.

Murphy-Burroughs Home

Call them hokey, but the 'living history' tours at this historic landmark home (☎ 332-6125), 2505 1st St, by the river, are still popular: you're led through the house with volunteers in the costumes and characters of Jettie and Mona Burroughs, daughters of Nelson Burroughs. Burroughs, a businessman (but not the electronics giant of the same name), bought the house from a Texas cattleman named Murphy in 1918, and the house remained in the family until it was donated to the city in 1983. Tours run Tuesday to Friday from 11 am to 3 pm every hour on the hour. On Saturday they host special events like weddings and meetings. Admission is $3 for adults, $1 for students; parking is available at the nearby Sheraton Harbor hotel.

Other Downtown Attractions

At the corner of Lee St and Edwards Drive, near the chamber of commerce, is the **82nd Airborne Memorial**, a monument to the Gulf Coast chapter of the army's 82nd Airborne Division.

In 1976, the town elders got together and made a **time capsule** of items readily available during that year, to be opened on July 4, 2076. The capsule is at the front corner of the City Hall property, on the corner of 2nd St and Broadway.

And every Thursday from 7 am to 3 pm there's a city **farmer's market** under the entrance to the Caloosahatchee River Bridge. It's kind of colorful. This is not to be confused with the **State Farmer's Market** (☎ 332-6910), 2744 Edison Ave, which is more a restaurant and hotel buyer's hangout than a public attraction.

Calusa Nature Center & Planetarium

This nature center (☎ 275-3435) has a series of boardwalks through their cypress swamp, an Audubon aviary and a faux Seminole village. Inside they have permanent and rotating exhibitions on the history and formation of southwestern Florida. But what the kids are really here for is the live poisonous snake exhibition, with daily snake and alligator demonstrations at 10.30 am and 1.30 pm. There are also weekly snake feedings (in May it was on Sunday at 11.15 am, but call first) and nature hikes around the grounds.

The planetarium (☎ 275-2183) features shows on the southwest Florida night sky and films like *Firstlight*, which tracks the development of the telescope from a clunky mirror in a tube to a clunky mirror aboard a billion-dollar spacecraft.

There are astronomy shows in the afternoon, and on Friday and Saturday nights, laser shows with rock music that's surprisingly current.

It's open Monday to Saturday from 9 am to 5 pm, Sunday 11 am to 5 pm. Admission to the museum and trails is $3 for adults, $1.50 for kids under 12; a combination museum, trails and planetarium ticket is $5/3. But they give out coupons left and right, so try showing them this listing to get $1 off a combination ticket. Go ahead: it's not like they said it's okay or anything, but it never hurts to try, right? Astronomy shows

SOUTHWEST

are $3/2, and laser shows are $5. The complex is at 3450 Ortiz Ave, north of the intersection of Ortiz Ave, Colonial Blvd and Six Mile Cypress Parkway.

Lakes Regional Park

This innovative park is home to two very original ideas: a Fragrance Garden (☎ 369-2003) and a miniature train village (☎ 275-3000). The Fragrance Garden was created in 1991 by Ed and Sylvia Blue to be a place where visually impaired and wheelchair-bound visitors could smell, feel and even eat herbs and flowers. It's fully wheelchair accessible, and signs are in print and Braille, but the park is open to everyone and it's a nice place for a picnic (tables are provided). The gardens were built up by volunteers from the Master Gardeners Club, Boy and Girl Scouts and students in the RISK program – those at high risk of quitting school – at nearby Cyprus Lakes High School. The garden is open every day except Christmas from 8 am to 6 pm.

There is also a miniature train (7½-inch gauge) in the park, where kids and adults can take a little tootle around the 1¼-mile track every 15 minutes. It runs Tuesday to Friday from 10 am to 2 pm, Saturday from 10 am to 4 pm and Sunday from noon to 4 pm. The cost for a ride is $2.50 for everyone over three years old; kids under three are free. The project is trying to raise money to restore the locomotive you'll see there, Atlantic Coast Line No 143, an 0-6-0 in horrendous shape. The rail line is closest to parking lot three.

You can rent boats here as well; Lakeside Marina (☎ 432-2017) rents paddleboats and canoes ($7 an hour) and canoes with electric trawling motors ($12 an hour) between 8 am and 4 pm. There are alligators in the lake and on the small islands – ask at the marina where the best areas are to see them. The park is in South Fort Myers; from downtown, take US Hwy 41 south to Gladiolus Drive; the park is at 7330 Gladiolus Drive on the right-hand side of the road. Parking is 75¢ an hour, or a maximum of $3 for the day.

Six Mile Cypress Slough Preserve

This preserve (☎ 338-3300) is a 2000-acre wetland that acts as a filter or drainage way collecting run-off water during heavy rains. The water is filtered by the slough, where sediment and pollutants settle or are absorbed by its plants, and the water finally makes its way out to the Estero Bay Aquatic Preserve. It's an eerie place to visit during the wet season from June to October, when water up to three feet deep flows through the area.

The preserve has a mile-long boardwalk trail lined with benches, a picnic area and an amphitheater used for interpretive meetings. On Wednesday and Saturday morning at 9.30 am, the Lee County Regional Park Program Office (☎ 432-2004) runs free tours through the preserve. Admission to the preserve is $3 per carload; bicycles and pedestrians are free. From downtown Fort Myers, take Cleveland Ave south to Colonial Blvd (Hwy 884) east, to Ortiz Ave and turn south. This road will become Six Mile Cyprus Parkway; the entrance is on the left, north of Daniels Parkway (Hwy 876).

Organized Tours

There's a 'tram' tour (☎ 334-7419) that runs a circle between the Burroughs Home, Fort Myers Historical Museum, Imaginarium and its depot at the Ford and Edison Estates. The tours run Tuesday to Saturday from 10 am to 4 pm; no tours Sunday or Monday. Tickets are $5 for adults, $2 for children, and include unlimited rides and discounts to the above attractions. They leave from the main entrance to the Edison Estate.

Eco-Tours The Lee County Parks & Recreation Department runs four-night, five-day, guided eco-tours (☎ 432-2004, 800-733-7935, ext 10), with local accommodations at hotels and resorts included with guided nature tours, in areas throughout southwest Florida and the Everglades. They're very expensive (about $650 per person, double occupancy), though perhaps you can find financial solace in knowing that the money goes to fund nature classes for children and adults at all the Lee County parks. Contact them for more information.

Air Tours Page Field, just south of downtown Fort Myers off of Cleveland Ave, is flight-tour central: Barnstormer Air (☎ 542-1768) operates a restored 1940 WACO UPF-7, open-cockpit biplane. (That's right, goggles, leather helmet and all!) They have three tours: half-hour flights over Fort Myers Beach are $100 for two people; 45-minute flights over Cape Coral, Captiva and Sanibel Islands and Fort Myers Beach are $160 for two; and the grand tour, a one-hour flight around the entire area and all the beaches, is $200 for two. Reserve the day before you fly (they fly every day from 9 am to 4.30 pm as well as at sunset) or on the morning of the flight. Could be fun.

Classic Flight (☎ 800-824-9464) does similar tours of the area in their 1990-built, 1935-designed, WACO YMF-5 open-cockpit biplane. Their two main rides are a half-hour 15-mile trip for $50 each and an extended 50-minute, 25-mile flight over the barrier islands for $85 each.

And if you're obscenely wealthy or want to act as if you are, take a Balloon Odyssey (☎ 458-5750) over the city: a champagne picnic breakfast is $125 per person. Launch locations vary based on weather, so call first. (Note that we did not make a hot air joke here. Talk about self-control.)

Special Events

The annual **Edison Festival of Light** (☎ 334-2999) takes place in the two weeks preceding Edison's birthday on February 11. There are dozens of mostly free events, block parties with live music and tons of food, high school band concerts, hymn sings, fashion shows and the Thomas A Edison Regional Science and Inventor's Fair, which features over 400 student finalists from within the southwest Florida school systems. Could be a blast – especially considering how Thomas himself blew up his railroad car/laboratory as a child. For information contact the Edison Festival of Light, 2210 Bay St, Fort Myers, FL 33901.

Places to Stay

Most people stay on Fort Myers Beach (see Around Fort Myers below), but business-people tend to gravitate toward the court-house-filled downtown area, where there are chain business hotels. There are three Holiday Inns (☎ 800-465-4329), including the *Holiday Inn Sunspree Resort* near the Edison and Ford estates at 2220 W 1st St, and at the Airport (☎ 482-2900), at 13501 Bell Tower Drive. The Sheraton Harbor Place (☎ 337-0300), 2500 Edwards Drive (near the Burroughs Home), and the Radisson (☎ 936-4300), 12635 Cleveland Ave, are here too.

There's a small cluster of motels downtown. We liked the *Townehouse* (☎ 334-3743), 2568 1st St, a few blocks from the Burroughs Home. It's got friendly staff and a small pool, and the rooms are pretty clean; singles/doubles are $28/30 in low season, $40/45 in the high season. The *Sea Chest Motel* (☎ 332-1545), 2571 1st St, has pleasant staff; small rooms with deep brown shaggy carpets and '60s vintage furniture are $30/45 to 75.

Along Cleveland Ave (US Hwy 41), there are some more, somewhat seedier motels. The *Fort Myers Inn Motel* (☎ 936-1959), 3511 Cleveland Ave, has not unfriendly staff and singles/doubles at $34/$38. Nearby, the friendly but cautious staff at the utterly unremarkable *Golf View Motel* (☎ 936-1858), 3523 Cleveland Ave, will let you into rooms for $32/60, if you're polite.

Places to Eat

A local favorite is the *Oasis Restaurant* (☎ 334-1566), 2222 McGregor Blvd (in the Edison-Ford Square shopping center, very close to the Edison and Ford Estates). They do a very good breakfast special for $1.99, including eggs, bacon or sausage, homefries, toast and coffee. At lunch, they serve great burgers ($3.85 to 5.25), chicken pasta salad ($5.45), a large fruit salad ($4.95) and sandwiches ($3.75 to 5.50).

Downtown Fort Myers has a couple of great and inexpensive restaurants that are almost worth the trip in and of themselves, and two flashier entries are very affordable at lunch, though prices skyrocket at night.

We followed our noses to 22 Patio de León, where *Ham Slam* (☎ 332-0112) blasts out sumptuous aromas: it's absolutely packed with downtown folks attracted by their freshly baked country ham and roast turkey sandwiches ($4.25).

The French Connection Café (☎ 332-4443), 2282 1st St, has great service and excellent salads including pasta, Caesar and Greek from $2.20 to 4.50. Big sandwiches or burgers are from $3.55 to 6.25. A killer French onion soup and daily soup specials are $2.20 (with a sandwich or salad it's $6). Carry-out is available.

The *Black Coffee Café* (☎ 332-3779), 2236 1st St, is a decent place for a quick bite as well.

Of the two stylish entries, *The Veranda* (☎ 337-1183), 2122 2nd St, wins for ambiance: it's in two beautiful houses that date to 1902 and have such intricate histories they practically tell the entire story of southwest Florida (see the back of the menu). And considering the quality, it's also a wonderful bargain at lunch (Monday to Friday from 11 am to 2.30 pm): offerings include baked onion soup ($2.95), sandwiches (from $4.50 to 6.50), Southern grit cakes ($5.95), fried green tomato salad ($7.50) and Florida crab cakes ($8.50).

Dinner (Monday to Saturday from 5.30 to 10 pm) is a far more serious and formal affair, and it's touted as 'Southwest Florida's most award-winning'. Entrees include roast duckling with roasted garlic and raspberry sauce ($19.95) and baked rack of New Zealand lamb with rosemary Merlot wine sauce ($24.95). At those prices we smelled but didn't taste, but for what it's worth, it smelled damn good.

Peter's La Cuisine (☎ 332-2228), 2224 Bay St, is the other flash place, very well known for its excellent continental food and its cool jazz upstairs (see Bars & Clubs below). At lunch, the menu's on the blackboard and the deals are pretty good: $8.95 gets you a three-course lunch of soup, salad and an entree.

But at dinner you'd better bring along Weimar Republic quantities of cash and put aside any vegetarian tendencies: among the appetizers is Beluga caviar for $65. But, hey, that includes warm *bliny*! Okay, okay, all the appetizers aren't that bad: crisp sautéed sweetbreads with white wine risotto, Madeira sauce and wild mushrooms is $9.95; carpaccio of lamb loin brushed with rosemary essence and parmesan cheese is $10.95; and terrine of cured salmon and sea scallops with fresh fennel and rémoulade sauce is $11.95. Main courses include pan-roasted salmon and grilled snapper; seared sesame striped tuna with balsamic sauce, fresh dill and tomato; and pan-roasted pork porterhouse with a green peppercorn cognac cream sauce (each $23.95). Roasted rack of lamb with a rosemary-infused reduced lamb stock sauce and black olive tapenade is $27.95, pan-roasted center-cut veal chop in natural sauce with garlic and fresh herbs is $32, and Chateaubriand for two is $49.95. Isn't this why they invented credit cards?

Entertainment

Theater & Performing Arts The biggest player in the area is the Barbara B Mann Performance Hall (☎ 481-4849, 800-440-7469) on the Edison Community College campus, just northwest of the intersection of Summerlin Rd and Cypress Lake Drive. It's host to visiting Broadway productions like *Grease*, visiting companies like the St Petersburg (this is *not* the Kirov) Ballet, and artists like James Taylor, Frank Sinatra, Jr, and Art Garfunkel. It's also home to classical and pops series from the Southwest Florida Symphony, and they hold a Community Concert Series with a diverse range of performances. Tickets are available at the box office or through Ticket Master.

Right downtown, the beautifully renovated Arcade Theater (☎ 332-6120), 2267 1st St, is underused at the moment, hosting not much more than the fall New Arts Festival (☎ 332-4643), which in 1996 featured *Cello*, a cello quartet playing classical, jazz and pop; Taylor 2 Dance Company; and, at the Canturbury School Theater

(8141 College Parkway between Winkler and Summerlin Rds), the Miller/Zoering Duo – a violin-cello tag team.

The Foulds Theater (☎ 939-2787), on Royal Palm Square Blvd (south of Colonial Blvd between Summerlin Rd and McGregor Blvd), is home to Theatre Conspiracy, a troupe that bills itself as going 'from the classics to the cutting edge'. Performances look interesting. Shows have included *Goodnight Desdemona, Good Morning Juliet*, which tells the story of a young woman transported back to a combination of *Othello* and *Romeo and Juliet*, making a farce of both, and Terrence McNally's *Frankie and Johnny in the Claire De Lune*. Tickets are $10.

Guess what's playing about a block away at the Broadway Palm Dinner Theatre (☎ 278-4422), 1380 Colonial Blvd at Royal Palm Square? Yup. Shows like *Nunsense*, *Cabaret* and *Forever Plaid*. Evening performances are Wednesday to Saturday at 8 pm and Sunday at 7 pm; matinees are Wednesday and Sunday at 1.15 pm. They do a buffet-style food service two hours before showtime (6 pm dinner, 11.45 am matinees, 5.30 pm Sunday dinner). Collared shirts and long pants are required for men (women, apparently, can wear what they like). Just a show costs $18; a meal and show combined is $28 for matinees, $31 on Wednesday to Friday and Sunday, and $34 on Saturday.

Seminole-Gulf Railway The Seminole-Gulf Railway (☎ 275-8487), founded in 1888, was a short line running between Arcadia and Naples with a second line running between Bradenton, Sarasota and Venice. Today it runs excursions and dinner tours on the line's restored trains. There are three-hour Sunday evening dinner rides ($29.75 for adults; $19.95 for children) and Thursday evening Jazz Trains ($10), with a cash bar and light snacks. They also operate murder mystery rides, two- and three-day packages and special events throughout the year; call for more information.

The terminal is located on the west side of the Metro Mall; from downtown take Cleveland Ave south to Colonial Blvd east until you think you'll run out of gas; the terminal will be on the left.

Bars & Clubs Downtown, *Peter's La Cuisine* (☎ 332-2228), 2224 Bay St, does jazz nightly in its upstairs lounge (see Places to Eat above). There's no cover for the house band, the Mambo Blues Brothers, and varying covers when national acts visit. The *Arcade Theater*'s just about a block away, and you can hit its downstairs bar for pre- and post-theater cocktails. The *Renaissance Jazz & Blues Club* (☎ 482-4459), 8695 College Parkway (at Winkler Rd), is a long haul from downtown, but it has jazz every night from 9 pm to about 1:30 am.

Check out the *Draft Haus* (☎ 337-7625), 1420 Dean St, which is a very popular watering hole; next door at 1414 Dean is Pulse, which apparently has seen better days. *Shooters Waterfront Cafe* (☎ 334-3434), 2220 W 1st St, next to the Holiday Inn Sunspree, is also popular, as is the *Indigo Room* (☎ 332-0014) in Patio de León. If you're into sports bars, hit *Shoeless Joe's* at the Holiday Inn Select, US Hwy 41 at Bell Tower Drive. For the local version of an after-hours club, where you BYO booze and pay small 'set up' fees, hit *Hollywood Underground* (☎ 433-1313), way down on US Hwy 41 just south of Gladiolus Drive.

Danceteria (☎ 332-1808), 2240 McGregor (just north of the Edison Estate), opened about a week before we went to press. They spent close to a million dollars on lighting and sound systems, and locals say it's excellent. It's open Thursday to Sunday; only people 21 or over are allowed in, except on Sunday, when anyone over 17 is welcome. The music is '70s, '80s and '90s mainstream. No shorts, hats or sneakers allowed. Danceteria is also organizing a ballroom dancing night, to allow seniors to take advantage of their 1200-sq-foot wooden dance floor. However, note that the club may be renamed by the time you arrive: the defunct New York club of the same name had a federal trademark on it.

Gay & Lesbian We only found two gay and lesbian clubs here, but there are bound to be more. Check out the *Bottom Line Lounge* (☎ 337-7292), 3090 Evans Ave, just north of Winkler Rd; all are welcome but it's predominantly gay and healthily lesbian. There are bartop dancers every night but Thursday, which is their traditional Sink or Swim night: unlimited draft beer ($5) or well drinks ($10) from 9 pm to closing. Sunday night they feature Kelly Anderson with a guest stripper, and on Friday there are shows with Vanessa Jackson. Also try *The Alternative* (☎ 277-7002), 4650 S Cleveland Ave, in the Montgomery Ward shopping plaza just south of Colonial Blvd.

Spectator Sports

City of Palms Park, 2201 Edison Ave, is the spring training home of baseball's Boston Red Sox (☎ 334-4700). Games are played here during March. Box seats are $9, reserved $8, general admission $5. The Minnesota Twins (☎ 768-4270) make the Lee County Sports Complex their spring home; it's just southwest of the intersection of Daniels Parkway and Six Mile Cyprus Parkway. During the regular season, the Fort Myers Miracle play here, which is the Minnesota Twins minor-league baseball farm team. Admission to Miracle games is free; call for Twins spring training game prices. Farm teams have become much more popular since the vilified major league baseball strike of 1994-95.

Things to Buy

The incredibly friendly people at Made on Earth (☎ 334-8300), 2976 Cleveland Ave, do great tie-dye and other hippie paraphernalia, along with smoking supplies. They're also good sources of local information.

The Edison Mall (☎ 939-5464), at the junction of Cleveland and Winkler Aves, is the largest shopping center in the area. Bell Tower Shops (☎ 489-1221), another mall, is at the corner of Cleveland Ave and Daniels Parkway, and the Sanibel Factory Stores (☎ 454-1616), about 60 close-out shops, are at Summerlin Rd and McGregor Blvd.

Getting There & Away

Air Southwest Florida International Airport (☎ 768-1000) is on Daniels Parkway east of I-75. It's becoming more important as the southwest section of the state experiences growth, and is currently served by airlines including America West, American (seasonal service), American Trans Air, Canada 3000, Canadian Air, Carnival, Continental, Delta, LTU, Northwest/KLM, TWA, United, USAir/British Airways and possibly Valujet, which served the airport before its suspension in 1996. In mid-1997, British tour operators are expected to begin charter service to the airport from London's Gatwick in summer months.

Bus The Greyhound station (☎ 334-1011) is at 2275 Cleveland Ave. Sample fares (one way/roundtrip) are listed below.

Destination	Price	Duration
Miami	$21/42	4 to 4½ hours
Tampa	$21/42	2½ to 4½ hours
Orlando	$36/72	5½ to 7½ hours

Train Amtrak (☎ 800-872-7245) has daily shuttle buses between Tampa and Fort Myers that pretend to be continuing rail service – see the Tampa Getting There & Away section for the daily train schedule between Tampa and Orlando.

Car Fort Myers is between I-75 and US Hwy 41 (the Tamiami Trail). It's about 140 miles from Miami and 123 miles from Tampa. Most major car rental companies have offices at the airport; see the Getting Around chapter for more information.

Getting Around

Because of the sadistic distances between everything you'll want to see, a car is key. But there is a decent public transport system that can get you around, if slowly. Within downtown and around the main Fort Myers sights, there's a trolley from Tuesday to Saturday (see Organized Tours above).

Bus LeeTran (☎ 275-8726) buses run throughout Lee County, though not to

Sanibel or Captiva Islands, and they take a while (like an hour and a half from downtown Fort Myers to Fort Myers Beach). The main downtown transfer center is at the corner of Monroe Ave and ML King Jr Blvd. Buses are divided by color, and fare is $1. From the transfer center, orange bus No 50 leaves every hour on the hour to Fort Myers Beach; green bus No 20 runs between the transfer center and the Edison and Ford Estates.

Car Downtown Fort Myers is about a 40-minute drive from Fort Myers Beach; the main connecting artery is Summerlin Rd (Hwy 869), which dead-ends into Colonial Blvd, an east-west running street. Another main connector between downtown and the beach is McGregor Blvd (Hwy 867), which forks away from Summerlin as it heads into downtown Fort Myers and becomes ML King Jr Blvd after it passes beneath US Hwy 41. Both Summerlin Rd and McGregor Blvd intersect with San Carlos Blvd, which continues to Fort Myers Beach and south.

Taxi Taxis in Fort Myers cost $2.70 flagfall, $1.70 for each additional mile. Companies include Yellow Cab (☎ 332-1055), Bluebird Taxi (☎ 275-8294) and Admiralty Taxi (☎ 275-7000).

AROUND FORT MYERS

The natural attractions in the area near Fort Myers are some of the best the state has to offer. From the excellent county parks to shelling on Sanibel and Captiva Islands to the area's gem – the undeveloped splendor of Cayo Costa Island off Pine Island and the Matlacha Pass Aquatic Preserve – you can spend days in nature kayaking or canoeing, watching the alligators, dolphins and manatees and really getting away from it all. On Estero Island, Fort Myers Beach manages to be both a party town (at its Times Square section) and a quiet beach resort (farther south near the Outrigger). Many people make this their base for exploring the area.

Lee County Manatee Park

Scheduled to open just after we went to press, Lee County Manatee Park (☎ 432-2004) is the newest Lee County park. There will be a manatee-viewing platform, picnic shelters, guided viewing programs and an 'Eco-Torium' with manatee displays and information. The park is along the Orange River off of Hwy 80, about eight miles east of downtown Fort Myers and about 1½ miles east of I-75 exit 25.

The park's hours are 8 am to 5 pm in winter and 8 am to 8 pm in summer. Admission is free, but there's a parking fee of 75¢ per hour to a maximum of $3 daily.

Corkscrew Swamp Sanctuary

Run by the National Audubon Society, Corkscrew Swamp Sanctuary (☎ 657-3771) is teeming with wildlife, including alligator, deer and over two hundred species of birds. The swamp is the world's largest subtropical-growth bald-cypress forest, and there's a two-mile-long boardwalk trail through the center of the action. The preserve is located northeast of the city of Bonita Springs; take I-75 to exit 17 (south of Bonita Springs) and go east on Hwy 846; follow the signs and the jig to the left.

The sanctuary is open daily: from December to April from 7 am to 5 pm, May to November from 8 am to 5 pm. Admission is $6.50 for adults, $5 for students, $3 for children aged six to 18.

Babcock Wilderness Adventures

A swamp buggy ride billed as an eco-tour (see the Everglades section for a discussion on swamp buggies and their effect on the environment), Babcock's Wilderness Adventures (☎ 338-6367, 800-500-5583) runs very popular nature tours through the enormous Crescent B Ranch on the Telegraph Cypress Swamp. Naturalist guides narrate the 90-minute tours, which promise alligators, panther, deer, wild turkey and boar. Reservations are required; the cost is $17.95 for adults, $9.95 for children. The ranch is northeast of North Fort Myers; take I-75 to exit 26 and take Hwy 78 east, then take Hwy 31 north for six miles.

Fort Myers Beach

Except for the beach, which is nice, a ton of hotels and condos and a few energetic bars, there isn't much here. But anyone who thinks that the sunsets at Key West are the bee's knees should get a gander at these. A great sunset celebration, and one far more genuine than the circus in Key West, is at the tiki bar at the Outrigger Beach Resort (see below), where the giant horn is blown by a different lounge lizard each night at the moment the sun disappears.

If you want turmoil, head to the **Times Square** area, a party area surrounding the Estero Island side of the Sky Bridge, which connects it to San Carlos Island and the mainland. Otherwise, prepare for broiling yourself in the sun, drinking, parasailing and scootering around.

Orientation & Information Estero Island is about a 40-minute drive southwest from downtown Fort Myers. It's a seven-mile long sliver of an island; the main drag – actually the *only* drag – is Estero Blvd. Estero Blvd eventually leads across another bridge to Lover's Key State Recreation Area (see below), Bonita Beach and US Hwy 41 – the Tamiami Trail.

The Greater Fort Myers Beach Chamber of Commerce (☎ 454-7500, 800-782-9283), 17200 San Carlos Blvd (about a mile north of the sky bridge to the beach), has a decent collection of pamphlets, handouts and menus. They can also help with hotel bookings and provide you with a voluminous list of time-share and rental condos along the beach.

If you need to do laundry, the Mid-Island Laundry and Car Wash (☎ 463-7452) is near the Outrigger Resort (see below). The little automatic car wash is right outside the laundry.

Places to Stay & Eat Note that there's camping not far south of here at the Koreshan State Historic Site and at Wood smoke (see Koreshan below). The only campground that's on the beach proper is the *Red Coconut RV Resort & Campground* (☎ 463-7200), 3001 Estero Blvd, between

Lovers Lane and Donora Blvd. They have sites in four rows on the beach itself, and many more on the 'park' side, across Estero Blvd. Parkside tent sites are $23.50/34 in low/high season; beach sites are $39 to 48/43 to 53.

The very friendly folks at *San Carlos RV Park* (☎ 466-3133), 18701 San Carlos Blvd (right before the bridge between the mainland and San Carlos Island), have tent and RV/van sites with electricity and water for $20/26 in low/high season. They also rent mobile homes by the week: they're $325/400 to 450.

There are hundreds of practically identical small motels in the $30 to 50 range; we stayed at the *Outrigger Beach Resort* (☎ 463-3131), 6200 Estero Blvd, to recuperate from a long, long journey and thought it worth the extra expense. Efficiencies in low/high season are $70 to 95/80 to 95, deluxe and gulf-front efficiencies are $95 to 135/115 to 135. Their beachfront tiki bar has great sunset celebrations. Several chains are represented here as well, including Best Western's *Pink Shell Resort* (☎ 463-6181) at 275 Estero Blvd (which isn't bad at all), *Ramada Beachfront Resort* (☎ 463-6158) at 1160 Estero Blvd, *Holiday Inn Fort Myers Beach* (☎ 463-5711) at 6890 Estero Blvd, and newly remodeled *Grandview All-Suite Resort* (☎ 765-4499) at 8701 Estero Blvd (formerly the Days Inn).

There's slightly less choice when it comes to food. Off the beach, about a mile and a half back toward Fort Myers at 17943 San Carlos Blvd, the *Split Rail* (☎ 466-3400) is a dependable source for breakfast ($2.75 to 4.95) and a weird mix of good Greek, Mexican and American food. Order Greek salads for $5.25, souvlaki for $5.95, Mexican beef burritos for $4.95, American grilled chicken breast for $7.50 and blackened rib-eye steak for $9.95.

Just by the sky bridge, get your German up at *Düsseldorf's on the Beach* (☎ 463-5251), 1113 Estero Blvd. Though it's known more for its beer – over a hundred kinds – and oom-pah-pah atmosphere than for its food, its meals are cheap (for the area) and good: a German sausage sampler or the Kassler Rippchen (smoked pork chop either fried or boiled in sauerkraut), both served with German potato salad, kraut and German bread, are $6.59. Sandwiches run $3.99 to 4.79, and a bratwurst, knockwurst or Polish kielbasa plate is $3.99.

Locals say great things about *Snug Harbor Seafood Restaurant* (☎ 463-4343), also right at the foot of the sky bridge, which does crab cakes or broiled chicken breast for $10.95, and broiled or fried grouper or shrimp scampi for $13.95.

Getting There & Away If you're driving from downtown Fort Myers, take McGregor Blvd to San Carlos Blvd and follow that over the sky bridge. From the south on US Hwy 41, turn west on Bonita Beach Rd at the southern end of Bonita Springs.

By bus, orange bus No 50 leaves the downtown Fort Myers transfer center every hour on the hour. The fare is $1.

Getting Around A tram runs between the Pier (opposite the sky bridge) and Bowditch Point Regional Park at the northwestern end of the island all the way southeast to Villa Santini Plaza at the 7000 block of Estero Blvd. The tram costs 25¢ and runs about every half hour from around 7 am

to around 9 pm. At Villa Santini Plaza you can catch a second tram that runs south between Fort Myers Beach and Bonita Beach, past Lover's Key.

Lover's Key State Recreation Area
Lover's Key (☎ 597-6196) is a state recreation area between Fort Myers Beach and Bonita Beach; there's a wooden walkway and bridge from the parking area across Inner Key out to the Gulf beach at Lover's Key itself. It's quieter than Fort Myers Beach to the north, but that's about it. It's open sunrise to sunset. Admission is $3.25 per carload, $1 for pedestrians and bicyclists; follow Estero Blvd straight south, the park's on the right.

Koreshan State Historic Site
The settlement of the Koreshan Movement is now a state historic site (☎ 992-0311) on US Hwy 41 at 8661 Corkscrew Rd, Estero, with access to the Estero River Canoe Trail. The Koreshans, led by Cyrus R Teed, were a religio-scientific movement that settled in the area in 1893 to build a New Jerusalem (see sidebar).

In 1961, the last four Koreshans donated the group's 305 acres of land to the state of Florida in exchange for a promise to maintain the buildings of the settlement in

SOUTHWEST

The Koreshans

Inspired by a vision, Cyrus R Teed changed his name to Koresh (Hebrew for Cyrus, 'the anointed of God', and with no connection to the ill-fated movement lead by David Koresh in Texas). The Koreshans believed, among other things, that while the earth was indeed round, it was concave, not convex; humankind lived inside the earth and viewed the solar system within it. Under this theory (they never argued the belief that the earth was 25,000 miles in circumference) that would have placed the sun – at the center of the earth – about 4000 miles from the inner crust on which people lived.

While a lot of pseudo-scientific mumbo-jumbo involving the use of a 'Pullman-built rectilineator' was used to explain this theory, the Koreshan Unity Foundation (see description in text) explains that the religious foundation for the theory was that the universe was God's greatest creation: talk in scientific circles of a 'limitless universe' disturbed the group, which felt that to confine the universe to a fixed area was to define it in their terms.

Their religion was based (as was the Shakers') around a biune God (one of male and female essences), and adherents practiced community of goods and effort and a restricted form of celibacy. To simply join the cooperative effort, members could maintain a family; to join the advanced ecclesia, and be allowed to live within the confines of the settlement, members had to impart their personal property and live a celibate life. ■

perpetuity. The last Koreshan died in 1982.

Inside the park stand the remains of the settlement, including such buildings as the members' cottage, machine shops and the art hall. In winter, rangers conduct campfire programs around the campfire ring, and there are slide programs every week.

The park is open from 8 am to sunset every day; admission is $3.25 per carload or $1 for bicyclists and pedestrians.

Canoeing The Estero River Canoe Trail passes through the northern end of the park, and you can rent canoes here for $3.18 an hour or $15.90 for five or more hours, including tax. The canoe trail is about 1½ miles upriver and 1¾ miles downriver to its junction with Estero Bay.

Mound Key Mound Key is an interesting destination if you're canoeing the Estero River; it's a mile into Estero Bay from the junction of the river (about 4¼ miles from the Koreshan site). Surrounded by forests of mangroves, the island is almost totally made of mounds of discarded oyster shells left by Calusa Indians who lived in the area. These folks ate a *lot* of oysters: many of the mounds that make up the key (which supported at least a thousand homes) are over 30 feet high! The area is now a state archeological site.

On the largest of the mounds was the town of Calos, which researchers think was the capital of the Calusa Indians' region. In 1567, Jesuit missionaries founded the San Antonio de Carlos mission on one of the mounds – the Calusa were not amused and the mission failed.

You can paddle here from the Koreshan site; tides are generally calm enough, but check with rangers before you make the trip. It's illegal to remove any of the shells, as it's a working archaeological site.

Camping There are 60 tent and RV sites (back-in, not pull-through) in the Koreshan site's Scrub Oak Camping Area. There is thick vegetation between the sites for privacy, and each has a picnic table, ground fire ring and hookups for water and electricity. Sites are $10.90 without hookup, $13.02 with, including tax. There are hot showers and a washer and dryer ($1 each). You must return to the campsite before sundown.

Reservations are essential on holiday weekends or when there are scout troops staying; reservations are accepted (with a Visa or MasterCard) up to 60 days in advance.

If they're full up at Koreshan, the nearest commercial camping in the area is *Woodsmoke Camping Resort* (☎ 267-3456), where tent sites are $17.50, RV sites $23.44 in summer, and both are 'about' $29 in winter. It's just south of San Carlos Park, about two miles north of Estero and nine miles south of Fort Myers at 19551 S US Hwy 41 (Tamiami Trail).

Getting There & Away The site is on the west side of US Hwy 41 (Tamiami Trail); from I-75 take exit 19, which becomes Corkscrew Rd. Go west two miles; Corkscrew Rd ends at the main park entrance. From Fort Myers Beach, take Estero Blvd south past Bonita Beach and over to US Hwy 41; go north to Corkscrew Rd, then west.

Koreshan Unity Foundation, Inc

Across the street from the Koreshan State Historic Site, the Koreshan Unity Foundation, Inc (☎ 992-2184), 8661 Corkscrew Rd (at the corner of US Hwy 41), is a continuation of the original colony preservation society. The foundation no longer offers lectures, but it holds two festivals a year. The first is in April; it's a lunar festival held on the weekend closest to the 11th, the birthday of Annie Ordway, the first president of the Koreshan Unity (1903). The second festival is in October, on the weekend closest to the 18th, the birthdate of Cyrus Teed. The celebrations include musical events and guest speakers on men's and women's roles in society today and at the turn of the century, communitarianism and other topics.

They've recently built a theater on their grounds and are planning concerts and activities in the future; call for what's up when you visit.

Tribute to songwriter Stephen Foster

From Tampa to Georgia

BILL BACHMANN

Suwannee River Bridge

The tranquil and glassy Steinhatchee River

Palm Beach doorway

BILL BACHMANN

Sunshine Skyway Bridge over Tampa Bay

Steinhatchee River

Oldest wooden schoolhouse, St Augustine

KENNETH DREYFUSS

Bloomin' bougainvillea

Garden Gate, Key West

Sanibel & Captiva Islands

The southernmost Gulf barrier islands, Sanibel and Captiva are excellent day trips, though staying in the luxury resorts out here is prohibitively expensive. Everyone's here for the beaches, which are both glorious and one of the Western Hemisphere's best spots for shelling – as in shelling so good and so diverse that they've even got an enormous shell museum. But there's also good kayaking and canoeing around the islands and in the JN 'Ding' Darling National Wildlife Refuge.

Orientation & Information Unless you're coming here by boat or helicopter, there's only one way to get here: the Sanibel Causeway (Hwy 867), which has a $3 toll for cars, $1 for motorcycles. At the end of the causeway, follow Periwinkle Way to its end, at Tarpon Bay Rd (look for the post office), turn right, and then left onto Sanibel-Captiva Rd; the shell museum will be on the left-hand side, and the entrance to 'Ding' Darling Refuge on the right. It seems to take forever and you'll think you've missed it, but you haven't.

The Sanibel Island Chamber of Commerce (☎ 472-6374), 1159 Causeway Blvd, hands out pamphlets and information; it also operates a trolley on the island, which runs between the chamber and the South Seas Plantation from December to April.

Bailey Matthews Shell Museum This museum (☎ 395-2233), 3075 Sanibel-Captiva Rd, is dedicated to just what it says. It's a serious effort: upstairs is a library (with everything from a *Seashore Coloring Book* to *Synopsis Omnium Methodica Molluscorum Generum*) and a computerized research center with an enormous conchological data bank and a 35-mm slide collection. Downstairs, the main exhibition halls have a huge range of exhibits, including displays on the edible scallops of the world, on the medicinal – and poisonous – properties of mollusks, on shells from around the world – including the Pacific Northwest, Japan, Saudi Arabia and South Africa – and on shells in tribal art. There's a very neat sculpture – made from shells, of course – called *Horse Racing at a State Fair* by Rolland McMurphy. At the front desk is a basket of shells collected from the island – grab a few on your way out.

The museum's open Tuesday to Sunday from 10 am to 4 pm, closed Monday. Admission is $4 for adults, $2 for children aged eight to 16.

JN 'Ding' Darling National Wildlife Refuge

Named for cartoonist Jay Norwood 'Ding' Darling, an environmentalist who helped establish over 300 sanctuaries across the USA, this wildlife refuge (☎ 472-1100) is a fascinating area at the northern end of Sanibel Island. Home to a huge variety of fish and wildlife, including alligators, green-backed and night herons, red-shouldered hawks, spotted sandpipers, roseate spoonbills, pelicans and anhinga, the refuge has canoe trails, a five-mile wildlife drive (on which you can take a naturalist-narrated tram tour), alligator observation platforms and walking trails. Note that shelling is prohibited here.

The Wildlife Drive tram tours (☎ 472-8900) leave from the parking lot at the visitor center on Monday to Thursday and Saturday at 10.30 am and 2 pm and on Sunday at 2 pm.

Get interpretive materials at the visitor center, which is open Saturday to Thursday from 9 am to 4 pm, closed Friday. The Wildlife Drive is open to bicycles and pedestrians Saturday to Thursday from sunrise to sunset. Cars are allowed in from 7.30 am. Admission is $4 per carload, $1 per family walking or bicycling.

Canoeing & Kayaking On Captiva Island, just north of the refuge, the 'Tween Waters Marina (☎ 472-5161) at the 'Tween Waters Inn rents canoes for $7 an hour, $12 for four hours and $17 for eight hours, no reservations necessary. It's close enough to the refuge to paddle down from the marina, but ask if you'll be fighting heavy winds or tides, or check the *News-Press* weather section. Even if you stay around the resort, you can zip right across to Buck Key where there are two canoe trails. They also offer 3½-hour guided kayak tours at Buck Key for $35. The resort is at the southern end of Captiva Island – huge signs are everywhere and you can't miss it.

On the grounds of the refuge, Tarpon Bay Recreation (☎ 472-8900), 900 Tarpon Bay Rd on Sanibel Island, rents canoes and kayaks for $20 for two hours, $5 each additional hour. They offer group trips through the refuge for $20 for adults, $10 for children under 12, or private tours for $35 per person.

Beaches & Shelling The main beaches are Bowman's Beach ($3 parking), Sanibel Lighthouse (75¢ an hour), Turner Beach (free but limited parking) and Gulfside Park (75¢ an hour). You can't go into the wooden **Sanibel Island Lighthouse**, but there's a fishing pier there and parking lots. The East, Middle and West Gulf Drives are the Gulf beach accesses.

There are about 160 varieties of shells on those beaches, and though it's so cliché it's embarrassing, people around here really *do* refer to the act of bending over to pick them up as the 'Sanibel Stoop'.

The best time to go out is at low tide, preferably low tide in winter, and the best time of all is low tide in winter after a storm. There will invariably be other people out there looking with you, and locals will cheerfully offer advice and counsel on strategy. But just walking down the beach, you'll run into beautifully colored shells without even trying.

Anything that's dead is yours for the taking, but make certain that nothing's living inside your shell – taking live shells or sand dollars, sea stars or urchins is grounds for a $500 fine *and* up to 60 days in jail for the *first offense*. That same penalty applies to any shells taken from the 'Ding' Darling Refuge, where shelling is prohibited. These people are incredibly serious about enforcement, so use your head.

If you're really interested in shelling, the Bailey Shell Museum has tons of pamphlets, and they may still have copies of Joan Scribner's *Shelling Basics*, which des- cribes all the varieties of shells and techniques for collecting, cleaning, preserving and showing them.

Places to Eat *Loco's Island Grill & Cantina* (☎ 395-0245), 975 Rabbit Rd, has great Mexican food, and live bands stop in now and then. Happy hour is Tuesday to Sunday from 4 to 7 pm, and appetizers like nachos and chili with cheese are $5.95, quesadillas or jalapeño poppers are $5.25, and main courses average about $8. Next door is the *Sanibel Island Comedy Club* (☎ 472-8833), which if you stick around can definitely be worth it. They get headline acts like Killer Beaz, Kevin Nealon, and comedians who write for folks like Dave Letterman (Jeff Stilson and Jim Hannah) and Howard Stern (Pat Godwin). Admission ranges from $10 to 20.

The Bubble Room (☎ 472-5558), 15001 Captiva Drive, has got to be seen to be believed: the place is packed with memorabilia from the 1930s and '40s, flashing lights, movie photos, bric-a-brac and hoohas. It's worth a stop even if you just have a drink – it's totally insane. Appetizers include She Crab soup (crab and cream) for $4.95 and four large Gulf shrimp in garlic butter for $6.95; main courses are expensive, though, averaging from $15 to 25. But fill up on appetizers and have a drink or two.

Gilligan's (☎ 472-0606), 2163 Periwinkle Way, is a very casual place with a raw oyster bar – $3.25 a half dozen, $5.95 a dozen – and sandwiches from $5.95 to 7.95, big salads from $2.25 to 7.95 and seafood entrees from about $9 to 15. Another casual place is *The Lazy Flamingo* (☎ 472-6939), which has a great raw oyster bar – $3.95 a half dozen, $6.95 for a bakers dozen (13). They also have smoked fish ($4.95) and sandwiches like mesquite-grilled grouper ($7.95) and grilled chicken breast ($5.95). They have two locations: on Sanibel at 1036 Periwinkle Way and on Captiva at 6520C Pine Ave.

Pine Island & Matlacha Pass

Just north of Captiva Island, the gorgeous barrier islands that surround the pristine

Matlacha (mat-la-SHAY) Pass Aquatic Preserve can be explored by kayak and canoe. The preserve, along with the Pine Island Sound Aquatic Preserve, covers 90 sq miles and over 70 miles of coastline, and it's made up of islands, mangrove swamps, lagoons and bays.

Pine Island, at 17 miles long, is the largest in the area, and while it's officially broken up into several communities, everyone calls the whole thing Pine Island. It's been spared development by its location and by Florida state height and density zoning limits.

The communities include the tiny fishing village of Matlacha, with a permanent population of between 300 and 600; Bokeelia (bow-KEEL-ya), at the northern tip of Pine Island, which is the commercial fishing center and home of the *Tropic Star* (see below); and Pine Island Center, the commercial district at the center of the island.

The island was inhabited by Calusa Indians from 300 to 1513 AD, when Ponce de León landed here – after which the Indians who weren't killed by soldiers were killed by disease.

Orientation Pine Island is due west of North Fort Myers, and there's no public transportation out to the area. By car take either US Hwy 41 north to Pine Island Rd (Hwy 78) or I-75 north to exit 26 (Bayshore Rd, which becomes Pine Island Rd). Follow Pine Island Rd west till you get there; you'll pass Matlacha and Little Pine Island.

Gulf Coast Kayak The absolute best way to see the entire area is through the very friendly folks at Gulf Coast Kayak (☎ 283-1125, see Online Services appendix), 4882 NW Pine Island Rd on Little Palm Island, Matlacha. Run by Frank Stapleton and Cindy Bear, two experienced and friendly nature lovers (Cindy teaches environmental education in Lee County schools), they offer several different tours year round as well as kayak and canoe rentals for self-guided trips.

Every day except Monday they run four-hour Matlacha Pass Excursions through the area. From October to April they leave at 9 am and from May to September at 8 am; the cost is $35/17 for adults/students.

On Tuesday and Thursday in winter they offer a 2 pm, two-hour tour through the area for $19/9. And on at least two Fridays a month in winter they run a TGIF tour to watch the sunset. It's a 2½-hour trip with snacks, drinks and champagne toasts; the cost is $25/10.

There are lots of other trips and special events throughout the year, so you should call for information.

Canoe and single kayak rentals are $17/25 for a half/full day; double kayaks are $19/35. You can take these canoes for several days at a time if you want; it's great for camping trips to Cayo Costa State Park (see below). Reservations are recommended.

Places to Stay & Eat There are two camping options in the area; *Fort Myers/Pine Island KOA* (☎ 283-2415, 800-992-7202) has tent sites for $22/25.95 in summer/winter; RV and van sites with full hookups are $29/32.95. Kamping Kabins are $39.95 year round. From I-75, take exit 26 and go west on Hwy 78 to the first four-way stop sign, turn left, and the KOA is five miles down Stringfellow Rd on the left-hand side. The other option is at Cayo Costa (see below), but there are a couple of good motel options – and some are more on the water than others: the *Bridgewater Inn* (☎ 283-2423), 4331 Pine Island Rd, is a way-cool building built directly on a pier. It has motel rooms and five large efficiency apartments; the two corner efficiencies have huge sliding-glass doors that look out directly onto the aquatic preserve and the waterfront, and dolphins and manatees swim by regularly. Rooms run from $39 to 79 in summer, $49 to 89 in winter, and there's a sandwich shop on the property.

Knolls Court (☎ 283-0616), 4755 Pine Island Rd, has efficiencies in summer for $50/60 on the roadside/waterside, in winter for $60/70. All rentals are weekly by arrangement.

There are a bunch of restaurants in walking distance of the motels, all along

SOUTHWEST

Pine Island Rd NW: they are mom-and-pop operations in Florida cracker decor, with a low tourist tolerance and consistently reliable seafood and burgers.

If you're here, a stop at *Burger Hut* (☎ 283-3993), 4590 Pine Island Rd, should be mandatory if only for the experience: it's a '50s-style diner, with burgers made from meat that's ground fresh every day. It's open daily year round from 7.30 am to midnight – Burger Jim, the owner, who cooks and cleans everything personally, hasn't had a day off in 15 years. A quarter-pound hamburger is $2.45; $2.50 with cheese.

The best pool table and biggest local hangout is *Mulletville* (☎ 283-5151), 4597 Pine Island Rd. The *Matlacha Oyster House* (☎ 283-2544), 3930 Pine Island Rd, does seafood specials for lunch and dinner every day: at lunch, grouper fingers are $7.50 and seafood stuffed flounder is $7.95, and at dinner, poached salmon is $13.50 and seafood strudel is $14.50.

Sandy Hook Fish & Rib House (☎ 283-0113), 4875 Pine Island Rd, is as good as its name: baby back ribs are $9.50, and combination platters like grouper and baby back ribs run around $13.95. It has excellent views of the water.

Cayo Costa State Park

West of Pine Island and north of Captiva Island, Cayo Costa Island is home to Cayo Costa State Park (☎ 964-0375), one of the largest completely undeveloped barrier islands in Florida.

The park offers incredible shelling, swimming, kayaking and canoeing opportunities, and Atlantic bottle-nosed dolphins live in the area and frolic just offshore. This

Bottle-nosed dolphins are commonly spotted around Cayo Costa Island.

is probably one of the best deals in the state in terms of getting down to the sun and fun of Florida beach life: white sand, sabal palms, gumbo-limbo hammocks, clear water and cheap accommodations. The only problems (if you could in any way call them that) are that you have to bring your own food (though cooking and picnic facilities are available) and there are no telephones or hot water in the cabins (though there are sweet-water showers). Tent camping is $13 per night (no reservations required), and cabins (reservations required), which have six bunk beds, cost $20 a night for four people, $5 for each additional person. Bring your own linen, utensils, and definitely insect repellent.

Getting There & Away The island is only reachable by boat. The main dock is on the bay side; rangers run a tram between the island dock and the camping area, or you can walk – it's about a mile from the dock area. Gulf Coast Kayak (☎ 283-1125) rents kayaks (see above) as well as tents and other camping equipment, and they also run guided tours for groups of six or more to the park, which include everything you'll need except a toothbrush and sleeping bag; prices vary depending on length of stay.

The *Tropic Star* (☎ 283-0015) leaves from the Four Winds Marina (☎ 283-0250) in Bokeelia (at the northern tip of Pine Island) every day at 9.30 am for a cruise of the area, including a stop at Cayo Costa (where you can get off and camp) and Cabbage Key Inn (see below). The cruise (or the ferry ride, if that's what you're using it for) costs $19 for adults, $10 for children under 12, roundtrip; if you get off at Cayo Costa and camp, the $19/10 includes your return whenever you get around to coming back. The pickup at Cayo Costa is at 3 pm, and the boat returns to Four Winds at 4 pm.

The other option is a private water taxi; these also leave from Four Winds, and boats hold about six people. The cost is generally $15 per person one-way, $25 roundtrip, with a minimum of $50 each way; try Captain Coleman (☎ 283-1150) or ask the marina for a list of all available boats.

Cabbage Key Inn

The list of luminaries who have stayed at the Cabbage Key Inn (☎ 283-2278) is diverse to the point of weirdness, from Carson-sidekick Ed McMahon to Ernest Hemingway. Built on a Calusa shell-mound, southeast of Cayo Costa, the home was built by writer Mary Rinehart in 1938. The atmosphere is rich-goofy in a '21 Club' sort of way: lots of stuff hanging everywhere and twenty to thirty thousand dollar bills festoon the walls.

The story of the bills – the hotel says – goes like this: in the 1940s, commercial fishermen used to eat here, and when they were feeling fat they autographed a dollar and stuck it to the wall. When they felt broke, they could always yank one down from the wall and buy themselves a bowl of chowder. Today, many guests do the same.

Gulf Coast Kayak (see above) runs lunch tours here from October to May; the price is \$49 for adults, \$29 for students, lunch included. The cheaper (if less original) way to go is aboard the *Tropic Star* (see Cayo Costa above), which also stops here for lunch on their daily cruise.

The Cabbage Key Inn's menu at lunch is darn reasonable – burgers are \$5.75 to 6.95, large salads are \$6.95 to 8.95 and hot steamed shrimp with potato salad and coleslaw is \$6.95. Prices go up at dinner, and if you're not staying here, you'll have to factor in the \$50 minimum for a water taxi (see Cayo Costa above). Appetizers include marinated char-grilled shrimp, shrimp cocktail (\$5.95) or local stone crab for two (\$18.95). Main courses start at \$15.95 for Gulf shrimp on angel hair pasta with scampi sauce, and they include blackened grouper or mahi mahi (\$17.95) or New York strip steak (\$18.95). Key lime pie is \$3.95, and they have a whole bunch of specialty drinks at around \$5.

Spending a night here, in one of their six rooms or six cottages, is cheaper than we would have thought, but reserve early: rooms are \$65, a four-person suite is \$130 and two-bedroom cottages are \$145. On weekends and holidays there's a two-night minimum stay required.

SARASOTA

• *pop 55,000* ☎ *941*

The largest city between Fort Myers and Tampa-St Petersburg, Sarasota is an affluent but welcoming place with some first-rate attractions, great beaches, good restaurants, lots of live music and one of the best bookstores in the south.

Many travelers skip it because it looks too expensive, but appearances can be deceptive. While you can pay as much as you want for luxury around here, you can stay in the area pretty cheaply without too much inconvenience, and there are heaps of restaurants doing great and inexpensive food. The Mote Marine Laboratory is a must-see tourist attraction, as is the Ringling home and museum – John Ringling's circus may have made him famous, but he also gathered one heckuva fine art collection. And Lido Beach offers some primo broiling territory.

We were wondering why everyone was being so nice to us here: 'Yes, Mr Selby, right away.' 'No, Mrs Selby, but I'd be happy to help you find it.' And then we noticed the signs everywhere: 'Selby Library', 'Selby Gardens', 'Selby Gallery', 'Selby Park'. Sarasota is indeed Selbyville, and we were, for the first time in months, in our element (well, okay, the element of the wealthy Selby family – to which we're not related – that to this day commits random acts of philanthropy throughout the area).

Orientation

The Tamiami Trail (US Hwy 41) zooms north straight as a die from Venice to the southern end of Sarasota, then it zips left near Wood St, follows the southwest curve of downtown and skirts Bay Front Park along the east coast of Sarasota Bay, then slashes northwest toward Tampa. Within town it's called N Tamiami Trail north of Gulf Stream Ave and S Tamiami Trail south of Bay Front Drive.

Downtown Sarasota is a standard grid layout: streets and roads run east-west, avenues and boulevards run north-south. Downtown is bordered on the north by 10th St, on the south by S Tamiami Trail, on the

SOUTHWEST

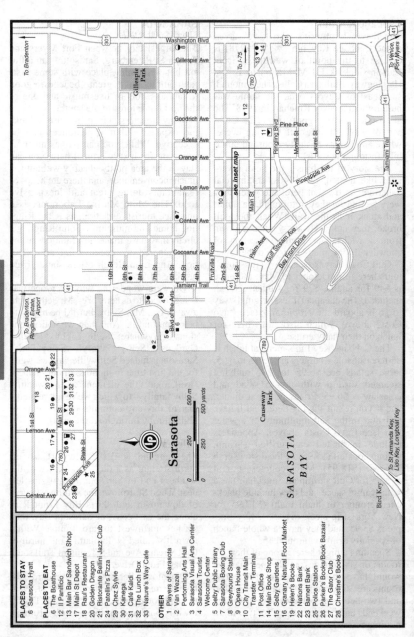

SARASOTA BAY

Sarasota

To St Armands Key,
Lido Key, Longboat Key

Bird Key

Causeway
Park

To Bradenton,
Ringling Estate,
Airport

To Bradenton

To Venice,
Fort Myers

Tamiami Trail

To I-75

PLACES TO STAY
6   Sarasota Hyatt

PLACES TO EAT
6   The Boathouse
12 Il Panificio
13 Main Bar Sandwich Shop
17 Main St Depot
18 Raul's Restaurant
20 Golden Dragon
21 Ristorante Bellini Jazz Club
24 Patelini's Pizza
29 Chez Sylvie
30 Kanega
31 Café Kaldi
32 The Lunch Box
33 Nature's Way Cafe

OTHER
1   Players of Sarasota
2   Van Wezel
    Performing Arts Hall
3   Sarasota Visual Arts Center
4   Sarasota Tourist
    Welcome Center
5   Selby Public Library
7   Sarasota Boxing Club
8   Greyhound Station
9   Opera House
10 City Transit Main
    Transfer Terminal
11 Post Office
14 Main Book Shop
15 Selby Gardens
16 Granary Natural Food Market
19 Helen's Books
22 Nations Bank
23 Barnett Bank
25 Police Station
26 Parker's Books/Book Bazaar
27 The Gator Club
28 Christine's Books

west by N Tamiami Trail, and on the east by N Washington Blvd (Hwy 301). The main drag downtown is Main St, which runs northeast from Bay Front Park then due east from Central Ave.

The Ringling Estate, Bellm Cars & Music of Yesteryear and the airport are north of downtown; Myakka State Park is southeast of downtown (see Around Sarasota below). The beach, St Armands Key, Mote Marine Laboratory and Pelican Man's Bird Sanctuary are on Lido Key, west of downtown.

Maps The CVB sells copies of the House of Maps' *Street Map of Sarasota* ($2.50).

Information

Tourist Offices The Sarasota Convention & Visitors Bureau (☎ 957-1877, 800-522-9799) has a Tourist Welcome Center at 655 N Tamiami Trail, and the Sarasota Chamber of Commerce (☎ 955-8187) is at 1551 2nd St. Both hand out reams of pamphlets and information on the area's attractions, included *See Sarasota*, which has a slew of hotel and motel coupons and more. For recorded information on music, jazz and film festivals, call the Sarasota Arts Council's ARTSline at ☎ 953-4636, ext 6000.

Money Barnett Bank has about 10 locations in town; the Barnett Plaza Office is at 240 S Pineapple Ave, and there are branches at St Armands, 30 N Blvd of Presidents; and Siesta Key, 1237 Stickney Point Rd. American Express has two offices: one is at Around the World Travel (☎ 923-7579), 8383 S US Hwy 41, and the other at Key Travel (☎ 388-3975), 540 Ringling Blvd.

Post The main post office is at the corner of Ringling Blvd at Pine Place.

Bookstores Sarasota is good book-hunting country, with several shops on Main St. The Main Bookshop (☎ 366-7653), 1962 Main St, is a fantastic place – one of the best in the state – with four floors of new, remainder and used books, an enormous selection of maps and LP titles, the LP newsletter and a first-rate Florida section. The fourth floor is the bargain section.

Have a cup of free coffee and enjoy the very cool atmosphere (say hi to the cats, Byron and Misha). There are free poetry readings every Wednesday at 8 pm. It's open every day from 9 am to 11 pm.

Other book shops along Main St include Book Bazaar (☎ 366-1373), 1488 Main St, with used and out-of-print books, Christine's Books (☎ 365-0586), 1502 Main St, Parker's Books (☎ 366-2898, 800-247-2321), 1448 Main St, and Helen's Books & Comic Books Shoppe (☎ 955-2989), 1531 Main St.

Libraries The Selby Public Library (☎ 951-5501) is at the western end of Blvd of the Arts (which is 6th St west of US Hwy 41) at No 1000, opposite the Sarasota Hyatt.

Media The main daily is the *Sarasota Herald-Tribune*, which is owned by the New York Times. *Pelican Press* has local news and covers city and county commission meetings. NPR is at 89.7 FM from Tampa, but you can still get it at 90.1 FM from Fort Myers here.

Gay & Lesbian We didn't find a community center, but the *Gay & Lesbian Information Line – Sarasota* (☎ 923-4636) has information on several matters of interest to gay, lesbian and bisexual travelers. The Sun Coast Cathedral Metropolitan Community Church (☎ 484-7068), 3276 E Venice Ave in Venice, holds all-welcome services every Sunday at 11 am. The Southwest Florida Business Guild (☎ 952-0884) meets on the third Monday of the month; call them for more information on gay-owned and -friendly businesses in the area.

Toilets All the beaches have public toilets, and there's one at the Main Book Shop.

Laundry We liked the people at the Colonial Laundry Center (☎ 366-5852), 290 N Lime Ave. Also try Violet Ray Laundry (☎ 954-1348), 2287 Lime Ave.

Medical Services The biggest hospital in the area is Sarasota Memorial Hospital (☎ 917-9000), 1700 S Tamiami Trail.

Ringling Estate

The winter estate of railroad, real estate and circus baron John Ringling and his wife, Mabel, is now open as a museum (☎ 359-5700) at 5401 Bayshore Rd. Ringling and his wife traveled extensively and apparently never came home empty handed: they were avid art collectors, and over the years they built up a collection of works by artists including Cranach, Rubens, Poussin, Hals, Van Dyck and others. Ringling began work on a fine arts museum in the early 1920s, and it was donated to the state of Florida after his death. You can also tour Ringling's home, Cà d'Zan, and the enormous Circus Museum that was built in Ringling's former garage.

The museum and grounds are open every day except Thanksgiving, Christmas and New Year's Day from 10 am to 5.30 pm. Admission to the grounds (including access to the museums and Cà d'Zan) is $8.50 for adults, $7.50 for seniors over age 55. Florida students are admitted free, and admission to the art museum only (not the Circus Museum or Cà d'Zan) is free on Saturday.

Ringling Museum In an enormous and imposing Venetian Gothic and Italian Renaissance building, the John & Mabel Ringling Museum of Art (1929) has a first-rate collection of 17th century, late medieval and Renaissance French, Dutch, Spanish and Baroque paintings, sculptures and tapestries.

The Ringlings opened the museum to the public in 1930 and bequeathed it to the state of Florida in 1936.

It's a wonderful place, and for once we weren't the only people frantically scribbling: dozens of art students make the rounds here regularly. Leave at least two hours to walk through the galleries and the sculpture garden properly.

The 21 galleries run in a horseshoe shape, and the sculpture garden courtyard is in the center. Highlights include several Rubens, including *The Departure of Lot and his family from Sodom* and the massive *The*

Four Evangelists; a late medieval room with several wacky and weird pieces; 16th- and 17th-century Italian rooms, with works by Francesco da Ponte, Bernardo Strozzi and Giovanni Francesco Barbieri's unmissable *The Annunciation*; the 17th-century French room, with Nicolas Poussin's lovely *Ecstasy of St Paul* and Claude Jaquet's pretty intense *Harpsichord* (1652); the large tapestries of the 17th-century Flemish room, especially Justus van Egmont's (designer) and Guillam van Leefdael's (weaver) *The Defeated Pompey Flees from Caesar*; and the Astor rooms, which contain decorative arts, including fans, frames, a Flemish cabinet with scenes from the Old Testament and vases.

There are also rotating exhibits of modern art and the **Asolo Theater** (not to be confused with the Asolo Center for the Performing Arts; see Entertainment, below), a horseshoe-shaped, 300-seat theater that was originally built in the castle of Asolo, Italy, in 1798. In 1930, the theater was dismantled piece by piece to clear the way for a movie theater, and it was bought by the museum from a Venetian antique dealer in 1950. Today it's open only for concerts, films, and special events; contact the museum before you come to see if any are on during your visit.

Cà d'Zan Cà d'Zan (1924-26), said to be 'House of John' in Venetian dialect, was the grand winter home of John and Mabel Ringling. Fronting Sarasota Bay, it's a pretty spectacular combination of Italian and French Renaissance, Baroque, Venetian Gothic and Modern architecture. It's unbelievably lavish; there's a catwalk around the 30-foot-high Court, or living room, on which very fine tapestries rub elbows with folks from Paramus, New Jersey, who are saying 'Oooh . . . Aahh.' The house has a ballroom, dining room, taproom (with vaulted ceilings and stained-glass panels); the ballroom and playroom had their ceilings painted by Willy Pogany, a set designer for the Ziegfield Follies. Upstairs, following the stairs to your left as you enter the house, is John's bedroom, with an eight-piece mahogany bedroom set and an enormous ceiling painting, *Dawn Driving Away the Darkness* by Jacob de Wit. The bathroom contains such necessities as a bathtub hewn from a solid block of Siena marble, which also covers the walls.

You can tour most of the house, but the playroom is closed to the public.

Circus Museum We loved the circus museum, which contains the fascinating Barlow Animated Miniature Circus, original circus wagons, the cannon used to blast the Flying Zacchinis into low orbit, and dozens of circus posters and lots of paraphernalia. Narration near the miniature circus is full of interesting tidbits (though the narrator's voice is like a router). Circus fans will be pleased to know that the spirit of the circus is still alive and kicking in this city, though it is no longer the winter home of Ringling Bros Circus: see the Sarasota Sailor Circus under Entertainment below.

Selby Gallery
The Selby Gallery (☎ 351-4614) is at the Ringling School of Art Design (on ML King Jr Way, just east of 2700 N Tamiami Trail), and it runs rotating exhibitions on contemporary and historical art and design-related works. The gallery is open Monday to Saturday from 10 am to 4 pm when exhibitions are being held (call to see what's on during your stay), closed Sunday and holidays. Admission is free.

Selby Gardens
The Marie Selby Gardens (☎ 366-5730), 811 S Palm Ave, are an 11-acre botanical garden specializing in orchids (they have over 6000) but with a wonderful selection of other botanical attractions. There's a hibiscus garden, an area dedicated to cacti and succulents, a tropical display house, cycad collections, a bromeliad display, a bamboo pavilion, waterfall garden and, our favorite, the tropical food gardens, where everything's edible. There is a Bay Walk Sanctuary here – a boardwalk over red, black and white mangrove (not to be confused with the Sarasota BayWalk, see below).

The gardens are open every day except Christmas from 10 am to 5 pm. Admission is $6 for adults, $3 for children aged six to 11. There are free wheelchairs and strollers available at the ticket office.

Mote Marine Laboratory
One of the USA's premiere organizations for shark study is the Mote Marine Laboratory (☎ 388-4441, 800-691-6683, see Online Services appendix), 1600 Ken Thompson Parkway, just east of the drawbridge between Lido and Longboat Keys. It operates the Mote Marine Aquarium, an educational museum with programs for children and adults.

Volunteers expertly guide you through the museum, where you'll see sea turtles (along with photos of sea turtles hatching), Florida lobsters, skates, nurse sharks (and explanations of cancer research using sharks and skates), a lot of shark jaws and a 135,000-gallon shark tank containing bull sharks, barracuda and grouper. There's also a 1000-gallon touch-tank filled with creepy things like horseshoe crabs. The glass is minimizing – look at the tank from above and everything gets bigger. Other exhibits include cutaways of the Myakka River ecosystem, Florida reef systems and lots of other fish tanks, including sea horses, squid, octopi and fireworms. (Don't tap on the glass: it scares the squid and octopi and they ink, poisoning their water.)

There's a small café at the aquarium where you can get a bagel with cream cheese ($1.60), muffins ($1.25) or a tuna sandwich ($4.25).

The aquarium is open daily from 10 am to 5 pm, except on Easter, Thanksgiving and Christmas. Admission is $8 for adults, $6 for kids four to 17 and $3 for kids under four. There's regular bus service from downtown Sarasota (see Getting Around below).

Goldstein Marine Mammal Center
Included in the price of admission to the Mote is a visit to the Ann and Alfred Gold-

Research at the Mote

The Mote's biomedical program concentrates primarily on researching the shark's immune system. The researchers are trying to understand the role that the immune system plays in conferring sharks and skates with a natural resistance to diseases, such as cancer, and they hope to use their findings to advance immunology research in humans. Since a shark's skeletal structure is made of cartilage, not bone, it has no bone marrow, which is the source of immune cells in mammals.

But in the years since the program began in 1990, Mote scientists have established the existence of thymus glands in sharks, skates and rays as well as the existence of T-cells – thymus-derived lymphocytes; discoveries which have encouraged researchers looking for clues to human immune systems. Other research programs include work on coastal resources, fisheries and aquaculture, environmental assessment and enhancement and marine mammals and sea turtles.

The Mote Marine Aquarium is the outreach program run by the laboratory to get the public more involved in its work. ■

stein Marine Mammal Center, which is dedicated to research and rehabilitation of marine mammals. In the visitor's center you can watch on the video screens as volunteers and staff work with injured dolphins. The screens also list the mammal's specific ailments and give an assessment of their progress. The mammal center is across the street from the museum just past the boat yard.

Airport Mote Exhibit If you're flying out of the Sarasota-Bradenton airport, check out the fish tank in Airside B, just before the security gate; it contains spadefish, leopard shark, soldier fish and porkfish. It's an interesting diversion before you catch your plane.

Sarasota BayWalk

The Sarasota BayWalk (☎ 361-6133) is a series of shell paths and boardwalks circling a series of ponds and jutting against red, black and white mangroves. It's next to the Mote Marine Laboratory next to the bridge between Lido and Longboat Keys. Though interesting, it's not exactly naturally occurring: the lagoons were excavated by the Sarasota Bay Natural Estuary Program to different depths to attract different animals.

Pelican Man's Bird Sanctuary

The Pelican Man is Dale Shields, and he established this sanctuary (☎ 388-4444) to rehabilitate injured wildlife; it's just east of the Mote Marine Laboratory on the south side of Ken Thompson Parkway. It's best known for pelicans (90% of all injured pelicans are hurt by fishing line) but all injured animals are helped, and since its inception in 1985 (with a pelican in Shields' bathtub), the sanctuary has grown to the point where it rehabilitates 4000 to 7000 animals a year. To date they have rehabilitated over 60,000 animals.

On display here are about 250 rehabilitated birds, including hawks, owls, storks, pelicans and other indigenous area wildlife; they are animals that have gone through the hospital process but for various reasons are non-releasable. The sanctuary has 10 paid staff who are assisted by 300 volunteers, and the entire organization is run on donations. We urge you to visit (admission is free) and make a donation; 100% of donations go directly to helping injured animals.

The sanctuary is open every day of the year from 10 am to 5 pm.

St Armand's Circle

John Ringling bought this plot of land on St Armand's Key from Charles St Armand with the intention of developing it into exactly what it is today: an upscale shopping center surrounded by posh residences. Ringling employed circus elephants to help haul timber for the construction of the causeway between the mainland and the key, and the area was opened to the public in 1926. Today, St Armand's Circle (☎ 388-1554) is a shopping center built on a glorified traffic circle, filled with shops too rich for our blood. As far as we're concerned, it's a handy transfer point between buses that head off to the beach (bus No 4) and over to the Mote Marine Laboratory and the Pelican Man's Bird Sanctuary (bus No 18).

Beaches
The area's excellent, white sand beaches are located on barrier islands to the west of town, including Lido Key and Siesta Key. Beaches on Lido Key include Lido Beach and north and South Lido Beaches, on Siesta Key there are Turtle, Siesta and Crescent Beaches. Parking is generally a snap; there are public lots, and there's public transport available from the mainland; see Getting Around below for bus and trolley information and non-repetitive driving directions.

Sarasota Jungle Gardens
We thought this place was so cheesy, so cynical and so reprehensible that it could have been a tourist trap out of a Carl Hiaasen novel. Sarasota Jungle Gardens (☎ 355-5305), 3701 Bayshore Rd, off N Tamiami Trail, represents, to us, the worst side of zoos. We got so angry at the conditions here and the 'who-cares' attitude we experienced from recalcitrant and disinterested staff that we stormed out after seeing the 'Butterflies of the World' collection. Some butterflies had ripped or missing wings and there were some pins stuck in the wall impaling the shattered tatters of remains of butterflies that had obviously been yanked off in a hurry. As we stormed out, we saw two miserable black leopards who were retching, had patches of fur missing and were pacing nervously in their cages.

Admission is $9 for adults and $5 for kids.

Bellm Cars & Music of Yesteryear
Bellm (pronounced bell-em) Cars & Music of Yesteryear (☎ 355-6228), 5500 N Tamiami Trail just south of the airport, is

an interesting place, though we're not certain it's worth the price of admission.

Cars here include a 1905 Rapid Depot Wagon, a '48 Jeepstar, a groovy '68 Volkswagen bus, an '81 DeLorean, and that most sought-after transporter, a 1976 Plymouth Voyager Van – which by extension means that everyone who lives in the city of Weehawken, NJ, could open their own museum. Okay, okay, there are also cool things here, like a 1932 Auburn speedster and a teeny 1955 Metropolitan.

The music room opens on the hour and contains hundreds and hundreds of radios, turntables and other noisemakers. The guided tours looked painfully detailed. We watched as one poor victim had to take it alone! The game room is very fun if you're over 40 – these are the arcade games of your childhood, and anyone who's seen the movie *Big* will recognize the swami (25¢). Some games work, some don't, and no signs let you know not to put your quarter in.

The museum's open every day from 9.30 am to 5.30 pm. Admission is $8 for adults, $4 for kids six to 12, and kids under six or adults over – we *swear* – 89 years are free; a family gets in for $25. You can't miss it as you drive north on US Hwy 41: look for the Flintstone's car outside.

Spanish Point
Spanish Point is a museum and archaeological site (☎ 966-5214) that crams about 4000 years of history into a 1½-hour, mile-long tour. The 31-acre site contains an Indian burial mound, two 1867 pioneer homesteads (with a reconstructed citrus packing plant), and five formal gardens created when the land was part of the winter estate of a Mrs Parker around 1913.

The new visitors center, at 500 N Tamiami Trail, is open Monday to Saturday from 9 am to 5 pm, Sunday from noon to 5 pm. The park itself is open Monday to Saturday from 10 am to 4 pm (with guided tours at 10.30 am and 2.30 pm) and Sunday from noon to 4 pm (guided tours at 12.30 and 2.30 pm). Admission is $5 for adults, $3 for children; on Monday seniors pay only $3.

Places to Stay

It's always cheaper to stay in or just outside of downtown as opposed to on the beaches, but the beach options give good value for the money.

Hotels & Motels

N Tamiami Trail (US Hwy 41) About halfway between the airport and downtown Sarasota on N Tamiami Trail is a spate of motels. The motel run by TCB Properties of Sarasota is set to become a *Super 8 Motel* (☎ 355-9326), 4309 N Tamiami Trail, with predictably Super 8-ish rooms for $19.95/24.95 a single/double year round.

The *Sunset Terrace Resort* (☎ 355-8489, 800-889-4776), 4644 N Tamiami Trail, has studio efficiencies for $34/45 to 55 in summer/winter, two-room suites are $45/55 to 65.

Rainbow Motor Lodge (☎ 355-7616) at 4200 Tamiami Trail N, looks nicer from the outside than it does on the inside; their medium-clean rooms have fridges and run $45 to 50/54 to 66 in summer/winter.

We thought the *Cadillac Motel* (☎ 35-7108), 4021 N Tamiami Trail, was a perfectly reasonable option, with singles/doubles for $26/28 in low season, $50/52 in high season; there's a decent pool, and rooms were very clean and smelled fresh.

Nothing but the price thrilled us about the *Allamanda Motel* (☎ 35-4764), 4014 N Tamiami Trail, with singles/doubles at $23/27 in summer, $49/59 in winter. None of the rooms have private bathtubs and all have yellow, blue and orange doors.

The friendly and family-run *Sundial Motel* (☎ 351-4919), 4108 N Tamiami Trail, is one of the best deals in town. Rooms run $22.95 in low season, $25.95 in mid-season and $45 in high season. It's very clean and safe.

For a few dollars more, try the older but clean *Best Western Golden Host Resort* (☎ 355-5141), 4675 N Tamiami Trail, where the rooms are $44 to 54 in summer, $54 to 64 in December and January and $79 to 89 from February to April. Rates include donuts, juice and coffee in the morning. All the rooms have in-room safes, and some have fridges and coffeemakers.

The newish *Red Carpet Inn* (☎ 355-8861), 8110 N Tamiami Trail, north of the airport, says that most of their rooms are $24.95 except on certain holidays; it sounds like a come-on to us but they say it's legit, so check it out.

Sunshine Motor Lodge (☎ 365-0350), 811 S Tamiami Trail just south of downtown, seemed friendly enough, with efficiencies from $38 to 48 in summer, $68 to 75 in winter. There's a laundry room and free coffee and donuts in the morning. It's popular with businesspeople.

On Lido Key The *Surf View Resort Hotel* (☎ 388-1818, 800-833-1818), 1121 Ben Franklin Drive, has very clean rooms and tons of extras – like free morning breakfast bar, newspaper, bicycles and two-person kayaks, beach chairs, beach mats and free laundry, including detergent and ironing board. Motel rooms are $45/280 a day/week in summer, and $55 to 75/350 to 500 in winter; efficiencies and studio apartments are also available.

The *Gulf Beach Motel* (☎ 388-2127, 800-232-2489), 930 Ben Franklin Drive, has clean motel rooms with fridges for $50/325 a day/week in summer, $60 to 75/395 to 485 in winter. The grounds have barbecue grills and a laundry.

B&Bs On Siesta Key, the *Crescent House* (☎ 346-0857), 459 Beach Rd opposite Beach Access No 8, has a large wooden sun deck and four different themed rooms. Breakfast is scones, orange juice, coffee, tea, muffins, yogurt, fruit and cereal. Rooms are $57 to 85/350 to 525 a day/week in summer, $82 to 110/560 to 735 in winter.

The enormous *Harrington House* (☎ 778-5444) on Anna Maria Key, north of Longboat Key, is about what you'd expect from an excellent beachside B&B: large rooms, good beaches and lots of extras – including kayaks, canoes and bicycles. Many of the rooms have balconies overlooking the water. They have a full hot breakfast that changes daily. Room rates are $89 to 119 on summer weekdays, $119 to 159 on summer weekends and $139 to 189 in winter. Call for directions.

Places to Eat

For the most part, you need look no further than a two-block stretch of Main St for a good place to eat. However, on your way to and from Ringling, a great place to use up your daily saturated fat allowance is *Mel's Drive Through* (☎ 359-2586), 2030 N Tamiami Trail. It's easy to recognize – the place is shaped like a gigantic ice cream cone: hamburgers or cheeseburgers are $1.59, cheese fries $1.50, chili and nachos $1.50 and sundaes $2.09. It's open daily from 11 am to 11 pm.

Patellini's Pizza (☎ 957-6433), 1410 Main St, has excellent New York-style slices ($1.30) and overstuffed calzones ($3.99). We thought this was some of the best pizza in the southwest. A 14-inch pie is $9.99, and do try their white pizza, topped with spinach, tomatoes, garlic, ricotta and mozzarella cheese ($10.99).

Main Bar Sandwich Shop (☎ 955-8733), 1944 Main St, has been here since 1958; they have a large selection of sandwiches and salads from $3 to 5.25. All the ingredients looked and smelled very fresh. *Main St Depot* (☎ 944-3112), at 1 Lemon Ave, is also good for snacks and quick bites, but is better known for its entertainment; see below.

The wonderful *Granary Natural Food Market* (☎ 366-7906), 1451 Main St, has a great salad bar ($3.39 a pound); pre-made sandwiches are in the cooler ($3 to 6). They also sell a huge range of organic fruits and veggies and other health foods.

For Chinese, the *Golden Dragon* (☎ 951-0077), 1537 Main St, has a $4.75 all-you-can-eat lunch buffet, Monday to Saturday from 11:30 am to 2:30 pm. Daily dinner specials are $6.95; other dishes run from $5.75 to 8.75.

For a quick snack or light meal, we only hear good things about *Kanega* (☎ 957-0813), 1528 Main St, where sandwiches run from $5.25 to 5.75, and they have great

hummus and pita ($4.25). A tomato and mozzarella salad is $4.25. They also have live music here (see Entertainment below).

Raul and Bertha Boeras have been serving up Mexican and Cuban food since 1968 here at *Raul's* (☎ 955-1844), 1544 1st St. It's the kind of place in which a dominoes game doesn't look out of place. Very friendly staff and inexpensive food: at lunch, arroz con pollo is $4.95, a southwest burrito $5.50. Dinner entrees come with bread, salad or soup; entrees include trout la russa (with eggs, pimento, parsley and garlic butter) for $8.95, Cuban-style roast pork $8.65.

The very good *Il Panificio* (☎ 366-5570), 1703 Main St, bakes *really* good bread and has a limited range of prepared Italian food. A 20-inch pizza is $10, large focaccia bread (10 to 12 inches) is $6, sandwiches range from $3 to 6 and excellent pastries are $1.75. Closed Monday.

If you just want some coffee and/or pastry, *Café Kaldi* (☎ 366-2326), 1568 Main St, has a large selection of coffees ($1.50 to 3) in a cozy atmosphere. They host a variety of live music (see Entertainment below).

The Lunch Box (☎ 951-2171), 1578 Main St, is a simple place. Breakfast is served till 11 am and runs around $3.25; sandwiches are $3.74 to 5.25, and salads are $2.25 to 3.99. It's open Monday to Friday from 7:30 am to 3 pm.

Nature's Way Cafe (☎ 954-3131), 1572 Main St, is yet another branch of this good health-food chain: sandwiches are $4.50 to 4.75, salads $2.75 to 5.75, vegetable pasta small/large $3.50/4.95, shakes $1.75 to 2.95.

The Boathouse (☎ 953-1234), 1000 Blvd of the Arts, is behind and belonging to the Hyatt, so we expected dainty portions for lots of bucks. Wrong: We had an orgy of nachos with the works for $5.35; other dishes include vegetable lasagne for $6.25 or chicken burgers at $7.10. There are huge portions and good service.

For a treat, hit *Chez Sylvie* (☎ 953-3232), 1526 Main St. It's owned by a French woman with an unbelievable accent who is quick to point out that all the ingredients are 100% organic and free of chemicals, and the meat is from free-range animals. What do we know? The food's very good but it's expensive: dinners start at about $25 and go up from here. They have a large French wine selection.

Entertainment
Asolo Center for the Performing Arts
The performing arts center (☎ 365-9629), 5555 N Tamiami Trail on the Ringling Estate (but not to be confused with the Asolo Theater in the Ringling Museum, about a hundred yards away), is a regional arts theater with plays by their Asolo Theater Company as well as visiting companies. Past performances have included *Jane Eyre, Noises Off* and *The Taming of the Shrew*. Tickets run from $10 to 32 for matinees, $14 to 33 for performances from Tuesday to Thursday and $15 to 34 on Friday and Saturday. Students with ID may show up on the day of the performance may be able to get a $5 ticket. Tours of the center are available (when performances are scheduled) on Wednesday to Saturday at 10, 10.30, 11 and 11.30 am.

Florida West Coast Symphony
This symphony (☎ 953-4252) performs classical concerts at two main venues in Sarasota and one in nearby Bradenton. Guest conductors include David Wroe, Joel Revzen and Eduardo Diazmuñoz, and the orchestra also holds several series, including masterworks (with the full 60-piece orchestra), ensemble performances with the Florida String Quartet, and morning musicales, concerts featuring a variety of ensembles along with coffee and pastries. Tickets range from $8 to 30.

Players Theater
The Players of Sarasota (☎ 365-2494), 838 N Tamiami Trail at 9th St, is a highly regarded nonprofit local theater organization that puts on six performances of well-known plays each year. Last year the list included *Dreamgirls, Sweeney Todd, Annie, Man of La Mancha, West Side Story* and *The Pajama Game*. Tickets for all seats and all performances are $16.

Sarasota Opera
The Sarasota Opera Association (☎ 953-7030) performs operas during their season, from February to March, at the opera house, 61 N Pineapple Ave. Tickets are $10 to 15.

Sarasota Concert Band
The Sarasota Concert Band (☎ 955-6600) plays a wide range of music at their home in Van Wezel Hall, 777 N Tamiami Trail. Music can range from big band to opera, classical to pops.

Gallery Walks
There are free gallery walks through the city's 25 art galleries on the first Friday of the month from November through May. Eight galleries are along Palm Ave and six are on Main St, and a handful are in other areas of downtown's southwestern quadrant.

Sarasota Film Society
Among its year-round offerings, the Sarasota Film Society (☎ 388-2441) holds the annual French Film Festival in November at the Asolo Center on the Ringling Estate (see above). Tickets are $7. Write them for a schedule of the upcoming films at the Asolo Center, 5555 N Tamiami Trail, Sarasota, FL 34243.

Sarasota Sailor Circus
Under a big blue-and-white dome top, the Sarasota Sailor Circus (☎ 361-6350), 2075 Bahia Vista St east off S Tamiami Trail, is nothing short of wonderful. It's made up of students, aged eight to 18, who attend school in Sarasota County. It's an extracurricular school activity, like after-school football, and you'll see high-flying, tumbling, clowning and a 95-piece band. The $250,000 arena was paid for through donations and gate receipts, and the circus performs during its regular season from late March to the end of school and then tours. It's been to Japan, Alaska and around the USA.

Rehearsals are free and open to the public; they're from October to March in the late afternoons beginning at about 4.30 pm. Tickets for performances are $6 in center ring, $5 for other seats.

Sarasota Boxing Club Well, why not? Amateur boxing matches take place at the Sarasota Boxing Club (☎ 362-3547), 532 Central Ave at 6th St, on an irregular schedule. It's a tiny, sweaty youth center that teaches boxing and community responsibility to high school kids to keep them off the street; so it's worth dropping by to show your support. If you're lucky, you'll see Johnny 'Ghetto Blaster' Williams. They try to work in three fights a month – call and see if one's on.

Clubs & Live Music *Ristorante Bellini Jazz Club* (☎ 365-7380), 1551 Main St, does jazz until midnight and blues after midnight on Monday, Friday and Saturday and various live acts on Thursday. There's usually no cover. The restaurant is pretty expensive; most people just go for the music.

Outside *Main St Depot* (☎ 944-3112) at the corner of Lemon and Main St (see Places to Eat, above), an outdoor stage is erected on Friday and Saturday nights and various bands show up and jam.

There's live music every night at the *Gator Club* (☎ 366-5969), 1490 Main St. Rhythm & blues happens Monday to Saturday at 9.30 pm and jazz is heard on Sunday at 8 pm. No cover for any of the shows.

There's occasionally live jazz on Thursday night at *Kanega* (☎ 957-0813), 1528 Main St (see Places to Eat above).

Café Kaldi (☎ 366-2326), 1568 Main St (see Places to Eat above), is a coffeehouse that has acoustic guitar – sometimes rock, sometimes jazz, sometimes classical, never loud – Wednesday to Saturday from 8 pm to midnight. It's a great place to spend an evening talking – too bad they only have skim milk for the coffee.

Getting There & Away
Air Sarasota-Bradenton International Airport (☎ 359-2770) is served by American, Canadian Airlines International, Continental, Delta, Northwest, TWA and USAir. It's located at 6000 Airport Circle; take N Tamiami Trail north to University Ave (near the Ringling Estate), and turn right.

Bus The Greyhound station (☎ 955-5735) is at 575 N Washington Blvd at 6th St. Sample routes are listed below; prices are one way/roundtrip.

Destination	Price	Duration
Miami	$41/81	7 hours
Tampa	$12/23	2 hours
Fort Myers	$16/31	2 hours

Car Sarasota is 60 miles south of Tampa and about 75 north of Fort Myers. The main roads into town are the Tamiami Trail (US Hwy 41) and I-75. The most direct route from I-75 is exit 39 to Hwy 780 west for about eight miles; Hwy 780 turns into Fruitville Rd.

The usual suspects rent cars at the terminal: take University Ave west to US Hwy 41, then south straight into downtown.

Getting Around
To/From the Airport If you're driving from the airport, take University Ave west to US Hwy 41, then south straight into downtown. Bus 10 runs between the airport and downtown via the Ringling Estate; buses are once an hour Monday to Saturday from 6.50 am to 5.50 pm, no service Sunday or major holidays. From the downtown transfer point, buses leave on the same days once an hour from 6.15 am to 6.15 pm. By taxi, count on spending about $10 between the airport and downtown, $17 to the beaches.

Bus Sarasota County Area Transit (SCAT, ☎ 316-1234) runs buses around the area; the fare is 25¢, no transfers. From the main transfer terminal downtown at Fruitville Rd and Lemon Ave, buses 4 and 18 go to St Armand's Key; bus No 4 then goes to south Lido Key and the beach, and bus No 18 goes north on City Island Rd, near the Mote Marine Lab and Pelican Man's Bird Sanctuary, and up to Longboat Key. Bus 4 leaves downtown at 15 past the hour, bus Nos 18 at 45 past. Note that the last bus back from the beach leaves South Lido Key at 6.30 pm. Bus 10 goes between downtown and the Ringling Estate (past Bellm Cars & Music) at 15 minutes past the hour – it stops right at the entrance to the Ringling Estate.

Car Parking's a snap, driving's a breeze, the streets are pretty safe and it's a happy situation for drivers. To get to the beaches, take the John Ringling Causeway (Hwy 789) in front of Golden Gate Point and Bay Front Park west, around St Armand's Circle and then follow Ben Franklin Drive. For the Mote Marine Laboratory and Pelican Sanctuary, turn right off the circle and right again just before the drawbridge to Longboat Key.

Trolley Siesta Key Trolley (☎ 346-3115) runs two routes between the Sarasota, Siesta Key and Lido Keys from Tuesday to Saturday between 9.30 am and 6 pm. The trolleys are 2½-hour guided tours that cost $2 for adults, free for children under six. The trolleys make three loops of the circuit daily; call for specifics, which are plentiful (option 3+pound key gets you to information about this trolley on their hateful automated telephone system).

Taxi For a cab, call either Diplomat Taxi (☎ 355-5155), Green Cab Taxi (☎ 922-6666) or Yellow Cab of Sarasota (☎ 955-3341).

AROUND SARASOTA
Myakka River State Park
Myakka River State Park (☎ 361-6511) is an almost 47-sq-mile wildlife preserve of dense woodlands and prairies about 14 miles from Sarasota. The big draw here is the 70-person airboat ride (rangers say that the airboat, which stays in the upper lake area of the park, does not damage wildlife, but it sure is loud) and a nature tram tour. The airboat rides leave at 10 and 11.30 am and 1.30 and 2.30 pm (no 2.30 pm tour in summer), and the wildlife tram leaves at 1 and 2.30 pm. The cost for the tours is $6 for adults, $4 for kids five to 12.

There are ranger interpretive programs from Thanksgiving to Easter, including courses in beginning birding on Saturday morning, campfire programs on Saturday night and Sunday morning nature walks.

You can also canoe along the Myakka River; the park rents canoes for $10 for two hours, $18 for four and $25 for eight hours.

If you would like to camp, tent and RV/van sites are $11.99 without electricity, $14.13 with, and cabins with kitchens and linens are $55.

Admission to the park is $2 for one person, $4 for two or more. To get here from downtown Sarasota, take US Hwy 41 south to Hwy 72 (Clark Rd) and head east for about 14 miles; the park is on the left-hand side of the road, nine miles east of I-75.

Crowsley Museum & Nature Center Just outside the back gate of the Myakka River Park, the Crowsley Nature Center (☎ 322-1000) is on the grounds of an old Florida homestead. The center offers nature walks, and there are environmentalists on hand to speak about native flora and fauna. You must be on a tour to see the grounds; tours are given at 10 am on Saturday and Sunday only. From Sarasota, take Fruitville Rd east from the interstate for about 11 miles; turn right at the stop sign and in 2½ miles the entrance is on the left hand side of the road.

Venice Beach
Venice Beach, unlike its California counterpart, is a quiet, lovely stretch of white sand along the Gulf Coast, and it happens to be the shark's tooth capital of the state. Shark's teeth have washed up on the shores for centuries due to coastal contours, and finding them is as easy as stepping into the water up to your ankles, reaching over and grabbing a handful of sand after a wave rushes in. If you don't have at least one tooth after 10 minutes, people, even the lifeguards, will make fun of your incompetence as a shark's tooth hunter – they're that plentiful. We found three in 10 minutes but had to leave; on the way out we saw a kid with a *bag*ful.

In August, the annual Shark's Tooth and Seafood Festival is a beachside party with lots of food, games and tooth hunting. If you're really lazy, you can buy bags of teeth at a bunch of roadside stands and in some tourist shops.

Most people come to the beach for day trips only (the City of Venice is, shall we say, mostly harmless), but there are some decent motel deals to be had if you decide to stick around for the night. And if you're driving through and like old-fashioned root beer, don't miss stopping at the Frosted Mug (see Places to Eat, below).

Places to Stay The best deal we found was the clinically spotless yet comfortable and welcoming *Gondolier Inn* (☎ 488-4417), 340 S Tamiami Trail. Run by a registered nurse with a yen for clean comfort, the place has all new mattresses, separate smoking and nonsmoking buildings (the nonsmoking rooms are nicer) *and* lower prices than the competition: singles/doubles are $30/35 in summer, $48 to 58/63 to 72 in winter. Breakfast (two kinds of bagels, three of cereal, juice, coffee, tea and cocoa) is included, and the seventh day is free. Highly recommended.

The Gulf Tide Motel (☎ 484-9709), 708 Granada Ave, also has very clean rooms, with fridge, stove, coffee machines and cable TV, for $49 to 89 in summer, $85 to 139 in winter.

The *Inn at the Beach Resort* (☎ 484-8471, 800-255-8471), 101 Esplanade, has such a complicated seasonal price scale that, for the sake of sanity, we'll say that rooms – depending on when you visit – cost somewhere between $60 and 115, efficiencies between $75 and 145, and suites between $110 and 220.

Places to Eat *PJ's Restaurant & Pizzeria* (☎ 486-1912), 391 S Business 41, does dependable chicken fajitas for $5.75, and good large pizzas (17-inch) for $11.25; sandwiches and hoagies run from $3.25 to 4.15.

Uncle B's Coney Dogs (☎ 484-7243), 602 S Tamiami Trail, does a good breakfast from $1.45 to 4.25. At lunch and dinner, burgers and sandwiches are $2 to 3, and, of course, large hot dogs are $1 to 2.

Papa Chico's (☎ 488-2806), 120 Indian Ave, is open for breakfast and brunch only (Monday to Saturday from 6 to 11 am,

Sunday from 7 am to 2 pm). Eggs with home-fries or grits, toast and coffee are $1.75 to 3.25, omelets and house specials $3 to 4, pancakes $1.75 to 3.25.

Althea's (☎ 484-5187), 220 W Miami Ave, does salads from $2.25 to 5.75; a veggie burger is $4.25, chicken enchiladas $5.95 and hot sandwiches $3.60 to 5.25.

South of Venice, on the way out of town, stop off at the roadside root beer stand *The Frosted Mug* (☎ 497-1611), 1856 S Tamiami Trail. It's been here since 1957 and serves real frosted mug root beer, and even root beer floats, for $1/1.90. For the uninitiated, a float is a mug of root beer with a scoop of vanilla ice cream floating on top, and root beer is a traditional American soda that some love and some say tastes like carbonated toothpaste – there's no accounting for taste. Even if you hate root beer, they do an excellent fish sandwich for $4 and a very good veggie burger for $2, along with the standard burgers, fries and dogs. Definitely worth a stop, if just for the ambiance.

Getting There & Away By car, take US Hwy 41 south from Sarasota for about 25 miles and turn west to the beach. Parking at the lots there is free. Greyhound has three buses a day between Sarasota and Venice (35 minutes, $7 one-way, $13 roundtrip).

Tampa-St Petersburg

The Tampa-St Petersburg area is becoming one of the hottest tourist draws in the southern section of Florida. St Petersburg has three excellent museums that together rival anything the state has to offer. St Pete Beach and, especially, Clearwater offer sunny, white sand beaches that are great for relaxing and shelling; the Gulf islands around Clearwater make for superb kayaking and canoeing. Tampa also has several high-quality museums and attractions, with the revitalization of the historic – and now very hip – Ybor City district at its heart.

Further north, the mermaid shows at Weeki Wachee Springs are an interesting

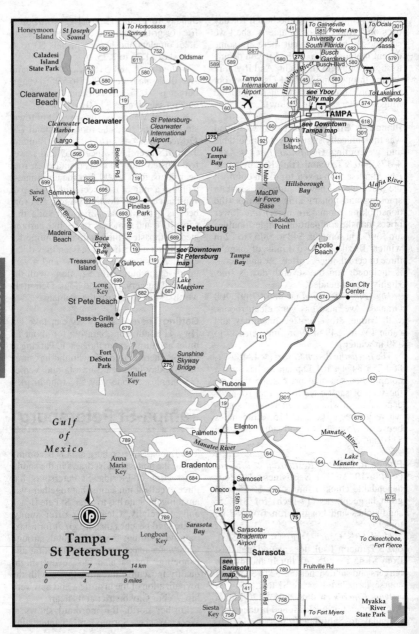

day trip, or visit Homosassa Springs State Park for a close-up look at some of Florida's wildlife. The tourist trap of Tarpon Springs is less than an hour away, but we consider it a waste of time: a once quaint town now entirely made up of tourist shops, junk stands, crap-stalls, expensive parking lots and exhibits on the sponge industry that are cheesy and overpriced – as is everything else.

ST PETERSBURG
• *pop 238,629* ☎ *813*

St Petersburg is in the middle of a rejuvenation, at the center of which is a collection of museums that together form what may be the state's cultural powerhouse. The St Petersburg Fine Arts Museum has one of the finest collections in the state; the Dali Museum is the largest collection of that artist's works outside Spain; and the Florida International Museum's blockbuster rotating exhibitions have brought St Petersburg to national attention with groundbreaking international shows like Treasures of the Tsars, Splendors of Egypt and now, Alexander the Great.

Orientation
St Petersburg is a typically sprawling southwest Florida town. Though it's not as spread out as Fort Myers, it's still a good 20-minute to half-hour drive to the beach in the best of traffic. St Petersburg is about 20 miles southwest of Tampa across Old Tampa Bay; St Pete Beach is about 10 miles southwest of downtown St Petersburg.

The city is oriented on the ever-familiar grid: avenues run east-west and streets and boulevards run north-south. The north-south dividing line is Central Ave, and 34th St (Hwy 19) is the east-west divider, though people usually ignore the east-west designation. The directional indicator is placed after the street, and street numbers indicate cross avenues, so the Greyhound station (☎ 898-1496) at 180 9th St N, would be at 3rd Ave S between Arlington and Burlington. Avenues count upward away from Central Ave, so 1st Ave N is one block north of Central, and 1st Ave S is one block south.

Downtown St Petersburg is the area roughly bordered by the bay at the east, ML King Jr Blvd (9th St) at the west, 10th Ave N at the north and 17th Ave S at the south.

Maps The usual suspects, AAA, Dolph and Rand McNally, all print maps to the area; the St Petersburg Chamber of Commerce gives out a Dolph Map that's excellent.

Information
Tourist Offices The St Petersburg/Clearwater Area Convention & Visitors Bureau (☎ 582-7892) is the best source for advance information, though their location in the ThunderDome, 1 Stadium Drive, is a little inconvenient for dropping in. They run a visitor line (☎ 800-345-6710), where you can get area information, order a visitors guide, make hotel reservations and more.

For pamphlets, city maps and coupon magazines, the St Petersburg Area Chamber of Commerce (☎ 821-4715), 100 2nd Ave N, is the best place; it also has information booths at the Pier and at 2001 Ulmerton Rd.

Money Barnett Bank has branches downtown at 3100 Central Ave and 6201 Central Ave. American Express is represented by Shouppe Bowen Travel (☎ 894-0623), 100 4th St S.

Post The open-air post office (☎ 323-6516), 76 4th St N, is the most convenient in downtown (see the Postal Museum below). The main post office is at 3135 1st Ave N.

Bookstores Haslam's Book Store (☎ 822-8616), 2025 Central Ave, has a good Florida section, a midsize LP book selection and new and remainder books in addition to their core used-book selection.

Attic Bookshop (☎ 344-2398), 6601 1st Ave S, has books, sheet music and comics. Lighthouse Books (☎ 822-3278), 1735 1st Ave N, has sections on Florida and the Caribbean as well as rare and unusual books, maps and prints.

The Age of Reason (☎ 821-0892), 401 1st Ave N, opposite the open-air post office, has a good selection of used books (including LP) and friendly service.

The Oriental Book Shelf (☎ 867-7978), 6940 9th St S, has books on Japan and Asia.

Libraries The main library (☎ 893-7724) is at 3745 9th Ave N. Downtown, the Mirror Lake Branch (☎ 893-7268) is at 5th St and 3rd Ave N.

Media The major daily is the excellent *St Petersburg Times*, which runs a very good website (see Online Services appendix) that has photographs, walking tours and information on major exhibits at the area's museums. NPR is at 89.7 FM.

Gay & Lesbian Affinity Books (☎ 823-3662), 2435 9th St N, is a gay and lesbian bookstore with books, videos, cards and music. Ask them about Healthy Lifestyles, a coming-out support group for adults 21 and over.

The Line (☎ 586-4297) is an information and a crisis hotline. They also run True Expressions, a coming-out support group for teens. Weekly recreational and social support groups are organized for youth aged 14 to 18 and 18 to 26 – you don't need to be gay to attend.

For up-to-date club, bar and social organization information, pick up a copy of *Encounter*, and *Womyn's Word* (a lesbian newsletter). Both of these are available at Affinity.

Laundry Try Snowhite Laundry (☎ 822-9021), 1117 4th St N (about nine blocks north of downtown).

Medical Services All Children's Hospital (☎ 898-7451), 33 6th St S, is the largest in the area. There's also Bayfront Medical Center (☎ 823-1234), 701 6th St S.

Salvador Dali Museum

One of St Petersburg's star attractions – with the largest collection of works by Salvador Dali outside Spain – is the Salvador Dali Museum (☎ 823-3767, see Online Services appendix), 1000 3rd St S.

While many of the galleries in the museum contain rotating exhibitions, there is always a permanent retrospective of Dali's works on display from the museum's large collection.

Dali is best known for his surrealist works, but the museum's collection covers the entire range of the artist's work: from his early works (1914 to '27, which included Impressionism, Cubism, still lifes and landscapes) and his transitional period (1928) through Surrealism (1929 to '40) and back to classical works from 1943 to '89 and a collection of masterworks – 18 major oil paintings produced between 1948 and '70.

You never know what will be up when you visit, though we were lucky enough to catch *Dali Under the Sun: World Premiere of the Florida Collection*, which displayed all of the museum's 94 oil paintings.

Guided tours ($5 for adults, $2 for students) are given between five and nine times a day; ask at the ticket counter for more information. There's no photography allowed in the galleries, and you must check cameras and unbagged video cameras.

The Master Gallery has four excellent oil on canvas paintings: *The Discovery of America by Christopher Columbus* (1958-59); *The Ecumenical Council* (1960); *Galacidalacidesoxiribunucleicacid* (1962-63); and (our favorite) *The Hallucinogenic Toreador* (1969-70).

Elsewhere in the museum, when we visited, we saw works including *Enchanted Beach with Three Fluid Graces* (1938), *Three Young Surrealist Women Holding in Their Arms the Skins of an Orchestra* (1936), *Tristan Fou* (1938-39), *Old Age, Adolescence, Infancy (The Three Ages)* (1940) and *Morphological Echo* (1936).

We loved the pencil and ink works (1923 to '56), including *Female Nude* (1926), and sketches, including *Male Head with Child* (1924-25), *Manuel de Falla* (1924-25) and the quintessential Dalian *The Nostalgic Echo* (1935).

We thought their gift shop was fantastic – a museum gift shop with style – and prices are reasonable.

The museum is open Monday to Saturday from 9.30 am to 5.30 pm, Sunday from

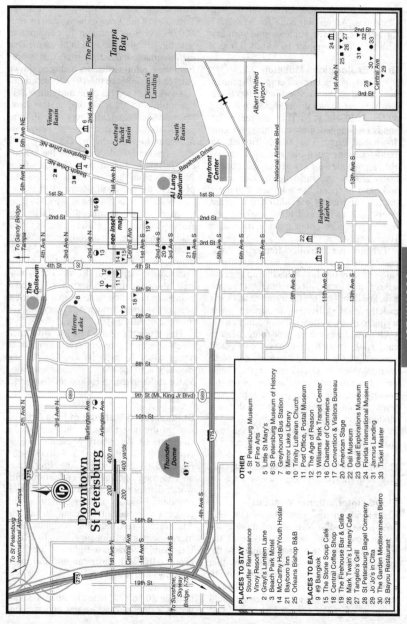

Tampa Bay

The Pier

Vinoy Basin

Central Yacht Basin

South Basin

Demen's Landing

Albert Whitted Airport

Bayboro Harbor

National Airlines Blvd

Al Lang Stadium

Bayfront Center

Bayshore Drive

Mirror Lake

The Coliseum

Thunder Dome

Downtown St Petersburg

To Gandy Bridge, Tampa

To St Petersburg International Airport, Tampa

To Sunshine Skyway Bridge, I-75

9th St (ML King Jr Blvd)

Burlington Ave

Arlington Ave

see inset map

PLACES TO STAY
1 Stouffer Renaissance
  Vinoy Resort
2 Gray's Lantern Lane
3 Beach Park Motel
14 McCarthy Hotel/Youth Hostel
21 Bayboro Inn
25 Orleans Bishop B&B

PLACES TO EAT
9 #9 Bangkok
15 The Stone Soup Café
18 Central Coffee Shop
19 The Firehouse Bar & Grille
26 Mark Twain's Literary Cafe
27 Tangelo's Grill
28 St Petersburg Bagel Company
29 Jo Jo's in Citta
30 The Garden Mediterranean Bistro
32 Bayou Restaurant

OTHER
4 St Petersburg Museum
  of Fine Arts
5 Little St Mary's
6 St Petersburg Museum of History
7 Greyhound Bus Station
8 Mirror Lake Library
10 Trinity Lutheran Church
11 Post Office, Postal Museum
12 The Age of Reason
13 Williams Park Transit Center
16 Chamber of Commerce
17 Convention & Visitors Bureau
20 American Stage
22 Dali Museum
23 Great Explorations Museum
24 Florida International Museum
31 Jannus Landing
33 Ticket Master

SOUTHWEST

noon to 5.30 pm, closed Thanksgiving and Christmas. Admission is $8 for adults, $7 for seniors, $4 for students and military with ID; children under 10 admitted free.

Great Explorations Museum

If the kids get squirmy being led through the Dali Museum, the best next stop is the nearby Great Explorations Museum (☎ 821-8992), 1120 4th St S. This is a really fun hands-on science museum that gets kids down and dirty. The Touch Tunnel, an eight-foot-long pitch-black maze, is (probably a poor idea for claustrophobics but) a really creepy and fun way for kids seven and older to spend five minutes. You enter the tube and crawl over different textured floors as it twists and turns, making you feel as if you're going much farther than you actually are.

The museum also offers interactive computer games, and everyone had fun with the safe-cracking display – kids line up to guess a three- and four-digit combination to open a locked door (we're still trying to work out exactly what skills this demonstration is trying to instill in the future of America).

Other features are a reptile room, a hurricane room (which simulates a condensed version of a Category-3 hurricane complete with a hysterical Dick Fletcher, the Channel 10 weatherperson), slapping pipes and coolest of all, the cone pyramid: put your finger in the hole and your pulse drives a cloud maker.

The museum's open Monday to Saturday from 10 am to 5 pm, Sunday from noon to 5 pm. Admission is $6 for adults, $5 for children four to 17, $5.50 for seniors; children under three are free.

Florida International Museum

The Florida International Museum (☎ 822-3693), 100 2nd St N, is an enormous exhibition space that's home to some of the most spectacular temporary exhibits in the country. And for all of you who think that guidebook writers get to experience it all, consider that our research schedule plopped us down in the city at a time when we could see none of it! The one we just missed was

their debut, the incredibly well received Treasures of the Tsars exhibit, seen by over 600,000 visitors and run in conjunction with the Kremlin museum in Moscow. That exhibit marked the first time that works from the Kremlin museum had been shown outside Russia since the 1917 Revolution.

As we went to press, the museum was in the middle of their second major show, Splendors of Ancient Egypt, run in conjunction with the Roemer-und Pelizaeus-Museum in Hildesheim, Germany. The show featured works depicting the historical, religious and artistic aspects of the Pharaohs from the close of the predynastic period to the end of the Roman Empire.

Scheduled to begin just as we go to print is an equally anticipated exhibition on Alexander the Great, with two major Greek exhibitions: one organized by the Greek Ministry of Culture, and the second as an extension of the Greek exhibition by the Fondazione Memmo of Rome. The exhibit will show sculpture, mosaics, jewelry, manuscripts and coins to form a historical perspective from Bronze Age Macedonia to the time of Alexander.

The museum hours change with each exhibition, and there are several exhibitions a year, so call for more information. Admission is $14.50 for adults, $13.25 for seniors, $5 for children five to 16, and children under five are free.

St Petersburg Museum of Fine Arts

One of the best fine arts museums in the state, the St Petersburg Museum of Fine Arts (☎ 896-2667, fax 894-4638), 255 Beach Drive NE (near the Pier), has an enormous permanent collection with works that as a whole make up a very well rounded art history of diverse cultures. The collection is made up of Asian, Indian and African art, pre-Columbian sculpture, photographic works from superstars like Jerry Uelsmann, Cycladic sculpture of the third-century BC and American and European paintings and sculpture.

Rotating exhibits are held in Galleries 17 through 20 and 22; when there are no temporary exhibits, these rooms contain con-

Highlights of the Museum of Fine Arts

Following is a highlights tour of the St Petersburg Museum of Fine Arts collections:

Gallery 1 Ancient Greek and Roman works include lots of body parts: *Head of Augustus*, *Head of a Man* and *Torso of Aphrodite*. Don't miss the 6th- to 5th-century Phoenician blue, core-formed glass and the tiny *Pair of Amphoriskoi*.

Galleries 2 & 3 Renaissance and works through the 18th century, including a crown from a bishop's miter, 14th- and 15th-century embroidery in silk and gold thread, Conrad Faber von Creuznach's oil *Albanus Wolfhart of Lindau* and Bertel Thorwaldsen's marble *Mercury About to Slay Argus*.

Galleries 4 & 5 19th- and 20th-century American works include Frederick Mac Monniess bronze sculpture *Young Faun and Heron*, Louis Comfort Tiffany's glass and bronze *Ten Light, Drop Cluster Pond Lily Table Lamp* and such Modern paintings as Theodore Stamos' *Garden of Eden*, Samuel Edmond Oppenheim's *Head of a Boy* and Carroll Cloar's *Pool Room*.

Gallery 6 Pre-Columbian art has as its centerpiece *God of Death – Micatlantecuhtli*, and also includes the excellent *Two Guardians with Spears*.

Gallery 7 African, European and Native American works include masks and arts from West Africa, such as gold weights and brass works; pottery by Pueblo potter María Martínez; and a Native American Zuñi pueblo *Water Jar*.

Gallery 8 Asian art includes a 17th-century Indian bronze *Shiva as King of Dancers*, a Siamese bronze *Head of Buddha*, and 18th- to 20th-century Japanese prints, including *Hinazuru* by Kitagawa Utamaro.

Gallery 9 Late 18th- and 19th-century European works (under renovation when we visited), includes Claude Monet's *Road to the Village of Vetheuil, Snow* and Jacques-Emile Blanche's *Contemplation*.

Gallery 13 The Jacobean room sure does look the part, with period prints from Renaissance and Baroque eras. **Gallery 14**, Hanna's Gallery, has Rodin bronzes on loan from the Cantor Foundation. **Gallery 15**, the Georgian room, has a Fragonard watercolor.

Gallery 16 Steuben glass works include Steuben glassmasters including James Houston – the spectacular *Arctic Fisherman*, *Ice Hunter*, *Elephants of Kilimanjaro*, *Apple of Eden* and *Excalibur* – as well as Peter Aldridge and Jane Osborne Smith's *Swan Bowl* and Donald Pollard's *David Livingstone*.

In the **Great Hall**, don't miss two easy-to-miss paintings hanging on the wall separating the hall from the entry to the toilets: on the left, Louis Silvestre the Younger's *Perseus Rescuing Andromeda from the Sea Monster*, and on the right, *Thetis at the Forge of Vulcan*. ∎

temporary art and photography exhibits from the museum's collection. The **Morgan Membership Garden** and the **Stuart Memorial Garden** host various events such as teas, and the **Marly Room** is home to concerts, plays and films: contact the museum to see what's happening in these areas during your visit.

The exhibitions are all on the main floor (see aside on gallery highlights). While signs in the museum are very clear, the room numbering is somewhat confusing: pick up a floor plan and catalogs of rotating exhibitions at the ticket desk. Tours of the galleries are included in the price of admission and run Tuesday to Friday at 10 and 11 am and 1, 2 and 3 pm. On Saturday, tours are at 11 am and 2 pm, and on Sunday at 1 and 2 pm.

The museum is open Tuesday to Saturday from 10 am to 5 pm, Sunday from 1 to 5 pm; closed Monday, Thanksgiving Day, Christmas Day and New Year's Day. On the third Thursday of each month it stays open until 9 pm. Admission is $5 for adults, $2 for students, $3 for seniors and groups of 10 or more, children under six are free. Admission is free to all on Sunday.

St Petersburg Museum of History

At the foot of The Pier (see below), the St Petersburg Museum of History (☎ 894-1052), 335 2nd Ave NE, has a great display on the early days of aviation – St Petersburg was the take-off site for America's first scheduled airline flight on January 1, 1914. The plane used for that flight, the Benoist Airboat (restored in 1984), now hangs in the Flight One Gallery, which also has some very interesting early aviation artifacts.

The Timeline Gallery is what you'd expect, beginning with native cultures, the Spanish Conquistadors, early settlers, Seminole Indians and the colonial frontier. There's a Cracker store replica complete with an ice maker, explanations on how people made a living before the advent of the railroads and a description of the founding and development of the city. One exhibit that manages to be both fun and cheesy is the historical closet: period costumes are on pullout vertical drawers near a mirror, so you can 'try on' things like a WWI aviator get-up, a 1920s wedding dress and flapper dresses.

The museum's open Monday to Saturday from 10 am to 5 pm, Sunday from 1 to 5 pm. Admission is $4 for adults, $3.50 for seniors, $1.50 for children seven to 17 and children under six are free.

The Pier

The Pier (☎ 821-6164), 800 2nd Ave NE, is something of a tourist trap but it's a focal point of downtown. It's, well, a long pier, with a square fishing platform at the end, in the center of which is a five-story shopping mall with shops and restaurants. There's an aquarium on the 2nd floor.

At the baithouse you can feed the pelicans, who are standing around waiting for you: five fish are $2, 15 are $5. Lazier pelicans you'll never see. You can also rent a fishing rod here for $10 a day with a $30 deposit; the rental price includes a bucket and bait.

Waterworks Pierside Rentals (☎ 363-0000) rents bicycles for $5 an hour, $10 for a half day and $15 for a full day. Hydro bikes – streamlined, foot-powered, very fast paddleboats, not those clunky ones you usually see – rent by the hour for $10 for a one-person bike, $15 for a double.

The Pier is open Monday to Saturday from 10 am to about 9 pm, Sunday from about 11 am to 9 pm. Pier parking is $2, and there's a shuttle tram that runs between the parking lots and the action. Valet parking is $5; valets work from 11 am till the last car is gone.

HMS Bounty The very same 18th-century tall ship used in the 1962 film *Mutiny on the Bounty* parks at the Pier for the winter; it's summer home is in Fall River, Massachusetts (see LP's *New England*). You can tour the boat, which has sailed over 70,000 miles (including a one-year trip to Tahiti where the film was shot), Tuesday to Saturday every half hour from noon to 5.30 pm, Sunday from noon to 6 pm. Guided tours (the only way to get on board) cost $5 for adults, $4 for seniors, $3 for children over five. The ship is here from around October 30th to early May.

Little St Mary's This is perhaps the only toilet in the state of Florida that is also a historic landmark. Our story begins when Henry Taylor was stiffed on payment for his work as the designer of St Mary's Church, 515 4th St S. Taylor built the Romanesque-revival toilet as a miniature of the church, and dubbed it Little St Mary's. It's at the western end of the Pier.

Demen's Landing Facing the Pier to its south is Demen's Landing, Bayshore Drive

SE at 1st Ave S, a waterfront park with picnic facilities. Each spring the American Stage in the Park (☎ 822-8814) presents its Shakespeare Festival here.

Postal Museum
It's a little much to call the itty-bitty display case at the rear of the downtown St Petersburg post office (☎ 323-6516), 76 4th St N, a 'museum', but these postal types are a shameless lot. However, the Mediterranean-revival building it's in was the nation's first open-air post office, and it's a glorious thing, with a keystone arched open front. The 'museum' contains postal paraphernalia such as stamps, inkwells, a numbering device, and so on. There used to be a large postal museum on the 2nd floor, but it was closed when we visited: the brochure promised that it 'contains artifacts of postal memorabilia of the St Petersburg area which is sure to delight young and old'. Okay. It's still a fully functioning post office.

Feeling philatelic? No worries: the St Petersburg Stamp Club meets monthly at Trinity Lutheran Church (☎ 822-3307), 401 5th St N.

First United Methodist Church
Built in 1925 and located in the heart of downtown, this Gothic-revival church (☎ 894-4661), 212 3rd St N, is listed in the National Register of Historic Places. There are some pretty nice Tiffany-style stained-glass windows. Sunday services are held at 8.30, 9.45 and 11 am.

Tampa Bay Holocaust Memorial
The Tampa Bay Holocaust Memorial & Educational Center (☎ 392-4678) is a haul and a half from downtown, but it's worth it. Outside is an original boxcar used to transport prisoners to the Auschwitz concentration camp near Kraków, Poland, on spikes and rails from the camp at Treblinka. The car transported Jews, Poles, homosexuals and other victims of Nazi aggression to the camp in groups of 100 to 120. One side has the original lock.

Inside there are exhibits not just of the Holocaust but of Jewish life throughout the world, with rotating exhibits on a number of subjects. When we visited, we saw a fascinating look at Ethiopian Jewry, their clothing and daily lives. Rotating art exhibitions take place in their gallery; when we visited it was *Journey into Darkness* by Frank Root: chillingly dark, three-dimensional works depicting suffering during the Holocaust, including *Kristallnacht I*, *Fasanenstrasse Synagogue* (one of a thousand destroyed during Kristallnacht), *Where are we going?* and *The Train*.

In the shop area are exhibits of instruments used by Dr Mengele, who conducted sadistic experiments on camp inmates, and examples of Star of David armbands the Nazis forced Jews to wear.

The museum is open Monday to Friday from 10 am to 4 pm and Sunday from noon to 4 pm. Admission is $6 for adults, $5 for senior citizens, students and children free. It's at 5001 113th St N. From downtown, take I-275 north to exit 15, get on Park Blvd (Hwy 694) going west until 113th St N, turn left, and the memorial is about a mile and a half on the left-hand side of the street in the Jewish Community Center. The sign says JCC.

Suncoast Seabird Sanctuary
The Suncoast Seabird Sanctuary (☎ 391-6211) is the largest wild bird hospital in North America (1½ acres), and it was founded by Ralph Heath, Jr, in 1971. About 40 different species of crippled birds have found a home here, and there are usually between 400 to 600 sea and land birds being treated and recuperating. Whenever possible, the birds are released back into the wild.

It's open daily from 9 am to dusk. Guided tours take place Wednesday and Sunday at 2 pm. Admission is free, but please leave a donation. It's at 18328 Gulf Blvd (south of Indian Shores on Sand Key); from downtown take I-275 north to exit 15, take Hwy 694 west to the Gulf, then turn left onto Gulf Blvd – the entrance is about a quarter mile south.

Sunken Gardens
Opened in 1935, Sunken Gardens (☎ 896-3186), 1825 4th St N, is a five-acre tropical

garden, with a walk-through aviary that's home to colorful birds, lots of exotic flowers and other flora and fauna. There's even a wax museum containing biblical figures. It's open daily from 9 am to 5.30 pm; admission is $14 for adults, $8 for children three to 11.

Gizella Kopsick Palm Arboretum

The Gizella Kopsick Palm Arboretum (☎ 893-7335), at N Shore Drive and 10th Ave NE (just north of the North Shore Pool, see below), contains about 200 different palms and cycads representing about 45 species from all over the world. Examples include such wildly diverse entries as the jelly palm, the windmill palm, the triangle palm and, of course, your garden variety gru gru palm. Guided tours take place about once a month; call to see if one's on during your visit.

North Shore Pool

The North Shore Pool (☎ 893-7727), 901 N Shore Drive NE, in North Shore Park, is an Olympic-size swimming pool. It's open to the public Monday to Saturday from 9 am to 4.30 pm and Sunday from 1 to 4.30 pm. Admission is $1.85 for adults, $1.30 for children ages three to 16 and $1.60 for seniors. They offer classes, like water aerobics, for $20 a month; classes are held twice a week for one hour. **North Shore Park**, on N Shore Drive from 7th to 13th Aves, also has a public beach, tennis courts and picnic areas.

Boyd Hill Nature Park

Boyd Hill Nature Park (☎ 893-7326) is a 245-acre park on Lake Maggiore with over three miles of nature trails and boardwalks. There's a picnic area with grills and sheltered tables and a playground northeast of the nature center. Bicycles are permitted, but not pets, in-line skates or skateboards.

There are six primary trails within the park: on the Willow Marsh Trail you'll likely hear young alligators squeaking, but there are many more animals, including pig frogs, bald eagles, snowy egrets, box turtles

and opossums, which can be found among the live oaks, cypress trees and ferns.

The friendly rangers here offer night hikes, bird walks, wildflower walks and ecology walks; daily tram tours take off at 1 pm. Night hikes take place at 8.30 pm on the second Monday night of the month, from April to October, at 7.30 pm during other months. Hikes take about one to 1½ hours; you'll explore the nature trails while rangers point out the different habitats and nocturnal animals that populate the place. Other walks are available, call for more information.

The park is open from 9 am to 5 pm; from April to October they stay open till 8 pm on Tuesday and Thursday. Admission is $1 for adults, 50¢ for children three to 17, and all activities in the park are included in the price. The park is at 1101 Country Club Way S on Lake Maggiore; from downtown take I-275 to exit 4, turn east onto 54th Ave S to ML King Jr Blvd S, then north to the first traffic signal (Country Club Way S) and turn left (west) to get to the park entrance. Parking is free.

Fort DeSoto Park

This 900-acre county park (☎ 866-2484), on Mullet Key south of downtown, has self-guided nature and recreational trails for biking, blading, walking and hiking, and about three miles of swimming beach. The fort was built during the Spanish-American War, and if you tire yourself out after a day of fun in the sun, you can camp here as well (see Places to Stay below). To get here, take I-275 south to exit 4 and follow the signs; it's at 3500 Pinellas Bayway S. There is a 85¢ toll on the approach road, but park entry is free and it closes at dusk.

Sunshine Skyway Bridge

Okay, it's not exactly an attraction, but it's impressive nonetheless: the four-mile-long Sunshine Skyway Bridge spans Tampa Bay south of St Petersburg. It's the continuation of I-275, which meets up with I-75 on the south side of the bay. The toll is $1 to drive across. Built to replace the old span, which was destroyed in 1980 when a ship, the *Summit Venture*, rammed into its base, the Sunshine Skyway is a shimmering modern bridge – and each of its supports are surrounded by 'dolphins': gigantic shock absorbers that are capable of withstanding the force of an 87,000-ton vessel traveling at 10 knots. The *Summit Venture* weighed 34,500 tons and was traveling at 8 knots when it struck the old bridge.

Much of the old bridge still stands, and the plan is to convert it into the world's largest fishing pier. When completed (parts of it are already open to the public), it will span almost two miles.

Organized Tours

Pierside Sight Seeing (☎ 363-0000), 800 2nd Ave NE, runs three two-hour tours of historic St Petersburg daily.

Caribbean Queen (☎ 895-2628), at the Pier, does 1½-hour dolphin sightseeing excursions. They leave the Pier at 11.30 am and 1, 3 and 5 pm. Tickets are $10 for adults, $8 for seniors over 55 and for teens 12 to 17, and $5 for children three to 11.

Gray Line Sightseeing Tours (☎ 535-0208, 800-282-4051) does one-, two- and three-day tours to such places as Walt Disney World, Busch Gardens, Sea World, Cypress Gardens and the Kennedy Space Center. Call for prices (which are more complicated than writing this book) and reservations.

Places to Stay

Camping *Fort DeSoto Park Campground* (☎ 866-2662), 3500 Pinellas Bayway S (see park description above), has 235 campsites for $17.75 per night (tents or RVs), electric and water included.

There's also a big *KOA St Petersburg/ Madeira Beach* near Madeira Beach. See Places to Stay under St Pete Beach for more details.

Hostels The non-HI (no matter what they tell you) *St Petersburg International Youth Hostel* (☎ 822-4141), 326 1st Ave N, is in the McCarthy Hotel, three blocks from the Pier. Dorm as well as semiprivate rooms

are available, as is a kitchen, common room and laundry facilities. Dorm rooms, which are clean enough but not the cheeriest in the world, are $11 for HI members, $15 for nonmembers; linen hire for those without a sleep sack is $2. Hostel rooms have no air-conditioning or cable TV, but you can rent a TV from the desk. They occasionally put hostelers in the hotel rooms (see Hotels & Motels below) when it gets too hot. The manually controlled elevator closes at 5 pm. The common area, above the lobby, has a TV, coffee, tea and a swell library.

Hotels & Motels The *Banyan Tree Motel* (☎ 822-7072), 610 4th St N, has clean rooms and fine service. Rooms include free cable TV and HBO, and they have refrigerators and phones. In summer, rates for the day/week are $27/125; in winter day/week/ month rates are $32/165/650.

The *McCarthy Hotel* (☎ 822-4141), 326 1st Ave N, home of the St Petersburg International Youth Hostel (see above), has decently renovated rooms and very nice staff. The rooms are spartan but basically clean, and many have a view of adjacent brick walls. The newly renovated wing on the higher floors are much cheerier. It's on the National Register of Historic Places, but it still has some of the best prices in downtown: singles/doubles are from $32 to 45/36 to 49; weekly rates from $205 to 290/230 to 315.

The *Beach Park Motel* (☎ 898-6325), 300 Beach Drive NE, has older but spotless rooms with fridges, coffee pots and other nice amenities. Singles/doubles are $40/45 in low season, $50/55 in high; efficiencies are $50/55 low season, $60/65 high.

Stouffer Renaissance Vinoy Resort (☎ 894-1000, fax 822-2785), 501 5th Ave NE, is a large pink hotel on the bay and the most flash offering in downtown. It has opulent dining and entertainment areas, and rooms include three telephones, a stocked 'refreshment center', bathrobes and two televisions. Rooms with very nice views of the bay go for just $115 to 169 in low season, $169 to 249 in mid-seasons and $249 to $289 in high season.

St Petersburg Bayfront Hilton (☎ 894-5000, 800-774-1500) at 333 1st St S, has Hilton-ish rooms from $119 to 145. It's got a great location downtown, and restaurants and bars inside, as you'd expect.

B&Bs *Bay Shore Manor* (☎ 822-3438), 635 12th Ave NE, is certainly the least expensive B&B in town. They do a German-style breakfast (coffee, tea, milk, orange juice, bread and rolls, cold cuts, cheese, eggs, cereal), and each room has a TV, coffeemaker, microwave and mini-refrigerator. Singles/doubles are $49/59.

Rooms at the very New Orleans-looking *Orleans Bishop Hotel* (☎ 894-4312, 800-676-4848), 256 1st Ave N, are very nice: all have clawfoot bathtubs and are tastefully decorated. All size beds (twin through king-size) are the same price, but the place has both B&B and standard hotel rooms. B&B rooms are $65 to 75 a night; breakfast is on their great terrace. Single/double hotel rooms cost $35/45.

Bayboro House (☎ 823-4955), 1719 Beach Drive SE, is a very nice Old South-themed place. Free wine is served in the parlor each evening; each room has a private bath and includes beach chairs, beach towels and a morning newspaper. No children or smoking. Two-day minimum during holidays and special events. On summer weekdays, rooms are $85 to 95, Friday and Saturday $95 to 105. In high season, weekdays are $100 to 110, Friday and Saturday $110 to 120.

Built in 1922, *Grayl's Lantern Lane* (☎ 896-1080, 800-880-7600), 340 Beach Drive NE (right across from the bay), has rooms with gorgeous four-poster beds and sitting rooms for $80 a night including continental breakfast.

Bayboro Inn & Hunt Room (☎ 823-0498), 357 3rd St S, is a historic house with theme rooms, like Renaissance, Egyptian and Key West. No smoking, no pets; free wine in the evenings. Rooms are $75 per night.

Places to Eat
Breakfast & Cafés *St Petersburg Bagel Co* (☎ 822-4092), 249 Central Ave, has great bagels for 40¢, sandwiches from $2 to 5, salads 75¢ to $3.50. It has another location (☎ 522-3377) at 7043 4th St N.

There's breakfast all day at the *South Gate Restaurant* (☎ 823-7071), 29 3rd St N. Dinner's from 4 to 9 pm daily, and during the day they do sandwiches for $2.95, a good Greek salad for $4.25 and meatloaf $4.25.

Central Coffee Shop (☎ 821-1125), 530 Central Ave, does breakfast and lunch Monday through Friday from 6 am to 1.45 pm, Saturday from 6 am to 11 am. Said to be excellent and cheap.

Torts & Ports (☎ 898-0800), 243 Central Ave, is a chi-chi sandwich place: Continental Combinations (those'd be sandwiches) are $4.25 or build your own baguette for $2.50 and up. Free delivery.

Mark Twain's Literary Cafe (☎ 821-6983), 260 1st Ave N, serves daily lunch specials, sandwiches and pasta from $4.50.

Tangelo's Grill (☎ 894-1695), 226 1st Ave N, does Cuban-style sandwiches like roast pork on grilled Cuban bread ($3.75) or Spanish grouper ($4.75).

Vegetarians will like the *Tamarind Tree Café* (☎ 898-2115), 537 Central Ave. It serves about seven kinds of salads (Greek $4.69, salad sampler of three with pita bread $5.19) and things like hummus ($3.69), vegetarian chili ($1.85/2.75) and sandwiches ($3.39 to 5.19).

We liked the *The Stone Soup Cafe* (☎ 895-1493), 27 4th St N, if only to reread the lovely story of stone soup on the menu. Main courses include wild mushrooms and chicken over rice with salad and muffin for $5.75, curried chicken salad for $4.95 and pebble burgers (three small burgers) with grilled onions, cheddar, honey mustard and potato salad for $4.95. Lots of salads from $4.25 to 4.75, and stone soup du jour is $1.75. It's open Monday to Friday from 8 am to 4 pm.

Restaurants *Number 9 Bangkok* (☎ 894-5990), 571 Central Ave, has good Thai food. Eleven choices for lunch include yellow curry with beef, chicken and pork for $3.95. Dinners are $4.95, house specials $7.95.

The *Fourth Street Shrimp Store* (☎ 822-0325), 1006 4th St N, is good for quick dinners from $3.99; fresh grouper dinner is $8.99.

The *Firehouse Bar & Grille* (☎ 895-4716), 260 1st Ave S, does soups, salads and sandwiches for around $5. It's open Monday to Thursday from 11 am to 9 pm, Friday and Saturday from 11 am to 11 pm, closed Sunday.

Another place worth looking into is *Dåc Biêt Phòl Mai* (☎ 894-2427), a Vietnamese place (who would have guessed) just west down the street from Thunder Alley Café & Sports Bar (see Entertainment below). It certainly looked authentic, and duck curry and beef soup goes for $4.95.

One of our favorite places was *The Garden Mediterranean Bistro* (☎ 896-3800), 217 Central Ave. At lunch they do an excellent pesto pasta ($4.95) and Lebanese sampler ($5.75), and daily lunch specials are $5.25. At dinner, dishes include grilled lamb chops at $9.75 or wild mushroom pasta for $10.50; dinner pastas range from $8.75 to 11.95, seafood dishes from $9.95 to 13.95. It also has 'theme nights' and hosts live jazz (see Entertainment below).

Ted Peter's Famous Smoked Fish (☎ 381-7931), 1350 Pasadena Ave, on the way out to St Pete Beach, has been smoking fish for something like 3500 years (well, for 45 at least). They do absolutely succulent freshly smoked salmon ($11.95 per pound), mackerel ($6.50) and mullet ($5.50) in the little smokehouse; next door is a restaurant where they serve seafood specials and drink lots of beer. A smoked fish dinner (salmon is $13.95, mackerel $9.95, mullet $8.95) includes German potato salad, rye bread and butter, pickles, onion, lemon and coleslaw. Sandwiches range from $1.50 to 4.20. Good for a picnic: take-away German potato salad is $3.75 a quart; smoked fish spread is $2.15 for a half pint, $4.25 a pint and $7.95 a quart. It's gooood.

The smells emanating from *Jo Jo's in Citta* (☎ 894-0075), 200 Central Ave, lead us to believe that their somewhat pricey Italian food is pretty darn good: think about baked pasta at $8.75 or veal picatta for $13.95. They also do much cheaper subs.

Bayou Restaurant & Bar (☎ 895-2968), 16 2nd St N, was in the process of opening when we visited. It will serve Cajun, Louisiana and Creole in a cavernous place with exposed brick and wooden archways. The manager and chef are from Los Angeles (as if that's a selling point), and at lunch they plan on shrimp Creole for $8.95, jambalaya for $6.95, gumbo $6; dinner will range from $6 to 12. From 10 pm on, there will be live music Thursday to Saturday. In the courtyard is Jannus Landing, a concert venue (see Entertainment below).

Entertainment

The St Petersburg entertainment scene is less exciting than that of its Russian counterpart, and that says a lot. For recorded information on upcoming events call the St Petersburg Entertainment Hotline (☎ 825-3333).

Theater The American Stage (☎ 822-8814), 211 3rd St S, is the oldest professional theater ensemble in the Tampa Bay area. It stages American classics and Broadway shows.

The St Petersburg Little Theater (☎ 866-1973), 4025 31st St S, is a community theater that puts on plays and musicals.

Bayfront Center (☎ 892-5767, 892-5700), 400 1st St S, houses both the Bayfront Arena and the Mahaffey Theater. The complex holds Broadway shows, ice skating performances, concerts and some sports events.

Concerts The Coliseum (☎ 892-5202), 535 4th Ave N (also called the Palace of Pleasure), opened in 1924 and over the years big bands, classical orchestras and rock bands have played here. It's been host to indoor tennis matches, and in 1985, it made its film debut in *Cocoon* – that incredible ballroom scene. If you're here on a Wednesday, definitely hit the **big band dance** sessions; they begin at 12.30 pm. Most events are BYOB (and hey, coolers are welcome).

The St Petersburg ThunderDome (see

below) also hosts concerts; call for information while you're here.

Bars & Clubs What was once Club Detroit is now *Jannus Landing* (☎ 896-1244), 16 2nd St N. It's an outdoor courtyard behind the Bayou Restaurant & Bar (see Places to Eat above), and there are several concerts of local and national bands every week. It's very casual – shorts, T-shirts and jeans. There is a full cash bar, and all ages are admitted – but you'll be proofed to the gills if you look under 30 and try to buy alcohol. They also serve burgers, hot dogs and such. Tickets are generally under $15, and of 10 about $10. You can get tickets from Ticket Master.

The Big Catch (☎ 821-6444), 9 1st St NE, has been around forever. It has live bands, usually modern rock, on Friday and Saturday with a $3 cover and no minimum. It's open Thursday to Saturday from 8.30 pm to 2 am.

The Garden (☎ 896-3800), 217 Central Ave (see Places to Eat above) does Get Togethers – set price dinner and wine tasting evenings – with themes like belly dancing, Spanish nights with tapas and a show – for $39.50. It also has live jazz outside with the Buster Cooper Jazz Trio every Friday and Saturday from 8.30 pm to 1.30 am.

Thunder Alley Café & Sports Bar (☎ 823-4417), 1113 Central Ave, is a friendly neighborhood place with a pool table and at least one big-screen TV. People across the street at the *Silver King Tavern* (☎ 821-6740), 1114 Central Ave, seemed a little rowdier, if equally jolly. It has happy hour daily from 4 to 8 pm, and it's open from 11.30 am to 2.30 am.

Psychic Espresso 'Add a psychic flavor to your coffee' at *Espresso Yourself* (☎ 822-6646), 111 2nd Ave NE in the Plaza Courtyard. It's a coffee bar that does psychic readings with Alexandra every Friday and Saturday from 11 am to 4 pm.

Spectator Sports
The St Petersburg ThunderDome (☎ 825-3333), 1 Stadium Drive, is home to the Tampa Bay Lightning hockey team. It also hosts concerts, car races and other events. Parking is at 10th St and 4th Ave S.

Al Lang Stadium (for tickets ☎ 822-3384), 230 First St S, is home to minor-league baseball's St Petersburg Cardinals, a St Louis Cardinals farm team.

Things to Buy
The big shopping mall in the area is Tyrone Square (☎ 345-0126), 66th St and 22nd Ave N, with 155 stores, including Burdines, Dillard's, JC Penney, Sears, Kookla Fran & Ollie and many more. **Antique stores** litter downtown St Petersburg, especially along 4th St: Antique Alley Mall (☎ 823-5700), 1535 4th St N, has several sorts of antique places.

Getting There & Away
Air St Petersburg-Clearwater International Airport (☎ 535-7600 for the most annoying recorded voice in the world) is served by several major carriers as well as cheapies like SunJet. It's at the intersection of Roosevelt Blvd and Hwy 686 in Clearwater. However, if you're flying into the region, you're more likely to land in Tampa; see the Tampa Getting There & Away section below.

Bus The Greyhound station (☎ 898-1496) is at 180 9th St N. There's regular service here from all over Florida; sample routes are listed below; prices are one way/roundtrip.

Destination	Price	Duration
Miami	$29/39	7 to 8 hours
Tampa	$7/14	½ to 1 hour
Orlando	$17/34	3½ to 4¾ hours

Train There's an Amtrak (☎ 800-872-7245) continuing rail shuttle bus link between Tampa and St Petersburg; it'll drop you at the Pinellas Square Mall at 7200 Hwy 19 N. See Tampa Getting There & Away for more information.

Car Several major car rental companies have offices at the airport.

It's 289 miles to Miami, 84 miles to Orlando. From Tampa, the best route is I-275 south, which runs right through downtown St Petersburg and continues across the Sunshine Skyway Bridge; it connects with I-75 and US Hwy 41 (the Tamiami Trail) on the south side of Tampa Bay. From Sarasota, take I-75 north to I-275 across the Sunshine Skyway. From Orlando, take I-4 south to I-75 to I-275.

Getting Around

To/From the Airport There's no local bus service directly to the airport; the closest you can get to it is about a half mile away at the corner of 49th St and Roosevelt Blvd, served by bus No 52 or 79. By car to downtown, take Roosevelt Blvd (Hwy 686) south, across the jig on Ulmerton Rd, to I-275 south. To Clearwater, take Roosevelt Blvd north to the Bayside (49th St) Bridge and go west on Gulf to Bay Blvd. Taxi fares from the airport to St Petersburg run between $15 and 20.

Bus Pinellas Suncoast Transit Authority (PSTA, ☎ 530-9911) has a downtown transit service center at Williams Park, on 2nd Ave N between 3rd and 4th Sts; it's open Monday to Saturday from 7 am to 5.45 pm, Sunday from 8 to 11.30 am and 12.30 to 4 pm. They sell daily/monthly unlimited-ride Go Cards ($2.50/40) and give transit information.

While there is public bus service between St Petersburg and places like Clearwater and Tarpon Springs, there is no PSTA service between St Petersburg and St Pete Beach – you'll have to take bus No 35 to Pasadena (25 minutes) and then transfer for a BATS bus to St Pete Beach. The trip takes about an hour total; bus No 35 leaves the Williams Park station once an hour. Regular bus fare is $1, bills accepted.

Trolley The five major museums in town – the Dali, Fine Arts, Historic, International and Great Explorations – along with a couple of hotels and the Pier have teamed up to provide a free (and pink) trolley ser-

vice called the Looper, which loops around downtown, all the museums, the retail district of downtown and the Pier. The service runs every day between 11 am and 5 pm.

Car Getting around and parking in St Petersburg by car is a cinch. To get to St Pete Beach, take I-275 to Hwy 682, which connects to the Pinellas County Parkway and west to the beach, or take Central Ave due west to either the Treasure Island Causeway or turn south on 66th St to the Corey Causeway.

Bicycle It's flat, but everything is very, very far apart. Lock your bike tightly and note that drivers are not used to people like you. Bikes can be rented at the Pier (see above).

ST PETE BEACH
• *pop 9200* ☎ *813*

With a great white sand beach and clear blue water, St Pete Beach (they officially changed their name a couple of years back) makes a great day or overnight trip from St Petersburg or Clearwater. But unless you're camping, you'll do much better to stay in the Clearwater Hostel (actually the beach is better there anyway) and do day trips from there – hotels on St Pete Beach are either expensive or not worth the money they charge.

Orientation & Information

St Pete Beach is on Long Key, about 10 miles west of downtown St Petersburg across the Corey Causeway or the Pinellas County Bayway. The island is long and narrow, and the main (and only) artery is Gulf Blvd (Hwy 699).

The St Pete Beach Welcome Center (☎ 360-6957), 6990 Gulf Blvd, hands out tons of pamphlets and discount coupons. It's open Monday to Friday from 9 am to 5 pm. Change money at one of Barnett Bank's two locations on the beach: at 4105 Gulf Blvd and 7500 Gulf Blvd.

Wash clothes at the Washboard Coin Laundry (☎ 360-0674) at 6350 Gulf Blvd.

Don CeSar Beach Resort

Don CeSar Beach Resort (☎ 360-1883) is probably the first thing you'll notice when you pull into St Pete Beach: built in 1928, this monster of a hotel was a hot spot for such characters as F Scott Fitzgerald, Clarence Darrow, Lou Gehrig and Al Capone. The enormous pink building was bought by the US Army in 1942 and turned into a hospital and convalescent center for army personnel. Stripped of all its splendor, the Veterans Administration, which had taken it over after the war, abandoned the building in 1967. It was reopened in 1973, and from 1985 to 1989 it was completely restored. Today it's open as a resort hotel, though its room rates make it a bit unapproachable: low season rooms run $165 to 195, and in high season they go up to $265 to 300.

Gulf Beaches Historical Museum

This new museum (☎ 360-2491), 115 10th Ave at Pass-a-Grille Beach (about two miles south of the Don CeSar Hotel), is located in the building that housed the Pass-a-Grille Church (1917) – the first to be built on a west coast barrier island. The museum has a large collection of photographs and artifacts from the beaches dating from the early 1800s. As yet they've got no Indian artifacts, but they're working on it. They have a good selection of interesting old postcards and church memorabilia as well. It's open Thursday and Saturday from 10 am to 4 pm and Sunday 1 to 4 pm, closed Monday to Wednesday and Friday. Admission is free, donations accepted. Take Gulf Blvd south past the Don CeSar; the road becomes Pass-a-Grille Blvd, which runs into 10th Ave.

Rentals & Tours

Cycle & Scooter (☎ 367-3882), 7116A Gulf Blvd, rents bicycles by the hour/day for $7 to 10/19, roller blades for $5/20, scooters $13/48. They also offer guided trips to Fort DeSoto Park for $24; tours last four to five hours and the price includes bicycle rental and pick up/drop off at the park.

Totally! Active Sports (☎ 367-7059), 7859 Blind Pass Rd, has windsurfing rentals and lessons. Dolphin Landings Charter Boat Center (☎ 367-4488, 360-7411), 4737 Gulf Blvd, does two-hour dolphin-watching trips at 9.30 am, noon and 2.15 pm ($25 for adults, $15 for kids under 11) and sunset sails from 7 to 9 pm ($25 per person). Both include free soft drinks, and reservations are required.

Places to Stay

Camping Camping is the best deal (unless you're staying at the Clearwater Hostel): the *KOA St Petersburg/Madeira Beach* (☎ 392-2233, 800-848-1094) is about two miles from Madeira Beach, which is north of St Pete Beach. It has tent sites for $21.95, or $24.95 with water and electric. RV and van sites are $27.95 with full hookup, or $24.95 with water and electric. One-room Kamping Kabins are $29.95, two rooms $36.95. To get there from downtown St Petersburg, take I-275 north and get off at 38th Ave N, go west for 5½ miles and take a left onto 66th St, take a right onto Tyrone Blvd, and go 1½ miles to 95th St. Turn right and it's about a half mile ahead at 5400 95th St N.

Motels & Hotels The chains along the beach include *Howard Johnson Lodge*, *Radisson Resort*, *Quality Inn*, *Best Western* and *Holiday Inn*. *The Florida Dolphin* (☎ 360-7233), 6801 Sunset Way, is clean enough but unspectacular; rates range from $45 to $65 depending on the month. The *Osiris Motel* (☎ 360-6052), 620 68th Ave, and the *Gulf Tides Motel* (☎ 367-2979) at 600 68th Ave, are both pretty much exactly like the Florida Dolphin.

The Alden Beach Resort (☎ 360-7081, in FL 800-262-3464, outside FL 800-237-2530, fax 360-5957), 5900 Gulf Blvd, is one of the nicer places to stay on the beach, with a pool and good service; rooms start from $61 in off season and escalate quickly.

The spotless *Colonial Gateway Resort Inn* (☎ 367-2711, 800-237-8918), 6300 Gulf Blvd, has very nice rooms from $67 to 95 in low season and $95 to $115 in

Lake Okeechobee

Pelicans on St Petersburg pier

Manatee

Steinhatchee River dwellings

KIM GRANT

Key West style

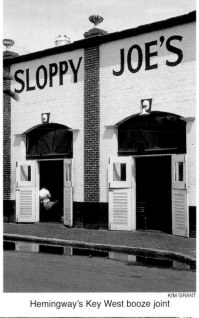

KIM GRANT

Hemingway's Key West booze joint

KIM GRANT

True Conch living

high season. Another place like it is the *Coral Reef Beach Resort* (☎ 360-0821 fax 367-2597), 5800 Gulf Blvd; rates start at $75 per night off-season, about $100 in high season.

Places to Eat

The *Sea Dragon Restaurant* (☎ 360-0992), 7390 Gulf Blvd, is a Chinese place that does a lunch buffet from 11.30 am to 3 pm for $4.95 and a dinner buffet from 5 to 9 pm for $6.95 (including a soup and salad bar). Early-bird specials ($5.95) are available from 4 to 6 pm. Regular dinner dishes include Szechwan vegetables for $5.95 and hot and spicy shrimp for $8.95.

The *Ice Cream & British Tea Shop* (☎ 367-2748), 4765 Gulf Blvd, does full British breakfasts from 8.30 am, and pub-style lunches and dinners cost $2.99 to $5.99.

Aunt Heidi's Italian Restaurant (☎ 367-3448), 6340 Gulf Blvd, is good for a quick bite; hoagies are $3.75, a baked ziti dinner $6.50, and they also have pizza and beer and wine.

Sunset Beach Cafe (☎ 367-3359), 9701 1st St E, serves reliable seafood, pizza and salads. Grilled shrimp Caesar salad is $6.95, and baby back ribs are $9.95.

Bruno's (☎ 367-4420), 432 75th Ave, is a well-spoken-of Italian place open daily for lunch and dinner. Main courses include fettuccine primavera ($10.95) and veal rollatini ($15.95) and chicken cacciatore ($12.95).

We were very pleasantly surprised at *PJ's Oyster Bar and Seafood Restaurant* (☎ 367-3309), 7500 Gulf Blvd. It has generous portions of seafood and friendly service. A half-dozen oysters are $3.75, clams $4.95, and main courses like baked grouper are $10.95. Twelve-ounce Delmonico or eight-ounce sirloin steaks are $9.95. It's open for lunch and dinner.

Fetishes (☎ 363-3700), 6690 Gulf Blvd, is less expensive than you'd think but it can still get up there: we hear good things about their coq au vin, $12.95. Curried lobster Lorraine appetizer is $6.95.

The Maritana Grille (☎ 360-1882), 3400 Gulf Blvd, is expensive but good; main courses from $17.50 include Atlantic salmon with a horseradish crust, shrimp fricassee and lobster beurre blanc ($22). Prix fixe dinner to two is $46.50.

There's karaoke and dancing at *Shell's Seafood* (☎ 360-0889), 6300 Gulf Blvd, from 9 pm to about midnight or 2 am. Happy hour is Monday to Friday from 4 to 7 pm in the restaurant bar and from 8 to 10 ·pm in their Bambooz bar.

Getting There & Away

See the St Petersburg Getting Around section for information on how to get here by bus and car. BATS buses ply Gulf Blvd with frequent service.

TAMPA
• *pop 285,000* ☎ *813*

Tampa is a city on the rise. At the center of its revitalization is Ybor City, the historic heart of the old cigar industry that once dominated this town. But Busch Gardens is undeniably a strong draw, as it combines an excellent zoo with some of the best roller coasters you'll ever encounter. Tampa also offers a great hands-on science museum, a wonderful and interesting new aquarium, several high-quality art museums (including an excellent one dedicated to African-American art), one of the largest performing arts centers on the East Coast and the elegant but haunted Tampa Theater.

History

An Indian fishing village when Hernando de Soto arrived in 1539, Tampa wasn't really settled by Europeans (who drove off and killed – by war or disease – most of the natives) until the late 18th century, and it didn't become a city of consequence until 1855, when Fort Brooke was established here.

At the turn of the century, Cuban cigar makers moved into the area en masse, and over the next 50 years, the city would be known as the Cigar Capital of America. The two men who put Tampa on the cigar-making map were Vicénte Martínez Ybor and Ignacio Haya. In 1885, they moved their considerable cigar factories – *Principe de Gales* (Prince of Wales) and *La Flor de la*

SOUTHWEST

Ybor City became the US cigar capital in 1885 when namesake Vicénte Martínez Ybor moved his factory here from Key West, dealing a blow to unionized labor.

Sanchez y Haya, respectively – to present-day Ybor City, a section of Tampa. Haya's factory actually opened first, in February 1886, and Ybor's soon after. (Ybor's opening had been delayed due to a strike by factory workers.) The move from Key West – which had until that time been the cigar-making capital of the USA for its proximity to Cuba – was precipitated by the strong organization of workers there: the cigar barons decided that moving was the only way to break the union's grip on their factories.

Workers were imported to the new (and un-unionized) factories from Key West and directly from Havana. And as if to send a message to Key West that its cigar-making days were over, a fire broke out there on April 1, 1886, that destroyed several cigar factories, including Ybor's Principe de Gales Key West Branch. Ybor City became the largest functioning production facility, and the cigar business never looked back.

Cuban Influx & Martí As the factories drew thousands and thousands of workers – such as cutters and support staff, like packers and shipping personnel – Ybor City grew to have the largest concentration of Cubans outside Cuba. These Cubans, well aware of the revolutionary fervor whipping up in the homeland, began organizing into leagues and clubs – notably *El Liceo Cubano*

and *La Liga Patriotica Cubana* (the Cuban Lyceum and the Cuban Patriotic League). These organizations, and later others including the Ignacio Agramonte Cuban Revolutionary Club, would form the backbone of revolutionary organization through fundraising and propaganda.

José Martí himself became a member of the Patriotic League (there is a statue of Martí across the street from the Ybor Cigar Factory building today), and he stayed in Tampa when not traveling around Florida. In mid-November 1892, agents of the Spanish government attempted to assassinate Martí by poisoning him.

Immigrants & Health Insurance The prosperity of the area was making it attractive to other immigrant groups, and Italians were chief among them. Blacklisted from working in the Cuban factories, the Italians founded their own 'buckeye' factories, in which they manufactured cheap cigars known as cheroots (see any Clint Eastwood film made prior to 1976 for more information).

In a note that should be interesting to American politicians who complain of immigrants coming to the USA to take advantage of 'the greatest health care system in the world', these Italians, along with Cubans and Spaniards, created Mutual Aid societies to provide health care for the workers. In the earliest example of cooperative social health care in the USA, several societies – among them *El Porvenir, El Circulo Cubano* and *L'unione Italiana* – provided medicine and hospitalization to their members.

Other large immigrant groups that migrated to the area included Spanish, Germans and Jews from various countries.

Wars in Cuba & Decline During the Cuban Revolution and the Spanish-American War, Tampa was an important staging area for revolutionaries and troops to Havana, since it had the most developed communication with the island due to the well-established steamship routes that had evolved to supply the area with Cuban tobacco.

Ybor City remained America's cigar-making capital until the Castro Revolution in 1959 and the resulting US embargo of Cuban products. Over the next three decades, Ybor City, and the entire city of Tampa, hit the skids but good; crime increased and the abandoned factories and housing became dangerous and dilapidated.

Tampa Today Tampa's resurgence of late is due in large part to the renovation, rehabilitation and gentrification of historic Ybor City, which was named a National Historic Landmark District in December 1990. More and more residents are pouring into the little community (especially since the Miami area has become so overcrowded), and it currently has a population of about 3000. Ybor City is now one of the centers of Tampa nightlife. But additionally, the presence of Tampa's excellent museums and Busch Gardens and the popularity of nearby beaches along the Gulf are turning southwest Florida's oldest city into a prime tourist destination once again.

Orientation
Tampa is criss-crossed by major highways and interstates; US Hwy 41 (the Tamiami Trail) flies straight north through the center of the city. Northeast of Tampa, I-275 breaks off from I-75 as it goes south into downtown, running parallel to US Hwy 41, until it meets up with I-4 – this intersection is lovingly referred to by local motorists as Malfunction Junction. I-4 runs east and then northeast to Orlando and on to meet I-95 on Florida's east coast. I-275 runs west, across the Howard Franklin Bridge over Tampa Bay, south through St Petersburg and on to Sarasota.

The Hillsborough River runs through the western side of the city before cutting across to the east; it runs roughly north-south through downtown.

Downtown Tampa is bordered by I-275 at the north, the Hillsborough River at the west, Garrison Channel at the south and

Meridian Ave at the east. Franklin St, in the center of downtown, is a pedestrian zone. Between 6 am and 7 pm Marion St is closed to all vehicular traffic except buses.

Davis Island, home of Tampa General Hospital, and Harbour Island are situated in Hillsborough Bay, south of downtown.

Maps The best map of the area is the cheapest one you can find, as they're all about the same. Check with the CVB's visitor center (see below) for handout maps, which you can also get at car rental companies at the airport.

Information
Tourist Offices Tampa/Hillsborough Convention & Visitors Bureau (☎ 223-1111, 800-826-8358) 111 Madison St, Suite 1010, has a visitors center that's crammed with helpful information and discount magazines. The Ybor City Chamber of Commerce (☎ 248-3712, see Online Services appendix), 1800 E 9th Ave, is a good source of information for the Ybor City historic district. The Greater Tampa Chamber of Commerce (☎ 228-7777) at the Sun Trust Building, 401 E Jackson, doesn't handle tourist information at all.

To find out the weather, call ☎ 645-2506.

Money Barnett Bank has tons of offices; their Barnett Plaza office (☎ 225-8111) is at 101 E JF Kennedy Blvd. In Ybor City there's a branch at 1701 E 7th Ave. American Express (☎ 273-0310) is at One Tampa City Center, and it's also represented by Shouppe Bowen Travel (☎ 963-1962), 14853 N Dale Mabry Hwy.

Post The main post office (☎ 877-0746) is at 5201 W Spruce St; the downtown office (☎ 221-3002) is at 925 N Florida Ave. There's a post office in Ybor City (☎ 248-2543) at 1900 E 12th Ave.

Bookstores The Old Tampa Bay Book Co (☎ 209-2151), 507 N Tampa St downtown, has a huge selection of used books, with a much smaller collection of remainder and new books. Books for Thought

SOUTHWEST

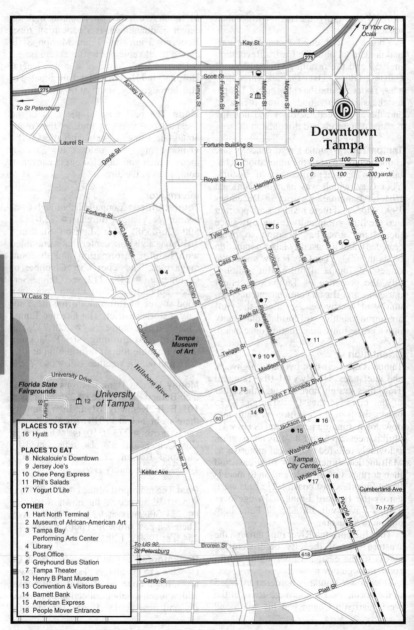

Downtown Tampa

Tampa Museum of Art

University of Tampa

Florida State Fairgrounds

PLACES TO STAY
16 Hyatt

PLACES TO EAT
8 Nickalouie's Downtown
9 Jersey Joe's
10 Chee Peng Express
11 Phil's Salads
17 Yogurt D'Lite

OTHER
1 Hart North Terminal
2 Museum of African-American Art
3 Tampa Bay Performing Arts Center
4 Library
5 Post Office
6 Greyhound Bus Station
7 Tampa Theater
12 Henry B Plant Museum
13 Convention & Visitors Bureau
14 Barnett Bank
15 American Express
18 People Mover Entrance

SOUTHWEST

(☎ 988-6363), 10910 N 56th St at White-way (two blocks south of Fowler Ave), specializes in books by or about African Americans. Tomes and Treasures (☎ 251-9368), 202 S Howard Ave, is a gay and lesbian bookshop.

Libraries The main downtown library (☎ 273-3652) is at 900 N Ashley St. In Ybor City, there's a branch library (☎ 272-5547) at 1505 Nebraska Ave.

Media The major daily is the *Tampa Tribune*, though the *St Petersburg Times* and the *Miami Herald* are available everywhere as well. Get community information and club/pub/going-out listings in *Weekly Planet*, and also in *Hyde Park Metro*. NPR is at 89.7 FM.

Gay & Lesbian The gay and lesbian scene in Tampa is enormous but hard to pin down. The editor of the biggest gay newsmagazine said things are in a constant state of flux, and we found that many phone numbers even a few years old had been disconnected.

The first stop any gay or lesbian traveler should make is to M/C Film Festival (☎ 870-6233), 3601 W JF Kennedy Blvd, between Himes Ave and Dale Mabry Hwy. Dubbed the Gay Mart of Tampa by none other than the director of *Hello Dolly*, it has the largest collection of nonpornographic gay videos in the USA and gay and lesbian interest films (which include everything Marlene, Keanu, Joan and Bette ever did). It's the site of meetings of the Florida Human Rights Task Force (the first Wednesday of each month); on Thursday in spring and summer they show selections from the Pride Film Festival. It has a 35-foot-long bulletin board with local events and happenings, as well as a coffee and juice bar. There's a bus stop right in front; any bus going west on Kennedy Blvd stops here – look for the pink triangles and rainbow signs out front.

There are three main periodicals available around the city: *The Gazette* – a monthly with the most up-to-date and solidly reliable listings of gay, lesbian and bisexual community groups and resource centers – *Stonewall* and *Watermark. Womyn's Words* is a monthly lesbian newsletter available at M/C Film Festival.

Laundry We used the Busch Laundromat (☎ 932-8145), 1216 Busch Blvd E. But check this one out: Laundromat Express (☎ 837-9100) is a coin laundry at Phar Mor Plaza, 4306 Dale Mabry Hwy S, that's open from 7 am to midnight and has pool tables, snacks and beer.

In Ybor City, there's a coin laundry at the corner of 7th Ave and 25th St.

Medical Services The biggest hospital in the area is Tampa General Hospital (☎ 251-7000), south of downtown on Davis Island. University Community Hospital is at 3100 E Fletcher Ave.

Museum of Science & Industry (MOSI) Tampa's absolutely enormous Museum of Science & Industry (☎ 987-6000, recorded information 987-6100), 4801 E Fowler Ave, is one of the biggest draws around, and it's definitely in contention for the best hands-on science museum in the state.

Downstairs there are traveling exhibits, a good gift shop and a very cool hot-air balloon exhibit: push the button and hot air fills the little balloon, which zooms skyward on its guidewire.

Upstairs there are exhibits on electricity and power, a cool infrared camera display, and one of our favorites, the Energy Pinball machine. Turn the giant screw to lift a giant steel ball to the top and send it on its journey through a wire pipe, which sends it through several different routes, each one demonstrating potential, trajectory, momentum or energy transfer. Which are fancy ways of saying that the ball makes an awful racket and resembles a giant Rube Goldberg contraption.

The Gulf Coast Hurricane exhibit is another favorite: you sit in a room that simulates 75 mph winds and watch as the indicator lights move slowly up to that speed – it's pretty amazing.

SOUTHWEST

There are some cool circuit and current experiments and a huge Tesla coil – no, it's not a crappy Czech-made television but, essentially, a huge capacitor. Nikola Tesla (1857-1943) devised a method of transferring electric current not with electric wires but with – for God's sake – highly charged pulses that he bounced off the ionosphere. The Tesla coil takes about a half hour to charge and then sends a ZAP against the glass. Far out.

And farther upstairs there's a great echo tube, a ham radio station (MOSI's station is KE4ZRS), and you can send Morse code or light signals.

There are exhibitions on the human body and Florida, and one of Corinna's favorites was the one that shows the amount of garbage the average American generates every year.

MOSIMAX is the museum's IMAX cinema, which shows several IMAX films.

The museum's open Sunday to Thursday from 9 am to 5 pm, Friday and Saturday from 9 am to 9 pm. Admission is $8 for adults, $7 for seniors, students and kids ages 13 to 18, $2 for children two to 12. Admission to MOSIMAX is $6/5/4, and a combination ticket is $11/9/7.

Museum of African-American Art

We highly recommend a visit to this lovely museum (☎ 272-2466), 1308 N Marion St, which holds works by and about African Americans that study and describe black life in America from slavery to the present day. There are two floors, and while exhibitions rotate (about 15% of the museum's holdings are on display at any given time), much of the smaller 2nd floor is dedicated to the permanent collection.

When we visited, there were woodcuts by Elizabeth Catlett on the role of black women in the world. We also saw a temporary exhibition of wood sculptures by Leroy Jackson, Sr, who feels that his works should be a tactile, as well as a visual, experience, and he encourages viewers to 'touch the wood and feel the marks'.

Upstairs is the Barnett-Aden Gallery, named for the mother of Alonzo Aden.

Aden was curator at the Howard University Art Gallery in Washington DC, along with James Herring, who founded the Howard University Fine Arts Program. Adolphus Ealey, who worked with Aden and Herring, brought the core collection to Florida. There's a portrait of Aden above the round desk in the gallery, and a portrait of Herring above the video monitor. Also in the gallery are works including Irene Rice Pereira's *Heavenly Twins*, Adolphus Ealey's strange *Night Flight*, Aaron Douglas's *Nashville* and Norman Lewis's *Study in Blue*.

The museum, funded by the Florida Education Fund, is very involved in Tampa community projects and holds lectures and special workshops, like one for children with Jackson demonstrating wood-cutting techniques. They have a partnership with the nearby Brighter Horizons Day Care Center, whose kids come by once a month for storytelling by members of the community, from teachers to postal workers.

The museum is open Tuesday to Friday from 10 am to 4.30 pm, Saturday from 10 am to 5 pm, closed Sunday and Monday. Admission is $3 for adults, $2 for children and seniors.

Tampa Museum of Art

The Tampa Museum of Art (☎ 274-8130), 600 N Ashley St, has rotating exhibitions throughout its enormous new building, and shows span a wide range – from avant garde to old masters, to sculpture, photography and works by emerging Florida artists.

Their permanent exhibition in the Barbara and Costas Lemonopoulos Gallery has antiques from Greece and Rome, including *Grave Altar of L Caltilius Diadumenus* (circa 160-170 AD), a very impressive collection including miniature vessels, Levantine oil lamps, a large collection of southern Italian vases and theater artifacts, and the ceramic Amphora trophy, given to winners of horse races around 540 BC.

The glassed-in Terrace Gallery, overlooking the Hillsborough River, is an incredible backdrop for sculptures, including the chromed steel, metal and glass *Multiple Faces* by Richard Stankiewicz and a very funky and *Untitled* aluminum work by Carol K Brown.

The museum shop is excellent, with a good selection of books, colorful ties, jewelry and T-shirts.

The museum's open Tuesday and Thursday from 10 am to 5 pm, Wednesday from 10 am to 9 pm, Sunday from 1 to 5 pm, closed Monday. Admission is $5 for adults, $4 for seniors and students, $3 for children aged six to 18. On Wednesday between 5 and 9 pm and Sunday from 1 to 5 pm admission is free.

Florida Aquarium

Tampa's newest star attraction, the Florida Aquarium (☎ 273-4020), 701 Channelside Drive, has exhibits over three floors that trace how water travels from its source to the open sea.

Take the elevator to the top to start at the beginning, Florida Wetlands, which has some very neat mist-covered water, itty bitty fish, cool turtles, a limestone cavern and a canopied tree area. You'll see alligator hatchlings in the marshes, and there's a great Wetlands Lab where you can look at (but not touch) diamondback turtles, red-bellied sliders and a three stripe mud turtle. There's a mangrove forest here as well.

In Bays & Beaches, an especially nice exhibit shows sea horses up close in the lab, along with a Caribbean reef octopus. The beach (which is indoors) is complete with dunes, waves, sea oats and live seabirds.

The best of their exhibits is the coral reef, which is in a 500,000-gallon tank with 12-inch-thick walls. It's teeming with colorful coral and thousands of fish, and divers jump in and speak to the open-mouthed crowds via intercom several times a day from 11 am to 3 pm. It's interactive: the audience asks questions of the diver, who swims around pointing out the answers, grabbing sharks and so on – kids love it. There's also an exhibit on ocean drifters, like moon jellyfish, and plankton under a microscope.

Channelside Drive is northwest of downtown between downtown and Ybor City.

From I-4, get off at exit 1 and follow the signs. From downtown, signage is plentiful. Jackson St, heading east, is the quickest route to Channelside Drive. From either starting point, there are large blue and accurate signs pointing the way. The aquarium is open daily from 9 am to 5 pm. Admission is $13.95 for adults, $12.55 for seniors and kids 13 to 18, $6.95 for children three to 12; parking is $3. You could rent an audio guide for $1, but we say spare yourself. They rent wheelchairs and strollers for $2.

Tampa Theater

The Tampa Theater is an extremely beautiful, atmospheric movie palace (☎ 274-8286, recorded information 274-8981), 711 Franklin St Mall. It was built in 1926 by John Eberson – 1996 was their 70th anniversary – and it was placed on the National Register of Historic Places in 1978. Today it shows independent and classic films, but it also holds concerts and other special events. It's the place that locals bring their out-of-town friends to show off historic Tampa.

There are stars painted onto the ceiling (though no star formations), some of which – 'wishing stars' – twinkle. All the furniture in the 1446-seat theater is original, and, oh yes, the place is haunted by one Hank Fink, a projectionist here for 25 years who died in the late 1960s. People claim to have seen apparitions, and one story says that a projectionist quit because he heard strange noises in the booth; other staff members have heard creepy things like keys rattling.

Come early to hear the mighty Wurlitzer organ, which is played before every movie by central Florida theater organ society volunteers; it features sirens, boat horns, cymbals, sleigh bells and other kooky sounds.

The old intercom unit in the back of the theater is neat, as is the Columbus statue on the left side of the stage. Other statues include figures from Greek and Roman mythology.

Admission prices are the cheapest in town: $5.50 for adults and $3.50 for children, seniors and students.

Henry B Plant Museum

Railroad magnate Henry Plant's Tampa Bay Hotel, which opened in 1891, was one of the most luxurious places imaginable in the early days of the city, when Tampa was about as remote a place as was Miami at the southern tip of the state. All the rooms had private baths and electricity, and the hotel was furnished as extravagantly as possible, with items that included the furniture, sculptures and mirrors Plant's wife had collected during their travels.

After the hotel failed in the early part of the 20th century, the city of Tampa took it over, and today the National Historic Landmark building is open as the Henry Plant Museum (☎ 254-1891), 401 W JF Kennedy Blvd, across the river from downtown on the University of Tampa campus. You can gawk at the luxury and tour the hotel's grand salon, guest room, solarium and lobby, among others. The museum is open Tuesday to Saturday from 10 am to 4 pm, Sunday from noon to 4 pm; closed Monday. Admission is free, though they ask for a $3 donation from adults, $1 from children 12 and under.

The annual Victoria Christmas Stroll takes place from December 1 to 21, and it includes dramatizations of fairy tales by actors in period costume in different rooms of the hotel. Tickets are $6 for adults, $3 for children aged three to 12.

Lowry Park Zoo

The best exhibit at the Lowry Park Zoo (☎ 935-8552), 7530 North Blvd, is their manatee and aquatic center; when we visited they had a 960-pound manatee called 'New Bob', though he may have been set free by now. There's an exhibit on panthers (Corrie and Butch), and alligators and bison can be seen in the Florida wildlife center.

In the Asian domain you'll see one of only two thousand remaining Indian rhinoceros. There's an 18,000-sq-foot, free-flight aviary and, of course, a petting area in the children's village. The strangest exhibit is that of the naked mole rats – the only mammal known to live in a social structure similar to that of ants and termites (one queen and a few breeding males). They live underground and are native to northeast Africa.

The zoo is open daily from 9.30 am to 5 pm. Admission is $6.50 for adults, $5.50 for seniors, $4.50 for children three to 11. Every year around Christmas they have Illuminations, a night festival; admission is $3.75 per person, children under two are free. To get to the zoo from downtown, take I-4 west to I-275 north to exit 31; go west on Fly Ave to North Blvd, turn right, and the entrance is about 200 feet ahead on the left.

Children's Museum of Tampa

The Children's Museum of Tampa (☎ 935-8441), 7550 North Blvd in Lowry Park (next to the zoo), has rotating, hands-on interactive displays and, outside, a very slick, permanent, 45,000-sq-foot exhibition that kids love: child-size replicas of 24 downtown Tampa buildings. Peddle cars cost $1 every 15 minutes, and Lowry Park has picnic tables.

It's open Monday to Thursday from 9 am to 4.30 pm, Friday from 9 am to 3 pm, Saturday from 10 am to 5 pm and Sunday from 1 to 5 pm. Admission is $2.50, children under two are free.

Contemporary Art Museum

The University of South Florida's Contemporary Art Museum (☎ 974-2849), on the USF campus at 4202 E Fowler Ave, runs six to eight exhibitions of works by university students and alumni. The museum is open Monday to Friday from 10 am to 5 pm, Saturday from 1 to 4 pm. Admission is free.

Ybor City

Until recently a dangerous and scary ghost town, Ybor City (EE-bore) is in the middle of a renaissance that rivals that of South Miami Beach. We found most of the people in Ybor City to be quite friendly, and the area is a must-see for its energy and its history (see above).

Ybor City is in the northeast section of Tampa. 7th Ave (La Septima) is the main drag which is closed to vehicles on Friday and Saturday from 9 pm to 4 am. The area is roughly bordered by 23rd St at the east, 13th St at the west, Palm Ave, between 10th and 11th Aves, at the north and the railroad tracks along 6th Ave at the south. 14th St is also called Avenida Republica de Cuba.

The folks at Creatures of Delight (see below) are wonderfully helpful and know the area well.

Ybor City State Museum Taking up about half a city block, the Ybor City State Museum (☎ 247-6323), 1818 9th Ave, is located in the former Ferlita Bakery building. The museum grounds include three reconstructed cigar workers' houses, the original brick ovens from the bakery, and nearby, La Casita, a separate historical museum, 1804 9th Ave.

The Ybor City State Museum has displays of the city's history, including fascinating photographs of the cigar factories and of turn-of-the-century Ybor City. Tours of La Casita (you need a guide to get in) leave every 30 minutes from 10 am to 2.30 pm. The museum is open Tuesday to Saturday from 9 am to 5 pm; La Casita is open from 10 am to 3 pm. Admission is $1, including the tour.

Ybor Square Mall Taking up the block between 13th and 14th Sts and 8th and 9th Aves, the Ybor Square Mall (☎ 247-4497) is in the former headquarters of the Ybor Martínez Cigar Factory. Today it's a shopping mall and drinking spot, and it's the launching point for free tours of the area (see Organized Tours below). You'll see the warehouse (home today to an Italian restaurant), stemmery house and factory. There's a statue of Queen Isabella of Spain on the 2nd floor of the mall to the left of the tour office; the statue was made in the 1880s by Ybor himself, and he dragged it around the world as an advertisement for his Principe de Gales cigars. See the Places to Eat and Nightclubs sections below for information on the mall's café, restaurants, jazz club and bar.

Friends of Martí Park The *Parque Amigos de José Martí*, across the street from Ybor Square Mall, contains a white (and not very good) monument to Martí that was dedicated by Martí's son, actor Cesar Romero. The park is at the site of the house of Paulina Pedroso, where Martí stayed after the Spanish government attempted to assassinate him in 1892.

SOUTHWEST

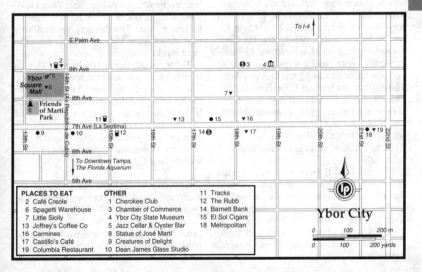

PLACES TO EAT	OTHER	11 Tracks
2 Café Creole	1 Cherokee Club	12 The Rubb
6 Spagetti Warehouse	3 Chamber of Commerce	14 Barnett Bank
7 Little Sicily	4 Ybor City State Museum	15 El Sol Cigars
13 Joffrey's Coffee Co	5 Jazz Cellar & Oyster Bar	18 Metropolitan
16 Carmines	8 Statue of José Martí	
17 Castillo's Café	9 Creatures of Delight	
19 Columbia Restaurant	10 Dean James Glass Studio	

Ybor City

0   100   200 m
0   100   200 yards

José Martí

José Martí (1853-1895) was born in Havana, and was exiled in 1870 to Spain for 'opposition to Colonial rule'. Eventually Martí would travel and write extensively in North and South America. His anti-racist writings were vast, and he relentlessly pursued his vision of a free Cuba, stirring up anti-Spanish sentiment wherever he could.

Martí traveled throughout Florida, and while he was allowed to return in 1878 to Cuba, he was quickly booted out again by angry Spanish authorities. In 1895, Martí returned to Cuba to take part in the war for Cuban independence, and was one of the first to die in the conflict.

Martí is considered to be one of Cuba's leading writers and a hero of its independence. The Friends of Martí Park in Ybor City commemorates the assassination attempt that took place here in 1892. ■

Cigar Shops In this former cigar capital of America, there's only one place in which you can see cigars being made, and shops that don't do it anymore will tell you that 'no one in Florida does that anymore,' which is complete balderdash – see the Miami Little Havana, Miami Beach and Key West chapters. Tampa Rico Cigar Co (☎ 247-6738, 800-892-3760) in Ybor Square Mall carries Honduran and Dominican-made cigars, and it does cigar-making demonstrations from 11 am to 3 pm daily. The oldest cigar store in Ybor City is El Sol (☎ 248-5905), 1728 E 7th Ave, which has been around since 1929. They sell Floridian, Honduran and Dominican cigars. Metropolitan (☎ 248-3304, 800-607-3304), 2103 E 7th Ave, is a cigar shop that also sells coffee.

The most well-known of the Tampa brands is Havatampa, whose mass-marketed Tampa Sweets are available in supermarkets and tobacco shops throughout the state and the country. Their factory is on the outskirts of Tampa, in the area of Sable Park, and they discontinued tours several years ago.

Ybor City Brewing Company In the former cigar factory of Seidenberg & Co (1894), the Ybor City Brewing Company (☎ 242-9222), 2205 N 20th St, is a microbrewery that produces 60,000 barrels of beer every year, including their Ybor Gold, Ybor Calusa Wheat, Ybor Brown Ale and Gaspar's Ale. The brews are available throughout Ybor City as well as throughout Florida.

Thirty-minute tours of the brewery (which does not have a restaurant or bar) are given Tuesday to Saturday from 11 am to 3 pm on the hour, and they include a look at the brewing and bottling process, a history of the building and a beer tasting (it's not enough to get you drunk). Tours cost $2, $1 of which is donated to restoration projects within Ybor City.

Creatures of Delight We say that the weird and wonderful world of Creatures of Delight (☎ 248-4167), 1325 E 7th Ave, is a definite highlight in Ybor City. Two guys (Tom and David) have teamed together to produce some incredible-looking creatures, made from rubber plush and painted in the most screaming colors, one sweeter and cuddlier than the next. If you're English and have ever opened a box of Rice Krispies to discover a latex monster that's both cute and terrifying, you've seen their work. Tom and David's workshop is in the back, and they don't mind if you watch them create, or – even better – attend one of their workshops (every Sunday at 2 pm). You pick one of their many creatures from the shelves and use the original mold to create your own; the charge, from $15 to 25, includes all supplies. It's a really fun place to stop.

Dean James Glass Studio Dean James Glass Studio (☎ 248-3132), 1401 E 7th Ave, is a working studio where you can watch glass being blown. They blow Monday to Friday from 9 am to 5 pm, and also during Gallery Walks.

Organized Tours The Ybor City State Museum (☎ 247-6323), Ybor City Chamber of Commerce (☎ 248-3712) and the Ybor Entertainment and Arts Association (get this acronym: YEAA! ☎ 247-6363) offer free guided walking tours through the district from January to April on Tuesday, Thursday and Saturday at 10.30 am, and from May to December on Thursday and Saturday at 10.30 am. They leave from the Ybor Square Mall (see above). The guides are very knowledgeable about the history and development of the area. Gallery Walks, sponsored by YEAA and several local galleries, take place periodically, though not as regularly as in other Florida cities, like Miami or Pensacola. Check and see if there are any on when you visit.

Places to Eat Since most people gravitate to Ybor City and stay through the night, we've included the area's eateries and nightspots here. There are new places opening all the time, but Ybor City's most eagerly awaited entries, we're certain, are those by stunt legend Evel Knievil and wrestling marvel Hulk Hogan. Knievil's place has been under construction for what seems like forever, and Hogan announced his recently. Let's watch, shall we?

Castillo's Café (☎ 248-1306), 1823 E 7th Ave, is a great spot for breakfast. Two eggs with ham and grits or hash browns is $2.65, omelets $3.50, chicken and yellow rice $3.95 and roast pork (Spanish style) $4.50.

Joffrey's Coffee Co (☎ 248-5282), 1616 E 7th Ave, is a New York-style coffee shop; they have croissant and bagel sandwiches ($4) and lots of coffee and tea, cakes and pastry. It's nonsmoking.

Three cheers for *Ybor City's B-Man's BBQ* (☎ 247-1966), a shack at 1604 N 17th Street (between 6th and 7th Aves), that has a few tables outside and stays open till 3 am on Friday and Saturday. Grab a chicken dinner with two sides and bread for $4 (!!); a ribs dinner is $6.50, half a slab of ribs is $7 and a full slab $13. They have draft beer for $1.50.

There are tons of choices for Cuban food, but for Cuban sandwiches, we liked *Carmine's* (☎ 248-3834), 1802 E 7th St, where you can watch through the window as they make mountains of sandwiches. A Cuban sandwich is $2.95 for half, $3.95 for a whole one; they also do pasta dishes from $3.95 to 5.95 and burgers from $3.95 to 5.95. Very cool service.

Little Sicily (☎ 248-2940), 1724 8th Ave E, is a great Italian-style deli with a few small outside tables. Huge sandwiches are from $2.89 to 5.79, good calzone is $3.99, ziti is $2.99, and, again, very friendly service. The Creatures of Delight crew says it's their favorite lunch spot.

Cephas Gilbert, who showed up in America in 1982 with $37 in his pocket, now runs *Cephas* (☎ 247-9022), 1701 E 4th Ave, a piece of Jamaica in Ybor City. It may look a little run down when you enter, but check out the back garden: it's lush, jungly and very Jamaican. Service is very friendly – note the sign outside that says 'respect due whether you're black or white' – and a huge plate of jerk chicken wings, curry goat chicken, brown stew, fish or vegetables (which Cephas says he grows himself) is $7. They also serve Red Stripe and Royal Stout beers. It's open 8 am to 3 am.

We had great food at the *Spaghetti Warehouse* (☎ 248-1720), 1911 N 13th St, but it seemed like service was a bit hit or miss, depending on whether your waiter was having a bad day. However, the spaghetti (from $4.19 to 6.99), fettuccine ($5.99) and eggplant parmigian ($6.99) was very good indeed, with fresh-made tomato sauce. It's a nice atmosphere in the renovated warehouse behind Ybor Square Mall, with tables inside and outside.

If you like Japanese, do hit *Samurai* (☎ 248-5829), 1901 N 13th St in Ybor Square Mall opposite the Spaghetti Warehouse. It serves great and cheap lunch specials: their Samurai Lunch includes hibachi chicken and sukiyaki ($5.95), or hibachi shrimp or scallops ($6.95), along with Japanese pasta, vegetables, steamed rice and salad with a killer ginger dressing. Other combinations, like steak and chicken or chicken and shrimp, are $7.95. Prices go up at dinner, but they have good sushi.

Said to be the oldest restaurant in Florida, the *Columbia Restaurant* (☎ 248-4961), 2117 E 7th Ave, is a gaudy, glitzy place that most people peg right away as a tourist trap. The interior is gorgeous, very Cuban-feeling, with a fountain at the center, and staff are attentive in a 'What you wan?' sort of way. We were unimpressed with the lunch we had (set prices from $5.95 to 8.95 for dishes like quesadillas, grouper and sautéed shrimp), though the salads were excellent. To be fair, we didn't come back for dinner, which is said to be better. Entrees at dinner include sautéed steak fillet for $13.95, cazuela de mariscos (shrimp, calamari, mussels and clams flambéed in brandy) for $15.95, and roast pork loin à la Cubana – marinated pork – for $12.95.

Probably the nicest place to eat in Ybor City in terms of atmosphere, *Café Creole & Oyster Bar* (☎ 247-6283), 1330 E 9th Ave (in the renovated El Pasaje Plaza), is a very chic and yuppified place with good beef and chicken dishes, though we were (and we feel grouchy saying it) totally upset at the fish dishes, which we felt were disastrous. Service was very good, and they have a good wine list and desserts. Expect to pay about $25 per person with a drink and tip. It has live jazz on Friday and Saturday nights.

Bars & Nightclubs Ybor City is Tampa nightlife central, and clubs are opening and closing all the time. On weekends expect intense crowds and partiers reveling into the wee hours – locals say that the best bet is to show up really early, get your hand stamped and then come back later and push through the crowds like a celebrity. Check flyers on walls and lampposts – they're the most reliable source of up-to-date party, concert and nightclub information.

The Castle Bar (☎ 247-7547), 2004 16th St at 9th Ave, was the 'in' nightclub while we were doing our research; it gets an artsy and interesting mix of people. No cover but you must be over 21 to get in.

The Rubb (☎ 247-4225), 1507 7th Ave E, gets a more mature crowd; it's an eclectic rock, jazz, blues club with live bands on weekends.

The Jazz Cellar (☎ 248-1862) has decent jazz every night. There's a $3 per person cover, but no minimum. It's behind the Ybor Square Mall – technically at 1916 14th St, but the basement entrance is on 9th Ave between 13th and 14th Sts.

Oak Barrel Tavern (☎ 247-1164) in the Ybor Square Mall is a very popular drinking spot – sort of an English pub thing. A half pint is $2.50, pints are $3.50 and liters are $5.95. There's a happy hour Monday to Friday from 4 to 7 pm, and they have bar food like soup ($1.95/2.75), chili ($2.50/3.25), a cheese platter ($6.95) and bratwurst ($3.95). It's open Monday to Saturday from 11 am to 3 am and Sunday from 1 pm to midnight.

Cherry's (☎ 247-4541), 1512 E 7th Ave, is a bar/restaurant popular with a younger crowd interested in drinks with vaguely lewd names.

Empire (☎ 247-2582), 1902 7th Ave, is alternative to industrial, with a diverse straight and gay crowd.

Vertigo (☎ 241-8300), 1505 Palm Ave E, has alternative music that's gothic and industrial.

Luna (☎ 248-3460), 1802 7th Ave E, sort

of a lounge club sans piano player and martinis, is a dark-ambient kind of place that's mixed gay and straight.

Gay & Lesbian Clubs With irony both heavy and satisfying, the *Cherokee Club* (☎ 247-9966), 1320 E 9th Ave (upstairs from Café Creole & Oyster Bar), is a predominantly lesbian club that was once a 'gentleman only' club. It has dancing and, infrequently, live music, and it's open Friday and Saturday from 8 pm to 3 am. Note the finger in the blue oval sign out front: it's a holdover from the old days in which it was the Chi Chi Club, and the gentlemen who frequented it included such luminaries as José Martí, Winston Churchill and Teddy Roosevelt. Bully, ladies!

Tracks (☎ 247-2006), 1430 7th Ave E (and if it isn't called Tracks there will still be *something* here), is a gay club in the former Hotel de la Havana building with drag shows on weekends and a rollicking atmosphere.

Busch Gardens
The area's biggest theme park, the 335-acre Busch Gardens (☎ 987-5171, recorded information 987-5082) is an African-themed thrill park with the best roller coasters in the state and one of the state's best zoos with about 2800 animals – though we wish you could get a little closer, especially to the more exotic ones in the Serengeti Plain. Still, a day at Busch Gardens is, we think, worth the price of admission, though it's more worth it if you get a combination ticket to Busch Gardens/Adventure Island (see below).

The park is open from 9.30 am to 6 pm. Admission prices are $36.15 for adults, $29.75 for children aged three to nine; children two and under are free. It's at 10000 McKinley Drive, accessible from both I-75 and I-275, both of which have Busch Blvd exits; from I-75 head west at the exit, from I-275 head east. The entrance to the park is on McKinley Drive, which juts north from Busch Blvd.

Orientation & Information The park

sprawls northward from the main entrance, which leads to the Moroccan Palace theater. There are about nine main areas, and they are described below in rough walking or transport order. See individual listings below for the easiest way to get to adjacent regions.

Just past the main entrance in Morocco, **Guest Relations** is to the left, as are toilets and telephones. You'll find **toilets** throughout the park (they're well signed). If you need **baby services**, most of the toilets have diaper-changing tables, and there's a nursing area in the Land of the Dragons (see Bird Gardens below). Stroller rentals ($2 to 5) are just to the right of the entrance.

As far as **handicapped services**, wheelchair rentals ($4) are also to the right of the entrance, and most rides are ADA compliant – though wheelchairs aren't allowed on some, and they're not allowed on the Skyride. Check with Guest Relations for a brochure describing all the park's restrictions.

First aid is available in the infirmary, next to Das Festhaus in Timbuktu.

Several of the rides have **height restrictions**, which vary from 42 to 56 inches, and these are noted with the individual rides below. You'll find that **lines** at Busch Gardens are far, far shorter than at Orlando parks; on a high-season summer day the wait for Kumba, currently the most popular ride at the park, was about 10 minutes.

As far as getting around the park, in addition to the monorail and Skyride described under Crown Colony below, there's a **train** that circles around the Serengeti Plain, across the north of the park, south around Stanleyville, and around Timbuktu with stations at Nairobi, Congo (disembark only) and Stanleyville.

And, of course, you'll never be at a loss for a gift shop, and cafes are dotted around. There's even a **bakery** in Morocco.

Shows & Performances Check at Guest Relations or the ticket window for the day's shows and activities. Craft demonstrations and live entertainment take place in the Marrakesh Theater, the Tangiers Theater and the Moroccan Palace. Various animal acts occur all over, including shows starring alligators (Morocco), elephants and tortoises (Nairobi), orangutans and warthogs (Stanleyville) and tigers (Congo). The schedule changes often, but when we visited shows (their titles are pretty self-explanatory) included:

Hollywood Live on Ice
　30 minutes, the Moroccan Palace Theater
Dolphins of the Deep
　25 minutes, Dolphin Theater
World of Birds
　30 minutes, Bird Gardens
Marrakesh Theater Entertainment
　Song and dance shows Latin Heat and
　Heart of the Country, 20 minutes, Morocco
Harris & Co
　A live local TV broadcast shot Monday
　to Friday at the Tangiers Theater, Morocco
Das Festhaus
　Bavarian dancing for those in need of
　a *Schuhplattl'n* fix, 20 minutes, Timbuktu
A Dragon's Tale
　Roaming dragons in the Land
　of the Dragons, Bird Gardens

Crown Colony Northeast of Morocco is the Crown Colony, from where you board the air-conditioned monorail (the bumpiest in the free world), a circular ride over the Serengeti Plain, and the Skyride – a ride across the western edge of Serengeti, past Timbuktu, to the border between Stanleyville and Congo and back. You can use it as an orientation tour or get off at either end.

The Crown Colony House Restaurant is in a Victorian-style building overlooking the Serengeti Plain. In here you'll also find the highly welcome Hospitality Center, where you can get a 10-oz cup of Anheuser-Busch beer (limit two per person per day, 21 and older). In the Clydesdale Hamlet you can see the trademark Budweiser Clydesdale horses.

Questor is a simulator ride that takes you through mountain formations, down a waterfall and past crystals inside the earth (minimum height 42 inches). The ride was a bit more rattling than others we've taken, and we thought the narration was way too loud and picture quality could be better. Seats toward the back are the better bet.

Egypt Adjacent to Crown Colony is the park's newest attraction, Egypt. The star of the show may well be the new star of the park: Montu, the world's largest inverted steel roller coaster. Because it opened on the day we went to press, we didn't get into Egypt, but it sounds pretty terrifying. This is a three-minute ride featuring an 'Immelman', or inverse, loop – a 104-foot vertical loop that is the world's largest on an inverted coaster. But there are also two more vertical loops at a 45° angle. Speeds on the coaster reach 60 mph, and the G-force hits a maximum of 3.85 (minimum height 52 inches).

Other attractions in Egypt include a replica of King Tutankhamen's tomb, a gigantic wall inscribed with hieroglyphics, and a Sand Dig area, where children can discover Egyptian antiques in the sand. There are, of course, shopping bazaars and Egyptian-costumed characters roaming around.

Myombe Reserve Also called the Great Ape Domain, this is a three-acre area landscaped to resemble the western lowlands, where the six gorillas and seven chimpanzees are from. It feels very tropical, complete with waterfalls and piped-in tropical fog. From here a pathway takes you north into Nairobi.

Nairobi This is home to the Animal Nursery, the petting zoo and the Nocturnal Mountain exhibit, which kids adore: nocturnal animals can be viewed. Other exhibits here include the Show Jumping Hall of Fame, Reptiles, a tortoise display (six Aldabre tortoises) and an elephant display. The Kenya Kanteen serves ice cream and snacks.

Timbuktu This area is home to Scorpion – a 50-mph ride with a 360° loop and 62-foot drop (minimum height 42 inches) – as well as Phoenix, a boat-swing ride (minimum height 48 inches). There are also kiddie rides in this area, as well as – parent alert! – a video-game arcade. The Dolphin Theater stages live entertainment, and Das Festhaus (in Timbuktu?) is an oom-pah-pah restaurant and entertainment complex, with a shopping bazaar. The infirmary is adjacent to Das Festhaus.

Serengeti Plain The Serengeti Plain lies north of Crown Colony, east of Nairobi and Timbuktu. It's an 80-acre habitat populated by about 500 animals, who can be seen best from the monorail and pretty well from the Skyride and the steam locomotive. But protecting the animals, which include zebras, giraffes, kudus, hippos, lions, camels and buffalo, by giving them free range makes viewing them very difficult. We can't think of a better way to do it, but we were a little disappointed at the distance from the animals, which themselves are fantastic. The bumpy monorail ride lasts about 15 to 20 minutes. We liked the Skyride much better – it's more peaceful, you can hear the wind and animal sounds, and it's much more natural and relaxed.

Congo Everyone is trying to get here, to the northwest corner of Busch Gardens, for one reason: Kumba, which is the star of the Congo area and one of the best roller coasters you'll find. It's a crazy ride, featuring a diving loop that plunges from a height of 110 feet, a camelback loop (spiraling 360° and creating three seconds of weightlessness) and a 108-foot vertical loop. In addition, there are ducks, dips and swirls around pedestrian walkways and a generally terrifying vibe (minimum height 52 inches).

But it's not that scary. Nick, who has been quite cautious about riding on coasters since the movie *Rollercoaster* finally mustered the courage to get on. His thoughts:

I was most surprised that despite the high speeds and the wicked twists and turns (especially the corkscrew plunge leading into a corkscrew loop after the first big hill) the ride was in fact very gentle, and not at all jarring. The loops are best viewed with your eyes wide open. The only side-effect was that with the high winds and the fact that people are smiling, it looks at the end of the ride like all the people on it are doing a Rod Serling impersonation, with their gums stuck to their upper teeth by the wind!

Having procrastinated getting on for the better part of an hour, I came out of the exit and walked right back into the entrance for another go! Highly recommended!

The other roller coaster ride here is the relatively tame (ha!) Python, a double spiral corkscrew that hits speeds of 50 mph (minimum height 48 inches). Rafts take you down the Congo River Rapids (height restriction 38 inches, or at least two years old), but beware that you *will* get wet: if not from the current splashing against the raft, from the water cannons that line the route. People actually *pay* to shoot water at innocent rafters as they float by.

Claw Island is home to absolutely heartbreakingly beautiful white and yellow Bengal tigers – there are feeding times posted near the fence, and it's gruesomely fascinating to watch these fluffy, elegant creatures ripping into lunch. There are more kiddie rides here, the Ubanga-Banga Bumper Cars and the seasonal (winter) Vivi Restaurant.

Stanleyville Stanleyville lies south of the Congo, west of Timbuktu. It's an African village featuring the Tanganyika Tidal Wave – a boat ride that plunges riders over a 55-foot waterfall (minimum height 42 inches). There's also Stanley Falls, a log-flume ride with a 40-foot drop.

Shows are presented in the Zambezi Pavilion and the Stanleyville Theater. You can walk through the Orchid Canyon, where there are orangutans and warthogs, the Stanleyville Smokehouse and the Bazaar Café.

Bird Gardens Originally, the park began here at Bird Gardens, which was a minor detour from the main action at the Anheuser-Busch Brewery tour: you'd guzzle some free beer and walk outside to see the birds. It was from this area that the attraction grew into what it is today. And it's interesting to note that the brewery not only doesn't offer tours anymore, but it may even be closing altogether, its work distributed to other breweries around the state and country.

The first area you enter is Land of the Dragons, an interactive children's area. It's an enchanted forest filled with colorful dragons, starring one called Dumphrey who romps around with the kids. There is a three-story-tall tree house to climb around in, slides, a Ferris wheel, a flume ride and a waterfall and dragon carousel (kids' rides have 56-inch height restriction). There's a nursing area here as well.

Other attractions within Bird Gardens include exotic birds and birds of prey, which can be seen in the lush, walk-through aviary. Bird shows are staged at the Bird Show Theater, flamingos and pelicans abound. The koala habitat has Australian animals, including Queensland koalas.

Adventure Island

Adventure Island (☎ 987-5600) is a water park that's also run by Anheuser-Busch. The 36-acre complex has 17 areas, and it's at 10001 McKinley Drive, adjacent to Busch Gardens (see Busch Gardens for directions).

The newest attraction is *Key West Rapids*, on which rafters go down a six-story twist ending in a 60-foot-long pool. Other slide rides include the Aruba Tuba (portions are in total darkness, others in daylight) and Rambling Bayou, where you go through weather 'effect' areas (parts are foggy, others have heavy rain). There's also a 9000-sq-foot swimming pool with waterfalls, diving platforms and translucent tube slides. And don't forget the 76-foot, free-fall body slide, Tampa Typhoon.

Admission is $18.95 for adults, $16.95 for children three to nine. Parking is $2. A combination ticket of Busch Gardens and Adventure Island is $40.60 for adults and $30.90 for children; you get one day at each park.

Organized Tours

Tampa Town Ferry Service (☎ 223-1522) runs a one-hour cruise daily around the Hillsborough River. The cost is $10 for adults, $9 for seniors, $6 for students. They run a one-hour sunset cruise as well (four person minimum) for which reservations are required; bring a cooler with food and drink. From April to September sunset cruises leave at 7 pm, from October to March they leave at 5.30 pm. All tours leave from the Tampa Town docks in front of the Florida Aquarium at 801 Channelside Drive.

The Big Red Balloon (☎ 969-1518) does one-hour balloon tours at sunrise – every day, weather permitting – for $150 per person, with a champagne brunch after the flight. It's at 16302 E Course Drive, in the city of Northdale, but the central meeting point is at Dale Mabry Hwy and N Dale Blvd. Reserve about a week ahead on weekends, about a day or two ahead on weekdays.

Gulf Coast Gray Lines (☎ 535-0208) does trips from Tampa to Walt Disney World, Sea World, and other locations in Florida; rates are impossible to summarize (but generally not bad deals if you don't have a car), so call for more information.

Suncoast Helicopter (☎ 872-6625) at Tampa International Airport is on call 24 hours a day, and for these prices we would be, too: they'll take three adults and one child up in their choppers for a half-hour flight around the area – either around downtown and up to Busch Gardens or out to the beaches – for $350.

Activities

Canoeing The least expensive canoeing in the area is at Clearwater Beach, where hostel guests can do it free, but closest to Tampa there's great and inexpensive canoeing at Hillsborough River State Park (see Around Tampa below).

Bicycling Contact the Tampa Bay Freewheelers (☎ 685-7209), Tampa Bay Bicycle Sport (☎ 938-5691) or the University of South Florida Bicycle Club (☎ 974-3193) for information on events, meets, races or riding groups during your stay.

Ice Skating Yup. Cool off the old-fashioned way: on a sheet of ice. Town and Country Skateworld (☎ 884-7688) is open year round and has afternoon and evening sessions from Tuesday to Saturday (call for specific times, as the schedule is a bit bizarre). Admission is $3 for afternoon sessions, $5 for evening sessions. What? Didn't bring your skates to Florida? Rental is $1. It's at 7510 Paula Drive, one block north of Hillsborough Ave. From downtown, take I-275 South to the Veteran's Expressway (Tampa International Airport exit off the interstate). Take the Veteran's to Hillsborough Avenue. Head west on Hillsborough to Hanley Road (about two miles). Turn right on Hanley Road; the rink is one block down on Hanley on the left side of the street. There is more ice skating in Clearwater.

Places to Stay

Unfortunately, there are no hostels in Tampa proper, but there's a good one in Clearwater Beach and a somewhat creepy one in St Petersburg – see those chapters for information. Both are easily accessible by car.

Family Value

Five or so cheers for the *Quality Suites USF Busch Gardens* (☎ 971-8930, 800-786-7446), which has excellent rooms, a nice pool, friendly, helpful and attentive staff and enough perks to make staying in a hotel fun even for the most grizzled of families or business travelers and the most cranky of guidebook writers. Everyone we spoke with here was happy, and why not? Rooms range from $89 to 129 from May to December and $109 to 159 January to April. All rooms have at the very least two televisions, a refrigerator, a microwave, a VCR, a boom box, and a bedroom and a living room. Breakfast – a hot, Southern breakfast – is an all-you-can-eat buffet that includes eggs, hash browns, grits, biscuits, bacon, sausage, muffins, cereal, juices, coffee and tea. Not convinced? They also give out free unlimited beer, wine *and* cocktails, and potato chips and pretzels, from 4 to 7 pm every day – and that's not a typo! It's at 3001 University Center Drive at 30th St and Bougainvillea (less than a mile from Busch Gardens). ■

Camping *KOA Tampa East* (☎ 659-2202, 800-872-3562) is 12 miles east of Tampa. All sites have water and electric; tent sites are $22.95; full hookup sites (for tents or RVs and vans) are $25.95; Kamping Kabins are $32.95. Take exit 9 off of I-4, then take McIntosh Rd south a quarter mile to Hwy 92, it's at 12870 Hwy 92.

There's also cheap and good camping at Hillsborough River State Park (see Around Tampa below).

Motels & Hotels There's a surprising lack of midrange hotels in Tampa other than the chains, all of which are represented; most of the more inexpensive options are near Busch Gardens. There are no hotels in Ybor City yet, though the chamber of commerce is trying.

There are really two main choices downtown: the enormous *Hyatt* and an *Economy Inn* (☎ 253-0851), 830 W JF Kennedy Blvd, near the University of Tampa and the Henry B Plant museum. The inn is very clean, and rooms in low/high season are $30 to 35/45 to 60. HBO is free.

Near the airport are *Westshore Airport Hotel*, *Embassy Suites*, *Double Tree*, *Marriott*, *Ramada* and *Crown Plaza*.

Near Busch Gardens and the University of South Florida, you'll find the most options (see especially the Quality Suites sidebar). Along Fowler Ave (Hwy 582) you'll find a *Holiday Inn*, *Motel 6*, *Quality Inn* and *Scottish Inn* – along with a bunch of chain restaurants like Red Lobster, Chili's, TGI Fridays and so on, as well as chain stores like Sports Authority, Circuit City and Pier 1 Imports.

Along Busch Blvd (Hwy 580), you'll find another slew of cheap but decent options. The clean and nice *Friendship Inn* (☎ 933-3958), 2500 E Busch Blvd, has singles/doubles for $27/33 in the low season, and singles or doubles for $38 in the high season; during special events rooms are $48. There's a pool, laundry and free coffee, but local calls are 40¢.

The *Red Roof Inn* (☎ 932-0073), 2307 Busch Blvd, has singles/doubles for $30/38; during the high season they're $44/48 (an additional person is $8). It has a pool and free coffee, local phone calls and *USA Today* daily.

The *Economy Inn* (☎ 933-2665) at 1810 E Busch Blvd has low/high-season rooms for $30/50, single or double (discount coupons are available from local restaurants), with free continental breakfast.

Econo Lodge (☎ 933-7681) at 1701 E Busch Blvd above the Steak Depot, charges $34 to 39 in the low season and $44 to 49 during special events and high season.

Budget Inn (☎ 932-3997), 2001 E Busch Blvd, has rooms for $33 during the week and $37 on weekends (single or double); during special events and in the high season it goes up to $50. Efficiencies are $5 more. Breakfast of coffee, juice and doughnuts is free, and they have a pool.

Places to Eat

Ybor City is really the place to head if you want an interesting meal (see its coverage above). If you're downtown, you'll find more standard lunch places. But if you want a meal to remember, reserve a table at Bern's Steak House (see aside).

Downtown *St Petersburg Bagel Company* (☎ 221-5103), 210 E Madison St, is a gourmet coffee and bagel place with over 30 coffees, an espresso bar, pastries and lunch specials. Bagels with cream cheese are $1, as are muffins and pastries.

Yogurt D'Lite (☎ 840-0247), 115 Whiting St (underneath the People Mover, across from the Hyatt), does cups of soft yogurt for $1.15/2.19, cones $1.45/1.75 and muffins $1.50.

Chee Peng Express (☎ 222-0065), 508 N Franklin St, is a lunch place with a fast-food atmosphere. It has a hot food buffet table (from $4.50 to 5.95, soup and salad included), or platters – like sweet and sour chicken, teriyaki beef, shrimp with vegetables – from $3.99 to 4.99 (including fried rice, noodles or mixed vegetables). It's open Monday to Friday from 10.30 am to 4 pm.

Wired (☎ 254-2699), 221 Davis Blvd E (on Davis Island), is a coffeehouse that's about as totally funked-out as you can get –

it's packed with nouveau bohemian Euro-trash. It's furnished with garage-sale items painted in day-glo colors, and your seat may be a toilet.

We had a really good feeling about *Phil's Salads* (☎ 228-0598), 505 N Florida Ave. Their lunch box special consists of California rolls, Asian pasta, bean sprouts, fried wonton and fruit for $4.50; sandwiches are from $3.50 to 3.75; and the salad bar (40 different items) is 24¢ an ounce. It's open Monday to Friday from 7 am to 3 pm.

Jersey Joe's (☎ 223-7373), 505 N Tampa St, is a sandwich place (from $2.50 to 10.35) that also has pizza by the slice ($1.50) and whole 16-inch pies ($7.99).

Four Green Fields (☎ 254-4444), 205 W Platt St on the edge of downtown, looks like a traditional Irish cottage (with, yes, a thatched roof), and it has Irish cooking, Irish music and, of course, Irish drinks.

Nickalouie's Downtown (☎ 229-7799), 604½ N Franklin St, does good Italian lunch specials from 11 am to 3 pm; ziti, lasagna and the like are $5.75. There's more variety at dinner, with main courses like lamb chops, seafood and manicotti from $8.95 to 13.95. Happy hour is Monday to Friday from 4 to 7 pm. It's a casual place with brick walls and wooden tables.

CK's (☎ 878-6500) is kind of a neat place: it's a revolving restaurant at the top of the Marriott Hotel at the airport. Lighter meals, like vegetarian moussaka or baked ziti are $12.95, and main meat and poultry dishes range from $18.95 for grilled filet mignon brushed with garlic butter and served with eggplant crouton with polenta to $22.95 for a veal and flank steak rolled in sun-dried tomatoes and pesto, topped with red wine sauce and served with herbed mashed potatoes. It has a medium-size wine list. Early-bird dinner specials, include soup or salad, are served from 5 to 6 pm, and range from $10.95, to $13.95 for Dijon rubbed and five-spice drenched pork chops and mashed potatoes.

Along Fowler Ave *Taj* (☎ 971-8483), 2734-B E Fowler Ave, serves delicious-

Bern's Steak House

Bern's Steak House (☎ 251-2421), 1208 S Howard Ave, is Tampa's landmark restaurant if ever there was one. The clever owner figured that allowing guests to fiddle about after their meal over dessert and coffee meant nothing but keeping other warm (paying) bodies waiting outside, so he came up with the ingenious idea of forcing diners to get up and *move* to a separate room upstairs for dessert – and that's even touted as a special feature! Bern says he also wanted guests to be able to enjoy a cigar over dessert and coffee without provoking gunplay. Both the cigar-friendly dessert room and the main dining room are very slick places, and the steaks, as they say, are some of the best east of the west and north of the south.

Downstairs the atmosphere is heavy on red velvet, gold leaf and statuary; upstairs the dessert tables are made from redwood wine casks.

Their wine list has over six thousand labels, and their cellars hold between half a million and a million bottles of wines from all over the world – predominantly American, French and Italian, but with a good representation of South American, Aussie and Chilean. But, if you're broke, there's always the Romanian section (blech). Steaks start at a six-ounce filet mignon for $18.50. The 20-ounce Chateaubriand serves two for $52.80, and the 60-ounce strip sirloin serves six for $156.02. However, chicken dishes range from a mere $14.91 to 16.51.

Upstairs in the dessert room (you can, by the way, come here just for dessert), prices range from a $2 scoop of vanilla ice cream to $15 flaming desserts like cherries jubilee, baked Alaska or bananas Foster.

The restaurant is open for dinner only. Reserve in advance – especially on weekends – as sometimes it's so full that they can't accommodate walk-ins for the dessert room, where dinner guests have priority on seating.

Howard Ave is in the Hyde Park area of Tampa. It runs parallel to Armenia St, but each runs one way, so take Bayshore Blvd from downtown to Howard Ave, and then turn right on Howard. Bern's will be on your right. ∎

smelling Indian food. It has an all-you-can-eat, $6.95 buffet on Tuesday to Friday from 11:30 am to 2:30 pm, on Saturday and Sunday till 3 pm. Dinner is from 5 to 10 pm. They have a fairly large vegetarian selection from $7.50 to 8.50; other dishes range from $9.95 to 15.95. It can get very crowded.

Nearby, *Lucy Ho's* (☎ 977-2783), 2740 E Fowler Ave, serves good Asian/Chinese food, and even with a smile; Friday and Saturday it's all-you-can-eat lunch buffet is $5.95, and dinner specials are $10.95. At other times, main vegetarian courses are $5.75 to 6.95, and meat dishes range from $7.95 to 8.95. There are lots of chicken dishes; try the garlic chicken ($7.95) or Phoenix and Dragon ($8.95) – chicken breast with shrimp, garlic, ginger, green onion and sautéed vegetables.

Entertainment

For cultural events, call the arts hotline run by the Hillsborough River Arts Council of Hillsborough County (☎ 229-2787).

Tampa Bay Performing Arts Center The largest performing arts center south of the Kennedy Center in Washington, DC, the Tampa Bay Performing Arts Center (☎ 229-7827, 800-955-1045), 1010 N MacInnes Place, is home to major concerts, plays, the Tampa Ballet and special events. There are four theaters in the complex; the Fest Hall (a 2500-seat venue where mainstay Broadway shows and headliners like Anita Baker perform), the Playhouse (1000 seats), the three-floor Cabaret and the 100-seat Off Center Stage, a 'black box' venue that's home to cutting edge performances by local and national artists and groups, and on some Monday nights, *Rough Stuff*, a jazz series. There are free guided tours of the backstage area from Wednesday to Saturday at 10 am by appointment.

Ticket prices range from $10 to 50 depending on the venue, the performance, the night and the seat.

Theater The Spanish Lyric Theater (☎ 223-7341), 1032 Coral St, does musical theater performances in English and Spanish, including Broadway musicals and Spanish zarzuelas.

The UT Falk Theater (☎ 253-6238), 428 W JF Kennedy Blvd, is a 900-seat theater operated by the University of Tampa.

Classical Music The 90-piece Florida Orchestra (☎ 286-1170) plays at the Performing Arts Center as well as in free park concerts.

The Tampa Bay Chamber Orchestra (☎ 874-8367) plays classical chamber music at the Tampa Museum of Art (see above).

Tampa Bay Gay Men's Chorus (☎ 837-4485), 1222 S Dale Mabry Hwy, Suite 602, is a community chorus that performs three major concerts a year at the Tampa Bay Performing Arts Center. All their concerts are interpreted for the hearing impaired.

USF School of Music (☎ 974-2311) on the USF Campus on Fowler Ave (accessible from Fowler Ave exits on I-275 and I-75) does a variety of concerts and recitals. Tickets are $3 per person, $2 for students and seniors; concerts at USF Theater 1 and 2 are $4 per person and $3 for students and seniors. The USF Theater also performs at both those theaters.

Rock & Jazz Also on the USF campus, the Sun Dome (☎ 974-3111), 4202 E Fowler Ave, hosts rock, jazz, pop and other concerts.

The Tampa Stadium (☎ 872-7977), 4201 N Dale Mabry Hwy, often presents concerts as well.

In South Tampa, *Bean There – a Traveler's Coffee House* (☎ 837-7022), 3203 Bay-to-Bay Blvd (take Bayshore Blvd from downtown to Bay-to-Bay, and turn right; it's on the right side of the road, past MacDill Ave) has live music on Tuesday, Thursday and Saturday; Thursday nights are open mike, and the music ranges from country to jazz to blues to accordion, and

even some spoken-word performances. The place is less a traveler's spot than it sounds, though there are maps and globes throughout, some travel books (including LP) and the big 'Where You Bean' bulletin board where guests put up photos, postcards and other travel mementos. Oh yeah, they serve coffee, espresso and cappuccino as well!

Bars & Nightclubs Ybor City is by far the place to go for nightlife – see the Ybor City Bars & Nightclubs section above for many more listings.

The Hub (☎ 229-1553), 701 Florida Ave N at Zack St near the Tampa Theater, is a fun local hangout that's not a whole lot to look at, but it serves up cheap drinks – maybe the cheapest in town. Looks like a hole in the wall, but this bar gets packed on weekends.

Two gay and lesbian places are *Impulse* (☎ 223-2780), 302 Nebraska Ave S (Hwy 45), which is a young adult gay club with high intensity dance music, and *Parthenon* (☎ 273-8799), which is right around the corner. It's an old-wave place with gay nights on Friday and Saturday, when it can get pretty wild; it's mixed gay and straight some of the time.

Spectator Sports

As in the rest of the state, sanity exits stage left as soon as sports are mentioned, and as usual, football is the major culprit. The Tampa Bay Buccaneers, taking a cue from television evangelist Oral Roberts (who once told viewers that God would kill him if he didn't raise $5 million), are threatening to leave the area unless, basically, every Tampa resident buys a season ticket. The drama is unfolding as we go to press, but it seems that for the short term they'll stay in Tampa.

Football The Tampa Bay Buccaneers (☎ 879-2827) play NFL football at, get this, Houlihan's Stadium (formerly Tampa Stadium but it's been bought by the restaurant chain of the same name) on N Dale Mabry Hwy. Take I-275 South from downtown to Himes Ave and turn west on Himes to the stadium. Games are played from August (pre-season) to December; single-ticket prices range from $20 to 30. Is it a coincidence they're known as the Bucs? We don't think so.

The Outback Bowl (☎ 874-2695) is an NCAA (National College Athletic Association) football game on New Year's Day at Tampa Stadium. If you've never seen an American college football game, this shouldn't be missed.

The USF Bulls (☎ 974-2125) are a Division I-AA football team that starts intercollegiate play in 1997. They'll play the first season at Tampa Stadium; tickets will be about $12.

Baseball The New York Yankees (☎ 875-7753) practice bobbles and whiffs during spring training games at Legend Field, near the corner of Dale Mabry Hwy and ML King Jr Blvd. It's a 10,000-seat stadium modeled after the House that Ruth Built, or Yankee Stadium, which is in the Bronx, New York (until that Steinbrenner character moves everything to New Jersey). Admission is free.

The Yankees' minor league team, the Tampa Yankees, play at Legend Field as well, from April to September. Tickets are $3 for adults and $2 for kids.

Soccer The Tampa Bay Mutiny (☎ 961-4625) are in the Division I League of Major League Soccer (or football, to the rest of the world). They play at Tampa Stadium from April to September; ticket prices are $7 to 22.

The Tampa Bay Cyclones (☎ 985-5050), the US Inter-regional Soccer League's Southeast Pro Division team, play at the USF Soccer Stadium from April to August. Tickets are $3 to 7.

Hockey The Tampa Bay Lightning play in a newly built arena in Tampa called the Ice Palace, an entertainment complex that will eventually be home to NHL hockey games, basketball games, concerts and ice shows. The stadium, which was not open as we went to press, is located in downtown Tampa in the Channel District near the Florida Aquarium.

Getting There & Away
Air Tampa International Airport (☎ 870-8700) is about 13 miles west of downtown off of Hwy 589. It's the major airport in the region, and most flights to the Tampa area (except the real cheapies on SunJet) land here – as opposed to at St Petersburg-Clearwater International Airport, the area's other big player. Tampa is served by over a dozen major carriers including Air Canada, Air South, America West Airlines, American Airlines, British Airways, Carnival Airlines, Continental, Delta, LTU International Airways, Northwest, Trans World Airlines, United, USAir and Valujet.

Bus Tampa's Greyhound station (☎ 229-2112) is at 610 Polk St. The schedule below reflects number of roundtrip buses per day and prices one-way/roundtrip.

Destination	Price	Duration
Miami	$29/39	6½ to 9 hours
Orlando	$17/34	2 to 4 hours
Sarasota	$11/22	2 hours
Gainesville	$25/50	3 to 4 hours
St Petersburg	$7/14	½ to 1 hour

Train The Amtrak terminal (☎ 221-7600) is at 601 Nebraska Ave N. Amtrak trains arrive from Orlando daily at 11.17 am, and leave for Orlando at 4.38 pm.

Car Tampa is 245 miles northwest of Miami, 135 miles southwest of the Space Coast and 85 miles south of Orlando. Take I-4 between Tampa and Orlando. Between Tampa and Miami the fastest way is to take I-75 to Fort Lauderdale and I-95 south, though the more scenic route is US Hwy 41 (Tamiami Trail) south to Everglades City and due east to Calle Ocho in Miami. Major rental agencies are located at the airport.

Getting Around
To/From the Airport HART bus No 30 picks up and drops off at the Red Arrival Desk on the lower level. From the airport, buses run to the downtown North Terminal

(see below) about every half hour from 5.51 am to 8.35 pm. The trip takes about 40 minutes. From the North Terminal to the airport, buses run about every half hour from 5.15 am to 7 pm. Shuttle services ply the road outside the arrival areas; they generally cost from $11 to 12 to areas in Tampa.

All major rental agencies have desks at the airport. By car, take I-275 to Ashley St, turn right and you're in downtown. A taxi from the airport to Busch Gardens should cost about $25, to downtown about $12, to St Petersburg about $35 to 45.

Central Florida Limousine Service (☎ 396-3730) runs vans from the airport to major hotels. The cost is $7 to 15 for two people.

Bus HART (Hillsborough Area Regional Transit, ☎ 254-4278) buses converge on the downtown North Terminal at 1414 N Marion St, under I-275 at Scott St. Buses cost $1.15 and transfers 10¢. To take your bike on the bus you'll need to go to the North Terminal and be subjected to a 10-minute safety video telling you how to do it, after which you'll need to buy a photo ID card ($1). From that moment on, you can bring bikes aboard HART buses at no extra charge. Here are some popular destinations by bus (all leave from the North Terminal):

Destination	Bus No	Departs
Ybor City	8, 46	½-hourly
Busch Gardens & USF	5	½-hourly
Lowry Park Zoo	7	½-hourly
Plant Museum	30	½-hourly
	17	hourly
MOSI	6 to University Transit Center*	hourly

*note there are two routes on bus No 6, so check the destination

There are also commuter buses during rush hours between Tampa and the coast: bus No 100x goes to St Petersburg and bus No 200x to Clearwater.

Trolley The Tampa-Ybor Trolley (☎ 254-4278) runs daily from 7.30 am to 5.30 pm several times an hour. Fare is 25¢ for adults, children under four and seniors ride free. The trolley route is as follows:

From the Marion St Transit Parkway at Fort Brooke Station, west on Whiting St, north on Ashley St, east on Jackson St, then south down Franklin St, across the Garrison Channel, east on Knight's Run, north back across the channel, past the Florida Aquarium and north to Ybor City. In Ybor City it runs east along 7th Ave from 12th St to 22nd, then west along 8th Ave and reverses the circuit.

People Mover The Harbour Island People Mover is a teeny putt-putt of a transportation system. The computer driven cars connect downtown with Harbour Island, an horrifically ugly little island just south of the city. The computer-controlled cars run Monday to Saturday from 7 am to midnight, Sunday from 8 am to midnight. The fare is 25¢, but you'll need to buy a token from the little machines at the station, which is on the 3rd level of the Old Fort Brooke Garage, on Whiting St between Franklin Mall and Florida Ave.

Taxi Meter rates are 95¢ flagfall, and $1.50 per mile. Companies include Yellow Cab (☎ 253-0121), Tampa Bay Cab Co (☎ 251-5555) and United Cab (☎ 253-2424). All offer senior discounts, but you'll have to ask.

Water Taxi Tampa Town (☎ 223-1522) offers a water taxi service from about 11 am to 5 pm daily around the downtown area. You can stay on the boat for the 35-minute ride (making it a minicruise) or get on and off at these locations: Florida Aquarium, Tampa Convention Center, Quality Hotel Riverside, Performing Arts Center, Plant Museum & University of Tampa, Tampa General Hospital and the Curtis Hixon Docks (near the Museum of Art).

Roundtrip fare is $6 for adults, $5 for seniors, $4 for students. You can pick up the ferry at Tampa Town's docks at 801 Channelside Drive, in front of the Florida Aquarium, or call them from any of the above stops and they'll come and pick you up. The taxi is on an air-conditioned, 40-passenger ferry with indoor and outdoor seating.

AROUND TAMPA
Hillsborough River State Park

This 3400-acre state park (☎ 987-6771) is nine miles north of the intersection of Fowler Ave and Hwy 301 at 15402 Hwy 301 N. It's a spectacular bit of greenery, and canoeing around here is a noble way to spend an afternoon or an overnight, as there's inexpensive camping here as well.

The park (admission free) is open daily from 8 am to sunset, and there are picnic facilities (grills and tables), nature and hiking trails and a new swimming pool ($1 admission). The pool's open Friday to Sunday in summer, daily in winter, from 10 am to 5 pm.

There are ranger-led nature walks through the park on advance request and, during the busy camping season in winter, campfire programs on Friday and Saturday evenings, like slide presentations or wildlife demonstrations. In winter there are also sometimes guided canoe trips.

To get here from downtown Tampa, take Fowler Ave east to Hwy 301, and go north for nine miles. There's no public transportation out here.

Canoeing The river's current is not at all challenging at this area, and you can rent canoes for $5 an hour (valid driver's license or a $10 deposit required). The current is highest from July to September, and when the river's high they don't rent canoes. Along the river you can see lots of wildlife, including, possibly, bobcats, white-tail deer, opossum, raccoons, gray foxes, red-tail hawks, osprey, lots of armadillos and water birds, and alligators – the best time to see them is early in the morning or in the evening.

The biggest commercial canoe rental company nearby is Canoe Escapes! (☎ 986-2067), near the Hillsborough River in Thonotosassa at 9335 E Fowler Ave, a half mile east of I-75. They rent canoes in two sizes, which can hold up to two adults and two children for two-, four- or six-hour tours. These are easy, self-guided adventures downstream along the Hillsborough River, and the tours have stops along the way where there are picnic facilities (bring a cooler).

They give you river maps and, if necessary, paddling instructions. The cost is $26 per canoe for the two-hour, and $30 for four- or six-hour tours, including transport to the river and back to their offices. It's open daily except Thanksgiving, Christmas Eve and Christmas. The first boat out on Monday to Friday is at 9 am, last out is 2 pm, last pick up from the river is 5 pm; on Saturday and Sunday they start an hour earlier, at 8 am, but last out and pick up are the same.

Fort Foster Also in the park is the Fort Foster Historical Site, a reconstruction of a fort that was originally built in 1836-37 as a bridge defense during the Second Seminole War, as the area was on a supply trail that ran from Fort Brooke in Tampa to Fort King in present-day Ocala. There were skirmishes here, but no major battles, and over the years the original fort deteriorated and was vandalized.

The fort's on the east side of Hwy 301. Access is an additional $1, payable on the honor system: put your money in an envelope, place the receipt in your car windshield and the envelope in the box. The fort's open for self-guided tours (weather permitting) on weekdays from 10 am to 3 pm, and on some (not all) weekends there are guided tours.

Camping Camping for tents, vans or RVs is $14.50 per night with water only, $16.63 with water and electric (including tax). There are no sewage hookups, but there is a dump station, and there are hot and cold showers. You can make a campfire, but you're not allowed to gather wood in the park. Bring your own or buy it ($4) from the ranger station.

CLEARWATER BEACH
• *pop 7000* ☎ *813*

Home to incredible white-sand beaches,

one of southwest Florida's largest fishing fleets and near enough to both Tampa and St Petersburg to be a base for either, Clearwater Beach is struggling to make a comeback to the powerhouse resort status it had up until about five years ago. And it's home to Florida's newest HI-member hostel, which is a superb, friendly source of local information and assistance.

The area's a great spot for canoeing and kayaking, shelling, bicycling and broiling yourself on the beach – which just about sums up the local 'tourist attractions'.

Backpackers will appreciate the scale of the island; unlike many Florida towns it's only 3½ miles long, and it's easy to get around by foot or bicycle.

Orientation & Information
Clearwater Beach is on a barrier island about two miles west of downtown Clearwater (a separate city on the mainland) over the Garden Memorial Causeway (Hwy 60), which to the east becomes Gulf to Bay Blvd between, you guessed it, the Gulf to the bay. There's a T-junction when Gulf To Bay hits the coastline; the road south is Gulf Blvd and north is Mandalay Ave, Clearwater's main drag. Pier 60 is right at the T-junction, as is the Clearwater Chamber of Commerce Welcome Center (☎ 447-9532). From St Petersburg, it's about a half-hour drive or a 1½-hour bus ride.

The welcome center and the Clearwater Hostel (see Places to Stay, below) are the best sources of local information. The fledgling Clearwater Beach Chamber of Commerce (☎ 447-4600) has a visitor desk at the time of writing in the Days Inn at 100 Coronado Drive.

Change money at the Barnett Bank at 423 Mandalay Ave.

Canoeing
The bay side of the beach is filled with mangrove islands, and it's great for canoeing. The calm waters of the Gulf also make it easy to paddle up to Caladesi Island (see below), which is a beautiful retreat.

The hostel has free canoes for its guests. Rent kayaks at Aqua Azul Kayak Tours

(☎ 530-7555), 17952 Alt US Hwy 19 N, on the east side of the Garden Memorial Causeway. They rent solo or tandem sea kayaks, with paddling instructions, for $12 an hour, or $35 a day for a solo, $45 a day for a tandem. They also do 4½-hour guided kayak tours for $42. There is a discount for hostel guests.

Sand Key
Sand Key Beach is a 65-acre park at the northern end of a long barrier island on the Gulf of Mexico, and it's a great spot for dolphin-watching, especially on the channel side. There's pretty good shelling here as well (best at low tide, especially during new and full moons and after storms). The beach is about a half mile long and the widest in the area. It's off the southern end of Clearwater Beach, connected by the Clearwater Pass Bridge. The Jolley Trolley (see below) goes here, or you can get here by bicycle.

Honeymoon & Caladesi Islands
Honeymoon Island State Recreation Area (☎ 469-5942), 1 Dunedin Causeway, began its life as a grand prize in a 1940s contest held by Paramount Newsreels and *Life* magazine. They were giving away all-expense-paid honeymoons on the island to newlyweds, who would come and stay in the 50 or so thatched huts that lined the beach. During the war, Honeymoon Island was a rest and relaxation site for exhausted war factory workers, and the place was never a honeymoon spot again. The road connecting the island to the mainland was built in 1964, and the state bought the land in the early 1970s.

The park today offers birding, swimming and great shelling. Coastal plant communities found on the island include mangrove swamps, virgin slash pine, strand and salt marshes. There are nature trails and bird observation areas here, as well as a ferry to Caledesi Island. Park admission is $4 per carload or $1 for pedestrians. To get here, take Hwy Alt 19 north to the city of Dunedin (dun-EDEN) and go west on Curlew Rd (Hwy 586), the Dunedin Causeway, which leads to the island.

Caledesi Island State Park (☎ 469-5918) is just south of Honeymoon Island. You can actually walk there from Clearwater Beach (a 1921 hurricane and a 1985 storm filled in the gap between north Clearwater Beach and the island), canoe there or take a ferry from Honeymoon Island. There are picnic pavilions, a concession stand and you can swim, shell and walk along nature trails or on the secluded, palm-lined three-mile beach. Wildlife you might see include armadillos, raccoons, snakes, turtles, pelicans, ibis, osprey, cormorants and others.

The Caledesi Connection (☎ 734-5263) is at the western end of Curlew Creek Rd (Hwy 586) in Honeymoon Island State Recreation Area. It runs ferries to Caledesi every hour on the hour on weekdays, and every half hour on weekends, starting at 10 am; the last departure from Caledesi is around 4.30 pm. The fare is $4 for adults, $2.50 for children, and free for those under age three.

Clearwater Marine Aquarium

The Clearwater Marine Aquarium (☎ 447-0980) is a nonprofit organization dedicated to the rescue and rehabilitation of marine animals. It currently is caring for two dolphins (named Sunset Sam and Halona), turtles (including loggerheads, Kemp's ripley and hawksbill), a huge variety of fish, sea otters and others.

It's open Monday to Friday from 9 am to 5 pm, Saturday from 9 am to 4 pm and Sunday from 11 am to 4 pm; admission is $5.75 for adults and $3.75 for children (under three free). It's at 249 Winward Passage, between Clearwater and Clearwater Beach, off the Memorial Causeway. The Jolley Trolley stops there, as does bus No 80, and it's about a mile walk from the hostel.

Sunset at Pier 60

This is Clearwater's version of the sunset celebration begun at Key West's Mallory Square. It takes place on the Pier from Thursday to Monday, two hours before and after sunset, and features jugglers, magicians, and craftspeople and artists set up stalls here as well.

Activities

Ice Skating Sun Blades (☎ 536-5843), 13940 Icot Blvd, at Alt US Hwy 19 N and Hwy 688, is an ice skating rink in the Icot Center building in Clearwater. Sessions are $5 to $5.50, and skate rental is $1.50. Afternoon sessions are Monday, Wednesday and Friday from noon to 2 pm, Saturday from 1.30 to 3 pm. Evening sessions are Wednesday from 8 to 9.45 pm and Friday and Saturday from 8 to 10.30 pm.

In-Line Skating The Transportation Station (☎ 443-3188) is right on the beach and rents skates for $5 an hour, $10 a half day and $20 a day; hostel guests get a 10% discount. Fritz's (☎ 445-1954), 700 Cleveland St in Clearwater, rents in-line skates for $8 an hour, $15 for half a day and $22 for the day, with a $100 cash or credit card deposit. Hostel guests get a 20% discount.

Bicycling You can bike along the beach or along the Pinellas Trail, a 47-mile bike path (see Around Clearwater below).

The hostel rents bicycles for $5 per day or $25 a week. The Transportation Station (see above) rents bicycles for $7 an hour and scooters for $13 to 18 an hour (depending on size); scooters are $47.95 to 65.95 for 24 hours. Hostel guests get a 10% discount.

Places to Stay

Hostel The HI-member *Clearwater Beach International Youth Hostel* (☎ 443-1211), 606 Bay Esplanade Ave, is a resort-style hostel with dorm rooms at $12 for members and $14 for nonmembers; rooms are $75/86 weekly. Private rooms are available at their adjacent *Sands Motel*; efficiencies are $34/46 and one-bedroom apartments are $41/56. There's a swimming pool surrounded by lush gardens, a picnic area and tiki huts, and it's only a three-minute walk to the beautiful (and very white) beach.

The hostel has kitchen and laundry

facilities ($1.25/1.50). You need at least a bottom sheet; they rent linens ($1 for a bottom sheet, $2 for a full set), and the whole place is air-conditioned. They have canoes available for free use (with a $50 deposit); there is table tennis, a shuffleboard, a barbecue, a library and a community and games room. Map and reference materials are available, and you can play tennis at the nearby tennis courts, as well as basketball and volleyball.

Motels & Hotels Chains along the beach include *Holiday Inn* at 521 S Gulfview Blvd (☎ 447-6461), and 400 Mandalay Ave (☎ 461-3222); *Days Inn* (☎ 447-8444), 100 Coronado Drive; *Best Western* (☎ 442-6171), 25 Belleview Blvd, and *Hilton* (☎ 447-9566), 715 S Gulfview Blvd.

The *Monaco Resort Motel* (☎ 443-6954), 648 Poinsettia Ave a block from the beach, has motel rooms for $30 in summer, $35 from December 1 to January 31, and $55 from February 1 to April 30; efficiencies, with fully stocked kitchens, are $36/40/65. There is a pool.

Amber Tides Motel & Apartments (☎ 446-0438), 420 Hamden Drive, is a nice, quiet place off the main drag. They have a great pool, and the charming Serbian owner speaks French, German, Spanish, Russian, Bulgarian and Serbian (among others) and constantly tells WWII stories. Room prices change by the month: the lowest prices, in June, are $35 for motel rooms and $37 for small efficiencies; the highest, in March, are $56/62. They have larger rooms, and up to three-bedroom apartments.

The friendly folks at the *Patio Motel* (☎ 442-1862), 15 Somerset St, have a clean motel room (yes, one, $36 in summer, $46 in winter), efficiencies and one- and two-bedroom apartments ($41 to 72/54 to 85). There's no pool, but it's right on the water (many rooms look right out on the Gulf) and has a private beach.

A friendly Swiss-German couple runs the *Dolphin Watch Motel* (☎ 449-9039), 607 Bay Esplanade. It's right on the bay and has a heated pool, a spa, a private dock and barbecue facilities. Efficiencies are

$49/59, larger one-to-four-person rooms are $65/85.

The *Bellview Mido Resort Hotel* (☎ 442-6171), 25 Belleview Blvd, off of Hwy 60 and Fort Harrison Ave, was built in the 1890s as a retreat for wealthy northeasterners. In the 1950s the Duke of Windsor, his dogs and possibly Mrs Simpson stayed here, and he even wrote part of his memoirs here while dancing with the bandleader's wife and all the staff – he was apparently a hit at costume balls. As was, we assume, Lady Thatcher, who stayed here recently. It's not exactly a backpacker's hangout: while the pool and spa may be charming, room rates are $150 to 410 in summer, $170 to 450 in winter.

If that's too rich for your blood, take a tour instead; there's one every day from 11 am for $5, or $13 including lunch at their restaurant, which is said to have the best $6 burger in town. You'll see the tunnels underneath the hotel, a museum and a section devoted to the Army Air Corps, which was stationed here during WWII. The spa is open to the public; it's $10 a day for their gym, whirlpool and sauna.

Places to Eat
The *Beach Diner* (☎ 446-4747), 56 Causeway Blvd, is a '50s- and '60s-style diner with wall murals of James Dean, Marilyn Monroe, Betty Boop, Superman and many others. Its free juke box is filled with '50s beach music. Saturday is Dime Day from noon to 3 pm, when they have 10¢ draft beers; raw or steamed oysters or clam or shrimp chowder are 10¢ as well – and there's no limit! There's a classic car show on the first and third Friday of the month. Been fishing? They'll cook up your catch (fried, grilled or blackened) and serve it to you with salad and potatoes or rice for $3.95. Burgers are $4.50, and their sublime milkshakes (made with Breyer's ice cream) are $3. And if you or your kids get bored, they have Legos on the tables. As one would imagine, the place is very popular with hostelers.

Golden Treasure (☎ 448-0372), 432 Poinsettia Ave, has excellent Chinese food at decent prices. Combinations of soup, egg roll and an entree, like kung poa chicken or Hunan beef, start at $4.50, and try their $3 hot and sour soup.

Rockaway Grill (☎ 446-4844), 7 Rockaway St, serves salads, burgers, seafood and Mexican food from $6 to 15. They make a great chimichanga, and we hear the she-crab soup is to die for. There is live music on Thursday to Sunday nights, pool tables and a happy hour.

Frenchy's Saltwater Cafe (☎ 461-6295), 416 E Shore Drive, is a seafood restaurant popular with locals. It's said to have a great grouper sandwich and mussels marinara.

The hostel folks say that *Los Mariachis* (☎ 448-0372), 1200 Cleveland St in Clearwater, is one of their favorites, with great margaritas, excellent fajitas and chimichangas. The portions are huge, they make their own tortilla chips, guacamole and salsa, and on weekends a Mariachi band plays. Entrees run from $6.95 to 15.

Frenchy's Shrimp & Oyster Cafe (☎ 446-3607), 41 Baymont, is 'the original hole in the wall'. It's a tiny place with picnic benches that's a great local hangout; specials include gumbo by the cup/bowl for $2.95/ 3.75 and crabby shrimp sandwiches for $5.35.

Entertainment
Shephards (☎ 441-6875), 601 S Gulfview Blvd, has reggae on Saturday and Sunday afternoons, and a beachfront tiki bar.

The *Bombay Bicycle Club* (☎ 799-1841), 2721 Gulf to Bay Blvd (Hwy 60), draws a young crowd; women drink free daily from 8 to 10 pm, and there are three-for-one drinks and two-for-one appetizers from 5 to 8 pm.

Storman's (☎ 571-2202), 2675 Ulmerton Rd, does a Friday night party from 5 to 8 pm, with two-for-one drinks and $3, 32-ounce draught beers and a free buffet from 6 to 8 pm.

Old New York New York (☎ 539-7441), 18573 US Hwy 19, is where singles mingle on Friday and Saturday nights.

Getting There & Away
Bus The Clearwater Greyhound station

(☎ 796-7315) is at 2811 Gulf to Bay Blvd at Hampton Rd. There are six buses a day making the half-hour trip from Tampa ($8 one-way, $15 roundtrip).

From Clearwater, take PSTA (☎ 531-0415) bus No 60 from the stop across Gulf to Bay Blvd westbound to the Park St Bus Depot, and change to bus No 80 to Clearwater Beach. Get off at the tennis courts at the corner of Mandalay Ave and Bay Esplanade, and it's about a two-minute walk to the hostel.

From the Tampa Amtrak station, take the courtesy bus to Pinellas Park and change for PSTA bus No 18, which you take to the Park St Bus Depot, where you catch bus No 80 to Clearwater Beach.

Getting to Busch Gardens by public transportation is the closest thing to hell on earth; a much better idea is to take the Gray Line (☎ 800-282-4051). It costs about $45, which includes the admission to Busch Gardens. If you consider that the admission is $36.15, Gray Line is essentially an $8.85 shuttle bus.

Car From Tampa take Hwy 60, the Courtney Campbell Causeway through Clearwater and straight west out to the beach. From St Petersburg, take Hwy 19 (34th St N) straight north to Hwy 60 and go west. From St Pete Beach take Gulf Blvd north.

Getting Around
The red Jolley Trolley (☎ 445-1200) runs all around Clearwater Beach from north to south and onward to Sand Key. Fare is 25¢ but said to be going up to 50¢. The beach route runs daily: Sunday to Thursday from 10 am to 10 pm, and Friday and Saturday from 10 am to midnight. A second Jolley Trolley runs between the beach and Clearwater's Park St Station; this route runs every hour from 10 am to midnight.

AROUND CLEARWATER
Heritage Park
Heritage Park (☎ 582-2123) is a 21-acre historical park and open-air museum. It has 22 structures, including the oldest house in the county, two Victorian houses, a school-

house, store, doctor's office, a mill, barn and a church. It's open Tuesday to Saturday from 10 am to 4 pm and Sunday from 1 to 4 pm; admission is free. It's at 11909 125th St in Largo, just south of the city of Clearwater. By car or bike (it's about 10 miles), take Alt Hwy 19 south to Ulmerton Rd, turn right, and left on 125th St. From Clearwater Beach, take bus No 80 to Park St Station and then change for bus No 52 or 61 to the stop at Walsingham and 125th St; the entrance is very close by.

Pinellas Trail

The Pinellas Trail is a paved, 47-mile county-run bicycle trail built on the track bed of the CSX railway. The path's very smooth – smooth enough for in-line skates or roller skates as well as bicycles – and it runs from St Petersburg to Tarpon Springs, though there is a gap at the north and south of Clearwater.

There are lots of stops along the way, with cafés, pubs, bike shops, skate shops, and fast-food places. As it's on the route of the old railway, the path cuts through widely varied terrain: sometimes you're in the middle of downtown (as in Dunedin), sometimes among orange groves (near Pinellas Park) and sometimes you're riding practically through backyards in bedroom communities.

To get there from the Clearwater Beach International Hostel, which rents bikes (see Clearwater Beach above), head down Gulf to Bay Blvd and over the causeway, and ride north on Fort Harrison Ave and east on Jones St for about three blocks. You'll pick up the southern end of the Clearwater to Tarpon Springs section of the path. It's 13.2 miles from Jones St to Tarpon Ave.

Contact the Pinellas County Planning Department (☎ 464-4751) for a copy of their free *Guidebook to the Pinellas Trail*, which lists rest stops and local attractions and has a mileage chart. It's the best guide to the trail. Also check with Rob at the Clearwater Beach hostel, who rides the trail all the time.

WEEKI WACHEE SPRINGS

• *pop 15* ☎ *904*

'The City of Mermaids', Weeki Wachee Springs (☎ 596-2062, 800-678-9335) is about 30 miles north of Clearwater, 80 miles northwest of Orlando, and 70 west of Ocala. Most people come here as a day trip from the Clearwater/Tampa area, but there's a Holiday Inn across the street from the park entrance. As have other attractions in Florida, like Marineland and Walt Disney World, Weeki Wachee Springs is now incorporated into its own city.

Hold it. Mermaids? Yup. Since 1947, families and celebrities like Esther Williams, Danny Thomas and Elvis Presley have been coming here to see the star attraction at this 200-acre theme park: the underwater show starring long-haired women in mermaid costumes who swim in the natural spring (there are also mermen).

The spring has a constant temperature of 72°F, measures about a hundred feet across and produces about 170 million gallons of water a day; it's the headwater of the Weeki Wachee River. The mermaids perform in the spring, alongside fish, turtles, otters, snakes and eels.

The shows here are the height of kitsch, a trip straight back to the 1950s. You watch the mermaids, about 20 of them, perform shows like *Pocahontas Meets the Little Mermaid* in an underwater theater – the audience watches through glass panels, making this the world's only underwater artesian spring theater. The theater was built in 1946 by Newton Perry, an ex-navy frogman. Remarkably, the mermaids flail and swim about with what appears to be the greatest of ease.

Don't be fooled. Performing underwater requires incredible stamina, and the breathing apparatus is tricky. There are submerged air hoses on the sides of the theater: the mermaids swim over, grab some air, hold their breath while swimming around performing and then zip back for more air – for *half an hour* at a time! They train first on land and then in the water without the tail, practicing the moves of the 30-minute shows. It takes about six to eight months to get the whole thing to look as effortless as it does, and if it looks easy, *you* try lip-synching to music underwater next time you're snorkeling!

The park also has a Wilderness River Cruise, a petting zoo with a pygmy goat, a fallow deer and a giraffe, and two bird shows: Birds of Prey, with eagles, hawks, owls and other raptors, and Exotic Birds, with macaws and cockatoos. To see all the shows, expect to spend at least five hours here. The Mermaid Galley sells burgers, hot dogs and the like.

The park's open from 9.30 am to 5.30 pm, a little later in summer and on holidays (note the totally campy and yet social-realist statue of two mermaids thrusting their arms skyward at the entrance). Admission is $16.95 for adults, $12.95 for children aged three to 10; parking is free.

To get there, drive north on Hwy 19 to the intersection of Hwy 50, about a half hour north of Clearwater; from I-75 take exit 61 and go west about 20 miles.

HOMOSASSA SPRINGS

Homosassa Springs (☎ 904-628-2311) is another spring to the north; this one, the headwater of the Homosassa River, is home to the Homosassa Springs State Wildlife Park, which amounts to the state's largest all-natural theme park.

The 168-acre park (actually it's 180, but some of it's submerged) does showcases and educational demonstrations of its diverse wildlife, which include manatees, black bears, bobcats, white-tailed deer,

alligators, American crocodiles and river otters. The area is made up of wetlands, hydric hammock and spring-run streams that bubble out of the 45-foot-deep Homosassa Spring. Staff here also rehabilitate injured manatees.

The area was formerly a for-profit theme park (Homosassa Springs Attraction), and the old owners had installed a floating underwater observatory – launched on ways of banana peels as opposed to grease to protect the fish. Today, the Fish Bowl observatory is still used to watch manatees and fish.

As you enter, you get on pontoon boats that take you on an orientation tour of the park, after which you're free to wander on the nature trails. There's a snack bar, and picnic tables are available. Plan on spending about three to four hours in the park.

There are a bunch of interpretive programs held every day, including two each of alligator and crocodile demonstrations, animal encounter programs on snakes or birds of prey, and manatees.

Daily educational programs include: the manatee at 10.45 am and 3.15 pm, the animal encounter at 11.30 am and 1.45 pm and the alligator at 12.15 and 2.30 pm.

The park is open daily from 9 am to 5.30 pm, ticket sales end at 4 pm. Admission is $7.95 for adults, $4.95 for children aged three to 12; there are AAA and AARP discounts and free kennels (no pets allowed in the park). The park is about 60 miles north of Clearwater, 75 miles north of Tampa; take Hwy 19 north right to the entrance of the park.

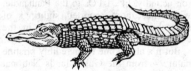

Northwest Florida & the Panhandle

The Florida Panhandle, which stretches almost 200 miles between the Alabama border at the west and Tallahassee at the east, is distinguished for three main features. First, its beaches are hands-down the best in the continental USA; the Apalachian quartz sand along Panhandle beaches is so white it's literally dazzling, and it's so fine that it 'barks' when you walk on it. The warm waters of the Gulf of Mexico are at various areas in the Panhandle brilliant turquoise or, astonishingly, emerald green, and they are always crystal clear.

Second, the Panhandle is known for Panama City Beach, called the Redneck Riviera for its popularity with visitors from nearby counties as well as nearby states like Alabama and Louisiana, where Spring Break never ends and the fact that it's legal to drink beer on the beach is touted by tourism officials as a selling point.

And third, the Panhandle is known for its hurricanes, which seem to gravitate to the area like UFOs to Midwestern RV parks (or, actually, like UFOs to the Panhandle, which has more reported sightings of spaceships than any other area in the country).

But it's also home to incredibly pristine nature – from the Gulf Islands National Seashore to the dazzling beauty of Black-water River State Park and Forest to the fascinating caverns at the Florida Caverns State Park in Marianna – as well as to interesting areas like Apalachicola, the state's Oyster Capital.

Many of the areas in the Panhandle can be explored as day trips, using either Pensacola, Panama City Beach or Apalachicola as a base.

Pensacola's history predates even St Augustine's (in fact, the two cities argue over which is the nation's oldest settlement), and the city has three gorgeous historic districts, some incredible beaches and the fantastic performances by the navy's Blue Angels precision-flying team, which make their winter home here at the Pensacola Naval Air Station.

Tallahassee is the state's capital, though don't expect to see busy legislators running around cutting deals – the hard-working Florida Legislature meets for only about 60 days out of the year (and you thought guidebook writers had a good scam going). And about 40 minutes east of the capital, you can find out just what type of fellow it was that has had generations of Americans and even foreigners singing about the Suwannee River, which slashes through extreme north central Florida and empties into the Gulf of Mexico.

NW & PANHANDLE

Even if you can't get out to the western stretches of the Panhandle, don't miss the opportunities to explore the nature along the Nature Coast, the coastline that stretches along the big bend of the state, where Steinhatchee Landing's superb restaurant and luxurious duplex cottages cost far less than they should.

PENSACOLA
- *pop 65,000, metro area 378,000*
☎ *904*

Pensacola is a surprisingly old city for the US. Europeans tried settling in the area in 1559, but a hurricane and lazy settlers forfeited the honor of first European settlement to St Augustine, in 1565. Pensacola was made a permanent settlement in 1568. Much of the downtown area today dates to the 1800s, though there are remnants of British and Spanish buildings dating to the late 1700s.

Today Pensacola's main attraction – despite three historic districts that have undergone extensive reconstruction and renovation – is its beach, and unfortunately much of it was badly damaged in 1995 by Hurricane Opal. But even right after the hurricane, it was obvious what a treasure this beach is: gently sloped, sugar-white sand lapped by calm blue waters, and plenty of room for everyone to get comfortable. As we went to press, the cleanup was entering its final stages, and by the time you read this, the area should be almost completely back to normal.

Pensacola's also a naval city: the enormous Pensacola Naval Air Station is home to thousands as well as to the Blue Angels, the navy's awesome precision-flying outfit. You can see them rehearsing here when they're in town, and the sight of the jets soaring up in tight formation and then breaking off and plummeting to earth is something even pacifists must admit is nothing short of spectacular.

History
Written record of the Indian population that made the area home for some ten thousand years is incredibly scant, and most historical accounts begin with its 'discovery' and exploration in the 1550s by Hernando de Soto, and the attempt in 1559 by Spanish explorer Don Tristan de Luna to settle the area. The settlement was a disaster: a hurricane wiped out much of it early on, and even though reinforcements arrived two years later, settlers opted to move on.

The relationship between the Spanish and the French, already testy, grew more openly hostile through the 17th century. The French had settlements at nearby Mobile, Alabama, and in 1719, the area was taken by the French and surrendered back to Spain four times.

During the period of British rule (1763-81), much of the planning of the city occurred, and remnants of British-built structures – including their government house and commanding officers' compound – can still be seen in the Seville Historic District, which the Brits laid out. When the Spanish took over again, the first thing they did was accept the street grids and change all the offensive names (any names having to do with the British Monarchy were nixed), thus the presence today of streets like Alcaniz, Palafox and Intendencia.

Andrew Jackson, the American general so keen on booting out Indians and colonial governments, swept unsanctioned into the area after the War of 1812 and just took it. During the war, Spain had allowed British ships to dock at Pensacola – and the Brits had assisted in training and supplying the Creek Indians Jackson was fighting. The US initially gave it back ('Oh, okay . . . *here*.'), but it was returned when the Spanish

---

Time
Get an extra hour of sleep free! The Panhandle is in two time zones: east of the Apalachicola River is on Eastern Standard Time, west of the Apalachicola River is on Central Standard Time. When it's 9 am in Apalachicola, it's 8 am in Panama City Beach and Pensacola. ∎

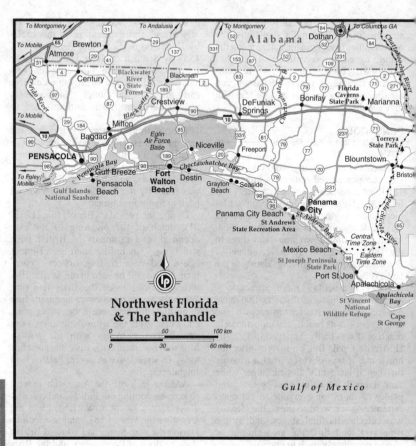

Northwest Florida & The Panhandle

0   50   100 km

0   30   60 miles

Gulf of Mexico

ceded Florida to the US in 1821. Andrew Jackson returned to Pensacola and became its first governor.

The city's deep harbor and geographical position were key factors in its development as a military city; construction of the first navy base was begun almost immediately after the US took control, and forts were built to defend Pensacola Bay from three sides.

Those forts would become a major focus of both Confederate and Federal troops during the Civil War, when fighting over them led to an enormous battle in the harbor,

which ended in stalemate. After the war and an epidemic of yellow fever, which had caused the population to dwindle, Pensacola went through a number of booms, probably the most important of which was lumber.

The navy, which had abandoned the Pensacola base in the early 1900s, reopened it as an air base in 1914, to train pilots for long-range flight and anti-submarine warfare. You can see the NC-4, the plane that made the first successful trans-Atlantic flight (it wasn't nonstop, nor was it solo) at the National Museum of Naval Aviation here.

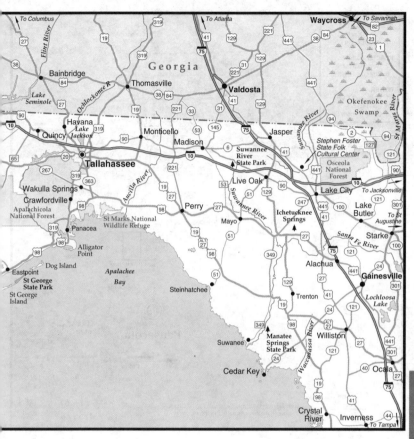

The area gained prominence again in WWII, when the US Navy's flight instruction school began working overtime, training thousands of American and foreign pilots. After the war, in the prosperous 1950s, Pensacola Beach, connected to the mainland by a three-mile-long bridge, became a popular tourist spot, and the area boomed.

Restoration of the historic districts was begun in the 1960s and '70s; North Hill was listed on the National Register of Historic Places in 1972. Today Pensacola is a city with a strong military economy, filled with gawkers and sun-worshipers. There's a vibrant arts scene developing, and despite the devastating blow that Hurricane Opal dealt to the city, it's coming back stronger than ever.

Orientation

The city's a typical Florida sprawler, and it's very difficult to get between places without a car, unless you're walking in downtown, just north of the Port of Pensacola, at the southeastern end of the city. Palafox St is the east-west divider, Garden St the north-south. Note that Palafox St is

NW & PANHANDLE

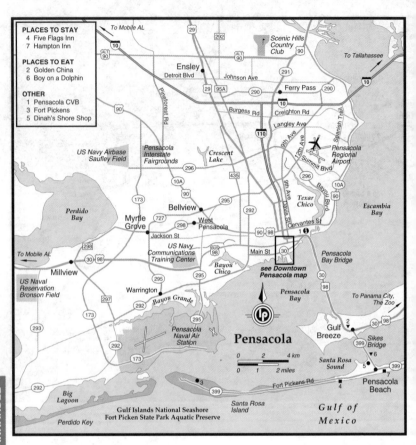

PLACES TO STAY
4 Five Flags Inn
7 Hampton Inn

PLACES TO EAT
2 Golden China
6 Boy on a Dolphin

OTHER
1 Pensacola CVB
3 Fort Pickens
5 Dinah's Shore Shop

Pensacola

0   2   4 km
0   1   2 miles

Gulf Islands National Seashore
Fort Picken State Park Aquatic Preserve

Gulf of Mexico

officially called Palafox Place south of Garden St, and there are attempts being made to register that section with the federal government as the Palafox Place Business District. But, confusingly, locals refer to it as simply Palafox, S Palafox Place, S Palafox Street or just Palafox St straight through. And even worse, commercially-bought and even locally obtained maps show different names for the street and several of the historic districts.

The North Hill Preservation District, about a mile northwest of downtown, is bordered by Palafox St to the east, Reus St to the west, Blount (pronounced 'blunt') St at the north and the northern side of Wright St on the south.

Much of the southeast quadrant of downtown Pensacola is taken up by the Palafox Historic District, a collection of smaller districts that have been combined into one large and growing preservation area bounded roughly by Cervantes St at the north, the waterfront at the south, Florida Blanca St at the east and Spring St at the west. Within the Palafox Historic District is Historic Pensacola Village, bordered by Government St at the north, Main St at the south,

Jefferson St at the west, and Alceniz St at the east.

The Naval Air Station (NAS) is in the southwest quadrant of the city.

Pensacola Beach is on Santa Rosa Island, southeast of Pensacola and Gulf Breeze. Gulf Breeze is connected to Pensacola by the three-mile-long Pensacola Bay Bridge (everyone calls it the Three Mile Bridge) and to Pensacola Beach by the Bob Sikes Bridge ($1 toll). An older series of bridges that run adjacent to Three Mile Bridge on its eastern side are now open as fishing bridges, and can be accessed by car only from the south side.

Maps The Pensacola CVB (see below) sells copies of Dolph's *Map of Pensacola* and gives out placemat-size free maps, which have the historic districts on one side and a simplified area map on the reverse. You can also find free handout maps of downtown at many downtown attractions.

Information

Tourist Offices The *Pensacola Convention & Visitors Information Center* (CVB, ☎ 434-1234, 800-874-1234), 1401 E Gregory St at the foot of the Pensacola Bay Bridge, has a glorious bounty of tourist information, with volunteers and staff who really know a lot about the area and do neat giveaways – when we went they laminated our business cards into luggage tags free and gave away Pensacola nail files made with the sparkling white sand from the beach (yeah, right). Other good sources of information are the *Pensacola Beach Visitors Center/Chamber of Commerce* (☎ 932-1500, 800-635-4803), 735 Pensacola Beach Blvd, and the Pensacola Chamber of Commerce (☎ 438-4081), 117 W Garden St. The Pensacola Historical Society Resource Center & Library (☎ 434-5455) at 117 E Government St opposite Seville Quarter, is just what it sounds like. There's a 24-hour arts information line at ☎ 438-8888, and for general help with things artistic, the Arts Council of Northwest Florida (☎ 432-9906) are of great help – see the Entertainment section below for more information.

Money Change money at the downtown Barnett Bank, 100 W Garden St. American Express has a representative office at Fillette Green Travel Service (☎ 434-2543), 313 Palafox Place.

Post The main downtown post office (☎ 434-3164) is at 101 Palafox Place.

Bookstores Page & Palette (☎ 432-6656), 106 Palafox Place, is the biggest bookstore in downtown, and it's an art gallery as well. The Arcade Newsstand (☎ 438-1796), 194 Palafox St, has magazines, newspapers, books, comics, and so on, and the suspicious folks at Toni's Pipe Rack (no phone), 4½ Palafox Place, sell tobacco, books, the *New York Times*, *Wall Street Journal* and other out-of-town stuff.

Libraries The main library (☎ 435-1760) is at 200 W Gregory St.

Media The *Pensacola News Journal* is the big daily; other papers include the *New American Press*, focusing on African-American news, and the *Gulf Breeze Sentinel*. NPR is at 88.1.

Laundry It's not easy finding a laundry in downtown Pensacola: on the beach, there's a coin laundry (☎ 932-3005) at 37 Via de Luna, and there's a huge one out toward the navy base at 43 S Navy Blvd.

Medical Services There are three hospitals in the area: Baptist Health Care (☎ 434-4011), 1000 W Moreno St, is the closest to downtown; Sacred Heart (474-7000), 5151 N 9th Ave; and West Florida Regional Medical (☎ 474-8000), 8333 N Davis Hwy.

Historic Pensacola Village

Historic Pensacola Village (☎ 444-8905) is a collection of old homes and museums that are open to the public. Half-hour guided walking tours of the area leave at 11.30 am and 1.30 pm from the main ticketing office at the **Tivoli House**, 205 E Zaragoza St, and include a history of many

NW & PANHANDLE

Erin & Opal – Tag Team Hurricanes

Just before we visited the Panhandle to research this chapter, the area was hit by the almost totally unexpected Hurricane Erin, which suckerpunched the beaches and caused $350 million in damages. A month later, Hurricane Opal moved through sooner than expected and with a ferocious destructiveness. We arrived a month after Opal hit, and we were still unable to gain access to several gulfside communities, including Destin, Fort Walton Beach, the gulf beaches and the state parks on St George Island and Panama City Beach (though accessed later), which were all sealed off by police, even, for a time, to residents. The entire western half of Pensacola Beach was buried under several feet of white sand – sand so white and so like snow that it made the Swedish-built snowplows that were brought in to assist with the cleanup right at home.

In Panama City Beach, perhaps the most devastated area in terms of impact on tourism, entire houses were carried off; solid-steel display signs were bent over as if they were made of tin foil. The southern end of the city's brand-new concrete fishing pier crumbled into the water, hotels were peeled from their frames, and rubble was thrown for hundreds of yards. Eighty percent of the city's motels and hotels were damaged and many were destroyed. Rubble was piled up along the entire length of Hwy 98, the main beach drag. It should come as no surprise, then, that even as we went to press the area was still partially crippled.

Tourism officials predict that the area will be back to normal in 1997, but much of the information here on the affected areas is necessarily vague. It's probably a good idea to contact accommodations before you arrive to double-check our prices, and contact the local tourist offices to get updates.

But don't be discouraged by all this: the Panhandle has some of the best beaches in the world, people are friendly, accommodations are inexpensive and nature opportunities abound. It should say something that surveys by the State Division of Tourism show that travelers who go to the Panhandle come back to Florida more often than those who visit other parts of the state. It's a wonderful area to visit. ■

of the buildings in the district, including the **Lavalle House**, 205 E Church St, and the **Julee Cottage**, 210 E Zaragoza St, the former home of freed slave Julee Paton, which features an exhibit on black life in Florida. It also includes the TT Wentworth, Jr Museum, the Museum of Commerce, Museum of Industry and Pensacola Historical Museum.

The district's buildings are open Monday to Saturday from 10 am to 4 pm, closed Sunday (unless otherwise noted below). Tours cost $5.50 for adults, $4.50 for seniors and military and $2.25 for children. Tickets for the tours are available at the Wentworth or at the Historic Museum store (see below).

Note that you don't have to go on a tour to see the buildings, and that one admission ticket gains you entry to all the buildings in the village. You can, however, opt to enter any of the museums included on the tour at a single admission price, but it doesn't really make sense to do it that way as the tour is a much better value.

TT Wentworth, Jr Museum The Wentworth (☎ 444-8586), 330 S Jefferson St, is made up of quirky exhibits that run the gamut from British and Spanish artifacts to a petrified cat.

The 3rd floor holds Discovery Kids Town, where kids can play with a totally neat television station set up with two functioning video cameras, a blue backdrop and a switcher that really works. The kids' post office has a little desk and rubber stamps.

The 2nd floor contains artifacts from Spanish and British rule, exhibits on colonial life, a Coca-Cola room (don't ask) and some funky machines (like a 1960 Associated Press photofax receiver and power unit, and a 1959 Philco Predictor TV).

The 1st floor, though, is our favorite, as it contains the 'curiosities': a wacky and eclectic collection of stuff including two stuffed

Kodiak bears looking very mean indeed, a Robert Wadlow's size-37 shoe, and – in a tie for most grizzly exhibit – the shrunken head of a 17-year-old Indian chief's son (found in 1926) and a petrified cat, dead since the 1850s (found in 1966).

Museum of Commerce This museum (☎ 444-8905), 201 E Zaragoza St, is a reconstructed 1890s period streetscape inside a brick warehouse. It has a horse-drawn buggy collection and, among others, a hardware store, a music store and a print shop (note the antique press collection).

Museum of Industry In the two joined warehouses across the street from the Museum of Commerce is the Museum of Industry (☎ 444-8905), 200 E Zaragoza St, which displays photographs, equipment and tools from the city's different industrial booms, including brickmaking, railroad and lumber.

Pensacola Historical Museum Once located inside the former Old Christ Church (1832) at 405 Adams St, the Pensacola Historical Museum lost its lease in late 1996. It is looking for new digs, but as we went to press had not yet located them. Check with the Pensacola Historical Society Resource Center & Library (☎ 434-5455, see Information, above) when you're in town to see if they've resettled: it has displays on (surprise, surprise) the history of the city, with exhibits on local geology, Indians, and the Spanish and British colonial and Civil War periods. It has a nice little book collection. In its first incarnation it was open Monday to Saturday from 9 am to 4.30 pm, closed Sunday. Admission is $2 for adults, $1 for children aged four to 16.

Pensacola Museum of Art The Pensacola Museum of Art (☎ 432-6247), 407 S Jefferson St, is housed in the Old City Jail (1906-8), and it holds about 18 different exhibitions a year; call for what's on when you're here. It's not part of the tour. It's open Tuesday to Friday from 10 am to 5 pm, Saturday from 10 am to 4 pm and

Sunday from 1 to 4 pm. Admission is $2 for adults, $1 for students and military.

Civil War Soldiers Museum
The small but interesting Civil War Soldiers Museum (☎ 469-1900), 108 Palafox Place, is an informative and interesting stop that's definitely worthwhile. Exhibits are in chronological order (begin on the wall to your left as you enter). Note the battlefield hospital (with it's utterly charming bloody arms and legs lying around) and photographs of field hospitals and amputation surgery. There are also exhibits on projectiles, shelters (a recreation of a soldier's campsite), uniforms, alcohol, tobacco and drugs, and currency. It's very well labeled and it's easy to get through; they have a small bookstore packed with offerings on local history and the Civil War. It's open Monday to Saturday from 10 am to 4.30 pm, closed Sunday. Admission is $4 for adults, $2 for children six to 12.

Veterans Memorial Park
Veterans Memorial Park is a moving monument to the veterans of all American wars on 5½ acres overlooking Pensacola Bay; it's at Bayfront Pkwy and 9th Ave (take Main St east from downtown and look for the navy helicopter). At the southern end is the Wall South, a replica of the Vietnam Memorial in Washington, DC, engraved with the names of the over 58,000 American soldiers who died in the war; among them are eight women, 'Angels on the Wall', who were nurses. To locate a name, there's a computer at the flag pole; type in the name and it will give you a tablet number.

Pensacola Naval Air Station
The Pensacola Naval Air Station (NAS, ☎ 452-0111) was where every US WWII pilot was trained, and today it's home to one of the best air museums in the world, along with thousands of navy staff, their families and countless support personnel, contractors and visitors. In fact, the place is so huge that it takes up almost three pages in the local phone book (which notes some interesting and unmilitary sounding entries,

NW & PANHANDLE

like 'Baskin Robbins', 'Choir Director', 'Student Analysis', 'Video Rental' and, chillingly, 'Trouble Desk' at the Naval Air Warfare Center).

Take Hwy 295 to the main entrance of the NAS, which is on the south side of the bridge at the end of Navy Blvd across the Bayou Grande. The checkpoint usually doesn't stop you from just driving in. Once inside, Navy Blvd becomes Duncan Rd (which cuts through that most essential of military perks: the AC Reed Golf Course, chock-full of crew-cut men resplendent in their golfing best); take it to Taylor Rd and turn right, which will lead you right toward the Advanced Redoubt Ruins and Fort Barrancas (see Gulf Islands National Seashore below), the National Museum of Naval Aviation and the lighthouse.

Museum of Naval Aviation One of the best air-space museums around, the National Museum of Naval Aviation (☎ 453-2389, 800-327-5002) is the largest of the navy's museums, and it's so good it's Florida's most attended museum of *any* sort – a million people come here each year, and that's expected to double over the next 10 years. The first thing you'll notice (unless you happen, as we did, to show up during a Blue Angels rehearsal, see below) are the four A-4 Skyhawk jets that the Blue Angels retired when they upgraded to F/A-18s. The museum was undergoing renovation when we went, and by the time you read this you should be able to see the new five-figured monument *Spirit of the Naval Aviator*, 9½-foot statues of naval aviators in WWI, WWII, Korea, Vietnam and Desert Storm uniforms. It's opening an IMAX cinema, featuring IMAX footage taken from the cockpit of Blue Angels jets running through maneuvers, landing and taking off on carriers and other ho-hum stuff like that. In the museum there are also dozens of aircraft, from vintage warbirds to a Harrier jump-jet.

Volunteers – many of them retired navy flyers – enchant with war stories and demonstrations, and kids can suit up and enter the cockpit of their 'test plane'. It also

plans to open a 15-seat flight simulator that will put you 'in the slot' with the Angels. The museum is also putting together the National Flight Log, a computer database of navy flyers that will allow visitors to touch a computer screen and see photographs and read and hear stories of flyers.

It's open daily from 9 am to 5 pm; closed Thanksgiving, Christmas and New Year's Day. Guided tours (in five languages) are available on request. Admission to the museum is free. The IMAX is planned to cost $4, and no price has yet been set for the flight simulator ride.

Blue Angels The Blue Angels (☎ 452-4784), who perform their spectacular air shows to about 6 million people a year, are a precision-flying team based at the NAS (they spend the months of January to March at the Naval Air Facility in El Centro, California). The Angels were organized in 1946, when they flew Grumman F6F Hellcat jets. Today the Angels, a navy publicity and recruiting tool, fly about 35 shows a year, during which four McDonnell-Douglas F/A-18 Hornet jet aircraft are flown in tight – *ooh* so tight – formation and perform rolls, swoops, dives and other precision maneuvers. Two other F/A-18s are used for solo flights, and the shows culminate with all six planes flying in their trademark Delta formation.

The Angels practice (quite a bit, actually – as you would if you were pulling stunts with $155 million worth of aircraft) over the NAS above Sherman Field, generally on Tuesday mornings at 8 am when they're not out of town for shows. To find out if there will be a practice during your visit, call the Blue Angels' Duty Office (☎ 452-2466) on Monday.

Shows are usually an hour long and given on Saturday and Sunday at about 2 pm; they can only be held if there are three nautical miles of visibility and a cloud ceiling of at least 1500 feet. With less than an 8000-foot cloud ceiling, the Angels can only perform a 'flat' show, with some rolls and other maneuvers; above 8000 feet they perform the whole shebang.

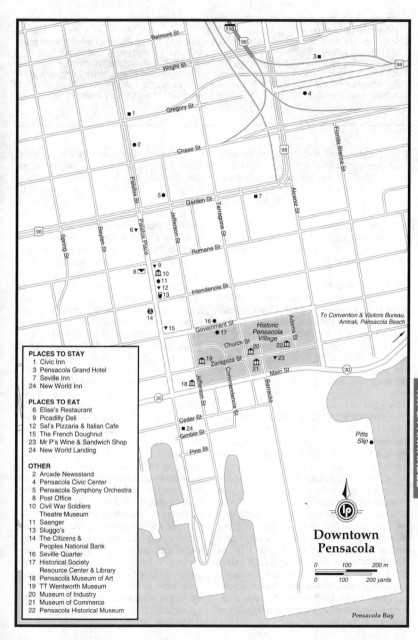

PLACES TO STAY
1 Civic Inn
3 Pensacola Grand Hotel
7 Seville Inn
24 New World Inn

PLACES TO EAT
6 Elise's Restaurant
9 Picadilly Deli
12 Sal's Pizzaria & Italian Cafe
15 The French Doughnut
23 Mr P's Wine & Sandwich Shop
24 New World Landing

OTHER
2 Arcade Newsstand
4 Pensacola Civic Center
5 Pensacola Symphony Orchestra
8 Post Office
10 Civil War Soldiers
   Theatre Museum
11 Saenger
13 Sluggo's
14 The Citizens &
   Peoples National Bank
16 Seville Quarter
17 Historical Society
   Resource Center & Library
18 Pensacola Museum of Art
19 TT Wentworth Museum
20 Museum of Industry
21 Museum of Commerce
22 Pensacola Historical Museum

NW & PANHANDLE

Downtown
Pensacola

0   100   200 m
0   100   200 yards

Pensacola Bay

How close is close?

Looking from a plane once, I was alarmed to see an Alitalia jet about a half mile from my LOT Polish Airlines Tupolev – I thought that was cutting things pretty darn close indeed. Then I spoke with the Blue Angels. During their Delta formation, the top of the right and left wingman's canopies – the door that covers the cockpit right over the pilot's head – are 36 inches below the chief's wingtips. Three feet, or about the distance of cars in adjacent lanes on an interstate highway, are all that stand between a glorious display of precision flying and several $18 to 26 million fireballs. ■

To see if a show will be on during your visit, contact the Blue Angels' events office at ☎ 452-2585; for an annual schedule, write to Public Affairs Office, Attention Schedules, Blue Angels, Naval Air Station, Pensacola, FL 32508-5508 (see Online Services appendix).

Admission to the shows is free; park in the parking lot next to the chow hall across from the Angels' hangar, No 1854.

Pensacola Lighthouse Florida's second-oldest lighthouse (it's on the site of the first) is now run by the US Coast Guard. You can only visit the Pensacola Lighthouse (☎ 492-0310), with 177 steps up to its original crystal, 1st-order lens, with a group of 10 or more by arrangement with the US Coast Guard Auxiliary on Sunday between noon and 5 pm. Admission is free.

The ZOO

The ZOO (☎ 932-2229), 5701 Gulf Breeze Pkwy (Hwy 98), about 10 miles east of Gulf Breeze), is a wonderful place that took quite a beating during Opal, but when we visited they had almost completely restored all services. We thought the best part of the place was the Farm, a petting area where you can feed the giraffes (you haven't lived until you've had a giraffe tongue slobbering on your arm), but there are lots of great animals like cougars, zebras, white tigers and snow leopards. You can take a 10- to 15-minute choo-choo train ($1.25 extra) through their nature preserve, and animals – including llama, brown deer, addax, scimitar-horned oryx, fallow deer and sable antelope – think nothing of walking right up to the cars as you pass.

Don't miss their water buffalo (who, at 1200 pounds, has earned the nickname 'Big Bubba'), and there are also white pelicans and wildebeest. On the down side, Colossus, their colossal gorilla, is on breeding loan to the Cincinnati zoo for the foreseeable future (it seems to be taking ol' Colossus a while to get interested).

From the end of November through January 1, they hold their annual 'Holiday Lights' festival, when the zoo is beautifully lit at night; admission is $3.50 per person.

The ZOO is open daily, weather permitting, from 9 am to 5 pm in summer and from 9 am to 4 pm in winter; closed Christmas and Thanksgiving. Call for Holiday Lights hours. Admission is $9.95 for adults, $8.25 for seniors, $5.25 for children three to 11.

Gulf Islands National Seashore

Covering many of the barrier islands for 150 miles between West Ship Island, Mississippi, and Santa Rosa Island, the Gulf Islands National Seashore (☎ 934-2600, 601-875-9057 in Mississippi) is a federally protected section of lands with many natural and historical attractions. In Florida, it covers two sections of Santa Rosa Island and extends to the NAS across the Fort Pickens Aquatic Preserve.

Unfortunately, when we visited, much of the area was completely gone – the entire western half of Santa Rosa Island, where one of the seashore's main attractions, Fort Pickens, is located, was completely buried under sand by Opal's storm surge. It took them until summer 1996 to shovel it all away, and when we went to press it had still not reopened.

The fort, and the section of the island on

which it sits, should definitely be reopened by the time you read this. The rest of the attractions in the area should all be open as well.

Fort Pickens Fort Pickens (☎ 934-2621) is a pentagonal-shaped brick fort, built in 1829-34, whose claim to fame is that it was the site of Geronimo's incarceration in 1886-87. Inside you'll see the officers' quarters, a mine battery room, mine chambers, the powder magazine, and Bastion D, which was destroyed in a magazine explosion on June 20, 1899. There's camping in the area around the fort (see Places to Stay below).

The Fort Pickens area also has swimming, nature and bike trails and used to have a fishing pier – all of these will be open when you read this. Operating hours and new admission prices had not been set when we checked, but it's likely to be about $3.25 per carload or $1 for pedestrians and bicyclists. There are guided tours Monday to Thursday at 2 pm; on Saturday and Sunday there's a rifle firing demonstration in the fort Parade. The rangers will also offer programs daily at 10 am, including:

Monday: Careful Camping – tips on
  ecologically sound camping
Tuesday: Hurricane Opal footage –
  30-minute video on the destruction
Wednesday: Snorkeling – one-hour
  class in how to view marine life
Thursday: Sand Castles – 'Not what
  you may think . . . but close'
Friday: Endangered Species – 30-minute
  talk on local endangered wildlife

USS Massachusetts Divers can get a close-up look at the remains of the *USS Massachusetts* at the Underwater Archaeological Preserve (☎ 487-2299) in the Fort Pickens State Park Aquatic Preserve. The ship is in 26 feet of water, 1½ miles south-southwest of the Pensacola Pass at latitude 30,17'45"N and longitude 87,18'45"W.

Fort Barrancas Accessed through the NAS, Fort Barrancas (☎ 934-2600) has

been built, destroyed, remodeled and occupied by Spanish, French, British, Confederate and American forces – there's been some incarnation of the fort on this sight since 1698. The British built a second fort, the Advanced Redoubt, nearby. The fort is open daily from 9.30 am to 5 pm, admission is free, as are the ranger artillery demonstrations every morning. Guided tours leave from the visitor center daily at 2 pm. Advanced Redoubt is open Saturday and Sunday only from noon to 2 pm.

From the main NAS gates, take Duncan Rd to Taylor Rd, turn right and the visitor center is straight ahead.

Naval Live Oaks Native American shell mounds and burial sites have been found here at Naval Live Oaks (☎ 934-2600), about six miles east of Gulf Breeze, but Americans found it very useful because of the super strong oak – ironwood – that grows here: it was the perfect strong material for the construction of war ships. The park has several nature trails, and the very helpful rangers at the visitor center will explain Indian artifacts and facts about the park and the region. They also run nature walks at various times of the year. If you're going to be hiking through the trails, bring a good insect repellent – the place is rife with bugs. There are picnic facilities, but camping is only allowed for youth groups. It's open from 8.30 am to 5 pm, admission is free.

Pensacola Beach
The beach here is majestic, and if you're in the area, it would be a crime to miss a day or, especially, a sunset. It's a gently curving shimmering white-sand beach, with stunningly clear gulf water. At night the sunsets are simply spectacular, though it's slightly disorienting to see a sunset to your right, as the beach faces almost due south.

However, beyond the very nice Hampton Inn and a couple of smaller places, there's not much else to see or do. Pensacola Beach's streets have mainly Spanish names; the main east-west drag, running from Fort Pickens all the way to the end of Pensacola

NW & PANHANDLE

Beach, is Via de Luna; from the foot of the Sikes Bridge to the end of town, Via de Luna is crossed by north-south running avenidas, numbered up to 23.

The Sign The '50s-era neon sign welcoming one and all to the 'World's Whitest Beaches' was originally constructed at the corner of Gregory and Palafox Sts, but it was moved to its present location at the entry to the Bob Sikes Bridge in the early 1960s. It's the height of kitsch – a 1950s sign of the future – and it's a beloved local landmark. That it survived Opal with nary a scratch should certainly be taken as an omen . . . of something or other.

UFO House On Pensacola Beach, one of the buildings that made it through the hurricane with flying colors is the UFO House, 1304 Panferio Drive. It's a saucer-shaped thing right out of *It Came From Planet 9*, complete with a ramp leading to the entryway. We knocked, but no one was home, and gawking in, all we saw were some musical gizmotronics indicating a home recording studio. Go to Rio Vista Drive, turn one block north to Panferio Drive, then go east.

Water Tower Modeled after the Sign, the Water Tower at Avenida 23 on Via de Luna is another beach landmark.

Places to Stay

Accommodations on Pensacola Beach were devastated by Opal with one major exception: the newly built Hampton Inn, which withstood the force with barely a creak. Nice rooms, too. Other area chain hotels include two *Motel 6*s, at 5829 Pensacola Blvd (☎ 477-7522) and 7226 Plantation Rd (☎ 474-1060); *Residence Inn By Marriott* (☎ 479-1000) 7230 Plantation Rd; two *Best Western*s, at 13585 Perdido Key Drive (☎ 492-2755) and *Best Western Pensacola Beach* (☎ 934-3300) 16 Via De Luna Drive; *Red Roof Inn* (☎ 476-7960) at the intersection of I-10 and Hwy 291; and *La Quinta Inn* (☎ 474-0411) at 7750 N Davis Hwy.

Camping The cheapest camping in the area is at *Big Lagoon State Park* (☎ 492-1595) and near the city of Milton at *Adventures Unlimited* (☎ 904-623-6197); see Around Pensacola below for both these listings.

Fort Pickens (☎ 934-2621), on the western tip of Santa Rosa Island, has camping sites with picnic tables, grills, showers and water and electric hookups. Sites without/with electricity are $12/16.

Downtown The *Civic Inn* (☎ 432-3441), 200 N Palafox St, is a fine option with typical motel-style singles/doubles for $32/36 in winter, $42/48 in summer. Watch those local calls at 35¢ a pop.

The *Days Inn* (☎ 438-4922, 800-325-2525), 710 N Palafox St, has all the usual features of a chain place, with rooms year round at $51/56.

Rooms at the *Seville Inn* (☎ 800-277-7275), 223 E Garden St, are okay, with singles/doubles for $39/49 in summer, about 'five bucks' higher in winter, including donuts and coffee in the morning.

Above and just as flashy as the New World Landing (see Places to Eat below) is the *New World Inn* (☎ 432-4111), 600 Palafox Place, with singles/doubles for $70/80. It has a great location, and nice clean rooms, but somewhat snooty staff.

With many parts of it built in 1912 as the L&N Railroad Depot, the *Pensacola Grand Hotel* (☎ 433-3336, 800-348-3336), 200 E Gregory St, is certainly that, and the prices reflect what you get: singles/doubles are $80 to 90/90 to 100 on weekdays, $78 for a single or double on weekends, and suites run $200 to 400. There's a nice Cavu Club lounge and a restaurant downstairs.

A nice B&B that's just west of the heart of downtown, *The Yacht House* (☎ 433-3634), 1820 Cypress St, is just across the street from the Pensacola Yacht Club. All rooms have a private bath and access to the screened-in porch. They do a 'Caribbean breakfast' – fresh tropical fruits, bagels, pastries, homemade jelly and English muffins and toast. Rooms range from $65 to 110 per night for a three-room suite with a private deck and hot tub.

Pensacola Beach The devastation of Opal made research difficult here, though there were a few options even then:

For us, the sight of the *Five Flags Inn* (☎ 932-3586), 299 Fort Pickens Rd, brought back fond memories of time we spent in Finland – especially as the ground all around it was covered by the snow-white sand dumped there by Opal. It's an institutional-looking building with friendly service and beachfront rooms at $45 in winter, $59 in fall and spring and $75 in summer. To get there, turn right at the traffic light after the bridge and go west for a bit; the hotel's on the left.

Clarion Suites Resort & Convention Center (☎ 932-4300, 800-874-5303), 20 Via de Luna, is a newish place right on the beach. Rooms from Sunday to Wednesday are $110, Thursday to Saturday $131 in summer, and as low as $67 in mid-winter. Rates include donuts, coffee and juice in the morning, and there's a pool.

The spanking new *Hampton Inn* (☎ 932-6800, 800-426-7866), 2 Via de Luna, is an excellent hotel, and cheaper than we would have thought for what you get. Rooms are from $65 to 71 in winter and $101 to 131 in summer (higher on special events). The place has excellent service, rooms are large and airy, and if you get a beach-view room (the higher priced ones), beautiful ocean views at sunrise and sunset. A good continental breakfast is included, and there's a pool out back (the only thing that was really damaged by the hurricane). It's right past the first traffic light on the way into the beach from Sikes Bridge.

Places to Eat
Downtown The cheerful and very popular *Elise's Restaurant* (☎ 432-5100), 11 Palafox Place, does breakfast from $1.50 to 4, but it's famous for its great, $5 lunch buffet – choose from two meats, four veggies, corn bread and salad bar ($4 without the meat). Lunch is daily from 11 am to 2.30 pm.

We loved the New Orleans-style food and service at *The French Doughnut* (☎ 434-1412), 212 Palafox Place. They

have enormous sandwiches, hickory coffee and daily seafood specials for about $4.75.

A very popular local place is *Mr. P's Wine & Sandwich Shop* (☎ 433-0294), 221 E Zaragoza St. It's in the Moreno Cottage, which is home of the daughter of Francisco Moreno, who is considered by many to be the father of Pensacola (he had 27 kids). The small, cozy place serves lunch specials like quiche ($5.50), sandwich platters ($4 to 5.50) and salads ($2.50 to 5.50).

Great sandwiches await at the *Picadilly Deli* (☎ 438-3354), 102 Palafox Place, including many vegetarian options from $2.75 and tuna sandwiches for $3.75. They have about 50 kinds of beer with which to wash them down.

Sal's Pizzeria & Italian Cafe (☎ 433-5385), 128 Palafox Place, sell slices for $1.50; spaghetti and chicken parmigiana is $4.99.

Founaris Bros Greek Restaurant (☎ 432-0629, 432-0639), 1015 N 9th Ave, is a good Greek and Italian place with a huge range of Greek pizzas from $4.85 all the way up to $15.25. Spanakopeta, an elaborate spinach pie with feta cheese in phyllo dough, is $2, Greek salads are $3.75, moussaka $6.50 and pasta dishes like veal parmigiana are $5.50. They have a whole bunch of sandwiches as well, from $3.50 to 4.75.

Billy Bob's Barbecue Company (☎ 484-5480), 6403 N 9th Ave, specializes in hand-pulled Carolina-style barbecue 'without the fat'. Daily specials include Uncle Grady's rib lunch for $4.99.

New World Landing (☎ 434-3736), 600 Palafox Place (downstairs from the New World Inn), is a very elegant place, with shrimp dishes for $13, filet mignon $15 and seafood fettuccine $14. They have patchy service – sometimes very good and sometimes pithy. It's open for dinner only, Tuesday to Thursday from 5 to 9 pm, Friday and Saturday from 6 to 10 pm; happy hour is 5 to 7 pm. It's closed Sunday and Monday.

Yamato (☎ 453-3461), 131 Warrington Rd, was closed when we visited but it's recommended. It is affordable for lunch, but prices skyrocket at dinner. At lunch, they

NW & PANHANDLE

have set meals, all with salad and rice: cashew chicken, sweet and sour pork or kushikatsu (deep-fried pork) are $4.95, sukiyaki and beef teriyaki are $7.50 and a seven-piece sushi sampler and a California roll is $9.95; other specials run $6.25. At dinner, entrees start at about $11.95 and go up to $21. They have a full sushi bar and hibachi tables.

Gulf Breeze *Golden China* (☎ 932-2511), 830 Gulf Breeze Pkwy (right near the north side of the Sikes Bridge), has some of the best Chinese food we've had outside New York (and those great cardboard boxes for take-out). Staff are really nice, and it serves a $5 lunch buffet Sunday to Friday from 11.30 am to 2.30 pm. Otherwise, most dishes are from $5.50 to 9 at lunch, $8 to 12 at dinner.

Chris' Seafood Grille (☎ 934-3500) is a very nice place at the foot of Three Mile Bridge in Gulf Breeze. Appetizers like an onion blossom or fried mushrooms are $4.95, shrimp or chicken quesadillas or onion rings are $4.50, and dinner main courses include chargrilled amberjack for $9.95, crawfish Alfredo for $10.95 and steaks and chicken dishes from $11.95 to 16.95. They do a catch-of-the-day lunch special for $7.95. Closed Tuesday.

Naval Air Station *Lighthouse Point* (☎ 452-3251), right in front of the Pensacola Lighthouse, does an all-you-can-eat lunch buffet for $4.95 from 10.30 am to 2 pm – great for the grumbles if you're spending time in the aviation museum, across the street.

Pensacola Beach The *Sun Ray Restaurante & Cantina* (☎ 932-0118) is in the *Jubilee Restaurant & Entertainment Complex* (☎ 934-3108, 800-582-3208), 400 Quiet Water Beach Rd (across the street from the Hampton Inn). It has $4.95 lunch specials daily from 11.30 am to 3.30 pm, such as shrimp and salad, quesadillas and mini-burritos. At dinner, burgers and sandwiches are from $5.95 to 6.95, Mexican stuff from $9.95 to 12.95. It's a very popular watering

hole, serving Mexican specialty drinks for $4 to 6. The entertainment complex itself has juggling, clowns and other live entertainment nightly.

Chan's Gulfside Café (☎ 932-3525), 2½ Via de Luna (next to the Hampton Inn) has a downstairs section for sandwiches, snacks and drinks and an upstairs section for sit-down meals.

We heard good things about *Boy on a Dolphin* (☎ 932-7949), 400 Pensacola Beach Blvd (on the east side of the bridge). It serves steaks, chicken and seafood dishes.

Entertainment

Saenger Theatre The gorgeous Spanish-baroque Saenger ('SAYN-ger') Theatre (☎ 444-7686), 118 Palafox Place, was reconstructed of bricks from the Pensacola Opera House, which was destroyed in a 1916 hurricane. It's home to Broadway road show productions (including *42nd Street, Will Rogers' Follies, Crazy for You* and *Forbidden Broadway*), as well as performances by the Northwest Florida Ballet and the Pensacola Symphony Orchestra and Pensacola Opera. Ticket prices change by performance. The box office is open Monday to Friday from 10 am to 5 pm in winter, 10 am to 4 pm in summer.

Pensacola Opera The Pensacola Opera (☎ 433-6737) performs two fully staged opera productions a year – using singers from all over the country – at the Saenger Theatre. The past two productions were Puccini's *La Bohème* and Verdi's *Il Travatore*. Call the opera when you're in town to see what's on, or the Saenger Theatre for ticket information.

Pensacola Symphony Orchestra This 70-piece orchestra (☎ 435-2533) has been performing since 1926. The season runs from September through April, with five concerts and a Christmas Holiday show, all held at the Saenger. Tickets (available through the Saenger only) are usually from $17 to 21.

Jazz Society The Jazz Society of Pensacola

(☎ 433-8382) is an appreciation society involved in a range of projects with local and national musicians. They hold an annual jazz picnic in June at the Pensacola Yacht Club, and they host events at Seville Quarter (see Bars & Clubs below), like Musical Gumbo on Friday night at Rosie O'Grady's and Sunday afternoon in the Seville Historic District in the fall and winter.

Gallery Nights The Arts Council of Northwest Florida (☎ 432-9906) is in charge of Gallery Nights, held in March, July and November. The nights, which are walks between openings at the area's art galleries, have been going on since 1991 and are gaining popularity and drawing power every year. The galleries are all downtown:

Schmidt's Gallery
8 Palafox Place (☎ 433-7717)
Jeweler's Trade Shop
26 Palafox Place (☎ 432-4433)
SOHO Gallery
23 Palafox Place (☎ 435-7646)
Page & Palette
106 Palafox Place (☎ 432-6656)
Good Design
121 Palafox Place (☎ 436-7772)
JD Hayward/Photography
122 Palafox Place (☎ 438-0416)
Benton-Foy
8 W Cedar St (☎ 433-9000)
The Billingsley Gallery
615 Palafox Place (☎ 433-1127)

The Arts Council has offices next to the Saenger Theatre, where you can pick up their annual Clearinghouse Calendar, which lists arts and cultural events for the entire year.

Bars & Nightclubs There will certainly be more options available, especially on the beach, when you get here. *McGuire's Irish Pub* (☎ 433-6789), 600 E Gregory St, is a local tradition. Happy hour is daily from 4 to 6 pm, it opens at 11 am and live entertainment starts nightly at 9 pm.

The third incarnation of *Sluggo's* (☎ 435-0543), 130 Palafox Place, is a down and dirty place with good, fun staff. It's open Tuesday to Saturday from 3 pm to 3 am.

Domestic beer is $1.75, imported $2.25, well drinks are $3.25 and call drinks $2.75; happy hour is from 3 to 8 pm and it's 25¢ off. You'll find books, Trivial Pursuit, chess and some neat typewriters scattered about. Upstairs are pool tables, air hockey, pinball and Ms PacMan. The 3rd floor is for live music; on Tuesday and Saturday cover is $3, and on Friday $4. Free drafts are served between 9 to 11 pm.

Bedlam (no phone), 15 E Intendencia St, is run by the same people as Sluggo's. It's an underground, techno-rave place (18 years and up) that's BYOB in order to take advantage of a loophole in Florida law that allows it to stay open until 4 am. Every other Thursday they have drag shows; the cover is $4. It's open Wednesday to Sunday from 11 pm to 5 am.

Seville Quarter (☎ 434-6211), 130 E Government St, is an entertainment and restaurant complex very much like Orlando's Church St Station. It houses numerous restaurants and bars, like *Rosie O'Grady's Goodtime Emporium, Lili Marlene's Aviator's Pub, End o' the Alley Bar, Palace Oyster Bar, Apple Annie's Courtyard, Phineas Phogg's Balloon Works* and *Fast Eddie's Billiard Parlor*. Open daily at 11 am, varying closing hours. Admission is $3; only people aged 21 and up are allowed in, except on Tuesday and Thursday when those 18 and older are welcome ($4 for 18 to 20 year olds).

Getting There & Away
Air Pensacola Regional Airport (☎ 435-1746) is served by Continental, Delta, American, Northwest and USAir. The airport is about four miles northeast of downtown, near the bay; the terminal is off of 9th Ave on Airport Blvd.

Train Pensacola is a stop for Amtrak's *Sunset Limited*, which pulls in at ungodly hours no matter which way you're going: from Los Angeles it arrives on Wednesday, Friday and Monday at 1.40 am; from Miami, it arrives on Monday, Wednesday and Saturday at 4.46 am. The Amtrak station (☎ 433-4966) is at 980 E Heinberg

St at 15th Ave, just north of the CVB visitor information center. See the Getting There & Away chapter for price information.

Bus The Greyhound station (☎ 476-4800) is at 505 W Burgess Rd. Bus service includes several buses a day to/from each of the following destinations; fares are quoted one way/roundtrip.

Destination	Price	Duration
New Orleans	$29/58	4 to 5¾ hours
Mobile	$15/30	1 hour
Panama City		
Beach	$21/42	2¼ hours
Tallahassee	$39/78	3½ to 5 hours
Jacksonville	$49/98	8¼ to 9½ hours
Gainesville	$57/114	7 to 8¾ hours
Miami	$89/178	16¼ to 20 hours

Car To New Orleans, Louisiana, or Mobile, Alabama, take I-10 west. To the rest of Florida and the Panhandle, take either I-10 east or the coastal route, Hwy 98, through Gulf Breeze, Fort Walton Beach and Panama City Beach. From Pensacola, it's about 200 miles to New Orleans, 650 miles to Miami, 103 to Panama City Beach, 191 to Tallahassee and 355 to Jacksonville.

Getting Around

To/From the Airport From the airport, take ECAT bus 2 to the downtown transfer station, and then bus 16 to downtown Pensacola (see below). A taxi should run from $11 to 13 to downtown, $18 to 20 to the beach. Driving, take Airport Blvd to 9th Ave or I-110 south, which go downtown and meet up with Hwy 98, which continues over the Three Mile Bridge to Gulf Breeze and Pensacola Beach.

Bus Escambia County Transit (ECAT; ☎ 436-9383 ext 611, ADA 12) has limited bus service around Pensacola, but it's not very convenient between tourist destinations – it doesn't go to the ZOO or to the beach. Bus 16 runs between Palafox St and the transfer station (also inconveniently located at the corner of Fairfield Drive, or Hwy 295, and L St, northwest of

downtown), from where you can catch bus 2 to/from the airport or bus 14 to the NAS. Fare is $1, transfers are 10¢.

Trolley The Tiki Trolley is a free weekend shuttle up and down Pensacola Beach that runs Friday and Saturday 10 to 3 am, Sunday 10 am to midnight. Stand by the trolley signs along Via de Luna and the trolley will pick you up.

Car There are a few one-way streets downtown, but otherwise driving is pretty straightforward and easy. It takes about 20 minutes to drive between Pensacola Beach and downtown. Several major car rental companies are at the airport, though not Value or Alamo.

Taxi Taxi rates in Pensacola are $1.50 flagfall, $1.20 each mile. Cab companies include Airport Express (☎ 572-5555), Yellow Cab (☎ 433-3333) and Green Cab (☎ 456-8294).

Bicycle On Pensacola Beach, Dinah's Shore Shop (☎ 934-0014) has bikes and skates for rent: bikes are $5 for two hours, $10 for eight hours; blades are $6 an hour, $15 for eight hours. It's at 715 A Pensacola Beach Blvd, just south of the toll booth on the beach side of the Sikes Bridge.

AROUND PENSACOLA
Big Lagoon & Perdido Key

Big Lagoon State Park (☎ 492-1595), 12301 Gulf Beach Hwy, is a 700-acre state park on the Gulf Intracoastal Waterway with nature trails, observation towers, a boat launch, camping and incredible spans of white sandy beaches. There are ranger-led interpretive programs on Saturday. Their adjacent satellite park, Perdido Key, has what's considered to be the finest beach in the area; boardwalks lead down to it. Admission to Big Lagoon is $3.25 per carload, $1 for pedestrians and bicyclists; admission to Perdido Key is $2.

Tent sites at Big Lagoon are $8.88/10.88 without/with electric and water. The camping fee includes admission to both Big

Lagoon and Perdido Key. It's about 12 miles southwest of Pensacola off Hwy 292.

Adventures Unlimited

Adventures Unlimited (☎ 623-6197, 800-239-6864) is a camping resort 12 miles north of the city of Milton, which is about 20 miles northeast of Pensacola, on the Coldwater River. They offer a huge range of canoeing and tubing options, with hourly to three-day trips on the Coldwater and Blackwater Rivers and on Sweetwater-Juniper Creek. The prices, which include canoe, paddles and preservers, are not out of line at all: short trips are $12, day trips are $13, special 18-mile, five-hour trips are $15. For overnight trips, you can rent a canoe with tent, sleeping bags, stove, cooking kit (but not food) and lantern for $24 per person for one night, $58 per person for two nights.

Camping at their campground is $15 for tents, or $29 in a camping 'tree house' (actually it's perched on stilts) with no air-conditioning. Basic bunk cabins with air-conditioning are $39, and fully equipped cabins (with kitchens and indoor bath-rooms) are from $59 to 89.

From Pensacola take I-10 east to Hwy 87 north to Hwy 90 west, turn right at the Burger King and go about 12 miles north – it's well signed. Their mailing address is Route 6, Box 283, Milton, FL 32570.

Blackwater River State Park

There's incredible canoeing and camping at Blackwater River State Park (☎ 623-2363), which is one of the clearest (yet tinted with tannin, which gives tea its color), sand-bottom rivers in the world. The shallow ends are clear because of the white sand bottom. And what's best is that if you're canoeing, you can camp anywhere along the riverbank you feel like it – the only regulations are the obvious ones: no cutting of live wood, gather only dead and down wood; bury human waste at least six inches deep; and take out what you brought in.

There are several nature trails throughout the park, and the rangers are trying to start some interpretive programs and campfire programs around the campfire ring, but at the moment they're understaffed.

The park is located in the Blackwater River State Forest, the state's largest, and it's mostly pristine wilderness. The forest runs south from the Alabama state line to just north of I-10, and the Blackwater River itself begins in the Conecuh National Forest in Alabama; its tributaries, the Sweetwater, Juniper and East Coldwater Creeks, run down through the Blackwater River State Park as well.

Canoeing Blackwater Canoe Rental and Outpost (☎ 623-0235, 800-967-6789) rents canoes for self-guided day trips along the Blackwater River for $13 per person and $19 overnight. You pay, get a receipt and they drive you upriver from four to 36 miles, and you paddle back downriver. For day trips, the canoe is yours until 6 pm. They also do a three-night overnight rental for $28 per person. For location, see Getting There & Away below.

Bob's Canoes (☎ 623-5457) runs canoe, kayak and tube trips on the Coldwater River: day runs start at $12 per person and overnights, which leave Bob's at 11 am and 2 pm, cost $20 per person; you camp along the riverbank. They also have kayaks ($17 for one-person, $30 for two-person) and inner tubes ($7) – and for $4 you can also rent a tube for your cooler (!).

From Pensacola take I-10 east to exit 10 (Hwy 87) north to Hwy 90 west, turn left at the Burger King and go for two traffic lights plus two blocks, and turn right on Munson Hwy (Hwy 191), for seven miles.

Camping Camping is available (30 sites) within the state park itself; tent and RV sites are $8.56 without electricity, $10.70 with, all sites have water.

Getting There & Away To get to the entrance to the park as well as to Black-water Canoe Rental from Pensacola, take I-10 east to exit 10 (Hwy 87), turn left, go north for one mile until you reach Hwy 90; turn right or east and go 5½ miles until you see the canoe/state park sign. Take a left

NW & PANHANDLE

(north), go 1½ miles and the Blackwater Canoe Rental and Outpost is on the right.

Air Force Armament Museum

The US Air Force Armament Museum (☎ 882-4062), outside the west gate of Eglin Air Force Base, will be of interest to real weaponry buffs but not to many others. Outside, the place is surrounded by aircraft, including an A-10A Warthog, an F-16A, a much cooler B-17 Flying Fortress and the SR 71-A Blackbird reconnaissance plane that set the transcontinental speed record, flying coast to coast in 68 minutes and 17 seconds. Inside there are tons of weapons, a Warthog simulator, a terrifying F-105 Thunderchief missile and this lovely entry:

The Sensor Fuzed Weapon (SFW), the first of a new class of smart munitions to enter production, provides multiple 'kills per pass' from a single weapon.

The gift shop has inflatable war planes, lots of model airplanes, many 'Made in China' bullet key chains and, inexplicably, seashells and hand-painted electrical outlet and light switch plates with nautical themes. The museum is open every day from 9.30 am to 4.30 pm; closed Thanksgiving, Christmas and New Year's Day. Admission is free. To get here from Pensacola, take I-10 east to exit 12 (Crestview), go south on Hwy 85 for a couple of miles to Hwy 123 (this bypasses Niceville). Take this for five miles and pick up Hwy 85 again for a couple of miles and follow the signs.

PANAMA CITY BEACH
• *pop 4400, beaches area 20,000*
☎ 904

The glorious, white, Apalachian quartz sand beaches of Panama City Beach (which is party central to generations of Southerners) were struck hard by Hurricane Opal. But as we went to press, remarkable progress had been made in restoring order. Of the city's hotel rooms, 14,000 of 18,000 were back open for the 1996-97 season, and the several properties that were forced to tear down and rebuild from scratch were in the process of doing that just. Two-thirds of

the city's concrete pier was washed away in the storm, and while the second fishing pier suffered less damage, it still lost the T at its end.

The impact of the storm was still visible at the western end of the beach, where the storm hit the hardest, and piles of rubble were lying along side streets as late as seven months after Opal had passed through.

But the beaches themselves, and those at St Andrews State Recreation Area, have been cleaned and groomed – in fact, they look better now than they have for years.

Panama City Beach's nickname, the 'Redneck Riviera', may be cruel, but it's also fitting. Locals refer to the ordinance allowing open cans of beer on the beach as a 'highlight'. And in contrast to the resorts along the Atlantic coast – where citizens have over the years demanded more and more cops to chase away college students on Spring Break (case in point, Fort Lauderdale, which pretty much outlawed the university ritual) – Panama City Beach doesn't just tolerate students partying on its beaches, it *recruits* them, as the Convention & Visitors Bureau boasts in an internet release:

Perhaps the best thing about spending Spring Break on Panama City Beach is, believe it or not, the police. You can party on the beach and the local constabulary will not hassle you. In fact, the police here go out of their way to make you feel welcome – unlike other places on the Atlantic coast of Florida – and will not hassle students.

But there's another side to the beach: it's home to a surprising number of religious – mainly Christian – retreats, and you'll find large groups of clean-cut, clean-living, upstanding citizens here as well, along with religious article and book shops. And while nightlife here is definitely in the 'party with thousands' category and fast-food places line the strip, there's some unspoiled nature here as well: St Andrews State Recreation Area at the island's eastern end was voted Best Beach in America by *Condé Nast Traveler* in 1995.

Orientation
Panama City Beach is located on a gulf

barrier island almost due west of the altogether separate city of Panama City, a military town based around the flygals and flyguys at Tyndall Air Force Base. Hwy 98, the main coastal road from the south, splits off at Panama City Beach and becomes Hwy 98 (at the north) and Hwy 98A at the south, along the beach, respectively known as Back Beach Rd and Front Beach Rd.

The island is about 27 miles long, spanning from St Andrews State Recreation Area at the east to the Philips Inlet Bridge at the west. Hwy 98 connects Panama City Beach to Panama City on the Hathaway Bridge, which crosses St Andrews Bay. The split of Hwys 98 and 98A occurs at the northeastern end of the beach, just south of the bridge, and cuts almost due west at Thomas Drive. Hwy 392 runs along the coast between Front Beach Rd and St Andrews.

Front Beach Rd is more than a little like Hwy 192 in Kissimmee (see Central Florida): it's lined with fast-food joints, motels, hotels, mini-golf and cheesy amusement parks – everything one needs to sit on a beach drinking beer.

Maps The easiest map to use is given away at the visitor center as part of a full-color brochure on general area attractions. The most accurate map of the beach is available through the Bay County Chamber of Commerce (☎ 785-5206), or by writing them at PO Box 1850, Panama City Beach, FL 32402.

Information

Tourist Offices The Panama City Beach Convention & Visitors Bureau (☎ 233-6503, 800-722-3224, fax 233-5072), 12015 Front Beach Rd, has a very helpful Visitors Information Center, which hands out pamphlets, dispenses good information, allows you to use their phone to make hotel and restaurant reservations and is generally very helpful. The modern building almost completely withstood the force of Opal, but look out the window at the pier, which didn't fare quite so well.

Money There are no (gasp) Barnett Bank offices in Panama City or Panama City Beach. Bay Bank & Trust Co has two branches on the beach: at 7915 Back Beach Rd (☎ 235-3333) and at 17255 Hutchinson Rd (☎ 235-4078). There are several private exchange places along Front Beach Rd. American Express doesn't have an office on the beach, but they do have a representative office in Panama City at Nervig Travel Service (☎ 763-2876), 569 Harrison Ave.

Post The biggest post office in the area is the General Mail Facility (☎ 747-4840), 1336 Sherman Ave in Panama City; the Panama City Beach post office (☎ 234-9101) is at 420 Churchwell Drive.

Bookstores The Book Warehouse (☎ 235-2950), 6646 W Hwy 98, has new and remaindered books, as well as some religious books.

Libraries Panama City Beach Public Library (☎ 233-5055) is at 110 Arnold Rd.

Media The *News-Herald* is the largest regional daily; it's published in Panama City. *Bay Arts & Entertainment* is a bimonthly with information on nightclubs and restaurants.

Laundry Beachside Laundry and Dry Cleaning (☎ 234-1601), 21902 Front Beach Rd, is open daily from 8 am to 8 pm. Long Beach Coin Laundry (no phone) is at 10444 Front Beach Rd.

Medical Services The two largest medical facilities in the area are in Panama City itself: the Bay Medical Center (☎ 769-1511) 615 N Bonita Ave, and Bay Walk-In Clinic (☎ 763-9744), 2306 Hwy 77.

Dangers & Annoyances See the Facts for the Visitor section for general hurricane preparedness information.

The waters off Panama City Beach are generally calm, though the city has devised a warning flag system to alert bathers of potentially treacherous conditions. Note that the absence of flags does not necessarily indicate safe seas. The flags are:

Red – Danger: undertow
Yellow – Potential undertow
Blue – Calm seas

Glass Bottom Boat

The Glass Bottom Boat (☎ 234-8944) runs three trips a day from May to August at 9 am and 1 and 4.30 pm; in other months call for their schedule. The trips, which last from 3 to 3½ hours, let you get a fantastic view of sea life through the clear water – you'll pass over sandy and grassy flats, and bottle-nosed dolphins will more than likely swim alongside and bark at you. The boat makes a stop at Shell Island, with its stretches of white sand and windswept dunes (it's imperative that you bring sunscreen); on the way back the crew lets out a shrimp net and identifies all the creatures they catch (they throw them all back), and you'll feed pelicans. It's a fun time on the water.

In summer the excursions are $13 for adults, $10 for children up to 12, children under two free; $1 less in winter. Note that you can get a $3-off coupon at the visitor center. The boat leaves from the marina at 3605 Thomas Drive.

Museum of Man in the Sea

The Museum of Man in the Sea (☎ 235-4101), 17314 Back Beach Rd, is actually a serious look at the history of diving. As you enter there are some neat (if cheesy) experiments: Ever wonder how those hand-pumped diving systems work? You can crank up a Siebe hand pump here, used for dives down to 30 feet. You can climb into what seems to be a precariously perched Beaver Mark IV submersible and see models of Sealab III, an underwater laboratory. Though the place has seen better days (several of the exhibits are a little ratty), the staff seem to really care about the displays, and it's certainly less cynical than some other tourist attractions. And with admission prices of $4 for adults, $2 for children six to 16, and discounts for seniors, naval personnel and others – why not? It's open daily from 9 am to 5 pm.

Zoo World

We were totally taken aback by the caring staff at Zoo World Zoological and Botanical Park (☎ 230-1243), 9008 Front Beach Rd, which is home to over 350 animals, including 20 endangered species. The zoo participates in the Species Survival Plan (SSP), which is governed by the American Zoological Association (though Zoo World is not yet a member). The plan brings together a network of zoos and parks to protect and breed endangered animals. Endangered animals here include jaguars, Sumatran orangutans, Bali myna, spectacled bears, siamangs (a large ape native to Borneo, Sumatra and Malaysia) and their golden lion tamarin – tamarins were one of the first species to be protected by the SSP.

Zoo World also has reptiles, chimpanzees and other primates, an aviary and a petting zoo that has a giraffe, a horse, a llama, goats, camels, deer, pot-bellied pigs and a gazelle (that'll let you pet it if you've got food in your hand).

The zoo is open daily from 9 am to dusk. Admission is $8.95 for adults, $7.50 for seniors, $6.50 for children aged three to 11.

St Andrews State Recreation Area

Voted the best beach in the USA by *Condé Nast Traveler* in 1995 – ahead of such shabby entries as the beaches on Oahu and Maui, Hawaii – St Andrews State Recreation Area (☎ 233-5140) is a 1260-acre park with nature trails, swimming, hiking and camping (see Places to Stay below). The park has lots of wildlife, including deer, fox, coyotes, snakes, alligators and all kinds of sea birds.

There is snorkeling available (rental prices were unavailable at press time), and every day from 10 am to 3 pm, the *Shell Island Shuttle* leaves every half hour from the park's jetty area to Shell Island, where you can broil on the beach or snorkel. A roundtrip ferry ticket is $7.50 for adults, $5.50 for kids under 12.

The park is at the eastern end of the island; from Panama City cross the bridge and turn left on Hwy 3031, across the Grand Lagoon and the entrance is on the left. From the beach, take Front Beach Rd to Thomas Drive as far as you can go.

Organized Tours

The *Island Queen* (☎ 234-3307 ext 1816), 4200 Marriot Drive (behind the enormous Marriot Bay Point Resort), is a Dixie-style paddlewheel riverboat, but as we went to press their docks had still not been repaired. When they work, they run from Tuesday to Sunday at 9 am and 1 pm. The whole trip takes about three hours, about half of which is spent on Shell Island. The cost is $10 for adults, $5 for children aged five to 12, $2 for children up to age four (half-price coupons are available at the visitor center).

Tropical Airbrush (☎ 234-3469) runs tethered hot-air balloon rides that will get you high enough to get good views of the whole beach. The rides cost $15 for one person, $26 for two, and they're piloted by – oh, this is too much – Captain Dudley Dooright (we're wiping tears of laughter from our eyes). It's open daily, weather (especially wind) permitting, and it's at 12386-D Front Beach Rd, just across the street from the County Pier, next to Wendy's, and behind Air Boingo Bungee.

Coastal Helicopter Charter Inc (☎ 769-6117) does short helicopter jaunts around the area beginning at $20; they park close to the visitor center.

Diving & Snorkeling

All of the following offer diving trips as well as snorkeling: Panama City Dive Center (☎ 235-3390, 800-832-4483), 4823 Thomas Drive, does boat rentals and dive charters – you can pay as low as $20 with gear, $15 if you bring your own. Boats leave daily at 10 am and 2 pm.

Aquastar (☎ 230-2800, 832-3909) does two three-hour snorkel trips daily at 11 am and 2 pm; the cost is $20 for adults, $15 for children 12 and under, and it includes snorkel gear. They leave from the Passport Marina off Thomas Drive.

Emerald Coast Divers (☎ 233-3355, 800-945-3483), 5121 Thomas Drive, charges $20 for a three-hour snorkeling trip to Shell Island.

Places to Stay

Camping *St Andrews State Recreation Area* (☎ 233-5140) has campsites for tents and RVs/vans for $8.68 for a non-waterfront site without electricity, $10.81 for non-waterfront sites with electric; $10.85 for waterfront nonelectric and $12.98 for waterfront with electric in summer; in winter the rates are $16.25/18.41/18.45/ 20.58, all including tax.

KOA (☎ 234-5731), 8800 Thomas Drive, has campsites in summer for $18.95 with water only, and $22.95 with full hookups. Winter rates are $13/17.95 a day, $99 a week and $235 a month. Kamping Kabins are $31.95 year round.

Hotels & Motels Note that due to the hurricane we were unable to check many of these places; we've counted almost exclusively on the CVB to compile this list of motels, many of which will be open when you visit. But prices may have changed, sometimes dramatically. There are chains here as well, including Marriott, Holiday Inn and Howard Johnson.

The Reef Motel (☎ 234-3396, 800-847-7286), 12011 Front Beach Rd, charges $35 to 75 for rooms with two double beds, $210 to 390 a week; efficiencies are from $39 to 89 a day, $240 to 450 a week.

Bright Star Motel (☎ 234-7119, 800-421-1295), 14705 Front Beach Rd, has single/double rooms from $30 to 49/40 to 75; efficiencies are $50 to 95 a day.

The Char-Bett Motel (☎ 234-3581), 291 S Hwy 79, has rooms from $20 to 35, efficiencies from $25 to 55.

Driftwood Lodge (☎ 234-6601), 15811 Front Beach Rd, charges $25 to 45 for singles, $30 to 65 for doubles; efficiencies are $40 to 90 and suites $85 to 160.

We stayed at the *The Palmetto Court* (☎ 234-2121), 17255 Front Beach Rd. Rooms here are $35 to 65 for a double; efficiencies are $45 to 70, which suffered some damage outside but remained open. It has rooms on the beachfront and across the road, which are clean and very comfortable; there is a nice indoor pool as well.

Osprey (☎ 234-0303, 800-338-2659), 15801 Front Beach Rd, is the sister motel of Driftwood Lodge; efficiencies are $45 to 90, suites $70 to 130.

Quality Inn Beachfront Resort (☎ 234-6636, 800-874-7101, fax 235-4202), 15285 Front Beach Rd, has doubles from $45 to 85, efficiencies from $55 to 95 and penthouses are $125 to 225.

Largo Mar (☎ 234-5750, 800-645-2746, fax 233-0533), 5717 Thomas Drive, has suites with a three-night minimum rental during high season: $65 to 105 for one bedroom, $85 to 125 for two bedrooms.

Places to Eat

As with motels, many restaurants were closed when we visited, and those that were open were not exactly in the best position to shine; the listings below are merely representative. Having said that, we weren't overly impressed with the offerings, though you won't starve. Seafood tends to be good – especially oysters, which are cheap and plentiful. Fast-food and chain places seem to thrive here. Check with the visitor center for up-to-date information on new restaurants; they also hand out a good selection of area restaurant menus.

Thomas Donut & Snack Shop (☎ 234-8039), 19210 Front Beach Rd, has 12-inch pizzas for $8; hot dogs and sandwiches are $2 to 3.50. *The Original Chicago Dawgs* (☎ 235-2800), 10812 Front Beach Rd, does $1 to $4 'meals on a bun'. The *Beach BBQ*

(☎ 230-1166), 2920 Thomas Drive, does plates and sandwiches from $2.50 to 6.

Pickle Patch (☎ 235-2000), 5700 Thomas Drive, does pita-bread sandwiches that average $4; Middle Eastern dinners run $5 to 7.50. *Sea Rock Cafe* (☎ 234-2838), 13006 Front Beach Rd, has a prime rib sandwich for $6, top sirloin for $10 and shrimp $13. Sandwiches served until 2 am, entrees until 10 pm.

Ms Crazy's Wine Dine & Daiquiris (☎ 230-6920), 16700 Front Beach Rd, is open from 11 am to midnight; it has salads from $1.50 to 5.50, sandwiches and burgers from $3 to 6 and chicken breast dinners are $7.

Shrimp City Seafood (☎ 235-4099), 3016 Thomas Drive, has fresh crabmeat, oysters and fish. A snow crab platter is $5.99.

Marina Grill (☎ 233-0008), 6426 W Hwy 98, has pasta jambalaya dinners for $14, lunches are $7.

KoKomo's Oyster Bar & Grill (☎ 230-8411), 3901 Thomas Drive, has a grilled fish sandwich for $4.25. They also do steamed shrimp, crab, oysters and wings.

Hamilton's (☎ 234-1255), at Thomas Drive and Grand Lagoon, does seafood as well; stuffed shrimp and most other dishes are $15. So does *Pier 77* (☎ 235-3080), 3016 Thomas Drive, serving a broiled seafood platter for two for $14. The *Boar's Head* (☎ 234-6628), 17290 Front Beach Rd, serves more expensive main courses, like stuffed grouper for $18.

Barefoot Beach Club (☎ 235-3100), 12705 Front Beach Rd, is a Caribbean grill and bar serving grilled fish and steaks; sandwiches are $5 to 7, fried oysters are $14.

The *Beach House Restaurant* (☎ 233-8800), 9851 S Thomas Drive, has grilled chicken for $9, salmon for $14 and seafood platters are $17.

Entertainment

Bars & Nightclubs Along the beach, every restaurant with a bar does some sort of happy hour and drink specials, especially during Spring Break, when really cheap beer flows freely. The two big nightclubs in town, *Spinnaker* (☎ 234-7822) and

Club La Vela (☎ 234-3866), adjacent to one another at 8795 and 8813 Thomas Drive, are famous around the Panhandle for their meat market, jam-packed, sleazy flesh-fests, including wet T-shirt contests, strip shows and a flirty pick-up-joint atmosphere. If that's the kind of thing you like, you'll like these kind of places.

Getting There & Away

Air The nearest airport is Panama City Bay County Airport (☎ 763-6751), served by ASA, Delta, Northwest Airlink and USAir Express. There's no public transport from the airport to the beach; a taxi or rental car is your only choice.

Train Amtrak's *Sunset Limited* stops at Chipley (57 miles away) on Monday, Wednesday and Saturday at 2.08 am from Miami, and on Wednesday, Friday and Monday at 4.10 am from Los Angeles.

Bus Greyhound has a flag stop in Panama City Beach at the stop light at Hwy 98 and Hwy 79; their station in Panama City (☎ 785-6111) is at 917 Harrison Ave. Greyhound runs several buses to/from each of the following destinations; fares are one way/roundtrip:

Destination	Price	Duration
Tallahassee	$23/45	2½ to 4 hours
Pensacola	$23/45	2½ to 4 hours
Miami	$83/168	13½ to 14½ hours
Gainesville	$48/95	5½ to 9 hours
New Orleans	$56/112	7 to 8½ hours
Jacksonville	$50/99	5½ to 6½ hours

Car Panama City is 287 miles from Atlanta, Georgia, 562 from Miami, 305 from New Orleans, Louisiana, 340 from Orlando, 98 from Tallahassee and 339 from Tampa. From the south, take Hwy 98 right into town; from the east or west take I-10 to either Hwys 231 or 79, which run south to the beach.

Getting Around

There's no public transportation on the beach. You'll either have to rent a car, bicycle or scooter, hire a taxi or limo or walk to get around.

To/From the Airport From the airport, a shuttle service (see below) will cost between $10 and $13 to the beach; a taxi will cost between $14 and 16. If you're driving, take Hwy 385 south to Hwy 98 west, and you're right on the beach.

Taxi Taxi meter rates are $1.50 flagfall, $1.25 each mile. The biggest is Yellow Cab (☎ 763-4691); others include Quality Transportation (☎ 267-7575) and Sea Coast (☎ 231-4050).

Limousine Affordable Limousine (☎ 233-0029) will pick up and drop off up to six people in a late-model luxury van or stretch limo anywhere on the beach – from bridge to bridge – for $10. Not a bad deal if there are a few of you. It's open and on call 24 hours. Other limo services include Deluxe Coach (☎ 763-0211), South East Shuttle Service (☎ 872-2011), Executive Limo (☎ 233-8299) and Bay Limo Service (☎ 235-3912).

Bicycle California Cycle Rentals (☎ 233-1391) rents bicycles for $10 a day, scooters are $9.95 an hour, or four hours for $25. It also rents motorcycles, but you must have a license; prices start at $20 an hour. They have five offices on Front Beach Rd, at No 10025, No 10624, No 14932 (main office) and No 17280.

APALACHICOLA
• *pop 2900* ☎ *904*

Florida's Oyster Capital, Apalachicola (it's in Eastern Standard Time) is a quaint old Southern town with the feel of a fishing village and, during their annual Seafood Festival in early November, the atmosphere of an old-fashioned carnival.

It's not really worth more than a day in itself, but its proximity to St George Island and its peaceful streets make it a far more tempting base for excursions out there than, say, Panama City Beach would.

Apalachicola is also the former home of

refrigeration pioneer Dr John Gorrie, who invented air-conditioning here (he was granted the first US patent on mechanical refrigeration in 1851). Gorrie got around: he was also at various times the city's mayor, postmaster, city treasurer, councilor, bank director and the founder of Trinity Church. Today Gorrie's house is open as a museum (albeit a mind-numbingly boring one).

Orientation & Information
Apalachicola is at the southern end of the Panhandle about halfway between Tallahassee and Panama City, south of the Apalachicola National Forest. Hwy 98 runs through the center of town and out toward St George Island (see below) and Panama City Beach. Downtown Apalachicola, and the Apalachicola Historic District, is on the eastern end of the spit leading toward the Gorrie Bridge (Hwy 98), and its streets are in a grid that's on a 45° angle to compass points.

Market St is the main southeast-northwest street; other streets west of Market St are numbered, beginning with 4th St. Streets are bisected by avenues, which are lettered beginning at Ave B, one block northwest of Bay Ave at the waterline. Ave E is the main drag, and the continuation of Hwy 98, running from Market St at the northeast all the way out of town and on to Panama City.

Get tourist information and city maps at the Apalachicola Bay Chamber of Commerce (☎ 653-9419), 84 Market St. If you're up for a bike, see the folks at Apalach Cruisers (☎ 653-9623) at the corner of Ave D and Market St.

Gorrie House Museum
Dr John Gorrie (1803-55) was one of the pioneers of refrigeration, which he developed to make conditions more comfortable for yellow fever patients. Today his house is open as a museum (☎ 653-9347), 46 6th St (one block south of Ave E), and in it you can see and use a model of his condensing pumps – though don't expect to understand *how* the thing worked unless you're already into physics (we are decidedly not). There are other displays on cotton and the cotton

warehouses that used to be in the city, trade along the Apalachicola River, and very tiny exhibits of tools, pine resin samples and sea sponges. The museum is open Thursday to Sunday from 9 am to 5 pm; closed Thanksgiving, Christmas and New Year's Day. Admission is $1 for adults, children under six free and free admission during the annual Seafood Festival.

Churches
The **Trinity Episcopal Church**, at the corner of 6th St and Ave E, may make you think that you've closed your eyes and woken up in New England, with its columns and large windows, and you're not far off: the church was originally built in New York state. It was cut into sections and sailed down the Atlantic Coast, around the Keys and up to this spot, where it was erected in 1836 (incorporated, with the help of Gorrie, in 1837). Services are held at noon on Wednesday and at 8 am and 10 am on Sunday.

St Patrick Catholic Church is another interesting old (1929) church, close to the Gorrie House Museum, on Ave C and 6th St. It holds Mass Saturday at 5 pm and Sunday at 10 am.

The **First United Methodist Church** building (1901), at the corner of Ave E and 5th St, replaced an even older church that had been at this location since 1846. It holds a Sunday service at 11 am.

Other Things to See & Do
The grand, columned and classic Southern plantation-looking **Raney House** (1838), at Market St and Ave F, was the home of David and Harriet Raney, a two-time former mayor of the city. It's open Saturday from 1 to 5 pm.

The **piers** at the waterfront are always interesting places to watch the boats coming in and out, and on the block between Aves D and F between Water and Market Sts are two interesting sites, the **Sponge Exchange** (1840) and the **Cotton Warehouse** (1838). And just strolling in the downtown area is a very nice way to spend an hour or two.

Places to Stay

Camping See St George Island below for nearby camping there. *Apalachicola Bay Campground* (☎ 670-8307), on Hwy 98 in Eastpoint (across the Gorrie Bridge from Apalachicola), has tent sites for $13, RVs and vans are $15; cable TV is $1. All sites have electricity and water; the RV/van sites also have sewer hookup.

Motels & Hotels The shabby and ramshackle but clean *Apalachicola Motel* (☎ 653-2116, 653-2117) on Hwy 98, just west of town, has singles/doubles for $26/30 in summer, $40/50 in winter; extra people $5.

Seabreeze Motel (☎ 670-8182, 670-8810) on Hwy 98, just east of the bridge leading into town, has very clean singles/doubles for $25/30 in summer, $35/40 in winter.

Rainbow Inn (☎ 653-8139), 123 Water St, has clean and friendly-looking beds, curtains and fabrics, but the baths and carpets are pretty worn. Rooms in the hotel's lower level are $54 to 64, on the upper level they are $59 to 69, and if you're far luckier than us, you can use their marina for a mere $15 a night.

B&Bs An enormous downtown centerpiece, the 1907 *Gibson Inn* (☎ 653-2191), 51 Ave C, has Victorian-style rooms from $55 to 75, including an American hot breakfast. There's a 10% discount for seniors and active military, though prices go up during the Seafood Festival. Its restaurant is open for lunch and dinner; entrees are $14 to 22, and happy hour is on Friday from 5 to 7 pm.

The spotless rooms at the *Coombs House Inn* (☎ 653-9199), 80 6th St close to the Gorrie House, are very comfortable and the place is newly renovated. Rooms run from $59 to $79, suites are $95. There's a large verandah, and breakfast is continental: pastries, fruit, juice, croissant, banana-nut muffins, coffee and so on.

Places to Eat

Risa's Pizza, 87 Market St, does salads from $2 to 3.50, subs $2.50 to 3, and 16-inch cheese pizzas for $7. We were dying to get into *Dolores' Sweet Shop*, 17 Ave E, which we had heard about and thought looked great, but it was closed when we visited. It's a very cute and old-fashioned ice cream parlor in a crumbling brick building – look for the large sign saying 'EAT'.

We had a good lunch at the comfortable, wrought-iron-and-wood *Apalachicola Grill* (☎ 653-9510), 100 Market St. Lunch specials include grilled chicken salad for $4.70, soup and sandwich combo $3.95, burger $3.50 and salmon salad $8. Dinner, which would earn the scorn of the American Heart Association, starts at 4.30 pm and has a special of all-you-can-eat fried fish for $8.95, or fried oysters with salad, potatoes, bread and veggies for $10.95. The ever-popular rib-eye steak is $13.95.

Roberto's (☎ 653-2778), 15 Ave D, is cozy in that checkered tablecloth, candles and Chianti kinda way. It serves lunch specials like fettuccine Alfredo for $5.95, grilled chicken penne for $6.95 and grilled shrimp for $7.95. At dinner, vegetable lasagne is $10.95, pastas are $12.95.

The *Rainbow Inn* (☎ 653-8139), 123 Water St, has a restaurant that serves things like chicken and scallop salad for $8.95, pasta Alfredo for $7.95, seafood pasta for $10.95, and broiled grouper for $14.95. It's open daily from 6 am to 10 pm.

Locals told us good things about *The Magnolia Grill* (☎ 653-8000), 133 Ave E. It's supposed to be a romantic place, where dinner for two with wine averages $29. It's open Monday to Saturday from 6 to 10 pm.

Getting There & Away

There's no Greyhound service within 50 miles of here, so the only way to get here is by car, and taking Hwy 98 is a great way to really get into rural Florida. On our trip here from Tallahassee, official highway department road signs carried these messages: 'Slippy When Wet' and 'You BEST Slow Down' (the BEST, of course, was flashing!).

AROUND APALACHICOLA
St Joseph Peninsula State Park

Battered by Opal, St Joseph Peninsula

State Park (☎ 227-1327) is nonetheless a spectacular place; a 2500-acre state park with 10 miles of wilderness trails, miles of beautiful beaches with dramatic dunes and canoeing and camping all make it worth a trip, if not an overnight.

Canoeing is very peaceful here; rent canoes from rangers for $15 a day, overnight rentals are at the ranger's discretion.

Camping is $15 per site, $2 extra for electricity, and there are furnished cabins for up to seven people that cost $55 per night (two night minimum) from October to February, $70 with a five-night minimum from March to September.

The park is open daily from 8.30 am to sunset. Admission is $3.25 per person, $1 for pedestrians and bicyclists. To get here from Apalachicola, take Hwy 98 west for about five miles and watch for a road veering off to the left before you get to the city of Port St Joe (if you hit Port St Joe you've missed it). Follow that left-veering road, called C-30, for about 10 miles. There will be a sharp turn, in the middle of which will be another left-veering road; take that (there's a sign saying St Joseph Peninsula State Park) to the end (about eight miles) and you're in the park.

ST GEORGE ISLAND
• *pop 700* ☎ *904*

Discovered by Europeans in the early 1500s, St George Island is a 28-mile-long barrier island that was, until Opal at least, one of the most paradisical islands in the Gulf of Mexico: secluded, away from the riff-raff across a long bridge, flat as a pancake and fringed with blindingly white sand. Opal damaged many homes on the island, but it wreaked total havoc on St George Island State Park, which was still closed when we researched.

Unless you're camping, St George Island isn't much of a budget traveler's destination – the cheapest room in the island's only motel is $45 in low season. But the camping, in either the state park or on Cape St George, the island to the west of St George, is excellent and the nature is spectacular.

Orientation & Information
The island is just south of the city of Eastpoint across a three-mile causeway. When you get to the beach, go straight until you can't anymore – this is known as Front Beach Drive, but also as Gulf Beach Drive. Yes, it's confusing.

St George Island State Park
This 1962-acre state park (☎ 927-2111) is at the northeast end of St George Island. There are hiking trails and boardwalks throughout the pine woods, marshes and live oak hammocks, and there's excellent swimming. At the campground here, tent sites are $12 without electricity and $14 with. Admission to the park is $4 a carload, $1 for pedestrians and cyclists. The park, which took a serious beating after Opal, is pretty much back to normal now: they've relocated about 1½ miles of the park's roadway, and removed about quarter mile of damaged or destroyed road.

Little St George Island
If you're looking for peace and quiet and to really get away from it all, this is the place for you: there is free camping on the eastern and western ends of the Cape St George Reserve (AKA Little St George Island), an uninhabited island just west of St George Island across Sikes Cut. The area is absolutely idyllic, and the only sounds other than the occasional passing motorboat during the day are of the area's wildlife, which include snowy plover, least tern, black skimmer willet and osprey, along with the standard Florida-issue raccoons.

Though the camping is free, there are absolutely no facilities on the island – bring everything you'll need, including a gallon of water per person a day and food in a strong, sealable plastic (not Styrofoam) cooler. Take all your trash with you – leave nothing – and only set campfires (use down and dead wood only) on the beach.

You don't need to reserve ahead, but the park rangers request that you let them know if you're going out there – they patrol for miscreants and also sometimes take out groups, so they like to know if they'll run into someone. Call the Apalachicola National Estuarine Reserve at ☎ 653-8063 to let them know.

But to get there you'll need to get yourself a boat; everything was up in the air when we were there because of the hurricane, but try Jeannie's Journeys (☎ 927-3259), 320 Patton St on St George Island. Expect to pay at least $80 for the ride until things normalize.

Places to Stay

Motel The *Buccaneer Inn* (☎ 927-2585, 800-847-2091), 106 Gulf Front, is the *only* motel on the island; rooms are $45 to 75 and $70 to 90 depending on the view and season; efficiencies are $65 to 85 and $80 to 100. The rooms are okay, though the kitchenettes have that Burger King feel to them. Pets are not allowed.

B&Bs The luxurious *St George Inn* (☎ 927-2903), at Franklin Blvd and Pine St, is sort of a hunting lodge on stilts. It's a B&B with singles/doubles for $60/70 year round. Rooms with two queen-size beds are $75 for two people; each additional person is $10. There's a restaurant here as well (see Place to Eat below).

Condos & Houses Lots and lots of people stay here in condominium apartments, cottages and houses, which rent for an average of $775 per week in the winter, $900 a week in fall, $1000 a week in spring and $1300 a week in summer. The biggest rental agents on the island for this type of accommodation are *Collins Vacation Rentals* (☎ 927-2900, 800-423-7418) and *Accommodations St George* (☎ 927-2666, 800-332-5196).

Places to Eat

The *Blue Parrot Oyster Bar & Grill* (☎ 927-2987), 216 W Gorrie Drive, is an oceanfront café and local hangout. A dozen raw oysters are $2.95, steamed $4.95. Sandwiches are $3.95 to 4.50, platters like chicken tenders are $7.50 and their seafood combo is $12.95. It's open daily from 11 am to 10 pm.

Paradise Cafe (☎ 927-3300), 65 W Gorrie Drive, has sandwiches for $4.50 to 7.50, burgers for $3.95 to 5.95 and entrees for $9.95 to 16.95. Happy hour is daily from 4 to 6 pm, and nightly specials (served after 5 pm) are $5.95 to 11.95.

The *Island Oasis* (☎ 927-2639), 29 E Gulf Beach Drive, has a daily happy hour from 4 to 6 pm: pitchers are $3.50, piña coladas and strawberry daiquiris $2.95. On Sunday from 11 am to 2 pm, it has a $5.95 brunch with $2.95 bloody marys and mimosas. Dinners come with baked potato or French fries, salad and garlic bread, and they run from $7.95 for smothered chicken breast to $14.95 for the seafood platter.

The *St George Inn* (☎ 927-2903), at Franklin Blvd and Pine St, also has a restaurant – 'southern-French bistro-style with a Cajun twist'. Dinner, in winter, is served Wednesday to Sunday from 6 to 9 pm; in spring, summer and fall it's served every day except Monday. Chicken Florentine is $12.95, crab-stuffed pork chops are $14.95 and oven-roasted grouper is $16.50. This place is very popular and crowded, so get there early.

TALLAHASSEE
• *pop 135,000* ☎ 904

When we think of capital cities, we tend to think of oppressively-scaled places with enormously wide streets and belligerent politicians speeding by in limousines, or worse, Brussels. But Tallahassee is charming in its fierce opposition to anything that might spoil its natural beauty: its streets are so tree lined – many are completely canopied – that when viewed from the air it looks more like a small settlement in the middle of a lush green forest than a center of political might.

Perhaps that's because the legislature works so rarely (see the New Capitol below). And yet, despite its unassuming appearance, this is a planned city – as much, perhaps, as Washington, DC – and a quick glance at a map reveals that 'all roads lead to Tallahassee': the capitol is at the hub of a loose network of roads that emanate from it in all directions.

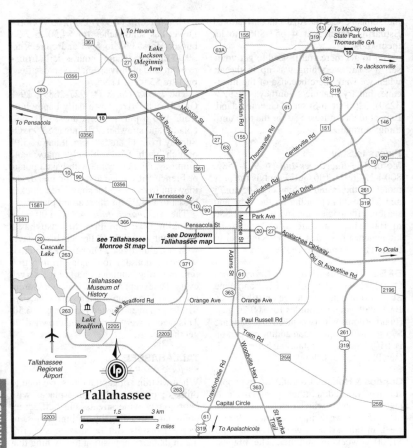

Tallahassee

Tallahassee was made the capital of the Florida territories in 1824, but not because of its own eminence. Tallahassee was a compromise between the two battling super-cities of the time, St Augustine at the east and Pensacola at the west. In an 'Oh, okay, let's just put it in the middle' decision, a heavily forested and hilly little settlement became the center of the state's business.

'Tallahassee' is an Apalachee word meaning 'old town'. The Apalachees, the original settlers of the area, were all killed off by disease or the Spaniards, who followed Hernando de Soto's arrival in 1539.

By the 19th century, the area was rich agriculturally, and it relied heavily on slaves to work the farms. During the Civil War, Tallahassee was the only Confederate city east of the Mississippi River that did not fall to Union troops – though there was a battle at nearby Natural Bridge (see History in Facts about Florida).

Today Tallahassee is a surprisingly pleasant town, except during FSU football games, when tens of thousands of unbelievably avid football fans descend with great vigor on the area, filling all the hotels and restaurants and driving in cars festooned with the team's politically incorrect flag and logo (see Campuses below).

But as a stop for a day or two, it's definitely rewarding. Despite the political intrigues at the capitol, the city has a slow pace that, at the end of the day, makes it a simply charming Southern city.

Orientation

The main drag is Monroe St, which runs north-south through downtown; it's the east-west dividing line for addresses. Tennessee St is the north-south divider. Tallahassee's downtown is pretty much in the center of the city, bounded by Tennessee St at the north, around Van Buren St at the south, the FSU campus at the west and Magnolia Drive at the east.

Thomasville Rd breaks off from Monroe St just north of Brevard St and runs northeast, up toward Maclay Gardens State Park.

The Civic Center is west of the Florida State Capitol and Old Capitol. The Florida State University campus is about three-quarters of a mile west of Monroe St; Doak Campbell Stadium is at the southwest corner of the campus, on the south side of Pensacola St.

Florida Agricultural & Mechanical University is south of downtown, bordered by Orange Ave at the south, Canal St at the north, Adams St at the east and Perry St at the west.

Maps There are somewhat useful tourist maps of the city at the Visitor Information Center (see below), and you can buy pretty much any map you'll ever need at the Map and Globe Store (☎ 385-8869), 2029 N Monroe St in the North Monroe Shops Mall.

Information

Tourist Offices The Tallahassee Convention & Visitors Bureau (☎ 413-9200, 800-628-2866, fax 487-4621, see Online Services appendix for e-mail address), 200 W College Ave, runs the excellent Visitor Information Center, which is inside the New Capitol Building, just to the right inside the main entrance (west side, plaza level, off S Duval St). They're very helpful on area informa-

tion. To the left as you enter the lobby is the Florida Welcome Center (☎ 488-6167), where Don Hardy, a six-year, steady-as-he-goes veteran with a friendly drawl, dispenses information, pamphlets, coupon books and flyers on attractions throughout the entire state – the information racks are broken up by region. It's open Monday to Friday from 8 am to 5 pm, Saturday and Sunday from 9 am to 3 pm. The Florida Welcome Center can also arrange free 30- to 40-minute guided tours of the capitol – you'll see the chambers, chapel and get a history of the building. There's a hotel reservation hotline – which might come in handy if you're showing up around the time of a football game – at ☎ 488-2337.

The Visitor Information Center also hands out two very helpful brochures, *Touring Tallahassee*, a walking guide to the downtown district, and *Canopy Roads and Country Lanes*, a driving tour to the county (see also Getting Around below for a list of canopy roads).

The Chamber of Commerce (☎ 224-8116), 100 N Duval St, is located in the Columns (circa 1830), Tallahassee's oldest surviving home; it's open Monday to Thursday from 8 am to 5.30 pm, Friday from 8 am to 5 pm. There's a (probably untrue) rumor that there is a nickel inside every brick. They no longer hand out general tourist information (but will help if you're thinking of moving to or doing business in the area).

Tallahassee also has one of the best World Wide Web home pages for practical information of any city in Florida, and the *Tallahassee News* is an internet newspaper on the city. See the Online Services appendix for website addresses.

Money Barnett Bank has a downtown branch at 315 S Calhoun St, and branches at 2262 N Monroe St and 1321 W Jefferson St. American Express has three representative offices, in the three branches of the Travel Center: at 703 N Monroe St (☎ 224-4464), FSU University Union, Room N-116 (☎ 561-9100) and at 1400 Village Square Blvd, No 11 (☎ 668-1360).

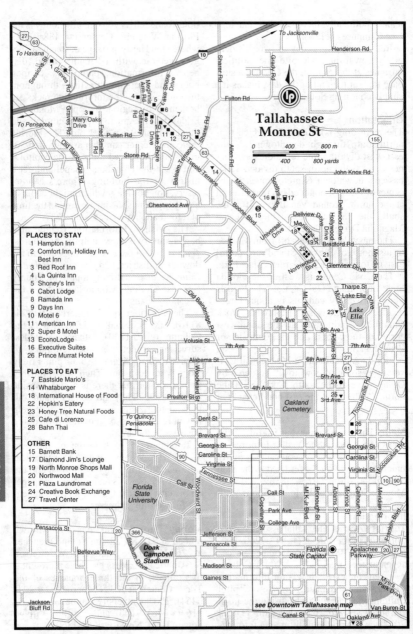

Tallahassee Monroe St

PLACES TO STAY
1 Hampton Inn
2 Comfort Inn, Holiday Inn, Best Inn
3 Red Roof Inn
4 La Quinta Inn
5 Shoney's Inn
7 Cabot Lodge
8 Ramada Inn
9 Days Inn
10 Motel 6
11 American Inn
12 Super 8 Motel
13 EconoLodge
16 Executive Suites
26 Prince Murat Hotel

PLACES TO EAT
7 Eastside Mario's
14 Whataburger
18 International House of Food
22 Hopkin's Eatery
23 Honey Tree Natural Foods
25 Cafe di Lorenzo
28 Bahn Thai

OTHER
15 Barnett Bank
19 Diamond Jim's Lounge
19 North Monroe Shops Mall
20 Northwood Mall
21 Plaza Laundromat
24 Creative Book Exchange
27 Travel Center

Post The main post office (☎ 216-4200) is at 2800 S Adams St; there's a more central location (☎ 385-4577) at 1845 ML King, Jr Blvd.

Bookstores Creative Books Exchange (☎ 222-5160), 1118 N Monroe St, has new and used books (which they buy and trade), a good kids section, an unexciting travel section, good fiction and decent politics. It's open Monday to Saturday from 10 am to 6 pm and Sunday from noon to 5 pm. Black Cat News Exchange (☎ 222-1920), 115 S Monroe St, has LP books, lots of mass print, and they will order you anything they don't have. Bill's Bookstore has two locations: at the northeastern end of the FSU campus at 102 S Copeland St (☎ 224-3178) and at 1411 Tennessee St (☎ 561-1495), both selling new and used books and a lot of textbooks. Barnes & Noble (☎ 877-3878), 1480 Apalachee Pkwy, has a café.

Libraries The main library (☎ 487-2665) is at 200 W Park Ave.

Media The (what else?) *Tallahassee Democrat* is the big daily paper of record. NPR is at 88.9 and 91.5 FM.

Campuses This is a major college town, with two universities. Florida State University (FSU, ☎ 644-2882) is a liberal arts school concentrating on sciences, computing and performing arts (and football), with undergraduate, graduate, advanced graduate and professional study programs. It's also well known for the political incorrectness of its athletics teams name, the FSU Seminoles – whose logo is an Indian warrior or squaw. Total enrollment is almost 30,000 students. From September to April there are free guided tours of the campus leaving from their Visitor Information Center (☎ 644-3246), 100 S Woodward Ave, on Monday to Friday at 10 and 11 am and 1 and 3 pm.

The city's second university, Florida Agricultural & Mechanical University (☎ 599-3000) – Florida A&M or FAMU (pronounced fam-you) – was founded in 1887 as the State Normal College for Colored Students, which had fifteen students and two instructors. Today, about 10,000 students of all races attend this university, which now includes the must-see Black Archives Research Center & Museum (see below).

Laundry Northwood Coin Laundry (☎ 385-9121), 1940 N Monroe St in the Northwood Mall, has tons of machines, a bunch of TVs and sassy service. Also try Plaza Laundromat (☎ 422-0262), 1911 N Monroe St.

Toilets There are public toilets in the Old and New Capitols.

Medical Services Tallahassee Memorial Regional Medical Center (☎ 681-1155), at Magnolia Drive and Miccosukee Rd, is the largest hospital in the area; it's northeast of downtown.

New Capitol

Welcome to the ugliest building in modern America: The New Capitol (☎ 413-9200), at Pensacola and Duval Sts, is a 22-story monolithic slab of a monstrosity that's home to the ever-hardworking Florida legislature – which toils mercilessly for an entire 60 days a year, from March to May. If you're here at that time, you can get a glimpse of the pure grit of American politics as . . . wait a minute . . . just what are these folks doing for the other *nine* months of the year?

The answer sure doesn't lie in the lobby, where their interactive 'Ask the Speaker' display has video of Rep Peter R Wallace answering questions you put forth via a touch screen – it's just inside the east entrance to the building. If the big swingers aren't here, at least take the free, 45-minute tour. It's every hour on the hour Monday to Friday from 9 to 11 am and 1 to 3 pm, Saturday, Sunday and holidays from 9 am to 3 pm.

Observation Deck You can see the view without the tour, just take the elevators. The Observation Deck affords a panoramic

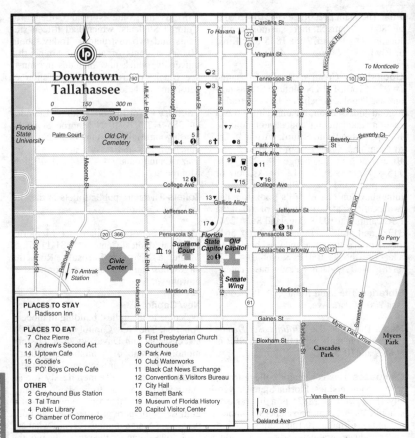

Downtown Tallahassee

0   150   300 m
0   150   300 yards

PLACES TO STAY
1 Radisson Inn

PLACES TO EAT
7 Chez Pierre
13 Andrew's Second Act
14 Uptown Cafe
15 Goodie's
16 PO' Boys Creole Cafe

6 First Presbyterian Church
8 Courthouse
9 Park Ave
10 Club Waterworks
11 Black Cat News Exchange
12 Convention & Visitors Bureau
17 City Hall
18 Barnett Bank
19 Museum of Florida History
20 Capitol Visitor Center

OTHER
2 Greyhound Bus Station
3 Tal Tran
4 Public Library
5 Chamber of Commerce

view that reveals just how much forest surrounds the city. You can easily make out landmarks like the Vietnam Veterans Memorial, the First Presbyterian Church and so on, and there is an art gallery with rotating exhibits here (as well as public toilets). Note that elevators 2 and 4 take you up all the way to the 22nd floor, and elevators 1 and 3 only take you to the 21st floor, from where you walk the last flight.

Chapel The Heritage Chapel is an odd and somewhat eerie exhibit on the history of religion in Florida, which is told through writings on brass plaques. The chapel is in the lobby just south of the Observation Deck elevators. There are three or four weddings here a month.

Old Capitol

Originally built in 1845 and restored in 1902, *this* is a capitol. The Old Capitol (☎ 487-1902) is a grand structure, and it's now open as a museum, not just of Florida legislative history (you'll see the House and Senate Chambers, Supreme Court and Governor's Suite), but also of state history, with rotating art works and shows: there's a mastodon, a Civil War display, early Florida weaponry and logging tools, but the highlight is the stained-glass dome and red candy-striped awnings.

The building is adjacent to the New Capitol at the corner of S Monroe St and Apalachee Pkwy. It's open Monday to Friday from 9 am to 4.30 pm, Saturday from 10 am to 4.30 pm, Sunday and holidays from noon to 4.30 pm; closed Thanksgiving and Christmas. Admission is free.

Vietnam Veterans Memorial
Opposite the Old Capitol on S Monroe St is a Vietnam War memorial honoring those Floridians who died, were injured and went missing in the conflict, and their names are inscribed on the monument. It's a huge towering American flag suspended between twin granite towers inscribed with the names of the 1942 Floridians listed as killed and 83 missing in action.

Black Archives Research Center & Museum
This museum (☎ 599-3020), in the Carnegie Library on the FAMU campus, has one of the country's largest collections of African-American and African artifacts, and it's a research center on black influence on US history and culture. There are exhibits on slavery and the treatment of slaves, a hands-on Underground Railroad exhibit for children, a 500-piece Ethiopian cross collection and a huge collection of papers, photographs, paintings and documents pertaining to black life in the USA. It's open Monday to Friday from 9 am to 4 pm. Admission is free. It's at the corner of Martin Luther King, Jr Blvd and Gamble St.

First Presbyterian Church
Tallahassee's oldest church, the Greek-Revival First Presbyterian (1835-38, ☎ 222-4504), 102 N Adams St, is open to the public. During the 19th century, it accepted slaves as members with or without their masters' consent, though seating was segregated.

Museum of Florida History
The Museum of Florida History (☎ 488-

1673), 500 S Bronough St in the RA Gray Building (1976), isn't the state's most spectacular, but hey, it's free. Its star attraction is its American mastodon skeleton, but it also has collections of Indian artifacts, artifacts from the Spanish period, the Civil War (including a reconstructed Confederate campsite from 1861), farm equipment from different periods, quilts, cigar box labels, old clothes and so on. This is also the home of the State Archives and State Library.

The hours are Monday to Friday from 9 am to 4.30 pm, Saturday from 10 am to 4.30 pm, Sunday and holidays from noon to 4.30 pm; closed Thanksgiving and Christmas. Free admission.

Odyssey's Exploration Station
Odyssey's Exploration Station (☎ 576-6520, fax 574-9874), 3950 W Pensacola St, was under construction when we visited, but it will be a three-story science museum with hands-on exhibits and Saturday morning science classes for kids. They also plan a special area for kids from six months to six years. It's scheduled to be open during classes on Saturday from noon to 3 pm (morning classes require special reservations). Call for hours when you're here.

Cemeteries
There are two cemeteries downtown, open sunrise to sunset: the **Old City Cemetery** (☎ 545-5842), which is bounded by Park Ave, Macomb and Call Sts and ML King, Jr Blvd; and **St John's Episcopal Cemetery** (1840), at Call St and ML King, Jr Blvd. There's a self-guided walking tour in the Old City Cemetery.

De Soto Archaeological Site
Just east of downtown and northeast of Myers Park, De Soto State Archaeological Site (☎ 922-6007) is said to be the sight of the first encampment of Spanish explorer Hernando de Soto. In December, there are reenactments of the First Christmas in the New World, but the park was under renovation as we went to press. It's just south

of Lafayette St, about 10 blocks east of Monroe St.

Other Museums

The **Knott House Museum** (☎ 922-2459), 301 E Park Ave, is a restored Victorian house that was occupied during the Civil War by Confederate, and after it by Union, troops. On May 20, 1865, Union General Edward McCook read out the Emancipation Proclamation from here; the date is still celebrated locally as Emancipation Day. In 1928, William V Knott, a local politico, bought the house. It's called 'the house that rhymes', because his wife, incorrigible teetotaler Luella Knott, wrote mainly insufferable temperance poetry that she attached to many of her furnishings, which are still here. Guided hour-long tours are given Wednesday to Friday from 1 pm to 4 pm and Saturday from 10 am to 4 pm. Admission is $3 for adults, $1.50 for children, or $7 for a family.

The **LeMoyne Art Foundation** (☎ 224-2714), 125 N Gadsden St, is a gallery of rotating exhibitions in the Meginnis-Munroe House (1852-53); there's a lovely garden. It's open Tuesday to Saturday 10 am to 5 pm and Sunday from 1 to 5 pm. Admission is free except at Christmastime, when it's $1 for adults.

Maclay Gardens State Park

A 20-minute drive north of downtown, the 1930s estate of financier Alfred B Maclay is now open as a state garden (☎ 487-4556), and during the peak blooming season from January to April, there are over 200 varieties of flowers. The gardens are open year round (when we visited in the fall there was a huge group of seniors having a picnic here), though the Maclay home is only open during the blooming season. There are nature trails and access to the lovely lake. Admission is free except during blooming season, when it's $3.25 per carload or $1 for pedestrians and bicyclists. It's at 3540 Thomasville Rd: from I-10, take exit 30 and take Thomasville Rd north, follow the signs – the entrance is on your left.

Tallahassee Museum of History

The Tallahassee Museum of History & Natural Science (☎ 576-1636, 575-8684), about four miles southwest of downtown near Lake Bradford, is a history museum with hands-on nature displays and a working 1880s farmhouse with animals. There are also wildlife demonstrations, and they run very creative programs throughout the year – such as sing-alongs with singers from all over the Panhandle and other shows like Spring Farm Days (which has demonstrations of turn-of-the-century farming techniques).

It's open Monday to Saturday from 9 am to 5 pm and Sunday from 12.30 to 5 pm. Admission is $6 for adults, $5.50 for seniors, $4 for kids four to 15. It's at 3945 Museum Drive: to get there take Gaines St to Lake Bradford Rd (Hwy 371), go south, then bear right at the fork and follow Orange Ave to Rankin Rd, turn left and follow the signs.

Courthouse & De Leon Park

This WPA-built building at 110 W Park Ave (1936) housed the US Courthouse and Post Office. Today it's open to the public, who can walk in to look at the building's neo-Classical columns and cupola, and the WPA murals. Just across the street is Ponce de Leon Park (circa 1880), a very pleasant bit of green with a fountain; it's the site of live jazz on Thursday nights as well.

St Marks Trail

The Tallahassee-St Marks Historic Railroad State Trail (☎ 922-6007) is a 16-mile, paved trail for bicyclists and skaters; it's totally flat and well paved the entire length. Bike rentals are $9 for two hours (minimum), $16 for four hours, and $35 for 24 hours; skates are $7 for one hour, $12 for two hours, $25 for 24 hours. The prices are discounted if you rent more than one. To get there from downtown Tallahassee, take Monroe St south, which will become Woodville Hwy (Hwy 363), and take that across Capital Circle; the park will be a hundred yards ahead on the right-hand side of the road. It's open April to October Monday to

Friday from 2 pm to 8 pm or dark, Saturday and Sunday from 9 am to 5 pm; November to March Monday to Friday from 10 am to 6 pm or dark, Saturday and Sunday 9 am to 5 pm. Admission is free.

Organized Tours

Captain Peper's Balloon Co (☎ 668-8200) offers hot-air balloon rides above the city. Southern Accent (☎ 297-0287, 800-365-9108, ext 4272) does a huge range of tours of the city and the region.

See the Old Town Trolley in Getting Around below for free orientation tours of the downtown area.

Places to Stay

Most of the hotels and motels in the area are clumped at exits along I-10 and are lined along Monroe St, between I-10 and downtown.

Camping About 10 minutes east of Tallahassee, the *Tallahassee RV Park* has sites with full hookups for tents and RVs/vans for $21.82. It's at 6504 Mayhan Drive (Hwy 90); from I-10, take exit 31A and go west for one mile on Hwy 90. About 15 miles farther east, there's a *Tallahassee East KOA* (☎ 997-3890) with tent sites for $14.50 with no hookup, $17.50 with water and electric, $19.50 for full hookups and Kamping Kabins for $22.50; all prices are year round, even during games. Take I-10 to exit 33, turn south on Hwy 19 for half a mile, then west for two miles on the little access road (Hwy 158), which dead ends into Hwy 259, and then turn north again for half a mile. See? Can't miss it.

The barbaric and insensitively named *Florida State University Seminole Reservation* (see the History section in Facts About Florida, ☎ 644-6083, 644-6892), 3226 Flastacowo Rd, is a 73-acre facility on Lake Bradford, but it no longer allows camping. They have rustic cabins (kitchens, but no TV or telephone) on the lake for $35 per night for nonstudents, $25 for FSU students (though you can try and get that rate with an ISIC). They also have two large dormitory-style cabins, each with about 12

bunk beds; the cost is $60 per night or $6 per person, whichever is greater.

Hotels & Motels Scour the Visitor Welcome Center for discount coupons, which abound and can save you a whole lot of money on area accommodations, except during football games, when no coupon in the world can help you. Most places offer free local calls and at least doughnuts and coffee in the morning.

The best motel deal in town (we thought) was the spotless if bland *Executive Suites Motor Inn* (☎ 386-2121, 800-342-0090), 522 Scotty's Lane. Rooms are from $29 with a coupon and $32 without (though you have to ask for that rate), and all have Jacuzzis (!) in the bathrooms. They are clean and roomy; the price includes doughnuts, coffee and juice in the morning; and there's a pool.

The *Super 8 Motel* (☎ 386-8818), 2702 N Monroe St, is a standard Super 8 in every respect, including price, which is $32.95/34.95 for singles/doubles.

We also liked the newly renovated and privately owned *American Inn* (☎ 386-5000), 2726 N Monroe St, with doubles for $40 ($45 at graduation and $55 during games). There's a pool, and they rent VCRs and two movies for $5.

Best Inn (☎ 562-2378), 2738 Graves Rd, has free cereal and milk at breakfast, and double rooms are $42 to 52; add $10 during special events.

Ramada Limited (☎ 224-7116, 800-272-6232), at the corner of Brevard and Tennessee Sts, has rooms for one to four people for $45, plus $6 each additional person (higher at special events).

La Quinta Inn (☎ 385-7172, 800-531-5900), 2905 N Monroe St, has rooms from $54 to 68; during football games all rooms are $80, and at graduation $89.

Other chains in town include the *Radisson Inn* (☎ 224-6000, 800-333-3333), 415 N Monroe St; *Shoney's Inn* (☎ 386-8286, 800-222-2222), 2801 N Monroe St; *Best Western Seminole Inn* (☎ 656-2938, 800-996-6537), 6737 Mahan Drive; and *Days Inn* (☎ 222-3219), 1350 W Tennessee St.

The clean and comfortable *Hampton Inn* (☎ 562-4300, 800-426-7866), 3210 N Monroe St, has singles/doubles for $54/59 to 65, though you can get coupons that will make doubles as low as $47. Rates include free large continental breakfast, HBO and friendly service.

B&Bs *The Riedel House* (☎ 222-8569), 1412 Fairway Drive, is a fairly nice B&B. Rooms are $75, and breakfast is fruit, muffins, breads, orange juice and coffee. Smoking is allowed outside only, no pets and no kids under 14.

The *Cabot Lodge* (☎ 386-8880, in Florida 800-432-0701, in US 800-223-1964), 2735 N Monroe St, is nothing too special, but it does have free cocktails. Rooms with two double beds are $59, with a king-size bed $65 (each extra person is $4), and during special events rooms are $75. All rooms include continental breakfast and free beer, mixed drinks and wine from 5.30 to 7.30 pm daily. Rooms could be cleaner, and the smoking rooms were very smoky.

Places to Eat

Hopkin's Eatery (☎ 386-4252), 1840 N Monroe St, is a terrific place with excellent garden sandwiches (spinach, mushrooms, tomatoes, sprouts, sunflower seeds and melted cheeses) for $3.50, tuna melts $3.75, vegetarian primo platters $3.99 and salads from $3.75 to 4.75. It's closed Sunday.

The *International House of Food* (☎ 386-3433), 2013 N Monroe St, is an East Asian/Middle Eastern food market with a deli counter: a feta sandwich is $1.79, gyros $2.89, falafel sandwich $2.79, platters $3.99 and dahl $3.49. And of course, they

sell all kinds of spices, chutneys, hot sauces and so on.

Honey Tree Natural Foods (☎ 681-2000), 1660-3 N Monroe St, is a health food store with everything you'd expect plus a juice and lunch bar. The menu changes every week; when we were there they had Moroccan stew over cous cous for $3.50, veggie lasagne for $4 and a salad bar for $4.95 per pound. Lots of different fresh-squeezed juices are $2. It's open Monday to Friday from 9.30 am to 7 pm, Saturday from 9.30 am to 6 pm.

PO'Boys Creole Cafe (☎ 224-5400), 224 E College Ave, serves Creole food like gumbo for $3 to 4.75; sandwiches are $2.50 to 5.80. Their specialty is shrimp pie ($5.65). It's open Monday to Friday from 11 am to 9 pm, Saturday from 10 am to 8 pm and Sunday brunch from 10 am to 2 pm. It also has live entertainment (see Bars & Nightclubs below). There's another location near FSU at 679 W Tennessee St (☎ 681-9191).

Uptown Cafe (☎ 222-3253), 111 E College Ave, is great for breakfast. For lunch they're particularly proud of their soups ($2), and sure enough, when we showed up at about 11 am it was sold out, so we had a sandwich ($3.20 to 4.75). They also make very, very good cookies for about 90¢. It's open Monday to Friday from 7 am to 3 pm.

Diagonally across the street, *Goodies Eatery* (☎ 681-3888), 116 E College Ave, isn't anywhere near as homey or comfortable, but it serves breakfast all day long and does sandwiches from $3.20 to 4.50; salads are $3.99 to 4.99. It's open Monday to Saturday from 7.30 am to 4.30 pm.

Cafe di Lorenzo (☎ 681-3622), 1002 N

Bahn Thai

Three cheers for *Bahn Thai* (☎ 224-4765), 1319 S Monroe St (south of the capitol), one of the state's best Thai places. Monday to Friday from 11 am to 2.30 pm there is a large (15 entrees, soup, rice and fruit), all-you-can-eat buffet for an incredible $4.85 per person, and regular entrees like pad thai for $6.95 (very good), curry (which they actually make spicy) for $8.95 and chow mein for $5.75. Dinner prices are slightly higher. This is a Tallahassee institution, and many customers have been coming here for years – so often that the chef knows regular customers by their orders. ∎

Monroe St, serves pasta, pizza and other Italian dishes for $8 to 11; if you carry out, prices drop to about $3 to 5.50.

Whataburger (☎ 386-6191), 2586 N Monroe St, is open 24 hours for burgers and the like from $1.50 to 3.50; grilled chicken salad is $2.99. Breakfast is served from 5 to 11 am.

Eastside Mario's (☎ 385-1774), 2756 N Monroe St, has brick-oven pizza and pasta for $6 to 9, chicken and meat dishes are $7 to 11, and eggplant parmigiani is $7.50. It also serves burgers and sandwiches.

Chez Pierre (☎ 222-0936), 115 N Adams St, is a cozy and not yet pretentious French place with a country setting. For what you get it is very inexpensive. Lunch entrees include crepes poulet for $4.50, ratatouille Nicoise at $5.25 and boeuf stroganoff for $6.95. They have homemade ice cream and sorbets daily. At dinner, prices are a bit higher, with entrees averaging $9.95 to 17.95. No smoking; reserve for dinner on weekends. They do lunch Monday to Saturday from 11 am to 2.30 pm, and dinner Tuesday to Saturday from 6 to 9.30 pm.

Andrew's Second Act (☎ 222-3444), 228 S Adams St, was in the middle of major renovation when we went to press, but it should be open again by the time you read this. Lunch at this elegant place is very cheap for what you get and very good – soups are $2.25 and main courses (fish and pasta dishes) run from $5.95 to 6.95. Prices shoot up at dinner.

Entertainment

Check the Friday Limelight section in the *Tallahassee Democrat* for theater listings.

Theater The FSU School of Theater (☎ 644-6500) has three venues. The Richard G Fallon Mainstage Theater in the Fine Arts Building, north of Call St on the campus, does large productions of plays and musicals, such as *Antigone* and *Lips Together, Teeth Apart* by Terrence McNally. Tickets are $16, $14 for senior citizens, $10 for all (not just FSU) students. The Studio, in the Williams Building on campus, does mainly free student productions and MFA-candidate works. Off-campus, at the corner of Lafayette and Copeland Sts, The Lab does a huge range of works from Shakespeare to *Grease* in their 150-seat thrust-stage setting. Tickets are generally $8 for adults, $6 for seniors, $5 for students.

The Tallahassee Little Theater (☎ 224-8474), 1861 Thomasville Rd, is a small community theater striving to break out of that mold; recently they performed *M Butterfly*, *Run for Your Wife*, *Wrong Turn at Lungfish*, *The Sisters Rosenzweig* and *The Boyfriend*. They do several productions a year.

FAMU Essential Theater (☎ 599-3000), on the FAMU campus, is said to be excellent (even by the FSU Theater Department). Their season is based around a 'Theater Unbound' schedule of shows; call for more information.

Classical Music The Tallahassee Symphony Orchestra (☎ 224-0461) performs at the FSU Ruby Diamond Auditorium at College Ave and Copeland St.

Concerts Most big-name concerts are held at the Leon County Civic Center (☎ 222-0400, 800-322-3602), just west of Monroe St at 505 W Pensacola St. There's live jazz on Thursday in Ponce de Leon Park, weather permitting, from 7.30 to 9 pm. If it's raining, they move to Waterworks (see below), and there's a $2 cover.

Bars & Nightclubs *Waterworks* (☎ 224-1887), 104½ S Monroe St, is a cool place. It has happy hour Monday to Friday from 4 to 7 pm with $1.75 Samuel Adams. There's jazz on Monday nights (no cover) and on Saturday ($2 cover); Friday is cha cha cha night. It's dimly lit, there are couches here and there, and it has a good beer selection.

PO'Boys Creole Cafe (see Places to Eat above) has live entertainment with a New Orleans Creole flare and big-screen sports. They serve beer and wine only, and they are open daily.

Diamond Jim's Lounge, 531 Scotty's Lane, is surprisingly fun; it's in the Silver Slipper restaurant across the street from the

Executive Suites Motor Inn. It's packed with locals and sometimes red-faced state legislators, and there's live country music Tuesday to Saturday.

Mustard Tree (☎ 893-8733), 1415 Timberlane Rd, is a yuppie dive with a two-for-one happy hour Monday to Friday from 5.30 to 7.30 pm.

The *Comedy Zone* (☎ 386-1027), 2900 N Monroe St at the Ramada Inn, has comedians with two shows on Friday and Saturday; it's a bar at other times.

The Palace Saloon (☎ 575-3418), 1303 Jackson Bluff Rd, is a sports bar near Doak Campbell Stadium with six satellite TVs, including a big-screen TV for NFL and FSU games. Live bands play Friday and Saturday, no cover.

Gay & Lesbian We looked, but all we could find was *Club Park Ave* (☎ 599-9143), 115 E Park Ave, just west of Monroe St. It's gay on Saturday and Sunday night (Sunday night there are drag shows) and straight on Wednesday and Friday; it's closed the rest of the week.

Spectator Sports The FSU Seminoles play football games to packed houses at the over 80,000-seat Doak Campbell Stadium on the FSU campus from September to November. Tickets (which sell out months in advance) are $21 no matter where you sit. They play baseball in the spring at Dick Howser Stadium; tickets are $6. For more FSU athletic information, call their athletic department (☎ 644-1830, 888-378-6653).

The FAMU Rattlers play football from August to November at Bragg Memorial Stadium (☎ 599-3141) on the FAMU campus.

Getting There & Away
Air Tallahassee Regional Airport (☎ 891-7800, 800 610-1995) is served by Delta, USAir, American Eagle and several smaller airlines. It's about five miles southwest of downtown, off of Hwy 263.

Train The Amtrak station (☎ 244-2779) is at 918½ Railroad Ave. The *Sunset Limited* arrives from Los Angeles on Wednesday,

Friday and Monday at 10.25 am, and from Miami on Sunday, Tuesday and Friday at 11.44 pm.

Bus The Greyhound station (☎ 222-4240) is at 112 W Tennessee, at the corner of Duval, opposite the downtown TalTran transfer center. Buses to/from Tallahassee include the following (there are around four a day for each); fares are one way/roundtrip:

Destination	Price	Duration
Panama City	$23/45	2¼ to 3¼ hours
Pensacola	$41/82	5 to 6 hours
Jacksonville	$30/59	3 to 4 hours
Gainesville	$33/66	3 to 3½ hours
Miami	$73/115	12 to 15 hours

Car It's 98 miles to Panama City Beach, 198 to Pensacola, 163 to Jacksonville and 463 to Miami. The main access road is I-10 from the east and the west, and to get to the gulf coast towns along the Panhandle, take Hwy 319 to Hwy 98. From Gainesville it's about 120 miles; take I-75 to I-10 west.

Getting Around
To/From the Airport There's no public transport to/from the airport. Annett Airport Shuttle Service (☎ 878-3216, 800-328-6033) charges $10 per person between the airport and Tallahassee; they like to have 24-hour notice, but if you forget, their vans cruise by regularly. Tropic Transit (☎ 222-3375) is another shuttle service in town. A regular cab will also cost about $10 to 12. By car, take Capital Circle Rd to Lake Bradford Rd, north to downtown.

Bus TalTran (☎ 891-5200) has a main transfer point downtown on Tennessee St at Adams St. Fare is 75¢, and transfers are free. Some popular routes include the following:

Bus No 15
    Museum of History & Science
Bus No 1
    Monroe St to I-10
Bus Nos 3, 23, 26
    Doak Campbell Stadium
Bus No 22
    De Soto Park

FSU shuttle, Bus Nos 14, 11, 5
    FAMU campus
Bus No 16
    North on Thomasville Rd to ¹/₂-mile
    south of Maclay Gardens State Park

Trolley The Old Town Trolley (☎ 891-5200) is a free shuttle service around downtown; it runs every 10 minutes Monday to Friday from 7 am to 6 pm. Look for the trolley signs. It runs as far north as Brevard St, then south to Madison St on Monroe St and around the Civic Center and back. Pick up route maps on the trolley or at the Visitor Information Center at the New Capitol.

Car There are several canopy roads (those almost completely covered by foliage) in the area, and the best way to see them is by driving. They are along Old St Augustine Rd, Centerville Rd, Meridian Rd, Miccosukee Rd and Old Bainbridge Rd.

Parking is an absolute nightmare in downtown, and $10 tickets are handed out like bad advice in a cheap bar. There's a two-hour, metered public parking garage at the corner of Duval and Bronough Sts, across from the New Capitol. The one-way system is also a challenge, so be prepared for a frustrating experience and follow the signs.

Taxi Taxi rates in Tallahassee are $1.20 at flagfall and $1.20 each mile. Companies include City Taxi (☎ 562-4222), Yellow Cab (☎ 580-8080) and Capital Taxi (☎ 942-1015).

AROUND TALLAHASSEE
Havana
The little town of Havana, about 12 miles north of I-10 on Hwy 27, is essentially a cute little antique mall. You'll find most of the shops along 7th Ave, off of Main St (called Hwy 27 in town). Most shops are closed Monday and Tuesday.

The Historical Bookshelf (☎ 539-5040), 104 E 7th Ave, has good selections of used books on history, aviation and political history, and a good Civil War section. Pepperhead Quarters (☎ 539-1554), 311 N Main

St, has about 350 hot pepper products; taste your way through (they also sell antiques and bric-a-brac) and chat for a while.

The big mall here is the Cannery (☎ 539-3800), 115 E 8th Ave, which is open Wednesday to Sunday from 10 am to 6 pm. It's filled with antique shops and other stores, like Southern Organic Provisions, which sells homemade sauces, spices and herbs, and two little cafés: *WYO Barbeque* (☎ 539-6222) serves barbecue chicken ($3.75) and pork ($4.25) sandwiches and changing Southern specials from $2 to 4.50 (the chicken goes first, so get here early). It's open Wednesday to Saturday from 11.30 am to 2.30 pm. *The Kitchen at the Cannery* (☎ 539-8956) does pastas with several sauces from $6 to 8, and quiche or chicken with rice and beans are $7.

The *Willow Cafe* (☎ 539-9111), 211 1st St, was very crowded when we visited: it has beautiful quilts hanging on the walls and serves light lunches like spaghetti pie ($6.95) and paella, veggie salad, shrimp and corn chowder. It's open Thursday to Saturday from 11.30 am to 2.30 pm and Sunday from noon to 3pm.

If you feel like staying, *Gaver's Bed & Breakfast* (☎ 539-5611), 301 E 6th Ave, is a decent B&B with singles/doubles for $55/65 and $75, and you can either have a full or continental breakfast. The house was built in 1907. No pets or kids under eight, no credit cards.

Natural Bridge Battlefield
Fifteen miles southeast of Tallahassee, the Natural Bridge Battlefield State Historic Site (☎ 922-6007) is on the site where a ragtag group of Confederate soldiers prevented Union troops from reaching Tallahassee in 1865 (see Facts about Florida). The park is peaceful, and it's free: open daily from 8 am to sunset, and don't miss the annual battle re-enactment on March 6. From Tallahassee, take Hwy 363 to Natural Bridge Road, in Woodville. The park is always open.

Wakulla Springs State Park
Edward Ball Wakulla Springs State Park (☎ 922-3633) is a 2860-acre park with a

natural spring that covers about three acres and produces at peak times 1.2 billion gallons of water a day. They do glass-bottom boat rides (when the water's clear) and a riverboat cruise. Both run daily from 11 am to 3 pm and are about 30 minutes; the cost is $4.50 for adults, $2.25 for kids under 12. There's also swimming and a six-mile hiking trail. Some of the underwater scenes from the old Tarzan movies were filmed here, as well as scenes from *The Creature from the Black Lagoon* and, hmmm . . . *Airport '77*.

Scientist Sarah Smith discovered the bones of an ancient mastodon on the bottom of the spring here in 1850; since then the remains of at least nine other Ice Age mammals have been found – you may be able to see some of the excavation sites near the waterfront or on the glass-bottom boat tours.

There's no camping allowed, but if you want to stay in the park, hit *The Wakulla Springs Lodge* (1937; ☎ 224-5950), an immense Spanish building with a huge dining room and a walk-in fireplace, and rooms with private marble bathrooms; double room rates are $69 to 85.

The park is about 17 miles south of Tallahassee. Take Hwy 319 south to Hwy 61 south and follow the signs; the entrance is on Hwy 267. Admission is $3.25 per carload, $1 for pedestrians and bicyclists.

APALACHICOLA NATIONAL FOREST

The largest of Florida's three national forests, the Apalachicola National Forest occupies almost 938 sq miles of the eastern Panhandle from just west of Tallahassee to the Apalachicola River. The forest is wet lowlands and slash-pine and longleaf pine in the higher areas; other areas are made up of oak and cypress hammocks.

Nature within the forest is diverse, with dozens of species calling the area home including mink, gray and red fox, coyote, eastern moles, half a dozen bat species, beaver, Florida black bear and unconfirmed sightings of Florida panthers, though the Florida Game and Fresh Water Fish Commission says there aren't any of those left.

While access to the forest is free and

there's free hiking, camping, boating and swimming throughout, note that it's also open to hunting.

Orientation & Information

Administratively, the park is dissected by the Ochlockonee River, which flows south right through the center of the park; the eastern half is controlled by the Wakulla Ranger District, the western by the Apalachicola Ranger District.

The Apalachicola Ranger Station (☎ 643-2282) is just south of the city of Bristol, northwest of the northwest corner of the park near the intersection of Hwys 12 and 20; the Wakulla Ranger Station (☎ 926-3561) is just north of the town of Crawfordsville on Hwy 319.

The forest's boundaries are Hwy 20 at the north, Hwy 319 at the east, the Franklin County line at the south and the Apalachicola River at the west.

Several highways transverse the park at various angles; the major ones are:

Hwy 65
    between Sumatra at the park's
    southwest and Telogia just north
    of the park's northern border
Hwy 267
    between Bloxhem and Hwy 319
Hwy 12
    Between Bristol and Wilma
Hwy 13
    east-west across the lower portion of the
    park between Crawfordsville and Wilma
Hwy 67
    runs mainly north south from just south
    of Bristol, at the northwest end of the
    park, down through Hitchcock Lake
    and down through Franklin County

Get maps of the forest – key equipment – at the Visitor Information Center at the New Capitol in Tallahassee, or either ranger station, which also give out pamphlets and sell topos. There are entrances to the park at the junctions of the above roads. Admission is free. Day use areas are open from 8 am to sunset year round.

Activities

The forest's filled with water and sinkholes,

but the best place to see both is at the **Leon Sinks Geological Area**, with interpretive materials and rangers to help explain the sinkholes; it's at the eastern end of the park just east of Hwy 319, about 20 miles south of Tallahassee.

The forest offers almost untouched wilderness for hiking, horseback riding, walking and canoeing, though note that power boats are permitted in the park. For information on canoe rentals, contact the ranger station.

On the western side of the forest, south of Tallahassee, is the **Munson Hills Loop**, a tough 7½-mile bicycle trail through the hilliest section of the forest in an area made up of a mixture of hammock, dunes, hills and brush. If you run out of steam halfway, you can bail out; take the Tall Pine Shortcut out of the trail for a total distance of 4½ miles.

Swimming is available at Camel Lake, Wright Lake, Silver Lake and Lost Lake.

Camping

All facilities are primitive, some with toilets, some not. With the exception of Silver Lake and Lost Lake, which charge $4, camping is free. There is camping available on the western (Apalachicola) side of the forest at Camel Lake (from Bristol, near the ranger station take Hwy 12 south for 11 miles and turn east on Forest Rd 105 for two miles); Cotton Landing (at the southwest of the forest; from Sumatra take Hwy 379 northwest for three miles then turn left on Hwy 123 for three miles, then left again onto Hwy 123 B for about half a mile); Hickory Landing (southwest of Sumatra off Hwy 101), Wright Lake, just northeast of Hickory Landing, and Hitchcock Lake, just west of the Ochlockonee River off Hwy 67.

In the eastern (Wakulla) section of the forest there's camping at Silver Lake (from Hwy 20 take Hwy 260 south to Silver Lake), Lost Lake (northwest of Leon Sinks; take Hwy 20 to Hwy 373 and follow it to the Lost Lake turnoff) and, at the southeast section of the park, Mack Landing (northwest on Hwy 375 from Sopchoppy) and Wood Lake (from Sopchoppy take Hwy 375 to Hwy 22 west, to Hwy 340 south to Hwy 338).

TORREYA STATE PARK

Fifty miles west of Tallahassee, this lovely little park (☎ 643-2674) along the Apalachicola River with its towering Torreya evergreen, elm and yew trees is home to the Gregory House, a pre-Civil War plantation mansion, and a seven-mile hiking trail. Tours of the house are available from Monday to Friday at 10 am, Saturday and Sunday at 10 am and 2 and 4 pm. The park is open daily from 8 am to sunset; admission is $2 per vehicle, $1 for pedestrians and cyclists. The Gregory House has a separate admission for the guided tour of $1 for adults, 50¢ for children.

The park is off Hwy 12, near Bristol; from Tallahassee, take Hwy 20 west, turn north on Hwy 12 and bear left at the fork, following the signs.

Tent **camping** is cheap here: $3 for adults, $2 for students or under 17 years old if accompanied by an adult. RV camping is $8 per site, $2 extra for electricity.

FLORIDA CAVERNS STATE PARK

Three miles north of Marianna are the fascinating caves inside Florida Caverns State Park (☎ 482-9598, 482-1228), a 1300-acre park on the Chipole River.

The lighted caves contain eerie stalactites, stalagmites, flowstones – the ones that look like rock waterfalls – and other formations that were made as calcite bubbled through the rocks. Only seven cavern rooms are open to the public, but there are many more. The Florida Parks Service zealously protects and safeguards these delicate formations, as well as the endangered gray bats that live in the caves. The other caves in the park are only open to scientists, biologists and archaeologists.

A nice surprise is the Chipole River, which actually dips underground for a couple of hundred feet within the park. But there is also **camping, canoeing** and **riding** (if you brought your horse along – there are no livery stables). The visitor center rents canoes year round for $10 per day (eight hours), $7 for half a day. To ride your horse along the trails costs $5 per person, or $12 for a family. To camp at one of the 30 sites within the park, it costs $8/10 without/with electricity from October to February, and it's $12/14 from March to September.

There are also five archaeological sites near the cavern and the fish hatchery area, and four natural stone Depression-era houses. Within the visitor center there are archives and artifacts taken from archaeological digs in the park.

One-hour guided tours of the caves leave the main ranger visitor center every half hour from 9 am to 4.30 pm daily. The cave tours are limited to 25 people at a time, and they sell out fast; go to the ticket office at the cave as soon as you arrive. Tours cost $4 for adults, $2 for children three to 13. Admission to the park is $3.25 per carload, $1 for pedestrians and cyclists.

FOSTER CENTER
About 40 minutes east of Tallahassee off I-10, the Stephen C Foster State Folk Cultural Center (☎ 904-397-2733) is a fine state park with exhibits and mementos honoring Stephen Foster, composer of Florida's state song, *Old Folks At Home* (see sidebar), and a man who never came near the area.

The center has a five-mile loop bicycle and hiking trail, an interpretive center, and a museum of Florida and Foster-related history. Free ranger-guided tours run frequently, sometimes with female rangers wearing antebellum dresses, and there are special events throughout the year culminating in the Florida Folk Festival every Memorial Day weekend.

Other annual festivals are the Folk Life Days in November, celebrating 19th-century homestead life, and Stephen Foster Day in January, with musical programs, caroling and recitals of Foster selections. There are also several Elderhostel programs held hear each year.

There's canoeing along the river, with canoe rentals available from American Canoe Adventures (☎ 397-1309). Tent camping is available here; the cost is $8 per site

(most have water hookups), and $2 extra for electricity.

The center is in White Springs, east of US Hwy 41 north. From I-10, take US Hwy 41 north just past White Springs and follow the signs. Admission is $3.25 per carload or $1 for pedestrians and bicyclists.

SUWANNEE RIVER STATE PARK
At the junction of the Suwannee and Withlacoochee Rivers, this 1800-acre state park (☎ 362-2746) offers a unique opportunity to see the confluence of rivers as well as bubbling springs. There's a scenic overlook, and you can still see the fortifications built by Confederates to protect the railroad bridge over the Suwannee the Confederates used to shuttle food supplies to the front (see History in the Facts about Florida chapter).

The park has canoe trails and rentals ($15 per day), and camping ($10 without electricity, $12 with). There are also interpretive nature signs along the Suwannee River Nature Trail through hardwood hammock, and the Sandhills Trail, which leads to the remains of the Columbus Cemetery and to the Old Stage Road, a major transport route between Pensacola and Jacksonville in the 18th and 19th centuries.

The park is open daily from 8 am to sunset. It's located 15 miles from the town of Live Oak on Hwy 90. Admission is $3.25 per carload, $12 for pedestrians and cyclists.

STEINHATCHEE
• *pop 800* ☎ *352*
This pristine, quiet little fishing village is about an hour southeast of Tallahassee along Florida's Big Bend section, which is one of the state's most beautiful. Your best bet for seeing this area is to contact Dean Fowler, who runs the Steinhatchee Landing Resort. This wonderful little place has duplex cottages with tons of amenities and absolutely excellent service, and they can arrange any number of nature trips throughout the region.

We took a half-hour tootle on the Steinhatchee River with Dean, and on the way we saw hawks, herons, egrets, alligators, raccoons, ducks and pelicans. The glasslike

Stephen C Foster

While Steven Collins Foster (1826-64) could in many ways be considered to be a true American legend (he was even born on the Fourth of July), his work in minstrel shows and popularity at the height of slavery ensures that his legacy is tainted with, to say the very least, political incorrectness.

Yet his performances, and variations on slave songs of the era, are undeniably offset by his contribution to American culture. It was Foster who brought us *Oh, Susanna!*, as familiar to listeners now as it was when released in 1846. And it was Foster who first brought the world's attention to the Suwannee River – a river Foster himself had never set eyes on.

The song is *Old Folks At Home*, with lyrics penned in simulated 'Darkie' dialect: 'Way down upon the Swannee Ribber, far, far away/Dere's wha my heart is turning ebber/ Dere's where the old folks stay'.

Foster apparently chose the Suwannee on a whim: he was said to have been considering the Pedee and the Yazoo rivers as well *(Way down upon the Yazoo River*?!?), but a misspelled map led to his selection of the 'Swannee', which runs from north to south through extreme north central Florida and empties into the Gulf of Mexico, for his song.

Despite its clearly racist tone and lyrics (a line from the chorus is 'Oh! darkeys how my heart grows weary/Far from de old folks at home') its worldwide popularity was such that it was adopted by the state of Florida as its official state song.

Today visitors to the Stephen Foster Center are treated to wildly disparate imagery: on one hand, the center is dedicated to the life and work of a man who spent most of his career writing 'plantation melodies'. On the other, the center itself is host to many fine programs that increase visitors' understanding of black and Indian culture and heritage.

In any event it's interesting to note that here, in the most southern of Southern states, this center is dedicated to the memory of a man who wrote a song of the South from his home in Allegheny, Pennsylvania. It could be worse – *Oh Susanna!* was written in Cincinnati, Ohio. ■

river is incredibly tranquil and beautiful – the trees growing alongside are totally awesome, with washed-out roots reflecting the strangest shapes in the water. This place really makes you feel that you're truly getting away from it all.

But remember, this is the countryside, and not only does it look like a redneck haven, in some ways it is – but once you get on the river, nothing else matters. In addition to the resort's cottages, there are two other motels.

Places to Stay & Eat

Cottages at the *Steinhatchee Landing Resort* (☎ 498-3513) all have screened-in porches, full kitchens, washer/dryers, dishwashers, TVs and VCRs, stereo systems, fireplaces and wood-burning stoves. One-bedroom, two-story houses are $110/125 in winter/ summer, two-bedroom houses are $115/ 130, two-bedroom townhouses $130/150, and three-bedrooms range from $190 to 225/215 to 255. Weekly rates are available, and during holidays there is a three-night minimum stay. See Getting There & Away below for directions on how to get here.

On the property there's badminton, a swimming pool, a playground, a jogging trail, free bicycles and canoes, a spa, a fish pond, walking paths, volleyball, tennis, shuffleboard and archery. It's a little expensive, but we thought it was well worth the price. There is also a vegetable garden, and guests are welcome to pick anything in it.

The resort runs trips (with lunch) to Manatee Springs State Park (see below) on the Suwannee River, as well as Steinhatchee River tours and fishing trips.

Steinhatchee Landing Resort also runs a motel, the *Steinhatchee River Inn* (☎ 498-4049), which has rooms for $50 to 60 in low season and $60 to 70 in high season. All rooms have TVs, a coffeemaker and a fridge; there are no phones, but you can make local calls from their office and the pay phone. If someone calls for you long distance, they'll bring you a cordless phone. The rooms upstairs all have full kitchens, and there are two suites downstairs ($10 per person extra). They're at 600 Riverside Drive.

Sexton's Riverside Motel (☎ 498-5005), 301 1st Ave NW, is run by very friendly people who keep their place quite clean and nice. All rooms have full kitchens, cable TV and a queen-size and two single beds (and if you need more, rollaways are available). Double rooms are $55, $12 for each additional person, $6 for children. There is also a dock, but you'll need to BYOB (bring your own boat) – they don't rent any.

Chef Jason Benavides runs the *Steinhatchee Landing Restaurant* (☎ 498-2345), and it's excellent. But don't just take our word for it: we met three other travel writers in the state who had been here and all spoke longingly of the food, and publicists at the State Division of Tourism told us that they promote Steinhatchee so they too can get down here to eat – it's *that* good: appetizers are from $5.25 to 8.95, and entrees include chicken supreme for $12.95, seafood pasta Alfredo for $13.75, gratin of grouper or salmon for $15.25 and the *awesome* crab cake dinner for $17.95.

Other than the Landing Restaurant, there's *Roy's* (☎ 498-5000), which is the most popular (maybe only) place in town. It has a great salad bar, and most seafood dinners are $10.75. It's about a mile west of the Landing.

Getting There & Away You can only get here by car. From Tallahassee, take Hwy 19 (also called Hwy 19/27 and, later, Hwy 19/98) to the city of Tenille and turn west on Hwy 51 and go west for about eight miles. Go past the horrific collections of mobile homes, and the Landing is on your left.

MANATEE SPRINGS STATE PARK
☎ 352

117 million gallons of crystal clear water gush from the Manatee Springs State Park (☎ 493-6072) springhead every day. The spring, in which diving and swimming is permitted, flows through cypress, maple and ash trees before emptying into the Suwannee River and finally into the Gulf of Mexico, about 25 miles downstream. There's an 8½-mile hiking and biking trail as well, but the best part of this wonderful park is the viewing platform and boardwalk; when we visited, a family of manatee was swimming just off the platform, and we saw an absolutely adorable little baby alligator swimming across the spring run.

There's canoeing along the spring run; canoes are available from the concession for $5 for the first hour, $4 each additional hour and here are discounts if you're camping in the park. Campsites cost $10 without electricity, $12 with, and it's an absolutely lovely place to stay.

The park is open daily from 8 am to sundown. Admission is $3.25 per carload, $1 for pedestrians and cyclists. It's at the end of Hwy 320, off Hwy 98, six miles west of Chiefland at 11650 NW 115th St.

CEDAR KEY
• *pop 700* ☎ 352

Once an important fishing port and the source of the wood for Eagle and Eberhard-Faber pencils – perhaps the most common brands in the USA – the town of Cedar Key was one of Florida's largest. At its heyday in the late 19th century, Cedar Key had the trade-oomph to become the western terminal of Florida's first transstate railroad (see the Amelia Island section in the Northeast Florida chapter for more information).

But the town and port were demolished by a hurricane in 1896; the factory closed and the port never regained its luster. Today Cedar Key is a pleasant, friendly little town (though it could be in danger of leaning towards a tourist trap), with some great nearby beaches, good seafood and a very good museum of local history. It's not jumping, but it's certainly worth a visit.

Orientation & Information
The Cedar Keys area is made up of 100 islands, 12 of which are home to the Cedar Keys National Wildlife Refuge. Cedar Key

is at the southwestern end of Hwy 24, which is 25 miles southwest of Hwy 19/98. The town is very compact, and most of the action centers around the Dock, at the southwest end of town. There are three noteworthy annual festivals, the Sidewalk Art Festival (April), the Fourth of July celebration and the October Seafood Festival.

The Cedar Keys Chamber of Commerce (☎ 543-5600) on Main St, is a good source of local information – though it's only open Monday, Wednesday and Friday from 10 am to 2 pm. A better source is the rangers at the Cedar Key State Museum (☎ 543-5350, see below), or Tom at the Island Hotel (see Places to Stay & Eat).

Cedar Key State Museum

The Cedar Key State Museum (☎ 543-5350) at 12231 SW 166th St (this address was formerly 1710 Museum Drive, but a reshuffling of the 911 emergency response addresses gave it its new moniker; most locals still call it Museum Drive), is an excellent collection of local and regional historical displays and the collections of St Clair Whitman, who arrived in the area in 1882 at the age of 14 and seemed to collect everything he saw. Displays include insects, butterflies, glass, sea glass, bottles, and what's billed as the largest seashell collection in Florida (this last claim may be challenged by the Bailey Matthews Shell Museum in Sanibel, see the Southwest Florida chapter). The museum is open Thursday to Monday from 9 am to 5 pm, closed Tuesday and Wednesday. Admission is $1 for adults, children under six free.

Cedar Keys National Wildlife Refuge

The Cedar Keys National Wildlife Refuge (☎ 493-0238) is on 12 islands in the Gulf of Mexico, about five miles from Cedar Key. Established as a breeding ground for colonial birds, today the refuge, which is home to 50,000 birds and 12 species of reptiles, is closed to the public except by advance arrangement by academics and researchers. Except for Seahorse Key, though, the refuge's beaches are open to the public during daylight hours. Seahorse

Key, including a 300-foot buffer zone around the island, is closed to all public entry from March 1 to June 30.

The Cedar Key Lighthouse, which no longer functions, is located on Seahorse Key, but it's used extensively by the University of Florida for research, and is generally closed to the public.

The keys can be accessed only by boat, and shallow water and mud flats makes them tough to get to. Contact the rangers' office or Wild Florida Adventures or Island Hopper (see below) for more information.

Organized Tours

We hear only good things about Wild Florida Adventures (☎ 528-2741, fax 528-2743) which conducts organized kayak tours of the entire area. Tour prices include the boat, paddles, life vests, drinking water and snacks for $45. Tom at the Island Hotel says he's recommended the tours to many visitors and all have raved, saying that it's definitely great value for the money. The four-hour tours run twice a day from October 16 to May 14, and a morning trip from May 15 to October 15. You can write for a brochure to Jeff and Renee Ripple, PO Box 142613, Gainesville, FL 32614-2613.

Island Hopper (☎ 543-5904) runs various pontoon boat trips throughout the region, and rents skiffs as well; call for price information.

Places to Stay & Eat

There's a very friendly campground in *Sunset Isle Park* (☎ 543-5375), on Hwy 24 one mile west of the first bridge from the mainland on the north side of the street. Sites for two people in tent or RV are $12, including water and electric hookups.

The *Faraway Inn* (☎ 543-5330) at 3rd and G Sts on the site of the Eagle Pencil mill, has double rooms from $40 to 75, and the price includes use of bicycles canoes and paddle boats.

The best entry in town for places to stay and eat is the *Island Hotel* (☎ 543-5111, see Online Services appendix) at 224 2nd St at B St. Formerly a general store (1859) that closed in 1910, it was converted to a

NW & PANHANDLE

hotel in 1915. Rooms here range from $75 to 95 year round, and staff is very friendly and helpful. At the restaurant, the specialties are locally caught seafood like softshell crab ($17.95) and stone crab claws ($19.95), and their house specialty heart of palm salad ($4.50) has a dressing made from (get this) vanilla ice cream, lime sherbet and *peanut butter*. They're open for dinner Wednesday to Monday from 6 to 9 pm, and breakfast (homemade poppyseed bread French toast or herbed eggs and bacon $7.50, crabmeat omelet $11.50) daily from 8 to 10 am, Saturday and Sunday from 8 to 11 am.

Two great places for seafood are along Dock St; *Seabreeze On The Dock* (☎ 543-5738), with its comfortable lounge complete with checkers, chess and tic-tac-toe games, serves great meat and seafood, with

most dishes in the $11 to 12 range and specials like baked chicken breast ($7.50) and a five-course mariners' feast for $20.25. Also on Dock St at similar prices is *The Brown Pelican Restaurant* (☎ 543-5428) with a specialty of soft-shell crab for $16.95.

Getting There & Away

There is no public transport to the area. Driving, take Hwy 19/98 or I-75 to Hwy 24 and follow it southwest to the bitter end. The area is very popular with private pilots, who land at George Lewis Landing Field (no phone), literally a strip of grass on the island of Cedar Key with no aviation services. Pilots: maybe this will make sense to you – the local taxi driver, Lester Ridgeway, monitors CTAF and will pick you up. The five minute ride from the air field costs 'whatever you think is fair'.

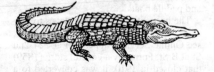

Appendix I – Online Services

For standard online services, the access
numbers are:

America Online
☎ 800 827-6364, local access ☎ 305-621-8500

CompuServe
☎ 800-848-8990, local access ☎ 305-262-9325

Prodigy
☎ 800-776-3449, local access ☎ 305-471-1500,
network symbol Q

MISCELLANEOUS

BBC worldservice.letters@bbc.co.uk

Council Travel
http://www.ciee.org/cts/ctshome.htm

Koblas
http://bin.gnn.com/cgi-bin/gnn/currency

Lonely Planet
http://www.lonelyplanet.com.au

Mobility International miusa@igc.apc.org

Q&A http://www.olsen.ch/cgi-bin/exmenu

QueerAmerica http://youth.org/outproud/

Queer Resources Directory
http://www.infoqueer.org/qrd

United Nations gopher://
gopher.undp.org:70/00/uncurr/exch_rates

zip code information
http://www.usps.gov/ncsc/aq-zip.html

AIRLINES

Aero Mexico
http://www.wotw.com/aeromexico

Aero Peru http://ichu.rcp.net.pe:80/aeroperu

Air Canada http://www.aircanada.ca

Air France http://www.airfrance.fr

Alitalia http://www.alitalia.it

American Airlines http://www.amrcorp.com

British Airways
http://www.british-airways.com

Carnival Airlines
http://www.carnivalair.com

Continental Airlines
http://www.flycontinental.com

Delta Air Lines http://www.delta-air.com

KLM Royal Dutch Airlines
http://www.klm.nl

LAN Chile http://www.lanchile.com

Lufthansa http://www.lufthansa.de

TWA http://www.twa.com

United Airlines http://www.ual.com

USAir http://www.usair.com

ValuJet http://www.valujet.com

Varig Brazilian Airlines
http://freesun.be/varig

Virgin Atlantic Airways
http://www.fly.virgin.com

OTHER TRANSPORTATION

Alamo http://www.freeways.com/bookit

Amtrak http://www.amtrak.com

Avis http://www.avis.com

Greyhound http://www.greyhound.com

MIAMI & MIAMI BEACH

**American Police Hall of Fame &
Police Museum** http://www.aphf.org

Breakwater Hotel breakw@aol.com

Eden Roc Resort
http://www.richnet.net/edenroc

Florida Shakespeare Theatre
http://www.afn.org/~theatre

**Historical Museum of Southern
Florida** natbrown@ix.netcom.com
http://www.gate.net/historical-museum

Holocaust Memorial
http://wahoo.netrunner.net/~holomem/

Jerry Herman Ring Theatre
http://www.miami.edu/tha

Miami Film Commission http://
www.hollywoodeast.com/mdtfp/expermit.html

Miami River Inn miami100@ix.netcom.com

Museum of Contemporary Art (MoCA)
http://gsni.com/moca-mia.htm

Single Source
http://thesinglesource.com/eventguide/mia/

SoBeNET riley@sobenet.net
http://www.sobenet.net

Virtua Cafe http://www.sobe.com/virtuacafe/

XS http://www.xso.com

FLORIDA KEYS

Atlantic Shores Resort
atlshores@aol.com

Banana Cabana PYDT60@Prodigy.com

Dolphins Plus
dolphins-plus@pennecamp.com
www.pennekamp.com/dolphins-plus

**Florida Keys & Key West
Visitor's Bureau** http://www.fla-keys.com

Key Largo Chamber of Commerce
klchamber@aol.com

Key West Business Guild
http://www.gaykeywest.com

**Marathon Visitors Center/
Chamber of Commerce**
http://florida-keys.fl.us/marathon.htm

Newfound Harbor Marine Institute
seacamp96@aol.com

newsgroup for Key lime pie recipes
alt.fan.jimmy-buffett

Pigeon Key Museum
pigeon-key@florida-keys.fl.us

SOUTHEAST FLORIDA

City of Fort Lauderdale
http://info.ci.ftlaud.fl.us

Floyd's Youth Hostel & Crew House
fecreamer@aol.com

**Greater Fort Lauderdale
Convention & Visitor's Bureau**
http://www.co.broward.fl.us

Palm Beach Police Dept
http://legal.firn.edu/muni/palmbch/

**West Palm Beach County
Convention & Visitors Bureau**
http://www.pwr.com/PBC/
http://www.florida.net/scuba/tourism/cvb.html

XS http://www.xso.com

CENTRAL FLORIDA

City of Orlando http://www.ci.orlando.fl.us/

Gainseville Civic Media Center
cmc@freenet.ufl.edu

Gainesville VCB acvacb@afn.org
http://www.afn.org/~acvacb

Gay & Lesbian Community Services
glcs@flamingopark.com
website http://www.flamingopark.com/glcs

Harry P Leu Gardens
http://www.tenkey.com/gardens/

HI Orlando Resort
103727.3100@compuserve.com

Universal Studios Florida
http://www.usf.com

**Unofficial Guide to
Universal Studios Florida** http://
members.gnn.com/tomtipton/greatday.htm

Sea World http://www.bev.net/education/
SeaWorld/homepage.html

Disney Official Sites
http://preview2.disney.com/DisneyWorld/
index.html

http://www.disneyworld.com/vacation.html

Disney Unofficial Sites

Ed Sterrett's Disney Links page http://
www.america.com/~dcop/tudlp/welcome.html

Gay Day at Disney
at http://www.gayday.com

Walt Disney World Made Simple
wdwms@jax.jaxnet.com

SPACE COAST

general information
http://www.space-coast.com

Kennedy Space Center Homepage
http://www.ksc.nasa.gov

KSC Visitors Center
http:///www.kscvisitor.com

NASA Homepage http://www.nasa.gov

Shuttle Homepage http://shuttle.nasa.gov

Space Station Homepage
http://liftoff.msfc.nasa.gov/station/
welcome.html

NORTHEAST FLORIDA

Amelia Island http://www.ameliaisland.com

Daytona Beach Area Convention & Visitor's Bureau DaytonaBea@aol.com
http://www.travelfile.com/get?/dbacvb

Daytona USA www.nascar.com

St Augustine http://www.oldcity.com

SOUTHWEST FLORIDA

Gulf Coast Kayak gckayak@gate.net

Mote Marine Laboratory
info@marinelab.sarasota.fl.us
http://www.marinelab.sarasota.fl.us

Salvador Dali Museum
qvbg71a@prodigy.com
www.highwayone.com/dali/

St Petersburg Times
http://www.sptimes.com

Ybor City Chamber of Commerce
http://www2.tia.net/ybor/

NORTHWEST FLORIDA & THE PANHANDLE

Blue Angels Public Affairs Office
bapao@aol.com

Island Hotel ishotel@gav.fdt.net

Tallahassee
http://www.stater.fl.us/citytlh/
http:www.co.leon.fl.us

Tallahassee Convention & Visitors Bureau vic@mail.co.leon.fl.us

Tallahassee News
http://www.polaris.ney/users-www/mikems/

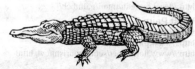

Appendix II: Climate Charts

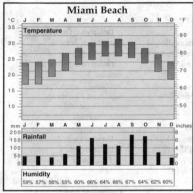

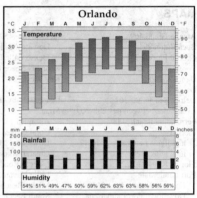

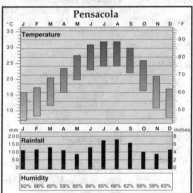

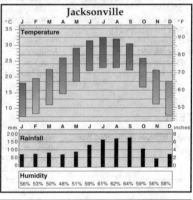

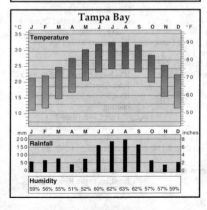

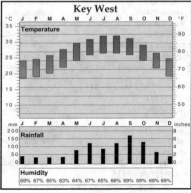

Index

MAPS

TEXT

LONELY PLANET JOURNEYS

LONELY PLANET JOURNEYS

JOURNEYS is a unique collection of travel writing – published by the company that understands travel better than anyone else. It is a series for anyone who has ever experienced – or dreamed of – the magical moment when they encountered a strange culture or saw a place for the first time. They are tales to read while you're planning a trip, while you're on the road or while you're in an armchair, in front of a fire.

JOURNEYS books catch the spirit of a place, illuminate a culture, recount a crazy adventure, or introduce a fascinating way of life. They always entertain, and always enrich the experience of travel.

'Idiosyncratic, entertainingly diverse and unexpected . . . from an international writership'
– The Australian

'Books which offer a closer look at the people and culture of a destination, and enrich travel experiences'
– American Bookseller

FULL CIRCLE
A South American Journey
Luis Sepúlveda
Translated by Chris Andrews

Full Circle invites us to accompany Chilean writer Luis Sepúlveda on 'a journey without a fixed itinerary'. Whatever his subject – brutalities suffered under Pinochet's dictatorship, sleepy tropical towns visited in exile, or the landscapes of legendary Patagonia – Sepúlveda is an unflinchingly honest yet lyrical storyteller. Extravagant characters and extraordinary situations are memorably evoked: gauchos organising a tournament of lies, a scheming heiress on the lookout for a husband, a pilot with a corpse on board his plane . . . Part autobiography, part travel memoir, *Full Circle* brings us the distinctive voice of one of South America's most compelling writers.

Luis Sepúlveda was born in Chile in 1949. Imprisoned by the Pinochet dictatorship for his socialist beliefs, he was for many years a political exile. He has written novels, short stories, plays and essays. His work has attracted many awards and has been translated into numerous languages.

'Detachment, humour and vibrant prose' – El País

'an absolute cracker' – The Bookseller

This project has been assisted by the Commonwealth Government through the Australia Council, its arts funding and advisory body.

LONELY PLANET TRAVEL ATLASES

Lonely Planet has long been famous for the number and quality of its guidebook maps. Now we've gone one step further and in conjunction with Steinhart Katzir Publishers produced a handy companion series: Lonely Planet travel atlases – maps of a country produced in book form.

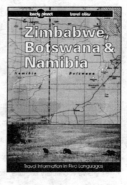

Unlike other maps, which look good but lead travellers astray, our travel atlases have been researched on the road by Lonely Planet's experienced team of writers. All details are carefully checked to ensure the atlas corresponds with the equivalent Lonely Planet guidebook.

The handy atlas format means no holes, wrinkles, torn sections or constant folding and unfolding. These atlases can survive long periods on the road, unlike cumbersome fold-out maps. The comprehensive index ensures easy reference.

- full-colour throughout
- maps researched and checked by Lonely Planet authors
- place names correspond with Lonely Planet guidebooks
  – no confusing spelling differences
- legend and travelling information in English, French, German, Japanese and Spanish
- size: 230 x 160 mm

Available now:
Chile & Easter Island • Egypt • India & Bangladesh • Israel & the Palestinian Territories •Jordan, Syria & Lebanon • Kenya • Laos • Portugal • South Africa, Lesotho & Swaziland • Thailand • Turkey • Vietnam • Zimbabwe, Botswana & Namibia

---

LONELY PLANET TV SERIES & VIDEOS

Lonely Planet travel guides have been brought to life on television screens around the world. Like our guides, the programmes are based on the joy of independent travel, and look honestly at some of the most exciting, picturesque and frustrating places in the world. Each show is presented by one of three travellers from Australia, England or the USA and combines an innovative mixture of video, Super-8 film, atmospheric soundscapes and original music.

Videos of each episode – containing additional footage not shown on television – are available from good book and video shops, but the availability of individual videos varies with regional screening schedules.

Video destinations include: Alaska • American Rockies • Australia – The South-East • Baja California & the Copper Canyon • Brazil • Central Asia • Chile & Easter Island • Corsica, Sicily & Sardinia – The Mediterranean Islands • East Africa (Tanzania & Zanzibar) • Ecuador & the Galapagos Islands • Greenland & Iceland • Indonesia • Israel & the Sinai Desert • Jamaica • Japan • La Ruta Maya • Morocco • New York • North India • Pacific Islands (Fiji, Solomon Islands & Vanuatu) • South India • South West China • Turkey • Vietnam • West Africa • Zimbabwe, Botswana & Namibia

The Lonely Planet TV series is produced by:
Pilot Productions
The Old Studio
18 Middle Row
London W10 5AT UK

For video availability and ordering information contact your nearest Lonely Planet office.

Music from the TV series is available on CD & cassette.

LONELY PLANET PHRASEBOOKS

Building bridges,
Breaking barriers,
Beyond babble-on

Nepali
phrasebook

Ethiopian
Amharic
phrasebook

Latin American
Spanish
phrasebook

Ukrainian
phrasebook

Greek
phrasebook

Vietnamese
phrasebook

Listen for the gems

Speak your own words

Ask your own
questions

Master of
your
own
image

- handy pocket-sized books
- easy to understand Pronunciation chapter
- clear and comprehensive Grammar chapter
- romanisation alongside script to allow ease of pronunciation
- script throughout so users can point to phrases
- extensive vocabulary sections, words and phrases for every situation
- full of cultural information and tips for the traveller

'...vital for a real DIY spirit and attitude in language learning' – Backpacker

'the phrasebooks have good cultural backgrounders and offer solid advice for challenging situations in remote locations' – San Francisco Examiner

'...they are unbeatable for their coverage of the world's more obscure languages' – The Geographical Magazine

---

Arabic (Egyptian)
Arabic (Moroccan)
Australia
  Australian English, Aboriginal and Torres Strait languages
Baltic States
  Estonian, Latvian, Lithuanian
Bengali
Brazilian
Burmese
Cantonese
Central Asia
Central Europe
  Czech, French, German, Hungarian, Italian and Slovak
Eastern Europe
  Bulgarian, Czech, Hungarian, Polish, Romanian and Slovak
Ethiopian (Amharic)
Fijian
French
German
Greek

Hindi/Urdu
Indonesian
Italian
Japanese
Korean
Lao
Latin American Spanish
Malay
Mandarin
Mediterranean Europe
  Albanian, Croatian, Greek, Italian, Macedonian, Maltese, Serbian and Slovene
Mongolian
Moroccan Arabic
Nepali
Papua New Guinea
Pilipino (Tagalog)
Quechua
Russian
Scandinavian Europe
  Danish, Finnish, Icelandic, Norwegian and Swedish

South-East Asia
  Burmese, Indonesian, Khmer, Lao, Malay, Tagalog (Pilipino), Thai and Vietnamese
Spanish (Castilian)
  Basque, Catalan and Galician
Sri Lanka
Swahili
Thai
Thai Hill Tribes
Tibetan
Turkish
Ukrainian
USA
  US English, Vernacular, Native American languages and Hawaiian
Vietnamese
Western Europe
  Basque, Catalan, Dutch, French, German, Irish, Italian, Portuguese, Scottish Gaelic, Spanish (Castilian) and Welsh

---

LONELY PLANET CITY GUIDES

City guides are pocket-sized and full-color. They're packed with useful information for travelers, whether they're visiting a city on holiday or business–irrespective of who's paying the bill!

They have reliable, inside information on transport, restaurants and accommodation–to suit those who want five-star comfort, as well as those who have tight budgets. There are extensive maps, background material, and comprehensive coverage of popular excursions.

- practical information for business and leisure travelers, whatever their budget
- convenient pocket-sized format, with superb color photos and color maps throughout
- fold-out maps on front and back (gatefold) covers
- background information on culture and sights
- high-quality mapping complementary to the text
- hundreds of recommendations for places to stay and eat
- detailed coverage of transport options
- comprehensive shopping suggestions
- information on day trips and walking tours
- high-quality paper and sturdy binding
- size: 184 x 85 mm

'Lonely Planet adheres to its tradition of offering tightly concentrated information in a cornucopia of small packages.'
                                                                                                    –Houston Chronicle

---

LONELY PLANET WALKING GUIDES

Walking guides cover some of the world's most exciting bushwalking and trekking routes. These informative and reliable guides are an invaluable resource for independent trekkers or those in an organized group–in fact for anyone who believes that the best way to see a country is on foot.

- written by experienced trekkers
- each guide includes walks of varying difficulty and duration
- detailed day-by-day route descriptions
- clear, reliable maps
- information on safety, preparation and planning, equipment, and hiring porters
- advice on the best time of year to undertake each walk
- what to take and where to get supplies on the way
- comprehensive health and first-aid sections
- superb color photographs
- size: 128 x 184 mm

'The trekking series, which covers many of the world's major mountain ranges, is exceptional.'
                                                                                                    –Backpacker

LONELY PLANET TRAVEL GUIDES

Lonely Planet travel guides provide comprehensive coverage of a single country or region for a wide range of budgets.

They have reliable, practical advice on transport, restaurants and accommodation to suit all tastes from five-star to five dollars a day. There are numerous maps, extensive background material, descriptions of sights both on and off the beaten track, and inside information on outdoor activities.

- practical information for every budget
- extensive background information on culture and sights
- high-quality mapping complementary to the text
- hundreds of good-value recommendations for places to stay and eat
- suggested itineraries to help planning
- details on a huge range of outdoor activities
- no-nonsense details on health and safety
- down-to-earth advice on everything from packing your bags to buying a ticket
- practical language sections
- extensive use of foreign scripts
- color photos
- high-quality paper and sturdy binding
- size: 128 x 184 mm

'The Lonely Planet travel survival kit is the traditional market leader and is still the best.' – Sunday Times

---

LONELY PLANET SHOESTRING GUIDES

Shoestring guides cover a number of countries and are packed with practical information for budget travelers.

They give travelers all the vital, relevant facts in a compact and economical format. They have reliable, first-hand advice on transport, restaurants and accommodation to suit those who want to make their money stretch as far as possible. These guides are written by experienced travelers in a no-nonsense, irreverent style.

- practical information for budget travelers
- high-quality mapping complementary to the text
- hundreds of good-value recommendations for places to stay and eat
- comprehensive coverage of transport options
- details on health and safety
- down-to-earth advice from packing your bags to buying a ticket
- practical language sections
- high-quality paper and sturdy binding
- size: 128 x 184 mm

'The instant appeal of LP guides is their refreshingly individual, independent voice . . . The tone is respectful and informative about the local culture and environment, is ecologically responsible and has a gutsy sense of travelers' survival humor necessary to experience other countries at ground level.' – The Age

PLANET TALK

Lonely Planet's FREE quarterly newsletter

We love hearing from you and think you'd like to hear from us.

*When...*is the right time to see reindeer in Finland?
*Where...*can you hear the best palm-wine music in Ghana?
*How...*do you get from Asunción to Areguá by steam train?
*What...*is the best way to see India?

For the answer to these and many other questions read PLANET TALK.

Every issue is packed with up-to-date travel news and advice including:

- a letter from Lonely Planet co-founders Tony and Maureen Wheeler
- go behind the scenes on the road with a Lonely Planet author
- feature article on an important and topical travel issue
- a selection of recent letters from travellers
- details on forthcoming Lonely Planet promotions
- complete list of Lonely Planet products

To join our mailing list contact any Lonely Planet office.

Also available: Lonely Planet T-shirts. 100% heavyweight cotton.

LONELY PLANET ONLINE

Get the latest travel information before you leave or while you're on the road

Whether you've just begun planning your next trip, or you're chasing down specific info on currency regulations or visa requirements, check out Lonely Planet Online for up-to-the minute travel information.

As well as travel profiles of your favourite destinations (including maps and photos), you'll find current reports from our researchers and other travellers, updates on health and visas, travel advisories, and discussion of the ecological and political issues you need to be aware of as you travel.

There's also an online travellers' forum where you can share your experience of life on the road, meet travel companions and ask other travellers for their recommendations and advice. We also have plenty of links to other online sites useful to independent travellers.

And of course we have a complete and up-to-date list of all Lonely Planet travel products including guides, phrasebooks, atlases, Journeys and videos and a simple online ordering facility if you can't find the book you want elsewhere.

www.lonelyplanet.com
or
AOL keyword: lp

LONELY PLANET PRODUCTS

Lonely Planet is known worldwide for publishing practical, reliable and no-nonsense travel information in our guides and on our web site. The Lonely Planet list covers just about every accessible part of the world. Currently there are eight series: *travel guides, shoestring guides, walking guides, city guides, phrasebooks, audio packs, travel atlases* and *Journeys* – a unique collection of travel writing.

EUROPE

Amsterdam • Austria • Baltic States phrasebook • Britain • Central Europe on a shoestring • Central Europe phrasebook • Czech & Slovak Republics • Denmark • Dublin • Eastern Europe on a shoestring • Eastern Europe phrasebook • Estonia, Latvia & Lithuania • Finland • France • French phrasebook • Germany • German phrasebook • Greece • Greek phrasebook • Hungary • Iceland, Greenland & the Faroe Islands • Ireland • Italian phrasebook • Italy • Lisbon • Mediterranean Europe on a shoestring • Mediterranean Europe phrasebook • Paris • Poland • Portugal • Portugal travel atlas • Prague • Russia, Ukraine & Belarus • Russian phrasebook • Scandinavian & Baltic Europe on a shoestring • Scandinavian Europe phrasebook • Slovenia • Spain • Spanish phrasebook • St Petersburg • Switzerland • Trekking in Spain • Ukrainian phrasebook • Vienna • Walking in Britain • Walking in Switzerland • Western Europe on a shoestring • Western Europe phrasebook

Travel Literature: The Olive Grove: Travels in Greece

NORTH AMERICA

Alaska • Backpacking in Alaska • Baja California • California & Nevada • Canada • Florida • Hawaii • Honolulu • Los Angeles • Mexico • Miami • New England • New Orleans • New York City • New York, New Jersey & Pennsylvania • Pacific Northwest USA • Rocky Mountain States • San Francisco • Southwest USA • USA phrasebook • Washington, DC & the Capital Region

CENTRAL AMERICA & THE CARIBBEAN

Bermuda • Central America on a shoestring • Costa Rica • Cuba • Eastern Caribbean • Guatemala, Belize & Yucatán: La Ruta Maya • Jamaica

SOUTH AMERICA

Argentina, Uruguay & Paraguay • Bolivia • Brazil • Brazilian phrasebook • Buenos Aires • Chile & Easter Island • Chile & Easter Island travel atlas • Colombia • Deep South • Ecuador & the Galápagos Islands • Latin American Spanish phrasebook • Peru • Quechua phrasebook • Rio de Janeiro • South America on a shoestring • Trekking in the Patagonian Andes • Venezuela

Travel Literature: Full Circle: A South American Journey

ANTARCTICA

Antarctica

ISLANDS OF THE INDIAN OCEAN

Madagascar & Comoros • Maldives • Mauritius, Réunion & Seychelles

AFRICA

Africa - the South • Africa on a shoestring • Arabic (Moroccan) phrasebook • Cape Town • Central Africa • East Africa • Egypt • Egypt travel atlas • Ethiopian (Amharic) phrasebook • Kenya • Kenya travel atlas • Malawi, Mozambique & Zambia • Morocco • North Africa • South Africa, Lesotho & Swaziland • South Africa, Lesotho & Swaziland travel atlas • Swahili phrasebook • Trekking in East Africa • West Africa • Zimbabwe, Botswana & Namibia • Zimbabwe, Botswana & Namibia travel atlas

Travel Literature: The Rainbird: A Central African Journey • Songs to an African Sunset: A Zimbabwean Story

MAIL ORDER

Lonely Planet products are distributed worldwide. They are also available by mail order from Lonely Planet, so if you have difficulty finding a title please write to us. North American and South American residents should write to Embarcadero West, 155 Filbert St, Suite 251, Oakland CA 94607, USA; European and African residents should write to 10a Spring Place, London NW5 3BH; and residents of other countries to PO Box 617, Hawthorn, Victoria 3122, Australia.

NORTH-EAST ASIA

Beijing • Cantonese phrasebook • China • Hong Kong • Hong Kong, Macau & Guangzhou • Japan • Japanese phrasebook • Japanese audio pack • Korea • Korean phrasebook • Mandarin phrasebook • Mongolia • Mongolian phrasebook • North-East Asia on a shoestring • Seoul • Taiwan • Tibet • Tibet phrasebook • Tokyo

Travel Literature: Lost Japan

MIDDLE EAST & CENTRAL ASIA

Arab Gulf States • Arabic (Egyptian) phrasebook • Central Asia • Central Asia phrasebook • Iran • Israel & the Palestinian Territories • Israel & the Palestinian Territories travel atlas • Istanbul • Jerusalem • Jordan & Syria • Jordan, Syria & Lebanon travel atlas • Lebanon • Middle East • Turkey • Turkish phrasebook • Turkey travel atlas • Yemen

Travel Literature: The Gates of Damascus • Kingdom of the Film Stars: Journey into Jordan

ALSO AVAILABLE:

Travel with Children • Traveller's Tales

INDIAN SUBCONTINENT

Bangladesh • Bengali phrasebook • Delhi • Hindi/Urdu phrasebook • India • India & Bangladesh travel atlas • Indian Himalaya • Karakoram Highway • Nepal • Nepali phrasebook • Pakistan • Rajasthan • Sri Lanka • Sri Lanka phrasebook • Trekking in the Indian Himalaya • Trekking in the Karakoram & Hindukush • Trekking in the Nepal Himalaya

Travel Literature: In Rajasthan • Shopping for Buddhas

SOUTH-EAST ASIA

Bali & Lombok • Bangkok • Burmese phrasebook • Cambodia • Ho Chi Minh City • Indonesia • Indonesian phrasebook • Indonesian audio pack • Jakarta • Java • Laos • Lao phrasebook • Laos travel atlas • Malay phrasebook • Malaysia, Singapore & Brunei • Myanmar (Burma) • Philippines • Pilipino phrasebook • Singapore • South-East Asia on a shoestring • South-East Asia phrasebook • Thailand • Thailand's Islands & Beaches • Thailand travel atlas • Thai phrasebook • Thai audio pack • Thai Hill Tribes phrasebook • Vietnam • Vietnamese phrasebook • Vietnam travel atlas

AUSTRALIA & THE PACIFIC

Australia • Australian phrasebook • Bushwalking in Australia • Bushwalking in Papua New Guinea • Fiji • Fijian phrasebook • Islands of Australia's Great Barrier Reef • Melbourne • Micronesia • New Caledonia • New South Wales • New Zealand • Northern Territory • Outback Australia • Papua New Guinea • Papua New Guinea phrasebook • Queensland • Rarotonga & the Cook Islands • Samoa • Solomon Islands • South Australia • Sydney • Tahiti & French Polynesia • Tasmania • Tonga • Tramping in New Zealand • Vanuatu • Victoria • Western Australia

Travel Literature: Islands in the Clouds • Sean & David's Long Drive

THE LONELY PLANET STORY

Lonely Planet published its first book in 1973 in response to the numerous 'How did you do it?' questions Maureen and Tony Wheeler were asked after driving, bussing, hitching, sailing and railing their way from England to Australia.

Written at a kitchen table and hand collated, trimmed and stapled, *Across Asia on the Cheap* became an instant local bestseller, inspiring thoughts of another book.

Eighteen months in South-East Asia resulted in their second guide, *South-East Asia on a shoestring*, which they put together in a backstreet Chinese hotel in Singapore in 1975. The 'yellow bible', as it quickly became known to backpackers around the world, soon became *the* guide to the region. It has sold well over half a million copies and is now in its 9th edition, still retaining its familiar yellow cover.

Today there are over 240 titles, including travel guides, walking guides, language kits & phrasebooks, travel atlases and travel literature. The company is the largest independent travel publisher in the world. Although Lonely Planet initially specialised in guides to Asia, today there are few corners of the globe that have not been covered.

The emphasis continues to be on travel for independent travellers. Tony and Maureen still travel for several months of each year and play an active part in the writing, updating and quality control of Lonely Planet's guides.

They have been joined by over 70 authors and 170 staff at our offices in Melbourne (Australia), Oakland (USA), London (UK) and Paris (France). Travellers themselves also make a valuable contribution to the guides through the feedback we receive in thousands of letters each year and on our web site.

The people at Lonely Planet strongly believe that travellers can make a positive contribution to the countries they visit, both through their appreciation of the countries' culture, wildlife and natural features, and through the money they spend. In addition, the company makes a direct contribution to the countries and regions it covers. Since 1986 a percentage of the income from each book has been donated to ventures such as famine relief in Africa; aid projects in India; agricultural projects in Central America; Greenpeace's efforts to halt French nuclear testing in the Pacific; and Amnesty International.

'I hope we send people out with the right attitude about travel. You realise when you travel that there are so many different perspectives about the world, so we hope these books will make people more interested in what they see. Guidebooks can't really guide people. All you can do is point them in the right direction.'

– Tony Wheeler

LONELY PLANET PUBLICATIONS

Australia
PO Box 617, Hawthorn 3122, Victoria
tel: (03) 9819 1877 fax: (03) 9819 6459
e-mail: talk2us@lonelyplanet.com.au

USA
Embarcadero West, 155 Filbert St, Suite 251,
Oakland, CA 94607
tel: (510) 893 8555 TOLL FREE: 800 275-8555
fax: (510) 893 8563
e-mail: info@lonelyplanet.com

UK
10a Spring Place,
London NW5 3BH
tel: (0171) 428 4800 fax: (0171) 428 4828
e-mail: go@lonelyplanet.co.uk

France:
71 bis rue du Cardinal Lemoine, 75005 Paris
tel: 1 44 32 06 20 fax: 1 46 34 72 55
e-mail: 100560.415@compuserve.com

World Wide Web: http://www.lonelyplanet.com
or *AOL keyword: lp*